BEDFORD BREVIARY. The Legend of Anne and Joachim.
(*See note in insert following* p. 492.)

THE DOGMA

OF THE

IMMACULATE
CONCEPTION

HISTORY AND SIGNIFICANCE

EDITED BY EDWARD DENNIS O'CONNOR, C.S.C.

UNIVERSITY OF NOTRE DAME

UNIVERSITY OF NOTRE DAME PRESS   •   1958

IMPRIMI POTEST:

Theodore J. Mehling, C.S.C., Provincial
May 31, 1958

NIHIL OBSTAT:

Albert L. Schlitzer, C.S.C., *Censor Deputatus*
May 31, 1958

IMPRIMATUR:

✠ Leo A. Pursley, D.D., LL.D., Bishop of Fort Wayne
August 22, 1958

University of Notre Dame Press

Paperback edition published in 2017

The Library of Congress has cataloged this book as follows:

O'Connor, Edward Dennis, *ed.*
    The dogma of the Immaculate Conception: history and
significance. [Notre Dame, Ind.] University of Notre Dame
Press, 1958.

        645 p. illus. 24 cm.
        Includes bibliography.

        ISBN 978-0-268-00082-0 (hardback)
        ISBN 978-0-268-16072-2 (paperback)

        1. Immaculate Conception.   I. Title.

BT620.O26   *232.93   232.1   56–9806 ‡

Library of Congress

To her whose heart
because untouched by sin
is both
Sanctuary of the Godhead
and
Refuge of Sinners

Preface

Of all the Catholic beliefs concerning the Blessed Virgin, that in her Immaculate Conception is, from several points of view, the most important and the most interesting. This is the belief that Mary is the unique exception (besides, of course, Christ Himself) to the law of Original Sin: the law that all of Adam's offspring come into this life in a state of sinfulness, which they inherit from their first parent, and from which they are not delivered except by an act of God's grace. Grace is believed to have intervened in Mary's life at the very instant in which that life began, preventing sin from touching her in any way, and so making her holy and immaculate from the moment of her conception.

Considered simply from a historical point of view, this belief has cut a far greater figure in the theology of the Church than any other Marian doctrine. In the first place, it has been the subject of far more controversy than any other. Most of the Marian doctrines were a firmly established element of Catholic piety long before theology gave them serious attention; and the work of theology, when it arrived, was to plumb the meaning of these doctrines rather than to enter into controversy over them.

In the early centuries of the Church's history, it is true, a few beliefs about Mary, such as her Divine Motherhood and perpetual virginity, did give rise to serious debate. However, the question at issue in the former case was chiefly Christological—the unity of person in the God-Man; Mary's title, *Mother of God*, was drawn in principally as an illustrative consequence. And both the Divine Maternity and the perpetual virginity were resolved after a relatively short debate, and were accepted thenceforward without question—at least within the confines of Christian orthodoxy.

The recently defined dogma of the Assumption, on the other hand, has never been the object of noteworthy theological controversy. Some voices were raised against it in the early Middle Ages, it is true, but they scarcely attained the level of scientific theology. Today, of course, there is a good deal of discussion about whether death was involved in Mary's Assumption; but this has to do with the mode rather than with the fact of the Assumption.

The doctrine of the Immaculate Conception, on the contrary, was raised as a question about the year 1100, and was not settled until 750 years later. In the meanwhile it occasioned what was perhaps the most prolonged and passionate debate that has ever been carried on in Catholic theology. The number of treatises written on it during that time would be practically impossible to ascertain, let alone catalog.

Furthermore, there is much more at stake in the Immaculate Conception than the doctrine itself, as we see when we inquire into the reasons for all the controversy. The basic difficulty lies in the fact that Scripture does not speak explicitly about the Blessed Virgin's conception. She appears in the Gospels only briefly, in connection with the life of Christ. She is like a meteor glimpsed in flight: where she came from and what she was destined for had to be calculated chiefly on the basis of the short segment of the trajectory recorded by the inspired authors. And the calculation had to be made, not by cold reason working with measurable data, but by the insight of loving hearts judging in the light of what God had revealed about His intentions respecting her, and His way of dealing with men. It is no wonder that, under such circumstances, different theologians came to different conclusions.

And not only was the doctrine of the Immaculate Conception handicapped by the lack of any clear Scriptural evidence (or even, for that matter, any explicit patristic tradition) in its favor, but it even seemed to go counter to the clear teaching of St. Paul, that all men have sinned in Adam (Romans 5), and Christ's own declaration that He had come to call "not the just, but sinners to repentance" (Luke 5:32). This is what motivated most of the theological opposition to the Immaculate Conception, once the issues had become clear.

In order to become an official dogma of the Church a truth must have been revealed by God and handed down to the Church by the apostles, who are the foundation on which she is built. Yet many of the greatest theologians of the past were unable to discover the Immaculate Conception in the fonts of revelation, and some of them even considered it to be heretical. And not only the theologians, but even popes, when at various moments pressure was put upon them to decide the question, replied that "the Holy Spirit has not yet opened to His Church the secrets of this mystery."[1]

When, therefore, Pope Pius IX in 1854 defined that the doctrine of Mary's Immaculate Conception "has been revealed by God and is therefore to be believed by all the faithful," he put the capstone on the most extraordinary evolution ever undergone by any of the Church's dogmas. After having been totally unthought of for many centuries (so far as history enables us to judge) and fiercely controverted for many more, after having been rejected almost unanimously by the greatest masters of the greatest century of theology—including, apparently, even him whose teach-

---

[1] See p. 306 of the present volume.

ings the Church has "made her own," as Pope Pius XI declared—this doctrine has now been canonized as dogma and declared to belong to the primitive deposit of revelation.

For anyone who thinks of the Church's doctrine as a set of propositions of equal clarity, held by her in exactly the same way from the beginning, such a history poses an insuperable problem. Much of the difficulty vanishes, however, once we realize that the truths revealed by Christ are divine mysteries which the Church, another Mary, keeps in her heart and comes to understand ever better and better over the centuries; and, on the other hand, that the history of the belief in the Immaculate Conception is not an erratic sequence of shifting fortunes in the struggle between conflicting views, brought finally to a halt by an arbitrary intervention of authority, but a steadily deepening realization of the holiness of the Mother of God, perceived dimly and imperfectly at first, but gradually asserting itself with increasing firmness and clarity. In this light, even the Parisian doctors of the thirteenth century are witnesses in favor of, rather than against, the Church's belief; for they too concurred in attributing to Mary the greatest possible holiness under Christ. It was only because they did not see how an immaculate conception could be reconciled with the universality of the Redemption that they were hindered from pursuing their conviction about Mary's holiness to its natural conclusion.

We can admit without difficulty Turmel's assertion that the Church's belief on this question has followed a course like that of a river tending toward the sea.[2] It has encountered obstacles that have retarded its advance and turned it to one side or the other; but it has never reversed its flow. Through all the windings which, under the Providence of God, the contingent circumstances of history have imposed upon its course, the belief in Mary's holiness has constantly obeyed the same law—the logic of its own implications, and has been driven by the same force—the impulse of the Holy Spirit, bringing it inexorably to the goal to which it had been destined from the beginning.

We are not here concerned with the many questions that are raised by the details of this history; they will be dealt with in the chapters that follow. For the moment, what interests us is simply the fact that the problem of the evolution of dogma was posed by the definition of 1854 with unprecedented force and clarity.

The Immaculate Conception has not, of course, been the only doctrine to undergo a significant development throughout the Church's history, nor

---

[2] "Les dogmes, comme les fleuves, ont un cours sinueux qui trompe tous les pronostics et où il semble que la seule logique soit celle du caprice. Il appartient à l'histoire de montrer que, sous l'apparence du désordre, se cache une logique profonde; que chaque dogme a réglé sa marche d'après les circonstances, et que toujours, ce qui est arrivé, c'est ce qui devait être." J. TURMEL (under the pseudonym, Guillaume HERZOG), *La Sainte Vierge dans l'histoire*, p. 162. Turmel's intention in coining this simile did not, of course, correspond exactly to that with which we here use it.

the first to be recognized as having done so. Nevertheless, at the moment of its definition, Catholic theologians had been for three hundred years occupied largely with defending the authenticity of the Roman doctrines against Protestant charges of innovation, and this had undoubtedly made them more attentive to the continuity in the Church's doctrine than to its development. One may even wonder whether they had not been influenced unconsciously by a rather Protestant conception of revealed truths as something to be preserved solely in their original formulation, incapable of entering into the life of the mind and there bringing forth new fruit. Whatever be the reason, most of the nineteenth century theologians seem to have been inclined to overlook or to minimize doctrinal development as much as possible. But the definition of the Immaculate Conception thrust upon their attention a striking example of such development which made imperative a reconsideration of the whole theory of the life-history of dogma.

No doubt, the problem would have called for attention even had the Immaculate Conception never been defined; Newman's *Essay on the Development of Christian Doctrine* had appeared in 1845—nine years before the definition of Pius IX. But this work which, it should be noted, was written before Newman's conversion, aroused suspicions of liberalism which would, perhaps, have grown still more intense had not the definition of 1854 served in some measure to ratify the theses of the Oxford convert. It is also true that the implications of the definition were not realized at once. Some of its most eager defenders put themselves in a false position by striving to pound out a chain of explicit testimonies to the doctrine reaching back as nearly as possible to apostolic times. Eventually, however, the realities of the situation imposed themselves, and the impulse imparted by the definition seems to have been in good part responsible for the work that has been done in the present century on the question of the evolution of dogma, as well as for much positive research into the history, not only of the doctrine of the Immaculate Conception, but also of Mariology generally. And doubtless the studies carried on in this area contributed in no small part to the over-all development of positive theology that has been so remarkable during the past hundred years.

Besides stimulating the growth of positive theology and the theory of doctrinal development, the definition of 1854 was significant as a kind of 'test case,' exhibiting the authority of the Church's *magisterium* in interpreting divine revelation. Döllinger regarded this definition as part of a strategy designed to prepare for the definition of the papal infallibility in 1870. His view was not altogether wide of the mark, for while the earlier definition was dictated by motives of an entirely different order from consideration of 'strategy,' nevertheless it did constitute an actual exercise of the authority that would be defined sixteen years later.

Moreover, the Immaculate Conception was a particularly significant point on which to exercise the papal *magisterium*: it involved not merely a public reaffirmation of what was obviously Scriptural teaching, nor a decision as to the precise sense in which a Scriptural text should be taken, but the assertion of a truth about which Scripture (as well as ancient patristic tradition) appeared at first sight to be quite mute. Hence, Pius IX was passing judgment, not only on the Immaculate Conception itself, but also on His own and the Church's authority to discern the most delicate meanings of God's Word, and to read aright the most implicit signs of God's intentions.

The Nicene Fathers had been reluctant to incorporate into the Creed the non-biblical term *homoousios*. Similarly, the Church had hestitated for centuries before defining the Immaculate Conception. In both cases there were many grave misgivings as to whether it was right to take this novel step. And just as the step taken at Nicaea proved to be not so much the termination of one journey as the commencement of another, so it appears the definition of the Immaculate Conception has opened a new era in Mariology, and perhaps in other areas also. It was the piety of Mary's clients that had 'discovered' the Immaculate Conception, through their loving meditation on the Mother of God. If this 'popular belief,' which the greatest theologians had once opposed, and which even now they find so difficult to defend, has proved to be an authentic insight into divine revelation, then it becomes obligatory to look with greater respect upon the beliefs of the faithful, and to be cautious about ascribing to legend, ignorance or superstition beliefs which may not have any obvious foundation in the fonts of revelation, but which seem to strike a responsive chord in the heart of the Christian people.

As a matter of fact, the definition of the Immaculate Conception has been followed, a century later, by that of the Assumption—a doctrine which is in a situation quite like that of the Immaculate Conception so far as its Scriptural justification is concerned. And there are strong indications that the Church is on the way towards a definition of Mary's Co-redemption and mediation of all graces. It would, of course, be presumptuous to anticipate the judgment of the Church in these matters; but the status of these beliefs in the common acceptance of the faithful today strikingly resembles that of the Immaculate Conception during the century preceding its definition. At any rate, it is no longer possible to dismiss these beliefs on grounds no weightier than those once urged against the Immaculate Conception.

Thus far, we have given reasons to indicate the historical importance of the belief in the Immaculate Conception. However, the importance of any doctrine does not lie chiefly in its history, but in its intrinsic significance as truth, and in its rank in the hierarchy of truth, which do not depend on historical contingencies. From this point of view, one might be tempted to look upon the Immaculate Conception as a minor dogma, inseparably bound up, no doubt, with the Catholic faith, but of no structural importance in its system. The big role it has played in the history of doctrine might be attributed to historic accidents rather than to its own merits. In fact, however, this doctrine is of the highest significance, for Mariology first of all, but also for Soteriology and Ecclesiology.

For the privileges of the Blessed Mother are not just startling jewels with which the Divine King has decorated His Mother and Queen; they are functional parts of an organic whole. "Mary is wholly in each of her privileges," declares Father Guérard de Lauriers, O.P., "in such wise that you cannot grasp any one of them adequately without grasping all the others in Mary herself."[3] What he says of her privileges in general applies pre-eminently to the Immaculate Conception, which precontained all the others as the germ from which they sprang, and which is fulfilled in them. From this it follows necessarily that the doctrine of the Immaculate Conception is not just a corollary but a basic principle of scientific Mariology.

Furthermore, the Immaculate Conception is an indispensable clue to the full dimensions of the Marian mystery. We do not begin to appreciate the work accomplished by grace in the Mother of God until we realize that, by an extraordinary intervention, it preserved her from the state of sin in which all others receive human nature, and thus made her, in a true sense, wholly a child of grace. Once we grasp the implications of this radical separation of her case from that of the rest of mankind, we may perhaps begin to glimpse the reason why so many Marian doctors have insisted that she is a kind of "divine world" in herself, a cosmos in which God takes more pleasure than in all the rest of creation together.

Far from being a peripheral element, therefore, the Immaculate Conception lies at the heart of the Marian mystery. Any synthesis of Mariology undertaken without it will inevitably be dwarfed, if not positively misshapen. Is not this one of the chief reasons why an adequate scientific Mariology did not even begin to be developed until after the definition of 1854 had made of the Immaculate Conception a certain *datum* on which theologians could build with security?

Our doctrine is also of the highest significance for the theology of the Redemption and of the Church, in which it constitutes a special chapter. It obliges us to distinguish, within the body of the redeemed, between those whose redemption follows the common pattern, and her who has been redeemed "in a more sublime way," It makes Mary first among the members of Christ, not merely by reason of her unique relation to the Redeemer, but also by reason of her unique relation to the Redemption itself. And thus it explains likewise why she alone should have been given a role in the very accomplishment of the Redemption.

The doctrine of the Immaculate Conception is, therefore, of the highest importance, whether viewed by the historian or the theologian. It is from

[3] M.-L. Guérard des Lauriers, O.P., "L'Immaculée-Conception, clef des privilèges de Marie," in *Revue Thomiste* 56 (1956), p. 84.

both these points of view that it has been studied in the chapters which follow. These are not merely a collection of miscellaneous essays on the subject; they have been organized with a view to treating all the major aspects of the doctrine, in order to provide not just interesting reading but a useful tool. For those not already familiar with the subject, the following summary may facilitate the use of this volume.

SUMMARY OF THE VOLUME

Introduction. Since belief in the Immaculate Conception has its roots in Sacred Scripture, it is with the texts of Scripture that our study begins. However, the great distance between the obscure allusions of the inspired writings, and the clear definition of Pope Pius IX, poses a grave problem. Although an adequate answer to this problem cannot be had apart from the history that is treated in the next six chapters, the problem itself is posed at the very outset, and the principles which must govern its solution are there indicated.

History. The Church's understanding of the holiness of the Blessed Virgin has passed through three major periods, divided by the two dates, 1066 and 1854. It was soon after 1066 that the question of Mary's initial holiness first became the object of acute theological scrutiny. The previous millenium had been a period of quiet incubation, during which the belief gradually took form in the Christian consciousness. The centuries between 1066 and the definition of 1854 were filled largely with the theological controversies over the orthodoxy of the belief, which controversies, however, abated towards the end as the belief gained nearly universal acceptance. The definition of Pope Pius IX in 1854 put a final end to these debates within the Church, and made the Immaculate Conception no longer a question to be argued but a treasure to be exploited.

The work of the first centuries of the Christian era (*chapter II*) was merely one of remote preparation, which consisted in the purification of the image of the Blessed Virgin in Christian piety. For the first Christians, who indeed gave little enough thought to the Mother of God, do not seem to have had any explicit belief that she was utterly free from sin. In fact, Origen saddled several centuries of Oriental thought with the doctrine that Mary's faith had failed at least once; and Tertullian taught a similar doctrine in the West. Not until St. Augustine do we find the notion expressed by any orthodox doctor that Mary had never committed any sin; and even Augustine speaks only tentatively.

At this time, Greek thought was in arrears of the Latin with respect to its sense of Mary's holiness; but almost at the moment of Augustine's death, the Council of Ephesus (431), in officially espousing the title *theotokos*—Mother of God, imparted to Greek piety an affection for the Holy Virgin which carried it far ahead of its western counterpart. From the seventh century onwards (*chapter III*), the great Byzantine preachers began to formulate, with increasing emphasis and distinction, the conviction that Mary was utterly free from sin, and in particular from that sinful state in which all of Adam's other descendants are born. The Greek doctors, whose theology of original sin had not been developed with great precision, seem to have found no difficulty in this belief.

In the West, things were quite different. St. Augustine had, indeed, sharpened the Latin sense of the holiness of the Blessed Virgin, which, after a long maturation, would be ready in the twelfth century to flower in the ardent Marian piety of St. Bernard—the equal of anything to be found in the East. But St. Augustine had also imprinted deeply on the western mind a strong and explicit realization of the universality of original sin; and this seems for a long time to have forestalled even the occurrence of the idea that anyone other than Christ had ever been conceived free from sin.

When we come to the eleventh century, the century of the great schism which was to divide the Eastern Church from the West, the Mother of God was the object of fervent veneration on both sides of the Aegean, but with a significant difference. In the East, her Immaculate holiness was fully realized by many, but was conceived in such a way as to risk separating her from the company of those redeemed by the blood of Christ. In the West, on the contrary, the 'conviction of sin' stood as an obstacle preventing the belief in Mary's holiness from attaining its full development. The two theologies needed to complete and rectify one another; and in fact, one of the last communications that occurred between East and West before the schism was the transmission of the idea that would ultimately liberate western Mariology from the bond which retarded its growth.

It was not, however, by a theological writing, but by the dissemination of a liturgical feast (*chapter IV*), that this idea was transmitted. For the Byzantine Church had for several centuries previous to this celebrated a feast in honor of Mary's conception. It was not precisely a celebration of the *immaculate* conception (it seems to have originated in imitation of the earlier feast of the Conception of St. John the Baptist); but in view of the general Christian conviction about Mary's sinlessness, it was bound to suggest the idea that, even in her conception, she had been free from sin. In the East, this idea had been accepted without difficulty; in the West, however, it would have to overcome resistance. The precise circumstances under which this minor Byzantine feast penetrated into the West are unknown; southern Italy, where Greeks and Normans lived in close proximity, seems to have provided the bridge. At any rate, it had mysteriously taken root in a few English monasteries and cathedrals shortly before the Norman Conquest of 1066, which opens a new period in the history of the belief.

The Normans, in reforming the English Church, suppressed the feast. Within a few decades it revived, but only against opposition, which meant that it could no longer be a mere innocent expression of filial piety towards the Mother of God; it had to be argued for or against. Reasons were produced on either side, and gradually but inevitably the debate focussed on the properly theological question, whether Our Lady had been free from sin in her conception (*chapter V*).

St. Bernard, who has done perhaps as much as anyone else in the history of the Church to foster devotion to the Blessed Virgin, was nevertheless unable to see how her conception could have been without sin. For a century and a half, his opinion seems to have prevailed on the continent, at least among theologians. Nearly all the Parisian doctors adopted it, including, apparently, St. Thomas Aquinas.

In England and Normandy, however, the feast became more and more strongly entrenched; and it was in England that the Immaculate Conception gained its greatest champion. Duns Scotus defended the belief, and his arguments won over the University of Paris, which remained thereafter one of its foremost strongholds.

From this time on, the Franciscans were the chief defenders of the Immaculate Conception, and the Dominicans its chief opponents (*chapter VI*). Not, however, until late in the fifteenth century was popular attention drawn to this theological question by a bitter conflict which broke out in northern Italy and provoked the first papal intervention in the matter. Pope Sixtus IV did not pronounce either for or against the doctrine itself; but he defended the right of anyone to believe in it without prejudice to his faith. This touched off a wave of popular enthusiasm for the belief, which found expression in liturgical and artistic creations.

The sixteenth and seventeenth centuries produced further debate and new papal interventions (*chapter VII*), the latter turning more and more markedly in favor of the belief. In the theological discussions, attention began to be given to the way in which the Immaculate Conception had to be visualized, and particularly to the question whether there must have been at least a "debt" of sin in Mary. The Protestant Reformation diverted attention to other matters, but the belief continued to strengthen its hold, and missionary expansion in the East and in America served to diffuse it. By the end of the eighteenth century, the opposition had nearly ceased, and shortly thereafter the Popes began to authorize the use of the expression, ". . . *in Immaculata Conceptione*," in the Mass for December 8, and of the invocation, "*Regina sine labe originali concepta*," in the Litany of Loretto. The rapidity with which these concessions were adopted clearly indicated the popular sentiment in favor of the belief. In 1830, the Blessed Virgin's apparition to St. Catherine Labouré, and the subsequent diffusion of the Miraculous Medal with its invocation, "Mary conceived without sin," gave new impetus to the movement that culminated in the definition of 1854.

Since the definition, and especially during the past 50 years, the meaning of the Immaculate Conception has been explored with greater profundity than before, particularly as regards its relations with the other Marian mysteries. An account of this development was to have been included in the present volume, but a series of accidents have obliged us to do without it. The missing chapter is partially replaced by the bibliography at the end of the volume, which will give at least some indication of the literature of the period.[4]

Theology. The theology of the Immaculate Conception implies not so much the amassing of arguments to show that it really has been revealed (a task which, in the present volume, has been undertaken in the first seven chapters), but rather penetration into the meaning of the mystery by a discernment of the reasons for it, the consequences that flow from it, and the relations in which it stands to the other mysteries with which it has been associated in the divine plan.

The essential notion of the Immaculate Conception is treated in *chapter VIII*. As Mary's exemption from original sin is the basic idea of this doctrine, the meaning of original sin must first be fixed with theological precision. Then the mystery itself is considered, first in the reasons which motivated it, secondly in the grace which effected it (with reference chiefly to Christ, the author and end of this grace), finally in the consequences which flow from it. These last are brought out chiefly by a contrast of Mary's grace with that of Adam and Eve, in whom freedom from original sin had not altogether the same implications as it had in the Blessed Virgin.

With the notion of the Immaculate Conception thus established as regards its intrinsic elements, it must next be situated in God's plan for the created world (*chapter IX*). This involves relating it both to creation (considered at the natural as well as the supernatural level) and to Redemption (considered in its source—Christ, in the act whereby it was accomplished, and in the Church which resulted from it).

Finally, special attention is given to some of the more significant consequences of the Immaculate Conception in Mary's own life. *Chapter X* relates the Immaculate Conception to several of Our Lady's graces and privileges, notably the Coredemption and the Assumption. For the former, the Immaculate Conception provides a basis, by situating Mary's grace in the hypostatic order, which is the source of the Redemption. As for the Assumption, if it be supposed simultaneous with the death of the Blessed Virgin, the Immaculate Conception provides a reason of the highest propriety for it, inasmuch as a life that begins in grace should end in glory.

Even the spirituality of the Blessed Virgin must have been profoundly affected by the Immaculate Conception, which shielded her soul from every trace of sin, and filled her with a grace of singular fullness and excellence. *Chapter XI* points out how it differentiated Mary's spiritual life from that of others, while at the same time explaining a certain communication of her spirit to souls formed under her influence.

---

[4] The papal teaching during this period has been studied by Eamon CARROLL, O.Carm., "Mary Immaculate in the *magisterium* since *Ineffabilis Deus*," in *Carmelus* 2 (1955), fasc. 1, pp. 3-53; and R. P. BARRÉ, "De Pie IX à Pie XII, l'Enseignement des Papes sur l'Immaculée Conception," in *L'Immaculée Conception (Congrès Marials Nationaux, VII Congrès, Lyon, 1954)*, Lyon 1954.

Supplementary and Auxiliary Studies. Although the present volume is concerned primarily with the theology of the Immaculate Conception and the history of the Church's belief in it, certain other materials have been added to provide background and enrichment.

The Moslem Koran offers one of the most interesting testimonies which the Blessed Virgin has ever received from outside the Church, in it famous *hadîth*: "Every Adam's son coming into the world is touched by sin, except the Mother of Jesus and her Son." Although the specialist whom we have invited to examine this document reaches the conclusion that the text cannot be interpreted properly as a belief in the Immaculate Conception (*chapter XII*), this *hadîth* is nonetheless a significant indication of the immaculist direction being taken by the Christian thought which influenced Islam at the time of its origin, in other words, the Near Eastern Christianity of the seventh century.

The chief vehicles of thought on the Immaculate Conception have naturally been theological and liturgical; nevertheless, it was inevitable that art too be pressed into service to pay homage to the mystery. Not, however, until after Pope Sixtus IV's interventions in defense of the belief (1477, 1482, 1483), did artistic representations begin to appear in great number. The difficulty of finding a suitable expression for this doctrine produced at the start a number of rather unhappily inspired efforts. Around the beginning of the sixteenth century, however, an unknown artist hit upon a formula which rapidly won wide acceptance: the image of a young girl encircled by some of the Old Testament symbols already in use to represent the graces and privileges of the Mother of God. The artistic inspiration of the next two centuries, in Spain above all, gradually softened the mechanism of the original formula by centering attention on the radiant purity of the Virgin, while letting the symbolic accompaniments drop out of sight. The development terminated in the work of Murillo, which has since then remained pretty much the type of the Immaculate Conception in art, and has not even been dislodged by the new forms under which the Immaculate Virgin herself has appeared in recent times. (*Chapter XIII*)

A few *documents* have been appended to this volume in order to represent some of the legends that had considerable influence in shaping the imagery of the feast in its artistic, liturgical and even doctrinal expression. Three are accounts of the birth of the Blessed Virgin taken from apocryphal writings. One is a twelfth-century sermon narrating two famous miracles which Mary was reported to have worked in favor of the cult of her Conception. The last is a hitherto unedited text from the twelfth century in which the application of Old Testament symbols to the Blessed Virgin is developed with exceptional fullness.

The *bibliography* lists essentially the more important books on our subject that have appeared since the definition, although it goes back as far as 1830 in order to include the literature that prepared the way for the definition.

Acknowledgments

We wish to thank cordially the many people who have helped prepare this volume. Those whose collaboration bore especially on a particular chapter will be mentioned in that place; here we will mention only those who had a more general part in the work.

Father Theodore Hesburgh, C.S.C., President of the University of Notre Dame, has been most generous in his support. Fathers Charles Schleck, C.S.C., and Francis Nealy, O.P., helped to prepare and organize the Marian Year Symposium held at Notre Dame, June 30-July 2, 1954, at which several of the papers in this volume were originally presented. Sister Mary Epiphany, R.G.S., of St. Paul, Minnesota, has helped in many different ways, always most fruitfully. Father Roland Soucie, C.S.C., was of great assistance with the correspondence that was required. Mr. Everett Warren, of Notre Dame's Audio-Visual Department, and Misses Eileen Connolly and Barbara Minehan of the University Library, all went out of their way to be of service.

The facilities placed at our disposal by Fathers Roland Simonitsch, C.S.C., and Louis Putz, C.S.C., head and member respectively of the Department of Theology and Religion of the University, and the assistance so kindly given by Mrs. Joseph Clements and Miss Pauline Kopzynski, considerably lightened the heavy burden of preparing the manuscript. In transmuting the manuscript into the printed page, Brother William Denton, C.S.C., and Messrs. Dwight Marsee, Eugene Guentert and Frank Plodowski of the Ave Maria Press were most faithful and cooperative. Dr. Frederick Crosson and Mr. Robert Rauch, faculty members of the General Program and the English department of the University of Notre Dame, corrected the proofs with generous care and remarkable accuracy. Finally, Mr. John Defant, Director of the University Press, has guided this publication with a cheerful patience that did much to make a difficult job pleasant.

It was at the request of the late Father Joseph Cavanaugh, C.S.C., then head of the Department of Theology and Religion at Notre Dame, that this work was undertaken. We would like the book that has resulted to be considered a small memorial to him, and a sign of the affection with which he is remembered by all who worked with him.

E. O'C.
December 8, 1957

Contents

Illustrations

FIGURES

NON-NUMBERED DRAWINGS

INTRODUCTORY CHAPTER

Scripture and the Immaculate Conception:
A Problem in the Evolution of Dogma

I

Scripture and the Immaculate Conception: A Problem in the Evolution of Dogma

CHARLES JOURNET*

This study is designed to answer two questions concerning the dogma of Immaculate Conception: 1) How is this dogma contained in the deposit of Faith? 2) Why, if it is really contained in this deposit, did it remain so long hidden or unobserved? We cannot, however, answer the first question until we have defined theologically the notion of the *deposit of Faith*. Hence, our study will have three parts: 1) How is the *deposit of Faith* to be understood? 2) What express elements of this deposit are at the source of the Church's later teachings on the holiness of the Blessed Virgin, particularly the doctrine of the Immaculate Conception? 3) What vicissitudes has this doctrine undergone?

I

THE DEPOSIT OF FAITH[1]

INCLUSION OF A TRUTH IN THE DEPOSIT
AND MANIFESTATION BY THE MAGISTERIUM

For a truth to be believed by divine faith, two elements are necessary, the one "ontological," the other "gnoseological."

It is necessary, first of all, that this truth be *really and truly included* in

* Professor of Dogmatic Theology at the Grand Séminaire, Fribourg, Switzerland, and editor of the review, *Nova et Vetera*. Monsignor Journet's paper was presented at a Symposium on the Immaculate Conception at the University of Notre Dame, June 30-July 2, 1954. Due to the limitations of the present volume, it was not possible to retain the original work in its entirety; the present chapter is a translation of the major part of it by Rev. James BUCKLEY, C.S.C., of the University of Notre Dame, and has been read and approved by the author. The original French text was published by Alsatia, Paris, in 1954, under the title, *Esquisse du Développement du Dogme Marial.—Editor's note.*

[1] The word deposit (παραθήκη) is scriptural in origin: "O Timothy, keep what has been *entrusted* to thee (τὴν παραθήκην), and keep free from profane novelties in speech and the contradiction of so-called knowledge" (I Tim. 6:20). "Hold to the form of sound teaching which thou hast heard from me: in the faith and love which

the primitive deposit of Faith, either *explicitly* and conceptually formulated, or at least *implicitly,* preconceptually and unformulated. In other words, it must be objectively (*quoad se*) revealed. This is the "ontological" element.

Secondly, it is necessary that the objective inclusion of this truth in the primitive deposit be *manifested* to us, not only by human authority (the exegetical, historical and philosophical sciences) but by an authority divinely assisted in an absolutely infallible manner. In other words, this truth must also be revealed subjectively (*quoad nos*). This is the "gnoseological" element.

To be the object of divine faith, therefore, a revealed doctrine supposes, first of all, a divine meaning or intellectual content, and secondly a "reading," i.e. a divinely authorized declaration of this meaning or content.[2] If we compare the roles played by these two elements in the evolution of dogma, we observe that the preponderance can pass from one to the other, and that successive reversals of their heuristic value occur. In many cases, the "ontological" element—the fact that a certain truth is contained in the deposit of Faith—is perceived first, and the "gnoseological" element, i.e. the definibility of this truth, appears as a consequence. This was the case with the dogmas of the divinity of Christ, the consubstantiality of the Word and the Father, the virginity of Mary, her Divine Maternity, the universality of the Redemption, the absolute necessity of grace, faith and charity for salvation, the resurrection of the body, etc.

---

are in Christ Jesus. Through the Holy Spirit who dwells in us, keep the good things *entrusted* to thee (τὴν καλὴν διαθήκην)" (II Tim. 1:13-14). There is a "deposit" which comes from the Holy Spirit and is kept in the Holy Spirit; such is the *deposit of faith* spoken of by the Vatican Council: The Holy Spirit, it declared, has been promised to the successors of Peter in order to help them, "not so that by His revelation they might make known a new doctrine, but that by His assistance they might sacredly guard and faithfully expound the revelation transmitted through the apostles, i.e., the deposit of faith—*traditam per apostolos revelationem, seu fidei depositum*" (Sess. IV, chap. iv, Denz. 1836).

When speaking of the 'deposit of Faith,' we must at once take care to avoid all trace of agnosticism. We could use this term to refer merely to the *realities* which have been transmitted to us by Christ and the apostles: God, the indwelling of the Holy Spirit, Christ, the Redemption, the Mass, the Eucharist, the Blessed Virgin, the Church, grace, the sacramental rites, etc. By their mystery, these realities overflow the conceptual expressions, exact though these may be, that we are capable of formulating for them. But we can also use the term *deposit of Faith* to refer to these realities, not by themselves, but taken together with their meaning, i.e. with the hold which the intellect has on them by means of propositions and judgments, the truth of which is divinely guaranteed for us. It is in this sense that we shall speak of the 'deposit of Faith' in this study. St. Thomas explains that the believer's act of faith terminates in the revealed *realities,* but in so far as these are attained by means of revealed *propositions* without which these realities would be unrecognized or inexistent for us (Cf. II-II, 1, 2). The deposit of Faith is the Mystery of Salvation taken together with the ensemble of divinely guaranteed truths which disclose to us its meaning, and through which this mystery is adhered to integrally by theological faith.

[2] Hence the first great division of theological sources into those in which revealed doctrine is contained (*loci continentes*), and those in which it is manifested or declared (*loci declarantes*).

In other cases, however, in which the truth is more secretly and implicitly contained in the deposit of Faith, it is the "gnoseological" element—the definability of this truth and the Church's consent to its definition—which is in the foreground, while the "ontological" element—the fact that it is contained in the deposit of Faith—is affirmed as a consequence. Thus it was, for example, when those two closely connected privileges of the Blessed Virgin, her Immaculate Conception and Assumption, were proclaimed. The greater part of the Bull *Munificentissimus Deus* is designed to establish the Church's accord on the doctrine of the Assumption, from which it can be inferred with certitude that this truth must have been included in the primitive deposit of Faith.[3] This has even resulted in some misunderstanding among non-Catholic theologians, who, having read the Bull too rapidly no doubt, reproached it with having scarcely bothered, in fact, to indicate the scriptural foundations of the definition.[4]

It would be easy to find analogous examples of dogmatic development, in which the Church's consent to a truth is more manifest than the inclusion of this truth in the primitive deposit of Faith. The Church progresses down through time according to the impulse imparted to her by the breath of the Holy Spirit, without always being able to choose for herself the paths of her progress. If the Spirit is pleased to unite the hearts of His faithful in a common belief, before manifesting to them the manner in which this belief was revealed, who shall prevent Him? We are simply confronted, in this case, with another application of the old axiom of St. Augustine and St. Vincent of Lerins, that the faith professed in common by the genuine adorers "in spirit and in truth" cannot be in error.

But while, in certain cases, this rule immediately and infallibly resolves the problem of the object of faith, it nevertheless leaves the mind of the believer unsatisfied, so long as he does not clearly see how the truths proposed for his belief are contained in the initial deposit of Faith, and, more generally, how this deposit is to be conceived. Doctrinal definitions such

---

[3] "Since this 'singular accord of Catholic prelates and faithful,' affirming that the Mother of God's bodily Assumption into heaven can be defined as a dogma of faith, is a manifestation of the concordant teaching of the ordinary *magisterium* of the Church and the concordant faith of the Christian people (which the same *magisterium* sustains and directs), it manifests by itself, with utter certainty and immunity to error, that this privilege is a truth revealed by God and contained in that divine deposit which Christ delivered to His Spouse. . . . From the universal agreement of the Church's ordinary *magisterium*, we have a certain and firm proof that the bodily Assumption into heaven of the Blessed Virgin Mary . . . is a truth that God has revealed, and that must, therefore, be believed firmly and faithfully by all children of the Church." Pius XII, *Munificentissimus Deus*, A.A.S. 1950, pp. 756, 757.

[4] E.g. Oscar Cullmann, *La Tradition*, Paris-Neuchâtel, 1953, p. 38. The Bull *Ineffabilis Deus*, which served as a model for *Munificentissimus Deus*, also insisted first of all on the Church's consensus regarding the doctrine of the Immaculate Conception; and while indicating the Scriptural texts invoked by ecclesiastical writers in favor of this truth, does not pause to scrutinize them or distinguish in them between what belongs to the literal sense and what to the derivative sense.

as those of the Immaculate Conception and Assumption necessarily give a
new orientation to the research of theologians and the reflection of the
faithful, who are obliged to consider the deposit of Faith in the light of the
new definitions.   Thus the Church is led—here we touch on an important
point—to acquire over the course of the centuries a more and more exact
awareness of the nature of the primitive deposit and of the riches it
contains.[5]

The Deposit of Faith in the Mind of the Apostles and in the Mind of the Primitive Church

The deposit of Faith results from a transmission (παράδοσις, *traditio*)—
not a human transmission, proceeding from men of the past to men of
the present,[6] but a divine transmission, proceeding from Christ and the
apostles to the primitive Church.   Two steps are to be distinguished in this
transmission, the first of which terminates in the apostles, and the second
in the primitive Church.

The terminus of the first step is the deposit of Faith as it was received
in the collective intelligence of the apostles, or the apostolic college.   All
that the apostles knew of revelation came to them from Christ.   As for
Christ's deeds or teachings, these were known to the apostles either immediately, by way of revelation (ἀποκάλυψις)—e.g. the Resurrection, of which
all of them, even St. Paul, were eye-witnesses; or mediately, by way of
transmission (παράδοσις) from one apostle to another—thus Christ's
apparition on Easter evening was recounted to Thomas by the other apostles
(John 20:25); and what St. Paul passed on to the Corinthians concerning
the apparitions of Christ was what he himself "had received" from the other
apostles (I Cor. 15:3).[7]

[5] A passage from the Bull *Ineffabilis Deus* might be cited here:
"Christi enim Ecclesia sedula depositorum apud se dogmatum custos et vindex,
nihil in his unquam permutat, nihil minuit, nihil addit; sed omni industria, vetera
fideliter sapienterque tractando, si qua antiquitus informata sunt et Patrum fides sevit,
ita limare, expolire studet, ut prisca illa caelestis doctrinae dogmata accipiant evidentiam, lucem, distinctionem, sed retineant plenitudinem, integritatem, proprietatem, ac
in suo tantum genere crescant, in eodem scilicet dogmate, eodem sensu, eademque sententia."—*Acta Pii IX*, I, pp. 606-607.

[6] Christ reproached the scribes and pharisees for putting the *"tradition* of men,"
i.e. ritual traditions of the rabbis, above the commandment of God (Mark 7:8;
Matt. 15:3).   Paul speaks of his excessive zeal for the *traditions* of Judaism (Gal.
1:14).   Peter reminds the Christians that they have been set free from the vain way
of life *handed down* to them by their fathers (I Peter 1:18).

[7] If St. Paul says that he has "received from the Lord" the account of the Last
Supper (I Cor. 11:23), it is because, in his eyes, the Lord Himself is at work in
that transmission by which the apostles instruct one another.   From this point of
view, one could attempt a preliminary explanation, albeit insufficient, of the text in
which St. Paul affirms that he received his Gospel "not from man . . . but by a
revelation (ἀποκάλυψις) of Jesus Christ" (Gal. 1:12).   Cf. Oscar Cullmann
(*La Tradition*, p. 26), who stops at this explanation.   But verse 17 makes it clear
that it is St. Paul's intention in verse 12 to exclude all mediation, even that of the
other apostles.   Cf. note 8.

However, the deeds and teachings of Christ were not proposed to the apostles merely according to their external contours and in their pure materiality; their interior meaning was also revealed by a prophetic light. This light came from Christ, and from the Holy Spirit whom Christ had promised to send when He had returned to His Father. It affects each apostle directly, and acts by way of *revelation*.[8] Thus, whatever be the part attributed materially to a *transmission* from apostle to apostle, the communication which Christ and His Spirit make to the apostles is formally, i.e. in its supreme and decisive light, a *revelation*. From this it is clear on what grounds the deposit confided by Christ to the apostles is called *deposit of revelation*. It is clear also—a point to which we shall return in a moment—what this deposit was *in the intelligence of the apostles*, where it was fully illumined by the direct prophetic light of a revelation.

The second step proceeds from the apostles and terminates in the deposit of revelation as received in the intelligence of the primitive Church. St. Paul writes to the Corinthians, "I, myself, have received of the Lord (what I also *delivered* to you) . . . " (I Cor. 11:23) "I *delivered* to you first of all, what I also received . . ." (15:3) Here there is no revelation ($\dot{\alpha}\pi o\kappa\dot{\alpha}\lambda\upsilon\psi\iota\varsigma$) but only transmission or tradition ($\pi\alpha\rho\dot{\alpha}\delta o\sigma\iota\varsigma$).[9]

The apostles, therefore, besides having a theological faith which was certainly holier than that of the common faithful,[10] also had a *prophetic light* unknown to the common faithful, in which the revealed deposit was known to them. Because of this light, the revealed formulas had a greater meaning for them than for the primitive Church. What did this meaning amount to?

We must be careful to distinguish, in divine revelation, between the formulas by which the revelation is made, and the meaning of these formulas. It is the latter which is formal.

---

[8] Only from this point of view is there an adequate explanation of St. Paul's declaration that he received his Gospel "not from man . . . but by a revelation of Jesus Christ" (Gal. 1:12) before he even had an opportunity to meet the other apostles (Gal. 1:17).

[9] This is the primary sense of the word *tradition*, which, when construed actively, denotes the act of transmitting a deposit—an activity which is accomplished through the Lord Jesus (Cf. I Thess. 4:2). The 'interapostolic tradition' is anterior to this; but for the reasons given above, it is reducible to the revelation by which it is perfected. In its primary sense, *Tradition* is a communication from the apostles to the primitive Church.

By extension, the deposit thus transmitted can also be called *tradition*, the word here receiving a passive construction. In this sense, it is used by St. Paul in both singular and plural: "Brethren, stand fast, and hold the *traditions* which you have learned, whether by word of mouth, or by letter from us" (II Thess. 2:14). "We charge you, brethren . . . to withdraw from every brother who lives irregularly and not according to the *tradition* received from us" (*Ib.* 3:6). *Tradition* means, in its primary and most comprehensive sense, the integral divine treasure which the apostles have transmitted to us.

[10] It is a commonplace in St. Thomas that the apostles surpassed the other saints in charity, whence the saying of St. Paul, "Be imitators of me as I am of Christ" (I Cor. 11:1).

For there to be a revelation at all, the prophet or inspired author must have at least some *explicit understanding* of the formulas used;[11] but it is not necessary that *the prophet or hagiographer* understand *everything* that God intends to signify by means of these formulas, and which is really contained in them.[12]   Had the author of the Protogospel an inkling of the dimensions which the drama opposing the offspring of the Woman and the offspring of the Serpent would later take on?   It can be said without hesitation that, thanks to the fuller doctrinal explanation given by Christ, the apostles and the Church, the meaning of the prophecies and revelations of the Old Testament is known to us today more explicitly than to the prophets themselves.[13]

The case of the apostles is different.   They penetrated the mystery of salvation more profoundly than the patriarchs or prophets had been able to do.   St. Paul writes:

> You can perceive how well versed I am in the mystery of Christ, that mystery which in other generations was not known to the sons of men, as now it has been revealed to His holy apostles and prophets in the Spirit. . . . To me, the very least of all the saints, there was given this grace, to announce among the Gentiles the good tidings of the un-fathomable riches of Christ, and to enlighten all men as to what is the dispensation of the mystery which has been hidden from eternity in God, who created all things (Eph. 3:4-9).

Being the foundation stones of the Church (Eph. 2:20), the apostles knew the economy of the law of grace as masters who were to teach all ages, with a knowledge which could never be surpassed or even equalled.   The future was revealed to them—cf. the visions of the destinies of the Church in the *Apocalypse,* and of the lot of the Jews in *Romans.*   Ordinarily, at least, their knowledge did not embrace the details of *contingent events;*[14]

---

[11] Pharaoh and Balthasar merely had visions; only Joseph and Daniel, who revealed the meaning of the visions, were prophets.

[12] Cf. F. MARIN-SOLA, O.P., *L'évolution homogène du dogme catholique,* Fribourg, 1924, I, chap. ii, p. 51 ff.

[13] "The very words of the inspired men of old have received, in the vast perspective of the divine plan, a richness and plentitude which their first authors did not conceive of, but which were to benefit future readers.   It is clear, for example, that those who were able to compare, centuries later, the messianic prophecies of Isaias, Jeremias and Daniel with one another, and even to confront them with their fulfillment in Christ, have a more lucid and profound understanding of them than did those to whom the revelations were originally made.   Thus God's Word gives a commentary on itself, and the ancient oracles are illumined by new ones, so as to acquire a deeper meaning, which is called the *sensus plenior* or *plenary sense."* P. BENOIT, *La prophétie,* Paris, 1947, p. 357; cited by F. M. BRAUN, "La Mère de Jésus dans l'oeuvre de saint Jean," *Revue Thomiste,* 1951, p. 64.

[14] Those to whom Jesus had said, "Go, teach all nations," could hardly fail to know that the Gospel was to be preached to the Gentiles, or that, after Christ's death, the observances of the Law were no longer binding.   Nevertheless, we see Peter hesitate when it came time to admit the first gentiles into the Church, or repudiate publicly the Mosaic observances.   Similarly, they could not have been unaware that Jesus

but everything that touched on the substance of the mysteries of Faith was fully revealed to them by the Holy Spirit. This does not mean, of course, that the apostles had in their minds the express formulation, automatically elaborated, of all the dogmas which should be promulgated in future centuries, and that they withheld this knowledge from their contemporaries. We wish to say merely that the faith of the apostles beheld the revealed truths in an infused prophetic light which they could not transmit as such to others. They had, therefore, to "translate" it for the use of the faithful, by a living and progressive effort of conceptualisation and formulation, which was, incidentally, conditioned by all sorts of historical circumstances.[15]

---

would preserve His Church "even to the consummation of the world," but they did not know "the times nor the moments which the Father had determined in His power," since that date was not included among the things which the Son of Man was to announce to the world. Cf. St. THOMAS I-II, 106, 4 ad 2.

[15] It is in the light of these considerations that we must understand II Cor. 12:4 and John 21:25. The apostles certainly did not have a knowledge of revealed truth *already expressed* in formulas which could be communicated to others, but they had a knowledge that was *capable immediately of being made explicit* by them in communicable formulas, to the degree that human language permitted. By way of illustration, let us suppose that, instead of provoking St. Paul to speak of marriage, idol-offerings and the Eucharist, the Corinthians had asked him whether original sin, in its universality, extended even to the Mother of God. In our opinion, the Apostle would not have avoided this question which would one day be put to St. Augustine by Julian of Eclanum, and would make the African doctor hesitate. (Concerning this incident, see chapter II of the present volume, p. 71 ff.) St. Paul would not have declared that he saw nothing in the revelation entrusted to him that permitted him to reply. Instead, strengthened by the light from above which illumined his view of the whole economy of the Mystery of Christ, he would have been able to affirm both the universality of Christ's Redemption and the spotless holiness of Her who was His Mother. Then we would have had an explicit revelation of the Immaculate Conception, but we would have been without certain points concerning the place of the Eucharist in the primitive Christian communities, and the condition of mixed marriages.

Theologians may well differ somewhat when they attempt to make precise determinations about the progress and modalities of the knowledge of the apostles. To our mind, what it is essential to hold is that the apostles, who were formed by Christ, taught by His Spirit and enlightened by the incommunicable prophetic light of direct revelation, had a knowledge of the Mystery of Christ that was total and exceptional, which embraced, though in a higher fullness, the explicit and immediately perceptible sense of the deposit of revelation as this was delivered by them to the primitive Church; and which, moreover, surpassed all that the Church could, with the help of the Holy Spirit, discover over the course of the centuries, by making explicit what was contained implicitly in the original deposit.

This doctrine, which is traditional, would find a confirmation today in an exegesis such as that of Père BRAUN, who, in *La Mère des fidèles, Essai de théologie johannique,* Tournai-Paris, 1953, invites us "to discover in the writings of the Apostle (John), not only what is revealed there explicitly, but also what is revealed obscurely or implicitly. This can be done by a more synthetic view, integrating the truths there affirmed with one another, conformable to the intentions more or less indicated by the Apostle" (p. 21). For example, there is the amplitude, too often unobserved, which the drama of the Protogospel assumes in the mind of St. John (pp. 94-96). The author calls *biblical theology* this attempt to clarify particular texts by relating

SCRIPTURE VS. TRADITION

The point of departure for the development of dogma, therefore, is the deposit of revelation, not as it was known to the apostles, who received it by *revelation,* but as it was known to the primitive Church, which received it by *tradition* simply.

A message can be transmitted either by the *spoken* word, which is fleeting, or by the *written* word, which endures. The apostles used both means, according to the occasion and the contingent circumstances. St. Paul recommends that the Thessalonians hold fast to "the traditions" which they had learned from him "whether by word or by letter" (II Thes. 2:15); he reminds the Corinthians by letter of "the Gospel" which he had first announced to them by word of mouth (I Cor. 15:1). In both cases, what is transmitted infallibly to the primitive Church, by speech or by writing, is a message freighted with divine meaning, a treasure of truth, a word of Christ which shall never pass away. It is the Gospel, the Good News, the Deposit of Revelation, Tradition, παράδοσις, in the initial sense of the word.

Having said this, we can legitimately distinguish between that truth which the primitive Church received from the apostles in writing, which we call *Scripture,* and that which was received by word of mouth, which we call *Tradition,* taking the word now in a second and restricted sense.[16] This distinction has a basis in St. Paul (who, however, uses the word *tradition* in the first sense only, for the whole message, whether oral or written), and is confirmed by the *magisterium* of the Church.[17]

But there are two ways to use the distinction: one is to insist especially on the *juxtaposition* of Scripture and Tradition, as two halves of the primitive deposit of revelation; the other is to insist more upon immediate *penetration* or transfusion of Tradition into Scripture, as a result of which, the true sense of Scripture is immediately evident to the primitive Church.

Those who use the distinction in the first manner begin by drawing up a list of the doctrines which evidently belong to the deposit of revelation.

---

them to others, and he adds that "the results obtained by the application of this simple method greatly surpassed his expectation" (p. 21). On the knowledge of the Apostles, cf. *L'Eglise du Verbe Incarné* I, Paris (1941), pp. 142-145 (English translation by A. H. C. Downes, *The Church of the Incarnate Word* I, New York-London, 1955, pp. 132-136); JOHN OF SAINT THOMAS on II-II, Q. 1, disp. 6, a.2 (ed. Vives VII, pp. 120 ff.); Guido MATTIUSSI, *L'assunzione corporea della Vergine Madre di Dio nel dogma cattolico,* Milano, 1924, p. 340.

[16] The Council of Trent recognizes this restricted sense of the word *Tradition* when, in Session IV, it distinguishes between "the written books and the unwritten traditions" received from the mouth of Christ or by the dictation of the Holy Spirit (Denz. 783).

[17] Cf. the preceding note. The Council "receives with equal respect . . . the books of the Old and New Testaments, since the one God is author of both, as well as the (aforementioned) traditions . . . as dictated either by Christ orally, or by the Holy Spirit" (*ibid.*).

When they come to doctrines that are not expressly formulated in Scripture, they think that these are to be sought for elsewhere, and that they will be found explicitly in that body of truths transmitted to the primitive Church by apostles orally, as distinguished from Scripture.[18]

The same theologians habitually insist on what they call the contingent and occasional character of Scripture. The apostles, they say, were sent to preach; they did not write, except when they were unable to exhort the churches by word of mouth. The questions to which they reply in their writings may have arisen often according to the whim of circumstances, or been occasioned by local incidents, etc. The classic theses of anti-Protestant apologetics are recognizable here.[19]

Those who use the distinction between Scripture and Tradition in the second manner affirm first of all that Scripture cannot be read torn out of the vital milieu in which it first appeared, and in which it was naturally and immediately understood according to its authentic sense. The oral preaching of the apostles was necessary to found the first churches, to open their minds to the *sensus fidei*, and to create a spiritual atmosphere in which Scripture would find its natural and indispensable context. This reading of Holy Scripture—as the primitive Church read it—in the light

---

[18] For example, the Canon of Scripture. God alone could reveal it, but St. John did not write it down, hence it must be sought in an oral revelation. Similarly the doctrine of the necessity of infant baptism: no scriptural text treats of it expressly, so again we must have recourse to an oral source. So, too, for the celebration of Sunday. After God had reserved the Sabbath to Himself, had anyone the right to replace it with Sunday, without a revelation?

It would be easy to find other examples of this same tendency. In *L'assunzione corporea della Vergine Madre di Dio nel dogma cattolico*, Milano, 1924, pp. 331 ff., Guido MATTIUSSI points out—in order to combat it—the tendency to try to base our knowledge of the Assumption on an express oral revelation through the apostles. The same tendency would lead us to say that the Immaculate Conception may have been revealed explicitly to the primitive Church through St. John. The difficulty would then be to explain how this truth was so late getting promulgated.

We would have no difficulty granting that, *as an apostle*, St. John must have seen in the Mystery of the Virgin the necessity of her Assumption; and on this point we would agree with Père Braun. It is quite another thing to say that this truth was *revealed explicitly to the primitive Church*, or even that it can be seen in Apoc. 12:6 and 14. Cf. F. M. BRAUN, *La Mère des Fidèles*, pp. 162, 183.

In his *De locis theologicis*, III, chap. iii (Padua, 1734, p. 90), Melchior CANO proposes some principles intended to establish theologically that there are divine traditions in the true Church of Christ: 1) Christian faith preceded the appearance of Scripture; 2) not all the truths of Christian doctrine are expressly contained in Scripture; 3) certain points are not found either openly or obscurely in Scripture, e.g. the Canon of Scripture and the doctrine that Confirmation and Holy Orders cannot be repeated. To this one could reply: 1) the first fact, which is incontrovertible, does not in any way exclude the possibility that the essential features of the oral tradition were later summed up in Scripture; 2) it is not necessary that the elements of Christian doctrine all appear expressly in Scripture, it suffices that they be there at least implicitly; 3) few theologians today would admit that the doctrine of the sacramental characters is not in any sense contained in Scripture.

[19] Note that Protestants can without difficulty recognize the priority of apostolic Tradition over apostolic Scripture. Cf. Oscar CULLMANN, *La Tradition*, pp. 41-42.

of the preaching of the apostles, surpasses all the readings we can make today with the help of our scientific data.[20]

The theologians of the first tendency would certainly not deny that Scripture is thus impregnated by oral tradition, but they seem to us to pay insufficient attention to the capital importance of this point. Their principal concern being to establish a parallel between Scripture and Tradition, rather than to show how Tradition penetrates Scripture, they are preoccupied with isolating and cataloging those truths which, to their minds, had no place in Scripture, and which they then proceed to refer exclusively to Tradition. They are determined to represent Scripture and Tradition as two *loci theologici* which are not only distinct, but separate, constituting the two halves of the deposit of revelation. But if, on the contrary, one were to insist upon the fact that Scripture was read by the primitive Church in the light of the apostolic preaching, which gave it its full meaning, one would be inclined to think, as we do, that *Scripture, especially towards the time of its completion, appears as containing explicitly, certainly not all revealed truths,[21] but at least the essential ones, the principles, the articles of faith from which the entire deposit of revelation could, with the help of the Holy Spirit, be made explicit later on.[22]*

[20] Père CONGAR puts it forcefully in connection precisely with the account of the Annunciation: "When someone tells us, for example, that the κεχαριτωμένη of Luke 1:28 means *graced* and not *full of grace*, and hence cannot serve as a foundation for the Catholic theology of the Virgin Mary, I reply: Philology is an excellent thing, and that science of exegesis which is founded on philology, archeology and history is necessary and good; but these are not the measure of divine revelation, of what has been confided to the Church and is testified to by the Bible. The one faculty adequate in fidelity and understanding to the gift of God is not the mind of the exegetes, but the *sensus ecclesiae,* the mind of the Church, that intelligence which the Holy Spirit fosters in her. I respect the knowledge of the exegetes and I interrogate it unceasingly, but I will not accept their *magisterium."*

The same can be said of the words *agape, Church, Covenant, justification,* etc. The author underlines "the fundamental error which would consist in believing that we could, from an exegetico-historical study of the notion of *agape,* determine what Christians must hold in this matter. For what Christians must hold is *id quod traditum est, id quod traditur,* that is, the Christian reality itself. . . . The same applies to *justification* and *justice.* . . . These are things that have been given to us *in their reality.* Sacred Scripture testifies to this reality, and its testimony has a decisive value; but even this testimony, which is already narrower than the reality, is to be sought in a broader field than that of *words.* For what is said of the life of Christ, of the gift and fruits of the Holy Spirit, etc., will affect also, even exegetically speaking, the biblical notion of justification, justice, etc."—*Vraie et Fausse Réforme dans l'Eglise,* Paris, 1950, p. 498-500. Lest we fall back into the misunderstanding cleared up above (n. 1), let us make clear that what Christians must hold are indeed these *realities,* namely *id quod traditum est,* but in so far as the *meaning* of these realities has been manifested, expressed, formulated by the apostles in the *propositions* which they transmitted to the primitive Church. Here is the apostolic παράδοσις.

With regard to κεχαριτωμένη, let us add that if the verbs in -οω signify a plenitude, it is hard to see how else to translate it than by *gratia plena.*

[21] Scripture itself tells us that Jesus did many things that have not been written down (John 20:30; 21:25).

[22] As to the question concerning the Canon of Sacred Scripture: How did the

Those who have followed us this far will not need to be told that when we come to the question of determining the first foundations of the Immaculate Conception and Assumption in divine revelation, we will not seek them in an oral tradition parallel to Sacred Scripture, but rather (with most and the better theologians) in Scripture itself, as a condensation of the apostolic tradition that was read by the primitive Church in the light of the Holy Spirit who assists her.

EXPLICITATION OF THE DEPOSIT

We have seen that the apostles had, by the incommunicable prophetic light of *revelation*, an exceptional knowledge of the mystery of Christ. It was in this light that they formulated, and that they themselves understood, the propositions transmitted by them to the faithful of their time. They penetrated these propositions in all their richness, and, had events demanded it, they would have been able to make explicit, to formulate and to express what they found as yet implicit, unformulated and unexpressed in them.

But this was not the case with the primitive Church. She had, it is true, received from the apostles the deposit of the Gospel, the oral and written παράδοσις, in its integrity. Up until then, this deposit had been receiving new enrichments and explicitations, not indeed heterogeneous and transformative, but homogeneous and continuous; for its meaning was so hidden and obscure in the beginning that it required *new revelations*, first to the ancient prophets, then to the apostles.[23] These reached their culmination

---

Church know that God was author of these books? She knew it in the general principle that every doctrinal book written or guaranteed by an apostle was normative. This is the *revealed* principle. It is taught expressly in Scripture, which speaks to us several times of the doctrinal authority of the apostles to found the Church: "You have been built on the foundation of the apostles and prophets" (Eph. 2:20; cf. Matt. 28:18-20; Apoc. 21:14; etc.). The primitive Church was *aided* so as to apply this principle rightly; therefore we must appeal to its infallible *magisterium;* but there is no need to recur to an oral *Tradition* parallel to Scripture. (There is a penetrating study of this question by M.-J. LAGRANGE, O.P., *Histoire ancienne du canon du Nouveau Testament*, Paris, 1933.) As for the necessity of infant baptism, is it not expressly contained in the following texts when they are read in a certain way— "taken seriously," so to speak?—"Go, teach all nations, baptising them . . ." (Matt. 28:18-20); "Unless a man be born again, he cannot enter the Kingdom of God . . . cannot see the Kingdom of God" (John 3:3 and 5); or the texts in which St. Paul speaks of incorporation into Christ by baptism. What is needed here is not recourse to another revelation outside of Scripture treating the express case of infants, but light on the meaning which the apostles put into these great texts. And if the Church is assisted in declaring this meaning, she does not need to appeal to an oral tradition parallel to Scripture. As for the third case: there is an obligation to celebrate the Lord's Day. But if it is revealed that Jesus is the Lord, that Redemption is a greater thing than creation, that the resurrection is the goal of creation, can the Lord's Day be any but Easter Sunday? No other revelation is needed; it suffices to understand the meaning of the one that is met on every page of Scripture. These examples could easily be multiplied.

[23] It is certain that all the articles of the Christian faith are contained in the first

in the visible missions of the Incarnation and Pentecost, which mark the center and the summit of the whole history of Salvation. From then on it was closed to new revelations.[24] However, the Church does not inherit from the apostles that infused prophetic light with which they had been endowed. The statements made by the apostles are principles for the Church. She sees a certain explicit, determinate and clear meaning in them; but, in addition, they are fraught with a sense that is implicit, undetermined and obscure. In proportion as a principle is the more profound, elevated and divine, the more virtuality, indetermination and obscurity it contains. Reciprocally, to the degree that a principle gains in clarity, fixity and determination, it loses in virtuality and fecundity, just as every force loses its potential in the measure that its energy is actualized. Hence, the propositions of councils, popes and theologians are clearer and more precise than those of the divine deposit; but the latter are more suggestive and pregnant, richer in truth and life.[25]

Thus the true point of departure for dogmatic progress is furnished by the apostolic formulas as they come from the mouths or the pens of the apostles, and as they were grasped by the faith and understanding of the Church when it was still under the *magisterium* of the apostles. For her faith and understanding, the hidden riches of these propositions were not capable of immediate explicitation, as they were for the apostles, but only of progressive explicitation. For all their virtualities to be developed, much time and many events would be needed. This is not progress in revelation, but progress in dogma, requiring an infallible assistance of the *magisterium* by the Holy Spirit.

But is there an infallible authority commissioned by Christ to protect the initial sense of the propositions deposited with the apostles, and to develop it in the course of time?[26] From the Catholic point of view, the reply is unhesitating: *"Go, teach all nations . . ."* The deposit of Faith was confided to the teaching authority which would succeed that of the apostles, the *magisterium* of the Church. This magisterial power is assisted by Christ until the end of the world: *". . . and behold, I am with you all days . . ."*

---

two *credibilia* revealed to Abraham, namely, according to Hebr. 11:6, that God exists and that He rewards those who seek Him. Cf. St. THOMAS II-II, 1, 7. But, *without the aid of new revelations,* we would never have been able to discover in these first two *credibilia* the dogmas of the Trinity and the Redemptive Incarnation.

[24] Cf. Proposition XXI condemned in the decree *Lamentabili,* "The revelation constituting the object of Catholic faith was not completed with the apostles" (Denz. 2021). Cf. the Vatican Council, sess. IV, chap. iv (Denz. 1836).

[25] Cf. MARIN-SOLA, *L'évolution homogène . . .* I, 58, p. 59; and 197, p. 295.

[26] For the reason why an infallible *magisterium* is necessary, see below, p. 29, n. 45. We have treated this point with regard to the thesis of OSCAR CULLMANN in our book, *Primauté de Pierre dans la perspective protestante et dans la perspective catholique* (Paris, 1953), chapters vii-ix (English translation by John Chapin, Westminster, Maryland, 1954).

The role of the *magisterium* is not to add new revelations to the deposit, the παράδοσις, which was complete by the death of the last apostle. All that the Word of God had to say was said by Himself and His apostles at the time of the foundation of the Church. The first Christians had no hesitation on this point. The whole mission of the *magisterium* is to *transmit the deposit of faith to future generations until the end of the world.* Here we meet the word *transmission,* παράδοσις, *tradition* (spelled now with a small *t*) in a new usage (third sense). There is no longer, as in the first two cases, a transmission to the primitive Church from the apostles, who received new revelations in order to instruct the Church. Here the transmission takes place entirely *within the body of the post-apostolic Church,* in which there are no more new revelations, but only new *explanations,* new explicitations, of the primitive deposit, given once and for all to the Church by Christ and His apostles.[27]

Transmission of the deposit entails its explicitation. For there are two kinds of deposits: those which are inert, such as nuggets of gold, which can be kept just as they are; and those which are alive, as a plant or a child, which cannot be kept in existence unless they are allowed to develop. If the Gospel deposit is classified among the second kind, it must be admitted that we cannot keep it except by developing it.

The Holy Spirit was promised to the successors of Peter, says the Vatican Council, so that they would "sacredly guard and faithfully expound—*ut sancte custodirent et fideliter exponerent* . . . the deposit of Faith."[28]

[27] Note that what the theology manuals call the *proof from tradition (probatur ex traditione)* is in reality a *proof from history*—a recourse to history in the attempt to discover, in the documents that have escaped the disasters of time, indications of the faith of the Church at each moment of its duration. Even in this endeavor, the theologian should interrogate history in the light of faith, in which the Church contemplated the revealed truths from the beginning, and has not ceased to contemplate them. The history of the early period will certainly be silent concerning later dogmatic explicitations, but at least it will never be able to establish that the Church as such, in the supreme act of its *magisterium,* has expressly opposed them. Rather, it will manifest the presence in the Church of the articles of faith in which the truths later defined were implicitly contained, in a preconceptual and unformulated manner. It will call attention to the explicitations as they appear.

[28] Session IV (Denz. 1836). When we say that the *magisterium* protects and explains the primitive deposit, and Sacred Scripture in particular, we do not thereby put the *magisterium* of the Church above this deposit, or above Scripture. This would be a grave error. It originates in the mistake already pointed out, of confusing the exceptional *magisterium* enjoyed by the Church when the apostles, the authors of Scripture and enlightened by revelations, were still present in it, and the *magisterium* of the post-apostolic Church, deprived of these revelations, and assisted solely in order to protect and explain the oral and written deposit of Faith.

The true doctrine is that Scripture, which *contains* the deposit, is above the *magisterium,* which manifests it. This was the reply of BossueT to the minister, Paul Ferry: "We do not say that the Church is judge over the Word of God, but we are sure that it is judge of the various interpretations that men give to the holy Word of God" (Part II, chap. iv; ed. Bar-le-Duc, V, p. 320. Cf. St. FRANCIS DE SALES, *Oeuvres complètes,* I, p. 206).

Thus, the Church's living *magisterium* unceasingly recalls what was *explicitly* contained in the primitive deposit, and she makes explicit, brings forth in a conceptual and formulated manner, what was contained there only *implicitly*, in a preconceptual and unformulated manner, as an obscure but powerful and irresistible exigency.[29]

If the implicit is *really* precontained in the explicit, it must be said without hesitation that the explicitation of a divine truth *conforms to a rigorous and ineluctable inner logic.* But however rigorous it may be, this derivation of one truth from another takes place wholly *in the night of faith.* It starts with a mystery grasped obscurely, preconceptually and, as it were, instinctively, and terminates at this same mystery grasped now distinctly, conceptually and clearly. The lights of human reason would not, by themselves, suffice to guide and guarantee this development. *The infallible assistance of the Holy Spirit* must be assured.

The instinct which senses the still unformulated truth hidden in one that is manifest, and can sometimes even predict its future promulgation, is the instinct of a loving faith. This it is which causes the "eyes of the mind" to be "enlightened," as the Apostle says (Eph. 1:18). When the objection was made to Newman, after his conversion, that, being subject to an infallible power which "at its own will imposes upon men any new set of *credenda* when it pleases," he could not say whether "to-morrow I may not have to give up what I hold to-day," he replied, as a Catholic theologian, that the infallible authority can never define anything which was not really contained in the primitive deposit:

> Nothing can be imposed upon me different in kind from what I hold already,—much less contrary to it.[30] The new truth which is promul-

---

[29] Hence, it can be said that the primitive Church "did not know" (i.e. explicitly) certain of our present-day dogmas; but it did know explicitly certain others in which the first are implicitly contained (Cf. MARIN-SOLA, *L'évolution homogène* . . . I, 173, p. 257). We can speak of "new dogmas" as long as we make it clear that they are not new in their *substance* or in their *principle,* but only in their *explanation* —and that, not by way of *extrinsic addition,* but by way of a purely *intrinsic manifestation* (MARIN-SOLA, *ibid.* II, 306, p. 16).

Here we must emphasize the decisive importance of the definition given by the *magisterium* in the course of the explicitation of a dogma. Before the infallible definition, anything contained only implicitly in the deposit of revelation is, by that fact, *really* revealed (*quoad se*), but not yet *manifestly* (*quoad nos*). After the infallible definition by the *magisterium,* what was already really revealed (*quoad se*), becomes also *manifestly* revealed (*quoad nos*). Before the infallible definition of the divinely assisted *magisterium,* what was implicitly revealed cannot be the object of any but a human consent, of the theological order; after the definition of the divinely assisted *magisterium,* the revealed truth, now divinely explicited, can be assented to by theological faith. Until the infallible definition of the *magisterium* intervenes, an error about what is implicitly revealed is still possible, even for the Fathers and theologians; after this infallible definition, error is no longer possible, except in the case of ignorance (MARIN-SOLA, *L'évolution homogène* . . . , I, 122, pp. 177 ff).

[30] This is the very distinction St. THOMAS makes in I *Sent.* divisio textus prologi: "Est apponere duplex: vel aliquid quod est contrarium vel diversum, et hoc est er-

gated, if it is to be called new, must be at least homogeneous, cognate, implicit, viewed relatively to the old truth. It must be what I may even have guessed, or wished, to be included in the Apostolic revelation; and at least it will be of such a character, that my thoughts readily concur in it or coalesce with it, as soon as I hear it. . . . Let me take the doctrine which Protestants consider our greatest difficulty, that of the Immaculate Conception . . . it is a simple fact to say, that Catholics have not come to believe it because it is defined, but that it was defined because they believed it.[31]

And if they believed it, it is because they sensed, obscurely, preconceptually, instinctively, that it was contained in the other truths of the deposit of revelation and was demanded by the ensemble of Christian doctrine.

II

THE FIRST PRINCIPLES OF MARIOLOGY
GIVEN IN THE DEPOSIT OF REVELATION

THE ANALOGY OF FAITH

It is impossible to discuss a Christian truth in isolation without ultimately distorting it in some way. Each truth needs to be situated in the ensemble of the Gospel message, in which Christ alone is the center, the Alpha and Omega. Everything begins with Him, is measured with respect to Him, is bound up with Him, and finds its perfection in Him. How, then, could we speak of the Blessed Virgin in isolation? Her person, her mission, her destiny will be unintelligible except in reference to Christ and to His work of salvation. Only then will she be sure to receive, without attenuation or exaggeration, the place which the entire context of Christian revelation mysteriously but inevitably requires that she have. This way of illuminating one truth of Faith through its integration in the ensemble of all the others, just as one organ of a living body is explained by its function with reference to the whole body, is what theologians call *recourse to the analogy of faith*.

The Gospel message, which was prepared for by the prophets long in advance, is the message of a God born in a stable and dying on a cross, in order that, by the outpouring of His superabundant gifts, He might form for Himself a people, a kingdom, a mystical body, a church.

Christ is God. He possesses a twofold sanctity: one, uncreated and incommunicable, by which He is the only Son of the Father, the Word made Flesh: "We have seen His glory, the glory as of the only-begotten of the

---

roneum vel praesumptuosum; vel quod continetur implicite, exponendo, et hoc est laudabile" (Cited by MARIN-SOLA, *L'évolution homogène* . . . , II, 306, p. 17).

[31] J. H. NEWMAN, *Apologia pro vita sua*, London, 1865, Part VII, pp. 278-279 (in later editions, chap. v).

Father, full of grace and truth" (John 1:14); the other, created and communicable, which He pours out upon men to conform them to Himself and to gather to Himself His people, His Kingdom: "And of His fullness we have all received, grace for grace" (John 1:16).

Between Christ and His Church, there is both infinite distance and profound union. Christ belongs to the hypostatic order, He is the Son of God by nature. The Church belongs to the order of created grace, to which the adoptive sonship and the indwelling of the Holy Spirit pertain. Salvation is in Christ as in its cause, source and principle; it is in the Church as in an effect, a derivation, a participation.

The relationships between Christ and the Church are comparable to the relationships between the head and body of a living organism. The head compared to the body, and Christ compared to the Church, have a position of both superiority and homogeneity: superiority, inasmuch as the head has life as the source from which it flows, while the body has it only dependently and by participation; homogeneity, inasmuch as it is the same life which descends from the head to be communicated to all parts of the body.

THE BLESSED VIRGIN—MEMBER OF CHRIST'S MYSTICAL BODY

If we ask now where the Blessed Virgin's place lies, there can be no hesitation. Only in Christ is Salvation found as in its Cause and Principle; it is in the Blessed Virgin after the manner of an effect, a participation. *Mary's place is with the people of God, the Church, the Mystical Body of Christ.*

We have here the *first principle* of the Church's Marian doctrine. It is a positive principle, for it allows us to attribute to the Blessed Virgin the grace of *Salvation derived from Christ,* the grace of the Mystical Body of Christ. It is at the same time a limiting principle, for it forbids us to attribute to the Blessed Virgin the grace of Salvation *as in its source.* Christ is the head of the Mystical Body; the Blessed Virgin is only a member. She is, in the Mystical Body, both a sign and an effect of the sanctity of Christ.

THE EXCEPTIONAL PLACE OF THE BLESSED VIRGIN IN THE MYSTICAL BODY AS MOTHER OF THE DIVINE SAVIOR

Does the Gospel give to the Blessed Virgin a privileged and pre-eminent place in the Mystical Body? And if so, how should we characterize it? This is our next question.

There is one title we could appeal to, to solve this question—that of *mother of Christ.* But this title is found in the Gospel at two different levels. In Matt. 12:50—"Whosoever does the will of my Father, who is in heaven, he is my brother, and my sister and my mother"—it denotes the spiritual motherhood of the Christian, inasmuch as he can give birth to others in the life of grace and form Christ in them (Gal. 4:19); and more generally the spiritual motherhood of the entire Church, which is more efficacious and universal than that of its individual children.

Elsewhere, the title, *Mother of Christ,* is reserved to Mary. She is the mother of God our Savior. Let it be pointed out at once that there is no question of stopping at the concept of motherhood considered abstractly in its purely material and physiological sense. This would yield absolutely no foundation for Mary's pre-eminent dignity. What we are concerned with is rather the concept of motherhood considered *concretely* and *existentially in the Gospel perspective.* In this perspective Mary is mother of God not only physically, but freely and consciously, with full knowledge of what was involved: mother in spirit even more than in body. She was proportioned, insofar as this is possible to a pure creature, to the holiness of such a mission. Mary is the *worthy Mother of God.* As soon as heresies oblige the Church to proclaim the divinity of Christ, Mary will be proclaimed *theotokos*—God-bearer. This is the concept on which the infallible *sensus ecclesiae* has pondered, and from which all of Mary's privileges are deduced, not by frail "arguments of fittingness," but by a genuine unveiling and "unfolding."[32]

As regards giving men birth in the life of grace and forming Christ in them, the saints do it more perfectly than other Christians, and the Church more perfectly than any of her children. There are various degrees of this spiritual motherhood; nevertheless, all are on the same plane.

The motherhood of the Blessed Virgin, however, puts us on a different plane. The holiness of giving birth to Christ's Mystical Body, and the holiness of giving birth to Christ, the Head of this Body, are incommensurable. The difference is not merely one of degree, but qualitative. It supposes a jump, equivalent to what mathematicians call "passing to the limit," for example, passing from the polygon to the circle. *Of this discontinuity, absolutely unique in the order of grace, we have in the Gospel itself a sign that is absolutely unique in the order of nature: the miracle of the virginal motherhood of Mary.*

To the question raised above, whether the Virgin Mary holds a privileged place in the Mystical Body, the Gospel replies that the relationship between Mary and the rest of the Church is the relationship between the holiness required to give birth to the Incarnate God, Head of the Mystical Body, and the holiness required to give birth to the members of this Body. Christ is the Head on whom all grace depends, by anticipation or derivation. Mary and the Church are the Body.[33] Whoever knows the Church's

[32] Cf. *L'Eglise du Verbe Incarné,* II, p. 389.
[33] Mariology is a part of Ecclesiology. To distinguish between Mary and the

holiness is on the way to knowing Mary's holiness, *but he cannot actually reach it except by a jump, an extrapolation, a "passing to the limit."* Here we have the second principle of the Church's Marian doctrine.

ALL THE GLORIES OF THE HOLINESS OF THE ENTIRE CHURCH ARE RECAPITULATED IN THE PERSON OF THE VIRGIN MARY ALONE

Christ appears at the center of the "Age of Salvation." The Church had existed before Him, beginning immediately after the Fall, in an inchoate form. This was the *Age of the Expectation of Christ.* After Christ, beginning on Pentecost, comes the *Age of the Holy Spirit,* through whom the grace of Christ is poured out upon the world, and by whom the Church, the Communion of the faithful, is established in the state of full development.

Except for Mary, the contemporaries of Christ belong either to the Age of the Expectation of Christ—as is the case of Elizabeth, Simeon, and John the Baptist, or to the Age of the Holy Spirit, as is the case of the apostles.

So far as chronology is concerned, the Blessed Virgin appeared before Christ, and was still present at Pentecost. She is contemporary with both the first saints of the Gospel, who live in the Age of Expectation, and the apostles, who belong to the Age of the Holy Spirit. But qualitatively, Mary belongs neither to the Age of the Expectation of Christ nor to the Age of the Holy Spirit; she stands *in the presence of Christ* at that moment when all the grandeurs of the hierarchy destined for the apostles were still held by Christ in reserve, whereas the grandeurs of holiness had already been bestowed upon her. All by herself Mary occupies an entire age in the life of the Church—the Age of the Presence of Christ. That is to say that the grace of Christ is granted to her according to a law or regime proper to her. While the distance between Christ, the Head, who is divine, and the Church, His body, which is a pure creature, remains infinite, the Blessed Virgin, being by her motherhood in an immediate relationship with the Person of the Redeeming Word of God, is the point or pole in the Church at which the attraction of the Redeeming Word of God is felt with the maximum of power. *The law of conformity to Christ is more intensively realized in the one Person of the Blessed Virgin than in the entire rest of the Church.*[34] We have here a new formulation of the second principle of the Church's Marian doctrine.[35]

Church is to distinguish between the Church, taken in its privileged part, and the Church, taken in its more common part. It is only for the sake of convenience that we use the term *Church* for what is really only a part of the Church.

[34] Cf. *L'Eglise du Verbe Incarné,* II, p. 439.

[35] This second principle shows how we must understand certain affirmations, well-intentioned, no doubt, but perhaps too facile, which are frequent in a type of popular preaching and devotional literature. They can easily cause irritation and provoke

FROM THE HOLINESS OF THE CHURCH TO
THE HOLINESS OF THE BLESSED VIRGIN

It is by pouring out upon men the superabundance of His holiness that Christ forms a body for Himself. What He possesses as source is found in His Church in a dependent and participated manner; and if what we have said be true, the Blessed Virgin is characterized by the same gifts, but pushed to their extreme limit.

Thus, Christ is the "Lamb of God Who takes away the sin of the world" (John 1:29). Total purity, without any stain, is found in Him as in its *source*. This same total purity exists elsewhere only in a *dependent and participated mode*. It finds one realization in Christ's Spouse, the Church, which is, as such, not indeed without sinners, but without sin. She belongs always and altogether to Christ. The Apostle shows her to us as "not having spot or wrinkle or any such thing, but . . . holy and without blemish" (Ephes. 5:25-27). However, this realization is that of a whole, of a *collectivity*, not in any individual person. No individual member of the Church is always and entirely free from sin, original as well as actual.

At its limit, however, this total purity finds a personal realization in the Virgin Mary, who "recapitulates" the entire Church in the presence of Christ. By reason of His influence, she is always and wholly without sin, even original sin.

Parallels could be drawn for the cases of Christ's redemptive work, His glorious resurrection, and His heavenly intercession.[36] All Ecclesiology, like Mariology, which is its privileged part, consists in discerning those

---

contradiction when they seem to be motivated by an eagerness to outdo all that has yet been said in praise of Our Lady; but they regain their true, profound and traditional meaning as soon as one takes care to justify them doctrinally, and to clarify them in the light of the principles just formulated. It may be said, for example, "Such and such a privilege becomes the Blessed Virgin; God is able to give it to her; therefore He did in fact do so: *decuit, potuit, ergo fecit.*" Or again, *"De Maria numquam satis."* Must we then attribute priesthood and the grandeurs of the hierarchy to the Blessed Virgin? Will she be said to have the same power that Christ has over the Church and the sacraments? (Cf. St. THOMAS, III, 64, 2 and 3). NEWMAN remarked already that certain expressions that burst out of the fervor of piety are, when formulated in meditations and exercises, "as repulsive as love letters in a police report." (*Certain difficulties felt by Anglicans in Catholic teaching, considered in a letter addressed to the Rev. E. B. Pusey, on occasion of his* Eirenicon *of 1864,* London, 1876, p. 80.)

E. NEUBERT proposes what he calls "the principle of analogy," for discovering the grandeur of Mary: "To the various privileges of the Humanity of Jesus, there correspond in Mary analogous privileges, according to the manner and the measure implied by the difference between Her condition and that of her Son" (*De la découverte progressive des grandeurs de Marie, Application au dogme de l'Assomption* (Paris, 1951, p. 56). Nevertheless, a little further on, he himself recognizes the inadequacy of such a principle: "To what extent is such and such a privilege of Christ found in Mary? The principle of analogy does not tell us, except in a general

[36] Cf. *L'Eglise du Verbe Incarné,* vol. II, pp. 393-453.

fashion" (p. 61).

gifts which reside in Christ as their source, but which He communicates to those associated with Him. They find, in the Mystical Body, two kindred but unequal realisations, one of which tends towards the other without ever being able to attain it: a collective realisation in the Church, which gives birth to the members of Christ, and a personal realisation in the Virgin Mary, who gives birth to Christ Himself.

As the Church, which counts many sinners among its members, grows more and more conscious of the divine gifts communicated to it—holiness without spot or wrinkle, a coredemptive mission, the glorious destinies towards which it draws all creation after it (Rom. 8:20-21), it likewise begins to grasp more and more explicitly the corresponding gifts in the Blessed Virgin, in whom they attain an unparalleled degree of perfection: her Immaculate Conception, her universal coredemptive mediation, her glorious resurrection and her Assumption. *Hence, the progress of the Church's doctrine on the Blessed Virgin parallels the concrete appreciation of its own mystery which the Church gradually attains in the course of time.* The solemn promulgations of the dogmas relating to the Blessed Virgin mark the principal stages of the Church's own development down through the ages. But whether the Church or the Blessed Virgin be under consideration, it is always the infinity of Christ and His redemptive work, of which they are but the finite result, which is concerned.

THE CHURCH'S INITIAL FAITH IN THE MYSTERY OF THE BLESSED VIRGIN

In the preceding paragraphs, we have attempted to explain *conceptually* the *obscure* and *instinctive* process by which the Christian doctrines concerning the Virgin Mary and the Church develop. These doctrines are found in Holy Scripture, but in an implicit, preconceptual and unformulated state. The force responsible for bringing them to light is secretly at work even in the simple faithful, inclining them to embrace these Christian truths even before the latter are promulgated, and giving them a presentiment of the Church's definitions.

We have also established the principle that the point of departure in all development of dogma is the understanding which the primitive Church had of the deposit of revelation. There is an initial intuition of faith, as it apprehends the inspired text, which perceives at once in the mystery of the Mother of the Incarnate God such a depth of content, that it embraces in advance—though of course in an obscure, preconceptual and veiled state—everything about this mystery that will be manifested in a conceptual fashion throughout the centuries. Likewise it excludes beforehand every misconception or mutilation of this mystery which will occur in the course of time. This is what is called the initial faith of the Church, the *sensus ecclesiae,* concerning the mystery of the Blessed Virgin. This faith, this "instinct," of the Church bears upon a primary *datum,* which truly and really contains, though in an implicit and unformulated state, everything that will later be defined concerning the Blessed Virgin's privileges. Hence the *magisterium* of the Church, in defining dogmas such as the Immaculate Conception and Assumption, can say that, "The Church has always believed," or "has always been convinced of" them.[37] It is somewhat as when you listen to a difficult question being debated, without being able to agree fully with either side; but when someone comes along who is able to distinguish the truth from error and thus solve the problem, you exclaim—and without any falsehood—"That is just what I always believed."

It remains now to determine the precise configuration of the initial datum upon which the faith of the primitive Church bore, and which constitutes the point of departure for the whole development of Marian doctrine. We will look for it in Scripture, that παράδοσις or tradition which was fixed by the apostolic writings. We will examine above all St. Luke and St. John. This initial datum will be marked by the following characteristics:

1)—It will have an *explicit* sense, capable, as it unfolds in the context of the analogy of faith, of giving birth to the whole ensemble of Marian doctrine.

2)—As seen, however, through the eyes of the primitive Church, it will not say anything already capable of manifesting expressly the dogmas of Mary's Immaculate Conception,[38] her coredemptive and co-dispensing mediation, or her Assumption.

3)—On the other hand, it will not contradict anything which will later be determined and promulgated in these dogmas.

4)—Furthermore, it will show itself vigorous enough to *overcome* the difficulties which will arise in the course of time to challenge it, as it were; and it will lead toward these later dogmas of the Church.

There is still a preliminary question that can be raised: In what sense can the faith in this initial *datum* grow more perfect and make progress, as it is explicited in the course of time? We would reply, in accordance with what has already been said above: a) The faith does not grow more perfect in *intensity,* holiness, or fecundity. The mystery of the Blessed Virgin is grasped at once by the primitive Church, in its relation to the mystery of the Incarnation, as a principle inexhaustibly rich in virtualities.

---

[37] "Perpetuus Ecclesiae sensus . . . persuasum semper fuit in Ecclesia Dei, ab ipso Ecclesiae initio . . ." Cf. MARIN-SOLA, *L'évolution homogène* . . . , I, 173, p. 257, and above, p. 16.

[38] It is in this sense that we must understand the words of St. Robert BELLARMINE in a *Votum* on the Immaculate Conception, pronounced in 1617 before Pope Paul V: "In Scripturis nihil habetur."—Cited by JUGIE, *L'Immaculée Conception* . . . , p. 41; see also chapter VI of the present volume, p. 252 f.

b) But the faith does grow more perfect in *clarity*, precision, and explicitation. The mystery of the Blessed Virgin manifests little by little the consequences which were hidden in it from the beginning. c) Nevertheless, neither the primitive Church, nor the Church of later times, will ever be able to recover all that the apostles put into Sacred Scripture, nor attain the exceptional knowledge that the apostles themselves had of the mystery of Christ, the Divine Savior, and consequently of the mystery of the Mother of the Divine Savior.

THE TEXTS OF ST. LUKE

Jesus declared what was required of his disciples if they were to have a spiritual motherhood over His Mystical Body: "Whoever does the will of my Father who is in heaven, he is my brother, and my sister, and my mother" (Matt. 12:50). And to the woman who had praised His mother, He replies: "Rather blessed are they who hear the word of God and keep it" (Luke 11:28). They must do His Father's will, hear His word, and keep it.

In the case of a spiritual motherhood with regard to Christ, the Head of the Mystical Body, these requirements as to sanctity must be pushed to their limit, as we have already said. But *is* Mary's motherhood a spiritual one? Will we find, in the mystery of this motherhood, a special will of the Father, heard with special attention, and carried out with a special obedience? It is to St. Luke that we turn for an answer. His testimony does not depend on one word alone—on the question, whether or not we may translate κεχαριτωμένη (Luke 1:28) by *gratia plena*, "full of grace"; it is incomparably more vast, rich and profound than that.

What we are seeking, let us repeat, is not the understanding of St. Luke which the resources of exegesis, philology and history alone could give, but rather the understanding of St. Luke that the primitive Church, as she read with the eyes of faith, attentive to that unimaginable mystery of the Son of God deciding to be born of the posterity of David according to the flesh (Rom. 1:3), and while in the form of God, taking the form of man (Philip. 2:6-7), Himself God blessed forever (Rom. 9:5). We reject *a priori* any understanding of St. Luke which loses sight of the unfathomable mystery of the Incarnation. The only admissible understanding of Scripture is the profoundest: that which is most aware of the holiness of the Incarnation and of all that it entails; in a word, that which is "mysterious" in the holiest sense.

Hence, in speaking of St. Luke's testimony, we do not by any means aim to construct a reasoned argument or undertake a verbal exegesis; still less are we concerned with apologetics.[39] We want to seize hold of an

---

[39] If there is "discourse" here, we would say, borrowing the expression of Père BRAUN, that it consists "in a discerning *rapprochement* of the texts, *not in order to*

intuition, a principle, a key-idea: not an intuition of the philosophical or artistic order, but the intuition of the primitive Church concerning the mutual relationships of Mary and her Divine Son. Principles are not demonstrated; either they are seen or they are missed. This is always true but with special reason in the domain of faith. The intuition of which we speak can be rediscovered by the faithful of today at the foundation of their personal belief in the grandeurs of Mary. It is from this starting point that the Marian doctrine can develop *according to a rigorous inner logic,* as we have already said, but always in the transluminous night of the faith, and with the assistance of the Holy Spirit. It would be absurd to think—though this is, perhaps, a frequent error in certain quarters, but not one which a theologian or a contemplative would ever make— that the dogmas concerning the Blessed Virgin can be derived from anything other than an initial mystery of faith, and to wish to derive them by a merely rational exegesis or an apologetic demonstration. We have the scriptural texts about Mary which were the object of the intuition of the primitive Church: above all the texts of St. Luke and St. John. And that these texts were read in the light of an intuition of faith, we know in another manner, and with another sort of certitude, as we know that the faith, given to the Church from its birth, will accompany it on its entire earthly pilgrimage and will never abandon it.

Did not the Blessed Virgin "hear" the word of God? Did she not "keep" it in her heart? Did she not "do" the will of the Heavenly Father? And did she not do all this, not just at any moment whatsoever, but at the most solemn moment in the history of salvation; in connection with an event not like those which go into the warp and woof of the Church's holiness, but one that was absolutely unique and incommensurable with all the other events of the era of the Redemption? If she did, then we must say that it is in a 'spiritual' and 'holy' manner that Mary is mother of Christ, the God-Man, the Head of the Mystical Body. And here we have precisely *a first equivalent form of that expression so dear to theologians and to the whole Church, as the principle of their entire Marian doctrine, that Mary is the 'Theotokos': that she is, insofar as this is possible for a pure creature, the worthy mother of the Divine Redeemer.*[40]

The Precursor—The account of the annunciation of the Precursor, of the Angel's visit to Zachary, of Elizabeth's miraculous conception and of her thanksgiving (Luke 1:5-25), prepares for the account of the Annuncia-

---

draw conclusions from them, but to make them explicit by integrating them with one another."—*La Mère des fidèles . . .* p. 188.

[40] Calling Mary the worthy mother of God does not mean that she merited the supreme grace of the divine maternity and the Incarnation of the Word: she did not merit it either *de condigno* or, properly speaking, *de congruo.* But because of the divine maternity, to which she is gratuitously predestined, she is given preparatory graces to 'proportion' her to that absolutely unique mission, somewhat as the gener-

tion of the Savior, the Angel's visit to Mary, her virginal conception, and her thanksgiving. The two accounts, however, are on different planes. The one belongs to the Age of the Expectation of Christ, when the Church, however pure it may have been, was able to give birth merely to members of the Mystical Body; the other account belongs to that privileged moment when the Church, represented by the Virgin Mary, gives birth to Christ Himself. Elizabeth's *miraculous* conception serves only as a sign of Mary's *virginal* conception (1:36-37).

Elizabeth's greeting (1:41-45) manifests the difference of planes. Elizabeth knows the mystery of Mary's motherhood; she acknowledges Mary to be mother of her Lord (1:43). And she understands that it is spiritually and with due holiness that Mary is mother: she proclaims Mary "blessed among women," blessed to have "believed the word of the Lord" (1:42, 45). Mary is the holy mother of the Savior of the world, of Him from whom flows the grace that causes John the Baptist to leap in his mother's womb (1:41, 44). *This is, in equivalent terms, the express acknowledgment of the* Theotokos, *of the worthy Mother of God.*

The Annunciation—(1:26-38) "And in the sixth month, the Angel Gabriel . . ." The sentence scarcely comes to an end of detailing the circumstances of the event. This is that event in the history of salvation in which God, Who is by essence invisible and a stranger to space and time, comes to dwell visibly in one point of space and time. Gabriel is the angel who, in the book of Daniel (8:16; 9:21), had explained the plans of God for the salvation of the world.[41] When he greets the Virgin, she has already been since time past the object of God's benevolence, κεχαριτωμένη,[42] even more than she herself knows, for she is troubled.

ative act prepares for the infusion of the immortal soul. When the Church says, in the *Regina Coeli*, that the Blessed Virgin merited to bear the Lord, *quia quem meruisti portare*, this means, explains St. Thomas (III, 2, 11 ad 3) that the first graces given to her elevated her to the degree of purity and holiness that became her who was to be God's mother. Cf. B. H. Merkelbach, O.P., *Mariologia*, Paris, 1939, p. 100; R. Garrigou-Lagrange, O.P., *De Christo Salvatore*, Torino, 1945, p. 504.

[41] "Gabriel appropriates to himself the function of revealing God. He brings the divine into the phenomenal world." A. Grieve, "Gabriel," in Hastings' *Dictionary of the Bible* (the five-volume edition of 1898-1904).

[42] In Eph. 1:3-6, it is said that God has chosen us "unto the praise of the glory of His grace, with which He has 'graced' us—ἐχαρίτωσεν—in His beloved (Son)." It is a theological principle that the divine love differs from human love in that it creates the being and the goodness of things (St. Thomas I-II, 110, 1). This is true of that love which God has poured into our hearts by the Holy Spirit, who has been given to us. The perfect tense—κεχαριτωμένη—signifies a state, whereas the aorist would signify the occurrence of an event.

There is a well-known commentary of Origen, *In Lucam*, homilia VI (*P.G.*, 13, 1815). "As the terms in which the angel greeted Mary are something new, the like of which I have not been able to find anywhere else in Scripture, a word must be said about them. For I do not recall having read elsewhere in Scripture the words that are spoken here: *Ave gratia plena*—in Greek, κεχαριτωμένη. Not even to a man is any-

And this first grace is but the announcement of a higher one: she will be the mother of Jesus, the Son of the Most High. But she is not unaware that God has accepted and ratified her vow of virginity. Hence her anxiety: how can she act without sin in such a choice? Gabriel replies that there will be a miracle, she will be a virgin-mother. (Cf. Matt. 1:18) From then on all is clear. She has listened to the entire word of God. She sees what is asked of her. Now it is up to her to believe, and to reply. The angel awaits her consent.

What amazes us in the story of the Annunciation is the infinite respect which God Himself shows towards Mary—towards her person, her intelligence, her vow of virginity, her uneasiness, her free decision. This is what gives to Mary's acceptance its unique importance and incomparable grandeur. Never had earth replied to heaven—nor will it ever be able to again—with a *yes* like this one. *Here we have the mystery that was grasped by the faith of the primitive Church, that was to be confessed by the title* Theotokos, *and that the theologians were to express by saying that Mary is the most holy Mother of God, that she has been made proportionate to the sublime mission of giving birth, not only to the members of the Mystical Body, but to the divine Savior Himself, in so far as it was possible for a purely human creature to be so proportioned. The absolutely unique holiness of the Virgin Mary in the hidden order of grace is symbolized in the visible order by the absolutely unique miracle of her virginal conception.* The salutation *gratia plena*—full of grace— is only a pale resume of these unimaginable favors.[43]

The Magnificat—Mary knows that she stands at the center of time, at the point at which all the promises of the Old Covenant, since the time of Abraham terminate, and from which flow all the graces of salva-

---

thing like this *Salve gratia plena* addressed; it is reserved for Mary alone. For Mary would not have been frightened by the strangeness of this greeting if she had known of one like it that had been addressed to someone else (and, remember, she was versed in the Law, and was holy, and meditated daily on the words of the prophets)." *And Origen justifies the unheard of character of this greeting by the unbridgeable gulf which separates Jesus from John the Baptist, the Savior of the world from His precursor.*

[43] It is in the light of this primordial intuition that we must read the entire Bull *Ineffabilis;* otherwise we run the risk of an erroneous perspective and continual misunderstandings: "When the Fathers and writers of the Church had carefully reflected on the fact that the Most Blessed Virgin was called *full of grace* by the angel Gabriel, in the name and by the order of God, at the moment when He announced the sublime dignity of the Mother of God, they taught that this singular and solemn salutation, elsewhere unheard of, showed that the Mother of God was the seat of all the divine graces, and adorned with all the gifts of the Divine Spirit; that she was indeed an almost infinite treasury and inexhaustible abyss of these gifts; so that, never having been under the curse, and participating with her Son in an everlasting blessing, she merited to hear from the lips of Elizabeth, under the impulse of the Divine Spirit, 'Blessed art thou among women, and blessed is the fruit of thy womb.' "—*Acta Pii IX,* p. 609.

tion for the future, even till the end of time. She knows her own nothingness, that of herself she is nothing, that she owes everything to the Almighty. But she knows too that He has not left her outside of this extraordinary effusion of His love, that His shadow has fallen upon her, that He has done great things *for her,* that He is *her* Savior, that Elizabeth was right in proclaiming her *blessed* and *mother of God,* and that from this day forward *all generations* will call her blessed. The Angel of the Annunciation had told her that from the beginning she had been the object of God's benevolence. She did not know to what degree, and she was uneasy. Every man is loved by God more than he knows: St. Anne knew that she was loved, but did not know all that her child would be; Mary knew that she was loved, but not that she would be the mother of her God. But now, after her *yes* at the Annunciation, by the great light of the holiness demanded by the mystery of Jesus, she sees in retrospect the holiness of the more remote divine preparations for the Incarnation—from Abraham to John the Baptist, and of the final preparations, beginning with God's benevolence towards her. We would think that it was at this moment that she became conscious, with wonderment in her heart, of her own Immaculate Conception.[44]

THE CHALLENGES OF THE GOSPEL

Here we touch upon a very mysterious aspect of the Gospel. While providing us with the great principles of our faith, it furnishes at the same time texts which seem to endanger them, and even to contradict them, texts which will be a cause of scandal and downfall for many. It teaches us that the Word made flesh is truly God (John 1:1) and at the same time we hear Jesus confess that the Father is greater than He (John 14:28), and complain that His God has abandoned Him (Mark 15:34). It assures us that Jesus is in the form of God (Philip. 2:6), and at the same time tells us that no one knows the day nor the hour of the end of the world, not even the Son (Mark 13:32). St. Paul teaches us that a man is justified by faith without the works of the law (Rom. 3:28), and James, that man is justified by works, and not by faith alone (James 2:24), etc. Why these "apparent contradictions," these genuine difficulties, which Arianism was to use to deny the divinity of the Savior,

[44] Karl BARTH recognizes that, even according to Scripture, Mary has a place apart. His reproach to the Catholic Church, therefore, is not that it gives her a special place, but that, instead of doing this in the Lutheran perspective of a grace that is merely imputed, covering sin without destroying it, the Church does so in the traditional perspective of a real created grace, which eliminates the stain of sin: "We must not be surprised at what has been made of Mary in the Roman Catholic Church. . . . We must not be surprised because, in Sacred Scripture also, the figure of Mary is unquestionably set apart. It is, nevertheless, due to a profound misunderstanding that Mary has been exalted . . ." ("Quatre études bibliques," in *Foi et Vie,* nn. 85, 86, Paris, August-October 1936, p. 487). In order to deny Mary's real holiness, Protestantism is forced to deny the real holiness of grace itself.

and Protestantism to deny the possibility of a transfiguration of human activity by grace? Since God saw into the future from all eternity, and knew how these texts would be abused, could He not have taken precautions beforehand, cleared up the obscurities and forestalled the misunderstandings? Certainly, to a degree at least, He could have.[45] Then why did He not do it?

This difficulty is posed not only at the level of the Gospel *teaching,* but at the very heart of the Gospel *life.* Jesus, who brings us the mysteries of salvation, seems deliberately to raise up obstacles along the paths which lead to Him. He speaks in parables, He takes pleasure in healing on the Sabbath. His manner of dealing with souls, especially the greatest among them, seems to be that of which He gives us a glimpse in the case of the woman of Chanaan, to whom He would not even listen, whom He was unwilling to regard as a "child," whom He compared to the little dogs, whom He repelled externally in every way possible, but who, by the grace which He was pouring secretly into her heart, triumphed over all these affronts, so that her love grew, like a river whose level rises when its flow is checked (Matt. 15:21-28).

Here we have the answer to the question we have asked. The obstacles which stand in the way of the otherwise clear teachings of the Gospel, and check their free flow, are designed to raise their level for us, to draw attention to their power, and to make the Gospel truths penetrate into the world as by wave upon wave. Blessed are those who, instead of being scandalized, are able to discover in each case the providential reasons! [46] It should now be clear what we meant by the "challenges" in the Gospel,

[45] We say "to a degree," because we know well that by reason of the congenital weakness of human thought and language, above all with regard to the mysteries of salvation, not everything can be expressed beforehand, and that what would have cleared up certain misunderstandings would be liable to create new ones, either in the future or even immediately. If God wished *publicly* to preserve the primitive sense of the deposit, oral and written, there could scarcely be, as far as we can see, any solution but this: to accompany the deposit *publicly* throughout the ages with a divinely assisted commentary. But this possibility remains inaccessible to Protestantism.

[46] Cf. PASCAL, *Pensées,* Ed. Br. n. 684: "You cannot draw a handsome face except by reconciling all our contrarieties; it is not enough to employ a series of attractive qualities without harmonizing them with their opposites. To understand the meaning of an author, it is necessary to reconcile all the contrary passages. *Thus to understand Scripture, it is necessary to have a meaning in which all the contrary passages harmonize.* It is not enough to have one which fits all the similar passages; you must have one which reconciles even the contrary ones. Every author has a sense in which all the contrary passages harmonize, or he has no sense at all. You cannot assert the latter of Scripture and the prophets; they had indeed too much sense. *Therefore you must look for a meaning that reconciles* all the contrarieties." And n. 575: "Everything turns to good for the elect, even the obscurities of Scripture; for they honor them because of the divine lights in them." This is an application to the plane of salvation of the principle that is already valid on the plane of culture, and which A. J. TOYNBEE characterizes by the remark of Socrates at the end of the greater *Hippias*: "Beautiful things are difficult."

a propos of St. Luke's revelations about the Virgin Mary. Let us examine them to see what they can teach us.

When the Child was twelve years old, His parents lost Him in Jerusalem and found Him again in the Temple. It was then that He said to them: "Why were you searching for me? Did you not know that I must be about my Father's business?" *"And they did not understand the word that he spoke to them"* (Luke 2:49-50). His mother was certainly not ignorant of the fact that He must be about His Father's business, for the Angel had told her that He would be the *Son of the Most High,* and that He would reign over the house of Jacob forever (1:32, 33). Simeon had added that He would be the glory of Israel and the light of the nations (2:32). How could she have forgotten that He was God's Son more than her own? But she could as yet only glimpse obscurely the exigencies of the mission that would make her the mother of a Divine Savior. Why should He, in order to attend to His Father's business, separate Himself thus from her? Why must He do this work *without her?* She experienced then a mysterious trial, a very sorrowful night. It would be necessary for her to be separated from him, somewhat as He was to be separated from His Father when he cried out, "My God, my God, why hast Thou forsaken me?" (Mark 15:34).

Saint Mark narrates that once when Jesus was in a house, surrounded by a great crowd, He was accused by his enemies of being possessed by the devil. "And when His own people had heard of it, they went out to lay hold of Him. For they said ('ἔλεγον), 'He has gone mad.'. . . And they said to Him, 'Behold thy mother and thy brethren are outside seeking thee.' And He answered and said to them, *'Who are My mother and My brethren?'* And looking round on those who were sitting about Him, He said: *'Behold My mother and My brethren. For whoever does the will of God, he is My brother and My sister and mother'* " (Mark 3:21, 32-35). These words contain a lesson for those who gather around Jesus. Above and beyond the bonds of earthly relationship appear the bonds of a new spiritual relationship so resplendent that the former vanish out of sight in its presence, like a candle flame in the sunlight. The earthly bonds are not suppressed: the bonds between husband and wife, parents and children, master and servants will remain and be ennobled. But over and above them, mysterious bonds will form among the children of the Kingdom, to the point where the earthly bonds must be broken whenever they go counter to the spiritual bonds: "If anyone comes to Me, and does not hate his father and mother, and wife and children, and brothers and sisters, yes and even his own life, he cannot be My disciple" (Luke 14:26). These words contain another instruction, however, for his Mother, who never did anything but the will of God. She had come in order to share with Him the bitterness of derision, to take her stand visibly by His side at the moment when He began to be attacked visibly. Why then does He crush this token of her love? It is because the moment of His public life has come when Mary must no longer act visibly on the plane of temporal care by helping and defending Jesus, but only on the plane of spiritual relationship, on which she retains the first place. Never again in fact, does the Blessed Virgin draw near to console Her martyred Son. He will be treated as a blasphemer once again, and the soldiers of the governor also will look on Him as one mad; but Mary will stay at a distance, leaving Him in His solitude. She has understood that such a solitude is required for the redemption of the world.

St. Luke tells us that another time an unknown woman coming to the defense of Jesus, cried out, *"Blessed is the womb that bore Thee and the breasts that nourished Thee."* But He said: *"Yea, rather, blessed are they who hear the word of God and keep it"* (Luke 11:27-28). To "hear the word of God and keep it," is exactly what this great-hearted woman has just done. And Jesus, in return, makes her understand that this is precisely what He loves in His Mother. The woman has glorified Mary, but does she know well enough what Mary is? She deserves to know more. From now on she must be able to greet Mary as Elizabeth did: "Blessed is she who has believed that the things promised her by the Lord shall be accomplished" (Luke 1:45), or as the Church does at the *Magnificat*: "Behold, henceforth all generations shall call me blessed (Luke 1:48).

If we know how to read aright the "challenges" we meet in the Synoptics, and grasp their true significance, we will see that, instead of obstructing, they bring out better the light of the great texts of the Annunciation, the Visitation, and the *Magnificat*, which show us in Mary, the Church's holiness carried to its limit, and proportioned to the office of begetting not merely the members of the Mystical Body, but Christ its divine Head. This great vision we will re-discover in St. John.

THE TEXTS OF ST. JOHN

The Protogospel (Gen. 3:15) taken by itself is too implicit and obscure to provide a point of departure for Mariology. According to the Hebrew, this text should be translated, "I will put enmity between thee and the woman, between thy offspring and hers. It (the offspring of the woman) shall bruise thy head and thou shalt bruise its heel." To take it as it stands, the least one can say of this passage is that it opens a messianic perspective into which the dogma of the Redemption, and even the dogma of the Immaculate Conception, can be inserted without conflict. The first woman, who till then had been immaculate, was led into sin by the demon. But the victory of the demon is not decisive. God does not abandon our first parents; He promises that they will be avenged, and declares that the Woman and her posterity will continue the struggle.

The Septuagint replaces this reference to the posterity of the Woman by a masculine pronoun, thus designating a son of the Woman as conqueror of the serpent:[47] "I will put enmity between you and the woman, and between your posterity and hers. *He* (αὐτός) will attack your head, and you will attack his heel." [48] Without any doubt this specification is important: it testifies to the progress of the messianic knowledge under the constant influence of the prophets.[49] Such is the text that must have been read by St. John, who cites the Old Testament habitually according to the Septuagint.

But insofar as John was an apostle, he could penetrate the meaning of the Protogospel more perfectly than the authors of the Septuagint. He can disclose to us the ultimate meaning, the profound literal sense, which it had in the mind of God from the beginning, but which had remained hidden until then.[50] This he does in the Apocalypse: here the prophecy of Genesis, placed under a higher light, discloses its hidden content. The

[47] Cf. Gal. 3:16. "The promises were made to Abraham and to his offspring. He does not say, *And to his offsprings,* as if there were many; but as of one, *And to thy offspring,* who is Christ."

[48] Hence the Christological interpretation of the Protogospel proposed by some of the Fathers, such as Irenaeus, Cyprian, Epiphanius, *et al.*
The Latin translation, no doubt influenced by the parallel that was early introduced between Eve and Mary, was to substitute a feminine pronoun for the masculine of the Greek: "I will put enmity between thee and the woman, between thy seed and her seed. *She* (*ipsa, the woman*) shall crush thy head, and thou shalt lie in wait for her heel." Cf. R. De Vaux, *La Genèse,* Paris, 1951, pp. 47, 48. Hence the direct application of this text to the Virgin Mary by some of the Latin fathers, who are, however, not very numerous. Cf. Martin Jugie, *L'Immaculée Conception* . . . , p. 44, note 1. For St. Augustine, the feminine in the Latin text signifies the Church: "*Ipsa tuum observabit caput, et tu ejus calcaneum. O Ecclesia, caput serpentis observa. Quod est caput serpentis? Prima peccati suggestio . . .*"—*Enarr. in Psalm.* CIII, Sermo IV, n. 6.
The preambles of the Bull *Ineffabilis* were intentionally restricted to general terms: "The Fathers and *ecclesiastical writers* . . ."—"Patres, Ecclesiaeque Scriptores . . . docuere, divino hoc oraculo clare aperteque praemonstratum fuisse misericordem humani generis Redemptorem, scilicet Unigenitum Dei Filium Christum Jesum, ac designatam beatissimam Ejus Matrem Virginem Mariam, ac simul ipsissimas utriusque contra diabolum inimicitias insigniter expressas."—*Acta Pii IX,* p. 607. Cf. chapter VII of the present volume, p. 314.

[49] The Church has recognized the translation of the Septuagint as *authoritative,* which means that its substantial integrity is guaranteed. The question has even been raised recently, whether we should not speak of the charism of *inspiration* in connection with insights for which we are indebted to it. Cf. D. B., *Revue Biblique,* 1952, p. 610; P. Auvray, "Comment se pose le problème de l'inspiration des Septante," *Revue Biblique,* 1952, p. 321.

[50] "No doubt it will appear superfluous to ask again, in what sense John understood Gen. 3:15. He understood it according to the interpretation of the Septuagint, in the strictly literal, but *plenary* sense: that is to say, if not according to a clear intention of the inspired author, at least according to the profound thought of God. The Serpent was Satan, and the offspring of the Woman was the Messias."— F. M. Braun, *La Mère des fidèles* . . . , p. 95. "When the Apostles, enlightened by the events of the Gospel period, and by the Spirit who was given to them for the understanding of Scripture, comment on the prophetic texts, the plenary interpretation which they give rests on a solid basis." *Ibid.* p. 187.

Apocalypse gives us the authorized interpretation, the apostolic exegesis, of the Protogospel.

Christ appears at the central point of the history of salvation. He ranks first, no doubt, in the order of values; but in the chronological order He is preceded by His Church which, by virtue of a mysterious anticipation, is already His work. The Church was created in order to give birth to the members of His Mystical Body; this was her work before Christ and after Him; but at one moment absolutely unique in her history, when she was represented by the Virgin Mary, she gave birth to Christ Himself. This is St. John's great vision, and is also at the roots of St. Augustine's work on the City of God.

The mysterious Woman who appears upon the screen of heaven, clothed with the signs of the divine power, yet pursued by the fire-colored Dragon, is the Church.[51] She has existed since the beginning of the world; but at the supreme moment of her existence, at the time of great trials and the "sufferings of the Messias," behold, in the person of Mary, the Church gives birth to Christ. (Apoc. 12:1-2)

The Dragon waits before the woman. He senses that the messianic Child is the supreme enemy announced by the prophecies (Gen. 3:15; Ps. 2:9). He will attack the Child: the Gospel shows us Satan trying to tempt Jesus in the desert (Matt. 4:1-11) and the Prince of this world plotting His death (John 14:30). But the child will escape from his clutches on the day of His Ascension, and the Church, transformed by its own birth, will then enter upon a new age, in which it will be no longer in the process of formation, but in the state of fulfillment. It flees to the desert, being *in* the world without being *of* the world (John 17: 16, 18). The desert, although a place of trial, is also the place where God provides and bestows His divine intimacies (Exod. 19:4; Osee 2:16). The Church will stay there all during the Messianic Era, which lasts from the Ascension to the Parousia, and which, measured from the time of her trials, is represented by the figure of 1260 days, or forty-two months, or three and one-half years (Apoc. 12:4-6).

Christ's Ascension into heaven to prepare a place for us (John 14:3) and send us the Paraclete (16:7) marks, on the one hand, the Church's entrance into the Age of the Holy Spirit, and, on the other hand, inaugurates the final downfall of the Dragon, who, understanding that his time is limited, prepares to intensify his violence (Apoc. 12:9-12). Pursued by him, the Church hides herself in the wilderness for the three and one-half years of the Messianic Era. The Dragon rages against her posterity, but God, Who watches over her, knows how to provide for her needs (Apoc. 12:13-17).

The final victory will come at the end of the Messianic Era, which,

[51] Cf. E. B. ALLO, o.p., *L'Apocalypse*, Paris, 1933, pp. 177 ff.

measured this time from the time of the Church's consolidation and interior fullness, is represented by the figure of a thousand years. Then, adorned like a bride going to meet her spouse, the Church, the Holy City, the new Jerusalem, will come down from heaven to meet the earth (Apoc. 21:1-4).

Here then is the Protogospel, i.e., the combat between the Woman and the Serpent, reinterpreted and transmitted (παράδοσις) by the Apostle, in the form in which it was contemplated by the initial faith of the Christian Church. No doubt the Apostle read his own text under the superior and incommunicable light of an immediate revelation (ἀποκάλυψις);[52] but even for us this text is immensely instructive, for it gives the whole history of Christian Salvation viewed in relation to the assaults of evil.

Three features of this grandiose vision are to be underscored:

The phases of the history of the Woman. The struggle between the Woman and the Serpent begins, the Protogospel informs us, the day after the fall. The struggle continues after the Ascension; the Woman remains in the world, without being of the world, to the very end of the Messianic Era, when she will be glorified. The history of the Woman, then, is the history of the Church, with three phases—one before Christ, one in the time of Christ, and one after Christ.

The mysterious solidarity between the cause of Christ and the cause of the Woman. They are together the object of a single hatred. They are united in the same struggle, the same destiny, the same victory—Christ as principle, the Woman as His handiwork. The struggle, the destiny and the victory of Christ are those of holiness in its source; the struggle, destiny and victory of the Woman are those of holiness participated. They possess the same weapons; that is to say, if Christ is purity and exemption from sin as their source, the Woman is purity and exemption from sin by participation; if Christ is the Redeemer, the Woman is called in Him and by Him to be co-redemptrix; if Christ rises from the dead in glory, the Woman is drawn after Him into glory.

The whole Church recapitulated in the Virgin Mary. Never is the Woman so close to Christ as at that incredible moment, center of the whole history of salvation, when, in the person of the Blessed Virgin, she must give birth to Christ Himself, aid Him during His childhood, and find Him again at the cross. At no other time is she so exceptionally holy, so entirely preserved from sin, so consciously co-redemptrix of the world, or so fully identified with Christ in His victory over death, the "last enemy."

Such is the intuition, translated, of course, into explicit terms, of the relationships which exist between Christ and His handiwork—the Church and Mary—which the faith of the first Christian communities was able to perceive *obscurely, instinctively,* yet *powerfully,* in the grand apocalyptic

[52] Cf. p. 6 ff.

vision, which is, in the same way as the story told by St. Luke,[53] at the beginning of the whole development of Marian doctrine.

Let us note here that there is no question of St. John's setting up a parallel between Eve, docile to the Serpent, and Mary, docile to the Angel, as the Fathers were soon to do in associating the Protogospel with the Gospel of St. Luke. St. John does not go back over the incident of the Fall; he simply reveals the destiny of that portion of the human progeny which, gathered together in Christ, takes up the struggle against the Serpent and ends by conquering him. There is indeed in St. John matter for a parallel, but it is the parallel between the Woman at the time when she can give birth only to the faithful, and the Woman at the unique moment when, in the person of the Blessed Virgin, she can give birth to Christ.

The Apocalypse brings out the mysterious solidarity, in the drama of salvation, between Christ and the Woman, in these two realizations of the Woman: one, collective, in which she gives birth to "those who keep the commandments of God and have the testimony of Jesus" (Apoc. 12:17), the other, personal and supereminent, in which she gives birth to the Messias and accompanies Him up to the moment of His Ascension. How then, can we be surprised to find the Virgin Mary in the Fourth Gospel? St. John records two solemn words of Jesus to His Mother: the first at Cana of Galilee, when He begins His public life (John 2:1-11); the second at the cross, when He completes it (John 19:25-27). Their relationship is too profound, and the Evangelist's intention of bringing them together too evident, for us to be able to explain them separately. They can be understood only when taken together.[54]

Cana.—The meaning of the drama of Cana overflows the confines of the letter, and disconcerts an immediate exegesis. One thing at least is clear. To us, as we read this story, Jesus seems to separate Himself from His mother and to rebuff her; Mary, on the contrary, understood immediately from her Son's words that her prayer was granted. Jesus' mysterious reply contains both an assertion of the distance between Him and her, and an assurance that her request will be granted. *Woman* is a solemn word. It indicates a distance. During the time of His hidden life, Jesus conducted Himself as the Son of Man, busied Himself with the things of earth, and was obedient to His parents. Now, as His public life is about to begin, He will act as the Son of God, busy Himself with the things of His Father, and take the initiative—as He had already done once, for a moment,

---

[53] Resemblances have been pointed out between the gospels of Luke and John which reveal a profounder relationship than is ordinarily supposed. They seem to be explained by a mutual influence: from John to Luke by oral tradition, and from Luke to John by way of Scripture. The two evangelists have common sources of information, which go back to Mary herself. Cf. F. M. Braun, *La Mère des Fidèles* . . . pp. 29, 114-115.

[54] Cf. *Les sept paroles du Christ en croix*, Paris, 1952, pp. 63 ff., the text of which is here summarized.

during His childhood (Luke 2:49). *And this will be, for Him and His Mother, the time of separation:* "*What is that to me and to thee?*" This lack of wine, these things on the level of earthly needs, what difference shall they make from now on for you and Me? I can indeed, if you wish, take this occasion to work a miracle, and advance the hour of my public life. The hour *to manifest myself* has not yet come, but because of your intercession I will anticipate it; by the same stroke, the hour of my death shall be anticipated. —Or there is another way to understand this text: My hour *to die* has not yet come—the hour when I will hear and even anticipate your every request (announcement of their future meeting on Calvary); but even now—since you have made this request—I can grant it to you.[55] In either of these readings—whether He refers to the hour of his manifestation or to the hour of his death, Jesus acquiesces to his Mother's request, and she understands: "*Do whatever He tells you.*" He works the miracle, He acts as God, He manifests His glory. Nothing else so great will ever be said about the intercessary power of the Blessed Virgin as the Gospel story of Cana. It is the hour of Mary's glory hidden in the glory of Jesus.

Calvary. The Apocalypse shows us the Woman as closely associated with Christ's combat and fully participating in it, especially when, in the person of the Virgin Mary, she is contemporaneous with the days that stretch from His birth to His Ascension. The supreme moment of Jesus' conflict with the one He calls the *Prince of this World* (John 12:31; 14:30), the hour which is His *par excellence* (12:23, 27) is that of His dying on the Cross in order to draw all men to Himself (3:14; 8:28; 12:32-33). How then could we think, even if we remained simply in the perspective opened by the Apocalypse, that the Blessed Virgin was not closely associated and wholly participant in the act of the Redemption of the world, during that decisive hour from Christmas to the Ascension?[56] According to St. Luke, God willed for Mary to be fully

---

[55] This is the interpretation of J. H. NEWMAN, *Certain difficulties felt by Anglicans in Catholic teaching, considered in a letter addressed to the Rev. E. B. Pusey, D.D., on occasion of his Eirenikon of 1864,* London, 1876, p. 72 f.: ". . . if on one occasion He seems to repel His Mother when she told Him that wine was wanting for the guests at the marriage feast, it is obvious to remark on it, that by saying that she was then separated from Him ('What have I to do with thee?') *because* His hour was not yet come, He implied that, when that hour was come, such separation would be at an end."

The very dense thought of St. IRENAEUS apparently seeks to embrace the two interpretations: "Everything is foreknown by the Father, but is accomplished by the Son (only) at the proper time, as is right and fitting. Hence, when Mary was over-eager for the marvelous *sign of the wine,* and wanted to partake of the *cup of the compendium* before the time, the Lord repulsed her untimely haste, saying, 'Woman, what is that to Me and to thee? My hour has not yet come.' He was waiting for the hour which the Father had foreknown." *Adversus haereses,* III, 16, 7 (*P.G.,* 7, 926).

[56] Père BRAUN, *La Mère des fidèles* . . . , pp. 77 ff., thinks it possible here to enter into exegetical precisions which must necessarily be of a conjectural and fragile char-

enlightened about the Mystery of Salvation, and to give it her holy consent as it began in the Incarnation. How then would He not will that she should be fully enlightened and give her holy consent to it at its consummation in the Redemption? We are not then surprised when St. John's Gospel shows us Mary at the foot of the cross. She is there with some companions and with the evangelist himself. With all the power of their souls they join in the supplication offered by Jesus. If Christians can have any part with Christ and in Christ in the redemption of the world, it is realized with special intensity in the Church assembled there around Jesus Crucified; and in Mary it is realized more intensely than in the others, and in fact, supremely. And it is precisely because Mary entered so deeply into the mystery of the world's redemption that Jesus, speaking now as we have seen Him do at Cana, as the Son of God solicitous about His Father's affairs, tells Mary that Her prayer has been heard; just as He gives men a rebirth into the life of love through the infinitely redemptive intercession of His Passion, so she too, the first among the redeemed, will be allowed, along with Him, to give birth to them through the coredemptive intercession, finite but nonetheless universal, of Her Compassion. Because She is the holy Mother of God our Savior, she is able in and with Him to become the Mother of the members of His Mystical Body, the Mother of the faithful, of the disciples of Jesus, even of the beloved disciple himself: "When Jesus therefore saw His mother and the disciple standing by whom He loved, He said to His mother: 'Woman, behold thy son.' Then, He said to the disciple, 'Behold thy mother'" (John 19:26-27).

These words indeed imply more than they say and are full of mystery. The prophetic light in which the Apostle himself read them is wanting to us. We are unable, we admit, to extricate their meaning, except by taking them in conjunction with what is given us in the Apocalypse, in the incident of Cana, and in the Gospel of St. Luke. The Church had to acquire through the ages an experimental consciousness of the coredemptive mission of Christians and of her own coredemptive mission with regard to the world, to be able to grasp the full sublimity and extent of Mary's coredemptive mission. Only then would Jesus' words reveal their hidden meaning. As we have said, the development of dogma can enable us to

---

acter. He sees in Cana (according to the second interpretation that we have indicated) the announcement of the future meeting on Calvary. He remarks that, in the course of his account of the Passion (19:17-42), St. John expressly recounts the episodes of the Passion of the Old Testament prophecies: the division of Christ's garments (24), the sponge dipped in vinegar (28), the burial (36-37). Would there not also be an Old Testament prophecy corresponding to the meeting of Jesus and His Mother (25-27)? If there is, the only possibility is the Protogospel: the Serpent is Satan, the Woman is Mary, the offspring of the Woman in combat with the Serpent is Christ. The Protogospel, reinterpreted by St. John in the Apocalypse, would then figure in the Fourth Gospel, not only as the background against which the entire drama of the Passion unfolds, but also as very precisely designated by John 19:25-27.

attain in some domains a knowledge of the deposit of revelation that is clearer and more explicit, not indeed than that of the Apostles, but than that of the primitive Church. It seems that the words of Jesus to His Mother can at last in our time shine with their full brilliance. For the faith of the contemporary Church, they glow like stars.

The Basis of Marian Doctrine in Divine Revelation

The fundamental revelation at the source of all Marian doctrine has been found to lie in the written Tradition as seen by the initial faith of the Church.

We have been careful constantly to respect the analogy of faith, never to isolate the data concerning the Blessed Virgin, but to give them their true place, and their full place, in the revelation of the doctrine of salvation. Christ alone is source. The entire work of salvation derives from Him. He is Head of the whole Mystical Body. This is the first principle of our Marian doctrine.

The work of salvation has two realizations: one collective, in the Church; the other personal, in the Virgin Mary. By hearing the Word of God and keeping it, by doing the will of the heavenly Father, by waging war against Satan, the Church is the holy mother of the members of the Mystical Body. Likewise, the Virgin Mary, by hearing the word of God and keeping it, by doing the will of the heavenly Father and waging war against Satan, is the holy Mother of the divine Messias, the Head of the entire Mystical Body; and by extension she is mother also of the disciples, even of the "beloved disciple." Because of this fact, Mary represents, in the Mystical Body, a holiness that cannot possibly be equalled. Between the holiness God has prepared for the bearing of the members of the Mystical Body, and the holiness He has prepared for the bearing of Christ Himself, there is a distance which cannot be traversed except by an extrapolation, by what is equivalent to a passage to the limit. A sign of this unprecedented discontinuity in the hidden order of sanctity is furnished by the gospel in the unprecedented and unrepeated miracle of the virginal motherhood. In a word, according to the testimony of Scripture, Mary alone, among all the daughters of men, is the holy Mother of the Divine Savior. This is the second principle of our Marian doctrine.

We are now in possession of the revealed foundation of Marian doctrine. This was expected, we recall, 1) to have an *explicit meaning;* 2) to *say nothing* explicitly, however, concerning the Immaculate Conception, the Coredemptive Mediation, or the Assumption; 3) to deny nothing which these dogmas would later formulate; 4) to be capable of *overcoming* the challenges it would meet in the course of time, *and thus to be explicited according to a rigorous logic, but at the interior of the transluminous night of faith, and thanks to the infallible assistance of the Holy Spirit.*

III

NOTE ON THE VICISSITUDES UNDERGONE BY THE DOGMA OF THE IMMACULATE CONCEPTION IN THE COURSE OF ITS EXPLICITATION

Cardinal Newman thought that the Immaculate Conception could be deduced from the parallel drawn by the Fathers of the Church between Mary and Eve. He recalled that, for the Fathers, grace was an interior reality and not, as the Protestants were to say, a purely extrinsic favor; he proceeded:

> . . . if Eve had this supernatural inward gift given her from the first moment of her personal existence, is it possible to deny that Mary too had this gift from the very first moment of her personal existence? I do not know how to resist this inference:—well, this is simply and literally the doctrine of the Immaculate Conception.[57]

What is to be thought of this proof? We believe that, in the form in which it is here presented, it has no value other than that of an argument of fittingness.[58] If one wished to go further and reach the true basis of the argument, it would be necessary to show *what is meant concretely in the Gospel perspective by the 'recapitulation' of Eve in Mary;* it would then be seen at once that Mary is the holy mother of our Divine Savior—which is the only solid foundation for the whole of Mariology.

Now, it is a central truth of Holy Scripture that salvation is offered to all men through the Redemption wrought by Christ, and that absolutely no one can be holy or saved except by the price of His death and the pouring out of His blood on the Cross. "Christ died for all, in order that they who are alive may live no longer for themselves . . ." (II Cor. 5:15).

Hence it must be held as an absolutely fundamental truth concerning the Blessed Virgin, that, if she is holy and is saved, this cannot be in any other way than by the Redemption. But compensation, expiation or redemption are possible only with reference to a sin. Hence arises the supreme challenge to Mary's holiness: if she was redeemed from sin, how can she be all-holy? This is the apparently insoluble problem which was to occupy several centuries of Christian theologians. Two questions were to be raised successively: 1) From what sin was Mary redeemed? 2) Is

---

[57] J. H. NEWMAN, *Certain difficulties felt by Anglicans in Catholic teaching, considered in a letter addressed to the Rev. E. B. Pusey, D.D., on occasion of his Eirenikon of 1864,* London, 1876, p. 45.

[58] We do not believe that an 'argument from fittingness' (which some call "argument from reason") has any value in itself. Its only value, which is that of a *sign,* consists in referring us to a more hidden, preconceptual, unformulated intuition, founded on the Gospel.

there any possible way for her to be redeemed from sin and yet be truly spotless and always in the state of grace?

With regard to the first question, the notion which comes immediately to mind when one speaks of sin is that of *personal* or *actual* sin. It was with this that the Oriental Fathers and writers were chiefly concerned. Those among them who posed the question: From what sin was Mary redeemed? —attempted to reply by seeking out an occasion when personal or actual sin could have entered into the life of the Blessed Virgin. But this put them in an impasse, for if Mary had been redeemed from personal and actual sin, from a sin which she had committed, it would be impossible, even contradictory, for her to have been always spotless and in the state of grace. As a result, these writers were compelled to minimize the Gospel testimonies about Mary's holiness, and so to isolate themselves on this point from the common teaching of the Church.[59]

The solemn proclamation of the absolute holiness of the *Theotokos* at the Council of Ephesus soon rendered this position untenable. Thereafter, the attempts to imagine defects in Mary became fewer and fewer; but when Greek thought began to praise the stainless purity of the *Panhagia*, and to exalt her altogether exceptional holiness and virtues, it did so without concern for the principle of the necessity of her redemption by Christ.

At first this was simply a matter of setting aside the question, or postponing it, rather than of giving it a negative answer; but the situation was liable, if prolonged, to create misunderstandings. There was danger that the delay might turn into forgetfulness, and silence into a denial. This is in fact what took place, precisely at the moment when, to explain the Blessed Virgin's gifts, a *theology of exception* was invented, *placing Mary outside the order of Redemption.* Mary, it was said, was foreseen by God from all eternity as one who would be all pure and without stain; but she pertains to a plan which separates her alone of all human beings from the compensation which Christ, dying upon the Cross, offered for the sin and for the salvation of the world: for she did not need to be redeemed by the blood of her Son. There was no longer any question of associating Mary with sin, *but neither was there question of her redemption.* It had become impossible to solve the initial problem, that is, to reconcile the universality of the Redemption with the absolute sanctity of Mary; and, in effect, it was the dogma of the universality of the Redemption which was abandoned in this case.

THE HOLINESS OF MARY IN GREEK THEOLOGY
DURING THE BYZANTINE AND DISSIDENT PERIOD

After Ephesus and the patristic era, during the period called Byzantine, the Greeks continued to proclaim Mary's exceptional holiness: "She has

[59] On the Immaculate Conception in the Fathers of the Eastern Church, see below, chaps. ii and iii.

always been in the state of grace before God"; "she was like Eve before the first sin"; "she was justified from her mother's womb"; "she was ever blessed, the unique blessed one." Father Jugie believes that he can find in such expressions a certain equivalent, positively expressed, of the doctrine of Mary's exemption from original sin from the first moment of her conception, which is more rigorously formulated in negative fashion.[60]

To praise the absolute holiness of the Blessed Virgin is equivalent to affirming that she was preserved from original sin, on condition that one believes in original sin. Did the Greek Fathers believe in this doctrine? Some have claimed that they were ignorant of it. Turmel wrote in 1907:

> At the time of St. John Damascene, the Greek Church was still in ignorance of the dogma of hereditary fault. It could not, then, have dreamed of exempting the Holy Virgin from a law it did not know of.[61]

Father Jugie, after enumerating the various expressions used by the Greek Fathers to describe the fallen state in which we are held from our origin, asks: "Do they not sufficiently express the idea of original culpability when they say that we have all been *accursed, condemned in Adam; that we all participate in the debt* which our first parent owes to the divine justice; that Adam lost for himself and for us divine grace and friendship?"[62] He points out that the word ἁμαρτία, which many of the Fathers reserve for actual sin, is the very one which the Cappadocians use to indicate the blemish we have from Adam.[63] He finds significant texts even in the first Fathers. Irenaeus writes:

> The Word was made flesh in order to destroy death and restore life to man. For we were in the bonds of sin, and came into the world covered with guilt and subject to death.[64]

According to Origen:

> Every soul born in the flesh is stained with sin and iniquity; hence it has been said . . . "no one is pure of stain, not even the child of one day." Moreover, since the Church baptises for the remission of sins, it can be asked why baptism is given to infants, in accordance with the Church's practice? For if infants had no need of remission or indulgence, the grace of baptism would seem to be pointless in their case.[65]

[60] M. Jugie, *L'Immaculée Conception dans l'Ecriture Sainte et dans la théologie orientale*, Paris, 1952, p. 473. (*Translator's note:* in the following pages reference will be made to this work in the case of texts given by it and which cannot be found in widely available editions.)

[61] Cited by M. Jugie, *ibid.*, p. 3.

[62] *Ibid.*, p. 28.

[63] *Ibid.*, p. 30.

[64] St. Irenaeus, *Proof of the apostolic preaching*, 37 (*P.O.*, 12, 775; cited by M. Jugie, *L'Immaculée Conception* . . . , pp. 28-29.

[65] Origen, *In Leviticum, Hom. VIII*, 3 (*P.G.*, 12, 496AB).

According to Basil: "Adam, eating what was forbidden, transmitted sin (to others)." [66] According to Gregory of Nyssa: "Man is soiled by sin, which is congenital to human nature, according to the word of Scripture, 'My mother conceived me in sin.' " [67]

After examining these texts and others as well in his article in the *Dictionnaire de Théologie Catholique,* Bishop A. Gaudel concludes:

> If the Greek Fathers, while affirming very explicitly that we all undergo the *punishment* of Adam's sin, were far less explicit in affirming that we inherit his *sin* itself, this is because they had not so clear a conception of the transmission of the guilt as of the punishment of the first sin. For most of them, it sufficed to acknowledge a mysterious envelopment of his descendants in the person of Adam, the sinner. We must add that men like Irenaeus, Origen, Didymus and Mark the Hermit had a more precise notion of the guilt transmitted by Adam to his descendants, one that approached that which the Church consecrated in opposition to Pelagianism. Only Theodore of Mopsuestia, in the Eastern Church up to the time of the Pelagian controversy, denies original sin. [68]

To the degree that this is so, the affirmation of the Blessed Virgin's absolute holiness by the Greek Fathers is equivalent to the recognition of the privilege by which Mary has been exempt from original sin from her conception. Her absolute holiness is acknowledged; however, nothing is said of her redemption by Christ. The latter is not denied, it is simply put in parentheses, and the dilemma, *holiness or redemption* of the Blessed Virgin continues to weigh silently on Christian thought.

When the dissident Greek Orthodox Church posed the question of original sin in Mary's case, an inclination began to take shape to explain her initial holiness, not by a purely gratuitous gift antecedent to all merit, but, on the contrary, by free meritorious acts, either of her ancestors or of herself. Thus the tendency to glorify the Blessed Virgin began to diverge from the Catholic line of thought not only by avoiding the problem of Mary's dependence on the Cross of Christ, but also by failing to see, at the source of Mary's greatness, a divine intervention anterior to all human initiatives.

No positive deviation is noticeable yet in Photius († 897); but according to Gregory Palamas († 1359) the purity of the Blessed Virgin is the result of the active holiness of her ancestors:

> . . . while the Virgin from whom is Christ according to the flesh, is of Adam's flesh and seed, she is also from the Holy Spirit, by whom (her ancestors), worthy men chosen out of each generation, were, from the beginning, purified in various ways. [69]

---

[66] St. BASIL, *Hom. VIII, 7 (P.G.,* 31, 324C).

[67] 'Ρύπος δὲ ἀνθρώπου ἡ ἁμαρτία, ἡ συναποτικτομένη τῇ ἀνθρωπίνῃ φύσει, 'ὅτι ἐν ἁμαρτίαις ἐκίσσησε με ἡ μήτηρ μου. *In Psalm VI (P.G.,* XLIV, 609D).

[68] A. GAUDEL, "Péché originel," col. 363.

[69] Gregory PALAMAS, *In Christi genealogiam,* 3 (SOPHOCLIS edition, 216; cited by M. JUGIE, *Immaculée Conception . . .* p. 228, n. 1).

According to Nicholas Cabasilas († after 1396), Mary had not received gifts superior to those of Adam or of other men to start with, but she succeeded in profiting to the fullest degree from the common grace, so that:

> . . . of all human beings in the past or yet to come, the Blessed Virgin alone preserved the human 'form' in all its splendor, pure of all alien 'form.' For none of the others, says the prophet, is pure of uncleanness.[70]

Another tendency, according to which Mary was not totally exempt from sin, found acceptance in the declaration of the Metropolitan Sergius of Moscow, Sept. 8-21, 1932:

> The Orthodox Church does not admit the Catholic teaching on the Immaculate Conception of the Virgin Mary; this conception is called 'immaculate,' not in a *particular* sense, but in a *relative* sense, just as every birth from saintly parents can be called immaculate coming as a result of their prayer and the blessing of God, with the empire of universal concupiscence almost suppressed in it. Faithful to the Word of God and to the universal tradition, Our Church seeks the foundation of the veneration of the Mother of God, not in the beginning of her earthly life, her *conception,* but on the contrary in her *dormition.*[71]

No doubt such a notion allows us to speak of Mary as being redeemed by Christ; but it implies that she was stained by original sin. Thus, at no time does Eastern thought succeed in reconciling the spotless purity of the Blessed Virgin, on the one hand, and the necessity of her redemption by Christ on the other. Hence we dare to say that the testimony which the Orient has rendered down through the ages to the spotless sanctity of the *Theotokos,* as moving and solemn and *authentic* as it indeed is, nevertheless implies, to our mind, a certain silence, and conceals a defeat on which Protestantism can capitalize under pretext of defending the rights of Christ. And only a reunion of the dissident Orient with the One Church could free the Marian doctrine of the East from all misunderstanding.

The Latin Church: Sinlessness and Redemption Reconciled

In the very period in which the dignity of the *Theotokos* was being proclaimed at the Council of Ephseus, there arose the Pelagian heresy, which soon obliged the faithful to attain a deeper awareness of the nature of original sin and of its transmission. In this development, the West, due especially to the genius of St. Augustine, had a preponderant part. From then on, the problem which had been posed by the Fathers of the Eastern Church shifted to a different ground. While Mary must have been

---

[70] Nicholas Cabasilas, *Homil. in Nativ.,* 6 (*P.O.,* 19, 482; cited by M. Jugie, *Immaculée Conception* . . . p. 250 n. 1).

[71] *Translator's note:* The English translation of this declaration has been made from the French translation given by Msgr. Journet, which was taken originally from *Unitas,* janvier-février 1953, p. 6, and reproduced also in *Nova et Vetera,* 1953, p. 67.

redeemed from sin, it was certainly not from a personal or actual sin, a sin *committed* by her—this would be incompatible with her dignity as Mother of God. The question could only be raised with reference to original sin, which is transmitted, and which—St. Paul assures us—affects all men. One had to reply without hesitation, that Mary was redeemed from it. But would this be possible if she had not previously contracted it? Here we have the ultimate challenge to Mary's sanctity—one which was not to be resolved in a day, and which was to receive its reply in the definition of the dogma of the Immaculate Conception.

The Pelagian heresy reduced all sin to actual sin, and consequently denied the possibility of a sin of nature transmitted from Adam by way of generation. In answer, St. Augustine pointed out that Adam had lost, not only for himself, but also for his descendants, the grace and holiness he had received from God. That is to say that his personal sin had brought about a sin of nature, an *original* sin.

This latter consists chiefly in the privation of grace; but what place is to be assigned in its definition to concupiscence? and how is its transmission to be conceived? These points were not yet sufficiently clear, and as a result misunderstandings arose to retard the progress of Marian doctrine.

The notion came to be accepted that the only way to escape original sin would be to be born not *"ex virili semine."* On such an hypothesis, the miracle of Mary's virginal motherhood would suffice to explain the initial purity of Jesus; but in order to affirm that Mary was exempt from original sin, one would be obliged, by the same principle, to suppose that Saint Anne was also a virgin mother. Neither St. Bernard[72] nor St. Albert the Great[73] would admit this.[74]

With Alexander of Hales, St. Bonaventure and St. Thomas, we are brought back to the heart of the problem. According to the first, "if the Blessed Virgin had not been conceived in sin, she would not have been a captive of sin . . . therefore she would not need redemption."[75] The idea of safeguarding the universality of the Redemption is likewise the master idea of St. Thomas. If he rejects the opinion that the Blessed Virgin "was never touched by the contagion of original sin," "had never incurred the original blemish," "was sanctified before the instant of her animation,"

[72] For the interpretation of St. BERNARD's letter (CLXXIV) to the canons of Lyons, see X. LE BACHELET, "Immaculée Conception," *DTC*, col. 1014; cf. col. 997.

[73] For the interpretation of St. ALBERT, *III Sent.*, dist. 3, A, art. 4 and art. 5, see Marie-Albert GENEVOIS, O.P., *Bible mariale et mariologie de saint Albert-le-Grand*, St-Maximin, 1934, pp. 183-184.

[74] This view was summed up in the maxim, *Quomodo peccatum non fuit, ubi libido non defuit?* Cf. chapter V of the present volume, p. 174.

[75] "Item, si B. Virgo non fuisset concepta in peccato, ergo non fuisset obligata peccato nec habuisset reatum peccati; . . . ergo ipsa non indigeret redemptione per Christum, quod secundum fidem catholicam non est ponendum." *Summa theologiae*, III, p. 1, tr. 2, q. 2 m. 2, c. 1, a. 2: "Utrum B. Virgo in conceptione potuerit sanctificari." Quarracchi ed., 4, p. 113e. Cf. St. BONAVENTURE *III Sent.*, dist. 3, p. 1, a. 1, q. 2.

it is because, according to that same opinion, the Blessed Virgin *"would not then have needed the Redemption and Salvation which comes through Christ."* [76]

It was at this moment that the dilemma of choosing between Mary's holiness and her redemption was most keenly felt. Those who opted for her holiness had had the time to erect a vast theology, according to which Mary, like Eve in the earthly paradise, stood apart from the entire plan for the Redemption of the world.[77] *A propos* of the Virgin Mary, they dared to contest the divinely revealed universality of salvation through Christ. They placed Mary outside and above the plan of Redemption. Unlike the Church, which exists only beneath the Cross of Christ, Mary is independent of the Cross, and thereby separated from the Church. The Blessed Virgin could be exalted endlessly in this way, but she would remain uprooted from redeemed humanity and disjoined from the Church: she would not be the first among the redeemed. Such a conception glorifies Mary only at the price of taking away from the Redemption its finest fruit.

Those who, on the contrary, forcefully reaffirmed the universality of the Redemption, were conscious of reacting against an aberration. But the question, whether Mary could be redeemed from original sin without having contracted it, could not be resolved until a clear distinction was made, first, within the notion of original sin, between the concepts of guilt (*culpa*)

---

[76] III, 27, 2. For an analysis of these texts, see Norbert DEL PRADO, O.P., *Divus Thomas et Bulla Dogmatica "Ineffabilis Deus,"* Friburgi Helv., 1919, p. 83.

More recently, it has been proposed to distinguish three periods in the thought of St. THOMAS. In the first he affirmed that the Blessed Virgin was exempt from both actual and original sin, *I Sent.,* dist. 44, qu. 1, a. 3, ad 3. In the second and longest period, he affirmed the universality of the Redemption wrought by Christ, but without being able to show how this could be reconciled with immunity from original sin in the Blessed Virgin. The third period is that of the *Expositio super salutatione angelica,* the critical edition of which shows that 16 out of 19 codices declare that Mary was exempt from all sin, even original. Cf. R. GARRIGOU-LAGRANGE, O.P., *De Christo Salvatore,* Turin, 1945, pp. 506-508. However, the text of the SPIAZZI edition, Rome, 1954, speaks of a purification of the Blessed Virgin: "Peccatum enim aut est originale, et de isto fuit mundata in utero . . ." (no. 1115).

[77] On the origins and historical destinies of this theology, one may consult X. LE BACHELET, *op. cit.,* col. 1019, 1020, 1022, 1042, 1044, 1063, 1074, 1075, 1077-78.

On the contents of this doctrine, its consequences, perspectives, and relations with the theology of the mystery of the Incarnation, see N. DEL PRADO, *op. cit.,* pp. 114-125, pp. 137-161. Scotus, he says, is its most illustrious representative. Starting from the principle that the Son of God would have become incarnate even if Adam had not sinned, "he thereby concludes, among other things: 1) that there are two types of merit in Christ, one of which is to be referred to the impassible Christ, the other to the suffering Christ; 2) that Christ is Mediator of angels as well as of men; 3) that the grace conferred on the angels and on our first parents is a grace derived from the merits of the impassible Christ; 4) that the predestination of both angels and men was dependent on the merits of Christ, but not on the Sacrifice of the Cross on Calvary; 5) that the election of the Blessed Virgin to the Divine Motherhood was joined in one and the same decree to the election of the man, Christ, anteriorly to the prevision of sin and of Calvary." *Ibid.* p. 138. Raymond Lull, Nicholas of Cusa, John of Segovia, Peter Galatin, Ambrose Catharinus, etc., followed in Scotus' footsteps. (As to how Christ is head even of the angels, without being their redeemer, see our study, "L'Univers antérieur à l'Eglise," *Revue Thomiste,* 1954, no. 1.)

and debt (*debitum*). Mary had to come personally under the universal
condemnation of which the Apostle speaks (Rom. 5:18). She contracted
the original debt, but not the stain. Secondly, within the notion of redemption itself, a distinction had to be made between a redemption conceived
as purifying from the stain of original sin, and one conceived as *preserving*
from it. Mary is redeemed from the debt of original sin not by *purification*,
but by *preservation*.[78]

It is to the honor of the Franciscan school of Oxford—of William of
Ware[79] and then Duns Scotus[80]—to have enunciated these distinctions.
Thanks to them, the apparently insoluble dilemma between the holiness
and the redemption of Mary was resolved. The way was now open for
the definition of the dogma of the Immaculate Conception.

In the *opusculum* which he wrote in 1515 for Leo X, and then in his
Commentary on St. Thomas, Cardinal Cajetan expounds the two
theses: 1) "The Blessed Virgin was *purified* from original sin"; and 2)
"The Blessed Virgin was *preserved* from the stain of original sin." He
himself adopts the former; but it is he also who best explains how those
who choose the second must understand it in order to remain faithful to
the Gospel teaching of the universality of the Redemption.[81]

---

[78] F. MARIN-SOLA, *L'évolution homogène du dogme catholique* . . . , t. I, p. 323.
Although *all* should die, *in fact* all will not die. Cf. I Cor. 15:51.

[79] X. LE BACHELET, *op. cit.*, col. 1060-1062. Cf. chap. V of the present volume.

[80] X. LE BACHELET, *op. cit.*, col. 1073-1078. Cf. chap. V of the present volume.
We may cite here the passage of SCOTUS, *III Sent.* dist. 3, qu. 1: "Per illud patet
ad rationes factas pro prima opinione, quia Maria maxime indiguisset Christo, ut redemptore: ipsa enim contraxisset originale peccatum ex ratione propagationis communis nisi fuisset praeventa per gratiam mediatoris, et sicut alii indiguerunt Christo
ut per eius meritum remitteretur eis peccatum iam contractum ita illa magis indiguit
mediatore praeveniente, peccatum ne esset ab ipsa aliquando contrahendum et ne ipsa
contraheret." Simply for having written those lines, Scotus' merit would be immense.
But this text does not represent his personal thought. For him the Blessed Virgin
stands apart from the plan for the Redemption of the world. See X. LE BACHELET,
op. cit., col. 1077-1078; and especially N. DEL PRADO, *op. cit.*, pp. 125 ff.

[81] The text of CAJETAN's commentary reads as follows: ". . . si tenetur Beatam
Virginem contraxisse originale peccatum, ut Sancti et antiqui doctores tenent, constat
omnia consona inveniri. Si autem tenetur Beatam Virginem, non ex vi conceptionis,
sed ex gratia singularissima in ipso instanti infusionis animae infusa illi animae, praeservatam ab originali peccato, quod tunc incurrisset nisi illa gratia affuisset: nihil
contra fidem tenetur, sed specialis modus redimendi ac salvandi a peccato originali
Christo attribuitur respectu suae matris. Sic enim ipsa Beata Virgo indiguit redimi et
salvari a peccato per Christum: quoniam ipsa tunc incurrisset peccatum nisi munus
gratiae praevenientis, non tempore sed natura, affuisset. Et ita puritas eius fuit maxima
sub Christo, qui nullo modo indiguit redimi, qui ex vi suae conceptionis fuit sanctus.
Fuitque in Beata Virgine *quod animale est* [I Cor. 15:46] prius natura, non tempore,
quam *quod spirituale est*: quoniam infusio gratiae in ipsius anima supponit produc-
tionem animae; quamvis, ut dictum est, praeveniat peccati maculam, quae tunc in-
currenda erat nisi gratia illam impedisset;—probabilis profecto opinio, nisi Sanctorum
antiquorum auctoritas obstaret, longe probabiliorem reddens contrariam positionem."
Commentaria in Summam theologicam Divi Thomae, III, 27, 2, no. vii.

CONCLUSION: THE ROLE PLAYED BY TIME AND EXPERIMENTAL
KNOWLEDGE IN THE DEVELOPMENT OF MARIAN DOGMA

The Church must first experience the effects of the Redemption in its own flesh, before it attains a full awareness of them and the ability to formulate them explicitly. And it was only after having experienced them and grown aware of them and enunciated them to herself that she was able, by the same movement and in virtue of a sort of knowledge by connaturality —by a kind of intuition—to understand what the effects of the Redemption could have been in Mary, who was the first among the redeemed, and was destined to give birth not only to Christians but to Christ Himself.[82]

The Church needs time and trials and the "challenges" addressed to her not only by her adversaries, but also by the ignorance, the awkwardness, the insufficiency and the sins of her children. More generally, the whole unfolding of history, with its progress and its catastrophes, is necessary to the Church to help her, and to compel her, to become progressively more extensively and explicitly aware of her own mystery.

In the same measure, the Church needs time, trials, "challenges," the unfolding of history, its progress and catastrophes, that she may know, as it were by way of inclination and affective knowledge, what she was when, in the presence of Christ, she was found entirely recapitulated in Mary; and also that she may know all that she is now through Mary. For it was necessary that the Church should once have been what she was in Mary, in order for her to be what she is in herself today. Viewed according to the greatness of holiness, which is the supreme greatness, Mary encircles Christ as the first wave of the Church, which produces all the others until the end of time.[83]

Hence we can understand why the definitions of Marian dogmas are in a hidden correspondence with the great events in the life of the Church. They mark the moments in which the Church, faced with the terrible "challenges" addressed to it by the world, must acquire through the faith a new awareness of the divine resources hidden in it from the days of its formation. In every instance, the cause of Mary will be the cause of the Church herself, and of the Christian people; in every instance, the cause of the Christian people will be Mary's cause; and both will always be, above all, the cause of Christ Himself.

At Ephesus, where the divinity of Christ and the divine maternity of Mary were defined, it was the nature of Christ, Head of the Church, that was at stake, and the nature of the two realizations of His Mystical Body, the one personal, in Mary, and the other collective, in the Church.

In defining the dogma of the Assumption, Pius XII wished that, at the

[82] See above, p. 21 f.
[83] Cf. *L'Eglise du Verbe Incarné*, II, Paris 1951, p. 428.

moment when the "myths of materialism" threatened to obliterate the life of men, "the sublime end to which our body and soul are destined should, in this glorious way, be put in a clear light before the eyes of all." [84]

In a civilization which, since the downfall of mediaeval Christianity, had denied sin, lost the sense of its dependence on Christ, and spoke of placing all its hope thereafter in the resources of the human adventure, the definition of the Immaculate Conception proclaimed the necessity of Christ's Redemption for all men, its holiness, the power of its effects in the Church and in Mary, in brief, the entire reality of that Kingdom which is not of this world.

[84] Pius XII, *Munificentissimus Deus,* in *Acta Apostolicae Sedis,* 1950, p. 770.

PART I

HISTORY

II

The Fathers of the Church
and the Immaculate Conception

GEORGES JOUASSARD*

The position of the Fathers of the Church in respect to the Immaculate Conception is difficult to determine, still more so to present. There are many reasons for this, of which the two primary are the following:

First, the documentation which has come down to us is far from being as ample as it should be. A great many works have disappeared, particularly from the ancient period, and frequently those which would have been most interesting for us are not among the ones which have been preserved. Such is the case, for example, with a number of sermons delivered on Marian feasts since the time when the Blessed Virgin began to be honored in her own name in the liturgy.[1]

In the second place, the Fathers, considered as a group, are far from having posed the problem of the sanctity of Mary in her conception. Most of them did not consider it at all. Some of them made pronouncements relative to her in such a way that their expressions have, in our eyes, a bearing on the problem; but then they usually did it in a rather indirect manner, often speaking of the Blessed Virgin only in connection with Jesus

---

* Dean of the Faculty of Theology of the University of Lyons, France. The present chapter, completed in October, 1954, and translated from the French original by Dr. Charles PARNELL, of the University of Notre Dame, has been read and approved by the author.—Editor's note.

[1] We shall not take up here the history of this liturgy, which is treated in Chapter IV of the present work. It is clear nevertheless that the liturgy has intervened considerably in the question we are here treating. Besides the influences that came relatively late, after the feast of the Conception of St. Anne had come into existence in the East, there were much earlier ones going back to the first celebration of feasts in honor of the Blessed Virgin in the East and West, and even to the celebration of certain feasts of Our Lord, such as Christmas and the *Hypapante* (the Greek equivalent of our February 2). The Fathers were often called upon to speak of Mary on these occasions. At present, only a very small portion of this literature is known; if we possessed all of it, it would be of prime importance for us, not only from the liturgical point of view, but also, and in certain cases still more, from the theological point of view. Hence, even here, we cannot fail to take account of as much of this literature as reaches us, whenever its authenticity is well assured.

51

or another person. It would therefore be an abuse of these statements to take them as if the Fathers had faced the problem with the intention of solving it.

In this respect we must distinguish between the Latin Fathers and those of the Eastern tradition. The former, beginning at least with Saint Augustine and the third decade of the fifth century, encountered the problem, and some of them attacked it more or less designedly. Up to the present time there is no evidence that their colleagues of the East did as much, either at that time or immediately afterwards. We must therefore distinguish between Latin tradition on one hand and Eastern tradition on the other.

With regard to the Eastern tradition, the limit assigned to this paper is the end of the sixth century; for the Latins, on the other hand, we have been asked to come down to the end of the eighth century, which we shall do. Since, however, during the first and second centuries, the Latin and Greek tradition are not yet separated from one another, the Fathers of that period being common to both, we shall consider these Fathers as a distinct group. We shall therefore study:

1. The beginnings of the patristic era, up to about the end of the second century;

2. The Eastern Fathers, from the end of the second century to the end of the sixth;

3. The Latin Fathers, from the end of the second century to the end of the eighth.

I

THE BEGINNINGS OF THE PATRISTIC ERA

If there is any period about which we are poorly informed in the Mariological sphere, it is this one. The evidence which has come down to us is so rare and says so little about our subject! Of the elements which stand out—ST. IGNATIUS OF ANTIOCH, the DIALOGUE WITH TRYPHO, and ST. IRENAEUS—the last-named is practically the only one we can really use. Ignatius considers nothing but the conception of Our Lord. It is this also which the *Dialogue with Trypho*, usually attributed to St. Justin,[2] has primarily in view, in the parallel which it draws between Eve and Mary (C, 4-6). For St. Irenaeus himself, the same point of view is important, even capital; but there is another in which he is still more interested when

---

[2] We use this expression designedly, for doubts have several times been raised about its authenticity, most recently by E. PREUSCHEN in *Zeitschrift für die neutestamentliche Wissenschaft*, 19, 1919-20, pp. 102-127. These doubts have never been resolved by a complete and decisive study of the problem.

he, too, develops the parallel between Mary and Eve. This is the anti-thesis between the two women, which he stresses.[3]

Indeed, if you examine the three passages in his work where such a parallel is now to be found,[4] and compare them with one another,[5] it will be clear that the Bishop of Lyons is contrasting two scenes which are in his eyes pivotal for the history of humanity: the temptation in the Garden of Eden and the Annunciation at Nazareth. What one woman did, the other undoes. Mary unties the knot so unfortunately tied by Eve. She accomplishes this by her obedience, by her reply to the divine message transmitted by the angel; whereas previously Eve, for her misfortune and ours, had believed Satan:

> And just as it was through a virgin who disobeyed that man was stricken and fell and died, so too it was through the Virgin who obeyed the word of God, that man, resuscitated by life, received life. For the Lord came to seek back the lost sheep, and it was man who was lost; and therefore He did not become some other formation, but He likewise, of her that was descended from Adam, preserved the likeness of formation; for Adam had necessarily to be restored in Christ, that mortality be absorbed in immortality, and Eve in Mary, that a virgin, become the advocate of a virgin, should undo and destroy virginal disobedience by virginal obedience.[6]

The Bishop's outlook does not extend expressly beyond these two scenes. Nowhere does he tell us what he believed the Blessed Virgin to have been before she received the visit of Gabriel.[7] Still, the fact that, through the account of St. Luke, he sees in her such a spirit of fidelity, docility and submission to the divine word, shows that he regards her as a sort of model of sanctity at the time of the Annunciation. His exegesis and theology, therefore, provide a start for developments which could move in the direction of the Immaculate Conception, and which rightfully tend towards it. We have no positive proof that he realized this himself; he said nothing

---

[3] On the differences between the ideas of St. Irenaeus and those of the *Dialogue with Trypho*, see our article, "Le parallèle Eve-Marie aux origines de la patristique," in *Bible et Vie chrétienne*, No. 7, Sept.-Nov. 1954, pp. 19-31.

[4] *Adv. haer.* III, XXII, 3-4 and V, XIX, 1 (*PG* 7, col. 958A-960A; 1175A-1176A); *Epideixis* 33 (*PO* XII, 5, col. 684 f.).

[5] As we have done in "La théologie de saint Irénée," in *L'Immaculée Conception* (*VIIème Congrès Marial National, Lyon, 1954*), Lyon, 1954, pp. 265-276, and in "La nouvelle Eve chez les Pères anténicéens," in *La nouvelle Eve I* (*Bulletin de la Société Française d'Etudes Mariales* 12, 1954), Paris, 1955, pp. 35-54.

[6] *Epideixis* 33, trans. by Joseph P. Smith, S.J., *Proof of the apostolic preaching* (*Ancient Christian Writers* 16), Westminster, Maryland, 1952, p. 69.

[7] In another passage of the *Adv. haer.*, III, XVI, 7 (*PG* 7, col. 926AB), St. Irenaeus alludes to the incident of the wedding feast of Cana, in such a way as to imply that in this case there was a certain reproach addressed to Mary by her Son. However, in *Recherches de Théologie ancienne et médiévale*, 20, 1953, pp. 189-191, P. NAUTIN would conclude that, according to the Bishop, the reproaches do not enter into the moral order properly so-called.

about it. At least, let us note this beginning, which is remarkable in view of the fact that we have to do with a man who was always careful to base himself on the apostolic teaching, and who is perhaps here expressing his views in continuity with that teaching.

Thus the period ends with a testimony which is valuable, even though we are quite unable to appreciate it at its true worth, or situate it against the background of contemporary theology. In reality, it should normally take its place there as a choice element, indeed, but as one element among many others, which are not now available to us.

II

THE EAST, FROM THE END OF THE SECOND CENTURY TO THE END OF THE SIXTH

By his origins, St. Irenaeus is directly connected with the Asiatic churches; he rightly liked to cite St. Polycarp as his authority. His writings could have influenced the Eastern communities just as they did those of the West; but, in reality, his influence seems to have been quite modest in the Greek-speaking lands. At present it is impossible to detect any trace of it in the domain of Mariology at the beginning of the third century. This is probably due largely to the fact that, at this date in the world then so Hellenistically inclined, the predominant influence suddenly passed into the hands of writers from Egypt: Clement of Alexandria and, above all, Origen. This was to have a singular and very important effect on our question.

While CLEMENT OF ALEXANDRIA seems, indeed, to have dealt with the Blessed Virgin in his writings only rarely, the same cannot be said for ORIGEN, who manifested more than once his great esteem for her.[8] He is particularly appreciative of her practice of virginity, even to the point of affirming that she could undoubtedly have had no carnal relations with St. Joseph after the birth of Jesus. From this point of view he presents her as a model for virgins:

> Those who say this (viz. that the "brothers and sisters" of Jesus mentioned in Matt. 13:55-56 were children of Joseph by a prior marriage) are motivated by the desire to maintain the dignity of virginity in Mary to the end of her life, so that her body, which had been chosen for the service of the Word, of Him Who had said, "The Holy Spirit shall come upon thee and the power of the Most High shall overshadow thee," which had received the Holy Spirit and had been over-

---

[8] On this point, see pp. 79-81 of the work to which we shall refer more than once, in *Maria*, t. I, pp. 79-81 (see the bibliography following the present chapter).

shadowed by power from on high, should not thereafter know man's embrace. And it seems to me reasonable to hold that Jesus was the first-fruits of chaste purity among men, and Mary among women; it does not sound right to attribute to anyone but her the first-fruits of virginity.[9]

Origen speaks, likewise, in delicate and evocative terms, of the confidence which Our Lord showed in entrusting His Mother to St. John.[10] Yet in spite of all this, he points out on numerous occasions and without hesitation certain sins against faith which he supposes the Mother of Our Savior to have committed.[11] He finds the indication of these sins particularly in the sword mentioned in the prophecy of Simeon, which, according to him, forecast that, at the moment of the Passion, Mary was to fall, even worse than the Apostles themselves.

> Then Simeon says, "And thy own soul a sword shall pierce." What is this sword, which pierced not only the hearts of others, but even Mary's? It is plainly written that at the time of the Passion, all the Apostles were scandalized, for the Lord Himself declared, "All of you will be scandalized this night." Therefore all were scandalized, so much so that even Peter, the Prince of the Apostles, thrice denied his Master. Are we then to think that when the Apostles were scandalized, the mother of the Lord was not? If she was not scandalized at the Lord's Passion, then Jesus did not die for her sins. But if "all have sinned, and have need of the glory of God," if all have been "justified" and redeemed "by His grace," then surely Mary also was scandalized at that time.
>
> And this is what Simeon now prophesies, saying, "And thy own soul a sword shall pierce." Although you know that you have begotten this child without man's concurrence, and although you heard Gabriel say, "The Holy Spirit shall come upon thee, and the power of the Most High shall overshadow thee," you will be transpierced by the sword of unbelief, you will be struck by the sword of uncertainty, your mind will be torn in two, when before your eyes He, Whom you heard called the Son of God, and Whom you know you begot without the seed of man, is crucified and dies, is subjected to human tortures, when He moans and weeps and says, "Father, if it be possible, let this chalice pass from me."[12]

---

[9] ... Οἱ δὲ ταῦτα λέγοντες τὸ ἀξίωμα τῆς Μαρίας ἐν παρθενίᾳ τηρεῖν μέχρι τέλους βούλονται, ἵνα μὴ τὸ κριθὲν ἐκεῖνο σῶμα διακονήσασθαι τῷ εἰπόντι λόγῳ, «πνεῦμα ἅγιον ἐπελεύσεται ἐπὶ σὲ, καὶ δύναμις ὑψίστου ἐπισκιάσει σοι,» γνῷ κοίτην ἀνδρὸς μετὰ τὸ ἐπελθεῖν ἐν αὐτῇ πνεῦμα ἅγιον, καὶ τὴν ἐπεσκιακυῖαν αὐτῇ δύναμιν· ἐξ ὕψους. Καὶ οἶμαι λόγον ἔχειν, ἀνδρῶν μὲν καθαρότητος τῆς ἐν ἀγνείᾳ ἀπαρχὴν γεγονέναι τὸν Ἰησούν, γυναικῶν δε τὴν Μαριάμ· οὐ γὰρ εὔφημον, ἄλλῃ παρ' ἐκείνην τὴν ἀπαρχὴν τῆς παρθενίας ἐπιγραψάσθαι. *Com. in Mt.*, X, 17 (*GCS* 40, pp. 21-22; *PG*, 13, col. 877A).

[10] *Com. in Joan.*, I, IV, 6, *GCS* 10, pp. 8-9 (*PG* 14, col. 29C-32C).

[11] Thus in *Hom. in Gen.*, I, 14, *GCS* 29, pp. 18-19 (*PG* 12, col. 158B); in *Lc.*, XIV, XVII, XIX and XX, *GCS* 35, pp. 94-102, 116-119, 125-130 and 132-133 (*PG* 13, col. 1833-1838, 1845A-1846A, 1849-1851, 1851B-1852B).

[12] Deinde Simeon ait: *et tuam ipsius animam pertransibit gladius*. Quis est iste gladius, qui non aliorum tantum, sed etiam Mariae cor pertransiit? Aperte scribitur, quod in tempore passionis omnes sint apostoli scandalizati, ipso quoque Domino di-

Did Origen perhaps find this idea in the official teaching of the Church in his time? There is no evidence that such was the case. Rather we seem here to be dealing with the statements of an exegete expounding Holy Scripture and trying to draw from it certain moral lessons for the use of Christians. It is nonetheless true that the exegete dared to do it in church, in homilies delivered in Palestine, perhaps even before bishops; and no one, so far as we know, ever protested. Hence we can conclude that during the first half of the third century, when this occurred and was repeated a number of times, there was scarcely any idea in the communities involved, or in those in which Origen's works were read, that such statements might be improper. This amounts to saying that at this time and in these communities, people were very far from believing in the Immaculate Conception of the Virgin Mary, since, as occasion arose, they candidly attributed grave sins to her, together, however, with singular virtue. Mary therefore appeared as a saint—to use the expression of a later age—but a saint who was subject to failings, just as so many others have been.

There was a danger that this image of the Blessed Virgin might be popularized throughout the churches of the Orient by the writings of Origen; and, in fact, this is exactly what happened. We know how much his writings were read there, and what an influence they had on succeeding generations of theologians and exegetes. Yet even in the third century there were some who managed to preserve themselves from being influenced excessively by Origen, and even reacted against him. METHODIUS is a typical example. Does this mean that we will find him thinking along quite different lines? In certain respects, yes; for in his work (or in that part of it at least which has come down to us so far) you do not find the type of accusation seen in Origen.[13] However, although Methodius exalts Mary as a virgin in his *Banquet,* he does not place her so very far above the others. We note even, to our surprise, that this man, who read St.

---

cente: *omnes vos scandalizabimini in nocte hac.* Ergo scandalizati sunt universi in tantum, ut Petrus quoque, apostolorum princeps, tertio denegarit. Quid putamus, quod scandalizatis apostolis mater Domini a scandalo fuerit immunis? Si scandalum in Domini passione non passa est, non est mortuus Jesus pro peccatis ejus. Si autem *omnes peccaverunt et indigent gloria Dei, justificati gratia ejus et redempti,* utique et Maria illo tempore scandalizata est. Et hoc est, quod nunc Simeon prophetat dicens: *et tuam ipsius animam,* quae scis absque viro peperisse te virginem, quae audisti a Gabriele: *Spiritus sanctus veniet super te, et virtus Altissimi obumbrabit tibi, pertransibit* infidelitatis *gladius* et ambiguitatis mucrone ferieris, et cogitationes tuae te in diversa lacerabunt, cum videris illum, quem Filium Dei audieras et sciebas absque semine viri esse generatum, crucifigi et mori et suppliciis humanis esse subjectum et ad postremum lacrimabiliter conquerentem atque dicentem: *Pater, si possibile est, pertranseat calix iste a me.—In Lucam Hom.* XVII, *GCS* 35, pp. 116-118 (*PG* 13, col. 1845A-C).

[13] This work of Methodius (formerly called Methodius of Olympus) is in a poor state; it comes to us mainly via ancient translations, through which it can be got at only with some difficulty.

Irenaeus, was very much inspired by him and is clearly dependent on him for his theological positions and vocabulary, took nothing, so far as we can see, from the parallels between Mary and Eve drawn by the Bishop of Lyons. One would be inclined to think that he was not acquainted with them; yet he could not possibly have failed to read them along with the rest. We cannot say definitely what the reason for this reserve was, but it is so striking that one can hardly avoid the suspicion that it was deliberate. At any rate, Methodius failed, unless we are mistaken, to make use of the opportunity that befell him, of developing the start made on this point by Irenaeus, as we noted above. Therefore the third century ends and the fourth begins, in the Greek world, without producing any continuation of what Irenaeus had started or any counter-weight to the accusations of Origen—not even from his occasional adversaries.[14]

Nevertheless, work destined to promote the cause of the Mother of God was being accomplished. First of all, the East began to call her *Theotokos*. ST. ALEXANDER OF ALEXANDRIA witnesses to this [15] about the time of the Nicene Council (325), and he uses the term without hesitating, or supposing that it might cause any difficulty. Moreover, he proposes Mary as an example to be imitated by the virgins of his time.[16] This had already been done by Origen, and by many others about the same time, and probably also before them. Still more were to follow. The important thing is that now the *hierarchy* is at the head of this tendency in Egypt, a fact which undoubtedly explains another, namely, that ST. ATHANASIUS went much further yet in this same direction, to the point of drawing a sort of portrait of the Blessed Virgin, which is already a model of its kind.[17] He does not rule out the possibility that Mary may have had certain imperfections; he even seems to imply as much, although without saying anything on the matter expressly. Nevertheless the portrait is remarkable, and was to have an influence.

Not everywhere in the East. It would even seem that most of the Greek Fathers of the fourth and also the fifth centuries were unacquainted

---

[14] Naturally, we take no account in this paper of works now recognized as apocryphal, as, for example, the Marian homilies attributed to St. Gregory Thaumaturgus, which are of a much later date. As to the authenticity of the documents edited in Migne, until something better is available, consult the list of corrections, already most useful, compiled by R. LAURENTIN in his *Court traité de théologie mariale*, Paris, 1953, pp. 119-173 (English translation, *Queen of heaven . . .*, Dublin, 1956).

[15] See this text in *Athanasius Werke*, OPITZ ed., III/1, p. 28 (*PG* 18, col 568C).

[16] Cf. *Maria* I, p. 86-87, following *Le Muséon*, 42, 1929, p. 259; cf. p. 256 ff.

[17] See *Le Muséon, loc. cit.*, pp. 197-275 and the explanations given in *Maria* I, p. 87. This work, which has come down to us in a mutilated condition and only in Coptic, is being more and more widely accepted as authentically Athanasian; it would be very useful if someone would make us a new edition and translation of it, taking into account the exceptional testimony given by St. Ambrose in Book II of his *De virginibus ad Marcellinam*, for it seems beyond a doubt that Ambrose read this text in Greek.

with it. The Cappadocians make no use of it; they follow Origen instead. This is well known as regards their theology in general; it also holds true in the particular field of Mariology.[18]   Neither St. Basil nor St. Gregory Nazianzen nor St. Gregory of Nyssa nor Amphilochius of Iconium hesitate to admit—in different degrees, however—sins in Mary. The first is even particularly clear on this point.[19]   He is directly dependent on Origen for the exegesis of Simeon's prophecy (with the result that, in our own time, whole pages of Basil's Greek on this question have been published under the name of Origen![20]) St. John Chrysostom, for his part, made similar statements, even in homilies to the people, which is still more significant.[21]   Moreover, he emphasizes and repeats his ideas, just as Origen had done, without provoking any more reaction than the latter had. It would seem, therefore, that, relative to the sanctity of the Mother of God, ideas had not developed much in the East since the first half of the third century. Rather, the early ideas must have spread, since now they are encountered just about everywhere. We have noted, however, that St. Athanasius showed himself to be more reserved than many others. The same is true of St. Epiphanius, who, in some of his views, is dependent on Irenaeus, whom he must have read in his study of heresy.[22]   On the other hand, the position of certain exegetes, such as Diodorus of Tarsus and Theodore of Mopsuestia, is more vague—for us, at any rate—and less radical than that of Chrysostom or St. Basil. In conclusion, the whole panorama leaves us with a mixed impression. At the turning from the fourth to the fifth centuries, the Blessed Virgin is far from being considered, except perhaps in a few cases, as a saint without fault or defect. Still less was there any idea of attributing to her an immaculate conception, except unwittingly and unintentionally in certain circles fond of apocryphal works, but which were of little influence in the theological world.

In such circles, in fact, there were current the writings[23] which ultimately came together to yield the conglomerate now known as the Proto-gospel of James. This apocryphal work speaks, among other things,

[18] Cf. the texts cited in *Maria* I, pp. 92-93. See also G. Söll, "Die Mariologie der Kappadozier im Licht der Dogmengeschichte," in *Theologische Quartalschrift*, 131, 1951, pp. 163-188, 288-319 and 426-457.

[19] In a private letter addressed to Bishop Optimos of Antioch in Pisidia in answer to a question by the latter: *Ep.* 260, 6-9 (*PG* 32, col. 964B-968B). Before reaching a decision, St. Basil had therefore the time to reflect on it amply.

[20] By Rauer in *GCS* 35, pp. 116-119, cf. *Maria*, I, p. 79, n. 5.

[21] For example, *In Mt. Hom.* IV, 4-5; *Hom.* XLIV, 1-2 (*PG* 57, col. 44-45 and 463-466); *In Joan. Hom.* XXI, 1-3; *Hom.* XXII, 1-2 (*PG* 59, col. 129-134 and 133-134). Cf. *Maria* I, pp. 94-97.

[22] See especially, in his letter to the Christian communities of Arabia inserted in *Panarion, Haer.* 78, nn. 18-19 (*GCS* 37, pp. 468-470; *PG* 42, col. 728C-732A). Cf. *Maria* I, pp. 91-92.

[23] Almost certainly there were more than one, originating doubtless at various times and in different circumstances. For the portion of this document that is relevant to our question, see p. 513 ff. of the present volume.

of the origin of the Blessed Virgin, and particularly of her conception by Anne. In certain manuscripts, this conception is represented not only as miraculous (Anne having been sterile up until then), but also (incidentally, and without insistence on the point), as virginal. This idea could go back to primitive times, as we shall see,[24] and although its source is more than questionable, it would merit our interest if the theologians of that time had given it any credit. But, as we shall likewise see, St. Epiphanius is the only one who spoke of it, so far as is known, and he did so only in order to reject it energetically. Such a notion was, in fact, incapable of winning much consideration in Catholic circles truly guided by the spirit of faith. It was not even used by Theoteknos of Livias, the new witness to the *Protogospel* recently brought to light by Father Wenger.[25]

Such is the state of affairs at this date in the Greek-speaking eastern world. Was it any different in communities of Syriac or Coptic tongue? It is difficult to judge with any precision, except for the case of the Syrians as represented by ST. EPHRAEM. Even with regard to him, one must take care to get his true ideas, to use only well attested writings, and to check the texts regularly against the manuscripts.[26] When this is done, one observes that, contrary to what has been said and is still being said, the Deacon of Edessa spoke of Mary as did the Greeks of his milieu—no more, no less.[27] He, too, esteems the Blessed Virgin, esteems her highly; never-

---

[24] Cf. what we say about the *Pseudo-Matthew*, p. 81 f., as well as the remarks of Msgr. AMANN in *Le Protévangile de Jacques et ses remaniements latins*, Paris, 1910, p. 17 ff.

[25] In particular, no. 6 of the text which Father WENGER has published in the thesis defended by him at Lyons, *L'Assomption de la T. S. Vierge dans la tradition byzantine du VIe au Xe siècle*, Paris, 1955, p. 274. According to the editor, this writer belongs, at the earliest, to the end of the period we are treating, probably between 550 and 650. It is to be noted that his acquaintance with the *Protogospel* and with Mary's "childhood in the Temple" does not deter him from attributing to Mary at the foot of the Cross sentiments which, although not carried quite so far, recall the ideas of Origen and others; cf. *ibid.* no. 7, pp. 274-276. Father Wenger had not at first remarked this last point, which, however, he acknowledged with good grace at the time of the defense of his thesis.

[26] This is what we had already maintained in *Maria*, I, p. 88, n. 9. Our views were confirmed by the study of Dom E. BECK (which, though only partial, is worthy of high esteem) in his work *Ephraems Reden über den Glauben (Studia Anselmiana* 33), Rome, 1953, pp. 95-107. Therein we see how necessary it is to control the work of L. HAMMERSBERGER, *Die Mariologie der ephremischen Schriften*, Innsbruck, 1948. —On the studies of MUELLER and Ortiz DE URBINA, cf. *Maria* I, p. 137, n. 5—On James of Sarug, who we are no longer quite sure should be classed among the Monophysites, two recent publications are to be noted: a translation of his Marian homilies by C. VONA, *Omelie mariologiche di S. Giacomo di Sarug*, Rome, 1953, and an article by P. KRÜGER, "Die Frage der Erbsündlichkeit der Gottesmutter im Schriftum der Jakob von Serugh," in *Ostkirchliche Studien*, 1, 1952, pp. 187-207.

[27] See *Maria* I, p. 95, n. 40. From now on, the commentary of Ephraem on the *Diatessaron* should be verified according to the Armenian edition and Latin translation which has just been published by Dom L. LELOIR. *CSCO* 137 and 145. It will be noted that, precisely for the scene of the Resurrection, the translator is not sure of the authenticity, or at least of the completeness, of the text which he has edited

theless he pictures her as fallible. It was his successors who expressed themselves otherwise, not he; or else, he has been interpreted in a sense which is not his.

The situation which we perceive just before the Council of Ephesus (431) is, therefore, rather general. There may have been exceptions, even more than we suspect. It is evident in any case that a considerable number of Eastern Fathers saw no objection to considering "the Holy Virgin" (although calling her by this name and with great respect) just as they did other characters of the Old or New Testament whose weaknesses are recorded in the Bible.

This situation does not change much at the time of the Council, nor immediately afterwards. We have a particularly typical proof of this, St. Cyril of Alexandria in person.[28]

One is justified in asking whether, before his encounter with Nestorius, St. Cyril was to be counted among those especially devoted to the *Theotokos*. Certainly, nothing in this name frightened him; but he seldom used it in his works. Nevertheless, he recognized its legitimacy so clearly, that scarcely had he received word that his new colleague in Constantinople was opposed to this *theotokos*, when he rose up against Nestorius and in favor of the term. Indeed, he began from then on to extol it and defend it against all possible attacks. For St. Cyril, the question was primarily one of Christology, as is evident from the remainder of the controversy, which bore precisely on the ensemble of Christological positions involved in the conflict, particularly the 'communication of idioms,' as we call it. Indeed this point constituted the first and principal stake in the debate. The fact remains that, devoted as St. Cyril was to the cause of the Mother of God, he had previously written lines about her—on the scene at Calvary, among others—which had undoubtedly been inspired by the exegesis of Simeon's prophecy by Origen and St. Basil.[29] And, in spite of the temperaments involved, he was not the least blunt of the three. Now these lines had been written just before, or at the beginning of, the conflict with Nestorius. The same ideas were repeated when the struggle was at its height, if not already over, this time in sermons addressed to the people on the Gospel of St. Luke.[30]

(cf. *CSCO* 145, p. 235 n. 6 of no. 27). However, what the commentary says of the doubts of the Virgin at the time of the Resurrection (*ibid.*, pp. 235-236) matches what it says of her attitude at Cana (*ibid.*, pp. 44-45).

[28] Cf. *Maria* I, pp. 98-99 and 139-140. See, in addition, our study, "L'interprétation par saint Cyrille d'Alexandrie de la scène de Marie au pied de la Croix," in *Virgo Immaculata* (*Acta Congressus Internationalis Mariologici-Mariani Romae anno MCMLIV celebrati*), Vol. IV: *De Immaculata Conceptione apud SS. Patres et scriptores orientales*, Romae, 1955, pp. 27-48.

[29] *Com. in Joan.*, Lib. XII (*PG* 74, col. 661A-666A, or better in the edition of Ph. Pusey, Vol. III, Oxford, 1872, pp. 89-93).

[30] *Hom.* IV. There exist two short fragments of this homily in Syriac, a Latin translation of which has finally just been published by Father Tonneau (*CSCO* 140,

Here the bishop is less expansive, and he seems to envisage the possibility of encountering some resistance; nevertheless, he continues on his way, expressing his mind as it is—though without imposing it—so that it may be shared by the members of his flock, and not merely for the benefit of a few readers of scholarly commentaries as had been the case before.

Such was the attitude of the Archbishop of Alexandria in the midst of the controversy, and after the Christian world had recognized the Blessed Virgin's right to be called the Mother of God. This position, on the part of the adversary *par excellence* of Nestorius, suffices to reveal the situation in Egypt at that time. It differed little from that of seventy years earlier in Cappadocia, or toward the beginning of the century in Syria and in Constantinople. It can even be asked whether there had not been a regression in Alexandria itself from the situation at the end of St. Athanasius' episcopate. At any rate we are far from hearing, even from the lips of Nestorius, statements like those which literary history has recorded from the pen of his illustrious opponent. (This applies, of course, to the question of Mary's sanctity, not to that of the Divine Maternity.) The difference is such that, whereas certain scholars have considered the possibility that Nestorius may have been inclined to admit the Immaculate Conception [31] —which, however, would still have to be proved—it seems quite improbable that the same hypothesis can ever be proposed seriously for Cyril. The latter had the great merit of establishing himself as the defender of the Divine Maternity; but he failed to perceive certain consequences of this privilege. In this he showed himself human, like all of us; nonetheless the Lord used him for His work, used him as he was.

This leads us to wonder how the situation developed in the East after the Council of Ephesus. The evolution was to take place slowly, as we can see—although none too clearly—from the elements now at our disposal.[32] Indeed, it is indubitable that the Council exercised a considerable

---

p. 6) as a continuation of the Lamy-Chabot edition which appeared in the same *CSCO* in 1912 (now no. 70 in the Collection). In addition we have the Greek of this homily and the one preceding it, more or less well edited, but with the two homilies joined together as though they were only one, in the AUBERT-MIGNE edition *PG* 77, col. 1040-1050.—For the other homilies which we find under the name of Cyril in this Aubert-Migne edition, some of which are primarily concerned with Mariology, it is well to be most reserved in attributing them to this bishop. In spite of the use which certain writers have made of them even recently, we maintain integrally the stand which we took in *Maria* I, p. 139, n. 17.

[31] Father JUGIE did not hesitate to express this idea, and to repeat it in his latest work, *L'Immaculée Conception dans l'Ecriture Sainte et dans la tradition orientale*, Rome 1952, pp. 86-87.

[32] These elements are, let us repeat, quite insufficient. A large number of the primary texts are lacking, particularly the sermons. As a result of the enormous investigations conducted by Msgr. EHRHARD, additional material will be made available, particularly by Father WENGER. Meanwhile we will often be left in doubt—all the more so in that critical problems frequently arise for certain texts, even when we are favored with some recent study, as is the case with Proclus of Constantinople (cf.

influence there in the Marian order, given, moreover, the fact that the Christological discussions pursued their development without ever again bringing seriously into question the legitimacy of the term *theotokos*. This influence seems to have been particularly great in the liturgy: [33] following the Council the number of holy days in honor of the *Theotokos* increased, and the cult spread everywhere in an official form, guaranteed by the hierarchy. In the field of theology, universal recognition was attained by such a privilege as Mary's complete virginity, i.e. her virginity *in partu* and *post partum* (her virginity *ante partum* had long since been admitted). This recognition, of which such patent evidence is provided by the acts of the Council of Chalcedon,[34] was not without repercussions on the question of Mary's sanctity, for in the minds of Christians at that time, the ideas of virginity and sanctity were more or less bound up together, particularly as regards the virginity *post partum*.[35] Little by little, therefore, there must have been a tendency in sermons and elsewhere to avoid or to soften a certain exegesis which earlier writers had thought permissible. The principle of the Divine Maternity had a similar influence, both encouraging the cult and exalting her who was its object.

We note this in the sermons of a certain number of men of the fifth century, whom Father Jugie has treated in detail,[36] e.g. THEODOTUS OF ANCYRA, BASIL OF SELEUCIA and ANTIPATER OF BOSTRA. They frequently used laudatory expressions which might make one think of the privilege of the Immaculate Conception, or which at least pointed people's minds in that direction. Alongside these expressions, however, certain others are to be noted which are more or less equivocal, and seem to recall the remarks of times past. Likewise, these orators had rivals, no less productive or less known than themselves, in whom we find a still more complex mixture of formulas of praise with others which imply rather directly, if not necessarily, a disavowal of the privilege. Among the latter are HESYCHIUS OF JERUSALEM and CHRYSIPPUS OF JERUSALEM, the former of whom was not only "slavishly bound to the Alexandrine exegesis," [37] but also such a stubborn disciple of St. Cyril that he was to fall into Monophysitism at the time of the Council of Chalcedon, and seems to have been allied personally with Eutyches.[38]

Maria I, p. 137). In every case, it goes without saying, one would do well to check LAURENTIN's table (cf. note 14, above), keeping in mind that it omits the rather numerous works not edited in Migne.

[33] This is not what it pertains to us here and now to record. As we said above, it suffices for us to point out the results of the new state of affairs, at least in so far as possible.

[34] *Maria* I, p. 138.

[35] *Ibid.*, p. 81.

[36] *Op. cit.*, pp. 77-94.

[37] *Ibid.*, p. 89.

[38] The case of Hesychius is particularly interesting in this respect, due to the fact that one finds in him a Monophysite speaking of the Blessed Virgin in the same way

A similar mixture of praise of the *Theotokos,* more intense than previously, with allegations scarcely compatible with the hypothesis of her perfect sanctity, seems to last on into the sixth century.[39] The evidence which has been found and studied so far is less abundant than that for the fifth century, but one can nevertheless get from it an idea of the situation, which was particularly striking in the case of ROMANOS MELODUS.[40] In the presence of the Christians assembled for the feast of the *Hypapante,* this poet caused to be sung a *kontakion* which the piety of later ages would have found difficult to accept exactly as it was.[41] True, the insinuations are attenuated, compared to what had been current previously. In interpreting the prophecy of Simeon, Romanos speaks only of a *doubt* which the Blessed Virgin experienced at the moment of the Passion, and from which her Son quickly healed her. Still the fact remains that he speaks of a doubt, in fact *sings* of it, and the Christian people with him. These Christians do not yet believe in the absolutely integral sanctity of the *Theotokos.* It is not possible that they believed in her initial sanctity either, or even gave it consideration, properly speaking. They were simply getting ready to consider and approve it at such a time as it should be presented to them by learned men of a later age. This was to be the contribution of the following period, the *Byzantine* period properly so-called, which is beyond the limit assigned to this chapter.[42]

The period which we have just studied did, in fact, prepare the way for the one which was to follow, despite appearances to the contrary. This can be seen from the homogeneity with which it developed. It gives, indeed, a singular impression of unity on the point with which we are concerned; from one end of the period to the other, more or less analogous charac-

---

as St. Cyril, and with equal candor. *A priori,* one would imagine exactly the contrary, and that it would be the Nestorians or defenders of Nestorius who would use such language, whereas the latter prove to be rather reserved in this regard, if we are to judge by documents now available. The indication is rather clear that among the Greeks in this case, it is not so much doctrinal orientation as affinities in the order of exegesis which are decisive. Furthermore, as far as exegesis is concerned, one cannot speak of the Alexandrian school as unfavorable to Mary's sanctity, for St. Athanasius in no way shared that attitude, and neither perhaps did his predecessor, St. Alexander of Alexandria. We observe furthermore that St. John Chrysostom greatly resembles St. Cyril of Alexandria, and also the Cappadocians. He might easily be the bridge between them, although he was on another side, as he shows in this case by the very detail of his exegesis.

[39] JUGIE, *op. cit.,* p. 95 ff.

[40] *Ibid.,* pp. 96-97; cf. *Maria* I, pp. 143-144.

[41] This text is to be found in G. CAMMELLI, *Romano il Melode, Inni,* Florence, 1930, pp. 121-155. See especially p. 146.—May we be permitted to refer to this work, although a liturgical one, because it concerns both the liturgy (since it was sung in church) and the history of theology (since Romanos composed it, and Christians repeated it after him, to express their sentiments).—Furthermore, we must note that another poem of Romanos, on Mary at the foot of the Cross, sounds quite different, although even here one feels that the poet is influenced by the exegesis of Origen; cf. CAMMELLI, *op. cit.,* pp. 329-361.

[42] See chapter III of the present volume.

teristics are encountered.   Unless we are mistaken, no one in the East at
that time clearly posed the problem of Mary's Immaculate Conception.
Most of the Fathers seem not to have considered it, even remotely, or to
have suspected its existence.   Likewise, the personal sanctity of Our Lady
did not constitute a problem for the majority of them either; those who
made a statement on the matter seem to have done so without facing the
problem squarely, and consequently without claiming to offer a solution—
let alone a definitive solution—to it.   They expressed, in passing, a personal
opinion which happened to have some bearing on the problem.   Sometimes
theologians influenced one another, especially in the field of exegesis.   This
is particularly noticeable in the case of Origen, followed by St. Basil, and
finally St. Cyril of Alexandria.   Through them the influence of a certain
exegesis made itself felt during the whole period, without, however, having
by any means the same effect on all the Fathers.   There is, on the contrary,
a marked difference in their reactions to the pressure of this exegesis. Some,
such as St. Athanasius, seem to have felt it very little; others, much more.
On the whole, its influence persisted until about the end of this period,
for it is still perceptible in Romanos; but, as we noted above, it had by
then diminished in intensity, it was losing its 'momentum.'   On the other
hand, as we also noted, the tendency was likewise growing to exalt the
Blessed Virgin, her greatness, her virtues and the excellence of her role.
It was like a slow, steady ascent, preparing the way for the future, even
though the preparation still seemed remote and the rise barely apparent,
somewhat like a child's imperceptible entrance into adolescence.

The state of affairs which we are to find in the West from the third to
the eighth centuries is considerably different, which provides further justification for the distinction which we have made for the purposes of this
study, between East and West after the period of the beginnings.

III

THE WEST, FROM THE END OF THE SECOND CENTURY, TO THE END OF THE EIGHTH

So far as the Immaculate Conception is concerned, the theology of the
East, considered as a whole, seems to have developed gradually, the way
a living being grows.   The Fathers drew progressively nearer to the idea,
without at first realizing it, and without having become clearly aware of it
even at the terminal date of our investigation.

In the West it was quite different.   The beginnings were similar—unless
every indication misleads us; but the ripening was far more rapid, so that
by the third decade of the fifth century, the problem of the status of the

Blessed Virgin at the time of her conception was to be raised—a fact which was without parallel in the East. Consequently, we must divide the Latin West into two periods, the first extending from the end of the second century to about the second decade of the fifth, the second running from thence to the limit of the period assigned to us, viz. the end of the eighth century.

FROM THE END OF THE SECOND CENTURY
TO THE PELAGIAN CONTROVERSY

The first period begins with TERTULLIAN, the first western writer known to have used Latin currently—although alongside of Greek—for theological writing. He knew St. Irenaeus, and even used the latter's parallel between Mary and Eve; but he did so in a rather different spirit from the Bishop of Lyons [43] and arrived at quite different opinions regarding the Blessed Virgin.[44]

First of all, there is for him no doubt that Mary had relations with Joseph after the Savior's birth: she had several children by him. This in no wise disturbs our African; he finds it quite natural. He does not envisage any other hypothesis, nor does he imagine that Jesus came into the world on Christmas day any differently from other babes. He believes only in the virginal conception of the Divine Master, and this he believes strongly, like all the Catholics of his time. Relative to the virginity of Mary, his beliefs go no further.

Furthermore, he associates Mary with the "brothers and sisters" of Jesus in their attitude towards Him. He declares of her and of all of them together that they had no faith in the Master when He set out on His apostolic journeys. Hence he considers Our Lord to have repulsed and disavowed His Mother in the incident of the interrupted sermon (Matt. 12:46-50); not as though He had denied that she was His Mother— quite the contrary; but that He brusquely repelled her from His company, and justifiably, because precisely of the incredulity which she manifested:

> Why does (Christ) deny His mother and brethren? . . . His brethren did not believe in Him. . . . Likewise His mother is not represented as adhering to Him, although Martha and Mary and other women were often in His company. Indeed, their unbelief is apparent in this very place; for although Jesus was teaching the Way of Life, preaching the Kingdom of God, and healing sickness and sin, and while strangers gave Him rapt attention, His nearest relatives stayed away. When they finally arrive, they stand outside, unappreciative of what is going on within. They do not even wait, as if bringing Him something He needs on account of His intense occupation; rather, they interrupt Him, and want to call Him away from His great work. . . . Christ was preaching and proving about God, fulfilling the Law and the prophets,

[43] Cf. "Le parallèle Eve-Marie aux origines de la patristique," cited in note 3.
[44] See *Maria* I, pp. 77-78.

dispelling the darkness of the long past ages; would you say that He undeservedly used the expression He did to strike at the unbelief of those who stood outside, or to be rid of the importunity of those who were calling Him away from His work? . . . when someone denies his parents out of indignation, he is not denying but rebuking them. . . . Just as He adopted those who attached themselves to Him, so in the same way He denied those who remained aloof. . . . His estranged mother is a figure of the synagogue, and His unbelieving brethren a figure of the Jews.[45]

This means that Tertullian considered Mary to be seriously at fault on this occasion—much more so than Origen was maintaining about this same time, or than the Easterners in general ever thought, it would seem. Thus Latin theology opens under strange auspices, so far as the Immaculate Conception is concerned.

When we examine closely these various positions of Tertullian's, however, we are compelled to acknowledge that they derive from his personal ideas, and in no wise from a tradition. A polemicist to extremes, he rushes headlong, piling argument on argument in order to vanquish his opponent, cost what it may. This is what he is doing in the case in question. There would hardly be grounds for taking account of his ideas if it weren't for the possibility of their having spread, and if they did not show that the church in Africa had apparently no teaching to offer in his day on these questions.

However, these ideas had no influence on such a person as St. Cyprian, whom we find nowhere repeating assertions of this type. Neither, however, do we see him react against them, or say anything precise that touches in

---

[45] Sed quotiens de nativitate contenditur, omnes, qui respuunt eam ut praeiudi-cantem de carnis in Christo veritate, ipsum dominum volunt negasse se natum, quia dixerit: *Quae mihi mater et qui mihi fratres?* . . . Sed quae ratio responsi matrem et fratres ad praesens negantis? Discat etiam Apelles. Fratres domini non crediderant in illum, sicut evangelio ante Marcionem edito continetur. Mater aeque non demon-stratur adhaesisse illi, cum Martha et Maria aliaeque in commercio eius frequententur. Hoc denique in loco apparet incredulitas eorum: cum Iesus doceret viam vitae, cum dei regnum praedicaret, cum languoribus et vitiis medendis operaretur, extraneis defixis in illum tam proximi aberant. Denique superveniunt et foris subsistunt: nec introeunt, non computantes scilicet quid intus ageretur, nec sustinent saltem, quasi necessarius aliquid afferent eo, quod ille cum maxime [*alias:* quo maxime ($=$ *quom maxime?*), tum maxime, tunc maxime] agebat, sed amplius interpellant et a tanto opere avocatum volunt. Oro te, Apelle, vel tu, Marcion, si forte tabula ludens vel de histrionibus aut aurigis contendens tali nuntio avocareris, nonne dixisses: 'Quae mihi mater, aut qui mihi fratres?' Deum praedicans et probans Christus, legem et prophetas adimplens, tanti retro aevi caliginem dispargens, indigne usus est hoc dicto ad percu-tiendam incredulitatem foris stantium vel ad excutiendam importunitatem ab opere revocantium? . . . cum indignatio parentes negat, non negat, sed obiurgat. Denique potiores fecit sibi alios et meritum praelationis ostendens, audientiam scilicet verbi, demonstrat, qua condicione negaverit matrem et fratres. Qua enim alios sibi adop-tavit, qui ei adhaerebant, ea abnegavit illos, qui ab eo absistebant. . . . Sed et alias: figura est synagogae in matre abiuncta et Iudaeorum in fratribus incredulis. . . . —*De Carne Christi*, 7, CSEL 70, pp. 208-212 (*PL* 2, col. 766A-768C); cf. *Adv. Marcionem*, IV, 19 CSEL 47, pp. 482-483 (*PL* 2, col. 404B-406A).

the least on our subject. As is well known, St. Cyprian's theology concerning the Blessed Virgin is rudimentary. In this, it confirms the indication given by Tertullian, that the official teaching on Mary was itself rudimentary at that time in Africa. Moreover, we note the same silence on the part of NOVATIAN, ARNOBIUS and LACTANTIUS. As for HIPPOLYTUS (if he was a Roman), he had been very discreet, showing himself uninclined, it seems, to develop the views of his master, St. Irenaeus, in the Mariological sphere, at least in a direction which could be of any real interest to us.

Thus we approach the Council of Nicaea with rather empty hands: and this council was not anything which would bring about much of a change in the West, where, as is known, it had at first little influence. Furthermore, Latin patristic literature was then in full decadence. It took the penetration of Arianism into the Latin countries to jostle the Fathers there out of their inertia.

ST. HILARY OF POITIERS was an exception. Before going to the East, he had expressed his views on the Blessed Virgin in his *Commentary on St. Matthew*,[46] in which he showed himself strongly opposed to Tertullian's idea that Mary had several children. He does not admit this, and, given his opinion of the Savior's Mother, he could not admit it. And yet, in this same commentary, when discussing the interrupted sermon, he represents the Blessed Virgin as the type of the synagogue.[47] Is this a reminiscence of Tertullian? It is possible; but the variation which we here note in the exegete's attitude leaves us in doubt about his real mind concerning Mary's sanctity, if, indeed, he had any well thought-out idea on the subject at that time. Once he had come into contact with the Eastern Fathers, he began to speak like several of them about a sanctification of the Blessed Virgin at the moment of the Incarnation, and of faults with which God reproached her at her death.[48] Christ alone, he affirms, was without sin, and this was possible because of His virginal birth.[49]

There is no shortage of contemporary Latin authors who expressed themselves very much like Hilary: e.g., GREGORY OF ELVIRA in Spain, MARIUS VICTORINUS in Rome, and AMBROSIASTER.[50] Others, on the contrary, such as ZENO OF VERONA and the mysterious author of the CONSULTATIONES ZACCHAEI,[51] seem rather to have praised the Blessed Virgin, although the former, by an odd turn which reminds one of St. Hilary, speaks of vices from which Mary had to be freed before the Incarnation.[52] Zeno

---

[46] I, 3-4 (*PL* 9, col. 921A-922B).

[47] XII, 24 (*ibid.*, col. 993AB).

[48] See particularly *De Trinitate*, II, 26 (*PL* 10, col. 67B-68A) ; *In Ps.* 118, III, 12 (*CSEL* 22, pp. 384-385; *PL* 9, col. 522C-523A).

[49] Cf. *Maria* I, p. 102, note 7.

[50] *Ibid.*, pp. 102-103.

[51] *Ibid.*, pp. 103-104. P. COURCELLE is now inclined to regard the *Consultationes* as an African work of about the year 412. *Revue de l'Histoire des Religions*, 146 (1954), pp. 174-193.

[52] *Tractatus, Lib.* I, *Tract.* XIII, 10 (*PL* 11, col. 352AB).

himself, therefore, is far from the idea of the Immaculate Conception: or, rather, his statements rule out the possibility of it, although we must note that he never met the problem directly.

It is doubtful whether St. Ambrose was any more aware of this problem than the others. At least, however, at the beginning of his episcopal career, he drew a portrait of the Virgin Mary, in which he speaks only of her sanctity and of the example she could afford for Christian virgins.[53] No restrictions qualify the portrait thus presented. This is all the more remarkable in that the author who inspired the Bishop of Milan's description was, we now suspect, St. Athanasius himself.[54] We saw above that St. Athanasius had undoubtedly left a few smudges on the ideal portrait he had drawn; in the mouth of St. Ambrose, from the beginning of his career to the end, and without any perceptible lapse,[55] there is nothing but praise for Mary. We conclude from this that he thought her sanctity was perfect, or nearly so. Up to now, no predecessor of St. Ambrose has been discovered who spoke of the Blessed Virgin as he did; and we know how much authority he acquired even in his own times, not only in Italy but quite far in the Empire and just about everywhere.

Moreover, St. Ambrose's influence in the field of Mariology was supported and reinforced by men who were themselves of the highest caliber.[56] There was, first of all, St. Jerome, who, by 384 at the latest, had attacked and destroyed Helvidius. Neither the Immaculate Conception nor even Mary's personal sanctity was directly at issue in this debate; indirectly, however, her sanctity was involved, for St. Jerome had vociferously maintained it, insisting that it was very great. In the public opinion, as well as in the eyes of the ecclesiastical authorities, he had been victorious; and from then on, detractors of Mary's virginity were in for trouble, be their names Jovinian or Bonosius—the latter a bishop, and of Illyricum, therefore belonging *de jure* to the eastern world. Jerome and his henchmen, and still more St. Ambrose, made things difficult for them, or reduced them to silence. St. Augustine was soon to join the company and before long, at

---

[53] *De virginibus ad Marcellinam, Lib.* II, c. II-III, nn. 6-19 (*PL* 16, col. 208B-211C, or better yet in the Faller edition, Fasc. 31 of the *Florilegium patristicum,* Bonn, 1933, pp. 47-52). This 'portrait' dates at the latest from the third year of St. Ambrose's episcopacy. There is no doubt that it is taken from a sermon given before a group of Christian virgins prior to that date. We presented this text in "Un portrait de la Sainte Vierge par saint Ambroise," *La Vie Spirituelle,* mai 1954, pp. 477-489.

[54] On this point cf., in addition to what was said above, *Maria* I, p. 104, note 18.

[55] We could cite only one possible example of a lapse of this kind; it is found in the *De mysteriis,* III, 13 (*PL* 16, col. 393AB, or the Botte edition in *Sources chrétiennes* 25, p. 111). In fact one must manifestly understand the *denique supervenit* which one reads there as a justification of what had just been said, since *denique* here has the force of *in fact,* which was classic at that time. There is nevertheless a very marked difference between St. Ambrose and the Orientals at that date; cf. *Maria* I, pp. 112-113.

[56] Cf. *Maria* I, p. 106 ff.

least after the death of St. Ambrose (397), to play the major role, surpassing even St. Jerome. It was only during his controversy with the Pelagians, however, that Augustine was to encounter the problem of Mary's conception. This opens the second part of the history of the Latin Fathers.

FROM THE PELAGIAN CONTROVERSY TO
THE END OF THE EIGHTH CENTURY

PELAGIUS had been a very influential spiritual director in Rome, where he was an important figure among what might be called the *ascetics,* a group to which St. Jerome himself was also attached, and whose adherents were urged to an especially intense and virtuous Christian life. Unfortunately, Pelagius insisted too much, in his teachings, on the human effort to be made for the attainment of virtue; he lost sight of the primordial action of God and of grace in the realization of the Christian ideal. This unfortunate neglect was to lead him into heresy and into conflict with the African bishops, the most important of whom was the Bishop of Hippo. The immediate occasion of the conflict was furnished by the bad times, which brought Pelagius and a number of his followers to Africa when the barbarians threatened and finally took Rome in 410. The controversy began almost at once.[57]

Pelagius was very soon led to bring the Blessed Virgin into it. He esteemed her very highly, as the ascetics did readily; he admired particularly her eminent virtue. When the Africans argued that all men, except Our Lord, have been or are subject to sin, Pelagius replied by citing the saints of the Old and New Testaments who are praised in the Bible. He cited particularly the Mother of Our Savior, judging it conformable to the faith and imposed by it to consider her as absolutely holy, free of the least fault. Thus did he express himself in his *De Natura,* according to ST. AUGUSTINE.[58]

This was a direct and telling blow to the Bishop of Hippo, who was himself inclined to exalt the Blessed Virgin very much. He had even proclaimed her a specially blessed mother, in his *De virginitate,*[59] for having merited from her Son this praise: "Whoever does the will of my Father in heaven, he is my brother and sister and mother." (Matt. 12:50)[60] St.

---

[57] *Ibid.,* p. 114 ff.

[58] We no longer have the text of PELAGIUS' *De natura;* we are informed of the heretic's argumentation here in question only by the *De natura et gratia,* XXXVI, 42, of St. AUGUSTINE (*CSEL* 60, pp. 263-264; *PL* 44, col. 267). Here is the essential of what the Bishop of Hippo writes on this subject: . . . *ipsam etiam domini ac saluatoris nostri matrem "quam" dicit (Pelagius) "sine peccato confiteri necesse esse pietati."*

[59] V, 5 (*CSEL* 41, p. 239; *PL* 40, col. 399).

[60] Note that this text is the one which closes, in the Gospel, the incident of the interrupted sermon, from which incident Tertullian and others drew quite different conclusions relative to the Mother of Jesus. St. Augustine's point of view was quite

Augustine had added that Mary, because she did the will of God, was not only the Mother of Christ in the physical sense, but also His "sister" and His "mother," in a spiritual sense. He believed furthermore that she had consecrated her virginity to God by a true vow.[61] In short, he considered her a truly exceptional person, from the standpoint of sanctity.

In such circumstances, how was he going to react to Pelagius' objection? He seems to have meditated deeply on the embarrassing case which was objected to him. The following is the solution which, at least, he proposes in replying to the heretic in his *De natura et gratia*. The saints cited by Pelagius as proof of his thesis had all, without exception, sinned, declared the Bishop of Hippo, according to the text of St. John: "If we say that we have no sin, we deceive ourselves and the truth is not in us." (I John 1:8) But St. Augustine does not dare apply this principle to Mary; for the honor of her Son, therefore because of her position as Mother of God, he is willing to admit that she was privileged in this regard. But it does not follow, in his eyes, that Pelagius is right, even in this case; for if the Blessed Virgin thus avoided sin, it was by pure grace, affirms Augustine, and not as an effect of her will:

> . . . except for the holy virgin Mary, about whom I do not wish any question to be raised when sin is being discussed—for whence do we know what greater grace of complete triumph over sin may have been given to her who merited to conceive and bear Him Who was certainly without any sin? . . .[62]

Therefore the principle which he defends remains absolute, despite the personal and, in principle, unique exemption which he admits in Mary's favor.

This solution of the problem is extremely important. It is the saint's own work, as he readily admits; he is far from claiming to speak here in the name of the Church and in virtue of a common teaching. But although the pronouncement is his own, it is equally clear that, in giving this solution, and admitting such a privilege for the Blessed Virgin, he feels that he is speaking according to the mind of the Church. As a matter of fact, he is here merely bringing to maturity the ideas and anticipations of his

---

other than theirs, and under the influence of his master, St. Ambrose, he naturally took a very different direction.

[61] *Op. cit.*, IV, 4 (*CSEL* 41, p. 239; *PL* 40, col. 399).

[62] *De natura et gratia*, XXXVI, 42 (*CSEL* 60, pp. 263-264; *PL* 44, col. 267); excepta itaque sancta virgine Maria, de qua propter honorem domini nullam prorsus, cum de peccatis agitur, haberi volo quaestionem—unde enim scimus quid ei plus gratiae collatum fuerit ad vincendum omni ex parte peccatum, quae concipere et parere meruit, quem constat nullum habuisse peccatum—hac ergo virgine excepta, si omnes illos sanctos et sanctas, cum hic viverent, congregare possemus et interrogare, utrum essent sine peccato, quid fuisse responsuros putamus? Utrum hoc quod iste dicit, an quod Joannes apostolus, rogo vos. Quantalibet fuerint in hoc corpore excellentia sanctitatis, si hoc interrogare potuissent, una voce clamassent: si dixerimus quia peccatum non habemus, nos ipsos decipimus et veritas in nobis non est.

master, St. Ambrose—the whole being bound up, for both of them, with the principle of the Divine Maternity.[63]

The Pelagians did not leave St. Augustine in peace after this triumph. The discussion continued, bearing more and more on original sin and the doctrine relative to it. Mary was again involved in the debate; but this time it was not Pelagius himself who brought her name into the arena, but his follower and quite audacious disciple, the deposed ex-bishop JULIAN OF ECLANUM.[64]

In the fourth book of his *Ad Florum*, written about 421, Julian opposes the case of Mary to St. Augustine's principle of the universality of original sin. "You are worse than Jovinian (the heretic)," he cries, in an effort to embarrass the Bishop of Hippo; "He (Jovinian) destroyed Mary's virginity by the manner (in which he conceived) of her giving birth;[65] you deliver her over to the devil by the condition in which (you affirm) she was born."[66] Indeed it goes without saying that Julian was convinced that, for St. Augustine, the Blessed Virgin was born in sin. Julian himself refused to admit such a notion, which he considered even more abominable than his adversaries' claim that all men were born with sin. He, personally, rejected this latter assertion, and he was even less willing to admit what he thought they claimed about Mary, namely, that she had been subject to a like disgrace.

This time the problem was posed before the mind of St. Augustine. It was not directly the problem of the Immaculate Conception as it presents itself to us, since Julian believed neither in original sin nor in its universality. The heretic was simply using the case of the Blessed Virgin as the starting point of an argument *a fortiori;* in no wise did he envisage an exception, properly speaking, on her behalf, which is what the Immaculate Conception really is. Still he might have been able to bring St. Augustine to the idea of an exception and thence to the very notion of the privilege, seeing that a similar process had taken place a few years earlier in connection with Pelagius and the case of the personal sanctity of the Mother of God. Would St. Augustine react this time as he had to the *De natura,* arguing

---

[63] See pp. 488-489 of the article mentioned in note 53 (in *La Vie spirituelle*).

[64] Cf. *Maria* I, p. 116 ff.

[65] The heretic Jovinian had been condemned by St. Ambrose because, among other things, he maintained that the Mother of Our Savior had lost her virginity in giving birth to Him.

[66] This fragment is taken from a long tirade in which Julian of Eclanum pours forth his bile against St. Augustine, who quotes it in his *Opus imperfectum adversus Julianum,* IV, 122 (*PL* 45, col. 1417-1418). Here are the lines which are essential for us: Ille quippe (Jovinianus) dixit boni esse necessitatem; tu, mali: ille ait per mysteria homines ab errore cohiberi; tu vero, nec per gratiam liberari: ille virginitatem Mariae diabolo partus conditione dissolvit: tu ipsam Mariam diabolo nascendi conditione transcribis: ille meliora bonis aequat, id est, integritatem connubio; tu vero commixtionem conjugii morbidam vocas, et castitatem foedissimae rei collatione depretias . . .

again that the Blessed Virgin had enjoyed an exemption?   Not at all; in the answer he gave, not a single word tended in this direction.[67]

It was a tardy reply, for it had so happened that the *Ad Florum* was not communicated to St. Augustine at the time of its publication, but fell into his hands only much later, just a few years before his death.   Then he was to labor long on it, and death would intervene to prevent him from refuting it from beginning to end as he had undertaken to do.   However, the fourth book is included in what remains of this unfinished refutation, or *Opus imperfectum adversus Julianum*.   The answer is famous, and for several centuries it has given rise to laborious exegesis and heated discussion.[68]   The ancients, for their part, saw no reason to understand it other than as a rejection of Julian's invitation in favor of Mary; therefore, she was born in sin, according to the Bishop of Hippo; she could not have been born otherwise.   Nevertheless, he would not yield her up to the devil's dominion (that is, in virtue of her birth), as Julian claimed followed necessarily from Augustine's hypothesis.   Augustine's reason, however, was simply the fact that her original unhappy state had been resolved by the grace of rebirth which she had received:

> See, I do not say that evil is necessary, because neither did Ambrose; and yet I say that infants are reclaimed from evil, as did Ambrose. **And the reason why evil is not necessary is precisely this, that God is able to heal what has been transmitted by nature**—and how much more, that which has been added on by our free will!   I do not say that men are not made free by grace (and God forbid that Ambrose should have said such a thing!); but we say—what you do not wish— that it is only by grace that they are freed: not only in the sense of being forgiven their sins, but also in being kept from temptation.   We do not deliver Mary over to the devil by the condition in which she was born; but for this reason, that this condition is changed by grace.[69]

[67] It is to be noted well that in Augustine's reply there is no question this time of a privilege in favor of the Mother of Our Savior. Yet it would have been easy for him to answer along such a line if he had had any idea of such a privilege, since earlier he had considered a solution of this sort for the problem of her personal sanctity.

[68] There is a whole body of literature dealing with the single sentence, *Non transcribimus diabolo. . .* Some idea of it can be had from Ph. FRIEDRICH, *Die Mariologie des hl. Augustinus*, Cologne, 1907, p. 199 ff. For the more recent interpretations of MUELLER, CAPELLE, HOFFMANN and GÖTZ, see *BTAM* I, no. 989, 1932, p. 508; II, no. 119, 1933, pp. 59-60; no. 318, 1933, p. 175; no. 573, 1934, p. 310; cf. *RTAM* 4, 1932, pp. 361-370; *BTAM VII*, no. 1674, 1956, p. 418.

[69] *Op. cit., ibid.*, col. 1418-1419. We give likewise the essence of St. Augustine's reply: Ecce ego non dico mali esse necessitatem, quia nec Ambrosius; et tamen dico parvulos a malitia reformari, quod et Ambrosius: et ideo mali nulla est necessitas; quia et illud Deo sanabile est, quod trahit nativitas; quanto magis quod addit voluntas?   Non dico, nec per gratiam homines liberari; quod absit ut dicat Ambrosius: sed quod non vis dicimus, nonnisi per gratiam liberari, non solum ut eis debita dimittantur, verum etiam ne in tentationem inferantur. Non transcribimus diabolo Mariam conditione nascendi; sed ideo, quia ipsa conditio solvitur gratia renascendi.   Non tanquam malo bonum, sed tanquam bono melius, virginitatem nuptiis anteponimus . . .

The explanation is labored, the thought is not clear. Apparently it is to be understood in reference to St. Augustine's general views on the birth of men and the rights thereby conferred on the devil.[70] In this light, it is quite true that, according to the Bishop of Hippo, concupiscence entails sin and condemns all men who are born in the normal way to be sinners, because concupiscence is involved in their conception. The fact remains, however, that God and not the devil retains sovereign rights over these sinners. God manifests His sovereign domain precisely by causing them to be born again, which is what took place in Mary's case.

From this explanation, one would have to conclude that Augustine considered the Blessed Virgin as born in sin like all of us. In fact, his immediate successors understood him in this way, and more than one repeated it after him, as we shall see. All this was presumably a consequence of excessively strict theories on the transmission of sin and of a particular theology relative to concupiscence, which was to be called precisely *Augustinian.*

Hence, if our interpretation and that which was current in Latin patristic literature from that time on is correct, St. Augustine tried, intentionally or not, to subject Mary to the law of sin, so far as her origin is concerned. In his *De natura et gratia,* however, he had formulated a principle which could have been liberating in this connection: *The honor of Christ, and therefore that of Christ's Mother.* He had made an exact application of this principle to the case of the personal sins which some had attributed to Mary, which application the Latin Fathers were practically to ratify. He failed, however, to apply it *hic et nunc* to the sin of origin. Was he perhaps afraid that his adversaries might abuse such a concession? But he had managed to make such a concession in the other case, while still binding up his opponents so firmly in the network of Catholic dogma that they could not get free. *De jure* he could just as well have done it this time, and silenced them in the same way; but he failed to do so, thereby showing (what was, at bottom, his thesis) that all men are fallible, even the greatest, when they are not guided by the sovereign authority of the Holy Ghost and the infallible hierarchy through which the Holy Ghost directs and quickens the Church.

It is true, indeed, that on this point as on the preceding, St. Augustine was stating his personal views. There was no official teaching of the Roman Pontiff or even of the Bishops of the African church, taken as a group, which could serve him as norm. He was all alone in the face of a new problem, and trying, as a theologian, to find a solution for it. He resolved it by himself, therefore, to the best of his ability and knowledge, but with the consequent liability to error, as he himself seems to be perfectly aware when he writes what we have seen in the *De natura et gratia,* relative to Pelagius.

[70] Cf. *Maria* I, pp. 118-119.

As a matter of fact, the Fathers who came after St. Augustine in the West adhered to his judgment concerning the personal sanctity of the Mother of God, without experiencing any difficulty about it, so it seems, and without even referring to it explicitly very often.   In general, they were content to speak of the Blessed Virgin as a saint who was never guilty of any fault.   This view was to become classical among the Latin Fathers, and remain the view of the Church.   To the Bishop of Hippo belongs the merit of having formulated it, even though he did so merely in his own name, and perhaps only *ad experimentum,* in order to obtain the evaluation and judgment of Christendom on it.

As for the other point, which interests us still more directly and concerns precisely our problem of the Immaculate Conception, it goes without saying that St. Augustine's opinion weighed heavily in the balance.   We have already noted that his successors tended to follow in his footsteps.   Certain of them, it is true, refrained from following him all the way, perhaps because they did not encounter the problem personally: St. Augustine himself had come up against it only at the end of his life, and even then treated it only in passing.[71]   This would undoubtedly explain why we do not find, in the writings of such men as St. Leo the Great, Prosper of Acquitaine, St. Caesarius of Arles, Cassiodorus, St. Gregory the Great and St. Isidore of Seville, any statement concerned with the Mother of God personally, in her relationship with original sin.[72]   These men, some of whom are among the most important of their time and of all times, were content to follow the Augustinian views on the transmission of sin by concupiscence.   Sometimes, it is true, they themselves happen to repeat that, for this reason, Christ alone was exempt from sin, which implies that, in their minds, Mary would not have been; but at least they abstain, so far as we know, from drawing this conclusion on their own.   This may have been only an accident, due to the fact that, as we were saying, the occasion never arose for them to draw the conclusion or express

[71] It is only too true that St. Augustine treated the Blessed Virgin's relationship to original sin only in passing, just as he had done for the question of her personal sins.   In both cases he was refuting the objections of his contradictors—Pelagius in the latter case, Julian of Eclanum in the former.   In no other work do we find him taking up these two questions again, either separately or together, to give them a thorough-going treatment.   This in itself is regrettable, for the conditions under which he actually treated them are not the best that one might wish for.   At any rate, the two passages are lost, so to speak, within immense treatises.   For several centuries now, theologians have been extracting them in order to focus attention on them and on this testimony of a master.   This in itself is somewhat arbitrary, at least if it is done in such a spirit as to give more importance to these answers than their author did.   There is no doubt that, historically, they exercised an influence on the successors of the Bishop of Hippo; but this was, at least as far as the immediate successors are concerned, more by the principles which they involve and imply, theologically speaking, than as answers *ad rem.*   We scarcely ever find them used directly as answers in the centuries that immediately followed St. Augustine.

[72] As to them, see *Maria* I, pp. 149 and 151.

themselves on the matter. Is not this the case, for example, with a man like CASSIAN, who could hardly be accused of excessive Augustinianism? In his *Collatio XXII* he declares: "To be without sin belongs to the majesty of Our Lord Jesus Christ alone. . . . He alone was never stained by the contact of anything impure." The reason alleged by Cassian to justify this affirmation is that Jesus had only "the likeness of sinful flesh." (Cf. Rom. 8:3)[73] By this we are to understand that He was born of a virgin. It is easy for us to divine what Cassian's idea about the Mother of the Savior would have been, even though he himself said nothing about her. On this question he is, beyond any doubt, in line with St. Augustine, as amazing as that may strike us.

The same line will be followed with all the more reason by such confirmed Augustinians as ST. FULGENTIUS OF RUSPE and the deacon, FERRANDUS, who, in fact, did take up the problem that had confronted St. Augustine, and did not mince words over it. The former discussed it in a sort of official document, an exposition of the faith which he composed in the name of several of his colleagues in the episcopate. Regarding the Incarnation of the Son of God, he wrote:

> This is the grace by which it happened that God, Who came to take away sins (for in Him there is no sin), became man according to the prophecy, and was born of sinful flesh and in the likeness of sinful flesh. For the flesh of Mary, having been conceived in sin, as is the condition of humans, was indeed sinful flesh, and begot the Son of God in the likeness of sinful flesh . . .[74]

It is expressly stated that Mary's was "sinful flesh," and that she was "conceived in iniquity." Hence the difference between her and Our Lord:

> The Son of God, sent (into the world), appeared "in the likeness of sinful flesh"—for in His truly human flesh, man's iniquity was not found, but only mortality.[75]

In this same perspective, Fulgentius added immediately[76] that if this

---

[73] IX (*CSEL* 13, pp. 627-628; *PL* 49, col. 1232A-C). Here Cassian is not thinking of any exception for Mary, even though his text deals directly with personal sins. On the other hand, in this text he connects Our Lord's privilege with His birth, which is Augustinian in spirit, and which one finds also in *Collatio*, V, V, *op. cit.*, p. 124 (*PL* 49, col. 614B-615A).

[74] Haec est gratia qua factum est ut Deus, qui venit peccata tollere, quia peccatum in eo non est, homo conciperetur atque nasceretur in similitudine carnis peccati, de carne peccati. Caro quippe Mariae, quae in iniquitatibus humana fuerat solemnitate concepta, caro fuit utique peccati, quae Filium Dei genuit in similitudinem carnis peccati . . . —*Ep.* 17, VI, 13 (*PL* 65, col. 458B). It is to be noted that what Fulgentius had in mind in this context was not the case of the Blessed Virgin but only that of her Son. The Bishop of Ruspe, unlike St. Augustine, was not confronted with a difficulty relative to the Mother of God; he gave an answer about her while speaking of her Son. He did it precisely in the spirit of a profoundly Augustinian theologian.

[75] In similitudine igitur carnis peccati Dei Filius missus apparuit, quia in ejus vera humana carne non iniquitas hominis, sed mortalitas fuit. (*Ibid.*, col. 458C)

[76] VII, 14 (*ibid.*, col. 458D-459A).

Virgin gave birth to God, it was not through any merit of her own, any human merit, but solely through the divine benevolence of the Son Whom she conceived.

With still greater emphasis, if that is possible, Ferrandus wrote in his turn, likewise on the question of the Incarnation:

> The flesh of Christ is taken from a mother; therefore it is all the more genuine; but it is altogether holy because purified by union with the divinity. The nature of our flesh is found in that of Christ, but our nature's guilt is not. Thus the flesh of Christ is in one way like Mary's flesh, and in another way unlike it: like it, inasmuch as it took its origin from it; unlike it, because it was not infected by its sinful (*viti-atae*) origin; like it in experiencing truly, albeit voluntarily, the infirmi-ties of flesh; unlike it, because committing no sins, whether voluntarily or through ignorance; like it in being passible and mortal, unlike it in being incorruptible and a source of life for the dead; like it in kind, unlike it in merit; like it as to species, unlike it as to power; like it because the likeness of sinful flesh, as the Apostle says: "God sent His Son in the likeness of sinful flesh." (Rom. 8:3) Thus we are taught that Mary was, in the natural order and according to the laws of human birth, the cause of the new existence of Christ's flesh; but the need of marital intercourse was eliminated, so that His flesh might not be sinful flesh, because it was to be the flesh of God; but that it might be the "likeness of sinful flesh," because truly born of mortal flesh; and that it might rightly be mortal because taking its matter from mortal flesh.[77]

No doubt it would be imprudent to judge the ideas of the Latin Fathers from the fifth to the seventh centuries, about Mary and her conception,

---

[77] Caro itaque Christi de matre sumpta est, ideo amplius vera est; sed plane sancta est, quia divinitatis adunatione mundata est. In carne Christi natura est nostrae carnis, sed non reperitur culpa naturae. Sic caro Christi carni Mariae et similis est, et dissimilis: similis, quia inde traxit originem; dissimilis, quia inde non contraxit vitiatae originis contagionem: similis, quoniam, licet voluntarias, tamen veras sensit infirmitates; dissimilis, quoniam nullas penitus neque per voluntatem, neque per ignorantiam commisit iniquitates: similis, quia passibilis et mortalis; dissimilis, quia incoinquinabilis, et vivificatrix etiam mortuorum: similis genere, dissimilis mer-ito: similis specie, dissimilis virtute: similis, quia similitudo est carnis peccati, dicente Apostolo: *Deus Filium suum misit in similitudine carnis peccati* (Rom. VIII, 3). Ecce quantum caro Christi docetur a Maria causam novae existentiae naturaliter assecuta secundum solemnitatem partus humani, sequestrata necessitate concubitus maritalis, ut non sit quidem caro peccati, quia caro est Dei; sit tamen similitudo carnis peccati, quia veraciter nata est de carne mortali: merito etiam mortalis, quia materiam traxit de carne mortali.—*Ep.* III, 4 (*PL* 67, col. 892A-C).

To write thus, Ferrandus and Fulgentius did not have to innovate, nor even to draw the logical conclusions from Augustinian theology, or make use of the ticklish text of the *Opus imperfectum*, IV, 122, which confounds theologians even today. St. Augustine had more than once made statements of this kind himself, for example in the *De Genesi ad litteram*, X, 32, PL 34, col. 422; in *Enar. in Ps.* 34, *Serm.* 2, n. 3, *PL* 36, col. 335. As a matter of fact, the Bishop of Hippo does not see how Our Lord Himself could have been born without sin if He had not been born of a Virgin and had not avoided the intervention of even the least degree of concupiscence in His birth; cf. *Serm.* 151, V, 5 (*PL* 38, col. 817); *Enchiridion* XXXIV (*PL* 40, col. 249).

from the samples which Ferrandus and St. Fulgentius have just furnished us. These two men were expressing, without any reserve, their own views, which were not necessarily the same as those of their colleagues, from whom we have found no statement on the precise point we are concerned with.[78]   One may well wonder, in fact, whether certain bishops such as St. PETER CHRYSOLOGUS and MAXIMUS OF TURIN, who seem to like to contrast Eve and Mary,[79] would not have adopted a slightly different orientation.[80]   How can we judge at present, since there are still unsettled questions about their works,[81] of which we are far from having satisfactory critical editions?[82]   The fact remains that, like the others including Cassian himself, as we have seen, they smack of Augustinianism; that a number of their contemporaries would have been capable, we may presume, of writing as Fulgentius and Ferrandus did; that the statements of these two disturbed no one, so far as we know, for no protest has been recorded. On the contrary, Fulgentius, as we have said, composed his work in the name of a group of about fifteen African bishops. Furthermore, he addressed it to some Orientals who had come to Rome to discuss dogmatic questions with the Holy See, and neither these nor the Roman circles which were able to become acquainted with the document reacted against it.   The fact is symptomatic enough to merit being pointed out.

Is our study of the Latin Fathers then to end with these observations? Not altogether, since we are to proceed to the end of the eighth century. Before reaching that date, we meet the VENERABLE BEDE, a man who is more original than many are willing to admit.   He is quite notably so on the subject of St. John the Baptist, at any rate—a point that scarcely seems to have been noticed.   In certain authentic homilies of his,[83] he takes a

---

[78] I.e., on the subject of the *caro Mariae*. However all of them have the same opinion as Augustine, Fulgentius, Ferrandus and Cassian himself as to the *similitudo carnis peccati*.

[79] For St. PETER CHRYSOLOGUS, see *Serm.* 140 (*PL* 52, col. 576B); for MAXIMUS OF TURIN, *Hom.* 6 (*PL* 57, col. 237B f.); *Hom.* 15 (col. 253C-254B).

[80] The mere fact of their having drawn a parallel between Eve and Mary in no way suffices to establish that their way of thinking differed from that of Ferrandus and St. Fulgentius. The text of ZENO OF VERONA mentioned above (cf. note 52) shows that it was possible in ancient times to draw from such a parallel something quite different from the idea that Mary had been holy. The texts cited under the names of CHRYSOLOGUS and MAXIMUS OF TURIN (cf. note 79) do not, it is true, seem to be of this kind.

[81] On the present status of the question of the authenticity of the texts, cf. the *Clavis Patrum Latinorum* in *Sacris Erudiri* III, 1951, and, in addition, the table of R. LAURENTIN, cited in note 14.

[82] One may question not only the authenticity of the writings, but also the critical worth of the text found in our present editions.

[83] For the distinction betwen the authentic and unauthentic works in Bede's homilary, i.e., *Lib.* I and II of the Migne edition, *PL* 94, one should refer to Dom G. MORIN, "Le recueil primitif des homélies de Bède sur l'Evangile" in *Revue bénédictine* 9, 1892, pp. 316-326; cf. R. LAURENTIN, *op. cit.*, p. 138. In the authentic works of the homilary, from which alone we quote here, the text is of Bede's own

position which is, in effect, opposed to that of St. Augustine. It is not so much by expressing the opinion that the precursor committed no personal sin.[84]   The Bishop of Hippo had had some hesitation on this point; and although, in the text quoted above from *De natura et gratia*[85] on Mary's exemption from all fault during her life, Augustine speaks as though this was, in his mind, a unique privilege; still, in the same work, just a few pages away, he admits that other holy persons might have enjoyed a similar grace;[86] it is sufficient for him (but this he insists on) that grace was involved.   Therefore Bede, in expressing his opinion relative to the Precursor more or less clearly, does not depart so far from St. Augustine's essential positions; rather, he applies the Bishop of Hippo's theology in a way that the latter had half-foreseen and tolerated in advance.   But Bede goes much further than Augustine when he speaks of a sanctification *in utero* for St. John the Baptist.[87]   He speaks of it as a veritable purification from original sin, whereas St. Augustine sees in it something quite different from justification properly so-called: a simple, transitory communication of the Spirit of God, designed to enable the Precursor to recognize from then on the Messias whom he was later to announce.   Indeed, for the Bishop of Hippo, it seems to be an absolute principle that it is impossible to be regenerated before being born;[88] according to him, therefore, John the Baptist would have come into the world just as we did, in sin.[89]   Bede, as is evident, has different views; and what is most remarkable is that he justifies them by the following argument: "It is certain, according to the

composition; that is why we cite them under his name. They are not older works which he caused to be included in a collection organized by him. The best edition to use from now on is that of D. HURST in *Corpus Christianorum*, Ser. Lat. CXXII, Turnhut, 1955.

[84] Hom. for the Feast of the Beheading of St. John the Baptist, Migne, *Lib.* II, *Hom.* XX (*PL* 94, col. 242D-243A; cf. *Corpus Christianorum, Lib.* II, *Hom.* 23, p. 356).

[85] See note 62.

[86] XLII, 49 (*CSEL* 60, pp. 269-270; *PL* 44, col. 271); cf. LX, 70 (*CSEL*, pp. 285-286; *PL* 44, col. 281-282). This shows that at that time St. Augustine was not so sure of what he had written earlier in the same work about the exception for the Blessed Virgin, i.e., that it was an exception unique in its kind. At least, he postponed examination of the question. We should not, therefore, try to draw too much out of the text today in this matter, without referring to the context and taking into account the subsequent development of the ideas of the Bishop of Hippo.

[87] Hom. for the Vigil of St. John the Baptist, *Lib.* II, *Hom.* XIII (*PL* 94, col. 208A-D; *Corpus Christianorum, Lib.* II, *Hom.* 19, pp. 325-326).

[88] *De peccatorum meritis et remissione*, II, XXVII, 43 (*CSEL* 60, p. 114; *PL* 44, col. 177). From this point of view, Augustinian theology encounters another obstacle in the way of the idea of the Immaculate Conception. Truly, in Augustinianism, the doors are shut on all sides against this idea.

[89] St. Augustine states this expressly, e.g. in *Serm.* 293, n. 12 (*PL* 38, col. 1335). He sees no possibility of an exception for John the Baptist, unless he should have had a virgin birth as did Our Lord. It goes without saying that the same principle holds for the Mother of Jesus.

dependable judgment of the Fathers, that the gift of the Holy Spirit is not bound by any law." [90]

If we have pointed out these assertions of Bede concerning St. John the Baptist, it is in no wise as though he had extended them to the case of Mary. No such inclination appears anywhere in his works. He simply reflected on the problem of the Precursor's sanctification *in utero* and expressed his opinion on the subject, nothing more. Nevertheless, a breach had been opened in the theology of St. Augustine, which is why we have called the attention of theologians to these texts, particularly to the principle which Bede formulates to justify his assertions. It is a liberating principle, which justifies the Immaculate Conception equally as well as, and even better than, the sanctification of St. John the Baptist before his birth. It is true, we repeat, that Bede did not apply the principle to the Blessed Virgin, or have any intention, apparently, of so doing; nevertheless, by this principle, he emancipated Latin theology from the vise in which strict Augustinianism then gripped it. Later centuries in the West were to receive instruction from Bede's homiliary,[91] and as they read and reread these texts they understood the case of St. John the Baptist better and better. The day was bound to come sooner or later when someone would conceive the idea of an *a fortiori* reasoning: If John the Baptist was sanctified before his birth, why not the future Mother of the Redeemer also, and she even earlier than he? St. Augustine had closed the passageway to precisely this sort of reasoning; now Bede unbolts the door. How could one fail to notice this, and the fortunate work he thus accomplished?

But let us not exaggerate. This was a long-range emancipation, of which Bede himself was undoubtedly quite unaware, if we are to judge by his homily on the Annunciation.[92] In it he praises the Mother of God very highly, putting her in a fine light in her opposition to Eve;[93] nonetheless he writes of the act of the Incarnation:

---

[90] Constat quippe veridica Patrum sententia quia lege non stringitur Spiritus sancti donum. (*Loc. cit.*, col. 208B; *Corpus Christianorum*, p. 325)

[91] Either directly—reading it as it was or with interpolations—or indirectly, through the inclusion of Bede's homilies in later homiliaries, which were more widely circulated than the original. It is not for us to trace this history, which extends beyond the limits of our subject; we should like however to point out that Bede's homily for the Vigil of St. John the Baptist found its way into the homily of PAUL THE DEACON; cf. F. WIEGAND, *Das Homiliarium Karls des Grossen*, Leipzig, 1897, p. 46. This indicates what a wide diffusion it must have had.—We shall abstain from studying this homiliary here and from making direct use of it, because it pertains properly to the field of the liturgy, being not an original composition but a collection, of which there were more than one at that time, made up of borrowed works.

[92] In reality, for the Ember Days of December, according to D. MORIN, *loc. cit.*, p. 325 (In *PL* 94, *Lib.* I, *Hom.* I, col. 9-14; *Corpus Christianorum, Lib.* I, *Hom.* 3, pp. 14-20).

[93] Cf. particularly col. 9A-11B. (*Corpus . . .*, pp. 14-16)

The power of the Most High overshadowed the Mother of God; for when the Holy Spirit filled her heart, he moderated the heat of carnal passion in it, cleansed it from the desire of temporal things, and with heavenly gifts consecrated her soul as well as her body.[94]

Following which, Bede comments thus on the words of the angel:

"Therefore the Holy One to be born of thee shall be called the Son of God": for because you are to conceive of the sanctification of the Spirit, that which is born will be holy. The birth is in keeping with the conception; as you conceive while remaining a virgin, contrary to the rule of human nature, so shall you transcend the human measure in giving birth to the Son of God. For we humans are all conceived in iniquity and born in sin, although all who are foreordained to eternal life by the gift of God are born again of water and the Holy Spirit. Our Redeemer, alone, Who deigned to become incarnate for us, was holy at the moment of His birth, because He was conceived without sin.[95]

Bede here forgets about St. John the Baptist, whom he has spoken about differently elsewhere, as we have just seen. Nor does he except Our Lady, the thought of whom ought to have stayed with him here and halted him, if he knew of the doctrine of the Immaculate Conception, and believed in it. Regarding her, he stays within the perspectives of Augustinianism, and expresses himself on the Incarnation as many Fathers had done before him.[96] His influence was to be exercised only indirectly, presuming he had an influence, by way of what we have called 'theological reasoning.'

He does not seem to have had any effect on his contemporaries or immediate successors: on ALCUIN, for example,[97] or AMBROSE AUTPERT. The latter would be very interesting for us if we could still attribute to him the composition of the famous *Cogitis me* of Pseudo-Jerome; but there can no longer be any question of this. Furthermore, there is still no collection of Ambrose's authentic writings. Several of the works attributed

---

[94] Obumbravit autem beatae Dei genitrici virtus Altissimi: quia Spiritus sanctus cor illius cum implevit, ab omni aestu concupiscentiae carnalis temperavit, emundavit a desideriis temporalibus, ac donis coelestibus mentem simul illius consecravit, et corpus. (Col. 12D-13A).

[95] Ideoque et quod nascetur ex te sanctum, vocabitur Filius Dei: quia quod de sanctificatione Spiritus concipies, sanctum erit quod gignitur. Congruit conceptioni nativitas, ut quae contra humanae conditionis morem virgo concipis, supra humanae consuetudinis modum Dei Filium generes. Omnes quippe homines in iniquitate concipimur, et in delicitis nascimur: quotquot autem donante Deo ad vitam praeordinati sumus aeternam, ex aqua et spiritu sancto renascimur. Solus vero Redemptor noster pro nobis incarnari dignatus, mox sanctus natus est: quia sine iniquitate conceptus est. (Col. 13A; *Corpus* . . . , p. 18).

[96] As for his ruling out concupiscence from the act of the Incarnation, he is in the Augustinian line. For the rest, it is not very likely that he followed certain Greek Fathers; rather, he probably depended on such people as St. Hilary or Zeno of Verona.

[97] However, to reach a final conclusion about Alcuin, it would be necessary to take into account his homilary, and therefore to have the text of it, and a dependable one. We have not yet reached this point.

to him by D. Winandy himself[98] are still contested.[99] In those that are of well established origin, we note that the author has a real devotion to the Blessed Virgin, and that he esteems her highly; [100] but, unless we are mistaken, he does not go beyond this.

To find something of this sort among the Latins before the end of the eighth century, just as for the Greeks up to the sixth century, it would be necessary, it seems, to have recourse to another series of witnesses, the APOCRYPHA.   In Latin we still read a certain PSEUDO-MATTHEW, as it is called, which is a story of the life of the Blessed Virgin more or less parallel to the *Protogospel of James,*[101] and more or less directly inspired by it or by its sources.   Now in several manuscripts which very well seem to correspond to the original,[102] this *Pseudo-Matthew* speaks of the conception of Mary by Anne as if it had been virginal (3:2 and 5).   This corresponds to what is found in some manuscripts of the *Protogospel of James,* which are perhaps rarer, comparatively speaking,[103] but which witness to a reading which must date quite far back in antiquity, since St. Epiphanius was acquainted with it and rejected it.[104]   Epiphanius could not admit that anyone but Our Lord could have been conceived virginally; and in this he was certainly right, and represented the Catholic mind.   The apocrypha did some inventing, embroidering no doubt in order to produce something of the extraordinary—which, apparently, is what seemed to them to be essential.   One cannot suppose, indeed, that either these authors or the copyists who reproduced their works with greater or less modifications all understood what this reading was leading them to, i.e. to a crude, although theologically ill-founded, idea of the Immaculate Conception. Did their readers understand this any better?   As far as the East is

---

[98] D. WINANDY, in his article, "L'oeuvre littéraire d'Ambroise Autpert," *Revue bénédictine,* 60, 1950, pp. 93-119, and in his work, *Ambroise Autpert moine et théologien,* Paris, 1953, pp. 10-12.

[99] Father H. BARRÉ would make some reservations relative to certain writings.

[100] For example: in connection with the prophecy of Simeon in the homily on the Purification, n. 12 (*PL* 89, col. 1301AB); or in the commentary of the beginning of chap. 12 of the Apocalypse, *Maxima Bibliotheca Patrum,* 13, Lyon, 1677, pp. 530 f.

[101] Cf. *supra,* p. 58 f. The two have been edited side by side by E. AMANN, *Le Protévangile de Jacques et ses remaniements latins,* Paris, 1910, but the manuscript tradition has never been thoroughly studied for either one. A more exhaustive study would undoubtedly bring out many peculiarities which we hardly suspect at present, even if we are aware of the surprises which await editors and critics when dealing with this very special type of literature. For the portion of the PSEUDO-MATTHEW relevant to our question, see p. 515 ff. of the present volume.

[102] Internal evidence makes it clear that the readers must have been disturbed by this idea of a virgin birth for the Mother of Jesus. It was presumably in order to eliminate this peculiarity that they emended the text.

[103] This reading is to be found in IV, 2 and 4. There are several witnesses for it, but the number of manuscripts of the *Protogospel* known and used is much greater than that of the corresponding manuscripts of the *Pseudo-Matthew.*

[104] In his *Panarion, Haer.* 79, nn. 5-7 (*GCS* 37, pp. 480-482; *PG* 42, col. 748B-752B).

concerned, this remains to be seen; in the West, there is a probability that a number of people, reading these things, may have envisaged the possibility of Mary having been born like her Son, and therefore without sin, because of the fact that ordinary conception and original sin were so bound up together for the Latin mind. This would explain why a few of the more learned copyists with Augustinian preoccupations seem to have rectified the (supposedly) original reading of the *Pseudo-Matthew*, not so much, it seems, to avoid the idea of the Immaculate Conception, as to reject the hypothesis that Mary, like Jesus, had been virginally conceived. The suspicion is justified, therefore, that until this time (and later on as well, if they found it in certain manuscripts), certain readers of the original version drew from it the conclusion that Mary had not known sin at her birth. But we do not see that such an idea made any headway in the world of theologians, properly so-called. We have found no trace of it in the East, where the reading was rather quickly eliminated from a very great number of the manuscripts themselves of the *Protogospel*. In the West, where it had a greater chance of survival, there is no indication that it influenced the least theologian before the end of the eighth century. This shows how little Latin thought before that date was orientated toward the idea of a holy conception and birth for the Mother of God. This idea seems to have attracted no one but a few Pelagians and, outside of them, a few poor souls at most, who perhaps did not very well understand what they were saying.

It is to be noted further that the eighth century was marked among the Latins by a rather sharp reaction of the theologians against the apocryphal literature, which movement was to be prolonged and strengthened by the Carolingians. St. Jerome was held in high esteem in this group, and, by means of a work composed in his name, he was even brought into the new crusade (belief in the Assumption, incidentally, was to suffer thereby). The *Pseudo-Matthew* in turn fell into neglect, and was replaced by the *Liber de nativitate Mariae*,[105] in which there was no longer question of Mary's virginal conception. Thus the curtain fell on an ill-starred idea which had had neither the time nor the means of getting a true hearing. It was a simple parasite which the historian today must mention, but merely as a curiosity.

*   *   *   *

In closing, let us try to take in at a single glance the centuries of history which we have attempted to cover. We will now be able to grasp clearly the difference between Latin and Eastern Fathers on the question of the Immaculate Conception.

---

[105] This other Latin revision has also been edited by Msgr. AMANN in the above-mentioned work.

The Latins collided ponderously with the dogma of original sin and got mired down in it, there to stay for centuries. To set them free, it took the long labors of mediaeval scholasticism, and especially the bold initiative of Duns Scotus.[106] In the East it was quite different: matters progressed calmly. Even though they had launched more than one audacious insinuation against the Blessed Virgin's sanctity, and some of them were continuing and would continue more or less to do so, the theologians began little by little to extol her virtues. The tendency strengthened, to the point where the derogatory remarks were progressively abandoned, or at least the expressions used were attenuated; however, the problem, properly so-called, of the original sanctity of the Mother of the Savior, was not clearly posed. Among the Latins, on the contrary, the problem of her personal sanctity was nearly solved in the early part of the fifth century, and was to remain so; while that of her original sanctity, raised almost immediately afterwards, is given a very different solution, at least for the moment. The Latins, therefore, were in the lead as regards the posing of this second problem, since they took it up under the negative aspect of original sin; but they were far behind as regards the preparation for its solution, which solution would lead to the definition of the Immaculate Conception. Indeed, considering the way things stood during the patristic period, the Latin Fathers had gotten so far away from the solution that it would seem as though they could never have attained it. But the Holy Ghost was present, watching over the seed; and He would be able to arrange everything in time—showing that the Lord disposes of centuries, and that God's ways are not those of men. Surely the Latins and Greeks could have helped one another with their beliefs and intuitions, if they had had more contacts at that time. A certain liaison indeed had been established with the Byzantines in numerous regions of the western world in the sixth century, and again at Rome in the seventh and eighth centuries, due particularly to a temporary resumption of a hellenizing tendency on the part of the Papacy; but this phenomenon did not go far enough to assure by itself the necessary interpenetration.

It is a fact that the Latins would have been in a position to help the Greeks by bringing them to pose the problem of Mary's conception, for the latter were still in the most elementary stages on this point at a time when some of the former were already deciding it definitely in the negative. The Latins were going ahead too fast, heedless of the complexity of the problem and of its various aspects; but at least they had felt more or less obscurely that one might wonder what the answer was, whereas their Eastern colleagues hardly suspected that the problem existed.

The deficiency on the part of the latter is easy enough to comprehend;

---

[106] Cf. chapter V of the present volume, p. 204 ff.; also chapter I, p. 45 f.

for while the Oriental theologians were not so ignorant of the doctrine of original sin as has been said,[107] still they did not give it so much attention as did the West, especially from the fifth century on. The outburst of Pelagianism crystallized the preoccupations of the Latins in this direction, and tended to orientate their theology a little too fixedly around it, as the later Augustinianism proves. For the same reason, the Westerners had great difficulty attacking the problem of Mary's initial sanctity according to its true dimensions. They had done much better with the problem of her personal sanctity, because here the Bishop of Hippo had prepared the way for them; but, precisely, Augustine was not so well placed to meet the problem of Mary's original sanctity, because handicapped by his views on the role of concupiscence in the transmission of sin. These views blocked the way for him and his successors, preventing them from admitting an exemption from the law of original sin in Mary's case, although they did admit such an exemption, through the operation of grace, from the con-cupiscence which she was thought to have inherited from her ancestors.

Finally, we might retain this lesson which Providence here gives us: our views are quite limited. Even those of the greatest theologians are some-times so. We are enveloped in mystery, a mystery that God allows our dull minds to penetrate slowly. May the Holy Spirit find it easier to work in us than He has occasionally elsewhere in the course of the centuries. Hence, let us open our souls to His action, and through it to the teaching of the *magisterium*. Furthermore, let us strive today to listen to all our brothers, including those of the Eastern Church, the ancient Fathers who once cast luster upon those lands. They spoke for us also. If our ancestors in the West had, in general, taken greater care to listen to them atten-tively[108] and to enter into a dialogue with them, they would undoubtedly have been spared more than one mistake. Let us retain this lesson also; it is a lesson in the Catholic spirit, and it is a view of the Church.

---

[107] Cf. chapter I of the present work, p. 41 f.; chapter III, p. 91 ff.

[108] We must not think that everyone neglected them. Without going back any further, we can say that St. Hilary borrowed much from them, as did St. Ambrose and St. Jerome. St. Augustine himself constantly urged St. Jerome to give the Latins numerous translations of choice works. He would have wished for many more of them than Jerome and Rufinus actually brought out. From the time of the Pelagian controversy on, the Bishop of Hippo considered it a duty, if he had to consult a patristic work written in Greek, to read in that language the part he needed if there was no Latin translation of the work. Would that all theologians had followed his example!

BIBLIOGRAPHY

An exhaustive bibliography of this subject is out of the question. We will list only those relatively recent works which seem to be the most directly usable because of the documentation they furnish. However, the value of this documentation will need to be verified in many cases.

X. LE BACHELET and M. JUGIE, "Immaculée Conception," *Dictionnaire de Théologie Catholique,* Vacant-Mangenot-Amann, VII, col. 872-984 (Paris 1923).

M. GORDILLO, *Mariologia orientalis,* Roma, 1954, pp. 88-149.

S. C. GULOVICH, "The Immaculate Conception in the Eastern Churches," *Marian Studies* 5 (1954), pp. 146-183.

M. JUGIE, *L'Immaculée Conception dans l'Ecriture Sainte et dans la Tradition orientale (Bibliotheca Immaculatae Conceptionis* 3), Rome, 1952.

F. S. MUELLER, "Die Unbefleckte Empfängnis der heiligsten Jungfrau im Bekenntnisse der koptischen und äthiopischen Kirche," *Orientalia christiana,* 35, 1934, pp. 157-192.

——, "Die Unbefleckte Empfängnis Marias in der syrischen und armenischen Ueberlieferung," *Scholastik,* 9, 1934, pp. 161-201.

——, "Die Unbefleckte Empfängnis der Gottesmutter in der griechischen Ueberlieferung," *Gregorianum,* 16, 1935, pp. 74-96 and 225-250; 17, 1936, pp. 82-115.

I. ORTIZ DE URBINA, "La Mariologia nei Padri Siriaci," *Orientalia christiana periodica,* 1, 1935, pp. 100-113.

——, "Lo sviluppo della Mariologia nella Patrologia Orientale," *Orientalia christiana periodica,* 6, 1940, pp. 40-82.

——, "Die Marienkunde in der Patristik des Ostens," in P. Sträter, *Katholische Marienkunde,* t. I, 2nd ed., Paderborn, 1952, pp. 85-118.

H. RAHNER, "Die Marienkunde in der lateinischen Patristik," in P. Sträter, *op. cit.,* pp. 137-182.

Virgo Immaculata. Acta Congressus Mariologici-Mariani Romae anno MCMLIV celebrati, Vol. IV, De Immaculata Conceptione apud Ss. Patres et Scriptores Orientales, Romae, 1955.

In addition, we have referred several times in the present study to the one which we published under the title, "Marie à travers la Patristique. Maternité divine, Virginité, Sainteté," in *Maria. Etudes sur la Sainte Vierge* edited by H. DU MANOIR, t. I, Paris, 1949, pp. 69-157.

CIVITAS DAVID

III

The Byzantine Church and the Immaculate Conception

FRANCIS DVORNIK*

One of the characteristic features of eastern Christianity is a deep and warm devotion to Our Lady, the Mother of Christ. Innumerable examples of this devotion are to be found in Eastern liturgies, in literature, in art, and in the spiritual life of simple believers. The Byzantine Church is particularly renowned for its devotion to Mary. This love of the Mother of God inspired Greek poets to compose hymns in her honor, hymns which are still sung in the Divine Office. And who does not know the numerous artistic representations of Mary, many of which still adorn Greek churches. Greek artists of the Byzantine period produced some masterpieces representing Our Lady, which inspired the piety of the faithful for centuries, were imitated by western artists, and still provoke admiration for the artists' achievements, and our humble homage by reason of their personal piety. The Byzantine Church inculcated in all the people whom it converted to Christianity, a profound devotion to Our Lady; and it was the Russian Church which became its best disciple in this respect. There also, in Kiev, Novgorod and Moscow, the iconography of Our Lady reached its greatest heights from the eleventh to the eighteenth centuries.

I

THE EASTERN CHURCH AND THE IMMACULATE CONCEPTION

In spite of that, it was not the Eastern Church but the Western Church which succeeded in defining the more clearly the great prerogatives which God bestowed on the One who should become the Mother of His incarnate Son. From the scholastic period on, the best western theologians worked

* Professor of Byzantine History, Dumbarton Oaks Research Library and Collection, Harvard University, Washington, D. C. The present article was completed in August, 1954.

ceaselessly on Mariology, and the result of their theological research permitted the highest authority in the Catholic Church to proclaim solemnly the two dogmas of the Immaculate Conception of Our Lady and of her Assumption after her death. Both doctrines are intimately connected. If it is true that Our Lady was exempted by a special privilege and in virtue of the future merits of the divine Saviour, from inheriting original sin, then it is logical to believe that God, in anticipating for her the resurrection of the body—a belief which is so dear to all Christians—exempted her from the corruption of the body which, with death, is one of the consequences of original sin.

MODERN EASTERN THEOLOGIANS

Eastern theologians of more recent times have not followed their western colleagues in their research into Mariology. Some of them have even expressed bewilderment over the proclamation of the two dogmas.[1] It seems, however, almost impossible to believe that the Church, which in the earlier stages of its development did so much for the spread of devotion to Our Lady, would have contributed nothing to a better understanding of Mary's prerogatives. The doctrine of the Immaculate Conception would seem to make a particular appeal to the genius of eastern Christianity. It appears fitting, therefore, to investigate the theology and liturgy of the Byzantine Church for any indications that some at least of its thinkers and theologians had envisaged the possibility, probability or certainty of God's granting this greatest privilege to Mary.

Such an investigation should be the more desirable, because the Byzantine Church was the heir and guardian of the patristic tradition to whose formation the greatest Greek thinkers of the first Christian centuries had contributed so much. It is in the patristic tradition that theologians have to find the necessary documentation for their doctrinal deductions.

THE PATRISTIC PERIOD

It is generally known that in the patristic period, Mariology was not especially cultivated.[2] The first great theologians were preoccupied with the definition and defence of other vital Christian doctrines. The divinity

---

[1] A detailed account of the attitude of modern Greek and Russian theologians toward the dogma of the Immaculate Conception is given by M. JUGIE in his book *L'Immaculée Conception dans l'Ecriture Sainte et dans la tradition orientale* (Rome, 1952), pp. 348-477. On the attitude of Serbian orthodox theologians see Ch. BALIĆ "L'Immaculée Conception de Marie dans la théologie contemporaine serbo-orthodoxe," *Revue des Études Byzantines*, 11 (*Mélanges Martin Jugie*, 1953), pp. 36-46. Numerous criticisms by modern Protestant and Orthodox theologians of the proclamation of the dogma of the Assumption are collated by Friedrich Heiler in the symposium "Das neue Mariendogma im Lichte der Geschichte und im Urteil der Oekumene" (*Oekumenische Einheit*, 1951, Heft 2).

[2] Cf. P. ORTIZ DE URBINA, "Le sviluppo della mariologia nella patrologia orientale," in *Orientalia christiana periodica* 6 (1940).

of Our Lord, the nature of the Holy Trinity, the two natures and the two wills in One Lord were attacked and needed explanation and clear definition. The role which Our Lady was chosen to play in our salvation was naturally left very much in the background. Nevertheless, the theological struggle for the true definition of the doctrine of the Holy Trinity, the Incarnation of Our Lord and His two natures helped the Church to clarify and to defend some other prerogatives of Our Lady: her perpetual virginity, her great sanctity and her title "Mother of God". The decision made at the Council of Ephesus that the Blessed Virgin was truly and verily *Theotokos*—Mother of God—was received with enthusiasm by the faithful and contributed greatly to the spread of the cult of Our Lady.

There are many indications that some theologians of the patristic period, when meditating on the degree of sanctity of the Mother of God, came very near to a belief in her Immaculate Conception. It was the comparison of Mary with Eve which suggested to some of them that Mary—the new Eve—was as immaculate from the beginning of her existence as Eve was when she was created. This, of course, suggests the idea of the Immaculate Conception, because Eve was also without original sin when she was created by God.[3]

II

THE SIXTH TO THE NINTH CENTURIES

These were the premises on which Byzantine theologians were working from the end of the fifth century on. The most important period for the study of this subject is that from the sixth to the ninth centuries. It was the time when Byzantine thinkers, stimulated by the fight against the monophysites, the monothelites and the iconoclasts, made important contributions to dogmatic theology in general. It is a period of consolidation of dogmatic theology in the Orthodox Church which must still be regarded as the great period of Greek dogmatic theology. It produced some ecclesiastical writers of great renown: Leontios of Byzantium, Anastasius of Sinai, stout defenders of Catholic dogma against the monophysites; Sophronius of Jerusalem and Maximus the Confessor, who explained the teaching on two wills in the person of Christ; Germanus of Constantinople, John of Damascus, Theodore of Studios and Nicephorus of Constantinople, who led the theological campaign against iconoclasm. The most important

---

[3] For details, see chap. II of the present volume; also G. JOUASSARD, "Marie à travers la patristique" in H. DU MANOIR, *Maria, Etudes sur la Sainte Vierge* (Paris, 1949), I, pp. 69-157; and M. JUGIE, *L'Immaculée Conception dans l'Ecriture sainte et dans la tradition orientale* (Rome, 1952), pp. 55-94.

of them all was St. John of Damascus, who was also the most prominent among Greek mariologists.

NEW MARIAN FEASTS

The cult of Our Lady and the theological speculation on the role she had played in our salvation, were greatly stimulated by the introduction of new Marian feasts into Byzantine liturgy. So far, the Eastern Church had recognised only one feast commemorating Mary in its liturgical calendar.[4] From the sixth century on, however, three other festive commemorations of the Blessed Virgin were introduced: The Annunciation (Εὐαγγελισμός) on March 25th, the Nativity of Our Lady on September 8th and the Κοίμησις or Dormitio, commemorating Our Lady's death, on August 15th. During the seventh century, the commemoration of St. Anne's conception was also introduced and celebrated on December 9th.[5]

For these new feasts, new offices had to be composed and new hymns were needed to celebrate the virtues and the merits of Mary. This period gave the Byzantine Church also one of the greatest Greek religious poets, the famous ROMANOS THE MELODIAN. He composed the hymns for the feast of the Annunciation, and for the Nativity of Our Lady.

ST. ANNE'S CONCEPTION

The fact that the Byzantine Church had introduced a special feast of the Conception of St. Anne has been interpreted by some western mariologists as a counterpart to the feast of the Immaculate Conception as the Western Church knows it. In reality the importance of this feast for the evolution of the doctrine of the Immaculate Conception should not be exaggerated. This feast was originally simply a counterpart to another similar commemoration—the feast of the Conception of St. John the Baptist. The introduction of the feast of St. Anne's Conception was inspired by the legendary account in the apocryphal Gospel of St. James[6] which described how the conception of Our Lady was announced to St. Anne and St. Joachim by an angel. Evidently this account is a reproduction of the narrative given in St. Luke when he speaks of the appearance of an angel to Zachary. The liturgies of the two feasts are very similar. It

---

[4] See M. JUGIE, "La Premiere fête mariale en Orient," in *Echos d'Orient,* 22 (1923), pp. 129-151.

[5] For details, see chapter IV of the present volume, pp. 114-123; also H. KELLNER, *Heortologie* (Freiburg in Br., 1911), 3d ed., pp. 182, 287, and S. SALAVILLE, "Marie dans la Liturgie Byzantine ou Gréco-slave," in Hubert DU MANOIR, *Maria, études sur la sainte Vierge* (Paris, 1949), I, pp. 249-326. Cf. also P. DE MEESTER, "La festa dell' Immacolata Concezione nella chiesa graeca," *Bessarione,* Ser. II, 7 (1904), pp. 89-102; A. SCHULTZ, *Der liturgische Grad des Festes der Empfängnis Mariens im byzantischen Ritus vom 8. bis zum 13. Jahrhundert* (Rom, 1941).

[6] E. AMANN, *Le Protoévangile de Jacques et ses remaniements latins* (Paris, 1910), p. 99 ff. Cf. chapter II of the present volume, pp. 58 f.; 81 f.; and especially the text cited on p. 513 ff.

should be pointed out here that the feast of Mary's Conception, which was introduced into England and Normandy during the eleventh century, also stressed the miraculous announcement of Mary's birth.[7] Eastern influences on the introduction of this feast are evident.

But besides the miraculous announcement of Mary's birth, the Byzantine Church also stressed, in the liturgy of this feast, the miraculous conception in the sterile womb of Anne and the beginning of life of the future Mother of God. In their poems and homilies Byzantine poets and orators insisted more and more on Our Lady's *passive* Conception, and on her holiness from the very beginning of her existence. So it happened that the introduction of this feast into the eastern liturgy contributed a great deal to the development of theological speculation on the greatest of Mary's prerogatives.

FEATURES OF BYZANTINE THEOLOGY

Before starting a more detailed study of the subject, certain particular features of Byzantine theological history, which differ considerably from the developments of dogmatic history in the West, must be recalled. First of all, the Eastern Church never witnessed among its theologians a struggle for the definition of Mary's prerogatives similar to that in the West. No Eastern theologian went so far as to deny explicitly Mary's prerogatives. Although the Eastern Church believed equally firmly in the existence of original sin, and in its consequences—concupiscence, death, the corruption of the body—its theologians were less interested than those of the West in the definition of the nature of original sin. The consequence of these facts was that the Eastern theologians never manifested such a lively interest in the Immaculate Conception of Our Lady as did their Latin colleagues. It would be wrong therefore to expect to find in the works of Byzantine theologians such clear declarations as are to be found in the treatises of western thinkers in favor of the solemn confirmation of this greatest privilege of Mary.

The starting point of Eastern theological speculation on Mary's prerogatives was different. The basis of this speculation on Mary's holiness was the dogmatic proclamation of the Council of Ephesus (431) that Mary was the Mother of God. This sublime fact presupposes a great degree of sanctity in the Blessed Virgin, and theological speculation in the Byzantine Church produced various estimates of this degree. Because all agree that God could not have chosen for His sojourn a body stained by sin, some of them at least, were induced quite logically to conclude that the Mother of God could not have been subject to original sin and its consequences. Because this speculation did not encounter any serious

---

[7] Cf. *infra*, p. 131; also F.-X. LE BACHELET, "Immaculée Conception dans l'Eglise Latine après le concile d'Éphèse," in *Dictionnaire de Théologie catholique* (Paris, 1923), VII, cols. 990-994; and M. JUGIE on the character of this feast, *ibid.*, cols. 956-960.

opposition, Byzantine thinkers were often uncertain about the moment when the Mother of God became exempt from original sin, but some of them rightly supposed that it should have been from the very moment of her passive conception.

In appreciating some declarations in Byzantine mariological literature, care must be taken not to attribute too much value to some titles given to Mary by poets and by some enthusiastic preachers. These writers liked to use metaphors, similes, and epithets which seem, at first sight, to express clearly the doctrine of her Immaculate Conception. In reality, however, they can only be connected with Mary's other privileges and give general expression to the high degree of her sanctity.

It will, therefore, be advisable to limit our research to theologians, and to panegyrists who have a solid theological background. It should, of course, be understood that even the panegyrists with their generalisations and flowery expressions of Mary's praises contributed considerably to the spread of Our Lady's cult in Byzantium, and that they stimulated speculation on the degree of sanctity God had bestowed upon the Mother of His Son.[8]

The most important sources for investigation are the theological writings of the famous Byzantine saints of the eighth century: St. Andrew of Crete († 740), St. Germanus, Patriarch of Constantinople († about 733) and St. John of Damascus († 749). They are preceded by St. Sophronius, Patriarch of Jerusalem, who died in 638.

The last-named is famous among eastern theologians for his Synodal Letter sent, after a synod held in Jerusalem in 634, to the Patriarch Sergius of Constantinople and to other patriarchs, in which he gave a very clear exposition of the Catholic doctrine on original sin and on the Incarnation. When speaking of the Incarnation, Sophronius uses the following words:

> I believe . . . that God the Word, the only Son of the Father, . . . descended into our lowliness . . . and became incarnate, entering the inviolate womb, resplendent with virginal purity, of the holy and radiant Mary, who was full of divine wisdom, and free from all contamination of body, soul and spirit. . . . He willed to become man in order to purify like by like, to save brother by brother . . . For this purpose, a holy

---

[8] Byzantine Mariology has, so far, been undeservedly neglected. The work of PASSAGLIA, *De immaculato Deiparae semper virginis conceptu Commentarius* (Roma, 1854-1855, 3 vols.), treats Byzantine Mariology very inadequately, and is lacking in critical sense. Th. TOSCANI and J. COZZA (*De Immaculatae Deiparae conceptione hymnologia graecorum,* Roma, 1862) limited themselves to Greek hymnology. The works of M. JUGIE, which are included or resumed in his latest book *L'Immaculée Conception dans l'Ecriture Sainte et dans la tradition orientale* (Rome, Bibl. Immac. Conc., 3, 1952) have opened new vistas in Byzantine Mariology. He made many unknown works accessible and he is certainly the most prominent specialist in Eastern Mariology. See also F. S. MÜLLER, "Die Unbefleckte Empfängnis der Gottesmutter in der griechischen Ueberlieferung," *Gregorianum,* 16 (1935), pp. 74-96, 225-250, vol. 17 (1936), pp. 82-115. For a complete bibliography on Eastern Mariology, see M. GORDILLO, *Mariologia Orientalis* (Roma, 1954), *Orientalia Christiana Analecta,* 141.

Virgin is chosen and is sanctified in soul and body; and thus, because pure, chaste and immaculate, she is able to serve in the Incarnation of the Creator.[9]

One thing seems clear to Sophronius, namely, that Mary was holy before the Incarnation of Our Lord. The plenitude of holiness on which Sophronius insists could perhaps be interpreted as exemption from original sin also. He suggests the same idea in an interesting passage of one of his homilies. When exalting Mary's holiness, Sophronius exclaims:

> Many saints appeared before thee, but none was as filled with grace as thou . . . No one has been purified in advance as thou hast been . . . Thou dost surpass all that is most excellent in man, as well as all the gifts which have been bestowed by God upon all others . . .[10]

The most important part of this passage is formed by the words: "None has been purified in advance," because they express the idea of Mary's being purified before her birth. It is thus legitimate to conclude that Sophronius was very near to belief in the Immaculate Conception, although he is not clear enough in his expression and fails to indicate the very moment when Our Lady "was exempted from all contamination of the body" and "when she was purified in advance."

Speculation about the degree of Mary's sanctity must have been spreading considerably in Byzantium in the seventh century, and the prevailing tendency was to attribute to her a privileged position before her birth. This is illustrated by the diffusion among the faithful of two erroneous beliefs concerning Mary, namely, that her conception was virginal and that she remained only seven months in her mother's womb.

These details may be learned from the writings of St. ANDREW OF CRETE,[11] a famous Greek orator and poet.[12] Eight of his numerous homilies and two of his poems celebrate Mary's sanctity and virtues.

---

[9] *Epistola synodica ad Sergium*, P.G., 87³, cols. 3160C-3161A: Πιστεύω . . . ὡς ὁ Θεὸς Λόγος, ὁ τοῦ Πατρὸς μονογενὴς Ὑιός . . . πρὸς τοὺς ταπεινοὺς ἡμᾶς καταβέβηκεν, . . . καὶ μήτραν εἰσδὺς ἀπειρόγαμον, παρθενίας ἀγλαϊζομένην ἁγνότητι, Μαρίας τῆς ἁγίας καὶ φαιδρᾶς καὶ θεόφρονος καὶ παντὸς ἐλευθέρας μολύσματος τοῦ τε κατὰ σῶμα καὶ ψυχὴν καὶ διάνοιαν, σαρκοῦται ὁ ἄσαρκος . . . Ἄνθρωπος γὰρ χρηματίζειν ἐβούλετο, ἵνα τῷ ὁμοίῳ ἀνακαθάρῃ τὸ ὅμοιον, καὶ τῷ συγγενεῖ τὸ συγγενὲς ἀνασώσηται, καὶ τῷ συμφυεῖ τὸ συμφυὲς ἐκλαμπρύνῃ. Διὰ τοῦτο Παρθένος ἁγία λαμβάνεται, καὶ σῶμα καὶ ψυχὴν ἁγιάζεται, καὶ οὕτως ὑπουργεῖ τῇ σαρκώσει τοῦ κτίσαντος ὡς καθαρὰ καὶ ἁγνὴ καὶ ἀμόλυντος.

[10] *Oratio II in Ss. Deiparae Annuntionem*, ch. XXV, PG, 87, col. 3248A. Cf. also ch. XLIII, *ibid.* col. 3273: "The Holy Spirit will descend upon thee, O Immaculate, in order to make thee more pure." Ch. XVIII (*ibid.* col. 3237D): "Thou art more radiant in purity than any other creature." There are similar eulogies in chs. XIX and XXXI (*ibid.* cols. 3240, 3241).

[11] *Canon in Beatae Annae conceptionem*, PG, 97, col. 1313A.

[12] For details on his work see S. VAILHÉ, "St. André de Crète," in *Echos d'Orient*, 5 (1901-1902), pp. 378-387. On Andrew's poetical works consult the important study by L. PETIT, in *Dictionnaire d'archéol. Chrét. et de Liturgie* (Paris, 1907), I. cols. 2034-2041.

Andrew is clearer than Sophronius in stressing Mary's sanctity before her birth. In the hymn which Andrew had composed for the feast of St. Anne's conception, it can also be clearly seen that this feast was becoming more and more the commemoration of the passive conception of Our Lady. Andrew terms the conception of Mary "holy" and her birth "venerable" and "immaculate." [13]

Moreover, Andrew introduced into Byzantium a new title for Mary— daughter of God, θεόπαις—which became very popular among Byzantine mariologists. Andrew gave this title a broader meaning by speculating as to whether God intervened in a special manner at the moment of her conception.[14]   In his homily in honor of Mary's birth, he says:

> Today, Adam presents Mary to God as the first fruits of our nature . . . Today, humanity recovers the gift it had received when first formed by divine hands, and returns immaculate to its original nobility.   The shame of sin had cast a shadow upon the splendor and charm of human nature; but when the Mother of Him who is Beauty itself is born, this nature recovers in her person its ancient privileges, and is fashioned according to a perfect model, truly worthy of God.   And this fashioning is a perfect restoration; this restoration is a divinization, and this divinization is an assimilation to the primitive state . . . In a word, the reformation of our nature begins today; the world, which had grown old, undergoes a transformation which is wholly divine, and receives the first-fruits of its second creation.[15]

These words are very eloquent and indicate clearly enough that Andrew regarded Our Lady as the first specimen, the beginning of our human nature recreated or brought back to its original status, when it was freed from the stain of original sin.[16a] Andrew often insists on this idea, calling Our Lady "the first fruit of our nature"[16b] or of our reformation, or "the first who was exempted (or freed) from the first transgression of our first parents."[16c] In another instance he designates the body of Mary as "the clay which was moulded by the hands of the divine artist."[17]

[13] Ibid. cols. 1309, 1313.

[14] Cf. M. Jugie, "Saint André de Crète et l'Immaculée Conception," Echos d'Orient, 13 (1910), pp. 129-133.

[15] Hom. I in Nativ. B. Mariae, P.G., 97, cols. 809D-812: Σήμερον ἐξ ἡμῶν ἀνθ' ἡμῶν ἀπαρχὴν ὁ Ἀδὰμ τῷ Θεῷ προσφέρων, τὴν Μαρίαν ἀπάρχεται . . . Σήμερον ἡ καθαρὰ τῶν ἀνθρώπων εὐγένεια, τῆς πρώτης θεοπλαστίας ἀπολαμβάνει τὸ χάρισμα, καὶ πρὸς ἑαυτὴν ἀντεπάνεισι· καὶ ἣν ἀπημαύρωσε τοῦ κάλους εὐπρέπειαν ἡ τῆς κακίας δυσγένεια, ταύτην ἡ φύσις τεχθείσῃ τῇ μητρὶ τοῦ ὡραίου προσέχουσα, πλάσιν ἀρίστην τε καὶ θεοπρεπεστάτην εἰσδέχεται. Καὶ γίνεται κυρίως ἡ πλάσις ἀνάκλησις· καὶ ἡ ἀνάκλησις, θέωσις· . . . Καὶ συνελόντι φάναι· σήμερον ἡ τῆς φύσεως ἡμῶν ἀναμόρφωσις ἄρχεται, καὶ ὁ γηράσας κόσμος θεοειδεστάτην λαμβάνων στοιχείωσιν, δευτέρας θεοπλαστίας προοίμια δέχεται.

[16a] Homil. III in Nativ. B. Mariae, ibid. col. 860B: ταύτην δὴ λέγω τὴν βασιλίδα τὴν φύσεως, τὴν ἀπαρχὴν τοῦ ἡμετέρου φυράματος.

[16b] Homil. IV. Ibid. col. 865A: ἡ ἀπαρχὴ τῆς ἡμῶν ἀναπλάσεως.

[16c] Ibid. col. 880C: ἡ πρώτη τοῦ πρώτου πτώματος τῶν προγόνων ἀνάκλησις.

[17] Homil. I. in Dormitionem, B. Mariae, ibid, col. 1068C: . . . ἡ θεογεώργητος γῆ . . .

Andrew is also one of the first Byzantine theologians to perceive that there is a logical connection between the Immaculate Conception and the Assumption of the body of Our Lady. On several occasions he ponders on the circumstances of the death of the Mother of God and comes to the conclusion that, if Mary had to die, it was because even Our Lord had to die, but that her death was different from the death of ordinary men. Death is the consequence of original sin. Andrew's words suggest the idea that because Mary was exempted from original sin, her death was also quite different. He does not go so far as to suggest the Assumption of her body, but he was well aware of the consequences to which his first supposition, namely that Mary was exempt from original sin, led.

St. Germanus of Constantinople was Andrew's contemporary, but it is improbable that he was influenced by the latter in his speculation on Mary's holiness. It is therefore all the more remarkable that St. Germanus insists in his writings, like St. Andrew, on the absolute holiness of Mary. One of his comparisons of Mary is particularly indicative. In his homily on the Presentation of Our Lady in the Temple, he lets Joachim and Anne apostrophize God as follows:

> Accept her whom you have chosen, predestined and sanctified, . . . her whom you have chosen as a lily among the thorns of our unworthiness.[18]

On another occasion, Germanus takes thorns as a symbol of our sins.[19] The comparison of Our Lady with a lily among thorns, suggests the idea that she alone was without sin. He also follows St. Andrew in his meditation on Mary's death and comes to the conclusion that Mary had to die like her Son, but that her body like that of her Son was exempt from corruption.[20] In his homilies St. Germanus also developed the idea of Mary's intermediary role in the distribution of supernatural gifts to men.[21]

τὸ πανόμοιον τῆς ἀρχικῆς ὡραιότητος ἴνδαλμα . . . ὁ θεοτελὴς τοῦ παντουργοῦ καὶ ἀριστοτέχνου πηλός.
A similar imagery is used by Andrew in his *Homil. I. in Nativ. B. Mariae*, ibid. cols. 813 sq. God chose an Immaculate Virgin for his Incarnation as he had formed the first Adam from an immaculate clay.

[18] *Homil. I. in Praesent. Ss. Deiparae* P.G., 98, col. 300D: ἀπολάμβανε, ἣν ἡρετίσω, καὶ προώρισας, καὶ ἡγίασας . . . ἣν ὡς κρίνον ἐξ ἀκανθῶν τῆς ἡμετέρας ἀναξιότητος ἐξελέξω.

[19] *Homil. in Dominici corporis sepulturam*, ibid. col. 253D: 'Αμαρτίας δὴ σύμβολον, ἄκανθα . . . .

[20] The most telling passage is in the *Homil. in Dormitionem Deiparae*, ibid., col. 345.

[21] On the authenticity of Germanus' Marian homilies see F. Cayré's study, "St. Germain, patriarche de Constantinople" in *Diction. de Théol. cath.* (Paris, 1924), VI, 1, col. 1306. The lessons of the Office of the Immaculate Conception are taken from Germanus' homilies. "A bon droit," says Cayré, "car si on n'y trouve pas ce dogme signalé en propres termes, il y est enseigné, sans aucun doute possible, au moins d'une manière indirecte. Tant dans des affirmations positives que dans d'innombrables comparaisons, Marie y est exaltée pour sa pureté incomparable écartant

The Mariology of St. John of Damascus is very important, because he is the leading theologian of the Orthodox Church, and his works still constitute for Orthodox theologians the basis of theological speculation. St. John, in his systematic exposition of the true faith, explained first of all, very clearly, the two great prerogatives of Our Lady: her Divine Maternity and her perpetual virginity. But this does not represent the sum of the great theologian's beliefs concerning the Blessed Virgin. Numerous expressions are to be found in his writings testifying to John's belief in the highest degree of Mary's sanctity, some of them pointing to his conviction that her sanctity, which means exemption from any kind of sin, had its beginning before her natural birth.[22]

St. John of Damascus' utterances on the sanctity of the Blessed Virgin in his greatest work, *On Orthodox Faith*, the first systematic work of dogmatic theology, should first be examined. He speaks there of the "holy and immaculate flesh and blood" of the holy Virgin from which the body of Jesus was formed,[23] characterizes her conception as unaccompanied by any sensual pleasure and the birth of Jesus as having been without pain.[24] The most conspicuous description of Mary's sanctity is, however, the following:

> And then, transplanted into the temple of God, and enriched by the Spirit like a fruitful olive tree, (Mary) became the dwelling of every virtue. She banished all worldly and carnal desires from her mind, and thus preserved her soul virginal, like her body, as befitted her who was to conceive God in her womb. . . . Thus, therefore, she pursued sanctity, and became a holy and admirable temple, worthy of the Most High God.[25]

John's description of Mary as a Virgin, not only in body, but also in soul, suggests the idea that she was free from any sin, including original sin. This is, however, only an indirect indication that John regarded Mary as exempt from any kind of sin from the time of her conception.

More positive testimonies to Mary's initial sanctity can be found in John's homilies on Mary.[26] In the homily on the Virgin's nativity John's

---

toute souillure, sans moindre restriction ni pour une tache quelquonque, ni pour un moment de son existence. Le péché originel est évidemment exclu aussi."

[22] On St. John of Damascus and his Mariology see the following studies: M. Jugie, "Saint Jean Damascène," in *Dict. de Theol. Cath.* (Paris, 1924), VIII, 1, cols. 693-751; M. Gordillo, "Damascenica," in *Orient. Christ.*, 3 (Roma, 1926), pp. 45-103; V. A. Mitchel, *The Mariology of St. John Damascene* (Kirkwood, U.S.A., and Proost, Turnhut, 1930), C. Chevalier, "La Mariologie de St. Jean Damascène," *Orient. Christ. Anal.*, No. 109 (1936), reviewed by Grumel in *Echos d'Orient*, 36 (1937).

[23] *De Fide orth.* IV, 14. *PG*, 94, col. 1160C; cf. also *ibid.* III, 1, col. 985B.

[24] *De Fide orth.* IV, 14, *PG*, 94, col. 1160D. Cf. *II hom. in Dormit*, 3, *PG*, 96, col. 728B.

[25] *De Fide orth.* IV, 14, *PG*, 94, col. 1160A.

[26] On the authorship of the homilies ascribed to St. John of Damascus see M. Jugie, *Saint Jean Damascène, op. cit.*, cols. 703 sq. Among the nine homilies which

most eloquent statement on this matter is to be found. In describing why Mary was born of a sterile mother, John exclaims:

> Nature was defeated by grace and stopped, trembling, not daring to take precedence over it (grace). Since the Virgin Mother of God was to be born of Anne, nature did not dare to precede the product of grace; but remained sterile until grace had produced its fruit.[27]

Then addressing Joachim and Anne, St. John makes his most clear and most advanced statement:

> O happy loins of Joachim, which had produced a germ which is all immaculate. O wondrous womb of Anne in which an all-holy child slowly grew and took shape . . .

This is the most eloquent statement and a direct proof that John regarded Mary as exempt from all sin from the very moment of her passive conception. In other words, the Catholic doctrine of the Immaculate Conception is clearly expressed in this statement.

Some other expressions can also be quoted which show, at least indirectly, that this was John's belief. According to John, Mary is all beautiful, nearest to God. She is above the Cherubim and Seraphim.[28] She is the lily which grew in the middle of thorns.[29] Here St. John uses the familiar comparison already found in the writings of other Fathers. The thorns are sins, and thus Mary is the only one without any sin. In another passage of the same homily, St. John says that the flaming visage of the enemy could not reach her and that she never knew the attacks of concupiscence.[30] All this confirms our impression that St. John believed in the initial sanctity of Our Lady. He merely failed to express his belief in her Immaculate Conception with the same clarity as we do, because in his time such a thing was not yet possible.[31]

Yet another fact must be adduced. St. John is known to have defined most accurately the orthodox doctrine on original sin. Thus he knew that death was introduced into the world by original sin and was the most

---

should doubtless be attributed to the Damascene, four are dedicated to Our Lady: one on the Nativity of the Blessed Virgin (*PG,* 96, cols. 661-680) and three on the *Dormitio* or Assumption. On the authorship of the hymn attributed to St. John see J. M. Hussey, "The Authorship of the Six Hymns attributed to St. John of Damascus," in *Journal of Theological Studies,* 47 (1946) pp. 74-96.

[27] *Homil. in Nativ. B. Mariae, P.G.,* 96, col. 664A, B: Ἡ γὰρ φύσις ἥττηται τῇ χάριτι, καὶ ἔστηκεν ὑπότρομος, προβαίνειν μὴ φέρουσα. Ἐπεὶ οὖν ἔμελλεν ἡ Θεοτόκος Παρθένος ἐκ τῆς Ἄννης τίκτεσθαι, οὐκ ἐτόλμησεν ἡ φύσις προλαβεῖν τὸ τῆς χάριτος βλάστημα· ἀλλ' ἔμεινεν ἄκαρπος, ἕως ἡ χάρις τὸν καρπὸν ἐβλάστησεν. . . . Ὦ ὀσφὺς τοῦ Ἰωακεὶμ παμμακάριστε, ἐξ ἧς κατεβλήθη σπέρμα πανάμωμον! Ὦ μήτρα τῆς Ἄννης ἀοίδιμε, ἐν ᾗ ταῖς κατὰ μικρὸν ἐξ αὐτῆς προσθήκαις ηὐξήθη, καὶ διαμορφωθὲν ἐτέχθη βρέφος πανάγιον! . . .

[28] *Ibid.* col. 676C, 669A.

[29] *Ibid.,* col. 669AB: ὦ κρίνον ἀναμέσον τῶν ἀκανθῶν . . . Ὦ ῥόδον ἐξ ἀκανθῶν . . .

[30] *Ibid.* col. 672B, 676A,C.

[31] For more details see Chevalier, *op. cit.,* pp. 130-148.

rigorous punishment for it.   But, on the other hand, John believes in the initial sanctity of Mary, which includes exemption from original sin, so he was led to explain why Mary had to die.   He did so in his three homilies on Mary's death.   He resolves this dilemma by explaining that Mary, as a daughter of Adam had to pay this death penalty because her Son, who is Life itself did not refuse to do so.[32]

> What could death have meant for her in whom the "sting of death"— sin [1 Cor. 15:56]—was slain?   It could only have been the beginning of a better and unending life.[33]

A little further on in the same homily, St. John expresses a very outspoken testimony to the Assumption of Our Lady.

Against this interpretation of John's doctrine on the Immaculate Conception, some theologians quote two passages, one from his main work, *On Orthodox Faith*,[34] and another from a homily[35] in which he says that the Holy Spirit descended on Mary in order to purify her.   These passages should, however, be explained in connexion with other declarations. From this comparison it is permissible to conclude that St. John had in mind, not the beginning but only the increase of sanctity in Mary through the Holy Spirit at the moment of her conception.[36]

Of the other Byzantine theologians of this period some declarations may be quoted from JOHN, BISHOP OF EUBOEA († about 750)[37] and ST. THEO-DORE OF STUDION († 826).   In his homily on the Conception of Mary, the Bishop used some phrases which confirm, at least, that on the initial sanctity of Mary, he had a very high opinion approaching that of the present day. This is the most expressive passage apostrophising Joachim and Anne:

> You are Earth, but she is Heaven.   You are earthly, but it is through her that the sons of the Earth become inhabitants of Heaven.[38]

---

[32] *Homil. II in Dormit. PG*, 96, col. 725C,D.

[33] *Homil. II in Dormit.*, *P.G.*, 96, col. 728C: ἐν ᾗ δὲ τὸ κέντρον τοῦ θανάτου ἡ ἁμαρτία νενέκρωτο, τί φήσομεν, ἢ ζωῆς ἀρχὴν ἀλήκτου καὶ κρείττονος;

[34] *De fide orthod.* III, 2, *PG*, 94, col. 985B.

[35] *Homil. I in Dormit. B. Mariae, PG*, 96, col. 704A.   Cf. on the controversy V. A. MITCHELL, *op. cit.*, pp. 113-125 and M. JUGIE *L'Immaculée Concept.*, pp. 120 seq., 126.   Cf. also F. S. MÜLLER, "Die Unbefleckte Empfängniss der Gottesmutter," *Gregorianum*, 16 (1935), pp. 232 seq.

[36] See M. JUGIE, *L'Immaculée Conception*, pp. 120 seq. CHEVALIER *op. cit.*, pp. 49-58 enumerates all figurative comparisons of Mary taken from the Old Testament, and which suggest the great degree of holiness the Damascene attributed to Mary.

[37] On the Bishop of Euboea see the recent study by F. DÖLGER, "Johannes von Euboia," in *Analecta Bollandiana*, 68 (1949), *Mélanges P. Peeters*, II), pp. 5-26. The author characterizes John as "das Beispiel eines provinziellen Homiletentypus" and publishes a new homily of John on the resurrection of Lazarus which shows many stylistic affinities with the Homily on the Conception of Mary.   John is often called in the manuscripts only "monk and priest," in others bishop, and he is often identified with John of Damascus.

[38] *P.G.*, 96, col. 1477B: Ὑμεῖς γὰρ γῆ ἐστε, αὐτὴ δὲ οὐρανός. Ὑμεῖς χοϊκοί, δι' αὐτῆς δὲ οἱ χοϊκοὶ ἐπουράνιοι.

The Creator himself made from the old earth a new heaven and a throne which defies the flames. He transformed the old image of man in order to prepare a new, all-heavenly dwelling for the Word. . . Sing and rejoice because here the devil, the tyrant over our nature, was defeated.[39]

St. Theodore of Studion in one of his homilies on Mary's Nativity, which used to be ascribed to St. John of Damascus,[40] uses a comparison similar to that of the Bishop of Euboea. The most telling passage deserves quotation:

Mary is the earth on which the thorns of sin did not grow. On the contrary, she brought forth a plant through which sin has been uprooted and taken away. She is an earth which was not cursed as was the first earth, fertile in thorns and thistles, but was blessed by the Lord; and her fruit also is blessed, as says the word of the Lord.[41] . . . She is the new dough that has been remade by God, the holy first-fruits of the human race, the root of that stem spoken of by the prophet.[42]

III

THE PHOTIAN PERIOD

With the second half of the ninth century a new period begins in Byzantine history and civilization. After the loss of the eastern provinces to the Arabs, the Byzantine Empire was at last able to stop their penetration further into the interior of Asia Minor and to take a stand in Sicily and southern Italy in order to block, at least temporarily, Arab penetration into Italy. Asia Minor became the backbone of Byzantine military, naval and economic power. Of its western provinces, Byzantium was able to keep only Greece, Thrace, a great part of Macedonia and the coastal cities on the Adriatic Sea, from Epirus to Zara and Venice. All the rest was engulfed by the Slavic masses which, during the period of migrations, had taken possession of what is now Jugoslavia and Bulgaria.

[39] *Ibid.*, col. 1485B, C: Αὐτὸς ὁ Δημιουργὸς ἐκ τῆς παλαιωθείσης γῆς ἐποίησεν οὐρανὸν καινὸν καὶ θρόνον ἀκατάφλεκτον, καὶ τὸν παλαιωθέντα χοϊκὸν εἰς ἐπουράνιον παστάδα μετέβαλεν . . . Ἰδοὺ γὰρ νενίκηται ὁ τὴν ἡμετέραν φύσιν τυραννήσας διάβολος.

[40] C. van de Vorst, "A propos d'un discours attribué à Jean Damascène," in *Byzantin. Zeitschrift*, 23 (1914-1920), pp. 128-132.

[41] *In Nativ. B. Mariae, 4*, P.G., 96, col. 685A: Γῆ ἐστιν, ἐφ' ἣν τῆς ἁμαρτίας ἄκανθα οὐκ ἀνέτειλε. Τουναντίον δὲ μᾶλλον διὰ τοῦ ταύτης ἔρνους πρόρριζος ἐκτέτιλται. Γῆ ἐστιν, οὐχ ὡς ἡ πρότερον κατηραμένη, καὶ ἧς καρποὶ πλήρεις ἀκανθῶν καὶ τριβόλων· ἀλλ' ἐφ' ἣν εὐλογία Κυρίου, καὶ ἧς εὐλογημένος ὁ καρπὸς τῆς κοιλίας, ὥς φησιν ὁ ἱερὸς λόγος.

[42] Ibid. col. 685D: Τὸ νέον φύραμα τῆς θείας ἀναπλάσεως, ἡ Παναγία ἀπαρχὴ τοῦ γένους, ἡ ῥίζα τοῦ θεοφράστου κλάδου.

For some other less important testimonies of St. Tarasius, Patriarch of Constantinople, Theodore Abou Dourra, the Monk Epiphanius and some anonymous writers, see M. Jugie, *L'Immaculée Concept.* pp. 128-135.

Unable to reconquer the lost territories, the Byzantines started a religious offensive in order to win over the new nations to Christianity and to subject them to their spiritual domination.   New bishoprics arose in Macedonia and Greece in place of others destroyed by the invaders; and the Slavs in these provinces were soon converted to Christianity.   This was the beginning of their complete assimilation by the Greeks.   About the middle of the ninth century, the Byzantines succeeded in establishing definitely their form of Christianity among the Bulgarians and the Serbs.   Their missionaries penetrated as far as the middle Danube and Moravia, where two Greek brothers, St. Cyril and St. Methodius, founded a Slavic Church subject to Rome, but using the Roman rite in a Slavic version.

This wide-spread activity betrays the penetration of the Byzantine Church by a new and vigorous spirit.   The victory won about the middle of the ninth century over the iconoclastic doctrine, gave the Byzantines a great self-consciousness and stimulated theological speculation.   At the same time, however, Byzantium was becoming more and more estranged from the West and from Rome.   The misunderstandings between Rome and Byzantium, which arose during the patriarchates of Ignatius and Photius, and which led to a short-lived schism, augured ill for the future and preceded the schism which broke out in the eleventh century.[43]

Because of the growing mistrust between the Christian East and the Christian West, it is all the more important to study the attitude of Byzantine theologians of this period to the question of the Immaculate Conception.   The victory over iconoclasm was, at the same time, a victory for the worship of saints.   In reality, Byzantine hagiography enjoyed one of its most flourishing ages in the ninth and tenth centuries.   It is natural to expect that with the veneration of the saints, the veneration of Mary, the Queen of Saints should increase.   And this is indeed what happened. The number of Our Lady's panegyrists increased considerably in this period. Because the whole tendency of Byzantine theologians from this period on was conservative, anxious to preserve intact the heritage of the past, venturing but rarely into new speculations, it can be presumed that their teaching on Mary's initial sanctity would tend to preserve inherited traditions.

The Byzantine cultural renaissance of the ninth century is dominated by the figure of the learned Patriarch PHOTIUS.   For some centuries he was regarded by Westerners as the main inspiration of the anti-Roman and anti-Western tendencies which started to manifest themselves in his time and was believed to have been the initiator of the great schism.   Recent researches have shown that this was not so.   He was a great Churchman, a very learned scholar, and in spite of his misunderstanding with Rome,

---

[43] On these problems see F. DVORNIK, *The Photian Schism. History and Legend* (Cambridge Univ. Press, 1948). Cf. also F. DVORNIK, "The Photian Schism in Western and Eastern Tradition," *The Review of Politics*, 10 (1948), pp. 310-331.

he stretched out his hand in reconciliation and died in communion with Rome.

Most recent studies have shown that, contrary to previous statements, Photius was mainly responsible for the liquidation of the last vestiges of iconoclasm.[44] This would indicate that Photius was also a promoter of the veneration of the saints, and especially of Our Lady. In fact we find among his homilies one on Mary's Nativity and two on the Annunciation. All, especially the two on the Annunciation are important for the study of the Immaculate Conception. A long passage from the second homily on the Annunciation deserves quotation, first of all. It provides moreover an example of Byzantine rhetoric and of the elaborate and difficult style of the learned Patriarch:

> The archangel comes to Mary, that fragrant and never fading flower of the race of David, that admirable, great and divinely fashioned ornament of human kind. For the Virgin, having been nourished, so to speak, from the very swaddling clothes on the virtues, and having grown with them, gave an example of an immaterial life on earth, and having opened the gates of the road to virtue, she made it possible for those who have an inborn and unquenchable desire to wait on the heavenly bridal chamber to tread [this road] by emulating her. Who has been from very childhood so self-controlled in the face of pleasures? . . . . . . Nay, the Blessed Virgin did not permit her thoughts even to tend towards any of those [pleasures], but was entirely possessed by divine love, showing and proclaiming in these and all other respects that she had been truly designated as a bride for the Creator of all, even before her birth. For, moreover, having also fettered anger, like some uncouth beast, with her impassive mind as with indissoluble threads, she made her whole soul a holy shrine of meekness, having with stable judgment at no time appeared to lessen the force of her courage, and even at the Lord's Passion, at which she was present, having let fall no word of blasphemy and indignation, such as distressed mothers are wont to do at such great suffering of their children. Her strength in this respect is sufficient evidence of the fortitude and courage which she possessed from the very beginning, and the exaltation of her soul grew like a noble plant. Her inimitable gift of sagacity and a clear understanding blossoms out in deeds and works, by means of which she prudently composed and adapted herself in divers ways against all the storms of life's temptations, and those which were roused by the violent hurricane of evil spirits, never allowing any of her pliant [emotions] even to touch the brink of evil.
> Thus while the Virgin by surpassing human standards showed herself worthy of the heavenly chambers, and brightened with her own beauty

[44] F. DVORNIK, "The Patriarch Photius and Iconoclasm," *Dumbarton Oaks Papers,* 6 (1953) pp. 67-97. Photius also provided the main inspiration for the artists who were engaged in redecorating the churches with ikons. One of his homilies was pronounced in the presence of the emperors in the Church of Santa Sophia when the first ikon of Our Lady was solemnly dedicated. Cf. F. DVORNIK, "Lettre a M. H. Grégoire à propos de Michel III et des mosaiques de Sainte-Sophie," in *Byzantion,* 10 (1935), pp. 5-9.

our unsightly aspect, which the pollution of our ancestors had stained, there appeared Gabriel, ministering to the mystery of the King's coming, and cried out, with unrestrained voice and tongue "Hail, much graced one, the Lord is with thee, delivering through thee the whole race from the ancient sorrow and curse." [45]

In the same homily Photius calls Mary:

. . . forever Virgin, the unblemished daughter of our race, chosen . . . among all others of the entire universe, alone as bride for the absolute King and Lord of all.

He apostrophizes Our Lady towards the end of this homily in the following way:

Mayest thou rejoice, furnace forged by God, in which the Creator, having leavened anew our nature with the most pure and virginal dough, has cleansed us of that sour and distressing staleness, renovating man into a new creature.

This passage alone expresses most clearly Photius' ideas on Mary's privileged position. Photius believed that Mary had been chosen before she was born, by a special act of God's predestination, to become the Mother of the Lord. He does not see in her any stain of original sin, because he says that she is the immaculate daughter of our human race, the furnace forged by God, the most pure and virginal dough with which God had leavened anew our nature and cleansed it. When he says that she knew no movements of concupiscence, that she completely dominated all human inclinations, he presupposes that she was without original sin, because concupiscence is one of its consequences. He also believes that Mary never committed the least offence against God.

This quotation with its parallels in the other two Marian homilies [46] is sufficient to show that this Patriarch who has hitherto been regarded with suspicion by Westerners, was not only a fervent worshipper of Mary, but also believed in her initial sanctity long before the dogma of the Immaculate Conception was proclaimed.

Attention should next be turned to a disciple of Photius who even surpassed his master in this respect—GEORGE, METROPOLITAN OF NICOMEDIA, who died at the end of the ninth century. George of Nicomedia was a particularly prolific homiletist. He wrote about 170 homilies, of which

---

[45] S. ARISTARCHIS, *Photii sermones et Homiliae* (Constantinople, 1901), 2, pp. 372-374. An English translation of the homilies by C. Mango is about to be published by Dumbarton Oaks. This extract is taken from his translation.

[46] See *ibid.*, pp. 334, 343, 348 seq. (*Homil. in Nativ. Deiparae*), pp. 236, 244 (*Hom. I in Annuntiat.*) Even J. HERGENRÖTHER (*Photius von Constantinople* Regensburg, 1867-1869, III, pp. 555 seq.) who presented Photius in a very bad light, had to confess that Photius had expressed sufficiently clearly his belief in the Immaculate Conception, although he knew only his homily on Mary's Nativity.

only ten have been published.[47] All but one of them are devoted to Mary and the homily on the Presentation in the Temple is the most important for our research. First of all, it provides the two comparisons of Mary which are to be found in the writings of Andrew of Crete and which point directly to the belief in Mary's initial sanctity, namely, "Mary, the holy and desirable soil," and "Mary, the magnificent first fruit of human nature offered to the Creator."[48] In one passage he seems to sense that this great privilege of Mary is expressed by the salutation of the divine messenger "Hail, full of grace."[49] He also thought that Mary did not know concupiscence, and he asserts firmly that she had never committed the slightest sin. These are his words:

> She is beautiful by nature. There is no stain in her . . . She was a closed garden, inaccessible to sinful thoughts . . . One could not find in her glorified body the least vestige of the corrupt clay.[50] . . . She was purified of all human habits and human passions . . . and elevated above the requirements of our nature.[51] . . . The heavenly food which the Immaculate Virgin received enriched her with divine grace . . . , but it did not bring about a cleansing from sins in her, because she who partook of it had no sins; she was pure and free from any stain.[52]

It is probable that among the unpublished homilies there are still some devoted to Our Lady. It would be worth while if a mariologist anxious to investigate the progress of speculation on Mary's prerogatives in Byzantium at this period, would go through the unpublished material and select the passages which prove that the Byzantines of the ninth century believed, at least implicitly, in the Immaculate Conception.

There is another writer of this period who can also be regarded as a supporter of Photius, because he acknowledged him as the legitimate Patriarch after Ignatius' death, St. Joseph, called the Hymnographer, who died in 883. He was a poet, and many of his religious hymns were incorporated into the Byzantine liturgy and the offices of the Saints. St. Joseph was very devoted to Our Lady and numerous expressions could be quoted from his poems to indicate, at least indirectly, that he believed in the initial sanctity of Mary, or in her Immaculate Conception. One would not be justified, however, in taking all the poetical expressions of the

---

[47] K. Krumbacher, *Geschichte der byzant. Literatur* (München, 1894), p. 166.

[48] *Orat. VI, In Ss. Dei Genitricis Ingressum in Templum, PG,* 100, cols. 1424D, 1444B.

[49] *Oratio VII, ibid.,* col. 1453B.

[50] *Orat. VI, ibid.,* col. 1425B, D, C: ἡ ὡραία τῇ φύσει, καὶ μώμου ἀνεπίδεκτος . . . τὸν κῆπον τὸν κεκλεισμένον τὸν λοχισμοῖς ἀνεπίβατον ἀμαρτίας . . . ἐν ᾗ τῆς ἐπιθολούσης ἰλύος οὐκ ἐφωράθη λείψανον.

[51] *Orat. VII,* col. 1449A.

[52] *Ibid.,* col. 1448B: 'Αλλ' ἐκείνη μὲν ἁμαρτημάτων κάθαρσιν οὐκ ἐνήργησεν ἡ τροφή· οὐδὲ γὰρ τούτοις ἡ μεταλαμβάνουσα ὑπέκειτο, καθαρά τε οὖσα, καὶ ῥύψεως ἁπάσης ἀνενδεής. . . .

hymnographer as arguments, even of an indirect nature, for our thesis. The same should be said concerning the hymns of Romanos the Melodian from the sixth century who was mentioned above. Of course, the works of these poets have a certain documentary evidence because they show how profound was the veneration for Our Lady in Byzantium and how widely it had spread among the faithful. Their praises for the prerogatives of Our Lady also contributed considerably to the spread of veneration for her, and to a better and more profound understanding of her prerogatives, including her initial sanctity.

Two passages may be quoted as evidence that St. Joseph the Hymnographer believed in what we call the Immaculate Conception. In the first passage, he apostrophizes the Virgin as follows:

> Thy spiritual bridegroom found thee as a very pure lily among the thorns and chose his sojourn in Thee.[53]

In another passage[54] the poet exclaims:

> Thou art dying now in consequence of a law which was not made for thee, thou, who art the only pure one.

When the meaning which was given to such expressions by other Fathers is recalled, then their value for our thesis is undeniable, even if they are repeated by a poet. They are already regarded as standard prerogatives of Our Lady.

This study of the theological writers of the Photian period may be closed with a short extract from a homily whose author is the monk THEOGNOSTUS, one of the fiercest enemies of Photius. In spite of that, his belief in the initial sanctity of Our Lady seems to be identical with that of his opponent. He expressed it most clearly in the following passage:

> She who, from the very start, had been conceived in the womb of a holy mother, through a holy prayer, in virtue of a sanctifying act . . . could not but be granted a holy death. For if the beginning of her life is holy, so, too, is its continuation, so is its ending; and thus her whole existence is holy.[55]

This passage suggests strongly our idea of the Immaculate Conception because the author presupposes a direct sanctifying act by God at the moment of Mary's passive conception.

[53] *Canon in festo ss. Samonae, Guriae et Abibi, PG,* 105, col. 1244B. Cp. *Canon in Ss. Chrysanthum et Dariam, PG,* 105, col. 1080C.

[54] *In pervigilio Dormit., Canon III, ibid.,* cols. 1000C, 1001D: Νόμους τῆς φύσεως λαθοῦσα τῇ κυήσει σου, τῷ ἀνομίμῳ νόμῳ θνῄσκεις, μόνη ἀγνή . . .

[55] *Homilia in Dormit. Mariae,* ed. M. JUGIE in *Patrologia Orientalis* (1922), 16, p. 457: . . . ἔπρεπεν ὄντως τὴν ἐξ ἀρχῆς δι' εὐχῆς ἁγίας εἰς μήτραν μητρὸς ἁγίας ἁγιαστικῶς ἐμβρυωθεῖσαν . . . τὴν κοίμησιν ἁγίαν κομίσασθαι. Ἧς γὰρ ἡ ἀρχὴ ἁγία, ταύτης καὶ τὰ μέσα ἅγια, καὶ τὸ τέλος ἅγιον, καὶ πᾶσα ἡ ἔντευξις ἁγία.

Cf. also M. JUGIE. "La vie et les oeuvres du moine Théognoste (IXe siècle). Son témoignage sur l'Immac. Concept.," in *Bessarione,* 35 (1918), pp. 162-174.

IV

THE TENTH TO THE FOURTEENTH CENTURIES

Numerous are the panegyrists from the tenth to the fourteenth centuries who glorified the Mother of God. Many of them used expressions which are highly suggestive, and which we have already analyzed in the writings of other Byzantine theologians and mariologists. For example, the figurative designation of Our Lady as the first fruit or ornament of the human race is used in panegyrics written by the Emperor Leo the Wise (886-912),[56] by John Mauropos,[57] by James the Monk,[58] by the hermit Neophytus († about 1220).[59] Leo the Wise,[60] Peter of Argos [61] (beginning of the tenth century) and the Patriarch Germanus II (1222-1240)[62] used the suggestive comparisons of Mary to the lily among thorns or to the fragrant rose. Of course, the contrast between Eve and Mary, the new Eve, is also used by John the Geometer [63] (end of the tenth century), by Psellos, the Archbishop Theophylactus [64] (end of the eleventh century) and Germanus II.[65] All this shows how popular these expressions, indirectly indicative of the original sanctity of Mary, were becoming in Byzantium.

Some passages from the writings of the above-mentioned authors deserve however to be quoted. It seems perhaps strange that the first author deserving of quotation should be not a theologian, but the famous Byzantine polygraph who was, at the same time, orator, philosopher, statesman, and panegyrist: MICHAEL PSELLOS (1018 to about 1079).[66] Among his numerous writings—over 200 in number—M. Jugie found a homily on the Annunciation[67] which he published, and which deserves the special attention

[56] *Homil. in Praesentat.*, PG, 107, col. 13A (also Mary, lily among thorns); col. 20C: Mary, root planted by God.

[57] *Homil. in Dormit.*, chap. 10, PG, 120, col. 1085A,B. See also chap. 4, col. 1080A: ἡ τοῦ γένους εὐγένεια.

[58] *Homil. in Nativit.*, 7, 15, P.G., 127, cols. 577D-588C: ... ἐγκαλλώπισμα τῆς φύσεως ... τῆς μόνης τοῦ ἀνθρωπείου γένους ... κεκληρωμένης προεδρίαν. Cf. also chs. 17, 18.

[59] *Homil. in Nativit.*, PO, 16, p. 530: ἀπαρχὴ τῆς ἡμῶν σωτηρίας.

[60] *Homil. in Praesent.*, PG, 107, col. 12D.

[61] *In concept. B. Annae*, PG, 104, col. 1352A; cf. also 1353A: ὁρῶντες τὴν τῆς ἡμετέρας εὐγένειαν φύσεως ἀρχομένην.

[62] *Homil. in Deiparae Annunciationem*, 9 (BALLERINI, A., *Syllagoge monumentorum ad mysterium conceptionis immaculatae Virginis Deiparae illustrandum*, Rome, 1855, II, p. 310).

[63] In the unpublished homily on the *Dormitio* (*Cod. Vatic. graecus* 504), quoted by M. JUGIE, *L'Immaculée Concept. op. cit.* p. 186 (folio 175). Cf. also his homily *In Annunt.* 8, PG, 106, col. 817B.

[64] *Enarratio in Evang. Lucae*, chap. I, vers. 26-30, PG 123, col. 701C-D.

[65] See below, p. 107.

[66] On Psellos see E. RENAULT's introduction to his edition of Psellos' *Chronography* (Paris, Collection G. Budé, 1926) I, pp. I-XLVIII and M. JUGIE's study in *Dict. de Théol. Cathol.* XIII, 1, (1936), cols. 1149-1158.

of mariologists. When interpreting the words with which Gabriel had saluted the Blessed Virgin, Psellos writes:

> Full of grace . . . Verily, from long ago she was filled with grace, completely united with God and favored from above with (increase of) graces and illuminations . . . Before the Virgin, our race had inherited the malediction of the first mother. Then a dam was erected against the torrent, and the Virgin became the wall protecting and delivering us from evil. . . . You are blessed among women . . . because you have not violated the precept and after being first divinized yourself, you have divinized our race.[68]

This passage indicates quite clearly that Psellos regarded Our Lady as free from original sin.

Theophylactus, Archbishop of Ochrida, the Greek head of the Bulgarian Church, also commented on the Archangel's salutation, but he did not see its profound theological significance.[69] In his homily on the Presentation, however, some words merit our attention. This passage shows that the Byzantines of his time believed in a legendary tradition, namely that the high priest, having contemplated the child presented to him by the parents, did not hesitate to introduce the infant Mary into the Holy of Holies, the most sacred part of the Temple. Commenting on this legend, Theophylactus exclaims:

> She who surpassed all nature in purity and holiness, and who was justified from her mother's womb, had to be exempt from a law made not for the just but for sinners.[70]

John Phournes, who lived at the beginning of the twelfth century, is an important witness testifying that the Byzantines believed in the Assumption of Our Lady; and he rightly connects this privilege with the fact that Mary was preserved from what he calls the mortal virus of corruption,[71] which can only be original sin. Another author of the same period— Theodore Prodromus—declared:

> It is absolutely impossible to suppose or to imagine in Mary the slightest stain of sin.[72]

---

[67] M. Jugie, "L'homélie de Michel Psellos sur l'Annonciation," in *Echos d'Orient*, 18 (1916-1919), pp. 138-140.

[68] *Homil. in Annunt.*, 3, *Patrologia Orientalis*, 16, p. 522: Τὸ χαῖρε προσθείς . . . Κεχαρίτωτο γὰρ πάλαι, ὅλη προσανακειμένη Θεῷ καὶ τὰς ἄνωθεν δεχομένη ἐλλάμψεις καὶ χάριτας . . . καὶ μεμένηκε μέχρι τῆς Παρθένου τοῦτο δὴ τὸ γένος κληρονομοῦν τὴν ἀρὰν τῆς προμήτορος. Εἶτα ᾠκοδομήθη τὸ ἔρυμα τῆς ἐπιρροῆς, καὶ γέγονεν ἐπιτείχισμα ἡ Παρθένος τῆς τῶν κακῶν ἐπιλύσεως. Εὐλογημένη σὺ ἐν γυναιξίν, ὡς μήτε τοῦ ξύλου γευσαμένη τῆς γνώσεως, μήτε παραβᾶσα τὴν ἐντολήν, ἡ αὐτή τε θεωθεῖσα καὶ τὸ γένος θεώσασα.

[69] *In Evangelium Lucae* I, *PG*, 123, col. 701C sqq. There he compares Mary with Eve.

[70] *Orat. in Praesentat.*, 6, *PG*, 126, col. 137A.

[71] Homily on the Assumption, published by G. Palamas (Jerusalem 1860), pp. 272 seq.

[72] *Theodori Prodromi Commentarii in carmina sacra . . .* , ed. H. M. Stevenson (Rome, 1882), p. 52.

Then there is the testimony of a very holy, but simple, almost illiterate monk—Neophytus—who spent many years of his life in strict isolation. In one of his simple homilies, Neophytus uses very adroitly the well-known designation of Mary as the first fruit of the human race. Inspired by the metaphor used by other Fathers—that of the clay from which God himself had fashioned Mary—he uses it in his own manner, imagining the divine Baker, choosing a piece of the dough, and sanctifying and transforming it.[73] The poor monk is certainly not a brilliant stylist and his comparison is expressed in a very awkward manner, but in spite of all these insufficiencies, his idea on the initial sanctity of Mary is clearly outlined, and deserves to be specially stressed.

Germanus II, the Greek Patriarch, who resided in Nicaea after the conquest of Constantinople by the Latins, also deserves special mention in a survey of Byzantine mariologists. He makes very original use of the traditional comparison of Mary with Eve, representing Eve as the bitter root and Mary as the fruit of this root which is sweeter than honey.[74] Then he repeats with great emphasis that the fruit of this bitter root received the gift of incorruptibility and, contrary to nature, communicated this quality to the root. In the same passage, Germanus also compares Mary to the lily among thorns, "whiter than snow, more fragrant than balm." These are only comparisons and figures of speech, but they are very illuminating.

Fourteenth and Fifteenth Centuries

In his book on the Immaculate Conception in the Eastern tradition, M. Jugie[75] devotes more than eighty pages to the study of ideas on the degree of Mary's sanctity expressed by Byzantine theologians of the fourteenth and fifteenth centuries, the declining period of the Byzantine Empire. It is the period he knows best and one which is very often neglected by western scholars and theologians. I would, however, hesitate to attribute to this period such great importance concerning the subject of the Immaculate Conception as does the learned theologian. The two centuries are characterized by a very lively intercourse between the Greeks and the Latins. The attempts at union made at the Councils of Lyons (1274), Constance (1315) and Florence (1439), generated a mass of polemical literature, and hostility against the Latins was constantly growing among the Greeks. In spite of that, many of the Greek theologians became well acquainted with Latin works on theology, and some of them perhaps

[73] *Homilia in Nativ. B. Mariae*, 3, *Patrol. Orient.*, 16, p. 530. Cf. *ibid.* p. 534 (ed. M. Jugie).

[74] In his homily *in Deiparae Annutiationem*, published by A. Ballerini in *Sylloge monumentorum ad mysterium concept. immac. Virg. Deiparae illustrandum* (Rome 1851), II, chap. 8, 9, p. 307, reprinted in *PG*, 140, cols. 684 seq. Most of Germanus' works are still unpublished. See K. Krumbacher, *op. cit.* p. 174.

[75] *Op. cit.* pp. 217-307.

with the controversy between the Franciscans and Dominicans concerning the doctrine of the Immaculate Conception. Both orders had monasteries in or near Constantinople and even counted some native members from among the Greek Uniates.

One of the first Greek theologians of this period—NICEPHORUS CALLISTUS who died about the year 1335—although violently anti-Latin, expressed, in the discussion on the Immaculate Conception, ideas similar to those of the Dominicans. Although he wrote beautifully on Mary's virtues and prerogatives, he thought that she was delivered from original sin only at the moment of the Annunciation.[76]

The homilies of ISIDORE GLABAS, metropolitan of Thessalonica, contain many passages which could be quoted in favour of the doctrine of the Immaculate Conception. In his homily on the Annunciation,[77] Isidore places Mary between the angels and God himself, and makes her co-operate with God for our salvation. In another homily[78] he lets Mary declare:

> I was not conceived in iniquity; I am the only one whose mother did not conceive her in sin.

In the homily on Mary's death,[79] we read, however, a passage containing a very clear declaration that Mary had inherited original sin. The editors of the homily think that this passage is an interpolation. This is possible, but the arguments are not entirely convincing. It is possible that the prelate, who died about 1397, had learned about the controversy concerning the Immaculate Conception and he seems uncertain what position he should take. His testimony is thus inconclusive.

The Uniate DEMETRIUS CYDONES,[80] who died in 1397 or 1398 in Crete, was a great admirer of St. Thomas Aquinas and translated the first two parts of the *Summa*. It is, therefore, the more interesting to see that Demetrius, although greatly influenced by Thomas' theology, hesitated to follow his master all the way in his opposition to the doctrine of the Immaculate Conception. In his unpublished homily on the Annunciation, there are several passages indicating that Demetrius, although believing that Mary should have inherited original sin like any other human being, thought that God had in a mysterious way, exempted Mary from this general law.[81]

---

[76] See M. JUGIE, *op. cit.*, p. 218, quotation from an unpublished Ms. (Oxford, Bodleian Lib. *Cod. Miscellaneous* 79, f. 192 v, and *Cod. Roe* 3, f. 147 v).

[77] *In Annunt.* 16, 22, *PG*, 139, cols. 96C., 104 B,C.

[78] *In Praesent. B. Mariae*, 13, *ibid.*, col. 52C: Οὐκ ἐν ἀνομίαις συνελήφθην, οὐκ ἐν ἁμαρτίαις ἐκίσσησέ με μόνην ἡ μήτηρ μου . . .

[79] *In Dormit.*, 33, *ibid*, col. 161B: προῆλθε μὲν τῆς ἰδίας μητρὸς, ὥσπερ ἄνθρωπος, καὶ διὰ τοῦτο τὸ ἀρχαῖον πάχος, λέγω δὲ τὴν προγονικὴν ἁμαρτίαν, μεθ' ἧς ἐγεννήθη.

[80] On this interesting figure of fourteenth century Byzantium, see the work of Cardinal G. MERCATI, *Notizie di Procoro e Demetrio Cydone di Manuele Caleca e Teodoro Meliteniota, ed altri appunti per la storia della teologia e della letteratura byzantina del secolo XIV* (Roma, 1931).

[81] Cf. M. JUGIE's study, "Le discours de Demetrius Cydonès sur l'Annonciation et

The learned Emperor MANUEL II PALEOLOGUS (1391-1425), who attended the Council of Florence (1439), seems also to have been influenced by western theologians, but, if this is so, he is inclined rather to follow the Franciscan school, although he does not express his view clearly about the moment when Mary became exempt from original sin.[82]

Among the representatives of the purely Byzantine tradition, Gregory Palamas, Nicholas Cabasilas and Joseph Bryennius deserve special mention. PALAMAS, who died in 1359, a mystic and a theologian of importance, was a defender and propagator of the *hesychast* [83] movement representing a kind of Byzantine mysticism, which preoccupied many Greek thinkers of this period.

It is to be expected that a mystic of Palamas' renown should have a profound devotion to Our Lady. He must often have meditated on the mystery of the Incarnation and on the purity of the Mother of God. Knowing that nobody is exempt from original sin and unable to imagine how the Word could take flesh from a body stained by sin, he imagined that God had chosen Mary from the beginning and had prepared her sanctity by purifying her ancestors and lastly Mary herself. He does not say exactly at what moment this last purification took place, but we can gather from his writings that he could not accept the idea of God taking his flesh from a body which had been even slightly stained with sin.[84] In another passage he expresses his idea even more clearly saying that the Lord needed for his Incarnation a flesh which was human, but was, at the same time, new. It was Mary who from her own substance gave him an immaculate nature.[85]

---

sa doctrine sur l'Immaculée Conception," *Echos d'Orient,* 17 (1913-1914), pp. 96-106. See the quotations from *Codex Parisinus graecus* 1213 in JUGIE's *L'Immaculée Conception,* 277-281.

[82] Cf. the Emperor's homily *In Dormitionem* published by M. JUGIE in *Patrol. Orient.,* 16. The most important passages are on pp. 552 seq., 555 seq., 559. A Latin translation of the homily was reprinted in *PG,* 156, cols. 91-108.

[83] For details see M. JUGIE's studies, "Palamas," and, "Palamite (Controverse)," in *Dict. de Théol. Cath.* XI, cols. 1735-1818.

[84]*Homil. in Christi genealogiam,* 2, 3, ed. SOPHOCLIS. Τοῦ ἐν ἁγίοις πατρὸς ἡμῶν Γρηγορίου τοῦ Παλαμᾶ ὁμιλίαι τεσσαράκοντα καὶ μία. (Athenes, 1861), pp. 213 seq. 216. Unfortunately the homilies which are most important for our subject are not reprinted in Migne's Patrology. It was a Czech Jesuit, Spaldák, who, in a study on the Greek Fathers and the Immaculate Conception, published in the Czech *Review of the Catholic Clergy* in 1905, first pointed out the importance of Palamas' Mariology.

[85]*Homil. in Praesent. Deiparae* 1 (ed. SOPHOCLIS, p. 120):   'Επεὶ σαρκὸς ἐδεῖτο προσλήμματος, καὶ σαρκὸς καινῆς ὁμοῦ τε καὶ ἡμετέρας . . . ὑπηρέτιν πρὸς πάντα πρεπωδεστάτην εὑρίσκει καὶ χορηγὸν ἀμολύντου φύσεως τὴν παρ' ἡμῶν ὑμνουμένην δειπαρθένον ταύτην. Cf. also *Homil. XIV. in Annuntiat.,* P.G., 151, col. 172A-C: Mary escaped the malediction of Eve. Free from the old servitude, she became the source of deliverance of men from it. In his homily XXXVII in Dormit. (*P.G.,* 151, col. 460 seq.), Palamas gives eloquent expression to his belief in Mary's Assumption. Palamas' Mariology impressed the modern Russian philosopher V. LOSSKY (*Essai sur la théologie mystique de l'Eglise d'Orient,* Paris, 1944, p. 136). He seems to accept Palamas' explana-

NICHOLAS CABASILAS († after 1396) seems to be an even more fitting representative of Byzantine tradition on Mary's initial sanctity than Palamas. His homilies were only published recently by M. Jugie, and that is the reason why Cabasilas was till then unknown, although he certainly deserves a prominent place among mariologists in general.

Considerations of space preclude more than a few short quotations from Cabasilas' writings, although his Mariological doctrine deserves more attention.[86] In one of his homilies Cabasilas describes the conception of Mary as a fruit of the fervent prayers of her parents. Many similar divine interventions happened in the past, but Mary's case supersedes all others.

> It was in consequence of this that nature was unable to contribute anything to the engendering of the all-holy (Virgin), and that God Himself did everything in her case, putting nature aside in order to form the Blessed Virgin Himself, without any intermediary, so to speak, just as He had created the first man. For, in a true and proper sense, it is the Virgin who is the first man, being the first and only one to exhibit what human nature really is.[87]

The passage praising Mary as the ideal type of humanity through the grace of God is very suggestive, but two others can be quoted which are even more clear. In another homily Cabasilas writes:

> The wall of separation, the barrier of enmity, did not exist for her, and everything which kept the human race away from God was removed in her. She alone made her peace (with God) before the general reconciliation; or rather she never needed reconciliation of any sort, because from the beginning she occupied the first place in the choir of the friends (of God).[88]

And the last quotation:

> Earth she is, because she is from the earth; but she is a new earth, since she derives in no way from her ancestors and has not inherited the old leaven. She is . . . a new dough and has originated a new race.[89]

---

tion of Mary's purification although he thinks erroneously that the dogma of the Immaculate Conception is alien to Oriental theology.

[86] Cf. M. JUGIE, "La doctrine mariale de Nicolas Cabasilas," *Echos d'Orient,* 18 (1916-1919), pp. 375-388.

[87] *In Nativitatem,* 4, *Patrol. Orient.,* 19, 469.

[88] *In Annuntiationem,* 3, *ibid.,* p. 486: Καὶ τὸ μεσότοιχον τῆς ἔχθρας καὶ ὁ φραγμὸς πρὸς ἐκείνην ἦσαν εὐδέν, ἀλλ' ἅπαν τὸ διεῖργον ἀπὸ τοῦ Θεοῦ τὸ γένος, τὸ ταύτης ἀνῄρητε μέρος· καὶ πρὸ τῶν κοινῶν διαλλαγῶν ἐσπείσατο μόνη· μᾶλλον δὲ σπονδῶν ἐκείνη μὲν οὐδαμῶς οὐδεπώποτε ἐδεήθη, κορυφαῖος ἔξαρχῆς ἐν τῷ τῶν φίλων ἱσταμένη χορῷ.

[89] *Homil. in Dormitionem B. Mariae,* 4, *ibid.,* p. 498: Γῆ μὲν, ὅτι ἐκεῖθεν· καινὴ δέ, ὅτι τοῖς προγόνοις οὐδαμόθεν προσῆκεν, οὐδὲ τῆς παλαιᾶς ἐκληρονόμησε ζύμης, ἀλλ' αὐτή, κατὲ τὸν τοῦ Παύλου λόγον (I Cor. 5:7) φύραμα νέον κατέστη, καὶ νέου τινὸς ἤρξατο γένους.

Cf. also *ibid.,* 3, 6, 8, pp. 500, 501, 502, 504, a clear declaration that Mary was the only one who was absolutely free from any sin.

It is interesting to see that JOSEPH BRYENNIUS, who died about 1435, and who was an avowed enemy of union with the Latins,[90] is, on the other hand, an outspoken believer in Mary's Immaculate Conception. Two short quotations will illustrate his belief clearly. In one homily on the Annunciation, he exclaimed:

> She who was inaccessible to any impurity and was free of any stain, merited to conceive the Word of God, which is immaculate by nature.[91]

Another passage is even more expressive:

> She who was to be more worthy and more pure than other (women) was sanctified by God from her mother's womb. . . . And the sovereign merit which she possessed consisted in being purified in advance by the Holy Spirit and made worthy to receive in herself the unapproachable divinity.[92]

From the context, it seems apparent that Bryennius had in mind a purification from the first instant of Mary's passive conception. This is what we call Immaculate Conception.

This survey of Byzantine mariologists may be terminated by a quotation from a treatise on the origin of the soul, written by GEORGE SCHOLARIOS, who became Patriarch of Constantinople after the conquest by the Turks and died about 1472. He is a very interesting figure, who was familiar with the work of all the great Latin theologians. Although he was himself a great admirer of St. Thomas Aquinas, and summarized the two *Summae* for his compatriots, he did not share Thomas' doubts, but expressed in a very clear way, his belief in the Immaculate Conception. It is the great merit of M. Jugie to have edited his works in collaboration with L. Petit and Siderides. This is what Scholarios has to say in the above-mentioned treatise:

> Inasmuch as she had been brought into existence through human seed, the most holy Virgin was not without part in the original sin. . . . But the grace of God delivered her completely, just as if she had been conceived virginally, in order that she might provide flesh entirely pure for the Incarnation of the Divine Word. Hence, because she was completely liberated from the ancestral guilt and punishment—a privilege which she is the only one of the human race to have received, her soul is altogther inaccessible to the clouds of (impure) thoughts, and she became, in body and soul, a divine sanctuary.[93]

---

[90] See the study by A. PALMIERI on Joseph Bryennius in *Dict. de theol. cath.,* II, cols. 1156-1161.

[91] *Homil. III in Annunt.,* ed. BULGARIS (Leipzig, 1768), II, p. 231.

[92] *Homil. II in Annunt., ibid.,* p. 152: Ἄλλη μὲν ταύτης οὐ προτετίμηται, ὅτι πάσας ὁ Θεὸς προγινώσκων, τὴν τῶν λοιπῶν ἐσομένην ἀξιωτέραν ἐκ μήτρας ἡγίασε στείρας· ἀπεβάλετο δὲ τὰς εἰς τοῦτ' ἀναξίας, ὥσπερ εἰκός· ἀρετῶν δὲ πασῶν ὑπερτέραν ἐκέκτητο, τὸ προκαθαρθῆναι τῷ Πνεύματι, καὶ δοχεῖον ἑτοιμασθῆναι δεκτινὸν τῆς ἀπροσίτου θεότητος.

[93] *Oeuvres completes de Georges Scholarios* (Paris, 1928-1936), I, p. 501: Ἡ δὲ Παναγία Παρθένος τῷ μὲν ἐκ σπέρματος γεγεννῆσθαι τῆς προγονικῆς ἁμαρτίας οὐκ ἂν ἀμέτοχος ἦν . . .

CONCLUSION

This is only a brief survey of Byzantine ideas on the greatest privilege of Our Lady. Even from this short and uneven account, however, it can be gathered how deeply many Greek theologians of the Middle Ages were convinced of the original sanctity of the *Theotokos*—Mother of God. Their Mariology is rich in ideas, profound and full of daring declarations which many would hardly expect from a Byzantine writer. It can be imagined how easy it would have been for their western confreres to disentangle their controversies and to clarify their doubts if they had known the works of Byzantine mariologists. In their own way, and almost without any opposition, the Byzantines came to similar conclusions on the degree of original sanctity of Mary, as did the western scholastics after laborious efforts and a protracted and passionate struggle.

All this shows how important the study of Byzantine theology is for western religious speculation. It has so far been undeservedly neglected, although Byzantine theologians are in many respects the continuers and guardians of our inheritance from the great patristic age. It is therefore eminently to be hoped that western specialists in dogmatic theology will in the future pay more attention to the works of Byzantine theologians.

ἀλλ' ἡ χάρις τοῦ Θεοῦ καθάπαξ αὐτὴν ἀπήλλαξεν, ὥσπερ ἂν εἰ καὶ χωρὶς ἐγένετο σπέρματος, ἵνα τῇ τοῦ θείου Λόγου σαρκώσει πάντη καθαρὰν ὑπόσχῃ τὴν σάρκα. Ὅθεν ὡς ἀπηλλαγμένη . . . καθάπαξ τῆς προγονικῆς ἐνοχῆς καὶ ποινῆς καὶ μόνη πάντων ἀνθρώπων τουτὶ λαβοῦσα τὸ δῶρον, ἀνεπίβατον καὶ τοῖς νέφεσι τῶν λογισμῶν ἔσχε παντάπασι τὴν ψυχήν, καὶ σαρκὶ καὶ ψυχῇ θεῖον οὕτω γέγονε τέμενος.

See also M. JUGIE's notice, "Georges Scholarios et l'Immaculée Conception," in *Echoes d'Orient* (1914-1915), 17. pp. 527-530.

IV

The Immaculate Conception
in the Liturgy

CORNELIUS A. BOUMAN*

The development of the doctrine of the Immaculate Conception is closely connected with the feast the Latin Church celebrates on December 8. It would be wrong, however, to interpret that history by concluding from the existence of the feast to the existence of the doctrine, or by looking upon the beginning of the feast as upon the first germs of that doctrine. In this respect some of the earlier authors on the subject, among whom at times Passaglia, were led astray by their zeal to trace the doctrine as far back as possible. As a matter of fact the feast, which up to 1854 A.D. had the simple name of *The Conception of the Blessed Virgin Mary*,† existed before theologians started worrying about the precise determinations of the sanctity and sanctification of the Virgin Mother which such a celebration seemed to demand. It is even permissible to state that the feast existed before one was clearly aware of any theological implications at all. In this instance, as in others, the instinct of Christian devotion preceded theological reflection and well-defined doctrine.

For this reason it is not enough to put together the heortological data concerning the origin and the spread of the feast of Mary's Conception.[1]

---

* The Reverend Mr. Bouman—an ordained deacon in the Byzantine rite of the Roman Catholic Church—has published numerous studies in the field of the history of the liturgy. He resides at Utrecht, Netherlands, and has taught at the University of Notre Dame several times as Visiting Professor in the Liturgy Program. The present article was completed in July, 1954.

† Cf. chapter VII of the present volume, p. 271 ff.

[1] A summary of the history of the feast of the Conception is given by K. A. H. KELLNER, *Heortologie*[3], Freiburg in Br. 1911, pp. 181-199 (the references in the present study are to the pages of the English translation, *Heortology*, London 1908, made from the second German edition, which, at least for the feast of December 8, contains substantially the same text as the third German edition). Furthermore, by X.-M. LE BACHELET in *Dictionnaire de Théologie catholique*, t. VII[1], col. 845-1218 (in collaboration with M. JUGIE), and in *Dictionnaire Apologétique de la Foi catholique*, t. III, col. 221-269; in both articles Father Le Bachelet gives extensive bibliographical notes. Works of more recent date, and those dealing with special heortological problems will be indicated in the following footnotes.—Some excellent notes on the liturgy of this feast may be found in the conference delivered by Father Bernard CAPELLE, O.S.B., at the seventh National Marian Congress of France, published in *Congrès Marials Nationaux*, Lyon 1954, *L'Immaculée Conception* (1954), pp. 147-161.

During a period of several centuries the entry we find in calendars at December 8 does not indicate clearly the real object of the feast. In order to understand its real meaning we have in each case to interrogate the documents, in the first place the liturgical formulas. By analyzing these formulas we can single out the different shades of devotional attitude, of theological reflection, of doctrinal precision and even the smaller sides of controversy, which have played a part in the development of this chapter of Mariology. And even then we have to proceed cautiously, always bearing in mind the phenomena peculiar to the development of liturgy itself, which in our case is sometimes in arrear of doctrinal precision.

It would be false to value the analysis of the liturgical texts exclusively as an illustration and corroboration of the history of dogmatic theology; for the prayer and meditation of the liturgy, as the daily expression of the Church's life itself, possess a value of their own and give utterance to perspectives which too often are lacking in theoretical and controversial treatises. The veneration of the mysteries of the Blessed Mother of God has not grown from cold speculation and penetrating arguments, but from the warmth of loving practice. And where could we find the traces of that practice better than in the prayer of liturgy?

Before the present formulas came into use (1863 A.D.), or at least up to the sixteenth century, there has existed a bewildering variety of them, so many that it would be useless as well as nearly impossible to list and analyze all the less important variants. For our purpose it will be sufficient to point out the main trends of liturgical tradition. In comparison with the vastness of the subject, we can only give, within the limits of an article, a brief outline. In the footnotes we will indicate the literature in which the student may find the material for a more thorough research into the different problems.[2]

I

THE BYZANTINE FEAST OF ST. ANNE'S CONCEPTION

The feast of the Conception was first celebrated in the East, or, to be more precise, in the Byzantine East.

The first trace of the Byzantine feast appears toward the very end of the seventh century,[3] when St. Andrew of Crete, probably at the time that

---

[2] Insofar as we have to deal with medieval liturgical texts we refer most of the time to the printed editions in which, in the course of the last eighty years, many of them have been made accessible. Although the number of published medieval texts is in many respects far from complete (there does not exist as yet, e.g., an edition which shows the development of the Breviary of the Curia), the main features of the liturgy of our feast are sufficiently represented to warrant a survey of the different motifs.

he was a deacon of Saint Sophia in the capital, wrote the *canon* of the feast which is still used in the morning office.[4] Up to the end of the Iconoclastic struggle, its celebration seems to have been restricted to monasteries; in the second half of the eighth century John of Euboeia says in a sermon that the feast is not known by all, but that it ought to be celebrated everywhere.[5] It became general about the year 850. The feast of December 9—on which day we invariably find it in the Greek *Minaea* and *Synaxaria*[6]—was for some time regarded as one of the notable festivals of the year. It is noted as such in the *Nomokanon,* found among the works of Photius;[7] Passaglia refers to a sermon by the emperor Leo VI the Philosopher, which equally presupposes a general celebration;[8] Manuel Comnenus gave it in 1166 all the splendor civil law could warrant. But it is equally true that since that time it has sunk back to the rank of a minor feast, in a way reminiscent of the feast of the Visitation of the Blessed Virgin in the Latin liturgy. At the time it was borrowed by the Latin West, however, the Greeks celebrated it as one of the notable festivals of the Blessed Virgin.

PIETY OF THE PHILOTHEOTOKOI

Tracing the origin of the Oriental feast to a precise period is not just a matter of historical accuracy.[9] For the characteristics of the period in the course of which the feast took form—the time immediately before and after the Iconoclastic struggle—give the key to the full understanding of the meaning of the feast. This period, so much more homogeneous spiritually than the preceding centuries, notwithstanding decades of official unorthodoxy, is to a large extent characterized by its devotion to the Blessed

---

[3] Cf. also chap. III or the present volume, p. 90 f.

[4] On this *canon,* see L. PETIT in *Dictionnaire d'Archéologie chrétienne et de Liturgie* I, 2036.

[5] *PG* 96, 1499.

[6] With regard to the fact that in the West the Byzantine date of December 9 has been replaced by that of Dec. 8, KELLNER, *o.c.,* p. 247, n. 1, offers as a probable explanation that, according to the Roman calendar, the writing of *VI Idus Dec.* is analogous to that of *VI Idus Sept.,* the traditional date of the feast of Mary's Nativity, whereas December 9 is written *V Idus Dec.*

[7] *Nomokanon* Tit. VII, c. 1; *PG* 104, 1070. GEORGE OF NICOMEDIA, a friend of Photius, refers to the crowds coming to church to celebrate the feast which had been instituted a long time before: *PG* 100, 1335 and 1351.

[8] C. PASSAGLIA and Cl. SCHRADER, *De immaculato Deiparae virginis conceptu,* 3 vol. Naples 1854/55, III p. 1750. Later scholars have been unable to find the ms. of the Sforza Library to which Passaglia referred.

[9] PASSAGLIA was wrong in tracing the origin of the feast of the Conception to the primitive version (ab. 485 A.D.) of the *Typikon* of the convent of St. Sabas near the Dead Sea. The mention of the feast, like many other passages in the famous *Typikon,* belongs to later interpolations. See Th. TOSCANI and J. COZZA-LUZI, *De immaculata Deiparae Conceptione Hymnologia Graecorum,* Rome 1867, p. xiv, and KELLNER, *o.c.,* pp. 243 and 447-448.

Mother of God. It is the piety known as that of the *Philotheotokoi,* of Germanus and Tarasius of Constantinople, of Sophronius and so many others, who wrote the innumerable sermons in honor of the Blessed Virgin from which many a lesson in the Roman Breviary has been borrowed. This piety is in fact so characteristic of the period that by judging its expression in a superficial way one could think that it amounts to a rather monotonous repetition of the same devotional motifs.

The dogmatic roots of the piety of the *Philotheotokoi* are, of course, older. They are the primordial comparison between Mary and Eve, and the joyfully accepted Ephesian doctrine of Mary as really the Mother of God. The main conclusions from these premises had already been drawn at an earlier time; the later flowering is undoubtedly linked up with the praises of the Virgin by Ephraem and by other Syriac authors whose writings have often come to us under the name of the famous deacon of Edessa. But only since the seventh century do we find the complete series of motifs which from that time onwards, with numerous variants, were to remain traditional in the Orient (equally in the non-Greek Orient, where they were borrowed from Melchitic use), and which also in the West, although doctrine and devotion would develop later there, always constitute the marrow of the authentic veneration of the Blessed Virgin. The misery caused by the disobedience of the first Eve and the salvation which followed the obedience of the second Eve; Mary's perfections, connected with her singular election as well as with her personal sanctity; the Blessed Virgin, universal advocate and protectress of Christianity; all these privileges and personal qualities seen as the consequences and essential elements of the central prerogative, that, as the well-known troparion *Axion estin* has it, Mary, "in uncorrupted virginity, has borne God the Word, that she is in truth *Theotokos."*

This is the piety which, in the monastic and other pious centers of the Empire, crystallized in the course of the sixth and seventh centuries and which forms the background of the new feasts of the Virgin-Mother, that of her Conception and that of her Presentation in the Temple.[10]

If we do not realize that the fundamental motifs of the liturgical formulas in honor of the Conception—the office of the *Proeortion* on December 8

---

[10] The older feasts of the Holy Mother of God, Annunciation (very soon celebrated as a feast of the *Theotokos*), Assumption and probably also Nativity, are clearly those of a former period. It may be true that their definitive liturgical formulas took shape under the influence of the standardizing tendencies of the fixed piety of the seventh and eighth centuries, but the feasts themselves are not properly Byzantine in the sense that the later ones are. The problem is that it remains extremely difficult to distinguish the primitive motifs in their liturgy from the later additions; the propers of these feasts were to a large extent remodeled during and immediately after the Iconoclastic struggle, when the lost office books had to be replaced by newly printed ones, and the new genre of the *canon* was introduced.—On the feast of the Presentation see M. J. KISPAUGH, *The feast of the Presentation of the Virgin Mary in the Temple,* Washington (Catholic University Press) 1941.

and that of the feast itself on December 9 [11]—are those of the *Philotheoto-koi,* we could easily be distracted by the apocryphal elements we find in those texts.

"THE CONCEPTION OF ST. ANNE"

That the feast is called "The Conception of Saint Anne, the Mother of the *Theotokos*" has to be explained by the fact that the Greek word σύλληψις, *conception,* is, as a rule (though not always), used in the active sense (and that consequently, in Greek texts, "The Conception of the Virgin" usually must be understood of the Conception of the Divine Word). It is true, however, that the story of Saint Anne, as it is given in the Protogospel of Saint James, plays an important part in the liturgy of the feast. But not an overwhelming part; the Greek rejected the naive additions found in the later recensions and variants of the Protogospel.[12] The apocryphal data they do use, Anne's sterility and the announcement by the Angel, serve to stress the real meaning of the feast. That there is a divine promise, miraculously promulgated, is not in itself the object of the feast, but it highlights the point that the Conception of the Virgin has to do with the mysteries of our salvation. To a certain extent the feast of December 9 is a *festum pio-historicum;* also in this respect it is true to the period, in which we also find the feasts of the Conception of Saint John the Baptist on September 23, and of the Presentation (of Mary) in the Temple on November 21. But a further analysis of the formulas shows that the feast of the Conception is firmly rooted in the piety of the *Philotheotokoi;* historical facts are recorded because they illustrate the greatness of the Mother of God and thus represent the beginning of the salvation of mankind achieved by the Incarnate Son.[13]

[11] The texts are found in the *Minaeon* of December at the 8th and 9th days of that month. In their *Hymnologia,* TOSCANI and COZZA have published them (Greek text and Latin translation) together with many *inedita* which makes their publication highly interesting. I doubt, however, whether the troparia for the second Ode of the Canon of St. Andrew (this Ode always being left out in the liturgical books), which they found in the ms. of the monastery of St. Elias at Carbone, are genuine. As a matter of fact these troparia are far shorter than those of the other odes.

[12] Cf. chapter II of the present volume, pp. 58 f., 81 f., together with the texts on p. 513 ff. (esp. notes of Docum. II). See also E. AMANN, *Le Protoévangile de Jacques et ses remaniements latins,* Paris 1910, pp. 198 and 294.—The *Synaxaria* (historical lessons read in monasteries during the morning Office, or the books containing these lessons) for December 9 always contain a warning against those apocryphal phantasies. In the *synaxarion* which is found in the current editions we read: "Our Lord and God, when He desired to prepare for Himself a living temple and a holy house for His dwelling place, sent His Angel to the just, Joachim and Anne . . . to announce the conception of the woman who was childless and sterile, and to determine the birth of the Virgin. Hence has been conceived the holy Virgin Mary and she was born, not after seven months as some say, nor without help of man, but after full nine months; her Conception was indeed foretold, but it happened with the assistance and from the seed of man . . ."

[13] This shows exactly the part which apocryphal motifs (already in existence at a far earlier time, of course) have played in the history of doctrine and piety. It may

This last idea, especially, is the main theme of the liturgy of the Byzantine feast. In this regard, the feast of the Conception is a duplicate of that of the Nativity of the Virgin; both celebrate the first beginning of salvation, the dawn announcing the rising of the Sun of Justice. All that is said about the privileges of the Blessed Mother and her sanctity culminates in her call—and her corresponding willingness—to be the Mother of God. So, for instance, we read in the Canon of the *Proeortion*:

> Today it is announced to us that the treasures of joy will be opened and that an end will be put to the sorrows of malediction, in the holy Conception of the Mother of God.[14]

St. Andrew of Crete alludes, in a Troparion of his Canon, to the paradise to which mankind will be restored through the *Theotokos*—the same paradise, as Christians then understood it—from which the first Eve had been driven; he extends this comparison between Eve and Mary by referring, in true Byzantine fashion, to the garden (paradise) in which Saint Anne implores God's help:

> While thou prayest in a garden (paradise), O pious Anne, the Most High hears thy voice and gives to thee, as the fruit of thy womb, Her who will open the gate of grace of Paradise.[15]

In the same Canon we find a wonderful allusion to the reality of the Incarnation; the heavenly *Basileus* will receive the flesh (the imperial purple He alone is allowed to wear) from the human being who has just been conceived:

> In thy womb, O Anne, begins the weaving of the royal purple in which God and the King of all will dress Himself, when He appears to the mortals and defeats the foes who are fighting against us.[16]

In the eighth ode of St. Andrew's Canon, the Blessed Virgin is honored as the protectress of Christianity:

> Anne exclaimed: Lo, I conceive in my womb the queen foretold by David, and I shall give birth to the Protectress of all the faithful, the future Mother of Christ, the King.

---

be true that to some extent the development of doctrine and piety has been furthered by those influences, but on the other hand we have to regard them as secondary phenomena (or rather: as the popular expressions) of authentic themes which were prior to them, and which remain the chief objects of the traditional liturgical formulas. For this reason we must reject what H. LECLERCQ wrote in the *Dictionnaire d'Archéologie chrétienne et de Liturgie*, X, 2040: "Les Orientaux commémorent volontiers tous les événements un peu extraordinaires de l'histoire évangélique."

14 The first Troparion of the first Ode: Χαρᾶς ἡμῖν σήμερον προκαταγγέλλονται ταμεῖα διανοίγεσθαι, καὶ ἀπεκλείεσθαι τῆς κατάρας αἱ λῦπαι, ἐν τῇ θείᾳ Συλλήψει τῆς Θεομήτορος.

15 The second Troparion of the third Ode: Ἐν παραδείσῳ εὐχομένης σου τῆς φωνῆς ἀκούει ὁ Ὕψιστος, Ἄννα θεόφρον, καὶ καρπὸν τῇ κοιλίᾳ σου δίδωσι, Παραδείσου τὴν ἀνοίξασαν τὴν θύραν τῆς χάριτος.

16 The second Troparion of the seventh Ode: Βασιλικὴ πορφύρα ἐν τῇ σῇ ἀπάρχεται, Ἄννα, ἐξυφαίνεσθαι γαστρί, ἣν ὁ Θεὸς καὶ Βασιλεὺς πάντων φορέσας τοῖς βροτοῖς ὀφθήσεται, καὶ ταπεινώσει ἐχθρούς, τοὺς πολεμοῦντας ἡμᾶς.

And then follows a litany of Scriptural names, which we find later on also in Latin hymns:

> In the womb of her mother now begins to blossom the earth which will be the dwelling place of the Creator of earth, the holy sceptre, the new ark, the vessel of manna . . . the bush which was not consumed by fire, the golden candelabrum, the living bridal room of the Lord God. . . .[17]

Many more examples could be given. They would represent a far richer variety of theologically founded meditations and praises, but they would not change sensibly the few conclusions we can draw at the end of this short survey.

THE SENSE OF THE FEAST

From the fact that St. Anne's conception is called 'holy,' we are not entitled to conclude to the existence of the idea of the Immaculate Conception in the later Western sense. Everyone who is acquainted with Byzantine liturgical texts knows that in them *holy* very often means nothing more than *venerable*. In the liturgy of September 23 the conception of the Baptist is called holy as well.

On the other hand, from the general acceptance of the feast in the Byzantine East, and from the wording of the liturgical formulas, it is clear that the pious faithful and theologians of that period *did not deny* the holiness of the Virgin's Conception in our sense of the term. On the contrary, the existence of the feast as such leads up to the later doctrinal precision in the West. The theological controversy in the West did not start in the way of an academic problem; it originated from the quarrel about the acceptance or non-acceptance of the liturgical feast. In the Greek Orient the rightful existence of that feast does not seem to have been seriously doubted.

In the liturgical texts we find no trace of any theological problem with regard to the relation between the holiness of Mary's Conception and the nature and universality of original sin. Or rather, the Greek concept of original sin did not clearly involve such a preoccupation. It would be an oversimplification to assert that the problem did not arise at all for Oriental theologians; but it is true that in general they treated the question of Mary's privileges and sanctity along other lines than those taken by later Latin theologians. It is difficult to define those lines; in order to do this we would have to compare the liturgical formulas with the entire

[17] The three Troparia of the eighth Ode:

Δαυΐδ ἦν προέφησε, Βασίλισσαν ἰδού, γαστρὶ ὑποδέχομαι, ἡ Ἄννα ἐκβοᾷ, καὶ τέξω τὴν πάντων προστασίαν πιστῶν, τὴν τὸν Βασιλέα Χριστὸν μέλλουσαν τίκτειν.

Ἡ γῆ ἦν κατῴκησεν ὁ γῆς Δημιουργός, τὸ σκῆπτρον τὸ ἅγιον, ἡ νέα Κιβωτός, ἡ Στάμνος τοῦ Μάννα, ἐν νηδύϊ μητρός, τῆς αὐτὴν τεκούσης, ἀπάρχεται βλαστάνειν.

Ἡ Βάτος ἡ ἄφλεκτος, Λυχνία ἡ χρυσῆ, ὁ ἔμψυχος Θάλαμος Κυρίου τοῦ Θεοῦ, ἡ ἔντιμος Ῥάβδος, ἐν γαστρὶ τῆς μητρός, τῆς αὐτὴν τεκούσης, ἀπάρχεται βλαστάνειν.

Oriental tradition as it is embodied in Syriac poetry and in Greek sermons and treatises. This much, however, is clear, that in Oriental Mariology we must always reckon with a tendency to regard the Blessed Virgin as 'paradise regained,' as creation restored to its primitive purity and therefore fit to become the meeting-point between God and mankind. This motif (which is not cosmological, but purely biblical, Mary being the 'spiritual paradise' as St. John Damascene has it, *viz.* the antitype of the creation described in the first chapters of Genesis) is seldom referred to openly in liturgical poetry, but it often underlies expressions which could hardly be understood without it.[18] As we shall see below, this theme is not entirely absent from later Latin formulas, although it never exercised an important influence on the development of Mariology in the West.—Also, we have to bear in mind that there was a tendency among Oriental divines to regard the sanctity of the Virgin Mary in function of her hallowing at the Annunciation. At a later time some Byzantine theologians would even treat the *sanctificatio in Annuntiatione* as a real *theologumenon;* during the period of the *Philotheotokoi* there existed at least a tradition which regarded the Virgin's sanctity in the perspective of what the Spirit wrought in her at the moment of the Incarnation.[19]

Without any doubt we are justified in deducing from the Greek liturgical formulas, that the Blessed Virgin at her conception is unhesitatingly venerated as the All-Pure One; that her immaculate purity (understood first of all of her perpetual virginity, but always denoting her entire freedom from sin) is connected with the part the *Theotokos* played in the economy of salvation; that her holiness involves a special privilege as well as personal sanctity.

OTHER ORIENTAL RITES

The feast of the Virgin's Conception in the Catholic branches of the other Oriental rites has been introduced by Latin influence. Therefore neither the existence of the feast nor the wording of the liturgical formulas as such are witness of an ancient tradition. Of far more interest for the history of our subject are the motifs of the old Marian texts, most of which were written for liturgical use, and passages of which are still found

---

[18] Cf. for instance the last of the quotations given from St. Andrew's *Canon:* "the earth which will be the dwelling place of the Creator of earth."

[19] Already St. James of Saroug, in a *Mimrâ* on the Virgin Mary (lines 381 f.), wrote: "He purified His Mother through the Holy Spirit, when He came into her, when without sin, He took from her a pure body."—Ed. J.-B. ABBELOOS, *De vita et scriptis sancti Jacobi Batnarum Sarugi in Mesopotamia episcopi,* Louvain, 1867, p. 238. When we compare these few lines to the rest of St. James' poem, it is clear that not too much can be deduced from them. The same holds for a troparion of the Seventh Ode from the Byzantine *Canon* for the feast of the Annunciation: "The coming of the Holy Spirit upon me has purified my soul, hallowed my body, and made of me a sanctuary enclosing God, a tabernacle adorned by God Himself, the pure Mother of Life."

in the propers of the feasts peculiar to those rites from ancient times. Also, the Marian strophes in the daily office are highly interesting in this respect.[20]

In most of these cases, however, owing to the fact that the greatest number of manuscripts available are of rather recent date, and that even the names of the authors, when given, are seldom a reliable indication, it is impossible to say anything definite with regard to the period in which these texts were composed. In many instances—as has been pointed out by students of the Coptic formulas—it is clear that later Melchitic influences are to be reckoned with. We may presume that the cult of the Blessed Mother of God in the Church of St. Cyril of Alexandria flourished at an early date, and that therefore a number of Coptic *Theotokia* stem from the very beginnings of the national patriarchate, but it is difficult to make this point any clearer.

When we study the Marian texts of the Western Syrian rite, viz. those of the Jacobites, the Catholics of the Antiochene rite, and the Maronites, we find ourselves on firmer ground. Many a passage from the hymns composed for the liturgy by the ancient Syriac poets is found in the printed liturgical books. It is true that modern scholars often hesitate to accept the authorship of St. Ephraem and his followers which the earlier editors asserted on the basis of indications in the manuscripts; but all agree that even the texts which might be spurious most often date from a period close

---

[20] For the *Coptic Rite* one may consult: DE LACY O'LEARY, *The Coptic Theotokia*, London 1923 (*cf. id.*, "The Coptic Theotokia," in *Coptic Studies in honor of W. E. Crum*, Boston 1950, pp. 417-420); J. MUYSER, *Maria's heerlijkheid in Egypte, een studie der Koptische Maria-literatuur*, I (the *Theotokia* during Advent), Louvain-Utrecht 1935.

For the *Ethiopian Rite*: A. GROHMANN, "Äthiopische Marienhymnen herausgegeben und übersetzt," in *Abh. der Philolog.-Histor. Kl. der Sächs. Akad. d. Wiss.* 33, Bd. 4, Leipzig 1919. A full bibliography of translations of Ethiopic hymns in honor of the Blessed Virgin in A. BAUMSTARK, *Liturgie Comparée*[3], Chevetogne 1953, pp. 255-6. An English translation (by S. A. B. MERCER) of the Ethiopic Anaphora of Our Lady in *Journal of the Society of Oriental Research*, 3 (1919) pp. 51-64; of less value is the abridged translation of the same text in J. M. HARDEN, *The Anaphoras of the Ethiopic Church*, London 1928, pp. 67-71.

For the *Armenian Rite*: *Laudes et hymni ad s.s. Mariae Virginis honorem ex Armenorum Breviario excerpta Mechitaristicae congregationis opera latinitate donata*, Venice 1877.

Very interesting is the responsory ('onithâ), sung on the feasts of the Blessed Virgin in the *Nestorian* Churches and found in many mss. of the 'Book of the Rose,' a collection of liturgical hymns mostly written by the Nestorian poet George Warda (thirteenth century). The opening lines give witness to the veneration of the Nestorians for the Blessed Mother, notwithstanding their denial of the Ephesian doctrine: "Who is able to grasp with his mind or to declare and proclaim that chaste, pure and holy, sanctified, unknown to man, unwedded and perpetual Virgin, who has been hallowed in the body of her mother and chosen from her mother's womb to be the dwelling place, the sanctuary, the resting place, the palace and the throne of the eternal God . . ." See G. P. BADGER, *The Nestorians and their Rituals*, London 1852, II pp. 51 ff.; cf. A. BAUMSTARK, *Geschichte der syrischen Literatur*, Bonn 1922, pp. 305-6.

to the classic epoch of Syriac Mariology, and present the characteristic themes known to us from writings of undoubted authenticity.

When we read in these liturgical hymns that the Blessed Virgin is without sin, pure and holy, we must keep in mind that the tendency to conceive Mary's holiness in the perspective of her sanctification at the time of the Incarnation is, in the ancient Syriac writings, even stronger than in the tradition of the Byzantine *Philotheotokoi*. It would be wrong to interpret this attitude as though the Syriac Fathers held some definite ideas about a *sanctificatio in Annuntiatione*, for many a passage implies the Virgin's holiness from the very beginning of her existence. But on the other hand we must bear in mind that most passages, when seen in context, have to be understood primarily as praises of the Virgin at her becoming and being the Mother of God. Thus, for instance, the first of St. Ephraem's hymns on the Blessed Virgin in Lamy's edition is a praise of the marvelous mysteries revealed to us through her Divine Motherhood. It is in that connection that the following stanza on Mary's perfections must be understood:

> Holy is her body, beautiful her soul, and pure her mind;
> Most resplendent is her thought,
> And most perfect her speech;
> She is chaste and wise, spotless and well proven,
>   full of all goodness.[21]

From other passages in the writings of the Syrian Fathers, however, it is clear that their idea of the Virgin's sanctity entails more than the above-mentioned would suggest. That goes for St. Ephraem[22] as well as for St. James of Saroug, to mention only the chiefs of Syriac poetry. Passages from the latter's writings are among the most eloquent Marian texts we find in the liturgical books. We quote only a few of them.

> Be in peace, O thou beautiful amongst women and full of splendor; peace be with thee, O veil spread out over creation; be in peace, O thou justice incorrupted; peace be with thee, O Eve who hast borne Emmanuel.[23]
> The most blessed among women is she, by whom the curse of the earth has been uprooted and the sentence of condemnation effaced; she is chaste and pure and wholly resplendent with sanctity; my mouth finds no words to proclaim the full measure of her praise.[24]

[21] T. J. LAMY, *Sancti Ephraem Syri Hymni et Sermones* II, Malines 1886, col. 519, stanza iv. The editor has found the text in four liturgical mss. dating from the ninth and tenth centuries. Passages from another liturgical hymn in Lamy's collection (*ibid.* col. 607-613) are to be found in M. L. ROUET DE JOURNEL, *Enchiridion Patristicum*[14], Barcelona 1946, n. 711.

[22] A Latin translation of the well-known stanza in *Carmina Nisibena* XXVII (never used in the liturgy, so far as I know) is found in ROUET DE JOURNEL, *o.c.* n. 719.

[23] *Officium feriale juxta ritum ecclesiae Syrorum*, Rome 1851, p. 292; part of a hymn generally ascribed to St. James of Saroug.

[24] *Officium feriale . . . Syrorum*, p. 125; *Officium feriale Syrorum Maronitarum,*

I speak about Mary with admiration, and I tremble with fear because a daughter of the earth has come to such an exalted state. Did grace bring the Son down to her, or is it because she was so pleasing that she became the Mother of the Son of the Holy One? It is clear that God came down to earth by grace, but Mary received Him because of her great purity. He regarded her humility, her sweetness and her purity, and He that loves to dwell in the humble took His abode in her.[25]

PENETRATION INTO ITALY

By way of southern Italy the Greek feast of the Conception and the idea it stood for came to the Latin West.

From the list of manuscripts Toscani and Cozza-Luzi collated for their edition of Greek liturgical texts of the Conception feast, it is clear that the calendar of the Greek communities in southern Italy (and Sicily) was in this respect conformable to Byzantine use. The earliest of these manuscripts, the *Minaeon* for December of the monastery of St. Elias at Carbone, seems to go back at least to the eleventh century. There is no need to doubt this, because we know that *Magna Graecia* was, during the last centuries of Byzantine rule, a stronghold of Greek orthodoxy, where the iconodule monks upheld all the uses of traditional piety. "We may conclude with practical certainty," wrote Edmund Bishop, "that in Greek monasteries newly founded or renewed in Lower and Middle Italy in the tenth and eleventh centuries both these feasts (i.e. Presentation and Conception) were already received and established as traditional." [26]

For the existence of the feast of the Conception in Byzantine Italy we have an indirect witness as early as the first half of the ninth century in the famous epigraphic calendar of Naples, two long slabs of marble, decorated on both sides, which were found in 1742 in the church of San Giovanni Maggiore, where they possibly had formed part of the colonnade in front of the sanctuary.[27] The Latin inscription gives a single item, for each day, like the freely combined calendar in many a modern prayer

Rome 1835, p. 393. It is a passage from the first *mimrâ* of St. James of Saroug on the Blessed Virgin (lines 35-38) edited by ABBELOOS, *o.c.*, p. 206.

[25] *Officium feriale . . . Syrorum*, pp. 264 f.; *Officium feriale Syrorum Maronitarum*, p. 149. It is likewise a passage from the first *mimrâ* (lines 91-98) edited by ABBELOOS, *o.c.*, pp. 210-212.

[26] E. BISHOP in the Supplementary Note to his "On the Origins of the Feast of the Conception of the Blessed Virgin Mary," reprinted in *Liturgica Historica*, Oxford 1918, p. 258.

[27] According to A. EHRHARD, "Der Marmorkalender von Neapel," in *Riv. di archeol. crist.* 11 (1934) pp. 119-150, the redaction of the calendar took place between 821 and 849 A.D.—There is a reproduction of the calendar in *Dict. d'archéol. chrét. et de liturgie* II, 1591/2.—Recent publications on the subject are D. MALLARDO, *Il calendario marmoreo di Napoli* (Bibl. Eph. Lit. 18), Rome 1947; and A. FERRUA, "Note sul testo del Calendario Marmoreo di Napoli," in *Miscell. lit. Mohlberg* I, Rome 1948, pp. 135-167.

book, and represents an artificial blending of the local and Oriental calendars. This at least is the conclusion reached by the Bollandist, H. Delehaye; he refuses to consider the Naples Calendar as a liturgical document, but considers it a kind of reduced martyrology borrowing its items from several sources.[28]   The situation at Naples, which up to 1050 A.D. belonged to the Byzantine realm across the Adriatic, makes it clear why one of the most conspicuous of those sources is the Greek use. This explains the date as well as the wording of the entry at December 9, C(on)CEPTIO.S. ANNE.MARIE.VIR.

There is no reason whatever to conclude that the feast was celebrated in Latin churches at Naples about 830, any more than the feasts of the Transfiguration of Our Lord on August 6, of St. Basil on January 1, or of the holy patriarchs of the imperial city and so many other Oriental saints who figure among the entries in the marble calendar.[29]   It is only two centuries later that we find the Conception for the first time in western liturgical documents, belonging to some monasteries in the South of England.

This observation must be understood exactly as it stands. It does not necessarily imply that the feast of the Conception was nowhere in the West celebrated at an earlier date; liturgical documents for this period are too scarce to permit us to make such a statement with absolute certainty. It only says that there is no proof for an earlier existence of the feast.

SPAIN

No one today accepts Passaglia's assertion that the Conception was celebrated in Spain as early as the seventh century.[30]   It would be interesting if it were true, for, as we know now, in the eighth and ninth centuries there existed relations between the Pyrenean peninsula and England which would have made a liturgical influence possible. But Passaglia merely relied on a biography of St. Ildefonsus of Toledo, which Mabillon had already proven to be false; and, moreover, he fell into the pitfall that besets the path of all who study the development of our feast and doctrine, by confusing the active and passive Conceptions of the Mother of God.[31]

[28] Hipp. DELEHAYE in *Analecta Bollandiana* 53 (1935), p. 392.

[29] There does not seem to be much system in this borrowing. Thus the Presentation of the Virgin is not mentioned, but we find the C(onceptio) S.IOH.BAP at Sept. 23 (the Byzantine date, St. Thecla being celebrated there on the 24th).

[30] PASSAGLIA (work cited in note 8), vol. III, p. 1755 ff.

[31] See KELLNER (work cited in note 1), p. 254, n. 2.—To complete the picture, there are no traces of a Conception feast in the Visigothic and Mozarabic liturgical books which since have been published by MORIN, FEROTIN, the Benedictine Fathers of Silos, and VIVES.—As to another document, alleged by PASSAGLIA, a deed dated at Cremona *in festo sanctae et immaculatae* (!) *Conceptionis b. Virg. Mariae* in the year 1047, it was fabricated by the forger Antonio Dragoni; see KELLNER, *ibid.*, p. 225, n. 1.

IRELAND

Far more impressive are the arguments, brought forward over and over again, in favor of the existence of the Conception feast in Ireland since the beginning of the ninth century. Especially fifty years ago, on the occasion of the Golden Jubilee of the definition of 1854, the question was fiercely debated. Fr. Herbert Thurston was the chief defendant, and Mr. Edmund Bishop the principal opponent in the case.[32] The witnesses are several entries in Irish Martyrologies.

In the first place, there is the *Félire of Oengus* (beginning ninth century) which reads at May 3rd:

Prímairec crainn chroiche	The first finding of Christ's Cross
Críst co n-ilur búade,	with its many virtues: the death of
bás Conláid cain áge,	Conlead, a fair pillar: the feast of
féil már Maire húage.	great Mary the Virgin.[33]

In the Martyrology of Tallaght (end ninth cent.—beginning tenth cent.) at May 3: *Crucis Christi inventio, Mariae virginis conceptio;* and at May 7 again: *Agnitio sanctae crucis, conceptio Marie i(d est) ut(ero).*[34]

Several versions of a poetical calendar (tenth cent.), written in England and largely depending on Irish examples, have at May 2: *Concipitur virgo Maria cognomine senis* (*senis* written for a misunderstood *VI,* viz. *nonas maias*).[35]

There can be no doubt, it seems, that the word *conceptio* is used here in the passive sense, because the active *conceptio Mariae* is invariably fixed at March 25. Moreover, the Latin commentary on the *Félire* (written by some scholars later than the tenth century) seems to present the key to the

---

[32] H. THURSTON, "The Irish Origins of Our Lady's Conception Feast," in *The Month* 103 (1904) pp. 449-465; *id.,* "England and the Immaculate Conception," in *The Month* 104 (1905) pp. 562-576; H. THURSTON and T. SLATER, *Eadmeri monachi Cantuariensis Tractatus de Conceptione Sanctae Mariae,* Freiburg in Br. 1904, pp. XXXII f.; E. BISHOP, "On the Origins of the Feast of the Conception of the Blessed Virgin Mary," an article which had been printed in 1886 and 1904 and which finally was published, with a lengthy supplement, in *Liturgica Historica,* Oxford 1918, pp. 238-259; *id., The Bosworth Psalter,* London 1908, pp. 51-52. See also A. NOYON, "Les origines de la fête de l'Immaculée Conception en Occident," in *Etudes de théologie,* 1904, and E. VACANDARD in his *Etudes de critique et d'histoire religieuse* III, Paris 1912, pp. 226-227, where the author follows, to some extent, the opinion of Fr. Thurston.

[33] Text from *The Martyrology of Oengus the Culdee,* ed. by W. STOKES (Henry Bradshaw Society 29), London 1905, p. 122. I have replaced the last line of Stokes' translation by that given by F. Ó BRIAIN, "Feast of Our Lady's Conception in the Medieval Irish Church," in *The Irish Eccl. Record* 84 (1948), p. 698.

[34] *The Martyrology of Tallaght,* ed. by R. I. BEST and H. J. LAWLOR (HBS 68), London 1931, pp. 39 and 40. That the abbreviation *.i.* has to be read: *id est* and not: *in* had been pointed out already by Fr. GROSJEAN in the article mentioned in the following note.

[35] The exact data are given by P. GROSJEAN, "Notes d'Hagiographie celtique," in *Anal. Boll.* 61 (1948), p. 92 n. 2.

riddle: *i*(d est) *haec inceptio eius, ut alii putant (sed in febru.o mense vel in martio facta est illa, quia post vii menses nata est, ut innaratur), vel quaelibet alia feria* (feast) *eius.*[36] In other words: this feast of the Blessed Virgin, wandering all through the first week of May, seems to be that of her Conception which, according to some apocryphal tradition (the same which is vehemently disallowed in the Greek Synaxaria), took place seven (or even four) months before her birth.

Fr. Thurston concluded to the existence of a liturgical feast of the Conception. Edm. Bishop considered the entries to be martyrological items, without any liturgical significance at all, due merely to the erudition of the compilers whose sources of information we are unable to trace.[37]

The Bollandist, Paul Grosjean, seems to have brought the final solution to this riddle.[38] In the first place he puts forward that the double mention of the *Inventio Crucis* in the Martyrology of Tallaght represents the two-fold recension of the *Martyrologium Hieronymianum,* that of the so-called second family and that of Epternach. In the shortened martyrology known in Ireland, one has read MARIAE, standing for MARIANI, MARCIANI or MARINAE, a martyr of Nicomedia, whose feast is indicated at May 3, 4 or 6. Oengus, who did not know very well what to do with the enigmatical entry "Maria," has written something vague about 'a' feast of Mary. Later on, others, knowing something of the apocryphal contents of the *Liber de Ortu B.Mariae et Infantia Salvatoris,* interpreted the feast mentioned by Oengus as that of Mary's Conception, a feast which in fact at that date never had existed. Máel Muire Ua Gormáin, who in the twelfth century compiled a metrical Martyrology far more extensive than those of his Irish predecessors, noticed the Conception at December 8 (Compert Maire more), but left out all allusions to a feast of the Virgin in the beginning of May, nor is there any mention of the feast in the Drummond Missal or in the *Missale Vetus Hibernicum* (eleventh and twelfth centuries).

It is possible, of course, that a feast of the Conception was celebrated in the Celtic Church before the eleventh century; but the external evidence

---

[36] W. STOKES, *o.c.,* p. 129.

[37] For the feast of the Blessed Virgin in May Fr. Thurston supposed an Oriental (Coptic) influence, without alleging, however, any solid argument for a Conception feast in May from an Eastern source. The influences with regard to the feasts of the Mother of God that we do find in the Irish Martyrologies are those represented in the different recensions of the *Martyrologium Hieronymianum,* one recension giving the Gallican tradition (feasts of Jan. 18 and Aug. 16) and the other giving the Byzantine tradition which in the course of the seventh cent. was introduced into the West (the feasts of Aug. 15 and Sept. 8); see BISHOP, "On the origins . . ." (cited in note 32), p. 252. Also it must be noted that all the mentioned Irish sources have at Sept. 24 the *Conception of St. John.* The Presentation, however, in the older documents the faithful companion to the Byzantine feast of the Conception of the Virgin, is lacking.

[38] P. GROSJEAN in *Anal. Boll.* 61 (1943) pp. 91-95. More particulars in the article by F. Ó BRIAIN, *l.c.* pp. 687-704.

for its existence seems to have been explained away conclusively, and we are altogether without internal arguments to explain why that feast should have been fixed on such curious dates and, above all, in what devotional background or influence it could have originated.

ENGLAND BEFORE THE CONQUEST

The oldest reliable traces of the feast in the Latin West are found in liturgical documents which were in use in the South of England during the last decades before the Conquest. They bear witness to the fact that, before the year 1066, liturgical functions were held in some English churches on December 8 to celebrate the feast of Mary's Conception. The texts in question are the following:

The entry at December 8: *Conceptio sanctae Dei genitricis Mariae,* in three calendars, found in as many manuscripts, written respectively in the monastery of Newminster (?), in that of Old Minster (Cathedral Priory), both at Winchester, and in St. Mary's Cathedral Priory at Worcester.[39]

The text of a pontifical blessing (i.e. one of the appropriate tripartite formulas we often find in non-Roman medieval service books, and which the bishops used in giving the blessing—according to old-Gallican and Spanish use—before Holy Communion during Mass) for the feast of Mary's Conception in a ms. which probably was copied from a Winchester original for the use of Bishop Leofric of Exeter (1046-1072).[40]

Another tripartite blessing formula, found in a pontifical and benedictional, written for the cathedral church of Canterbury between 1023 and 1066.[41]

Three prayers for the Mass of the feast (*vi id.dec.*) in the Leofric Missal. The texts are found in a part of the ms. which has been written by later hands; but according to the editor, F. E. Warren, the entire ms. was finished before Leofric's death.[42]

[39] F. WORMALD, *English Kalendars before A.D. 1100* (HBS 72), London 1934, resp. pp. 125, 167 and 223.

[40] Brit. Mus. Add. Ms. 28188. See BISHOP, *On the Origins . . .* , pp. 239-240. In this case and in the following, the date of the feast is without doubt that of the calendars, December 8, because the blessing formula follows that for the feast of St. Birinus (Dec. 3).

[41] *The Canterbury Benedictional,* ed. by R. M. WOOLLEY (HBS 51), London 1917, pp. 118-119.

[42] *The Leofric Missale as used in the Cathedral of Exeter* (1059-1072), ed. by F. E. WARREN, Oxford 1883, p. 268. Cf. F. MADAN and H. H. E. CRASTER, A summary catalogue of Western Mss. in the Bodleian Library at Oxford, vol. II, part I, Oxford 1922, pp. 487-489.

(Since the completion of these pages, I have had the opportunity to study the ms. for myself. I must confess that I do not understand why Warren was so certain that the formulas were added to the Missal during Leofric's lifetime. At any rate, the writing—a rather unsteady insular hand—and some features of subsequent insertions suggest that they were not executed much later.)

The texts of these formulas will be reproduced and analyzed below. Beforehand we have to deal with the heortological problem, how the connexion between the Byzantine and the Latin feast is to be envisaged. For there is no doubt that the feast of December 8 was borrowed from the Greek; in the calendars and in the Canterbury Benedictional mentioned above, the feast of the Presentation is indicated as well (at November 21, the date of the Greek *Minaea*); both feasts were introduced into the West at the same time.

Reestablishment after the Conquest

After having been celebrated at Winchester, Canterbury and Worcester (possibly also at Exeter), the feast of December 8 disappeared again in the turmoil following the Conquest (1066), and was re-established by Anselm the Younger and his pious friends at the beginning of the twelfth century, i.e. about the same time in which we find the first traces of the feast in Normandy. This, at least, is the account that is usually given.

Some facts, however, are unexplained in this way. In the first place, there is the circumstance that the three prayers of the Mass from the Leofric missal are found, usually with slight variants, in many later medieval missals. The Secret and Postcommunion especially are often repeated.[43] It is possible that those prayers were used again in the twelfth century because they were found in pre-Norman sacramentaries; but in view of the great changes Church life in England underwent in the second half of the eleventh century, this seems to be highly questionable. We might be inclined to suppose either that the feast never disappeared entirely in England, or that the first establishment as well as the re-establishment in southern England was caused by influences from abroad, viz. from Normandy.

One could allege, in favor of the first solution, the legend of Abbot Helsin from St. Augustine's at Canterbury, and afterwards from Ramsay—a story we find in a great number of redactions as *hystoria* in medieval breviaries: how Helsin was sent by William the Conqueror on a delicate diplomatic mission to Denmark, and was saved from shipwreck by the Blessed Virgin on account of his promise to celebrate henceforth the feast of her Conception.[44] The story is just another medieval legend, but Helsin is an historical person, and it is quite possible that the legend has preserved some nucleus

---

[43] The secret, *Sanctifica domine muneris oblati libamina,* even is still found, slightly altered, in the Roman Missal, in the masses of Our Lady of Mt. Carmel (July 16) and of Our Lady of Good Counsel.

[44] The story owed its success to the fact that it went under the name of *Sermo* or *Epistola b. Anselmi de Conceptione b. Mariae.* Three different versions are given in H. THURSTON and Th. SLATER, *Eadmeri monachi . . . tractatus,* pp. 88-98; according to Fr. Thurston, the earliest of these texts dates probably from the end of the twelfth century. Two other redactions in *PL* 149, 319-326, one of which is translated below, in Document IV, p. 522 ff.

of truth, viz. that the abbot played a part in the spreading of the new feast.

It is not necessary to repeat here all the facts concerning the re-establish-ment of the feast in England at the beginning of the twelfth century. The names and writings of the protagonists—Anselm the Younger of Bury (often mistaken for his uncle, St. Anselm, who for that reason was for a long time regarded as a champion of the cause of the Immaculate Conception, though he probably was not); Osbert of Stoke Clare of Westminster; St. Anselm's former secretary, Eadmer; and Warin of Worcester—appear whenever a survey is given of the development of the doctrine concerning the Conception during the Middle Ages. I should like, however, to put one question mark with regard to their activity. Is it true that they 're-established' the feast in all the monasteries where their influence was felt, or can we interpret the documents in this sense, that these men, invoking the devout custom of many places on the continent, propagated the celebra-tion of the feast which up to then had been known in only a few English centers? [45] The examples on the continent must have been those of centers of piety in Normandy. As a matter of fact, the inventories published by Leroquais show that the feast had spread in the monasteries and dioceses of Normandy at an earlier date than formerly supposed.

NORMANDY

Kellner took it for granted that the primitive English feast disappeared after 1066 and was reintroduced in the South of England by influences from Normandy, where the feast had originated in the meantime.[46] Maybe we could go even further. It is possible, I think, that the feast was already celebrated in Normandy before the Conquest. The manifold relations between Anglo-Saxon England and the duchy on the continent would

[45] The crucial text is the first part of Osbert's letter to Anselm of Bury (written c. 1128), where we read: "in multis locis celebratur eius vestra sedulitate festa con-ceptio . . . multi testimonium perhibuerunt quoniam et in hoc regno et in transmarinis partibus a nonnullis episcopis et abbatibus in ecclesiis dei celebris instituta est illius diei recordatio, de cuius summa redemptionis nostrae salutari processit exordio," THURSTON and SLATER (work cited in note 32), pp. 54, 55; in the ed. of Osbert's letters by E. W. WILLIAMSON, London 1929, pp. 65, 66.

[46] KELLNER (work cited in note 1), p. 252. BISHOP seems to reject all Norman influence: "The Normans in coming into England were disposed to treat in a con-temptuous fashion enough both English liturgical observances and English saints and relics; to them the feast of the Conception of the Blessed Virgin must have appeared specifically English, a product of insular simplicity and ignorance. Doubtless its public celebration was abolished at Winchester and Canterbury, but it did not die out of the hearts of individuals; the memory was kept up, and on the first favorable oppor-tunity the feast was re-established in the monasteries again, as in them it had had its rise." (Bishop, *On the Origins* . . . p. 246; cf. *supra*, note 32). It is difficult to reconcile this view with some of the facts: the relations which existed between the group of the two Anselms and their clerical friends in Normandy, and the rapid spread of the feast in Normandy, which seems to presuppose an acquaintance of longer standing. Lanfranc, who 'reorganized' the English Church after the Conquest, may have been an enemy to a use which was entirely strange to him, but it is also pos-sible that he knew the feast already from Normandy.

explain quite easily the fact that it was borrowed by monasteries in Winchester and Canterbury.   There are no documents to support this supposition, it is true; but it is equally true that liturgical documents from this period are so extremely scarce that it would be misleading to build a theory only on the data from the few liturgical manuscripts which have survived.

At any rate, the supposition that, before the Conquest, Normandy played a part in the origin of the Conception feast in the Latin West, would facilitate the solution of the question, how the Byzantine feasts of the Conception and Presentation, celebrated at that time in Greek monasteries in southern Italy, both became known in the environs of the Channel.   The Normans who, since the second quarter of the eleventh century, were settled in Italy (not as friends, it is true, but neither as invaders in the modern sense of the word), may have gotten acquainted with those feasts; and their well-known relations with the people at home may have influenced the monastic centers in the duchy on the Atlantic coast.   Of course, it is also possible that there existed relations between the ecclesiastical *milieux* of southern Italy and England; we know that they existed in an earlier period, but for the time under consideration they are not too clear.[47]   At any rate we have to suppose the active role of a very concrete relationship, for which the presence of the Normans in *Magna Graecia* may have created the conditions; otherwise it is not understandable why the example of the Greeks worked at such a great distance as it did, whereas there is no trace (with the exception of the academic entry in the Naples calendar) of any influence nearer to the Byzantine scene.

We must understand that this is not merely an historical question.   The probing of the relations between the Latin West and the Christian East is also for the fatal period of the year 1054—when only the bridgehead in southern Italy seems to present a meeting-point—of great importance for the understanding of the development of Western piety.   We know so little about that period that we must weigh every possibility.   Of course, a short note such as we are giving here tends to oversimplify the picture. In fact, the texture of liturgical or spiritual influence is always far more complicated than can be deduced from available historical data and from the few service books which have outlived a long time of use.   So, for instance, for the first years of the twelfth century, we have to reckon with the unknown quantity of the role St. Anselm played in the history of the feast of the Conception.[48]

[47] Edm. BISHOP, *On the Origins*, pp. 258 f., suggests several occasions on which English ecclesiastics could have come into contact with Byzantine use. None of these suggestions is very convincing.

[48] For a time it was thought that Anselm was familiar with Oriental Marian themes, since BLUME and DREVES attributed to him the poem, *Ave per quam orbis lapsi*, which contains the well-known refrain of the *Akathistos* Hymn, *Ave sponsa insponsata* (Χαῖρε Νύμφη ἀνύμφευτε)—*Analecta hymnica*, XLVIII, 103. However, WILMART, *Auteurs spirituels*, p. 154, n. 2, proved that the poem (eleventh cent.)

THE SENSE OF THE WESTERN FEAST

How has the feast of the Conception, borrowed from the Greek, been understood in the West? In order to find our way we must analyze the liturgical formulas, and in the first place those in the English documents of the eleventh century. They are the only sources we possess for that period, for the oldest non-liturgical Latin texts date from at least sixty years afterwards.

In the first place, there is the blessing formula from the Exeter Pontifical:

BENEDICTIO IN CONCEPTIONE SANCTAE MARIAE.[49]
Sempiterna(m) a Deo benedictionem vobis beatae Mariae virginis pia deposcat supplicatio, quam concipiendam Omnipotens, ex qua eius conciperetur Unigenitus, angelico declaravit praeconio, quam et vobis iugiter suffragari benigno, ut est benignissima, sentiatis auxilio. Amen.
Quique illam ante conceptum praesignavit nomine Spiritus Sancti obumbratione, vos divinam gratiam mente annuat concipere in sanctae Trinitatis confessione, atque ab omni malo protectos deifica confirmet sanctificatione. Amen.
Sancta vero Dei genitrix Maria vobis a Deo pacis et gaudii obtineat incrementum, ut quibus felix eiusdem beatae virginis partus extitit salutis exordium, sit etiam ipse Iesus Christus praemium in caelis vitae permanentis sempiternum. Amen.
Quod Ipse praestare dignetur (qui cum Patre et Spiritu Sancto vivit et gloriatur Deus per omnia saecula saeculorum. Amen.)

The blessing formula from the Canterbury Pontifical reads as follows:

BENEDICTIO IN DIE CONCEPTIONIS SANCTAE DEI GENITRICIS MARIAE.
Caelestium charismatum inspirator terrenarumque mentium reparator, qui beatam Dei genitricem angelico concipiendam praeconavit oraculo, vos benedictionum suarum ubertate dignetur locupletare et virtutum floribus dignanter decorare. Amen.
Et qui illam prius sanctificavit nominis dignitate quam edita gigneretur humana fragilitate vos virtutum copiis adiuvet pollere, et in nominis sui veneranda confessione infatigabiliter perdurare. Amen.
Obtineat vobis gloriosis intercessionibus prospera tempora, iocunda et pacifica, et post praesentia saecula gaudia sine fine manentia, cuius venerandae conceptionis frequentamini magnifica sacramenta. Amen.
Quod Ipse praestare dignetur.

And finally the three prayers from the Leofric Missal:

(*Collecta*) Deus, qui beatae mariae virginis conceptionem angelico vaticinio parentibus praedixisti, praesta huic praesenti familiae tuae eius praesidiis muniri, cuius conceptionis sacra solemnia congrua frequentatione veneratur. Per.

---

is not St. Anselm's work. According to G. G. MEERSSEMAN, it is modeled on a Latin translation of the *Akathistos* Hymn written about 800 A.D. (*Der Hymnos Akathistos im Abendland* I, Freiburg, Switzerland, 1958, pp. 77-86.)

[49] In order to facilitate the study of the liturgical texts, which are quoted in this article, the orthography of this and the following formulas has been made uniform and conformable to modern use.

Secreta. Sanctifica, domine, muneris oblati libamina, et beatae dei genitricis saluberrima interventione nobis salutaria fore concede. Per.

Ad complendum. Repleti vitalibus alimoniis, et divinis refecti mysteriis, supplices rogamus, omnipotens deus, beatae mariae semper virginis, cuius venerandam colimus conceptionem, pia interventione a squalorum erui inmanium dominatione. Per.

In all these texts we find the apocryphal motif of the angelic annunciation of the Virgin's birth and name, a theme which, in the blessing formula from the Exeter Pontifical, is used to stress the relation between Mary's Conception and the economy of salvation.[50]   This connexion is most extensively expressed in the first part of that blessing, where the Conception of the Virgin and the Incarnation are named together in one elegant phrase.   One could be inclined to consider the words *ex qua eius concipere-tur Unigenitus* as just another euchological amplification, evoked by the foregoing *concipiendam.*   However, when we compare those words with the redaction of the third part of the same blessing where the birth of the Virgin is called *salutis exordium,* it is clear that they have been used designedly.[51] A third element in the first clause of the Exeter manual is one that we find in all the pre-Conquest texts and, for that matter, in all later texts: the Virgin-Mother as advocate of the faithful.

These are the themes which equally figure in the Byzantine texts. But, of course, it would be wrong to suppose that the western feast was tributary to the Byzantine use with regard to its liturgical expression also.   The wording of the Latin formulas is so unlike the Greek that there is no sense in looking for any borrowing, even if we might suppose that Western scholars in the eleventh century could have had an intimate knowledge of Oriental liturgical texts, which is highly improbable.   We come nearest to the truth if we say that the feast as such was borrowed (together with the feast of the Presentation) and that it was accepted in its new surroundings because the Western atmosphere was at that time very much akin to that of the Greek centers.

Western piety, and especially devotion to the Blessed Virgin, had developed along the same lines as the Eastern, not necessarily because of direct influence (although there had been such an influence during an earlier period, at the time when the older feasts of the *Theotokos* were introduced into the Latin liturgical books), but because spiritual conditions were about the same and, above all, because the devotion was rooted in the

---

[50] Cf. *Evangelium de Nativitate S. Mariae,* chap. 3-4, in AMANN's edition (cf. note 12 above), pp. 346-350.

[51] Also, the fact that this third formula seems to have been borrowed from a blessing for the feast of Our Lady's Nativity is highly significant for the idea the compiler had of the Conception feast.—We do not know what other liturgical formulas, besides these blessings and the prayer from the Leofric Missal, were used. We may surmise that they were borrowed from the feast of September 8, according to the tradition of the Helsin legend and to constant later use.

same theological traditions. It is true that very soon, almost from the beginning, Occidental piety showed its own attraction towards concrete situations and towards the expression of human tenderness—tendencies which, in their Latin form at least, are alien to the Oriental mind. These tendencies do not start with St. Bernard; as a matter of fact they can be traced to a far earlier period. But on the whole, Western piety during the eleventh century was that of the post-patristic period, i.e. of that period during which Greek and Latin sensibility were so much closer to each other than in the following centuries.

Some tendencies towards the later Western development can, however, be discerned in the pre-Conquest formulas. A few expressions constitute a prelude to the important theme which would become the cause of the debate during the following period and ultimately that of the final doctrinal precision, *viz.* the theme of the connexion between Mary's conception and sanctification. It would be possible to evaluate the full importance of those expressions only by means of an examination of all the available written documents of the foregoing period—which would exceed the scope of our study; but it will be necessary to situate them in a general way in order to show their significance.

The first noteworthy expression occurs in the second formula of the Exeter benediction: *Quique illam ante conceptum praesignavit nomine Spiritus Sancti obumbratione.* The sense seems to be the following: the *conceptus* is Mary's active conception at the Annunciation (*Spir.S.obumbratione*), whereas *illam praesignavit nomine* refers to the Virgin's sanctification on the occasion of the giving of her name, as is indicated by the parallelism of the following petition: that God may grant to the faithful to conceive the divine grace . . . and that He may strengthen them . . . with His . . . hallowing. The right solution seems to be to interpret the 'giving of Mary's name,' not as a conventional allusion to the angelic *praeconium* of the Virgin's birth and name, but as an allusion to the angel's greeting at the Annunciation. In that case the apocryphal motif would be that of the ninth chapter of the Gospel of Mary's Nativity: *Ad hoc angelus . . . Spiritus enim Sanctus supervenit* [sic] *in te et virtus Altissimi obumbrabit tibi contra omnes ardores libidinis* (here: original sin).[52]

Also, the text of the second formula in the Canterbury book is not too clear. It says, rather elaborately, that the Virgin has been sanctified by the giving of her name before her birth. So we have here the current opinion, later on defended by St. Thomas (and often dependent on the idea, then general, that the human soul was united with the embryo some time after conception)[52a], which the redactor in the eleventh century could

---

[52] See AMANN, *o.c.*, p. 362.—Or must we suppose that the redactor is alluding to the theological speculations concerning the connection between Mary's sanctification and the Incarnation? This is hardly probable.

[52a] Cf. *Index* to the present volume, under the entry, *Conception, twofold.*

find worded in another chapter of the apocryphal gospel: *Anna uxor tua pariet filiam et vocabis nomen eius Mariam . . . et Spiritu sancto replebitur adhuc ex utero matris suae.* (IV, 1)

The difference between the meaning of these two liturgical formulas characterizes, I think, the uncertainty which existed before the twelfth century with regard to the prerogative of the Virgin's sanctification. On the one hand it is clear that the theme of Mary's conception, at the moment it enters into the orbit of Western piety, is confronted with the Western idea of original sin—an idea not too well defined as yet, but already of long standing; on the other hand, however, this first confrontation is rather hesitant, because it is mixed up with two different traditions concerning the Virgin's sanctification, both known from apocryphal texts which were current at that time.[53]

We find a far clearer attitude in the first half of the twelfth century in the writings of the champions of the new feast, as for instance in the letter of Osbert of Clare to Anselm of Bury-St. Edmund's: *Si enim beatus Ioannes, quem Deus Pater praecursorem misit Filio suo, angelo annuntiante conceptus est, et in utero matris suae sanctificatus, multo magis credendum est in ipsa conceptione eandem sanctificatam fuisse, de cuius carne sanctus sanctorum processit in mundo factus caro tanquam sponsus de thalamo suo.*[54] The traditional transition which Osbert makes from the sanctification of the Forerunner to that of the Blessed Virgin is weakened by his affirmation that the Virgin has been sanctified *in ipsa conceptione* (here clearly understood of the conception *"ante menses novem"*); but this affirmation itself is, without any equivocation, more explicit than most texts prior to the scholastic controversy. As a rule, these early texts manifest the notion of a sanctification *ante partum* (at the moment of, or shortly after the 'second' conception, that of the infusion of the human soul). The activity of Anselm's circle put the idea of the feast on a doctrinal footing which hitherto had been lacking. The opposition of their adversaries had compelled the 'friends' of the feast to elucidate their point.

The only indication as to the liturgical formulas that may have been used

---

[53] With regard to the second member of the Canterbury formulary Fr. CECCHIN draws attention to another variant of the Proto-Gospel, underlying the *Historia nativitatis* by Hrosvitha of Gandersheim (PL 137, 1066 ff.), in which the Virgin is said to have been sanctified eight days after her birth, when the priests came to give her a name; see Andrea M. CECCHIN, "La Concezione della Vergine nella liturgia della Chiesa occidentale anteriore al secolo XII," in *Marianum* 5 (1943) pp. 58-114, especially pp. 96-97. I must confess that I do not see the point; the syntax of the liturgical text is clear enough: *Et qui illam sanctificavit nominis dignitate priusquam* (scil. *illa) edita gigneretur . . .*

[54] THURSTON and SLATER (work cited in note 32), pp. 55-56. This is not the place to discuss the relation between Osbert's opinion and that of some earlier Western authors, such as Paul the Deacon and Paschasius Radbertus. Cf. chapter V of the present volume, pp. 163-165.

by the 'friends' is found in the Missal of Winchester (early eleventh century), in which the three prayers from the Leofric Missal are given, probably to be accompanied by the lessons and choral parts of the Mass of September 8.[55] The same seems to have been the case with the earliest use in Normandy.[56] Very soon, however, in Normandy as well as in England, other formulas appear; we shall deal with them in the following pages.

II

THE VARIETY OF MEDIEVAL LITURGICAL FORMULAS

OPPOSITION TO THE FEAST

This is not the place to give the whole history of the opposition to the doctrine and of the different stages of its growth in precision during the Middle Ages.[57] But we must stress the point that this history in large part centered around the fact of the feast and its liturgical expression.

The story of the oldest known incident, that of the celebration in Westminster Abbey Church on December 8 of the year 1127, brings us right into the picture. In his letter to Anselm the Younger, in which the details of the incident are told (notwithstanding the intervention of two bishops, the monks "proceeded with the office of the day, which had started already, and carried it through with joyous solemnity"), Prior Osbert relates the arguments of the opponents: the novelty of the feast, and the fact that "its establishment does not have the authorization of the Church of Rome." [58] The same arguments seem to be at the bottom of St. Bernard's opposition to the introduction of the feast by the canons of Lyons; the fact that their way of proceeding lacked the backing of rightful authority seems to weigh as heavily as the fact that he does not know how to reconcile the celebration with the idea then current on the continent of the Virgin's sanctification (*fuit ante sancta quam nata*).[59]

---

[55] On the Winchester Missal see LEROQUAIS, *Sacramentaires et missels* I, p. 191 (cf. *infra* n. 62).

[56] See A. NOYON, "Histoire de la théologie de l'Immaculée Conception," in *Bulletin de littérature ecclésiastique* (Toulouse) 21 (1921), p. 307.

[57] Cf. chaps. V, VI and VII of the present work.

[58] The Latin text in THURSTON and SLATER, *Eadmeri . . . tractatus*, pp. 54-55 (cf. *supra*, note 32); English translation and commentary by Edmund BISHOP, *On the origins . . .* (work cited in note 32), pp. 243-245.—It is to be noted, however, that at that time, and even for some centuries afterwards, the bishops exercised their right to fix their diocesan calendars, a right which gradually shrank to that of accepting or refusing new feasts introduced or tolerated by the Holy See, and which, after the Council of Trent, disappeared altogether.

[59] St. BERNARD, *Ep.* 184. Cf. note 27 of the following chapter. On the discussion provoked by St. Bernard's letter and on the identity of the Nicholas who wrote a most important answer to it, see C. H. TALBOT, "Nicholas of St. Alban's and Saint Bernard," in *Revue Bénédictine* 64 (1954) pp. 83-91. A critical edition of Nicholas' treatise is given *ibid.* pp. 92-117.

The same goes for the attitude of authors like Beleth and Sicardus of Cremona; their opposition is the unwillingness of traditionalists to accept a new feast which gives expression to an idea whose background seemed to be chiefly devotional.[60]

SPREAD OF THE FEAST

Notwithstanding the opposition, the feast found its way into the calendars of most dioceses and religious orders during the Middle Ages. The lines along which it spread seem to have been very erratic, and for many a minor heortological problem the historian awaits the publication of more local material.[61] We may find the feast at a rather early date in the calendars and liturgical books of churches which are at quite a distance from the centers where it was first in use. In general, we can say that it was widely known about the middle of the thirteenth century, as St. Thomas gives us to understand (*S. Th.* III, 27, 2 ad 3). This does not mean, however, that it was generally celebrated; in many dioceses the feast was introduced only in the course of the fourteenth or even fifteenth centuries (in the diocesan churches of Rome only during the pontificate of Sixtus IV).[61a]

Much material on the spread of the feast is to be found in the inventories of liturgical manuscripts in French public libraries, published by Leroquais, who has indicated in each case the salient items from the calendar, noting the feast of December 8 whenever it occurs.[62] Many similar items from sacramentaries and missals in Italian libraries are given

---

[60] BELETH, *Rationale Div. Off.*, c. 146; SICARDUS OF CREMONA, *Mitrale*, c. 43. DURANDUS speaks very cautiously about the feast in *Rationale* VII, c. 6, 3-4. RADULPH DE RIVO mentions only four or even three feasts of the Blessed Virgin (in the ed. of C. MOHLBERG, *Radulph de Rivo, der letzte Vertreter der altröm. Liturgie* II, Münster 1915, pp. 28 and 77 resp.); the feast is found, however, in a calendar that is probably contemporary, in the *Ordinarius* of the Chapter of Tongres to which Radulph belonged; see MOHLBERG, t. I, Louvain 1911, p. 244.—It is misleading when those authors are referred to most of the time as "liturgists"; a name such as "traditionalists" would be more apt.—Another clear instance of that "traditionalist" attitude occurs in *De Domo Dei* by BOTO OF PRÜFENING (not Potho of Prümm), where the author refers to the opposition of devout and well-intentioned persons in Rome (1152 A.D.) to the introduction of the new feasts of the Most Holy Trinity, of the Transfiguration of Our Lord and of the Conception of the Blessed Virgin (text in MABILLON, *Annales O.S.B.*, Paris 1739, t. IV p. 521).

[61] We have only to consult the book reviews in the leading reviews of Church History and in the *Jahrbuch für Liturgiewissenschaft* (since the last war, *Archiv für Liturgiewissenschaft*) to see how many notices on the subject may be collected from all kinds of monographs.

[61a] Cf. chapter VII of the present volume, p. 275.

[62] Especially the two series: V. LEROQUAIS, *Les sacramentaires et les missels manuscrits des bibliothèques publiques de France*, 3 vol., Paris 1924, and *id.*, *Les bréviaires manuscrits des bibliothèques publiques de France*, 6 vol., Paris 1934.—A list of the most interesting items from the former series is given in A. WILMART, *Auteurs spirituels et textes dévots du moyen-âge latin*, Paris 1932, pp. 46-47.

in Ebner's *Iter Italicum;* it is not clear, however, whether the author has compared all mss. according to the same heortological standards.[63]

1100-1300. RADIATION FROM NORMAN AND ENGLISH CENTERS

The information that can be gathered from the available inventories and monographs is far from complete. It enables us, however, to divide the period we are treating (roughly speaking, from c. 1100 to c. 1500) into two different parts, in order to get a better view of the historical development which must be compared with the liturgical use. The turning point between those two periods may be fixed at about the beginning of the fourteenth century.

For the former period it is clear from Leroquais' inventories that the feast radiated out from the English centers, from Normandy and, very soon, from the whole northern part of France. One gets the impression that at the beginning the main influence was exercised by the monasteries and churches of Normandy. That the feast was for a long time known as *la fête aux Normands* was not only because the corporation of Norman students in Paris celebrated it as their patronal feast, but equally because it was general throughout the duchy at an early date, possibly even earlier than in England.[64]

Outside the English centers, which never completely forgot the precise way in which the 'friends' of the feast had formulated the idea of the Virgin's Conception—it is significant that English thinkers, William of Ware and Scotus, paved the way for the definitive formula—the opinion with regard to the sense of the feast seems to have remained rather vague during this time. The general idea was that of the Virgin's sanctification, linked up unreflectively with the idea of her Conception *ante menses novem* which gave the feast its name. It would be wrong to stress exclusively the lack or the amount of theological speculation we find, or to characterize this period only by means of the scattered passages in the writings of St. Bernard and of the early Scholastics who attempted to determine the exact nature of Mary's privileges. The feast and its liturgy were at that time understood not so much by means of some theological formula (albeit that some of the opponents were fully aware that the current doctrinal

[63] A. EBNER, *Quellen und Forschungen zur Geschichte und Kunstgeschichte des Missale Romanum im Mittelalter, Iter Italicum*, Freiburg in Br. 1896.—For England must be consulted Fr. WORMALD, *English Benedictine Kalendars after A.D. 1100* (HBS 77 and 81), London 1938 and 1946.

[64] There is the well-known problem about the date of the introduction of the feast in the English dioceses. I leave it to others to decide on the value of the entries in some mediaeval chronicles asserting that the feast of the Conception had been introduced by a council of London of 1129 (cf. E. BISHOP, *On the Origins . . .* , pp. 242 and 247, n. 5), and on the trustworthiness of what is stated in *Can.* 2 of the Council of Canterbury of 1328, viz. that the feast was first established by "our predecessor," Anselm (cf. KELLNER, work cited in note 1, p. 258, n. 7).

formula did not agree entirely with the fact of the feast) as after the manner of an expression of piety, which was in advance of doctrinal precision.   In a general way we can say that the attitude of those who celebrated the feast of the Conception was that of the Greeks, with this exception, however, that among theologians reflection on the precise nature of the Virgin's privilege had already started.   Therefore the study of the euchology and of the general trends of devotion of that time is of even more importance for the understanding of the first spread of the feast than the thorough knowledge of all that may be found on this subject in the writings of theologians (though it is true, on the other hand, that the activity of the theologians was due mainly to the fact of the feast's existence).   In this regard much importance is to be attached to the part which the ever increasing devotion to St. Anne played, until after the Middle Ages, in furthering, on the level of popular piety, devotion to the Virgin's Conception.[65]

1300-1500 Religious Orders and Theological Precision

The second period—roughly speaking, that of the fourteenth and fifteenth centuries—is mainly characterized by the influence of the religious orders and by the fact that the idea of the feast gradually comes to be understood everywhere according to the precise interpretations, in whatever sense, formulated by the theologians.   Thus the feast of December 8 was called by the champions of the doctrine, that of the "Immaculate Conception of the Virgin Mary"—although it would bear for some centuries more the official name *Conceptio b. Mariae Virginis;* whereas the opponents of the doctrine, who nevertheless accepted the feast, preferred to call it the feast of the Virgin's *sanctification.*[65a]

The Franciscans especially, following Duns Scotus, were the promoters of the feast during this period.[66]   They celebrated it at Avignon with the express authorization of Pope Clement VII.[67]   At Basel, Father Petrus

[65] OSBERT of Stoke Clare wrote his sermon for the feast of the Virgin's Conception after having written one in honor of St. Anne. For other texts composed by him, see A. WILMART, *Auteurs spirituels,* pp. 261 ff.: "Les compositions d'Osbert de Clare en l'honneur de sainte Anne"; on other similar medieval texts cf. *ibid.* pp. 46 ff. and 202 ff. Cf. also B. KLEINSCHMIDT, *Die hl. Anna, ihre Verehrung in Geschichte, Kunst und Volkstum,* Düsseldorf 1930, and W. LAMPEN, "Verering der H. Moeder Anna in de Middeleeuwen," in *Historisch Tijdschrift* 2 (1924) pp. 221 ff.

[65a] Cf. chapter VII of the present volume, p. 279.

[66] But not earlier than since the beginning of the fourteenth century. On the strength of an entry in the *Memoriale Ordinis Minorum* under the year 1263, it has for a long time been thought that the feast was admitted by the General Chapter, held at Pisa in that year. It has been proven that this is not correct. See Hieron. GOLUBOVICH, "Statuta liturgica seu rubricae Breviarii auctore divo Bonaventura in Generali Capitulo Pisano an. 1263 editae," in *Archivum Franciscanum Historicum* 4 (1911) p. 66.

[67] Although this 'Pope' of Avignon must officially be ranked among the anti-popes,

Perqueri and his colleagues collected the material which underlies the famous *Allegationes VIa* and *VIIa*.[68] A pope of Franciscan extraction, Sixtus IV, set the doctrine of Scotus on an official footing and introduced the feast into the basilicas and title churches of Rome.[69]

The Benedictines also were, as a rule, champions of the cause of the Immaculate Conception, which had found its first defenders among them. The Cistercians received the feast into their calendar in the fourteenth century, together with that of St. Anne. Among the Carmelites, who had already been celebrating it at an earlier date, it found some persuasive apologists.[70]

The Dominicans followed the opinion of St. Thomas: *quia quo tempore sanctificata fuerit ignoratur, celebratur festum sanctificationis eius potius quam conceptionis in die conceptionis ipsius*.[71] Towards the end of the fourteenth century, however, they accepted the feast of December 8, but under the title of *Sanctificatio b.Mariae Virginis*.[72] The same name we find in Carthusian books, although the celebration of the feast had been received by the Chapter of 1334.[73]

The liturgical sources give us the same impression of the fourteenth and fifteenth centuries as we get from the controversial literature and from the facts of history (from which even fetters and dungeon are not entirely absent), *viz.* that with regard to both doctrine and devotion, the struggle was fought at times, and on both sides, with a narrow-mindedness in which the healthy activity of the new religious orders shrank to an attitude of petty provincialism. The simple circumstance of being a Franciscan or a Dominican was, it seems, enough to make one an ardent defender or an unshakeable opponent of the cause. The issue of the Immaculate Conception (like the propagation of certain devotions and pious practices

---

he belonged undoubtedly to the great churchmen of his time. He composed the Mass *Ad tollendum schisma*, which is still found in the missal.

[68] Cf. chap. VI of the present volume, p. 229 f.

[69] Cf. chap. VII of the present volume, p. 275.

[70] The most important of them is another Englishman, John Bacon or Baconthorp; see B. M. XIBERTA, *De Scriptoribus scholasticis s. XIV ex ordine Carmelitarum* (*Bibl. de la Rev. d'hist. ecclés.* 6), Louvain 1931, pp. 227-240. Cf. also chap. VI of the present volume, p. 220 f.

[71] S. Th. III, q. 27, a. 2 ad 3.

[72] For the first introduction of the feast of the *Sanctificatio* in the Dominican Order and the history of this feast during the fifteenth century, see W. R. BONNIWELL, *A history of the Dominican Liturgy, 1215-1945*[2], New York, 1945, pp. 227 ff., 254 and 256 ff. EBNER, *op. cit.* pp. 112 and 113, alleges two examples of manuscript Dominican missals in the National Library at Naples, where this title has been written on erasure.

[73] EBNER, *o.c.*, pp. 159 and 227.—In the earlier tradition of the Carthusians no trace of the feast is found. WILMART (as cited in note 62), p. 230 n. 1, notes the fact that the feast is not mentioned in the Constitutions written by Prior Hugh I (c. 1127), who was a great friend of St. Bernard and apparently shared his opinion with regard to the matter.

during a later period) had become an element of the tradition of religious orders, and mere touchiness at times took the place of speculation and argument. In the following sequence which Blume and Dreves ascribe to an unknown Franciscan poet of the fifteenth century there is as much quarrelsomeness as doctrine:

> Diem sacram celebremus,
> Odas laudis personemus
>   Festivando laetius,
> Qua beata mater Christi
> Est concepta, desit isti
>   Murmur indiscretius.
> Absit hic syllogizare,
> Lexis loram [i.e. lorum, *the bridle of the tongue*] non laxare
> Debes neque derogare
>   Theotocos honoribus. . . .[74]

THE TEXTS OF THE LITURGY

When we survey the liturgy of the feast of the Conception from its first spread to the introduction of the formularies of Sixtus IV and Pius V, we see that in general the liturgical expression has seldom been influenced by theological determinations of the doctrine. As a matter of fact, during that whole period of four or five centuries the liturgical texts for the feast have been borrowed over and over again from the same small stock of formulas. It would be wrong to interpret this state of affairs as though the liturgy had fallen in arrears; we must reckon with the well-known fact that ecclesiastical and especially liturgical use has always been very faithful to traditional formulas.

What was the liturgy of the feast during the Middle Ages?

Because the inventories and the heortological notes in monographs do not, as a rule, indicate which liturgical formulas are found in the service books, it is as yet impossible to trace even a provisional outline of the different uses (which might help to give a better picture of the various stages in the spread of the feast).[75] On the other hand, in the printed texts and in the mss. which have been published, the same formulas occur so often, and the unpublished mss., when one has the occasion to consult them, offer so invariably the texts which are known already from other sources, that we may safely surmise that there are no big surprises in store.

As it happens, we find very often in missals and office books no proper formulas at all, but the simple rubric that all the texts for the feast of

---

[74] BLUME-DREVES, *Analecta hymnica* IX, 54.

[75] It would be of no use to reproduce the lists I have made of the various uses, because they are necessarily incomplete and might lead to wrong conclusions. Once a complete list can be composed, it will serve to illustrate the relations between the liturgical uses of England and those of Normandy and Northern France.

December 8 are to be taken from the formulary of the *Nativitas b.Mariae Virginis,* except that the word *Conceptio* is to be inserted where the text for September 8 reads *Nativitas* or *Ortus.*[76] We may see in this the influence of the widely known Helsin legend, according to which the Blessed Virgin herself had ordered that the feast of her Conception be celebrated in that way.[77] The main reason, however, was doubtless the very idea of the new feast, and account must also be taken of the fact that for a long time the Church has been very slow in admitting anything new into the traditional antiphonaries.

Even in cases in which the prayers and lessons of the nocturns are proper to the feast, the choral parts of the Mass and Divine Office are invariably those of the Nativity, according to the various uses.[78] The lessons of the Mass also are always those of September 8: the Epistle *Dominus possedit me, Ego quasi vitis* or, occasionally, *O quam pulchra est* (York); and for the gospel, Matthew's *Liber generationis.*[79]

The liturgical formulas which may be found proper to December 8 are: the three orations of the Mass, a text for the pontifical blessing before Holy Communion, some lessons for Matins and a number of sequences.

ORATIONS OF THE MASS

Besides the orations from the Leofric Missal which (as we have already noted) were used over and over again, there appears at an early date, either in Normandy or in England, another set of orations found in several missals after the end of the thirteenth century.[80] These texts are, I think, the most expressive formulas of the whole period.

[76] We may assume, I think, that in some cases, when the feast was introduced, the text of this rubric was not inserted into existing service books, because its contents were known already. Therefore we must not deduce too much from the fact that the feast is not mentioned in the corpus of older books.

[77] "Et quo, inquit abbas [Helsinus], servicio utemur in ecclesiastico officio? Omne, inquit [Maria], servicium quod dicitur in eius nativitate dicetur et in conceptione, excepto quod nomen nativitatis mutabitur nomine conceptionis. Hiis dictis disparuit . . . ." THURSTON and SLATER, (work cited above in note 32), p. 91. Cf. Document IV appended below, p. 522 ff.

[78] For the Mass of Sept. 8 a great number of uses have been collected by J. Wickham LEGG in the index to his edition of the *Missale ad Usum Ecclesiae Westmonasteriensis* III (HBS 12), London 1897, pp. 1589-1590. With the exception of the Roman books, which have *Salve sancta Parens,* all the other alleged formularies give *Gaudeamus* (the old Introit of St. Agatha, which was widely used during the Middle Ages for many feasts); the other choral parts are a varying assortment of texts, most often taken from the Common of Virgins.

[79] Interesting is the Epistle—probably introduced only towards the end of the Middle Ages—which is found in the Missal of Westminster, ed. by J. Wickham LEGG; see fasc. III (HBS 12), London 1897, p. 1614: *Cum vidisset Balaam quod placeret* (*Num.* 24, 1-3.5-9.17-19). This passage harmonizes excellently with the prayers of the Westminster formulary for Dec. 8, which will be quoted below.

[80] Missal of Fécamp, Ms. 313 (290) of the library of Rouen; see LEROQUAIS, *Sacramentaires et missels* I, p. 196. Wickham LEGG refers in his edition of the Westminster Missal (III, pp. 1613-1614) to three mss. English missals. The Collect is

In the Collect we find the contrast between Eve's guilt and Mary's part in the redemption. We might think that the allusion to the conception of God's Only-begotten Son at the end of the prayer has been evoked, as in other texts, by the fact that Mary's conception is being celebrated; but probably here also the real comparison is that between Mary who conceived and bore her Son as a virgin (*virgo concepit et virgo peperit*) and Eve who, as tradition has it, fell into sin while she was a virgin:

> Deus ineffabilis misericordiae, qui primae piacula mulieris per virginem expianda sanxisti, da nobis quaesumus conceptionis eius digne sollemnia venerari, quae unigenitum tuum virgo concepit et virgo peperit, dominum nostrum.

In order to get the full meaning of this beautiful text we must bear in mind the intimate connexion which existed in post-patristic Mariology between Mary's purity from sin (i.e. her personal sanctity and her sanctification) and her spotless virginity as the Mother of God.

The Postcommunion expresses the theme of the Nativity, with unusual strength even; the Virgin's Conception is not merely the dawn of our salvation, but it is called its 'cause':

> Caelestis alimoniae vegetati libamine, quaesumus domine deus noster, ut nos gloriosae semper virginis mariae continua foveat protectio, cuius nostrae causa salutis extitit hodierna conceptio.

The motifs of these prayers have been elaborated in the proper preface which we find in the Fécamp Missal; it is a text which represents a real summary of Mariology:

> Vere dignum . . . Tuam domine clementiam et ab aeterno praescientiam admirando praedicare qua decreti chirographum unde subnixum est, inde vaticinando cassandum ipse promisisti. Hoc plasma tuum et imaginis transfusio ne periret, idem sexus qui corruperat reparavit; idem, sed alter, nam virtutum praerogativa praestantior; consimilis origo, sed originis dispar proportio. Mater humani generis eva corrupta mente vipereo livori succubuit, genitrix salvatoris mundi maria signato pudore caput eius comminuit. Quapropter maiestatem tuam suppliciter exoramus, ut cuius hodie conceptionem celebramus in terris, pro nobis exaudiat exorantem in caelis. Hanc enim sicut omnium dignitate praecessit fastigia meritorum, ita prae omnibus privilegiorum honore sublimasti. Merito iam caelestis eam curia submisse veneratur per quam restaurari diminutionis suae damna laetatur.

The theme of the sanctification *in secunda conceptione* (i.e. at the infusion of the human soul, which often was supposed to happen some time after the conception *ante menses novem*) occurs in the following prayer

---

found in the Monastic Breviary of Hyde Abbey (the former Newminster) at Winchester, ed. by J. B. L. Tolhurst, IV (HBS 78), London 1939. A. M. Cecchin (work cited in note 53) p. 98 n. 95, refers to a ms. missal of Aquilea from the beginning of the thirteenth century in the Archepiscopal Library at Udine.

from the printed Utrecht breviaries of the first half of the sixteenth century.[81] It is the theme we find developed in some later redactions of the Helsin legend, used as *hystoriae* for Matins (see below), but which otherwise is rarely expressed in liturgical texts, though sometimes presupposed.

> Deus qui in corpus gloriosae virginis mariae matris tuae animam divina inspiratione infudisti, praesta quaesumus, ut de tali conceptione animae ad corpus sic in terris iucundemur, ut post hanc vitam in regno caelorum cum maria caelestibus gaudiis perenniter perfruamur.

Other prayers to be found in medieval books are far less interesting.[82] In the first place there are the Collect and the Postcommunion of the type we find in the Missal of Westminster Abbey Church, written shortly after the year 1380.[83]

> *Collecta.* Omnipotens sempiterne Deus, qui per beatae mariae virginis foecunditatem et partum salutem generis humani fieri voluisti: da nobis ita conceptionis eius hodierna die digne celebrare mysterium, ut ad incarnati filii quem ipsa concepit et peperit mereamur pertinere consortium.
> *Postcommunio.* Per haec redemptionis sacrosancta mysteria nobis, quaesumus domine, caelestis gratiae benedictionem infunde, ut conceptionis eius gloriosa sollemnitas famulis tuis ad salutem prosit aeternam, quae sine viro virgo concepit et mundo peperit lucem et vitam.

Another prayer is the Collect from the printed missal (1515) of the Benedictine Casinese Congregation; the only original note in this formula is the emphasis which is laid upon the festive character of the feast: [84]

[81] In the edition of 1508 (Leyden) for all the hours. In the edition of 1504 (Leyden) the prayer is indicated *ad Laudes* only, whereas Vespers has the Collect of the Leofric type (like the Utrecht missals) and for Terce, Sext and None—according to a custom which is often followed for votive offices—still other, rather uninteresting, formulas are given.

[82] Students are warned that the Collect *Supplicationem servorum tuorum*, found in many medieval books (beyond the realm of influence of the Missal of the Roman Curia), is just another prayer for the feast of the Virgin's Nativity, still used as such by the Dominicans and the calced Carmelites. In the missals of those religious orders we find also at Aug. 15 the Collect *Veneranda*. Both formulas, *Supplicationem* and *Veneranda,* are found in the Gregorian Sacramentary as prayers for the procession before Mass; Radulph de Rivo was unaware of the fact that the Collect *Famulorum* on Aug. 15 and the Collect *Famulis* on Sept. 8, both found in the Roman books which were propagated by the Franciscans, are the old Roman Collects *ad Missam* (see MOHLBERG, work cited in note 60, I, p. 184).—P. BRUYLANTS refers in *Les Oraisons du Missel romain* I, Louvain 1952, no. 159, to the *Missale Curiae* (two mss. from the beginning of the fourteenth century) in which, for the Mass of the Conception, the three prayers of March 25 are given. This does not mean, of course, that the feast was celebrated before Sixtus IV in the Roman basilicas and title churches. The choice of the Annunciation formulas may give to understand that also in the Latin West at that time the speculation on the relation between the Virgin's sanctification and the mystery of the Incarnation influenced liturgical use.

[83] Ed. by J. Wickham LEGG (HBS 5) London 1893.—The Secret is that of the Leofric Missal, with an unimportant variant. On the Epistle of this Mass, see note 79.

[84] According to J. Wickham LEGG, *Miss. Westmon.* III, p. 1614. The author refers (for this prayer and for the other parts of the Mass: Secr. and Postcomm.

Maiestatem tuam, omnipotens deus, supplices deprecamur: ut qui hodie exultantibus animis beatissimae semperque virginis mariae conceptionis festum diem celebrare gaudemus: eius gloriosis precibus et meritis ab instantibus malis et a morte perpetua liberemur.

The same stress on the festive character is observable in the Collect of the formulary which bears the name of the Council of Basel, and which is found in a large number of missals before the Council of Trent, sometimes immediately after the Mass *Egredimini* of 'Sixtus IV.[85]   In other respects the prayer is not noteworthy at all; like other texts it states the object of the feast (adding, however, that God wants us to celebrate it) and contains the theme of the Virgin's powerful help:

Omnipotens sempiterne deus, qui conceptionis diem genitricis filii tui semperque virginis mariae voluisti sollemnitate annua venerari, tribue quaesumus, ut omnes qui eius implorant auxilium petitionis suae salutarem consequentur effectum.

Nor are the other prayers (Leofric type) or the lessons (*Deus possedit me* and *Liber generationis*) of the Basel formulary special.   Some of the choral parts, however, are interesting (the Introit *Gaudeamus* and the Gradual *Diffusa est . . . Propter veritatem* are from the Nativity Mass).   The verse of the Alleluja reads like a theological thesis: *Virginis sanctificatae miranda conceptio gratiae mundo collatae fuit ab initio exemplar et ratio.* The Offertory, like the Epistle in the Westminster Missal, is taken from the twenty-fourth chapter of Numbers (vs. 17 and 18): *Orietur stella ex iacob et consurget virga ex israel: et percutiet duces moab et erit idumea.* The Communion is from the Epistle: *Ab aeterno ordinata sum . . .*

A DOMINICAN COLLECT

The last prayer that we will cite for this period is the Collect of the Mass *in Sanctificatione b.Mariae Virginis* found in Dominican missals.[86]   The formula is an unmistakable witness of the attitude of the Dominicans, but

---

variants of the Leofric type, lessons and choral parts from the Nativity formulary) to the edition printed at Venice in 1515. These indications do not correspond with Fr. Leccisotti's note on the formulary in the first known edition of the printed Casinese Missal (of 1508): "La festa dell'immacolata Concezione ha le orazioni, l'epistola ed il Vangelo della messa cosidetta di Costanza (i.e. of Basel, the formulary mentioned below), il resto dal commune della Vergine."—Tomasso LECCISOTTI, "Il 'Missale Monasticum secundum morem et ritum Casinensis Congregationis alias Sancte Justine'," in *Miscell. Mercati* V (p. 5 of the off-print).

[85] In the index to LIPPE's edition of the *Missale Romanum*, H. A. WILSON (t. II, HBS 33, London 1907, p. 165) notes the Paris editions of the Roman Missal of 1530 and 1540.

[86] Wickham LEGG, *Missale Westmon.* III, pp. 1613-1614, indicates the texts according to the *Missale Predicatorum*, Venice 1504.   I have not had the opportunity to consult the study by S. CORBIN, *L'Office de la Conception de la Vierge (à propos d'un manuscrit du XVe siècle du monastère dominicain d'Aveiro*, Portugal), Coimbra 1949.

at the same time a clear proof of the fact that their devotion towards the Pure and Holy Virgin was not less than that of their theological adversaries:

> Deus, qui beatissimam virginem mariam post animae infusionem per copiosum gratiae munus mirabiliter ab omni peccati macula mundasti et in sanctitatis puritate postea confirmasti, praesta quaesumus, ut qui in honorem suae sanctificationis congregamur, eius intercessionibus a te de instantibus periculis eruamur.

It is to be noted that this prayer states clearly that the Blessed Virgin was not sanctified *at* the infusion of the human soul (which could easily be explained in the sense of the doctrine of the Immaculate Conception), but *after* that infusion.

The Secret and the Postcommunion in the Dominican formulary are those of the feast of September 8; the lessons are respectively *Ab initio* and *Missus est.*

An Episcopal Blessing

A very interesting theme is found in the text of the following episcopal blessing which seems to have been widely used:[87]

> Deus, qui conceptionem gloriosae virginis ad unigeniti sui ordinavit temporalem originem, cordibus vestris suae radicem inserat puritatis immobilem.
>
> Et sicut ipsa concepta secundum praedestinationem erat ad salutem omnium veraciter ordinata, ita vos laetificet per haec quamvis remota salutis nostrae primordia.
>
> Quo sicut insuper in matris utero per sanctificationis gratiam concepta est triumphanti ecclesiae, cui et nata est in assumptione, sic vos assumi suis precibus obtineat in gloriam pertransita huius miseriae peregrinatione.
>
> Quod ipse praestare.

The literal sense of the first part is that God may let the faithful partake in His own holiness; but according to this interpretation, the Virgin's Conception would be mentioned in the invocation alone, which is contrary to the usual structure of these formulas. Therefore it seems permissible to see in this petition (reading *eius* instead of *suae*) an allusion, curious for that time, to the theme known today in the devotion to the Immaculate Heart of Mary, i.e. to the unshaken purity of the Virgin as a model for ours: *Deus . . . cordibus vestris (eius) radicem inserat puritatis immobilem.* For the rest, the first two members represent the traditional idea of the relation between our salvation and the conception of her who was 'predestined' *ad salutem omnium.* But the most interesting motif is found in the third formula: the connexion between the sanctification of the Virgin (*in sinu matris*) and her Assumption, regarded respectively as her conception and

---

[87] See e.g. *Missale Westmon.*, ed. Wickham Legg, II, 654, and *The Benedictional of John Longlonde, bishop of Lincoln*, ed. by R. M. Woolley (HBS 64) London 1927, p. 44.

her birth to the heavenly Church.   The connexion which is made here
between the two mysteries of the Mother of God is not only a highly
important instance of theological speculation, but also a proof, I think,
of the efforts made to express the relation between the doctrinal motif of
the *sanctificatio in utero* and the name of the feast, which was somewhat
embarrassing for that doctrine.

THE LESSONS

The lessons of the breviary, usually the most eloquent texts of a proper,
are, for the period we are dealing with, disappointing in that, even when
they are not taken from the office of September 8, they do not contain
many elements which bear witness to doctrinal development.   We might
expect to find, at least in English breviaries, passages from that most eloquent document on the attitude of the 'friends' of the feast, Eadmer's
treatise, *De Conceptione sanctae Mariae,* which up to modern times was
regarded as a work of St. Anselm of Canterbury.[88]   A text from the same
period and *milieu* which we do find used, is that of the sermon on the
Conception written by Osbert at the request of Warin, dean of Worcester.[89]
In the accompanying letter, Osbert himself declares that he has not dared
to put down in the sermon all that he really thinks about the subject, and
as a matter of fact the document does not contain a clear statement like
those which can be found in Eadmer's treatise or in Osbert's letter to
Anselm the Younger.[90]   This does not alter the fact that, e.g., the very
freely chosen cento we find in the first and second nocturns of the breviary
of Hyde Abbey at Winchester (the former Newminster, transferred in 1111
to new buildings outside the walls of the city) contain some note-worthy
variants on the traditional themes:[91]

> *Lectio ii.*   Quod enim per tot saecula de beata virgine divina prae-
> dixerant oracula, gloriosae conceptionis eius ostendit sollemnitas
> hodierna.   Hodie lutum illud moabitidis ollae ex massa praevaricati-
> onis adae ad opus figuli assumptum est, ex quo christus de carne et
> veritas de terra orta est.
>
> *Lectio iii.*   Terra illa quae spinas et tribulos solebat germinare, mundi
> vitam et fructum salutis produxit aeternae.   Terram quae maledicta
> est in opere adam benedixit deus et per eam avertit captivitatem
> nostram.

[88] Ed. by THURSTON and SLATER (work cited in note 32), pp. 1-52; MIGNE, *PL*
159, 301C-318D.

[89] The entire sermon in THURSTON and SLATER, *o.c.,* pp. 65-83.

[90] "Dicere tamen non audeo quod de hac sancta generatione corde concipio;
quoniam caelestes non licet palam margaritas coram multis spargere, qui ad solis
claritatem densiores erroris sui tenebras sibi consueverant cumulare"; THURSTON and
SLATER, *o.c.,* pp. 61-62.

[91] The breviary, written c. 1300, has been edited by J. B. L. TOLHURST. The
office of December 8, which has the choral parts from the feast of the Virgin's Nativity, is in vol. IV (HBS 78) fol. 401-402 of the ms. For the passages from the
sermon used in the eight lessons of the first and second nocturns see in the ed. by
THURSTON and SLATER pp. 66, 74, 78-79 and 82-83, respectively.

Lectio iv. Terra ista beata est virgo maria de nostro semine, de hoc luto de adam; terra ista dedit fructum suum. Terra ista primo dedit florem et postea fructum. Iste enim flos fructus factus est, ut nos illud comederemus, ut panem angelorum manducaret homo.

Often, and in breviaries from all parts of western Europe, there are to be found as *historiae at Matins* (especially during the octave in books from the sixteenth century) one or other of the various redactions of the Helsin legend, sometimes under the title *Sermo* or *Epistola B.Anselmi de Conceptione B.Mariae.*[92] The most interesting part of the text as we find it in some late-medieval breviaries (as in those of Hereford and York) is that which follows the story itself. In the longest, but not earliest, redaction which Thurston and Slater give as the first of their series, this part is a simple peroration (pp. 91-92); but in the breviaries of Hereford and York these few lines have been elaborated into a whole sermon. Neither of these elaborations is very interesting, except for the passages which deal with the distinction between the two conceptions. The distinction between the first conception and the infusion of the human soul—a distinction which, of course, was used by theologians in order to defend and to explain the doctrine of the *sanctificatio in utero,* but which is remarkably seldom found in liturgical texts—is used in those *historiae* to combine the idea of the *sanctificatio* with the historical object of the feast; or rather, to offer a free choice between two different opinions with regard to that object. This theme is most clearly expressed in the Hereford Breviary:

Lectio iv. Erubescant igitur insensati qui tantum diem tantaque mysteria et sacramenta tenebris ignorantiae excaecati, et idcirco respuunt celebrare, quia viri ac mulieris copulatio in virginis fuit conceptione (*the* ardor libidinis *seen as an element of original sin*). Si enim eius conceptionem eo quod carnaliter extitit, stultis non placet hodie celebrare, tamen diem illam et noctem, diem quamvis multis incognitam, et tempus et horam specialiter eiusdem humilibus celebrare delectet obsequiis: quia ipse animarum creator suae matris animam dignam et sanctissimam virginali corpori angelis eius ministrantibus infundere complacuit. Quam etiam diem primam nostrae reparationis et salutis praeelegit et sanctificavit.

Lectio v. Quod autem sunt hominis duae conceptiones omnibus notum est peritis; una quae carnali viri ac mulieris copulatione agitur, alia spiritualis qua anima nova et pura deo cooperante corpori divinitus adunatur. Quibus ergo non placet carnalem dominicae matris celebrare conceptionem, placeat saltem spiritualem eius animae creationem corporisque cum animae copulatione(m) celebrare. Non est enim verus amator virginis, qui respuit hunc diem celebrare conceptionis.

[92] On the spread of this use cf. BISHOP, *On the Origins* . . . (as cited in note 32), p. 249 n. 2. Examples of later redactions of the legend in breviaries are found in *Brevarium ad Usum Insignis Eccl. Eboracensis,* ed. by S. W. LAWLEY, II (Publ. of the Surtees Society 75) 1882, col. 110-114, and in *The Hereford Breviary* (Rouen edition of 1505), ed. by W. H. FRERE and L. E. G. BROWN, II (HBS 40) London 1911, pp. 64-66.

Lectio vi. Sicut enim in sancta ecclesia eius nativitas, sic debet excolli (extolli) conceptio. Nisi enim conciperetur, nunquam nasceretur. . . .[93]

As lessons in the second nocturn of the feast, in the Breviary of Mayence (1507), the text of the decree of Basel is given.[94] Notwithstanding the fact that the Council of Basel was formally schismatic at the time the decree was promulgated, the decision and the text played a large part in the spreading of the doctrine of the Immaculate Conception.[95]

In some printed Utrecht breviaries (Leyden, 1504 and 1508) I have found as lessons for the first and second nocturns, passages from the letter of Pseudo-Jerome from which the lessons of the second nocturn in the present office have been taken.

The lessons for the third nocturn are, of course, always passages from homilies or commentaries on Matthew's *Liber generationis,* as those by Jerome, Bede or Hilary, the same we find indicated for the feast of the Virgin's Nativity. Invariably they contain the motifs of the *exordium salutis* and that of the lineage of Our Lord 'according to the flesh', but nothing special with regard to the doctrine of the Immaculate Conception.

HYMNS

To conclude our survey, we must say just a few words on the hymnology of the Immaculate Conception.

A single glance at the index to Chevalier's *Repertorium* suffices to show how abundant has been the poetry in honor of the Virgin's Conception (or specially used for the feast of December 8). A long list of sequences, hymns and tropes is there given.

For many of those texts it is not at all clear whether they have been used in the liturgy. Only a small number of sequences appear regularly in service books. Other proses and hymns have been sung in some churches and monasteries during Mass and Divine Office, but these belong only to the periphery of medieval liturgy, to that wide margin of religious poetry which is better treated under the heading of medieval Latin literature than under that of liturgical tradition. Moreover, we find in that flood of poetic texts very little which could be of interest to our subject. The long litanies of sweet names and scriptural images they present correspond to the *laudes* we find in medieval sermons. But it is seldom that we find an original or even a clear expression bearing on the precise sense of the doctrine of the Immaculate Conception.

Of the sequences which have been used regularly and which, for that

---

[93] The text of a Hereford *Historia de Conceptione b. M.* from the thirteenth century in A. T. BANNISTER, *A Descriptive Catalogue of the Mss. in the Hereford Cathedral Library,* Hereford 1927, pp. 34 ff.

[94] KELLNER (work cited in note 1), p. 260.

[95] Cf. chap. VI of the present volume, pp. 228 ff.

reason, must be accounted of traditional use, the best known is the one
we find in most medieval English and in very many continental missals:
Dies iste celebretur. We give the entire text; the different themes will easily
be discerned.

Dies iste celebretur,
In quo pie recensetur
   Conceptio Mariae.

Virgo Mater generatur,
Concipitur et creatur
   Dulcis vena veniae.

Adae vetus exsilium,
Et Joachim opprobrium,
   Hinc habeat remedium.

Hoc Prophetae praeviderunt,
Patriarchae praesenserunt,
   Inspirante gratia.

Virgo prolem conceptura,
Stella solem paritura,
   Hodie concipitur.

Flos de Virga processurus,
Sol de Stella nasciturus,
   Christus intelligitur.

O quam felix et praeclara,
Nobis grata, Deo cara,
   Fuit haec Conceptio!

Terminatur miseria;
Datur misericordia;
   Luctus cedit gaudio.

Nova mater novam prolem,
Nova stella novum solem,
   Nova profert gratia.

Genitorem genitura,
Creatorem creatura,
   Patrem parit filia.

O mirandam novitatem,
Novam quoque dignitatem!
Ditat matris castitatem
   Filii conceptio.

Gaude, Virgo gratiosa,
Virga flore speciosa,
Mater prole generosa,
   Vere plena gaudio.

Quod praecessit in figura,
Nube latens sub obscura,
Hoc declarat genitura
Piae matris: Virgo pura,
Pariendi vertit jura,
Fusa, mirante natura,
   Deitatis pluvia.

The comparison with Eve gives rise to a *jeu de mots* far more complicated than that which we find for instance in the hymn *Ave maris stella*:

Triste fuit in Eva vae!
Sed ex Eva format ave,
Versa vice, sed non prave;
Intus ferens in conclave
Verbum bonum et suave;
Nobis, Mater Virgo, fave
   Tua frui gratia.

Omnis homo, sine mora,
Laude plena solvens ora,
Istam colas, ipsam ora:
Omni die, omni hora,
Sit mens supplex, vox sonora;
Sic supplica, sic implora
   Huius patrocinia.

Tu spes certa miserorum,
Vere mater orphanorum,
Tu levamen oppressorum,
Medicamen infirmorum,
   Omnibus es omnia.

Te rogamus voto pari,
Laude digna singulari,
Ut errantes in hoc mari,
Nos in portu salutari
   Tua sistat gratia.

Another sequence which we sometimes find in the Mass of December 8 is *Ave praeclara maris stella,* ascribed (and, it seems, with good reason) to Herman Contractus.[96] This poet, who wrote in the abbey of Reichenau in the first half of the eleventh century, has, of course, nothing special to say about the Virgin's Conception; as a matter of fact this poetry is a general praise of the Mother of God which has been used as a sequence on other feast days also. The same goes for other well-known texts in honor of the Blessed Virgin, such as the hymn *Quis possit amplo famine praepotens* by Paul the Deacon, the friend of Charles the Great.[97]

A direct affirmation of the Immaculate Conception occurs in the late-medieval and otherwise uninteresting sequence *Cor devotum elevetur,* occasionally found in fifteenth-century French missals:

Haec concepta miro more
Est ut rosa cum nitore,
  Est ut candens lilium.

Ut fructus exit a flore,
Est producta cum pudore,
  Praeventa per Filium(!).

Sicut ros non corrumpitur,
Quando in terra gignitur,
  Elementi (*dust*) rubigine;

Sic Virgo non inficitur,
Cum in matre concipitur,
  Originali crimine.

In general, however, the expressions in poetry remain rather vague. At times it even happens that the poet mixes up the passive conception with the active conception of the Virgin, as in the vesper hymn in some French breviaries, which begins by announcing the object of the feast and then immediately continues with the praise of the Divine Incarnation:

Fulget dies specialis,
  Regia concipitur
Christi parens virginalis;
  Per hanc mors deprimitur
Culpae cunctis generalis,
  Hac homo reficitur. . . .

Haec est cuius in conclave
  Carne iuncto numine
Caro Verbum tam suave
  Fit non viri semine,
Et ex Eva format Ave
  Evae verso nomine.[98]

III

THE LITURGICAL FORMULAS
SINCE THE FIFTEENTH CENTURY

NOGAROLO AND DE BUSTI

It seems that the Fathers at Basel made a mistake when, in summing up all the extant arguments for the cause of the Immaculate Conception, they alleged the celebration of the feast of December 8 in the churches of

---

[96] The text is given in *Analecta hymnica* L, 313.
[97] *Ibid.,* L, 123.
[98] *Ibid.,* XI, 36.

Rome. As a matter of fact, it was celebrated chiefly in churches belonging to religious houses, which, however, were so numerous that the mistake is quite understandable.[99] The first official step toward the celebration in all the Roman churches was made by Pope Sixtus IV, a former Franciscan, who in the year 1477 promulgated the famous Constitution *Cum praeexcelsa* (followed in 1482 and 1483 by the injunctions *Grave nimis*) and at the same time inserted into the Roman service books an entirely new proper for the Mass and the Divine Office. The proper for the breviary, at least, had been composed by the apostolic prothonotary, Leonardo Nogarolo.[100]

The formulary of the Mass is interesting in many respects, not only because of the well-chosen redaction of the Collect (which since 1863 forms a part of our actual proper), but also because of the quaint way, very typical of the epoch, in which the texts of the choral parts were composed from different biblical sentences and expressions, taken most often from the *Canticle of Canticles.*

Introitus (cf. Cant. 3:11; Job 38:7 and Cant. 2:14). Egredimini et videte filiae Sion reginam vestram, quam laudant astra matutina, cuius pulchritudinem sol et luna mirantur et jubilant omnes filii Dei. *V.* Ostendat faciem suam, sonet vox eius in auribus nostris, quia eloquium suum dulce et facies decora nimis.

Oratio. Deus qui per immaculatam virginis conceptionem dignum Filio tuo habitaculum praeparasti: quaesumus; ut qui ex morte eiusdem Filii tui praevisa eam ab omni labe praeservasti, nos quoque mundos eius intercessione ad te pervenire concedas. Per.

Epistola. Dominus possedit me . . .

Graduale (cf. Cant. 5:10, 6:9 and 4:10). Qualis est dilecta nostra, carissimi, qualis est mater dicite domini, qualis et quanta sit soror et sponsa Christi. *V.* Dilecta nostra candida, immaculata quasi aurora consurgens. Alleluia. *V.* Veni regina nostra, veni domina in hortum odoris super omnia aromata.

Evangelium. Loquente Iesu ad turbas . . .

Offertorium (cf. Cant. 4:12-13; 5:5 and 7:1). Hortus conclusus, fons signatus, emissiones tuae paradisus, o Maria, manus tuae stillaverunt myrrham, mellifluique facti sunt caeli, dum manu domini fabricata es mater tanti Dei. Alleluia.

Secreta. Suscipere digneris per temetipsum benignitatis auctorem, rogamus Domine, matris ac domus tuae zelatorum devotas cum hilaritate supplicationes: ut, sicut ipsa tui gratia preveniente mundo hodie immunis apparuit, ita ipsi mundam de tuae matris munere, te concedente, exhibeant gratiarum actionem, per tempetipsum Iesum Christum Filium.

---

[99] Cf. chap. VII of the present volume, p. 274 f.

[100] Nogarolo's Office for the feast of Our Lady's Conception is found in the Roman breviaries between 1477 and 1568, either as a kind of votive or alternative office at the end of the book, or at its place in the Proper of the Saints. Cf. n. 93 on p. 296, below. All the varieties of the local liturgies continued to be used side by side ith the Sixtine proper until the end of the sixteenth century, when they were gradually replaced by the formulas of the Roman books of Pius V.

Communio. Gloriosa dicta sunt de te, Maria; quia fecit tibi magna qui potens est. Alleluia.

Postcommunio. Odorem, Domine, sacrificium huius suscipe suavitatis, et praesta, ut qui hodie Mariae conceptionem iubilando celebrant, eius salubri oratione fructum centuplum suae devotionis accipiant. Per.

The piety manifested by this proper is very different from that which we found represented in the older formulas. Here there is not so much a meditation on the place of the Virgin's privileges in the economy of salvation as a joyous praising of her immaculate splendor. The doctrine is stated with utmost precision, but the liturgical formulas have lost the full resonance which the older texts possessed. This resonance, however, can still be found in the Collect, in which, for the first time, the expression *immaculata Conceptio* is used. In some of the printed editions from the sixteenth century the words *ex morte eiusdem Filii tui praevisa* are missing, but it does not seem that we can draw any conclusion from this omission, since the idea these words stand for is clearly expressed in the Secret of the Mass (*tua gratia praeveniente*) and in the Invitatory of the Sixtine office: *Immaculatam Conceptionem Virginis Mariae celebremus, Christum eius praeservatorem adoremus Dominum.*[101]

The character of Nogarolo's Office is about the same as that of the Mass proper. The Office is best known for its lessons, a rich collection of *dicta sanctorum* (mostly of uncertain origin) in favor of the doctrine of the Immaculate Conception. These *dicta*, in turn, became widely used, thanks to the shortened edition of Nogarolo's Office published by another Franciscan, Cardinal Quignon, in his famous Breviary, known after the Cardinal's titular church as the *Breviary of the Holy Cross* and very popular for several decades (St. Francis Xavier used to recite his office out of this smallish book), until it was suppressed by the Fathers of Trent.[102] A number of quotations may show the character of this type of patched up lesson:[103]

Augustinus. Magnifica illum qui te ab omni peccato reservavit.[104] Quis enim inquit, dicere poterit: sine peccato sum natus? aut mundus sum ab omni iniquitate dicere audebit, nisi illa virgo prudentissima animatum templum Dei excelsi: quam Deus sic elegit et praeelegit

[101] As a rule the wording of the Invitatory is very illuminating for the way in which the feast was understood. In the Breviary of Pius V (1568) it fell back to: *Conceptionem Virginis Mariae celebremus, Christum eius Filium adoremus Dominum*

[102] Its use was abolished altogether by the Bull *Quod a nobis* of Pius V (1568): *Tollimus in primis et abolemus Breviarium novum a Francisco Cardinale praedicto editum.*

[103] The quotations are taken from the second, revised edition of Quignon's Breviary (since 1536) and are borrowed from the second, fourth and sixth lessons of Nogarolo's office. A critical edition of the revised Breviary of the Holy Cross was edited by J. Wickham Legg, *The Second Recension of the Quignon Breviary*, 2 vol. (HBS 35 and 42), London 1908 and 1912.

[104] The edition printed at Lyons in 1560 has the noteworthy variant *praeservavit*

ante mundi constitutionem, ut esset sancta et immaculata mater Dei
filia ab aeterno reservata incorrupta ab omni labe peccati.

Cyprianus. O virgo justa et omni iustitia plenissima, cuius conceptio
singularis.

Basilius. O Maria tu candoris et decoris forma, cui in terris non
est aequalis, nec in caelis ianua.

Origenes. Quae neque serpentis persuasione decepta, nec eius vene-
nosis afflatibus infecta.

Ambrosius. Haec est virga in qua nec modus originalis, nec cortex
venialis culpae fuit.

Bernardus. Caro virginis ex Adam sumpta, maculas Adae non
admisit.

Thomas. Maria ab omni peccato originali et actuali immunis
fuit.[105]

Dominicus. Sicut primus Adam fuit ex terra virgine, et numquam
maledicta formatus, ita decuit in secundo Adam fieri.[106]

We find an even larger series of *dicta* in the lessons of the proper (Mass
and Office) for the feast and its octave, composed by the Franciscan
Bernardino de Busti and approved by Sixtus IV in the year 1480.[107] In
this formulary the idea of the feast is even more isolated than in the Sixtine
proper. Characteristic in this respect is the text of the preface:

> . . . aeterne Deus. Qui dilectam Sponsam tuam gloriosam Viginem
> Mariam omnibus virtutibus ornatam fabricasti, et in purissima eius
> Conceptione ab originalis peccati macula illaesam praeservasti, ut
> totius esset innocentiae speculum, et exemplar sanctitatis, dignumque
> existeret habitaculum unigeniti Filii tui. Per quem . . .

REFORM OF PIUS V

Upon the publication of the Roman Breviary and Missal (1568 and
1570 respectively) by Pius V, the Sixtine formularies for the feast of
December 8 were suppressed, after having formed a feature of the Roman
service books for nearly a century. Except for the lessons of Matins, the
Mass and Office in the official Roman use were, from that time until

---

[105] The anger of MALDONATUS was roused especially by this quaint, so-called
quotation: Quisquis composuit breviarium illud . . . fecit lectionem unam conflatam
ex testimoniis omnium veterum authorum, ut persuaderet omnes sensisse B. Virginem
fuisse conceptam sine peccato originali: quod profecto fuit hominis imprudentissimi,
cum nemo eorum authorum quos citat ita senserit: et, quod amplius est, non poterat
ignorare D. Thomam esse in contraria sententia, tamen voluit persuadere nobis etiam
illum ita sensisse: quod non est bonam causam bene agere, sed perdere. Joh. MAL-
DONATUS, *Opera varia theologica,* Paris 1677, I: *Tract. theol. de peccato originali,*
Q. 4 p. 75.

[106] Cf. below, note 119.

[107] The complete text is given in *Acta Ordinis Fratrum Minorum* 23 (1904) pp.
402-420.—The office suffers from the over-adaptation we find later on in baroque
Officia parva. Thus the antiphons for the first Vespers are worded as follows: Dixit
Dominus Dominae meae: Sede a dextris innocentiae meae.—Laudate pueri Dominam
super omnes gentes in Conceptu gloriosam.—Nisi Dominus custodisset matrem suam,
angelus tenebrarum denigrasset eam. Etc.

1863 A.D., those of the feast of the Virgin's Nativity, with the usual changes of the words *Nativitas* and *Ortus* into *Conceptio*.[108]

It would not be right to attribute this change exclusively to the fact that Pope Pius V was a Dominican. We must also reckon with the aversion to all recent additions which was traditional in the *milieu* of the pope's collaborators. And this aversion must have been even stronger because of the fact that the Mass *Egredimini* and Nogarolo's Office were, on the whole, no liturgical masterpieces, while the return to the longstanding use of the Nativity formulary is entirely in keeping with the atmosphere in which the liturgical unification after Trent took place.[109]

Whatever was at the origin of the liturgical 'retrogression' in the books of Pius V (which eventually came to be accepted in place of most local service books), it most certainly was not indicative of an abatement in the cause of the Immaculate Conception. On the contrary, this cause had found new champions in the Jesuits who had a large share in giving it the peculiar emphasis it received in the devotional revival of the Counter-reformation. In the piety, cult and iconography (Murillo!) of the baroque period, the idea of the Virgin's Immaculate Conception becomes more and more an isolated theme, always understood but not always perceived in its fundamental relations to Incarnation and Redemption.[110]

This does not mean, however, that the opposition of theologians had died out completely. To cite only one incident which bears upon our subject: in the year 1678 the Dominican Raymund Capisucchi, then *Magister sacri Palatii*, forced through—to use no stronger word—a decree by which a votive office in honor of the Immaculate Conception was put on the Index.

---

[108] The proper lessons for Matins were the following: in the first nocturn *Ecclus.* 24: Ego ex ore Altissimi prodivi . . . vitam aeternam habebunt; in the second nocturn a passage from St. Ambrose's *De virginibus* II, 6-7: Sit vobis tamquam imagine descriptae virginitas . . . ut ipsa corporis species simulacrum fuerit mentis, figura probitatis; the homily of the third nocturn was taken from St. Augustine's *De consensu Evangelistarum* II, 2.

[109] It seems that the commission for the reform of the Missal and the Breviary under the pontificates of Clement VIII and Urban VIII drew up a plan for a new proper, or at least that Bernardo Gavanti, one of its best-known members, collected some material to that effect. According to S. BÄUMER, *Histoire du bréviaire* (French transl. by R. BIRON) II, Paris 1905, p. 287, these notes were probably used when the new office was composed under PIUS IX.—In a report by Baronius and Francolini to Clement VIII, mention is made of new office propers which Sixtus V had had composed for the feasts of the Conception, Visitation and Presentation and which, as they suggested, might be printed separately as long as the revision of the Breviary was not yet decided. See *DACL* IX, 1675.

[110] Anton L. MAYER, "Liturgie und Barock," in *Jahrb. für Liturgiewiss.* XV, p. 135: "Die Gottesmutter erscheint . . . immer in neuen, sich allmählich verselbständigenden Eigenschaften: Schmerzensmutter, liebliche Mutter, Mutter der Barmherzigkeit, Königin des Friedens, Königin des Rosenkranzes, Herrin des Skapuliers und, jede andere Schau überragend und überhellend, die Unbefleckte Empfängnis." On the iconography of the Immaculate Conception, see chapter XIII of the present volume.

Only by means of a very diplomatic procedure was it possible to save the reputation of the overzealous theologian as well as the office.[111]

Nor does the overwhelming devotion to the Immaculate Conception mean that the feast of December 8 was universally received at the beginning of the seventeenth century. Only towards the end of that century was it celebrated everywhere. In 1693 Innocent XII elevated it to the rank of a *festum secundae classis* (it had been *duplex maius* since Clement VIII) and extended the octave, kept already by some religious orders and in a number of Spanish dioceses, to the entire Church.[112] Finally, in 1708, Clement XI (persuaded by the Franciscan Francis Diaz) prescribed that the feast should be celebrated by all Catholics as a holy day of obligation.[112a]

THE EIGHTEENTH CENTURY

It has often been said and written that the religious atmosphere of the eighteenth century was not propitious to the cult of the Blessed Virgin, and to that of the Immaculate Conception in particular. This is not the place to go deeply into the matter, but we may say at least that in its generality this statement is not entirely correct, because the opposition (which existed indeed) was most often directed not so much against the doctrine and cult as such, as against the isolation of a devotional theme that had lost its connection with the doctrinal motifs from which it had sprung. Confining ourselves to the liturgical aspect of the subject, we may say that the opposition to the rank of the Conception feast and to its octave must not always be understood as an opposition to the idea of the feast. That the octave nearly fell victim to the activity of the Breviary Commission appointed by Benedict XIV [113] and that it was in fact suppressed in most of the new local service books in France and Germany, was simply the result of a general desire (not confined to that period only!) to reduce the excrescences of the liturgical calendar. It is true that in some of the new breviaries a number of texts in honor of the Blessed Virgin were changed according to the tendencies of an "enlightened" theology;[114]

[111] See chap. VII of the present volume, p. 278, n. 62.—A seemingly much debated prayer from the votive office in question, *Sancta Maria Regina caelorum* (and perhaps also the hymns of the office), can be found in the little votive office—with the same opening lines: *Eia mea labia nunc annuntiate / laudes et praeconia Virginis beatae*— which was approved by the Congregation of the Holy Office in 1838, and was printed in numerous Latin editions of the well-known prayer-book *Caeleste Palmetum*.

[112] The lessons which were chosen for the Matins of the octave have not been used in the present office. When one consults the editions of the Roman Breviary prior to 1863 one will see that they contained some highly interesting passages from patristic literature, such as the comparison between Mary and Eve in Irenaeus' *Adv. Haer.* (V, 19; the 6th lesson on Dec. 14) and a similar passage from Epiphanius' *Panarion* (III, haer. 78; read in the 2nd nocturn of Dec. 12).

[113] Cf. BÄUMER-BIRON, *o.c.*, II p. 380.

[112a] Cf. chapter VII of the present volume, p. 276 f.

[114] The breviaries of Münster and Cologne. Cf. BÄUMER-BIRON, *o.c.*, II pp. 355/6.

but it is equally true that at times the propers of the feast in the so-called neo-Gallican books witness to a very delicate understanding of the idea of the Conception. The invectives heaped by Dom Guéranger upon those local liturgies must not make us forget the profound and scriptural piety they may express.

ROUEN BREVIARY

The best example is, I believe, that which we find in the Rouen Breviary (since 1728). According to the puristic maxims of the period the texts of antiphons and verses are taken exclusively from the Bible. The effect is rather severe, and there is little tenderness in this formulary; but on the other hand we find here, along with the traditional biblical allusions, a large number of quite unexpected Scriptural texts which are very appropriate. So, among the antiphons of Vespers:

> Arca ferebatur super aquas, et aquae praevaluerunt nimis super terram (Gen. 7:18-19).
> Dominus faciens et formans te, ab utero auxiliator tuus (Is. 44:2).
> Ipsa est mulier quam praeparavit Dominus filio Domini mei (Gen. 24:44).

The Scriptural lessons are passages from Isaias (from chapters 11, 44 and 45) and, from the twelfth chapter of the Apocalypse, the passage (3-9, 13-17) about the dragon and the victory of the Woman.[115] As in other neo-Gallican breviaries, the Canon to be read at Prime is the passage from the decree of Trent on original sin in which the traditional doctrine about the Immaculate Conception is mentioned. An interesting instance of the way biblical texts were used, is furnished by a responsory from the second nocturn:

> R. Per unum hominem peccatum in hunc mundum intravit; et per peccatum mors, et ita in omnes homines mors pertransiit, in quo omnes peccaverunt (Rom. 5:12). V. Noli metuere: non morieris; non enim pro te, sed pro omnibus haec lex constituta est (Esther 15:12-13).[116]

THE FRANCISCAN OFFICE

The proper most widely used before 1863 was that of the Franciscans: the Sixtine Mass *Egredimini* and the Office beginning with the antiphon *Sicut lilium inter spinas*. Pope Clement XIV (1769-1774), a Franciscan Conventual, permitted it to be used in all the churches of the Spanish realm, where the feast of the Virgin's Immaculate Conception had been celebrated since the sixteenth century with unusual solemnity.[117]

---

[115] Curiously enough, not the first verse, *Mulier amicta sole* . . . , which had such a great influence on the iconography of the Immaculate Conception.—It is interesting to note that *Apoc.* 12, 1 was not used for the liturgy of the feast before the present office, where it serves in a responsory at Matins and as chapter at None.

[116] Cf. the responsory after the first lesson in the present office.

[117] Many permissions were granted during the seventeenth and eighteenth cen-

In the text of the Office, the idea of the Immaculate Conception is clearly expressed, as might be expected.[118] The invitatory at Matins is that of the Office of Sixtus IV: *Immaculatam Conceptionem Virginis Mariae celebremus, Christum eius praeservatorem adoremus Dominum.* The choral parts are well chosen, mainly from the Sapiential books, and from the canticle in the last chapter of Judith. As lessons for the second nocturn on December 8 we find the passage from the letter of Pseudo-Jerome (*Qualis et quanta*) which is used in the present formulary. On the octave day, as lessons for the second nocturn, there are a paragraph from Eadmer's (not Anselm's) *De excellentia Virginis;* the famous passage of *De conceptu virginali* c.18, in which St. Anselm comes very close to confessing the doctrine of the Immaculate Conception; and a short series of *Dicta sanctorum*, beginning with a curious *sentence* "by saint Andrew the Apostle," which is very much like that given by Nogarolo as St. Dominic's.[119]

MASS AND OFFICE OF PIUS IX

In 1854 Pius IX solemnly proclaimed the doctrine of the Immaculate Conception in the sense in which it had generally been understood since the fourteenth century. Nine years later, in 1863, a new proper for the feast was introduced into the Missal and the Breviary.[120]

---

turies for the recitation of the votive office of the 'Immaculate' Conception (taken from the Roman formulary) on Saturdays. The best known is that given by Benedict XIII *Universo clero, saeculari et regulari, in omnibus Regnis, Dominiis et Ditionibus Caesareae Maiestatis subiectis extra Italiam.* Cf. chapter VII of the present volume, p. 277 f.

[118] During the later centuries also, the Franciscans remained the promoters of the doctrine and the devotion. At their General Chapter of 1644 at Toledo the *Minores* had the Blessed Virgin, under the title of her Immaculate Conception, proclaimed as the patroness of their Order; their example was followed in 1719 by the Conventuals.

[119] The *"sentence"* of St. Andrew" (not found in the Acts of that Apostle) was borrowed by the redactor of the Franciscan proper from Louis Lippoman, probably from his *Catena* on Genesis. It reads: *Andreas Apostolus: Quomodo de immaculata terra factus fuerat homo primus, necessarium fuit, ut de immaculata Virgine natus Christus, vitam aeternam, quam omnes perdiderant, repararet.*—It would be interesting to trace the theme of the immaculate (virginal) paradise or first creation found in this apocryphal passage and in the sentence in Nogarolo's office ascribed to St. Dominic (see above), all through post-patristic and patristic literature. Cf. for instance St. Proclus of Constantinople, *Or.* 6, c. 8 (*PG* 65, 733). In the West, we find it as early as in the Benedictional of Freising, written in the ninth or tenth century, but reproducing a tradition which is at least a century older. The blessing formula for Thursday after Easter has: Deus qui e terra virgine Adam pridem condere voluisti et tu Adam caelestis quadam similitudine sed perfecte sine peccato de virgine nasci dignatus es. (*Diction. d'arch. chrét. et de lit.* VI, 501.) We may surmise, I think, that during the Middle Ages, the text from the Canticle of Canticles (4, 12) *Hortus conclusus,* so often used as an antiphon or responsory in the office of the Blessed Virgin, was understood in the sense of that theme.

[120] Already in 1855 Passaglia had composed a new proper which, according to BÄUMER (work cited in note 109) II, p. 411, found a place in the breviaries printed between that year and 1863. I have not had the opportunity to consult all the books

The tone of the Mass and Office is very festive and the various formulas are in exquisite taste. To some extent the present proper, like several of its predecessors since the fifteenth century, presents the idea of the feast and doctrine as an isolated theme: the splendor of the Immaculate Virgin, chosen by God and from the very beginning of her existence surpassing all other creatures by her unblemished purity. The connexion with related theological themes is not absent, however. Thus in the choral parts of the Mass and Office we find the motif of the Protogospel of Genesis: *hodie' contrita est ab ea caput serpentis antiqui.* The lessons from Genesis in the first nocturn of the feast were chosen for the same reason; another redactor' would have divided the pericopes differently in order to stress at one and the same time the motifs of the virginal paradise and of the comparison between the first and second Eve. The Gospel of the Mass, taken from Luke I, ends with the angel's greeting: *gratia plena . . . benedicta tu in mulieribus.* If a few more verses had been given, the relation between the Virgin's unique privilege and the mystery of the Incarnation would have found the expression it has in the Nativity formulary and which forms the theme of the Collect, borrowed from the proper of 1476: *Deus qui per immaculatam Virginis Conceptionem dignum Filio tuo habitaculum praeparasti.*

The most interesting feature of the proper is the rich use which has been made of the homilies of the Greek *Philotheotokoi* (chiefly to stress the link between the dogma of 1854 and early Christian doctrine, and perhaps also for oecumenical reasons). Kellner judges them rather harshly as "the homilies of the later Greeks, full of long-winded and empty exclamations." [121] But these exclamations are far from monotonous and empty, I think. Only, we must learn how to read them, by appreciating the background of the doctrine and piety they represent. Then we shall see that what might appear to be no more than poetic phrases are, in fact, allusions to the manifold biblical images in which the theologically founded piety of the patristic and post-patristic periods expressed all that can be thought and felt and venerated regarding the eminence of the All-pure Mother of God. [122]

---

printed during that period. A number of breviaries which I was able to examine contained only the formulary which had been traditional since Pius V. At any rate, after that of Passaglia had been withdrawn, a new proper was prepared according to a project, it seems, which had been drawn up by the Commission for the Breviary at the beginning of the seventeenth century (see note 109).

[121] See KELLNER (work cited in note 1), p. 198 of the third German edition.

[122] For the authorship of the homily in the third nocturn on December 15, cf. the list by G. MORIN in *Revue bénédictine* 1891, p. 270 ff.; Dom Morin proves that the sermon was not written by St. Epiphanius, but by his (homonymous) successor on the see of Salamis, Epiphanius of Cyprus (c. 870 A.D.). The learned author has proven equally that the "Letter of St. Jerome" (*Ep. 9 ad Paulam et Eustochium*) from which the lessons in the second nocturn on Dec. 8 are taken—passages which are found in some older breviaries at Dec. 8 and at August 15—must be ascribed to

The most recent addition (1879) to the liturgy of the feast of December 8 has been the Mass of the Vigil. The three prayers have been modeled on the prayers of the Vigil Mass of August 14. The Gospel is St. Matthew's *Liber generationis,* for many centuries read on the feast day itself. The choice of the Epistle, *Ego quasi vitis,* has its precedent in many medieval missals. Not that such a precedent is necessary—for the praise of God's chosen one in Ecclesiasticus is the eloquent expression of what Christians instinctively feel when they begin to celebrate the feast of the first dawn of their salvation, the great festival of their Mother and Protectress: *Memoria mea in saecula saeculorum . . . Qui elucidant me, vitam aeternam habebunt.*[123]

Ambrose Autpert or Ansbert. Previously MORIN (in *Revue bén.* 1888, p. 347 ff.) had suggested Paschasius Radbertus as the author, an opinion which Dom T. A. Agius sought to confirm in the *Journal of Theol. Stud.* 24 (1922-1923), pp. 176-183.

[123] Since the writing of the preceding pages, a decree of the Sacred Congregation of Rites (March 23, 1955) has reduced the formulary of the Mass of the vigil and the lessons of the octave to the status of historical documents. For the appreciation of the tradition regarding the liturgical celebration of the feast of December 8, the value of these texts remains, of course, unchanged.

SICUT CEDRUS EXALTATA

V

The Mediaeval Controversy over the Immaculate
Conception up to the Death of Scotus

Carlo Balić, O.F.M.*

While formerly it was held that Scotus was the first to have given a scientific presentation of the doctrine of the Immaculate Conception, nowadays this honour is claimed for many others, such as Peter of Compostella,[1] Eadmer,[2] Nicholas of St. Alban's,[3] Peter Paschasius[4] and Raymond Lull,[5] all of whom are described as the "first" theologians of the Marian privilege. Some of these lived at the beginning of the twelfth century, others at the end of the thirteenth; all of them, however, wrote before Scotus.

Some theologians even declare that there is no opposition between the doctrine defined by Pius IX in the Bull *Ineffabilis Deus* and the doctrine of the great doctors of the golden era of scholasticism, such as St. Thomas [6] and St. Bonaventure, even though in subsequent centuries the authentic representatives of the Thomist school denied the doctrine of the Immaculate Conception in the name of the Angelic Doctor, and the supporters of our Lady's privilege considered Scotus as their leader.

What has just been said gives an idea of the difficulty of the problem which we intend to discuss.

* President of the International Marian Academy and of the Scotist Commission, Rome, Italy. The present article was completed in April, 1955.

[1] Perez J. Cl., "El primer escolástico que propugnó el privilegio inmaculista de María fué un español, in *Ilustración del clero* 32 (1939), 17-20. 57-63. 90-95; Roschini G. M., "Il primo scolastico che propugnò il privilegio dell'Immacolata Concezione," in *Marianum* 4 (1942) 130-131.

[2] Cf. Del Marmol B., *La conception immaculée de la Vierge Marie (De conceptione sanctae Mariae) par Eadmer*, Lille-Paris 1923; Burridge W., "England and the Immaculate Conception," in *The Tablet* 11 (1954) 573.

[3] Cf. Mildner F. M., "The Immaculate Conception in the writings of Nicolas of St. Albans," in *Marianum* 2 (1940) 173-193.

[4] Mancini V., *Il primo difensore dell'Immacolata Concezione di Maria è stato un mercedario: S. Pietro Pascasio*, Napoli 1939.

[5] Cf. Bové S., *Lo Doctor de la Inmaculada*, cited by Avinyo J., *B. Raymundi Lulli, Liber de Immaculata Bmae Virginis Conceptione*, Barcinone 1901, 17-39; Pasqual A. R., *Vindiciae Lullianae*, I, Avenione 1778, 433.

[6] Del Prado N., *Divus Thomas et bulla dogmatica "Ineffabilis Deus,"* Friburgi 1919.

We will glance briefly through the fairly abundant literature of the first six centuries of the Middle Ages (from the eighth to the fourteenth), to discover what each theologian thought or at least wrote about the sanctification of the Blessed Virgin, without concerning ourselves at all with the question, whether their doctrine is, in itself, acceptable.

I

THE PREPARATORY AND INTRODUCTORY PERIOD OF SCHOLASTICISM (FROM THE EIGHTH TO THE BEGINNING OF THE THIRTEENTH CENTURIES).

First of all, it is to be noted that in the preparatory period of scholasticism (eighth to eleventh centuries), in which the Greek Church was definitely separated from the Latin Church on account of the schism of Michael Cerularius (A.D. 1054), and a scholastic period distinct from the preceding periods was inaugurated in the West, no trace is found of controversies concerning the Immaculate Conception.

Further, on account of the anti-Pelagian leaning which it had inherited from Saint Augustine, western theology from the very beginning places the emphasis on the absolute universality of original sin. In addition, the barbarian invasions and public disturbances of many different kinds were not favorable to study and speculation. Finally, it must be remembered that the Greek language was almost unknown in the West, and consequently the theologians in the West knew nothing of the development of ideas which had taken place in the Oriental church after the Council of Ephesus, concerning the complete sanctity of the Mother of God.

In the light of the foregoing facts, it is not to be wondered at if, in this first theological epoch, we find few or no explicit testimonies which coincide exactly with the doctrine of the dogmatic Bull, *Ineffabilis Deus*.

THE PREPARATORY PERIOD OF SCHOL-
ASTICISM: PASCHASIUS RADBERTUS . . .

Nevertheless, although the followers of the Augustinian school generally insist on the absolute universality of original sin because of the connexion between concupiscence and sin (i.e. that concupiscence directly affects the body, and indirectly the soul, of all those who are born by the ordinary union of the sexes),[7] the fact remains that even among the theologians of this first epoch, we find not only a number of documents in which the principles of the fullness of grace in the Mother of God are established

---

[7] Cf. BEDA, *Homiliae*, lib. 1 hom. 1, *In festo Annunt.* (PL 94, 13); ALCUINUS, *Adversus Felicis haeresim*, c. 24 (PL 101, 96): "Nos quippe sancti efficimur, non tamen

"because the gift of the Holy Ghost is not bound," [8] but we also find, in the twelfth century, the dawn, as it were, of the explicit teaching of the Marian privilege.

Affirmative propositions turn up now and again, as for example when an anonymous writer asserts, when comparing the Virgin to a nimbus, that she, symbolized by the cloud, "was never in darkness, but always in light." [9] Another example: Ambrose Autpert calls the Mother of God:

Immaculate because in no way corrupt.[10]

Paul Winfridus the Deacon says:

She was completely free from the bonds of wickedness.[11]

St. Fulbert writes that the soul and flesh of the Virgin were:

. . . utterly pure of all malice and uncleanness.[12]

All these testimonies merely continue the sayings of those authors of Christian antiquity who found Our Lady's unlimited sanctity in the idea of her Divine Maternity. The encomia they uttered certainly entailed the doctrine of the Immaculate Conception; but it is difficult to say whether these authors (for at the moment we prescind from others) had—we do not say a full awareness of the adequate concept of the Immaculate Conception as defined by Pius IX—but even a rudimentary idea that Mary had never been subject to original sin. This doubt can be raised with regard to the testimony of Paschasius Radbertus (ca. 850), about which some exclaim, "What could be more clear and more decisive!" [13] In my opinion, it would be wise to quote the text fully:

> Although Blessed Mary was born and begotten of sinful flesh, and was herself sinful flesh, she was such no longer, thanks to the grace of the Holy Ghost, when the angel hailed her as the most blessed of women. 'The Holy Ghost,' he said, 'shall come upon thee, and the power of the Most High shall overshadow thee.' For if she was not sanctified and cleansed by the same Spirit, how could her flesh be other than sinful flesh? And if her flesh came from the mass of original prevarication, how could Christ, the Word made flesh, be without sin . . . ? . . .

nascimur, quia ipsa naturae corruptibilis conditione constringimur, ut cum propheta dicamus: 'Ecce enim in iniquitatibus conceptus sum, et in delictis peperit me mater mea' " (Psal. L, 7). Ille autem solus veraciter sanctus natus est, qui, ut ipsam conditionem naturae vinceret, ex commixtione carnalis copulae conceptus non est . . ."

[8] Cf. chapter II of the present volume, p. 79, n. 90.

[9] ANONYMUS, *Breviarium in psalmos*, ps. 77, 4 (appendix to the works of Saint Jerome, PL 26, 1112).

[10] AMBROSIUS AUTPERTUS, *Epist. ad Paulam et Eustochium de Assumptione B. M. V.*, n. 9 (among the spurious works of St. Jerome, PL 30, 136).

[11] WINFRIDUS PAULUS, *In Assumptione B. M. V.*, hom. 1 (PL 95, 1567): "Vitiositatis nodis funditus carens."

[12] FULBERTUS CARNOTENSIS, *De nativitate B. M. V.*, sermo 4 (PL 141, 322).

[13] MALOU J. B., *L'Immaculée Conception de la Bienheureuse Vierge Marie*, II, Bruxelles 1857, 99.

How could she have failed to be without original sin at that moment when she was filled with the Holy Spirit, since even her glorious nativity is proclaimed blessed by everyone in the whole Catholic Church? If this feast were not blessed and glorious, it would certainly not be celebrated everywhere and by everyone. But because she is so solemnly venerated, it is certain from the authority of the Church that she was not subject to any sin at her birth, and that she had not contracted original sin in the womb in which she had been sanctified. Hence, while the birthdays of Jeremias and Job (Jer. XX, 14; Job III, 5) are called accursed, the day on which Mary's happy Nativity began is called blessed and is religiously venerated.[14]

To this text may be joined another in which the same theologian says:

Mary—since she was blessed—had not the corrupting stain (*culpa corruptionis*), and hence gave birth to Christ without sorrow or corruption.[15]

He also asserts that it is the mark of most ardent piety and the sign of virtue:

. . . to proclaim the purity of the Blessed Virgin incorrupt and untainted, and to declare it exempt from the contagion of our first origins.[16]

The authenticity of the principal text has been questioned, so that even Le Bachelet says that "Paschasius considers the sanctity of the child at her birth, and thence argues back to her original sanctity at her conception"; [17] and he concludes that "the final solution can be given only when we have a critical edition of this work." [18] But even if we were to admit that the text is genuine, the case is anything but clear. In the first place, some incorrectly translate the principal words, for example: ". . . sanctified in her mother's womb, she never contracted original sin." [19] Now, Paschasius

---

[14] Paschasius Radbertus, *De partu Virginis*, lib. 1 (PL 120, 1371): "At vero beata Maria licet ipsa de carne peccati sit nata et procreata, ipsaque quamvis caro peccati fuerit, non tunc jam quando praeveniente Spiritus sancti gratia ab angelo prae omnibus mulieribus benedicta vocatur. 'Spiritus sanctus,' inquit, 'superveniet in te, et virtus Altissimi obumbrabit tibi.' (Luke I, 35) Alioquin si non eodem Spiritu sancto sanctificata est et emundata, quomodo caro ejus non caro peccati fuit? et si caro ejus de massa primae praevaricationis venit, quomodo Christus Verbum caro sine peccato fuit . . . ? . . . Alias autem quomodo Spiritu sancto eam replente non sine originali peccato fuit, cujus etiam nativitas gloriosa catholica in omni Ecclesia Christi ab omnibus felix et beata praedicatur; enimvero si non beata esset et gloriosa, nequaquam ejus festivitas celebraretur ubique ab omnibus. Sed quia tam solemniter colitur, constat ex auctoritate Ecclesiae quod nullis, quando nata est, subjacuit delictis, neque contraxit in utero sanctificata originale peccatum. Unde et si Jeremiae dies atque Job maledicta pronuntiatur, dies, inquam, nativitatis eorum, dies tamen, quando inchoata est felix Mariae nativitas, beata pronuntiatur, et colitur religiose satis."

[15] *Ibid.*, (col. 1369).

[16] *Ibid.*, (col. 1375): ". . . eximiae pietatis honor est vobis et decus virtutis, beatissimae Virginis pudicitiam praedicare incorruptam et incontaminatam, et ab omni contagione primae originis confiteri alienam."

[17] Le Bachelet F. X., "Immaculée Conception," in *Dictionnaire de théologie catholique*, VII[1]; Paris 1927, col. 984.

[18] *Ibid.*, 985.

[19] Roschini G. M., *La Madonna secondo la fede e la teologia*, III, Roma 1953, 47.

says that the Blessed Virgin was sanctified in her mother's womb and that accordingly, when the Catholic Church celebrates universally the glorious nativity of the Virgin, she celebrates not only the nativity, in as much as it was an exit from the womb, but also its incipient stages, in which the infant was sanctified in the womb. But did Paschasius extend this incipient nativity or sanctification to the very first moment of conception, so as to imply that she never contracted original sin?

A further doubt arises here, because Paschasius asserts in the same context that Mary's flesh was sinful flesh, and that the Blessed Virgin was procreated and born of sinful flesh. Perhaps one might conjecture that, in the author's mind, flesh which had been tarnished by concupiscence or sin was cleansed before animation. But it would be difficult to reconcile this with the whole context, which suggests that the Blessed Virgin's flesh was cleansed at the Annunciation.

Since the author says that this "incipient nativity" of the Virgin was not accursed like that of Job (who cursed his first conception), nor like that of Jeremias (who was sanctified), we could conclude that he really did extend this sanctification to the very beginning of Our Lady's existence, because her flesh had been cleansed before her animation, so that the cause from which the stain would have derived was removed in advance. But even if this interpretation of Paschasius' mind be correct, we must not forget that, while according to the Bull *Ineffabilis Deus* the Virgin was preserved free "from all stain of original sin . . . from the first moment of her conception," Paschasius, speaking of sanctification at the time of the Annunciation, dares to speak of "uncleanness" (*sordibus*) from which the Virgin was purified; he claims that:

> When the Holy Spirit came to her, He cleansed and purified her completely, so that she was holier than the stars of heaven.[20]

To sum up, while Paschasius makes one of the first efforts among western theologians to discover the doctrine of the Immaculate Conception, he also abounds unfortunately in the obscure, incomplete and imperfect terminology which was to prevent the theologians, until the time of Scotus, from grasping and clearly expounding the mystery of Our Lady's preservation from all stain, as will emerge more clearly from the remainder of this history.

THE INTRODUCTORY PERIOD OF SCHOLASTICISM:
ANSELM, EADMER, OSBERT, NICHOLAS, BERNARD . . .

If we pass now from the preparatory period of scholasticism to the introductory period, which begins in the second part of the eleventh century and lasts up to the first decades of the thirteenth century, it becomes patent that the doctrine and cult of the Immaculate Conception progressed *pari passu* with sacred doctrine in general.

[20] PASCHASIUS RADBERTUS, *op. cit.* (col. 1372).

In this period there was widespread discussion about the nature of original sin and the manner in which it was transmitted. The Augustinian doctrine was the most widely accepted—namely, that the sin was concupiscence, or concupiscence together with ignorance, and that it was transmitted by the body, in the sense that the principal agent in transmitting original sin was not propagation as such, but rather the *libido* connected with the act of generation. And just as a contaminated vessel befouls the liquid which is poured into it, so also the soul, created by God, is soiled by its contact with the body.[21]

Since the expression *sin* has various significations in this century, so that Bandinelli can say: "By *sin* is understood a stain, an act of sin, guilt, fault and even punishment";[22] and since a stable terminology, generally speaking, is lacking, it is not easy to determine which authors taught that Our Blessed Lady contracted original sin and which held the contrary.

However, bearing in mind the diversity of expression and the circumstances of the time, especially the false ideas about original sin and the manner of its transmission, it seems that the Immaculate Conception was generally denied, either explicitly or implicitly, in this period.

Some, such as Geroch of Reichersberg,[23] Godfrey of Admont,[24] and Rupert of Deutz, said so clearly, affirming of Mary that:

[21] Cf. Martin R.-M., "Les idées de Robert de Melun sur le péché originel," in *Revue des sciences phil. et theol.* 7 (1913) 700-725; Lombardus P., *Sent. II*, d.31 c.4 n. 286 (Ad Claras Aquas, I², 1916, 469-470): "Caro enim per peccatum corrupta fuit in Adam, adeo ut, cum ante peccatum vir et mulier sine incentivo libidinis et concupiscentiae fervore possent convenire, essetque thorus immaculatus, iam post peccatum non valeat fieri carnalis copula absque libidinosa concupiscentia, quae semper vitium est, et etiam culpa, nisi excusetur per bona coniugii. In concupiscentia igitur et libidine concipitur caro formanda in corpus prolis. Unde caro ipsa, quae concipitur in vitiosa concupiscentia, polluitur et corrumpitur; *ex cuius contactu anima, cum infunditur, maculam trahit, qua polluitur et fit rea*, id est vitium concupiscentiae, quod est originale peccatum." *Ibid.*, c.6 n. 288 (I, 471): "Et quod vitium vel corruptio sit in carne ante coniunctionem animae, effectu probatur cum anima infunditur, quae ex corruptione carnis maculatur; *sicut in vase dignoscitur vitium esse, cum vinum infusum acesit.*" *Ibid.*, c.7 n. 290 (I, 472): "noster vero conceptus non fit sine libidine, et ideo non est sine peccato."

[22] Roland Bandinelli, *Die Sentenzen Rolands*, ed. Gietl, Freiburg i. Br. 1891, 132; cf. Le Bachelet, *art. cit.*, 1030.

[23] Gerhohus Reicherspergensis, *Commentarius in Psalmos*, Ps. 1 (PL 193, 639): "licet ipsa in peccatis more aliorum hominum fuerit concepta, tamen velut *hortus conclusus et fons signatus* (Cant. IV, 12) actualibus peccatis fuit inaccessibilis. Atque ipsa culpa originalis, sicut deficit fumus prae claritate solis, et sicut cera consumitur a facie ignis, in ea defecit, et consumpta est, illuminante pariter et inflammante illam Spiritu sancto, id est amore divino."—Cf. Honorius Augustodun., *Sigillum B. Mariae*, c.5 (PL 172, 509): "Sacra namque Virgo ostium fuit, per quod Christus in mundum introivit; pessulus autem erat moles peccatorum hominum, quod ideo ejus dicitur, quia et ipsa in peccatis nata creditur."

[24] Godefridus Admontensis, *Homiliae dominicales*, hom. 6 (PL 174, 51): "Ipsa namque nobilis illa terra erat quam totam nebula ista tegebat, et circumquaque obumbravit, ne eam, quae haereditaria peccati originalis labe processerat, actualis culpae macula . . . tangeret."—Cf. *ibid.* hom. 4 (PL 174, 40).—*Idem, Homiliae festivales*, hom. 31, *In festo Annuntiationis B. M. V.* (PL 174, 772): "Est autem peccatum ori-

. . . since she was of the mass which was corrupted in Adam, she was not free from the hereditary stain of original sin . . .[25]

Therefore she was conceived in sin like everyone else. Others seem to express the same idea indirectly, asserting that Christ *alone* was without sin,[26] or even speaking about a "purification from sin," which took place for Mary, either in her mother's womb by sanctification (St. Bernard,[27] Richard of St. Victor,[28]) or at the time of the Incarnation.[29]

It is difficult to understand exactly of what she was purified at the Incarnation; but if we bear in mind the very wide meaning of original sin, comprehending "guilt" in its true sense, and punishment in its improper sense, it seems that those who spoke about purification at the time of the Incarnation were really speaking about a purgation of the effects of original sin, supposing that the sin itself had been taken away when she was in her mother's womb. Although, for various reasons, this can be taken as the

---

ginale concupiscentia carnis et ignorantia animae. Hoc sane pallio, quia haec Virgo beata, utpote in peccatis concepta et nata, nequaquam caruit, audita quidem credidit, sed quomodo fieri possent, penitus ignoravit."—Cf. *ibid.*, hom. 63, *in vigilia Assumptionis B. M. V.* (PL 174, 957).

[25] RUPERTUS TUITIENSIS, *In Cantica Canticorum*, lib. 1 (PL 168, 841): "Et tu quidem veraciter dicere potueras: 'Ecce enim in iniquitatibus concepta sum, et in peccatis concepit me mater mea' (Psal. L). Cum enim esses de massa quae in Adam corrupta est, haereditaria peccati originalis labe non carebas."

[26] PETRUS DAMIANI, *Sermones*, sermo 23, *In nativitate S. Ioannis Bapt.* (PL 144, 628): "Quicumque de massa praevaricatrice mundum ingredimur, longam restem originalis peccati trahimus nobiscum. Solus ille qui peccatum non fecit (I Petri 2) excipitur, quem virginalis thalamus ignorante viro terris effudit. . . . Cum igitur omnes 'in iniquitatibus concepti sint' (Psal. L), neminem umquam mortalium intra materna viscera sanctificatum legimus, praeter Jeremiam et Joannem Baptistam; quamquam et de singulari Virgine nulla sit ambiguitas, quin ipsa maternis circumsepta visceribus, sublimiore sanctificationis genere mundata sit, utpote sacrarium illud, in quo Deus, Dei Filius, carnem fuerat suscepturus."—ZACHARIAS CHRYSOPO-LIT., *De concordia evangelistarum*, lib. 1 (PL 186, 55; from BEDE): "Nos etsi sancti efficimur, non tamen sancti nascimur, dicente Propheta: *In iniquitatibus conceptus sum* (Psal. L); Jesus vero singulariter natus est sanctus, quia ex commissione carnalis copulae conceptus non est."

[27] BERNARDUS, *Epist. 174* (PL 182, 334): "Quod itaque vel paucis mortalium constat fuisse collatum, fas certe non est suspicari tantae Virgini esse negatum, per quam omnis mortalitas emersit ad vitam. Fuit procul dubio et Mater Domini ante sancta, quam nata . . ."

[28] RICHARDUS A S. VICTORE, *Explicatio in Cantica Cantic.*, c.26 (PL 196, 482): "Beata Maria virgo tota pulchra fuit, quia sanctificata in utero. Ab utero quoque egressa nec mortale umquam nec veniale commisit. Et ante conceptionem quidem Filii Dei prius per gratiam custodita est a peccatis, post hanc vero ita confirmata est ex virtute Altissimi, obumbrata et roborata, ut peccatum omnino committere non potuerit . . ."

[29] HERBERTUS DE LOSINGA, *In die natali Domini*, sermo 1 (ed. GOULBURN E. M., in *The Life, Letters and Sermons of Herbert de Losinga*, II, London 1878, 1); cf. LE BACHELET, *art. cit.*, 1029 f.—PASSAGLIA C. in his well known work *De immaculato Deiparae semper Virginis conceptu commentarius*, Naples 1854, especially when quoting the "opinion of tradition about the Virgin," enumerates a large number of authors and passages which, if they are carefully examined, show that only a very few authors really thought that the blessed Virgin was preserved from sin, and not one of them attributed her exemption to preservation by the Redemption of Christ.

general rule, when we come to examine the individual authors, doubts arise as to what they actually taught.

Such a doubt occurs, in the first place, with regard to those authors who said nothing at all directly or explicitly about the conception of the Blessed Virgin, yet, when writing about original sin and its universal diffusion, and about the Incarnate Word, emphasize the purity of the Blessed Virgin. It is well known that the great Anselm, the father of scholasticism, is among those writers. Posing the problem, "How God took a sinless man from the sinful mass, that is, from the human race, which was totally infected with sin—as if getting unleavened bread out of leavened," Anselm speaks of the purity of the Blessed Virgin.[30] The question which he poses is solved in two ways: first, because Mary was purified, and secondly because Christ was conceived of a virgin. Then he goes on to say:

> I do not deny that there may be a higher explanation (*ratio*) of the way God took a sinless man from the sinful mass, like unleavened bread from leavened. If it is shown to me, I shall willingly accept it, and shall abandon my own arguments if they can be shown to be contrary to the truth, though I do not think they are.[31]

Whether that "higher reason" conceals what was taught by his secretary Eadmer, as we shall see later, namely the total purity, in body and in soul, of the Blessed Virgin, it is difficult to say. It does not seem that Anselm could have admitted that complete purity, because of his doctrine of the absolute universality of original sin. For Christ was "the only one" who did not sin in Adam and was not conceived in sin; because conceived by a virgin, He escaped the legacy of sin, whilst all who are born of "the nature and will of Adam" are necessarily conceived in sin.[32]

Therefore Mary, who "was brought into existence from Adam, in the same way as all others," [33] "was one of those who were cleansed from their sins by Him before He was born"; and in anticipation of the merits of Christ she was cleansed by his future death.[34]

Consequently, although Anselm seems to have considered original sin

[30] ANSELMUS, *Cur Deus homo*, II, c.16 (PL 158, 416; ed. SCHMIDT, II, 116).

[31] IDEM, *De conceptu virginali et de peccato originali*, c.21 (PL 158, 452; ed. SCHMIDT, II, 161).

[32] ANSELMUS, *De conceptu virg.*, c.3. 22 (PL 158, 433. 452-454; ed. SCHMIDT, II, 142.161-162); cf. JONES R. T., *Sancti Anselmi Mariologia*, Mundelein 1937, 39-40.

[33] ANSELMUS, *De conceptu virg.*, c.23 (PL 158, 455; ed. SCHMIDT, II, 164).

[34] ANSELMUS, *Cur Deus homo*, II, c.16 (PL 158, 419; ed. SCHMIDT, II, 119): "[Virgo] fuit de illis qui ante nativitatem eius per eum mundati sunt a peccatis . . ." —*Ibid.* c.18 (PL 158, 423; ed. SCHMIDT, II, 124-125): "Virgo quae per fidem munda facta est. . . . Veritas fidei Virginis non fuit causa, ut ille sponte moreretur, sed quia hoc futurum erat, vera fuit fides."—Cf. *ibid.* (PL 158, 420-423; ed. SCHMIDT, II, 119) —*Idem, De conceptu virginali*, c.18 (PL 158, 451; ed. SCHMIDT, II, 159): "Qualiter autem Virgo eadem per fidem ante ipsam conceptionem mundata sit, dixi, ubi aliam rationem de hoc ipso unde hic agitur reddidi."

to have been so absolutely and totally universal that no exception was possible, even for the Mother of God,[35] nevertheless he asserted the principles which, objectively considered, lead to the doctrine of the Immaculate Conception.   Hence it is that he not only salutes Mary as the "woman wonderfully and uniquely wonderful," through whom the elements are reborn and the demons trampled underfoot; as the "blessed and everblessed Virgin," and "holy, and after God uniquely holy among the saints"; who had "holiness above all, after her supreme Son"; [36] but he also asserts the principle that "it was fitting," that the conception of Christ should "be from a most pure mother":

> It was proper that she should shine with a purity such as none greater under God can be imagined—that Virgin to whom God the Father determined to give His only Son, whom He had begotten equal to Himself and loved as Himself, so that He should be the Son at one and the same time of God the Father and of the Virgin. . .[37]

It must be remembered too that similar tributes in honor of the Mother of the Redeemer occur not infrequently in those writers whom we have already mentioned as being contrary to the Marian privilege.   When commenting on the Canticle of Canticles, or explaining the *Hail Mary*, or speaking about the various Marian feasts, these authors mention here and there that Mary is "all beautiful," that "she alone is free from the universal malediction," without any stain because she had to be worthy to be Mother of God, exceeding all creatures in holiness, and so on.[38]

---

[35] Cf. JONES, *op. cit.*, 27.45: "Immaculatam Conceptionem non tenuit S. Anselmus. . . ."—SPEDALIERI F., S.J., "Anselmus per Eadmerum. De mente S. Doctoris circa Immaculatam B. V. Conceptionem," in *Marianum* 5 (1943) 205-219, tries to show that this has not been proved: "quae in contrarium adduci solent aliam interpretationem admittunt et quidem rectam, si unum excipias locum ex libro *De conceptu virginali* desumptum; in quo tamen ille dubius haeret, at quoad demonstrationem ex rationibus necessariis deductam, et quia clara et sufficientia testimonia, eo quod traditio de dogmate immaculatae conceptionis ista aetate parum nota erat, non inveniebantur" (*ibid.*, 219).

[36] Cf. ANSELMUS, *Oratio ad S. Virginem Mariam 50.52* (PL 158, 949. 953. 955).

[37] ANSELMUS, *De conceptu virg.*, c.18 (PL 158, 451; ed. SCHMIDT, II, 159): ". . . decens erat ut ea puritate qua maior sub Deo nequit intelligi, Virgo illa niteret, cui Deus Pater unicum Filium, quem de corde suo aequalem sibi genitum tamquam se ipsum diligebat, ita dare disponebat, ut naturaliter esset unus idemque communis Dei Patris et Virginis filius . . ."

[38] HONORIUS AUGUSTODUNENSIS, *Sigillum B. Mariae*, c.1 (PL 172, 501): "Maria vocatur amica, quia portavit Patris secreta, *ecce tu pulchra*, coram Deo in humilitate, *ecce tu pulchra*, coram hominibus in castitate. Pulchra virginitate, pulchra fecunditate, pulchra in virtutibus, pulchra in operibus. Pulchra hic laude hominum, pulchra in caelis laude angelorum. Pulchra bis praedicatur, quia sine interiori et exteriori macula declaratur." — FRANCO AFFLIGEMENSIS, *De gratia Dei*, lib. 6 (PL 166, 744): "Ipsa [Sapientia Dei] Mariam sibi in sponsam ab aeterno ordinavit, ipsa in plenitudine temporis castissimum Mariae uterum in tabernaculum sibi sanctificavit, ipsa templum suum in Maria omni gloria et decore super omnium creaturarum visibilium atque invisibilium pulchritudinem adornavit: quantum voluit et quantum nasciturum de ea decuit . . ."

When we read such testimonies in the works of authors who do not clearly deny the Immaculate Conception, e.g. Hervaeus of LeMans,[39], Aelred,[40] Herman,[41] Absalom,[42] and other pious abbots,[43] as well as Alan[44]

[39] HERVAEUS BURGIDOLENSIS, *In epist. II ad Cor.*, 6.5 (PL 181, 1048): "Omnes itaque mortui sunt in peccatis, nemine prorsus excepto, dempta matre Dei, sive originalibus, sive etiam voluntate additis, vel ignorando, vel sciendo, nec faciendo quod justum est." Cf. also *Commentaria in epistolas divi Pauli. Expositio in Epist. ad Rom.*, c.8 (PL 181, 698).

[40] AELREDUS REIVALLENSIS, *In nativitate B. Mariae, sermo* 19 (PL 195, 319): "Sine dubio beatissima Maria, vera scilicet Maria, cujus typum illa Maria tenebat, praecedit omnes. . . . Sed etiam in hoc praecessit, quia prima omnium transivit: illa enim prima fuit de omni humano genere, quae maledictionem primorum parentum evasit. Ideo audire meruit ab angelo: 'Benedicta tu in mulieribus,' (Luc. 1) id est cum omnes mulieres sub maledictione sint, tu sola inter eas mirabilem hanc benedictionem mereris." Cf. also BALDUINUS CANTUARIENSIS, *Tractatus de salutatione angelica* (PL 204, 476): " 'Benedicta tu in mulieribus.' Benedicta plane, primo quidem immunitate communis maledictionis."—It is obvious that these authors attribute to the Blessed Virgin the exemption from the effects of sin rather than exemption from the sin itself.

[41] HERMANNUS TORNACENSIS, *Tractatus de Incarnatione Domini*, c.8 (PL 180, 31): "Quod vero dicitur, 'et custodiret eum,' expositione non indiget, quoniam et priusquam in beata Virgine incarnaretur, et cum in ea clausus fuit, et postquam ex ea natus est, semper eam in omni sanctitate et munditia servavit."

[42] ABSALOM SPRINCKIRSBACENSIS, *In purificatione B. M. V.*, sermo 16 (PL 211, 97-98): " 'Mulier, inquit, si concepto semine peperit masculum' . . . Lex ista data est purificandae, non purificatae; peccatrici, non ab utero sanctificatae; mulieri, non virgini; corruptioni, non integritati . . . Nulla profecto opus est purificatione, ubi non praecessit aliqua macula culpae."

[43] PHILLIPPUS DE HARVENG, *Commentaria in Cantica Canticorum*, lib. 4 c.7 (PL 203, 366-7).—Cf. OGERIUS LUCEDIENSIS, *Sermones XV de sermone Domini in ultima coena*, sermo 13 (PL 184, 941): "Non est in filiis hominum magnus vel parvus, tanta praeditus sanctitate, nec tantae religionis privilegiatus honore, qui non in peccatis fuit conceptus, praeter Matrem Immaculati peccatum non facientis, sed peccata mundi tollentis; de qua, cum de peccatis agitur, nullam prorsus volo habere quaestionem."—AMEDEUS LAUSANNENSIS, *Homiliae de Maria virgine matre*, hom. 7 (PL 188, 1341): "[Maria] pulchra in cogitatu . . . pulchra in actu, pulchra ab ortu usque ad finem" Cf. *ibid.*, col. 1310. 1311-1318. 1338.—Cf. NOGUES D., *Mariologie de saint Bernard*, Tournai-Paris 1947, 38. 39-40.

[44] ALANUS DE INSULIS, *Elucidatio in Cantica Canticorom*, c.4 (PL 210, 80): " 'Tota pulchra es,' id est in corpore et in anima, 'amica mea,' per gratiam et per opera; 'et macula non est in te' venialis et criminalis. Quia nullum credimus in Virgine ante et post conceptum fuisse peccatum"; cf. *ibid.*, c.6 (col. 94): " 'Quae est ista, quae progreditur quasi aurora consurgens?' . . . Aurora solem antecedit, sed ipsa tamen a solis virtute procedit; sic Virgo veri luminis praevia, id est solis justitiae est praenuntia; sed tamen ab ipso spirituali gratia est illuminata. Et vere 'quasi aurora consurgens,' id est tota simul surgens; quia tota fuit sancta et corpore et spiritu splendens.—'Pulchra ut luna, electa ut sol.' . . . Et sicut est pulchra ut luna, imo plus quam luna, quia luna aliquando deficit, ista semper proficit . . . luna aliquam in se habet maculam, ista nullam, ideo 'electa ut sol,' qui in se nullum habet defectum luminis."—It is difficult to say whether Alanus taught the Immaculate Conception or not. In any case, when he says that Mary was without sin before and after conception, he is speaking of the conception of Christ. He says (*ibid.*, col. 61-62): " 'Dum esset rex' Christus . . . 'in accubitu suo,' id est, in me . . . 'nardus mea dedit odorem suum', id est caro mea fragilis, per nardum arborem humilem significata, adventu Spiritus sancti mundata, fomite peccati extincto, in ea dedit odorem suum . . .'"

and the Victorines[45] and in the psalters of the Blessed Virgin,[46] we are inclined to believe that these writers really admitted the pious belief that the Mother of the Redeemer was altogether without stain.

But whatever may be said about those who speak of the Conception, or rather sanctification and purity of the Blessed Virgin, only indirectly and in passing, it is well known that this period produced writings treating explicitly of this subject. When the feast of the Conception of Mary was first introduced, a great controversy flared up about the lawfulness of this feast.[47] Treatises, sermons and letters were written, in which various authors, such as Eadmer, Osbert, Nicholas Magister, Pseudo-Abelard, Pseudo-Peter Cantor, Pseudo-Peter Comestor[48] and others explicitly upheld

---

[45] RICHARDUS A S. VICTORE, *Explicatio in Cantica Canticorum*, c.26 (PL 196, 482)—ADAMUS DE S. VICTORE, *Sequentia in Assumptione B. Virginis* (PL 196, 1502):

> Salve, Verbi sacra parens,
> Flos de spinis, spina carens,
> Flos, spineti gloria.
> Nos spinetum, nos peccati
> spina sumus cruentati,
> sed tu spinae nescia.

—GUALTERUS A S. VICTORE, *Excerpta ex libris contra quattuor Labyrinthos Franciae*, ex libro tertio (PL 199, 1155).—Speaking of the immunity of the Blessed Virgin from all sin, he quotes Lombard, St. Anselm and St. Bernard. Finally, from the text of St. Augustine, "Excepta hac Virgine, de qua cum de peccatis agitur, nullam prorsus haberi volo quaestionem," he concludes: ". . . scimus quod ex omni parte peccatum vicerit." He then proceeds: "Hanc auctoritatem Petrus [Lombardus] positurus ex sensu suo volens pervertere, sicut et caeteras, praemittit. Ex tunc, inquit, id est ab incarnatione intelligenda est sine peccato vixisse. Sic Augustinus ait, excepta hac Virgine, etc. Certum est ergo quod Augustinus non ex tunc, sed absolute quandocumque de peccatis agitur, determinat illam omni modo et tempore debere excipere, contraria istis scholasticis evidentissime definiens, etc. . . . Quippe Spiritu sancto adhuc ex utero matris suae singulariter repleta . . ."

[46] Cf. LE BACHELET (article cited in note 17), 1026-1029; RIUDOR I., S.J., "La Concepción Inmaculada de Maria en la primera mitad del siglo XII," in *Estudios eclesiásticos* 28 (1954) 465-472.

[47] A number of papers dealing with the doctrine of the Immaculate Conception according to the writers of the twelfth century will be found in the *Acta* of the International Mariological Congress held in Rome in 1954 (*Virgo Immaculata*, vol. V: *De Immaculata Conceptione in epocha introductoria scholasticae*, Romae, Academia Mariana Internationalis, 1955). Among them is the work of Father Lucas MODRIĆ, O.F.M., "Doctrina de conceptione B. M. Virginis in controversia saeculi XII" (*ibid.*, pp. 13-73), a part of the doctoral thesis of the same name which he presented in the Pontifical Athenaeum of St. Anthony in 1954. Our special thanks are due to Father Modrić for placing at our disposal photostats of three sermons on the Immaculate Conception preserved in the library of Heiligenkreuz in Austria, cod. 14, f.70r-76r, here indicated as ANONYMUS I, II and III. All three authors treat of our subject in the treatise which they call *Sermo de conceptione Dei Genitricis et semper virginis Mariae*. We give their texts below in notes 122-124.

[48] We omit any reference to Peter of Compostella, who is sometimes mentioned as the first to assert the doctrine of the Immaculate Conception. This author wrote in the first half of the fourteenth century. Cf. MODRIĆ L., "De Petro Compostellano qui primus assertor Immaculatae Conceptionis dicitur," in *Antonianum* 29 (1954) 563-572.

the doctrine of the Immaculate Conception, and some of them undertook the task of refuting the arguments which St. Bernard had brought forward on the other side.

Now when we examine the doctrine of these authors and look for the three elements which were defined in the Bull *Ineffabilis Deus,* it will be useless to expect any explicit mention of the "first instant," [49] with exact distinctions concerning the priority of nature and of time in one and the same instant, or of preservative redemption from all stain of sin applied to the first instant of conception.

For example, Eadmer uses the expressions: *conceptio,*[50] *primordium conceptionis,*[51] *propagatio,*[52] *primordia creationis,*[53] *ortus,*[54] *conceptus.*[55] But if we wish to give an exact meaning to these terms, while it is quite certain that the author had a clear idea of active conception (i.e. of the seed), and incipient passive conception (i.e. of the flesh), it is not easy to determine whether he had a clear notion of conception considered in the first moment in which a person is constituted. And what is said of Eadmer holds for all the others with the possible exception of one or two.[56]

Pseudo-Cantor distinguishes the *generatio* from the *conceptio* which follows *generatio;* while *"generatio* takes place with the cooperation of both sexes, *conceptio* is the office of the mother alone." [57] Pseudo-Abelard says

---

[49] Pius IX, Bulla dogmatica *Ineffabilis Deus,* ed. Tondini A., in *Le encicliche mariane,* Roma 1950, 54.

[50] Eadmerus, *Tractatus de conceptione S. Mariae* (ed. Thurston H. et Slater T., Friburgi Br. 1904, n.9, p. 8): "cum ipsa *conceptio* fundamentum, ut diximus, fuerit habitaculi summi boni . . ."

[51] *Ibid.,* n.13 (p. 15): ". . . cum operante Spiritu sancto construeretur, fundamenti illius initium, *primordium conceptionis* beatae Mariae, quam ipsam aulam nominamus."

[52] *Ibid.,* n.9 (p. 10): ". . . si quid originalis peccati in *propagatione* Matris Dei et Domini mei extitit . . ."

[53] *Ibid.,* n.12 (p. 14): "Igitur si *primordia creationis* illius alio intuitu quam aliorum de propagine Adae prodeuntium considero . . ."

[54] *Ibid.,* n.8 (p. 7): "multis saeculis ante *ortum eius* vel conceptum . . ."

[55] *Ibid.,* n.18 (p. 22-23): "Te igitur, Domina, . . . crediderimne, quaeso, te morte peccati . . . in *tuo conceptu* potuisse praegravari?"

[56] Magister Nicolaus, *Liber de celebranda conceptione B. Mariae contra beatum Bernardum* (ed. Talbot C. H., in *Revue Bénédictine* 64 [1954] 114 lin. 40-45), distinguishes between conception and the infusion of the soul: "probabile videtur in animae virginalis infusione, carnem mundatam fuisse virgineam, quia in suscipienda carne Virginis talis munditia inesse debuit, qualis in suscepta carne Christi postea fuit, videlicet tam legis peccati, quam totius peccati nescia. Quae mundicia nec in conceptione Virgini collata est, quia forte in concupiscentia conceptio facta est, et lex peccati causaliter traducta, nec post animae infusionem dilata, quia tunc et lex causaliter et peccatum realiter inesset, et animam pariter et carnem maculasset. Quae in tantae mundiciae futurae contumeliam inessent, si forte pariter inessent."—For examples of *conceptio* used to signify both the engendering of the body and the infusion of the soul, cf. chapter IV of the present volume, pp. 133, 143, 148, and Document IV, p. 526.

[57] Petrus Ps.-Cantor, *Tractatus* [seu] *Sermo de conceptione beatissimae Virginis Mariae* (ed. Alva et Astorga P., in *Monumenta antiqua immaculatae conceptionis sacratissimae Virginis ex variis auctoribus . . . ,* I, Lovanii 1664, 107-117) 111.

that *"conceptio"* took place when the Virgin "did not yet exist." [58] Pseudo-Comestor writes: "there is *conceptus* and there is *conceptio*. There is the *conceptus* of the mother and the *conceptio* of the offspring." [59] Bernard seems to have used these terms with the opposite meaning, since he argues as follows:

> If she could not have been sanctified before her *conceptus,* because she did not yet exist; nor in the *conceptus* itself, because of the sin which was present; the only possibility remaining is that she received sanctification after the *conceptus,* when already existing in the womb; this sanctification made her nativity holy and free from sin, but not her *conceptio.*[60]

It would seem then that for St. Bernard, the term *conceptus* denotes the offspring, while *conceptio* denotes incipient conception (i.e., of the flesh). Accordingly, when he asks, "since this is so, what reason can be assigned to justify the feast of the *conceptio?*" he seems to take the beginning of her existence in the flesh as the object of the feast. In that case, the Mellifluus Doctor agrees with his adversaries. And even Eadmer himself proposes the difficulty urged by his adversaries against the celebration of the feast of the Conception as follows:

> Since the very process of the formation of her body and its appearance in this world [i.e. its birth] are venerated by all, it would be superfluous to pay honour to that still formless matter which often perishes even before acquiring human shape.[61]

Osbert says clearly:

> That glorious *flesh* of the Blessed Virgin Mary was conceived today, that it might be born into the world.[62]

[58] PETRUS PS.-ABAELARDUS, *Tractatus de conceptione beatae et gloriosae virginis Mariae* (ed. ALVA ET ASTORGA P., work cited above, in note 57, 118-138) 123.

[59] PETRUS PS.-COMESTOR, *Sermo in conceptione B. Virginis* (ed. ALVA ET ASTORGA P., in *Radii solis zeli seraphici . . . ,* Lovanii 1666, 614-623) 618.

[60] BERNARDUS, *Epistola 174* (PL 182, 333), begins by expressing his astonishment that the canons of Lyons had introduced a new feast "quam ritus Ecclesiae nescit, non probat ratio, non commendat antiqua traditio" (333); and he continues (335 f.): "Unde ergo conceptionis sanctitas? An dicitur sanctificatione praeventa, quatenus iam sancta conciperetur, ac per hoc sanctus fuerit et conceptus; quemadmodum sanctificata jam in utero dicitur, ut sanctus consequeretur et ortus? Sed non valuit ante sancta esse, quam esse: siquidem non erat antequam conciperetur. An forte inter amplexus maritales sanctitas se ipsi conceptioni immiscuit, ut simul et sanctificata fuerit, et concepta? Nec hoc quidem admittit ratio. Quomodo namque aut sanctitas absque Spiritu sanctificante, aut sancto Spiritui societas cum peccato fuit? aut certe peccatum quomodo non fuit, ubi libido non defuit?" Shortly thereafter follow the lines we have cited in the text: "Si igitur ante conceptum sui sanctificari minime potuit, quoniam non erat; sed nec in ipso quidem conceptu, propter peccatum quod inerat: restat ut post conceptum in utero jam existens, sanctificationem accepisse credatur, quae excluso peccato sanctam fecerit nativitatem, non tamen et conceptionem."

[61] EADMERUS, *Tractatus,* n.3 (p. 3).

[62] OSBERTUS DE CLARA, *Sermo de conceptione S. Mariae* (ed. THURSTON H. et SLATER T., in *Eadmeri monachi cantuariensis Tractatus de conceptione S. Mariae,* Friburgi Br. 1904, 65-83) 66.

Bernard, unable to see "how sin can fail to be present where concupiscence is not absent," [63] proposed the following dilemma:

> How, I ask, can a *conceptus* be styled holy, which is not of the Holy Spirit (lest I say, which is of sin);—or how can a feast be celebrated which is anything but holy? [64]

His adversaries were fully persuaded that God could ensure that the Virgin's flesh be sinless in its very beginnings, either by wiping out the morbid infection of the flesh, or by preserving it from infection. Osbert says that Mary was "purified even bodily from all stain." Indeed, he asks:

> Why should we be surprised if God sanctified the glorious matter of the Virgin's body in its very conception, when He willed to sanctify Jeremias and certain others while still in their mothers' wombs? [65]

Master Nicholas believes that her flesh was:

> . . . cleansed from the leprosy of corruption.[66]

Some speak of the sinlessness of Our Lady's parents and of their having intercourse without experiencing carnal pleasure. They also speak of a stainless cell of flesh which was transmitted from Adam down to them.

Apropos of this, Pseudo-Comestor writes:

> It can be believed that the flesh which was assumed by the Word existed in the first moment after the corruption of the whole human race, but was preserved free from all contagion of sin and remained so until the moment of its being assumed by the Son of God, and was never weighed down by the least burden of sin.[67]

This was highly fitting, because Mary's flesh was to a certain extent the flesh of Christ, and the opprobrium of the Mother redounds on the Son. Pseudo-Abelard says:

> There is no doubt that whatever the Son does to enhance the honor of His Mother conduces to His own praise.[68]

To sum up, let us say: the authors who in the twelfth century defended the liceity and opportuneness of the feast of the Conception of the Blessed Virgin, fixed as object of this feast the chaste and stainless beginning of her virginal flesh. Their argumentation is founded principally on the Divine Maternity, and also is expressed in the formula "Potuit, voluit, fecit"—'He could do it, He willed to do it, He did it.' The origin of

---

[63] S. Bernardus, *Epist. 174,* 335. (Cited in note 60, above)

[64] *Ibid.,* col. 336.

[65] Osbertus de Clara, *Epistola ad Anselmum* (ed. Thurston H. et Slater T. in *op. cit.,* 53-59) 56: "Et quid mirum si in ipsa conceptione omnipotens deus illam gloriosam materiam virginei corporis sanctificavit quando ieremiam quosdamque alios in utero materno constitutos sanctificare voluit?"

[66] Magister Nicolaus, *Liber,* 114.

[67] Petrus Ps.-Comestor, *Sermo,* 615.

[68] Petrus Ps.-Abaelardus, *Tractatus,* 136.

the Virgin's flesh should be celebrated because it is the beginning of our redemption. Pseudo-Cantor declares:

> All the faithful, with unanimous devotion, honor the venerable day of the most holy conception of the Mother of God, because through it the earth was freed from a darkening mist, and there gleamed a new dawn, productive of a new sun; through its instrumentality, a special grace of Providence bestowed a saving Pasch on the children of Adam who were sitting in the shadow of death.[69]

Eadmer expresses practically the same idea in the first words of his treatise:

> As I was about to meditate on the source from which salvation comes, there came into my mind the thought of the feast which is celebrated today in many places, in honor of the Conception of Mary, the blessed Mother of God.[70]

This is really the great joyous reason why the feast should be celebrated and retained, as Pseudo-Abelard says, "even though she was conceived in sin."[71] And he explains his opinion as follows:

> I do not think that anybody, were he to find the couch on which the Mother of God was conceived, would fail to show it reverence. Her sepulchre and the garments which clothed her holy body we regard as priceless relics, and venerate them profoundly; yet these do not participate in the glory of her resurrection and eternal beatitude, since they are extrinsic to her body. How great therefore should be the honour given to that seed of which Mary's and the Lord's bodies were formed; and should we not offer grateful thanks to God for the very beginnings of our redemption, in that He gave us this seed and caused it to be such a fruitful source of grace?[72]

Osbert exclaims:

> If the conception of the servant, John the Baptist, be celebrated, what should be done for that of the Mother of the Lord![73]

Though the question posed was not whether Our Lady was conceived in original sin, but rather, whether it was licit and becoming to celebrate the feast of the Conception; though, too, great confusion reigns concerning the precise meaning of the terms used, especially *conceptio, conceptus, generatio, ortus, sanctificatio, mundatio, purgatio,* etc.; yet it cannot be said that none of the above-mentioned authors who defend the feast of the Conception agree with the Bull *Ineffabilis Deus* that the Mother of God was immune "from every stain of original sin in the first instant of her conception." For Eadmer speaks about the *"exordium," "primordium"*

---

[69] Petrus Ps.-Cantor, *Sermo,* 107.

[70] Eadmerus, *Tractatus,* n.1 (p. 1): "Principium quo salus mundo processit mihi considerare volenti occurrit hodierna solemnitas, quae de conceptione beatae matris Dei Mariae multis in locis festiva recolitur."

[71] Ps.-Abaelardus, *Tractatus,* 123.

[72] *Ibid.,* 135.

[73] Osbertus de Clara, *Epistola ad Anselmum,* 56.

and *"primordia"* of the conception and the creation of the Blessed Virgin.[74] Osbert, too, uses the expressions *"in ipsa conceptione,"*[75] *"in ipso creationis et conceptionis exordio."* [76]   Others speak of *conceptio* as something distinct from *conceptus,* and of a *generatio* that is distinct from conception.   In all these cases, it is extremely difficult to show that the authors are thinking about consummated conception, namely that which is accomplished in the first instant in which a person as such begins to exist.   One thing at least is certain: they all wish to ward off from the Virgin every stain of original sin, from the very first beginnings of her existence.

Hence, while we must admit that these first defenders of the Marian privilege possess substantially the doctrine of Mary's exemption from all stain of original sin that has been defined in the Bull *Ineffabilis Deus,* it would be an exaggeration to seek in their works the technical terminology used in the Bull.   Thus, for example, Osbert writes:

> The Most High therefore sanctified His tabernacle and cleansed the virginal fabric and bridal couch that rests on the seven columns of the Holy Spirit *from all uncleanness in the first beginnings of its creation and conception in the mother's womb;* He so thoroughly purified and illumined it that He left no impurity in that flesh from which the flesh of our Redemption was destined to be taken.[77]

Noyon translates: "In the very moment when Mary was conceived and created, He preserved her from every stain." [78]   But there is question of "beginnings," not of a "moment"; and Osbert speaks of *cleansing,* not of *preserving*: he made clean that which was unclean.   The imperfection of terminology is manifest: withal it is possible to deduce the idea from it.

Likewise, when Eadmer excludes from the Virgin Mother everything savoring of original sin, using such expressions as:

> . . . with every stain of the human condition taken away . . .[79]
> Thou must have been purer than all.[80]
> Thou camest forth from the root of Jesse . . . untainted by any sin.[81]

—we may conclude that in his opinion the Blessed Virgin was conceived without original sin in the very moment that she was constituted a person.

[74] EADMERUS, *Tractatus,* n.3 (p. 3). Cf. *supra,* p. 173.

[75] OSBERTUS DE CLARA, *Epistola ad Anselmum,* 56.

[76] *Ibid.,* 57.

[77] *Ibidem.*

[78] NOYON A., *Les origines de la fête de l'Immaculée Conception en Occident,* in *Etudes* 41 (1904) 762.

[79] EADMERUS, *Tractatus,* n.13 (p. 16): ". . . remota omni labe conditionis humanae . . ."

[80] *Ibid.,* n.19 (p. 24).

[81] *Ibid.,* n.20 (p. 24): "Ego, piissima Domina, ego tuus qualiscumque servulus, ego scio, credo et confiteor quia inde ex radice Iesse pulcherrima, ac per hoc omni quod te aliquatenus decoloraret peccati vulnere aliena prodisti, et integerrima permanens florem speciosissimum protulisti."

But it would be an exaggeration to claim that Eadmer knows the terms *primum instans* and *preserved* as applied to the doctrine.[82]

If we turn now to the other fundamental question, the attribution of the Immaculate Conception to the merits of Christ, nowhere do we find a formula comparable to that of *Ineffabilis,* "preserved through the merits of Jesus Christ, Saviour of the human race."

We may legitimately suspect that this doctrine was held substantially by the first defenders of the Marian privilege, from what has been said about the doctrine of St. Anselm, whose subsequent influence was immense. He ascribed both the personal sanctity of those who were sanctified before Christ's Passion, and the purity of the Blessed Virgin, to the anticipated merits of Christ the Redeemer. After asserting that the Passion of Christ was so great and such that "its effects extend even to those who are absent in time and place," [83] he applies this principle to the Blessed Virgin, saying that she was pure through His future death [83a] and obtained her purity "through faith." [84]

This point is very important, particularly in view of the controversy which raged in the following century, with a negative result, as to whether the exemption of the Blessed Virgin from all sin was reconcilable with the universality of Christ's Redemption, on account of the universality of original sin. We must therefore proceed slowly, and carefully distinguish what is certain from what is spurious or doubtful. Although some of these first defenders did say that the Blessed Virgin owed her complete sanctity to her Son, nevertheless their teaching is so inconstant, so confused, and so casually mentioned, that no one ever thought of solving the great problem as to how Anselm's opinion, attributing the purity of the Blessed Virgin to the anticipated merits of Christ, could be reconciled with the opinion which held that she was not just pure and cleansed from sin, but in fact had never contracted sin at all.

Let us look first of all at the doctrine of Eadmer, in the passage which is usually quoted in favor of preservative redemption, namely:

> To this dignity, neither the most blessed of virgins, nor the throng of the elect, would ever have ascended if the Son of God had not descended from the bosom of the Father to destroy the sin of Adam by assuming human nature (*hominem*) from the Virgin.[85]

The context shows that we may not deduce the conclusion formulated by Vacandard, to wit: "the merits of her Son became applicable to her as

---

[82] Del Marmol (work cited in note 2), 50, is inexact when he translates the expression of Eadmerus "primordia creationis" as "the first instants of your creation." The same remark applies to the word *préservé* (p. 38. 43. 53), which does not exist in the Latin text of Eadmerus and ought not to appear in the French translation.

[83] Anselmus, *Cur Deus homo,* II, c.16 (PL 158, 418; ed. Schmidt, II, 118).

[83a] Anselmus, *Cur Deus homo,* II, c.16 (PL 158, 419; ed. Schmidt II, 119).

[84] Anselmus, *De conceptu virginali,* c.18 (PL 158, 451; ed. Schmidt II, 159).

[85] Eadmerus, *Tractatus,* n.25 (p. 32).

well as to other men, but they were applied to her at the very moment of her conception rather than later." [86]   Eadmer in the whole of this chapter proves how human nature would have been deprived of various dignities, "if the first man had not lost paradise on account of his sin." [87]   If Adam had not sinned, Christ would not have come, and consequently Mary would not have been the Mother of God.

In other passages, Eadmer asserts that nobody escaped damnation before the advent of the Son of Mary; [88] that the Son wished His mother to be pure; [89] that Mary was indebted to her Son for her Queenship; [90] that:

> He was able, from the sinful mass, to make a human nature free of all stain of sin, which He could take unto His person so as to be an integral human being (*homo*), without any diminution of His divinity.[91]

—that "the wisdom and power of God" which preserved the angels from sin "could keep His future mother free" also,[92] and so on.

From this some theologians conjecture that she was made clean and immune from sin by Christ Himself, the Redeemer of the human race.[93]

[86] VACANDARD E., *Études de critique et d'histoire religieuse,* IIIème série, Paris 1912, 249.

[87] EADMERUS, *Tractatus,* n.25 (p. 31).

[88] *Ibid.,* n.17 (p. 20).

[89] *Ibid.,* n.19 (pp. 23f.).

[90] *Ibid.,* n.25-28 (pp. 31-35).

[91] *Ibid.,* n.17 (p. 22): "Poterat ergo de massa peccatrice naturam humanam ab omni labe peccati immunem facere, unde in unam personam sui susciperet, ut homo integer esset et divinitati suae nihil minueret."

[92] *Ibid.,* n.13 (p. 16).

[93] Cf. DEL MARMOL (work cited in note 2), pp. 22 f.: "Vient enfin l'objection tirée de la Rédemption nécessaire à la Vierge aussi bien qu'aux autres hommes. . . . Eadmer auquel sans doute cette difficulté n'avait pas été proposée, n'exprimera pas encore dans toute sa clarté l'admirable explication adoptée par l'Eglise, mais il l'insinuera déjà en plusieurs endroits avec une intuition merveilleuse de ce mystère. La conception de Marie et la gloire de sa royauté qui en est le terme, il les attribue toujours au Fils incarné et rédempteur."
The same theory, more or less, was defended in the International Mariological Congress in Rome in 1954, by Monsignor H. F. DAVIS ("Theologia Immaculatae Conceptionis apud primos defensores, scil. in Anglia saec. XII" in the *Acta* of the Congress, *Virgo Immaculata,* vol. V, *De Immaculata Conceptione in epocha introductoria scholasticae,* Romae, Academia Mariana Internationalis, 1955, pp. 1-12) and Father G. GEENEN ("Eadmer, le premier théologien de l'Immaculée Conception," *ibid.,* pp. 90-136). But in that same Congress, Father B. DEL MARMOL declared ("Marie Corédemptrice.—Eadmer enseigna-t-il que Marie rachetante fut rachetée?" *ibid.,* pp. 194-201): "Comme Eadmer, quand il écrivit au XIIme siècle son traité de la conception immaculée de la Vierge Marie, la première et la meilleure apologie de ce privilège dont on n'aurait jamais dû s'écarter, on éprouve une répugnance absolue de parler de péché, en fait ou en droit, quand il s'agit de celle dont le docte et pieux moine de Cantorbéry disait si admirablement: 'Après Dieu on ne peut concevoir rien de plus grand que Marie' " (p. 199).
"Jésus Fils de Dieu et rédempteur et Marie Mère de Dieu Corédemptrice sont dans un ordre à part au-dessus de toutes les créatures. Ils ne peuvent être compris dans le décret de condemnation de la race d'Adam. Ils n'ont rien à voir avec le péché sinon pour le détruire, pour écraser la tête du serpent infernal. *Ils sont essentiellement*

But it is well to note that the words of Eadmer do not exclude the possible interpretation that the "Wisdom of God," to which he attributes the purity of the Blessed Virgin, is not the Incarnate Word, but the Godhead in general.[94] Indeed, Eadmer sometimes ascribes to the "Wisdom of God" those operations which are commonly attributed to God the Father, for example, the creation of man, instituting or decreeing the liberation of the human race from damnation, and so on.[95]

Further, when the author explicitly mentions the difficulties which arise from the universality of original sin, he does not say a single word about the efficacy or the anticipation of the merits of Christ, but, acknowledging his ignorance about the manner in which Mary was made free from original sin, he has recourse to the omnipotence of God: ". . . utterly free from any stain of sin, through a unique and—to human minds—inscrutable power and operation of God," and "in her conception, she was not bound by the same law as others." [96]

---

immaculés par la volonté toute libre et toute sainte de la divine Trinité." (p. 201).— It is important to differentiate between what we, in the twentieth century, conclude from the principles of the medieval authors, and what they actually taught. It is plain enough that the writers of the twelfth century had no sort of preservative redemption in mind! Consequently, any attempts to interpret their words as though they substantially admitted what we now call preservative redemption, are leading nowhere. In this respect we are gratified to note that our point of view is confirmed by Dr. Del Marmol, who held quite a different opinion about Eadmer in 1904, because the theological winds were then blowing in a different direction. We do not agree with Fr. Del Marmol about the main point at issue, but we do agree in interpreting the doctrine of Eadmer. Each one, right or wrong, has a right to his own opinion.

[94] Cecchin A., "Bulla Ineffabilis Deus et Eadmerus," in *Marianum* 7 (1944) 107: "Quod Eadmerus non cogitaverit de *praeredemptione* B. V. Mariae colligi potest etiam ex responsione data difficultati ex textu S. Pauli desumptae: *Omnes homines in Adam peccaverunt.* Auctor noster nedum non respuit veritatem huius sententiae, immo eam fortius affirmat. Nihilominus testatur Mariam *a lege naturae aliorum* liberam fuisse, et quidem non intuitu Christi Redemptoris, sed virtute divina, et utpote supra omnes creatas res constitutam."—Eadmerus *Tractatus*, n.17 (p. 21-22): "Necesse . . . fuit ut natura, de qua se hominem facere volebat [Deus], et humana et munda ab omnis peccati contagio esset. Quod ubi inveniret, cum, ut dixi, nihil incorruptum vitiata cunctorum radice existeret? Sed *qui humanae perditioni subvenire disponebat, Dei virtus et Dei sapientia nuncupatur.* Itaque ad omnia quae vult posse suppetit illi, nec sapientiae illius ullus est numerus, quae pertingit *a fine usque ad finem, cuncta disponens. Poterat ergo de massa peccatrice naturam humanam ab omni labe peccati immunem facere,* unde in unam personam sui susciperet, ut homo integer esset et divinitati suae nihil minueret. Praedestinata fuit et praeordinata in hoc opus mirabile . . . Maria . . . ab aeternae mortis interitu paventium ac sub eius praesidium confugientium tutum iuvamen atque redemptio."

[95] Eadmerus, *Tractatus*, n.17 (p. 20). See preceding note.—*Ibid.*, n.9 (p. 8): "Haec igitur Virgo, tanti Filii dignissima parens, cum in alvo suae parentis naturali lege conciperetur, quis non concedat Dei sapientiam, a fine usque ad finem pertingentem, cuncta implentem, cuncta regentem, novo quodam et ineffabili gaudio caelum, terram, et omnia quae in eis sunt, perfudisse."—Cf. *ibid.*, n.13 (p. 15).

[96] Eadmerus, *Tractatus*, n.12 (p. 12-13): "cum eminentiam gratiae Dei in te considero, sicut te non intra omnia, sed supra omnia quae praeter Filium tuum facta sunt, inaestimabili modo contueor, ita te non lege naturae aliorum in tua conceptione devinctam fuisse opinor, *sed singulari et humano intellectui impenetrabili divinitatis virtute et operatione ab omnis peccati admixtione liberrimam.*"

Again, Mary's body had to be free from all sin, because "the power of God" and "the power of the Godhead" predestined her to such a peak of perfection.[97] For since the almighty and all-wise God, "in the eternity of His counsel," [98] purposed to give His Son a most worthy, and therefore most pure, mother, he gave to this woman both the purest flesh and personal holiness, and adorned her in such a way with all gifts that the Word would choose her for His mother.

Finally, whatever may be said about a few passing expressions which seem to recall Anselm's opinion about the anticipated merits of Christ applied to His Mother, the main point is that Eadmer never even thought of the very serious problems which were to arise a century later about the sanctification of the Mother of God, as to how she was redeemed by Christ if she had not been conceived in sin.

This can be appreciated by the following consideration. It is known that mediaeval writers normally taught that one of the principal effects of the Redemption was the opening of the gate of heaven, which had been closed by the sin of the first parents, so that, since all their descendants contract the same sin, none of them can enter heaven, not even the holy patriarchs, nor John the Baptist, nor Jeremias, who had been sanctified and justified, until the Passion of Christ had really taken place. Thus John Duns Scotus asks the question: "If she had died before Christ's Passion, would she have been beatified?" (supposing that she had, in fact, been exempted from original sin through the merits of Christ's Passion).[99] The Subtle Doctor denies the consequence, teaching both that Mary was preserved from incurring the sin through the merits of the Passion of Christ, and that perhaps she would not have entered into heaven because God had ordained otherwise.[100] Eadmer poses the difficulty and solution in a different way:

> If it is said that, if you had died before the birth of your Son, you would not have avoided the law of sin any more than the rest of men [i.e. you would not have been able to enter into paradise] . . .

He considers this an idle question:

> . . . this is ridiculous, and not worthy of an answer.[101]

—considering not the Redemption, but the predestination and power of God. For if God decreed from all eternity that Mary was to be the

[97] *Ibid.*, n.18 (p. 22).

[98] *Ibid.*, n.13 (p. 16).

[99] I. Duns Scotus, *Theologiae marianae elementa* (ed. Balić C., in *Bibliotheca mariana medii aevi,* II), Sibenici 1933, 41.—For the edition of Scotus' texts on the Immaculate Conception, see below, note 209.

[100] *Ibid.*, 41-42.

[101] Eadmerus, *Tractatus,* n.19 (p. 23): "Quod si dicitur te, si ante partum beati Filii tui praeventa corporis morte fuisses, originalis peccati legem aliorum more evadere non potuisse, inepte dicitur, nec tanti est ut ei respondeatur."

mother of His Son, it is idle to ask what would have happened had she not actually become so, since God's eternal decrees necessarily come to pass.[102]

If even Anselm's secretary, in his defense of the Marian privilege, suffered from the grave lacuna of not endeavouring to reconcile the exemption of a creature from original sin with the universal Redemption of Christ, what shall we say about the doctrine of the others?

It is true that Osbert affirms, in reply to the infidels and heretics:

> The children of the Mother of grace do not celebrate the act of sin, but solemnly proclaim the manifold joys of the beginning of our Redemption.[103]

We read the words of Master Nicholas, that in Mary is the "fullness of grace" through Christ;[104] and he continues:

> For if she had contracted sin from her parents, she would have been founded on the old Adam and not on the newness of Christ. But, "He who was born in her was her foundation," so that the building should match the foundation, and with the new shoot wholly consonant with the root from which it sprang, the fruit should be like the tree that had engendered it."[105]

The quotation from Osbert does not suggest that he is saying anything different from what he says elsewhere, namely that the feast of the Conception was instituted because it is "the salutary beginning of our Redemption,"[106] namely, because then was conceived the flesh from which would be taken the flesh which was to suffer for us. This was the general idea of the defenders of the Marian privilege in the twelfth century, and it was the same idea that Eadmer laid down at the beginning of his treatise, when he spoke about "the source (*principium*) from which the salvation of the world proceeded,"[107] which Pseudo-Abelard expressed in the words,

---

[102] *Ibid.*, n.19 (p. 23): "Qualiter enim mater Dei futura praeordinata fuisses, si ad hoc te, qui praeordinavit, Deus, non perduxisset? Nam in Deo non est, est et non, sed simplex est in illo est. An mors valentior esse posset Deo, de cuius manu valet quiquam rapere nemo?

[103] Osbertus de Clara, *Epistola ad Warinum* (ed. Thurston H. et Slater T., in *Eadmeri Tractatus* as cited above, in note 50, 60-64) 63: ". . . filii matris gratiae non de actu peccati celebritatem faciunt, sed *de primitiis redemptionis nostrae* multiplicia sanctae novitatis gaudia solemniter ostendunt."

[104] Magister Nicolaus, *Liber* (as cited above, in note 56), 113: "Ego totus pulcher, quia in me et ex me omnis pulchritudo; tu tota pulchra, quia in te ex me gratiae plenitudo, et ex te per me gratiae plenitudo, et per te in omnes gratiae participatio."

[105] *Ibid.*, 112: "Si enim ex parentibus peccatum traduxisset, vetustas quidem Adae, *non novitas Christi eam fundasset*. Sed qui natus est in ea fundavit eam, ut edificio fundamento apte cohaerente et pullulante ramo propaganti radici per omnia consonante, talis esset fructus in ea natus, qualis arbor in qua natus est."

[106] Osbertus a Clara, *Epistola ad Anselmum*, 55: "celebris instituta est illius diei recordatio, de cuius summa redemptionis nostrae salutari processit exordio."

[107] Eadmerus, *Tractatus*, n.1 (p. 1). See above, note 70.

"the beginning of the salvation of mankind," [108] and which Master Nicholas had in mind when he spoke of "announcing the beginning of salvation through Mary." [109]

The last-named author, who is considered by many to be one of the greatest defenders of the Marian privilege,[110] indicates the purpose of the feast of the Conception thus, at the end of his disquisition:

> The reason for the [feast of the] Conception is the grace of our salvation which was announced in it, . . . the laying of the foundation of the temple in which the fullness of the Godhead dwelt bodily, . . . the construction of the bridal chamber in which God the Father joined the Church to His Son and celebrated their nuptials. The reason for the Conception is the unfathomable mystery of our Redemption, which indeed is contained principally in the Passion, Resurrection and Ascension of the Lord, but is adorned and, as it were, announced by certain preceding solemnities, such as the Annunciation and Nativity of the Lord. And these, in turn, are announced by the Conception and Nativity of her to whom the Announcement of the Redemption was made, and of whom the Redeemer was born.[111]

It will be worth while considering this text separately. In the beginning of his treatise, Nicholas had said that John the Baptist and the Blessed Virgin have certain particular solemnities "inasmuch as they fulfilled an office in connection with our Redemption," [112] and that in their conception and nativity, "the sacrament of our Redemption is begun." [113] He further describes how the reason (*causa*) for the Blessed Virgin's procreation was "the beginning of our salvation," because "the fountain of grace sprang from the soil of her flesh." [114] It is clear therefore that the solemnities which precede the feasts of the Passion and Resurrection of Christ are not celebrated because deriving their sanctity from the mystery of the Cross, but as the announcement and ornament of the Redemption.

---

[108] Ps.-ABAELARDUS, *Tractatus* (as cited above, in note 58), 127: "Unde ergo conceptionem Mariae magis quam adventum Christi poteris improbare, et non potius tam conceptionem quam nativitatem maxime commendare, in quibus consistere videtur totius *exordium salutis humanae?*"; *ibid.*, 128: ". . . *conceptio . . . ipsius atque nativitas totius naturae salutis facta est causa.*" Cf. *ibid.*, 133.

[109] MAGISTER NICOLAUS, *Liber,* 111: "in celebratione conceptae Virginis non nunciatae sanctitatis in ipsa, sed nunciandae salvationis per ipsam primordia, votivo gaudiorum festo excolimus."

[110] Cf. MILDNER F., "The Immaculate Conception in the Writings of Nicholas of St. Albans," in *Marianum* 2 (1940) 173-193.

[111] MAGISTER NICOLAUS, *Liber,* 116.

[112] *Ibid.*, 92-93: "Praecursor igitur pariter et mater Salvatoris non solum officii singularis, sed et meriti incomparabili insigniti privilegio, sicut naturae conditione ceteris hominibus similes, sed gratiae dono prae ceteris hominibus sublimati, etiam in merito ceteris dissimiles extitere, ita quasdam habere solemnitates eos contigit secundum quod communi lege humanitatis migraverunt a saeculo, et quasdam singulares secundum quod officium redemptioni nostrae congruum exercuerunt . . ."

[113] *Ibid.*, 93: "Porro ex officii privilegio Praecursori indultum est quod eius nativitas, matri vero Virgini quod eius conceptio simul et nativitas celebri cultu veneraretur, quia in *ipsis quodam modo initiatur nostrae redemptionis sacramentum.*"

[114] *Ibid.*, 93.

Further, Master Nicholas, after declaring that:

> the institution of a feast of the Conception is neither justified by holiness propagated in the conception, nor prohibited by sin, either committed actually by the parents, or contracted *originaliter* by the offspring, in the conception; [115]

and after admitting that Mary was probably quite stainless at all times so that there was never any sin in her; goes on to say that she was "sanctified by the Holy of Holies," [116] i.e., by her Creator.

If this was the doctrine of those who held Mary to have been born by natural generation, what teaching shall we expect to find in those writers, such as pseudo-Comestor and others, who speak of a healthy germ preserved in the body of Adam, from which the bodies of both Mary and Christ were formed, so that the Body of Christ cleansed the Blessed Virgin from any original sin in her very conception, sanctified and purified her in every way? [117] What shall we say of the opinion of pseudo-Abelard, pseudo-Cantor and others, who explained the Immaculate Conception by saying that the blessed Virgin was conceived without concupiscence and without lust? [118] Do any of these theories solve the problem whether, if Mary neither had nor could have had original sin, Christ could be called the universal Redeemer? How could Redemption be needed by one who neither had nor could have had sin, because not born in the ordinary way or by the concupiscence normal to human generation?

In brief, St. Bernard's opinion, that the Blessed Virgin was conceived in

---

[115] *Ibid.*, 116: "Institutionem festivae conceptionis nec sanctitas in conceptione propagata approbat, nec peccatum in conceptione vel actualiter perpetratum a parentibus, vel originaliter traductum a prole, reprobat."

[116] *Ibid.*, 112: "Tota pulchra es, quia nihil quod turpe est, in te est, quia a sapientia es aedificata; et tota pulchra es, quia omne quod pulchrum est, in te est, cum sis gratia plena, a Sancto sanctorum sanctificata, et macula non est in te, nec originis traducta, nec voluntate super ducta, quia a fundamento praeter quod non est aliud, es fundata."

[117] PETRUS Ps.-COMESTOR, *Sermo* (as cited above, in note 59), 615: ". . . in massa naturae nostrae corruptae in Adam, *divina gratia venam quamdam reservavit*, velut quoddam (ut ita dicam) arminium: illam videlicet patriarcharum et prophetarum progeniem, ex qua Dominus noster humanam dignatus est sine peccati corruptione naturam assumere. . . . Unde credi potest, carnem illam quae assumpta est a Verbo, post corruptionem totius humanae naturae in primo parente, ita tamen illaesam, et ab omni contagione peccati immunem custoditam, ut usque ad susceptionem sui a Dei Filio semper libera manserit, et nulli umquam peccato vel modicum pensum reddiderit. Non enim decuit, ut caro illa peccato se aliquando obnoxiam cognoverit . . ."—A similar notion is developed in ANONYMUS I, *Sermo* (as cited above, in note 47), 70ra-72va.

[118] PETRUS Ps.-ABAELARDUS, *Tractatus*, 129: "Quid enim nos impedit credere *hanc gratiam Dominum parentibus suae Genitricis posse et velle conferre*: ut absque omni carnalis concupiscentiae labe sanctissimum illud corpusculum generarent, quod solum sensuit dignum suae incarnationis honore?—Non dubitamus parentes primos sine peccato ad humani generis propagationem in paradiso filios esse procreatos [the original has here a false reading: *procuratos*]: et quicumque deinceps generaret, hanc habiturus gratiam, si priores illi inoboedientiae non incurrissent culpam. Quod ergo de omnibus esset commune, cur conferri non potuit parentibus Mariae?"

original sin and sanctified in the womb, was the general opinion in the twelfth century.[119] But some writers, although convinced of the universality of both original sin and the Redemption, found that their sense of piety and faith [120] would not allow them to admit that the Mother of God had been conceived in original sin.[121] They were motivated by the principles of fittingness [122] and analogy,[123] by the eternal predestination of the

[119] Regarding the doctrine of the Immaculate Conception in the twelfth century, Le Bachelet rightly observes, *art. cit.*, 1028-29: "Il y eut donc au XII siècle un progrés notable dans le développement de la croyance à la sainteté originelle de la mère de Dieu, mais il s'en faut de beaucoup que cette croyance ait été alors commune ou même prépondérante. La plupart s'en tenaient à la sanctification *in utero,* avec des nuances cependant. Les uns regardaient cette sanctification comme postérieure à la conception proprement dite, qu'ils supposaient faite dans le péché . . . D'autres affirment simplement que Marie fut sanctifiée dans le sein de sa mère, sans rien ajouter qui exprime ou suppose une relation de priorité et de postériorité entre la conception proprement dite et la sanctification . . . D'autres, enfin, ou parlent d'une façon dubitative . . . ou proposent même une disjonctive . . ."

[120] Cf. Balić C., "Il senso cristiano e il progresso del dogma," in *Gregorianum* 32 (1952) 106-134; *Idem,* "Il senso cristiano e i dogmi mariani," in *Studi frances-cani* 51 (1954) 187-209; Dillenschneider Cl., *Le sens de la foi et le progrès dogmatique du mystère marial (Bibliotheca mariana moderni aevi* II) Roma 1954.

[121] As a rule this thesis of the complete purity and holiness of Mary was put forward quite tentatively. For example, Nicholas of St. Alban's, *Liber,* 93-94, writes: "Modum vero propagationis, sicut et assumptionis eius, sub ignorantiae sigillo clausum tenere pietas elegit christiana . . . non tantum conceptionis occultum, sed et totius infantiae ipsius secretum, mater nostra universalis Ecclesia in sana doctrina reputat totum ex pietate ignorare, ne si ex traduce peccati doceat propagatam, in contumeliam fiat tantae integritatis, sin autem absque conscientia peccati, in prae-iudicium Verbi incarnandi singularitatis."—Eadmer himself writes (*Tractatus,* n.12, p. 13-14): "Quod si aliquis ipsam Dei genitricem usque ad Christi annuntiationem originali peccato obnoxiam asserit, ac sic fide qua angelo credidit inde mundatam . . . si catholicum est non nego, licet altior consideratio mentem meam ab hoc divel-lat . . ." Cf. *ibid.,* n.9 (p. 9 f.).

[122] Eadmerus, *Tractatus,* n.10 (p. 11): "Si Deus castaneae confert ut infra spinas a spinis remota concipiatur, alatur, formetur; non potuit dare corpori humano, quod ipse sibi templum [parabat], in quo corporaliter habitaret, et de quo in unitate suae personae perfectus homo fieret, ut licet inter spinas peccatorum conciperetur, ab ipsis tamen spinarum aculeis omnimodis exors redderetur? Potuit plane. Si igitur voluit, fecit"; *ibid.,* n.12 (p. 13): "Quia ergo ita fieri oportebat, Matrem de qua talis crearetur, mundam esse ab omni peccato decebat"; Anonymus I, *Sermo,* 70va: "Quare imprudenter attestaris Matrem Domini eo quod concepta est, fore com-munem iniuriam non solum Matris sed Filii, qui illam antequam esset, mundavit: iniuria matris redundat in filium et qui maledicit matri, maledicit et filio. . . . Nonne vides, cum Matrem Domini ob temporalem conceptionem a sanctificatione seiungis, dicens eius conceptionem qua ipsa concepta est, esse non sanctam nec celebrio dig-nam, in ipsum Deum, qui unum corpus erat cum Matre, te nimium incaute incur-risse?"; *ibid.,* 72ra: "Si 'ab initio et ante saecula creata sum,' id est praescita et praedestinata, ut eius caro et sanguis origo sit nostri Salvatoris, quomodo mox, ut ipsa sacratissima Virgo esse cepit, mundata in sua conceptione non esse . . . ?"; Petrus Ps.-Cantor, *Tractatus,* 116: "Non enim divinam decebat facetiam et puritatem, ut ex carne cicatrizata sibi nascendi materiam assumeret; quod quidem contigisset, si caro virginalis per peccati corruptionem in sui primordio vulnerata, tametsi postea sanata per sanctificationem, extitisset"; Petrus Ps.-Comestor, *Sermo,* 616: ". . . ve-risimile est, ut et Mater Christi solam carnem et nullam penitus maculam a parentibus contraxerit; praesertim cum una et eadem caro sit Matris et Filii, et qualis Agnus,

Blessed Virgin to be the Mother of God, by the purpose of the Incarnation —which was to destroy sin and open the gate of heaven to us all,[124] and by a number of biblical and patristic texts.[125]

---

talis et Mater Agni"; PETRUS PS.-ABAELARDUS, *Tractatus*, 135: ". . . quanto magis autem illi semini, unde tam Mariae quam Domini corpus est formatum, honorem nos convenit exhibere debitum; et de hoc ipso nostrae redemptionis exordio grates persolvere Domino, quod et ipsum semen dedit, et in tantam gratiam multiplicavit?"; cf. *ibid.*, 137. (For complete references to EADMERUS, ANONYMUS I, PETRUS PS.-CANTOR, PETRUS PS.-COMESTOR and PETRUS PS.-ABAELARDUS, see above, notes 50, 47, 57, 59 and 58, respectively.)

[123] Authors cite the example of Jeremias and St. John the Baptist.—Cf. EADMERUS, *Tractatus*, n.9 (p. 9): "Si igitur Ieremias, quia in gentibus erat propheta futurus, in vulva est sanctificatus, et Ioannes, Dominum in spiritu et virtute Eliae praecessurus, Spiritu sancto est ex utero matris suae repletus, quis dicere audeat singulare totius saeculi propitiatorium et unici Filii Dei omnipotentis unicum ac dulcissimum reclinatorium, mox in suae conceptionis exordio Spiritus sancti gratia et illustratione destitutum?"; OSBERTUS, *Epistola ad Anselmum*, 55 f.: "Si enim beatus Ioannes, quem Deus Pater praecursorem misit Filio suo, angelo annuntiante conceptus est, et in utero matris suae sanctificatus, multo magis credendum est in ipsa conceptione eandem sanctificatam fuisse, de cuius carne Sanctus sanctorum processit . . ."; PETRUS PS.-ABAELARDUS, *Tractatus*, 130: "Sufficeret tibi, iuxta opinionem tuam, eam Ioanni adaequare: ego vero ex ipso veritatis testimonio eam Ioanni praefero nec solum de conceptione . . ."; cf. also pp. 118-120, 128s.; PETRUS PS.-CANTOR, *Tractatus*, 115: "Et cum non modo beatus Ioannes, sed nec quisquam naturali lege natorum, aut valeat ei, aut debeat in aliquo comparari: necessario consequitur, ut eius generatio et conceptio aliorum omnium generationi et conceptioni incomparabiliter praefulgeant sanctitatis praerogativa singulari"; PETRUS PS.-COMESTOR, *Sermo*, 617: "Quomodo stare poterit ut statim ab utero Ieremias sanctificatus sit, Virgo Dei Genitrix diu in peccato iacuerit?"; ANONYMUS I, *Sermo*, 72vab: "Sed quaeso te, an beatus Ioannes . . . a Zacharia et Elisabeth per veteris plagam peccati corpus in hoc mortis communi de traduce satus, mundum cum originali peccato ingressus est, at si mortem illam . . . evadere non potuit? Cur in festivitatum cathalogo inseritur eius conceptio, si immunda est? . . . Quanto magis ergo conceptionem beatae Mariae et ipsam conceptam, per gratiam qua plena fuit mundatam, necessarium est confiteri esse sanctissimam. Ecce enim plusquam Ioannes haec"; ANONYMUS II, *Sermo*, 73vb: "Si igitur Salvator vulvam sanctificavit alienam . . . , ut nasceretur Ieremias propheta, quanto magis conceptionem, qua concepta est Maria, ipse Dei Filius, de qua natus est, inter omnes filios hominum sanctificavit, ut haberet nullam maculam vel rugam vel aliquid huiusmodi"; ANONYMUS III, *Sermo*, 75va: "Si sanctus Ieremias antequam exiret de vulva, sanctificatus est, si priusquam formatus esset in utero, a Domino est cognitus, quanto magis ista beatissima Virgo . . . ante conceptionem . . . a Domino est cognita et in utero sanctificata. . . . Si praecursor Domini Ioannes adhuc ex utero matris suae conceptus Spiritu sancto repletus [est], quanto magis haec gloriosa Virgo . . . Spiritu sancto repleta est."

[124] EADMERUS, *Tractatus*, n.8 (p. 7 f.): "De ipsa quippe, multis saeculis ante ortum eius vel conceptum, Isaiam Spiritu sancto afflatum dixisse constat: *Egredietur virga de radice Iesse, et flos de radice eius ascendet* . . . Haec itaque virga, quae talem ex se protulit florem, nullo dissentiente, Virgo Maria fuit; et flos, qui de radice eius ascendit, benedictus Filius eius, super quem et in quo omnis plenitudo divinitatis essentialiter requievit"; *ibid.*, n.17 (p. 22): "Praedestinata fuit et praeordinata in hoc opus mirabile et omnibus operibus Dei praestans et incomparabile, Maria, scilicet, illa magni maris nobilissima stella, hoc est totius saeculi illustratio . . ."; OSBERTUS, *Epistola ad Warinum* (as cited above, in note 65), 62: "Corde autem credo et ore confiteor quod ante saecula temporalia Deus sibi Matrem praeelegit Virginem, de cuius aula virginalis uteri faceret egredi mortalitatis humanae piisimum Redemptorem"; ANONYMUS I, *Sermo*, 71vb-72ra: "Ab aeterno enim et

As to how Mary's preservation from sin came about, they offer different explanations. Some, positing the certain universality of original sin and admitting the universality of the Redemption, prefer to have recourse to a special power and will of God beyond all human investigation, without even asking how Mary could have been without sin if she had been redeemed by Christ. In this connection, the following words of Eadmer are worthy of note:

> That teacher of pure truth [St. Paul] who was surnamed *Vessel of election* by thy Son, reigning in heaven, says that all men sinned in Adam. This is true, and I declare it sinful to contradict it. But when I consider the eminent degree of God's grace in thee, I see thee, not among, but above all created things (except for thy Son), and I believe that, in thy conception, thou wert not bound by the law of nature of others, but through a unique and—to human minds—inscrutable power and operation of God, wert [kept] utterly free from any stain of sin.[126]

We can learn nothing better from the other authors of the period. Even though it can be gathered from passing remarks of theirs that the Blessed Virgin owed her purity to her Son, the universal Mediator, no one thoroughly investigated the really difficult problem, how Mary's immunity from sin could be reconciled with the dogma of the universal Redemption.[127]

---

ante mundi constitutionem praescivit et praedestinavit de eadem sibi carnem assumere eamque sibi matrem facere et habitaculum plenitudinis gratiae in ea sibi praeparare. Eius quoque caro et sanguis origo fuit nostri Salvatoris, eius anima templum in quo factum est comercium nostrae redemptionis"; PETRUS PS.-CANTOR, *Tractatus,* 109: "Huic itaque tam gloriosae tamque admirabili et tam necessariae saeculis omnibus incarnationi suae, non fortuita, non casuali electione, electam sibi Genitricem aut voluit aut debuit habere Dei Filius: sed sicut ab incommutabili providentia disposito ordine, quod carnem susciperet, progressum est, ita et de qua carnem susciperet, ab aeterno praeelecta electione, provisum est"; PETRUS PS.-COMESTOR, *Sermo,* 615: "Quomodo enim aliquando corruptioni subiacuit, quae ab initio electionis gratiam suscepit, ut imminentem toti mundo ruinam consumeret, periclitantique naturae subveniret? Si electa est ab initio beata Maria, quod indubitanter verum non ambigimus, si ipsa (ut quidam fabulantur) similiter corrupta remansit, ad tergendam corruptionem corruptio electa fuit. Quod Dei sapientia indignum credere possumus, ut quod ad lumen gentium praedestinavit, tenebris pravitatis sineret involvi."

[125] The writers quote quite a number of Scriptural texts and examples, principally Gen. III, 15; Canticle of Canticles, IV, 7; Luke I, 28. The text of Genesis is cited by ANONYMUS I, *Sermo,* 70rb; by OSBERT, *Sermo* (as cited above, in note 62), 66. The Canticle is cited by ANONYMUS I, *Sermo,* 72ra; by MAGISTER NICOLAUS *Liber* (as cited above, in note 56), 112; by the Ps.-ABELARD, *Tractatus,* 126. The text of St. Luke is used by ANONYMUS I, *Sermo,* 71ra; and by PS.-COMESTOR, *Sermo,* 616.

From Patristic sources, a number of our authors quote the famous words of St. Augustine, ". . . de qua propter honorem Domini, nullam prorsus, cum de peccatis agitur, habere volo quaestionem . . ." (*De natura et gratia,* c.36 n.42; PL 44, 267). Among these are PS.-ABELARD, *Tractatus,* 125; PS.-COMESTOR, *Sermo,* 616; and MAGISTER NICOLAUS, *Liber,* 111. ANONYMUS I, *Sermo,* 71 vb, also has recourse to the text of HUGH OF ST. VICTOR, *De Sacramentis,* II, I c.5 (PL 176, 38)

[126] EADMERUS, *Tractatus,* n.12 (p. 12-13)—cited in note 96, above.

[127] When weighing the opinion of ancient writers, we frequently transport our own way of thinking into their times. Thus, for example, we might argue that if these

This defect in the whole elaboration of the theology of the conception of the Virgin in the introductory period of scholasticism was such that to the great scholastic doctors of the thirteenth century, Bernard's reasoning appears both clearer and truer than simple assertions uttered for "sublime reasons," but without a solid analysis of the terms used, and without a precise notion of the Virgin's immunity from sin, taking into account the universality of the Redemption accomplished by Christ.

II

THE GOLDEN AGE OF SCHOLASTICISM: THE THIRTEENTH AND EARLY FOURTEENTH CENTURIES

Scholastic theology reaches its peak in this period, which begins about 1230 and lasts until the early decades of the fourteenth century. The characteristics of the sacred science are clearly delineated and differentiated from those of the preceding period. This is particularly evident from a consideration of the writings of these authors who defend Our Lady's privilege of freedom from sin. Theology, utilising the philosophy of the ancients, adapted, perfected and corrected in accordance with Christian principles, is perfectly analytical, and at the same time absolutely didactic and indeed technical, so that the effusive and mystical expressions which were so much in evidence in the theological writings of the preceding period, especially in those dealing with the Immaculate Conception, disappeared.

In discussing the sanctification of the Blessed Virgin, the outstanding theologians now divide and subdivide the subject logically into single articles until they arrive at a clearly determined proposition; having stated this, they give the arguments for and against it; next the assertion is explained;

---

authors taught that no one could be saved without a Redeemer, and that even His Mother was cleansed by Him, it follows logically that they taught that Mary had been pre-redeemed. It is known now that some authors of the fourteenth century argued and asserted that the Blessed Virgin had no sin, but they also taught that she had not been redeemed. It will be sufficient to mention Scotus' own contemporary, William of Nottingham, who admitted the Immaculate Conception and then, in answer to the difficulties about the universality of the redemption, gave two replies, of which the first was, "cum dicitur quod, nisi contraxisset originale, non indiguisset morte Christi nec redemptore, posset forte dici quod, si non contraxisset, redemptore non indiguisset, sicut nec aliquis in statu innocentiae." Cf. EMMEN A., "Immaculata Deiparae Conceptio secundum Guillelmum de Nottingham," in *Marianum* 5 (1943) 257.

It must be remembered also that the scholastic doctors, such as Peter Lombard, Anselm, Hales, and others, distinguished between "liberation" and "redemption"; the first might have taken place without the passion and death of Christ, but the second could not. Cf. ALEXANDER DE HALES, *Glossa in III Sent.*, d.20, Quaracchi 1954, 230. 238.

and, if necessary, special difficulties are solved.   The general form of the question is as follows: When did the first santification of the Virgin take place—*before* or *after* animation (the infusion of a soul into a sufficiently evolved body)?—before conception, in conception, or after conception but before the infusion of the soul?—or did it take place in the soul; and if so, when?

THE COMMON OPINION CONTRARY TO THE IMMACULATE CONCEPTION: BONAVENTURE, ALBERT THE GREAT, THOMAS AQUINAS . . .

The great scholastic doctors of the thirteenth century were familiar with the pious opinions of some of their predecessors; they quote the arguments on which these opinions were based; they even analyse the way in which the Marian privilege was explained.   Nevertheless, as a rule, they prefer the opposite opinion held by St. Bernard, whom they salute as "the greatest lover of the Virgin and champion of her honor," [128] that is, the opinion that the Mother of God was sanctified in the womb and purified from the sin in which she had been conceived.

Thus St. Bonaventure mentions some who had held the opinion that "sanctifying grace forestalled the stain of original sin in the soul of the glorious Virgin in the instant of her creation," and he knew that this was taught both out of reverence for Christ—"that He should be born of a most pure mother,"—and out of respect for the "Virgin, who should have been immensely superior in holiness to all the other saints." [129]   The Seraphic Doctor further recalls that this pious opinion rests also on the authority of St. Anselm, who had asserted that "the Blessed Virgin was so pure, that "under God none greater could be imagined"; and that St. Anselm had also asserted that the pious opinion, far from being repugnant to Holy Scripture, was compatible with it.   Moreover, it was not contrary to the Christian faith, because it admitted that:

> . . . the Blessed Virgin was freed by grace, which depended on and derived from faith in Christ, the Head, like the graces of the other Saints. [130]

[128] BONAVENTURA, *Sent. III,* d.3 p.1 a.1 q.1 (Ad Claras Aquas, III, 63).

[129] *Ibid.,* q.2 (pp. 66 f.): *"quidam dicere voluerunt,* in anima gloriosae Virginis gratiam sanctificationis praevenisse maculam peccati originalis . . . Haec autem positio videtur posse fulciri multiplici congruentia, tum propter Christi praecipuum honorem, quem decebat de Matre purissima fieri; tum propter Virginis praerogativam singularem, quae debuit in dignitate sanctificationis ceteros sanctos et sanctas praeire."

[130] *Ibid.,* 67: "quasi mediam rationem huius multiplicis congruentiae voluerunt quidam apponere, addentes insuper illud, quod non repugnat veritati sacrae Scripturae et fidei christianae . . . Fidei etiam christianae, ut dicit positio praedicta, non repugnat, pro eo quod dicunt ipsam Virginem ab originali peccato liberatam per gratiam, quae quidem pendebat et ortum habebat a fide et capite Christo, sicut gratiae aliorum sanctorum."

Bombolognus of Bologna said shortly afterwards that the pious opinion was

For while the others were raised up after falling, the Virgin Mary was, as it were, supported in the act of falling and prevented from falling, so that we can say that she did not have the infection of original sin "in its effect, but only in its cause."

But in spite of this explanation of the pious opinion, Bonaventure agrees with the opinion of St. Bernard which is "more fitting, more reasonable and safer," and especially because it is more conformable to "piety and faith," for:

Although reverence and great devotion are due to the Mother, greater devotion is due to the Son, from whom all her honour and glory comes.

Consequently:

Since it pertains to Christ's surpassing dignity that He is the Redeemer and Saviour of all, and that He opened the door to all, and that He alone died for all, the Blessed Virgin is not to be left out of this universality (*generalitate*), for fear that, while the Mother's excellence was enhanced, the Son's glory should be lessened.[131]

No different is the teaching of Albert the Great,[132] St. Thomas Aquinas,[133] Alexander of Hales,[134] William of Militona,[135] Odo Rigaud,[136] Richard of Mediavilla,[137] Thomas Sutton,[138] Peter of Tarantasia,[139] Giles

---

"strange" and that "nobody holds it now" (BOMBOLOGNUS DE BONONIA, *Sent. III*, d.3, ed. PIANA C., "Questione inedita de sanctificatione B. V. Mariae di Bombologno da Bologna, O.P." in *Studi Francescani* 38 (1941) 185-196. Even Bonaventure says that none of those with whom he had spoken held this opinion. Hence we conclude that Bonaventure, like Albert the Great and most of the scholastic authors of the thirteenth century, referred to the opinion which had been taught in England in the twelfth century, merely changing the oratorical argument into technical terminology and illustrating it with new arguments.

[131] BONAVENTURA, *Sent. III*, d.3 p.1 a.1 q.2 (Ad Claras Aquas, III, 67 f.). On p. 67, where the edition has the word *communior* ("Hic autem modus dicendi communior est et rationabilior et securior,"), I am of the opinion that the abbreviation was misread, and that the reading should be *convenientior*.

[132] ALBERTUS M., *Sent. III*, d.3 a.4-5 (ed. BORGNET, XXVIII, 46-48).

[133] THOMAS, *Sent. III*, d.3 q.1 a.1 sol.1 (Parmae, VIII, 39-40); *Summa theol.*, III, p.27 a.2 (ed. Leon., XI, 290); *Quaestiones disp. de malo*, q.4 a.6 (Parmae, VIII, 292-293); *Compendium theologiae*, c.224 (Parmae, XVI, 65).

[134] ALEXANDER HAL., *Summa theol.*, III, q.76 n.75-78 (Ad Claras Aquas, IV, 112-118).

[135] GUILELMUS DE MILITONA, *De sanctificatione B. V. Mariae*, q.3 (Tolosae, bibl. municip., cod. 737, f.37va).

[136] ODO RIGALDUS, *Sent. III*, d.3 q.1 a.2 (Cod. Vat. lat. 5982, f.146).

[137] RICHARDUS DE MEDIAVILLA, *Sent. III*, d.3 a.1 q.1 (Brixiae 1591, 27).

[138] THOMAS SUTTON, *Sent. III*, d.3 q.1 (Oxonii, bibliotheca Collegii Magdalen., cod. 99, f.229).

[139] PETRUS DE TARANTASIA [Innocentius V], *Sent. III*, d.3 q.1 a.1 (Tolosae 1652, 18): "Gradus sanctificationis quadruplex potest intelligi: aut ita quod sanctitatem habeat quis ante conceptum et ortum, aut post conceptum et ortum, aut in ipso conceptu et ortu, aut in ortu non in conceptu, nam quod in conceptu et non in ortu est impossibile. Primus gradus non est possibilis: tum quia personalis perfectio, ut scientia vel virtus, non transfunditur a parentibus, tum quia in filiis non potest fieri esse gratiae ante actuale esse naturae super quod fundatur. Secundus gradus

of Rome,[140] Hannibaldus of Hannibaldis,[141] Bombolognus of Bologna,[142] William of Godino,[143] and the other great masters of the thirteenth century.[144] They all admit, as with one voice, the principles which Eadmer, Osbert, Magister Nicholas and certain others invoked in the twelfth century in teaching that Mary was entirely pure and without stain. They all admit that "under Christ, the Blessed Virgin was the purest of all," [145] and they think it reasonable that:

> . . . she who bore the only-begotten Son of the Father, full of grace, and truth, received greater privileges of grace than any other.

Hence, they say, the Blessed Virgin, who was chosen by God to be His mother, received a greater grace of holiness than John or Jeremias, who were chosen as special types of the sanctification of Christ.[146]

---

communis est omnibus secundum legem communem sanctificationis. Tertius singularis est Sancto sanctorum, in quo solo simul fuit omnis sanctificatio, conceptio, animatio, assumptio. Quartus ergo restat: hic vero quatuor gradus habet, quia potest intelligi foetus conceptus in utero sanctificari aut ante animationem, aut in ipsa animatione, aut cito post animationem, aut diu post animationem.—Primus gradus est impossibilis, quia secundum Dionysium de div. nominibus c.12, sanctitas est ab omni immunditia libera et perfecta et immaculata munditia: immunditia vero culpae non expellitur nisi per gratiam gratum facientem (sicut tenebrae per lucem), cuius subiectum non est nisi rationalis creatura.—Secundus gradus non fuit conveniens B. Virgini, quia aut non contraxisset originale, et sic non indiguisset universali Christi sanctificatione et redemptione, aut si contraxisset, simul culpa et gratia inesse possent. —Quartus item gradus non fuit conveniens Virgini, quia fuit aliis communis, ut Ieremiae et Ioanni (qui sexto mense fuit sanctificatus, Luc. I), et quia non convenit tantae sanctitati ut diu morata fuerit in peccato.—Tertius vero videtur conveniens et pie credibilis (licet de Scriptura non habeatur), *ut cito post animationem, vel ipsa die vel hora (quamvis non ipso momento) fuerit sanctificata.*"

[140] AEGIDIUS ROMANUS, *Sent. III*, d.3 pars 1 q.1 a.1 (Romae 1623, 96).

[141] HANNIBALDUS DE HANNIBALDIS, *Sent. III*, q.1 (THOMAS, *Opera omnia*, ed. VIVES, XXX, 459): "dicendum quod beata Virgo nec ante conceptionem nec in conceptione ante animae infusionem sanctificata fuit, quia proprium subiectum gratiae sanctificantis est anima. *Nec in ipso instanti infusionis animae*, quia sic non contraxisset originale, sicut nec Christus, et ideo omnibus non conveniret redimi per Christum; *sed tantum sanctificata creditur post infusionem, quia hoc aliis sanctis est collatum.* Et ideo Matri sapientiae maxime decuit hoc conferri, in quam nihil coinquinatum incurrit, ut dicitur Sap. VII."

[142] BOMBOLOGNUS DE BONONIA, *Sent. III*, d.3, see PIANA C., (article cited in note 130) 189: ". . . si B. Virgo non contraxisset originale, non indiguisset universali Christi sanctificatione et redemptione . . ."

[143] GUILLELMUS DE GODIN, *Lectura Thomasina Sent. III*, d.3 (Naples, bibl. nat. cod. VII, c.30 (s. f.): "non potest dici quod beata Virgo fuit sanctificata in primo instanti infusionis animae; fuit tamen sanctificata ante nativitatem, *in utero, quia celebrat Ecclesia nativitatem beatae Mariae Virginis.*"

[144] Cf. MASSON R., "De Immaculata Conceptione apud fratres Praedicatores," in *Angelicum* 31 (1954) 374; KOROSAK B., *Mariologia S. Alberti Magni eiusque coaequalium (Bibliotheca mariana medii aevi*, VIII), Romae 1954, 375-384; STORFF H., *The Immaculate Conception*, San Francisco 1925; FRANCISCO DE GUIMARAENS, O.F.M. Cap., "La doctrine des théologiens sur l'Immaculée Conception de 1250 à 1350," in *Etudes franciscaines* (N.S.) 4 (1953) 23-33.

[145] THOMAS, *Summa theol.*, III. q.27 a.2 ad 2 (ed. Leon. XI, 290).

[146] *Ibid.*, a.1. a.4. a.5. a.6 ad 1 (pp. 288-299).

But in spite of these principles, the pious opinion could not be admitted because there were not reasons enough to explain the Marian privilege. The theory that some cell, preserved from corruption in Adam, was passed down to the Blessed Virgin, is considered to be quite heretical, like any other explanation in which Mary would have been sanctified before animation. Albert the Great exclaims:

> We say that the Blessed Virgin was not sanctified before animation, and if any one says otherwise he is guilty of the heresy condemned by blessed Bernard in his letter to the Canons of Lyons, and by all the masters of Paris.[147]

Nor was it fitting that she should have been without sin in her conception or in "the instant of creation," because even this explanation is incompatible with the universality of the Redemption. Christ is our Head, because He redeemed us; all the members of Christ's Mystical Body depend on Him, because redeemed by His blood. If any person had not been redeemed, that person could not have been a member of Christ. And, for one who has not contracted original sin, such a redemption is impossible. Therefore, Mary had sin, at least for an instant; she contracted sin and was immediately liberated from it.[148]

---

[147] ALBERTUS M., *Sent. III*, d.3 a.4 sol. (ed. BORGNET, XXVIII, 47). Cf. THOMAS, *Commentarius in Evangelium S. Ioannis*, cap.3 lect.5 (Parmae, X, 355). —The Angelic Doctor examined some of the arguments with which his predecessors tried to prove the absolute purity of the Blessed Virgin, and he tore them to shreds with his irresistible criticism. Cf. THOMAS, *Sent. III*, d.3 q.1 a.1 sol. 1 (Parmae, VII, 37 f.): "*Nullo modo in parentibus sanctificari potuit, neque etiam ex ipso actu conceptionis eius.* Conditio enim specialis personalis a parentibus in prolem non transit, nisi sit ad naturam corporalem pertinens, ut grammatica patris in filium non transit, quia perfectio personalis est. Unde et sanctificatio parentum in beatam Virginem transfundi non potuit, nisi curatum esset in eis non solum id quod personae est, sed etiam id quod est naturae in quantum huiusmodi: quod quidem Deus facere potuit, sed non decuit. Perfecta enim naturae curatio ad perfectionem gloriae pertinet; et ideo sic in statu viae parentes eius curati non fuerunt ut prolem suam sine originali peccato concipere possent; et ideo beata Virgo in peccato originali fuit concepta, propter quod B. Bernardus (epist. 174) ad Lugdunenses scribit conceptionem illius celebrandam non esse, quamvis in quibusdam ecclesiis ex devotione celebretur, non considerando conceptionem, sed potius sanctificationem: quae quando determinate fuerit, incertum est."—*Idem, ibid.*, ad 3 (p. 38): "concubitus quo beata Virgo concepta fuit meritorius creditur, non per gratiam omnino purgantem naturam, sed per gratiam perficientem personas parentum; et ideo non oportuit quod in prole concepta, statim sanctitas esset, non propter repugnantiam actus matrimonii ad sanctitatem, sed propter repugnantiam vitii naturae nondum curati."—Cf. BONAV., *Sent. III*, d.3 p.1 a.1 q.1 (Ad Claras Aquas, IV, 62).

[148] We read in the *Summa Alexandrina:* "Item, si B. Virgo non fuisset concepta in peccato, ergo non fuisset obligata peccato nec habuisset reatum peccati; si ergo quod non habet reatum peccati, non indiget redemptione, quia redemptio est propter obligationem ad peccatum et ad reatum peccati, ergo ipsa non indigeret redemptione per Christum: quod secundum catholicam fidem non est ponendum." (ALEXANDER HAL., *Summa theol.*, III, n. 76—Ad Claras Aquas, IV, 113, e)—Similar ideas are expressed by ODO RAGAUD, *Sent. III*, d.3 (cod. Brugen. 208, f. 358rb-359ra) and GUILELMUS DE MILITONA, *De sanctificatione B. V. Mariae* q.3 (Tolosae, bibl. municip., cod. 737, f. 37va.)—ALBERTUS M., *Sent. IV*, d.6 a.9 q.2 ad 3 (ed. BORG-

As St. Thomas is the most outstanding of these theologians, it will be useful to glean from his works this fundamental argument opposed to Our Lady's immunity from original sin.   In his commentary on the third book of *Sentences,* after pointing out that the sanctification could not properly have taken place before the infusion of the soul, as Our Lady was not yet capable of receiving grace, nor in the actual instant of infusion in such wise as to preserve her from incurring original sin through the grace then conferred on her,[149] he goes on to say:

> Of all the members of the human race, Christ alone did not need redemption, because He is our Head; all others are to be redeemed by Him.   But this could not be, if there was ever another soul which never had the stain of original sin.   Therefore, this was not granted to the Blessed Virgin nor to anyone besides Christ.[150]

We read in the *Summa*:

> According to Catholic Faith we must firmly hold that all of Adam's descendants contract original sin from him, except Christ; otherwise all would not need redemption through Christ, which is erroneous.[151]

And in Question 27 of the same work, where he expressly treats of the sanctification of the Mother of God, we read:

> If the Blessed Virgin had been sanctified in any way before animation, she would never have incurred the stain of original sin, and therefore she would not have needed that redemption and salvation through Christ, of which Matt. 1 says "He will save his people from their sins." But it is altogether unbecoming that Christ be not "the Saviour of all men," as I Tim. 4 says.   Hence the sanctification of the Virgin must have taken place after her animation.[152]

NET, **XXIX**, 138): ". . . ille qui sic conciperetur [that is, without sin], non esset sanctificatus ex hoc, sed esset in statu innocentiae primae; et hoc non esset decor justitiae, sed esset deformitas, quod unus indigeret redemptore et alter non."

[149] Thomas, *Sent. III,* q.1 a.1 (Parmae, VII, 36-38).

[150] *Ibid.,* q.7 a.1 sol. 2 (Parmae, VII, 38): "dicendum quod sanctificatio beatae Virginis non potuit esse decenter ante infusionem animae, quia gratiae capax nondum erat, *sed nec etiam in ipso instanti infusionis, ut scilicet per gratiam tunc sibi infusam conservaretur, ne culpam originalem incurreret.* Christus enim hoc singulariter in humano genere habet ut redemptione non egeat, quia caput nostrum est, sed omnibus convenit redimi per ipsum. Hoc autem esse non posset, si alia anima inveniretur quae numquam originali macula fuisset infecta; et ideo nec beatae Virgini, nec alicui praeter Christum hoc concessum est."

[151] Thomas, *Summa theol.,* I-II, q.81 a.3 (ed. Leon., VII, 90).

[152] Thomas, *Summa theol.,* III, q.27 a.2 (ed. Leon., XI, 290): "quocumque modo ante animationem beata Virgo sanctificata fuisset, numquam incurrisset maculam originalis culpae: et ita non indiguisset redemptione et salute quae est per Christum. . . . Hoc autem est inconveniens, quod Christus non sit *salvator omnium hominum,* ut dicitur I Tim. 4. Unde relinquitur quod sanctificatio B. Virginis fuerit post eius animationem."—*Ibid.,* ad 2: "si numquam anima beatae Virginis fuisset contagio originalis peccati inquinata, hoc derogaret dignitati Christi, secundum quam est universalis omnium salvator. Ed ideo . . . beata Virgo contraxit quidem originale peccatum, sed ab eo fuit mundata antequam ex utero nasceretur.—Cf. *idem, Sent. IV,* d.43 q.1 a.4 sol. 1 ad 3 (Parmae, VII, 1056-1057; cited below, in note 159).

Aquinas repeats the same idea in the *Quodlibet*, insisting that:

> We must not attribute so much to the Mother as to detract from the
> honour due to her Son, who is "the Saviour of all men," as the Apostle
> says.[153]

He says the same in his *De Malo* [154] and in the *Compendium Theologiae*,
asserting that the Blessed Virgin is necessarily conceived with original sin:

> . . . because if she had not been conceived with original sin, she would
> not have needed to be redeemed by Christ; then Christ would not be the
> universal redeemer of man—which would take from His dignity.[155]

From the foregoing, it is quite obvious that, for the Angelic Doctor as for
the other scholastics, to contract original sin in one's own person, and to be
redeemed from it, are correlative: the second cannot occur without the
first.

In order to understand this opposition of the scholastic doctors to the
Immaculate Conception, it is necessary to bear in mind exactly what they
meant by *redemption*. St. Thomas says:

> Insofar as He snatched us from the devil's power, He is said to have
> redeemed us, as a king redeems his kingdom from the possession of an
> enemy by the effort of battle; insofar as He appeased God with regard
> to us, He is said to have redeemed us, as paying the price of His satis-
> faction for us, that we might be freed from punishment and sin.[153]

[153] THOMAS, *Quodlibet* VI, a.7 (Parmae, IX, 545-546): "Est ergo consideran-
dum quod unusquisque peccatum originale contrahit ex hoc quod fuit in Adam
secundum seminalem rationem . . . Omnes autem illi in Adam fuerunt secundum
seminalem rationem qui non solum ab eo carnem acceperunt, sed etiam secundum
naturalem modum originis ab eo sunt propagati. Sic autem processit ab Adam B.
Virgo, quia nata fuit per commixtionem sexuum, sicut et ceteri; et ideo concepta fuit
in originali peccato, et includitur in universitate illorum de quibus Apostolus dicit
ad Rom. 5, 12: *In quo omnes peccaverunt;* a qua universitate solus Christus excipitur, qui in Adam non fuit secundum seminalem rationem; alioquin si hoc alteri conveniret quam Christo, non indigeret Christi redemptione. Et ideo non tantum debemus dare Matri quod subtrahat aliquid honori Filii, qui est salvator omnium hominum, ut dicit Apostolus, 1 ad Tim. 4.—Quamvis autem B. Virgo in originali concepta fuerit, *creditur tamen in utero fuisse sanctificata, antequam nata . . . ,* in ipsa
sanctificatione copiosius ceteris munus gratiae accepit, non solum ut purgaretur a
peccato originali, sed ut tota eius vita redderetur immunis ab omni peccato tam
mortali quam veniali, ut dicit Anselmus."

[154] THOMAS, *De malo*, q.4 a.6 (Parmae, VIII, 292-293).

[155] THOMAS, *Compendium theologiae*, c.224 (Parmae, XVI, 65): *"Nec solum a
peccato actuali immunis fuit, sed etiam ab originali, speciali privilegio mundata.*
Oportuit siquidem quod cum peccato originali conciperetur, utpote quae ex utriusque
sexus commixtione concepta fuit. Hoc enim privilegium sibi soli servabatur ut virgo
conciperet Filium Dei. Commixtio autem sexus, quae sine libidine esse non potest
post peccatum primi parentis, transmittit peccatum originale in prolem. Similiter
etiam quia si cum peccato originali concepta non fuisset, non indigeret per Christum
redimi; et sic non esset Christus universalis hominum redemptor: quod derogat dignitati Christi. Est ergo tenendum quod cum peccato originali concepta fuit, sed ab
eo quodam speciali modo purgata fuit . . . Quod autem praestitum est Christi Praecursori et Prophetae, non debet credi denegatum esse Matri ipsius, et ideo *creditur
in utero sanctificata, ante scilicet quam ex utero nasceretur . . .* Beata Virgo tanta

Again:

> In order to have redemption, two things are required: the act of payment, and the price paid.[157]

> Because He is our Head, He delivered us (as His members) from our sins by His Passion, which He underwent out of charity and obedience —as if the Passion were a price He paid.[158]

The great Aquinas writes:

> Anyone conceived without original sin would have no need of the Redemption which came through Christ, and thus Christ would not be the Redeemer of all.[159]

---

abundantia gratiae sanctificata fuit, *ut deinceps ab omni peccato conservaretur immunis . . .*"

[156] THOMAS, *Sent. III*, d.19 q.1 a.4 (Parmae, VII, 204).

[157] THOMAS, *Summa theol., III*, q.48 a.5 (ed. Leon., XI, 468).

[158] *Ibid.*, q.49 a.1 (ed. Leon., XI, 471).

[159] THOMAS, *Sent. IV*, d.43 q.1 a.4 sol. 1 ad 3 (Parmae, VII, 1066 f.): "Ad tertium dicendum, quod hoc est erroneum dicere, quod aliquis sine peccato originali concipiatur praeter Christum; quia ille qui sine peccato originali conciperetur, non indigeret redemptione quae facta est per Christum, et sic Christus non esset omnium hominum redemptor. . . . Oportet autem ponere, quod quilibet personaliter redemptione Christi indigeat, non solum ratione naturae. Liberari autem a malo, vel a debito absolvi non potest nisi qui debitum incurrit, vel in malum dejectus fuit; et ita non possent omnes fructum dominicae redemptionis in seipsis percipere, nisi omnes debitores nascerentur, et malo subjecti, unde dimissio debitorum et liberatio a malo non potest intelligi, quod aliquis sine debito vel immunis a malo nascatur, sed quia cum debito natus postea per gratiam Christi liberatur."

In the International Mariological Congress held in Rome in 1954, twenty learned theologians of the Order of Preachers delivered papers on St. Thomas' doctrine on the Immaculate Conception. These have been published in volume VI (*De Immaculata Conceptione in ordine S. Dominici,* 1955) of the *Acta* of the Congress (*Virgo Immaculata,* Romae, Academia Mariana Internationalis). Some of these theologians hold the negative thesis, namely that the Angelic doctor never taught the Marian privilege, because he clearly distinguished between conception in original sin and sanctification later in her mother's womb; others held an alternative thesis, namely that the Angelic doctor first of all held the Marian privilege explicitly, then denied it, and at the end of his life returned to the affirmative opinion; others maintained that St. Thomas clearly expounded the principles in which the doctrine is contained; and some even held that the Angelic doctor explicitly held that the Blessed Virgin was without original sin. In this last sense there is a recent work by John F. ROSSI, C.M., *Quid senserit S. Thomas Aquinas de Immaculata Virginis Conceptione,* Piacenza 1955, with a preface by Fr. Cornelius Fabro. Father Rossi, who has already published other work on this subject, depends principally on three texts which he considers clear *and which are to be used to clarify the obscure texts,* namely: a) "talis fuit puritas B. Virginis, quae peccato originali et actuali immunis fuit" (*Sent.* I, d.44 q.1 a.3 ad 3); b) "Spiritus sanctus in beata Virgine duplicem purgationem fecit; unam quidem quasi praeparatoriam ad Christi conceptionem, quae non fuit ab aliqua impuritate culpae vel fomitis" (*Summa theol.,* III, q.27 a.3 ad 3); c) the Blessed Virgin "nec originale nec mortale, nec veniale peccatum incurrit" (*Expositio Salutationis Angelicae*).

There is no reason to tarry over these well known texts; see SYNAVE, "Le commentaire de Saint Thomas sur l'Ave Maria et la doctrine de l'Immaculée Conception," in *Bulletin thomiste* 9 (1932) 563-584; DE BLIC J., "Saint Thomas et l'Immaculée Conception," in *Revue apologétique* 57 (1933) 25-36.

Everybody knows that in the texts quoted above, the Angelic Doctor was not treating the sanctification of the Blessed Virgin *ex professo,* and it is unusual, to say the very least, to take these as our guide in interpreting the other texts where he does treat *ex professo* of the subject. In any case, these texts are anything but clear, because when St. Thomas says that Mary was immune from sin, he does not say when she obtained this immunity—whether it was in the first instant of the infusion of the soul, or whether it was in her mother's womb after she had been in a special way cleansed from original sin (See above, notes 158, 156).—St. Thomas' disciples themselves admitted that they gathered his teachings from his oral delivery, as stray ears of corn are gleaned after the harvest; and anyone familiar with the medieval *reportationes* will hesitate to insist on isolated words or expressions which occur in the propositions therein formulated. The correction of the three codices which say that the Blessed Virgin "ab originali in utero matris sanctificata fuit, nec mortale nec veniale incurrit" (ROSSI, *op. cit.*, 92) is quite arbitrary; ingenuous is the only word for the note added in the Madrid codex (*ibid.* 86): "quod beata Virgo non incurrit maculam originalis peccati sed tamen contraxit ut patet supra, sed licet contraxerit quia in illo concepta fuit, non incurrit quia prius quam exiret de ventre fuit purificata." It will surprise nobody who knows these medieval *Reportationes*, that the reporter could have formulated the proposition as it is found in the greater number of codices, even though this did not correspond exactly with what St. Thomas had said in his sermon.

Let each one adhere to his own opinion. But there are some points put forward by Rossi as certain, which no one else even suspects. Among other things, we may mention the historical context as depicted by the author on page 77: "Nessuno dei maculisti, prima della controversia suscitata del Monzon, aveva pensato di invocare a sostegno della propria tesi l'aiuto di San Tommaso." He adds that when the authority of St. Thomas was invoked against the Immaculate Conception for the first time in 1387, Peter d'Ailly immediately silenced his adversaries by claiming St. Thomas on his own side; hence, says Father Rossi (p. 6), "nell'università di Parigi S. Tommaso era considerato fautore esplicito del privilegio mariano"!

Unfortunately this is nothing but a romance without a shred of truth behind it. It is the very opposite of the truth. As soon as the traditional and common opinion, that Mary was conceived in original sin, was attacked by John Duns Scotus and R. of Hotot in the beginning of the fourteenth century, the authority of St. Thomas, as expressed in III Sentences and his work *De malo*, was invoked *against* the innovation (see chapter VI of the present volume, p. 214 ff.; also IOANNES DE POLLIACO et IOANNES DE NEAPOLI, *Quaestiones disputatae de Immaculata Conceptione*, ed. C. BALIĆ, in *Bibliotheca mariana medii aevi*, I, Sibenik, 1931, 12-13). Further, when Montson and the Dominicans appealed to the Pope against the condemnation of fourteen propositions of Montson, including four which referred to the Immaculate Conception, Peter d'Ailly, wishing to demonstrate to the Holy See that the condemnation was reasonable, says clearly and expressly that "quaestionem utrum B. Virgo fuerit in peccato originali concepta hic disputari non proponimus, nam praedictae et tres sequentes condemnantur non obstante probabilitatae huius quaestionis" (Cf. D'ARGENTRÉ, *Collectio iudiciorum de novis erroribus*, I, pars 2, Paris 1728, 107). In other words, even though St. Thomas had said in III Sentences, "quod fuit concepta in originali," he never said what Montson affirmed and for which he was condemned, namely that the opposite opinion was "expresse et expressissime contra fidem" (*ibid.*, 107; for an account of the Montson controversy, see chapter VI of the present volume, p. 223 ff.).

And what is to be said to the assertion that "maiorem partem Fratrum Praedicatorum inter principaliores tum sanctitate tum doctrina" were in favor of the Immaculate Conception (ROSSI, *op. cit.*, 11)? In a recent article (cited above, in note 144), Father MASSON enumerates 132 writers of the Order of Preachers, who wrote about the Immaculate Conception up to the seventeenth century, and he could not claim even one fifth of them in favor of the doctrine. The classical commentators, such as Cajetan and Sylvester of Ferrara, whose commentaries are published together with the text of St. Thomas in the Leonine edition, and who wrote after the Popes had spoken in favor of the pious opinion, are still opposed to it. Father GUIMARAENS, (in the article cited in note 144, above), 174, justly observes that "on ne connaît

Hence it must be asserted that everyone needed to be redeemed by Christ personally, and not only by reason of his human nature.

We have quoted these testimonies rather fully, especially those of St. Thomas, principally to show that the real reason why the great scholastic doctors did not admit the doctrine of the Immaculate Conception was the central idea of Christ as Head and universal Redeemer. Christ died for all without exception: He is the Redeemer and Saviour of all, to whom he opened the gates of paradise. Now it is not easy to see how the Virgin was indebted to Christ for her redemption, if she was exempted not only from actual sin but also from original sin. Accordingly:

> . . . the Blessed Virgin is not to be left out of this universality, for fear that, while the Mother's excellence was enhanced, the Son's glory should be lessened.[160]

If, in addition to this principal argument, we keep in mind other arguments, adduced by authorities such as Bernard [161] and Peter Lombard,[162] based on the universality of original sin and its transmission through seminal generation, it is easy to see why not a single doctor of the Franciscan Order who wrote in this period—and from St. Anthony of Padua [163] to Duns Scotus and William of Ware, there were more than forty—held that Our Lady was immune from original sin. Some of them were persuaded that God in his absolute power could have granted such a privilege to Our Lady, but they all agreed with Saint Bonaventure that:

> It was not becoming for this favour to be granted to anyone save to Him alone through whom the salvation of all mankind was accom-

---

aucun dominicain de la première moitré du XIV siècle qui ait embrassé la doctrine de l'Immaculée Conception." Thomas Sutton, Hervaeus Natalis, John of Naples, and other Dominicans in the first decades of the fourteenth century make use of the same fundamental arguments as St. Thomas Aquinas in attacking the Marian privilege and combating the arguments of Scotus.—St. Thomas is to be interpreted in his historical context, remembering what Hannibaldus de Hannibaldis clearly said in the work printed among the *Opera omnia S. Thomae*, ed. Vivès, XXX, 459, namely that grace was given to Mary "post animae infusionem, *quia hoc aliis sanctis est collatum*" (See above, note 141).

[160] Bonaventura, *Sent. III*, d.3 p.1 a.1 q.2 (Ad Claras Aquas, III, 68). See above, note 131.

[161] Bernardus, *Epistola 174* (PL 182, 336).

[162] Petrus Lombardus, *Sent. II*, d.30 c.1 n.267 and d.31 c.1 n.286 (Ad Claras Aquas, I, 460. 469).

[163] For the doctrine of St. Anthony of Padua on the Immaculate Conception, see Romeri C., *De Immaculata Conceptione B. M. V. apud S. Antonium Patavinum*, Romae 1939; di Fonzo L. "La Mariologia di Sant'Antonio," in *S. Antonio dottore della Chiesa*, Città del Vaticano 1947, 126-139; p. 138: "S. Antonio, perciò, da quanto ci rimane del suo pensiero scritto e da quanto esposto, a nostro modesto parere, non è nè un assertore esplicito o corifeo (ad es., come Scoto), nè propriamente un assertore implicito (un S. Efrem) dell'Immacolata; non precisamente un negatore— perchè non ha mai negato niente in proposito—nè tanto meno un oppositore (come, ad es., un S. Bernardo o S. Tommaso) . . ."

plished, namely, the Lord Jesus Christ, so that no flesh should glory in His sight.[164]

Indeed, some did not even hesitate to style the opinion of those who taught that "the Virgin was preserved by Christ's grace from all sin and concupiscence," [165] "heretical, impious and blasphemous." [166]

It is true that Catholic theologians, in order to satisfy their devotion to the Blessed Virgin, gradually tried to reduce this subjection to original sin as far as possible. Not only did they all admit that she was sanctified "before being born," they also formed the pious opinion that this happened "soon after" the contracting of original sin—"on the same day or in the same hour, though not in the very instant," [167] and in fact some went so far as to use the traditional argument, *Potuit, decuit, fecit*, in order to prove that the Blessed Virgin was in a state of original sin only for a fleeting instant.[168]

SOME SPECIAL OPINIONS: HENRY OF GHENT, 'GERARD OF ABBEVILLE,' ROBERT GROSSE-TESTE, PETER PASCHASIUS, RAYMOND LULL.

Henry of Ghent, arguing from the undeniable premise that God had the greatest love for the Virgin and that He gave such holiness and purity to

[164] BONAVENTURA, *op. cit.*, 69.

[165] Cf. DOUCET V., "P. I. Olivi et l'Immaculée Conception," in *Archivum franciscanum historicum* 26 (1933) 562; JURIC I., "Franciscus de Mayronis Immaculatae Conceptionis eximius vindex," in *Studi francescani* 51 (1954) 237-238.

[166] DOUCET, *art. cit.*, 563.

[167] Cf. RICHARDUS DE S. LAURENTIO, *De laudibus B. V. Mariae*, lib.10 c.30 (ed. BORGNET, in *S. Alberti Opera omnia*, XXXVI, 519): "sanctificatio Virginis in utero matris cito, ut creditur, post conceptionem."—ALBERTUS M., *Sent. III*, d.3 a.5 sol. (ed. BORGNET, XXVIII, 48): "Dicendum quod ante nativitatem ex utero sanctificata fuit; sed *quo die vel qua hora* nescire quemquam hominem nisi per revelationem; nisi quod probabilius est quod cito post animationem conferatur, quam longe exspectetur."—RICHARDUS DE MEDIAVILLA, *Sent. III*, d.3 a.1 q.1 (Brixiae 1591, 27): ". . . *eodem die, cito post constitutionem naturae* eius pie creditur esse factum."—AEGIDIUS ROM., *Sent. III*, d.3 pars 1 q.1 a.1 (Romae 1623, 96): "pie creditur quod *valde modica* fuerit morula inter animae infusionem, vel eius conceptionem, et eius per gratiam sanctificationem: idcirco dici potest quod semper fuit sancta."—PETRUS DE TARANTASIA, *Sent. III*, d.3 q.1 a.1 (Tolosae 1652, 18): "videtur conveniens et pie credibilis (licet de Scriptura non habeatur), ut cito post animationem, *vel ipsa die vel hora* (quamvis non ipso momento) fuerit sanctificata."—THOMAS, *Quodl. VI*, a.7: "Creditur enim quod *cito post* conceptionem *et animae infusionem* fuerit sanctificata."—GERARDUS DE ABBATISVILLA, *op. cit.*, 284; "creditur parum fuisse in originali culpa et statim post infusionem animae Deus per immissionem gratiae sanctificavit illam."—BOMBOLOGNUS DE BONONIA, *Sent. III*, d.3 (ed. PIANA, 190): "Creditur . . . quod *statim post* animationem fuerit sanctificata." See notes 139. 141, above.—SCHULTER A., "Die Bedeutung Heinrichs von Gent für die Entfaltung der Lehre von der unbefleckten Empfängnis," in *Theologische Quartalschrift* 110 (1937) 312-340. 437-455.—LE BACHELET, *art. cit.*, 1058: "tous admettent et requièrent un intervalle réel, ne fût-il que d'un instant, entre la conception consommée et la sanctification de la bienheureuse Vierge."

[168] Cf. IOANNES DE POLIACO et IOANNES DE NEAPOLI, *Quaestiones*, Prolegomena, pp. XLV-LIV.

His Mother that none greater could be found in creatures, came to the conclusion that the greatest indication of His great love would have been to sanctify the Virgin and purify her from sin as soon as possible.[169] Hence the great Belgian theologian of the thirteenth century concludes:

> If, therefore, it was possible for her to be sanctified and cleansed from sin in such wise as to have been in sin only for an instant or moment . . . one may hold that this was the case.

But almighty God, with His divine power, was able to dispose that the Blessed Virgin should be in a certain condition (i.e. in original sin) for an instant only. Original sin would have both its beginning and its end in that instant, but each in a different 'aspect' of the instant (*"secundum aliud et aliud signum illius instantis"*); its beginning, in so far as this instant was the end of the preceding period of time; its end, in so far as this instant was the beginning of the following period of time.[170]

According to this theory, Mary would have been pure from the beginning, and immediately at the beginning of her creation, just as Eadmer and others had said in the twelfth century, but after being conceived in sin; and this because the Catholic faith teaches that the Redemption is universal, and therefore original sin also must extend to all men.

Henry of Ghent's opinion about the purgative sanctification of the Blessed Virgin exercised considerable influence, for at the end of the thirteenth century there seems to have been some sort of compromise between the pious opinion held in the twelfth century, and the negative opinion of the solemn masters of the University of Paris. Discussions are heard about the potential existence of original sin, and the relations between instant and time. Henry's fellow-countryman and contemporary, Godfrey of Fontaine, attacks his opinion, but admits that Mary was in sin for a short and almost imperceptible time: it is piously believed that the time was very short indeed; consequently one can say that she was always holy.[171] Some even defend, despite St. Bernard, the opinion that the flesh of the Virgin might have been purified so that her soul should have no sin; they call this cleansing her "preservation" from sin. And although this was possible by God's "absolute power," several reasons were adduced to show that such "preservation" did not in fact take place.

In the question of the Immaculate Conception which is sometimes attributed to Gerard of Abbeville, we read that it would not have been right for the divine justice, or the divine clemency, power or wisdom, to preserve the Blessed Virgin from sin:

[169] Cf. Goicoechea y Viteri I. M., *Doctrina mariana de Enrique de Gante*, Lima 1944, App. XIII.

[170] *Ibid.*, XVII: "Videtur mihi quod originale in Virgine per solum momentum instantis fuisse potuit, rerum natura non repugnante"; p. XXI: "pie credo quod macula originalis in Virgine non fuit nisi in instanti et in potentia . . . Et si macula originalis non fuit in Virgine nisi in instanti, non sequitur quin Virgo aliquando fuerit in macula originali . . ."

God did not will to preserve her from sin, He willed to cleanse and purify her from sin in order to declare His justice; to show the severity of the divine justice against that mass which had been damned on account of the sin of the first parents.[172]

For since the Virgin was entirely present in the common father of all, as regards both her bodily substance and the *ratio seminalis,* she underwent the sentence of condemnation and contracted the sin from him.

Further, through original sin and its cleansing, God wished to show his greater mercy.

> For although it is a greater benefit to preserve someone from falling than to raise him up and cleanse him after he has fallen, yet it is a sign of greater clemency to raise him up and cleanse him after the fall.

In the present case, "after the fall into original sin," God raised up the Virgin because He wanted her not only as His mother but as "Queen of heaven and earth" also.[173]

Finally, the power and wisdom of God are shown more clearly if it is said that Mary was cleansed from sin instead of being preserved, because by her falling and being raised again it is seen how God "knows how to bring forth good from evil; which would not appear so clearly if He had preserved her from sin."[174]

Robert Grosseteste, the founder of the Franciscan School at Oxford, had proposed the hypothesis that Our Lady could have been:

> . . . cleansed and sanctified in the very infusion of her rational soul. In this way, there would have been a purification, not from a sin which had at one time been present in her, but from one which would have

---

[171] GODEFRIDUS DE FONTIBUS, *Quodl. VIII,* q.4 (ed. HOFFMANS, in *Les philosophes belges,* IV, 54-55.

[172] GLORIEUX P., "Une question inédite de Gérard d'Abbéville sur l'Immaculée Conception," in *Recherches de théologie ancienne et médiévale* 2 (1930) 261-289 (the text in question is found on pages 268-286).—A. DENEFFE published another redaction of the same question after Glorieux ("Deux questions médiévales concernant l'Immaculée Conception," in *Recherches de théologie ancienne et médiévale,* 4 (1932) 402-404), and joins Pelster in doubting the attribution of this question to Gerard of Abbéville. Glorieux holds, however, that the III Sentences contained in *cod. lat. 15.906* of the Bibliothèque Nationale in Paris is to be ascribed to Gerard. The fact that this work, at d.3 q.1 (fol. 40ra), denies the possibility of Mary's preservation from sin, which the above mentioned *Questions* admit, increases our doubt about the authenticity of the *Questions.*

[173] GERARDUS DE ABBATISVILLA (ed. GLORIEUX, cited in preceding note), 276-277.

[174] *Ibid.,* 277. Gerard puts the question clearly: "Utrum Virgo gloriosa originale peccatum habuit et concepta fuerit in peccato originali." (*Ibid.,* 268) He begins his answer by saying that there were two erroneous positions on the question: "dixerunt enim aliqui quod Virgo gloriosa concepta fuit omnino sine originali; et haec positio contrariatur dictis sanctorum . . . Alii posuerunt quod fuit concepta in originali, in tantum quod aliter non potuit fieri nec concipi innitentes illi verbo Bernardi . . ." The author therefore holds that by God's absolute power, "potuit semen illud, ex quo formatum est corpus Virginis, purgari," but that this was not fitting! (*Ibid.,* 274 f.).

been in her if she had not been sanctified in the very infusion of her rational soul.[175]

This hypothesis, however, had yet to be developed before it would actually have a notable influence.

Nor is it without significance that two of the great defenders of the Immaculate Conception at the close of the thirteenth century did not think of reconciling their opinion with the universality of Redemption, but invoked instead in Mary's favour a special grace granted by God Himself, rather than a grace obtained for His Mother by her Son, the Redeemer.

Thus, we read in a dialogue between Mary and her Son, composed at the end of the thirteenth century by Peter Paschasius:

> Thou art that maiden chosen by God in whom there is no sin, venial or mortal, original or actual, or any other kind. And this is why Adam was created innocent and sinless.[176]

And again we read:

> Some, O Mother, hold that thou art stained with original sin, but what they say is erroneous and iniquitous; for, as we have already said above, before Adam was created, My Father chose thee pure and sinless, that His Son might take flesh from thee.[177]

It seems, therefore, that this author, who is styled by some "the first defender of Mary's Immaculate Conception,[178] does not build his argument for Mary's preservation from all sin upon the merits of Christ the Redeemer—the Christ who suffered—but rather upon an act of will of Almighty God.[179]

---

[175] ROBERTUS GROSSATESTA, cited by E. LONGPRÉ, "Robert Grossetête et l'Immaculée Conception," in *Archivum franciscanum historicum* 26 (1933) 551: "*Tota pulchra es, amica mea et macula non est in te.*—Non fuit in beata Virgine macula, originalis peccati in ortu suo. Qualiter enim sancta Ecclesia celebraret ipsius nativitatem si in peccato nata fuisset? Purgatam itaque credimus eam ab originali in utero matris, quae purgatio potuit altero duorum modorum fuisse: uno videlicet, ut ipsa vere haberet originale peccatum aliquamdiu post infusionem animae rationalis, ante ortum tamen ex utero matris, operatione Spiritus sancti, purgata et sanctificata fuisset; alio autem modo ut in ipsa infusione rationalis animae esset mundata et sanctificata et hoc modo esset purgatio, non a peccato quod aliquando infuit, sed quod infuisset nisi in ipsa infusione rationalis animae sanctificata fuisset. Congruit autem ut ipsa nasceretur sine peccato . . .*"
This text is taken from an unpublished sermon in the British Museum, MS. Royal VII. F.2, fol. 48va-49va (and is also found in MS. Royal VI. E.5, fol. 84vb-85rb).
[176] PEDRO PASCUAL, *Istories religioses*, II, n.13 (ed. ARMENGOL VALENZUELA, P., *Obras de S. Pedro Pascual*, I, Roma 1905, 24).
[177] *Ibid.*, n.14 (I,24).
[178] Cf. MANCINI, *op. cit.*, *passim*.
[179] PEDRO PASCUAL, *Disputa del obispo de Jaén contra los Judíos sobre le fé catolica*, tit. 48 n.2 (ed. ARMENGOL VALENZUELA, *Obras*, II, Roma 1907, 223-224). It seems that the text of Paschasius has not been critically established; some passages belong to the abbreviator of the saint's work. See *op. cit.*, II, p. 224 note 2.

Raymond Lull was of a similar opinion. Having first asserted that he who imagines sin in the Virgin "thinks of darkness in the sun," [180] and that there could not be anything evil in the Mother of God, because "she was completely good," [181] he then claims that it was necessary that "her conception should correspond to that of her Son." [182] But when discussing the difficulty of the universality of original sin ("the entire human race was corrupted by original sin") [183] and the difficulty arising from the universality of redemption ("the Blessed Virgin would have had no need to be re-created through her Son"),[184] Raymond applies his theory of predestination from all eternity and recurs to "the infinite power" [185] of the Son of God or of the Holy Spirit, making no mention of either the Passion or the Redemption.[186]

This, therefore, is how the problem stood when Duns Scotus and Raymund Lull were at Paris together. The doctors almost unanimously held that Mary was conceived in original sin, and they did so to save the excellence and pre-eminence of Christ the Redeemer.

This unanimity, at least in Paris (the *Mater scientiarum*), was such that St. Bonaventure could declare:

> None of those to whom we have been able to listen with our own ears has ever asserted that the Blessed Mary was immune from original sin.[187]

And in the beginning of the fourteenth century, when the pious opinion was being taught at the University of Paris by Duns Scotus and Robert of Hotot, John of Pouilly declared it to be heretical: "Until the present time, no doctor whose writings have been published in the Paris *studium*, has dared to hold this opinion." [188]

---

[180] RAYMUNDUS LULLUS, *Blaquernae anachoretae interrogationes et responsiones CCCLXV de amico et amato,* Parisiis 1632, 159s.

[181] RAYMUNDUS LULLUS, *Liber de laudibus beatissimae virginis Mariae qui et ars intentionum appellari potest,* c.2, Parisiis 1499, 5s.

[182] RAYMUNDUS LULLUS, *Disputatio Eremitae et Raymundi super aliquibus dubiis quaestionibus Sententiarum Magistri Petri Lombardi,* q.96 (*Opera,* IV, Moguntiae 1729, 83).—The same question has been transcribed and published by B. SALVÁ in *Analecta tertii ordinis regularis S. Francisci,* 2 (1934) 171-172.

[183] *Ibid.,* 84 (ed. SALVÁ, 172).

[184] *Ibidem.*

[185] *Ibidem.*

[186] *Ibidem.*

[187] BONAVENTURA, *Sent. III,* d.3 p.1 a.1 q.2 (Ad Claras Aquas, III, 68): "Nullus autem invenitur dixisse de his quos audivimus auribus nostris virginem Mariam a peccato originali fuisse immunem."

[188] IOANNES DE POLLIACO, *Quodl.* III, q.3 a.1 (ed. BALIĆ, 13): "Neque etiam aliquis doctor hactenus ausus est dicere contrarium, cuius scripta sunt in Studio Parisiensi publicata."—It is known that the scholastic doctors used to hand over their works to the University of Paris, which undertook the task of multiplying and circulating them. The name of "stationers" was given to those who today are known as book-sellers and publishers. No work of Duns Scotus was published in this way, because he was still revising and perfecting them when overtaken by his untimely

Since an entirely new epoch opens at the beginning of the fourteenth century with the intervention of the Subtle Doctor, we must dwell more fully on his teaching. And since Scotus was taught by William of Ware, who taught the pious opinion at the same time, we can consider their opinions together in a special section.

III

THE INTERVENTION OF JOHN DUNS SCOTUS AND HIS MASTER, WILLIAM OF WARE

WILLIAM OF WARE.

Having briefly and clearly posed the single question, "Whether the Blessed Virgin was conceived in original sin," [189] Ware examines successively three hypotheses, the first of which is that of Henry of Ghent: "that she was conceived in original sin and was cleansed and sanctified in the same instant, although in a different aspect of the instant (*in alio . . . signo eiusdem instantis*)"; [190] the second is the common opinion: "that she was conceived in original sin and not cleansed in the same instant," [191] and finally the third hypothesis, that she did not contract the original stain.[192] This last hypothesis, the author attempts to prove, proving first the possibility,[193] then the suitability,[194] and lastly the fact, of preservation of the Blessed Virgin from sin.[195]

Ware accepts the Augustinian explanation of the transmission of sin.[196] He asserts, however, that while the flesh from which Mary's body was to be formed was infected—due to its source—with the *qualitas morbida*, it could have been purified at the moment of insemination.[197] Hence, while

---

death. This explains why he is rarely quoted between 1300 and 1308, which was the time of his greatest activity. John of Pouilly had some *Reportatio* of Scotus' lectures on the Sentences, made by one of the students who had attended them. Peter Sutton, Thomas Sutton and others had copies of the *Ordinatio* immediately after 1308. Cf. BALIĆ C., "La valeur des citations des oeuvres de Jean Duns Scot," in *Mélanges Auguste Pelzer*, Louvain 1947, 351-356.

[189] GULIELMUS GUARRA, *Sent. III*, quaestio *De conceptione beatae Virginis*, in Fr. GULIELMI GUARRAE, Fr. I. DUNS SCOTI, Fr. PETRI AUREOLI, *Quaestiones disputatae de Immaculata Conceptione B. V. Mariae*, Ad Claras Aquas 1904, 1.

[190] *Ibid.*, 2; cf. GOICOECHEA (DE) Y VETERI I. M. (work cited above, in note 169), App. XXI.

[191] GULIELMUS GUARRA, *op. cit.*, 3.

[192] *Ibid.*, 4: "Alia est opinio, quod non contraxit originale."

[193] *Ibid.*, 5 f.

[194] *Ibid.*, 6.

[195] *Ibid.*, 6 f.

[196] *Ibid.*, 4 f.

[197] *Ibid.*, 5: "Illa massa carnis ex qua corpus Virginis fuit formatum, simul fuit seminata et mundata." *Mundata*, not *sanctificata*, which can be said only of a rational nature. Cf. text cited below, p. 204, at note 206.

Jesus was conceived *mundus de munda,* and the rest of us *immundi de immundis,* Mary was conceived *munda de immundis.*[198]

Now since the Son is purity itself, it was suitable that He should give His Mother such purity as He could; He had therefore not only to liberate, but to preserve her from all stain. God could create a sinless being; if Mary were tainted with sin, she would be inferior to such a being.[199] Hence he concludes:

> What He could do, it was fitting that He should do and from this it follows that He did do it; for the Son should honor the Mother.[200]

In reply to difficulties, amongst which one of the most important is that concerning the redemption of the Most Blessed Virgin, Ware affirms that Mary:

> . . . needed the Passion of Christ, not on account of any sin that was in her, but on account of that which would have been in her, had her Son not preserved her through faith. Thus Augustine, in his sermon on Magdalen,[201] says that there are two kinds of debts—those that are contracted and paid, and those that are not contracted, but could have been.[202]

Ware desires to hold the pious opinion, because:

> If I must err—seeing that I am not certain about the opposite position —I would rather err by excess in giving a privilege to Mary, than by defect, diminishing or taking from her a privilege which she had.[203]

As regards the feast itself, not only does it deserve to be celebrated because of the fact that, "all is pure in this conception so far as the Virgin herself is concerned," [204] but, "it could still be celebrated even if she had contracted original sin." [205]

---

[198] *Ibid.,* 6.

[199] *Ibidem.*

[200] *Ibidem:* "quod potuit, congruum fuit quod fecerit; et ex hoc sequitur quod ita fecerit, cum Filius debeat matrem honorare."

[201] AUGUSTINUS, *Sermo 99,* c.6 n.6 (PL 38, 598).

[202] GULIELMUS GUARRA, *op. cit.,* 10: "Ad aliud, cum dicitur: si fuisset sine peccato, non indiguisset redimi per passionem Christi, dico, quod sic; quia tota munditia Matris Virginis fuit a Filio; dicit enim Anselmus, II *Cur Deus homo* c.16, ubi quaerit discipulus quomodo Christus fuit mundus per se, si accepit munditiam a matre, et respondet Anselmus: 'Quoniam Matris munditia, per quam mundus est, non fuit nisi ab illo; ipse ergo per se ipsum et a se mundus fuit.' Unde tota munditia Matris fuit ei per Filium suum; unde indiguit passione Christi non propter peccatum, quod infuit, sed quod infuisset, nisi ipsemet Filius eam per fidem praeservasset. Et ideo dicit Augustinus in sermone *De Magdalena,* quod duplex est debitum, scilicet vel commissum et dimissum, vel non commissum, sed possibile committi; 'nullum enim peccatum facit unus homo, quod non posset facere alius homo, nisi praeservaretur a Deo.' "

[203] *Ibid.,* 4.

[204] *Ibid.,* 8: "Et ex hoc sequitur quintum, quod, ex quo totum mundum est quod est a parte Virginis in conceptione, festum conceptionis est celebrandum."

[205] *Ibidem:* "Et supposito, quod contraxisset originale, adhuc posset celebrari, in quantum illa massa debuit esse originale principium corporis Christi, non in quantum vitiata."

This manner of treating and solving the question recalls the apologists of the twelfth century whom we have listed above. The difficulties which had accumulated in the thirteenth century are solved briefly by Ware. He rejects the argument of St. Bernard and others on the grounds that they falsely identified purification with sanctification:

> for flesh and irrational nature are susceptible of cleansing, but not of sanctification.[206]

He also affirms the idea of a redemptive preservation; but not only does he fail to develop or elucidate this idea as applied to the Blessed Virgin, he even speaks of a sort of preservation "through faith." [207]

In the designs of Providence, it was Scotus who was destined to elucidate it at length. "This key idea of the theology of the Immaculate Conception will henceforth defy the attacks of its adversaries; it attains all its perfection in Scotus. If Ware found the formula which expresses preservative redemption and the *debitum* at one and the same time, Scotus has the honor of elucidating and justifying it happily and definitively." [208] We shall now take up the opinion of Scotus, who has been justly styled the Doctor of the Immaculate Conception.

John Duns Scotus

The doctrine of Duns Scotus on the Immaculate Conception, like that of Ware, is aptly designated by the axiom, *"Potuit, decuit, fecit,"* although it does not occur literally in his writings. In fact, it would be more in accord with Scotus' arguments to say, *"Decuit, fecit, potuit,"* or, better still, *"Voluit, fecit, potuit."* His arguments hinge on three points. The first comes to this:

> God was able to ensure that she should never be in original sin.[209]

Because:

> Everything is possible to God which is not manifestly contradictory in itself, and does not lead necessarily to a contradiction.[210]

The second principle is borrowed from the Fathers and other great doctors, but especially from St. Augustine and St. Anselm. With the

---

[206] *Ibid.,* 10.

[207] See note 202, above.

[208] Cavallera F., "Guillaume Ware et l'Immaculée Conception," in *Revue Duns Scot* 9 (1911) 154.

[209] I. Duns Scotus, *Ordinatio*, III, d.3, q.1, in *I. Duns Scoti, Theologie marianae elementa* (ed. Balić C., in *Bibliotheca mariana medii aevi,* 2) Sibenici 1933, 28: "Deus potuit facere, ut ipsa numquam fuisset in peccato originali . . ."
The work just cited will be referred to henceforth simply as Balić, *Elementa,* All the texts of Scotus bearing on the Immaculate Conception have recently been brought together in one small volume entitled *Ioannes Duns Scotus Doctor Immaculatae Conceptionis,* I. *Textus auctoris,* in *Bibliotheca Immaculatae Conceptionis,* V, Rome 1954. The work is quoted here as Balić, *Ioannes Duns Scotus.*

[210] I. Duns Scotus, *Ordinatio,* IV, d.10, q.2, n.5 (ed. Vivès, XVII, 193).

former he says: "when sin is being discussed, I do not wish there to be any question of Mary, on account of the reverence due to the Lord." [211] And with St. Anselm he adds, "It was altogether fitting that the Virgin should be resplendent with a purity than which no greater under God can be conceived." [212]   And Scotus faithfully echoes the views of both Augustine and Anselm when he says:

> With regard to honoring Christ I would rather err by excess than by defect if, through lack of knowledge, I am forced to fall into one or other. [213]

The third principle also is taken from Augustine: "Whatever course of action reason shows to be better, know that God has followed it rather than not." [214]   Then he notes:

> It seems probable to ascribe the more excellent prerogative to Mary, provided that the authority of the Church or of Scripture oppose no veto.[215]

Scotus was, moreover, mindful of the difficulties proposed by his predecessors, and he solved them adequately.   In answer to the objection that it was not fitting for the Blessed Virgin, begotten through seminal generation,[216] to have been sanctified either before the infusion of the soul (since she was not yet capable of receiving grace),[217] or in the first instant of the infusion of the soul (so that by means of the grace then infused she would be preserved from incurring original sin),[218] Scotus replies: "God was able to ensure that she should never be in original sin." [219] "For," he argues:

> . . . grace is equivalent to original justice, so far as God's approval of the soul is concerned; for, by reason of this approval, original sin does not reside in a soul that has grace. God could have conferred as much grace on her in the first moment of her soul's existence as He does on another soul at circumcision or baptism; in that moment, then, the soul would not have had original sin, as it would not have it afterwards when the person was baptized.[220]

---

[211] Augustinus, *De natura et gratia,* c36 n.42 (PL 44, 267); cf. Balić, *Elementa,* 20. 45. 197. 224. 336. See also chapter II of the present volume, p. 70.

[212] Anselmus, *De conceptu virginali,* c.18 (PL 158, 451).   Cf. Balić, *Elementa,* 20.

[213] I. Duns Scotus, *Ordinatio,* III, d.13 q.4 n.9 (ed. Vivès, XIV, 463).

[214] Augustinus, *De libero arbitrio,* III, c.5 n.13 (PL 32, 1277); Cf. I. Duns Scotus, *Ordinatio,* III, d.13 q.4 n.9 (ed. Vivès, XIV, 463).

[215] Duns Scotus, *Ordinatio,* III d.3 q.1 (Balić, *Elementa* 31): "Quod autem horum trium quae ostensa sunt possibilia esse, factum sit, Deus novit; sed si auctoritati Ecclesiae vel auctoritati Scripturae non repugnet, videtur probabile, quod excellentius est attribuere Mariae."

[216] *Ibid.* (21).

[217] *Ibid.* (29).

[218] See above, notes 141 and 152.

[219] Duns Scotus, *op. cit.* (Balić, *Ioannes Duns Scotus,* 11, 19-20).

[220] *Ibid.* (29).

Scotus proceeds to recall the following arguments against the Immaculate Conception: "Mary was not righteous in the first moment of her natural existence; therefore she was non-righteous;" [221] "By nature the Blessed Virgin is first and foremost a daughter of Adam," therefore, she is a child of wrath, and accordingly has sin.[222] Scotus answers that there is nothing repugnant in the soul's being created, united with the flesh and adorned with grace, all in the same instant.[223]

Again, it is argued that Mary "was *naturaliter* a daughter of Adam prior to being justified." Scotus concedes that, given the nature which Mary had, and the way in which it was conceived, the natural consequence was for her to be a daughter of Adam and without grace in the first instant of nature. "But," he maintains, "it does not follow that she was deprived [of justice] in that instant of nature (speaking of the absolutely first instant) :

> For, by the priority here concerned, nature is just as much prior to the privation of justice as it is to justice itself. All that can be inferred is that it pertains intrinsically to nature to be naturally the foundation of Adamic filiation; and that neither justice nor the lack of it is included in nature thus considered. This I grant.[224]

---

[221] *Ibid.* (40): "non est iusta in primo instanti naturae: ergo in illo instanti naturae est non iusta, ex II Periherm."

[222] Cf. *ibid.* (38-40).

[223] *Ibid.* (29; 38-41).

[224] *Ibid.*, 18, 9-19: "Quando igitur arguitur quod 'prius naturaliter fuit filia Adae quam justificata—concedo quod illam naturam in primo instanti naturae sic conceptam consequebatur esse filiam Adae et non habere gratiam in illo instanti naturae. Sed non sequitur: ergo in illo instanti naturae fuit privata, loquendo de omnino primo instanti, quia secundum illam primitatem natura ita naturaliter praecessit privationem iustitiae, sicut ipsam iustitiam; sed tantum potest hic inferri, quod de ratione naturae est, quod est naturaliter fundamentum filiationis Adae: nec in ea ut sic includitur iustitia, nec eius carentia, quod concedo." Cf. Michel A., "Duns Scot et l'Immaculée Conception," in *L'Ami du Clergé* 64 (1954) 355: "C'est la distinction qui, chez les théologiens immaculistes postérieurs, deviendra classique . . ." P. 353: "Il est certain que le jeune théologien franciscain opéra une réaction profonde contre la thèse patronée par les plus grandes autorités de son temps . . ." P. 354: ". . . le jeune docteur d'Oxford, par ses répliques et ses distinctions pertinentes, se place au départ de l'explication du dogme de la conception immaculée."—Marin Sola F., O.P., *L'évolution homogène du dogme catholique*, I², Fribourg 1924, 322-331, deals with the dogma of the Immaculate Conception.—P. 323: "Le doute et la discussion n'ont porté que sur la mineure *de raison* suivante: 'Or on peut être à la fois *conçu sans péché originel et racheté* par Jésus-Christ'. Tel est le point central des controverses relatives au développement du dogme de l'Immaculée Conception."—P. 324: "C'est au célèbre Scot et à son école, sur ce point, immortelle, que revient, sans nul doute, la gloire d'avoir *amorcé* la vraie solution du problème . . ." The author confesses that, "sans vouloir diminuer le moins du monde le mérite incontestable de Scot en cette question," Scotus only had the merit "d'avoir amorcé la vraie solution du problème," because he does not speak clearly enough about the "debitum personnel ou prochain sans lequel il semble presque impossible de sauvegarder une véritable et légitime rédemption personnelle." (P. 325, in note)—On this question of *"debitum personale,"* see Balić C., *De debito peccati originalis in B. V. Maria. Investigationes de doctrina quam tenuit Ioannes Duns Scotus*, Rome 1941.

Moreover, according to the mind of the Subtle Doctor this priority is privative rather than positive, i.e., a priority discovered by reason which in no way affects the real being of the Virgin.[225]

But Scotus' chief title to fame was the fact that he reconciled the truth of the Immaculate Conception not only with the dogma of original sin but also with that of Christ, the universal Redeemer:

> (If she had been without sin) Mary would have had the greatest need of Christ as Redeemer; for by reason of her procreation, which followed the common mode, she would have contracted original sin had she not been kept from it by the grace of the Mediator, and just as others are in need of Christ for the remission, by His merit, of sin which they have already contracted, so Mary would have been in still greater need of a Mediator preventing her from contracting sin.[225a]

As a matter of fact, the reasoning employed by Scotus permitted him to go so far as to say that the opinion denying the Immaculate Conception really derogated from Christ's eminence as the most perfect Redeemer. For everybody agreed that Christ was a most perfect Redeemer; that being so, He ought to have saved at least one person from contracting original sin, to wit, his Mother:

> The most perfect mediator exercises the most perfect act of mediation possible with respect to some person for whom he mediates: therefore Christ had the most perfect form of mediation possible with respect to someone for whom He was Mediator. But for no one did He exercise a more excellent form of mediation than for Mary; therefore, etc.

> But this would not be so if He had not merited to preserve her from original sin.[226]

---

[225] Cf. Balić C., *De debito peccati originalis* 86; Bonnefoy J. Fr., "La negación del 'debitum peccati' en María. Síntesis historica," in *Verdad y Vida* 12 (1954) 103-171; Alcantara P., "La redención y el débito de María. Siglos XVII-XVIII," *ibid.*, 1-48.

[225a] Duns Scotus, *Ordinatio*, III d.3 q.1 (Balić, *Elementa*, 35,9 - 36,3): Per idem patet ad rationes factas pro prima opinione quia Maria maxime indiguisset Christo ut redemptore; ipsa enim contraxisset originale peccatum ex ratione propagationis communis, nisi fuisset praeventa per gratiam mediatoris; et sicut alii indiguerunt Christo, ut per eius meritum remitteretur eis peccatum iam contractum, ita illa magis indiguit mediatore praeveniente peccatum, ne esset aliquando ab ipsa contrahendum et ne ipsa contraheret.

[226] Duns Scotus, *Ordinatio*, III d.3 q.1 (Balić, *Elementa*, 22, 6-23, 4): "*arguitur ex excellentia Filii sui*, in quantum redemptor, reconciliator et mediator fuit, *quod ipsa non contraxit peccatum originale*. Perfectissimus enim mediator perfectissimum actum habet mediandi possibilem respectu alicuius personae pro qua mediatur,—ergo Christus habuit perfectissimum gradum mediandi possibilem respectu alicuius personae respectu cuius erat mediator; respectu nullius personae habuit excellentiorem gradum quam respectu Mariae; ergo etc. Sed hoc non esset nisi meruisset eam praeservare a peccato originali . . ."

Ibid. (25, 6-8): "si Christus perfectissime reconciliavit nos Deo, istam poenam gravissimam meruit ab aliquo auferre,—sed non nisi a matre; ergo etc."

Scotus proves this fundamental thesis of his by means of various arguments: "first, with reference to God to whom [Christ] reconciles; secondly, with reference to the evil from which He liberates; thirdly, with reference to the obligation incumbent on the person whom He had reconciled." [227]   In this diffuse and subtle reasoning we find assertions such as the following:

> Christ would not have placated the Trinity in the most perfect manner possible for the fault incurred by Adam's descendants, if He did not prevent [at least] one person from offending the Trinity and if the soul of [at least] one of Adam's children had not been without that fault.[228]

> It is a more excellent benefit to preserve a person from evil, than to permit him to fall into it and then deliver him from it.[229]

The exemption of the Blessed Virgin is plain if we consider, on the one hand, the gravity and malice of original sin, and, on the other hand, the relation of mother to son. Theologians were unanimously agreed that Mary was free from actual sin; from this the Subtle Doctor argued that she was also free from original sin.[230] For if Mary had not been exempt from original sin, the angels would have been purer and holier than she; and while some creatures would be indebted to Christ for the remission of original sin, others for the remission of mortal and venial sin, no human creature would be indebted to Him to a supreme degree for the gift of innocence. If we bear in mind that we are not considering actual sin, but original sin, i.e. sin "contracted from another," [231] it will be plain that the common opinion which places Mary in the power of the devil is not reasonable and that preservative redemption is more reasonable.

From the entire reasoning it is quite clear that:

> The Blessed Mother of God . . . was never at enmity [with God] either

---

Ibid. (26, 9-10): "nulla persona summe tenebitur Christo ut mediatori si nullam praeservavit a peccato originali."

Ibid. (35,14-36,3): "sicut alii indiguerunt Christo ut per eius meritum remitteretur eis peccatum iam contractum, ita illa magis indiguit mediatore praeveniente peccatum, ne esset aliquando ab ipsa contrahendum et ne ipsa contraheret."

Ibid. (41, 2-7): "patet quod ianua fuit sibi aperta per meritum passionis Christi, praevisae et acceptatae specialiter in ordine ad hanc personam, ut propter illam passionem numquam huic personae inesset peccatum, et ita nec aliquid propter quod ianua clauderetur, cum tamen sibi ex origine competeret unde ianua sibi clauderetur, sicut aliis."

[227] *Ibid.* (23).
[228] *Ibid.* (24).
[229] *Ibid.* (27).
[230] *Ibid.* (26).
[231] *Ibid.*, 8, 10.—Dom Capelle B., "La fête de la conception de Marie en Occident," *VIII Congrès marial national, 1954, Immaculée Conception*, Lyon 1954, 154, writes: "L'idée d'une rédemption préservatrice avait déjà été suggérée avant lui, mais nul n'y avait ajouté ce qui suit: 'De plus, si le Christ a mérité qu'une multitude d'âmes lui soient débitrices de leur grâce et de leur gloire, pourquoi n'y en aurait-il aucune qui lui soit débitrice de son innocence? Et pourquoi, puisque les saints anges sont là-haut innocents, n'y aurait-il dans la patrie aucune autre âme humaine innocente que celle du Christ.' "

actually—on account of actual sin, or *originally*—because of original sin. She would have been [at enmity with God] had she not been preserved [from original sin].[232]

Thus far we have considered only the *Ordinatio*—the work which Scotus wrote with his own hand or dictated. It was the last work of his life, and was, in fact, unfinished and unpublished when he died. But the argument from the most perfect Redeemer is also present in all five forms of the *Reportationes,* which represent various lectures given by him in Paris and Oxford. Moreover, it is also frequently asserted in each of the *Reportationes* that Mary did not contract sin. It is not a matter of a mere hypothesis in Scotus' mind, or of the "fittingness" of the doctrine; he flatly asserts that Christ ought to have preserved His Mother, that He willed to do so, and that He actually did so! [233]

---

[232] I. DUNS SCOTUS, *Ordinatio* III d.18 (BALIĆ, *Ioannes Duns Scotus,* 21): "Est etiam [scil. in caelo] beatissima mater Dei, quae numquam fuit inimica 'actualiter' ratione peccati actualis, nec 'originaliter' ratione peccati originalis; fuisset tamen nisi fuisset praeservata."

As to the historical value of the story of Scotus' disputation about the Immaculate Conception in Paris, I have treated the matter at length in the work *Ioannis Duns Scoti Theologiae marianae elementa,* pp. xcvii-cxx. I showed that the explicit assertion of this disputation dates from about the year 1430, that the story became more embellished with the passage of time and reached its final form in the *Annals* of Wadding. However, I came to the conclusion that Scotus did have some form of disputation with his adversaries, because Scotus' mind on the third distinction of the third book of Sentences, as portrayed in the Valencia codex is so different from the other five forms in which his thought is preserved for us; it begins without giving arguments *"Quod sic"* and *"quod non,"* and straight away proposes the thesis to be defended after quoting twenty-four authorities comes to the determination: "De conceptione autem arguitur sic: *Celebranda. Quaere alibi."* It is evident that this was no "solemn" disputation, and that Duns Scotus did not admit in it any more than he had admitted in the Third Book of the Sentences, and it is easy to understand why his contemporaries did not pay any special attention to it. Besides, we have several testimonies from the second decade of the fourteenth century, including that of Petrus Aureoli in 1314, that "many outstanding doctors preached in Paris and in England, and still preach every year that the Virgin Mary did not contract original sin." (Cf. FR. GULIELMI GUARRAE, FR. I. DUNS SCOTI, FR. P. AUREOLI . . . , as cited in note 189, above, 72). We only know one of those many doctors anterior to the year 1314. Consequently we can see that there is no weight in the argument from silence which is constantly being brought against Duns Scotus' disputation; the critics are not thinking of a simple disputation, but of a solemn and spectacular and decisive public disputation, which we readily agree to have been a legend.

[233] Thus, in the so-called *Opus Parisiense,* III d.3 2.1, we read: ". . . si Christus est perfectissimus mediator, praevenit omnem offensam in matre sua"; ". . . si debet mater summe obligari Filio, debet Filius praevenire omne peccatum originale." (BALIĆ, *Ioannes Duns Scotus* 29, 6-22; cf. *ibid.,* lines 35 f.; p. 30, 35-38)

The same ideas occur in the *Troyes* codex of the *Reportationes.* The argument begins with the following statement: "Quia ehim Christus fuit redemptor universalis, ideo sequitur quod Maria non habuit peccatum originale." (*Ibid.,* 39, 28-30) In the *probatio,* the following reasoning occurs: "Item, redemptio Christi et mediatoris Dei et hominum maxime fuit propter peccatum originale; sed ista mediatio pro persona Virginis praeservavit ab omni peccato actuali, manifestum est; ergo magis ab originali." (*Ibid.,* 40, 19-22; cf. 42, 19-23)

In the *Reportationes* preserved in the *Barcelona* and *Valencia* codices, the affirma-

To sum up briefly: in the argument based on the most perfect manner of redeeming considered with regard to God and to the person preserved, Scotus did not wish to impose an obligation on God, who always acts most freely. But, since God cannot will things which are contrary to right reason (which would be the case were it true that the Mother of God had original sin), it follows that He achieved (*"fecit"*) what it behoved him to accomplish (*"decuit"*), and what he could accomplish (*"potuit"*).[234]

*   *   *

Scotus' intervention had widespread repercussions both in England and on the continent. Even during the lifetime of the Subtle Doctor, his

---

tion of the Marian privilege is still more outspoken. The former contains the following expressions: ". . . actus perfectissimus mediandi requirit vel immunitatem ab omni peccato vel praeservationem ab omni peccato.—Sed in Virgine fuit huiusmodi praeservatio, a Christo . . ." (*ibid.*, 53, 31-33); "[Christus] Deum praevenit merito passionis ne inesset culpa matri suae, quam contraxisset nisi prius pro ea placaret offensum pro offensione quam incurreret de se, ut sic ex complacatione mediatoris numquam esset inimicus vel inimica, quae tamen de communi iure successionis esset inimica nisi placatio praeveniret . . ." (*ibid.*, 54, 17-22); ". . . praeservavit matrem suam ut paenam istam numquam incurreret" (*ibid.*, 55, 1-2); "Item, perfectissimus mediator debet mediare tam pro originali quam pro actuali peccato; sed mediavit in Maria, eam praeservando ab actuali,—ergo et ab originali" (*ibid.*, 55, 9-11).

The *Valencia* codex argues thus: ". . . cum . . . dicitur . . . 'Christus fuit mediator vel redemptor universalissimus, vel mediator perfectissimus,' [dico quod verum est], sed ad talem pertinet ut praeservet a culpa ne insit . . ." (*ibid.*, 67, 14-17); ". . . ad mediatorem et reconciliatorem perfectissimum pertinet quod eum qui offendit 'non ex culpa sua actuali sed aliunde contracta' praeservet ne offendat" (*ibid.*, 17-19); "Item, non est perfectus mediator qui non impetrat remissionem paenae maximae; sed culpa est maior paena quae possit inesse animae . . . ; igitur Christus matrem suam ab ea praeservavit, si mediator perfectissimus et reconciliator fuit" (*ibid.*, 68, 1-6); ". . . sicut aliis remittitur culpa per meritum passionis Christi, sic Mariae collata fuit gratia praeservans a culpa, quae culpa ei infuisset nisi sic praeservaretur; . . ." (*ibid.*, 68, 26—69, 1; cf. 69, 15-25; 70, 19-20).

Finally, the *Lectura Completa* repeats that ". . . non est perfectissimus mediator et reconciliator qui non obtinet remissionem maximae paenae; . . . igitur praeservavit eam a culpa originali" (*ibid.*, 87, 25-31); "Ex quo tunc probabile est quod beata Virgo sibi summe tenetur, sequitur quod nullam umquam culpam habuit,—ut sic tota Trinitas, ab aeterno praevidens passionem Christi, placata fuit ratione illius, ut beata Virgo praeservaretur semper ab omni culpa, tam actuali quam originali" (*ibid.*, 88, 7-11; cf. *ibid.*, 89, 1-4; 96, 17-20; 98, 26-28).

[234] Replying formally *ad quaestionem* in the *Ordinatio,* Scotus placed among the "possible" solutions, the opinion that Mary did not contract original sin, together with the opposite opinion, and the third which held that she remained in sin for an instant only. He did indeed declare: "Quod autem horum trium quae ostensa sunt possibilia esse, factum sit, Deus novit,—sed si auctoritati Ecclesiae vel auctoritati Scripturae non repugnet, videtur probabile, quod excellentius est, attribuere Mariae." I. Duns Scotus, *Ordinatio* III, d.3 q.1, ed. Balić, *Ioannes Duns Scotus,* 13, 11-14).

But if anyone reading these words were to doubt whether Scotus had demonstrated only the possibility or also the fact of the Marian privilege, he would show himself familiar only with the externals but ignorant of the real Scotus. It suffices to continue reading further and see how Scotus answers each and every one of the difficulties which are raised on grounds of Scripture, patrology, physiology and philosophy. Then, having demolished that hypothesis, which had been introduced

former teacher, Master William of Ware, had already modified the previously accepted proof of the fact of the Immaculate Conception, and had come to the conclusion that Mary was *certainly* conceived without sin.[235] Richard of Bromwich, about 1306, transcribes the whole argument drawn from the infinite perfection of the Redeemer, and consequently adheres to the pious opinion.[236]   In Paris, after Scotus had successfully attacked the arguments which St. Thomas, St. Bonaventure, St. Bernard and Peter Lombard had brought against the Immaculate Conception, Ralph de Hotot ventured to preach the Marian privilege in a public university sermon.[237]

But although the immunity of the Blessed Virgin from all sin appears as the necessary postulate of the perfection of Christ, who is God and man, *"Summum opus Dei,"* as the Subtle Doctor puts it, nevertheless, the passage of centuries and much discussion were necessary before this truth, which seems so elementary to us now, appeared clearly to all Catholic theologians. No sooner had the pious opinion been clearly expounded by Scotus in Oxford and Paris, than the authority and arguments of St. Thomas and

---

by the word "if," Scotus sees only the fact of the preservation of the Blessed Virgin, which he had already proved from the excellence of Christ.

Neither is there any indication of the contrary in his words, "nihil assero," in the *Reportatio* (Balić, *Ioannes Duns Scotus*, 32, 22) if we remember that he used similar expressions with regard to all the propositions which form the very basis of the Scotistic system.   Did he not say of the formal distinction, "dico sine assertione et praeiudicio melioris sententiae" (cf. I. Duns Scotus, *Ordinatio*, I d.2 n. 389, ed. Vaticana (Città del Vaticano 1950), II, 349)? With regard to the brief proposition in Theorema 14, proposition 27, it is well known that this Theorema belongs to those fifty-seven propositions about beliefs (e.g. the Blessed Trinity, the Incarnation, interior life in God, etc.) about which Scotus rightly says that they cannot be proven necessarily and evidently, *by mere reason*, and abstracting from revelation. Consequently, the Theoremata cannot be quoted as a source when discussing whether or not, according to Scotus, the Immaculate Conception can be proved.

Cf. Kaup J., *Duns Skotus als Vollender der Lehre von der Unbefleckten Empfängnis*, in *Beiträge zur Geschichte der Philosophie und Theologie des Mittelalters*, Supplementband, III, 2, Münster 1935, 991-1008; Roschini G. M., *Mariologia²*, II, pars 2, Romae 1948, 69; de Guimaraens F., "La doctrine des théologiens sur l'Immaculée Conception de 1250 à 1350," in *Etudes franciscaines* 4 (1953) 31-33; Koser K., "Die Immakulatalehre des Johannes Duns Scotus," in *Franziskanische Studien* 36 (1954) 337-384; Arcangelo da Roc, *Il Dottore dell' Immacolata*, Roma 1955; P. Migliore, "La dottrina dell' Immacolata in Guglielmo de Ware, O. Min. e nel B. Giovanni Duns Scoto, O. Min.," in *Miscellanea francescana* 54 (1954) 433-538.

[235] Guilielmus Guarra, *Reportatio in III Sent.*, d.3 q.1 (Bordeaux, bibl. municip., cod.163, 162vb): "Ex quo enim Filius tenebatur ad honorem Matris et possibile contrarium fuit sic fieri quod esset sine peccato, per consequens sic debuit facere, et *credo certe quod fecit"*; "Ideo credo quod sic factum sit" (Firenze, bibl. naz. conv. A. IV. 42, 121vb) ". . . sicut debuit facere, fecit"; "Ideo credo quod sic sit factum."

[236] Richardus de Bromwich, *Sent. III*, d.3; Worcester, bibl. cathedr. F.139, 181v.

[237] Cf. Ioannes de Polliaco (work cited above, in note 159) 1; Doucet V., "Raoul le Breton défenseur de l'Immaculée Conception . . ." in *Archivum franciscanum historicum* 47 (1954) 448-450.

others were urged against it.   The pious opinion was already known as the *Opinio Scoti* in the first half of the fourteenth century,[238] and within a short time the opposite opinion came to be known as *opinio Thomae*.[239] Under these two leaders and with these two banners the controversy continued until 1854, when both schools—those who supported and those who denied the Marian privilege—laid down their arms in the embrace of the truth which all Catholic theologians had always sought and longed for.

It was the merit of Duns Scotus that when the opinion contrary to the Immaculate Conception was in possession in both Oxford and Paris, he obliged all his contemporaries to re-examine the question and ask themselves not merely whether Mary might have been in sin only for an instant, but whether she had ever been in sin at all.   His merit lay in proposing the question properly, using the correct terminology, proving the Marian privilege from the dignity of Christ, and showing that there was no impossibility on account of her natural generation and the transmission of original sin.   On account of his learning and the influence which he exercised as the best known and the acknowledged head of one of the schools, the title of "Doctor of the Immaculate Conception" was given to him; and since this mystery is, after the Divine Motherhood, the most important part of Mariology, he rightly became known simply as the "Marian Doctor."

---

[238] Cf. IOANNES DE POLLIACO, *op. cit.*, 64; BACONTHORPE I., *Sent. II*, d.30 q.unica a.2 (ed. SAGGI L., "Ioannis Baconthorpe textus de Immaculata Conceptione," in *Carmelus* 2 [1955] 219-223).

[239] Cf. THOMAS DE SUTTON, *Sent. III*, d.3, bibl. apostol. Vaticana, cod. Ross. lat. 431, 111v; IOANNES CAPREOLUS, *Defensiones theologicae divi Thomae Aquinatis in III Sent.*, d.3 q.1, Tours 1904, V, 26-40; GABRIEL BIEL, *Repertorium generale super Sent. III*, d.3 q.1 a.1 (Lugduni 1519), s. fol.).

VI

The Controversy over the Immaculate Conception from after Scotus to the End of the Eighteenth Century

Wenceslaus Sebastian, O.F.M.[*]

Historians acknowledge Scotus as the herald and champion of the Immaculate Conception.[1] Yet if it is true that he gave the thirteenth-century controversy a decisive turn, he did not by any means immediately compel universal acceptance of the doctrine. After his death, in fact, and almost to the very moment of the proclamation of the Dogma of Mary's Immaculate Conception, a long and often very bitter conflict persisted between theologians of opposite schools. Though the struggle was not free from the passion and rivalry inherent to all things human, it nevertheless was the providential means God used to clarify and establish the principles, terminology and doctrinal grounds of Our Lady's glorious prerogative. It stimulated research, led to greater precision in academic circles, and produced more persuasive eloquence in the pulpit. Thus, as the centuries rolled by, the teaching of the Church's official *magisterium* gradually became more explicit, and the faith of its members grew stronger and more universal; until finally belief in Mary's freedom from original sin was like a swelling tide that swept away all opposition and compelled unfailing acceptance in the whole Catholic world.

It is our purpose in this paper to trace the doctrinal history of the Immaculate Conception through the period which begins with the death of Scotus and ends with the close of the eighteenth century. We shall divide our dissertation into two parts, of which the first will deal with the interval between Scotus and the Constitutions of Sixtus IV, and the second with the period from Sixtus IV to Pius VI.

[*] Professor of Dogmatic Theology, Regina Cleri Seminary, Regina, Saskatchewan, Canada. The present study was completed in June, 1954.
[1] G. Alastruey, *Tratado de la Virgen santisima*, 2 ed., Madrid 1947, p. 198. "Juan Duns Escoto es el heraldo y propugnator glorioso de la concepción inmaculada de María."

I

BETWEEN SCOTUS AND SIXTUS IV

Scotus' opinion was a novelty in an academic world which, ever since Bernard of Clairvaux, had been told that to accept Mary's Immaculate Conception was tantamount to denying the universality of the Redemption. The young Friar's explanation of the perfect redemption, clear as it was, could not dispel all suspicion and distrust even in the most unbiased minds; and it had the effect of antagonizing those who had sworn allegiance to St. Thomas, the "angel of the School." Thus it was not long before controversy was in the ascendant.

EARLY CONTROVERSIES

Opposition to the doctrine of the Immaculate Conception in the fourteenth century came to a considerable extent from the Order of Preachers.[2] As early as 1313, at the General Chapter of Metz, the Order of St. Dominic had been urged to follow the doctrine of St. Thomas: "Cum doctrina . . . fratris Thomae de Aquino sanior et communior reputetur, et eam ordo noster specialiter prosequi teneatur." [3] When in 1323 the Angelic Doctor was solemnly canonized, it was only natural that the Dominicans should consider his doctrine as officially sanctioned by the Church.[4] It is therefore not surprising that theologians like Herveus Natalis,[5] Durandus de S. Porciano,[6] Petrus de Palude[7] and John of Naples[8] should unanimously rally behind St. Thomas and take their stand against the teaching of the Immaculate Conception.

John of Naples, a master in the University of Paris around 1317, was evidently influenced by John of Pouilly, of the diocesan clergy, who had taught in the same university around the year 1309. Both vehemently attacked the doctrine of the Immaculate Conception as taught by Scotus and his followers,[9] of whom, as Pouilly insinuates, there seems even at

---

[2] D. A. MORTIER, *Histoire des maîtres généraux de l'ordre des Frères Prêcheurs,* vol. 3, Paris 1907, p. 617, note 2.

[3] A. DUVAL, O.P., "La dévotion mariale dans l'ordre des Frères Prêcheurs," in *Maria,* II, Paris 1952, p. 756, note 99.

[4] P. MANDONNET, O.P., "La canonization de saint Thomas d'Aquin (12 juillet 1323)," in *Mélanges thomistes* (Bibliothèque thomiste, III), Paris 1923, p. 1-48.

[5] Herveus NATALIS, Quodl. IV, art. 15; VII, art. 12. Cf. GLORIEUX, *La littérature quodlibétique de 1260 à 1320,* Le Saulchoir, Kain, 1925, vol. 2, p. 204, 206.

[6] DURANDUS DE S. PORCIANO, Quodl. III (1314), art. 12; GLORIEUX, *op. cit.,* vol. 2, p. 73.

[7] Petrus de PALUDE, in *III Sent.,* d.3, q.1, Erlangen, bibl. univ. cod. 338.

[8] IOANNES DE NEAPOLI, *Quodl.* I [VI], q.11; *Quodl.* IX, q.14, in C. BALIC, *Ioannis de Polliaco et Ioannis de Neapoli Quaestiones Disputatae de Immaculata Conceptione Beatae Mariae Virgins,* Sibenici 1931, p. 71-95.

[9] C. BALIC, *op. cit.,* p. XLIX-LIV.

that early date to have been a considerable number.[10]   In the writings of
both theologians we discover flagrant accusations against proponents of
Mary's preservation.[11]   Against such who presume to teach this doctrine,
says Pouilly, one ought to proceed not with arguments, but otherwise:
"Qui si praesumeret, non argumentis sed aliter contra ipsum procedendum
esset." [12]

In their refutation of Scotus, John of Naples and John of Pouilly follow
the traditional arguments.   Christ alone was preserved from original sin
because He was born of a Virgin and was to be our Mediator and
Redeemer.[13]   Since the redemption by Christ was, according to Scripture,
to be universal, all without exception were necessarily subject to sin.[14]

---

[10] *Ibid.*, p. LI.

[11] IOANNES DE POLLIACO, *Quodl.* III, q.3 a.3, ed. Balic, p. 70: "Si aliqui illud
praedicaverint pseudopraedictatores fuerunt, haeresim praedicantes"; IOANNES DE
NEAPOLI, *ibid.*, p. 84.   [12] BALIC, *op. cit.*, p. 13.   [13] *Ibid.*, p. XLIII.

[14] IOANNES DE NEAPOLI, *Quodl.* I: "Undecima quaestio est, utrum beata Virgo
contraxerit peccatum originale? . . .

"Respondeo: In hac quaestione sunt duae opiniones. Quidam enim dicunt, quod
non fuit concepta in peccato originali. Et primo probant, quod hoc decuit; secundo,
quod ita de facto fuit. . . .

"Alii dicunt oppositum, scilicet quod concepta fuit in peccato originali. Quam
opinionem tamquam magis consonam dictis sacrae Scripturae et sanctorum ad praesens teneo. Ad cuius evidentiam probanda sunt tria per ordinem:

"Et primum est, quod de potentia absoluta Dei potuit praeservari ab omni peccato originali sic quod numquam contraxisset illud. . . .

"Secundo probandum est quod hoc non decuit. Quod probatur sic: Non decuit
aliquem purum hominem excipi a generali omnium redemptione et salute, quae est
per Christum, de quo dicitur, Math. 1, 21: *Salvum faciet populum suum a peccatis
eorum;* et I ad Timoth. 4, 10: *Qui est Salvator omnium, et maxime fidelium.* Sed
beata Virgo esset a tali redemptione et salute excepta, si numquam peccatum originale contraxisset: ergo etc.

"Maior declarata est, minor probatur. Quia cum redemptio seu salus non sit,
nisi existentis, sicut nihil proprie habet esse, cum solum est in causa sua, nisi habeat
esse in se ipso, sic nec proprie potest dici aliquis redemptus vel salvatus existens sub
spirituali servitute, quae est per culpam, solum in suis parentibus et non in propria
persona. Unde Augustinus, in libro, *De perfectione iustitiae* cap. utimo: 'Quisquis
fuisse vel esse in hac vita aliquem hominem, vel aliquos homines putat, excepto uno
Mediatore Dei et hominum, quibus necessaria non fuerit remissio peccatorum. con-
trarius est divinae Scripturae, ubi Apostolus dicit: *Per unum hominem peccatum intravit in mundum, et per peccatum mors, et ita in omnes homines pertransiit, in quo
omnes peccaverunt;* et necesse est, ut ipsa contentione asserat posse esse homines, qui
sine mediatore Christo liberante et salvante liberi sint salvique a peccato.' Quantumcumque ergo beata Virgo fuisset praeservata, non tamen potuisset dici vere esse
redempta et salvata a Christo, nisi quandoque fuisset subiecta servituti peccati in
persona propria et non solum in persona parentum.

"Et confirmatur ratio, quia redemptio seu salvatio importat quandam mutationem
seu transitum a culpa ad gratiam, sicut dealbatio importat mutationem de nigredine
in albedinem . . . ergo nullus proprie potest dici vere esse salvatus vel redemptus a
Christo qui numquam fuit subiectus servituti peccati.

"Tertio probandum est, quod de facto subiecta fuit peccato originali. Quod patet:

"Primo per auctoritatem Apostoli ad Rom. 5, 12, ubi loquens qualiter per primum
hominem intravit peccatum in mundum, dicit, quod in ipso *omnes peccaverunt;*..."
—ed. BALIC, pp. 73-79 cf. p. XLIV.

Because Mary was born in concupiscence, she necessarily underwent in her soul the infection inherent in her body.[15] The Blessed Virgin was subject to original sin at least for a time and was sanctified only after her conception.[16]

The importance of John of Naples and John of Pouilly can hardly be overstressed since their arguments were quoted by nearly all opponents of the Scotistic opinion in after years. Peter of Alva y Astorga took the trouble to check the writings of such authors as Capreolus, Torquemada, Bandelli, St. Antoninus, Peter of Vincentia and others, only to find that they quoted our two theologians verbatim.[17] Under the leadership of the latter, opposition to the immaculist opinion not only continued through the second half of the fourteenth century but it became uncompromising and aggressive; so much so that prior to the Council of Basel, John Capreolus expressed the common opinion of his order when he wrote: "Beata Virgo fuit concepta in peccato originali."[18] The popularity of the maculist opinion is all the more evident if one considers that three of the popes of the fourteenth century either adopted it frankly or at least failed to reject it.[19]

Even the Friars Minor had their opponents to the new doctrine in those early years. Thus Bertrand de Turre († 1334), a renowned preacher and successively archbishop of Salerno and cardinal of Frascati, prefers to hold the common opinion of Alexander of Hales and St. Bonaventure: "sicut tenet scola communis."[20] Another illustrious Friar, Alvarus Pelagius, an apostolic penitentiary under John XXII and later bishop of Silves in Portugal, writing to the court of Avignon around 1330 professed allegiance to the traditional doctrine and chided the "new" theologians who departed from the common view: "licet quidam novi theologi a sensu Ecclesiae recedentes communi . . ."[21] Yet the "quidam novi" were far more numerous than Pelagius suspected, at least if we may judge by Holzapfel's *Bibliotheca Franciscana*.[22] Among them there were important theologians, such as Peter Aureoli, John of Bassolis, Peter Thomas, Francis Mayron, Peter of Aquila, Francis de Marchia and William Rubio.[23] Let us give closer attention to a few of them.

Peter Aureoli, who read the Sentences in Paris in 1316, and was, on

---

[15] *Ibid.*, p. 6, 80.   [16] *Ibid.*, p. 49.   [17] *Ibid.*, p. XXIV, XXXV.

[18] Ioannes Capreolus, *Libri defensionum theologiae divi doctoris Thomae de Aquino in libros Sententiarum*, I, III, q.3, a.1 (Tours 1900, vol. 5, p. 26).

[19] See chapter VII of the present volume, p. 293, and especially notes 83, 86.

[20] *Sermo 1, de Nativitate et de Conceptione*, quoted by Alva et Astorga, *Radii solis*, col. 1141.

[21] Alvarus Pelagius, O.F.M., *De planctu Ecclesiae*, 1. 2, c.52, Venice 1560, p. 110.

[22] H. Holzapfel, *Bibliotheca Franciscana de immaculata Conceptione*, Quarrachi 1904.

[23] X. Le Bachelet, "Immaculée Conception," in *Dict. de theol. cath.* 7, col. 1081; P. Pauwels, *Les Franciscains et l'Immaculée Conception*, Malines 1904, p. 79.

the injunction of John XXII, granted the Master's degree in theology in 1318,[24] wrote two treatises on the Immaculate Conception. The first, *Tractatus de Conceptione Mariae Virginis,* consists of six chapters in which Aureoli systematically expounds the opinions and arguments of both schools, concluding that Mary's preservation from original sin can be maintained without danger of heresy, and that neither opinion is *de fide* until the Church defines it as such.[25] Peter's second treatise, *Repercussorium editum contra adversarium innocentiae matris Dei,* is an answer to William Gannati, O.P., who had attacked Aureoli's *Tractatus de Conceptione.*[26] Aureoli concludes by stating that any sin, be it original, mortal or venial, is repugnant to the Mother of Grace, since sin and grace are contradictory. Pious ears would be horrified to hear of a stain of sin in the fountain of grace. Wherefore, until the Holy Roman Church expressly determined what belief should be held concerning the conception or the sanctification of the Immaculate Virgin, he, Peter Aureoli, would not abandon what he had begun to teach; nor did his conscience reproach him on his stand.[27]

One of Aureoli's contributions to the development of the theology of the Immaculate Conception consists in a distinction he places between contracting original sin *de iure* and incurring it *de facto.* Everyone who descends from Adam "libidinose," "per viam propagationis et seminis," contracts original sin *de iure.* By the very nature of his birth he becomes liable to contract original sin. Whether he contracts it *de facto* depends on God's will to preserve or not to preserve him. It would be impossible for a person to contract original sin *de facto,* even though *de iure* he were bound to contract it, if God by His grace and condonation preserved him from doing so. In the case of the Blessed Virgin there is no doubt that *de iure* she was a "child of wrath" and contracted original sin, born as she was by way of natural propagation; but whether she contracted it *de facto* is the point at issue. Aureoli then goes on by lengthy arguments to prove that God could and very becomingly would preserve her; and he concludes

---

[24] *Fr. Gulielmi Guarrae, Fr. Ioannis Duns Scoti, Fr. Petri Aureoli Quaestiones Disputatae de Immaculata Conceptione Beatae Mariae Virginis,* Quarrachi 1904, p. XVIII.

[25] *Ibid.,* p. 71: "absque fidei periculo potest teneri, quod Deus eam praeservavit de facto; nec una pars vel alia est de necessitate fidei, donec per ecclesiam determinatum fuerit, quid tenendum."

[26] *Ibid.,* p. XVIII. Both Aureoli's treatises are edited in these *Quaestiones Disputatae* of Quarrachi.

[27] *Ibid.,* p. 152: "omne peccatum repugnat matri gratiae, sive sit originale sive mortale vel veniale, cum peccatum et gratia opponuntur. Propter quod aures piae aliqualiter exhorrescunt in fonte gratiae maculam culpae." *Ibid.,* p. 153: "Donec itaque sacrosancta romana ecclesia sic expresse determinaverit, sicut ista expressa sunt quid de conceptione aut sanctificatione immaculatae Virginis tenendum, iustificationem eiusdem Virginis, quam tenere coepi, non deseram; neque enim reprehendit me cor meum."

by expressing his adherence to the teaching of her Immaculate Conception.[28]

Francis Mayron, one of Scotus' pupils, known as *Doctor Illuminatus,* deserves mention for his efforts to explain how Mary was preserved from original sin. In his *Tractatus de Conceptione B. M. Virginis*[29] he enumerates four methods of explanation prevalent in his day. Some theologians, identifying original sin with a 'morbid quality' inherent in the sensitive powers of the body, affirmed that the Virgin was preserved by being cleansed of this infection. Others, though they did not admit the formal presence of original sin in the flesh of the Blessed Virgin, advocated a causal or virtual presence, and made preservation consist in the removal of this causality or virtuality. A third group stated that Our Lady's preservation came about when God by a special privilege enabled her parents to generate her in such a way that the universal decree which bound all who were born of woman by seminal propagation would not affect her. A fourth school held the opinion that God, from the very first moment of her conception, "by a singular dispensation," preserved Mary from contracting original sin. Mayron rejects the first two opinions on the grounds that the fact of carnal infection is in no way related to the question of Mary's preservation.[30] Hence the third and fourth explanation alone are plausible.[31] In his commentary on the third book of the Sentences, Francis Mayron, again touching on the manner of Mary's preservation, remarks that though she was preserved, she can be said in some way—"aliquo modo"—to have contracted original sin "propter dicta sanctorum."[32]

Of considerable importance in the fourteenth century controversy are the writings of four Spanish Franciscans.[33] The first, the Catalan Peter Thomas, composed a treatise, entitled *De conceptione B. M. Virginis,*[34] while he was teaching in Barcelona, probably between 1316 and 1320. A contemporary of Thomas, Anthony Andreas, also a Catalan, expressed his views on the Immaculate Conception in his commentary *In quattuor*

[28] *Ibid.,* p. 47-48.
[29] Franciscus de MAYRONIS, O.F.M., *Tractatus de Conceptione B. M. Virginis,* ed. ALVA ET ASTORGA, O.F.M., *Monumenta antiqua seraphica pro Immaculata Conceptione Virginis Mariae,* Louvain 1665, p. 289-290. Cf. C. BALIC, *De debito peccati originalis in B. Virgine Mariae,* Roma 1941, p. 4.
[30] BALIC, *ibid.:* "quia talis infectio nihil facit ad propositum."
[31] *Ibid:* "ideo remanet tertius et quartus modus."
[32] Franciscus DE MAYRONIS, O.F.M., *Commentarius in III Sent.* dist. 3, q.2, art. 4, Venice 1517, fol. 7va. Cf. BALIC, *op. cit.,* p. 5.
[33] An excellent monograph on the doctrine of these theologians has been published by the Academia Mariana, Rome: Antonius BRAÑA ARRESE, O.F.M., *De Immaculata Conceptione B. V. Mariae secundum theologos Hispanos saeculi XIV,* Rome 1950.
[34] This treatise has been edited by P. De ALVA ET ASTORGA, O.F.M., *Monumenta antiqua seraphica,* Louvain 1655, p. 212-274.

Sententiarum libros longe absolutissimum.[35] Another Friar of approximately the same period, William Rubio, is known for his *Disputata et decisa in quattuor libros Sententiarum.*[36] Finally, near the turn of the fourteenth century, John Vitalis played a decisive role in the controversy between the University of Paris and the Dominican John Montson, of whom we shall speak shortly. He wrote a sermon on the Immaculate Conception entitled *Tota pulchra es amica mea,* and a treatise, *Defensorium B. V. Mariae.*[37]

To explain the manner of Mary's preservation from original sin, these theologians begin with a definition of original justice. Though original justice co-existed with sanctifying grace,[38] it was essentially distinct from grace.[39] It constituted man's natural relationship with God before the fall, and its effect was an easy, felicitous subjection of man's sensitive powers to his free will, and of his free will to God.[40] Original justice was some sort of gift superadded to nature. According to Peter Thomas it was a natural gift, perfecting nature;[41] according to Andreas, Rubio and Vitalis, it was supernatural, surpassing in its effects what nature left to itself could attain.[42] All the natural descendants of Adam, according to Thomas, Andreas and Vitalis, are born with an obligation to possess original justice; and the lack of this justice since the fall constitutes original sin.[43] Rubio, on the other hand, denies the obligation to possess original justice, and states that original sin is no real sin, but merely a "poena damni" or a "non praemiatio."[44] All affirm that sanctifying grace is the ordinary means of moral rehabilitation.[45]

All likewise admit what was then known as the "lex communiter conceptorum"; namely, that every natural descendant of Adam contracts

---

[35] Edited in Venice in 1578, and found in manuscript form in ms. 70 of Oriel College, Oxford.

[36] P. De ALVA ET ASTORGA, *Monumenta antiqua seraphica*, p. 8087; 89-185.

[37] P. De ALVA ET ASTORGA, *Monumenta antiqua seraphica*, p. 80-87; 89-185.

[38] W. RUBIO, *II Sent.* d.29, q.1, ed. Iodocus Bodius Ascensius, Paris 1518, p. 357vb.

[39] A. ANDREAS, *II Sent.* d.20, q.1, Venice 1578, p. 72vb; W. RUBIO, *II Sent.* d.30, q.1, p. 359vb; J. VITALIS, *Defensorium B. V. Mariae,* I, q.1, ed. De ALVA et ASTORGA, p. 90. This seems to have been the opinion likewise of St. Thomas, St. Bonaventure, Richard of Middleton, etc. For references see A. BRAÑA ARRESE, *op. cit.* p. 7, note 7.

[40] P. THOMAS, *op. cit.,* I, pars 2, c.I, p. 217; VITALIS, *Defensorium,* I, q.1, p. 89.

[41] P. THOMAS, *De conceptione B. M. Virginis,* I, pars 2, c.1, p. 217; II, pars 1, c.8, p. 227; III, c.15, p. 271.

[42] A. ANDREAS, *II sent.* d.20, q.1, p. 72vb; W. RUBIO, *II Sent.* d.30, q.1, p. 359vb; J. VITALIS, *Defensorium,* I, q.1, p. 90.

[43] A. ANDREAS, *II Sent.* d.32, q.1, p. 78va; P. THOMAS, *op. cit.,* I, pars 2, c.2, p. 217; J. VITALIS, *op. cit.,* II, q.3, p. 110.

[44] W. RUBIO, *II Sent.* d.30, q.2, p. 361ra-rb; *III sent.* d.3, q.1 et 2, p. 16va-17ra.

[45] A. ANDREAS, *II sent.* d.32, q.1, p. 77vb; d.28, q.1, p. 76vb; P. THOMAS, *op. cit., II,* pars 2, c.4, p. 231; W. RUBIO, *III Sent.* d.3, q.1 p. 19va; J. VITALIS, *op. cit.* IV, c.1, p. 149.

original sin.[46] Yet they are careful to note that the will of the legislator has always the right and the power to grant the privilege of exemption from the law.[47] This God can do either by dispensing the Blessed Virgin before her Conception from the obligation of possessing the original justice lost by Adam,[48] or more probably by granting her the possession of original justice in the first instant of her conception and independently of the sin of Adam.[49] Rubio, in accordance with his definition of original justice, says that God could preserve Mary from original sin by dispensing her "in primo instanti" from the "poena damni," or by making her capable of the beatific vision.[50] All agree that God could keep the Blessed Virgin from contracting original sin by pouring sanctifying grace into her soul in the first instant of her conception; for grace is either equivalent to original justice, or incompatible with sin.[51] As for the objection that Mary was conceived by way of seminal propagation, Thomas and Vitalis reply that the bond between concupiscible generation and original sin is not so unbreakable that the two cannot be separated by the power of God.[52]

These are some of the more important Franciscan theologians. Their influence gradually made itself felt in other religious orders, particularly among the Carmelites and Augustinians. For a time the Carmelites adhered to the traditional teaching of St. Bernard, St. Thomas and St. Bonaventure. Such renowned masters as Gerard of Bologna († 1317), Guy of Perpignan († 1342), and Paul of Perugia felt that they could not safely adopt the new theory, although their reaction against it was rather moderate.[53] Guy of Perpignan was unable to conceal a deep sympathy for the doctrine of Mary's Immaculate Conception, but he felt the evidence of authority was against it: "Ista opinio, propter reverentiam beatae Virginis, multum mihi placeret, nisi auctoritatibus canonis et sanctorum obviaret."[54] However, after 1340 the Order of the Carmelites reversed its allegiance, thanks to one of its most renowned masters, John Baconthorp. John had at first misunderstood the position of Scotus and of Peter Aureoli,

---

[46] P. Thomas, *op. cit.*, I, pars 2, c.3 et 4, p. 218-219; II, pars 2, c.10, p. 234. Cf. Braña Arrese, *op. cit.*, p. 19: "Lex communiter conceptorum profuse ab omnibus adhibetur et invocatur ut principium regens totam metaphysicam peccati originalis."

[47] A. Braña Arrese, *op. cit.*, p. 22-23.

[48] P. Thomas, *op. cit.*, II, pars 1, c.2, p. 223.

[49] *Ibid.* also p. 217.

[50] W. Rubio, *III Sent.* d.3, q.1, p. 18vb and 19ra.

[51] A. Braña Arrese, *op. cit.*, p. 32.

[52] P. Thomas, *op. cit.*, II, pars 1, c.4, p. 224-225. Cf. A. Brana Arrese, *op. cit.*, p. 35-39.

[53] X. Le Bachelet, "Immaculée Conception," in D. T. C. vol. 7(1), col. 1082. Elisée de la Nativité, O.C.D., "La Vie Mariale au Carmel," in *Maria*, vol. 2, Paris 1952, p. 845; Gabriel ab Annuntiatione, "De fide in Immaculatam Conceptionem apud Carmelitas," *Analecta O.C.D.*, vol. 5, p. 31-44; 81-87.

[54] Guy de Perpignan, O.C.D., *Quodl.*, I, III, q.14, in P. De Alva et Astorga, *Radii solis*, Louvain 1666, col. 1026.

and consequently in his Quodlibeta I, III, XIII, and XIV, as well as in his commentaries on the first three books of the Sentences, he had taken a stand against the doctrine of the Immaculate Conception, qualifying it as "nimis adulatoria." But when he began the fourth book of the Sentences he avowed that he had been won over to the Scotistic opinion. From then on he devoted his entire energy to the defense of the Immaculate Conception. "After Bacon [thorp]" writes Father Doncoeur, "the pious belief triumphed among the Carmelites; during the second half of the century they provided the cause of the Virgin with outstanding defenders." [55]

The Augustinian teaching on the Immaculate Conception follows much the same trend as that of the Carmelites. Until 1340 the masters of the Order followed the traditional opinion of Mary's sanctification; after that date they began to adopt the immaculist theory. The intellectual activity of the Order in the early part of the century was dominated by Giles of Rome, whom the chapters had recognized as *the* theologian to be followed by masters and students. Giles died archbishop of Bourges in 1316.[56] His position on the negative sanctity of Mary was that of the Victorines. "The Blessed Virgin," he says, "was the object of a twofold sanctification: the first in the womb of her mother; the second after her birth. In the womb of her mother she was personally purified of the original stain and preserved from all actual sin. At the Annunciation, the source of sin (*fomes peccati*) was extinguished in her . . . so that what was born of her was free from all infection." [57]

Theologians in Giles' day conceived of three possibilities as regards original sin in Mary: "vel quod non possit contrahere nec contrahat; vel quod possit contrahere et contrahat; vel medio modo, quod possit contrahere et non contrahat." Giles contends that the middle way is impossible. The Virgin, like all the other children of Adam, was conceived in and contracted sin; only Christ was the beneficiary of a virginal conception. It is because she contracted sin that she was redeemed and became a member of Christ. Not to count her as a member of Christ would be to rob Mary of glory. Giles likewise refutes the opinion of those theologians who taught that although the Blessed Virgin did contract sin she possessed grace in the first instant of her conception. Such a view is metaphysically impossible. The Virgin was in sin for a time, even though it was brief and imperceptible. She is the counterpart of Lucifer: "non plus fuit in hac infectione quam fuerit Lucifer in veritate." She

[55] P. DONCOEUR, S.J., "Les premières interventions du Saint-Siège relatives à l'Immaculée Conception," in *Revue d'Hist. Eccl.*, vol. 9, p. 908; p. 283.

[56] A. SAGE, A.A., "La doctrine et le Culte de Marie dans la famille Augustinienne," in *Maria*, vol. 2, Paris 1952, p. 694.

[57] AEGIDIUS A ROMA, *Ad Romanos, Lect. 24*, Rome 1553. See also *In II Sent.* d.29, q.1, a.3, Venice 1581, p. 385; d.31, q.1, a.2, p. 447; *In III Sent.* d.2, pars 1, q.1, a.3, Rome 1623, p. 67; d.3, pars 1, q.1, a.3, p. 111-115.

was justified sooner and more perfectly than the Precursor, and that was her privilege. One might say in a broad sense that her purification coincided with her conception, and affirm that she was always holy. In this way it would be quite legitimate to celebrate a special feast in honor of her Conception.[58]

Giles' influence on his order lasted until after the middle of the century, although a number of Augustinians rallied to the doctrine of the Immaculate Conception as early as 1340. Such authors as Albert of Padua († 1323), Augustine Trionfo († 1328), Henry Vrimach († 1334), and Gerard of Sienna († 1336) repeated Giles' arguments and theses.[59]   Even after 1350 there were still disciples of Giles.   Gregory of Rimini, who died in 1358, continued to teach that Mary was conceived in original sin; but the space he devotes to answering the objections of immaculist theologians gives evidence to their increasing numbers.[60]   Yet despite growing opposition Giles' doctrine found adepts as late as the last quarter of the fourteenth century.   Jordan of Saxony, who died in 1380, contends that Mary, according to the sayings of the Saints (dicta sanctorum), contracted original sin.[61]

Meanwhile, however, an opposite trend had developed among the Augustinians.   As early as 1340 Herman Schildis had defended the privilege of the Immaculate Conception.   In a treatise entitled *De Conceptione gloriosae Virginis Mariae,* he chooses the following as the topic of one of his chapters: "Quomodo . . . Deus benedixit conceptae virgini creando animam illam sanctissimam quae post Caput nostrum immediate ab ipso Capite esset omnis gratiae receptiva."   In the course of the treatise he proves that the effects of original sin are incompatible with the Divine Maternity.[62] Simon Fidati de Cassia († 1348) follows the same trend of thought.[63] Thomas of Strasbourg († 1357) accepts the thesis of the Immaculate Conception without the least hesitation.   He employs the typical argument "potuit, decuit, fecit."   If the Blessed Virgin was preserved from all actual sin on account of the honor of Christ, he reasons, a fortiori ought she to be immune to the much more grievous sin which infects our nature.   There is no reason for a second cleansing sanctification, since the Virgin was not stained by the "fomes peccati."   Thomas then concludes from Mary's peerless beauty to her supereminent dignity: *"Et sic Maria infra dignitatem*

---

[58] AEGIDIUS A ROMA, Quodl. VI, q.20: "Utrum B. V. primo instanti suae conceptionis habuerit gratiam?" Louvain 1646, p. 418-424.

[59] A. SAGE, *art. cit.,* p. 695.

[60] GREGORIUS A RIMINI, *In II Sent.,* d.31, q.2, Paris 1482. Cf. Sage, *ibid.*

[61] IOANNES A SAXONIA, Ms. lat. n. 596, Municipal Library, Lyon.

[62] HERMANNUS A SCHILDIS, *De Conceptione gloriosae Virginis Mariae,* pars II, c.4, in P. ALVA ET ASTORGA, *Monumenta antiqua seraphica,* vol. 1, p. 139.

[63] SIMON FIDATI de Cassia, *In 4 Evangelistas,* lib. II: *De virgine Maria,* c.1, Cologne 1540, p. 41.

solius Filii sui omnes alios homines magnifice praecellebat." [64]   Raymond Jourdain († 1381) greets Mary as "all beautiful in her conception . . . *et macula peccati sive mortalis sive venialis sive originalis non est in te."* However the source of sin ("fomes peccati") still remains in her, but without burning her, like the fire of the bush of Moses.[65]

JOHN MONTSON AND THE UNIVERSITY OF PARIS (1387-1389)

From the brief account we have given of the controversy so far, we are aware of the increasing popularity of the doctrine of the Immaculate Conception.   By the end of the fourteenth century, at least three great orders have definitely chosen to profess and defend Mary's glorious prerogative. Before the century closed, however, the controversy was brought still more noticeably into the open, and universities as well as ecclesiastical authorities were called upon to take sides.   The disputes which had thus far been tempered with moderation now became more aggressive and tempestuous.

The attitude of the University of Paris towards the controversy at the end of the fourteenth century was tolerant and non-committal.   Both schools were free to expound and defend their opinions, provided a proper respect was given the pious belief adopted by a large number of masters. In conformity with the mind of the university, the Franciscans who taught in Paris were prudent and reserved in their statements.   Thus Peter of Candia, the future Alexander V, simply affirmed that the opinion which stated that the Blessed Virgin was "preserved by a singular dispensation" was more common and more reasonable.[66]   If there were a question of choosing between the two opinions, he said, without presuming on the decision of Mother Church, he would for no other reason than his personal devotion firmly believe that Mary was never stained by original sin, and exhort all the faithful to share the same belief.[67]   However, all were not so reserved, and the University felt compelled to check their indiscretion. In 1362 two Friars Preachers, John l'Eschacier and James of Bosco, proclaimed from the pulpit at Châlons-sur-Marne, that the opinion which supported the privilege was false, heretical and condemnable.   They even

---

[64] THOMAS AB ARGENTORATO, *In III Sent.*, d.3, q.1, Venice 1564, p. 8 ss.

[65] Raymundus JORDANUS, *Contemplationes Idiotae de Virgine Maria,* pars 2, Paris 1654, p. 245, 242.

[66] PETRUS DE CANDIA, O.F.M., *Tractatus de Conceptione B. Virginis Mariae,* ed. ALVA ET ASTORGA, *Monumenta antiqua seraphica,* p. 207. Cf. BALIC, *op. cit.,* p. 5.

[67] PETRUS DE CANDIA, *ibid.,* p. 211: "Quae autem praedictorum opinionum sit eligenda, dico sine praeiudicio determinationis sanctae matris Ecclesiae . . . et nulla ratione ad hoc me cogente, sed sola devotione purissima firmiter credo et simpliciter fateor quod beatissima Virgo Maria . . . nunquam fuerit sordibus originalis criminis deturpata . . . et sic credendum omnes christifideles exhortor." Cf. SERICOLI, O.F.M., *Immaculata B. M. Virginis Conceptio iuxta Xysti IV constitutiones,* Rome 1945, p. 20.

stated that, had Mary died before her Son, she would have been damned.[68] The ecclesiastical authority proceeded against them and exacted a retraction.[69]

A much more serious incident occurred in June 1387. John Montson, a Dominican of the diocese of Valence in Aragon, in his thesis for the master's degree, advanced a number of objectionable conclusions. Four of the fourteen propositions found offensive had a bearing on the conception of the Blessed Virgin. They are as follows:

> 10. It is expressly against the Faith to deny that every man except Christ contracts original sin through Adam.
> 11. It is expressly against the Faith to deny that the Blessed Virgin Mary, Mother of God, contracted original sin.
> 12. It is no less against Holy Scripture to say that one man outside of Christ was really exempt from original sin than to extend exemption to ten men.
> 13. It is more expressly against Holy Scripture to affirm that the Blessed Virgin was not conceived in original sin than to affirm that she was at once in the state of the blessed and in that of wayfarers, from the moment of her conception or sanctification.[70]

Montson referred to St. Thomas as his principal authority. Indeed Pope Urban VIII had declared the doctrine of St. Thomas as true and Catholic, and the Bishop of Paris had especially recommended it in 1326.[71] Against John Vitalis, who stated that Aquinas had expressed two contradictory opinions as regards Mary's conception, John Montson angrily replied that St. Thomas had never openly favored the immaculist opinion, and wherever he spoke of the Virgin he had asserted that she was conceived in original sin.[72] According to Vitalis, Montson was supported and encouraged in his stand by his master and confrere John Thomas.[73]

The faculty of theology had Montson's fourteen propositions examined, particularly those which concerned Our Lady's conception, and gave orders to the Franciscan John Vitalis to compose an apologetic treatise, his *Defensorium B. Virginis Mariae,* of which we have already spoken. In five books Vitalis treats of original justice, original sin, the original purity of the Mother of God, and the controversy then at issue. Particularly noticeable are questions based on Montson's propositions and queries on the authority of the faculty of theology and of St. Thomas. Thus question 10 of chapter 3 in book 1 reads: "Utrum puritatem virginis Mariae dicere

---

[68] A. DUVAL, *ibid.,* p. 757.

[69] D. A. MORTIER, *ibid.,* p. 619; H. DENIFLE, *Chartularium Universitatis Parisiensis,* vol. 3, n.1272 p. 99; A. Brana ARRESE, *op. cit.,* p. 92.

[70] X. LE BACHELET, *art. cit.,* col. 1084.

[71] *Ibid.*

[72] J. VITALIS, *op. cit.,* IV, c.2, p. 153.

[73] J. VITALIS, *op. cit.,* IV, c.9, p. 167; Cf. DENIFLE, *ibid.,* vol. 3, p. 618; MORTIER, *op. cit.,* vol. 3, p. 629.

non fuisse originali obnoxiam, sit expresse contra fidem?" Question 1 in chapter 5 of book 1 is: "Utrum ad facultatem theologiae pertinet doctrinaliter inquirere . . .?" And question 5 of same chapter: "Utrum doctrina sancti Thomae de Aquino sit censenda sic veridica et approbata, ut non ei liceat contraire?" [74]

On July 6 the University pronounced judgment. More than thirty theologians unanimously agreed that the four propositions referring to Our Lady should be retracted as false, scandalous, presumptuous and offensive to pious ears.[75] However the decree admitted the 'probability' of the contrary opinion, expressing its wish to maintain all the reverence due to St. Thomas and his doctrine: "Salva in omnibus reverentia sancti Thomae nec non doctrinae suae." [76]

When John Montson refused to submit to the judgment of the University, the case was referred to the Bishop of Paris, Peter d'Orgemont who ratified the censure of the faculty of theology. He placed a penalty of excommunication *ipso facto* on anyone who would teach, preach and advocate the fourteen propositions, whether publicly or privately.[77] Yet Montson was not vanquished. He went to the palace of Avignon to plead his cause with Clement VII. Seeing this, the University of Paris sent a delegation of four doctors, headed by the chancellor Peter d'Ailly, who presented a juridical memoir entitled: *Apologia facultatis theologiae Parisiensis circa damnationem Joannis de Montesono.*[78] In it he reproaches Montson, in regard to Mary's conception, for having qualified as a formal error against the faith what so many saints, approved doctors and prelates of Catholic churches hold, affirm, and approve openly. If the opposition considers it absurd that St. Thomas should have advanced a proposition expressly contrary to the faith, *a fortiori* can the same reasoning be applied to the large number of saints, doctors and other Catholics who profess belief in the Immaculate Conception. The general approbation given the doctrine of St. Thomas does not of its very nature declare it free from all errors of detail. Besides, if one compares St. Thomas' teaching in the *Summa* with that of his commentary on the *Sentences,* one becomes aware of at least an apparent discrepancy between the two.[79]

After hearing both sides Clement VII appointed three cardinals to investigate the case very carefully. John Montson, afraid that the issue

[74] X. Le Bachelet, *art. cit.,* col. 1085.

[75] Denifle, *op. cit.,* vol. 3, n.1559, p. 491; cf. Le Bachelet, *ibid.,* "revocanda est tanquam falsa, scandalosa, praesumptuose asserta et piarum aurium offensiva."

[76] Denifle, *op. cit.,* p. 493ss; Le Bachelet, *ibid.*

[77] P. Doncoeur, S.J., "La condamnation de Jean de Monzon par Pierre d'Orgemont, évêque de Paris, le 23 août 1387," in *Revue des questions historiques,* Paris 1907, vol. 82, p. 184.

[78] P. De Alva et Astorga, *Monumenta antiqua ex variis authoribus,* vol. I, p. 576ss.

[79] X. Le Bachelet, *art. cit.,* col. 1085.

would not be to his advantage, secretly departed from Aragon and left the obedience of Avignon for that of Rome.[80]   Summoned three times by the court of Avignon, he was condemned as contumacious and excommunicated at the pontifical see January 27, 1389, and in Paris on March 17th.[81]

The decision of Avignon, considered independently of the legitimacy of Clement VII's pontificate, did not bear on the question whether Mary's Conception was immaculate or not, but rather on the expediency of declaring it false, heretical and condemnable.   The censures were of a disciplinary rather than of a doctrinal nature.   Nevertheless, for all practical purposes the University emerged victorious from the controversy.   As a consequence it felt powerful enough to issue a decree whereby all aspirants to degrees and academic privileges would henceforth have to subscribe to the University's action in condemning the fourteen propositions of John Montson.[82]   Moreover the University imposed formal retractions on the Dominicans who had been involved with John Montson, or who had preached against the Immaculate Conception.   The first and most spectacular case was that of William of Valan, the Bishop of Evreux, who retracted on Feb. 17th, 1389, at the Louvre in the presence of Charles VI and members of the University.   The same year other retractions followed; namely, those of John Thomas, Adam of Soissons, Geoffrey of Saint-Martin, Johne Ade, Peter of Chancey and John of Nicolai.[83]

One of the unpleasant aspects of the Montson controversy was that it created opposition between two mendicant orders which had been founded side by side in an atmosphere of peerless friendliness.   But on the other hand it accentuated the tendency among the masters of the University of Paris to adhere to the teaching of the Immaculate Conception.   The number of sermons on Mary's glorious privilege bears witness to the fact.   Among these is a sermon by John of Mandeville († 1372),[84] and another by John Vitalis, on the text, *"Tota pulchra es, amica mea, et macula non est in te."* [85]   Most noteworthy of all was the sermon *Tota pulchra es, amica mea,* preached in 1401 by the chancellor of the University, John

---

[80] This occurred during the Great Western Schism. Clement VII was the French antipope at Avignon, while Urban VI reigned in Rome.

[81] Denifle, *op. cit.,* vol. 3, n.1567, p. 506ss.

[82] *Ibid.,* p. 496, note 8.

[83] *Ibid.,* n.1571ss., p. 515ss.

[84] P. De Alva et Astorga, *Monumenta antiqua ex variis authoribus,* vol. 1, p. 249.

[85] P. De Alva et Astorga, *Monumenta antiqua seraphica,* p. 80, gives 1389 as the date of this sermon.   Max Liebermann, in a treatise entitled *Gersoniana. A Latin sermon on the Immaculate Conception of the Virgin Mary ascribed to John Gerson* (New York, mimeographed, 1951), concludes that this sermon "was written by Jean Vital, perhaps for the Feast of the Immaculate Conception, December 8, 1387, but more likely between February 14 and March 28, 1388, new style." (p. 66)

Gerson, at Saint-Germain l'Auxerrois.[86] The arguments set forth by Gerson were not particularly new, but they were presented with such piety and simplicity that they could not fail to leave a lasting impression. In the first part of his sermon he enumerated the reasons which should excite or strengthen in pious souls the belief in Our Lady's glorious privilege. Should not a good son seek to honor his mother in every way possible? Always a virgin in her body, was it not becoming that Mary should always be a virgin in her soul? If a prince can exempt his subjects from the laws he promulgates, is it not logical to conclude that God can dispense Mary from His laws? God had wanted Mary to beget our Lord virginally and without the pains of childbirth; was this less directly against the laws of nature, than to create her soul pure of all sin? The Almighty had wrought miracles on less important occasions in favor of Josue, Moses, Elias and Daniel; could He not sanctify His Mother in the first instant of her existence? He sanctified Jeremias and John the Baptist in the womb of their mothers, and He would do nothing more for Mary! Such were some of the pious considerations advanced by Gerson. However, he made it clear in a sermon for the feast of the Purification, preached at the Council of Constance in 1415, that he did not consider as heretical the opinion which denied Mary's Immaculate Conception. Both beliefs were opinions, and nothing more.[87]

Nicolas Eymeric and the Lullists (1357-1399)

John Montson had a rival in a Dominican of his own nationality, Nicolas Eymeric, born at Girone in Catalonia around 1320. He was the Inquisitor General of the Kingdom of Aragon from 1357 to 1360, and from 1366 to 1399. In several of his writings [88] he vigorously attacked some of the teachings of Raymond Lull,[89] particularly the doctrine of the Immaculate Conception. He did not hesitate, in 1366, to qualify the latter as heretical and to express his intention of treating as heretics all who defended it. As the followers of Raymond Lull were in favor at the court of Aragon, they had Eymeric exiled twice, and better still, on March 13, 1393, they obtained from King John I a pragmatic sanction in which his majesty formally expressed his adherence to the pious doctrine: *"Firmiter credimus et*

---

[86] J. GERSON, *Opera Omnia*, Antwerp 1506, vol. 3, p. 1322ss. Cf. X. LE BACHELET, *art. cit.*, col. 1087.

[87] *Ibid.*, vol. 2, p. 287.

[88] A. DE ROSKOVANY, *Beata virgo Maria in suo conceptu immaculata ex monumentis omnium saecularoum demonstrata*, Budapest 1873, vol. 1, p. 236.

[89] Raymond LULL, a member of the Third Order of St. Francis, was an ardent defender of the Immaculate Conception. He wrote several treatises on the subject, and taught in Paris before Duns Scotus. Historians are not in agreement as to whether Lull's teaching had any influence on Scotus. Cf. X. LE BACHELET, *art. cit.*, col. 1062-1064; and chapter V of the present volume, p. 201.

tenemus quod praefatae huius sanctissimae Virginis sancta fuit penitus et electa conceptio." As a consequence the king forbade all missionaries and preachers to expound or proffer anything that could in any way be prejudicial to the purity of Mary's blessed conception. The following year the decree was extended to the principality of Girone.[90]

A good result of this Aragonian controversy was the appearance of several important treatises on the Immaculate Conception in answer to the attacks of Eymeric. Probably the most remarkable was written by Francis Martin, a Carmelite from Barcelona. In his *Compendium veritatis immaculatae conceptionis virginis Mariae Dei genitricis,* composed around 1390 and published by Alva y Astorga,[91] he presents one of the most complete expositions of the question as treated and discussed at that time.

THEOLOGIANS AT THE COUNCIL OF BASEL (1431-1449)

The action of Avignon against John Montson had not brought a positive decision on the fundamental issue of the controversy, but the desire to have the doctrine of the Immaculate Conception defined still remained. As early as 1417 Alphonsus V, the king of Aragon wrote several times to Emperor Sigismund asking him to promote the twofold cause of the belief and feast of the Immaculate Conception. Since his request had met with no results at the Council of Constance, he reiterated his appeal in 1425 through John of Palomar, who had already been appointed as papal delegate to the forthcoming Council of Basel. He entreated Sigismund to see to it that in the Council the universal and perpetual celebration of the most pure conception of Mary might become a reality, in fulfilment of the requests that had several times been made.[92]

There is no indication that during the first three years of the Council the Fathers of Basel actively studied the question of the Immaculate Conception, although they solemnly celebrated the feast of the Conception each year and had sermons preached in honor of the mystery at that occasion.[93] However, in 1435, a canon of Puy, by the name of John Roceti,[94] presented a treatise or sermon on the Immaculate Conception of the Blessed Virgin Mary Mother of God. In his discourse, the text of which was *"Tota pulchra es, amica mea, et macula non est in te,"* Roceti declared that the Mother of God was preserved from the original stain in her venerable

---

[90] X. LE BACHELET, *art. cit.,* col. 1088; F. D. GAZULLA, "Los reyes de Aragon y la purisima Concepción," in *Boletin de la Real Academia de Buenas Letras de Barcelona,* III (1905-1906) *passim,* especially pp. 52. 55-56. 59-63.

[91] P. DE ALVA et ASTORGA, *Monumenta antiqua ex novem auctoribus antiquis,* p. 1-215.

[92] ". . . ut in dicto generali concilio dictae purissimae Conceptionis universalis et perpetua celebratio ad effectum perveniret toties supplicatum." Cf. FITA Y COLOMAR, *Tres discursos historicos. Panegirico de la Inmaculada Concepción, app. Collección diplomatica,* 2nd ed., Madrid 1909, p. 82ss, 85, 88, 92ss; SERICOLI, *op. cit.,* p. 22.

[93] X. LE BACHELET, *art. cit.,* col. 1109.

[94] *Ibid.,* col. 1109

conception, at least in the instant when her soul was united to her body: *"ab exordio saltem infusionis animae in corpore, ab originali praeservatam."* In proof of his thesis the author presents four main arguments: the figures of the Old Testament, patristic authorities, theological reasons of the doctors, and the miracles wrought in confirmation of the doctrine. The most important part of the discourse was an exhortation to the Fathers of the Council to deign finally to bring about the exaltation of the Immaculate Virgin and to formulate conclusions that could be discussed in the venerable assembly.[95] He himself suggested as the aim of these discussions the canonization of her conception and the declaration that she was conceived without original sin.[96]

The appeal was heard. Before the end of the year Cardinal Louis of Aleman, the Cardinal Archbishop of Arles, who was then the president and "iudex fidei" of the Council suggested that all the libraries of Christendom be searched for documents in favor of or against the Immaculate Conception.[97] From then on the question of our Lady's preservation became the subject of lengthy discussions. Among the principal antagonists of the doctrine was John of Montenegro, the General of the Friars Preachers. Roskovany lists a treatise written by him, which has not come down to us, or has not yet been discovered.[98] The substance of it is probably contained in the work of John of Torquemada. Moreover John of Segovia says that in his *Allegationes* he follows the same plan as Montenegro in order to refute his arguments.

John of Segovia was the outstanding protagonist of the immaculist opinion. A canon of Toledo, he was sent by the king of Castile for the express purpose of promoting the cause of the Immaculate Conception. Segovia is the author of three treatises, of which the third was not presented at the Council. The first, his *Septem Allegationes*,[99] follows the traditional method of proving that Mary could have been preserved, that it was fitting she should be preserved, and that consequently she must have

---

[95] *Ibid.*, col. 1110: ". . . atque ad exaltationem conceptionis immaculatae Virginis conclusiones aliquas eliciendi, proponendas in sacris disputationibus."

[96] *Ibid:* ". . . si munus ei obtuleris suae conceptionis canonizandae simul et declarandae immunitatis eius ab originali."

[97] J. SEGOVIA, *Septem allegationes et totidem avisamenta pro informatione patrum Concilii Basileensis, praesidente tunc iudice fidei DD. Cardinali Arelatensi A.D. 1436, circa sacratissimae V. Mariae Immaculatae Conceptionem eiusque praeservationem a peccato originali in primo suae animationis instanti—Studio et labore* P. DE ALVA ET ASTORGA, Brussels 1664, p. 1, *Ad Lectorem:* ". . . et proposuerunt, quidquid pro sua opinione undique corradere potuerunt et facere putaverunt. Cardinalis vero Arelatensis qui erat pro tunc Praeses dicti concilii et fidei iudex duo fecit: Primum et scrutatis omnibus Bibliothecis Christianitatis, ad Concilium adferrent omnia acta et scripta reperta pro vel contra."

[98] *Relatio sive allegationes de conceptione beatae virginis pro sua opinione de sanctificatione virginis Mariae post contractionem originalis maculae.* Cf. ROSKOVANY, *op. cit.*, vol. 1, p. 285.

[99] J. SEGOVIA, *op. cit.*; cf. chapter IV of the present volume, p. 139.

been preserved. Segovia makes copious use of the writings of John Vitalis and of Peter Thomas.[100]   In his fourth allegation, after enumerating the different ways in which Mary's preservation had been explained by theologians, he expresses his preference for the opinion which explains her preservation by a sanctification in the first instant of her existence in virtue of a prevenient grace: "Praedictus modus ponendi sanctificationem beatissimae Virginis per gratiam praevenientem est multo rationabilior."[101]   An argument Segovia borrows from Peter Thomas is the pseudo-Augustinian rule of Mary's conformity with Christ: "In omni propositione quae Christum a peccato excipit, intelligitur excipi Virgo Mater."[102]   In his *Septem Avisamenta*,[103] Segovia devotes the sixth section to arguments taken from theological reason, Scripture, the piety of the faithful and the doctrine of the saints.[104]   He expressly abstains from using as arguments private revelations and miracles as Vitalis had done, because such adversaries as Montson had argued that only proofs drawn from Scripture and the authority of the saints had any value.[105]   It is for that reason, too, that he did not present to the Council a third treatise he had already written: *Pulcherrima miracula ab eodem auctore collecta de conceptione beatissimae virginis Mariae.*[106]   On the other hand he makes much of the argument of the general consensus of the faithful.   For a long time already, he remarks, the opinion which opposes Mary's Immaculate Conception, has become so disagreeable to the people that they can no longer tolerate it.[107]

A personage of no less importance at the Council, though for entirely different reasons, was the renowned Dominican John of Torquemada. He was at that time the Master of the Sacred Palace, and he later became a cardinal.   As he himself tells us, he had been asked by the Council to present a complete *summa* of all the arguments contrary to the doctrine of the Immaculate Conception, so that the Fathers of the Council might weigh both sides of the question before pronouncing final judgment.[108]   He very

---

[100] A. Braña Arrese, *op. cit.*, p. XVII, 41, 110.

[101] J. Segovia, *op. cit.*, Alleg. 4, e. Alva et Astorga, p. 111.

[102] *Ibid.*, alleg. 6, p. 210-211; P. Thomas, *op. cit.*, III, c.2, p. 259; Braña Arrese, *op. cit.*, p. 146-147.

[103] Alva et Astorga published the *Avisamenta* along with the *Allegationes* as can be seen in the title in note 97 above.

[104] J. Segovia, *op. cit.*, "Avisamentum VI: In quo summario declaratur, quomodo doctrina de sancta conceptione sit multum conformis rationi, sacrae Scripturae, pietati fidei et sanctorum doctrinae."

[105] J. Segovia, *op. cit.*, alleg. 7, p. 349.

[106] Ed. P. De Alva et Astorga, Brussels 1664.

[107] J. Segovia, *op. cit.*, alleg. 1, docum. IV, p. 21ss.

[108] J. Turrecremata, *Tractatus de veritate conceptionis beatissimae Virginis, pro facienda relatione coram patribus concilii Basilieensis, anno Domini M.CCCC.XXXVII, mense julio, de mandato sedis apostolicae legatorum, eidem sacro concilio praesidentium, compilatus*, Rome 1547, p. 8: "Omnia autem dicturus sum, omnia vestrarum paternitatum judicio submitto, protestans quod in hac relatione non explico adhuc votum meum, nec quod de materia praesenti sentiam, sed tantum vestrarum dominationum mandata suscipiens, quod doctores quos legere potui sentire cognovi."

carefully protests that he intends neither to affirm nor to deny anything contrary to the universal judgment of Mother Church.[109] His *Tractatus de veritate conceptionis* comprises thirteen sections or parts, divided into chapters which added together number 351. Everything that could be said against the Immaculate Conception was gathered together into the treatise. Of particular interest is the fourth chapter of section VII, in which Torquemada enumerates ten reasons why the order of St. Dominic was at that time opposed to the immaculist opinion.[110] Strangely enough the authority of St. Thomas is not given as a reason. Torquemada presents nothing more than the ordinary arguments of the maculists, namely, the universality of original sin, the testimonies of Fathers and councils who taught that Christ alone was sinless and that the Blessed Virgin was stained by sin; the honor of Jesus Christ who alone should be endowed with this privilege; the necessity of the redemption; the advice given by St. Dominic to his sons always to follow the doctrine of Scripture and of the Fathers, and to be on guard against novelties; the absence of solid proofs to support the pious belief of Mary's preservation.[111]

Despite its elaborate preparation Torquemada's treatise was not presented at the Council. The Avignon experience and the history of the years of schism had given rise to the wildest theories about the source of ecclesiastical authority. The idea that the Council was superior to the Pope was gaining ground, and in no small measure contributed to the withdrawal of Eugene IV's legates from Basel in September 1437. Another reason for the dissolution was the arrival of the Greeks in view of discussing reunion with Rome, and the failure of the delegates at Basel to agree on the most suitable location for the meeting with the delegates from the Orient. The upshot of it all was that the papal legates left, and John of Torquemada with them. His manuscript was not even studied at the Council.[112]

Cf. J. B. MALOU, *L'Immaculée Conception de la Bienheureuse Vierge Marie considérée comme Dogme de Foi*, Bruxelles 1857, vol. 2, p. 477.

[109] *Ibid:* "Quare quidquid fuerit, quod ex aliorum sententiis et dictis retulero, protestor quod nihil intendo asserere, in hac facienda relatione, nisi quod asserendum est; nec negare quod negandum est, secundum universalis Matris Ecclesiae."

[110] *Ibid.*, p. 128: " In quo assignantur decem rationes, quare professores ordinis praedicatorum hanc doctrinam, videlicet quod Virgo Maria concepta fuerit in originali peccato, communiter prosequuntur."

[111] *Ibid.;* cf. MALOU, *op. cit.*, vol. 2, p. 476.

[112] J. TURRECREMATA, *op. cit.*, pars XIII, p. 276v: "Completo hoc opere, cum ego praefatus Magister Joannes de Turrecremata, apost. sacri palatii Magister, in plena congregatione concilii Basileensis me obtulissem paratum ad faciendam relationem mihi injunctam . . . responsum est mihi per organum Rev. D. Cardin. S. Angeli Legati apostolici et praesidentis S. D. N., quod cum patres sacri concilii in praesentiarum circa adventum Graecorum plurimum forent occupati, non possent pro nunc intendere praefatae materiae Conceptionis B. Virginis . . . Ego vero cujus erat majorum parere praeceptis, hac responsione audita, supersedi ab ulteriori requisitione audientiae. Mansi tamen post, per plures Menses basileae . . . Tandem vero orta gravissima et scandalosa dissensione inter patres aliquos Basileae residentes et S. D. N. Eugenium, super loco ad quem Graeci venturi essent, recedentibus dominis legatis

Meanwhile the proceedings of the Council were carried on, without a pontifical mandate, by a group consisting of the one Cardinal of Arles, about eight archbishops and bishops, a dozen prelates and about three hundred priests and doctors. John of Segovia was in the group. He was also one of the seventeen-member committee to which was entrusted the final discussion of the documents for and against the doctrine of the Immaculate Conception, and the formulation of the decree which was published Sept. 17, 1438 in the 36th session. The following is the dogmatic section of the decree:

> . . . We define and declare that the doctrine according to which the glorious Virgin Mary, Mother of God, by a special effect of divine preventing and operating grace, was never stained with original sin, but has always been holy and immaculate, is a pious doctrine, conformable to the cult of the Church, to Catholic Faith, to right reason and Sacred Scripture; it must be approved, held and professed by all Catholics; furthermore, it is no longer allowed to preach or teach anything contrary to it." [113]

The tenor of the decree would seem to indicate that the Fathers of Basel really intended to define the doctrine of the Immaculate Conception, though their intention was of little importance, since at the time of the definition the assembly no longer had an ecumenical status. Still the significance of Basel cannot be overlooked.[114] It contributed to the spread of the pious belief, since a number of countries, such as Switzerland, Savoy, Germany, Aragon and France, considered the synod as legitimate even after the withdrawal of the papal legates.[115] Indeed in September 1457 a provincial synod of Avignon ordained that the decree of Basel be unfailingly observed and that a penalty of excommunication be imposed on anyone who dared attack the doctrine of the Immaculate Conception either in the pulpit or

---

et praesidentibus, aliisque probis viris, quibus temeritates Basileensium plurimum displicebant, ego etiam recedere ab eis, tamquam a male in Christi fide sapientibus, decrevi ad sedem apostolicam . . . cum libro relationis meae me conferens. Ex his apertissime intelliget quisque doctus, quod vacua et invalida sit determinatio quam in materia Conceptionis B. Virginis factam quidam aiunt . . . Tum quia facta est post recessum RR. Cardinalium legatorum et dominorum praesidentium, et ita per quosdam acephalos, tum secundo quia facta est post translationem concilii factam de Basilea in Bononiam . . ."

[113] "Nos doctrinam illam disserentem gloriosam Virginem Dei Genitricem Mariam praeveniente et operante divini numinis gratia singlari nunquam subiacuisse originali peccato, sed immunem semper fuisse ab omni originali et actuali culpa, sanctamque et immaculatam, tanquam piam et consonam cultui ecclesiastico, fidei catholicae, rectae rationi et sacrae scripturae, ab omnibus catholicis approbandam fore tenendam et amplectendam definimus et declaramus, nullique de cetero licitum esse in contrarium praedicare seu docere." J. D. Mansi, Sacrorum Conciliorum nova et ampliccima collectio, vol. 29, Florence 1759, col. 182ff.; J. A. Robichaud, S.M., "The Immaculate Conception in the Magisterium of the Church before 1854," in *Marian Studies*, vol. 5, Washington 1954, p. 94.

[114] Cf. chapter VII of the present volume, note 231.

[115] Sericoli, *op. cit.*, p. 23.

in public discussions.[116]   And even as early as December 1, 1439, only three months after its promulgation, Queen Mary of Aragon had the decree of Basel published in her kingdom.[117]

Loyalty to Basel is likewise reflected in a number of writings of that century. Thus Gabriel Biel, († 1495) a professor at Tübingen brings in the authority of the Council as an argument in favor of the Immaculate Conception: "Praeterea determinatum est in concilio Basiliensi." [118]   In Belgium, Dionysius the Carthusian († 1471) expressed a similar allegiance. In his commentary on the third book of the Sentences, he states that the definite truth on the Immaculate Conception must not be sought in the disputes of the schools, but rather in the decisions of the Church. Now in the latest general Council the Church has put an end to all discussions on the matter: "quae in novissimo concilio universali finem (ut dixi) his discussionibus imposuit." [119]   In the same context Dionysius writes: "We would be horrified to affirm that she who was to crush the head of the serpent was ever crushed by him (quandoque ab eo contritam), and that the future Mother of Our Lord had been a daughter of the devil."[120]

Though they do not mention the Council of Basel in their writings, three great Italian saints who lived in the first half of the fifteenth century deserve a mention here. The first, St. Antonine of Florence († 1459), did not profess the doctrine of the Immaculate Conception, but loyally adhered to the teaching of the masters of his own order, the Dominicans. The second, St. Lawrence Justinian, the first Patriarch of Venice († 1455), openly proclaimed Mary's preservation from original sin.[121]   Finally, St. Bernardine of Siena, an ardent promoter of the spirit of the Franciscan Order, strangely enough seems on most occasions to be rather reticent and noncommittal as regards the controversial question of Mary's Conception. In fact, in one passage he clearly expresses his will to be free of all scholastic disputes on the matter: "Dismissis autem scholasticis bellis circa Virginalem conceptum, triplicem sanctificationem ad praesens discutamus . . ." [122]

[116] P. De Alva et Astorga, *Armamentum seraphicum et regestum authenticum universale pro tuendo titulo Immaculatae Conceptionis intemeratae Virginis Mariae,* Madrid 1649, vol. 2, p. 297, 299; Fita y Colomar, *op. cit.,* p. 46, 107, 113, 117; J. Mir y Noguera, *La Inmaculada Concepción,* Madrid 1905, p. 129ss.

[117] The statute can be found in E. Martène, *Thesaurus novus anecdotorum,* vol. 4, Paris 1717, p. 381; D. Mansi, *op. cit.,* vol. 32, col. 183; cf. Sericoli, *op. cit.,* p. 23.

[118] X. Le Bachelet, *art. cit.,* col. 1116. G. Biel, *De festis divae Virginis Mariae varii atque eruditi sermones,* Brescia 1583, p. 4a; also his commentary *in III Sententiarum,* d.3, q.1.

[119] *Opera Omnia Dionysii, In III Sent.,* Tournai 1904, vol. 23, p. 98A.

[120] *Ibid.* Besides his commentary on the Sentences, Dionysius wrote two treatises on the Blessed Virgin: *De praeconio et dignitate Mariae: Opera Omnia,* vol. 35, book 2, art. 13, p. 486: *De dignitate et laudibus B. V. Mariae; Opera Omnia,* vol. 36, book 1, art. 7, p. 26. Cf. Dom Yves Gourdel, "Le Culte de la très sainte Vierge dans l'ordre des Chartreux" in *Maria,* vol. 2, Paris 1952, p. 643.

[121] X. Le Bachelet, *art. cit.,* col. 1116-1117.

[122] *S. Bernardini Senensis Ord. Min. Opera* (ed. Pietro Rodolfi da Tossignan,

However on a few occasions Bernardine lets us see his true sentiments. Thus in one of his Latin sermons, commenting the words of Christ, "Non surrexit inter natos mulierum maior Joanne Baptista," (Mat. 11:11) he remarks that Our Lord rightly says, "non surrexit":

> Because no one is said to get up or rise, who has not fallen; but since Christ, as also the Blessed Virgin, did not fall into any sin of conception or into any actual sin, they are consequently not under that rule, because they have not fallen in the manner mentioned. Therefore they are not said to rise, as all the other humans from Adam on, who fell and are falling through original sin. However the statement that the Virgin was conceived in original sin is not condemned by the Church; yet it is more pious to believe that she was not conceived in sin than contrariwise.[123]

Bernardine had written these lines before the Council of Basel. His prudence in not condemning the contrary opinion is remarkable. He holds a similar attitude in one of his vernacular sermons, preached in Florence in 1424:

> "The second star was that she was conceived without original sin, and was preserved from sin. O, what if you held the contrary? You would not be condemned, because the Church has not yet approved it [the immaculist opinion]. But what should the devout mind hold? That she was conceived without original sin. O, if St. John and so many saints were sanctified in the womb of their mother, how would God not have done a greater honor to His Mother than to the others?"[124]

Sixtus IV and Vincent Bandelli

The period between the decree of the Council of Basel (1438) and the accession of Sixtus IV (1471) was marked by an ever-increasing dissension between theologians regarding the conception of our blessed Lady. On the one hand those who advocated the legitimacy of the definition of Basel accused the maculists of heresy. Thus, for instance, in 1457 the doctors of the Sorbonne punished as a heretic a certain Dominican who publicly asserted that Mary was conceived in original sin.[125] Theologians, on the other hand, who rejected both the doctrine of the Immaculate Conception and the decision of Basel, because they considered them contrary to Scripture, the Fathers and the teachings of the Pontiffs, accused the immaculists

---

O.F.M. Conv.), vol. 2, Venice 1591, p. 510H. Cf. Lorenzo Di Fonzo, O.F.M. Conv., *La Mariologia Di S. Bernardino Da Siena*, Rome 1947, p. 67.

[123] *S. Bernardini Sen. Opera* (ed. Tossignano), vol. 4, p. 272CD: ". . . non dicuntur surgere, sicut omnes caeteri homines qui ceciderunt et cadunt ab Adam citra *per peccatum originalem*. Tamen utrum beata Virgo fuerit concepta in peccato originali, Ecclesia non damnat: sed magis pium est credere, quod non fuerit in peccato concepta, quam credere quod sic."

[124] S. Bernardino Da Siena, *Le Prediche Volgari Inedite*, Firenze 1424, 1425—Siena 1425 (ed. Dionisio Pacetti, O.F.M.), Siena 1935, p. 329-330.

[125] C. Du Plessis D'Argentré, *Collectio iudiciorum de novis erroribus qui ab initio duodecimi saeculi post incarnationem Verbi usque ad annum 1713 in Ecclesia proscripti sunt et notati*, Paris 1724, vol. 1, p. 252.

of schism and defection in the faith. Thus in 1441 Raphael of Pornasio, O.P., affirmed that the doctrine of Mary's conception in sin was "a defined article of Faith necessarily to be believed, an unfailing, clear truth, the Catholic faith, of which it was wrong to doubt." [126] Around 1470 Gabriel of Barleto, O.P., made similar statements.[127] Meanwhile Rome remained silent on the issue. The decree of Basel had very little influence in Italy, since its legitimacy had never been recognized there. Besides the pontiffs were gravely preoccupied with political concerns over the war against the Turks. Even Sixtus IV in his early years thought it more prudent not to intervene until positions were more clearly defined.

However the situation was soon altered. Around 1474 the controversy crossed the Alps and began to rage on the Italian peninsula. The principal, if not the only, instigator of this new movement was Vincent Bandelli, O.P. If Torquemada's attitude was tempered with prudence and moderation, Bandelli's vehemence knew no bounds. Endowed with a brilliant mind and a scintillating eloquence, he made use of every artifice of erudition and of daring to combat the protagonists of the Immaculate Conception, so much so that he came to be known as the "adversariorum Goliath." [128]

The first time Bandelli appeared as an adversary of our Lady's preservation was in a public debate held at Imola probably in 1474 or 1475.[129] Shortly afterwards, in Milan in 1475, he published his *Libellus recollectorius auctoritatum de veritate Conceptionis B. V. Mariae*, in which he expounds in systematic order what he had said in the debate.[130] The treatise, divided into four parts, attempts to prove by negative and positive arguments, especially from the Fathers, of whom he quotes over two hundred, the falsity of the teaching of Mary's preservation. The tone of the whole treatise is bitingly polemic. He qualifies the immaculist system as erroneous, impious, temerarious, more dangerous than the heresies of Pelagius, Celestius and Julianus; as a wicked, pestiferous, execrable, diabolical dogma; as a lie spoken by raging lips; as a false assertion that undermines the founda-

---

[126] P. De Alva et Astorga, *Radii solis,* col. 1945: ". . . articulum fidei definitum de necessitate credendum, veritatem certam, claram, catholicam fidem, ut nefas sit de ea dubitare christianum."

[127] *Ibid.,* col. 1952 ss.

[128] L. Schönleben, *Palma virginea sive Deiparae Virginis Mariae de adversariis suae Immaculatae Conceptionis victoriae omnium saeculorum aerae christianae succincta narratione representatae,* Salzburg 1671, p. 62.

[129] P. De Alva et Astorga, *Radii solis,* col. 1679 ss; T. Strozzi, S.J., *La Controversia della Concezione della beata Vergine Maria descritta istoricamente,* Palermo 1703, p. 377.

[130] This work, which at first appeared anonymously, is very rare. Cf. *Gesamtkatalog der Wiegendrücke herausgegeben von der Kommission für den Gesamt-Katalog der Wiegendrücke,* vol. 3, Leipzig 1928, p. 306. That it belongs to Bandelli is affirmed by the author himself in his *Tractatus de singulari puritate et praerogativa conceptionis salvatoris nostri Iesu Christi,* Bologna 1481. Cf. Quétif-Echard, O.P., *Scriptores Ordinis Praedicatorum recensiti notisque historicis et criticis illustrati,* Paris 1721, vol. 2, p. 2; Malou, *op. cit.,* vol. 2, p. 479.

tions of the faith and resists a well-founded belief, etc.   The advocates of the pious opinion are indiscrimately designated as adulterous, devoid of all knowledge and full of wind, stupid, seducing the people under the pretext of piety and in the hope of lucre and favor, depraving holy Scripture, condemning the holy Fathers, extolling the Blessed Virgin with false honors, nefariously slandering the Blood of Christ, prating and howling against the divine truth.[131]

The excesses of Bandelli and his followers who preached far and wide on the Italian peninsula incited the advocates of the Immaculate Conception to answer in kind.   The result was hatred, heated and disgraceful discussions which rejoiced the enemies of the Church, saddened the hearts of the pious, and scandalized the faithful.   It was not long before the matter was brought to the attention of Sixtus IV, who, desirous of ending the conflict and preventing greater harm, gave orders that a solemn disputation be held in Rome between theologians from various regions.   The debate took place at the beginning of 1477, in the presence of the Pontiff. The arguments against the preservation of Our Lady were eloquently and diffusely expounded by Bandelli; evidence in favor of the glorious privilege was advanced by Francis Insuber of Brescia, the Minister General of the Friars Minor.   The latter manifested such facility and dexterity in answering and annihilating the arguments of his adversary, that Sixtus IV surnamed him Samson, a name that clung to him so well that he was thenceforth known as Francis Samson.[132]

Encouraged by the success of Francis Insuber, two pious authors, Leonard Nogarolo, a protonotarius apostolicus, and Bernardine de Bustis, O.F.M., composed offices of the Immaculate Conception, which were approved by Pope Sixtus IV.[133]

---

[131] V. BANDELLI, O.P., *Libellus recollectorius auctoritatum de veritate conceptionis B. V. Mariae,* Milan 1475; *praefatio:* "Inter ceteros autem errores contra veritatem ille longe periculosior est qui beatissimam Virginem a Christi redemptione segregare mollitur . . . Isti [immaculatistae] divinarum litterarum ignari, B. Virginem Dei genitricem sub specie pietatis falsis honoribus extollunt, Christi dignitati nefandissime detrahunt, sanctas Scripturas perverse exponunt, SS. Patrum sententias spernunt et tandem per humanum favorem ac terrenum lucrum novos errores configunt . . . catholicae veritate deiecta . . . [In hoc quidem opere] perfacile erit ipsum quem tam emphatice sustentare conantur errorem . . . ut mortalem, ut fugiendum ut falstitate plenum refellere: impium quoque fore ac profanum utpote fidei divinisque litteris adversatissimum hunc perniciosum errorem obstinata fronte credere aut defensare." P. 2: "Tales [immaculatistae] profecto Scripturas sacras perniciose depravant et haeresim Pelagii, Caelestii, et Iuliani suis expositionibus defendunt: adversus quos beatus Augustinus . . . fortiter exclamans dicit: o malum dogma, quod pacis inimicus adinvenit: o dogma pestiferum per quod scinditur unitas matris Ecclesiae; o dogma pessimum, quod sub nomine pietatis evertere et mutare nititur Ecclesiae Christi fundamenta; o dogma nefandum . . . Quis haec quae dicitis catholicorum sapientissimus feret? . . ." P. 2: "Igitur asserere beatam Virginem non contraxisse originale peccatum . . . est impium et etiam haereticum."

[132] L. WADDING, O.F.M., *Annales Minorum seu trium Ordinum a S. Francisco institutorum,* Quarrachi 1931-33, vol. 14, p. 195.

[133] See chapter IV of the present volume, p. 150 ff.

If for a time after these papal interventions the adversaries of the Immaculate Conception were somewhat more cautious, they soon took courage again and renewed their attacks under the pretext that Sixtus IV did not express his mind clearly and did not issue a precept that the feast be celebrated everywhere. Consequently they either did not celebrate the feast-day at all, or they interpreted the word *"conception"* as denoting Mary's sanctification. This attitude was brought out most glaringly in another public debate held in Ferrara after the Lent of 1481, under the auspices of Herculus Estensis, the governor of the state. The discussion lasted six hours. The speakers in favor of the Immaculate Conception were Bartholomy Bellati of Feltre, O.F.M. Conv.,[134] Baptista of Ferrara, O. Carm.,[135] and a certain Caesarius, O.S.M.,[136] who were all masters of sacred theology. Their principal adversary was again Vincent Bandelli, who somewhat later in the year published his arguments in a new treatise, *Tractatus de singulari puritate et praerogativa conceptionis salvatoris nostri Iesu Christi.*[137]

The treatise is of the same vehement tenor as his earlier publication. The arguments, too, follow the usual pattern. The only new element is Bandelli's interpretation of Sixtus IV's Bull *Cum praeexcelsa.*[138] If the Roman Church has instituted the feast of the Conception and has granted an indulgence to those who recite the office of Nogarolo, he asks, how can the opinion which ascribes original sin to the Virgin still be considered as probable? To this objection Bandelli gives a lengthy and subtle reply. The mind of Sixtus in approving the feast and granting indulgences was not to exemplify the natural conception or the preservation of Mary from original sin, but rather to stress her spiritual conception, or her sanctification after the first instant of her animation. Hence it still remains true that the immaculist theory is hertical, erroneous, superstitious, impious, a wickedness hitherto unheard of, a detestable crime, a madness of iniquity, a deadly virus, a pernicious pestilence.[139]

---

[134] V. BANDELLI, O.P., *Tractatus de singulari puritate et praerogativa conceptionis salvatoris nostri Jesu Christi,* Milan 1512, p. 74b-82a. J. B. MALOU, *op. cit.,* vol. 1, p. 63, and X. LE BACHELET, *art. cit.,* col. 1122 mistakenly list Bernardine of Feltre, O.F.M., as a protagonist on this occasion instead of Bartholomew of Feltre. Cf. H. SBARALEA, O.F.M., Conc., *Supplementum et Castigatio ad scriptores trium ordinum S. Francisci a Waddingo aliisve descriptos,* vol. 1, Rome 1936, p. 118.

[135] Cf. Bernardinus DE BUSTIS, O.F.M., *Mariale de singulis festivitatibus B. Virginis per modum sermonum tractans,* pars 1, serm. 4, Lyons 1525, p. 16ra.

[136] He published in 1502 a treatise entitled, *Pro Immaculata Virginis Conceptione et eius immunitate a peccato originali rationes contra V. Bandellum,* cf. A. ROSKOVANY, *op. cit.,* vol. 1, p. 350.

[137] V. BANDELLI, *op. cit.*

[138] V. BANDELLI, *Tractatus,* ed. Milan, p. 59b-67b.

[139] *Ibid.,* p. 1a-3b: ". . . oppositam partem ut quoddam nefarium detestandum sacrilegium utpote fidei divinisque litteris ac SS. Patrum et clarissimorum doctorum testimoniis aperte repugnans e christiana religione exstirpandam, ejiciendam, audaci animo validissime comprobant." Of the immaculist opinion he writes: "O scelus inauditum! O facinus detestandum! O stultas mentes! O pectora coeca! O deliramenta nequitiae!" And on p. 52b-53a: "Illud quod doctores sancti et famosi dicunt esse

The audacity of the writer could not have been greater. He was attacking the very dignity and authority of the Holy See by misrepresenting the mind of the Pope. It is not surprising, therefore, that Sixtus IV should have reacted energetically in the Bull *Grave Nimis* of 1482. In this document the Pope, with strong words, condemns the members of different Orders who are deputed to preach the word of God in the different cities and towns of Lombardy, and who are not ashamed to affirm publicly, before crowds of people, that anyone who holds Mary's preservation from original sin is to be considered a heretic, and that the Roman Church celebrates only Mary's spiritual conception or sanctification. However, the Pope did not decide the question of the objective truth of the Immaculate Conception. On the contrary, he fulminated an excommunication against anyone who should call either the maculist or the immaculist opinion heretical.[140]

Even though Sixtus did not mention Bandelli's name, he indicated clearly enough that he had him and his writings in mind. The Constitution was addressed to the regions of Lombardy, where Bandelli was then residing as vicar of the province of Lombardy,[141] and where he had held some of his debates and published his books. Moreover the propositions condemned by the Pontiff were exactly those contained in Bandelli's last book. The latter understood that he was aimed at, for from then on he kept complete silence and never again appeared in any debates.

However, Bandelli's silence did not put a stop to the effect of the ideas he had expressed. Wherever he had spoken he had obtained a following, and gradually the radius of his influence had spread far beyond the confines of Lombardy.[142] As word came to Sixtus IV of further excesses in regions other than Lombardy, he issued another Bull on September 4, 1483, also entitled *Grave nimis.* The tenor and style of this document is much the same as that of the first *Grave nimis,* but it is addressed, not merely to Lombardy, but to every state and land.[143]

II

THE CONSENSUS OF THE CHURCH

The approval granted by Sixtus IV to the doctrine of the Immaculate Conception gave a new impetus to its diffusion all over Christendom. By

---

erroneum, superstitiosum et haereticum, non est pium sed impium; sed quod B. Virgo vel alius praeter Christum non habuerit aliquod peccatum, sancti et doctores famosi dicunt esse erroneum, etc., ergo . . ."

[140] SERICOLI, *op. cit.,* p. 156-158; J. A. ROBICHAUD (article cited in note 113, above), p. 100. Cf. chapter VII of the present volume, p. 298, especially note 106.

[141] SCHÖNLEBEN (work cited in note 128), p. 63.

[142] I. CLICTHOVAEUS, *De puritate Conceptionis beatae Mariae Virginis,* Paris 1513, p. 25r.

[143] See chapter VII of the present volume, p. 299.

the beginning of the seventeenth century the belief in Mary's preservation had become so general that Vincent Justinian Antist, a Spanish Dominican, acknowledged that, "at present in Spain, in the Indies, in France, and almost all over Europe, to preach, write or teach against this devotion would be like trying to carry a millstone in one's arms to the top of a mountain."[144]

However, the papal intervention did not immediately stamp out all opposition. In 1494, at Venice, there appeared a treatise composed by Peter of Vincentia, a Dominican, entitled, *Opusculum de veritate conceptionis beatissimae Virginis Mariae,* in which the author quotes 216 doctors in support of the maculist opinion. Both the doctrine and the method of the treatise reflected the tradition which had begun with John of Naples and reached its apex in Vincent Bandelli. In his *Monumenta Antiqua Seraphica,* Alva y Astorga enumerates some twenty authors who at this occasion rose in defense of Mary's preservation and refer to Sixtus IV's documents. Among them are Louis della Torre,[145] Anthony Cucharo,[146], and John Clicthovaeus.[147] Most of these writings add nothing new to what had already been advanced in the past. They are popularizations of the teaching in schools of theology. However, though they acknowledge the liberty of opinion allowed by Sixtus IV,[148] they are not slow to point out that the Church celebrates the feast of the conception and not that of the sanctification.[149]

The Universities

The universities gradually rallied to the doctrine of the Immaculate Conception. Already in 1507, Cucharo, in his *Elucidarius,* states that the universities of Paris, Oxford, Cambridge, Toulouse and Bologna had been won over to the pious teaching.[150] The Sorbonne had decreed on March 3, 1497 that all candidates for academic degrees would henceforth have to take the oath to defend the Immaculate Conception of Mary.[151] The decree was published on August 28, and the oath was taken on Septem-

---

[144] V. J. Antist, O.P., *De la Inmaculada concepción de la Virgen* . . . Madrid 1615, in De Alva et Astorga, *Monumenta dominicana . . . pro immaculata Virginis Conceptione,* Louvain 1666, p. 518.

[145] L. Della Torre, *Tractatus de conceptione beatae virginis Mariae,* Brescia 1486, in De Alva et Astorga, *Monumenta antique seraphica,* p. 377.

[146] A. Cucharo, O.F.M., *Elucidarium de Conceptione incontaminata Virginis gloriosae,* in De Alva et Astorga, *op. cit.,* p. 535-993. In the first part the author enumerates Bandelli's authorities, and in two other parts he presents arguments in favor of Mary's preservation and answers to objections raised against the pious doctrine.

[147] J. Clicthovaeus, *op. cit.*

[148] L. Della Torre, *op. cit.,* p. 438.

[149] D. Bollandi, *Tractatus de immaculata Virginis conceptione,* in De Alva et Astorga, *Monumenta antiqua ex variis authoribus,* p. 320.

[150] A. Cucharo, *op. cit.,* p. 630.

[151] C. Du Plessis D'Argentré, work cited in note 125, p. 234.

ber 17 by 112 doctors whose names are listed by John Trithemius.[152] Forty-seven of the doctors belonged to religious orders: 8 Benedictines, 3 Cistercians, 1 Premonstratensian, 13 Dominicans, 8 Franciscans, 7 Augustinians, 5 Carmelites, and 1 Servite.

The German universities began to adopt the practice of imposing the oath as a result of two controversies. The first arose when George Frickenhausen headed a Dominican group in their attack against the doctrine of the Immaculate Conception at Leipzig in 1489 and 1490.[153] Frickenhausen asserted that there was a distinction between a heretic and a heresy. Sixtus IV, he explained, had not intended to excommunicate those who declared that the immaculist opinion was a heresy, since in reality it was contrary to Sacred Scripture and the Fathers. The Pope's purpose was merely to excommunicate those who labelled the advocates of the immaculist opinion as heretics, because the Church had not yet condemned and reproved that opinion.[154] The chief opponents of the Dominicans and Frickenhausen were the Franciscans, and the Faculty of Law of the university which was headed by Sebastian Brandt.[155]

The starting-point of the second controversy was a book written by the pious John Trithemius, entitled *De Laudibus S. Annae matris beatissimae Dei genitricis et virginis Mariae,* in chapter 7 of which the author defends the Immaculate Conception and accuses of arrogance, presumption and temerity those who deny the privilege.[156] The accusation aroused the adversaries who, with the Dominican Wigand Wirth as their spokesman took up the challenge. Wirth spoke at the University of Frankfort in 1494, at Heidelberg in 1501 and at Strasbourg in 1510. He declared that

---

[152] J. TRITHEMIUS, *De purissima et immaculata conceptione virginis Mariae, et de festivitate sanctae Annae matris eius,* Argentinae 1506. The list of these doctors is found at the end of the book. Cf. X. LE BACHELET, *art. cit.,* col. 1126.

[153] G. FRICKENHAUSEN, O.P., *Repetitio disputationis de Immaculata Conceptione Virginis gloriosae in florentissimo studio Lipsiensi cum responsionibus et replici in qua fundatis iuribus et theologicis rationibus evidentissime ostenditur quid dicta disputatio veritatis in se contineat cum bulla apostolica,* in De ALVA ET ASTORGA, *Radii solis,* p. 1673. Cf. G. M. LOHR, "Die Dominikaner an der Leipziger Universität," in *Quellen und Forschungen zur Geschichte des Dominikanerordens in Deutschland,* vol. 30, Vechta 1934, p. 64-66.

[154] *Op. cit.,* p. 1673. Sericoli, *op. cit.,* p. 100.

[155] S. BRANDT, *Disputatio brevissima de Immaculata Conceptione Gloriosae Virginis in florentissimo studio Lipsiensi die martis post festum S. Luciae Virginis in scholis iuristarum publice facta et pronuntiata,* in P. De ALVA et ASTORGA, *Radii solis,* p. 1672.

[156] J. TRITHEMIUS, *De Laudibus S. Annae matris beatissimae Dei genitricis et virginis Mariae,* Mayence 1499, ch. 7: "Scimus hanc purissimam Conceptionem in signum positam, cui a multis usque in hodiernum diem contradicitur, qui dum naturae consuetudinem volunt defendere, gratiam Dei non verentur impugnare. Quid stolidi latrant? Quid imperiti murmurant? Annon licet Deo quod vult facere? Ecce Conceptionem Deigenitricis sine macula puram veneratur Ecclesia; ecce festum celebrat devotione annua, et homines captiosi eam temeraria praesumptione maculare laborant! . . . Nec errorem tuum, ô nicator, damno, sed arrogantiam, sed temeritatem, sed prasumptionem." Cf. MALOU, *op. cit.,* vol. 2, p. 151.

whoever dared exempt Mary from the stain of original sin was a heretic. As a result he met with reprisals, not only from Trithemius, but also from the University of Cologne, and especially from the faithful who heard him preach.[157]

These controversies turned to the advantage of the belief in Mary's preservation. In 1499 and 1500 the Universities of Cologne and Mainz followed the example of the Sorbonne by imposing on their faculties and student personnel the oath to profess the doctrine of the Immaculate Conception. From then on a number of other German and Austrian universities included the oath in their statutes: Vienna in 1501, Ingolstadt in 1653, Tyrnau in 1656, Salzburg in 1697. The University of Cracow, in Poland, also adopted the oath.[158]

In Spain the University of Valencia was the first to impose the oath, in 1530. Barcelona and Osuna were the next to follow suit. And from then on universities vied with each other in their zeal to require that their students profess faith in Mary's Immaculate Conception: In 1617 the oath was adopted by Granada, Alcala, Bacza, Santiago, Toledo, and Saragossa; in 1618 it was Salamanca; in 1619 Huesca. The universities of Coimbra and Evora, in Portugal, also had their turn. Even in territories under Spanish influence the oath was enforced; thus in Naples and Palermo in 1618, and in Douay in 1662. Kösters remarks that by the end of the seventeenth century nearly 150 universities or colleges had expressed themselves in favor of the pious belief, and about a third of that number had included the oath in their statutes.[159] The attitude of the universities played a considerable role in spreading the belief of Mary's Immaculate Conception, since these centers of learning provided apostles and defenders of the glorious privilege.

THE RELIGIOUS ORDERS IN THE SIXTEENTH AND SEVENTEENTH CENTURIES

We need not insist here on those religious orders who had in preceding centuries rallied to the doctrine of the Immaculate Conception—namely, the Franciscans, the Carmelites, the Augustinians and the Servites. Their theologians and their saints continued in the tradition of their confreres of the past. Such glorious names as St. Peter of Alcantara, St. Paschal Baylon and St. Joseph Cupertino among the Friars Minor; St. John of the Cross and St. Theresa of Avila among the Carmelites; John of Sahagun and St. Thomas of Villanova among the Augustinians always remain on the pages of those who treasured Mary's original purity. To these ancient orders were added the Clerics Regular, namely the Theatines, the Barnabites, the Somaschi, the Jesuits, the Clerics Regular of the Mother of God.

[157] A. DUVAL, O.P., *art. cit.*, p. 761; X. LE BACHELET, *art. cit.*, col. 1128-1129.
[158] X. LE BACHELET, *art. cit.*, col. 1129.
[159] L. KÖSTERS, *Maria, die unbefleckt Empfangene*, Ratisbon 1905, p. 125.

Then there were such ecclesiastical congregations as the Oratorians, the Mission Fathers, the Eudists, and the Sulpicians. All without exception adhered to the pious belief of Mary's preservation. The Jesuits particularly manifested a great zeal for the doctrine. Among them there were illustrious defenders of Mary's privilege. We shall merely mention some of them here, with the intention of referring to them later as the occasion demands. Lainez, Salmeron, St. Peter Canisius, Toletus, St. Robert Bellarmine, Gregory of Valencia, Vasquez, Suarez—all were loyal supporters and promoters of Mary's preservation. As early as 1593 in its fifth general congregation, the Society of Jesus officially adopted the belief in the Immaculate Conception: "De conceptione autem B. Mariae. . . . . sequantur sententian quae magis hoc tempore communis, magisque recepta apud theologos est."[160]

Though the Order of St. Dominic opposed the teaching of the Immaculate Conception up to the sixteenth century, it gradually began to join the general movement which favored Our Lady's original preservation. One of the most ardent defenders of Mary's privilege in Italy was Ambrose Catharinus († 1553). We shall speak of him at some length in a later section. A century later, another Dominican, Thomas Campanella († 1639), in his *Tractatus de immaculata beatae Virginis conceptione*[161] strongly exhorted his order to rally to the common opinion. Surprisingly enough, he uses the argument John Vitalis had employed against Montson in the fourteenth century, namely that St. Thomas had taught Mary's Immaculate Conception, and that consequently the pious belief owes its origin to the Dominicans rather than the Franciscans. If in one passage the Angelic Doctor seems to be denying Our Lady's privilege, he is in reality merely quoting the opinion of another. Aquinas' real thought is to be sought in his commentary on the first book of the Sentences, where he clearly teaches that the Blessed Virgin was preserved from original sin. Other Dominican theologians of that time stated that the two passages in St. Thomas could be reconciled if one understood the first as referring to the act, and the second to the debt or original sin. Thus Capponi of Porrecta,[162] and John of St. Thomas.[163] The latter, however, was reprimanded by the Master General, Nicolas Ridolfi, for his attempt to list St. Thomas among the protagonists of the Immaculate Conception. He was ordered to continue his commentary on the Angelic Doctor, but to delete from the books he had not yet sold and to omit from future editions the passage

---

[160] X. Le Bachelet, *art. cit.*, col. 1130.

[161] Published in Naples in 1624. The treatise is contained in De Alva et Astorga, *Monumenta dominicana*, p. 571-624. Cf. also: L. Firpo, "Appunti campelliani XVI. Il 'de conceptione virginis' ritrovato," in *Giornale critico della filosofia italiana*, vol. 29, 1950, p. 68-77.

[162] S. Capponi a Porrecta, O.P., *Tertia pars de Salvatore divi Thomae de Aquino, Angelici et S. Ecclesiae doctoris almi Ordinis Praedicatorum, cum elucidationibus formalibus*, Venice 1596.

[163] Joannes a S. Thoma, O.P., *Tractatus de approbatione et auctoritate doctrinae angelicae D. Thomae, Cursus theologicus*, ed. Solesmes, vol. 1, 1931, p. 265ss.

Figure 1. THE FRIARS AGREE ON THE IMMACULATE CONCEPTION, (1649).

(*See p. 507*)

in which he had tried to show that Aquinas had exempted Mary from the *act* of original sin.[164]

However, the authorities of the Order of Preachers, becoming concerned over the hatred, rivalry and scandals occasioned by the controversy, prescribed measures of prudence. In 1519 the Province of Saxony bade its preachers speak of Mary's sanctity "sine opinionum narratione."[165] In 1524 Albert de las Casas, a provincial of Andalusia, acknowledges that the practice and authority of the Church should outweigh the testimony of the individual doctors, quoted in favor of the maculist opinion.[166] In Paris the diplomatic submission of the Dominican doctors tends to become an interior acquiescence; some of the Friars Preachers even recite an office of the Immaculate Conception, at least privately.[167] William Pepin (1533) preaches the privilege openly,[168] and Peter Doré, a regent at Saint-Jacques, exposes the immaculist doctrine in his *Image de vertu*.[169] In Spain the General Chapter of Vallodolid in 1605 asks the preachers of the Order to abstain from any saying that could scandalize the faithful as regards original sin and the Blessed Virgin.[170] Finally, on June 24, 1618, while Philip III was negotiating with Rome regarding a definition of the Immaculate Conception, a petition was sent to the Pope by the Dominican province of Spain, entreating the Holy Father to order their province to celebrate the Feast of the Conception as it is celebrated in the Church, and to compel them to preach that the Virgin was conceived without sin.[171] Mir y Noguera[172] mentions about ten illustrious Dominican orators who spoke

---

[164] "8 Decembris 1640 scriptum est Patri Magistro F. Joanni a Sancto Thoma ipsique sub precepto formali iniunctum, ut prosequatur scribere super Summam Sancti Thomae et quod deleat sive tollat ex exemplaribus quae hactenus non vendidit, vel ab illis quae excudet (si iterum excudi contingat primus thomus primae partis) quod est defensorium Divi Thomae in materia de Conceptione." Quoted in *Archivum fratrum praedicatorum*, vol. 1, 1931, p. 398-399.

[165] G. M. LOEHR, *Die Kapitel der Provinz Saxonia im Zeitalter der Kirchenspaltung 1513-1540*, in *Quellen und Forschungen zur Geschichte des Dominikanerordens in Deutschland*, vol. 26, Vechta 1930, p. 110-111.

[166] ROSKOVANY, *op. cit.*, vol. 1, p. 408: "Quia Ordo proedicatorum solitus est Sanctorum doctrinae adhaerere, sustinuit hucusque opinionem B. Hieronymi, Augustini, Ambrosii, Bernardi, Gregorii, Bonaventurae, et aliorum SS. Doctorum, quod B. Virgo fuit concepta in originali: sed iam de hoc non est curandum, cum sit materia nullius utilitatis et valde scandalosa, praesertim cum tota fere ecclesia, cuius usus et auctoritas secundum B. Thomam praevalet dicto Hieronymi vel cuiuscumque alterius doctoris, iam asserat, quod fuit praeservata."

[167] Such an Office is found at the end of *Horae beatae Mariae Virginis ad usum ff. Praedicatorum*, Paris 1529. Cf. ROSKOVANY, *op. cit.*, vol. 1, p. 408.

[168] P. De ALVA ET ASTORGA, *Monumenta dominicana*, p. 536-570.

[169] P. DORÉ, O.P., *L'image de vertu demonstrant la perfection et saincte vie de la bienheureuse vierge Marie Mère de Dieu, par les Escriptures tant de l'ancien que du nouveau Testament*, Paris 1540.

[170] *Monumenta Ordinis Fratrum praedicatorum historica*, Rome 1896, vol. II, p. 68.

[171] ROSKOVANY, *op. cit.*, vol. 2, p. 16-17. M. CANAL, "El padre Aliaga y la Inmaculada Concepción," in *Archivum fratrum praedicatorum*, vol. 1, 1931, p. 136-157.

[172] J. MIR Y NOGUERA, *La Inmaculada Concepción*, ch. 14, Madrid 1905.

favorably of the Immaculate Conception, the most noteworthy of whom is St. Louis Bertrand († 1581).

SHEPHERDS OF SOULS

The general consensus of the Church was evidenced in the sixteenth and seventeenth centuries in the large number of confraternities established even in villages and hamlets to honor Our Lady's Immaculate Conception, in prayer books and in the dedication of Churches and places of worship to Mary Immaculate.[173] Everywhere the faithful manifested a tender piety toward Our Blessed Mother's unsullied purity. To a great extent this piety was aroused and nourished by the sermons of their pastors and by the official teaching of their bishops. Even a mere catalogue of such sermons would lead us far beyond the scope of this paper. However, a mention of at least a few important bishops is called for here.

St. Thomas of Villanova († 1555), archbishop of Valencia and a member of the great Augustinian family, beautifully expressed his belief in Mary's preservation:

> It was becoming that the Mother of God be wholly pure, stainless, and sinless, and that consequently she be holy not only in the womb of her mother, but also most holy in her conception (*et in conceptione sanctissima*). For it was not fitting that there be the least stain in her who was the sanctuary of God, the dwelling place of the divine Wisdom, the reliquary of the Holy Spirit, the urn of the celestial manna.[174]

In Italy, St. Charles Borromeo († 1584), preaching in his metropolitan church on the nativity of Our Lady, shows that Mary's first sanctification was superior to that of St. John the Baptist, since she was endowed with the plenitude of grace from the very beginning of her existence. The sublimity of that plenitude is known to Him alone who wished to make of His Mother a dwelling place worthy of Himself.[175]

In France, a Doctor of the Church, St. Francis of Sales, extolls Mary's Immaculate Conception. In a sermon on the Presentation, he writes:

> Since this glorious Virgin was born of a father and a mother like other children, it would seem that like them she, too, would be stained with original sin; but divine Providence ordained otherwise, reaching out His hand to hold her back, so that she might not fall into this miserable precipice of sin.

[173] Cf. X. LE BACHELET, *art. cit.*, col. 1133-1136.

[174] *Serm. III de Nativitate virginis Mariae*, quoted by J. MIR Y NOGUERA, *op. cit.*, p. 478; LE BACHELET, *art. cit.*; see also A. SAGE, *op. cit.*, in *Maria*, vol. 2, Paris 1952, p. 700.

[175] *Homilia*, edited by J. G. SAXIUS, Augsburg 1758, p. 614, 617. Cf. LE BACHELET, *art. cit.*, col. 1137: "Nam Joannes quidem sexto post conceptionem mense fuit in utero sanctificatus, haec vero ab ipso statim conceptionis exordio gratiae plenitudinem accepit . . . Solus tu, Christe, qui eam tibi domum parasti, qualiter paraveris, nosti."

Some theologians say that while St. John the Baptist was still in his mother's womb, Our Lord sanctified him and granted him the use of reason.

> Now if Our Lord granted such a grace to him who was to be His precursor, who can doubt that He not only granted the same grace, but that He accorded a much greater privilege to her whom He had chosen as His Mother? Not only did He sanctify her in the womb of St. Anne, as He had sanctified St. John in the womb of St. Elizabeth, but He made her all holy and pure from the very instant of her conception.[176]

Another sacred orator and bishop who marvelously expounded the doctrine of the Immaculate Conception to the faithful was Bossuet. Between 1652 and 1669 he preached the panegyric for the feast of the Immaculate Conception on five different occasions. The first two sermons especially contain his doctrine. He acknowledges the difficulty of preaching on this subject, for if he says too little the piety of his audience will remain unsatisfied, and if he resorts to an undue elaboration he risks going beyond the limits dictated by the canons of the Church which demand circumspection and restraint.[177] However, he feels encouraged at the thought that the University of Paris, his *alma mater,* obliges its members to defend this doctrine. Moreover, though the Church does not compel the faithful to believe in the Immaculate Conception, she at least insinuates that such a belief is very agreeable to her. By obeying the commandments of the Church, we give proof of our obedience; by doing what she insinuates we manifest our affection.[178]

Bossuet's method of exposition consists primarily in refuting the objections that are ordinarily raised against the doctrine of the Immaculate Conception. He believes that Mary's preservation is one of those truths which naturally appeal to the mind once the difficulties to its acceptance are removed. Profound reasoning and tricks of rhetoric are not required to convince the faithful of the soundness of this teaching.[179] To the objec-

[176] *Oeuvres Complètes de Saint François de Sales,* vol. 2, *Sermons depuis la Pentecôte jusqu'à la veille de Noel,* Paris 1834, p. 411: "Ne la sanctifiant pas seulement dès le ventre de Ste Anne, comme S. Jean dans celuy de Ste Elizabeth; mais la rendant de plus toute saincte et toute pure, dès l'instant mesme de sa conception." See F. Vincent, *Saint François de Sales,* in *Maria,* vol. 2, Paris 1952, p. 993-1004.

[177] *Oeuvres de Bossuet,* vol. 3, Paris 1845, p. 386: "De tant de diverses matières que l'on a accoutumé de traiter dans les assemblées ecclésiastiques, celle-ci est sans doute la plus délicate. Outre la difficulté du sujet, qui fait certainement de la peine aux plus habiles prédicateurs, l'Eglise nous ordonne de plus une grande circonspection et une retenue extraordinaire. Si j'en dis peu, je prévois que votre piété n'en sera pas satisfaite. Que si j'en dis beaucoup, peut-être sortirai-je des bornes que les saints canons me prescrivent."

[178] *Ibid.,* p. 398: "[L'Eglise] a un sentiment fort honorable de la conception de Marie: elle ne nous oblige pas de la croire immaculée; mais elle nous fait entendre que cette créance lui est agréable. Il y a des choses qu'elle commande, où nous faisons connoitre notre obéissance: il y en a d'autres qu'elle insinue, où nous pouvons témoigner notre affection."

[179] *Ibid.,* p. 386: "Il y a certaines propositions étranges et difficiles, qui, pour être

tion that Mary was born by seminal generation and was therefore subject to the universal law of sin, Bossuet answers that indeed Mary would have contracted original sin, had not God's Omnipotence preserved her with prevenient grace. If God made an exception to the laws of the universe in the miracle of Josue and in delivering the three young men in the fiery furnace, He can dispense Mary from the universal law of sin.[180] If he could dispense Mary from the pains of childbirth, the fires of concupiscence, the necessity of actual sin, and the corruption of the tomb, why could He not dispense her in this case? [181] That Mary's preservation would derogate honor from Christ is not a valid objection either. Christ is innocent by nature, Mary by grace; Christ is innocence par excellence, Mary by a special privilege; Christ is pure because He is the Redeemer; Mary owes her innocence to the redeeming power of His precious Blood.[182]

Neither can the fact of Mary's redemption be invoked as an argument that she contracted original sin. Bossuet's answer reminds one of Scotus. Our Lord's victory over Satan would not be complete had He not exercised His power in preserving from original sin. If Satan reigns in the souls of the new-born infant, Christ triumphs over him through baptism. But that is not all. The devil through original sin penetrates into the very maternal womb; yet even there Christ triumphed over him by sanctifying St. John before his birth. And still there is one more instance where the devil seems invincible: the moment of conception. Bossuet at this point addresses the Savior in these words:

> "Arise, Lord, and let Thine enemies be scattered: and let them that hate Thee flee before Thy face." (Ps. 67:1) . . . Choose at least one creature whom Thou wilt sanctify from her very beginning, from the first instant of her animation. Show the great envious one that Thou canst preclude his venom by the power of Thy grace; that there is no place which his infernal darkness has penetrated, from which Thou canst not dislodge him by the all-powerful splendor of Thy light. The Blessed Mary offers Thee the occasion. It is worthy of Thy bounty and of the grandeur of so excellent a Mother that Thou make her experience the effects of Thy special protection.[183]

---

persuadées, demandent que l'on emploie tous les efforts du raisonnement et toutes les inventions de la rhétorique. Au contraire, il y en a d'autres qui jettent au premier aspect un certain éclat dans les âmes, qui fait que souvent on les aime, avant même que de les connoître. De telles propositions n'ont pas presque besoin de preuves. Qu'on lève seulement les obstacles, que l'on éclaircisse les objections, s'il s'en présentent quelques unes, l'esprit s'y portera de soi-même et d'un mouvement volontaire. Je mets en ce rang celle que j'ai à établir aujourd'hui."

[180] *Ibid.*, p. 388-390.
[181] *Ibid.*, p. 391.
[182] *Ibid.*, p. 392.
[183] *Ibid.*, p. 393-394: "Choisissez du moins une créature que vous sanctifiiez dès son origine, dès le premier instant où elle sera animée; faites voir à notre envieux que vous pouvez prévenir son venim par la force de votre grâce; qu'il n'y a point de lieu où il puisse porter ses ténèbres infernales, d'où vous ne le chassiez par l'éclat

A mention must be made here of two Jesuit saints who also taught and defended the doctrine of the Immaculate Conception: St. Peter Canisius and St. Robert Bellarmine. The former devotes chapters 5 to 8 of his *De Maria Virgine incomparabili* to the pious teaching.[184] In his *Summa doctrinae christianae,* while commenting on the "Hail Mary," he declares that Our Lady was not only a Virgin before, during and after the birth of Our Lord, but she was also free of all stain of sin, *ab omni peccati labe libera . . .* quae *sicut lilium est inter spinas.*[185] St. Robert Bellarmine in his larger catechism, explaining the words *gratia plena,* writes:

> Our Lady was full of grace. For . . . she was not infected by the stain of any sin, whether original or actual, mortal or venial.[186]

The first edition of Bellarmine's catechism, published in Italian in 1598, was that very year approved by Clement VIII and recommended to all the bishops.[187]

From the facts we have briefly outlined or alluded to in this section we have at least an idea of the almost universal acceptance of the doctrine of the Immaculate Conception by the middle of the seventeenth century. Universities, religious orders, the faithful and shepherds of souls eagerly proclaimed that Mary was preserved from original sin. The Jesuit Vasquez writes:

> Since the time of Scotus, this opinion has been so widely spread not only among scholastic theologians but also among Christians at large, and has gradually become so deeply rooted in their minds, that one can no longer make anyone abandon or turn away from it.[188]

Even Cajetan acknowledged that:

> This opinion has now become so common, that almost all the Catholics of the Latin Church believe they are rendering homage to God by following it.[189]

---

tout-puissant de votre lumière. La bienheureuse Marie se présente fort à propos. Il sera digne de votre bonté, et digne de la grandeur d'une Mère si excellente que vous lui fassiez ressentir les effets d'une protection spéciale." A similar reasoning recurs on page 410 of the same edition.

[184] P. Canisius, S.J., *De Maria Virgine incomparabili, et Dei Genitrice sacrosancta, libri quinque: atque hic secundus liber est Commentariorum de verbi Dei corruptelis, adversus novos et veteres sectariorum errores nunc primum editus,* Ingolstadt 1577. Cf. X. Le Bachelet, "Le B. Pierre Canisius," in D. T. C., vol. 2(2), col. 1528.

[185] P. Canisius, S.J., *Summa doctrinae christianae. Per quaestiones tradita, et in usum christianae pueritiae nunc primum edita,* Vienna 1554, q. XVIII.

[186] R. Bellarminus, S.J., *Christianae doctrinae copiosa explicatio,* in *Opera Omnia,* vol. 7, col. 1262, Cologne 1617.

[187] R. Bellarminus, S.J., *Dichiarazione piu copiosa della dottrina cristiana,* Rome 1598. Cf. X. Le Bachelet, "François-Robert-Romulus Bellarmin," in D. T. C., vol. 2(1), col. 583, and chapter VII of the present volume, p. 297.

[188] G. Vasquez, S.J., *Commentariorum ac disputationum in tertiam partem S. Thomae tomi duo,* disp. 117, c.2, Lyon 1618, p. 20: "ita percrebuit et cum hominum saeculis inveteravit, ut nullus iam ab ea deduci vel dimoveri possit."

[189] Th. (De Vio) Caietanus, O.P., *Tractatus primus de Conceptione B. M. Vir-*

This common consensus of the Church could not fail to impress theologians who grappled with difficult scriptural and patristic texts in their efforts to demonstrate the doctrine of the Immaculate Conception. The learned Petau wrote:

> What impresses me most and inclines me most strongly in that direction is the common opinion of all the faithful, who bear engraved on their minds, and attest by all sorts of manifestations and acts of homage their conviction that among the works of God nothing is more chaste, more pure, more innocent, more free from all stain and blemish than the Virgin Mary; that there is nothing in common between her and the devil or his agents, and that consequently she has been exempt from every offense of God and from every cause of condemnation.[190]

III

THEOLOGICAL CLARIFICATION DURING THE SIXTEENTH AND SEVENTEENTH CENTURIES

The growing consensus in favor of the Immaculate Conception and the petitions made to Rome to have the doctrine defined induced theologians to seek greater precision on certain aspects of the question of Mary's preservation. First of all, what degree of certitude could be ascribed to what had now become the *opinio communior*? Was it a truth of divine faith, or of divine Catholic faith? Or was it at least definable? If the answer was yes, then it would be necessary to show how Mary could be Immaculate and yet redeemed by Christ; in other words, it became imperative to clear up the question of the debt of sin in the Blessed Virgin. Then, too, there was the problem which arose from Mary's being born by seminal propagation. Did she, because of her manner of birth, contract the "fomes peccati"? In this section we shall therefore see how the theologians of the sixteenth and seventeenth centuries resolved the three problems of: 1) the definability of the doctrine of the Immaculate Conception; 2) the debt of sin in Mary; 3) the precise object of Our Lady's privilege.

The Definability of the Doctrine

Even after Sixtus IV's *Grave Nimis* the University of Paris continued to hold that the doctrine of the Immaculate Conception was of defined faith

---

ginis ad Leonem X, Pont. Max., c.5, Lyon 1558: "ita ut omnes fere catholici latinae Ecclesiae arbitrentur obsequium se praestare Deo in hujusmodi sequela opinionis." Cf. X. Le Bachelet, "Immaculée Conception," *loc. cit.,* col. 1141.

[190] D. Petavius, S.J., *Opus de Theologicis dogmatibus, De Incarnatione Verbi,* lib. 14, c.2, n.10, ed. Thomas (1868), vol. 7, p. 245: "Movet autem me, et eam in partem sim propensior, communis maxime sensus fidelium omnium; qui hoc intimis mentibus, alteque defixum habent, et quibus possunt indiciis officiisque testantur, nihil illa Virgine castius, purius, innocentius, alieniusque ab omni sorde, ac labe peccati procreatum a Deo fuisse. Tum vero nihil cum inferis, et horum rectore diabolo, adeoque cum qualicumque Dei offensa, et damnatione commune unquam habuisse."

ever since the Council of Basel. In 1496, the Dominican John Veri, a doctor of the Sorbonne, declared in a public sermon on the feast of the Immaculate Conception that those who asserted that the Virgin Mary was conceived in original sin did not sin mortally nor were heretics; indeed all who accused them of sin, or heresy were excommunicated by a certain Bull of Sixtus IV. The Sacred Faculty replied that the first part of Veri's statement was false, impious, and offensive to pious ears; it detracted from the devotion of the faithful to the Immaculate Conception of the glorious Virgin Mary, Mother of Our Lord Jesus Christ; it was contrary to ecclesiastical worship, right reason, Scripture and the faith, and should consequently be revoked and repaired publicly. The second part of the statement was qualified as temerarious and scandalous. As for the third part, the University replied that it was not likely Sixtus had intended to excommunicate those who called the advocates of the maculist theory heretics.[191] Again in 1521 when Luther asserted that to deny Mary's preservation from original sin was not condemned, the Sorbonne declared that he had ignorantly and impiously proffered a false statement against the honor of the Immaculate Virgin.[192] Even as late as 1543 the University qualified as heretical and injurious to the Virgin the thesis of a Dominican who declared that Mary needed a liberative redemption.[193]

It seems strange that the Sorbonne took this stand after Sixtus IV had so clearly declared that all who accused advocates of the opposite opinion of heresy or sin were excommunicated. The reason probably is that the University was either completely unaware of the second *Grave Nimis,* or it was not convinced of its authenticity.[194] The attitude of Paris finally came to a showdown in 1574, when John Maldonatus, S.J., in a lecture on the Incarnation held at the Jesuit College of Clermont severely rebuked the Faculty of the Sorbonne for compelling its members, even after *Grave Nimis,* to hold *de fide* that the Blessed Virgin was preserved from original sin.[195] The University referred the matter to Peter of Gondy, the Bishop

[191] J. TRITHEMIUS, *De purissima ac Immaculata Conceptione Virginis Mariae et de festivitate sanctae Annae matris eius,* Strasbourg 1506, *post epistolam prooemialem,* s. fol: "Asserentes V. Mariam esse in peccato originali conceptam non peccant mortaliter nec sunt haeretici, immo omnes qui dicunt ipsos sic dicendo mortaliter peccare vel esse haereticos, excommunicantur a Xysto per quamdam bullam." . . . "Quantum ad primam partem est falsa, impia et piarum aurium offensiva, a devotione fidelium de Immaculata Conceptione gloriosae Virginis Mariae, matris Domini nostri Jesu Christi retractiva, cultui ecclesiastico, rectae rationi, Scripturae et fidei dissona, revocanda publice et reparanda; secunda pars est temerarie praedicta et scandalosa; quantum ad tertiam partem non est veresimiliter credendum sanctissimum dominum papam Xystum taliter dicentes excommunicasse."

[192] C. DU PLESSIS D'ARGENTRÉ, *op. cit.,* I, II, p. 369: "Contradictoria huius propositionis: Beata Virgo est concepta sine peccato originali, non est reprobata."—"Haec propositio est falsa ignoranter et impie contra honorem Immaculatae Virginis asserta." Cf. SERICOLI, *op. cit.,* p. 111.

[193] C. DU PLESSIS D'ARGENTRÉ, *op. cit.,* II, I, p. 138.

[194] Cf. SERICOLI, *op. cit.,* p. 112-115.

[195] The text of Maldonatus' lecture on our Lady's Conception is conserved in the

of Paris, who declared that nothing in Maldonatus' teaching was heretical or contrary to the Catholic Faith. No condemnation was obtained either when the case was taken to Gregory XIII in Rome. Nevertheless the University of Paris did not completely change its attitude. In a treatise published around 1705, it admits the Roman See has not yet decided that the Immaculate Conception is *de fide;* nevertheless the same Holy See has not forbidden particular groups to hold the doctrine as *de fide.*[196] Even though the doctrine is not *de fide catholica,* some say it is *de fide gallicana,* binding all those who belong to France,[197] because of a particular revelation made to the Church of France, and not yet made to other churches.[198] According to Villaret the University of Paris was severely condemned by Rome on its particularistic stand, and would even have incurred excommunication had Maldonatus not intervened.[199]

The upshot of the controversy was that the doctrine of the Immaculate Conception could not yet be considered *de fide catholica.* The next move was to determine whether it could ever be defined. A group of Dominicans flatly denied the definability because according to them the doctrine of Mary's preservation was contrary to Revelation, and therefore heretical. Spina was the principal propounder of this opinion. Following in the footsteps of Frickenhausen, he declared that by imposing a censure on those who taxed advocates of the Immaculate Conception as heretical, Sixtus IV in no way insinuated that the immaculist opinion was immune from heresy, but he wished the good faith of the individual immaculists to be respected. For the Pontiffs could not declare non-heretical what in reality was heretical.[200] Indeed to say that Mary was preserved from

---

Vatican Library, cod. lat. 6433, fol. 24r-29r: *"Dictata a Maldonato Jesuita circa Conceptionem Immaculatam Virginis Mariae."* Maldonatus merely denied that the doctrine of the Immaculate Conception was of defined faith; he did not reject the doctrine itself. Indeed, he qualified it as *paulo probabilior.* Cf. X. Le Bachelet, "Immaculée Conception," *loc. cit.,* col. 1151.

[196] *Tractatus de fide sacrosanctae Facultatis theologicae in universitate Parisiensi circa Immaculatam Virginis Matris a peccato originali Conceptionem et contentionum circa eamdem olim ortarum et earum quae inter D. et Rev. episcopum Parisiensem, D. Iesuitas et ipsam Facultatem anno superiori et isto millesimo quingentesimo septuagesimo quinto motae sunt.*—The treatise is in ms. in Archiv. Vat., Miscell. arm. II tom. II ff. 478-500.

On fol. 496ra and 497v: "Universitatibus manet liberum sane . . . illam [partem] amplecti, quae fide credit Conceptionem esse de fide in se seu revelatam esse a Deo quamdiu nondum esset revelata omnibus ecclesiis . . . Licet Sedes Romana nondum deciderit esse de fide, non improbat tamen particulariter credentes vel decidentes sibi esse de fide . . . cum nec prohibere possit revelationes divinas particulares, ex quibus in singularibus nascitur fides."

[197] Quoted by X. Le Bachelet, *art. cit.,* col. 1152: "Respondent quidam non esse de fide *catholica,* sed de fide *gallicana,* certa tamen et necessaria . . . non esse quidem de fide in aliis provinciis, sed esse in Gallia."

[198] *Ibid.,* "ob revelationem Ecclesiae gallicanae factam quae nondum aliis facta est."

[199] E. Villaret, S.J., "Marie et la Compagnie de Jésus," in *Maria,* vol. 2, Paris 1952, p. 949.

[200] B. Spina, O.P., *De universali corruptione generis humani ab Adam seminaliter*

original sin is contrary to Sacred Scripture and the Councils.[201] Grysaldus,[202] and Montagnolius[203] used the same arguments as Spina. Melchior Cano is a typical example of those who denied the definability of the Immaculate Conception:

> The Sacred Books, taken literally and in their true sense, nowhere affirm that the Blessed Virgin was totally exempt from original sin. On the contrary they enunciate the law of sin in general terms, without any exception, for all those who descend from Adam through carnal propagation. Nor can one affirm that the belief came to us by tradition from the Apostles. Indeed, the traditional beliefs could have come to us only through the medium of the Bishops, successors of the Apostles. Now it is manifest that the early Fathers did not receive from the Apostles the doctrine of the Immaculate Conception; for if they had received it, they would have transmitted it to their successors.[204]

Among those who did not absolutely deny the definability of the doctrine of the Immaculate Conception, but rather admitted it in a restricted sense was St. Robert Bellarmine. He asserted that Our Lady's privilege could be the object of a definition, but only as a pious belief or as a theological conclusion, not as a truth of faith. In his *Votum pro Immaculata B. Virginis Conceptione* of August 31, 1617, he writes:

---

propagati, in *Opuscula Omnia,* vol. 5, Venice 1535, p. 74ra-74vb: "Contra statuta Patrum aliquid condere vel mutare nec huius [Apostolicae] quidem Sedis potest auctoritas . . . Hoc enim non subest potestati Papae ut; quae haeretica est opinio, faciat sua voluntate non haereticam."

Ibid., p. 74ra: "Si Xystus in sua extravaganti contrarium sentiret aut sentiendum praeciperet, procul dubio haereticus esset et consequenter a pontificali dignitate deiectus tam quoad Deum quam quoad Ecclesiam, cum haec omnia sint ab Ecclesia iam vulgata et in conciliis sub anathematis damnatione determinata; et nullum ligaret ab eo fulminata sententia."

[201] *Ibid.,* p. 74ra: "Omnes homines ab Adam seminaliter propagatos contrahere de facto peccatum originale secundum Augustinum ad fidei fundamenta pertinet; quo remoto cum removeatur Christum esse omnium hominum redemptorem, salus hominum et beatitudo tolleretur, et ex consequenti ad fidem directe pertinet. Qui enim hoc negaret iam sacris litteris sacrisque conciliis contradiceret et esset formalis haereticus."

[202] P. GRYSALDUS, O.P., *Decisiones fidei catholicae et apostolicae ex sanctorum Scripturarum, BB. Rom. Pontificum diplomatum, sacrorum conciliorum fontibus ac Sanctorum gestis deductae et in uno alphabetico ordine collectae,* Venice 1587, p. 247: "Imo Bartholomaeus Spineus . . . probat alteram opinionem . . . esse haereticam et hanc nostram tamquam de fide sequendam."

[203] I. D. MONTAGNOLIUS, O.P., *Defensiones theologiae angelicae ac thomisticae a recensioribus theologis universam theologiae divi Thomae summam complectentes,* Naples 1610, p. 435: "Nec etiam verum est quod Xystus IV definiat praeservationem [B. Virginis] non esse contra fidem; sed tantum definit quod qui tenet alterutram opinionem non est haereticus nec mortaliter peccat, cum tamen in re ipsa altera sit contra fidem vel erronea, quoniam circa Scripturae sensum materia haec versatur."

[204] Melchior CANUS, O.P., *De locis theologicis,* lib. 7, c. 3, conclusio 4, Bassano 1776, p. 159. Cf. X. LE BACHELET, *art. cit.,* col. 1153; cf. B. MEDINA, O.P., *Expositio in tertiam D. Thomae partem,* Venice 1582, q.27, a.2, p. 347.

One could define that all the faithful should hold as pious and sacred the belief in the conception without stain of the Virgin, so that henceforth no one may be permitted to say the contrary without temerity, scandal or suspicion of heresy.

And before that, in his second conclusion, he remarks: "It cannot be defined that the opposite opinion is heretical." [205] Why this restriction? Evidently because the saintly Cardinal did not believe that there was enough evidence in Scripture and Tradition to prove that the doctrine of the Immaculate Conception was divinely revealed. This seems also to have been the opinion of Maldonatus, for he objects:

> What is of faith must have been revealed by God immediately or mediately, explicitly, that is in plain words *(in propria forma verborum)*, or implicitly; namely, in the language of theologians, in virtue of a logical or necessary consequence *(in necessaria et bona consequentia)*. But that the Blessed Virgin was conceived without sin is an assertion which in no one of these four ways appears as revealed by God.[206]

Among those who contended that Mary's preservation could be defined, there was a group who based themselves on the axiom, *Lex orandi, lex credendi*. They argued that when the Church institutes a feast in honor of a saint or a mystery and invites the faithful to celebrate the feast, she canonizes the sanctity of that saint or mystery. It would be very temerarious to suspect the Church of error in such a canonization, or even to think that she did not act on the basis of perfect certitude. Therefore the approbation accorded by Sixtus IV to the feast of the Immaculate Conception proves that the doctrine of Mary's preservation has a supreme degree of certitude just short of *de fide divino-catholica*.[207] Such were the arguments of Giles of the Presentation,[208] Catharinus,[209], Albertinus,[210], Wadding,[211] Nieremberg,[212] and others.

[205] V. Sardi, *La solenne definizione de dogma dell'Immacolata Concepimento di Maria santissima*, vol. 1, Rome 1904, p. 10-17. Cf. X. Le Bachelet, *art. cit.*, col. 1153.

[206] Vatican Library, cod. lat. 6433, fol. 44. Cf. X. Le Bachelet, *art. cit.*, col. 1153.

[207] Sericoli, *op. cit.*, p. 119.

[208] Aegidius De Praesentatione, O. E. S. A., *De immaculata B. Virginis Conceptione ab omni originali peccato immuni*, Coimbra 1617, p. 301ss.

[209] A. Catharinus Politi, O.P., *Disputatio pro veritate Immaculatae Conceptionis B. V. Mariae ad Patres ac Fratres Ordinis Praedicatorum*, Senis 1532, lib. 3, test. 4, (ed. s. fol.); *Idem, Disputatio pro veritate Immaculatae Conceptionis B. Virginis et eius celebranda a cunctis fidelibus festivitate ad S. synodum Tridentinum*, Rome 1551, pars 2, p. 92ss.

[210] A. Albertinus, O.P., *Tractatus solemnis et aureus de agnoscendis assertionibus catholicis et haereticis*, Venice 1571, q. 17, p. 54r-57r.

[211] L. Waddingus, O.F.M., *Legatio Philippi III et IV catholicorum regum Hispaniarum ad SS. DD. NN. Paulum PP. V et Gregorium XV de definienda controversia Immaculatae Conceptionis B. Virginis Mariae, per Ill. et Rev. Dom. D. F. Antonium a Treio Ep. Carthag. . . . ex Ordine Minorum*, Louvain 1624, p. 309ss.

[212] I. E. Nieremberg, S.J., *Opera parthenica de supereximia et omnimoda puritate Matris Dei*, Lyon 1659, p. 77. 93ss.

The weakness of their argument was pointed out by Salazar and Miranda. To determine the degree of certitude of a mystery of which the Church approves the feast, they remark, two things must be adverted to: first, the manner in which the Church sanctions the feast, and secondly, the degree of certitude the Church herself attributes to the mystery celebrated. If the Church solemnly commands the feast to be celebrated in the whole world, the degree of certitude will undoubtedly be very great; if however she merely approves, confirms and commends the feast without any precept that it be observed, the certitude will be far less.   Moreover, since public worship is always a practical expression of the doctrine of the Church, one must advert to the degree of certitude she ascribes to the truth in question; namely, either a certitude of divine Catholic faith, or a certitude just short of Catholic faith, or a certitude of mere probability.   Attention must also be paid to the manner in which she condemns the opposite opinion; whether, for instance, she condemns it as heretical, or temerarious, or absolutely improbable, or merely less probable.[213]   That is why, according to Suarez, the only conclusion to be drawn from Sixtus IV's approbation of the feast, is that the doctrine of the Immaculate Conception is more probable than that of the opposite opinion.[214]

The true basis for a *de fide* definition of a doctrine is clearly indicated by the Oratorian Louis Crespi de Borgia. He makes a distinction between extrinsic arguments (*externa adiumenta*), which can motivate the *magisterium* of the Church to proceed to a definition, but are in themselves insufficient to warrant an *ex cathedra* pronouncement; and intrinsic arguments which provide a sufficient basis for a dogma. The extrinsic arguments are such things as miracles, papal approval of religious orders, silence imposed on advocates of the opposite opinions, the wish of religious communities, the suffrages of renowned academic circles, the greater probability of a doctrine, the piety of princes, the insistence and wishes of the people. These can serve to confirm the certitude of a doctrine. Yet the real arguments are intrinsic; namely, the testimony of Sacred Scripture, ecclesiastical tradition, and the authority of the Fathers.[215]

Those who advocated the definability of the Immaculate Conception generally acknowledged that the doctrine could not be defined unless it were contained in Sacred Scripture or Tradition. However it is sufficient, they

[213] F. Q. DE SALAZAR, S.J., *Pro Immaculata Deiparae Virginis Conceptione defensio*, Alcala 1621, p. 443ss.

[214] F. SUAREZ, S.J., *In tertiam partem D. Thomae.—Opera Omnia*, vol. 19, Paris 1860, q.27, a.2, disp. 3, sect. 6, p. 48: "Addo neque ex festi celebritate colligi posse tantam certitudinem quanta in alicuius Sancti canonizatione esse solet, quia ipsemet Pontifex qui hoc festum approbat, declarat se solum probare sententiam illam ut piam magisque probabilem."

[215] L. CRISPI A BORGIA, *Propugnaculum theologicum definibilitatis proximae sententiae negantis beatissimam virginem Mariam in suae conceptionis primo instanti originali labe fuisse infectam*, Valentia 1653, p. 413.

remark, that it be contained implicitly. We believe truths of faith today, writes Suarez, which the Church formerly did not believe with an explicit faith, although they were implicitly contained in the primitive teaching of the *magisterium.* And often, in virtue of her authority, and with the guidance of the Holy Spirit, the Church has resolved controversies similar to that of the Immaculate Conception.[216] An anonymous author of the time warns theologians not to insist too much on the literal presence of a doctrine in Scripture and Tradition, lest they fall into the error of the Reformers. In the case of the Immaculate Conception, since the vast majority are in favor of its definition, the Church could manifestly use her authority to determine the true meaning of Holy Scripture, *declarando utra pars congruat menti Spiritus Sancti.*[217]

In regard to the argument from Tradition some authors, especially in Spain, tried to prove that a formal belief in the Immaculate Conception existed from the time of the Apostles;[218] but their opinion was based on legends and apocryphal literature. Others, like the Franciscan Christopher Davenport (Franciscus a S. Clara), acknowledge that the existence of a primitive oral tradition cannot be established by positive proof; but they are of the opinion that it can be deduced from the constant belief of the Church.[219] The weakness of their reasoning lies in the difficulty of establishing the constant belief of the Church. Others, finally, make a distinction between an *apostolic* and an *ecclesiastical* tradition, both of which are valid bases for a dogmatic decision. Thus Crespi de Borgia.[220] The strength of their argumentation began to be realized when such

---

[216] F. SUAREZ, S.J., *In tertiam partem D. Thomae.—Opera Omnia,* vol. 19, Paris 1860, disp. 3, sect. 6, n.4: ". . . saepe Ecclesia sua auctoritate, assistente sibi Spiritu sancto, similes controversias definivit, absque nova revelatione expressa, ut potest manifestis exemplis ostendi, in quaestione de habitibus infusis, de canonica auctoritate aliquorum librorum sacrae scripturae, de carentia omnis peccati venialis in ipsamet Virgine. Addi etiam potest exemplum de resurrectione, de gloriosa assumptione, et de sanctitate nativitatis ejus: ex his enim aliqua jam sunt de fide, alia vero sunt fidei proxima, et nullus dubitat, quin tandem possint definiri. Ad hanc definitionem satis est, ut aliqua supernaturalis veritas in traditione, vel scriptura implicite contenta sit, ut crescente communi consensu Ecclesiae, per quam saepe Spiritus sanctus traditiones explicat, vel scripturam declarat, tandem possit Ecclesia definitionem suam adhibere, quae vim habet cujusdam revelationis, respectu nostri, propter infallibilem Spiritus sancti assistentiam."

[217] Bruxelles, Bibliothèque Royale, ms. 7289, fol. 139: "Porro cavendum ne qui *tam rigide* exigit ad definitionem, ut ex scriptura vel ex traditione res definienda colligatur, faveat haereticis qui multa definita minoris momenti in se quam sit praeservatio ab originali peccato, negant et rident, quia non deducuntur ex Scriptura, et de iisdem traditio incerta sit." Cf. X. LE BACHELET, *art. cit.,* col. 1155.

[218] F. BIVAR, O.Cist., *De festo immaculatae conceptionis beatae Virginis in Hispania celebrato a tempore apostolorum,* Lyon 1627.

[219] FRANCISCUS A S. CLARA, O.F.M., *De definibilitate controversiae immaculatae Dei Genitricis opusculum seu disputatio,* Douay 1651, p. 58: "Perpetuus sensus Ecclesiae et Conciliorum et Patrum sanctorum cogit fideles supponere traditionem oris, ubi in scriptis non invenitur."

[220] L. CRISPI A BORGIA, *op. cit.,* p. 58.

authors as Alva y Astorga [221] and Wangnereck [222] published the testimonies of the post-Ephesian Greek writers in favor of the Immaculate Conception. Two centuries later the Bull *Ineffabilis* brought to light the full value of their reasoning.

THE DEBT OF ORIGINAL SIN IN MARY [223]

We have already seen some of the attempts of fourteenth century theologians to reconcile Mary's preservation with her redemption by Christ. In answer to the question *how* Mary was preserved they resorted to various distinctions of doubtful precision. Thus Francis Mayron asserted that she contracted sin *"aliquo modo"*; Andreas stated that she incurred it *"in quantum ex se est"*; whereas Aureoli affirmed that she sinned *"de iure,"* but not *"de facto."* From the context of their writings it is evident that these authors did not place any real sin in Mary, but rather a liability to sin, from which she was preserved. Their terminology was considered insufficient by theologians of the sixteenth and seventeenth centuries.

A new development was initiated when Cajetan made a distinction between the *act* and the *debt* of original sin. His problem was to conciliate our Lady's Immaculate Conception with her redemption by Christ. To those theologians who taught that the Mother of God was *totally* exempt from original sin, he replied that their opinion would not only free her from all debt of sin, but also make her incapable of any redemption. Hence, to say that Mary was preserved from all debt of original sin, *in propria persona*, would be contrary to the Faith.[224] Del Prado remarks that Cajetan exacted a debt *in propria persona*, and not merely a debt common to the human race, in order to make it possible for her to be reconciled and redeemed.[225]

---

[221] Between 1648 and 1660 Peter DE ALVA ET ASTORGA, O.F.M., wrote some 40 volumes in folio, most of which contain testimonies in favor of or against the Immaculate Conception. A number of his manuscripts were not published, and a few of his books were placed on the Index because of the vehement and polemic tone of his arguments. However, his writings are one of the richest sources available on the controversy of the Immaculate Conception. Cf. the abbreviation ALVA at the end of chapter VII of the present volume, p. 321.

[222] S. WANGNERECK, *Pietas mariana graecorum*, Munich 1647.

[223] In this section we are making use of Father BALIC's excellent study, *De debito peccati originalis in B. Virgine Maria*, Rome 1941, p. 2-24.

[224] Thomas (De Vio) CAIETANUS, O.P., *Tractatus de Conceptione B. Mariae Virginis ad Leonem X Pont. Max.*, in *Opuscula*, Bergomi 1590, p. 180-181: "positio dicens B. Virginem esse praeservatam a peccato originali et reatibus, etc., est contraria fidei catholicae, quoniam repugnat his, quae in Sacra Scriptura et aliis documentis certis et necessariis continentur. Oportet namque de B. Virgine firmiter credere quod Christus est mortuus pro ipsa, et quod ipsa est mortua morte peccati."—"Positio vero dicens B. Virginem praeservatam solum a macula peccati originalis et iis quae a macula sunt inseparabilia (ut est reatus aeternae poenae damni), non negat B. Virginem carnem habuisse infectam; ac per hoc in propria persona debitum contrahendi maculam originalis."

[225] N. DEL PRADO, O.P., *Divus Thomas et Bulla Dogmatica "Ineffabilis Deus,"*

Cajetan's position was attacked by his own confrere, Catharinus. Although the latter does not always express himself very clearly, he would seem to belong to those who either deny all debt of original sin in Mary or at least completely minimize it. Catharinus admits that according to the condition of her nature the Blessed Virgin should have contracted sin (*"habere debuerit"*) ; [226] but, on the other hand, he asserts that she was excepted from the pact whereby the cause of Adam's descendants was joined with that of their first parent, because she had been chosen as the first-born daughter, the most loving spouse and a mother worthy of all honor.[227] Indeed, Catharinus does not hesitate to affirm that, absolutely speaking, Mary did not have any debt of contracting original sin: "Quoniam vero gratia in Virgine, Dei futura Matre, superavit naturam, ideo non dicitur absolute contraxisse peccatum neque debitum contrahendi."[228]

Cajetan and Catharinus set the stage for a new controversy on the Immaculate Conception. There is no longer a question of denying that Mary was preserved from original sin, but rather of determining *how* she was preserved. Two opposite tendencies, stemming from the two Dominicans just mentioned, run through the whole literature of the sixteenth and seventeenth centuries on the debt of sin in Mary. On the one hand theologians teach that Our Lady contracted a real, personal and proximate debt of sin; on the other hand their opponents either deny any debt soever, or at most admit a remote debt of sin.

What complicates the controversy is a glaring lack of uniformity in the terminology and interpretation of the different writers. They generally agree that the debt of original sin consists in some sort of moral obligation or necessity of contracting sin and the privation of grace; [229] but since this

---

Friburgi Helvetiorum 1919, p. 96: ". . . quoniam si debitum aut initium peccati originalis non ponitur *proprium* illius qui concipitur, sed commune, iam non salvaretur quod illa persona esset *mortua, redempta, reconciliata,* etc."

[226] A. CATHARINUS, O.P., *Annotationes in Commentaria Caietani,* Lugduni 1543, p. 290.

[227] A. CATHARINUS, O.P., *Disputatio pro veritate Immaculatae Conceptionis et eius celebranda a cunctis fidelibus festivitate, ad Sanctam Synodum Tridentinam,* Rome 1551, p. 14: "Quoniam vero gratia in Virgine, Dei futura Matre, superavit naturam, ideo non dicitur absolute contraxisse peccatum neque debitum contrahendi. Non enim tam erat in illa respicienda natura quam gratia; immo propter summam gratiam et privilegium singulare despicienda erat natura."

[228] *Ibid.*

[229] Franciscus DEL CASTILLO VELASCO, O.F.M., *De Incarnatione Verbi divini et praeservatione Virginis Mariae ab originali,* Antwerp 1641, p. 488; F. Q. DE SALAZAR, S.J., *Pro Immaculata Deiparae Virginis Conceptione defensio,* Alcala and Paris 1621, p. 14 and 15; T. F. DE URRUTIGOYTI, O.F.M., *Certamen Scholasticum expositivum argumentum pro Deiparae Immaculata Conceptione,* sect. 9, n.197, Lyon 1727, p. 197: [debitum est] "quaedam *obligatio* trahendi carentiam iustitiae ab Adamo praevaricatore quatenus Adamus non solum perdidit sibi sed toti posteritati statum innocentiae"; B. BELLUTI, O.F.M. Conv., *Disputationes de Incarnatione Dominica ad mentem Doctoris Subtilis,* disp. 16, q.1, a.2, Catana 1645, p. 273; "Sciendum est quod *debitum,* in praesenti nihil aliud significat nisi necessitatem et exigentiam alicuius formae in aliquo subiecto."

debt of sin is related to the sin of Adam, it could be conceived as more or less proximate or remote, thus necessitating a subdivision of the concept of debt. It is here that authors go into a maze of distinctions and a complexity of subdivisions that becomes bewildering. They speak of an absolute and a conditional debt; a debt *simpliciter* and *secundum quid;* a physical and a moral debt; a debt *in actu* and *in potentia,* etc. However most commonly they distinguish between a proximate and a remote debt of sin.

Yet even here, as Salazar remarks,[230] uniformity is lacking in the interpretation given the two words *proximate* and *remote.* According to some theologians, the remote debt of sin consists in this that we, being solidary with Adam, *could* by a divine decree be made responsible with him for the sin he committed. Authors of this definition consider humanity before God decrees to include us with Adam in sin. The proximate debt of sin is a necessity of contracting the sin at conception, because of the pact God made with Adam rendering him responsible for the whole human race. The remote debt, consequently, precedes the divine pact; the proximate debt follows it.[231] Others consider man's debt of original sin in reference to the actual stain to be incurred in his own person, rather than in reference to the actual sin of Adam. The proximate debt is said to exist in the person when it is generated; the remote debt exists not in the person itself, but in its ancestors traced back to Adam.[232] For a third group the remote debt of sin is a passive obligation to contract the sin with Adam and in Adam if and when he sins; the proximate debt is an active necessity in Adam's descendants of contracting the stain of sin as their own as soon as they exist.[233] Finally, a fourth group calls the proximate debt a *debitum*

---

[230] F. Q. DE SALAZAR, *op. cit.,* c.1, n.61, p. 17: "Celebratissima est hac nostra aetate divisio debiti peccati originalis in remotum et proximum: sed non est apud omnes utriusque debiti eadem acceptio."

[231] J. LEZANA, O.Carm., *Liber apologeticus pro Immaculata Conceptione,* Madrid 1618, p. 143: "Unde etiam (et est maxime advertendum) *duplici* debito adstricti concipimur omnes ad contrahendum originalem maculam in propriis personis. Primum est *radicale,* et *remotum* in eo consistens, quod per seminalem propagationem ab Adam actum ducamus: ex eo enim provenit, ut sicut Adae filii, et membra sumus, ita eodem, quo ipse, qui caput est, crimine inficiamur . . . Secundum *debitum est proximum,* et *immediatum,* ortum scilicet ex eo, quod, quia in pacto a Deo cum Adamo inito comprehensi sumus, peccante eo, pactumque transgrediente, nos etiam cum illo peccaverimus, ac per consequens *debitum proximum* contrahendi tale peccatum in propriis personis, cum conciperemur, haberemus."

[232] BALIC, *op. cit.,* p. 12.

[233] F. Q. DE SALAZAR, *op. cit.,* n.62, p. 18; *Aegidius a Praesentatione, op. cit.,* p. 78; S. MONTALBANUS, O.F.M.Cap., *Opus theologicum tribus distinctum tomis in quibus efficacissime ostenditur Immaculatam Dei Genitricem . . . fuisse prorsus immunem ab omni debito,* Palermo 1723, n.259, vol. 1, p. 260: "Dico eapropter **quod** debitum *conditionatum,* seu (si ita velis) *remotum,* est necessitas quaedam passiva, moralis quo ad rem, naturalis seu veluti naturalis quo ad modum, vel etiam est quaedam relatio vinculi seu nexus passive capti, moralis quo ad rem, naturalis aut veluti naturalis quo ad modum, vi cuius Adae posteri obstricti fuere ad peccandum *cum Adamo in Adamo,* ut capite suo morali, sub conditione, quod ipse in subiecta materia peccaret . . . Debitum autem *absolutum,* seu (si ita velis) *proximum,* in

exercitum which supposes the person as actually existing, and incurring the debt of sin because of its seminal dependence on Adam. The remote debt, called *debitum signatum,* takes place before the actual sin of Adam and the divine pact with Adam, at the moment when God decrees that mankind will descend from Adam by seminal propagation. By the very fact of their solidarity with Adam, all men incur the possibility of becoming solidary with him in sin.[234]

Differences of opinion regarding the debt of sin stemmed from the purpose authors had in mind. The majority, intent on exempting Mary from any share in the sin of our first parents, conceived the remote debt of sin as prior to the actual sin of Adam. On the other hand, a smaller group, who were not too concerned about Our Lady's preservation, placed both the remote and proximate debt of sin after Adam's transgression.[235] Further differences arose when theologians brought in the question of Mary's predestination with Christ. According as they believed in the absolute predestination of Christ and His Mother or not, authors determined the moment of her preservation and of the various debts of sin.[236]

The question of the debt of original sin led to an unpleasant incident. In 1615 a group of Franciscans in a disputation with Dominicans in Toledo, declared that they wished to have no part in any statement which attributed a debt of original sin to Our Lady. Their opinion was referred to the tribunal of the Sacred Inquisition and condemned; and the Friars Minor were forbidden in future to defend it. However, when an inquiry was made among theologians at Burgos, Seville, Cordova, Granada and Salamanca, a large number of them declared that they were in favor of the Franciscan opinion which they considered entirely irreproachable. Their written testimonies were sent to the Inquisition, with the result that the Cardinal of Toledo, acting as Supreme Inquisitor, decreed that the opinion of the Friars Minor could thenceforth be freely held and defended.[237] One of the consequences of this decision was that Suarez, who had until then

---

ordine ad culpam originalem ut habitualem, est *necessitas moralis* passiva et quidem moralis quo ad rem, naturalis aut quasi naturalis quo ad modum: seu relatio vinculi et nexus . . . , vi cuius Adae posteri ex eo quod peccaverunt in Adam obstricti sunt ad absolute contrahendam in propria persona illius peccati, ut *moraliter proprii,* maculam, cum primum realiter extiterint."

[234] F. DEL CASTILLO VELASCO, *op. cit.,* c. 1, 490. For a thorough discussion of these four opinions, see BALIC, *op. cit.,* pp. 11-15.

[235] F. DEL CASTILLO VELASCO, *op. cit.,* c.i, n.20, p. 490.

[236] A good discussion of this source of differences can be found in D. KOCHANOWSKI, O.F.M., *Novus asserendae Immaculatae Conceptionis Deiparae Virginis nodus,* Casimiriae ad Cracoviam 1669, p. 16-17. Cf. BALIC, *op. cit.,* p. 15.

[237] Carolus LANTERIUS, O.F.M., *Tractatus de SS. Incarnationis mysterio,* disp. VI: *De peccato originali in ordine ad Virginem,* Naples 1665, p. 262; F. DEL CASTILLO VELASCO, *op. cit.,* n.3, p. 525-526; *Aegidius de Praesentatione, op. cit.,* p. 79-82; Ioannes Antonius VELASQUEZ, S.J., *Dissertationes et adnotationes de Maria Immaculate concepta,* Lyon 1653, p. 290.

taught that the denial of the debt of sin in the Blessed Virgin was deserving of censure, now admitted that the opinion could be considered as 'probable'.[238]

THE QUESTION OF THE "FOMES PECCATI"

Though authors in the sixteenth and seventeenth centuries generally agreed that Mary's Conception was immaculate and free from concupiscence (*"fomes peccati"*), they were not in agreement in their manner of explaining this absence of physical infection. According to Giles of the Presentation, Toletus, Suarez, and the majority of the theologians, the *fomes peccati* was extinguished at the moment of Our Lady's first sanctification. Others, like Clicthovaeus[239] and Nicole Grenier[240] contended that there could be no question of purification, since the *fomes peccati* either never existed in Mary or was destroyed before the infusion of her soul. In the mind of these theologians concupiscence was some sort of "morbid quality" inherent in the flesh. According to Clicthovaeus a grace of preservation at the occasion of seminal conception made the Blessed Virgin immune to all concupiscence. Others admitted a sanctification or purification of the flesh prior to its animation by the soul.[241] Still others denied the validity of the very theory which identified original sin with a "morbid impression" or an infectious virus of the flesh.[242] The controversy, however, had little consequence, since even the dogmatic definition of the Immaculate Conception by-passed the issues of the *fomes peccati*.

IV

FURTHER CONTROVERSIES, AFTER SIXTUS IV TO THE END OF THE EIGHTEENTH CENTURY

LEO X's PROJECT OF DEFINITION

The discussions which took place after the death of Sixtus IV determined Alexander VI to confirm the sanctions of *Grave nimis* by means of the Bull *Illius qui* of February 22, 1502. Ten years later, at the occasion of the

---

[238] SUAREZ' original opinion can be read in *In III partem D. Thomae*, disp. 3, sect. 2, *Opera Omnia*, ed. Vivès, vol. 19, p. 28-29. His retraction is found in *Opera Omnia, ed. cit.*, vol. 4, p. 615. Cf. BALIC, *op. cit.*, p. 17-18.

[239] I. CLICTHOVAEUS, *De puritate Conceptionis beatae Mariae Virginis*, Paris 1513, lib. 2, c.10.

[240] N. GRENIER, *Bouclier de la Foy*, Paris 1549, vol. 2, c.29.

[241] D. BOLLANI, *Tractatus de immaculata Virginis conceptione*, c.14, in P. DE ALVA ET ASTORGA, *Monumenta antiqua ex variis authoribus*, vol. 1, p. 321: "Dicamus ergo quod postquam fuit formatum corpus virgineum physicum in ventre matris gloriosissimae Virginis, virtute Spiritus Sancti illud sacratissimum corpus ante infusionem animae intellectivae fuit mundatum atque purificatum, ut esset vas aptissimum ad recipiendam animam illam sanctissimam."

[242] I. DE MEPPIS, *Tractatus de immaculata Virginis conceptione*, in DE ALVA ET ASTORGA, *op. cit.*, p. 92: "Sed iste modus implicat peccatum originale esse qualitatem morbidam in sensitivis viribus complantatam, quod alias improbatum est."

Fifth Lateran Council (1512-1517), Pope Leo X, wondering whether he should not place the question of the Immaculate Conception on the agenda of the Council, consulted Cardinal Cajetan on the advisability of the project. Cajetan's answer came in the form of a treatise, his *Tractatus primus de Conceptione B.M. Virginis ad Leonem X, Pont. Max.*[243] In this dissertation the learned cardinal gave evidence of extreme prudence and moderation. Neither of the two opinions, he remarked, is of faith, since neither the Scriptures, nor the patristic tradition, nor the definitions of Popes and Councils contain an explicit statement that Mary was or was not conceived without sin. The doctrine of the Immaculate Conception can be held without danger of heresy as long as it bears on Mary's preservation from sin alone, and does not assert that she was free from all debt of sin. However, if the immaculist opinion is tolerable, the opposite opinion seems more probable because of the large number of important doctors and saints who held it in the past. On the contrary, the arguments in favor of the Immaculate Conception do not seem convincing. Cajetan quotes only fifteen saints, from St. Ambrose to St. Vincent Ferrer, in support of the Dominican opinion, but he refers to the writings of Torquemada and Bandelli for further testimonies. He admits that the number of authorities in favor of Our Lady's privilege is almost infinite (*sunt numero infiniti*), but these testimonies are all recent, and compared to the ancient authorities which deny the Immaculate Conception, their probability is very weak (*valde exigua est*). Let the Pope decide with his infallible authority. Let him choose between fifteen saints and a countless number of ancient doctors, on the one hand, and the moderns as well as the mass of people who support them with their clamors on the other. In any case, the writings of theologians and the sermons of sacred orators should be kept in check on the question of Our Lady's Conception, according to the precept of Sixtus IV.[244]

Despite Cajetan's moderation, his treatise induced Leo X to abandon the plan of having the question of the Immaculate Conception discussed at the Fifth Lateran Council. However the cardinal's conciliatory stand on the probability of the two opinions caused a reaction in his own order. Bartholomew Spina, who later became the Master of the Sacred Palace (1542-1546), in a treatise inspired both by the doctrine and the vehmence of Vincent Bandelli,[245] attempted to demonstrate that Cajetan's

---

[243] Thomas (de Vio) CAIETANUS, *op. cit.* (cf note 224, above).

[244] G. BOSCO, O.P., *L'immacolata Concezione nel pensiero del Gaetano e del Caterino*, Florence 1950, p. 32; Thomas Caietanus, *op. cit.*, p. 139b: "coercendae sunt praedicatorum linguae scriptorumque manus in hac quaestione; et neutram partem debent damnare ut erroneam, ut fidei, ut Sacrae Scripturae, aut Ecclesiae determinationi contrariam; sed sobrie scribere et loqui debent, et non plus sapere quam oportet, iuxta Apostolicae Sedis praeceptum a Sixto IV editum"; X. Le Bachelet, *art. cit.*, col. 1165.

[245] B. SPINA, O.P., *Tractatus contra opusculum Caietani de Conceptione*, in *Opuscula omnia*, Venice 1535.

middle way was illogical, dangerous, insufficient, contrary to Sacred Scripture and the spirit of the Church as well as to the Dominican Order and its most outstanding doctors. This was not the first time Spina had attacked Cajetan. As early as 1526 he had taken exception to the latter's commentary on I-II, q.81, art.1 of the *Summa,* in which Cajetan had asserted that one could in good faith admit that not all descendants of Adam by way of seminal propagation contracted original sin *de facto,* but they were subject to it only *de iure,* having a debt or an obligation to contract it because of the manner of their origin.[246]   After drawing arguments and testimonies from Bandelli's writings, Spina concluded that the evidence he had adduced from the Sacred Scriptures and the holy doctors was such that it could not be denied *"absque praejudicio veritatis Catholicae Fidei."*

If Spina reproached Cajetan for his excessive concession to the Immaculist opinion, another of his confreres, Catharinus, took him to task for not completely subscribing to the doctrine of Mary's preservation. Ambrose Catharinus Politi, O.P., had long since become notorious among his Dominican confreres for his uncompromising support of the doctrine of the Immaculate Conception. In 1526, when attacked by Florentine troops, the Sienese authorities had, on the advice of Margaret Bichi, a saintly Franciscan tertiary, taken the vow of solemnly celebrating the feast and octave of the Immaculate Conception each year if victory were accorded them. Their prayers were crowned with success, and they forthwith decreed that the whole city should take part in a procession and solemn mass in honor of Mary Immaculate. Everyone obeyed the decree except the two Dominican monasteries, whose superiors gave as an excuse certain censures imposed by the two major authorities of the Order on all those who adhered to the doctrine of Our Lady's preservation. The same refusal was repeated each year at the anniversary of the victory and on the 8th of December. Catharinus, appointed superior of S. Spirito in 1528, strenuously endeavored to persuade Michelozzi, the superior of the other monastery in Siena, and Zenobius Pieri, the vicar general in Florence, to yield to the Sienese authorities. His correspondence with these two Dominicans has recently been published by Father Giacinto Bosco.[247] His efforts for a long time met with no success, despite a brief of Clement VII which confirmed the Sienese vow and declared the Dominican censures not binding for the Friars at Siena. Finally Catharinus was withdrawn from his office as superior and obtained permission to live in Rome. It was around that time that the Dominican Cardinals Cajetan and Garcia de Loaysa advised the Dominican authorities to allow the Sienese Friars to celebrate the Mass of the Immaculate Conception.[248]

[246] Thomas (de Vio) Caietanus, O.P., *Commentarium in Summam Theologiae S. Thomae* (I-II, q.81 and III, q.27), ed. Leonina, vol. 7 and 11, Rome 1892, 1903; B. Spina, O.P., *De universali corruptione generis humani ab Adam seminaliter propagati,* Venice 1535.   [247] G. Bosco, *op. cit.,* p. 51-84.

[248] For a detailed and very interesting account of all these events see Bosco, *op. cit.,* p. 7-50.

Encouraged by this concession and by the conciliatory tone of Cajetan's treatise to Leo X, Catharinus, though persecuted and held under extreme suspicion by his confreres, decided in his retirement in Rome to make every effort to bring his Order around to the belief of the Immaculate Conception. At the General Chapter of the Dominican Order, held at the monastery of the Minerva May 19th 1532, Catharinus personally presented the first edition of his *Disputatio pro veritate Immaculatae Conceptionis* to the capitular Fathers.[249] In the third book of this treatise he expounds in seven chapters the arguments of Sacred Scripture, the testimonies of doctors and universities, the popular devotion and the practice of the Church, strenuously refuting the objections raised by Cajetan.[250]

In 1542 Catharinus published a second edition of his *Disputatio*.[251] This time his purpose was mainly to refute the *De universali corruptione generis humani* of Bartholomew Spina,[252] who had declared the immaculist opinion heretical, despite the sanctions of Sixtus IV and Alexander VI. Among other things, in the second book Catharinus makes an interesting analysis of the mind of St. Thomas on the Immaculate Conception. In book three he elaborates on the arguments which substantiate Our Lady's preservation. Perhaps the most cogent of these are the consensus of the people and the authority of the Roman Church in approving the feasts in honor of the Immaculate Virgin. The common consent of the people, which arises as it were from a spontaneous instinct, can have no other origin than the infallible motion of the Holy Spirit who is always present and operative in the Church. It is the fruit which had its germ in patristic thought and the sentiment of the early Church regarding Mary's sanctity. Hence it has a true value of Tradition, since it is an explication and a reflected consciousness brought to maturity of the implicit faith of the primitive Church, the Fathers and the ancient writers.[253] Of still more value to Catharinus is the authority of the Church, manifested with ever-increasing clarity and emphasis, from a tacit approval to the solemn sanctioning and celebration of the feast in honor of the Immaculate Conception. He repeats this argument over and over again, and considers it as more solid even than the scriptural and patristic arguments. If it were not, one would have to doubt the very promise of inerrancy made by Christ to His Church.[254]

Catharinus published still another edition of his *Disputatio* in 1551, when he was already a bishop.[255] The occasion was the publication by Spina

---

[249] A. Catharinus Politi, O.P., *Disputatio pro veritate Immaculatae Conceptionis B. Virginis ad Patres ac Fratres Ord. Praed. eiusdemque expositio controversiae inter ipsum et quosdam de Patribus eiusdem Ordinis exortae*, Siena 1535.

[250] G. Bosco, *op. cit.*, p. 42.

[251] A. Catharinus Politi, O.P., *Disputatio pro Immaculata Divae Virginis Conceptione*, in *Opuscula Omnia*, Lyon 1542, Tract. V.

[252] See note 246, above.

[253] Bosco, *op. cit.*, p. 45.   [254] *Ibid.*, p. 46.

[255] A. Catharinus Politi, O.P., *Disputatio pro veritate Immaculatae Concep-*

of Torquemada's treatise, presented in manuscript form to the Council of Basel. Under the pretext that the manuscript had been changed by succeeding scribes, Spina rewrote it completely according to his own fancy. His contention was that the feast of the Immaculate Conception should be suppressed because its object was contrary to the letter and the spirit of Sacred Scripture and the Fathers, and a dishonor to Jesus Christ and Our Lady. Catharinus vigorously defends the feast and urges that it be celebrated by all the faithful. This was his last publication. He died in November 1553, while on his way from Conza to Rome to be created a cardinal by his former student, Julius III.[256]

AT THE COUNCIL OF TRENT (1546)

The question of the Immaculate Conception came up more or less unexpectedly in the fifth session of the Council of Trent. The Fathers of the Council had successfully completed their work on Holy Scripture and Tradition in the fourth session, which ended April 8, 1546, and were intent on further fulfilling their objective of solving the problems that had arisen with the Protestant Reformation. It was at this time that a delegation arrived from Emperor Charles V requesting the Council to omit all dogmatic questions and to deal solely with matters of ecclesiastical reform. The emperor's object was to avoid anything that could further stir up the animosity of the Protestants and complicate political issues.[257] His request, however, was not granted. Pope Paul III, wholly bent on the good of the Church, gave orders that dogmatic questions resulting from the Reformation take precedence over other matters, and that the dogma on original sin be elaborated at once.[258] Thus it was that on May 24, 1546 the article on original sin was proposed to the venerable assembly.

In the preparatory session of theologians, May 24 and 25, when the text of Rom. 5, 12 was brought up in support of the universality of original sin, John Morello remarked that not only was Christ to be declared exempt from the common law of guilt, but that the Blessed Virgin also was piously believed to have been preserved from it in virtue of a special privilege.[259] However, his observation seems to have aroused little atten-

tionis B. V. Mariae et eius celebranda a cunctis fidelibus festivitate, ad S. Synodum Tridentinum, in *Enarrationes in quinque priora capita libri Geneseos,* Rome 1552, Tract. V.

[256] BOSCO, *op. cit.,* p. 48-49.

[257] CALENZIO, *Saggio di storia generale de Trento sotto Paolo III,* Roma-Torino 1869, p. 42. Cf. M. TOGNETTI, S.M., "L'Immacolata al Concilio Tridentino," in *Marianum* vol. 15, Rome 1953, p. 305.

[258] *Concilium Tridentinum. Diariorum, actorum, Epistolarum, Tractatuum nova collectio,* Friburgi Brisgoviae, 1901, vol. 5, p. 107.

[259] *Concilium Tridentium,* vol. 12, p. 557: "creditur etiam excepta Beata Virgo, et pio quodam in illam affectu, non quod peccatum non habuerit jus in illam, sed quod ex privilegio creditur, misericordiam et gratiam Dei praevenisse occupationem peccati, dum conciperetur."

tion. It was not until the General Assembly convened May 28 that the question of the Immaculate Conception really came to the fore. When the Cardinal Legate asked the Fathers whether the order and method of dealing with original sin was satisfactory, Cardinal Pacheco, the head of the Spanish bishops, rose and observed that the Council must give thought to the Conception of Our Lady, a topic to be dealt with and solved now, in connection with the question of original sin.[260] The greater part of Christendom, he added, piously believed in the Immaculate Conception, and a definition would be most pleasing to Spain and France.[261] The Cardinal acted on the advice of his counsellor, the Franciscan theologian Andrew de la Vega.[262]

Pacheco's suggestion met with a volley of objections from the Dominican bishops, whose chief spokesman was Peter Bertano, the bishop of Fano. The latter, without attacking the immaculist doctrine directly, tried to smother the question from the start. His reasons, like those of Pacheco, were of a practical rather than of a speculative nature. First of all, he remarked, both opinions were pious *"et a sanctissimis doctoribus hinc et inde suas partes comprobatos";* and if the Council decided in favor of one, it would necessarily condemn the other.[263] His reasoning was rather specious, since it was a known fact that not only the greater part of Christendom, but even the vast majority of the Fathers of the Council were convinced that Mary was immaculate. Furthermore, added Bertano, the matter of Our Lady's Conception is a difficult one, which the Church herself has been unable to unravel.[264] If the Council decides to discuss this matter, it will take months to come to a conclusion, and this would be playing into the hands of the Protestants and would bring dishonor upon the assembly.[265] Wherefore, suggested Bertano, the most sensible thing would be to impose perpetual silence on all who would henceforth wish to speak on this question.[266] He was supported by the Bishop of Sanciano, who likewise advocated silence because both opinions were pious.[267] Even the Bishop of Bitonto, the Franciscan Cornelius Musso, thought it more prudent not to discuss the matter, since the Immaculate Conception was already accepted by the consent of the whole Church.[268]

[260] *Ibid.*, vol. 5, p. 166: "sed cogitandum est quid agendum de Conceptione B. Virginis, quae quaestio omnino tractanda nunc est, cum de peccato originali agamus, et a sacra synodo terminari omnino debet."

[261] RAYNALDUS, *Annales ecclesiastici,* Luca 1755, vol. 14(1546), num. 72, p. 154: "maximam enim Christiani orbis partem pie ita sentire remque Hispanis et Gallis fore gratissimam."

[263] *Concilium Tridentium,* vol. 1, p. 120.   [262] PAUWELS, *op. cit.,* p. 142.

[264] RAYNALDUS, *op. cit.,* p. 154: "Addo rei difficultatem."

[265] *Concilium Tridentium,* vol. 5, p. 168: "dicentibus omnibus nos quae decidenda sunt omittere et silenda decernere."

[266] *Ibid.,* vol. i, p. 65: "propterea hac in re laudarem, ut perpetuum silentium imponeretur omnibus."   [267] *Ibid.,* vol. 5, p. 168.

[268] A. THEINER, *Acta genuina S.S. Oecumenici Concilii Tridentini ab Angelo Massarello servata,* Zagabriae 1874, vol. 1, p. 112.

At the General Assembly of June 8, a provisory text of the five canons on original sin was presented for discussion. It made no mention whatever of the Blessed Virgin, and Pacheco again protested. The Immaculate Conception is a truth which cannot be denied, he said, "since it is approved by the Roman Church, celebrated by the universal Church and held by all the universities." [269] If the Synod has decided not to define the doctrine, at least let it be prudent enough not to condemn it.[270] Pacheco's warning caused a moment of tenseness in the assembly. Something had to be done to save Our Lady's privilege. Several bishops insisted that the text of the cannons should make it clear that Our Lady is not included in the common law of original sin. Finally Cardinal De Monte, the president of the assembly, suggested "that in the decree the Blessed Virgin should be excepted by a few words" (*ut in decreto aliquibus verbis excipiatur Virgo*).[271] Bertano, however, warned that were anything added to the decree, care should be taken that neither of the two sides be offended, and that the matter be maturely discussed.[272]

The question now was to find the proper wording for the amendment. Pacheco was the first to suggest an addition, namely the clause: *"nisi alicui Deus ex Privilegio aliud dederit, prout in B. Virgine."*[273] This was considered unacceptable, since it implicitly condemned the maculist opinion. The Bishop of Torres then suggested the words, *"a qua lege pie creditur B. Virginem exceptam."*[274] Again the clause was rejected as implying that the opposite opinion was impious. Finally, after a great deal of bickering by the members of the Council, Cornelius Musso, the Bishop of Bitonto, struck upon a formula that suggested a new procedure. He expressed the opinion that a paragraph be added to the canons to state that the Council had no intention to pronounce itself in favor of one or the other opinion regarding Our Lady's Conception, but rather to abide by what the Holy Roman Church and the other Churches and universities held.[275]

In the session of theologians that followed, on June 10, the importance of making an exception for Our Lady was still more forcefully brought out by the Jesuit Lainez. He observed that the adversaries based their stand on the fact that the Fathers of the Church and several great scholastics, while commenting on the text of St. Paul concerning the universality of original sin, made no mention of Our Lady. Lainez denied that the silence of

---

[269] THEINER, *op. cit.*, vol. 1, p. 131.

[270] *Ibid.*

[271] THEINER, *op. cit.*, vol. 1, p. 136; *Concilium Tridentium*, vol. 5, p. 203.

[272] *Concilium Tridentium*, vol. 5, p. 201: "si aliquid est addendum, advertatur ne aliqua pars offendatur."—"Id cum maxima discussione et disputatione fiat."

[273] *Ibid.*, vol. 5, p. 199.

[274] *Ibid.*

[275] *Ibid.*, p. 202: "de conceptione explicet synodus quod non est suae intentionis ulli parti derogare, sed relinquatur quod S. Romana et coeterae Ecclesiae et Universitates tenent."

these ancient writers was an argument against the privilege of the Blessed Virgin. However, he continued, today the situation is different. In an age when the controversy over the Conception of the Virgin is at its height, it becomes urgent to define precisely what extension is to be given the words of St. Paul. If the Council wishes to maintain intact the pious belief of Mary's preservation, it must absolutely except her from the common law of the universal propagation of original sin.[276] Lainez was seconded by Salmeron, another renowned Jesuit, as well as by the Franciscan Jerome Lombardello and other Friars Minor.[277]

On June 13, the task of amending the decree was given over to a special committee which finally drafted a paragraph that was in substance accepted by the Council in its general assemblies of June 14, 16 and 17, although Pacheco still protested that justice had not been done to the question of the Immaculate Conception. The Council simply declared that it did not intend to include in its decree on original sin, "the Immaculate Virgin Mary"; and it renewed the constitutions of Sixtus IV concerning this question.[278]

THE JANSENIST OPPOSITION

Two further controversies arose, which for a time seemed again to threaten the realization of the final victory. The first of these controversies no longer stemmed from theologians and churchmen who bore allegiance to the Holy See, but rather from a group who pretended to reform the Church from within and yet adhered to heretical tenets. They were the Jansenists. Jansenius himself did not write Marian theology; but his doctrine on the transmission of original sin by means of concupiscence inherent in all natural generation logically led to the negation of the Immaculate Conception.[279] It is not surprising, therefore, that a certain Doctor Marias, on the instigation of his friend, John Launoy, denied the privilege in a discourse at the college of Harcourt, December 8, 1672. He was compelled by the bishop to retract his statement.[280] The following year a more subtle attack was made on the doctrine by Adam Widenfeldt, a lawyer and recent convert from Protestantism, in his *Monita salutaria B. Mariae V. ad cultores suos indiscretos,* which was soon translated into French by Dom Gerberon.[281] Without directly mentioning them, the

[276] MANSELLA, *Il dogma dell'Immaculata Concezione de Maria Vergine,* Rome 1866, p. 176-177.

[277] PAUWELS, *op. cit.,* p. 143.

[278] For the text of this decree, see chapter VII of the present volume, p. 305, note 139.

[279] X. LE BACHELET, *art. cit.,* col. 1176.

[280] *Ibid.*

[281] C. DILLENSCHNEIDER, *La Mariologie de S. Alphonse de Liguori, son influence sur le renouveau des doctrines mariales et de la piété catholique après la tourmente du protestantisme et du jansenisme,* Fribourg 1931, p. 41.

booklet slyly attacked the doctrines of the Assumption and the Immaculate Conception in the following brief passage:

> Love that is contentious is not beautiful. Stop devouring one another in your wrangling over my privileges; it serves no purpose except to upset the listeners. And why do you presume to decide what has been neither revealed by God nor defined by the Church? Deal with the word of truth, and avoid profane and empty talk.[282]

The author's intention of attacking the Immaculate Conception did not escape the notice of orthodox writers and orators. Bourdaloue, for example, denounces the attitude of minimizers in his second sermon on the Assumption. After the definition of the Divine Maternity, he argues, there is no privilege we should dare deny Our Lady.[283] And even if these privileges have not yet become the object of a dogmatic definition, is it not enough that they have been acknowledged by the most learned men of the Church, authorized by the common belief of the faithful and substantiated by the most solid arguments and testimonies?[284] The censors of a so-called indiscreet devotion would, by a pretense of reform, destroy all the feasts in Mary's honor and reduce religion to a dry and cold speculation.[285]

Two ardent partisans of the Jansenist doctrine were Launoy and Baillet. The former, in 1676, published a book entitled *Prescriptiones de Conceptu B. Mariae V.*[286] He develops the argument of prescription used by Tertullian in defense of Christianity.[287] If the Church for thirteen centuries has taught that Mary was conceived in original sin, that doctrine remains definitely acquired by prescription and can no longer be changed.[288] The texts Launoy used to establish the continuity of the maculist tradition were either unauthentic or not pertinent to the question. Baillet, in *La dévotion à la Vierge et le culte qui lui est dû . . . ,*[289] eagerly defends Widenfeldt, and categorically denies the doctrine of the Immaculate Conception. He was refuted by the venerable Archdeacon Boudon, who wrote *Avis catho-*

---

[282] *Ibid.*, p. 47.

[283] *Oeuvres de Bourdaloue*, vol. 4, Paris 1840, p. 214, 215-216: ". . . moi, j'avance et je soutiens que depuis que l'Eglise universelle, par le plus solennel de ses décrets, qui fut celui du concile d'Ephese, a maintenu la Vierge dont je défends ici la gloire, dans la possession du titre de Mère de Dieu, que l'hérésiarque Nestorius lui disputoit, il n'y a point de titre d'honneur qui ne lui convienne, ni de qualité éminente qu'on puisse sans indiscrétion lui contester."

[284] *Ibid.*, p. 216: "N'est-ce pas assez que ce soient des privilèges reconnus par les plus savants hommes de l'Eglise, autorisés par la créance commune des fidèles, appuyés, sinon sur des preuves évidentes et des démonstrations, au moins sur les plus fortes conjectures et les témoignages les plus solides et les plus irréprochables?"

[285] *Ibid.*, p. 217.

[286] LAUNOY, *Opera Omnia*, Cologne 1731.

[287] D'ALÈS, *Théologie de Tertullien*, Paris 1905, p. 261.

[288] LANNOY, *ibid.*, p. 9-43.

[289] BAILLET, *La dévotion à la Vierge et le culte qui lui est dû, avec l'Avis salutaire de la Vierge à ses dévots indiscrets et une Lettre pastorale de M. Choiseul, évêque de Tournai, sur cet Avis*, Paris 1694.

liques touchant la véritable dévotion de la bienheureuse Vierge.[290] Baillet's Marian doctrine was furthermore condemned by two decrees of the Holy Office, August 4, 1694 and July 6, 1701.

MURATORI'S OBJECTIONS

Another threat to the definition of the doctrine of the Immaculate Conception was contained in the writings of Louis Anthony Muratori. In 1714 he edited a manual to help critics discern the truth in religious controversies. It was published under the pseudonym *Lamindus Pritanius,* and was entitled, *De ingeniorum moderatione in religionis negotio.*[291] This was followed by three other books: *De superstitione vitanda,* in 1740;[292] *Fernandi Valdesii Epistolae,* in 1743;[293] and *Della regolata divozione de' cristiani* in 1747.[294] His chief complaint seems to be the practice, rather common in his day, of taking a vow to defend the Immaculate Conception even at the cost of one's life. Muratori calls the pious practice the *"votum sanguinarium."* One does not shed his blood for a simple opinion, he affirms. Even though it is true that the Church has a right to define the doctrine of the Immaculate Conception, she would not do so until the doctrine was proven to be well founded on Sacred Scripture and Tradition. Such proofs do not seem available. Indeed, despite insistent demands of devotees, the Church has not proceeded to a definition, and her silence shows that the doctrine is not definable.[295]

Muratori's writings gave rise to a number of apologetic treatises in favor of the Immaculate Conception. Authors like Bernard Moraës in Portugal, Stephen Vargyas and Joseph Petzler in Austria, George Lienhart in Germany, Francis Burgio, Francis Anthony Zaccaria and Joseph Anthony Milanese in Italy took up the defense of Our Lady's glorious privilege.[296] At Palermo, Benedict Plazza published a remarkable reply to Muratori in his *Causa immaculatae conceptionis,* in which he established the theological certitude of the doctrine of the Immaculate Conception, to conclude that the Church could define it as a dogma of faith.

Perhaps the most outstanding apologist of Our Lady's preservation in the Muratori controversy was St. Alphonsus of Liguori. As early as 1748, two years before the publication of his *Glorie,* St. Alphonsus inserted into the first edition of his Moral Theology a dissertation on the Immaculate Conception. Later on he revised this treatise for his second edition of

[290] BOUDON, *Oeuvres Complètes,* Migne, vol. 2, col. 327-377.

[291] Lamindus PRITANIUS, *De ingeniorum moderatione in religionis negotio,* Paris 1714.

[292] Antonius LAMPRIDIUS, *De superstitione vitanda sive censura voti sanguinarii in honorem Immaculatae Conceptionis Deiparae emissi,* Paris 1740.

[293] *Fernandi Valdesii epistolae,* Paris 1743.

[294] Lamindus PRITANIUS, *Della regolata divozione de' cristiani,* Venice 1747.

[295] DILLENSCHNEIDER, *op. cit.,* p. 70-71.

[296] X. LE BACHELET, *art. cit.,* col. 1181.

the *Theologia Moralis*. In 1750 he incorporated it in his dogmatic sermon on the Immaculate Conception in his *Glorie di Maria*.[297]

St. Alphonsus knew that the weakness of Muratori's theories lay in his failing to understand the living Tradition of the Church; hence he stressed that point in his arguments rather than the evidence of Holy Scripture and the Tradition of the Fathers. The two reasons which should convince us of the truth of the pious doctrine, he writes, are the universal consent of the faithful, and the feast of the Immaculate Conception celebrated in the whole Church. In support of the first reason St. Alphonsus refers to testimonies of Giles of the Presentation, of the Bull *Sollicitudo* of Alexander VII, and of the learned Petau. The second reason, in the mind of the holy Doctor, is even more cogent than the first. Pope Alexander declares that in celebrating the feast of the Conception the Church renders homage to Our Lady's exemption from original sin. Now the Church cannot give the honors of religious worship to anything that is not holy or that is erroneous. Therefore the feast of the Immaculate Conception is one of the strongest proofs of the certitude of the pious belief.[298]

CONCLUSION

In the pages that precede we have attempted to trace a summary history of the controversy over the doctrine of the Immaculate Conception from the death of Scotus to the end of the eighteenth century. Needless to say a great many details of history and a good number of authors have had to remain unmentioned because of space limitations. However, what has been said is sufficient to describe the atmosphere of incertitude and strife that accompanied this turbulent phase of doctrinal development. Through it all the *magisterium* acted as the secure and infallible guide of theologians and faithful. Like a prudent pedagogue, the supreme teaching authority of the Church supervised the attempts of her children to fathom the mystery of Mary's Conception, now containing their impatience, now encouraging deeper study, until finally, under the enlightenment of the Holy Spirit, the full splendor of the Revelation broke through the darkness of human ignorance. Thus, more perhaps than in any other doctrinal controversy, the assertion of Pope St. Hormisdas was clearly verified: "In the Apostolic See the Catholic religion has always been kept unsullied." [299]

[297] DILLENSCHNEIDER, *op. cit.*, p. 290.

[298] Saint Alphonse DE LIGUORI, *Gloires de Marie*, Paris 1945, p. 229-230.

[299] DENZINGER, H. *Enchiridion Symbolorum*, n. 171. (English translation by the Jesuit Fathers of St. Mary's College, *The Church Teaches*, St. Louis (Herder), 1955.

VII

RENE LAURENTIN[*]

The Role of the Papal Magisterium
in the Delevopment of the Dogma
of the Immaculate Conception

TRANSLATED AND ABRIDGED BY
CHARLES E. SHEEDY, C.S.C.,[†] AND EDWARD S. SHEA, C.S.C.[‡]

INTRODUCTION

In 1907, Herzog wrote, under the name Turmel:

> When one runs through the series of Pontifical acts touching on the
> Conception of the Virgin, one's first impression is that of amazement.
> What one pope does, another undoes; today's work is destroyed tomor-
> row. It is like Penelope's weaving. . . . As a result, the section of the
> *Bullarium* consecrated to the feast of December 8 and to its object is
> distinguished by its *inconsistencies.* Now when you get to the bottom
> of these inconsistencies, you find that most of them were committed
> out of consideration for St. Thomas: the Popes *contradicted* themselves
> in order to spare the holy doctor.[1]

The impressive 'erudition' with which Turmel supported this accusation
was largely second-hand; and the bias of his arguments quickly becomes
apparent. Nevertheless, many historians of this dogma experience a certain
tension and uneasiness when they confront their own, apparently mini-
mizing conclusions, with the assertions of the Bull *Ineffabilis.* There are

[*] Professor of Dogmatic Theology, University of Angers. The original article was
written in French, and has been published in volume II of *Virgo Immaculata, Acta
Congressus Mariologici-Mariani Romae 1954 celebrati,* Romae, Academia Mariana Internationalis, 1956, pp. 1-99, under the title, "L'action du Saint-Siège par rapport au
problème de l'Immaculée." Because of the length of the original work, it was deemed
advisable to abridge it for present purposes by the omission of some details. The
author has examined the present translation as regards the principal matters dealt
with, and has approved it; the conclusion has been revised by him for this edition.
† Dean of the College of Arts and Letters of the University of Notre Dame.
‡ Member of the Department of Modern Languages of the University of Notre
Dame.
[1] G. HERZOG, "L'Immaculée Conception," in *Revue d'Histoire et de Littérature
religieuse,* 12 (1907) p. 599.

those, for example, who are afraid to confront the late adoption of the Feast of the Conception at Rome, or the difficulties encountered at Rome by the proponents of the immaculist doctrine during the seventeenth century, with Pius IX's assertion that "the Roman Church has held nothing more dear (*nihil potius habuit*) than to profess, protect, promote and defend, as eloquently as possible, and with every available means, the doctrine and the cult of the Immaculate Conception." [2]

What these problems demand is not to have a veil thrown over them, but to be solved once and for all.[3]   Too many well-intentioned writers have constructed their "defense and illustration" of the dogma with the same precipitate selectivity that Turmel used in drawing up his indictment.   The present paper has been written with the intent of casting the fullest possible light on the objections that are raised against the *magisterium* in the historical order.   We will undertake to study the papacy's action with regard to the Immaculate Conception precisely insofar as this action has been immersed in the complexities of history and has developed amid, and in vital contact with, the vicissitudes of time.

The documentation of such a study involves considerable difficulty. Although the problem of the Immaculate Conception was not raised until relatively late, and did not become the object of any decision on the part of the Holy See until the fifteenth century, the quantity of documents from that moment on is considerable.   A systematic research among the collections of documents has resulted in a list of over a thousand acts—major or minor—attributed to the Holy See.

These collections are of two sorts.   First, there are the official collections, to be found in the Roman archives, of papal bulls and decrees of the

---

[2] *APN* 1a, p. 599. (See table of abbreviations below, p. 322). This difficulty is taken up at the end of part III of the present article.

[3] The principal general treatments of these questions are the following:

X. Le Bachelet, "Immaculée Conception" in *DTC* 7, 979-1215. On the whole, this remarkable article retains its value, but it has been superseded on a number of points. Its global references are difficult to use.

A. Robichaud, "The Immaculate Conception in the Magisterium of the Church before 1854," in *Marian Studies* 5 (1954) 73-146. A clear essay with precise references, but often dependent on secondary sources.

C. Sericoli, "De praecipuis Sedis Apostolicae documentis de B.M.V. Immaculata Conceptione," in *Antonianum* 29 (1954) 373-408. A good synthesis, well documented, although his criticism of his sources could be improved on here and there, and his global references sometimes prove to be disappointing when verified. I would not agree with his negative interpretation of the pontificate of St. Pius V. He is inclined to exaggerate the contrast between this Dominican Pope and the Franciscan Popes, Sixtus IV and Sixtus V. I would readily believe that their personal opinions differed from one another (although we are poorly informed about the mind of Pius V). Sericoli's ingenious observations give us a glimpse of the differences among these pontiffs, but the accord and continuity of their *acts* as such are absolutely perfect.

B. Llorca, "La autoridad eclesiastica y el Dogma de la Inmaculada Concepción," in *Est. Ecl.* 28 (1954) 299-322. A rapid resume of the grand lines of the development.

various Roman congregations, notably the Congregation of Rites and Indulgences.[4] This series, which includes all the major acts, poses no problem of authenticity.

The same does not hold, however, for the other series of acts, (equal in number but infinitely less in importance) transmitted in the enormous collections published by the immaculists of the seventeenth and eighteenth centuries—notably Alva y Astorga and Gravois, and in the smaller and better compilations made by the maculists.[5] The quantity of dubious or false documents contained in these unofficial collections is considerable; not that the compilers were counterfeiters, but their zeal had made them credulous regarding the most extravagant frauds. In many cases, the disappearance of archives makes it impossible for us to reach any firm conclusion.

The activity of the *magisterium* lay along three distinct but connex lines, dealing respectively with the *feast,* its *name,* and the *doctrine* which was its object. In the present paper, each of these three lines of development will be considered separately. This is not an artificial division: the facts impose it. There are three distinct series of papal decisions. Those which are concerned with the feast generally avoid committing themselves with regard to the title and doctrine, and vice versa. The inconsistency which Turmel likes to perceive in the decisions of the *magisterium,* and which certain Catholics unwittingly admit, is caused in large measure by their attributing doctrinal import to disciplinary or liturgical decrees, whereas it is precisely such a meaning that the Holy See carefully avoided giving them.

We will, therefore, consider successively the *feast,* the *title,* and the *doctrine* of the Immaculate Conception, insofar as they were the object of papal activity. In each case, we will discover a steady, unbroken progress, and a gradual transition, from total silence to prudent watchfulness, to discreet encouragement, to the definitive decisions. It is thus that, little by little, this feast, title and doctrine assumed the place which they hold in the Church today.

---

[4] The principal collections are indicated in the table of abbreviations p. 321 ff.

[5] For the immaculists, see, in the table of abbreviations: ALVA, CALDERON, GRAVOIS, MARRACCI, LOSSADA, as well as the authors indicated below, note 49.

For the maculists, BANDELLI (Cf. table of abbreviations) has established the fundamental dossier, a list of 260 authors opposed to the Immaculate Conception, among whom are eleven popes (Cf. notes 82 and 86 below). The references are inexact and the texts often interpolated. The work of J. LAUNOY (*Prescriptions touchant la Conception de Notre Dame,* which appeared anonymously, with no indication of the place or date of publication, in 1676, and was republished in his *Opera omnia,* Coloniae Allobrogorum, 1733, t. 1a, pp. 9-43) is more precise and more reliable in its erudition, but often biased in its interpretations.

We cite only those authors who give a new and first-hand documentation. There is no use mentioning those who merely transmit the sources which we have examined directly.

I.

THE FEAST

It was the feast that provoked all the other questions about terminology and doctrine, besides providing the setting in which their solutions were gradually worked out. Since the history of the feast is traced elsewhere in the present volume,[6] it will suffice to point out only a few facts here.

Although the first approval of the feast by the Holy See has been attributed to various popes from John X (†928) to John XXII (1316-1334), the facts are clear. Until about 1330, a continuous series of reliable and well-informed witnesses assure us that "the Roman Church does not celebrate this feast": Osbert of Clare:[7] then St. Bernard about 1130;[8] St. Thomas Aquinas about 1272-1273;[9] John of Naples about 1360;[10] Peter Auriol several times between 1315 and 1318.[11] Towards the third decade of the fourteenth century, this situation changes: John Bacon, about 1330;[12] Thomas of Strasbourg, in 1339 or 1340;[13] and John

---

[6] Chapter IV.

[7] *Eadmeri . . . tractatus de Conceptione,* Freiburg in B., Herder, 1904, p. 58. Cf. the commentary of P. Doncoeur, in *Rev. d'hist. eccl.* 8 (1907) pp. 268-269.

[8] Letters to the Canons of Lyons, PL 182, 333A: "novam celebritatem quam *ritus Ecclesiae nescit,*" and 336BC: "*contra Ecclesiae ritum* praesumpta novitas." Cf. 336C: "*Romanae* praesertim *Ecclesiae auctoritati* atque examini totum *hoc reservo.*" All these remarks imply that the feast was not observed at Rome at the time when St. Bernard was writing.

[9] "Licet quod Romana Ecclesia Conceptionem B.V. non celebret, tolerat tamen consuetudinem aliquarum Ecclesiarum illud festum celebrantium." *Sum. theol.* III, q. 27, art. 2, ad 3.

[10] "Illud festum non facit Ecclesia Romana . . . ab Ecclesia Romana tolleratur fieri in aliquibus Ecclesiis." Quodlibet I (VI), q. 11, edited by C. Balić, Joannis de Polliaco et Ioannis de Neapoli, *Quaestiones disputatae de Immaculata Conceptione,* Sibenici, Kacic, 1931, p. 89, lines 7-8 and 14-15. Cf. D. Doncoeur, in *Rev. hist. eccl.* 8 (1907), p. 282-285, and Francisco de Guimaraens (art. cited below, in note 89), in *Et. franc.* 4 (1953), p. 173, note 191.

[11] In 1314, in the *Tractatus de Conceptione,* c. 6 (edited in *Quaestiones disputatae de Immaculata Conceptione,* Quaracchi 1904, p. 93). Cf. *Repercussorium,* Conclusio VIII, ib. pp. 142, 150.

In his Commentary on Book III of the Sentences, composed at Paris, about 1317-1318, d. 3, q. 1, a. 5, he writes: ". . . licet non faciat Ecclesia Romana, tamen permittit, ut apparet in Ecclesiis solemnibus et cathedralibus ut Lugduni et in Anglia et in multis aliis locis; nec etiam Ecclesia Romana colit festa omnia," ed. P. Alva y Astorga, *Monumenta antiqua seraphica,* Lovanii 1665, p. 74.

[12] "Publica et diuturna consuetudine celebratum est hoc festum in Curia Romana . . . et haec duraverunt tempore multorum romanorum Pontificum usque in praesens tempus . . . Et . . . bene noverunt . . . Summi Pontifices et Sedes apostolica, et per consequens haec est sancta et catholica religio." I. Baco, *Radiantissimum opus super quattuor Sententiarum libros,* Lib. 4, d. 2, q. 4, a. 3, ed. Cremona 1618, p. 316. Cf. *Quodlibeta fertilissima,* III, 13, ed. Venetiis (1527), fol. 60 a: Papa scit hoc festum celebrari in Curia publice." Evidently it is a private celebration that is referred to: Bacon says that the popes *are acquainted with* this usage, not that they *celebrate* the feast.

[13] "Sancta Romana Ecclesia festum Conceptionis ipsius Virginis gloriosae solet solemniter celebrare," Thomas ab Argentina, *Commentaria in quattuor libris Sententiarum,* Lib. 3, d. 3, a. 1, ed. Venetiis 1564, II, 9.

Tauler, in 1350,[14] attest that the feast is celebrated by the Roman Curia.

There might seem to be some friction between the last negative testimonies and the first positive ones. Whereas Peter Auriol denies the existence of the feast in 1318, John Bacon, less than fifteen years later, represents it as an ancient custom: *"diuturna consuetudo."* [15]

This apparent contradiction is explained by the prudent and progressive character of the adoption of the feast. Its celebration by the Roman Curia was at first occasional. The feast was widespread from the end of the twelfth century, and various popes on journeys had occasion to associate themselves with its celebration in the dioceses or monasteries which had adopted it. It is not unlikely that Innocent IV acted thus at Mâcon, December 8, 1245, and at Anagni about the same date. It is certain that Boniface VIII, while passing through that same town on December 8, 1295, enriched the feast with indulgences. At Avignon, the Pope and his entourage acquired the habit of assisting at this feast in the Carmelite monastery, and in time it came to be celebrated at the papal court. This usage became fixed not long before 1330. Beginning about the middle of the fourteenth century, the Conception is found in the Calendar, the Breviary and the Missal of the Roman Curia, but still has an unofficial and private character. The official pontifical acts continue to take no note of the feast for about half a century. They restrict themselves to the enumeration of the *four* ancient Marian feasts; the Nativity, the Purification, the Annunciation and the Assumption.[16]

Sixtus IV (1471-1484) marks a new era. This Franciscan pope was the first to recognize and officially to confirm the feast,[17] to celebrate it personally, publicly and solemnly in the Curia itself. He approved two new proper offices,[18] accorded an octave to it, and enriched it with numerous indulgences. In brief, he was the first pope to engage the *authority* of the Holy See officially in favor of the Feast of the Conception, but without, however, going so far as to prescribe the celebration of it for the entire Church, as has often been affirmed.[19]

---

[14] I. Thaulerus, O.P., *De decem coecitatibus Ecclesiae,* in *Opera omnia,* Cologne, 1615, p. 873, repeats almost word for word the remark of the preceding author. On this whole question, see Doncoeur, in *Rev. d'hist. eccl.* 8 (1907) 696-697 and Sericoli, p. 13.

[15] See above, note 12. Bacon exaggerates a little in favor of his thesis.

[16] On all this matter, see P. Doncoeur, *Rev. d'hist. eccl.* 7 (1907), pp. 277, 693, 699-700; Sericoli, pp. 9-10, note 34, 13-14; *DTC* 7, 1100-1101.

[17] On Sixtus IV see the excellent monograph of Sericoli pp. 57-70; on the role of Sixtus IV in the institution of the feast, see p. 61.

[18] One of these offices, that of Nogarolo, was inserted in the Breviary and Missal of the Curia. Cf. chapter IV of the present volume, pp. 150-153.

[19] Jean de Varenne, *apostolic auditor,* had asked the anti-pope, Benedict XIII, to extend the feast to the Universal Church. E. Martenne, *Veterum scriptorum et monumentorum historicum, dogmaticorum, moralium amplissima collectio,* Parisiis, 7 (1733) 580. This extension was promulgated by the Council of Basel, following its definition of the Immaculate Conception. (I. D. Mansi, *Sacrorum Conciliorum, nova*

In this respect it was a Dominican pope who took the next step. On July 5, 1568, by the Bull, *Quod a nobis postulat,* Pius V realized the reform of the Divine Office which the Council of Trent had asked for in 1558. In the revised breviary, which abolished all feasts which had been in existence for less than two centuries, the Feast of the Conception is found at December 8 as a double, but without an octave. In other words, the feast receives an increased extension, counterbalanced by a reduction in solemnity, in a measure designed to introduce greater uniformity into the Church's liturgy.

Under Clement VIII, on May 10, 1602, the Feast of the *Conception* is elevated along with eleven other feasts to the rank of major double.[20] The octave of the feast was restored gradually. At first it was granted to particular groups as a privilege, beginning with the Franciscans in 1569.[21] On May 15, 1693, its observance, which was by then more or less general, was extended by Innocent XII to the entire Church,[22] the feast itself being raised to the rank of double of the second class.

Only with some difficulty was the feast made a holy day of obligation. The list of thirty-seven obligatory feasts promulgated by Urban VIII, September 23, 1642, with the intention of restricting the excessive number of holy days instituted by individual bishops for their dioceses, did not include that of the Conception. However, the insistent efforts of the king of Spain obtained permission for this feast to be celebrated as of obligation in his country (October 29, 1644), and twenty years later this permission was extended to all the Spanish possessions in Europe and America. Meanwhile, Louis XIV had obtained the same privilege for France on June 15, 1657, although the requests of less important personages during this same period met with categorical refusals.[23] Gradually, however, the exceptions became more

---

et amplissima collectio, Venetiis 29 (1788), col. 183. Cf. ROSKOVANY I, 114). But the Council was no longer legitimate, and the measure did not take effect.

[20] Brief *Cum in Ecclesia,* 10 Mai 1602.

[21] ALVA, *Nodus,* 664-673; and GRAVOIS II, 25-26, give an abundant documentation concerning this *"oraculum vivae vocis,"* the authenticity of which was disputed by the adversaries. (GRAVOIS examines an entire series of breviaries from 1573 to 1604 which take advantage of this concession.) The permission given orally by Pius V, was officially confirmed by his successor, the Franciscan pope, Sixtus V (*Ineffabilia,* March 30, 1588; published in ALVA, *Armam.* II, 173. Cf. *Indic.* 2, 259, n. 12, which gives the date, *March 20;* ROSKOVANY I, 149, who gives *May 30*).

[22] ". . . ut officium et missa ejusdem B.M.V. Immaculatae cum octava . . . ubique terrarum ab omnibus . . . qui ad horas canonicas tenentur de praecepto recitetur . . . mandamus et decernimus." *In Excelsa,* 15 Mai 1693. *Bull. Coq.* 9, 304. *Bull. Taur.* 20, 522a. Cf. BOURASSE 7, 322-324. ROSKOVANY II, 397, n. 296.

[23] The following answer was received by the Bishop of Mariana (Corsica), Carlo Fabrizio Giustiniani (*Hierarch. Catholica,* Münster 4, 1935, p. 232), who had bound himself by solemn vow to make the feast of the Conception a holy day of obligation in his diocese: "Sacra Congregatio, *ut alias* in similibus respondit: Praeter festa quae ab universali Ecclesia servantur Carolum Fabritium Justinianum *particulariter sese* voto adstrictum ad celebritates et jejunia praedicta servanda teneri, caeteros vero ad ea non teneri, nec cogendos esse." GARDELLINI I, 317, n. 1871.

general, and on December 6, 1708, Clement XI "in order to favor the cult of the very glorious Virgin whose Conception was an announcement of joy to the entire world," inscribed December 8 among the feasts of obligation for the universal Church. The final step was the elevation of the feast to the rank of double of the first class. Certain orders or churches had already requested,[24] and sometimes obtained it,[25] when, on December 5, 1879, Leo XIII extended this usage to the Universal Church,[26] at the same time prescribing the observance of the vigil.[27]

A more complete study of this question would have to consider also various favors granted (or refused) over the course of these centuries, such as midnight Mass,[28] indulgences,[29] certain privileges,[30] and above all the

[24] On December 7, 1680, the request of the Diocese of Cordova was refused in the following terms: "Lectum. Et in posterum . . . non proponatur alla instantia Sanctissimae Conceptionis inconsulta S. Congregatione S. Inquisitionis." *AJP* 8 (1865) col. 1231, n. 2150.

[25] The Spanish church of St. James in Rome obtained this privilege by the Brief *Sanctae et Immaculatae,* November 26, 1631. The Capuchins obtained the same favor from the Congregation of Rites, March 10, 1714, in connection with their adoption of the Blessed Virgin in her Immaculate Conception as their principal patron.

According to GRAVOIS II, 49, the Third Order of St. Francis obtained the same privilege on February 16, 1726; the Diocese of Cordova in 1727; Ceuta (Marocco) November 24, 1731; Malta and Teruel, April 6, 1737; the Order of Mercy, July 27, 1742.

[26] Litt. apost. *Annus iam quintus et vicesimus, Acta Leonis XIII* I, (1881) 307-308. Cf. *AJP,* 1881, p. 255.

[27] *Ibid.* The vigil had been instituted by Pius IX for use in certain localities by the Brief, *Quod jampridem,* September 25, 1863 (*APN* 1c, 629).

[28] Permission for Mass at midnight between December 7 and 8 seems to have been granted for the first time by Leo X (*Pia Christi fidelium,* February 18, 1518) to the town of Molina in the diocese of Seguenza (Aragon). The text of this indult, based on the archives of Molina, was published by ALVA, *Arman.* II, 141-142 (cf. *Milit.* 256, *Nodus,* p. 85, *Nodus* 1663, p. 122a, *Indic.* n. 20; A. CALDERON, *Pro titulo Immaculatae Conceptionis,* Matriti, D. Diaz, 1650, pp. 265-269 and 651-653). But a refusal of the Sacred Congregation to confirm this privilege, December 11, 1627, suggests that the Congregation may have doubted the authenticity of the indult (cf. *AJP* 7, 1864, col. 199, n. 813).

[29] An enormous number of indulgences are attributed to the Holy See, especially by ALVA, *Armam., Nodus,* and above all *Indic.* Cf. GRAVOIS II, 56-57. A few are repeated by ROSKOVANY. Most often, their authenticity is impossible to verify. The official collections of the Sacred Congregation of Indulgences list very few indulgences associated with the Immaculate Conception. A few can also be found mentioned in various *bullaria.* Cf. figure 3, p. 279.

[30] Hundreds of benefices, chapels, chaplaincies, altars and confraternities are mentioned in ALVA, *Armam., Nodus, Funic.* and especially *Indic.* Here, too, verification is called for. The favors most commonly listed in the official collections are of the following sorts: permission to celebrate the Mass of the Conception on certain days other than the feast; confirmation of constitutions that provide for certain prayers relative to the Conception; approval of the Immaculate Conception as patroness (with which went certain liturgical privileges in many cases) of the Capuchins in 1714 (see note 25, above), of the Franciscan Conventuals in 1720, of Spain in 1760 (see note 72, below), of various towns (according to GRAVOIS II, 49-50), of the United States of America in 1846 (*Acta et decreta sacrorum Conciliorum recentiorum. Collectio Lacensis,* Freiburg im Br., t. 3, 1875, col. 101c—decision of the Sixth Provincial Council of Baltimore; *ibid.* 106c—papal approval. Cf. also P. GUILDAY, *A history of*

Saturday votive Mass of the Conception.   Permission for the latter was granted for the first time to the Franciscan Observants, January 20, 1609, and was the object of numerous decrees thereafter.[31]

II.

THE TITLE

Over the question of the title to be given to the feast of December 8, papal prudence encountered far more serious difficulties.   This was the point around which the battle centered.

CONCEPTION AND SANCTIFICATION

The first conflict revolved around the two designations, *sanctification* and *conception*.   The latter was the more ancient: the only one known to the Greeks, and the only one used in the twelfth century.   The other was invented by the 'maculists,' taking off, doubtless, from the statement of St. Thomas[32] and of St. Bonaventure:[33] "It is Mary's *sanctification,* rather than her conception, that is celebrated."   The use of this term, however,

---

the councils of Baltimore (1794-1884), New York, 1932, p. 149; *Pareri* P. 3, vol. 6, p. 597), of the Congo Free State in 1891 . . . , the insertion of the invocation, *Mater Immaculata* (after 1839: *Regina sine labe originali concepta;* see note 75, below) in the Litany of the Blessed Virgin; the granting of scapulars and other habits in honor of this mystery; and finally, processions.   (Numerous specific examples of all these types of privilege are given in LAURENTIN, note 78)

[31] The Franciscan Observants received permission to use the Office of Nogarolo by an *oraculum vivae vocis,* dated variously at January 19, 20 and 21, 1609.   (See chapter IV of the present volume, p. 150 ff.   The privilege was confirmed November 11, 1641 (*AJP* 7, 1864, col. 278, n. 1280.   Cf. ALVA, *Milit.* 1135) ; other communities had obtained the privilege in the meantime.   But there are a number of instances in which the same privilege was refused to other communities, especially of sisters, during the seventeenth century.

On July 19, 1673, permission was granted by Pope Clement IX to Queen Catherine of England (the Portuguese—and Catholic—spouse of Charles II) for the votive Mass, *"Sanctissimae Conceptionis Immaculate Virginis Mariae"* to be celebrated every Saturday of the year (except Holy Saturday, the Vigil of Pentecost, and the vigil and feast of Christmas) in the royal chapel "of the Immaculate Conception" at Somerset Palace. *AJP* 8 (1865) col. 1181, n. 1973. GRAVOIS II, 52 (cf. I, 155, n. 171; BOURASSE 8, 388) ; ROSKOVANY II, p. xxxii.

See also p. 156 of the present volume, note 117.

[32] "Celebratur festum *sanctificationis* ejus potius quam Conceptionis ipsius."—St. THOMAS AQUINAS, *Summa theologiae* III, 27, 2 ad 3. St. Thomas was preceded by HUGH OF ST. CHER, *In Ecclesiasten* 7, c. 7, ed. Lyon 1669, t. 3, fol. 92B: "B. Virgo originali habuit, propter quod ejus conceptio non celebratur, tamen qui celebrant debent habere respectum ad sanctificationem."

[33] "Potest etiam esse quod illa solemnitas potius refertur ad diem sanctificationis quam Conceptionis."—St. BONAVENTURE, *III Sent.,* d..3, P.1, art.1, q.1, ed. Quaracchi III, 63a. This affirmation is common among the scholastics of the thirteenth and fourteenth centuries. See FRANCISCO LEITE DE FARIA, "L'opinion d'Henri de Gand sur la Conception," in Marianum 16 (1954) pp. 291-295. Cf. FRANCISCO DE GUIMARAENS (article cited below in note 89, *passim*).

Figure 2. THE APOCALYPTIC VIRGIN, WITH PRAYER "OF SIXTUS V."
Fifteenth century.

was quite restricted.[34]   In all the acts of the Holy See, no other term than that of *Conception* is used. Humanly speaking, Pope Pius V, being of Dominican origin, should have favored the term *sanctification* which was in use in his Order; but when, in 1568, he reformed the Breviary, he chose the more ancient and more general usage in preference to that of his own community: he retained the title of *Conception* for the feast. By the terms of his decree, only those could keep the other title who had used it for 200 years.[35]

The last exceptions were eliminated on May 24, 1622, by a new decree occasioned by the insistent representations of the king of Spain: Gregory XV forbade the use "of any other title than that of *Conception*," [36] which was used by the Roman Church. This decision was intended to strengthen the unity of the Church, divided by the conflict of differing usages.

The maculists were at this time virulent and powerful. They held positions of authority, especially in the Inquisition, the flexible and secretive methods of which offered particularly efficacious possibilities of action. The decree of Gregory XV, by suppressing the only term able to give comfortable shelter to the *sententia affirmans*,[37] provoked a lively commotion among them. They intensified their activity, attempting to erect one last barrier— not without a logical argument: the Pope had made it clear that he did

---

[34] The feast was celebrated under this name by the Dominicans (ALVA *Armam.* II, 220-233). The Carthusians who had at first introduced the feast *ad libitum* under the name of *Conceptio* in 1333, adopted that of *sanctificatio* in 1341, and in 1471 returned again to the original name (*DACL*, article *Chartreux* 3a, 1059).

The title *sanctificatio* was used by the Church of Gerona in Catalonia, according to I. de TURRECREMATA (*Tractatus de veritate Conceptionis beatissimae Virginis pro facienda relatione coram Patribus Concilii Basileense, anno Domini 1437*, Romae 1547, P. VI, c. 14, fol. 107 r. Reedited by E. B. PUSEY, Oxford, Parker, 1869, pp. 298b-299). The manuscript breviaries of Gerona (fourteenth-fifteenth centuries) confirm this. G. DREVES, *Analecta hymnica medii aevi*, Leipzig, 16 (1894), p. 40: *In sanctificatione Conceptionis;* 17 (1894) pp. 22 and 25; cf. 34 (1900) p. 65.

ALVARUS PELAGIUS, *De planctu Ecclesiae*, Lib. 2, c. 52, Venetiis, ex officina F. Sansovini, 1560, fol. 110v claims to have seen this name employed in a missal of St. Mary Major's. However the Spanish ambassador, during the embassy of 1618-1622, declared that he had found no trace of such a usage in the archives of this church. L. WADDING, *Legatio Philippi III*, Orat. 6, No. 3, Lovanii 1624, p. 155 (On Wadding's work, see note 141, below).

[35] *Quod a nobis postulat*, July 9, 1568, *Bull. Coq.* 4c, pp. 22-23. *Bull Taur.* 7, 685a-688a.

[36] "Sanctitas sua . . . mandat ac praecipit ut in sacrosanctae missae sacrificio ac divino officio celebrandis, tam publicae quam privatim, non alio quam *Conceptionis* nomine uti debeant." Decree *Sanctissimus*, No. 4, May 24, 1622, *Bull Coq.* 5, p. 46, *Bull. Taur.* 12, 689b. BOURASSE 7, 222.

[37] In the jargon of the controversy, the SENTENTIA AFFIRMANS designated the opinion *affirming* that the Blessed Virgin was *conceived in sin,* while the SENTENTIA NEGANS (also called PIOUS BELIEF) designated the opinion which denied it (and hence *affirmed the Immaculate Conception*). We have avoided using these expressions, convenient as they are, because they tend to confuse the uninitiate. The terms *maculist* and *immaculist*, although less elegant, are more immediately comprehensible.

not intend to settle the debate or to harm their opinion,[38] and that his aim was peace and unity.[39]   Hence they concluded: Since Gregory XV does not settle the question, he is using the word *conception* in a very broad sense; he does not determine whether the first or second instant of conception is meant: thus he leaves room for the opinion that the Blessed Virgin was purified from sin only in the second instant.[40]   And since the Pope's action is prompted by a desire for peace and unity, it implies the elimination, not only of the word *sanctification,* but also of any other determination that would stir up new discussion, above all, of affixing the adjective *immaculate* to the term *conception.*   Over this adjective a new war was about to break loose.[41]

1622-1655. ORIGIN OF THE DECREE OF 1644.

Prior to the decree of Gregory XV, the expression *Immaculata Conceptio* had indeed been used in papal documents, but only with great rarity,[42]

---

[38] ". . . Per hoc tamen Sanctitas sua non intendit reprobare hanc opinionem (the maculist opinion) nec ei ullum prorsus praejudicium inferre . . . ," Decree *Sanctissimus* of May 24, 1622 (cited above, note 36, and below, note 125), No. 2. *Bull. Taur.* 12, 689b.

[39] ". . . ut cultus esset magis uniformis." (*ibid.*)

[40] Cf. the *libella* mentioned in note 49, below. The first begins thus: "Ad agnoscendum quam provide S. Romana et universalis Inquisitio decrevit titulum Immaculatae non esse addendum Conceptioni sed Virgini, annotanda maxime est diversa acceptio hujus nominis *Conceptio* ante Gregorium XV et post illum. Licet enim nomen Conceptio in suo proprio significatu solum importet formationem foetus in utero, ante Gregorium tamen apud multos idem valuit usus hujus nominis Conceptio quod Conceptio Immaculata . . . Contenderunt fautores Immaculatae Conceptionis apud eumdem Gregorium ut praeciperet omnibus quod in celebratione solemnitatis non alio quam Conceptionis nomine uterentur. Quod Pontifex, ut cultus esset magis uniformis, concessit, innuens nomen Conceptionis esse de se indifferens ad utramque sententiam. Quod ut magis etiam insinuaret, declaravit expressis verbis per hoc nullum praejudicium inferri alterutri parti . . . Quod si declarasset nomine Conceptionis *Immaculatam Conceptionem* intellexisse, declarasset Gregorium sibimet fuisse contrarium, dum ex una parte asserit se nullum praejudicium inferre velle opinantibus B. Virginem in peccato conceptam, et ex alia parte plusquam notabile praejudicium ipsis inferret jubendo quod Ecclesia universalis Conceptionem Immaculatam Celebraret." [T. TURCO,] Libellus I, edited by ALVA, *Armam.* I, col. 7-8 and CALDERON, pp. 18-19.

[41] Note well the point of the discussion:

1.   The maculists did not object to positive epithets (Conceptio *sancta, sanctissima, pura,* etc.) such as occurred in the liturgical office (see below, p. 296) but only to the negative epithet *im-maculata,* which strictly implied the negation of every stain. In his second anonymous libellum (note 49, below) T. TURCO wrote: "Vox *sancta* in sensu ab Ecclesia intento . . . abstrahit a primo vel a secundo (instanti conceptionis), et cum sit terminus positivus, sufficit ut in altero instanti verificetur. Vox autem immaculata exprimit sanctitatem . . . per negationem . . . Ideo videtur excludere maculam pro quocumque instanti . . ." etc. (ALVA, *Armam.* I, col. 18-19. CALDERON p. 29).

2.   They did not object to the ancient and traditional usage which attributed the name immaculate *to the Blessed Virgin,* but only to calling her conception immaculate.

[42] The complete list of texts is given in LAURENTIN, pp. 31-34.

and most often indirectly. Furthermore, apart from a few minor documents, generally meant for Spain, the expression is so used as in no wise to implicate the authority of the Holy See. The attitude of the latter is, in fact, distinctly one of reserve; for in various documents, certain confraternities,[43] or orders [44] under the patronage of the *Immaculate Conception* are referred to merely as orders or confraternities *of the Conception,* the controversial adjective being omitted. It is not proscribed or treated as suspect, but out of prudence the popes are unwilling to attach their authority to it, so long as the substance of the debate is not settled.

As the authority of the Holy See was not yet committed, the two opposing parties made use of every possible means to win it over to their side: shrewdness, diplomatic pressure and the exploitation of surprise and weariness. Urban VIII († 1644) succeeded, although not without difficulty, in maintaining the delicate line of conduct of his predecessors. He tolerated the expression, *Immaculata Conceptio*—most often in citations—in a few minor documents usually destined for Spain; but he held himself aloof from any really important implication of his authority, in order not to provide fuel for the disputes he was trying with all his might to quell. Thus, when he approved the order of knights founded by the Duke of Nevers under the title of the *Immaculate Conception,* he took the adjective away from the Conception and gave it to the Virgin, and so approved the order under the title of *The Conception of the Immaculate Virgin.*[44]

This conduct was not without precedents of a sort; but soon events of a newer order occurred. At the beginning of October, 1626, some posters announcing the promulgation of an indulgence granted by the Pope in honor of the laying of the first stone of the Franciscan church of the *Immaculate Conception* were torn down by order of the Master of the Sacred Palace, because of the appearance of this name on the posters.[45] Likewise, on January 19, 1640, the Holy Office suppressed all confraternities of the *Stellarium Immaculatae Conceptionis,*[46] which was, according to the *Libretti* of the society: "la corona propria dell'Immacolata Concezione." Finally, in the towns that had a strict Inquisitor, it was impossible

---

[43] ALVA gives a typical case, relative to a conceptionist confraternity (*Armam.* II, 144-153). The confraternity was erected, he says (col. 153) *sub titulo* IMMACULATE *Conceptionis,* but the document designates it constantly *sub titulo Conceptionis* (col. 146).

[44] Cf. ALVA, *Armam.* I, col. 21; cf. col. 415. LAUNOY, *Opera omnia,* Coloniae 1733, t. I, pp. 20b-21a, and the Constitution *Imperscrutabilis,* of February 12, 1624 (*Bull. Taur.* 13, 114-116. *Bull. Coq.* 5e, 181-194).

[45] The documents relevant to this curious affair (it was Urban VIII himself who laid the first stone of the church in question) have been edited by ARCHANGELUS A ROC, "Ioannes Maria Zamoro," in *Collect. Francisc.* 15/19 (1945) pp. 185-187; cf. 148.

[46] On this *Stellarium,* and the history of its suppression at Bologna, see the study made directly from the archives by C. PIANA, "I Padri conventuali di Bologna e l'Immacolata," in *Archiv. francisc. histor.* 39 (1946), pp. 203-218.

to publish books bearing this *title*,[47] and several works which had managed to get around this obstacle were subsequently put on the Index.[48]

The official acts behind these various measures are minor ones, done in the name of the Congregation, and *not in that of the popes*; furthermore, they do not concern themselves explicitly with the *title* in question. Behind these measures, we can detect the cunning and precautious activity of those who were quietly preparing the way for the Decree of 1644.

The first act leading up to this decree, about which much passionate literature was to be written,[49] took place on February 23, 1627. On the testimony of Gravois—who is all the more worthy of credence in that he would much rather avoid these facts if he could:

> The Vicar of the Holy Office of Cesena—a Dominican—forbade the use of [this title] for certain conclusions which were to be debated in this town, and referred the matter to the Holy Office. His letter [was] read in the course of the general meeting held on February 23 of the same year, in the palace of his Eminence, Cardinal Bandini, in the presence of three cardinals and several Dominican Consultors. The following resolution was adopted: "The eminent cardinals deem that the Vicar of the Holy Office at Cesena has done well in not allowing

[47] This conclusion is based on a vast inventory, 1) of the numerous *manuscripts* consecrated to the Immaculate Conception during this period; 2) of the printed works in which we notice that in certain places, the title dear to the immaculists is missing during these years.

[48] These works remained on the Index until the revision of Leo XIII. The preface of the revised edition declares: "Delere . . . placuit *non pauca opera quae de Beatae Virginis Immaculata Conceptione* recte quidem sed intemperantius vel cum adversariorum nonnulla offensione tractant." *Index librorum prohibitorum P. N. Leonis XIII Summi Pontificis recognitus* (various editions, beginning with 1900) ed. Rome, typ. Vaticanis, 1925, Praefatio, p. XVII.

[49] BIBLIOGRAPHY OF THE ESSENTIAL LITERATURE ON THE DECREE OF 1644. This decree gave rise to an abundant controversial literature. A number of *anonymous manuscript libella* were written in its defense. The manuscripts and the best informed authors attribute all of them to T. TURCO, fiftieth Master General of the Dominicans, who died December 1, 1649. The grossest mistakes have often been made about these *libella*. ROSKOVANY lists them twice (t. III, p. 369, nn. 8436-8440) and is also in error about both the author and the contents (ib. p. 469, n. 9474). The correct list follows. As they have no fixed title, we designate them by their *incipit*:

    1. Incipit. *Ad agnoscendum quam provide* . . . (Cf. note 40, above.)

    2. Incipit. *De titulo Immaculatae tribuendo.*

The text of these two *libella* is given at the beginning of the works of ALVA, *Armam.* I, 7-11, and CALDERON pp. 18-38, which were written to refute them. Another refutation was written by Amadaeus SALIUS, theologus Haeteveranus [=pseudonym of Theophile RAYNAUD], *Dissertatio de retinendo titulo Immaculatae Conceptionis adversus Linum et Cletum* [=pseudonyms for the authors of the above-mentioned *libella* whose names are unknown to RAYNAUD], *contendentes reformatum a Gregorio XV dictionarium,* Coloniae 1651, re-edited in *Opera,* Lugduni, Boissat, 1665, t. 7, 305-332. Cf. also Joannes A FONTE, *Allegatio pro informando Sanctissimo Domino Nostro Innocentio X et Sancta Inquisitione Romana universali circa scrupulos emergentes de non continuando nec retinendo titulo Immaculatae Conceptionis B. M. Virginis,* Conchae, ex mandato ordinarii apud Salvatoris [sic] a Viader (Roma, Bibl. naz. Misc. B. 716, 5).

    3. Incipit. *Foelici sydere admirabilique Dei consilio crediderim.* It is contained

the use of the title *Immaculate Conception,* but rather that of the *Conception of the Immaculate Virgin."* They ordered that this decision be observed.[50]

The same day in the general meeting held in the palace of Cardinal Bandini the Cardinal Inquisitors established a general decree:

It shall not be permitted to confer the title *Immaculate Conception;* one is to say simply *Conception of the Immaculate Virgin.*[51]

---

in the ms. Cl. II, 1 NA, of the Biblioteca communale Ariostea, fol. 1r-35v, and twice in the Mc. Casanatense (Roma) 2651, fol. 1r-34v and 39-61v (which last seems to be the autograph) under the title *(Tractatus) pro decreto S. R. Universalis Inquisitionis de titulo Immaculata non addendo Conceptioni B.M.V.* ALVA, *Radii,* 2097-2107, gives a resume with long extracts, under the title *De Conceptione SS. Deiparae Virginis Mariae. Opus . . . compositum Romae et SS. D. N. Innocentio Papae et Sacrae Cardinalium Congregatione S.R.E. et Generalis Inquisitionis exhibitum.*

4. A fourth libellum is mentioned by GRAVOIS (I, 116), "in codice Ghisiano 120 signato, fol. 95." He remarks that it is *"fere eadem"* (as the above mentioned libella).

In the eighteenth century, nearly all the works on the Immaculate Conception consecrate a chapter to the Decree of 1644. The most important are the following:

H. MARRACCI, *Tiara Pontificia mariana,* Ms. conserved at Rome, Santa Maria in Campitelli, Lib. III, q. 10 et 15.

V. FASSARI, *Immaculata Deiparae Conceptio commissa trutinae . . .* Lyon 1666, disp. 9, div. 3, No. 12.

T. STROZZI, *Controversia della Concezione della Beata Vergine Maria descritta istoricamente,* Palermo, Gramignani, 2a edizione 1703, Lib. X, pp. 565-581.

D. LOSSADA, O.F.M. Obs. *Discussio theologica super definibilitate proxima mysterii Immaculatae Conceptionis Dei Genitricis,* Matriti, typis Ven. Matris Mariae a Jesu de Agreda, 1733 (based upon a manuscript *Relatio historica* conserved at Madrid) *Appendix* [not paginated], Anno 1664, n. 59-83.

Among the more recent studies, those which give an original documentation are PIANA (cited below, note 53) and IPARRAGUIRE (cited in note 141), who cite the documents of archives. The monographs of ARCHANGELUS A ROG, "J. M. Zamoro (1579-1649)," in *Collect. francisc.* t. 15/19 (1945/49) pp. 144-158 and R. PAZELLI, *L'Immacolata Concezione di Maria in P. Francisco Bordoni T.O.R.* (1595-1671), Roma 1951, Extractum ex *Analecta Tertii Ordinis Regularis Sancti Francisci* 5 (1950/51), especially pp. 46-51, show well how the authors whom they study found themselves at grips with the Decree of 1644. Finally, *La embajada a Roma de 1659 y la Bulla Sollicitudo de Alejandro VII,* special issue of *Miscellanea Comillas* 24 (1955) 480 pp. 8°, is a work of capital importance. It gives the 177 documents relevant to the matter (p. 85), as well as the three preparatory drafts of the Bull *Sollicitudo* (pp. 458-469), which date respectively from the beginning of May, the end of June and the beginning of August, 1661.

[50] GRAVOIS I, 114, n. 118 (ed. BOURASSE 8, 362). The archives give us the precise text: "Visum fuit DD. Cardinalibus optime se Vicarium gessisse ac *melius fecisset, si titulum Immaculatae postposuisset Virgini,* et ita Sacra Congregatio responderi et observari mandavit." *Arch. post.* [5]. The point is that the expression *Conceptionis Virginis Immaculatae* is not so ambiguous as the expression *Conceptionis Immaculatae Virginis.*

[51] "In generali Congregatione Sanctae Romanae et Universalis Inquisitionis habita in Palatio Illustrissimi Domini Cardinalis Bandini in Regione Campi Martii coram Illustrissimis et Reverendissimis Dominis Cardinalibus contra haereticam pravitatem Inquisitoribus generalibus a Sede Apostolica deputatis, Illmi. et Rmi. Cardinales Generales Inquisitores praedicti decreverunt, quod quando agitur de tribuendo titulo Immaculatae Conceptionis Beatissimae Virginis, nullo modo permittatur, sed solum dicatur Conceptio *Immaculatae Virginis,* et ita observari mandarunt." *Arch. post.*

Eleven years later, the Franciscans of Ancona announced by posters and printed invitations an academic debate on the *Immaculate Conception.* The Inquisitor asked the Holy Office for instructions. On April 28, 1638, this Congregation transmitted to him the text of the decree of 1627, enjoining him to conform his conduct to it.[52]

A similar incident occurred at Bologna in 1644. The decree was then confirmed by the general assembly of the Inquisition, and it is from this confirmation that it gets its usual name of "Decree of 1644." [53] From then on it was applied more strictly, particularly in Italy, but it remained unpublished.[54] It was only three or four years later that its authors—who represented an influential part of the Inquisition, but not the whole Congregation—considered themselves strong enough to publish it. At that time the Jesuits in Rome were holding a convention on the question of the Immaculate Conception. When they applied for an *Imprimatur,* the Master of the Sacred Palace refused to grant it, and printed the Decree of 1644 on which his decision was based.[55] At the same time there were put into circulation two anonymous manuscript booklets explaining with an impassioned argumentation the basis of the decision. Their author was the General of the Dominicans, T. Turco (see note 49 above).

A lively commotion followed. Antonio de Ribera, Commissary at the Roman Curia of the Franciscans of the Strict Observance in Italy, went to see Innocent X and aroused the Christian princes. On September 1, 1648,[56]

[7.] I. IPARRAGUIRE, in *Est Ecl.* 28 (1954) p. 618, likewise cites Bibliotheca Chigi, Roma, Ms. B.V. 73. The objections raised by ALVA (*Radii,* col. 2098) against the existence of this first decision are not convincing.

Analogous interventions occurred at Milan (February 28, 1630), at Narni (February 13, 1636), at Faenza (July 28, 1638) and at Florence (September 5, 1646). *Arch. post.* [5] et [6].

[52] GRAVOIS I, 114, n. 118 (ed. BOURASSE 8, 363). These facts are confirmed by C. PIANA, O.F.M., "Attivita e peripezie dei Padri del convento di S. Francesco in Bologna per la difesa e la propagazione del culto dell'Immacolata Concezione nel seicento," in *Archiv. Franc. Hist.* 29 (1946) pp. 221-227. According to I. IPARRAGUIRE, "La definibilidad," in *Est. Ecl.* 28 (1954) 618, and ALVA, *Radii,* Col. 2098, the date should be April 28, 1638, and not April 29, 1639, as GRAVOIS maintains.

[53] "Feria quarta vigesima Januarii, in Congregatione generali S. Romanae et Universalis Inquisitionis habitae in Conventu Sanctae Mariae super Minervam, coram Em. DD. Cardinalibus contra haereticam pravitatem Generalibus Inquisitoribus a Sede Apostolica deputatis, Eminentiss. ac Rev. Domini Cardinales Inquisitionis praedictae decreverunt: Quando agitur de tribuendo titulo Immaculatae Conceptionis Beatae Virginis nullo modo permittatur sed solum dicatur Conceptio Immaculatae Virginis et ita observari mandarunt . . . Ioannes Andreas Thomasius S. R. Inquisitionis Notarius." This is the complete text as given by ALVA, *Radii* 2098, citing the third manuscript *libellum* of T. TURCO (see above, note 49). GRAVOIS (I, 115), BOURASSE (8, 363), and numerous other authors give the same text more or less abbreviated.

[54] Cf. I. IPARRAGUIRE, in *Est. Ecl.* 28, 1954, p. 621.

[55] Cf. D. LOSADA, *Discussio* (cited above, note 49).

[56] His letter is reproduced in H. MARRACCI, *Caesares mariani,* Romae, Barnabo, 1656 (ed. BOURASSE 10, 1442).

Philip IV of Spain sent for an explanation. What happened thereafter remains in part obscure, for everything was conducted in the greatest secrecy. On March 18, 1649, Pope Innocent X invited the General of the Dominicans to present his views,[57] which the latter did in a third booklet (*supra,* note 49), dying shortly thereafter. The King of Spain received a benevolent, but somewhat dilatory answer. Innocent put off to gain time, and by many oral directives called upon both parties to have patience and moderation. The situation remained unchanged, except for two slight differences: on the one hand, the application of the decree was henceforth less rigid and less belligerent; on the other hand, greater care was taken in the acts of the Holy See not to use this expression which aroused so many discussions.[58]

In the pontificate of Alexander VII (1655-1667), however, a new step was taken. Led by Philip IV of Spain, who had early been informed by his ambassador of the new Pope's favor for this doctrine, the partisans of the Immaculate Conception called attention to the strong measures that had been used in one place or another, in a spirit entirely contrary to the decisions of 1617 and 1622, against those who favored the pious belief. The Pope summoned the Master of the Sacred Palace (who was responsible by his office for the publications in the Papal States), and ordered him personally to grant an *imprimatur* to two works bearing this title, the publication of which had been prohibited for some years.[59] He was further directed not to bother anyone again on this score.

Henceforth the expression, *Immaculate Conception,* already in common usage, could spread without hindrance.[60] A few minor incidents con-

---

[57] *Arch. post.* 6: Texts edited by I. IPARRAGUIRE, *loc. cit.,* p. 622. Cf. GRAVOIS I, 115, n. 120. But what these authors add must be rectified. Contrary to the interpretation of most authors, T. TURCO did in fact send an answer to the Pope, but he sent it under the seal of the secret of the Holy Office. And because of his death the same year, the same question was posed again to his successors. (ALVA puts the death of Turco on *December 9,* no doubt because he sees there the sign of a judgment of God. The official documents of the Order give the date, *December 1.*)

[58] ALVA and GRAVOIS did not find any act of Innocent X (1644-1655) in which the expression, *Immaculata Conceptio,* occurs.

[59] *Arch. post.* [6] to [9] and GRAVOIS II, 28-30. The two works published at Rome where, for a long time, no book had appeared under this title, were: 1. Martinus DE ESPARZA, S.J. (professor at the Roman College), *Immaculata Conceptio Virginis deducta ex origine peccati originalis,* Romae 1655. 2. Lucas WADDING, O.F.M., *Immaculatae Conceptioni B. Virginis non adversari ejus mortem,* Romae, Ap. N.A. Tinassium, 1655. Cf. D. LOSSADA, *Discussio* (cited above, note 49), Appendix, n. 83.

[60] On November 6, 1655, the Inquisitor at Faenza is directed to make no more objections to the printing of holy pictures and pious writings by Franciscans, bearing the title of the Immaculate Conception. (GRAVOIS, II, 29) *Arch. post.* [8] and [9]. At Bologna, the Inquisitors who had received the order to permit the printing of this title in the case of sermons and other pious writings, prohibited "the discussion and printing" of theological conclusions. The correspondence on this subject between the Inquisitor of Bologna and the Holy Office is published by C. PIANA (article cited in note 127), in *Archiv Franc. hist.* 39 (1946) pp. 225-226.

tinued to occur: in 1668,[61] 1678,[62] 1712,[63] 1734,[64] and 1738; [65] but they terminated in victory for the immaculists whenever appeal was made to the Pope.

Let us try to situate clearly the attitude of Popes Urban VIII (1622-1644) and Innocent X (1644-1655) regarding the Decree of 1644. They permitted the Inquisition to apply the decree, which, it must be remembered. was not in itself directed *against* the *Immaculate Conception*. In their minds—and it is thus that it was represented to them—the decree was a measure of prudence and peace. One was free to use the title privately and discreetly; but in a tense situation that was not yet clear, it was only normal that an expression of such great import should not be diffused hastily and spectacularly at a time when the Holy See had not yet decided anything. Applied with tact, this decree could have served as an instrument of peace. It left the immaculists free to express and to mature their opinion, provided they did not give public provocation to their adversaries, who had lost, since 1622, all right to express themselves.

In sum: 1) This measure was intended by the popes to bring divided Christians into accord on the basis of a provisory terminology, until the distant time when decisions should have ripened.

2) The popes were not implicated personally either in a formal appro-

---

[61] Not long after the death of Alexander VII, the Inquisitors of Bologna and Parma had forbidden the printing of the expression, Immaculate Conception. Upon an appeal from the General of the Franciscan Conventuals, the Holy Office replied: "Rescribatur Inquisitori Bononiae quod in dictis conclusionibus non continetur aliquid repugnans Constitutionibus Apostolicis: Idcirco illas currere relinquat. Idemque significetur Inquisitori Parmensi." GRAVOIS II, 43, n. 17 B et *Arch. post.* [10]: cf. [7]: A summary of the text is given by I. IPARRAGUIRE, *Est. Ecl.* 28 (1954) p. 624.

[62] On February 17, 1678, a decree of the Master of the Sacred Palace, Raymond Capisucchi (claiming, without justification, to act in the name of the Pope) prohibited an immaculist office. After a very complicated series of maneuvers, Innocent XI had the office submitted to a commission of four members, including Capisucchi. Instead of being suppressed, the expression *Immaculata Conceptio* was twice added.

The principal texts relating to this affair are published in Dom G. MORIN, "Un curieux épisode de l'histoire du culte de l'Immaculée Conception en Allemagne au XVIIe siècle," in *Historisches Jahrbuch* 62-69, 1949, p. 709. Cf. GRAVOIS II, repeated by ROSKOVANY, II, 395.

One of the letters published by Dom MORIN (*Ibid.* p. 712), dated August 25, 1678, reveals the efforts made in Germany to propagate the Decree of 1644, which was no longer in force: "Etiam hic . . . circumferunt PP. Dominicani decretum a S. Palatii Magistro impressum. Indignantur cultores piae sententiae..." (*Ibid.*, p. 711.)

[63] According to GRAVOIS I, 172, n. 184; BOURASSE 8, 398. The Inquisitor of Bologna argued from the fact that, in the Brief *Commissi nobis* which had made the Conception a holy day of obligation, Clement XI did not call it "festum *Immaculatae Conceptionis*," but "festum Conceptionis B. M. Virginis Immaculatae."

[64] GRAVOIS I, 172, n. 184 gives no details concerning this incident which he dates at January, 1734.

[65] Cf. GRAVOIS I, 172, n. 184. BOURASSE 8, 398.

bation or in the application of the Decree, which does not figure in any official collection. There is no denying, however, that the popes' intentions were overstepped here and there by the virulence with which the rule was applied by the maculists who severely tested its serviceableness in the interests of peace.

THE PAPAL ATTITUDE FROM 1655 TO 1844.

Even after the abolition of the Decree of 1644 by Alexander VII, the Holy See remained faithful to the rules of prudence which had long been in use. Alexander VII himself,[66] the champion of the Immaculate Conception, and likewise his successors, abstained from using the expression *Immaculata Conceptio* and limited themselves strictly to *Conceptio Virginis Immaculatae*.[67]

At times the application of the rule went very far: the papal documents generally refrained from designating by name those groups or persons which had adopted the name, *Immaculate Conception.* Sometimes the titles of these latter are modified in the official documents, even at the risk of creating confusion.[68] Sometimes *Immaculata Conceptio* is to be found in

[66] Cf. ARCHANGELUS A ROC, O.F.M.Cap., (*Collect. Francis.* 15/19, 1945/1949, p. 186, note 33). In the Bull *Sollicitudo,* the decisive act for the cause of the Immaculate Conception, he does not employ the disputed expression (Cf. No. 4, *Bull. Coq.* 6e,182b. *Bull Taur.* 16, 740: "Sancta Romana Ecclesia de Intemeratae *Virginis Mariae Conceptione* festum solemniter celebrat"). In his acts, the expression *Immaculata Conceptio* is systematically replaced by *Conceptio ImmaculatAE Virginis.* Thus, in the Constitution *Majestatis tuae* of June 18, 1661, addressed to Philip IV, he speaks of the "Moniales Conceptionis Beatae Mariae *Virginis Immaculatae*" (*Bull. Coq.* 6e, 150b. *Bull Taur.* 16, 692), whereas, in reality, these sisters bore the name of "Moniales Immaculatae Conceptionis." In the Decree *Exponi nobis* of December 12, 1661, he makes a similar change in the name of a Franciscan province: "Custos et definitores provinciae Conceptionis B.M. *Virginis Immaculatae* fratrum minorum ordinis sancti Francisci Recollectorum nuncupatorum" No. 1, (*Bull. Coq.* 6e, 184b; *Bull. Taur.* 16, 742b). Likewise, in 1664 and 1667, he grants to the King of Spain, and then to three other princes or states "Officium et Missa Conceptionis B.M. *Virginis Immaculatae* cum Octava."

[67] Expressions such as *Sancta* and *Sanctissima Conceptio* are also to be found in the Decrees of the Roman Congregations but, as we have said, these adjectives, based on the liturgy of the Church, were not attacked by the opposition. I have not found the expression in the Roman *Bullarium,* but it occurs in numerous decrees of the Congregation of Rites (not signed by the pope) from 1662 to 1732: GARDELLINI I; 373, n. 2197; 392, n. 2293; 411, n. 2411; 429, n. 2501; II: 77-78, n. 3120; 82, n. 3133; 203, n. 3915; 334, n. 4008. See also *AJP* 8, 1865, col. 1142, n. 1780; col. 1181, n. 1973. *Bull Cap.* I, 151; cf. *Bull. Min.* 7a, p. 44.

[68] A particularly clear case is that of the *Custodia of the Immaculate Conception* of Rio de Janeiro, which was separated from the Province of St. Anthony and erected as the Province of the *Immaculate Conception,* on December 20, 1675. This province was the object of numerous acts in which the functioning of the following laws can be observed: 1) In all the non-pontifical documents, and in the titles given by the Franciscan *Bullarium,* this province is regularly designated under the title, *Provincia IMMACULATAE CONCEPTIONIS* (*Bull. Min.* contains six cases between 1683

the questions asked, but not in the answers. There are cases in which the contrast between the petition, which speaks about the Immaculate Conception, and the reply, which has recourse to other terms signifying the same thing, is quite striking.[69] Such reticence is obviously intentional.

Again we must not conclude to a hostility on the part of the Holy See toward the title; that would be to return to the sophism of the eighteenth century maculists. If it were a matter of opposition on principle, the Holy See would have eliminated this expression from the statutes and constitutions which it approved; whereas the expression occurs there frequently. More generally, it occurs in documents inserted in the pontifical decrees, as distinguished from the *text of the decrees* properly so called.[70] In other words, the Popes refrain solely from using it on their own initiative and on their own responsibility; but they permitted others to use it, and approved

and 1734). 2) In all the pontifical briefs, this title is changed into that of *Provincia Conceptionis Beatae Mariae* VIRGINIS IMMACULATAE: under Clement X, in 1675 (twice) and 1676; under Innocent XI, in 1688; under Clement XI, in 1717; under Benedict XIV in 1743.

The same thing occurs also in the case of the *Provincia Immaculatae Conceptionis* erected in Castille. It is designated by this title three times in the decision of the Order dated August 8, 1744 (*Bull. min.* 4, 567-570). Benedict XIV inserts this document into the confirmatory brief, *Militantis Ecclesiae*, January 29, 1745; but in the part in which he speaks in his own name, he says, "novam provinciam sub titulo Conceptionis B.M. Virginis Immaculatae." (*Bull. min.* 4, 466-472) Another case is that of the *Provincia Immaculatae Conceptionis* of la Beyra. It is called by its proper name in the title given by the *Bullarium Minorum* (3, 133) but the official document itself, the Brief *Nuper pro parte* (April 24, 1705) reads five times "provincia conceptionis."

This seems to have occurred in the following cases also: 1) The "provincia immaculatae conceptionis of the Franciscan Observants of Portugal (Clement XIII, *Exponi nobis,* November 17, 1732. 2) The "Confraternitatis *sub titulo . . . Conceptionis B.M. Virginis Immaculatae . . .* in Ecclesia ordinis ejusdem B.V. de Mercede . . . in Indiis occidentalibus" spoken of by Clement XI (Brief *Cum sicut dilecti,* June 23, 1703. Cf. Bourasse 7, 337). 3) The "Provinciae Conceptionis B.V. Immaculatae" of the Franciscan Observants spoken of by Clement XII in the Brief *Exponi nobis* of November 17, 1752.

[69] In 1712, the General of the Capuchins requested of the Congregation of Rites that the Blessed Virgin be named patroness of the Order, "sub titulo Immaculatae Conceptionis," and that the Feast of the Immaculate Conception might be celebrated by them as a double of the first class. The favor was granted on March 10, 1714, but the reply says "Sanctissimae Conceptionis." (*Bull. Cap.* 1, 150-151)

[70] In all the Roman decisions examined, I have found only two exceptions to this rule—cases in which the expression, *Immaculate Conception,* was employed in the question or petition, and was repeated in the text of the response. Neither case seems to be of particular significance, and in neither case is the rescript signed by the Holy Father. One case is that of the indulgence granted to the Franciscan Conventuals *pro festo Immaculatae Conceptionis,* on November 30, 1762 (*Decreta authentica C. Congregationis Indulgentiis sacrisque reliquiis praepositae ab anno 1668 ad annum 1889 edita jussu . . . Leonis XIII,* Ratisbonae, Pustet, vol. 2, 1885, n. 210, p. 173). The other case is a response of the Congregation of Rites, July 23, 1736, to a question concerning the votive office of the Immaculate Conception (Gardellini 2, p. 357a, n. 4044, quest. 27).

this usage within communities in which it was traditionally and peacefully accepted.[71]

The application of this rule was sometimes ingenious and subtle, as when, in 1760, Charles III asked Clement XIII to name the Immaculate Conception official patroness of Spain. There were precedents; on July 12, 1720, Clement XI had approved the Constitutions of the Friars Minor Conventual, in which "the ever-blessed Virgin, under the title of the Immaculate Conception," was declared to be their principal patron. The king had no doubt that an analogous favor would be accorded to him without difficulty, and in his request, dated August 28, he used the expression *Immaculata Conceptio* with extreme insistence.[72]   The chancery found itself in a very embarrassing position. It could not deny to the king what had been granted to others; but since there was question here, not merely of approving some constitutions in which the term occurred, but of a special act regarding the term itself, the Holy See was in danger of implicating itself directly in regard to the title. There is no difficulty, however, from which diplomacy cannot find an outlet; in this case, the King's request to have the "Immaculate Conception" as patroness of Spain was incorporated into the reply with warm praise; but the pontifical decision itself spoke merely of the *"praedictum mysterium."*

The King's disappointment can easily be imagined. The following year he introduced a new request which likewise called for the use of the term so carefully avoided. He began by thanking the pope for having granted as patroness of Spain, "the ever-blessed Virgin in the sacred mystery of her *Immaculate Conception,"* and ended by requesting the office *Sicut Lilium* for the feast-day of the same *Immaculate Conception.* Once again the chancery incorporated the letter into its reply, and granted the favor while speaking only of *"said mystery."* [73]

In 1767, however, on the occasion of another request, the title so dear to the monarch—and to so many Christians—passed over into the reply. By his apostolic authority, the Pope accorded to Spain the faculty to celebrate every Saturday—with a few exceptions—*"the proper office of the Immaculate Conception."* [74]   Nothing however is more tenacious than the habits of the chancery. Partly out of prudence, partly out of routine, the

----

[71] In their zeal for the cause of the Immaculate Conception, the eighteenth century immaculists made every effort, by an abstract dialectic, to get away from this prudential distinction, which was motivated by the desire to avoid giving rise to quarrels, or committing the future irrevocably. (See, for example, GRAVOIS p. 182, n. 192a) It is important that the distinction be recognized; otherwise the conduct of the Holy See appears inconsistent and vacillating, whereas, once we perceive the principle behind it, we can only admire the coherence and sureness of its slow but unfaltering progress toward the goal.

[72] Cf. BOURASSE 7, 389. ROSKOVANY II, 515-518, n. 451.

[73] Cf. BOURASSE 7, 392-394. ROSKOVANY II, 519, n. 453.

[74] Cf. BOURASSE 7, 398-399. ROSKOVANY II, 520-521, n. 454.

old caution continued to be observed for many years after this exception.

The decisive and definitive turning point came only at the beginning of the nineteenth century. On May 17, 1806, under Pius VII, the Franciscans obtained permission to add the word *Immaculata* to the expression *et te in Conceptione* of the preface for December 8. On September 6, 1834, Gregory XVI granted the same privilege to the diocese of Seville. In 1838, in a general measure, he granted it to whatever orders or diocese should ask for it. From then on, the requests poured in. In the course of that same year, fifty-seven requests were recorded. By the end of his pontificate, the number 300 was almost reached.[75]

This measure started a sort of consultation, and furnished the occasion of a discreet appeal to put an end to the last opposition. In the long list of the recipients of this privilege, the Dominican Order appears.[76] It was doubtless due to some pointed invitation from the Holy See itself, that Father Angelo Ancarani, Master General of the Order, took this initiative on December 10, 1843. He did it without consulting the General Chapter of his Order, and not without some apprehensions; for in spite of the progress of the pious belief among the sons of St. Dominic, many still persisted in their opposition to it. The Master General's decision was debated; some thought it was not binding so long as the General Chapter had not confirmed it; others alleged that their oath of fidelity to the doctrine of St. Thomas forbade them to pronounce such a formula. On June 14, 1845, a rescript from the Congregation of Rites side-stepped these objections; a second rescript, approved by Pius IX, July 17, 1847, put an end to further appeals.[77] Thus the last centers of resistance disappeared honorably and quietly.[78]

[75] All the documents relative to this affair have been published in an *Appendix* by J. PERRONE, S.J., *De Immaculato B.V. Mariae Conceptu,* ed. Avenione, Seguin, 1848, pp. 353-385, and reproduced by BOURASSE 7, 605-628.

Beginning in 1839, the Holy See began to grant a new permission, which, up until then, *had always been refused* (even as late as January 7 of that same year the Holy Office had intervened against the Capuchins who had adopted the practice, *Bull. Cap.* 7a, p. 44). From then on it was permitted to add to the Litany of the Blessed Virgin the invocation: *Regina sine labe originali concepta.* By a new decree of 1844, the two additions were to be granted together to all who should ask for them from then on. (The Decree and a list of the beneficiaries are given by PERONNE and BOURASSE in the works cited at the beginning of this note.)

[76] PERONNE (work cited in the preceding note) List 2, n. 192, p. 378. Complete text of the document *ib.,* pp. 385-386. (A French translation is given by BOURASSE 7, 619 and 623-624.)

[77] The rescript recapitulating the whole affair has been published by J. PERONNE, *De Immaculato B.V. Mariae Conceptu,* Appendix, ed. Avenione 1848, pp. 387-392, and reproduced in BOURASSE 7, 624-628.

[78] GRAVOIS gives a different impression of this history, and is followed by ROSKOVANY. According to X. LE BACHELET (*DTC* 7, 1188), who follows them, the title *Immaculate Conception,* was frequently (*couramment*) used in the decrees of the Congregation of Rites after the incident of 1712. Besides the fact that LE BACHELET

III.

THE DOCTRINE

We come now to the essential point: the decisions of the *magisterium* concerned not merely with the feast or the title, but with the *doctrine* underlying them.

PREHISTORY

Previous to the twelfth century, the dogma has only a 'prehistory,'[79] since the question of the *conception* had not yet been explicitly raised.[80] The papal writings of this time testify solidly to two complementary positions which would mark, as it were, the two boundaries of the channel down which the formulation of the dogma was to make its way. On the one hand, the Virgin is without stain: *immaculata*[81] (although this epithet was not reserved exclusively to her); on the other hand, she is

---

is confusing the *toleration* of this title by the Holy See with its adoption, which comes much later, these authors have misrepresented the documents. In a number of cases, GRAVOIS writes *Conceptio Immaculata* where the *Bullarium* reads *Conceptio Virginis Immaculatae*. In other cases, the texts cited follow the rule formulated above, i.e. the title does not occur in the text of the rescript proper, but only in a document inserted into it.

[79] See chapters II-VI of the present volume.

[80] The Conception of the Virgin began to be spoken of in the East, towards the end of the seventh or the beginning of the eighth century, but the problem it involves was not *explicitly* considered (See chapter III of the present volume). In the West, Eadmer and Osbert of Clare clearly pose the problem at the beginning of the twelfth century (see chapter V of the present volume). No act of the Holy See refers to it prior to Sixtus IV. Nevertheless, we encounter a considerable mass of apocryphal documents purporting to come from epochs in which the question had not been raised. Two such examples are mentioned in note 135, below.

[81] For example:

HONORIUS I (625-638), Epist. "Scripta fraternitatis vestrae" ad Sergium, in 634: "Christum enim . . . sine peccato conceptus de Spiritu Sancto, etiam absque peccato est partus de sancta et *Immaculata* Virgine Dei Genitrice." (G. D. MANSI, *Amplissima Conciliorum collectio*, Florence 1765, XI, 539C. PL 80, 472AB. DENZINGER 251.)

St. MARTIN I, in Canon 3 of the Lateran Council (649), calls Mary: "Genitricem sanctam semperque Virginem et *Immaculatam* Mariam." (MANSI X, 1151-1152. C. J. HEFELE, *A history of the councils of the Church,* transl. by W. CLARK, Edinburgh, 1896, V, p. 110 DENZINGER 251.)

At the Council of Rome in 680, St. AGATHO gave global approval to the Acts of the preceding council (*PL* 87, 1224. Cf. HEFELE V, pp. 146-147) and called Mary *Immaculata* in a letter which would be read at the ecumenical Third Council of Constantinople (*PL* 87, 1220-1221. Cf. MANSI, XI, 290C and DENZINGER, n. 288, note 2).

A letter of St. Sophronius of Jerusalem, in which also Mary is called *immaculate,* was approved at the Sixth Ecumenical Council (*PG* 87c, col. 3160-3161 and M. JUGIE, *l'Immaculée Conception, Rome, Academia mariana,* 1950, pp. 99-105; HEFELE, *ibid.,* p. 164) and confirmed, along with the other acts of this council, by Leo II, Pope from 682 to 683 (*ib.,* pp. 178-181). However, in the same letter, Mary is also said to have been sanctified, without any indication of the precise moment when this occurred.

included in Adam's posterity, which is universally affected by original sin. With regard to this latter point, an exception had been formulated for Christ, but not yet for Mary.[82]

The fact cannot be concealed, that in accordance with the tendencies of the period, a number of popes from the twelfth to the fourteenth centuries were led to place the accent on the universal extension of original sin—a fact which weighed heavily on the earliest development of the belief. After having listed eight popes who affirmed the universality of original sin, without making any direct or explicit reference to Mary,[83] Father Sericoli, summarizing the conclusions of Father Doncoeur,[84] declares:

> [Many] predecessors [of Sixtus IV] denied Mary's privilege in a more direct and explicit fashion, but only as private doctors, and [85] exclusively in sermons and treatises composed before their accession to the papal dignity. Hence it was their intention to declare only their own personal opinion, not that of the Holy See. In this group belong Innocent III (1198-1216) . . . Innocent V (1276), John XXII (1316-1334), Benedict XII (1334-1342) . . . On the other hand, prior to Sixtus IV, we do not find any document of the Holy See in favor of the Immaculate Conception.[86]

[82] Thus, for example:

St. Leo I, (440-461), *s. 24, de Nativ.* 4, c. 3, *PL* 54, 206A: "Terra carnis humanae quae in primo fuerat praevaricatore maledicta *in hoc solo* B. Virginis *partu germen* edidit benedictum et *a vitio suae stirpis alienem"; s. 25, de nativ.* 5, *ib.* col. 211C: *"Solus . . . inter filios hominum* Dominus Jesus innocens natus est, quia *solus* sine carnalis concupiscentiae pollutione conceptus." Similar assertions are to be found in the *s. 21, in Nativ. Domini 1,* c. 1, *PL* 54, 191A and *s. 22, in Nativ. 2,* c. 3, *ib.,* col. 196C.

Gelasius I, *Ep. 7 ad ep. Provinciae Pincenum, PL* 59, 36A.

St. Gregory the Great, *Moralia in Job,* L. 18, c. 51, *PL* 75, 89B comments thus on *Ps.* 50, 7: "Solus (Christus) veraciter *sanctus natus* est quia . . . *ex commixtione copulae conceptus non est." Homil. in Ev.* Lib. 2, hom. *39,* n. 8, *PL* 76, 1299A.

Cf. also Honorius III, cited in note 86.

[83] "Talis est casus Innocentii I (402-417), Zozimi (417-418), Bonifacii I (418-423), s. Leonis I (440-461), s. Gregorii (590-604), Innocentii II (1130-1143), Clementis V (1305-1314) et Eugenii IV (1431-1444). Ceteri vero septem praedecessores [Sixtus IV] utique mariale privilegium magis directe ac explicite negarunt ast solum qua privati doctores atque unice in tractatibus ante adeptam pontificiam dignitatem compositis . . . Ad quam classem reducunter Innocentius III (1198-1216), Honorius III (1216-1227), Innocentius V (1276), Johannes XXII (1316-1334), Benedictus XII (1334-1342), Clemens VII (1342-1352) et Bonifacius IX (1389-1404)." Sericoli, p. 17.

[84] *Rev. hist. eccl.* 8, (1907) 706-714. A thorough study limited to a few popes.

[85] It would be better to say *or* rather than *and,* for it is not certain that the sermons of Innocent III and John XXII were written before they became pope.

[86] According to Sericoli (as cited in note 83), *"seven" popes* "directly and explicitly" denied the Immaculate Conception. From this number, we have dropped three, for whom this assertion has not been established, namely, Honorius III (1216-1227), Clement VI (1342-1352) and Boniface IX (1389-1404).

1) On Honorius, Sericoli's only source of information is Alva *Radii,* col. 712-715. But the latter says that he could find none of the four maculist texts invoked

This account need not shock us. Theology asks us to distinguish carefully between the *man* and the *pope,* and there are other facts of Church history which also call for the use of this important distinction.[87]   It would be shabby to camouflage the above-mentioned facts as if they could embarrass us.   As a matter of fact, they should have the very contrary effect, for they enable us almost to lay our fingers on the action of God, who did not permit any of these popes who were personally attached to the maculist opinion, ever to express this opinion in the exercise of the *magisterium.*   This is a fact of high apologetic value.   And it is all the more striking in that the popes of this period were at times requested to "confirm that the virgin was

---

by Bandelli, which he considers suspect. In Horoy's edition of the *Opera Honorii III* (*Medii aevi bibliotheca patristica,* Paris, 1879), we have not been able to find the two *explicit* maculist texts invoked by Bandelli (p. 49; see below, p. 298 ff.). The sermons *in Purif.* and *in Assumpt.* (Horoy ed., I, 1, col. 17 and 54-86) contain *similar passages.* We look there in vain for the assertions that God "purified Mary from original sin." (Bandelli was not beyond an interpolation or two.) In the other two sermons invoked by Bandelli (vaguely and without citation: *"Idem dicit* in sermone Johannis Baptistae *et* Dominicae de Passione"—4729, P.I., c.8, p. 50), I have found the following sentence three times in the same words: "Beata Virgo non peperit carnem peccati sed peperit carnem in simulitudinem carnis peccati, quia *Ipse solus est sine peccato quia conceptus* est de Spiritu Sancto." (Horoy ed., t. 2, col. 201, 218 and 815) This statement gives us to understand that Honorius III (who was doubtless still Concius Sabellus) did not make Mary an exception to the universal law of original sin. It is not very likely that he ever envisaged such an exception, but this does not permit us to say that he denied the Immaculate Conception *directly and explicitly.* Hence he should be put in the first list (cf. note 82, above), with the popes who affirmed the universality of original sin without making an exception for Mary even though she was mentioned in the context.

2) Clement VI, while still Pierre Roger (sermon *Erunt signa in sole,* Ms latin 3293 Bib. Nationale de Paris, published by Alva, *Radii,* col. 689-692) expressed indeed the opinion that the Blessed Virgin "fuit *per modicam morulam in culpa* et postea semper in gratia." But this opinion remained *conditional:* "ex unione animae cum carne contrahitur peccatum originale, a quo beata Virgo, *si contraxit,* fuit statim sanctificata." See P. Doncoeur, in *Rev. hist. eccl.* 8 (1907) p. 714-715 and Francisco de Guimaraens in *Et. Francisc.* 4 (1953) p. 185. Cf. *DTC* 7, 1080-1081.

3)   Concerning Boniface IX, Bandelli (P. I, c. 18, p. 51), copied by several other authors (cited in Alva, *Radii,* 575) declares: "Idem tenet Bonifacius III in privilegio Visitationis," and he cites a text affirming the universal extension of original sin. He has in mind the privilege *Superna benignitas,* November 9, 1389 (*Bull. Coq.* 3b, p. 378). Numerous other *bullaria* are cited by B. Plazza, *Causa Immaculatae Conceptionis,* Coloniae, F. de Tournes, 1752, Act. 5, art. 1, XI, p. 387, note 1). We note at once that the pope concerned is Boniface *IX* (not Boniface *III* who lived in the seventh century!), and that the date is 1389 and not 1383, as Bandelli says. Finally, the latter is citing a corrupt text, in which Alva was able to point out (not without some ingenuity) over twenty errors in less than ten lines. The original text contains *nothing* which is even remotely opposed to the Immaculate Conception.

Sericoli is correct in mentioning the other four popes; but it will be useful to make his global references more precise and more complete, for the works he cites (Alva, *Radii,* 674-684; 686-709. Roskovany I, 190, 192, 203, 208, 216, Doncoeur, *op. cit.*) are not satisfactory on all counts. Here, as briefly as possible, are the basic data and studies:

1.   Innocent III, *sermo in Purif.* PL 217, 506C-506D ". . . in utero matris *animam ejus* (=Mariae) *ab originali peccato mundavit"; Serm. 28 de Ass.* 2: "Illa

stained by original sin," [88] yet took no account of these requests, in spite of the apparently strong position of the maculist opinion by reason of its almost unanimous acceptance among thirteenth century theologians.[89]

The main point to be noted about the papal decisions is that before Sixtus IV there was nothing, on a doctrinal plane, except an attitude of watchful waiting; thereafter, an involvement, at first quite discreet, begins to be observable. This takes place along three distinguishable lines which we will treat successively: first, a body of approbations and condemnations which involves the *magisterium* only indirectly; next, the great series of decisions concerned formally with the Conception; finally, the plans for the definition, and the definition itself.

(=Eva) fuit sine culpa producta sed produxit in culpa. Haec (=Maria) *fuit in culpa producta* sed sine culpa produxit." (See also *s. 16, ib.,* col. 531B) Cf. ALVA, *Radii,* 677-685.

2. INNOCENT V, while still Peter of Tarantasia, *In III Sentent.,* dist. 3, q. 1, art. 1 corps: Mary was "cito post animationem sanctificata," ed. Tolosae, apud Colomerium, 1652, p. 18a; cf. ad. 2, art. 2: "decuit ut Virgo habuerit quidem originale peccatum sed nunquam commiserit actuale" *ib.,* p. 19a. Cf. ALVA, *Radii* 704-709 and *DTC* 7, 1050.

3. JOHN XXII, Ms lat. 3290, Paris, Bib. Nle, *serm. in Nativ.,* fol. 28ra: "anima Beatae Virginis . . . fuit creata et infusa . . . sine originali justitia et sic originale (peccatum) eam dicimus contraxisse, sed statim post animae infusionem gratiam superveniens eam sanctificavit et ab originali purgavit" and *serm. in Ass.*: "B. Maria fuit in originali peccato concepta . . . Mundavit tamen eam Dei Filius et levavit eam de luto peccati originalis antequam nasceretur" (*ib.,* fol. 20rb) etc. The proof of the authenticity of these sermons has been established by Noël VALOIS, in *Histoire Littéraire de la France,* Paris, 34 (1914) 537-539. Cf. ALVA, *Radii* 2122-2124. P. DONCOEUR, in *Rev. hist. eccl.* 8 (1907) 706-707. *DTC* 8, 638. FRANCISCO DE GUIMARAENS, in *Et. Francisc.* 4 (1953) n. 11, pp. 184-185.

4. BENEDICT XII, while still Jean FOURNIER, *serm. de Concept.* Ms. lat. Vat. 4006, fol. 422r: "Inter illos autem qui per Christi gratiam mundati sunt a peccato in utero, excellentior fuit beata Virgo . . . quia non solum fuit mundata et purgata a peccato originali sed etiam fomes, id est concupiscentia . . . in ipsa fuit sopita et quasi exstincta." Cf. P. DONCOEUR, in *Rev. hist. eccl.* 8 (1907) 707-709 and FRANCISCO DE GUIMARAENS, in *Et. Francisco.* 4 (1953) p. 185.

[87] Pope John XXII's retraction is a noteworthy example. Cf. *DTC* II, 663-668.

[88] In 1455, the Master of the Sacred Palace, Jacques Gilles, O.P., addressed such a request to his compatriot of Aragon, Pope Calixtus III, composing to this effect a memorandum entitled, "Summa tractuum praescriptorum in duabus conclusionibus." The first of the "two conclusions" was expressed thus: "Quod Sedes Apostolica Beatam Virginem peccato originali sicut et caeteros fuisse obnoxiam debet confirmare." Cf. R. CREYTENS, "Les ecrits de Jacques Gilles, O.P.," in *Archivum Praedicatorum* 10 (1940) pp. 162-165.

[89] FRANCESCO DA LEIRE (=FRANCESCO DE GUIMARAENS) "La doctrine des theologiens sur l'Immaculée Conception de 1250 a 1350," in *Etudes Franciscaines* 3 (1952) 181-204 and 4 (1953) 23-52, 167-188. From this very careful inventory it can be seen that after the great immaculist development of the twelfth century, the pious belief lost ground in the whole theological world during the latter half of the thirteenth century. It was in the fourteenth century, with William of Ware and Duns Scotus, that the thesis of Eadmer, Osbert of Clare, and Nicholas of St. Alban's reappeared at the University and made its way there with lightning-like rapidity. Cf. chapter V of the present volume, pp. 165 ff., 188 ff., 202 ff.

EARLY APPROBATIONS AND CONDEMNATIONS INDI-
RECTLY RELATED TO THE IMMACULATE CONCEPTION

The mass of documents pertaining to the first series is abundant and complex. There are first of all, approbations given to offices, constitutions, and books which contain the immaculist doctrine. We must be careful not to exaggerate the import of such acts, which are in no wise definitive or irreformable.[90] Nevertheless when a doctrine is approved on numerous occasions, during several centuries, the papal decisions, taken all together, acquire a considerable weight.

With regard to the *offices*, it is to be noted that the earliest usage of the Roman Curia—prior to the adoption of the feast by Sixtus IV—did not correspond to any very precise design. The Office of the *Nativity* of Mary was simply taken over, with the word *Nativity* being changed wherever it occurred, to *Conception*.[91] All the same, this procedure gave the occasion for a positive doctrinal orientation; for since the Nativity of Mary had been called *dignissima* in the Antiphon for the *Magnificat,* and *Sancta* in the eighth response at Matins, the Conception took on the same properties:

Gloriosae Virginis Mariae NATIVITATEM DIGNISSIMAM recolamus.	Gloriosae Virginis Mariae CONCEPTIONEM DIGNISSIMAM recolamus.
Sentiant omnes tuum juvamen quicumque celebrant tuam SANCTAM NATIVITATEM.	Sentiant omnes tuum juvamen quicumque celebrant tuam SANCTAM CONCEPTIONEM.

The two Offices approved by Sixtus IV[92] were committted to the doctrine much more formally. That of Leonard Nogarolo, approved February 27, 1477,[93] was adopted by the Roman Church, and survives partially in our present Office (the Oration, most noteworthily, being

---

[90] Plácido de Tosantos, emissary sent by King Philip III of Spain to Pope Paul V, for the purpose of obtaining a definition of the Immaculate Conception (see note 141, below, addressed to His Holiness a memorandum entitled, "Utrum ex eo quod Ecclesia celebrat festum Conceptionis B.M.V., colligatur eam sine originali peccato conceptam fuisse." (Archivo de la Postulación S.J., *De Conceptione B.M.V. Vari Argumenti,* cited by I. IPARRAGUIRE in *Est. Ecl.* 28, 1954, 613) Tosantos proposed an affirmative reply; but this was not the mind of Paul V. Another emissary of the same Philip III, sent for the same purpose, received a reply from the Pope which he transmitted to the king in the following terms: "Su Santidad . . . replicó que en cuanto a las fiestas, la Santa Iglesia las proponía no como cosa de fé y necesaria para creer, sino para observarlos como cosa pía."

[91] *Breviarium . . . sec. usum curiae romanae,* Paris, Bib. Nle, ms lat. 1277, (fourteenth century) for. 323 (cited by P. DONCOEUR, in *Rev. d'hist. eccl.* 8, 1907, p. 700, note 4): ". . . omnia fiant ut in nativitate ejus mutato nomine nativitatis . . . in nomine Conceptionis."

[92] Cf. chapter IV of the present volume, p. 151.

[93] By Sixtus IV, in the Bull, *Cum praecelsa,* February 26, 1477 (*O.S.*: 1476). Critical edition by SERICOLI, pp. 153-154. There is a study of the Bull *ib.,* pp. 26-36.

The texts of the Mass and of the Office are given in ALVA, *Armam.* II, 55-70. On the spread of this office in the printed breviaries, see GRAVOIS II, 24-25.

retained). That of Bernardine De Bustis,[94] poorer in quality and less warmly approved,[95] never enjoyed wide diffusion.

Other immaculist Offices,[96] constitutions of religious orders or universities which had a special devotion to the Immaculate Conception, or which imposed on their members a vow to defend this doctrine,[97] various private revelations which expressed the doctrine [98]—these form the subject matter of other approbations.

Under the heading of approved books, the most important instance is that of the *Dottrina Breve,* published in 1597 by St. Robert Bellarmine in which Mary was declared "exempt from all sin, *original or actual.*"[99] This *opusculum* was warmly praised in a brief of Clement VIII, July 15, 1598. The Pope imposed it as the catechism to be used in all the dioceses of the Papal States, and expressed the desire that it be adopted universally. Benedict XIV repeated this wish on February 7, 1742. Between them, in a brief of February 22, 1633, Urban VIII had recommended the use of it in the missions of the Orient.[100] This little book, which owed its circulation to the papal authority, instilled into many generations, notably at Rome, the belief in the Immaculate Conception.

However, these approbations did not bear upon the Immaculate Conception itself except indirectly. The same holds for the condemnation of the errors of Baius, drawn up by Pius V,[101] promulgated by Gregory XIII in 1579,[102] and renewed by Urban VIII in 1641.[103] The seventy-third of the condemned propositions is expressed as follows:

[94] The text of this office was inserted into the *Mariale* of Bernardino de Bustis, between Part I and Part II (Lyon edition, A. du Ry, 1525, fol. 43b-50b) and reproduced in ALVA, *Armam.* II, 70-105, and *Acta Ordinis fratrum minorum* 23 (1904) 401-420. Cf. SERICOLI pp. 36-37.

[95] By Sixtus IV in the Brief *Libenter,* October 4, 1480 (critical edition by SERICOLI, p. 155; there is a study of the Brief *ib.,* pp. 36-40).

[96] This point would require a special monograph. One case has been examined above, notes 57-62.

[97] A list of constitutions in which the expression *Immaculata Conceptio* occurs is given by LAURENTIN, note 152. The expression of the same belief is found in other constitutions which do not use this term, for example, those of the Order of Mercy, approved by Alexander VIII, in the Brief *Ex injuncto,* December 7, 1691.

[98] The immaculists often made much of the approbation of the Revelations of St. Bridget which were favorable to the Immaculate Conception (*Revelationes sanctae Birgittae,* L.6, c.49 and 55, Romae, ap. L. Grignanum, t. 2, 1628, pp. 92 and 112), by Gregory XI (1370-1378) and Urban VI (1378-1379)—ALVA, *Milit.* 558. However, these revelations are not by that fact exempt from error (P. POURRAT, "Brigitte," in *Catholicisme* 2, 271-272).

[99] "nullius peccati macula nec originalis aut actualis nec mortalis aut venialis infecta fuit," cap. 5 (numerous editions). Cf. p. 248 of the present volume.

[100] The texts of these different approbations are given by GRAVOIS II, 57-63. Cf. *DTC* 2, 584-585 and *Catholicisme* 1, 1383-1385.

[101] *Ex omnibus afflictionibus,* October 1, 1567.

[102] *Provisionis nostrae,* January 29, 1579, *Bull. Coq.* 4c, p. 426a-429b. *Bull. Taur.* 8, 318b-319a. Cf. DENZINGER 1073, 73rd proposition.

[103] *In eminenti Ecclesiae,* March 6, 1641, *Bull. Coq.* 6b, p. 272a. *Bull. Taur.* 15, 97ab.

No one but Christ is without original sin; therefore the Blessed Virgin died by reason of sin contracted from Adam, and all of her afflictions in this life, just as in the case of the other just, were penalties for sin, original or actual (*ib.*).

It is difficult to say what exactly is condemned in so complex a proposition. It could not be maintained that the maculist opinion, held at that time by so many authors, was the object of the condemnation, inasmuch as certain of the propositions listed could be held "in a certain sense."[104] Hence nothing precise can be derived from this measure.

BULLS CONCERNED WITH THE CONCEPTION ITSELF

We come now to the series of documents which have Mary's Conception as their direct object. They are disciplinary decrees, in which a doctrinal orientation favorable to the Immaculate Conception becomes more and more pronounced.

First on the list, and quite dominating it, are the two bulls *Grave nimis* issued by Sixtus IV in 1482 and 1483. They were occasioned by the campaign of the influential Bandelli, then provincial of the Lombardy Dominicans, against the immaculist thesis, at a time when this thesis was drawing new strength from the liturgical decrees (discussed above) of this Franciscan pope. In writing and by word of mouth, Bandelli violently condemned the pious belief:

Unheard-of wickedness! Detestable crime! Foolish minds! Blind hearts! Evil madness! [105]

As such declarations, propagated by many preachers, were a source of disturbance to souls, the Pope condemned the condemners of the pious belief. He censured the two following assertions as "false, erroneous and alien to the truth":

The Roman Church celebrates the feast merely of the spiritual conception and sanctification, of the Virgin.

Those who believe that the Mother of God was preserved from the stain of original sin in her conception are guilty of heresy . . .[106]

---

[104] *Ibid.* (DENZINGER 1080).

[105] "O scelus inauditum! O facinus detestandum! O stultas mentes! O pectora caeca! O deliramenta nequitiae!" BANDELLI, *Praefatio*, p. 3. For further texts and details, cf. chapter VI of the present volume, pp. 234-238, and especially notes 131 and 139.

[106] Bull *Grave nimis* prior, 1482; critical text edited by SERICOLI, pp. 155-157: ". . . Assertiones praedicatorum . . . qui affirmare praesumerent . . . Romanam Ecclesiam de spirituali dumtaxat Conceptione et sanctificatione ejusdem Virginis gloriosae festum celebrare, et eos qui crederent et tenerent eamdem Dei Genitricem ab originalis peccati macula in sua Conceptione praeservatam fuisse, propterea alicuius haeresis labe pollutos fore, utpote falsas et erroneas et a veritate alienas . . . auctoritate apostolica . . . reprobamus et damnamus." (P. 157, lines 29-38)

He pronounced an excommunication reserved personally to the Holy
See agains the fomenters of such assertions. But he subjected

> to the same condemnation . . . those who should have the presumption
> to declare . . . heretical [the belief] that the Virgin . . . had not been
> preserved from original sin.[107]

In brief, it was forbidden to call either opinion, maculist or immaculist,
heretical. The decree appears to be above all a disciplinary measure,
intended to establish peace in a matter not defined.

The activity of Bandelli was thereby brought to a halt in Lombardy;
but the attacks launched in this province against the Immaculate Conception had already spread much further. Hence, on September 4, 1483, the
Pope promulgated the second Bull *Grave nimis,* which extended the decision
of the first to the whole Church.[108] Besides this universal extension, the
following modifications were introduced into the text: 1) The condemnation of the first proposition (according to which Mary's sanctification was
the object of the feast) disappeared. 2) Not only was it forbidden to call
either of the two opinions heretical, it was also prohibited to accuse their
defenders of *grave sin.*[109] 3) Absolution is no longer reserved personally
to the Pope (this is explained by the extension of the measure to the whole
Church at a time when the means of communication were slow and
uncertain). 4) Finally, a new clause is added, declaring that the question
"has not yet been decided by the Roman Church and the Apostolic See."[110]
In brief, in extending the measure to the universal Church, the Pope
situates it more clearly on the level of discipline: he no longer commits
himself directly concerning the object of the Roman feast, and he makes
it clear that the question remains open.[111]

What is the doctrinal import of this act? According to the maculists, it
placed the two opinions on an equal footing, whereas the immaculists saw
in it a kind of definition of their thesis. The truth is more complex than
either of these positions. On the disciplinary level, strict equality is maintained between the *prohibitions* and the *penalties* inflicted on both parties.
However, the circumstances make it clear that the measure was enacted
to protect the doctrine of the Immaculate Conception against attack; and,
from a different point of view, the preambles of the document suggest a

---

[107] *Ib.,* pp. 157-158, lines 54-57: "Pari damnationi et censurae subjicientes illos
qui praedicare . . . praesumerent haereticum fore eamdem Virginem gloriosam a
peccati originalis macula praeservatam non fuisse."

[108] Critcal edition by SERICOLI, pp. 158-161.

[109] "Alicujus haeresis labe pollutos" (note 106, above) becomes: "*mortaliter peccare* vel esse haereticos." SERICOLI, p. 159, lines 17-18.

[110] "Cum nondum sit a Romana Ecclesia et Apostolica Sede decisum." *Ib.,* p.
160, 52-53.

[111] SERICOLI, pp. 92-94, with some ingenuity, has gotten around the reduced
commitment characteristic of the second bull.

solidarity of the Holy See with the pious belief. It is by reason of the fact that the Roman Church celebrates the feast publicly and has established a special Office for it,[112] "that it is forbidden to call the immaculist opinion (expressed in that Office) heretical, whereas it is merely because "the question has not yet been decided by the Roman Church," that the other opinion may not be called heretical.

With all this, the conflicts did not cease, and later popes often had to recall, reinforce and add further determinations to the decisions of the second Bull *Grave nimis*. On March 1, 1502, Alexander VI cited it in full and urged that it be applied.[113] On August 7, 1570, Pius V made it more severe, prohibiting all discussion of the question:

> Let no one dare to find fault, whether openly or secretly, with those who do not think as he does . . . but let him either keep silence altogether (and this would be better and safer) or . . . let him expound his own opinion with due moderation and without attacking the contrary opinion.[114]

Bishops are required, under penalty of suspension *latae sententiae*, to imprison transgressors, and keep them in custody until the Holy See, to which the cases must be referred, decides upon the penalty to be inflicted (§3).

Three and a half months later, on November 30, 1570, in the Bull *Super Speculum*, all of these prohibitions (which, because of their absolute character, had been difficult to apply) received a form that was more restricted, but was juridically more precise, and therefore more efficacious. The prohibition of disputes is restricted to popular gatherings and vernacular writings.[115]

---

[112] "Cum sancta Romana Ecclesia de intemeratae semperque Virginis Conceptione publice festum solemniter celebret et speciale ac proprium super hoc officium ordinaverit."—*Grave nimis* posterior, SERICOLI, p. 159, 10-12.

[113] Bull *Illius qui se pro Dominici gregis salvatione*, March 1, 1502, given in ALVA, *Armam*. II, 118-122; *Radii* 1661; ROSKOVANY I. 133, n. 191; *DTC* 7, 1164.

According to GRAVOIS I, 78, n. 82 (BOURASSE 7, 340) Leo X likewise renewed the Constitutions of Sixtus IV by the Bull *Sacrosanctae*, August 18, 1515, in which he instituted the feast in Poland.

[114] ". . . Interdicimus et prohibimus ne quis post hac vel in concionibus ad populum, vel in publicis aut privatis disputationibus, vel quovis alio modo quaestionem hanc tractando, verbum ullum adversus eas constitutiones facere, nec rationis argumenta auctoritatisve . . . confirmandi refellendive causa proferre, neve aliquem a se dissentientem palam vel occulte reprehendere . . . audeat . . . sed hac de re omnino sileat, id quod sane rectius ac tutius fuerit, aut . . . quod sibi probabilius videbitur, ea quae decet modestia, exponat, CONTRARIAM NON IMPROBANDO SENTENTIAM." *Bull. Coq.* 4c, 120-121. *Bull. Taur.* 7, 845-846. ROSKOVANY I, 141-142.

[115] "Mandamus quatenus nemo . . . in popularibus concionibus . . . de hujus controversiae alterutra parte disputare vel vulgari sermone scribere praesumat," *Super Speculam*, No. 2, *Bull. Coq.* 4 c, 138-139, *Bull. Taur.*, 8, 872. Cf. BOURASSE, 7, 73. ROSKOVANY I, 145-146, n. 207; *DTC* 7, 1171; *Ami du Clergé* 32 (1910) 101.

In academic discussions . . . and where there is no occasion of scandal, learned men may argue the question . . . so long as neither side is declared to be erroneous.[116]

Sixtus IV's measures for peace are thus strengthened: it is forbidden to make the accusation, not only of heresy or sin, but even of error, against either side. However, on the disciplinary level, the two parties remain equally balanced, and on the theological level there is no progress.

Pius V confirmed the Bull of Sixtus IV without restriction. He did not, it is true,[117] repeat explicitly those considerations in the Bull in which we have noted a certain immaculist tendency; but it was merely because their implicit and indecisive character gave rise to every possible discussion, that he, the man of government, omitted them, so as to render his decisions as efficacious as possible.

In spite of the pontifical measures, the disputes kept up. On July 6, 1616, in the Constitution *Regis Pacifici*, Paul V had to recall the earlier prohibitions, and increase the penalties provided for.[118] The next year— an embassy sent from Spain by Philip III had meanwhile intervened[119]— the Pope took a step forward. On September 12, 1617, he prescribed that:

Hereafter, until the matter . . . is defined by the Holy See, or until a different directive is given, no one is to affirm . . . in *public acts* of whatever sort, that the Blessed Virgin was conceived with original sin.[120]

It was also forbidden, under the same penalties, to attack the maculist opinion. Nevertheless, the balance between the adversaries, maintained until this time on the disciplinary level, was now destroyed, since the one side could express itself publicly, while the other could not. The maculists could indeed point out that the Pope had declared in the same decree that

[116] "Liceat viris doctis in publicis academiae disputationibus, sive generalium aut provincialium capitulorum, vel ubi alias intersunt qui rem capere possunt nec scandali ulla subest occasio de illa quaestione disserere et argumentis utramlibet partem asserere vel impugnare dum neutra veluti erronea praedicentur." *Ib.*, No. 3.

[117] "Pius V aliquatenus certe *obscurasse* visus est objectum festi a Xysto determinatum." (SERICOLI, p. 145; cf. p. 146: "Obscurans objectum festi"; and in *Antonianum* 29, 1954, p. 386). *Obscurasse* appears to me to be too strong a term to apply to Pius V, as does *determinatum* also for Sixtus IV (although I in no wise intend to qualify what I said of the great merits of this book in reviewing it in *Vie Spirituelle* 89, 1953, 286-288).

[118] Cf. ALVA, *Armam.* II, 174a-179b. BOURASSE 7, 200-204. ROSKOVANY II, pp. 2-5, n. 356.

[119] On the history of this legation, see the studies of L. FRIAS and of I. IPARRAGUIRE cited below, note 141.

[120] "Ut in posterum, donec articulus . . . fuerit definitus . . . non audeant IN PUBLICIS concionibus, lectionibus, conclusionibus et aliis quibuscumque ACTIBUS asserere quod eadem B. Virgo fuerit concepta cum peccato originali." Constit. *Sanctissimus*, September 12, 1617, No. 2, *Bull. Coq.* V, 4, pp. 234-235. *Bull Taur.* 12, 396b-397b. Cf. ALVA, *Armam.* II, 180-182. BOURASSE 7, 209. ROSKOVANY II, p. 5, n. 214.

he ". . . did not intend to condemn (their) opinion or in any way prejudice it, but to leave it in its present status." [121]   They could use the second part of the Decree [122] as a powerful weapon against their adversaries, for it is indeed difficult to affirm one opinion without in some way denying the other.   But their thesis, henceforth deprived of any possibility of public diffusion, was condemned to a slow but sure death.

Upon this success, Philip III dispatched to Rome a new embassy (1618-1620) in an attempt to obtain the ultimate decision.[123]   His delegation pointed out that the half-measure of 1617 had in no wise restored peace—which was true—and that the only way to put an end to the matter was to define the Immaculate Conception.   Paul V resisted until his death the assaults of the tireless ambassador,[124] who continued his lengthy discourses with the new Pope, Gregory XV.   On May 24, 1622, the latter took a new step forward.   He extended to *private acts* (oral or written) the prohibition against expounding the maculist thesis.[125]   Like his predecessor, he added that he did not intend to condemn or prejudice this opinion;[126] but this time, deprived of every possibility of expression, the latter was really doomed.   The Dominicans, however, obtained, on July 28, a final concession—that of being permitted "to discuss this question freely among themselves, in private discussions and conferences, but not with others." [127]

An important development occurred in the pontificate of Alexander VII (1655-1667).   In 1655, Philip IV of Spain, aware of the new Pope's predilection for the pious belief, dispatched to him an ambassador who

---

[121] ". . . Sanctitas Sua non intendit reprobare alteram opinionem nec ei ullum prorsus praejudicium inferre, eam relinquens in eisdem statu et terminis in quibus de praesenti reperitur."—No. 4.

[122] No. 5 gives the following prescription for the immaculists, under the same penalties: "aliam opinionem *non impugnent,* nec de ea aliquo modo agant seu tractent." (*Ib.*)

[123] The references are given below in notes 141, 142.

[124] For another incident involving the pontificate of Pope Paul V, see chapter VI of the present volume, at note 171.

[125] "Hoc suo presente decreto . . . extendit et ampliavit etiam ad privata colloquia et scripta mandans et praecipiens omnibus ne de caetero . . . neque etiam in sermonibus et scriptis privatis audeant asserere quod eadem B. Virgo fuerit concepta cum peccato originali nec de hac *opinione affirmativa* [see above, note 37] aliquo modo gerere seu tractare, exceptis tamen quibus a Sancta Sede Apostolica fuerit specialiter indultum." Bull *Sanctissimus,* May 24, 1622, No. 2. *Bull Coq.* 5f, pp. 45-46. *Bull. Taur.* 12, 688a-690a. Cf. ALVA, *Armam.* II, 183-187. BOURASSE 7, 1172-1173. ROSKOVANY II, 348-349, n. 254. *Bullar. Ordinis praed.* 6, 13-14, etc. Cf. *DTC* 7, 1172-1173.

[126] *Ib.* The terms are exactly those of Paul V, cited above, note 121.

[127] "Ut in privatis eorum colloquiis seu conferentiis inter se dumtaxat, et non inter alios aut cum aliis, de materia . . . Conceptionis B.M. Virginis disserere et tractare absque ullo poenarum . . . incursu libere et licite possint et valeant . . . concedimus et impartimur." *Eximii,* July 28, 1622. *Bull. Coq.* 5e, p. 46. *Bull. Taur.* 12, 717. Cf. BOURASSE 7, 222-224. ROSKOVANY II, 350, n. 255.

made much of the fact that the papal decrees had remained ineffectual:
attacks on the immaculist opinion, although more sly, were not less ener-
getic than before.   Alexander then issued the Bull *Sollicitudo,* of December
8, 1661,[128] in which he recalled and strengthened the prescriptions of Sixtus
IV, Paul V and Gregory XV.   Above all, instead of favoring the immaculist
doctrine as his predecessors had done, merely by the slant of his disciplinary
measures, he took up the doctrinal orientations insinuated by Sixtus IV and
carried them still further.   In terms which Pius IX would use again in
1854, Alexander praised the antiquity of the pious belief that:

> By a special grace and privilege of God, and in view of the merits of
> Jesus Christ, . . . Redeemer of the human race, [Mary's] soul was
> preserved from the stain of original sin, in the first instant of its creation
> and infusion into her body.[129]

The Pope proceeds to declare that this doctrine represents the sentiment
of the Church at Rome, where it is in the tranquil possession of the faithful; [130] then, using his pontifical authority to determine the profound meaning of the decrees of this three predecessors, he declares that they had been
issued:

> . . . *in favor* of the thesis which affirms that the soul of the Most Blessed
> Virgin was, in its creation and infusion into her body, endowed with
> the grace of the Holy Spirit and preserved from original sin.[131]

"Careful to preserve in the flock of Christ the unity of the Spirit in the
bond of peace, and to allay all rancor and quarrels," [132] the Pope further
tightens the restrictions imposed by his predecessors: he forbids any attack
on the belief favored by the Holy See, upon any pretext (examination of
definability, interpretation of Scripture or the Fathers) or in any way (in
writing or orally) whatsoever; and he adds to the penalties already
decreed.[133]

---

[128] *Bull. Coq.* 6e, pp. 182-184. *Bull. Taur.* 16, 738-742. Bourasse 7, 251-255.
Roskovany II, pp. 381-384, n. 281. Cf. *DTC* 7, 1174-1175. This decree gave rise
to an abundant literature. See Roskovany, t. 3, n. 6195, 6436, 6451, 6460, 6461,
6467, 6469, 6474, 7857, 7865, 7872, 7877, 7890, 8387, 8389, 9194 (e), 9834, 9835,
9837, 9849, 9850, 9855, 9862, 9863, 9867, 9869, 9898. Roskovany's references call,
in many places, for correction and supplementation—for which, however, there is
not space enough here.

[129] No. 1, *Bull. Taur.* 16, 739. The Latin text is given below, in note 171.

[130] The Pope reproved the adversaries pointed out by Philip IV, who "Ecclesiam
Romanam huic sententiae . . . favere negant, pios Christi fideles a sua pacifica quasi
possessione deturbare conando . . ." 3, *Bull. Taur.* 16, 740a.

[131] "Constitutiones et decreta . . . a Romanis Pontificibus . . . et praecipue a
Sixto IV, Paulo V, et Gregorio XV edita *in favorem sententiae asserentis animam
beatae Virginis* in sui creatione et in corpus infusione . . . *a peccato originale praeservatam fuisse* . . . innovamus." 4, *Bull. Taur.* 16, 740b.

[132] No. 3, *ib.,* p. 740a.

[133] No. 5, *ib.,* p. 741a.

Nevertheless, this doctrinal commitment is not equivalent to a definition:

> In accordance with the Constitution of Sixtus IV, we forbid anyone to affirm that, in consequence of this [decree], those who hold the contrary opinion—namely, that the glorious Virgin Mary was conceived with original sin—are guilty of heresy or of mortal sin; for the Roman Church and the Apostolic See have not yet decided about this, and we ourselves do not wish or intend to decide it now.[134]

Transgressors of this prohibition, said the Pope, will be subject to "even graver penalties" than had been inflicted by Sixtus IV and his successors.

EARLY ATTEMPTS TO OBTAIN A DEFINITION.

Nearly two centuries were yet to pass before the definition for which this last measure paved the way was actually realized by Pius IX. But before examining the work of the latter, we must retrace our steps a little to note the previous attempts that had been made to obtain a definition.[135]

We need not go into the definition made by the Council of Basel (September 17, 1439), which, although formal, was made at a time when the Council was in schism with the Holy See.[136] Its action is of interest merely as evidence of the strength that had already been gained by the 'pious belief' since the profound crisis of the thirteenth century.[137]

---

[134] No. 6, *ib.*, "Vetamus autem, Sixti IV Constitutionibus inhaerentes, quempiam asserere quod propter hoc contrariam opinionem tenentes—videlicet gloriosam Virginem Mariam cum originali peccato fuisse conceptam—haeresis crimen aut mortale peccatum incurrant cum a Romana Ecclesia et ab Apostolica Sede nondum fuerit decisum, prout nos nunc minime decidere volumus, aut intendimus." The terms employed are copied from Sixtus IV, as cited above, notes 109, 110. But Alexander does not repeat the clause of Paul V and Gregory XV: "Sanctitas Sua non intendit reprobare hanc opinionem (the maculist opinion) nec ei ullum praejudicium inferre." (supra, notes 121 and 126).

[135] In this matter also there are some imaginary documents that must be set aside. Chief among them is one which many seventeenth century writers never failed to bring up—an explicit definition, made by the twelve apostles, in plenary council: "Concilium Hierosolymis habitum de Apostolis Christi Domini haec pro Immaculata Virginis Conceptione decrevit: *Illa Virgo, illa Maria, illa praeservata fuit a peccato originali in primo instanti suae conceptionis et libera ab omni culpa, et qui ita non senserit non consequetur vitam aeternam.* Ita in libris plumbeis S. Montis Granatensis in Curia Romana existentibus a F. Bartholomaeo Pectorato latine traductis." ALVA, *Milit.*, p. 296. Cf. J. A. VELASQUEZ, S.J., *De Maria Immaculata Concepta*, Lugduni, Anisson, 1653, Lib. IV, Diss. I, adn. I, p. 309, etc.

According to ALVA, the antipope Clement VII (1378-1394) and Pope Innocent VII (1404-1406) condemned the maculist thesis of John Montson (*Milit.* pp. 294 and 696; cf. the observations of P. DONCOEUR, "La condamnation de Jean de Monzon," in *Rev. des quest. hist.* 82, 1907, 176-187). Also according to ALVA, Alexander V (1409-1410): "determinavit controversiam circa mysterium Conceptionis quod fuit verum." (*Milit.* 31, citing with some hesitation Daniel AGRICOLA, *Corona Doctorum* fol. 176. Cf. the observations of SERICOLI, pp. 19-21.)

[136] Cf. chapter VI of the present volume, pp. 228-234.

[137] Cf. chapter VI of the present volume, pp. 232-234, and H. AMERI, O.F.M., *Doctrina theologorum de Immaculata B.V. Mariae Conceptione tempore Concilii*

Between 1512 and 1517, Leo X was occupied with the question, with a view to making a definition at the Council of the Lateran. But the opposition of Cajetan, appointed to examine the matter, put a stop to the undertaking.[138]

In 1546, at the Council of Trent, the problem of the Immaculate Conception was raised in connection with the decrees on original sin, and gave rise to a lively discussion. The Council arrived, not without difficulty, at a compromise which set aside the case of the Blessed Virgin without deciding anything about it:

> This holy Council declares that it does not intend to include in this decree on original sin, the Blessed and Immaculate Virgin Mary, Mother of God; but that the constitutions of Pope Sixtus IV . . . are to be observed, under the penalties contained in those constitutions, which [the present Council] renews.[139]

If we look back, in the perspective adopted by Pius IX, who considers each step in view of the term towards which the Holy Spirit was orienting it, we can say that, by implication, this decree favors the Immaculate Conception;[140] but in the minds of those who drew it up (especially those who were of the opposition), the formula was neutral.

In the course of the seventeenth century, numerous authorities, both lay and religious, put pressure on the Holy See to obtain a definition. Notwithstanding these repeated assaults, despite the power of the King of Spain and the ardor of his ambassadors, the popes opposed a firm negative to all demands for a final decision.[141]

Basilensis, Roma, Academia Mariana, 1954. His principal conclusion is summed up as follows: "Quo tempore decretum suum emisit Concilium Basilense jam non erat legitimum. Attamen ejus decretum, licet omni canonica et juridica auctoritate carens, magnum momentum habet ut monumentum . . . moraliter universalis piae fidei de glorioso Virginis privilegia." Cf. also Sericoli, pp. 21-23.

[138] Cf. chapter VI of the present volume, p. 260 f.

[139] "Declarat tamen haec ipsa sancta Synodus, non esse suae intentionis, comprehendere in hoc decreto, ubi de peccato originali agitur, beatam et immaculatam Virginem Mariam Dei genitricem . . ." Session V, *Decretum de peccato originali,* No. 6. Mansi, t. 33, col. 39. Denzinger 792. On this text, as well as that of Sess. VI, Canon 23 (Mansi, t. 33, col. 42; Denzinger 833), see the monographs of M. Tognetti, O.S.M., "L'Immacolata al Concilio Tridentino," in *Marianum* 15 (1953) pp. 304-374 and 555-586, and of J. Sagues, "Trento y la Inmaculada. Natura del dogma mariano," in *Est. ecl.* 28 (1954) 323-368.

[140] *APN* 1a, p. 606.

[141] Concerning the Spanish King's first delegation, the initiative for which originated in Seville, and which was directed by Plácido de Tosantos, former general of the Benedictine Order, see the monograph of L. Frias, "Felipe III y la Inmaculada Concepción," in *Razon y Fé* 10 (1904) 145-46; 293-308; 11 (1905) 180-198; 12 (1906) 322-336; 13 (1907) 62-75. This work has been judiciously summarized and supplemented by I. Iparraguire, "Pareceres encontrados sobre la definibilidad de la Inmaculada en el Siglo XVII," in *Est. Ecl.* 28 (1954) 611-612.

The second delegation (1618-1622) was at work during the reigns of Philip III and Philip IV, and during the pontificates of Paul V and Gregory XV. Its *acts*

We will cite only the answer of Paul V in the first audience which he gave to the Spanish ambassador, December 23, 1618:

> This is a difficult question, and at present I am not inspired by God or directed by my conscience to do anything more than what I have already prescribed.[142]

Gregory XV, faced with similar demands, used similar language in replying to a Spanish princess:

> The Holy Spirit, although besought by the most constant prayers, has not yet opened to His Church the secrets of this mystery . . .[143]

According to a document produced by Gravois, it was unanimously decided (*firmatum*), at a general meeting of the Holy Office on January 28, 1627, during the pontificate of Urban VIII, in favor of the opinion affirming the Immaculate Conception. The same body is also said to have agreed that the predecessors of Urban VIII had already gone so far that there was no other possibility except to define the question or to do

---

(consisting essentially of twelve long discourses of the legate, together with the reports which he sent to the King after each audience) have been printed by L. WADDING, ΠΡΕΣΒΕΙΑ *sive Legatio Philippi III et IV catholicum regum Hispaniarum ad SS. DD. NN. Paulum PP. V et Gregorium XV de definienda controversia Immaculatae Conceptionis B.V.M. per Illustriss. et Reverendiss. Dom. D. Fr. Antonium a Trejo ep. Carthaginensium Regium consiliarium et oratorem ex ordine minorum continens exactissime omnia in hac materia desiranda ac consideranda qua theologica historica,* Lovanii, ex officiana Henrici Hasterii, 1624. The popes' replies at the first nine audiences as summarized by the ambassador from his own point of view, are also given there, and have been reprinted in ROSKOVANY II, nn. 230, 234, 236-242.

[142] "S. Pater audivit et magnopere se laudare et aestimare respondit Vestrae Mai. pietatem, attamen difficilem videri rem hanc quam postulat nec aliud modo sibi a Deo inspirari nec a conscientia dictari praeter illud quod ante praeceperat . . ." WADDING, pp. 40-41. ROSKOVANY II, 18-20, n. 230.

At the end of the Spanish mission, soon after April, 1620, the Pope added: "Sibi displicere non posse se in his quae proposita sunt regiis votis et pietati adesse . . . verumtamen quod postulabatur ex illorum genere non esse quae diligentia humana clauduntur vel quae ob necessitatem aut mundanas instantias, aut Regum potentias liceat illico concedi; donec Spiritus ex alto infuderit quid in controversia gravi et duiturna graviter et mature debeat deliberari . . ." WADDING, p. 424. ROSKOVANY II, 345, n. 256.

[143] *Epist. ad monialem Regis catholici amitam,* 4 Junii 1622. The text is given in ROSKOVANY II, 351, n. 256.

In the Brief *Dilecti,* addressed to Philip IV of Spain, June 4, 1622, the Pope declares: "Spiritus Sancti enim voci auscultare, non humanarum rationum ponderibus, rem examinare debemus, qui in divinae Sapientiae Cathedra Christiano orbi a Deo praefecti sumus. Quare cum nondum aeterna Sapientia Ecclesiae suae tanti mysterii penetralia patefecerit in Dei Romanorumque Pontificum autoritate, debent fideles populi conquiescere."—H. MARRACCI, *Pontifices mariani,* Roma 1642, c. 94, p. 232. Ed. BOURASSE 10, 750-751.

The same Pope wrote to the King of Poland in 1624: "Nondum enim Spiritus Sancti lux pontificiae menti affulget, coeleste hoc arcanum hominibus detegens." ROSKOVANY II, 361, n. 266, citing THEINER, *Vetera monumenta Poloniae et Lithuaniae,* Romae, 1863, III, 373.

something equivalent to a definition.[144] Gravois' document is highly suspect.[145] This is probably one more case of a big story being built out of scanty facts by the zeal of a document-hunter; perhaps a private conversation among some immaculist inquisitors was at the bottom of it.

The popes do not seem to have made any plans for a definition during the seventeenth century, when the opposition between maculists and immaculists reached its highest pitch. In this atmosphere of strife and confusion the question was not yet ripe.

In the eighteenth century peace returned. The decrees of Alexander VII won a steadily increasing number of adherents to the immaculist thesis. The popes gave discreet approval to this trend, but none of them seems to have thought seriously of making a definition, despite a number of proposals, the most important of which was that of St. Leonard of Port Maurice.[146] There is extant a plan for a bull, submitted to Benedict XIV in 1742 by André Budrioli, S.J. We cannot believe (although there are those who do) that this pontiff, a man of great ponderation, took very seriously the project which the learned and ardent religious presented to him with a naivete of which the latter's own account has left us an undeniable image.[147] Pope Benedict's own position is more surely attested in his personal writings, in which, prior to his pontificate, he enunciated three affirmations about which he never seems to have altered his views: the Apostolic See manifests a unanimous inclination in favor of the Immaculate Conception; he, personally, is attached heart and soul to this opinion, which is confirmed by the "common sense, as it were, of the faithful"; but it is not yet a certitude of faith.[148]

At the beginning of the nineteenth century, the campaign of petitions

[144] GRAVOIS II, 63, n. 25, repeated by ROSKOVANY II, 362, n. 268. A more complete text is given in *Arch. Post.* [4]—Cf. *DTC* 7, 1174.

[145] SERICOLI (article cited in note 3), in *Anton.* 29 (1954) p. 396, calls this document "mirum et curiosum"; an examination of the sources leads us to add: *dubium.* On a similar document attributed to the pontificate of Paul V, August 28, 1617, cf. L. FRIAS "Felipe III," in *Razón y Fé*, 10, 1904, p. 304.

[146] Cf. *DTC* 7, 1186-1187. See above all the famous letter 66 (in the Italian edition, 26) at the end of tome I of his *Oeuvres complètes*, Paris, Casterman, 1858. The saint recounts his appeals to Clement XII (p. 584), and Benedict XIV (p. 584).

[147] BUDRIOLI's account and his draft of a bull are printed in A. BALLERINI, *Silloge*, Rome, t. 2 (1856), p. 835; SARDI II, 1-22, and ROSKOVANY II, 453-461, n. 444-445. On the work of A. Budrioli, see the *anonymous* article of P. TACCHI VENTURI, S.J., "Per la storia del domma dell'Immacolata Concezione ai tempi di Benedetto XIV," in *Civiltà Cattolica*, 1905, vol. 4, pp. 513-527. See also A. BUDRIOLI, *Della Papal Capella per le festa della Immacolata Concezione*, Padova, Stamperia del Seminario, 1752 (Rome, Bib. Nazionale 32. 8. H 4/1), and the entry *Arch. post.* in our table of abbreviations, p. 322, below.

[148] The two works in which P. LAMBERTINI, the future Benedict XIV, treats the question, are the following: 1. *De servorum Dei beatificatione et beatorum canonisatione* (1st ed., Bononiae 1734-1738) Lib. 1, c. 42, n. 14, in *Benedicti XIV opera omnia*, Prati, Aldina, t. 1 (1839) p. 308, and Lib. 3, c. 19, n. 12-17, t. 3 (1841) pp. 193-195 (on the "*votum sanguinarium*"). 2. *De festis B.M.V. signanter de festo Conceptionis* (1st ed., in Italian, Bononiae, 1740), No. 186-188, 200, 208-210. No.

began again with new strength, emanating no longer from princes or from states (which latter were becoming more and more laicized), but from bishops and religious orders.

The three immediate predecessors of Pius IX favored this movement. They did not feel that the ground was ready for the final step,[149] but they prepared for it effectively by introducing immaculist formulas into Christian prayer and into the liturgy, thus cutting off the roots of whatever opposition was still alive. In this connection, the introduction into the Dominican Preface of the formula, *et te in Immaculata Conceptione*—the circumstances of which have been reported above[150]—was an important episode.

PREPARATION OF THE DEFINITION

It was Pius IX who was to take the decisive step.

First act, 1847: In a series of coverging measures, the new Pope openly encouraged the doctrine of the Immaculate Conception. On the one hand, by confirming a rescript of the Congregation of Rites, he cut the Gordian knot proposed to Alexander VII (1655-1667) by Alva y Astorga: of those who affirm that the Virgin is without stain and those who affirm that the doctrine of St. Thomas is without error (even where he says that Mary was conceived in original sin) which are right?[151] Alexander had not responded to this summons. Leo XII (1823-1829) may have taken a step in this direction, for he is said to have declared that those who had vowed to defend the doctrine of St. Thomas might, without fear of perjury, defend the Immaculate Conception.[152] In any case, on July 17, 1847, Pius IX approved a rescript of the Congregation of Rites in which the two following points were made: 1) The vow does not authorize the omission of the word *Immaculata* added to the Preface. 2) "Insofar as there be need, his Holiness is to be consulted for a release [from the vow]."[153]

---

210 is the "declaratio auctoris in hac controversia": "Toto nos animo Immaculatae Conceptionis B. Mariae sequi sententiam, Ecclesiae Sedisque Apostolicae *propensionem* in eam sententiam demisse venerari . . ." etc.—*Opera omnia*, Lib. 2, c. 16, n. 25, tome 9 (1843), p. 311 (reproduced in ROSKOVANY II, 444-449, n. 439).

[149] See Gregory XVI's declaration to Msgr. Clement Villecourt, Bishop of La Rochelle in 1843, in ROSKOVANY 4, 706. Cf. *DTC* 7, 1193.

[150] See note 76, above.

[151] ALVA, *Nodus* (cf. table of abbreviations). This book touched off so violent a controversy that it was put on the Index along with all those that attacked it, in a measure that was purely disciplinary. It was withdrawn from the Index in the revision of Leo XIII (see note 48 above).

[152] This decision is attested without reference in an otherwise well-documented *votum* of the Bishop of San Marco and Bisignano (Italy): "Leo XII an. 1824 declaravit eos qui jurejurando se obstrinxerint ad tuendam S. Thomae doctrinam posse sine periurii timore Immaculatam B.M.V. Conceptionem defendere." (*Pareri*, t. 7, appendix, p. LXLVII, note)

[153] ". . . et quatenus opus sit consulendum Sanctissimo pro absolutione." The text of this response is given in GARDELLINI 4, 114-116 (but is incorrectly dated 1846, for the decree is confirmed by Pius IX). J. PERRONE, *De Immaculato B. V. Conceptu*, Appendix II, ed. Avenioni, 1848, p. 392. BOURASSE 7, 626.

On October 28 of that same year, the Pope congratulated the Jesuit, J. Perrone upon his book, *De Immaculato B. V. Conceptu,* the design of which is clearly summarized in the subtitle: *An dogmatico decreto definiri possit?* [154]

Second Act: Inquiry and consultations. On June 1, 1848 the Pope proposed the question of definition to twenty theologians; seventeen favored it. Meanwhile, the Pope had to leave Rome for Gaeta, where he continued the inquiry. A preliminary congregation was set up on December 6, 1848.[155] Two questions were proposed: *should we define,* and *how?* The first question was answered affirmatively; as for the second, a recommendation was made that the Bishops of the Universal Church be consulted. For this purpose Pius IX issued the Encyclical *Ubi Primum* from Gaeta, on February 2, 1849.[156] Of 603 Bishops consulted, 546 favored definition; 56 or 57 opposed it for various reasons; only four or five opposed *definability;* 24 were undecided on the question of opportuneness; about ten desired an indirect definition, without condemnation of the contrary opinion as heretical. A final group would make no judgment. The Pope, now back in Rome, ordered the publication of the *Opinions of the Bishops,*[157] and proceeded to take further consultations. On September 20, 1850, three theologians were invited to give their views. One of them, Monsignor Tizzani, Bishop of Terni, was opposed to the definition; the others favored it. On July 28, 1851, the Pope named three new consultants, and on August 4, 1851 he named three more; all were favorable.[158] Meanwhile, with great secrecy, Pius IX had instructed Father Perrone, S.J., to draw up the first plans for a bull. These were transmitted to His Holiness on March 26, 1851.[159]

In November and December of the same year, the Pope held five audiences with Dom Guéranger, Abbot of Solesmes, whose *Mémoire sur la question de l'Immaculée Conception,*[160] published the year previous, had been called by the Pope, "the best thing he had seen . . . on the

---

[154] Brief *Nihil certe,* reproduced at the beginning of the Avignon, 1848, edition, pp. 1-2 and in BOURASSE 7, 627-628.

[155] The documents concerned in this phase of the development are published in SARDI I, 1-554 (cf. p. 957) except where otherwise indicated. Sardi is the chief source of the material of the following paragraphs. Detailed references are given in LAURENTIN, notes 264-275. See also *DTC* 7, 1196 ff.

[156] *APN* t. 1a, p. 162. Cf. A. TONDINI, *Le Encicliche mariane,* Roma 1950, pp. 2-7. SARDI I, 571.

[157] *Pareri* (cf. table of abbreviations), in ten volumes, distributed as they were published (1851-1854) to the members of the theological commission. SARDI I, 778-779.

[158] SARDI (I, 755-778) publishes only one of the last three opinions—that of Antonio de Rignano. But it is well known that the other two—Perrone and Passaglia —were favorable.

[159] 1st schema, *Deus Omnipotens,* printed in SARDI II, 22-38.

[160] Paris, Lecoffre, 1850, 147 pp. 80.

subject."[161]   On February 6, 1852, Guéranger obtained from Pius IX, Perrone's schema, which he revised and submitted to Passaglia who annotated it.[162]   The two of them together put it in final shape, and a printed copy was ready for Pius IX on March 24.[163]

From May of 1852 through August of 1853 a special commission appointed by Pius IX reviewed the entire question analytically, and drew up a 'synopsis' of arguments destined for the elaboration of the future bull.[164]   These arguments were drawn largely from the book of Passaglia, who was a member of the commission.

After March of 1854, the Commission moved faster and more intensely. Sometime between the end of 1853 and May of 1854 a third schema, *In mysterio,* was composed by Passaglia.   On March 22, the Pope appointed a consultative assembly comprising twenty-one cardinals and numerous theologians.

Between the beginning of September and the end of November, five new schemas [165] were discussed.   Meetings, papers and printings succeeded one another at a constantly accelerating rate.   December 8 drew near, yet the discussion continued.   When the bishops who had come for the definition were invited to give their views, this only started the arguments all over again, in ways which were sometimes quite interesting.[166]   The Pope decided it was time to put an end to preliminaries which might have gone on indefinitely.   On December 1, presenting the eighth and last schema, he cut short considerations of detail and brought the attention of the assembled Cardinals to the essential question:

> Do you agree that we enact (*proferamus*) the decree concerning Immaculate Conception?

[161] Manuscript diary of Dom GUERANGER (archives of the Abbey of Solesmes), at November 24.   This document was discovered by Dom FRENAUD, who has published a detailed study of Dom Gueranger's contribution in the Acta of the Congressus mariologicus internationalis of 1954, *Virgo Immaculata,* vol. 2, Romae, Academia Mariana Internationalis, 1956, pp. 337-386.

[162] The manuscript, conserved at Solesmes, has been edited by Dom FRENAUD *op. cit.,* pp. 366-386.

[163] Five copies were printed, one of which is conserved at Solesmes. This is the second schema, *Quemadmodum Ecclesia,* edited by SARDI II, 60-76, who attributed it to Passaglia.

[164] The *Silloge degli argumenti da servire all'estensore della Bolla* is published in SARDI II, 46-54.

PASSAGLIA's work is entitled *De Immaculato Deiparae Virginis Conceptu,* Roma, Typ. de Propaganda fide, 1855, three parts in one large volume of 2104 pp. 8°.

[165] These schemas, and the dates of their transmission, were as follows:

4th Schema. *Sapientissimus,*	September	2. 1854.	(SARDI II, 103-118, n. 12.)
5th Schema. *Deus cujus viae,*	October	31, 1854.	(SARDI II, 125-142, n. 17.)
6th Schema. *Deus cujus viae,*	November	3, 1854.	(SARDI II, 151-167, n. 20.)
7th Schema. *Ineffabilis,*	November	?, 1854.	(SARDI II, 177-194, n. 23.)
8th Schema. *Ineffabilis.*	December	1. 1854.	(SARDI II, 259-274, n. 32.)

[166] SARDI II, 244-258. Cf. R. AUBERT, "La Proclamation de l'Immaculée Conception," in *Coll. Mechl.* 36 (1951) p. 595.

The consent of the cardinals brought the debate to an end. The Pope fixed December 8 as the date of the definition and discharged the commissions. On December 4, and on one of the following days, he conferred with four Cardinals (Wiseman, Brunelli, Caterini and Santucci(chosen from among the eighteen who had sent observations on the eighth schema. The final revision, he reserved to himself, assisted only by his secretary, Pacifici. Here is what we know of this last phase:

> From then on, His Holiness, reserving the matter entirely to himself, instructed Pacifici to develop the bull according to the first plan: he should set forth first the comportment of the Church [with regard to this doctrine], and then, *as far as was fitting,* [the teaching of] the Fathers.[167] In other words, the first and second parts of the Bull [as arranged in the more recent schemas] were to change places. Then the Pope directed Pacifici that everything concerning the actual belief of the Church and the Popes, as well as the expressions of the Fathers of tradition, etc., should be presented *in globo,*[168] as in the first plan.[169] At the same time he told him that when the work was finished it was to be submitted to His Holiness alone, who reserved the matter exclusively to himself. He did not wish to hold any more consultations or hear any more opinions (*altri sentimenti*). Pacifici followed the Holy Father's instructions scrupulously, and the latter, after going over the work together with his venerable secretary, directed him to have the bull printed.[170]

The bull was not ready by December 8; on that day the Pope read only the *Decree.* The writing of the bull was probably terminated in the early days of January, for the first copies were in the mail soon after January 14.

THE BULL INEFFABILIS.

The official definition of the dogma was formulated in the following terms, borrowed substantially from the bull of Alexander VII: [171]

[167] ". . . ordinò al Pacifici che stendesse la Bolla nel modo sin dal principio ideato, che avesse prima posto il fatto della Chiesa a quindi, quanto si deceva, dei padri . . ." The only document which corresponds to this description is the second schema, *Quemadmodum,* that of Dom Guéranger.

[168] The suggestion that tradition should not be spoken of except *in globo* in order to avoid the historical problems and the misunderstandings that it was liable to lead to had already been made by the anonymous author of the *Dichiarazioni,* n. 11, last line (SARDI II, 60).

[169] Here there is no longer question of Dom Guéranger's schema, but of the *first* draft submitted to the consultative assembly named on March 22, that is to say the fourth schema, the only one in which the documents of tradition are mentioned globally (SARDI II, 103-121).

[170] *Relazione circa la redazione finale* published in Italian in SARDI II, 300. Pacifici served as secretary for nearly all the assemblies preparatory to the definition.

[171] In order to grasp the process of this elaboration, it is best to consider the third schema:

ALEXANDER VII, *Sollicitudo* (*Bull. Taur.,* 16, 789)	SCHEMA III (SARDI II, 69)
. . . ejus *animam* in *primo* instanti *creatio*nis	. . . *animam* Beatissimae V. Mariae cum *primum* fuit *creata*

... we declare, pronounce and define that the doctrine which holds that the most Blessed Virgin Mary was preserved from all stain of original sin in the first instant of her Conception, by a singular grace and privilege of Almighty God, in consideration of the merits of Jesus Christ, Savior of the human race: has been revealed by God, and must, therefore, firmly and constantly be believed by all the faithful.[172]

The two great traditional requirements are here satisfied with all desirable clarity: from the very first moment, Mary is *absolutely exempt* from all stain of *original sin*. Yet, this daughter of Adam has been *saved by Jesus Christ.* The great difficulty of reconciling these two demands lay in the order of time: how was it possible for Mary, conceived in the ordinary way, not to have incurred *even for an instant* the sin of the *race* to which she belonged? And how could she have been saved *before* Christ had redeemed the world? This difficulty is resolved in two words: *preservation, pre-vision*: the Blessed Virgin was *preserved* from original sin, in *pre-vision* of the merits of Jesus Christ.[173]

In this text, remarkable for its precision and concision, by contrast with the more ample style of the remainder of the bull, the Pope restricts himself to the most certain doctrine; his definition prescinds from all particular questions and opinions of schools. In the course of the preliminary discus-

---

et *infusionis in corpus* *fuisse* speciali *Dei* *gratia et privilegio* *intuitu meritorum Jesu Christi,* ejus filii, *humani generis* Redemptoris a macula peccati *originalis* *praeservatam immunem.*	et *in* suum *corpus infusa* *fuisse* singulari omnipotentis *Dei* *gratia et privilegio* *intuitu meritorum Christi Jesu* Salvatoris *humani generis* ab omni *originalis* culpae labe *praeservatam immunem.*

Alexander VII commended this doctrine as a pious belief, whereas Pius IX *defined* it as a truth of faith. The adjective *singulari* in the place of *speciali* accentuates the unicity of the privilege.

No noteworthy change occurred in the following schemas. Two of the cardinals who made observations on the last schema expressed the desire that the *very terms* of Alexander VII be repeated (SARDI II, 277 and 280), notably that the *first instant* be mentioned. In his final revision of the text, the Pope granted their wish, but he suppressed the specific references to the body and soul of the Virgin, and referred the privilege to her person (cf. note 177, below).

[172] "Definimus doctrinam quae tenet beatissimam Virginem Mariam *in primo instanti* suae Conceptionis fuisse singulari omnipotentis *Dei gratia et privilegio intuitu meritorum Christi Jesu* Salvatoris humani generis ab omni originalis peccati culpae labe *praeservatam immunem* esse a Deo revelatam . . ." APN 1a, p. 616. We have italicized the words taken from the Bull of Alexander VII, cited in the preceding note. Note that the text of Alexander VII is explicitly cited in an earlier paragraph of the Bull *Ineffabilis, APN* 1a, 604-605.

[173] ". . . praeservation . . . intuitu meritorum Christi"—text of the definition (*APN* 1t, 616). Cf. the body of the Bull, *APN* 1a, 605: "Sanctissimam Dei Genitricem Virginem Mariam ob PRAEVISA Christi Domini Redemptoris merita . . . PRAESERVATAM omnino fuisse ab omni originalis peccati labe et idcirco sublimiori modo redemptam . . ."

sions, questions about the *debitum*,[174] preservation from concupiscence,[175] and the manner in which the dogma had been revealed, had been set aside.[176] Finally, the Pope himself, in the last revision of the text, had eliminated distinct references to the body and soul of the Blessed Virgin, attributing the privilege instead to her person *in globo*.[177] The formula was thus stripped down to a pure expression of revealed doctrine, abstracting from all particular systematizations.

In the body of the bull, the meaning and the reasons for the definition are explained. These reasons are not the adequate causes of the definition; they are merely tokens indicating in a global fashion the ensemble of reasons on which the definition is based. They are not covered by the papal infallibility. Furthermore, these explanations are even more loosely attached to the definition proper than is the case with other similar documents, since the "justifying" considerations were not determined until *after* the definition, and were intentionally designed in such a way as not to settle many still unresolved discussions.

This does not mean that the ordinary *magisterium* is not involved in a most special way in the composition of such a document, which provides the most authoritative explanation of the definition. Here again we encounter the protective action of the Holy Spirit. As there is not space here to treat everything, we will single out only the point which is of special interest in the perspective of the present study: the Pope's approach to the historical question.

The third schema, which served as the initial basis for the discussions of 1854, contained innumerable patristic references, swarming with apocryphal passages, about which Passaglia was poorly informed. In the discussion which followed, criticisms were directed against certain inaccuracies which it was possible to detect even in the state of science at that time. It was also pointed out that the meaning of certain texts was not very obvious.[178] Several Cardinals observed, no less judiciously, that the Bull, as it stood, had the appearance of a dissertation rather than an act of the *magisterium*. As a result, the references were first shifted into the foot-

---

[174] SARDI I, 528, 532. Bianchini's proposal that the Blessed Virgin's exemption from the *debitum* be affirmed found no echo.

[175] SARDI II, 242-243. Letter of the Bishop of Unguento.

[176] In November, 1854, Archbishop Kenrick of Baltimore observed that *most Catholics* (Plerique catholici) did not believe in an explicit revelation (expressam ... revelationem). SARDI II, 231.

[177] This correction had been proposed by the Bishop of Unguento on November 24, 1854, but in an altogether different context (SARDI II, 242). On December 1, 1854 (SARDI II, 292), Cardinal Pecci proposed it much more formally with very judicious arguments: "Quoad verba Dogma . . . definientia, illa vitanda putarem quae quomodocumque redolerent Scholam, animam in Conceptione a corpore seiungentia: ita ut *definitio respicerit personam Mariae quemadmodum Ecclesia festum Conceptionis ejusdem celebravit hucusque de persona, non de anima tantum.*"

[178] SARDI II, 278, 288-289, 295 *et passim*. Cf. *DTC* 7, 1201-1202.

notes, and ultimately disappeared altogether.[179]   Thus was eliminated a documentation, the inaccuracies of which would have been embarrassing. Moreover, Pacifici was directed, in the last revision—that made by the Pope himself—to speak of the Fathers only with great reserve, and to present the data of Tradition *in globo*.   Meanwhile, it had been agreed that all explanations relative to the adversaries of the dogma—St. Bernard and the thirteenth century scholastics—should be suppressed.   Finally, care was taken not to speak of Scripture (the testimony of which was so vague), except in reference to the interpretation of Fathers and Doctors taken *in globo*.   In short, the presence of the dogma in the fonts of Revelation (which had to be affirmed, in order to make it clear that there was no question of a new revelation, but of a doctrine constantly held by the Church) was presented in the most general way.   Thus, little by little, the Bull, which had started out as the work of a professor—and of a professor in a period when scientific methods were as yet unknown—ended up by finding its true ground, as well as a literary *genre* adapted to the nature of the Act and to the knowledge of the period.   It was thus preserved from the errors with which the historical deficiencies of the time would normally have riddled it.

The Bull Ineffabilis, and History

This raises the question, how the viewpoint of the Bull *Ineffabilis* is related to that of the historian in the handling of historical materials.   There is a real problem here which has often given rise to forced assertions and artificial harmonisations.   We would say, in brief, that it is a matter of a different perspective and a different lighting.

A first difference has to do with *duration*.   The historian is concerned with the progress of the doctrine in time, with its development as such. The Pope, on the contrary, is concerned with that which has permanent validity.   The historian does not deny the fundamental permanence, and the Pope does not deny the progression;[180] but the one plunges immediately into the complexity of this latter aspect, while the other goes immediately to the substance of the matter, which he would like to establish definitively.   The historian is concerned with the *movement* and the imperfect processes through which the explicitation of the object is gradually realized.   The Pope is concerned with the *term,* that is to say, with the definition which crowns this sometimes hesitant progress, and gives it its meaning.

Two distinctions must be made here to avoid any equivocation.   First, we must take care not to exaggerate the difference between the two atti-

---

[179] The names of the Fathers appeared in the text of the first three schema; they disappeared in the fourth, reappeared in notes in the fifth to eighth, and disappeared in the Bull.

[180] See below, note 182.

tudes. On the one hand, the historian must not lose sight of the end, or he will become a simple collector of documents (that is why, in the present work, we have insisted on situating the facts in lines which showed the direction the development was taking). On the other hand, while Pius IX could disregard certain facts (those, namely, which were not oriented towards the term: notably the dossier of the opposition, of which he was by no means unaware, as well as the manifestations of prudence and reserve by his predecessors), the historian must consider them all. Pius IX considered, in the various stages of the development, only their reference to the end, whereas the historian is concerned with their value as limited stages.

Here we must point out a second distinction. What we have said holds in a general way for all solemn acts of the supreme *magisterium;* to it must be added some observations relative to the particular case of the Bull *Ineffabilis.* Pius IX lived before the development of the modern science of history. He was not interested in historical development as such; rather he would have been irritated by all this temporal conditioning, and have looked upon it as a hindrance. At the same time, he would have been warned by a sure spiritual instinct (illumined both by the labors of the commissions and the light of the Holy Spirit) of the dangers of error involved in entering into this complex domain. Therefore he voluntarily and consciously made abstraction, as far as possible, from time and from all that is bound up with time. This explains the instruction given to his secretary, to cite the Fathers only *in globo.* The way in which he recalls the interventions of his predecessors is most significant. The eighth schema had enumerated them with great precision in chronological order. Pius IX suppressed all the names, except that of Alexander VII, and listed all the acts without giving any indication of their date or of the temporal succession among them.[181] Without by any means denying that there is progress (on the contrary he points this out several times,[182] but only

---

[181] The following passages will give a more concrete idea of the corrections made on the eighth schema:

SCHEMA VIII (SARDI II, 267-268) PIUS vero V . . . edixit ut	DEFINITIVE TEXT (SARDI II, 301) Romani Pontifices . . . Summopere laetati sunt decernere
ab omni Ecclesia festum Conceptionis	*Conceptionis festum ab omni Ecclesia* esse habendum
eodem censu ac numero quo festum *Nativitatis* haberetur; ac praeterea INNOCENTIUS XII legem tulit qua *festum idem cum octava ab* *Universa Ecclesia celebrandum* constituit. Neque id satis. CLEMENS namque XI voluit ut festum Conceptionis *inter ea quae praecepta sunt* *ab omnibus* haberetur.	*eodem censu ac numero quo festum* *Nativitatis* *idemque* Conceptionis festum *cum octava* *ab Universa Ecclesia celebrandum* et *ab omnibus* *inter ea quae praecepta sunt* sancte colendum.

obliquely) he adopts, as far as possible, an a-temporal perspective.   By way of contrast, Pius XII, without relinquishing a perspective that transcends time, has incorporated into the Bull *Munificentissimus* important distinctions relative to the order of time and to the progression which takes place in it.[183]

A second difference between Pope and historian appears in their approach to a text or document.   There is a principle of St. Thomas' which sheds light on this difference.   *"The believer's act of faith terminates,"* he says, *"not in the statement, but in the reality."* [184]   The Pope is concerned with the *realities* which are the objects of faith, and which it is his task to *define*.   The historian, on the contrary, is concerned with statements precisely as such; he endeavors to ascertain their literal meaning, taking great care not to make this more explicit than the terms allow. Thus, the feast of the Conception was celebrated by the faithful for many centuries with ideas that were vague and often quite alloyed with adventitious elements; all the same, it was the total reality of the mystery that their faith attained in its liturgical *elan*.   The Pope is concerned with this ultimate reality, in the light of which he illumines in retrospect the profound intent of the earlier acts of the *magisterium*.   Thus, he sifts the testimony of history, disregarding what is aberrant, consecrating whatever pertains to the authentic tradition, and discerning in the most implicit expressions the total reality to which they correspond.   In short, in defining the term, he reveals the profound meaning of the earlier approximations to it, giving them a value which they truly have in the intentions of the Holy Spirit, but which exceeds the explicit awareness which their authors could have had.

Here too we must distinguish what is peculiar to the point of view of Pius IX.   Absorbed by the light of the definitive truth, he made no particular effort to determine the literal meaning of the declarations of Scripture and the Fathers; and he made frequent use of such terms as *luculentissime*,

---

[182] "Hanc de Immaculata Beatissimae Virginis Conceptione doctrinam QUOTIDIE MAGIS gravissimo Ecclesiae sensu, MAGISTERIO, studio . . . EXPLICATAM, declaratam, confirmatam" etc. *APN* 1a, p. 606. There follows a very free and implicit citation of St. VINCENT of LERINS, *Commonitorium* n. 28, *PL* 50, 668 and 669 (the borrowings are given here in italics): *"Ecclesia ita limare, expolire studit, ut prisca . . . dogmata, accipiant evidentiam, lucem, distinctionem . . . ac in suo . . . genere* CRESCANT." Cf. p. 598: "Catholica Ecclesia *magis in dies explicare*, proponere ac fovere nunquam destitit"; 599: *"promovere";* p. 600: *"augere . . . promovere, amplificare . . . quotidie magis";* p. 601: "amplificantes"; cf. p. 602: "declaravit." The references to time are adventitious and quite global.

[183] On the differences between the Bull *Ineffabilis* of Pius IX and the Constitution *Munificentissimus* of Pius XII, see the interesting article of M. PEINADOR, "De Bullis 'Ineffabilis Deus' et 'Munificentissimus' ad invicem comparatis," in *Ephem. mariol.* 4 (1954) pp. 181-200.

[184] "Actus . . . credentis non terminatur ad enuntiabile, sed ad rem." *Summa theologiae*, II-II, 1, 2 ad 2.

clare, aperte, etc., [185] in connection with documents which, in many cases, were not very explicit. Pius XII, on the contrary, has adhered more precisely to the literal meaning of the text, stating clearly that the testimonies of early ages have merely the value of *indications* and *traces.*[186]

The two differences that we have pointed out between the Pope and the historian have their explanation in a third, namely, that the latter has neither authority nor a charism; he is simply a disciple in the school of facts. The Pope, although he does not fail to make an historical investigation, acts less as a *student* than as a *maker* of history: he has the authority to define its meaning and its bearing.

With this is associated an accessory difference, pertaining to literary *genre*. In the act which brings to its term the laborious process of the explicitation of the dogma of the Immaculate Conception, the Pope is carried on the crest of an *elan* that had been raised by the breath of the Holy Spirit. Hence he speaks with an enthusiasm, and emotion normally expressed by a more lyrical tone: the tone appropriate to a proclamation or celebration. By comparison, the historian appears cold and stingy in his appreciation— somewhat as a chronicler in comparison with an epic poet.

In this regard also, *Ineffabilis* has its own peculiarities: Pius IX gave free rein to his feelings. The lyricism which was already pronounced in the last schema, was still further accentuated in the definitive revision, which is rich in superlatives,[187] and in poetic over-simplifications which need to be exegeted according to the facts and in the general spirit of the document.[188] Finally, it bears to some degree the mark of its times, and even that of its principal editor, Passaglia, who had the habit of presenting

---

[185] Note the frequency of these expressions in the Bull *Ineffabilis* SARDI, pp. 302 (luculentissime, eloquentissimis quibuscumque modis, apertissime planissimeque), p. 303 (manifestissime, clare aperteque), 304 (luculentissimis) etc. Very typical is the *clare aperteque* concerning the designation of Mary in Genesis 3:15 according to the Fathers (SARDI II, 307, *APN* 1a, 607, and the *insigniter* in reference to the immaculist meaning of the biblical figures of the Blessed Virgin according to "the same Fathers" (SARDI II, 308; cf. *APN* 1a, 608).

The *Silloge degli argumenti* (SARDI II, 48-49; see above, note 164) had declared: "Ceterum priores Ecclesiae aetates, etsi NON testimonia PERSPICUA ET LUCULENTA de Immaculata Beatae Mariae Conceptione, quaedam tamen INDICIA et quasi VESTIGIA piae . . . sententiae . . . suppeditant." Because he wished the Bull to have the character of a purely doctrinal affirmation, Pius IX omitted from it the observations so clearly formulated in the preparatory labors.

[186] "Per saeculorum decursum manifestantur testimonia, INDICIA atque VESTIGIA" *AAS* 42 (1950) p. 757. Were these two terms taken from the *Silloge (of the preceding century)* cited in note 185?

[187] While the Bull *Ineffabilis* and the Constitution *Munificentissimus* are equal in length, I have counted 96 superlatives in the former and only 45, that is to say half as many, in the latter. (But even this latter number surpasses what would be found in an historical work.)

[188] "Ex stylo et modo redigendi, quoddam exegeticum criterium eruere possimus, ut videlicet prioris documenti (=Bullae *Ineffabilis*) neque verba neque expressiones nimis premantur." C. PEINADOR, as cited in note 183, p. 185.

particular facts under the guise of generalities. Pius XII, without abandon-
ing the lyricism [189] suitable to a proclamation, subordinated it to the
modern demands for moderation, and especially for precision.[190]

It is evident, therefore, that in its matter of treating historical data,
the Bull *Ineffabilis* differs in important respects from the modern historian.
The differences derive from two factors, one of which is essential to the
magisterium as such, while the other is peculiar to Pius IX, and connected
with a particular condition of science and of style. Whereas Pius XII, in
1950, was able to integrate the laborious conquests of the historical method
into the exercise of his *magisterium,* Pius IX, in 1854, could only rise
above the weakness of the science of his day by the use of generality and
even imprecision. This imprecision was intentional, being commanded by
an awareness of the complexity of history, and a refusal to enter lightly
into it; it was also optimistic, being commanded by assurance of the truth
which had come to light so laboriously down through the centuries. As a
result, the historian of the dogma of the Immaculate Conception cannot
be content to gather the decisive lights that have been shed by the *magisterium* on the development of the dogma; he must also make precise what
the Bull, with its rapid and global exposition, gave only approximately, and
he must supply what the Bull by-passed.

We can see, therefore, why the historian's doctrine often appears mini-
mizing in comparison with that of the Bull *Ineffabilis;* but it should also
be evident how the historian's humble point of view harmonises profoundly
with the higher, charismatic point of view of Pius IX, without either
contradiction or 'concordism.'

ACTIVITY OF THE MAGISTERIUM SINCE THE DEFINITION

Before terminating, we must note a final phase of the activity of the
magisterium that has taken place *since* the definition: the Popes continue
to propagate, protect, and promote the defined truth, the consequences of
which pursue their development both in the theoretical order, and in the
life of the Church.[191] The feast and the doctrine of the Immaculate Conception have been enriched, notably on the occasion of the anniversaries
of the definition.[192] The fiftieth and hundredth anniversaries have given
rise to liturgical and doctrinal acts of particular solemnity. The year

[189] Cf. note 188, above.

[190] "Pro stylo oratorio et diffuso Bullae *Ineffabilis* habemus in Bulla *Munificentissimus* stylum sobrium."— M. PEINADOR, as cited above, in note 183, p. 200. Cf.
also note 187, above.

[191] On this point see the thorough study of H. BARRÉ, "De Pie IX à Pie XII,
L'enseignement des Papes sur l'Immaculée Conception, in *L'Immaculée Conception.
Compte rendu . . . des travaux du . . . VIIe Congrès marial et national 1954*, Lyon,
5 rue de Mulet, 1954, pp. 95-112.

[192] For the twenty-fifth anniversary, Leo XIII wrote the Apostolic Letter, *Annus
iam quintus et vicesimus, Acta Leonis XIII*, 1 (1881) pp. 307-308. Cf. *AJP* for the
year 1881, p. 255.

1904,[193] saw the granting of numerous indulgences,[194] the Encyclical *Ad diem illum*[195] and an international congress;[196] in 1954, the Marian Year, with its indulgences and privileges, was promulgated,[197] the Encyclical *Fulgens Corona* was written,[198] and another international Marian congress was held.[199]

GENERAL CONCLUSION

If we now look back over this entire history, we cannot fail to be struck by a remarkable continuity and consistency in the activity of the *magisterium* (which Turmel, with his accustomed superficiality, failed to perceive).

We have examined three series of documents, referring respectively to the feast, the title, and the doctrine of the Immaculate Conception (the last of these series being itself composed of several inter-connected sub-series). In all three cases, there could be seen a somewhat irregular progress, in which three phases were discernible: first, an attitude of prudent watchfulness; then a series of interventions designed to maintain peace amid the conflict of opinions; finally, an authoritative decision (preceded in some cases by judicious measures designed to eliminate the last resistance).

It is true that some slight retrogression was observed on two minor points (the reduction of the liturgical rank of the feast in the sixteenth century, and the systematic restriction of the use of the title *Immaculata Conceptio* in pontifical acts from the mid-seventeenth to the early nineteenth century); but in both cases, this retrogression was connected with progress in a different order (extension of the feast, in the first case, and the ripening and

[193] See especially: Leo XIII, *Da molte parti*, May 26, 1903, in *ASS* 35 (1903) 715; *Acta Leonis XIII* 22 (1903) 349-350 (setting up the commission of Cardinals for the celebration of the fiftieth anniversary). Pius X, *Se è nostro dovere*, September 8, 1903, in *Acta Pii X*, 1 (1905) pp. 29-30; and the Letter *Ad omnium instaurationem*, *ib.*, 393-394.

[194] Apostolic Letter, *Universis christifidelibus*, December 7, 1903 (*Acta Pii X*, 1 (1905) pp. 92-94). Cf. the Indulgence of March 23, 1904, in *Enchiridion Indulgentiarum*, Rome 1951, pp. 239-240; Apostolic Letter, *Oblatis nobis*, *ASS* 7 (1904) 11-12.

[195] *Acta Pii X*, 1 (1905) 147.

[196] *Atti del Congresso mondiale tenuto in Roma l'anno 1904 . . . compilati p. c. di Monsignore* G. M. Radini Tedeschi, Roma, Tip. San Guiseppe, 1905.

[197] Cf. the decrees, *Quo Solemniori*, *AAS* 35 (1953) p. 808 and *Mariano anno*, November 29, 1953, *AAS* 35 (1953), p. 819.

[198] September 8, 1953, *AAS* 45 (1953) 576-592. Cf. the *Adnotationes* of M. Peinador, in *Ephem. mariol.* 4 (1954) 20-24. Let us recall also the Encyclical *Ad coeli Reginam* of October 11, 1954 (*Osservatore Romano*, October 24, 1954, pp. 1-2) and the Allocution on the occasion of the coronation of image of the Blessed Virgin, "*Salus Populi Romani*," (*ib.*, November 2-3, 1954, p. 1). Cf. R. Laurentin, "Salve Regina," in *Vie Spir.* 92 (1955) 82-89.

[199] Congressus mariologico-marianus internationalis, Rome, October 24-November 1, 1954. The proceedings of the congress, under the title *Virgo Immaculata*, are being published at Rome, Academia Mariana Internationalis, 1955 ff., under the direction of Father Carlo Balic, President of the *Academia*.

assimilation of Alexander VII's doctrinal commitment, in the other).

The consistency seen in each line of the papal activity considered separately, is matched when the three lines are compared with one another. They did not keep pace, but advances in one domain provided support for those that were made later in another. The liturgy was the pilot factor, both raising the problems and establishing the climate in which the solution would be worked out. The popes who increased the solemnity of the feast were indirectly paving the way for the doctrinal solution. The question of the title was the last to be decided, after a long and prudent deliberation.

This consistency, maintained over a period of centuries, transcends the view that any one pope could have had. Behind the human wisdom and individual lights of Peter's successors, we catch glimpses of a higher wisdom, conferring on the whole process a unity superior to that intended in any particular decision, however wise it may have been.

Finally, the consistency of the Holy See's activity becomes further manifest when contrasted with the impassioned efforts made over a period of four centuries, by every conceivable means, to entice, pressure or surprise a Pope into an untimely decision. These efforts would normally have involved the Holy See inextricably in contradictions, especially since certain popes were humanly bound to one side or other of the controversy. But those whose opinion had been maculist before their elevation to the papacy did not introduce their personal views into the acts of their *magisterium;* and the alternation between Franciscans and Dominicans on the papal throne produced no fluctuation in the line of conduct pursued by the Holy See. The contradictions of which Turmel accuses the latter (see above, p. 271) existed only in the form of pressures which, by any human calculation, ought to have produced contradiction, but in fact did not.

It is important to note the motives that inspired the papal decisions. Here, a new contrast appears. Legations and petitions represented to the popes the glory that would accrue to their name and the material benefits (health, prosperity . . .) they would receive from Our Lady, if they would make the desired decision.[200] But these irrelevant and unworthy considerations were steadily disregarded by the pontiffs, whose motives were rather: in the disciplinary order, sollicitude for peace and unity; in the doctrinal order, a desire to adhere to the tradition of the Church and to the line

___

[200] See the references given in notes 141-144. In the eighteenth century, André BUDRIOLI, S.J., told Pope Benedict XIV that if he would define the dogma, the Blessed Virgin would not fail to obtain better health for him as she had done for Alexander VII after the publication of the Bull *Sollicitudo.* (SARDI II, p. 6, cf. p. 2. See also note 147 above). The same Pope was assured by St. LEONARD OF PORT MAURICE that he would make his name immortal by defining the Immaculate Conception. The Pope replied, that a ray of light must first be given from heaven; if this did not take place, it was a sign that the moment fixed by Providence had not yet arrived. (Reference in note 146, above)

followed till then by the Holy See; and over and above all else, docility to the Holy Spirit. It was, in fact, to the latter, that Peter's successors constantly (and often explicitly) referred, not only their commitments, but also their silence, their delays, and their refusals.

In the light of history, therefore, the definition of 1854 appears, not as one man's achievement, or the result of a few years' labor, but as the work of the Holy See, slowly matured over the course of centuries. And the ultimate explanation of the continuity of this work is the Holy Spirit. He is the reason for the order and harmony among the papal decisions which no individual pope could have envisioned, and which still less could have been expected from the tumultuous course of events in which it was realized.

ABBREVIATIONS

AAS—Acta Apostolicae Sedis, Roma, Tip. Vaticana, 1909 ff.

AJP—Decreta authentica sacrorum rituum Congregationis; in *Analecta juris Pontificii,* volume IV, series 7 (1864) col. 1-383 and series 8 (1865) col. 1138-1387—A collection of unedited decrees and responses emanating from the Congregation of Rites, from the beginning to the year 1700. Edited anonymously by Monsignor CHAILLOT. The first twelve years (1588-1599) are lacking from the archives and their reconstitution is very fragmentary.

ALVA—Pedro de ALVA y ASTORGA, O.F.M. (†1667)—The most learned of all the authors who have ever studied the Immaculate Conception. He traveled everywhere, kept numerous secretaries at work, and founded at Louvain a *Typographia Immaculatae Conceptionis.* His information is usually dependable but his interpretations are often passionate and biased. We will designate his principal works by the following abbreviations:

ALVA, *Armam.—Id., Sacra cismontana familia ordinis minorum exhibet Armamentarium Seraphicum et Regestum universale pro tuendo titulo Immaculatae Conceptionis,* Matriti, typ. Regia, 1659. Two volumes in one, in folio:
  I. *Armamentarium,* 467 pp.
  II. *Regestum,* 718 pp. plus indices.—This book was composed in reply to the Decree of 1644 and to the first two *libella* written in defense of the Decree (see above, note 149).

ALVA, *Funic.—Id., Funiculi nodi indissolubilis,* Bruxellis, P. Vleugaert, 1663. This is a re-edition of the *Nodus* mentioned below. The two works were put on the Index, July 22, 1665, as were those which combatted them. They were removed from the Index in the revision of Pope Leo XIII in 1897. See note 48, below.

ALVA, *Indic.—Id., Indiculus Bullarii Seraphici ubi Litterae omnes apostolicae, quae a principio Religionis Minorum, a Summis Ecclesiae Pontificibus, pro tota Seraphica S.P.N. Francisci Familia tam in communi, quam in particulari, hucusque expeditae fuerunt, breviter recensentur,* Roma, ex typ. R. Camerae Apost. 1655. A chronological list designating bulls and briefs touching upon the Franciscan family in some way. The author indicates briefly their date, *incipit* and object. In our citations—for example II, 176, n. 39—the Roman numeral designates the tome, the second numeral the page, and the third, the number of the document in its order in the year under consideration.

ALVA, *Milit.*—*Id., Militia Immaculatae Conceptionis Virginis Mariae,* Lovanii, typ. Immaculatae Conceptionis, 1663—Alphabetical dictionary of the authors and documents relative to the Immaculate Conception. This is the most defective of ALVA's works, due to the part played by his collaborators in it.

ALVA, *Nodus*—*Id., Nodus indissolubilis de conceptu mentis et conceptu ventris hoc est: inter immunitatem ab omni defectu et errore angelicae doctrinae s. Thomae Aquinatis et ejus exclusionem ab illis universalibus regulis: omnis homo mendax . . . et praeservationem ab omni culpa et macula purissimae animae Virginis Dei Matris Mariae et ipsius exceptionem ab istis: Omnes in Adam peccaverunt . . . ac de utriusque approbationibus Apostolicis Ecclesiasticis atque revelatis . . . ligatus a Petro de Alva y Astorga,* Bruxellis, P. Vleugaert, 1661.

ALVA, *Radii*—*Id., Radii Solis Zeli Seraphici coeli veritatis pro Immaculatae Conceptionis mysterio Virginis Mariae discurrentes per duodecim classis auctorum vel duodecim Signa Zodiaci,* etc. . . , Lovanii, typ. Immaculatae Conceptionis, 1666.

APN—*Acta Pii noni, Pontificis Maximi,* Roma, tip. Vaticana, 1854 et ss.

Arch. post—*Decreta et resolutiones Inquisitionis de Conceptione B.M.V.* 1616-1668. A collection of documents unequal in value drawn up by Andrea BUDRIOLI, postulator of the Society of Jesus (1679-1763), and conserved in the *Archives de la Postulation generale,* Borgo Santo Spirito, Roma, under the title, *De Immaculata Conceptione B. M. Virginis. Miscellanea I*—a collection in which neither the documents nor the pages are numbered. The *decreta* comprise ten folios (267x 190 mm.) which are found about four-fifths of the way through the volume. For the sake of convenience we have given a number in brackets [1], [2] . . . to each of the nineteen pages. For a microfilm of this material I am indebted to Père E. Lamalle, S.J.

ASS—*Acta Sanctae Sedis,* Roma, Tip. Vaticana, 1865-1908.

BANDELLI—V. BANDELLI, *Tractatus de singulari puritate et praerogativa Conceptionis Salvatoris N.J.C. ex auctoritatibus duocentorum sexaginta Doctorum, ad exemplar impressum Bononiae, 1481,* place and date of publication not given viii, 211 pp. 8° (Paris, Bib. Nle. D. 4729).—Bandelli's treatise underwent many editions under various titles. Therefore we will cite the *part* and the chapter, the page being that of the edition indicated above. The first edition of the work appeared at Milan, published by Valdarfer, 1475.

BOURASSE—J. BOURASSÉ, *Summa Aurea,* Paris, Migne, 1862-1866, 13 vol.

Bull. Cap.—*Collectio Bullarum, Brevium, Decretorum, Rescriptorum, Oraculorum* etc. . . . *quae a Sede Apostolica pro ordine Capucino emanarunt . . . Jussu RR. Patris Bonaventurae a Ferraria . . . variis notis, et scholiis elucubrata a P. F. Michaele a Tugio in Helvetia,* Tomus primus, Romae, Typ. Joannis Zempel Austriaci prope Montem Jordanum, 1740, 7 volumes.

Bull. cont.—*Bullarii Romani continuatio, summorum Pontificum Clementis XIII, Clementis XIV, Pii VI, Pii VII, Leonis XII et Pii VIII, Constitutiones, Litteras in forma brevis, epistolas . . . atque alloquutiones complectens,* Romae, typ. Rev. Camerae Apostolicae, 20 vol., 1835-1857.

Bull. Coq.—*Bullarium privilegiorum ac diplomatum Romanorum Pontificum amplissima collectio . . .* ed. COCQUELINES. Romae, H. Mainardi, 14 vol., 1739-1764. Certain volumes comprise several tomes, which I distinguish by the letters a, b, c, etc.

Bull. min.—*Bullarium fratrum ordinis minorum Sancti Francisci strictioris observantiae discalceatorum . . . ab Alexandro VI hispano Pontifice maximo usque ad . . . Benedictinum XIV a P. Fr. Francisco Matritensi . . . sub auxpicio I.C.V.M.,* Matriti, E. Fernandez, 5 vol. 1744-1749.

Bull. Prati.—*Bullarii romani continuatio,* Prati, typ. Aldina, 1839-1856, 23 volumes.— The titles and division into volumes of this work present a certain complication: Volumes 1-14 bear the title, *Benedicti XIV Opera omnia* and contain the private works of Benedict XIV; volumes 15-17 bear the title, *Benedicti XIV Bullarium* and contain the official acts of the same pope. Subsequent volumes bear the title, *Bullarii romani continuatio* and contain the official acts of his successors. Two independent systems of numbers (sometimes decorated with errors, which we have corrected) are given at the back of this *Bullarium* parallel to the various titles. We will give both numbers joined by an equal sign. For example: "*Bull. Prati.* t. 3b = vol. 17" designates *tomus III, Pars secunda Clementis XIII* which is vol. 17 of the collection.

Bull. Taur.—*Bullarium diplomatum et privilegiorum sanctorum Romanorum Pontificum Taurinensis editio locupletior facta . . . a s. Leone Magno usque ad praesens* (=years 440-1740), Augustae Taurinorum, s. Franco, 1857-1872, 24 vol.

CALDERON—A. CALDERON, *Pro titulo Immaculatae Conceptionis Beatissimae V.M., adversus duos Anonymi Libellos. Lib. unus. Philippo Quarto Regi Catholico O.D.C.*, Matriti, typ. Diegum Diaz de la Carrera, 1650 8° de 692 pp.—On the object of this work see below, note 49.

DACL—F. CABROL, H. LeCLERCQ et I. MARROU, *Dictionnaire d'archéologie chrétienne et de liturgie*, Paris, Letouzey, 1903 ff.

DENZINGER—H. DENZINGER, *Enchiridion symbolorum definitionum et declarationum*, Freiburg im Br., Herder, 1937.

DTC—*Dictionnaire de Théologie catholique*, edited by Msgr. AMANN, Paris, Letouzey (completed in 1951).

GARDELLINI—A. GARDELLINI, *Decreta authentica Congregationis Sacrorum rituum*, Rome, typ. S.C. de Prop. Fide, 4 vol., 1856-1858.

The *second.* edition which abridges and *continues* the first, was published *sub auspiciis . . . Leonis Papae XIII*, ib., 1898. We will designate it as GARDELLINI 1898. It has a double system of numerotation, the first proper to this edition, the second conformable to the preceding edition.

GRAVOIS—M. A. GRAVOIS, a Franciscan Recollect of the province of France, *De Ortu et progressu cultus ac Festi Immaculati Conceptus Beatae Dei Genitricis V.M.* We cite according to the *editio secunda, priore auctior et emendatior.*, Lucae, typ. J. Riccome, 1764. Two tomes in one volume:

I. *Articuli* (republished in BOURASSE 8, 289-458, which we will also cite).

II. *Summarium seu documentorum regestum* (a compilation of texts omitted in BOURASSE's re-edition)—The author's erudition is rich and careful, but sometimes inaccurate; his interpretations are still more so.

LAURENTIN—R. LAURENTIN, "L'action du Saint-Siège par rapport au problème de l'Immaculée," in *Virgo Immaculata*, vol. II, Romae, Academia Mariana Internationalis, 1956, pp. 1-99. This is the original work of which the present chapter is an abridgement and translation; cf. the editor's note on p. 271 of the present volume.

Pareri—*Pareri sulla definizione dogmatica dell'Immacolato Concepimento della Beata Vergine Maria*, Roma, tip. della Civiltà Cattolica, ten volumes published from 1851 to 1854, containing the Bishops' replies to the Encyclical *Ubi Primum* of Pius IX.

PG—*Patrologiae cursus . . . Series graeca*, Paris, Migne, 1857-1866.

PL—*Patrologiae cursus . . . Series latina*, Paris, Migne, 1844-1864.

Reg. Vat.—*Regestum Vaticanum.* This abbreviation is used by GRAVOIS (II, 88-89) in citing this collection. It designates the Latin manuscript registers kept in the secret archives of the Vatican and containing a copy of the Pontifical Bulls.

ROSKOVANY—A. ROSKOVÁNY, *Beatae Virgo Maria in suo conceptu immaculata ex monumentis omnium saeculorum demonstrata; accedit amplissima literatura*, Budapestini, typ. Athenaei, 1873-1881, 9 vol. A rich but very mediocre compilation, based on secondary sources, mixing documents of value with the most fantastic apocrypha (the Marian writings of St. Paul and the twelve apostles!), and too rarely indicating its sources.

SARDI—V. SARDI, *La solenne definizione del dogma dell'Immacolato Concepimento di Maria Santissima. Atti e documenti pubblicati nel cinquantesimo anniversario della stessa definizione*, Roma, tip. Vaticana, 1904-1905, 2 vol. 963 et 723 pp. Edition of the archives of the definition of the Immaculate Conception deposited at the Secretariat of Briefs by Monsignor Pacifici, who was the secretary of Pius IX and of nearly all the preparatory commissions.

SERICOLI—C. SERICOLI, O.F.M., *Immaculata B.M. Virginis conceptio iuxta* XYSTI IV *constitutiones* (Bibliotheca Medii Aevi V), Kacic, Sibenici-Romae, 1945.

Note: This study has been based as far as possible on original sources. Hence we cite only official collections and the authors who transmit unpublished documents. But to facilitate the task of the reader who wishes to examine the context, we will also cite BOURASSE and ROSKOVANY wherever possible, as being more accessible than the original collections.

On the few inevitable technical expressions (pious belief, *sententia affirmans, ententia negans*), see above, note 37.

PART II

THEOLOGY

VIII

The Meaning of the Immaculate Conception in the Perspectives of St. Thomas

MARIE-JOSEPH NICOLAS, O.P.*

Many disciples of St. Thomas have sought and still seek to show that it was not the Immaculate Conception itself which their master denied, but only a certain explanation of it which would have separated Mary from the Redemption wrought by Christ. Our only intention here is to present the theology of the Immaculate Conception in the general framework of St. Thomas' doctrine. Doubtless this study will result in the impression that the answers to St. Thomas' objections are provided by his own theology; but that is not what we are chiefly interested in showing. We are attempting to construct a synthesis, and it is in the Thomistic theses on original sin, grace, and the Redemption, as well as in the principal foundations of its Christology and Marian doctrine, that the means are to be found.

First of all, we must make clear the true nature of original sin and the manner of its transmission; the history of the controversies over the Immaculate Conception shows how necessary this is. And this will enable us to understand how and under what conditions the preservation of a human being from original sin can be conceived. The very heart of our subject will then come into view: why it was fitting for the Mother of God to be conceived without contracting original sin, and what effects this exemption had in her soul and in her entire being. At the end of this study, the connection of the Immaculate Conception with all Mary's other privileges will be so vividly apparent that the importance of this doctrine, the necessity of its dogmatic definition, and the fecundity of all study and meditation on it, will be better understood.

I

ORIGINAL SIN

Before we can understand the nature and significance of exemption from

* Professor of dogmatic theology at the Institut Catholique de Toulouse. The present article was completed in May, 1955.

original sin, we must have a clear idea of the common condition of mankind with regard to this sin.

Faith obliges us to believe that from our mother's womb, before the awakening of conscience or the performance of any personal act, but by the simple fact of being born in human nature, we are sinners. More precisely, it obliges us to believe that we are sinners *by the fact of the sin of Adam,* who was the first man and the source whence human nature descended. The miseries of our human condition and, precisely, death, suffering (which is the announcement and presage of death), and the inborn disorder of our instincts and emotions, especially those that have to do with sex: this whole aggregate of evils is caused by Adam's sin and does not affect any of us except insofar as this sin becomes ours.

How is this possible? How can one be punished, and, still more, become a sinner, through an act one has not committed?

Certain theologians have sought to be satisfied with imagining a sort of pact between God and the first man, according to which the sin or fidelity of the latter would be imputed to all his offspring. This pact is conceived as a purely moral entity, constituting Adam a sort of ambassador and juridic representative of humanity, in such wise that his acts count for us as the acts of a plenipotentiary legate count for the one who sent him. Of course, this delegation would not have been conferred on Adam by the human race or any of its members, but solely by the will of God. In any event, Adam's quality as our representative would not properly be based on anything in his acts or in his being.

This pact theory obviously makes it very easy to explain the Immaculate Conception. According to it, it would suffice to say simply that Mary was an exception to that solidarity which had been created by a free act of the divine will.

That there was, at the origin of the whole economy of creation and the fall, a divine act of will creating a solidarity of destiny between Adam and his offspring, is certainly admitted by St. Thomas. But for him, this divine will had a very real effect *in human nature,* and this solidarity was inscribed in Adam's very being.

We must beware of images here. Because sin is a stain, and because the sexual act which is at the origin of the human being appears as particularly stained, some were led to think that human flesh itself was stained by its origin, and that the soul, in being united to the body, contracted this stain by a sort of contagion. Such a notion does not stand up under analysis. If we were to suppose that the sexual act was evil even in marriage (and why should we?), this would not make sinners of anyone but the parents.

The "physical" theories also entailed another exaggeration: in trying to include Adam's descendants in their sinning father in a real manner, and being unable to include our wills in his (physically, this would be impossible; morally, it would mean that we had voluntarily made Adam our vicar, which is equally impossible), they imagined that, at the moment of Adam's sin, there was contained in Adam's body a material portion of each one of us, which was to be transmitted through generation. Even if this were so, how would that flesh have been infected by Adam's sinful act, and how would it have infected our souls?

All of these explanations, which, because of the value of their imagery, have frequently been used in sermons (traces of them are to be found even in Bossuet), make the mistake of trying (unsuccessfully, as a matter of fact) to represent us as actually and personally present in Adam and conniving in his sin, whereas, in truth, only our nature is present in him.

This is what St. Thomas insisted on with admirable force, showing thereby that, if original sin is truly a sin, it is a sin of nature, not a personal sin; and, above all, that original sin cannot be understood until original justice is.

The first man was created *in grace;* that is to say, in that participation in the divine nature which, without destroying human nature, elevates it as regards what is most basic in it—its intrinsic finality. By grace, God in His interior life becomes the object of the soul's activity. This could not take place except by an ontological transformation of the soul's intimate structure, and a new kind of presence of the Divinity. But *being created in grace* meant more than merely being created *in order to receive grace;* it implied that grace was, if not natural, at least *'native.'* No ordination, intrinsic or extrinsic, to any natural end, could have preceded the divine destination of the being that was created in a divinized state. Moreover, in this divine economy, nature was so ordained to grace that it was endowed with gifts designed to ensure this ordination with perfection. These gifts are called 'preternatural,' because they did not arise from the principles of nature, even though they corresponded to its aspirations. They were not supernatural in essence, but they were destined to make the human being 'connatural' to a supernatural end. Chief among these gifts were immortality and the spontaneous submission of the passions and emotions to the reason.

It is essential for us to understand that the source and principle of these gifts was the submission of man's spirit to God which was realized by grace, but so perfectly achieved as to produce in turn the submission of man's sensible faculties to the spiritual, of the body to the soul, and even of the exterior world to man. What must be grasped here is that human nature was transformed by divine grace in its very structure, even insofar as it was sensible and corporal; and that this transformation was in view of the full and harmonious development of grace.

Another point of capital importance is that this grace was given to nature as such, i.e. as regards what is specific in it.   It was Adam, indeed, who received it; but he received it for the whole race.   The proper subject of this gift of God was nature *as specific and transmissible;* that is why it affected the psychological structure and physiological destiny of this entire new race which, in the very instant of its creation, had been placed beyond all the hopes of an ordinary biological evolution.

Naturally, grace itself, the principle of the state of original justice, would not have been transmitted by generation; [1] nor would the spiritual soul. What was to be transmitted was the body, but a *human* body, calling for a spiritual soul as its proper form.   In this state of original justice, the pro-creative act, in order to attain a term truly "like unto its principle," tended intrinsically to a spiritual soul in the state of grace, the proper form of a "preternatural" body.

Let us stop a moment to reflect on the divine plan.   Human nature alone, among all created natures, resembles the divine nature in that it implies a profound community among distinct persons.   Among the angels, you do not find a community of specific nature, giving rise to an intimate material, psychological and social interdependence; and among animals there is not a community of spiritual and immortal *persons* capable of self-awareness, of love and of inter-relations.

In founding this community of natures on a common origin—which would not have been the case if the human race had been created through polygenesis—God had already accentuated this communal trait, and thereby the resemblance of human nature to the divine.   But in giving it *grace* —that is to say, in causing it to participate in His own nature—*in common* and *as a species;* in uniting this multitude of persons to Himself *by means of their common nature and common origin,* God seems to have exploited to the utmost the unique resources of solidarity, and of unity in diversity, which the human essence offered Him.   He corrected the weaknesses which were liable to make life according to grace difficult for human nature, but He accentuated the importance and the role of generation as a factor of spiritual communion.

Only this positive aspect of the divine plan can give us a glimpse of the consequences of original sin.

Sin is a voluntary separation from God, a turning to creatures, or rather, to oneself, as an 'end,' as the total and exclusive object of one's love.   This is what constitutes the essence and evil of sin.   Such was Adam's sin: if it entailed the loss of grace, this was not as a punishment, but by its very essence, by the contradiction it implied to the very nature of grace, which ordains us to God as to our end.

---

[1] This is why St. Thomas attributed to Adam an office of unparalleled teaching authority and spiritual influence over his offspring—thereby magnifying, incidentally, his paternal role.

What was unique in Adam's sin was that it destroyed grace *in the very mode in which grace had been given,* i.e., not only for Adam, but for the entire race. This grace, whose subject was the being in its profound, specific and transmissible nature, was contradicted and destroyed by the personal will of Adam.

This does not mean that Adam's merits counted for his descendants. What is communicated to us is certainly not his personal demerit, as if it were ours, but the loss of grace included in his personal sin, which loss pertains to human nature as such, inasmuch as common and transmissible. But because grace was the principle of the entire human equilibrium, this equilibrium was lost with it. The spirit was separated from God, the emotional area of the soul recovered a quasi-autonomy with regard to the spiritual, and the mysterious power of surmounting death which had been possessed by the body, or rather by the soul informing the body, was automatically suppressed.

The transcendent character of the Fall becomes apparent when you consider that man, after having been created with grace and with those gifts which were conferred for the sake of grace, fell back to a state of nature, stripped of everything that was not essential to nature; that is to say, to the status of a spirit existing in the animal order, that has just barely attained the level of spirituality The Fall appears still more dramatic when you recall that man had not been given any natural end to unify his being, and that none is given him by sin. The "absurd" and incomprehensible character of the human condition is thereby explained.

It is easy enough to see that the procreative act transmits nature in this impoverished condition. Since the Fall, that which the procreative act calls for, that to which it tends as to a term connatural to its principle, is a soul without grace: *"sine Deo in hoc saeculo."*

To be conceived in the state of original sin, therefore, is to be conceived without grace and, by that very fact, in a condition essentially characterized by the union in one being of two metaphysical contraries which nothing serves to harmonize: the animal being and the spiritual being, of which the former is itself profoundly divided by the very complexity of its faculties and the native incoherence of its personality.

What could seem much more difficult of understanding, is how our being conceived without grace through Adam's fault makes us participate in his sin and even acquire the character of sinners. In order for there to be sin, it is not sufficient that there be privation of God; this privation must in some way be voluntary. But in a human being who is now conceived in the state of privation of God, this state is not voluntary; it was voluntary only in Adam. Nevertheless, the absence from God which was included in Adam's sin affects the entire nature, and each new person, in individualizing that nature, individualizes this state and makes it his own. This he does in that moment of dependence upon the procreative act which is the formal moment of his "personalization"; and the procreative act arises from the specific nature as such and joins the new being to Adam—not only to Adam begetting his first son, but, anteriorly to that, to Adam losing by his sin the power to beget sons of God.

Original sin is a fault, therefore, insofar as we are all one in the nature of him who lost grace. The mystery of original sin is a mystery of solidarity. We are all in Adam when he sins; or rather—since we do not exist in him at the moment of his sin—we enter into that unity in receiving from him the nature which was deprived of the state of grace by his sin. Just as each sinful act leaves a stain in us, so, as a consequence of our conception (by which we have not indeed, sinned, but have contracted a solidarity with Adam's sinful act), there remains in each of us a *stain*, a privation of God, which constitutes a state of sin.

This enables us to understand the role of the procreative act in the transmission of original sin. It transmits sin because it transmits nature without God, and because it transmits it in virtue of a power and a privation, both of which ultimately derive from Adam, the first man. The pleasure and the disorder which often accompany this act, the animality which frequently triumphs in it (although at quite different degrees), are not the proper cause of its malefic power, but the symptom and effect of a disorder in the nature itself which transmits and is transmitted.

II

THE TRUE SENSE OF THE IMMACULATE CONCEPTION

At the time of the great mediaeval controversies, everyone admitted that the animation of a human fetus, that is, the creation by God of a spiritual soul, did not take place until several weeks after the conception of that fetus. The name *active conception* was given to the procreative act, or at least to the "informing," by the semen of the man, of the matter provided by the woman. The name *passive conception* was given to the coming into existence of the new being thus begotten. Hence, properly speaking, the latter was *conceived* before receiving a spiritual soul; but even in this transitory form, the fetus already bore in itself that 'call' for the creation of the soul of which we have spoken. For this reason, many authors did not consider the passive conception as accomplished until the instant the soul was created, that is to say, until animation. As a result, the proposition, *Mary was conceived without sin,* could be taken in three different senses:

1. In the first sense, it would refer to the 'active conception,' that is to say, to the procreative act of the parents. But since the sinful character of this act was not in question, its 'purification' could only mean the

suppression of its power to transmit original sin.[2] If what we have already said has been well understood, it will be clear that this would mean precisely that the power to transmit, or rather to postulate grace, had been restored to the act. This would be altogether inexplicable, because such a power supposes that grace has been given to *nature as such,* inasmuch as transmissible. Hence, in this case, it would be necessary to hold that Joachim and Anne themselves, before begetting their child, had received original justice, the grace of Adam and Eve.

2. In the second sense, the proposition would refer to the 'passive conception'; but at this moment, the fetus, being not yet animated by a spiritual soul, cannot be a subject of grace—or of sin either, for that matter. In virtue of the procreative act, it merely calls for the creation of a purely natural soul. Its 'purification' could be conceived only as a transformation of this 'call' or exigence. By some mysterious gift the flesh would be intrinsically ordained to a soul in the state of grace. In the perspective of St. Thomas, this is inconceivable. But it is likewise altogether inconceivable, in his perspective, to speak of the flesh, in this embryonic and not yet personal state, as "stained." 'Stain,' like holiness, can be taken here only in a moral sense. But human nature does not even exist yet in this embryo, which contains human nature only in germ; and although this 'being in the state of becoming' tends, by all its interior reality and dynamism, toward a nature that is stained and sinful, no person is yet there who could be called the subject of this tendency, or who could contract this stain even germinally and in its cause. It is proper to original sin that it does not become the sin *of someone* except by the emergence, in the "stained" nature, of a determinate person. Before the creation of a spiritual soul there can be neither sin nor grace. Before the creation of Mary's soul, that which was to become her body shared the common lot; but before the creation of her soul, *Mary* did not yet exist.

3. In the third sense, our proposition would be taken with regard to the moment of animation. Then it would mean quite simply that Mary's soul was created in the state of grace; for the state of original sin is the state of privation of grace insofar as this is imputable to the procreative act. Note well that, of itself, this act tended to transmit a nature deprived of grace; hence, for Mary's soul to have been created in grace, there would have to have been in its creation some intention positively saving it from that to which it was destined by the carnal act which called it into existence: that is to say, something saving it from original sin. And if it was *saved*

---

[2] Unless, of course, you were to say that Mary was conceived virginally—the idea against which St. Bernard reacted so violently in his letter to the canons of Lyons. Cf. chapter I of the present volume, p. 44.

from sin, this was, as we shall see, in consideration of the redemptive merits of Christ.

But when the matter is so presented, can you say that Mary was saved in the proper sense of the word, and *personally* redeemed? St. Thomas thought that the very *person* of Mary had contracted that from which Christ saved and redeemed her, and this was, without any doubt, the objection which held him back. But Scotus was to answer it: by the union of her soul with the flesh issued from Adam, Mary had personally contracted the natural incompatibility with grace which was inscribed in his flesh, and which made her grace doubly gratuitous. Scotus went even further, distinguishing between that metaphysical moment in which the soul is created and begins to constitute, with the body, one nature and one person, and a second moment in which it receives grace. He did not mean that there were two successive moments, but only that there is an order between that which comes from nature and that which comes from grace. It is certain that grace *presupposes* the nature which reecives it. In that first instant of nature, prior to the instant in which grace is possible, there is neither grace nor privation of grace, but only a natural ordination not to have grace. This is what Mary contracted, and from which she is saved.[3]

Later theologians called this ordination not to have grace *debitum peccati*. The only excuse for the expression is the difficulty of replacing it. It is indeed calculated to give rise to equivocations and disputes; for since original sin consists essentially in the privation of grace and, consequently, in a sort of *debitum gratiae* (*privatio = carentia boni debiti*), the *debitum* of this *debitum* is liable to appear as something sinful. It is hard to avoid the impression that Mary would have been purer if she had not contracted this 'debt.' To call the state of the flesh prior to animation, or the disorder of the procreative act, a 'stain' or an 'infection,' ultimately provokes the same repugnance. The fact is, there is no stain except where there is the possibility of grace; up to this point there is only the threat of stain, and this threat is not properly a *debitum* because not a moral reality. But what is it to be called? Throughout this exposition, we have used the terms, *interior exigence, call, ordination to*. Cajetan spoke of a *necessitas contrahendi peccati*. What is essential is that, in the midst of these terminological difficulties, we agree on what we mean. Nothing resembling a moral stain was ever, at any conceivable instant, contracted by Mary: *sine ulla labe peccati concepta*.

We have situated our exposition in the ancient perspective which distinguished between passive conception and animation. Today it is generally agreed that the spiritual soul is created at the very moment when the initial

---

[3] For further details concerning the doctrine of Scotus, see chapter V of the present volume, p. 204 ff.

cell of the new being comes into existence as a result of the fusion of the spermatozoid and of the ovulum. No essential change is thereby introduced into the doctrine; the procreative act simply becomes immediately connex with the creative act corresponding to it. The procreation tends of itself to the creation of a purely natural soul, without grace; contrary to this tendency, and in virtue of something other than it, it is a soul full of grace that is created.

III

THE REASON FOR THE IMMACULATE CONCEPTION

THE GENERAL REASON

Christian instinct sensed that Mary's purity would have been less, and her grace less perfect, if she had been conceived in original sin. It also sensed that she could not have been less dependent on Christ and on His redemptive sacrifice than other human beings were—not only for Christ's honor, but also for that of Mary herself. If one were to succeed in reconciling these two exigencies of the Church's living tradition, how could one hesitate?

A being that has been redeemed can, it is true, rise to a sanctity higher than that from which it had fallen. But if innocence too often engenders pride or tepidity, it is because this innocence is rather the absence of faults than the intensity of charity. In reality, as St. Thomas says, "Innocence is, in itself, more perfect than repentance." [4] And from the point of view of the gift of God and the gratuity of His love, Mary's immaculate innocence is not a lesser grace than that which is given to the entire race, for it is given to her despite her origin. As St. Therese of Lisieux says, "A child owes much more to his father when the latter takes the stones out of his path, than when he picks the child up and heals him after a fall." And what St. Thomas says in a more general way can very well be applied to the case of Mary: "Of two equal graces, that which is bestowed on a penitent who had deserved to be refused it is more of a gift than that which is bestowed on an innocent person who had not so deserved." [5] For Mary was born in a human nature which had "demerited" grace, and she received in her conception what her conception did not merit.

---

[4] The text of St. Thomas deserves to be cited in its entirety: ". . . sive sint innocentes, sive poenitentes, illi sunt meliores et magis dilecti, qui plus habent de gratia. Ceteris tamen paribus, innocentia dignior est et magis dilecta. Dicitur tamen Deus plus gaudere de poenitente quam de innocente, quia plerumque poenitentes cautiores, humiliores et ferventiores resurgunt. Unde Gregorius dicit . . . 'quod dux in praelio eum militem plus diligit, qui post fugam conversus, fortiter hostem premit, quam qui nunquam fugit, nec unquam fortiter fecit.' Vel, alia ratione, quia aequale donum gratiae plus est, comparatum poenitenti, qui meruit poenam, quam innocenti, qui non meruit. Sicut centum marcae maius donum est, si dentur pauperi, quam si dentur regi." (I, 20, 4 ad 4)

[5] *Ibid.*

There have been some who minimized the necessity of the Immaculate Conception because they minimized the importance of original sin as a moral stain. It is, after all, the human race in its entirety which sins, and not any particular person. Would it not suffice for Mary's purity if the stain with all its consequences had been totally expunged immediately after having been contracted through the procreative act by which the person becomes solidary with the mass?

It is difficult to understand how a Thomist could ever have seen things in this light. Exemption from original sin is not a mere negation; on the contrary, it is original sin which is a negation and an absence. To be exempted from original sin is to receive grace at the very moment of the creation of one's soul, to be loved and set apart from Adam's sin—and, as we shall see, through a union with and an ordination to Jesus Christ. How can one fail to see that a true fullness of grace implies being given at that first moment and in this fashion? We will see better shortly to what degree, being given in the very act of creation, as in the case of Adam, implies being rooted in nature. We will see also that preservation from personal sins, if it is to be radical and, as it were, inscribed in the will itself, supposes the abolition of the consequences of sin. But how much more radical and more perfect as a gift of God it is if the consequences do not need to be abolished because their source does not exist!

The Proper Reason for the Immaculate Conception: Predestination to the Divine Motherhood

We could stop at the point just reached: the greatest purity possible in a human creature [6] for her "whom God loves more than the totality of His creatures;" [7] a perfection and fullness of grace as great as can be conceived in anyone who has been redeemed. This would be sufficient to prove the Immaculate Conception, and is, furthermore, nothing but the formulation in precise terms of the living Tradition of the Church, for which Mary has always been the "Virgin" in the total sense, "holy" without qualification.

But the theologian is not satisfied with reasons that are too general; they prove a conclusion, but do not always make it fully understood. In reality, *the proper and formal reason for the Immaculate Conception is Mary's predestination to the Divine Motherhood.*

Predestination is the ordination of a being from all eternity by God to *an end* for which it was willed and created. Predestination commands the means which will lead to this end, that is to say, essentially, the totality of graces which will be given to the being in question. But predestination

---

[6] St. Anselm.
[7] The Bull *Ineffabilis.*

also embraces the faults into which, by its own initiative, but with the divine permission, the creature will fall, and from which it will have to be raised again. Not until it is finished will the tissue of acts with which a life is filled be understood; then it will be seen from God's point of view, from the point of view of His will and His grace. But in the divine eternity, it always appears as fully accomplished. The destiny of each individual forms part of an ensemble: there is only one universe, one Church, and one Divine Plan in which each being has its place.

Mary's predestination differs from that of other Christians in that, *whereas the others are predestined essentially to beatitude, i.e. to the eternal possession of God, the term of Mary's predestination is the Divine Motherhood.*

Mary's motherhood is not merely one event in her life of grace; it cannot even be called a *mission* in the order of grace, like the apostolate or priesthood. It represents the closest bond there is between a creature and God, and, because all predestination is in Christ, the greatest possible proximity to the Incarnate Word. By it Mary attains to the hypostatic order, on which every order of grace and glory depends. It can truly be said that *Mary is created, willed and predestined in order that she may be the Mother of God—the Beatific Vision and Love being, in her case, ordained in God's plan to her state of Mother of God.* Evidently this could not be said of the Divine Motherhood considered only in its biological reality; it must be taken as including all that the mystery of procreation calls for by way of spiritual life (consciousness and love). To say that Mary is predestined to be the Mother of God is to say that she is predestined to be so not only in her flesh, but also in her soul, whence alone can spring a charity similar to that with which the Father loves the Son. From this it can be understood why she had not yet attained the term of her predestination at the instant of the Incarnation, even though she was already Mother of God. She was still 'en route' and in the process of development. Her entire earthly life would be necessary for her to attain the fullness of the spiritual state of Mother of God. At her death, she was able at last to grasp her Son and possess Him according to His Divinity, according to His personal being, in a perfect and eternal correlation with Him. Grace, charity and the beatific light are in her only means or effects, in comparison with the state of Mother of God which calls for them and finds, thanks to them, the fullness of its perfection. From this it follows that the order of grace attains its summit in Mary for the very reason that she transcends it.

More precisely yet, it follows that *Mary is included in the decree of the Incarnation; that her predestination is indissociable from that of Christ.* The other saints also are predestined *in Christ;* He is the model and cause of their predestination. Mary is predestined *for Christ:* Christ himself is *her proper end.* All beings are ordained to Christ; she alone *attains* Him by her *personal being and acts.* She alone is constituted in her supernatural and eternal being by the Incarnation of the Word.

This is the sense in which it can be said of her, and of her alone, that she is included with Christ in one sole and unique decree of predestination. This refers, of course, not only to her physical being, which is the condition of that of Christ, but to the total ordination of her being and grace to the total being of Christ.

But we must go still further. *Mary's motherhood is ordained to the Incarnation of the Word to such a degree as directly to constitute a part of its realization.* Her grace and innocence, having as their direct purpose to make her a more perfect mother, are directly for Christ; her holiness, as also her virginity, add to the beauty of the Incarnation. To say that Mary is ordained to Christ by her grace as well as by her being is to say that she forms part of the predestination of Christ: "Under predestination comes not only that which is to be done in time, but also the mode and order according to which it is to be fulfilled in time." [8] Just as the humanity assumed by the Word in the Incarnation has to be holy and perfect, so also its origin, and the mother from whom it issues, must be holy and perfect. All this is designed *for His sake,* directly for *His sake.* Mary's grace belongs to the *coassumpta,* i.e. to the perfections due to the humanity of Christ. This is the profound meaning of the reason which St. Thomas gives for her freedom from all personal sin: *"Honor parentum redundat in prolem"*— "The parents' honor reflects upon the children." [9]

This reason must be taken very formally. In human affairs, the race, the social position, the respectability of parents reflect upon their children. This applies, in Mary's case, to the very perfection of her quality as a human being; because the Word, in making Himself man, wished to assume everything that was in man except sin.

One might be tempted to think that Mary's holiness matters to the Incarnate Word only at the moment of the Incarnation, or from that moment on; but this is not so. The person of the Son exists even before that of the Mother, and in the first moment of her existence, He already loves her as His Mother. He chooses and creates her for Himself. That first instant in which Mary's person received its existence was the proper effect of the Eternal Love preparing for the Incarnation of the Word. How would it be possible for divine grace not to have been bestowed on her at the same time as natural existence? To speak more formally, the first moment of Mary's existence was also that of her belonging to Christ.

---

[8] "Sub praedestinatione . . . aeterna non solum cadit id quod est fiendum in tempore, sed etiam modus et ordo secundum quod est complendum ex tempore." (III, 24, 4)

[9] III, 27, 4.

Her motherhood was yet to come; but it was already present to Him Who was to be her Son and Who was creating her for this very purpose. "Daughter of your Son," said Dante. Could it be said better or more profoundly?

IV

THE GRACE OF MARY IMMACULATE

The Grace of Mary and the Grace of Christ

If it is true that Original Sin consists essentially in the privation of grace, we must beware of speaking of the Immaculate Conception in negative terms. Light drives out or keeps out darkness; Mary's soul is born in the light. But, as we have seen well enough, it is the light of Christ, the grace of Christ that she receives. She is not only a preparation for the coming of Christ, but also its first effect. If it is true that every grace is a participation in that of Christ's human soul,[10] it is especially true of Mary, because she receives grace by reason of her predestination for the sake of Christ, and in order to be conformed and "fitted" to Him. Mary is an advance reflection of Christ, the dawn before the sun. If she is created in grace, therefore, it is *because of Christ*. The word *because* must here be taken in its strongest sense, so that the sentence means, *in consideration of the coming merits of Christ*—for merit can act in advance, and for all eternity. Although the charity of Christ began in time, it is nevertheless eternally present to the divine mind; and it is in the name of this charity, and of the sacrifice which it inspired, that all grace is given on earth, even before the Incarnation. It would not be right, of course, to say that Christ merited His mother's existence, because the latter is presupposed to His Humanity; but it was due to His merits that her motherhood was holy, full of grace, and of such a character as to unite her to His person. And while this was supremely fitting for the greatness of the Incarnation, it was not actually *necessary;* it was even naturally impeded by Mary's necessarily carnal origin. The Bull *Ineffabilis* states this clearly: If Mary was exempted from original sin, it was "by reason of the foreseen merits of Jesus Christ, Savior of the human race." [11] For if we are to say that Mary herself was redeemed, it is not sufficient that her original grace have been given *in spite of* the origin of her flesh, it had to be given her also in the name of the sacrifice of Jesus. But at the same time it was precisely for the sake of this redemptive sacrifice that the Word was to become incarnate,

---

[10] III, 7, 9: "Sic . . . recipiebat anima Christi gratiam ut ex ea quodammodo transfunderetur in alios. Et ideo oportuit quod haberet maximam gratiam; sicus ignis, qui est causa caloris in *omnibus* calidis, est maxime calidus." Likewise: ". . . conferebatur ei gratia tanquam cuidam universali principio in genere habentium gratiam. Virtus autem primi principii alicuius generis *universaliter* se extendit ad omnes effectus illius generis."

[11] "Intuitu meritorum Christi Jesus Salvatoris Humani Generis."

and that He created for Himself this human mother. Mary was both ordained to Christ from the first instant of her existence, and *the first* to receive from Him all that the rest of the human race would receive.

But once the Word had become incarnate in her womb, the grace of Christ no longer acted merely as exemplary final and meritorious cause. The very source of grace was now present in Mary, filling her with grace by an ineffably direct communication of the fullness of Christ. The "marvellous exchange," in which God takes our humanity and gives us His divinity is realized first of all between Mary and Jesus. This shows Mary's absolute priority in the ranks of those who have grace, in other words, in the Mystical Body of Christ. As St. Thomas says, "Being the closest to Christ's Humanity, from which all our grace derives, she receives a greater plenitude of grace than anyone else." [12]

THE GRACE OF MARY AND THE "ORIGINAL JUSTICE" OF ADAM AND EVE

If Mary's grace is a Christian grace (or "Christique," as some authors say), it would be expected to differ in some way from the *original grace,* that is, from that which Adam and Eve received. And if this is so, can one truly say that Mary has been entirely exempted from original sin?—for the latter, as we have seen, consists precisely in the privation of that grace originally given to human nature.

If Adam had not sinned, we would have received grace, along with nature, in virtue of and in the name of the procreative act that united us to him. Now it is far from being in the name of the act which engenders her that Mary receives grace; on the contrary, it is in spite of it, and directly from God—from God insofar as He is to become her son, consequently, from Christ. The New Eve is created after the image of the New Adam, not, directly, of the old. Indirectly, however, she is after the image of the old Adam, and eminently so, if this expression may be permitted, because obviously Christ's grace contains in its fullness all the perfection of Adam's grace, and, very specially, that perfection which consists in being rooted in nature, whereby nature is ordained to grace. The original grace and more yet is restored to man in the New Adam.

It is true that Baptism does not communicate grace to us in this state of perfection; or rather, St. Thomas tells us, it communicates it to us only *virtute,* in germ. Baptism is a birth, a beginning. When the "new man"

---

[12] "Quanto aliquid magis appropinquat principio in quolibet genere, tanto magis participat effectum illius principii; . . . Christus autem est principium gratiae: secundum divinitatem quidem auctoritative; secundum humanitatem vero, instrumentaliter; unde et Joan. I (17) dicitur: 'Gratia et veritas per Jesum Christum facta est.' Beata autem Virgo Maria propinquissima Christo fuit secundum humanitatem, quia ex ea accepit humanam naturam. Et ideo prae caeteris majorem debuit a Christo gratiae plenitudinem obtinere." (III, 27, 5)

attains "the fullness of the age of Christ," the total restoration of the state of original innocence will be accomplished, at least as regards what is essential and "eternalizable" in it (for the exceptional earthly conditions which characterized the time of human merit and becoming in the primitive plan of God will be eliminated).

Many theologians think that the privilege of the Immaculate Conception did not necessarily imply that Mary enjoyed all the perfection of original grace, but that she, like those who are baptised, had to submit to all the conditions of fallen nature, except, of course, concupiscence.

To solve this problem, we must take some steps backwards. As we have said, grace was accompanied in Adam by gifts called "preternatural,' such as the perfect rectitude of the passions and emotions (and hence, the absence of concupiscence), and also immortality. The pain and suffering of this life, including death itself, evidently comes to man from without, and could not have been avoided, as one day it will be, except by a transformation of the general order of things. On the contrary, whatever pertains to the interior harmonization of nature with grace depends on nothing but the perfection of the latter,[13] and entails none of the biological, physical or, for still greater reason, cosmic transformations which Christ has evidently reserved for the time of the Resurrection.

The important and, incidentally, difficult [14] text which we have cited in the last note invites us to another consideration. The soul of the first man was *created in grace,* because otherwise his nature would not have been

---

[13] Cf. I, 95, 1 (Utrum primus homo fuerit creatus in gratia): ". . . quod fuerit conditus in gratia . . . videtur requirere ipsa rectitudo primi status, in qua Deus hominem fecit, secundum illud Eccle. VII (30): 'Deus fecit hominem rectum.' Erat enim rectitudo secundum hoc quod ratio subdebatur Deo, rationi vero inferiores vires, et animae corpus. Prima autem subiectio erat causa et secundae et tertiae; quandiu enim ratio manebat Deo subjecta, inferiora ei subdebantur, ut Augustinus dicit. Manifestum est autem quod illa subiectio corporis ad animam, et inferiorum virium ad rationem, non erat naturalis; alioquin post peccatum mansisset . . . Ex quo datur intelligi, si deserente gratia soluta est obedientia carnis ad animam, quod per gratiam in anima existentem inferiora ei subdebantur."

[14] It would appear from this text that *the submission of the spiritual faculties to God* which was accomplished by grace in its perfect state *caused* the submission of the emotional faculties to the spiritual, and of the body to the soul. But even for the harmonization of the emotions it seems necessary to admit some sort of gifts innate in them, a kind of instinct to submit to the reason, such as virtue can confer after a period of time. But can such gifts or such an instinct be *caused,* properly speaking, by the union of the soul with God? With still more reason—can the submission of the body to the soul, even to the point of immortality, be an effect, properly so-called, of grace? The truth seems to be that in the state of original justice nature was so completely *designed for grace,* and the latter exercised its role of second nature so perfectly, that, in virtue of the profound and admirable laws of interior finality, everything in the structure of such a nature, as well as in its exterior circumstances, concurred providentially in favor of man's harmonious development. Hence the harmonious equilibrium of all the faculties under the rule of the mind; hence the creation of means unknown to us, capable of assuring victory over death.

created in that state of harmony with grace which only grace could confer on it. Mary's soul was also created in grace. . . . This does not mean merely that, in her case, grace began to exist simultaneously with nature; as in Adam's case also, there is involved that total and fundamental ordination of nature to grace which is the characteristic mark of original innocence.

The reason why the grace of baptism does not bestow original innocence is, as St. Thomas tells us, that it heals only the person, and not the nature. When the last human person has been called to salvation, nature will be healed in its entirety, collectively and inasmuch as specific nature, although in virtue of baptism.[15] In Mary's case, on the contrary, nature as such is saved at the same time as the person; it is precisely this which is meant by preservation from the sin of nature.

As a matter of fact, even when theologians doubted the Immaculate Conception, they all agreed that the source of concupiscence had been suppressed in Mary. This was a somewhat negative fashion of expressing the perfect purity of her senses, emotions and will. The state of innocence is not easy for us to picture: powerful faculties, none of which however, is attracted by any object which has not first been taken up and put in its place by the light of the mind; a heart which always loves in due order, and yet spontaneously and ardently, and with an absence of egoism which is innocence itself; a promptitude of one's entire being in following the impulses of grace; a constant fidelity of one's fervor. . . . And Mary had even more than is implied in the state of innocence, for she was preserved from all fault, imperfection or spiritual slackening by the same power which willed that she should be without sin, and which is nothing other than the hand of Christ placed upon her in advance. Above all, grace had on her soul an intense effect, comparable to nothing that may occur in any other, because it was designed to prepare her to meet the Incarnate Word. The 'first movements' of her soul are not only good, they are divine. She belongs to God not only in the sense implied by grace, but more than anything else which can exist in the created universe. Her virginity, and the invincible consecration of her heart to God, are the expression of a purity and sanctity which is not merely that of original innocence. Furthermore, her purity was, according to St. Thomas, so great and so contagious that, in spite of her beauty, no one who saw her ever had any sensual desire for her.[16]

---

[15] Cf. III, 69, 3 ad 3: ". . . peccatum originale hoc modo processit quod primo persona infecit naturam, postmodum vero natura infecit personam. Christus vero converso ordine prius reparat id quod personae est, et postmodum simul in omnibus reparabit id quod naturae est."

[16] Speaking of the "sanctificatio . . . prima, qua in utero sanctificata fuit," he says: ". . . gratia sanctificationis, ut dicitur, non tantum repressit motus illicitos in ipsa, sed etiam in aliis efficaciam habuit; ita ut quamvis esset pulchra corpore, a nullo unquam concupisci potuit." (*Scriptum super sententiis,* in Lib. III, D. III, q.1, a.2, q.1, resp.)

As regards the sufferings of this life, and what theology calls the *defectus humanae naturae*, Mary's case was like that of her Son. Of Himself, Christ would not have been subject to them; the state of the Transfiguration would have been more natural to Him than that of suffering and obscure pain. But He assumed them *voluntarily*, and used them as the instrument of His charity and of our salvation. When it is Jesus Who undergoes them, human sufferings cease to be penal or simply inevitable, and become a source of redemption. Likewise, it was by the will of Jesus and in no sense *"ex debito peccati"* that Mary assumed these sufferings and humiliations of mortal flesh; and she consented whole-heartedly to this will of Christ in order to be more like Jesus, and work with Him for the salvation of mankind. Christ's will is, in her case too, purely redemptive; for she too had "received human nature without sin and in all the purity of the state of innocence." [17] The sufferings she thus voluntarily accepted went even to that extreme point of maternal affliction in which the "thou shalt bear children in sorrow" found its most cruel realization, not at Bethlehem but at Calvary, not as a punishment or consequence of the fallen state of feminine nature, but as a fruitful redemption.

Among these *defectus humanae naturae* there is mortality, which is also the culmination of all the others, all suffering being already a *responsum mortis*. With regard to it, the principles we have just laid down need only be applied. Like Jesus, Mary was mortal, but only in spite of the claim to victory over death which was implied in her grace of innocence. If she died, this would have been conformable to the laws of her nature, materially speaking. But her grace had elevated her above these laws, and only a redemptive intention could have subjected her to them. Many theologians even think that no principle of sickness or aging is conceivable in the body of Jesus, so that His death could not have come except from an external cause.[18] If that is so, the same thing would have to be said about Mary, and it would then follow that she could not have died except by the excess of a divine love that united her to Christ so powerfully that her separation from Him could not endure.

[17] III, 14, 3. St. Thomas says this of Christ, not of the Blessed Virgin, of whom, on the contrary, he affirms in the *ad primum* that her flesh was naturally subject to these miseries. But St. Thomas thought, alas, that Mary had been conceived in sin, and it is explicitly for this reason that he recognizes that she had "contracted" the consequences of original sin. It is faithful to St. Thomas' thought on this point to say that since Mary was not conceived in original sin, she was spared its consequences. And it is evident what a marvelous answer could have been given to the objection in question, "Christus simul cum natura humana defectus et infirmitates corporales per suam originem traxit a matre, cujus caro hujusmodi defectibus subjacebat." By His origin *ex matre,* Christ could receive only a flesh delivered of all the enslavements and consequences of sin.

[18] Perhaps the gift of immortality enjoyed by the first man was nothing other than that. But in the state of original innocence, there would have been no exterior cause of death.

But if the meaning of Mary's death lies in her union with Christ for the salvation of men, how could she fail to be associated with His Resurrection? The definitive restoration of humanity need not be awaited in order for her to rise again like Christ: her resurrection and assumption are inscribed in the very reason for which it was fitting that she should die: death, which, for other men, is a consequence of original sin, was for her only the means of conformity to Christ and of participation in His redemptive activity. And this is not accomplished except in her resurrection and in her reigning with Christ at the head of the Universe and of the Church.[19]

It is evident to what degree Mary can be said to be Woman restored to her first splendor. She does not belong to the primitive order, but to that of Christ, which is that of Redemption: in her you find innocence, indeed, and still more, divine and total purity; but not ease, harmony and human happiness; rather, the holiness of suffering and the exaltation of love to the supreme gift, which is death. This New Eve assumes the sufferings of humanity, and does not become the Mother of the Living except in sorrow and in the tears mysteriously predicted for her ancestor in all her childbearings.

V

THE IMMACULATE CONCEPTION AND THE COREDEMPTION

It would take too long to show the profound connection between the privilege of the Immaculate Conception and Mary's mediative and co-redemptive role. This question is so important that it is the object of a special study in the present volume. We desire only to call attention to what follows immediately from what we have already said.

First of all, it becomes easy to see how Mary, who is herself one of the redeemed, can contribute to the redemption of the human race. For she is redeemed apart from other men and before them, being predestined before them and with Christ, who is the cause of their salvation.[20] Further-more, not only can Mary play a role in the redemption of the human race; the meaning of the grace of the Immaculate Conception would be incomplete if she did not. Her destiny embraces not only original innocence, but also the suffering and pain from which this innocence ought to have dispensed her, were she not called, like Jesus and with Him, to deliver us by suffering them innocently and holily. By this grace of perfect innocence which she alone, among men, can receive, she is, in fact, wholly ordained to the healing of men's sin, with something which is proper to her and which

---

[19] It is not a matter of faith that Mary died; and at the present time a theological movement, of rather recent origin, it is true, tends to affirm the contrary. But such a position could not be based on the exigencies of original justice, because in this regard Mary merely participates 'in Jesus,' Whom Himself passed through death.

[20] When anteriority in predestination is spoken of, there is question of an order of nature and of dependence among the various objects of the divine will.

makes its special contribution to the modality of mankind's salvation. For Jesus, although the son of our race, did not have in any sense the least possibility of sin. Mary *ought to have* been born in sin, and she is made of nothing but humanity. She is, in her origin, solidary with this nature of ours, which is for us precisely a source of sin. In her, grace is so purely grace, so little due—I do not say in virtue of any merit, but even in view of her natural origin, that there is necessarily in her heart a sister's pity for the sin of men, a mercy without measure. She is saved from among men; she is truly the Advocate *par excellence*. One would be inclined to say that Christ does not assume His role and power as Judge without first assuring Himself of an advocate before His tribunal who can base her prayer, not on our merits, but precisely on that misfortune of ours from which she has been spared.

This suggests a beautiful thought. One could ask whether Mary's virginity, admirably suited though it is to the ends of the Incarnation, does not make Christ a little less united to the human race, a little less directly son of man. If so, it is also through Mary that He recovers total solidarity with us. In this association between the Incarnate Word and the Virgin Mary, she 'confers' on Him something in the order of union to the human.

A spontaneous and wholly simple devotion to the Blessed Virgin existed in the Church long before the justification which we now give for it. That the doctrines of the Immaculate Conception and Coredemption have become more explicit in the Church has been due, perhaps, to the fact that for many centuries sinners called upon the most pure being they could imagine to purify them of their stains. It is these movements of the soul, which often find expression only slowly and painfully, and of which the Church in her interior life is the theater, that explain the surprising developments of ideas whose marvellous logic can sometimes be admired by reason only *post factum*.

PLANTATIO ROSAE

IX

The Immaculate Conception in God's Plan of Creation and Salvation

Urban Mullany, O.P.*

The precise question with which this paper is concerned is this: what is the place of Mary's Immaculate Conception in divine truth as a whole? More theologically put, the question is: how does God, in His causative view of the vast universe, look upon this initial privilege of Mary? To answer, we must attempt to see the pattern of Mary's grace of conception subtly intertwining itself in all the works of God from that beginning of time when God said "Be light made" even to that unending eternity in which predestined men and angels shall forevermore live by the light and love that is God. Briefly, then, we ought to look to the influence of Mary's privileged grace in God's plan of (1) creation, (2) predestination, (3) the Incarnation, (4) Redemption, and (5) that mystical Body which is the Church. In this undertaking we shall simply presume understanding of the inner nature and meaning of that preventive grace which constitutes Mary's Immaculate Conception.

The Immaculate Conception and the Mystery of Creation

> In the beginning God created heaven and earth . . . And He said: Let us make man to our own image and likeness: and let him have dominion over the fishes of the sea, and the fowls of the air, and the beasts, and the whole earth . . . And God created man to his own image . . . And God blessed them saying . . . fill the earth and subdue it and rule. (Gen. I, 26-28)

From these God-inspired words of Genesis, two great truths stand out clearly. The first is that God in creating produced order in the universe, an order whereby all lesser things were ordained to the service of man. It is not anthropomorphism grown exaggerated, but divinely guaranteed truth

---

* Professor of dogmatic theology, Dominican House of Studies, Washington, D. C. Co-editor of *The Thomist.*

that man is a certain final cause of all infra-rational creation. St. Thomas is merely summarizing traditional Christian understanding when he writes, "All bodily things are believed to have been made for the sake of man": God has indeed set man in dominion as master of all lesser creation; and all lesser creation is *propter hominem* in so far as it is intended simultaneously to perfect him in bodily life, and to whisper to him of divine truth. As St. Paul says, "All things are yours." (I Cor. III, 23)

But, secondly, the Scriptures indicate not merely that man is the end and master of all lesser things; but also the *why* of man's mastery. "Let us make man to our own image and likeness," and—by way of consequence— "let him have dominion."

For all things have been made unto the honor and glory of God.[2] Yet formally speaking only the image of God can give to God glory, for this requires that altogether spiritual knowledge and affection in which consists the image of God's being and life. Because man, the very image of God, can know and love the Creator, man uniquely within the bodily universe, achieves the goal of all. Lesser things give honor to God mutely, materially, rather in their service of man than in any formal sense.

But of men, and therefore of all things else, Christ, even in His humanity, is a certain goal. We have the words of St. Paul that Christ "is the head of all principality and power," (Col. I, 10) and again that Christ is set:

> . . . in the heavenly places above all principality and power and virtue and dominion and every name that is named, not only in this world, but also in that which is to come. And He hath subjected all things under His feet. (Eph. I, 20)

Even more clearly the great Apostle writes that Christ is:

> the image of the invisible God, the first born of every creature; for in Him were all things created in heaven and on earth, visible and invisible . . . and He is before all, and by Him all things consist. And He is the head of the body, the Church, who is the beginning, the first born from the dead. (Col. I, 15)

Note that these words are said of the God-*Man,* for Christ is "head of the Church," He is "first born from the dead," according to His humanity.

Basing themselves on such texts, the *Salmanticenses* write—and this is the teaching of Thomists commonly, a teaching in no way opposed to the truth that the motive of the Incarnation is man's redemption from sin— "God so intended the Incarnation . . . that He decreed Christ as the *primo volitum* to whom all other things . . . would be ordered as to their

---

[1] *Summa Theologiae,* Suppl., 91, 1.
[2] Cf. Proverbs XVI, 4.

end." [3] They cite especially St. Paul's words to the Colossians, "He is the first born of every creature. For in Him were all things created . . . and He is before all," and so forth.[4] Since this primacy, asserted of the man Christ, is not, they argue, in the order of execution (since in that order Christ comes after a whole multitude of creatures), then "we must have recourse to priority according to God's intention whereby He willed Christ first and all other things on account of Him, ordering all things to Christ as to their end." They cite once more the words of St. Paul, "He chose us in Him (Christ) before the foundation of the world" (Eph. I, 4); and the authority of Cyril of Alexandria and Rupertus Abbas, the latter phrasing the doctrine very clearly: "on account of this man (Christ), God created all things."

This clear Christian truth is briefly stated by the *Salmanticenses* in these words:

> Christ was the *primo volitum* as the end of all divine works; so in the genus of final cause He precedes (all other things) in the orders of nature and of grace . . . For where many things are willed together it is in accordance with reason and nature that that be looked to as the end which is the most perfect of all. But Christ is far more excellent and dignified than all other things . . . Therefore it seems true that He was intended as first and as the end *cujus gratia* of divine works, and all other things were willed for His sake.[5]

The speculative reasons for this truth can, I think, be summarized thus: "The Lord hath made all things for himself," as the Scripture says (Prov. XVI, 4), in the sense that He most lovingly determined to make things to be by freely giving things a varied sharing of His fullness of perfection. Created reality exists for the glory of God: but this means that for their welfare, not God's, existent realities share more or less in God's own perfection, both in the order of being and in the order of activity.

The most perfect and most divine of God's perfections is intellectuality: therefore the greatest manifestation of God's glory is the imaging of God which is intellectual life and love. In this, infra-rational creation cannot share, so it achieves its glorification of God, its manifesting of His divinity

---

[3] *Tract. de Incarnatione*, Disp. II, dub. 1, n.4: "Deum intendisse Incarnationem . . . ita ut decreverit Christum tanquam primo volitum in quo omnia alia . . . ordinarentur sicut in finem."

[4] Cf. *supra.*

[5] SALMANTICENSES, *l.c.*, n.26: "dicendum est Christum fuisse primum volitum et intentum per modum finis omnium operum divinorum; atque ideo praecessisse in genere causae finalis ordinem nature et gratiae . . . Nam ubi plura volita concurrunt consonum est rationi et naturis rerum quod illud respiciatur . . . per modum finis quod est inter omnia perfectissimum. Christus autem longe excellit in perfectione ac dignitate cuncta quae disposuit Deus. Ergo . . . verosimilius est quod fuerit primo intentus per modum finis cujus gratia operum divinorum et quod omnia fuerint volita propter ipsum."

or wisdom, in its order of service of God's image; for order is the manifestation of wisdom.

But the intellectual creature, the created image of God, whether angelic or human, images God's life only in a participated way. Through the Incarnation there is One, a Man, Who is the image of the Divine Father not merely by participation, but in Person; a Man Who not only knows and loves God but Who *is* God.

Him God must set as the measure, the end, of all other images; the measure, because always that which is by participation is measured by that which is such by essential right; the end, because what is by participation is tendential toward that which is such in plenary fashion.

In the order of operation, too, Christ is the end of all other images. Because this Man is infinite in Person, the actions of this Man, even His human actions of actually knowing, loving and glorifying the Divine Father, are acts of infinite value. Christ therefore gives to the Father infinite honor and glory; He exhausts, so to say, the possibilities of creatures' glorifying of God.

The glory given to God by the entire universe—the achieving of its end— is therefore but a certain sharing of the glorification achieved by Christ. It follows that our Lord is a fullness, a norm, a rule. He *is* the end of the world, concretized, achieved. That is why in the Mass, our supreme act of glorifying God, we say that it is through Christ our Lord that even the very "Angels praise God's majesty, Dominations adore" and so forth.[6] And again at the closing of the Canon of the Mass we profess that "through Christ and with Him and in Him is to Thee, Father almighty, in the unity of the Holy Ghost all honor and glory." Christ is the end of all because in Him all things find their purpose realized.

Apply now these principles and similar reasoning to our Lady immaculately conceived. Her Immaculate Conception constituted her as, simply speaking, the most perfect of all pure creatures. After Christ and dependently on Christ, she even, by her original grace, achieved the imaging of God far more perfectly than all the rest of the universe taken together, because by that grace she manifests God's perfection more brilliantly than all other creatures singly or collectively considered. For this we have the words of Pius IX. Writing of her original grace he says:

> On her God showered more love than on all other creatures, and so with her alone, He was pleased with a most loving complacency. He therefore filled her, far more than all the angelic spirits and all the saints, with an abundance of all heavenly gifts . . . that all beautiful and perfect, she might display such fullness of innocence and holiness, that under God none greater is known, and which, God excepted, none can attain even in thought.[7]

6 *Praefatio communis* of the Mass.
7 Bull, *Ineffabilis Deus,* 8 Dec. 1854.

She is then, with respect to all other pure creatures, a certain maximum of manifestation of Divine life and goodness. Can we conclude thence that she is, in some admittedly less perfect sense, an exemplar and end of all things beneath her?

From the principle enunciated by so many Christian theologians, *viz.*, "when many things are willed together, that one is regarded as end which is most perfect of all," or, "the lower is for the sake of the higher," such a conclusion would certainly follow.

Lending assurance to the conclusion, however, is the point made by Pope Pius IX:

> The Church understands that the inspired words referring to Christ's primacy have some true reference to and verification in Our Lady. So to her the Church of God applies, for example, the words of Ecclesiasticus (XXIV, 5) "I came out of the mouth of the most High, *the first born before all creatures*"; and those of Proverbs "the Lord possessed me in the beginning of his ways, before he made anything from the beginning. I was set up from eternity and of old before the earth was made . . . *I was with him forming all things*" . . . (VIII, 22, 23, 30).

Thus the Church understands that in some real sense Mary is the first of all pure creatures, the model having true influence upon the formation of all others. This is intelligible clearly in the order of exemplary casualty, since she most adequately among creatures mirrors God's life and love. But the exemplar is also a certain final cause with respect to what it effects, because the whole drive of the thing exemplified is to the exemplar in which it is achieved. The goal—the end—of its activity consists in assimilation to its own ideal: and so the whole universe has in Mary's sanctity—which is substantially her Immaculate Conception—a certain proximate, or intermediate goal.

Christian tradition expressly states this. St. Bernard puts it that "for the sake of Mary . . . the whole world was made." [8] Even among the ancient Jews there was a tradition that the Messias and the Virgin were the final cause of the whole world. Cornelius a Lapide quotes Jewish authority for this proposition, "God created heaven and earth out of love for the Virgin. The world was not only created but is sustained out of love for her." [9]

Such statements taken in themselves could easily seem exaggerations, as Mariologists are quick to admit. We have then this difficulty. Tradition, expressed also in the Church's liturgy, does teach that Our Lady, her

---

[8] *Sermo III in Salve Regina,* P.L., 184:1069: "Propter hanc totus mundus factus est."

[9] Cornelius a LAPIDE, *in Prov.* VIII, 22. (Pelagaud edit. vol. III pars I^a p. 194)

grandeur, is a certain final cause of creation. Yet to state flatly, "Mary is the final cause of the whole created universe," can most surely be scandalous and difficult doctrine, especially since Scripture expressly teaches that God is the goal or final cause of all things. What is the reconciliation of these two propositions, both of which pertain to Catholic doctrine?

I should like to suggest that it is by reference to the teachings of sound philosophy that we shall find the solution.[10]   Philosophers distinguish between *finis ut assequibilis* and *finis ut imitabilis* and add that the exemplar as such (and Our Lady is actually the first-born among creatures primarily as an exemplar of creaturely perfection) is *finis non ut assequibilis sed ut imitabilis.*

The distinction means this: What is rightly designated *finis ut assequibilis* is an existing thing, the true possession or enjoyment of which is the end of whatever is finalized by it; *finis ut imitabilis* designates a finalizing idea or a formality rather than a total existent.

Note that the *finis ut imitabilis* can never be that numerical reality which is the principal *finis cujus gratia.* For the exemplar or *finis ut imitabilis* can only be either a *ratio* as abstract, or a *ratio* concretized in some complex existent. The first, a mere idea or abstraction, can never be the principal final cause since real agents are perfected by real things. The second, or ideal as concretized in an individual, can never be the principal final cause for the reason that it is, in its numerical identity, unobtainable by the thing it exemplifies. Because the exemplar and the *exemplatum* are distinct individual things, the *exemplatum* can only become like to the exemplar according to those *rationes* in which the exemplar exercises causality; but those very *rationes* because they are individualized in and by the exemplar can never be possessed by the *exemplatum.* For example, we can say that George Washington was an exemplar of good citizenship. As such he should have directive influence over our actions. But our end is not the possession of the physical reality of George Washington, or even of that reality which was his special virtue, because his numerical qualities cannot possibly be ours. The end envisioned is merely specific similarity as to determined qualities.

Thus the *finis ut imitabilis* is never the true end *cujus gratia* precisely because its possession by the agent is impossible. The true *finis cujus gratia* is by definition one which so finalizes that possession of it is the very goal of activity of that which it finalizes. Therefore the exemplar is at best only relatively an end; it speaks to us of a further end which is obtainable by us; but the exemplar is not the reality which is that end.

When we say then that Mary is a final cause of creation the sense cannot be that she is an existent reality which finalizes the entire universe, the

---

[10] Cf. JOHN OF ST. THOMAS, *Cursus Philosophicus,* P.I.ª, Ques. XI, art. 3 (Reisner edit. vol. 2, pp. 240 ff.)

finis cujus gratia of cosmic being and activity. Emphatically she is not that. But since her own holiness is the most perfect created likeness of God, those qualities which make her that, constitute her a true *finis ut imitabilis,* so that the more God's many creatures do approach to her beauty and grandeur, the more are they perfected in themselves, the more do they become in fact conjoined to the perfecting end which is not Our Lady, but Him whose ideal created image she is.

In the order of activity, too, Our Lady, is a certain end of all things else, as we have already seen Christ also, in a more perfect way, to be. The implication here is that since all created activities have for their goal the glorification of God; and since, secondly, among all pure creatures, Mary's acts of glorifying God are a limit of perfection for all things beneath her, including angels and men; therefore the activities of all lesser things achieve their purpose to the degree that they imitate Mary's activities. But here, too, Our Blessed Mother is *finis mere ut imitabilis,* for the one Whom above all we glorify for His own sake is God. Mary is indeed one to the glorification of whom our efforts must, by God's determination, be directed; but what we, please God, do and shall forever glorify in her is not her own by any title proper to her. Of herself alone she is not even the handmaid of the Lord. What we love and glorify in Mary is the great things that "He that is mighty" has accomplished in her. Reverencing her, we reverence God really; for what we reverence in her is God imaged and even brought forth by her.

It remains only to point out that what constitutes Our Lady *finis ut imitabilis,* or exemplar, is really her Immaculate Conception and not, for example, her Divine Motherhood; with the result that it is the same thing to say "Our Lady is the end of all creation," and, "The Immaculate Conception is the end of all creation." I say that Mary's own holiness—substantially identical with her Immaculate Conception— and not her Divine Maternity, constitutes her our exemplar, for the reason that in her maternity of God no creature can specifically imitate or be like her; whereas in her likeness to God all things, but especially intellectual creatures, can and should be like to her. Evidently then it is in her imaging of God that she is *imitabilis.*

In fine, God made all things for Himself as His own revelation asserts; but God made all things for Mary, too, in the sense that through her, by imitation of her, all things attain God's purpose and their own perfection.

In God's view then Christ and she stand as the center of His great universe. In them is the reason for all else, the meaning of all else, the definitive achievemnt of the purpose of all else. Because they more than accomplish the goal of all things in their glorifying of God, they are the end with respect to all else. And of Mary it is true that, already by her Immaculate Conception, by that splendor of personal sanctity, she is raised to that height in God's plan and view. It is true that a far greater dignity was one day to be hers; but even taken alone the magnificence of her original holiness is sufficient to make her the most faithful "mirror of justice," the most accurate created image of God, and that created person in whom God's purpose for all is at last fulfilled.

THE IMMACULATE CONCEPTION AND THE MYSTERY OF PREDESTINATION

Coming now specifically to the supernatural order and, more restrictedly, to the mystery of predestination, can we discern in the whole order of the predestination of other created persons a definite influence of Mary's Immaculate Conception? Is this immaculate daughter of God a certain cause of the predestination of the elect?

Here the tradition is even more explicit than in the question of creation. The traditional answer is emphatically affirmative. There is, first, the saying of the Fathers, especially the Greek Fathers, that Mary is *sola electa;* [11] not, as Cardinal Lépicier points out, that other saints were not elected, but because election is, so to say, appropriated to Mary since she is *par excellence* the elected among all creatures.[12] By this very fact Our Lady is exemplar of the predestination of all men; for the grace of her conception to which she was predestinated "filled her," again to quote Pius IX, "far more than all the angelic spirits and all the Saints, with an abundance of heavenly gifts," so that her grace, her holiness, is such that "under God none greater is known." Thus her original grace—her Immaculate Conception—is full measure of the grace of any and every pure creature. It is an ideal, an exemplar, we can but approach by the eternal determination of the eternal God.

Is it also a *final* cause of our predestination? That Mary herself is such a cause seems clear, and this is taught by Mariologists generally. But can we say that her Immaculate Conception, apart even from her maternity of God, is the final cause of our predestination? The question is equivalent to asking whether, in the plan of God, the grace and glory of all the elect is, in some true sense, for the sake of Mary formally because of her own personal holiness? We must answer cautiously.

In the order of intention, God's intention, Mary's predestination to the Immaculate Conception is an end of our predestination to grace. For while her grace is of the same species as ours, it is, according to Papal teaching, a limit which contains and indescribably exceeds all our holiness. It follows that the grace to which we are predestined is a certain assimilation of us unto Mary; and this God intends, since it is He Who set her as a certain exemplar with respect to us.

In ordine executionis, in the working out of our predestination, every

---

[11] Cf. G. M. ROSCHINI, *Mariologia,* Rome, 1947 vol. 2 p. 52.
[12] LEPICIER, *Tract. de Beatissima V. Maria,* Rome, 1926, p. 27.

advance in grace and every good act of ours is, even objectively speaking, a greater assimilation to the grace of Mary's Immaculate Conception. In that order also, therefore, Our Lady's grace of conception is a certain goal of our predestination.

Yet it would be a frightful aberration to imagine that Mary is the end of our predestination in the sense that her Immaculate Conception or anything else about her is the object terminating and specifying our predestination; in other words, to imagine that our grace is a formal participation of Mary's life, our glory a participation of her glory. Very decidedly it is not. The end which (*finis qui*) terminates our predestination is God alone, the divine life alone. Both *in ordine intentionis* and *in ordine executionis*, Our Lady is said to be a certain *finis* in the sense of *finis ut imitabilis, non assequibilis*. This is most clearly true since the grace of her conception is in fact incommunicable to others: to it, as to something to be possessed by us in whole or in part, not even God's absolute power could ordain us, for God cannot make the numerically one to be numerically many.

It is, therefore, by way of specific likeness, not by way of formal communication, that our Blessed Mother's predestination is the cause of our predestination. In the endlessness of eternity, the elect shall indeed exult in the glorification of Mary, herself predestined, and the cause of their predestination. But in this they shall exult even more: that their predestination, like unto Mary's, is predestination to life intrinsically and properly divine.

Other aspects of Mary's casuality of our predestination are discernible. Since, however, they are dependent upon prerogatives other than her Immaculate Conception, consideration of them would be pointless here for our purposes.

THE IMMACULATE CONCEPTION AND THE INCARNATION

That there is connection between these mysteries is Papal teaching. Pius IX indicates that Mary's original grace was divinely ordered to the enfleshing in her of God's own Son.

> In view (of the Incarnation) God chose and appointed a mother for His only-begotten Son. . . It was quite becoming, that so venerable a mother should be ever adorned with the splendor of most perfect holiness . . . because she it is to whom God the Father willed to give His only Son.[13]

The Scriptures themselves imply this connection. God's messenger, Gabriel, first greeted in Our Lady the sanctity that was the identical sanctity

[13] Bull, *Ineffabilis Deus*, 8 Dec. 1854.

of her conception: "Hail, full of grace," and then, "Fear not, . . . thou hast found grace with God. Behold thou shalt conceive in thy womb and shalt bring forth a son." God's own word implies the nexus here, a divinely decreed nexus between Mary's grace and God's advent through her as the uniquely graced one.

An insight into the nature and importance of this nexus between Mary's grace and the Incarnation is given us by St. Thomas. The greatness of the saints, he writes, is this, that grace sanctifies their souls; now, he adds, "the soul of the Blessed Virgin was so full that from it grace overflowed into her flesh, so that from her flesh she conceived the Son of God."[14] In another place he expresses the same thought in these words: "From her soul, grace overflowed into her body, for through the grace of the Holy Ghost not only was the mind of the Virgin perfectly united to God . . . but her womb was supernaturally impregnated by the Holy Ghost."[15]

In God's plan, therefore, the Immaculate Conception in itself was a certain *sine qua non* with respect to the Incarnation. For God would be incarnate not of any flesh, not of any woman; but only of flesh sanctified by the touch of supernatural grace, only of a woman whose very body could be a true temple of the all-holy God. This, God's reverence to Himself decreed.

In the Immaculate Conception we must distinguish its substance, divine grace, from its mode, preservation. Both were involved in Mary's preparation for the Incarnation. According to St. Thomas as we have just seen, her grace, her holiness, as it were drew down God Himself to her to fashion in her the living garment of His Son's humanity. According to the Holy Father her freedom or preservation from the sin of our nature was no less requisite. "It was quite right that, as the only-begotten had a Father in heaven whom the Seraphim extol as thrice holy, so He should have a Mother on earth who would never lack the splendor of holiness."[16]

For His supreme gift to man, God demanded supreme worthiness in man; that worthiness of soul and body that is the sinlessness of Mary's origin. Without her, without her Immaculate Conception, we should not be the brethren of God's own Son; through her grace of conception God has reached to us in the one way that He would take. The spotless love of Mary's conception, that mirror of God's own spotless love, already whispers of the substantial advent among us of true God. In God's view, that grace of her conception is like the hush of daybreak, when all the powers of nature stand poised to exult in the life of new day. Mary's conception is

---

[14] Opus. VI, *In Salutationem Angelicam Expositio:* "anima Beatae Virginis ita fuit plena quod ex ea refudit gratiam in carnem, ut de ipsa conciperet Filium Dei."
[15] *Expositio in Joannem* c.1 lect. 10: "ab anima ejus gratia redundavit in carnem; nam per Spiritus sancti gratiam non solum mens Virginis fuit Deo per amorem perfecte unita, sed ejus uterus a Spiritu Sancto est supernaturaliter impraegnatus."
[16] Bull, *Ineffabilis Deus,* 8 Dec. 1854.

man's readiness, man's hushed and reverent silence, as he awaited the enlivening light and warmth of that Sun of Justice who should bring to men the everlasting day of God's light and love.

THE IMMACULATE CONCEPTION AND THE MYSTERY OF REDEMPTION

Inseparable from the mystery of the Incarnation, because it gives internal character to that mystery, is the mystery of our Redemption. Is the Immaculate Conception of Mary in any true sense a part of that mystery, an interior element of its constitution? Again, in the teaching of Popes, Fathers of the Church, and theologians, that Mary is our Coredemptrix, we have assurance that the holy Virgin herself is a true part of this mystery; but our question here concerns Mary precisely and only as to the preservative grace of her conception.

Of our redemption, the Immaculate Conception is first the exemplar, the extreme limit beyond which redemption cannot *de facto* reach. Since all human predestination is predestination in the Divine Redeemer, the preeminence of Mary's redemption is of course implicit in the preeminence of her predestination. Yet it is worth noting that a greater redemption than Mary's grace of conception is, in the present order, impossible. For the substance of that privilege was the sanctity earned for her by Christ; and it is a sanctity "such that a greater under God cannot be conceived." So, because her original grace immeasurably exceeded the sanctity lost in Adam, her redemption did not merely restore what had been lost, but gave far in excess of that measure. Again, the mode of Mary's grace of conception, the mode that is preservation, implies a certain maximum in her redemption, for in the whole range of possibility there cannot be a greater deliverance from inherited evil than not to inherit that evil.

In the eyes of God, the Immaculate Conception of Mary is the first fruit and the greatest achievement of man's redemption. For Mary's preservation from sin was, in order and in nature, prior to our redemption. It was prior in order or dignity because preservative rather than liberating and because of the nobler holiness it conferred. It was prior in nature in this sense, and for this reason, that in the offering of Christ and in the acceptance by the Eternal Father, the passion and death of Christ were offered, first, as the price for Mary's preservation, and, secondly, and as a somewhat distinct effect, for our redemption from sin. The reason is that the preservative redemption of Mary is a greater good than the redemption of all the rest of mankind; so it was divinely loved and willed, according to priority of nature. That is why Our Lady, herself redeemed by the Passion of Christ, could cooperate in His redeeming Passion. Herself she could not and did not coredeem, because, as Coredemptrix, she needed to be already *de jure* a friend of God through redemption. She cooperated only in the secondary aspect of Redemption, that is, in so far as it was a redemption from the stain of sin actually found in all other human persons. Thus the grace of Mary's preservative conception was literally the noblest achievement of Christ's death: an achievement of the redemptive Incarnation greater in itself than the redemption of all other men taken together.

We must say, then, that Mary's Immaculate Conception is a certain term of accomplishment in the mystery of Redemption, an exemplar that we, in the working out of our redemption, only approach.

Thus, in God's view, the Immaculate Conception stands as a certain redemption from all evil. In the initial grace given Mary, God sees a God-likeness greater by far than the good that might have been bestowed on man through the fidelity of Adam. Mary conceived without sin is God's plan of redemption vindicated, personalized.

The role of the Immaculate Conception in the actual work of our redemption, both objective and subjective, we have treated elsewhere.[17] In summary we can say that the Immaculate Conception is involved in Mary's work as Coredemptrix (in objective redemption) and distributrix of graces (in subjective redemption) not only as exemplar but also as the principle efficiently elicitive of her activities for our redemption, and a material disposition enabling her to perform those activities. And Mary's redemption by way of her Immaculate Conception is even the end of our redemption in the sense already admitted, namely, that our redemption is an imitation of hers.

It would seem then that, in the God-view, the Immaculate Conception makes Mary to stand among the redeemed, unique. In such fashion has redemption reached to her that by it she is exalted above all others. Upon her, first, has the redeeming Blood of Christ fallen; marking her with her Immaculate Conception, that Blood has set her apart, so that thenceforth redemption shall reach to others only through the express cooperation of her grace of conception. God, coming substantially among us, came only on condition of, and through the grace of, Mary's Conception; and God, coming by grace within us now and forever, will come only on condition of, and through that same grace of, Mary's Conception. And so in every sacramental administration, in every Mass, in each good work we do, or prayer we offer, in each offer of grace, actual or sanctifying, from the grace of conversion unto the grace to gasp out for the last time the names of Jesus and of Mary—in all these the Immaculate Conception is at work for our salvation, for our eternal joy in the embrace of God.

---

[17] Cf. "The Meaning of Mary's Compassion" in *The American Ecclesiastical Review*, vol. 125 p. 1 ff; pp. 120 ff; pp. 196 ff; also "The Queen of Mercy" in *The American Ecclesiastical Review*, vol. 126 pp. 412 ff. and vol. 127 pp. 31 ff. See also chapter X of the present volume.

THE IMMACULATE CONCEPTION AND
THE MYSTERY OF THE CHURCH

By the Church is meant here the Mystical Body of Christ, that is, the body of the baptized faithful living in Apostolic unity, which body is, through the instrumentality of Christ's Passion and death, animated by the Holy Ghost unto the glory of God and of our Lord and Savior.[18]

Our aim here is briefly to consider each of the four causes of the Mystical Body of Christ in relation to the role, if any, the Immaculate Conception has with regard to that cause. From such an examination should emerge, at least in broad outline, some picture of the place of Mary's Immaculate Conception in the Church and its life.

First, as to the membership of the Church or its "body." What special place is to be assigned to Mary within the Mystical Body of her Son? Retaining the inspired figure of the Church as a living body, theologians have described the role of our Blessed Mother by assigning to her a function similar to that of certain parts of the body, especially the neck and the heart. More recently the latter analogy has found greater favor, though there is very great authority for the figure of the neck.

This much both analogies have in common: they attribute to Mary, first, a certain preeminence or primacy within the Church and, secondly, a vital role in the transmission of the enlivening grace of God to all the other members of the Body. Both analogies teach a true dependence of the rest of the Body on Mary's universal mediationship.

By what activity does Mary bring divine life to others, now and in every generation? She did so objectively by co-offering Christ on Calvary; she does so at every instant by her intercession for men to God and by her distributing divine grace from God to men. And the principle, the source of this activity so necessary to the Church, is the love, the sanctity, of Mary's soul, the sanctified love which constituted her sinlessness of conception. Thus Mary's role relative to her own eminent place in the Mystical Body is in fact inseparable from her Immaculate Conception. That preeminence is given her by her Immaculate Conception is clear from this that it involves the greatest grace given a mere creature.

Secondly, the soul of the Church is that divine Person who is the Holy Ghost. With respect to His coming to animate the Mystical Body of Christ, does Mary's grace of conception have any special function?

Since this is a question of the mission of a Divine Person there can be no question of Mary's role only in the order of what is called dispositive

[18] This description of the Church is taken from the Encyclical *Mystici Corporis* of Pope Pius XII, 29 June 1943 (*A.A.S.* vol. XXXV pp. 193 ff.) in the sense that it gathers into one formula the principles of the Church as they are described in that document.

causality. Most obviously Our Lady could not be a formal, or efficient, or a final principle of any divine mission. But the point is that Our Lady, through her Immaculate Conception *is* a certain material or disposing cause with respect to the Holy Spirit's inhabiting the Mystical Body. It is Papal teaching that on that first Pentecost the Holy Spirit came not upon Mary—her He had already uniquely "overshadowed"—but upon the Church, in answer to Mary's pleas. The works of God are without repentance. As the Holy Spirit came of old upon the Apostles because of her, so is He with those apostles all days because of her.

And whence sprang and spring Mary's groanings that the Spirit of her Son shall dwell within the Mystical Body of Her Son? For all ages they spring from the love, the sanctified love of Mary's soul, the love that is her Immaculate Conception. Until time shall no more be, it is the grace of her Conception, active in her pleas, which as it were produces in God's Church such disposition, such need, as to constitute a true exigency of the presence of the Spirit of God. In human generation there is a certain perfection of material condition or disposition which demands of God the Creator the infusion of a human soul. Supernaturally, in the Church, the plea which springs from Mary's unaltered grace of conception is a similar disposition which God shall not ignore. It, too, cries out for the coming of a soul, the soul that is God's Spirit.

Thirdly, the instrumental, efficient principle of the Church is, as the Holy Father teaches, the Passion and death of the Savior; for by His death the Son of Man won title for mankind to the grace which is poured abroad in our hearts by the Spirit dwelling within the Church. So, as instrument, Christ builded His Church by His death; for He thereby merited in most strict right the enlivening of His Body by His Spirit.

But in that passion of the Lord, Mary was cooperator. Whatever He by most strict title merited, she merited by congruity. I do not imply that Our Lady is, like Christ, a physical instrument in the divine animation of the Church; but it is clear that she is at least a moral instrument without whose direct cooperation the Church would not have been established.

And if we should ask what this has to do with her Immaculate Conception, the answer is already evident. Mary's cooperation in the suffering of the Lord had for its efficient principle that grace, obedience, and love of her soul which constituted her original sinlessness. In that instant in which the Church began to be, then were the powers, the virtues of Mary's Immaculate Conception alive, and again drawing down the Spirit of God among men, that the Christ whose physical body has sprung of her, should fashion to Himself a new, a mystical body sprung also of her, through her immeasurable original sanctity.

Last of all, the purpose, the end, of God's Church is the glory of God and of Christ. Since that glory consists in sharing—in creaturely fashion—something of God's own splendor of light and love, then by her Immaculate Conception Mary achieves that end more fully than all the rest of the Church taken together, because by her Immaculate Conception she is greater in grace not only than all men but greater even than all angels and all men. The Church, apart from her, is far less than the glory of her Conception; far less in splendor, in beauty, in God-likeness. Thus, the Immaculate Conception is intimately involved in all four causes of the Church.

In brief, at the moment of creation, at the moment of the Incarnation, and at the moment of Redemption, at this moment, and forever it is Mary's sanctity which God requires and shall eternally require as the indispensable condition of His dwelling within us, and among us. Only in her by God's decree, is mankind worthy of man's God.

May we one day grasp the wisdom and the beauty of what God has required: the wisdom and the beauty that is Mary conceived without sin ...

---

[19] Cf. Leo XIII, Encyclical, *Jucunda semper*, 8 Sept. 1894. (*A.A.S.* vol. XXVII p. 17).

X

The Immaculate Conception and the Divine Motherhood, Assumption and Coredemption

CHARLES DE KONINCK*

INTRODUCTION

One may wonder how a study on the connection between the Immaculate Conception, the Divine Motherhood, and the Assumption, viewed specifically in the light of the doctrine of Coredemption, could find a suitable place in a Symposium in commemoration of the dogma defined by Pius IX in the Constitution *Ineffabilis Deus* of a century ago. Our aim is to show that the Immaculate Conception is not an isolated privilege. The Divine Motherhood—than which, in the entitative order and in the line of *esse personale,* there is nothing greater in all creation this side of the hypostatic union itself —is its very foundation: the seat of all the Virgin's graces and privileges. Furthermore, the Immaculate Conception not only renders the person of Mary incomparably more worthy of her Son; it means that her habitual grace belongs to the hypostatic order and, therefore, that a mere human person was able to share actively and worthily in the fulfillment of the very purpose of the Incarnation, by way of coredemption. In other words, that privilege makes her more worthy of her Son specifically *qua* Redeemer. Without it, she could not have become the universal Coredemptrix that she is. The intimate connection between Mary's singular fullness of grace and the fact that the Mother of the Redeemer, the new Eve, did *crush the head* of the Serpent, according to the prophecy in Genesis III, 15, is actually the main theme of the Constitution *Ineffabilis Deus.*

More recently, the bull *Munificentissimus Deus,* which proclaimed the Assumption as a dogma of faith, establishes a further connection between the Immaculate Conception and the victory over the Enemy, on the one hand, and the complete glorification of Mary's person at the term of her earthly life, on the other:

* Member of the Faculties of Philosophy and Theology at Laval University, Quebec; member of the Roman Academy of St. Thomas; president of the Canadian Academy of St. Thomas. The present article was completed in June, 1955.

We must remember above all (*maxime*) that since the second century, the Virgin Mary has been designated by the holy Fathers as the new Eve, who, although subject to the new Adam, is most intimately associated with Him in that struggle against the infernal foe which, as foretold in the *protoevangelium,* finally resulted in that most complete victory over the sin and death which are always associated in the writings of the Apostle of the Gentiles. Consequently, just as the glorious Resurrection of Christ was an essential part and the final sign of this victory, similarly that struggle which was common to the Blessed Virgin and her divine Son should be brought to a close by the glorification of her virginal body, for the same Apostle says: *when this mortal thing hath put on immortality, then shall come to pass the saying that is written: Death is swallowed up in victory.*

Hence the reverend Mother of God, from all eternity joined in a hidden way with Jesus Christ, in one and the same decree of predestination, immaculate in her conception, a most perfect virgin in her divine motherhood, the noble associate of the divine Redeemer who has won a complete triumph over sin and its consequences, was finally granted, as the supreme culmination of her privileges, that she should be preserved free from the corruption of the tomb and that, like her own Son, having overcome death, she might be taken up body and soul to the glory of heaven where, as Queen, she sits in splendour at the right hand of her Son, the immortal King of the Ages.[1]

In other words, just as the final cause of the Incarnation of the Son of God is, in fact, none other than the redemption of mankind and the glory of the elect, the fulfillment of this end is no less the first cause of the Divine Motherhood, and of the Immaculate Conception perfecting beyond all measure that same motherhood with regard to the mode of achieving our redemption. This privilege—this gift of divine mercy, bestowed upon her by the prevenient piety of her Son, raising her above the common law— enriches the Mother with that spiritual fecundity from which, in the Compassion, we are born to the life of her Son's very Godhead. It is in this fuller sense that the Assumption is "the crowning and complement of that prior privilege [the Immaculate Conception]."

> . . . For the greatest possible glorification of her virgin body is the complement, at once appropriate and marvelous, of the absolute innocence of her soul, which was free from all stain; and just as she took part in the struggle of her only-begotten Son with the utterly wicked serpent of hell, so also she shared in His glorious triumph over sin and its sad consequences.[2]

---

[1] *Munif. Deus, A.A.S.,* Nov. 4, 1950, pp. 768-769. We quote the English translation from *Papal Documents on Mary,* compiled and arranged by William J. Doheney, C.S.C. and Joseph P. Kelly, S.T.D., The Bruce Publishing Co., Milwaukee, 1954. We shall henceforth refer to this volume by the initials P.D.M. (The present passage is on p. 237) Here and there we have changed a word in order to bring the English closer to the original, whenever this seemed feasible—though usually at the expense of felicity of style.

[2] *Fulgens Corona, P.D.M.,* pp. 258-259.

If, then, by her Assumption, the Blessed Virgin shared in the triumph of the new Adam, it was not because of her Immaculate Conception considered merely as an effect of the merits of Christ: it was, more properly, owing to this perfect innocence, inasmuch as in virtue of it she could and did take part in the victorious struggle of her Only-begotten Son with the Enemy who held mankind in bondage. It was by reason of this active participation that Mary won the title of Coredemptrix, and that her Assumption was "an essential part and a final sign" of the "common" struggle and victory. There exists, therefore, a strict parallel between the Incarnation of the Word and its actual purpose, viz. the redemption of man, on the one hand; and, on the other hand, the Immaculate Conception of the Mother of God and its ultimate purpose, viz. the Coredemption. Only the *causa causarum* of the Word's becoming flesh can provide the proper and adequate light in which we must endeavor to consider every truth of faith concerning the person of Mary: the real meaning of the Immaculate Conception is to be found in its *finis cujus gratia*—the Redemption itself.

Now, the Constitution *Ineffabilis Deus* not only confirmed that the Virgin was immaculate in and from the first instant of her existence; in the very opening sentence of that solemn document, this singular privilege is referred to what is, in fact, the ultimate purpose of

> God ineffable, whose ways are mercy and truth, whose will is omnipotence itself, and whose wisdom *reacheth from end to end mightily, and ordereth all things graciously* ... ; [of God Who] decreed, by a plan concealed from the centuries, to complete the first work of His goodness by a mystery yet more wondrously hidden [*sacramento occultiore complere*] through the Incarnation of the Word. . .

What was this purpose? The same sentence goes on to state:

> this He decreed in order that man who, contrary to the plan of divine Mercy, had been led into sin by the cunning malice of Satan, would not perish; and in order that what had been lost in the first Adam would be gloriously restored by the second Adam.[3]

If, then, Mary's active share in the universally redemptive mission of her Son depends not only upon the Divine Motherhood as such but upon the Mother and new Eve inasmuch as she was conceived entirely free of all contagion of sin, it follows that the Immaculate Conception is the proximate principle in virtue of which the second Eve, "while subject to the new Adam," could achieve the redemption of mankind in what the Constitution on the Assumption and the Encyclical *Fulgens Corona* call their "common" struggle and victory. Hence, unless we consider the Immaculate Conception, not only in the line of formal causality with respect to the person of Mary, but further, as a *principle*, indeed a universal one, pertaining to the

[3] *P.D.M.*, pp. 9-10.

order of efficient causality, we fail to see this privilege of the Mother of God in the light of its ultimate reason: the active share of a mere human person in the salvation of mankind.

Such is the reason why we believe that, instead of distracting us from what the Immaculate Conception really is, the doctrine of the Coredemption provides the truly proper perspective in which Mary's fullness of grace must be viewed; subject to Christ, it is a fullness from which we have all received through the merits of "the one and only daughter, not of death but of life; the child, not of anger but of grace." [4]

If the doctrine of the Coredemption is the light in which we ought to consider the Immaculate Conception, we must explain first of all what that doctrine is; and, for the sake of further clarification, we shall envisage some of the difficulties to which it may give rise (part I).

But the Immaculate Conception was bestowed upon Mary as Mother of God; for "she obtained this unique privilege, never granted to anyone else, because she was raised to the dignity of Mother of God." [5] We must try to show, in particular, why it is that "from this sublime office of the Mother of God seem to flow, as it were from a most limpid hidden source, all the privileges and graces with which her soul and life were adorned in such extraordinary manner and measure." [6] We must therefore endeavor to catch some glimpse of what it means to be the Mother of God and show the reason why this motherhood is essential to the coredemption; we shall point out why the assimilation of Christ and Mary in the order of nature is basic to all her privileges and graces. Then we must show how the Immaculate Conception, conferred upon Mary as Mother of God, renders her proximately and properly able to share in Christ's redeeming Passion, for the good and honor of all—*honorificentia populi tui* (part II). Finally, we must try to show why the Immaculate Conception and the Assumption are "most intimately bound to one another"; on what condition there can exist a strict correspondence between the two, and how the latter can be called a reward of the former (part III).

I

THE MEANING OF COREDEMPTION

The Dignity of Man and the Motive of Redemption

The first thing we must call to mind here is that, without any injustice whatsoever, God might well have forgiven man without redeeming him. [7]

---

[4] *Ineff. Deus, P.D.M.*, p. 20.
[5] *Fulgens Corona, P.D.M.*, p. 255.
[6] *Ibid.*, p. 256.
[7] "Even this justice depends on the Divine will, requiring satisfaction for sin from the human race. But if He had willed to free man from sin without any satisfaction,

There was no need for God to sacrifice His only-begotten Son, *laying on Him the iniquities of us all, to bruise Him in infirmity.* (Isa. liii 6, 10) Nor was it even necessary that He should expose the Church, the body whose head is Christ, to the contempt and hatred of the world, letting its vanquished Prince, *liar* and *homicide from the beginning,* feign victory until the end of time. God willed freely that the sound and the fury should go on until the day of His choice. *He who does wrong, let him do wrong still, and he who is filthy, let him be filthy still.* (Apoc. xxii. 11)

Yet it was more in keeping with both His mercy and His justice that God should exact satisfaction for the sin of the human race, and let all share in the sacrifice.[8] Thanks to the Incarnation, man himself, in the Person of Christ, can render justice to God and be cause of his own redemption.

> For it is far more to the glory of man that he himself should fully satisfy for the fault he had committed, rather than being forgiven without atonement. . . For whatever one obtains by merit, one achieves by oneself, in the measure that it is deserved. In like fashion, by satisfying for his fault, the one who satisfies is somehow the cause of his own cleansing. . . Because God willed man to be redeemed by way of satisfaction, His mercy is revealed in a most perfect manner; for He wanted, not only to remove the fault, but also to restore human nature wholly to its original dignity.[9]

He would not have acted against justice. For a judge, while preserving justice, cannot pardon fault without penalty, if he must punish fault committed against another —for instance, against another man, or against the State, or any Prince in higher authority. But God has no one higher than Himself, for He is the sovereign and common good of the whole universe. Consequently, if He forgive sin, which has the formality of fault in that it is committed against Himself, He wrongs no one: just as anyone else, overlooking a personal trespass, without satisfaction, acts mercifully and not unjustly. And so David exclaimed when he sought mercy: *To Thee only have I sinned* (Ps. i. 6), as if to say: *Thou canst pardon me without injustice.*" St. THOMAS AQUINAS, *Summa Theologiae, IIIa Pars,* q. 46, a. 2, ad 3. — We use, throughout, the English Dominican translation of the *Summa* (Benziger Brothers edition, 1947). But we have made some changes. For instance, "distinguuntur ratione" is not the same as "a distinction of reason between them."

[8] "With his justice, because by His Passion Christ made satisfaction for the sin of the human race; and so man was set free by Christ's justice: and with His mercy, for since man of himself could not satisfy for the sin of all human nature, as was said above (q. 1, a. 2), God gave him His Son to satisfy for him, according to Rom. iii. 24, 25: *Being justified freely by His grace, through the redemption that is in Christ Jesus, whom God hath proposed to be a propitiation, through faith in His blood.* And this came of more copious mercy than if He had forgiven sins without satisfaction. Hence it is said (Ephes. ii. 4): *God, who is rich in mercy for His exceeding charity wherewith He loved us, even when we were dead in sins, hath quickened us together in Christ.*" IIIa Pars, q. 46, a. 1, ad 3.

[9] *In III Sent.,* d. 20, a. 1, sol. 2.—This does not mean, of course, that by redemption, man was merely restored to his original dignity; for man's worthiness, his *bonitas propter se,* is now far greater than it might have been had Adam never sinned. PIUS XI, *Lux Veritatis:* "With this dogma of truth [i.e. the hypostatic union] placed be-

The Incarnation, therefore, is a unique manifestation of God's Wisdom and Power—*reaching from end to end mightily and ordering all things graciously* (Wisdom, viii. 1). For in the Person of Christ are united the extremes of rational nature, the Godhead and man—*in se reconcilians ima summis.* As to mercy, considered in itself,

> it takes precedence of other virtues, for it belongs to mercy to be bountiful to others, and, what is more, to succor others in their wants, which pertains chiefly to one who stands above. Hence mercy is accounted as being proper to God: and therein His omnipotence is declared to be chiefly manifested.[10]

However, to God, in His Divinity, only the effect of mercy can be attributed, and not the affection of passion.[11] Yet, thanks to the Incarnation, the Second Person of the Blessed Trinity, the Image of the Father, stoops down to us and takes upon Himself our misery; *He humbled Himself, becoming obedient to death, even to death on the cross.* And that is the very reason why *God has exalted Him and has bestowed upon Him the name that is above every name.* (Philipp. ii. 8)

By denying the oneness of the Person of Christ, and, therefore, the reality of the Incarnation, the Nestorians, while pretending to exalt the Godhead in His infinite perfection above all creatures, ignored His power to stoop down to and exalt the lowly; they strained the quality of *mercy in which God's omnipotence is chiefly manifested.*[12] That denial of His superabundant goodness and power to unite in His Person the lowly nature of man, to achieve in it the work of universal redemption, was, therefore, a negation of what God is—of the very transcendence of the Godhead. Yet, *God hath made foolish the wisdom of this World* (I Cor., i. 20), *by showing,* a gloss adds, *those things to be possible which it judges to be impossible.* He did so, more especially, by demonstrating how much He can do with how little. For, *the weakness of God is stronger than men. . . But the foolish things of the world has God chosen to put to shame the "wise," and the weak things of the world has God chosen to put to shame the strong, and the base things of the world and the despised has God chosen, and the things*

---

yond the realm of doubt, it is easy to conclude that the entire aggregation of human beings and earthly creatures has, by the mystery of the Incarnation, been invested with a dignity greater than can be imagined, far greater than that to which the work of creation was raised. Among the offspring of Adam, there is One, namely Christ, who attained everlasting and infinite divinity, and who is united with it in a mysterious and most intimate manner; Christ, We repeat, our Brother, possessing human nature, but God with us, or Emmanuel, who by His grace and merits has brought us back to the divine Author and recovered for us that heavenly blessedness from which we had fallen away by original sin. Let us therefore be grateful to Him, obey His precepts and imitate His example. In this way we shall be partakers of the divinity of Him *who deigned to partake of our human nature.*" P.D.M., p. 171.

[10] *IIa-IIae,* q. 30, a. 4, c.

[11] *Ia Pars,* q. 21, a. 3.

[12] Collect for the Tenth Sunday after Pentecost.

that are not, lest any flesh should pride itself before Him. (I Cor. i. 25)
The wisdom of the world had been defined and judged once and for all
by the words: *For my thoughts are not your thoughts, nor your ways my
ways, saith the Lord.* (Isa. iv. 8)

This rejection of God's merciful might underlies every heresy down to
our own time when God is most frequently denied because, in His designs,
He tolerates *that very great evil among all things that are done under
the sun, that the same things happen to all men.* [Eccl. ix. 3][13] In each
and every instance, the one who elects his own self protests against some
special work of divine mercy, especially against the Virgin Mother of whom
the Church says that *She alone destroyed all heresies.*[14] For she, too, was
to be *a sign that shall be contradicted.* (Luke ii. 34) Yet, that Mary
should have been raised to such heights, which naturally arouses protests
among those who would compass God's designs with their own measure,
is expressly attributed by her to the Lord's merciful might:

> *My soul magnifies the Lord, and my spirit rejoices in God my Savior;
> Because He has regarded the lowliness of his handmaid; for, behold,
> henceforth all generations shall call me blessed; Because He who is
> mighty has done great things for me, and holy in His name; And His
> mercy is from generation to generation on those who fear Him. He has
> shown might with His arm, He has scattered the proud in the conceit
> of their heart, He has put down the mighty from their thrones, and
> has exalted the lowly.* (Luke i. 46)

CHRIST AND MARY, THE OBJECT OF ONE
AND THE SAME DECREE OF PREDESTINATION

The extent to which God willed Mary to share in the work of salvation
He first made known to the head of all evil by a prophecy of predestination
(Gen. iii. 15): *I will put enmities between thee and the woman, and thy
seed and her seed: she* ('he', 'it'?) *shall crush thy head, and thou shalt lie
in wait for her* ('his'?) *heel.* The plural *enmities* makes it plain that the
opposition is one of adversaries mutually recognized as such and active,
much as in the contrary case, viz., "to be friends, [people] must be mutually
recognized as bearing good will and wishing well to each other."[15] In
other words, *enmities* already implies that each party deliberately desires,
and acts for, the defeat of the other. Whichever may be the correct read-

---

[13] *There are just men and wise men, and their works are in the hands of God:
and yet man knoweth not whether he be worthy of love, or hatred.—But all things
are kept uncertain for the time to come; because all things equally happen to the just
and to the wicked, to the good and to the evil, to the clean and to the unclean, to
him that offereth victims, and to him that despiseth sacrifices. As the good is, so
also is the sinner: as the perjured, so he also that sweareth truth. This is a very
great evil among all things that are done under the sun, that the same things happen
to all men.* (Eccl. ix, 1-3)

[14] Tract of the Mass *Salva Sancte Parens.*

[15] ARISTOTLE, *Ethics*, VIII, 2, 1156a.

ing of the pronouns in the next part of this verse, the sense is much the same.[16]

What is important to us is the way in which the Church understands the implications of this text. That Mary's role in the struggle against the enemy and in the achievement of victory was indeed an active one we find clearly stated in the Apostolic Constitution *Ineffabilis Deus*:

> [The Fathers and writers of the Church] in quoting the words by which at the beginning of the world God announced His merciful remedies prepared for the regeneration of mankind—words by which He crushed the audacity of the deceitful Serpent and wondrously raised up the hope of our race, saying, *I will put enmities between thee and the woman, between thy seed and her seed*—taught that by this divine prophecy the merciful Redeemer of mankind, Jesus Christ, the only-begotten Son of God, was clearly foretold; that His most blessed Mother, the Virgin Mary, was prophetically indicated; and, at the same time, the very enmity of both against the Evil One was significantly expressed.—Hence, just as Christ, the Mediator between God and man, assumed human nature, blotted out the handwriting of the decree that stood against us, and fastened it triumphantly to the cross, so the most holy Virgin, united with him by a most intimate and indissoluble bond, was, with Him and through Him, eternally at enmity with the evil Serpent, and most completely triumphed over him, and thus, crushed his head with her immaculate foot.—This sublime and singular triumph of the Blessed Virgin, together with her most excellent innocence, purity, holiness, and freedom from every stain of sin, as well as the unspeakable abundance and greatness of all heavenly graces, virtues, and privileges—these the Fathers beheld in that ark of Noah, which was built by divine command and escaped entirely safe and sound from the common shipwreck of the whole world.[17]

The second prophecy of the same nature was made to Mary herself at the Presentation in the Temple (Luke. ii. 34-35): *And Simeon blessed them, and said to Mary His mother, "Behold, this child is destined for the fall and for the rise of many in Israel, and for a sign that shall be contradicted, and thy own soul a sword shall pierce—that the thoughts of many*

---

[16] Cf. Cornelius a Lapide, *Comm. in Scripturam Sacram*, t. I, Paris, 1866, pp. 106-108. Cf. F. M. Braun, O.P., *La Mère des Fidèles*, Paris, 1953; "En dépit de la leçon *ipsa conteret caput tuum*, qui ne se lit que dans la *Vulgate*, la victoire à vrai dire dépendait, non pas directement de la *Femme*, mais de son descendant. Etablie en état de guerre ouverte vis-à-vis du Serpent, la *Femme* était cependant destinée à y participer personnellement. A cet effet, il était indispensable qu'elle fît cause commune avec son enfant. C'est pourquoi il n'a pas suffi à Jean, comme à Matthieu et à Luc, dont il est cependant si proche, de faire entrer Marie dans le plan du salut simplement pour avoir donné le jour au Sauveur. La présence de Marie au Calvaire l'avait introduit dans un autre mystère. Il n'a pas craint de faire entendre qu'au moment où Jésus consommait son sacrifice la maternité de Marie avait acquis une nouvelle dimension." (p. 91). See also chapter I of the present volume, p. 31 f.

[17] P.D.M., pp. 17-18.

hearts may be revealed." [18] This prophecy manifests the unity of the Passion of Christ and of the Mother's Compassion. Such a unity, as we shall see, was possible only because of the complete enmity between the Woman and the Serpent, because of her total preservation from every stain of sin in the first instant of her conception.

To see how fitting it was that God should bestow upon the person of His Mother such a unique role, we must recall that in the Incarnation God's aim is to bring about the salvation of man by way of merit, atonement, sacrifice and redemption.[19] In this He shows His mercy, raising human nature to the utmost dignity. Now the Incarnation might have been wrought in the manner in which the first man was formed, i.e. not by way of birth, but immediately by God from an irrational nature; or even by mere creation of the human nature as a whole. Thus, just as God could have forgiven man without exacting the debt, He might have assumed our nature without any dependence whatsoever upon the offspring of the father of all men. Yet, "His power being thereby made more manifest, He assumed, from a corrupt and weakened nature, that which was raised to such might and glory." [20] To this end He chose to proceed from human nature by way of birth, i.e. as a substantial image of the one to whom He is assimilated in His temporal origination, even as in His eternal procession the Son is assimilated to the Father. That same Son was joined with the very person of His mother *in one and the same decree of predestination.*[21]

It is thanks to this singular election that Christ's human nature was united to the Godhead by way of birth. Because of this, Mary belongs to the order of the hypostatic union. It is by reason of "the grace of union [which is wholly of the entitative order] that man is God, and that God is man." This union was predestined from all eternity. For "predestination, in its proper sense, is a divine preordination from eternity of those things which are to be done in time by the grace of God." [22] Now, "eternal predestination covers not only that which is to be accomplished in time, but also the mode and order in which it is to be accomplished in time." [23]

---

[18] On this verse 35, M.-J. LAGRANGE, O.P., observes: "La première moitié du verset n'est pas une parenthèse; elle se soude à ce qui précède, tandis que la seconde moitié s'applique à tout ce qui est antérieur." *Evangile selon saint Luc,* Paris, 1921, p. 88.

[19] "Christ's Passion, according as it is compared with His Godhead, operates in an efficient manner: but in so far as it is compared with the will of Christ's soul it acts in a meritorious manner: considered as being within Christ's very flesh, it acts by way of satisfaction, inasmuch as we are liberated by it from the debt of punishment; while inasmuch as we are freed from the servitude of guilt, it acts by way of redemption: but in so far as we are reconciled with God it acts by way of sacrifice." *IIIa Pars,* q. 48, a. 6, ad 3.

[20] *IIIa Pars,* q. 4, a. 6, c.

[21] PIUS IX, *Ineffabilis Deus;* PIUS XII, *Munificentissimus Deus.*

[22] *IIIa Pars,* q. 24, a. 1, c.

[23] *Ibid.,* a. 4, c.

It is therefore natural that this same predestination should extend to the grace of motherhood, which is likewise of the entitative order, owing to which the Son of God is also and truly the Son of Man.

Predestination, however, refers all that is done in time by the grace of God, to the ultimate, supernatural end of the rational creature. Since this end exceeds all proportion and faculty of created nature, and thus cannot be attained by the power of nature alone, it must be directed to it by another, as the arrow is directed by the archer towards a mark.

> Hence, properly speaking, a rational creature, capable of eternal life, is led towards it, directed, as it were, by God. The reason of that direction pre-exists in God; as in Him is the type of the order of all things towards an end, which we proved above to be providence. Now the type in the mind of the doer of something to be done, is a kind of pre-existence in him of the thing to be done. Hence the type of the aforesaid direction of a rational creature towards the end of life eternal is called predestination. For to destine, is to direct or send. Thus it is clear that predestination, as regards its objects, is a part of providence.[24]

Christ and Mary are joined by nature in a way that is wholly unique. But they are also united in the order of sanctifying grace which, in them, belongs to the hypostatic order. Now, all grace is ordered to the state of glory. Since Mary was predestined not only to be the Mother of God, but a Mother such as to be, in glory, far above any or all other created persons, she is also most intimately conjoined to the Godhead in the order of glory, i.e. of "clear knowledge with praise," in a fashion that is again wholly unique. For not only is her Son glorified there, seeing God by His created intellect, viz. according to the nature which He received from her, and in which he saved mankind; this same Son of hers, this Person, is at the same time the Word in Whom the blessed see God, and Who is God.

THE PROPHECIES OF PREDESTINATION CONCERNING MARY'S COREDEMPTION

The prophecies of the divine motherhood were prophecies of predestination. *I will put enmities between . . . thy seed and her seed.* (Gen. iii. 15) *Behold a virgin shall conceive and bear a son: and his name shall be called Emmanuel.* (Isa. vii. 14) *Behold, thou shalt conceive in thy womb and shalt bring forth a son; and thou shalt call his name Jesus.* (Luke i. 31) This, however, did not prevent Mary's consent from being most perfectly free. Indeed, "a prophecy of predestination is fulfilled without the causality of our will, but not without its free consent."[25] They act in greatest freedom who readily and unfailingly fulfill the will of God.

[24] *Ia Pars*, q. 23, a. 1, c.
[25] *IIIa Pars*, qu. 30, a. 1 ad. 1.

But Mary's share in the act of Redemption was also implied in the prophecies of predestination in Genesis iii. 15, and Luke ii. 35. What, then, is the relationship between the object of this prophecy and that elevation of human dignity far above anything it might have been in the order of original justice? We have seen that, thanks to the nature assumed by the Word, in which He satisfied for our sins, man is a *causa suae purgationis*. In this regard, however, the *human person* as such is not a cause, since the Person of the Incarnate Word is Divine. Therefore, although man, in this respect, did save himself (for Christ is a man), the human person did not redeem himself. But if Mary, thanks to her offspring, did crush the head of *the one by whose envy sin and death came into this world,* then the human person, too, shared in delivering man from enslavement.

In Adam, original sin was both an actual or personal sin, and a sin of nature, which is derived from the former. In him, "the person corrupted the nature, and by means of this corruption the sin of the first man is transmitted to posterity, inasmuch as the corrupt nature corrupts the person." [26] But we do not therefore distinguish a twofold grace, one corresponding to the nature, the other to the person, as in Adam we distinguish the sin of the nature and the sin of the person. For, "grace is not vouchsafed us by means of human nature, but solely by the personal action of Christ Himself." [27] Yet, thanks to Mary, in whom those prophecies were fulfilled, the New Order, too, is derived from a human person. Children of Eve, we derive our corrupt nature from the person of Adam. But Adam had fallen through the mediation of Eve already seduced by the serpent to sin against both God and her neighbor. Adam preferred to offend God rather than resist the elated will of Eve. So too in the order of Redemption, mankind owes its spiritual regeneration not only to the Divine Person who is Christ, but also to a human person, to the second Eve from whom the New Adam was formed, and who conformed her will to that of the Father and her own Son. For

> When the supreme hour of the Son came, beside the cross of Jesus there stood Mary, His Mother, not merely occupied in contemplating the cruel spectacle, but rejoicing that her only Son was offered for the salvation of mankind; and so entirely participating in His Passion, that, if it had been possible "she would have gladly borne all the torments that her Son underwent."—From this community of will and suffering between Christ and Mary, "she merited to become most worthily the reparatrix of the lost world" and dispensatrix of all the gifts that our Savior purchased for us by His death and by His blood.[28]

As we shall see, this kind of participation of the human person in the work

---

[26] *IIIa Pars*, q. 8, a. 5, ad 1; q. 69, a. 3, ad 3.
[27] *Ibid.*
[28] St. Pius X, *Ad diem illum*, *P.D.M.*, p. 140.

of universal Redemption was possible only because the Mother of God had been conceived immaculate.

One of the reasons for the Angel Gabriel's mission was "to show that there is a spiritual wedlock between the Son of God and human nature. Wherefore in the Annunciation the Virgin's consent was besought in lieu of that of the whole of human nature." [29]   In his *Commentary on the Sentences*, St. Thomas calls this consent an "actus singularis personae in multitudinis salutem redundans, immo totius humani generis." [30]   Leo XIII, referring to this teaching of the Angelic Doctor, uses the expression: "Ipsius generis humani personam quodammodo agebat." [31]   So too, at the foot of the Cross, in her Compassion, "generis humani personam quodammodo agebat."

It is true that her compassion was natural inasmuch as the *Man of sorrows* was her own Son by nature, and that compassion is not necessarily meritorious.   Even the Passion of Christ was not meritorious in virtue of its outward principle, namely the will and actions of His persecutors, but because of an inward principle, inasmuch as He bore the Passion willingly.[32] Now, in giving consent, at the Annunciation, to be the Mother of the Savior, the Virgin, full of grace, freely consented to compassionate Him. It was therefore willingly that she accepted to share the suffering of her Son.   Furthermore, that the sword of His Passion would *pierce her own soul,* that He *must be about His Father's business,* were things that she had *kept carefully in her heart.* (Luke ii. 35, 49, 51)   It was she, then,

> who, free of all personal and inherited sin, ever most intimately united to her Son, offered Him to the Eternal Father, as well as the sacrifice of her maternal rights and motherly love, even as a new Eve, for all the children of Adam, deformed by his fall.[33]

The Habitual Grace of Mary belongs to the Hypostatic Order and is a "Gratia personalis in alios redundans"

The habitual grace of Christ,—which is ordained to an act (viz. the operations which attain God, as He is in Himself, by knowledge and love, to which it is necessary for human nature to be raised by grace),[34]— follows, "as a natural property," upon the grace of union, which is not ordained to an act, but to the personal being.[35]   It follows naturally, first of all because the nearer a recipient is to the inflowing cause, the more

---

[29] *IIIa Pars*, q. 30, a. 1, c.
[30] *In III Sent.*, d. 3, q. 3, a. 2, ad 2 qu., obj. 3.
[31] *Octobri mense, P.D.M.,* p. 56.
[32] *IIIa Pars*, q. 48, a. 1, ad 1.
[33] Pius XII, *Mystici Corporis,* Epilog.
[34] *IIIa Pars*, q. 7, a. 1, c.
[35] *Ibid.,* a. 13, ad 2; q. 8, a. 5, ad 3.

it receives; therefore, the soul of Christ, which is more closely united than all other rational creatures, to God, the cause of all grace, receives the greatest outpouring of His grace. Secondly it follows by reason of the very purpose of the grace of union, of the Incarnation itself, namely that Christ be the Mediator between God and men. (I Tim. ii. 5) It is therefore natural that Christ's habitual grace should overflow to each and all according to every operation, and to all effects of grace, i.e. the virtues, gifts, and the like; it follows, as a natural property, that His personal grace should be such as to have the nature of a universal principle in the genus of such as have grace. *And of His fullness we have all received, and grace for grace.* (John i. 16) [36] Because of the unparalleled nearness of His soul to the outflowing cause of grace and because the grace of any other man is compared to His own as a particular to a universal power, Christ possesses grace in a pre-eminent way.[37]

The habitual grace of Mary, too, belongs to the hypostatic order,[38] inasmuch as it is proportioned to and was destined, by privilege, to follow from the Divine Maternity in which she attains to the hypostatic union. For

> God gives to each one according to the purpose for which He has chosen him. And since Christ as man was predestinated and chosen to be *predestinated the Son of God in power . . . of sanctification* (Rom. i. 4), it was proper to Him to have such a fullness of grace that it overflowed from Him into all, according to Jo. i. 16: *Of His fullness we have all received.* Whereas the Blessed Virgin Mary received such a fullness of grace that she was nearest of all to the Author of grace; so that she received within her Him Who is full of all grace; and by bringing Him forth, she, in a manner, dispensed grace to all.[39]

That all Mary's graces and privileges have the Divine Maternity as their seat is plainly taught in the following pontifical texts:

---

[36] *Ibid.,* q. 7, a. 1, c.; a. 9, c.

[37] *Ibid.,* q. 8, a. 5, c.

[38] Cf. l'abbé Maurice DIONNE, "La grâce de Marie est d'ordre hypostatique," *Laval théologique et philosophique,* 1954, vol. X, n. 2, pp. 141-145: "Nous disons 'ordre hypostatique' car il faut distinguer *union* hypostatique et *ordre* hypostatique. Cette distinction s'impose déjà à propos du Christ: il n'y a pas que le grâce d'union qui soit d'ordre hypostatique; la grâce habituelle du Christ, qui est une grâce capitale, est propre à cet ordre. La grâce habituelle du Christ se distingue de toutes les autres, non par un simple degré d'intensité mais par un mode éminent qui s'enracine dans l'union hypostatique. De même, toute proportion gardée, la grâce de Marie se distingue de la nôtre. Notre grâce est une grâce commune, effet de la rédemption réparatrice, et qui obéit à la *loi commune.* En revanche, la grâce de Marie est toute singulière, privilège qui soustrait la Mère de Dieu à la loi commune. *Non enim pro te, sed pro omnibus haec lex constituta est.* (Esther xv. 13) Et non seulement la grâce de la maternité divine appartient à cet ordre, mais aussi la grâce "gratum faciens" de Marie. En d'autres termes, la grâce de Marie se distingue-t-elle encore de la nôtre, par un mode éminent propre à l'ordre hypostatique." (p. 142)

[39] *Ibid.,* qu. 27, a. 5, c.

When the Fathers and writers of the Church meditated on the fact that the most blessed Virgin was, in the name and by the order of God himself, proclaimed *full of grace* by the Angel Gabriel when he announced her most sublime dignity of Mother of God, they taught that this singular and solemn salutation, never heard before, shows that the Mother *of God is the seat of all divine graces* and is adorned with all gifts of the Holy Spirit.[40]

. . . *From this sublime office of the Mother of God seem to flow, as it were from a most limpid hidden source, all the privileges and graces* with which her soul and life were adorned in such extraordinary manner and measure.—For, as Aquinas correctly states: "The Blessed Virgin, because she is the Mother of God, has a certain infinite dignity from the infinite Good, which is God." And a distinguished writer [Cornelius a Lapide] develops and explains this in these words: "The Blessed Virgin . . . is the Mother of God; therefore she is the purest and the most holy, so that under God a greater purity cannot be understood." [41]

Although Mary's habitual grace does not follow upon her Motherhood as a natural property, it is, nevertheless, connatural to her.

The Blessed Virgin is said to be full of grace, not on the part of grace itself—since she had not grace in its greatest possible excellence—nor for all the effects of grace; but she is said to be full of grace in reference to herself, i.e. inasmuch as she had sufficient grace for the state to which God had chosen her, i.e. to be the mother of His Only-begotten. So, too, Stephen is said to be full of grace, since he has sufficient grace to be a fit minister and witness of God, to which office he had been called. And the same must be said of others. Of these fullnesses one is greater than another, according as one is divinely pre-ordained to a higher or lower state.[42]

Hence it is the clear and unanimous opinion of the Fathers that the most glorious Virgin, for whom *He who is mighty has done great things*, was resplendent with such an abundance of heavenly gifts, with such a fullness of grace and with such innocence, that she is an unspeakable

---

[40] *Ineffabilis Deus*, P.D.M., p. 19.

[41] Pius XII, *Fulgens Corona*, *P.D.M.*, p. 256.

[42] *IIIa Pars*, q. 7, a. 10, ad 1.—That Mary did not have all the effects of grace, St. Thomas explains, *ibid.*, qu. 27, a. 5, ad 3 in the following terms: "There is no doubt that the Blessed Virgin received in a high degree both the gift of wisdom and the grace of miracles and even of prophecy, just as Christ had them. But she did not so receive them, as to put them and such like graces to every use, as did Christ: but accordingly as it befitted her condition of life. For she had the use of wisdom in contemplation, according to Luke ii. 19: *But Mary kept all these words, pondering them in her heart.* But she had not the use of wisdom as to teaching: since this befitted not the female sex, according to I Tim., ii. 12: *But I suffer not a woman to teach.* The use of miracles did not become her while she lived: because at that time the teaching of Christ was to be confirmed by miracles, and therefore it was befitting that Christ alone, and His disciples who were the bearers of His doctrine, should work miracles. Hence of John the Baptist it is written (Jo. x, 41) that he *did no sign;* that is, in order that all might fix their attention on Christ. As to the use of prophecy, it is clear that she had it, from the canticle spoken by her: *My soul doth magnify the Lord.* (Luke, i. 46)

miracle of God—indeed, the crown of all miracles and truly the worthy Mother of God; that she approaches as near to God Himself as is possible for a created being; and that she is above all men and angels in glory.[43]

She dispenses grace with a generous hand from that treasure with which from the beginning she was divinely endowed in fullest abundance that she might be worthy to be the Mother of God. By the fullness of grace which confers on her the most illustrious of her many titles, the Blessed Virgin is infinitely superior to all the hierarchies of men and angels, the one creature who is closest of all to Christ. "It is a great thing in any saint to have grace sufficient for the salvation of many souls; but to have enough to suffice for the salvation of everybody in the world, is the greatest of all; and this is found in Christ and in the Blessed Virgin." [44]

The last quotation as well as several of the preceding ones make it plain that Mary, too, in her own way, has the eminence of a universal principle in the order of grace—a cause universal *in causando*.

The Person of Mary, an Instrumental, Voluntary Cause of Universal Redemption

Since the Godhead alone is the principal efficient agency of grace and salvation, the humanity of even Christ Himself can be no more than the instrumental cause of the Godhead in this regard.[45] Hence "all Christ's actions and sufferings operate instrumentally in virtue of His Godhead for the salvation of men." And since the instrumental cause belongs, properly and exclusively, to the order of efficient agency, "Christ's Passion accomplishes man's salvation efficiently." [46] Nevertheless, "it is proper to Christ as man to be the Redeemer immediately," though not principally, for it is His blood and bodily life which were the price he paid for our redemption.[47]

Now the Person of Christ, in His Divinity, could not be an instrument in any sense, for it belongs to the very nature of an instrument to move *qua* moved: *movens motum*. We must note, however, that while

the humanity of Christ is the instrument of the Godhead, [it is] not, indeed, an inanimate instrument, which nowise acts, but is merely acted upon; but an instrument animated by a rational soul, which is so acted upon as to act.[48]

But the very person of Mary, being a mere creature, can be such an instru-

---

[43] *Ineffabilis Deus, P.D.M.,* pp. 19-20.
[44] Leo XIII, *Magnae Dei Matris, P.D.M.,* pp. 69-70.—The passage quoted in the text is from St. Thomas' *Super Salutatione angelica 'Ave Maria.'*
[45] *Ia-IIae,* qu. 112, a. 1.
[46] *IIIa Pars,* qu. 48, a. 6, c.
[47] *Ibid.,* a. 5, c.
[48] *Ibid.,* qu. 7, a. 1, ad. 3.

mental cause, that is, a living, rational instrument, which is not only moved, but also moves itself by its will, freely acting for a purpose, in subjection to the principal agent—as when a man is so acted upon by the Holy Ghost that he also acts himself, insofar as he has a free will.[49]

Hence, just as the Virgin Mary's consent to become the Mother of the Savior was an "actus singularis personae in multitudinis salutem redundans," so was her act of sacrifice and Compassion on Calvary. Thanks to this share in the act of universal redemption, not only human nature, in the Person of Christ, but a mere human person too, while dependent on Him, was a cause of man's salvation.

> The sorrowful Virgin took part in the work of redemption along with Jesus Christ; and, being made the Mother of mankind, she took into her arms the children entrusted to her by the testament, as it were, of divine charity, and she protects them with the greatest love.[50]

THE SUBORDINATION OF MARY'S UNIVERSAL CAUSALITY TO THAT OF CHRIST

There is no point in trying to evade the difficulty which is frequently raised at this juncture, by both Catholic and Protestant authors—though to the former it is rather a question of understanding the *how* than of contesting the fact. It is a real one, and should be faced squarely. How could Mary be Coredemptrix when she too was in need of redemption? There is no shying away from the plainly stated truth: *For there is one God, and one Mediator between God and men, himself man, Christ Jesus.* (I Tim. ii. 5) *Furthermore, it is by one offering* [that] *He has perfected forever those who are sanctified.* (Hebr. x. 14)

Christ has grace fully in every respect: viz. its totality and perfection, understood as regards both intensive quantity—which is none other than the maximum of quality[51]—and power. He has the fullness of grace as regards intensive quantity, since, by reason of the hypostatic union and of His mission, He has as much grace as can be had.[52] Likewise, as regards

---

[49] *Ia IIae*, q. 68, a. 3, ad 2.

[50] Pius XI, *Explorata res*. See also the text of Benedict XV, cited below, in note 72.

[51] *Ia IIae*, qu. 52, a. 1.

[52] *IIIa Pars*, qu. 7, a. 9, c.—The translation of the *Summa* by the Fathers of the English Dominican Province renders the last words of the sentence, "puta si dicam aliquem plene habere albedinem, si habeat eam *quantumcumque nata est haberi*," by: "If he has as much of it as can naturally be in him." This is somewhat confusing inasmuch as it converts St. THOMAS' argument into a vicious circle; whereas in applying the analogy to grace, he means that to have it totally and perfectly according to intensive quality is to have grace as much as it can be had, without reference to any particular subject, viz. the fullness of grace "ex parte ipsius gratiae." True enough, Christ is the only one who can have grace to this extent—*quod erat demonstrandum*. As it is shown in article 10 of the same question, the Blessed Virgin did not have the fullness of grace "ex parte ipsius gratiae," but only to the extent that she could have the fullness of it, i.e. as much as can naturally be *in her*.

the fullness of power, "grace was bestowed on Him, as upon a universal principle in the genus of such as have grace." Now, whatever is first in any genus, is principle and cause of all that is contained within that genus. "Hence the [fullness of grace as to power] is seen in Christ inasmuch as His grace extends to all the effects of grace . . ." [53]

From this it is plain that grace could not be in Mary as fully as it can be "on the part of grace itself"; nor can she be a universal cause of all that is contained within its genus. This is proper to Christ, in virtue of the hypostatic union upon which His habitual grace follows "as a natural property." But this does not prevent the relative fullness of Mary's grace from extending to each and every one, except to her Son Himself.

Two distinctions must be called to mind, in this connection. The first distinction was already implicit in the Constitution of Alexander VII, *Sollicitudo omnium Ecclesiarum,* of December 7, 1661. The passage is quoted in the Bull *Ineffabilis Deus.* We refer to the belief as expressed in the following terms: "Beatissimam Virginem, *praeveniente* scilicet Spiritus Sancti gratia, a peccato originali *praeservatam* fuisse." Now this grace should not be equated with common prevenient grace. For inasmuch as it cleanses the soul—its first effect—grace is called prevenient with respect to its second effect: the desire of the divine good; and inasmuch as it causes this desire, grace is called subsequent with respect to its first effect.[54] Now the prevenient grace which preserved the Blessed Virgin from the stain of original sin should be specified by this latter particular effect which, natural in Christ, is in Mary a unique privilege, bestowed upon her in virtue of the future merits of her Offspring, the Redeemer—whose merits are present to God in His Eternity—that she might be a Mother worthy of such a Son. As a result, Pius IX goes on to say, the Mother of God was "redeemed in a more sublime way—*sublimiori modo redempta"; she is:

> . . . the one and only daughter not of death but of life, the seed not of enmity but of grace, which [seed] by the singular providence of God has always flourished, budding from a corrupt and infected root, contrary to the settled and common laws—*praeter statas communesque leges.*[55]

This grace, given her thanks to the merits of the Redeemer, preserves Mary from the common lot of man, and is therefore rightfully called *gratia praeservatrix* in a sense that is unique to her, whereas all other human persons, subjects as they are to the general law, born with a corrupt nature, are in need of healing grace, *gratia sanans;* for the corruption is already there, in the individual, and must be removed by grace. For this reason, all

[53] *Ibid.*
[54] *Ia-IIae,* qu. 111, a. 3.
[55] *Ineffabilis Deus.* We have followed for this text the translation of *Official documents connected with the definition of the dogma of the Immaculate Conception . . . ,* Baltimore, Murphy & Co., 1855, p. 84. Cp. *P.D.M.,* p. 20.

others first need a gratuitous strength from God in order to be healed from the infection that is already in them.[56]   Hence, with respect to us, grace has first of all the character of what restores the health.   Our nature is a fallen one, and is in need of being saved from a condition in which we were born and that was ours until we were baptized—not omitting the *fomes peccati* that remains.   The grace that is common to all who are under the law, is in this exact sense rightly called *gratia reparatrix*.   Yet grace, whether *praeservatrix* or *reparatrix,* is derived from the Redeemer.

The second distinction to be borne in mind concerns "universal cause."   God alone is the *causa universalis totius entis*.   Christ, in his humanity, cannot be a universal agent to such extent, neither in the order of nature nor in that of grace.   By a universal agent we mean a cause which is one and extends to many; not in a confused manner, as when we say that *art* is the cause of the house, but in a determinate fashion, as a single art which could produce the particular effects of diverse arts.   In the natural order, no human being can achieve the status of a truly universal agent.   The reason is that our general knowledge is confused; e.g., the concept *animal* does not represent in their distinction and diversity the things of which animal can be said—such as horse, man, this rabbit, etc.   And this again is due to the abstractive nature of our reason.   But the separated substances all have means of knowing, intelligible species, that are universal *in repraesentando;* somewhat as if in our general concept *animal* were represented, at the same time and distinctly, all the kinds of animals and each one that exists.   Because a purely spiritual substance, viz. an angel, does have species that are universal in representation, such an agent can be a universal *in causando,* though always dependent on something already given—as the sculptor on the stone.

Now, according to his degree of specific perfection one angel has intelligible species that are more universal and distinct than those of another, and can therefore be more universal in his agency—in the manner in which the direction by the general manager of a factory extends to more persons and works than the direction by the head of one department. This comparison, however, is most inadequate, because a truly universal cause is, at the same time, more cause of the particular effect than the particular cause. The comparison is nearer to the truth when we consider the example of a worker who makes, as directed, this particular part of a machine without knowing how it fits in with other parts, what its function is in the whole, and what is the purpose of the whole that requires the parts to be such and such; whereas those who planned this kind of part and that, would know better what the particular worker is making than the latter does himself. The

[56] *Ia-IIae,* qu. 109, a. 2, c.

comparison fails, however, inasmuch as the former do not actually *make,* *hic et nunc,* this particular part to be this *kind* of part in *this* thing.

The angelic hierarchies, and the orders within each of them, are distinguished according to degrees of universal agency in the order of divine government by means of subordinate causes.[57] What should be pointed out, as relevant to the present subject, is that a more universal and primary cause attains the proper effect of a particular cause with greater force (*vehementius*) and intensity than the particular cause itself; nevertheless, the more universal cause does not render superfluous a less universal cause extending to an effect that is the same in number. Otherwise, as some believed, only God would be the agent cause of anything that comes about.[58]

The reason for divine government by subordinate causes—which is confined to the order of execution—is to be found in the very nature of the good as *diffusivum sui.* For whatever God produces is for the sake of manifesting His own goodness.

> Now it is a greater perfection for a thing to be good in itself and also the cause of goodness in others, than only to be good in itself. Therefore God so governs things that He makes some of them to be causes of others in government; as a master, who not only imparts knowledge to his pupils, but gives also the faculty of teaching others.[59]

In other words,

> if no creature exercises an action for the production of an effect, much is detracted from the perfection of the creature; because it is due to the abundance of its perfection that a thing is able to communicate to another the perfection that it has. Therefore [the opinion that no creature has an active part in the production of things] detracts from the divine power.[60]

Furthermore,

> it is better that the good bestowed on someone should be common to many than that it should be proper to one; since *the common good is always considered more godlike than the good of one only.* But the good of one becomes common to many if it flows from the one to the others,

---

[57] *Ia Pars,* qu. 108.—We realize that most modern Scholastics tend to ignore or even reject (e.g. the late Father Joseph Gredt) the reality of created universal agency. This attitude is modern inasmuch as it is in keeping with the neglect, or denial, of the very idea of "good" and its proper causality; and with the consequent assumption that a scientific explanation of whatever comes about should proceed "ex causis prioribus in esse, quae sunt movens et materia," inasmuch as with respect to future events their necessity is *a priori.* (Cf. St. Thomas, *In II Phys.,* lect. 12-15).

[58] On this error, and for its refutation, see *Contra Gentiles III,* cc. 69, 70, 77).

[59] *Ia Pars,* qu. 103, a. 6, c.

[60] *Contra Gentiles III,* c. 69. For quotations from this book we use the translation of *Basic Writings of St. Thomas Aquinas,* Anton Pegis, Random House, N. Y., vol. II.

and this can be only when the one, by its own action, communicates it to them; but if it has not the power to transmit it to others, that good remains its own property. Accordingly, God communicated His goodness to His creatures in such wise that one thing can communicate to another the good it has received. Therefore it is derogatory to the divine goodness to deny to things their proper operations. Again, to take order away from creatures is to deny them the best thing they have, because, though each one is good in itself, together they are very good because of the order of the universe; for the whole is always better than the parts, and is their end. Now if we take away action from things, the order among things is withdrawn; because things differing in nature are not bound together in the unity of order, except through the fact that some are active and some passive. Therefore it is unfitting to say that things have not their proper actions.[61]

A last point to be noted is that the effect of the most universal agent and the effect of a less universal cause may be numerically one with that of a particular cause, such as *this* man or *this* tree; each agent attaining in its own mode the same effect—the more deeply according as the agent is a cause less restricted to this particular effect.[62]

> . . . The action of the lower agent must not only proceed from the lower agent through the agent's own power, but also through the power of all the higher agents, for it acts by the power of them all. Now just as the lowest agent is found to be immediately active, so the power of the first agent is found to be immediate in the production of the effect; because the power of the lowest agent does not of itself produce this effect, but by the power of the proximate higher agent, and this by the power of a yet higher agent, so that the power of the supreme agent is found to produce the effects of itself, as though it were the immediate cause, as may be seen in the principles of demonstration, the first of which is immediate. Accordingly, just as it is not unreasonable that one action be produced by an agent and by the power of that agent, so is it not unreasonable that the same effect be produced

---

[61] *Ibid.*—In view of the objection that *we* have recourse to intermediaries when we ourselves cannot perform a task alone, as the head of a state, in need of ministers; whereas God does not need such help, St. Thomas repeats that divine providence "governs things inferior by things superior, not on account of any defect in His powers, but by reason of the abundance of His goodness; so that the dignity of causality is imparted even to creatures." (*Ia Pars*, qu. 22, a. 3, c.)—Hence the respect in which God's government by intermediaries differs from that of a king. "It pertains to a king's dignity to have ministers who execute his providence. But the fact that he has not the plan of those things which are done by them arises from a deficiency in himself. For every operative science is the more perfect, the more it considers the particular things with which its action is concerned." (*Ibid.*, ad 1)—Nevertheless, "that an earthly king should have ministers to execute his laws is a sign not only of his being imperfect, but also of his dignity; because by the ordering of ministers the kingly power is brought into greater evidence." (*Ia Pars*, qu. 103, a. 6, ad 3).

[62] *Ia Pars*, qu. 104, a. 1; *Contra Gentiles III*, c. 65; *Q. D. de Potentia*, qu. 3, a. 7; qu. 5, a. 1.

by the inferior agent and by God, and by both immediately, though in a different way. It is also evident that there is nothing superfluous if a natural thing produce its proper effect and God also produce it, since a natural thing does not produce it except by God's power. Nor is it superfluous, if God can produce all natural effects by Himself, that they should be produced by certain other causes, because this is not owing to the insufficiency of His power, but to the immensity of His goodness, by which it was His will to communicate His likeness to things not only in the point of their being, but also in the point of their being causes of other things. For it is in these two ways that all creatures in common have the divine likeness bestowed on them, as we proved above.—In this way, too, the beauty of order is made evident in creatures. It is also clear that the same effect is ascribed to a natural cause and to God not as though part were effected by God and part by the natural agent; but the whole effect proceeds from each, yet in different ways, just as the whole of one and the same effect is ascribed to the instrument, and again the whole is ascribed to the principal agent.[63]

Let us now apply these distinctions.—The redeeming grace of Christ has a twofold effect, one of which is proper to Mary, who, conceived Immaculate, is above the common law. *Thou shalt not die: for this law was not made for thee, but for all others.* (Esther xv. 13). Redeemed in a fashion "more sublime," she *"came forth from the mouth of the Most High* (Ecclus. xxiv. 5) entirely perfect."[64] From her very Conception she was confirmed in the good; and while she was still *walking by faith and not by sight* (I Cor. v. 7) her grace, in her initial sanctification, was already, as Suarez suggested, "intensively more perfect than the supreme grace in which the blessed angels and men have attained their end." [65] The other effect is common to all who are under the law.

Mary's habitual grace is, indeed, a grace of redemption, merited by her Son. Yet it differs from our own by the scope of its purpose: namely, that she be a worthy mother of the Savior Himself, highest in glory of all creatures.

Now the Blessed Virgin did not conceive the eternal Son of God merely in order that He might be made man, taking His human nature from

---

[63] *Contra Gentiles III,* c. 70.

[64] *Ineffabilis Deus, P.D.M.,* p. 19.

[65] SUAREZ, *In IIIam Partem,* qu. 27, disp. 4, sect. 1, n. 4 (edit. Vivès) t. 19, p. 57: "Quarto addo, pium et verisimile esse credere gratiam Virginis in prima sanctificatione intensiorem fuisse quam supremam gratiam, in qua consummantur Angeli et homines. Solet ad hanc veritatem accommodari illud Ps. 86: *Fundamenta ejus in montibus sanctis,* quia fundamenta sanctitatis Virginis posita fuerunt ubi alii Sancti consummantur: *Quia diligit Dominus portas Sion, super omnia tabernacula Jacob;* neque mirum, *quia Altissimus, qui illam fundavit, in ea factus* est homo; . . ." Regarding this opinion Suarez points out, further on, against Cajetan, that St. Thomas refers Mary's grace to "the state for which God had chosen her, i.e. to be the mother of His Only-begotten Son." This places her above, and apart from, all other created persons.

her, but also in order that by means of the nature assumed from her He might be the Redeemer of men.[66]

Just as Mary, having conceived of the Holy Ghost, and giving birth to the Son of the Eternal Father, attains (*attingit*) to the hypostatic union, so her habitual grace was ordained to the end that she might be a worthy dwelling place of the Word Incarnate, the Savior of all mankind. For this reason, her habitual grace belongs, as we saw, to the hypostatic order. Hence, it is not only the Divine Motherhood as such that sets her apart from all others; but even her habitual grace, considered on the part of its subject, as connatural to the Mother of the Redeemer, is above that which is given to those who are under the common law, i.e. each and everyone excepting the Son and the Mother.

Christ, then, is a universal principle with respect to every grace bestowed upon the human race because of His merits: the plenitude of grace that is proper to Mary, and the grace which is common to all under the law, viz. of both preservative and reparative grace. And by this may be defined the universal causality that is proper to Him, even according to His humanity, extending as it does to graces of such widely different modes. First, according to a priority of nature, Christ merits the singular grace of Mary—"*sublimiori modo redempta*"—in virtue of which she alone, of all created persons, belongs, even as to habitual grace, to the hypostatic order, in which the entire order of redemption has its root. The words *Ego sum radix*, are attributed to both Christ and Mary. Secondly, His meritorious action extends simultaneously to the grace of all who are under the common law.

Now there is nothing to prevent Mary from being, in virtue of her singular plenitude of grace, a universal principle with regard to common grace, which is not of the hypostatic order but presupposes it. By the choice of Mary to be his Mother, and bestowing upon her, *de congruo*, such fullness of grace, Christ assimilates the Blessed Virgin to Himself, in the hypostatic order, as regards both nature and grace.

> Hence it is the clear and unanimous opinion of the Fathers that the most glorious Virgin, for whom "He who is mighty has done great things," was resplendent with such an abundance of heavenly gifts, with such a fullness of grace and with such innocence, that she is an unspeakable miracle of God—indeed, the crown of all miracles and truly the worthy Mother of God; that she approaches as near to God Himself as is possible for a created being; and that she is above all men and angels in glory.

As a result, her greatness is such that only God can know fully the "sublimissima Dei matris dignitas."

---

[66] St. Pius X, *Ad diem illum, P.D.M.*, p. 139.

Above all creatures did God so love her that truly in her was the Father well pleased with singular delight. Wherefore, far above all the angels and all the saints, so wondrously did God endow her with the abundance of all heavenly gifts poured from the treasury of His divinity that this Mother, ever absolutely free of all stain of sin, all fair and perfect, would possess that fullness of holy innocence and sanctity than which, under God, one cannot even imagine any thing greater, and which, outside of God, no mind can succeed in fully comprehending. And indeed it was by all means fitting that so wonderful a mother should be ever resplendent with the glory of most sublime holiness and *so absolutely free from all taint of original sin that she would triumph completely over the ancient serpent.*[67]

In other words, the Son of God assimilated Mary so faithfully to Himself, in nature and in grace, not merely for her sake in view of His own dignity, but also in view of His mission as Redeemer. *Full of grace,* she is Mother of *Jesus*: the Savior. As near "to God Himself as is possible for a created being," she approaches, in that measure, the source of all good and mercy, from which she—"in qua totius boni posuit [Deus] plenitudinem"—[68] derives all that she is, all that she has, and all that she does even as to its very mode. Now, if such is her perfection, it is entirely in keeping with the divine rule, that her goodness should overflow into others, to all who, born in sin, are in need of spiritual regeneration. And this demonstrates the superabundant fecundity of God's own Goodness.

Wherefore in the same holy bosom of His most chaste Mother, Christ took to Himself flesh, and united to Himself the spiritual body formed by those who were to believe in him. Hence Mary, carrying the Savior within her, may be said to have also carried all those whose life was contained in the life of the Savior. Therefore all who are united to Christ, and as the Apostle says, are *members of his body, of his flesh, and of his bones,* have issued from the womb of Mary like a body united to its head. Hence, in a spiritual and mystical fashion, we are all children of Mary, and she is Mother of us all; "the Mother spiritually indeed, but truly the Mother of the members of Christ, who we are." [69]

It is in virtue of such an incomparable assimilation to Christ that Mary can be a worthy principle of reparative grace in us. For, once established in the hypostatic order to that fullness, there seems to be no reason why she could not merit *de condigno*, with her Son, in dependence upon Him, all graces for those who are beneath the common law.[70] In other words, when

---

[67] *Ineffabilis Deus, P.D.M.*, pp. 19-20; p. 10.

[68] Leo XIII, *Supremi Apostolatus.*

[69] St. Pius X, *Ad diem illum, P.D.M.*, p. 139.—The quotation at the end of this passage is from St. Augustine, *De sancta virginitate*, c. 6.

[70] Leo XIII, in his Encyclical Letter *Magnae Dei Matris*, adds his authority to the following passage from St. Thomas' *Expositio super Salutatione angelica*: "It is a great thing in any saint to have grace sufficient for the salvation of many souls; but

we refer our salvation to the remote principle of Mary's own universal causality—namely God who, in virtue of the merits of Christ, bestowed upon her, *de congruo*, the singular privilege of such fullness of grace—we say that she merited our redemption *de congruo*. But if we refer our salvation to the proximate cause, i.e., to Mary as regards the state in which she was established and wholly confirmed in the good, by way of congruous privilege, it seems we ought to say that—dependent on her Son, as her Compassion on His Passion—she merited with Christ our redemption *de condigno.*[71]

> She suffered and almost died with her suffering and dying Son; for the salvation of mankind, she renounced her mother's rights over Him; to appease the divine justice—insofar as this depended on her—she sacrificed her Son; hence it can rightfully be said that, together with Christ, she redeemed the human race.[72]

It is sometimes objected that Mary's cooperation would divide the redeeming act of Christ, which is contrary to the *one offering,* taught by St. Paul. (Hebr. x. 14) This would be true enough if Christ acted in the mode of a particular cause, whose agency is divided according to the multiplicity of its effects. But just as an intelligible species that is universal in representation is in no way divided by the specific or numerical diversity of its objects, neither is the action of a universal cause divided by the

---

to have enough to suffice for the salvation of everybody in the world, is the greatest of all; and this is found in Christ and in the Blessed Virgin." (*P.D.M.*, pp. 69-70) Now, if the grace is "sufficient for the salvation of everybody in the world," whoever possesses that grace is also a free and sufficient cause—though dependent—with regard to "the salvation of everybody in the world." To be such a cause is proper to Christ and to Mary. In this she differs from all other saints taken together, *quasi genere.*

[71] The well-known text of St. Pius X does not seem to present any difficulty in this matter: ". . . She merits, as the expression is, *de congruo* what Christ merits *de condigno* . . ." (*Ad diem illum, P.D.M.*, p. 141) For Christ, "by His nature is the Mediator between God and man." (*Ibid.*, p. 140). In other words, Mary does not share in mediation by her Motherhood considered in itself and apart from the fullness of grace that is hers by privilege, except in a remote way inasmuch as she "is in truth and by nature the Mother of Christ." (*IIIa Pars*, qu. 5, a. 3, c.) Yet, by reason of the singular grace bestowed upon her without absolute necessity, but only *de congruo* by a special mercy of the Almighty, she can, on this condition and in virtue of what the theologians call "necessitas immutabilitatis" (*De Verit.*, qu. 23, a. 4, ad 1), merit for us in justice, i.e., *de condigno.*

[72] "Ita cum Filio patiente et moriente passa est et paene commortua, sic materna in Filium iura pro hominum salute abdicavit placandaeque iustitiae, quantum ad se pertinebat, Filium immolavit, ut dici merito queat Ipsam cum Christo humanum genus redemisse." BENEDICT XV, *Inter Sodalicia.* Our translation of *paene commortua* by "almost died with . . ." could be misleading, if interpreted to mean literally that Mary was actually near death. The meaning intended seems to be—*salvo meliori judicio*—that in her Compassion she willingly renounced the good of her temporal life, in such wise that the merit was the same as if God had permitted her to die.

diversity of its effects—not even when the latter are universal agents in their turn.[73] Nor does the agency of the subordinate universal cause follow upon that of the higher in a succession of time.

Finally, we must consider the opinion of those who, distinguishing between the private person of Mary and her *persona publica,* suggest that she was pre-redeemed and sanctified by the grace of Christ in her private person; but that she was coredemptrix only in her social person, in which respect she is not, they claim, dependent on the influence of the grace of Christ, but of the grace of God, directly. It follows that, in this respect, her causality would not be subordinate to that of Christ, but coordinated with it. But it is difficult to see how such a position can be reconciled with the *one offering* by which Christ *has perfected forever those who are sanctified.* Such an opinion divides the Order of Redemption at its very head.

And why should the grace of the private person and that of the *persona publica* be distinct any more than in notion? To the question whether the grace of Christ, as Head of the Church, is the same as His grace inasmuch as He is an individual man, St. Thomas replies:

> Since everything acts inasmuch as it is a being in act, it must be the same act whereby it is in act and whereby it acts, as it is the same heat whereby fire is hot and whereby it heats. Yet not every act whereby anything is in act suffices for its being the principle of acting upon others. For since the agent is nobler than the patient, as Augustine says (*Gen. ad lit.* xii. 16) and the Philosopher (*De Anima,* iii. 19), the agent must act on others by reason of a certain preeminence. Now it was said above, grace was received by the soul of Christ in the highest way; and therefore from this preeminence of grace which He received, it is from Him that this grace is bestowed on others,—and this belongs

[73] The now current distinction between "objective" and "subjective" redemption, tends to favor an otherwise already widespread confusion of what is universal *in repraesentando,* or *in causando,* with what is universal *in praedicando* or *inessendo* (as opposed to *in essendo*). E.g., it is sometimes said that Christ, during His life on earth, merited our salvation in a "global" way, as when a man stores up wares with only a general idea of those to whom they are to be allotted; as if the treasury of graces were like a general store-house, whose goods are unlabeled and the addresses still undetermined. This is all wrong in as much as it implies that the act of distribution and application, by means of the sacraments, is the first cause of distinction; as if grace received thereby a determination which the universal cause did not provide. The lack of determination is on the part of the recipient and its particular cause; not on the part of the universal agency inasmuch as it is universal *in causando.* In other words, the terminology "objective" and "subjective" redemption lends itself all too readily to Father Th. DE REGNON's understanding of universal causality in his *Métaphysique des causes* (Paris, 1886). What it should mean is the distinction between Christ's Passion as a "universalis causa salutis," and the application of this universal cause to each in particular by means of the sacraments—the "remedia quibus universalis causae virtus pertingit ad homines." (*Contra Gentiles IV,* cc. 53-54; *IIIa Pars,* q. 49, a. 1, ad 4).

to the nature of head. Hence the personal grace, whereby the soul of Christ is justified, is essentially the same as His grace, as He is the Head of the Church, and justifies others; but they are distinct in notion.[74]

Furthermore, because the personal grace of Christ and the grace which overflows to others are essentially the same, the Mystical Body of Christ is also more one and divine.

> . . . Grace was in Christ not merely as in an individual, but also as in the Head of the whole Church, to Whom all are united, as members to a head, who constitute one mystical person. And hence it is that Christ's merit extends to others inasmuch as they are His members; even as in a man the action of the head reaches in a manner to all his members, since it perceives not merely for itself alone, but for all members.[75]

Now Mary's singular plenitude of grace, bestowed upon her in virtue of the merits of her Son, sanctifies her own person, but in such a preeminent way that, essentially the same, her grace overflows to others. This personal preeminence does not set the Mother apart from her Son, as if she were henceforth a first principle all by herself, acting in extrinsic coordination with Him—*quasi duo trahentes navim.* On the contrary, in her very difference as Mother and Spouse, it renders her more perfectly subordinate to His purpose, and more one with Him in His redeeming action. The nature of this subordination is illustrated by the analogies, quoted from St. Bernard, in the Encyclical Letter *Ad diem illum* (1904) in which St. Pius X commemorated the fiftieth anniversary of the Proclamation of the Dogma of the Immaculate Conception:

> But Mary, as St. Bernard justly remarks, is the "channel" or, if you will, that connecting portion by which the body is joined to the head and by which the head exerts its power and its virtue: "For she is the neck of our Head by which He communicates to His Mystical Body all spiritual gifts." [76]

In this way, the Order of Redemption is itself more perfect and one; just as God's creation in general is more assimilated to Him when a thing is able to communicate to another the perfection that it has, and especially when

> the good of one becomes common to many [flowing] from the one to the others, and this can be only when the one, by its own action, communicates it to them; but if it has not the power to transmit it to others, that good remains its own property.[77]

---

[74] *IIIa Pars,* q. 8, a. 5, c.
[75] *Ibid.,* q. 19, a. 4, c.—"For, just as the natural body is one, though made up of diverse members, so the whole Church, Christ's mystic body, is reckoned as one person with its head, which is Christ." (*Ibid.,* q. 49, a. 1, c.)
[76] *P.D.M.,* pp. 140-141.
[77] *Contra Gentiles III,* c. 69.

That God might have governed all without subordinate universal causes, does not imply that we can behave as if He actually does.

Thanks to the person of Mary, the dignity of every human person graced by God is raised in a most merciful way, such as would not have been without her. This is in keeping with God's will to renew this dignity to the utmost. Now such is indeed the case when man owes his redemption not only to the God-man, but to a human person as well: deriving all grace from

> the new Eve, who, although subject to the new Adam, is most inti-
> mately associated with Him in that struggle against the infernal foe
> which, as foretold in the *protoevangelium,* finally resulted in that most
> complete victory over the sin and death which are always associated in
> the writings of the Apostle of the Gentiles.[78]

Now that we have seen, in general, what is meant by Mary's Coredemption, it remains to be shown more concretely how the fullness of grace, to the extent of Immaculate Conception, is the proximate, formal and perfecting cause of that "arctissima conjunctio" between the new Adam and the person who was chosen as a *help like unto himself,* the second Eve, as well as of the "perpetual enmity between her and the serpent, spoken of from earliest tradition down to the time of the solemn definition of the Immaculate Conception." [79]   For it was in virtue of this most intimate union that Mary could take part, as she did, in the struggle of her Son, *to crush the head of the Serpent,* and share in the new Adam's glorious triumph by her Assumption.   However, as we have quoted from both *Ineffabilis Deus* and *Fulgens Corona,* Mary's Divine Motherhood is the *sedes* and *fons* of all her privileges and graces.   Hence, before considering in particular the Immaculate Conception as achieving, with regard to the final cause of the Incarnation, the fullest possible assimilation between the new Adam and the second Eve, we must note that (as remains to be shown in the following chapter) in virtue of the *Divine Motherhood* there already exists in the entitative order, by priority of nature, a unique assimilation between the Virgin and her only-begotten Son—an assimilation which is the basic prerequisite of all the privileges and graces bestowed upon Mary as Mother of God.   It is in virtue of this natural assimilation, presupposed to the Immaculate Conception as nature is to grace, that the evil inflicted upon the Son affected the Mother as a personal one—as a *malum proprium.* Then we can show, specifically, that because of her Immaculate Conception, Mary's assimilation to the Son *qua* Redeemer, was such that she could take an active, universally meritorious part, in the Redemption of all who are under the general law.

---

[78] Pius XII, *Munificentissimus Deus, P.D.M.,* p. 237.
[79] *Fulgens Corona, P.D.M.,* p. 254.

II

THE IMMACULATE CONCEPTION AND THE FULLNESS OF MARY'S MOTHERHOOD WITH RESPECT TO THE PURPOSE OF THE INCARNATION

A Divine Person is the image of Mary

As Mother of God, Mary does not derive her greatness merely from the excellence of Christ's human nature considered in itself, but from the fact that the temporal generation of the Son of God must be attributed to the Divine Person. For "nativity is attributed to the person or hypostasis as to the proper subject of being born, but not to the nature." [80] For the Virgin to be *Dei Genitrix*, requires that the Divine Person should proceed from her "by way of similitude in the same specific nature." [81] Now that which proceeds from another, like to it in species, has the nature of true image.[82] But Christ was conceived of the Virgin Mary "unto likeness of species. For this reason He is called her Son." [83] In other words, in His temporal birth, the Word of the Father proceeds as the image of Mary who thereby has the nature of "origo Dei." [84]

We must note, then, that the Word, in His humanity, is not simply "in the image" of the Mother, but *He* is her image, just as He is her Son. The reason for this is that Christ is univocally a man [85] and proceeds by way of generation *in quarto modo dicendi per se*—that is, in the same mode in which, according to His Godhead, He proceeds as the image of the Father.

Furthermore, since the human nature of Christ is the term of his temporal procession, and not 'that which' is born, it is not the humanity of Christ which is the image of Mary, but the very Person of her Son, *according to His humanity.*[86] Thus, if we said, absolutely speaking, that the Blessed Virgin is the origin of Christ's human nature formally as the *subject* of generation, we could not say that she is true Mother of God. In the same way, if we said that it is the human nature of Christ which is the image of Mary, and not the Person Himself, according to His humanity, the Son of the Eternal Father would not be the Offspring of Mary, nor would God have been *born* man.

It follows, therefore, that Mary, in generating the Son of the Father—

---

[80] *IIIa Pars*, q. 35, a. 1, c.
[81] *Ia Pars*, q. 27, a. 2, c.
[82] *Ibid.*, q. 35, a. 1, c.
[83] *IIIa Pars*, q. 32, a. 3, ad. 1.
[84] Cf. St. ALBERT, *Mariale*, q. 145, (edit. Borgnet) t. 37, p. 206a. (It has recently been shown that St. Albert is not the author of this work, which nevertheless enjoys great authority, as we noted in *La Piété du Fils*, pp. xi-xii.)
[85] *IIIa Pars*, q. 2, a. 5, c.
[86] *Ibid.*, q. 35, a. 4, c.

Deum verum de Deo vero—assimilates Him to Herself according to the nature in which He proceeds from her. For assimilation is of the very notion of generation: *assimilatio viventis a principio vivente conjuncto;* and it is precisely 'what proceeds' that is assimilated to its orign, with respect to which whatever proceeds by way of similitude has the nature of image.

THE DIVINE MOTHERHOOD AS A NATURAL BASIS OF FRIENDSHIP BETWEEN GOD AND MAN

The kind of assimilation we have just considered is provided by the operation of nature, inasmuch as "the Blessed Virgin Mary is in truth and by nature the Mother of Christ." [87] We must now return to this assimilation, and consider it with regard to the order of action, as a natural basis of that similitude which is the *per se* cause of friendship.[88] For, since the child is the image of the parent, nature provides the basis for a friendship that is "abiding and excellent." [89] It is, more particularly, the love of a mother for her child that is the most natural and striking expression of what is also most perfect in friendship, namely loving rather than being loved.[90] Aristotle shows that it is by referring to motherly love that the basic traits of friendship are defined, such as to grieve and rejoice with one's friend—"and this too is found in mothers most of all."[91]

While it can be said of every true friend that he is, as it were, another self, to the parent the child is, by nature, another self in a way that is unique.

> For parents love their children as being a part of themselves, and children their parents as being something originating from them. . . Mothers love more than fathers do. Parents, then, love their children as themselves (for their issue are by virtue of their separate existence a sort of other selves), while children love their parents as being born of them, and brothers love each other as being born of the same parents; for their identity with them makes them identical with each other (which is the reason why people talk of the 'same blood,' 'the same stock,' and so on). They are, therefore, in a sense the same thing, though in separate individuals.[92]

We should not fail to note that, even from this point of view, the friendship between the Virgin, as "vera naturalis mater," and her Son, is unique inasmuch as Mary gave free consent to become mother of the One whose

---

[87] *IIIa Pars*, q. 35, a. 3, c.
[88] St. THOMAS, *In VIII Ethicor.*, lect. 4, n. 1588.
[89] "When children render to parents what they ought to render to those who brought them into the world, and parents render what they should to their children, the friendship of such persons will be abiding and excellent." ARISTOTLE, *Ethics*, VIII, c. 7, 1158 b 20.
[90] *Ibid.*, c. 8, 1159 a 25.
[91] *Ethics IX*, c. 4, 1166a.
[92] *Ibid.*, VIII, c. 12, 1161 b 25.

Name and purpose she knew, thus conforming to the rule: "We must not make a man our friend against his will." [93]

THE DIVINE MOTHERHOOD AS THE REASON WHY EVIL INFLICTED UPON GOD CAN AFFECT A HUMAN PERSON AS A "MALUM PROPRIUM"

The proper object of sorrow is *one's own evil,* i.e. the evil inflicted upon one's own person—*dolor est tristitia de malo proprio.*[94]   But one may sorrow for an evil that is not one's own; "and thus we have *pity,* which is sorrow for another's evil, considered, however, as one's own—*misericordia . . . est tristitia de alieno malo, inquantum tamen aestimatur ut proprium."* [95]

Mercy or pity, like justice, is directed, properly speaking, towards another. It is said of the sorrow for one's own evil in a figurative way only, as when we speak of justice towards oneself, according as a man is considered to have various parts, as in the text: *Have pity on thy own soul, pleasing God.* (Ecclus. xxx. 24)   In fact, as Aristotle observes, our pity extends only to people who are not very closely related to us.[96]   However, "in the case of those persons who are so closely united to us, as to be part of ourselves, such as our children or our parents, we do not pity their distress, but suffer [dolemus] as for our own sores." [97]

Therefore, owing to the natural bond of Mary's motherhood and to Christ's temporal filiation, a purely human person can suffer, naturally, as his *own* evil, the very Passion of the Son of God.   Hence, it is in the strictest sense that in the liturgy Mary's Compassion should be called *dolorosa,* founded, as expressly stated throughout both Offices commemorating her Sorrows, upon the relationship of *Genitrix* and *Genitus, Mater* and *Filius; Parens, Parturiens* and *Partus.*   The Blessed Virgin's Motherhood, as we shall see, is an essential and incommunicable disposition to share as Coredemptrix in the Passion of her Son.

---

[93] *Ibid.,* c. 13, 1163 a.

[94] *Ia-IIae,* q. 35, a. 8, c.

[95] *Ibid.,*—Cf. "The Compassion of the Virgin-Mother, and the Prophecy of Simeon," *Laval théologique et philosophique,* 1950, vol. VI, n. 2, pp. 314-327.

[96] "The people we pity are: those whom we know, if only they are not very closely related to us—in that case we feel about them as if we were in danger ourselves. For this reason Amasis did not weep, they say, at the sight of his son being led to death, but did weep when he saw his friend begging: the latter sight was pitiful, the former terrible, and the terrible is different from the pitiful; it tends to cast out pity, and often helps to produce the opposite of pity." *Rhetoric II,* c. 8, 1386 a 15. W. R. Roberts transl.

[97] *IIa-IIae,* q. 30, a. 1, ad 2.—The same kind of union in sorrow is true of husband and wife, as St. Thomas points out elsewhere, for they too are part of one another, even in virtue of the sole "indissolubilis conjunctio animorum." This union in sorrow applies to Christ and Mary as new Adam and second Eve.

The union of grace between the Son of God and His Mother

As the true natural Mother of Christ, Mary, in her very person, is as near to God as can be in the order of nature. Yet, as St. Augustine says, "Mary is more blessed in receiving the faith of Christ, than in conceiving the flesh of Christ. . . Her nearness as a Mother would have been of no profit to Mary, had she not borne Christ in her heart after a more blessed manner than in her flesh." [98] We should note here, that all graces and privileges bestowed upon Mary are proportioned to her Motherhood of the Savior. The fullness of grace was hers *"ut esset propinquissima auctori gratiae—* in order to be as near as possible to the Author of grace, and to receive within her Him Who is full of all grace; so that by bringing Him forth, she, in a manner, might dispense grace to all." [99]

Unlike that of any other saint, the grace of Mary was not confined to her soul. "It is a great thing indeed to have so much grace that it sanctifies the soul. But the soul of the Blessed Virgin was so replete that grace overflowed from her soul into her flesh, in order to conceive from it the Son of God. . . *Behold, thou shalt conceive in thy womb and shalt bring forth a son . . . the Son of the Most High."* (Luke, i. 31) [100]

In Christ we distinguish the grace of union—ordained as it is to His *esse personale*—from His habitual grace, which is both personal and ordained to others. Likewise, in Mary, we distinguish the grace of Divine Motherhood from her habitual grace which may, nevertheless, also be called grace of motherhood inasmuch as it is ordained to her Maternity. But the grace of Motherhood in the first sense, is something of the physical order, of the *esse personale* of Mary herself inasmuch as in and by her nature of Mother she is a principal agent and the generating cause of her Son according to His humanity, to Whom she is referred by a real relation. And this is what St. Thomas calls the "affinitas quam habet ad Deum," [101] which is the basis of the cult of hyperdulia. "This affinity belongs to the Blessed Virgin alone," Cajetan adds in his commentary, "for she alone attains to the confines of the Deity by her own operation."

Now the habitual grace of Mary, which by its nature is ordained to the operations of mind and will with regard to the supernatural end, viz. God in His very Godhead, is also called grace of Motherhood because it was bestowed upon her as Mother of God, who, even in the order of nature, "ad fines deitatis . . . attigit." Thereby, her nature as a whole, soul and

---

[98] *De Sancta virginitate,* c. 3. Quoted by St. Thomas, *IIIa Pars,* q. 30, a. 1, c.
[99] *IIIa Pars,* q. 27, a. 5, c.
[100] St. Thomas, *Expositio super Salutatione angelica 'Ave Maria,' Opuscula,* (Edit. Mandonnet), t. IV, p. 458.
[101] *IIa-IIae,* q. 103, a. 4, ad 2.

body, is singularly sanctified, and not just the person by reason of a part, namely the soul alone.

Grace is a participation of the Divine Nature. While singularly adapted to her person as Mother of God, Mary's sanctifying grace does not in any way divert from the final cause of grace. To the Blessed Virgin, this end is none other than union with the Godhead of the One Who is her only-begotten Son. This is entirely proper to her, inasmuch as her sanctifying grace perfects the divine Motherhood with respect to the final cause of all grace. Her grace is likewise singularly proportioned to the means designed by God for the sake of this end, viz. the mission of the Word: His birth, life, and death among us, to redeem man that, by grace, he may again be child and friend of God—a mission which she shares both as Mother and as new Eve.

MARY'S MOTHERHOOD AS THE NATURAL BASIS OF HER UNIQUE FRIENDSHIP OF VIRTUE WITH GOD

Friendship is a mutual love between persons, founded on some kind of communication. When love is based on the communication between God and man, inasmuch as He communicates to us the happiness which is proper to Him as God, it is essentially a love of friendship—the one, "of which it is written: *God is faithful: by Whom you are called unto the fellowship of His Son* [I Cor. i. 9]. The love which is based on this communication, is charity: wherefore it is evident that charity is the friendship of man for God." [102] But Mary, both by nature and by grace, is united to this Son as her own—to Him Who is charity by His nature.

Love, as such, is a unitive force—*amor est virtus unitiva*—[103] and friendship is one kind of love. For lack of words to express the union between friends, proverbial sayings refer to "a single soul," "another self," and "what friends have is common property." [104] Now charity is the friendship of man for God. Indeed the archetype of the union of charity is none other than that which exists, by nature, between the Divine Persons. *Holy Father, keep in thy name those whom thou hast given me, that they may be one even as we are. . . . That all may be one, even as thou, Father, in me and I in thee; that they also may be one in us. . .* (John, xvii, 11, 20) This union is such that if it were to be achieved naturally between created persons, it would imply their mutual destruction.[105]

This most intimate of unions must be had in mind when we consider Mary's Compassion—but never in separation from her nature as Mother

---

[102] *Ibid.*, q. 23, a. 1, c.
[103] *Ibid.*, q. 25, a. 4, c.
[104] *Ethics*, IX, c. 8, 1168 b.
[105] Cf. PLATO, *Symposium*, the discourse of Aristophanes, 189a, et sq.; ARISTOTLE, *Politics*, I, c. 4, 1262 b 10.

of God and of new Eve, for while the union of grace surpasses beyond measure every natural union, it does not destroy, nor even by-pass nature, but perfects it. It is for this reason that the order to be observed in charity respects the order of nature, such as loving one's own parents more than those of another.[106] Likewise, the vision of God does not consume the mind of the blessed, but raises it to its highest perfection in conformity with its own nature, whereas excessive light would destroy the very organ of sight.

In the order of nature, Christ's temporal filiation, unlike the filiation of any other child of man, is wholly undivided, since, in this procession according to human nature, He is brought forth exclusively in the image of the Virgin, who is the only generating principle of His birth among us. For, though she conceived of the Holy Ghost, Christ did not proceed in the image of His active principle of generation, and in no wise should He be called the Son of the Holy Ghost.[107] It is because of her that the Incarnation of the Word is a generation in the strictest sense of this term. The assimilation of one human nature to another could not be more complete and undivided. Hence, the same evil that befalls her Son in His Passion, at the same time attains undivided her own person—of a passible nature. It is not as when parents share the sorrow for their child in distress.

Whatever the implication of the epithet *Woman* at the Marriage Feast of Cana, the sole assertion of Christ, *"My hour has not yet come,"* (John, ii. 4) is sufficient to warrant St. Augustine's teaching on this point, which St. Thomas makes his own.[108] The power to work miracles belongs to Christ's Godhead, not to the nature He received from the Mother. St. Augustine explains that Christ will acknowledge Mary publicly as His Mother when the weakness of the nature which He owes to her shall be exhibited upon the Cross, where, at the same time, her spiritual motherhood shall be made known to all. *Behold thy Mother.* (John, xix. 27) We may understand, therefore, that the Son of Man and new Adam designed this solemn manifestation to express at once the unity between her natural motherhood with regard to Him and—owing to her fullness of grace and union with the Savior in His sacrifice—the new Eve's spiritual fecundity with regard to us.[109]

Mary, then, compassionated the Redeemer not only because He was her Son by nature, but immeasurably more so because to this Son of hers by nature, she was singularly united in most perfect innocence, by her

---

[106] *IIa-IIae*, q. 26.

[107] *IIIa Pars*, q. 32, a. 3. Although the Holy Ghost is a principle of this generation, He is not a generating principle, for the latter implies assimilation.

[108] St. Augustine, *In Joannis Evangelium*, Tract. 8, c. 9; Tract. 119, cc. 1-3. St. Thomas, *In Joann.*, c. ii, lect. 1; c. xix, lect. 4.

[109] Cf. *Mystici Corporis*, Epilogue.

grace of the hypostatic order. This means that she was one with her Son *qua* Redeemer, as a second Eve, subject to the new Adam.

In this regard, our spiritual regeneration is the fruit of Mary's singular union with Christ in His Passion, a oneness of Passion and Compassion which could not have been without the Virgin-Mother's "most complete innocence," i.e. without the Immaculate Conception.

THE NOBILITY OF CHRIST'S FRIENDSHIP, AS CAUSE OF THE VIRGIN'S SHARE IN THE REDEMPTION OF MANKIND

Friendship must involve at least an equality of proportion. But justice, too, involves such a proportion. Yet there is a difference between them, for whereas justice reduces inequality to equality, the latter having the nature of a term, in friendship the equality of persons has the nature of a principle. As Aristotle points out:

> Friendship and justice seem . . . to be concerned with the same objects and exhibited between the same persons. . . . And the extent of their association is the extent of their friendship, as it is the extent to which justice exists between them. And the proverb, "what friends have is common property," expresses the truth; for friendship depends on community. . . . And the demands of justice also seem to increase with the intensity of the friendship, which implies that friendship and justice exist between the same persons and have an equal extension.[110]

There is still another point, in Aristotle's treatise on friendship, that may be used in connection with our subject:

> It is true of the good man too that he does many acts for the sake of his friends and his country, and if necessary dies for them; for he will throw away both wealth and honors and in general the goods that are objects of competition, gaining for himself nobility; since he would prefer a short period of intense pleasure to a long one of mild enjoyment, a twelve-month of noble action to many trivial ones. Now those who die for others doubtless attain this result; it is therefore a great prize that they choose for themselves. . . . Rightly then is he thought to be good, since he chooses nobility before all else. *But he may even give up actions to his friend; it may be nobler to become the cause of his friend's acting than to act himself.* In all the actions, therefore, that men are praised for, the good man is seen to assign to himself the greater share in what is noble. In this sense, then, as has been said, a man should be a lover of self; but in the sense in which most men are so, he ought not.[111]

Because of her singular fullness of grace, Mary is the most perfect and most worthy of God's friends. *Tota pulchra es amica mea, et macula non*

---

[110] *Ethics, VIII,* c. 9, 1159 b 25. (Ross transl.)
[111] *Op. cit.,* IX, c. 8, 1169 a 15-35.

est in te. (Cant. iv. 7) The friendship between the Son and the Mother, between the new Adam and the second Eve, being what it is, it is entirely natural according to the doctrine quoted above, that the most Noble of friends should have become the cause of Mary's acting for the sake of His own end as Redeemer. Thus the Virgin's share, instead of detracting from the Savior's power, shows it more fully: whatever she does is performed in virtue of His friendship. And though He is the cause of His friend's acting, the Friend is truly a cause nevertheless. To underrate the proper worth of this action would amount to belittling the power and nobility of the Redeemer Himself, as well as His Wisdom in the choice and making of His most worthy friend. Thus, in bestowing upon Mary the character of a *help like unto Himself;* in causing her to act universally for the sake of His mission on earth, the Savior demonstrated His divine nobility in the mode which we recognize as proper to the perfect friend.[112] That is why we may say that the perfection of Christ's friendship for the Mother and new Eve—and, through her person, for all mankind—is the cause of her role as Coredemptrix.

MARY'S INITIAL SANCTIFICATION, AS ORDAINED
TO THE PURPOSE OF THE INCARNATION

The Order of Redemption is not merely a restoration of the Order in which man had originally been established. In God's plan, reaching from end to end, the old was ordained to the new; an occasion, as it were, "to complete, by a plan concealed from the centuries, the first work of His goodness by a mystery yet more wondrously hidden through the Incarnation of the Word." [113] Before time began:

> the eternal Father chose and prepared for His Only-begotten Son a Mother . . . [whom] He so loved that truly in her was the Father well-pleased with singular delight. Wherefore, far above all the angels and all the saints, so wondrously did God endow her with the abundance of all heavenly gifts poured from the treasury of His divinity that this Mother, ever absolutely free of all stain of sin, all fair and perfect, would possess that fullness of holy innocence and sanctity than which, under God, one cannot even imagine anything greater, and which, outside of God, no mind can succeed in fully comprehending.[114]

---

[112] "Et dicit [Philosophus], quod contingit quandoque quod virtuosus etiam actiones virtuosos concedit suo amico: puta si sit aliquod opus virtutis faciendum per ipsum vel alterum, *concedit quod fiat per amicum, ut ex hoc proficiat et laudetur.* Et tamen in hoc etiam accipit sibi id quod est melius. Melius est enim et magis virtuosum, quod ipse sit causa amico suo talia faciendi, quam etiam si ipse faceret: praesertim cum sibi remaneat opportunitas, alias talia vel majora faciendi. Sic ergo patet, quod virtuosus plus sibi tribuit de bono quantum ad omnia laudabilia, et sic maxime amat seipsum." St. THOMAS, *In IX Ethic.*, lect. 9 (edit. Pirotta), n. 1883.

[113] *Ineffabilis Deus, P.D.M.*, p. 9.

[114] *Ibid.*, p. 10.

In the following few lines, Pius IX states plainly the reasons why it was most fitting that such sanctity should have been conferred upon the Mother of the Redeemer:

> And indeed it was by all means fitting that so wonderful a mother should be ever resplendent with the glory of most sublime holiness and so absolutely free from all taint of original sin that she would triumph completely over the ancient serpent. To her did the Father dispose to give His Only-begotten Son—the Son whom, equal to the Father and begotten by Him, the Father loves from His heart—and to give this Son in such a way that He would be the one and same common Son of God the Father and of the Blessed Virgin Mary. It was this venerable Mother whom the Son Himself chose to make His mother. And the Holy Spirit who proceeds from the Son willed and brought it about that of Mary should the Son be conceived and born.[115]

The New Order did not make a clean sweep, so to speak, of the Old. Not only was the greatest good of the latter elicited from the "lamentable wretchedness" that resulted from Adam's sin;[116] the first Eve was the figure of the Woman, as the first Adam was the figure of the New. The "plan concealed from the centuries" embraces both orders even as to their proper principles: *It is not good for man to be alone; let us make him a help like unto himself.* (Gen. ii. 18) Since our purpose, in the present chapter, is to show how the Virgin's Immaculate Conception is essential to the Order of Redemption as God chose it to be, even as to the manner in which its end is achieved, the most pertinent words, in the passage just quoted from *Ineffabilis Deus,* are those of the very first sentence: "So absolutely free from all taint of original sin that she would triumph completely [*amplissimum . . . triumphum referret*] over the ancient

---

[115] *Ibid.*

[116] The good that is proper to the order of Redemption, as distinguished from the state of original justice, is of the kind "which could not be elicited except from some evil, such as the good of patience which comes about from the evil of persecution, and the good of penance from the evil of fault; nor does this deny the weakness of evil with regard to the good, for such things are not elicited from evil as from a *per se* cause, but accidentally, so to speak, and materially." St. Thomas, *Q. D. de Veritate,* q. 5, a. 4, ad 5. Evil is subject to God's *providentia concessionis,* as distinguished from the *providentia approbationis.* (*Ibid.,* c.) *For God has shut up all in unbelief, that he may have mercy upon all.* (Rom. xi. 32) Since God does not permit any evil except inasmuch as He can ordain it to a greater good, does it not follow that we should, *as some calumnously accuse us of teaching, do evil that good may come from it? The condemnation of such is just.* (Rom. iii. 8) "To commit evil for the sake of good is reprehensible in man, nor can such be attributed to God. But to ordain evil to the good, is not contrary to goodness; hence, to permit evil for the sake of some good to be elicited from it, this is attributed to God." (St. Thomas, *loc. cit.,* ad 10) The fact that the incomparable perfection of the order of Redemption presupposes the concession of an evil does not make its goodness depend upon an evil as upon a *per se* cause; on the contrary, it demonstrates the excellence of the *per se* cause, which can ordain not only good to good, but evil as well to an even greater good. This latter good owes its greater perfection not to the evil as to a *per se* cause, but wholly to the *per se* cause of the greater good that it is.

Serpent." Note the sequence of ideas, as the Bull goes on to say: "To her did the Father dispose to give His Only-begotten Son. . ." In other words, by reason of the Immaculate Conception, bestowed in virtue of the merits of her Son, intuited by God in His eternity, she is not only most wondrously assimilated to the Father as to the nature of generating principle with regard to the same Son, as well as to the Holy Ghost from Whom she conceives, and Who proceeds from the same Father and Son; she is there, at the very principle of the Order of Redemption, with active regard to its final cause by her ability to triumph completely over the head of all evil, and to free us from enslavement to him. The same relationship will be repeated over and again in this solemn document.[117] " . . . By divinely given power she utterly destroyed the force and dominion of the evil one." [118] "All our hope do we repose in the most Blessed Virgin—in the all fair and immaculate one who has crushed the poisonous head of the most cruel Serpent and brought salvation to the world."

Now that we know, most explicitly, with divine certitude, that in the very first instant of her conception, Mary was already freed from every subjection to the Serpent, we see that the Order of Redemption is, universally, both more divine and human, comprising at its very root a mere human person raised to the dignity of *a help like unto* the Savior. How radically different this order would have been if, for no matter how brief a time, Mary had been subject to the hereditary fault, as St. Thomas believed, and thus under the dominion of the one whose name is *Enemy*.[119] Though by her Motherhood she would have attained, nevertheless, to the hypostatic union, her habitual grace would not have been of the hypostatic order; the Virgin would not have been conceived a second Eve as *a help like unto* the new Adam. No human person would have been that close to Him in sanctity, at the very foundation and principle of the Order of Redemption; nor would the Woman have been so one with her seed in complete enmity against the *father of all liars*. A more merciful design towards mankind is inconceivable.

THE IMMACULATE CONCEPTION AND THE UNITY OF THE ORDER OF REDEMPTION

In His Encyclical Letter *Fulgens Corona*, of September 1953, Pius XII pays heed to the accusation that, on account of the Immaculate Concep-

---

[117] E.g., *P.D.M.*, pp. 17-18.

[118] *Ibid., P.D.M.*, pp. 20, 26.

[119] "Now, if at any time, the Blessed Mary were destitute of divine grace even for the briefest moment, because of contamination in her conception by the hereditary stain of sin, there would not have come between her and the Serpent that perpetual enmity spoken of from earliest tradition down to the time of the solemn definition of the Immaculate Conception, but rather a certain subjection." *Fulgens Corona, P.D.M.*, p. 254.

tion, "the Redemption by Christ was lessened, as if it did not extend to the whole race of Adam: and that, therefore, something was taken away from the office and dignity of the divine Redeemer." To this objection, the Holy Father replies:

> . . . if we carefully and thoroughly consider the matter, we easily perceive that Christ the Lord in a most perfect manner really redeemed His Mother, since it was by virtue of His merits that she was preserved by God immune from all stain of original sin. Wherefore, the infinite dignity of Jesus Christ and His office of universal redemption is not diminished or lowered by this tenet of doctrine; rather it is greatly increased.[120]

But why could the Blessed Virgin not have been preserved from the stain of original sin by a grace bestowed upon her immediately by God, without dependence on the merits of Christ, as was the case of the original grace of Adam and of the angels? This might have been, but God chose otherwise. Thanks to the redeeming grace of Christ, Mary belongs, entirely and intrinsically, to the Order of Redemption. If God had chosen the other method, the Virgin would have been, in the order of grace, not only alien to us, but to her own Son as well. The Order of Redemption would have been divided at its very root. Mary would not have been assimilated as she is to her Son the Redeemer. This union in His Passion would not have been what it was; nor would she have been, in the strictest sense, the Mother of our spiritual regeneration. She would not have been the spouse of Christ as Eve was the spouse of Adam.

The first Eve received from God her nature formed from Adam. *For Adam was formed first, then Eve.* (I Tim. ii. 13) In the order of nature, Adam was prior to Eve, though she was not his daughter. But in the order of spiritual evil, it is Eve who was first. *And Adam was not deceived, but the woman was deceived and was in sin.* (*ibid.*, 14) Conversely, in the order of generation, the new Adam receives his human nature from the second Eve, and therein she precedes Him. But in the order of the good, namely of grace, the new Adam is prior to her, inasmuch as it is in virtue of His merits that she is preserved from the stain of the first man's sin. Thanks to this preservation, the new Adam proceeds from a wholly spotless nature. He can therefore be the more freely assimilated to her in the order of nature itself, she being an origin more worthy of the One who is her Image. The Immaculate Conception is therefore a work of supreme piety and friendship. Of *pietas,* the virtue which extends to the principles of our origination, to whom we owe homage and duty inasmuch as we are in debt towards those who gave us life;[121] of perfect friendship,

---

[120] *P.D.M.,* pp. 256-257.
[121] *IIa-IIae,* q. 101, a. 1.

too, inasmuch as, owing to His merits, He causes Mary to assimilate Himself, as to His human nature, more entirely to her own. Here again applies the rule that it is nobler to be the cause of one's friend's acting. And this mutual assimilation— of the Mother to the Son in the order of grace, of the Son to the Mother in the order of nature—is sealed, "in a hidden way, by one and the same decree of predestination." [122]

The Bull *Ineffabilis Deus* teaches that because of the singleness of this decree of predestination: "the very words with which the Sacred Scriptures speak of Uncreated Wisdom and set forth His eternal origin, the Church, both in the ecclesiastical offices and in the liturgy, has been wont to apply likewise to the origin of the Blessed Virgin." [123]

Thanks to "her most excellent innocence, purity, holiness, and freedom from every stain of sin, as well as the unspeakable abundance and greatness of all heavenly graces, virtues and privileges," [124] Mary, in her Compassion, can experience the depth of the abyss which separates the sinful creature from its Maker. For "the pain of the innocent sufferer is more intensified by reason of his innocence, in so far as he deems the hurt inflicted to be the more undeserved. Hence it is that even others are more deserving of blame if they do not compassionate him; according to Isaias, lvii. 1: *The just perisheth, and no man layeth it to heart.*" [125] Christ is the innocent victim by His very nature, even in his human nature united to the Godhead, and this makes His Passion the more intense. Now the pure of heart have a better understanding of innocence than they who themselves bear guilt. They can compassionate the one who suffers undeservedly in a manner more selfless and understanding. Hence, the Mother of God could not have been so intimately one with Her Son in His Passion had she herself not been conceived in perfect innocence, had she at some time borne guilt. Otherwise, how could she have offered her Son in perfect dignity?

Pius XII, in a text we have already quoted, states explicitly that "it was she who, *free of all personal and inherited sin,* ever most intimately united to her Son, offered Him to the Eternal Father, as well as the sacrifices of her maternal rights and motherly love, even as a new Eve, for all the children of Adam, deformed by his fall." [126]

---

[122] *Munificentissimus Deus, P.D.M.,* p. 237.

[123] *P.D.M.,* p. 11—Even in some Christians there remains a spark of that envy to which LUTHER gave vent when protesting against the Church's use of *Proverbs xii* for the Epistle of the mass of the Nativity of Mary; he considered it a blasphemous lie to apply those words to Mary. "We are the equals of the Mother of God," he proclaimed, "and just as holy as she is, except that we cannot be mothers of God, as she was." Cf. CANISIUS, *De Maria Deipara Virgine,* Lib. I, c. 12, (edit. Ingolstadii, 1583) p. 84; *De corruptelis Verbi Dei,* c. 10, p. 121.

[124] *Ineffabilis Deus, P.D.M.,* p. 18.

[125] *IIIa Pars,* q. 46, a. 5, ad 5.

[126] *Mystici Corporis,* Epilog.

By this mode of redemption, all who are under the common law derive incomparable dignity from Mary's Immaculate Conception, inasmuch as their reparative grace derives both from Christ and, subject to Him, from a human person whom God had made worthy of that share in the work of salvation.

WOMAN, BEHOLD THY SON

It is more than a theological opinion that "the most holy Virgin is the Mother of all Christians, whom she bore on Mount Calvary in the supreme torments of the Redeemer." [127]   The Church has made it plain that this is the very meaning of Christ's last words from the Cross: *Woman, behold thy son.* (John, xix, 27)

> The mystery of Christ's immense love for us is clearly shown in the fact that the dying Savior bequeathed His Mother to His disciple John in the memorable testament: *Behold thy son.*   Now in John, as the Church has constantly taught, Christ designated the whole human race, and in the first rank are they who are joined with Him by faith.   It is in this sense that St. Anselm of Canterbury says: "What dignity, O Virgin, could be more highly prized than to be the Mother of those to whom Christ deigned to be Father and Brother?" [128]

The words of Christ to His Mother *Woman, behold thy son,* and to the disciple *Behold thy mother,* are therefore the formal and solemn proclamation made by God Incarnate at the consummation of His redemptive Passion, of the fact that "from this community of will and suffering between Christ and Mary 'she merited to become most worthily the reparatrix of the lost world' "; [129] that "she who was bodily the Mother of our Head, became spiritually, by a new title of suffering and glory, the Mother of all His members." [130]

This is, essentially, the doctrine of the Coredemption.

III

THE "PLENISSIMA GLORIFICATIO" OF MARY'S PERSON

THE DEATH OF THE BLESSED VIRGIN

Owing to the future merits of Her Son, the Virgin was "the first and especial work of God—*proprium* Dei opus primum." [131] ". . . It was fitting that she be conceived as the first-born, from whom *the first-born of every creature* would be conceived."   By that fullness of grace which is proper

---

[127] Leo XIII, 'Quamquam pluries,' *P.D.M.,* p. 48.
[128] Leo *XIII*, '*Adiutricem Populi,' P.D.M.,* p. 102.
[129] St. Pius X, *Ad Diem illum, P.D.M.,* p. 140.
[130] Pius XII, *Mystici Corporis,* Epilog.—cf. F.-M. Braun, O.P., *op. cit.,* chap. IV.
[131] *Ineffabilis Deus, P.D.M.,* p. 21. Unless otherwise indicated the subsequent quotations are taken from the same document, pp. 20, 21.

to the Mother of God, Mary was "the one and only daughter not of death but of life, the child not of anger but of grace." "Never in darkness but always in light," she was exempted from the general law, having "only nature in common" with us. *Thou shalt not die: for this law is not made for thee, but for all others.* (Esther xv. 13)   By virtue of her Immaculate Conception and her consequent share in the work of Redemption, Mary was likewise exempted from the law of common death.   According to this law:

> the bodies of even the just are corrupted, and only on the last day will they be joined, each to its own glorious soul.   Now God has willed that the Blessed Virgin Mary should be exempted from this general rule.   She, by an entirely unique privilege, completely overcame sin by her Immaculate Conception, and as a result she was not subject to the law of remaining in the corruption of the grave, and she did not have to wait until the end of time for the redemption of her body.[132]

The first part of the Apostolic Constitution on the Assumption shows that, in the mind of the faithful as well as in fact, these two privileges are "most closely bound to one another—*arctissime . . . inter se connectuntur.*"[133]   The reason for this most intimate bond has been somewhat simplified by those who suggest that, in virtue of her Immaculate Conception, the Mother of God had a right to immortality, such that, at the term of her earthly life, she was glorified without passing through death.   However, there is sufficient evidence that, in the mind of the Church, Mary really died.   On the other hand, it is not less certain that her death was unlike that of all who are under the common law.   This is plainly stated in the same Constitution:

> Christ's faithful, through the teaching and the leadership of their shepherds, have learned from the sacred books that the Virgin Mary, throughout the course of her earthly pilgrimage, led a life troubled by cares, hardships, and sorrows, and that, moreover, what the holy old man Simeon had foretold, actually came to pass, that is, that a terribly sharp sword pierced her heart as she stood under the cross of her divine Son, our Redeemer.   In the same way, it was not difficult for them to affirm that the great Mother of God, like her Only-begotten Son, had actually passed from this life [quemadmodum jam Unigenam suum, ex hac vita decessisse].   But this in no way prevented them from believing and from professing openly that her sacred body had never been subject to the corruption of the tomb, and that the august tabernacle of the Divine Word, had never been reduced to dust and ashes.[134]

The teaching of this solemn document is so plain that we fail to see

---

[132] Pius XII, *Munificentissimus Deus, P.D.M.,* p. 222.
[133] *Ibid.,* p. 221.
[134] *Munificentissimus Deus, P.D.M.,* p. 225.

how the question whether Mary died or not could still be a problem in theology. That she did pass through death, "even as her Only-begotten Son before her," becomes a matter of principle beyond all doubt—whether we understand the reason and the how of it or not. The reader must be made aware of our position on this point, lest he gather the impression that in the course of the present discussion we are trying to show why Mary was actually subjected to death (in itself a legitimate question, even though we are quite certain that she did die); whereas our purpose is to examine how the fact of her death is compatible with the privilege of the Immaculate Conception: how, at the very term of her earthly life, and in virtue of that privilege, she was fully glorified, notwithstanding the reality of death.

THE SIMULTANEITY OF MARY'S DEATH AND ASSUMPTION

The person of Mary, being merely human, depends, for its reality, upon the actual union of body and soul. If, then, her soul had been maintained in a *state* of separation; if, during some course of time, she had been in death, she would have ceased, for that time, to exist as a human being, as a person, and as Mother of God. Such a state would mean that, during some lapse of time, however brief, the grace of Motherhood—the seat of her habitual grace and of all her privileges as Mother of God—would have been withdrawn. Now, "what is bestowed through God's grace is never withdrawn except through fault." But Mary, conceived Immaculate and wholly confirmed in the good, could never have committed the slightest of faults. For this reason, we have argued elsewhere [135] that no lapse of time occurred between Mary's death and Assumption, in which her soul would have been in a state of separation from her body; but that, on the contrary, her resurrection from death took place in the same instant as her death itself. We will not repeat here the arguments we have already presented in other writings, but will give only the following points of explanation.

Death, understood *proprie et essentialiter,* cannot occur but in the instant, the indivisible of time. Since there can be no such thing as a before-last instant, but only a last time, the last instant of Socrates' life is the first in which he already no longer exists. Death, in the most proper sense of the word, is verified of that instant alone, and never of a course of time, either before or after. It is a case of *fieri et simul factum esse.* Now resurrection, too, is wrought in the instant. The first instant, here, is one in which the person is already resurrected; it is the only one of which resurrection can be verified essentially. All this is common doctrine. Now the question is: does the reality of death and resurrection require an interval

---

[135] *La Piété du Fils,* Les Presses Universitaires Laval, 1954, chapters V and VI, which had appeared in *Laval Théologique et philosophique* under the title, "La mort et l'Assomption de la Sainte-Vierge," 1952, vol. VIII, n. 1, pp. 9-86; *ibid.,* "La personne humaine et la résurrection," 1954, vol. X, n. 2, pp. 199-221.

of time, to distinguish them? [136] Is it really necessary that resurrection take place after death, according to an *after* of time? If so, how long after? You might suggest: at least one instant later. But this postulates the possibility of a next-after instant which again involves a contradiction since any two instants must be separated by an interval of time.

The general doctrine involved was fully developed by Aristotle in Book VI of the Physics, as well as in chapter 8 of Book VIII. St. Thomas applies it consistently, as the only possible solution, wherever he discusses the instantaneous character of absolute generation and corruption, of transubstantiation, and of justification. As regards justification, the last instant of the fault is the first in which there is no longer fault, and the first in which there is already grace. The last instant of the bread is the first in which the bread no longer is, and the first in which the body of Christ is already present. The last instant of St. Peter's life was the first in which his soul was already separated from his mortal body [*corpus animale*]. The first instant of his future life will be one in which his soul is already reunited to his glorified body [*corpus spiritale*]. Now, considering things absolutely, there is no reason why the last instant of one's earthly life, the one in which body and soul are already separated, could not be the same instant in which the glorified soul is already reunited to the body now immortal. The only difficulty of this doctrine arises from the fact that we imagine the last instant of the earthly life as still occupied, as it were, by the person who in reality has already ceased to be; yet, if this were so, nothing could cease to be, nor could anything new become.[137]

But, you might say, if such were the case: if (as St. Augustine actually believed) a person might die and be resurrected *in ipso temporis puncto*,[138] he would not have died really; for the same instant in which he ceased to exist, would be exactly the one in which he already exists anew. True enough, there would be not a single instant in which he did not exist; there would be neither a time nor even an instant in which the man, the very person, did not live. But there would have been—and this is the crux of the matter—a last instant of his life according to the union of corruptible

[136] This would be necessary if we were expected to establish their truth by experience; which is wholly extrinsic to what is possible in itself. And who, furthermore, has ever had an experience of the indivisible of time? Whatever we experience is always in part no longer and in part not yet. The indivisibility of the instant can be established by demonstration only.—Thus, in the case of Christ, "to confirm our faith regarding the truth of His humanity and death, it was needful that there should be some interval between His death and resurrection." *IIIa Pars*, q. 53, a. 2, c.

[137] Hegel, for this very reason, declared that "to begin," or "to end," implies a contradiction. We have examined this problem in an article entitled, "Un paradoxe du devenir par contradiction," in *Doctor Communis*, Rome, n. III, 1954, pp. 133-188.

[138] *De Civitate Dei*, XX, c. 20.—On the various meanings and paradoxes of death, *ibid.*, XX, cc. 9-11. That by *punctum temporis* St. Augustine meant the indivisible of time, can be seen in the *Confessiones*, XI, cc. 15 and 28.

body and soul, viz. the first instant of the *primum non esse* of earthly life, which is death *proprie et essentialiter;* and there would have been a first instant, the same as the latter, in which glorified soul and body were already reunited, viz. the instant of the *primum esse* of the glorified life of the person, which is resurrection essentially.

But would this not imply that, in the same instant, a person would be both dead and alive? be and not be? Does not the principle of contradiction object to that sort of thing? Indeed it does preclude the possibility of being simultaneously dead and alive according to the same kind of life; of being and not being in the same respect. But that is all.[139]

Except in the case of Christ and Our Lady, death achieves at least a partial victory inasmuch as "by reason of the common law [generali lege], God does not will to grant the full effect of victory over death to the just until the end of time shall have come."[140] In view of this it might be objected that by deferring until the third day the full effect of victory over death in His own humanity Christ Himself to that extent apparently submitted to the common law. Hence, it would seem that the mode of Mary's resurrection, such as was suggested above, would make her triumph over death more complete than that of Christ; a circumstance hardly honoring Him Who is the Resurrection and the Life (John xi. 25)—This difficulty is easily disposed of, for

> Christ was not held fast by any necessity of death, but was *free among the dead*: and therefore He abode a while in death, not as one held fast, but of His own will, just as long as He deemed necessary for the instruction of our faith.[141]

Christ, then, was not even in the state of death if by this we mean a time during which one is kept down by the bonds of death (*mortis nexibus*). Nor did the reality of His death ever affect the very Person in His Godhead, to which both body and soul remained united. And He arose from the dead through His own power—the same by which He shall raise all the elect who are in the bonds of death. But in His Mother He showed without delay the fullness of their common victory over death by leaving her at no time in the bonds of death. As the ancient prayer has it: "Venerable to us, O Lord, is the festivity of this day on which the Holy Mother of God

---

[139] Whoever is familiar with the doctrine that the generation of one thing is the corruption of another in the same instant of time, should have no difficulty with this other application. In generation and corruption, it is the subject that is permanent. In death and resurrection, the form is permanent; the proper subject is reproduced one in number. All one has to do is to turn the whole thing upside-down—with a qualification.

[140] *Munificentissimus Deus, P.D.M.,* p. 222.

[141] *IIIa Pars,* q. 53, a. 2, ad 2.

suffered temporal death, but still could not be kept down by the bonds of death, who has begotten Thy Son Our Lord incarnate from herself." [142]

The "marvelous and fitting conformity" between Mary's Conception and Assumption

In the *Encyclical Fulgens Corona*, of Pius XII, there is a line which calls to mind a particular comparability between the Immaculate Conception and the Assumption. We quote it in its context:

> Henceforth, it seems that the faithful can with greater and better reason turn their minds and hearts to the mystery of the Immaculate Conception. For the two dogmas are intimately connected in close bond. And now that the Assumption of the Virgin Mary into heaven has been promulgated and shown in its true light—that is, as the crowning and complement of the prior privilege bestowed upon her—there emerge more fully and more clearly the wonderful wisdom and harmony of the divine plan, by which God wishes the most blessed Virgin Mary to be free from all stain of original sin.
>
> And so these two very singular privileges, bestowed upon the Virgin Mother of God, stand out in most splendid light as the beginning and as the end of her earthly journey [*ut terrestris ejus peregrinationis ortus ita et occasus fulgentissima emicuere luce*]; to the absolute innocence of her soul, which was free from all stain, did correspond, with a marvelous and appropriate conformity [*mirabili quadam congruentique ratione respondit*] the most complete glorification of her virgin body; and just as she took part in the struggle of her Only-begotten Son with the wicked serpent of hell, so also she shared in His glorious triumph over sin and its sad consequences.[143]

We assume that the words *ortus* and *occasus* are aptly chosen and deserve to be weighed. *Ortus* refers to Mary's Conception, to the very first instant of her earthly life. *Occasus* first means a going down, as in *ab ortu ad occasum*, from sunrise to sundown; and, finally, downfall, destruction, death, as in *post obitum occasumque vestrum*, or *occasus interitusque rei publicae*. It was never used to mean a final term in general. Now, it is thanks to the Assumption that the *occasus* of Mary's earthly journey stands out in fullest light—*fulgentissima luce*. But this can be literally true only if the *occasus* is somehow overshadowed and enclosed by the Assumption. Then, death itself might be called glorious. And that is exactly how St. Amadeus (1110-1159) of Lausanne—"that most pious man" of the earliest period

---

[142] Quoted in *Munificentissimus Deus, P.D.M.*, p. 227.—This prayer is still used in the Dominican rite.

[143] *P.D.M.*, pp. 258-259.—We have changed in part the last paragraph of the English translation we use, to bring out the idea of correspondence in the Latin original. *Ratio*, in this context, means conformity or proportion.

of Scholastic Theology, as Pius XII calls him in the Constitution on the Assumption [144]—did phrase it.

> She passed away with a glorious death—if, indeed, a passing to life can be called death. To speak truly, it is life, in which death alone dies, and 'the body of this death' is laid aside.
>
> * * *
>
> The heavenly hosts find her rising rather than dying, departing rather than perishing . . .
>
> * * *
>
> (Her death) does not bring on the darkness; it opens the way to eternal light. It does not take away the life which it sends to the Author of life.[145]

The statement, in *Fulgens Corona*, which follows immediately upon the one we have just examined seems to confirm our understanding of Mary's death as a glorious one. For not only does her *occasus* "stand out in most radiant light"; we are told that the Assumption corresponds, in a marvelous and fitting proportion, to the Immaculate Conception. Now the "true object" of the latter belief is Mary's "Conception considered in its first instant." If her *occasus* involved a certain amount of time—an interval between death and "the most complete glorification of her virgin body" [146] —the comparison would fail in this respect, for there can be no true proportion between instant and time. If, on the other hand, we compared the first instant of a glorification some time after death, with the instant of Conception, the correspondence would hardly be "mirabili quadam congruentique ratione." The comparison, as we understand it, implies the following: just as in the first instant of her Conception Mary was already preserved from every stain of sin, though conceived by the natural process of generation; so, in the last instant of her earthly life [*expleto terrestris vitae cursu*]—which is naturally the instant of the *primum non esse* of that life of the person—she was preserved from the 'state of death' inasmuch as the same instant was that of her *primum esse* according to the life of glory.

---

[144] *P.D.M.*, p. 232.

[145] Hac *morte gloriosa* migravit, si transitum ad vitam mortem liceat nominare. Imo, ut verum fatear, vita est, ubi sola mors moritur, ubi corpus mortis exuitur [. . .] Ibi *orienti* magis quam morienti, et *abiturae* plus quam obiturae occurrunt castra Dei [. . .] Nec tenebras inducit, quae lumen aeternum aperuit, *nec vitam tollit*, quam dirigit ad auctorem vitae.—Hom. VII, *P.L.* 188, col. 1340-1341. For further significant quotations taken from this author, cf. *La piété du Fils*, pp. 156-157; or "La mort et l'Assomption de la Sainte Vierge," in *Laval théologique et philosophique*, 1952, vol. VIII, n. 1, pp. 84-85.

[146] We must note that if the preservation from corruption was due to the "amplissima virginei corporis glorificatio," this could not have been achieved before reunion with the soul since the formal cause of the glory of the body is none other than what St. Augustine calls the "plenissima beatitudo" of the soul. Cf. St. THOMAS, *In I ad Cor.*, c. xv, lect. 6.

Now in this, and on this condition only, can she be compared to her son, Whose Person, in death, was nevertheless the Person of her Son.

THE ASSUMPTION AS THE REWARD OF COREDEMPTION

Although the Assumption—as well as the "glorious death" which it implies—was due to her in virtue of the Immaculate Conception, the Blessed Virgin merited, nonetheless, her complete glorification, and this, specifically by reason of her role as Coredemptrix. Here, besides the one we have just quoted from *Fulgens Corona,* is a crucial text on this subject, taken from the Constitution *Munificentissimus Deus:*

> We must remember most of all that, since the second century, the Virgin Mary has been designated by the holy Fathers as the new Eve, who, although subject to the new Adam, is most intimately associated with Him in that struggle against the infernal foe which, as foretold in the *protoevangelium,* finally resulted in that most complete victory over the sin and death which are always associated in the writings of the Apostle of the Gentiles. Consequently, just as the glorious Resurrection of Christ was an essential part and the final sign of this victory, similarly that struggle which was common to the Blessed Virgin and her divine Son should be brought to a close by the glorification of her virginal body, for the same Apostle says: *when this mortal thing hath put on immortality, then shall come to pass the saying that is written: Death is swallowed up in victory.*
>
> Hence the revered Mother of God, from all eternity joined in a hidden way with Jesus Christ in one and the same decree of predestination, immaculate in her conception, a most perfect virgin in her divine motherhood, the noble associate of the divine Redeemer who has won a complete triumph over sin and its consequences, was finally granted, as the supreme culmination of her privileges, that she should be preserved free from the corruption of the tomb and that, like her own Son, having overcome death, she might be taken up body and soul to the glory of heaven where, as Queen, she sits in splendor at the right hand of her Son, the immortal King of the Ages.[147]

The Constitution *Ineffabilis Deus,* of Pius IX, had already made quite explicit the relationship between Mary's Immaculate Conception and the meaning of the prophecy: *I will put enmities between thee and the woman*:

> Also did they [the Fathers] declare that the most glorious Virgin was the Reparatrix of her first parents, the giver of life to posterity; that she was chosen before the ages, prepared for Himself by the Most High, foretold by God when he said to the Serpent, "I will put enmities between thee and the woman"—an unmistakable evidence that she has crushed the poisonous head of the Serpent. And hence, they

[147] *P.D.M.*, p. 237.

affirmed that the Blessed Virgin was, through grace, entirely free from every stain of sin, and from all corruption of body, soul, and mind; . . .[148]

The Constitution *Munificentissimus Deus* and the Encyclical Letter *Fulgens Corona* have now established beyond doubt the intimate relationship between Mary's Coredemption and her Assumption: between "that struggle which was common to the Blessed Virgin and her divine Son," and "the glorification of her virgin body."

Because of her redeeming Compassion—for which she was prepared in the Divine Motherhood graced by the Immaculate Conception establishing between her and the Serpent that complete and perpetual enmity—she is now there in her own person: that merely human person through whose *consortium* in the work of Redemption as willed by ineffable Wisdom and Mercy, we who are subject to the common law become *partakers of the divine nature*. (II Peter i. 4)

MARY'S PRESENT QUEENSHIP

It is significant that, in the Constitution on the Assumption, the Holy Father should point out, in a passage quoted on a preceding page, the relation between Mary's Coredemption, her Assumption, and her Queenship. ". . . Like her Son, having overcome death, she [was] taken up body and soul to the glory of heaven where, as Queen, she sits in splendor at the right hand of her Son, the immortal King of the Ages."

Mary is not only the Mother of the One Who is King in the most proper sense of this name [149] and Who conquered the Kingdom in His Passion and death: by her sorrowful Compassion she shared in His victory, even as a new Eve; for she "who corporally was the Mother of [Christ] our Head, through the added title of suffering and glory became spiritually the mother of all His members." [150] It was foretold to her, at the Annunciation, that her Son, with Whom she is the object of a single decree of predestination now fulfilled, would be given, by the Lord God, *the throne of David His father*—David His father thanks to her Motherhood; that *He shall be King over the house of Jacob forever; that of His Kingdom there shall be no end*. (Luke i. 32)   In their "common struggle" they conquered the Kingdom—she as Mother of the King, but also as the new Eve and, therefore, as His Spouse.

At the marriage feast of Cana, Mary interceded on behalf of the guests as Mother of the Son—*gessit . . . mediatricis personam;* [151] whereas she

[148] *P.D.M.*, pp. 20-21.
[149] "La perfection de la royauté du Christ," *Laval théologique et philosophique,* 1950, vol. VI, n. 2, pp. 349-351.
[150] *Mystici Corporis*, Epilog.
[151] St. THOMAS, *In Joannem*, c. 2, lect. 1.

first intercedes as Queen, while still on earth, after the death of the Savior. For it was through her mediation that, at Pentecost, the fullness of the Holy Ghost, which is ours at Confirmation, was bestowed upon the Church newly born.[152]   When we reflect that Confirmation, conferring as it does both spiritual maturity and full citizenship in the City of God, is appropriately called the Sacrament of the Kingdom, Mary's role of Queen becomes strikingly evident.

It is thanks to the Assumption that Mary is now present as Queen.   If her soul alone were in heaven, she herself would not be there in her person, nor, therefore, as Queen.   It is essential for a King that he be one in nature with his subjects, although he should be superior to them by his goodness.[154]   Owing to His humanity the Person of Christ is a King in the proper sense of this title.   A separated soul could not have the nature of either King or Queen, in the strict meaning of the names.

We must note, too, that the King and Queen of the Kingdom of God are universal agencies *in causando* who attain to each and every person in particular, no matter how contingent the circumstances of their life, ordaining all to the supreme common good which is none other than the King Himself in His Godhead.   In this too, the Kingdom of Christ is wholly unlike any other.   For, in it, the common good of the realm and the proper good of the King are one and the same.   To Christ, considered in His Godhead, the divine good is a strictly personal good, His own by nature.   Considered in His human nature, that same good is to Him a common good, as it is to everyone but God Himself in his Godhead.   For the soul even of Christ does not see the divine essence comprehensively. Now in this He is one with his subjects, but first of all with the Queen of the realm, whose vision of the Godhead is, intensively and extensively, nearest to His own according to the humanity in which He is her image— He the Word in Whom all comprehensors, angel or man, enjoy the glory of divine fruition.

Sapientis est ordinare.   The Wisdom that founded the Kingdom of Christ is shown in its hierarchy, reaching as it does *from end to end mightily and ordering all things graciously.* (Wisdom viii. 1)   Truly King, He is nonetheless a Divine Person.   Considered in His Godhead alone, He is

---

[152] "Ipsa fuit, quae validissimis suis precibus impetravit, ut Divini Redemptoris Spiritus, iam in Cruce datus, recens ortae Ecclesiae prodigialibus muneribus Pentecostes die conferretur." *Mystici Corporis, ibid.*

[153] Cf. Msgr. Ferdinand VANDRY, "The nature of Mary's Universal Queenship," *Laval théologique et philosophique,* 1954, vol. X, n. 1, pp. 60-64.—On the relationship betwen Christ and Mary as King and Queen, see, especially, M.-J. NICOLAS, O.P., "La Vierge-Reine," in *Revue Thomiste,* January-March, 1939, pp. 1-29; April-June, 1939, pp. 207-231.

[154] St. THOMAS, *In I Polit.,* lect. 10.

too lofty to be our King: [155] His Person is King because He is also a man. Yet His reign is aimed at the Godhead. Now it is only in virtue of grace, conveyed by the sacraments—the mercifully humble, sensible things and words—that we can become children, friends of God, and fellow-citizens in His realm. In His Godhead, the King works in the sacraments by authority; yet even as man, His operation conduces to the inward sacramental effects meritoriously and efficiently, inasmuch as His humanity is the instrument of His Godhead.[156] Thus, the dominion which extends to all created persons is that of One Who is also a man. Without lowering His Godhead, the rule of the One *Who is the head of every Principality and Power* (Col. ii. 10), is most connatural to us—owing to His Kingship.

Thanks to the Queen of this same indivisible realm, whose grace is one of pre-eminence and who—in a fashion entirely her own, viz. in her character of Woman, Mother, Spouse and Queen—shares in Christ's power of excellence with regard to the sacraments,[157] the governance of God's Kingdom is at once as mercifully human as can be, to the greater dignity of man's person, which by nature is the lowliest of all. *Nigra sum, sed formosa.* (Cant. i. 4) For Mary, by right of conquest seated at the right of her Son, is entirely near to us inasmuch as she is a merely human person—the Handmaid of the Lord, truly Mother of God, Spouse of the new Adam, Queen of the One Who was given the throne of David, His father, owing to His descent from *a virgin betrothed to a man named Joseph, of the House of David.* (Luke i. 27) And of their *Kingdom there shall be no end.*

[155] As ARISTOTLE said: "but when one party is removed to a great distance, as God is, the possibility of friendship ceases." *Ethics,* VIII, c. 7, 1159 a.
[156] *III Pars,* q. 64, a. 3.
[157] Cf. *III Pars,* q. 64, a. 4.

XI

The Immaculate Conception and the Spirituality of the Blessed Virgin

Edward D. O'Connor, C.S.C.*

The "spirituality of the Blessed Virgin" can be spoken of in reference either to her personal life, or to that of others insofar as they are devoted to and influenced by her. Since, however, Mary's personal spirituality is the basis and pattern of her influence on others, it is natural and advantageous to treat these two subjects in conjunction; and that is what we shall undertake in the present paper, endeavoring to see what light the dogma of the Immaculate Conception sheds on Marian spirituality taken in this twofold sense of the term.[1]

It might seem preposterous to propose to make a theological treatise concerning something so free and personal as the inner life of an individual soul, especially in the case of an individual about whom only the briefest snatches of information are available. Nevertheless, we maintain that certain aspects of the interior life of the Blessed Virgin, if treated in the proper spirit and perspective, can be the object of genuine theological consideration.[2]

* Member of the Department of Theology and Religion, and of the Institute of Mediaeval Studies, of the University of Notre Dame.

[1] We will presuppose the exposition of the dogma given in the preceding chapters of this volume, particularly that of chapter VIII.

[2] The classical work along this line is that of SUAREZ, *Mysteria vitae Christi* (=*De Incarnatione,* pars secunda), especially Disp. IV, XVIII, XIX and XX.

In modern times, this approach to the spirituality of the Blessed Virgin has been cultivated particularly by the French Dominicans. Cf. R. GARRIGOU-LAGRANGE, O.P. *Mariologie, La Mère du Sauveur et notre Vie intérieure,* Lyon, 1941 (Engl. trans. B. Kelly, *The Mother of the Savior and our interior life,* Dublin [1948]); M.-J. NICOLAS, O.P., "Essai de synthèse mariale," in H. DU MANOIR, S.J., *Maria* I (Paris 1949); T. PHILIPPE, O.P., *Les tresors du Coeur Immaculée de Marie* (retreat conferences transcribed, mimeographed and distributed by the Couvent du Coeur Immaculée, Bouvines par Cysoing, Nord, France). See also Timothy SPARKS, O.P., "The Immaculate Conception and the Immaculate Heart of Mary," in *The Thomist* xix (1956), pp. 239-249, and Dom FRÉNAUD, O.S.B., "La grace de l'Immaculée Conception," in *L'Immaculée Conception (Congrès marials nationaux,* VII), Lyon 1955, pp. 221-249.

By the proper perspective, we mean, above all, in the light of Catholic theology, and particularly the Catholic understanding of sin and grace. Obviously, a theology which denied the objective reality of original sin and divine grace, as immanent in the human soul and profoundly affecting its activities, would preclude the very basis of a study such as the present one. In the second place, the perspective here presupposed assumes as authoritative the doctrine of the classical mystical theologians — St. John of the Cross in particular — on the development of the life of grace.

If, in such a perspective, it be granted that the Virgin Mary was, by the grace of God, preserved from original sin and its effects, it inevitably follows that her interior life must have been profoundly differentiated from that of Adam's other descendants, who were not so preserved. It will be possible to point out some of the differences, just as it is possible to predict some of the differences between the paths of two projectiles, one of which passes through a vacuum, and the other through a resisting medium.

But even granted the perspective of official and traditional Catholic theology in the sense just indicated, we do not claim that all that we shall say is patently deducible from definite theological principles by a syllogistic process. There will be questions about which only conjectures of greater or lesser probability can be made. (Hence it is to be understood that what we say is proposed in each instance with no more assurance than the evidence in the particular case permits.)

Furthermore, each science must be developed according to its proper spirit. Mariology is not like algebra, with an inexorable march of logic imposing itself on the intellect regardless of one's personal attitude toward the subject. There is, in fact, no area of theology in which the full implications of the Catholic faith are apparent to any passer-by who peers curiously into it. Its doctrines must be lived, the mysterious realities with which they deal must be embraced and assimilated into one's own life, before many aspects of their meaning begin to be realized. If this is true of theology in general, it is especially so in the case of Mariology. For the mysterious role in the economy of Redemption which Divine Wisdom has conferred on the Virgin whose name was Mary is intelligible only from the point of view of the maternal relationship that obtains between her and the entire Mystical Body — Head and members; and such a relationship can be adequately appreciated only from the interior — by those involved in it.

Mariology depends, moreover, upon a right interpretation of some of the most delicate implications and suggestions of Divine Revelation. These are inaccessible to the type of theology which thinks to attain complete objectivity by grappling onto the text of Scripture and applying to it semi-mechanical procedures of exegesis, heedless of shades of meaning, subtle implications, and the spirit in which a word is uttered. Its preoccupation with the text blinds it to the realities which transcend what can be said of them; and its busyness leaves no room for an inner silence in which the Spirit of God might make Himself heard over the clacking of the mental machinery. Such a theology will be quite unable to discover even the first principles of Mariology; and if it accepts them from elsewhere, it will begin at once to make clumsy constructions out of them, instead of allowing them to bear their natural fruit.

Only a heart schooled in the wisdom of the Holy Spirit is capable of discovering the more hidden implications of God's word, with flashes of insight that far outstrip the lumbering processes of conscious reasoning. It has well been said that "there are certain matters in which a necessarily hesitant argument needs to be confirmed by the insight of the heart of the saints."[3] Accordingly, while attempting to employ as rigorous a theology as possible, and to avoid ever substituting rhetoric for reason, we will nevertheless be obliged at times to rely on those insights into the soul of the Blessed Virgin which are to be encountered in the writings of the great Marian saints, or in the common acceptance of the faithful. They are not matters of faith or, generally speaking, theologically demonstrable; but are nevertheless well authenticated by the fact of their being accepted there where the Spirit of Truth most assuredly breathes. Our method will sometimes consist merely in pointing out how the doctrine of the Immaculate Conception provides an intelligible explanation for such insights.

I

MARY'S PERSONAL SPIRITUALITY

The Immaculate Conception was the beginning of the life of grace in Mary, the seed out of which her entire supernatural life sprang. The character of this initial grace, therefore, provides one of the chief keys to the character of what might be called her supernatural personality. As the genesis of a being imparts to it its most fundamental traits, so the Immaculate Conception, prolonging itself in the Immaculate Heart of Mary, stamps her spirituality with many of its most distinctive features.

The fact that Mary was free from original sin from the first moment of her existence, and that the supernatural life began simultaneously in her with the natural life, distinguishes her from the rest of Adam's descendants, who come into existence deprived of grace by original sin and need to be born again of water and the Holy Ghost in order to enter into life.

---

[3] "On a besoin, en certaines matières, de confirmer un raisonnement forcément hésitant, par la divination du coeur des saints." M.-J. NICOLAS, O.P., "Le concept intégral de la Maternité Divine," in *Revue Thomiste* N.S. 20 (1937), p. 69, n. 12.

The difference is not merely one of time — of Mary's receiving her redemption some nine months earlier than ordinary human beings. It is the difference between being holy *to start with,* and receiving holiness *through a subsequent purification;* the difference between one who has ever been a beloved daughter of God, and those who are at first "children of wrath" (Eph. 2:8) before being admitted to the divine friendship. The length of the interval between conception and sanctification, in those who are conceived in sin, is quite secondary. John the Baptist was not three months closer to having an immaculate conception because he was sanctified while yet only a foetus of six months. The mediaeval theory propounded as a substitute for the doctrine of the Immaculate Conception, namely, that Mary, after being conceived in sin, was sanctified an instant later,[4] was not even a close approximation of the true doctrine, missing, as it did, the essential point — that Mary was *never* in need of God's pardon, that there was never an instant in which she was, and was not holy.

We are those whom God has "rescued from the power of darkness and transferred into the kingdom of His beloved Son." (Col. 1:13) Although we are now true citizens of the Kingdom, the fact remains that we are immigrants who have had to be naturalized. Mary, on the contrary, is native-born. It is only to be expected, then, that whereas we never fully divest ourselves of the accent and mannerisms that betray our alien origin, Mary should be fully at home in the Kingdom of grace, and should live in it with a naturalness and appropriateness contrasting sharply with our awkwardness there.

In fact, it might be said that she receives grace in a *quasi-natural* manner, whereas the rest of us receive it later on through a 'remaking' of a nature constituted at first without it. Not that the basic distinction between the natural and supernatural orders is effaced in her any more than in others; but the supernatural is conferred on her *after the manner* of a natural constituent. Hence, she stands in a different relation to grace from us, possessing it as her own to a degree we never can. It follows that the development of grace followed very different patterns in her and in us. We will try to show this more concretely by considering first the negative, then the positive aspects of the Immaculate Conception.

THE SINLESSNESS OF
MARY IMMACULATE

In its negative aspect, the Immaculate Conception excludes sin and the results of sin from the life of the Blessed Virgin. To exclude original sin is, of course, of the very essence of this privilege, which thereby imparts to Mary's sanctity a certain splendor by comparison with those from whom

---

[4] Cf. chapter V of the present volume, pp. 191, 198.

the tarnish of original sin must first be removed. Actual sin is not excluded by the simple fact of Mary's having been conceived free from original sin; Adam, for example, fell from an originally 'immaculate' state. It was the grace of impeccability that kept Mary from falling into actual sin. However, Mary's impeccability did not come from a grace supplementary to that which preserved her from original sin; rather, the grace conferred at the instant of her creation was preservative from all sin, actual as well as original.

When we say that Mary was preserved also from the *results* of sin, we refer only to those results which occur in the sinner himself, and are intrinsically bound up with his having sinned. It is evident that the Blessed Virgin was affected by the results of sins committed by others; for she, too, suffered. Also, the absence in her of certain privileges conferred on Adam, such as the gift of immortality,[5] was *de facto* a consequence of sin — Adam's sin — although not *de jure* connected with sin, since these privileges were not absolutely demanded either by nature or by grace. The results of sin about which we are speaking here, therefore, are simply those disorders left by sin in one who has been guilty of it.

Freedom from sin and its results is one of the most distinctive features of Mary's spirituality, for sin and sinfulness is a major factor in the lives of all other human beings, even of those extraordinary saints whose holiness was displayed *"ab incunabilis."* The human soul retains to the end of its life the imprint of the state of sin in which its life began: a congenital proneness to sin that persists even after actual sinfulness is effaced. The natural inclination to virtue, while not indeed eradicated, is weakened and obstructed; in a practical sense, at least, it appears to have been supplanted in large measure by inclinations to evil which original sin has released. The rebellion of the lower faculties against the higher can be suppressed only by great effort and constant vigilance, which are never wholly successful.

This state is particularly tragic in that we are drawn in spite of ourselves toward that which we recognize as evil:

> I do not understand what I do, for it is not what I wish that I do, but what I hate, that I do. . . . For I do not the good that I wish, but the evil that I do not wish, that I perform. (Rom. 7:15, 19)

We are men divided:

> The flesh lusts against the spirit, and the spirit against the flesh. (Gal. 5:17)
> For I am delighted with the law of God according to the inner man, but I see another law in my members, warring against the law of my

---

[5] We suppose that she was not given this gift; cf. chapter VIII of the present volume, p. 341 ff. If one were to suppose the contrary, then the point we are making—Mary's preservation from the results of sin—would, of course, be strengthened.

mind, and making me prisoner to the law of sin that is in my members. (Rom. 7:23)

A part of us has been betrayed into the hands of the enemy; we are "sold into the power of sin" (Rom. 7:14); so that in order to attain our own good, we must do battle against a part of ourselves. Though we muster all our strength to say *No* to temptation, there is something in us which continues to say *Yes*. Strive as we may, we are incapable of a total gift of ourselves to God: something is always withheld. And the gift once made must often be made over, because it gets taken back.

The struggle would be difficult enough if the line of division lay clearly between our lower and higher faculties; in fact, however, it extends even into the will itself. There are recesses of evil so deep within us as to be beyond the reach of our own efforts at reform; for the taint of sin attains the very core of our psychological and moral being, leaving in us no utterly pure faculty from which a wholly righteous movement of reformation could proceed.

With regard, therefore, to his moral and spiritual life, man is not only dependent on the initiatives of divine causality, he is prostrate, miserable and guilty before the throne of divine justice, redeemable only by the divine mercy. He needs grace, not only to elevate him to the supernatural order, but first of all to heal him. And the grace that is given does not sanctify him totally from the outset, but establishes only a 'beachhead,' from which it extends its conquest over the human soul only gradually, against a constant and resourceful resistance that is never completely exterminated until the light of glory completes what the power of grace began. The greater part, therefore, of man's moral effort — at least in the early stages of spiritual development, in which most people spend most of their lives — is occupied with the avoidance of sin and the doing of penance for sins already committed; and there is no hope of attaining in this world a state in which there is no longer any need of purification.

By the Immaculate Conception, Mary is exempted from this condition.[6] There was nothing in her life to be regretted, corrected, or overcome. Hence, the practice of *penance* or *mortification* had no place in her spirituality.[7] Accordingly, her virginity was in no wise ordained to the

---

[6] It is true that the simple fact of being conceived without original sin did not of itself imply impeccability as regards actual sin; else Adam and Eve could not have fallen. But Mary's initial sinlessness at least made it possible for her to live sinlessly, by preserving her from the roots of evil that make sin inevitable in others. Moreover, the preservation of Mary from original sin was a sign of God's intention to preserve her from every trace of sin, and the first act in the execution of this intention. And if we consider in the Immaculate Conception, not merely the freedom from original sin, but the concrete grace by which this was effected, it is generally admitted that impeccability was included in it.

[7] In making this remark, we have no intention of taking a stand on the question,

conquering of concupiscence: even had she lived a normal wedded life, no inordinate carnal movements would have disturbed in the least her constant union with God. For the same reason, no self-conquest was involved in the maintenance of her virginal state. Mary's virginity must have had the significance only of a positive consecration, and its merit derived, not from the resistance which it overcame, but solely from the love which it expressed.[7b]

Similarly, the *sufferings* she endured had a different sense from ours. In the Providence of God, our own purification is one of the principal ends to which our sufferings are ordained; but the Dolors of Mary must be understood solely as a means of communion with her Suffering Son — a kind of sacrament — and of participation in His redemptive work.

As for the question, whether the Blessed Virgin ever underwent *temptation,* the Immaculate Conception clearly implies that she was not subject to any temptations arising from within herself, for these would have presupposed disorder and involved some trace of sin.[8] But the temptations proposed from without by the devil are compatible with perfect sanctity, as is evidenced by the temptations undergone by Christ. Whether His Mother, like Him, was subjected to such assaults, or whether, by an exceptional grace, He shielded her from them, is a question to be decided on other bases than that of the Immaculate Conception. But, even supposing she did undergo exterior temptations, she would never have responded interiorly to them, nor have felt any attraction, even of an involuntary sort, towards evil.

Hence it can be said that Mary's life not only attained a higher degree of spirituality than ours, but moved at a different tempo, with a rhythm peculiar to itself. Our lives revolve around the three poles, *nature, grace* and *sin*; hers had only two: *nature* and *grace*. In her life, therefore, occurred none of the drama created in that of others by the struggle between sin and grace for the possession of their souls. Much of the light shed in the Church by the Magdalenes and Augustines seems to have been generated by the resistance of their natures to grace — a fact that is indeed consoling and encouraging to us. However, the light that comes from these saints is murky and lurid in comparison with Mary's serene

---

whether Mary could have had the *virtue* of penance, but only of pointing out the obvious fact, that she was not in need, as others are, of atoning for past sins, or of "chastising the body, and bringing it into subjection," in order to forestall future ones.

[7b] Cf. the suggestive remark of Dom Frénaud in the article cited in note 2 above: "I would have liked to show to what extent the Immaculate Conception initiates (*engage Marie dans*) the virginal consecration which makes Mary from this moment on the perfect spouse of God." (p. 241)

[8] "Tentatio autem quae est a carne non potest esse sine peccato." St. Thomas, *Summa Theologiae*, III, 41, 1 ad 3. Cf. his explanation in q.3 a.2 of his commentary on *II Sent.*, D. 24.

purity, which is nothing else than the *candor lucis aeternae* reflected in her without diminution or distortion.

THE HARMONY AND EQUILIBRIUM OF MARY'S LIFE

So far we have considered only the 'negative' effect of the Immaculate Conception: preservation from sin. When we turn to the positive effects, it is necessary to distinguish between grace itself, which is principal, and a certain harmony or equilibrium of Mary's moral organism, which is of a lower order than grace, although closely connected with it. It is this latter effect which we will consider first, reserving the treatment of grace itself to the following section.

Being a composite of many disparate elements bound together in a perilously frail unity, man is by his very nature liable to disintegration and disorder. The body alone is an extremely complex organism. Its union with the soul, however intimate and natural it may be, obliges man to live in two worlds — the corporeal and the spiritual — together, and makes necessary, in addition to the faculties required by each of these two lives, the complex psychological equipment necessary for communication and collaboration between the two. And the complexity which man has in himself is further compounded by the ties of dependence and friendship that bind him to his material and social environs.

Daily experience makes us all aware of the stresses and perversions that arise from disequilibrium among these various factors in us. It is not easy to say precisely in what measure such disequilibrium is a result of original sin, and in what measure the very structure of our nature makes us liable to it.[9] It is the Thomistic view, at any rate,[10] stemming from an insight of St. Augustine's,[11] that Adam's freedom from any disorders of this sort was due to the grace given him: not, that is to say, to grace simply as possessed by human nature (for then all who are in the state of grace would be preserved from such disorders), but the effect of grace in Adam was due to its having resided in him from the beginning of his existence, exercising uninterrupted dominion over all that belongs to his nature. Perhaps, also, there was a special perfection in Adam's grace, or in the mode of its insertion into human nature.[12]

In any case, if grace had such an effect in Adam, it would surely have

---

[9] On this question, cf. CAJETAN, *Commentaria in summam theologicam divi Thomae*, on I-II, 109, 1; and JOHN OF ST. THOMAS, *Cursus theologicus*, on I-II, Disp. 19, No. 12.

[10] Cf. ST. THOMAS, *Summa theologiae* I, 95, 1.

[11] In the article just cited, St. Thomas quotes ST. AUGUSTINE, *De Civitate Dei* XIII, 13 (*PL* 41, 386; *CSEL* 40, 631 f.). Cf. also *De Pecc. Remiss. et Bapt. Parv.* I, 21 (*PL* 44, 120; *CSEL* 60, 20 f.); *De Nat. et Grat.* 28 (*PL* 44, 260 f.; *CSEL* 60, 254)

[12] Cf. chapter VIII of the present volume, p. 340 ff., especially notes 13 and 14.

had an equal effect in the Immaculate Virgin. She, too, was subject to grace from the beginning, and received it, we may presume, in a mode no less perfect than that of Adam. And even those who might be disposed to question the connection posited by St. Augustine and St. Thomas between grace and the gift of integrity, generally seem willing to admit that by reason of the *fullness* and *perfection* of the grace given to Mary in her conception, the confusion, tension and disorder that mark *our* lives would have been replaced in her by a tranquil, stable harmony and equilibrium.

First of all, there must have been harmony between her soul and body, such that each found its natural complement in the other, without a trace of strain or conflict of interests. As Garrigou-Lagrange has said, "Her body did not weigh down her mind, but rather served it."[13] Perhaps we may go so far as to say that what took place in the one would always have had its corresponding resonance in the other. This would help to explain why her motherhood could never have been a purely corporeal relationship to her offspring: she had to be maternal in soul as well as in body.[14]

Was it not out of an instinctive appreciation of this equilibrium between soul and body that the faithful of the early centuries instinctively insisted that Mary's virginity was preserved in childbirth, even as regards mere corporeal integrity? Perhaps those who argue that this latter is a trivial thing, the loss of which would not have detracted from Mary's virginity in a 'legal' or 'medical' sense, are missing the significance that was plain and important to simpler minds, of the due proportion between body and soul which ought to exist in every human being, and was realized at least in her in whom sin had no part.

A second harmony conferred on the Blessed Virgin by the Immaculate Conception lay within her soul itself. The complexity of the human soul, and the resultant bewildering web of confusions, betrayals and self-deceptions in which it finds itself caught, are a familiar subject to modern thought. It is the work of human virtue to reduce the various parts of the soul to "friendly harmony" and "bring order into the inner life," so as to make a man "at peace with himself," and "no longer many, but one entirely temperate and perfectly adjusted nature."[15]

Due to the Immaculate Conception, the development of virtue in Mary must have been enormously accelerated. We have already seen that the perverse inclinations which make virtue difficult and at times even re-

---

[13] R. Garrigou-LaGrange, O.P., work cited in our note 2, p. 48 of the English translation.

[14] Cf. the article of M.-J. Nicolas, O.P., cited above in note 3.

[15] Plato *The Republic* (Jowett translation), IV, 442 f.

pugnant for us, were eliminated in her, so that moral growth would have taken place as the spontaneous and even eager movement of her soul towards its natural fulfillment. Beyond this, the grace of the Immaculate Conception would itself have included all the infused virtues to an eminent degree. We can be sure, therefore, that whatever virtues there are to be had, Mary had them — saving only such as presuppose sin or moral imperfection.

The detailed account of Our Lady's virtues presented in certain types of devotional literature sometimes leads us to ask in dismay what the author's source of information could have been. However, the doctrine of the Immaculate Conception provides at least some degree of justification for these works, inasmuch as it guarantees that in all the circumstances of her life, Mary acted with perfect virtue. Thus, for example, while Scripture does not speak explicitly of the courage with which she faced her Son's death, we are sure of it *a priori,* and can rightfully take her "standing" at the foot of the Cross as symbolic of it.

But even the concept of the "sum of all virtues" does not adequately represent the harmony which the Immaculate Conception effected in Mary's soul. Unity and coordination among a plurality of agents or energies can derive only from their subordination to an end, as only an inspiring leader can hold a multitude of men together in a team. Our directionless era has learned from experience the need, on the social as well as the individual plane, of total commitment to an end capable of gathering man's various "drives" under its empire. In Mary, the natural finality of human nature was mightily supplemented and subsumed by an ardent charity, which every fibre of her being served in simple obedience. Saints who have attained the state of 'transforming union' have experienced the unity and wholeness that comes from being totally consumed by the love of God.[16] In their case, it was won at the price of a purifying action by the fires of love, consuming all inordinate attachments and inclinations; whereas in Mary's case it was the condition in which her life began.

> The heart of the sacred Virgin was a true earthly paradise, in which there was no war, disturbance, or disorder of any sort, but rather a marvellous peace, tranquility and order, in a continuous activity of adoration, praise and blessing for Him who had established His throne in that paradise. For all the passions there were wholly subject to reason and to the Spirit of God; in perfect union with one another, they unceasingly blessed and praised Him, with admirable harmony in the variety of their different movements, uses and functions, which were all directed by one same Spirit, and had likewise only one end: to glorify His Divine Majesty.[17]

[16] Cf. St. John of the Cross, *Spiritual Canticle,* stanzas 26 and 28 (17 and 19 of the first redaction).

[17] St. John Eudes, *Le Coeur admirable de la Très Sacrée Mère de Dieu,* ed. LeBrun, Paris 1935, p. 133.

Because this unity and harmony are the fruit of the Holy Spirit rather than the construction of a human intellect, they are characterized by simplicity rather than complexity. The creature is by nature complex, and man more than any other creature; but Mary's spirituality was one of divine simplicity, embracing all without derangement or confusion.

Thirdly, it would seem that the Immaculate Conception must have produced in Mary a certain harmony between nature and grace not found in others. It is true that God adapts His grace to our natures, elevating and building on them rather than suppressing or disregarding them. At the same time, however, there often seems to be a certain disharmony between grace and nature — the latter being taken concretely for the moral and psychological configurations fallen nature has acquired. The direction in which the Holy Spirit leads a soul sometimes appears quite counter to what human considerations would indicate. As we see in the example of the Curé of Ars, one's supernatural vocation does not always correspond with his natural qualifications. Especially in the case of conversions (not only conversions from unbelief to faith, but also from sin to virtue and from mediocrity to fervor), grace seems to burst in upon nature with a certain violence, disrupting the patterns that were formed in it, as was the case with St. Paul.

Grace worked no such violence in the soul of the Blessed Virgin. It entered quietly, disturbing nothing, sanctifying everything. Her development had been presided over by grace from the beginning; consequently, there was nothing in her that resisted grace, there were no configurations requiring revision. With regard to grace, her nature was purely a receptacle. Even more, there was a radical and positive orientation of nature to grace,[18] producing between the two a faultless harmony that made Mary, after the Sacred Humanity of Christ, the supreme work of Divine Wisdom. Hence we can say with assurance that all her natural instincts, on the one hand, were elevated by grace, and that her spirituality, on the other hand, had a distinctively feminine and maternal character, corresponding to her natural condition.[18b]

Finally, we must take note of the harmony in Mary's relationships with the world around her — particularly the world of human beings. The disorders that occur in men's dealings with one another, like the disorders interior to each individual, are the result of sin; the sinless Virgin was, therefore, as free from the one kind as the other. Her life fitted into its place in the cosmos and in human history like a stone cut exactly for its place in a construction, because her activity was inspired by the same Divine Wisdom which governs the universe and orders all things to its

[18] Cf. chapter VIII of the present volume, p. 341, note 14.

[18b] We have developed this point more fully in an article, "The womanliness of the Blessed Virgin," in the review, *The Age of Mary*, May-June, 1958, pp. 60-63.

ends. Indeed she is, together with Christ, the end to which the universe is ordained,[19] the jewel of which it is the setting; but prescinding from that fact, in all that depended on her initiative she was docile and responsive to every divine inspiration, through the Gift of Wisdom bestowed 'n her conception.

Externally, her life appears as a violent mixture of contraries; what poles could be farther apart than Nazareth and Calvary? But the interior of her soul underwent no corresponding reversals. She met changing fortunes with an unchanging faith and adherence to God that was a reflection of God's own unalterability. The turmoil, confusion, crises and anguish of a soul that has lost its bearings, she never experienced.

This steadfastness was not achieved, however, by an armor plating of indifference; on the contrary, her soul was more sensitive to the values of each new situation than are those that have been clouded over by sin. Her alarm at Gabriel's approach, her affection for her Babe, her grief on Calvary — were genuine and deep human emotions.[20] But the fundamental constancy of her spirit underlying these feelings was no more disturbed by them than the depths of the ocean are by a breeze over its surface, because each event in her life was a new encounter with God under the veil of a creature. She sensed the mystery of each moment, its meaning as a sign from the Beloved. Thus, both joys and sorrows nourished her soul, and each darkness and light made its peculiar contribution to her spiritual development.

It might be objected that, while Mary herself was flawless, the world she lived in was full of disorders which would have forced their way into her life. For a person's life is not simply the product of his own activity, but is also the result of interchanges between himself and his environment. As a matter of fact, Mary's life certainly was affected by the disorders of the world: her sufferings were due precisely to the intrusion of the world's sin into the cosmos of her own sanctity. But just as the Divine Wisdom is not thwarted by the evil of creatures, but rather triumphs over it, using it in the accomplishment of a still greater good, so Mary, thanks to the Divine Wisdom that unfailingly directed her, was able to assimilate into the pattern of her life even the apparently alien elements proceeding from the sin of others. It was more true of her than of anyone else that "God makes all things work together unto good for those that love Him." (Rom. 8:28) Thus, for example, by accepting in a sacrificial and compassionate spirit the sufferings that bruised her heart, she cooperated in the Redemption.

---

[19] Cf. chapter IX of the present volume, p. 347 ff.

[20] Pope Pius XII speaks of the "joys which affected her deeply," and of her "distress and atrocious suffering." *Fulgens Corona gloriae, A.A.S.* 45 (1953) p. 584.

THE GRACE OF THE
IMMACULATE CONCEPTION

Thus far, we have considered nothing but *consequences* of the Blessed Virgin's initial grace: her being kept from sin and put in a condition that permitted an extraordinary degree of spiritual perfection. These points are easier to grasp, and they distinguish her spirituality from ours more palpably. However, it is in the grace itself bestowed by the Immaculate Conception that we must look for the principal determinant of the spirituality of the Blessed Virgin.

Theologians are unanimously agreed that the grace of the Immaculate Conception, being Mary's primordial ordination to the Divine Motherhood, was altogether exceptional in comparison with the graces given to other pure creatures.[21] There is, however, not such unanimous agreement as to the exact measure of this exceptional grace. Some want to say that it surpassed in value the sum of all the graces ever bestowed on other creatures; others will not go so far, but will say, for example, that it surpassed only the highest grace attained by any single angel or saint.

We need not get involved in such a question here.[22] It is sufficient foundation for what we have to say, that Mary's grace was, on the one hand, the same in its essential structure as that given to other human beings in this life; and, on the other hand, that it was of an altogether exceptional perfection. Like all grace, it was a share in the divine nature and life. Like the graces normally given to human beings, it had to be lived, at first, in *faith*. Christ had the beatific vision even during His life on earth, for He was the head and teacher of His Mystical Body; by His strength others were to be raised to the vision He already possessed. Mary, although a cooperator in Christ's work, was fundamentally His member and disciple; accordingly, she too lived in this world by faith in His vision.

This is a capital point for Marian spirituality, for it means that Our Lady was, like us, subject to the trials and darkness intrinsic to faith,

---

[21] There is, in fact, an exceedingly strong papal statement to this effect. In the opening paragraph of *Ineffabilis Deus*, Pius IX declared that Mary was loved by God "above all creatures," endowed with heavenly gifts "far above all the angels and saints," so as to possess a sanctity which was greater than any under God's, and beyond the power of any creature's comprehension: ". . . tantoque prae creaturis universis est prosequutus amore, ut in illa una sibi propensissima voluntate complacuerit. Quapropter illam longe ante omnes Angelicos Spiritus, cunctosque Sanctos coelestium omnium charismatum copia de thesauro divinitatis deprompta ita mirifice cumulavit, ut Ipsa ab omni prorsus peccati labe semper libera, ac tota pulchra et perfecta eam innocentiae et sanctitatis plenitudinem prae se ferret, qua maior sub Deo nullatenus intelligitur, et quam praeter Deum nemo assequi cogitando potest." *Acta Pii IX*, Pars Prima, p. 597-598.

[22] Cf. R. GARRIGOU-LAGRANGE, O.P., as cited in note 8, Engl. transl. p. 79-88, together with the sage observations of M.-J. NICOLAS, O.P., "Essai de synthèse mariale," in H. DU MANOIR, *Maria I* (Paris 1949), pp. 726-727, and Dom FRÉNAUD, as cited in note 2, above, pp. 229-240.

and to the law of spiritual progress through merit. If proof be necessary that her life was passed in the darkness of faith, her questions ("How shall this be done . . . ?" "Son, why hast thou done so to us?" — Luke 1:34; 2:48), and her inability to understand "the word that He spoke to them" (Luke 2:50) would seem to be decisive.

This is not said with the intention of denying the belief held by many, that Mary, at certain moments during her life on earth, was given brief 'glimpses' of the beatific vision. But such temporary incursions into the regime of the next world, if they occurred, would not have suppressed the faith which was the ordinary rule of her life; on the contrary, they would have accentuated its darkness.

That Mary's first grace was, on the other hand, a 'fullness' quite surpassing any attained by others, is due principally to its being ordained to the Divine Motherhood and Coredemption — offices altogether out of proportion with the vocations of other saints; and it is from these points of view that this grace is usually considered. But we may note that the Immaculate Conception is at least indicative of the surpassing dimensions of the grace therein conferred. Since grace was given to Mary, not merely as a gratuitous endowment, but *as triumphing over and excluding* the sinful condition which otherwise would have been passed on to her from her forebears, it had to have a certain power not found in the grace of Adam (which did not need to perform such a role) or that of Adam's other descendants (which fails to perform it).

Furthermore, the Immaculate Conception also shows that grace has a certain primacy in Mary that it has not in others. For her case does not follow the law of nature (of nature, that is, in its fallen condition); she does not inherit the "law of sin" (Rom. 7:23) engrafted on human nature; rather, in virtue of a higher law triumphing over that of fallen nature, she is born a pure child of grace. Thus, grace is, in a certain sense, more primordial in her than nature itself; and this first moment sets the pattern of her entire life, which will always be more the work of grace than of nature: her motherhood will be brought about by the Holy Spirit rather than by human agency; and, at the end of her life, her body, instead of following the natural law of decay, will, in accordance with the law of grace, be transfigured with glory.

The Immaculate Conception is also indicative of the immensity of Mary's grace inasmuch as it manifests God's predilection for her. Not wishing her to be separated even for an instant from the influence of His love, He intervened miraculously to preserve her from the stain of sin she was destined by her lineage to inherit. Of all His adopted children, she is the favorite, for whom He does not hesitate to go to any length. Hence the profound basis of the Suarezian maxim, thus phrased by Pope Pius XII:

. . . the mysteries of grace which God has wrought in the Virgin must be measured, not by the ordinary laws, but by the divine omnipotence.[23]

The greatness of Mary's initial grace helps to explain the tendency of Mariologists for many centuries to want to maintain that she was given the use of reason — through infused knowledge — from the instant of her conception, being thus enabled to receive that first grace itself by a voluntary and meritorious acceptance, and to render thanks and adoration to her Creator from the moment of her creation. "Mary was created in contemplation," it has been said.[24] For if God did not wish her to exist even for a moment deprived of the radical power of responding to His love, and if this power, this grace, was of an intensity unparalleled in the universe, it seems repugnant that it should have been bestowed on one who was totally unaware of it and who would have been incapable for exercising it for a considerable length of time.[25]

Whatever be the moment when Mary's conscious life began, and however high the degree of holiness with which she started, it must not be imagined that the Immaculate Conception fixed her spiritual life on so high a plane that she remained thereafter at the same level. Only the soul of Christ, in permanent possession of the beatific vision, remained at the same level throughout His earthly life — because it began at a height that was unsurpassable. All other spiritualities are governed by the law of merit and growth.

[23] Pius XII, *Munificentissimus Deus* (at note 43; *A.A.S.* 42 [1950], p. 767. The text of Suarez reads as follows: "Mensura enim privilegiorum Virginis potentia Dei dicitur, quae parcendo maxime et miserando manifestatur, et decuit singulari modo manifestari in matre." (Work cited above, in note 3) Disp. III, sect. 5, n. 31.

[24] Thomas Philippe, O.P., work cited in our note 2, VIII, p. 3.

[25] R. Garrigou-LaGrange, O.P., remarks that for Mary's surpassing fullness of grace, virtues and gifts to have remained inactive at the beginning of her life "would appear opposed to the sweet and generous dispositions of Divine Providence in favor of the Mother of the Savior." (—Work cited in our note 8, Engl. transl. p. 94). But many people find the notion of Mary's having received the use of reason while still a foetus in the maternal womb highly repugnant; and it has been pointed out that this would seem difficult to reconcile with the simplicity and "littleness" that also seems to characterize the dispositions of Providence regarding Mary. (Cf. M.-J. Nicolas, O.P., article cited in our note 22, pp. 729-730). Perhaps these seemingly opposed 'exigencies' of Divine Providence regarding Mary could be reconciled, and the repugnance eliminated, if we were to suppose that what was given to Mary in the Immaculate Conception was not the use of reason in the way even that a child has it, but only an infused notion of the dimmest and most obscure sort of the existence of God, which did not involve discursive activity of reason, (as infused contemplation does not involve it), but sufficed for an act of love of extraordinary intensity. By it, her soul would have been actually adherent to its Creator and Divine Spouse from the first moment of its existence, and yet would still have to undergo in all simplicity the normal development of an infant intellect.

As a matter of fact, the Immaculate Conception gives reason for maintaining that Mary developed spiritually at an extraordinarily rapid rate. Following a suggestion of St. Thomas,[26] a law of spiritual growth has been formulated,[27] according to which, the greater a soul's union with God, the more rapidly does it tend to grow in this union. That is to say, as a soul advances in holiness, its rate of advancement tends constantly to accelerate, like the speed of a falling body. It is implied in this principle — and seems indeed to be confirmed by the testimonies of the saints — that a holy soul, cooperating generously with grace, will, in a given length of time, make incomparably greater spiritual progress than a mediocre soul. If, therefore, it be granted that the point from which the Blessed Virgin started lay well beyond the peaks attained by the greatest saints, her spiritual growth from moment to moment must have been stupendous. In addition, there is the fact that Mary's ascent was not retarded by the 'gravitational force' or evil inclinations and disorders that weigh upon all those conceived in original sin. She was capable, as has already been pointed out, of a total and constant gift of self to God; hence her actual love of God could always be maintained at the full measure of the sanctifying grace she possessed. She was able to press forward steadily, without ever lapsing into "remiss" acts.

Suarez maintained that Mary's life was an endless repetition of acts of charity, each so intense as to merit an increase of grace equal to that already possessed. In other words, each act had a meritorious value equal to the sum of all that had preceded it, so that the final burst of love with which she passed from this life was rewarded with an increase of grace equal to the totality of grace conferred on her throughout her whole life.[28] Whatever judgment is to be passed upon the arithmetic of such calculations, there seems to be no doubt that we must conclude with Suarez that, at the term of Mary's spiritual growth, her perfection was such "that it could scarcely be comprehended by the human faculties."[29]

Any attempt, therefore, to form an idea of the grace of the Blessed Virgin must be made with the greatest caution. As the metaphysician dares not speak of God except in the most chastened language, renouncing all pretense of circumscribing the divine being with his human concepts, so, too, the Mariologist, due proportion guarded, is obliged to use an almost metaphysical purification of the concept of grace when applying it to

---

[26] Commentary on Hebrews 10:25 (end of lectio 3); cp. *Summa Theologiae* III, 35, 6, and the commentary on *I De coelo*, vii (end of lectio 17).

[27] R. GARRIGOU-LAGRANGE, O.P., *Perfection chrétienne et contemplation* I, 4th ed., Paris (1923) p. 237 ff. The application to Mary is made here, and again in his *Mariologie* (cited in note 2), Engl. trans. p. 98 ff.

[28] SUAREZ (work cited above, in note 2), Disp. XVIII, sect. 4 (ed. Venetiis 1746, p. 153a).

[29] ". . . in fine augmenti tanta erit perfectio, ut vix possit humano ingenio comprehendi." *Ibid.*

Mary. We are more familiar with the action of grace in its relatively rudimentary forms, and as received into natures that must be healed as well as elevated. Hence, when dealing with the case of the Blessed Virgin, we have to strip our concept of grace of all non-essentials, and then posit it in a condition of maximum perfection.

In everyone who receives it, grace is a *divinization* and elevation of the creature, making him share in the nature and life of the Creator. This is the great mystery of divine grace announced by St. Peter when he assured the early Christians that it had been granted to them to become "partakers of the divine nature." (I Peter 1:4). Grace is not merely, as we so often tend to think of it, a forgiveness of sins and a help to lead a good life; it is literally a participation in the nature of God. It does not make us identical with God, since it is only a participation, and always remans distinct from our own proper nature. Only God possesses the divine nature in its fullness and as His proper nature; we receive only a kind of reflection of it. But this 'reflection' is so strong and so real that we can say in simple truth, and without any exaggeration, that whoever has received even the least degree of sanctifying grace is *divinized* by it. Even in the infant who has just been baptized, this is so; and in no one can grace be anything more than this — for what is above the divine? There are different degrees of grace and holiness, but these are merely variations in the extent and intensity of the divinization. Hence, in Mary, too, grace consisted simply in a sharing of the divine nature and life; but in her case this took place with a fullness, both intensive and extensive, which is without parallel among pure creatures.

Perhaps we can be even more precise. St. John of the Cross says that it is impossible for anyone in this life to rise higher than the state of "transformation in God" or "spiritual marriage."[30] Yet within this state itself he distinguishes various degrees, and remarks that "with time and practice the soul may become more completely perfected and grounded in love."[31] If these words be taken in the absolute sense in which they seem to have been meant, it would seem that we are not obliged to postulate for the Blessed Virgin a state of soul with no correspondence whatsoever to those described by mystical writers; but rather that we can apply to her what is said of the transforming union, keeping in mind that in her case it would have been realized with a perfection that has never been approached by anyone else, and that utterly surpasses our power of appreciation.

Of the "new life, which begins when the soul has reached . . . perfection of union with God," St. John of the Cross gives the following account, which one would not know how to modify in order to make it apply more suitably to the Blessed Virgin:

[30] St. John of the Cross, *Spiritual Canticle,* stanza 26 (17 in the first redaction), on the text, "In the inner cellar." E. A. Peers translation.
[31] St. John of the Cross, *Living Flame of Love,* Prologue.

. . . as each living creature lives by its operation, as the philosophers say, the soul, having its operations in God, through the union that it has with God, lives the life of God, and thus its death has been changed into life — which is to say that animal life has been changed into spiritual life.

For the understanding, which before this union understood in a natural way with the strength and vigour of its natural light, by means of the bodily senses, is now moved and informed by another and a higher principle, that of the supernatural light of God, and the senses having been set aside, it has thus been changed into the Divine, for through union its understanding and that of God are now both one.

And the will, which aforetime loved after a low manner, that of death, and with its natural affection, has now been changed into the life of Divine love; for it loves after a lofty manner with Divine affection and is moved by the power and strength of the Holy Spirit in Whom it now lives the life of love, since, through this union, its will and His will are now only one.

And the memory, which of itself perceived only figures and phantasms of created things, has become changed through this union, so that it has in its mind the eternal years spoken of by David. And the natural desire, which had only capacity and strength to enjoy creature pleasure that works death, is now changed so that it tastes and enjoys that which is Divine, being now moved and satisfied by another and a more living principle, which is the delight of God; for it is united with Him and thus it is now only the desire of God.

And finally, all the movements and operations and inclinations which the soul had aforetime, and which belonged to the principle and strength of its natural life, are now in this union changed into Divine movements, dead to their own operation and inclination and alive in God. For the soul, like the true daughter of God that it now is, is moved wholly by the Spirit of God, even as Saint Paul teaches, saying: "That they that are moved by the Spirit of God are sons of God Himself."

So, as has been said, the understanding of this soul is now the understanding of God; and its will is the will of God; and its memory is the memory of God; and its delight is the delight of God; and the substance of this soul, although it is not the Substance of God, for into this it cannot be substantially changed, is nevertheless united in Him and absorbed in Him, and is thus God by participation in God, which comes to pass in this perfect state of the spiritual life, although not so perfectly as in the next life.[32]

It is in the light of such a description that we must understand the expression, *"the divine Mary,"* used without hesitation by some of the

[32] *Ibid.,* stanza 2 (second redaction), on the text, "In slaying, thou hast changed death to life." E. A. PEERS translation.

great Marian doctors of past centuries,[33] although at times it alarms people today. It does not mean 'divine by essence,' or imply that the Blessed Virgin ranks with the Trinity. Her 'divinization' is only an accidental modification of the creature such as is received by all the just; but if the effect of grace is truly to *divinize* there is no other adjective adequate to describe one in whom grace achieved its work with incomparable fullness.

We can see likewise that there is a certain rectitude in the sentiments of the letter, once highly credited among Marian writers, which purported to have been sent by Dennis the Areopagite to St. Paul the Apostle. Dennis declares that when he had been brought into the presence of the exalted Virgin by the Apostle St. John:

> Such an immense divine splendor encompassed me exteriorly, and illumined me still more fully interiorly, such a fragrance of all perfumes overwhelmed me, that neither this unhappy body, nor even my spirit, was able to bear the *"insignia"* of such great happiness. My heart failed, my spirit failed, under the weight of such great glory. God, who was present in the Virgin, is my witness that if I had not been instructed by your teaching, I would have believed her to be the true God; for the glory of the blessed could never surpass that felicity which I, now unhappy, but then most blessed, experienced.[34]

SOME CHARACTERISTIC TRAITS OF THE
SPIRITUALITY OF THE IMMACULATE VIRGIN

Our treatment of Mary's spirituality thus far has been rather abstract, whereas Christian piety has always sought to obtain a more concrete knowledge of the Blessed Mother. From earliest times, the faithful have wondered about the unrecorded details of her life, her part in the events recorded by Scripture, and even the traits of her countenance. It is natural that they should also want to know the traits of her spiritual 'physiognomy' more particularly than we have given them.

This is not the place to attempt to satisfy such a desire; but we may at least point out that the Immaculate Conception gives us certain general indications as to the elements that must go into a true portrait of Mary's interior life. It warns us, first of all, against two opposite errors sometimes committed by those who attempt such a portrait.

One consists in making her too ordinary, for want of due appreciation for the transcendent dimensions of the mystery of grace in her. Thus we sometimes see attributed to her a little too readily the feelings which the

---

[33] It occurs in the works of ST. GRIGNION DE MONTFORT (e.g. *Traité de la vraie dévotion à la Sainte Vierge*, Introduction, and ch. V, art. 5, towards the end of section 3) and St. John EUDES (e.g. the work cited in our note 17, p. 175).

[34] Translated from the Latin text given by A. ROSKOVÁNY, *Beata Virgo Maria in suo conceptu Immaculata. . .* I, Budapest 1873, p. 4 f.

ordinary woman experiences in similar circumstances. Is not Péguy thus guilty when he writes of Mary and Joseph:

> They found him sitting in the temple in the midst of the doctors.
> Sitting in the midst of the doctors.
> And the doctors listening religiously.
> He was teaching, at the age of twelve, he was teaching
>   in the midst of the doctors.
> How proud they felt.[35]

Between Mary's heart, incandescent with the presence of the divinity, and the 'average' human heart, tepid, dark and heavy; scarred — if not actually laden — with sin, there is an incommensurability that should make us exceedingly wary about projecting an image from one to the other. Not only were her attitudes and reactions free from the traces of egoism, exaggeration and aimlessness that normally mar ours; they were never even merely human. Her entire psychology moved on the plane of the theological virtues. The "total divinization" of the perfect soul, of which St. John of the Cross speaks in the long passage quoted above, extends even to the soul's 'first movements,' according to the saint's explicit testimony.[36] And St. John Eudes writes of the Blessed Virgin in a way that sounds almost like a direct application of the doctrine of John of the Cross to her case:

> . . . the spirit of the New Man, which reigned perfectly in Mary's heart, had such absolute dominion over all her passions that they never stirred except on its order. Thus, she never used them except as led by the Spirit of God, and solely for the glory of His divine majesty.[37]

An opposite misunderstanding of Mary's spirituality consists in filling her life with astounding miracles, as was done, for example, in the ancient apocryphal lives of the Virgin. This comes from a naive misconception of holiness, which substitutes the visible marvels of divine power for the greater but invisible work of divine love assimilating the creature to itself. The instinct of the faithful has, over the course of the centuries, reacted against attributing any spectacular peculiarity to the Mother of God, and has grown in the conviction that the external pattern of her life would have

---

[35] Péguy, *Le mystère de la charité de Jeanne d'Arc*, trans. Julian Green.

[36] St. John of the Cross says of the soul "betrothed" to God: ". . . even as a maiden that is betrothed sets not her love upon another than her spouse, nor directs her thoughts or her actions to any other, even so the soul in this estate has no longer any affections of the will or acts of knowledge of the understanding, nor any care or action which is not wholly turned to God, together with its desires. It is, as it were, Divine, deified, so that in even its first movements it has naught whereto the will of God is opposed, insofar as it can understand." *Spiritual Canticle*, stanza 27 (in the first redaction, 18), "There I promised him to be his bride." E. A. Peers translation.

[37] St. John Eudes, work cited above in note 17, p. 132 f.

been a simple one, like that of her fellow-countrywomen.[38] The doctrine of the Immaculate Conception confirms this instinct, by presenting Mary's essential greatness as belonging to the hidden order of grace, rather than to the external order of the miraculous.

But we must likewise note that the divinization brought about by grace in Mary did not detract from her humanness. Rather, it is sin that is inhuman; in being shielded from it and endowed with a human nature free from the flaws which affect this nature in others, Mary was enabled to be *more human* than anyone else.[39]

An adequate presentation of the spirituality of the Blessed Virgin would have to give lengthy consideration to her office as Mother of God, with individual attention to the great mysteries in the life of her Son, which were the substance of her own life. Without attempting to do this, we may make three general observations about the relation of the Immaculate Conception to the Divine Motherhood.

The first is that the Immaculate Conception prepared Mary for this office by giving her a spirituality proportionate to it. Her close association with the All-holy God demanded an unblemished holiness of her. The Divine Wisdom was willing to integrate itself into a sinful people, and even to employ sinners as ministers of its grace to that people, but it required that at least the point of contact between itself and the rest of the race should be without sin — and not only without sin, but transfigured with a sanctity which, by its splendor, should be in some sense congruous with the divine holiness. This sinlessness and sanctity were the direct effect of the Immaculate Conception.

The second observation to be made concerning the Immaculate Conception as a preparation for the Divine Motherhood is that it disposed Mary for this office in its specifically maternal character, and not merely as one of close association with God. That is to say that, from the beginning, Mary's grace was pointed toward the motherly office to be conferred on her; and if this was true of her grace, it held likewise for the spirituality springing from that grace. On this basis, may we not ask whether her spirituality had not a maternal character even before the Annunciation? This does not imply that she knew beforehand that a Divine Person would

---

[38] "We should not say unlikely or uncertain things about her," declared St. THERESA OF THE CHILD JESUS. ". . . For a sermon on the Blessed Virgin to bear fruit, it must portray her real life, as the Gospel lets us glimpse it, not her supposed life; and we can divine that her real life, at Nazareth and later, must have been quite ordinary. . . 'He was subject to them'—how simple that is."—*Novissima Verba*, p. 154 ff., as cited by M.-J. NICOLAS, O.P., in the article cited in our note 3, pp. 69-70, note 12.

[39] It follows that the development of Mariology presupposes not only a profound and rigorous theology of grace, as was mentioned above, but likewise a rich and sure appreciation of authentic human values.

be born of her, but only that she was inspired by the Holy Ghost with a love of God that was, without her knowing why, motherly in spirit. In this case, Gabriel's message would have come less as a surprise than as the natural culmination of her spiritual history up to that point, and as the explanation of the mysterious presentiments which she had already felt without knowing their meaning.

Our third observation is that the Immaculate Conception not only gave Mary a spirituality proportionate to the Divine Motherhood, but also enabled her to draw fully on the spiritual resources contained in that Motherhood. For Mary's life was one of such total devotion to Christ that she had, in a sense, no life of her own: His life was hers. The Sacred Mysteries of His life were the nourishment on which her soul lived, and of which her spirituality was a simple reflection. It was, therefore, from the Divine Motherhood, even more than from the Immaculate Conception, that her spirituality received its characteristics; but it was only because of the Immaculate Conception that she was a material plastic enough to receive the full imprint of Christ's image without blemish. By preserving her from any disorders or self-centeredness, the Immaculate Conception enabled her to have a spirituality which had no features but those derived from her Son.

In the case of certain particular virtues, the influence of the Immaculate Conception on Mary's spirituality is especially evident.

Purity is the virtue that people most spontaneously associate with Mary, because of her sacred virginity. Properly, however, purity is a quality of soul rather than body; and it was the Immaculate Conception, preserving Mary from concupiscence, that was the true source of the purity of which her virginity was an external expression. This very fact sometimes leads people to think that there was little merit in her virtue, since she was not tempted against it. We tend to calculate the worth of a virtue by the struggle that must be made to attain and preserve it. In reality, however, a virtue is a positive quality, the perfection of which is measured by the perfection of the activity it brings forth. From this point of view, the flawless purity of the Immaculate Virgin is of immeasurably greater value than any attainable to those who must develop it against the resistance left by original sin.[40]

Because of Mary's purity, an overly-human calculation might be led to feel that she was somewhat lacking in that *fire of love* that imparts a self-transcending greatness to the human soul; for it is almost a rule in

[40] Cf. M. J. NICOLAS, O.P., article cited in our note 15, p. 730: "There was less merit in her rejection of evil, to which nothing attracted her; but not less in the free and powerful aspiration of her entire being toward the good, and towards God."

human life that great lovers are great sinners. As we lay flowers, therefore, at the feet of the Virgin Most Pure, we may be inclined to dissociate from her the intensity of a heart burning with love.

Nothing could be further from the truth. Saving always the case of her Divine Son, there was never a human heart that loved so intensely as Mary's. The principal obstacle to the growth of love is selfishness, of which she was utterly free. Her heart is Immaculate, not out of coldness or indifference, but through the incandescence of a fire dampened by no dross. We who are accustomed to measure the intensity of love by its aberrations have still to learn that a fire is not burning hottest when it is making the most smoke.

The fact that her love was chiefly for God does not mean that it was less genuine or less ardent. If the love of God leaves us cold, it is not because God is unlovable, but because we do not know what God is — nor, by the same token, what love is. And Mary not only loved God in Himself; she loved all creatures in God. Especially since that moment at the foot of the Cross when she was told to admit all mankind into that place in her heart kept hitherto for her Son, her immaculate love has embraced all the children of God with an affection so intense and so tender, that all the passion of this world's lovers is tepid beside it.

There is one virtue at least in which we might think that others could surpass the Blessed Virgin: *humility* — since her sinlessness deprives her of one of the greatest motives of humility that others have. But in this also, the wisdom of man is inadequate to scrutinize the things of God. Humility comes chiefly from the knowledge of God, and is proportionate to one's nearness to Him. Mary, therefore, having a clearer vision and a more intimate contact with God than anyone else, was more keenly aware of His majesty and of her dependence on Him.

It is true that sin becomes an additional motive of humility when it is repented of; nevertheless, every sin involves an act of pride, a setting of oneself in the place of God. And while the consciousness of sin can move us to humility in moments when our complacent hearts are insensible to other motives, it leads to a humility less pure, less truly humble. Other saints humbled themselves at the view of their own misery; Mary's immaculate humility consisted in her having no eyes for herself, but only for God. "She is the only saint who never looked at herself."[41]

We must keep in mind that humility is necessary to let oneself be loved, and to accept a favor. The humiliation involved in accepting a divine invitation to a friendship surpassing his natural right made Lucifer prefer hell to heaven. Mary, who, already in the Immaculate Conception, and still more in the Incarnation, was the recipient of a divine favor more

---

[41] Cf. Thomas PHILIPPE, O.P., work cited in our note 3, I, esp. p. 6.

gratuitous and unmerited than that bestowed on any other creature, needed, by that fact, to have the greatest humility of all.

Humility was likewise demanded for the cooperation with God to which Mary was called. The ultimate barrier to a soul's cooperation with its Creator is the egocentricity deposited in it by original sin. It puts its taint on the labors of the holiest saints, for it is the last stain to be removed by the purgative action of divine grace. Mary was kept altogether free from it by her Immaculate Conception in order that she might be able to respond with an undeviating *fiat* to every divine invitation to her to take part in the work of the Redemption.

This transparent humility, which was one of the most characteristic effects of the Immaculate Conception, became, in turn, a kind of prolongation of the Immaculate Conception. For if Mary were ever to have sinned, her first sin could only have been one of pride;[42] her humility, in forestalling this, maintained her in that sinlessness in which her original grace had engendered her.

As *faith* is the foundation of the entire supernatural structure in a soul, Mary's faith must have been proportionate to the edifice built upon it. Her belief in the miracle announced by Gabriel is sometimes taken as representative of her extraordinary faith; but belief in God's power to work such a miracle was easy in comparison with the supernatural mentality Mary needed in order to be interiorly at the level of the divine mysteries among which she lived. Christ Himself prayed for Peter's faith, because the Church would be built on it; yet Peter was only the messenger and dispenser of the mysteries of God, whereas Mary had an intrinsic part in the mysteries themselves. Her faith, therefore, had to surpass Peter's by far, both in the constancy and totality of her acceptance of the divine light, and in the intensity of her adherence to the mysteries proposed. The Immaculate Conception made her capable of such faith by giving her a spirit undisturbed in its inner integrity, and wholly docile to divine truth.

Accordingly, her faith would not have been half-hearted in any respect, but would have manifested in its own way the wholeness and unity that are everywhere characteristic of the Immaculate Virgin's inner life. She did not suffer the anguish of those whose belief is still too hesitant to assert itself firmly against the claims of the wisdom of the world, or the agony of those whose weak faith has been partially supported by inferior motives, from which the Spirit of God must wean it. Her faith was crowned with an ardent charity and perfected by the Gifts of the Holy Ghost, making her ever conscious of the divine presence, and receptive of every ray of light let fall by the Divine Teacher. Hence, she viewed all things in a steady supernatural light; and nevertheless her faith endured a blacker darkness

---

[42] Her case would have been analogous to that of Adam before the fall. Cf. St. Thomas, *Summa theologiae*, II-II, 163, 1.

than any ever experienced by a John of the Cross. The disparity between that which faith disclosed, and the divine reality itself, was only too sensible to her whose heart yearned for the definitive, unveiled presence and possession of the God she loved.

It is not easy for us to appreciate this *longing for God* that must have sprung up in the heart of the Immaculate Virgin, for we cannot know the intensity of a soul that was perpetually directed towards God with all its energies. God had made her for Himself in a way that is true of none other. All rational creatures have been invited to a personal fruition of Him in a hyper-fulfillment of their capacities of love and contemplation to which they could never, by nature, aspire; but she has been called to a uniquely intimate and personal union with Him as mother and sponsal associate in the mystery of the Redemption. And her heart was capable, because of its purity, of feeling to the full the attraction of her Divine Spouse, and incapable, because of that same purity, of being distracted, even momentarily or secondarily, from a total response to His call. And yet her ardent longing for God was without impatience or anxiety, waiting in peace of spirit for the moment appointed by her Beloved.

The disparity between Mary's faith and love—that is, between what was given her in faith and what was demanded by her love — gives some idea of the strength of her *hope,* which had to close the gap between the two. In regard to it, the Immaculate Conception had a twofold effect. It purified her reliance on God from any inclination to replace Him with secondary causes and powers; and it gave to her trust in Him a peculiar note of confidence in His love of predilection for her. The benevolence which hope presupposes in the 'mighty one' on whom it relies was, in her case, the incredible love lavished by the Creator on His elect creature from the beginning of her existence.

II

THE IMMACULATE CONCEPTION
AND OUR SPIRITUAL LIVES

Up to now we have considered the influence of the Immaculate Conception on the Blessed Virgin's own life; but it is also of radical importance for the role she plays in the life of others. For, in the distribution of grace, God uses some of His creatures as instruments in the sanctification of others. Sometimes He uses inanimate beings — as in the case of the sacraments — or He uses human beings independently of any intention of theirs. But the highest kind of instrumentality is that of those who freely and consciously serve Him. For such service, sin makes a man a defective instrument, while holiness makes him specially apt. The Immaculate Conception, therefore, makes Mary God's most perfect instrument among pure human beings, the only one without a flaw. She is the one channel through which grace can flow without encountering any resistance whatsoever.

Mary serves in the sanctification of others in two ways: as model and as helper. By the Immaculate Conception, she is uniquely qualified to serve as our model, because her spirituality is of the same order as ours (for she, too, walks "by faith, and not by sight" — II Cor. 5:7), but is perfect in that order. She is "first among the faithful," not only *de facto,* but *de jure*: her primacy cannot be supplanted. The saints can be taken as models only with some caution, for not all that is in them is imitable; besides their faults, each has a grace and a vocation that is, to a degree, peculiar to himself. Yet Mary, whose grace is utterly unique, is offered as a model to all, and in all things. For priests, laymen and religious, for those in the active and those in the contemplative way of life; in joys and in sorrows, in works and in prayer, she is model. This is because her grace, being the highest, is also the simplest and purest, the most accessible to all approachers, the least restricted to particular categories. She is the faultless *Mirror of Justice,* reproducing without distortion, yet in a form adapted to our weak eyes, the perfection of the Heavenly Father, and of Christ, the Sun of Justice.

One might fear that, precisely because of her perfection, she is a model less suited to us than those saints who began their lives as sinners; that just as Christ's grace of vision places Him in an order above us, so too, in lesser measure, does Mary's immaculateness place her above us. No doubt it is true that the saints who began with faults like ours give us a certain concrete example of how to rise from them, as well as inspiration and confidence to imitate them. At the same time, however, there is less in them that can be imitated; and a model is imitable primarily by reason of its excellence. The Blessed Virgin is proposed to us as an example, not because she was imperfect like ourselves, but because she has the virtues we stand in need of. Her example may not be so appealing as Magdalene's, but it has a greater power to draw us from our sins. If the appeal is less human, it is more divine — and the divine is more powerful than the human.

The Blessed Virgin's importance as model in the spiritual life, however, lies chiefly in the fact that she is not merely a model, but has *power* to help our attempts to imitate her. This power is exercised both by intercession and by direct intervention; and in both respects the Immaculate Conception provides a basis for it.

Her intercessory power depends upon her Immaculate Conception, as making both her petitions, and herself as petitioner, agreeable to God: the former because all her desires are in conformity with the will of God; the latter, because she has never been an object of offense to Him, but has always been the object of His fondest love. Her requests to Him are sure in advance of being granted. Pius IX, in the encyclical defining the Immaculate Conception, declared:

What she seeks, she finds; [her prayer] cannot be in vain.[43]

Hence the significance of the Miraculous Medal invocation:

O Mary, conceived without sin, pray for us who have recourse to thee.

The sinner knows that his petition has a better chance of a favorable hearing when it comes from her pure lips, rather than from his own.

But Mary's power to help does not seem to be limited to her intercession; many theologians, at least, believe that the role of "chief minister of the graces to be dispensed,"[44] which she merited by communing in the Passion of Christ,[45] includes the power to intervene directly and personally in the lives of the faithful. As "dispenser of all the gifts that Jesus purchased for us,"[46] she bestows these gifts as she sees fit.

Such a function can, of course, only be ministerial, as the expressions just quoted from Pope Pius X indicate. However, it is not as an inanimate instrument, but as a person, free and responsible in making decisions, that God employs His handmaiden. She is steward of divine grace itself. This responsibility could not be entrusted to her if there were the least flaw in her conformity to the will of God; and it is the grace of the Immaculate Conception which ensures this conformity.

By the same token, the Immaculate Conception makes her the *Virgin Most Powerful* in her interventions on behalf of those devoted to her. She acts with all the power of God, because she is purely an instrument and channel through which *it* acts. Hence Pius IX, in the closing paragraphs of the encyclical on the Immaculate Conception, calls her:

---

[43] ". . . coeli terraeque Regina a Domino constituta, ac super omnes Angelorum choros Sanctorumque ordines exaltata adstans a dextris Unigeniti Filii Sui Domini Nostri Iesu Christi maternis suis precibus validissime impetrat, et quod quaerit invenit, ac frustrari non potest." Pius IX, *Ineffabilis Deus* (*Acta Pii IX*, Pars prima, p. 618; W. J. Doheny-Kelly, *Papal documents on Mary*, Milwaukee 1954, p. 27).

[44] ". . . princeps largiendarum gratiarum ministra." Pius X, *Ad Diem Illum* (A. Tondini, *Le Encicliche Mariane*, Roma 1954, p. 314; W. J. Doheny-Kelly, *op. cit.*, p. 141).

[45] "Ex hac autem Mariam inter et Christum communione dolorum ac voluntatis, 'promeruit' illa 'ut reparatrix perditi orbis dignissime fieret,' atque ideo universorum munerum dispensatrix, quae nobis Iesus nece et sanguine comparavit." Pius X, *Ad diem illum* (A. Tondini, *op. cit.* p. 312; Doheny-Kelly, *op. cit.* p. 140).

[46] *Ibid.* Cf. St. John Eudes: "Jésus a versé dans le coeur de Marie les trésors de sagesse et de science qui sont cachés dans le sien. Mais outre cela, il y a mis encore tous les trésors des grâces des miséricordes qu'il a acquis par son sang et par sa mort, et il lui a donné le pouvoir de les distribuer, *cui vult*, dit saint Bernard, *quando vult*, et *quomodo vult:* à qui il lui plaît et en la manière qu'il lui plaît. *In manibus tuis*, dit le pieux et savant Denys le Chartreux, *sunt omnes thesauri miserationum Dei.*"
—Work cited in note 17, above, p. 466.

> . . . the most safe refuge and reliable helper of all who are in danger;
> . . . the impregnable stronghold of the holy Church . . . who has
> snatched the faithful peoples and nations from all sorts of the most
> dire calamities, and has freed Us also from so many threatening
> dangers.

The Pope then concludes His letter with the recommendation:

> Let (all the children of the Catholic Church) fly with utter confidence
> to this most sweet Mother of mercy and grace, in all dangers, difficulties,
> needs, doubts and fears. With her as guide and patroness, with her
> favor and protection, nothing is to be feared, nothing is hopeless.[47]

Mary's contribution to the sanctification of others, whether as model or
as helper, has always a maternal character to it. Hence, we must also
ask whether the Immaculate Conception prepares her for this specifically
maternal role.

One point is obvious from the outset: that since her motherhood regarding
Christ is the basis of her motherhood regarding the Christian,[48] the grace
which prepared her for the one prepared her for the other also. And
insofar as her spiritual motherhood consists in the giving and fostering of
the life of grace, what has already been said about her instrumental service
in the sanctification of others applies directly here also.

But a mother caring for the wants of her children is not merely a
stewardess, faithfully distributing the Lord's goods in due season. Hence,
over and above her instrumental function, Mary's spiritual motherhood
entails a mother's affection for her children. And as the Immaculate Conception prepared her heart for the maternal love she was to give to Christ,
so did it also prepare her to love Christ's members maternally.

There is a great difference, however, between the two cases. Christ's
lovability, infinitely surpassing Mary's power to love, called forth the love
from her heart, and constantly inspired her to ever greater bursts of affection. But her other children, those whom her Son took in off the highways
and byways and brought home to her heart, are comparatively meager
objects of love. Not only are they far less lovable than Christ; they are
altogether unworthy of the Mother's heart that embraces them with a
divine affection which they neither deserve, nor are able to requite or even

---

[47] Pius IX, *Ineffabilis Deus* (*Acta Pii IX*, Pars prima, pp. 617-618; Doheny-
Kelly, *op. cit.* p. 26 f.)

[48] Cf. Pius X, *Ad diem illum* (Tondini, *op. cit.* p. 310; Doheny-Kelly, *op. cit.*
p. 139): "An non Christi mater Maria? Nostra igitur et mater est. . . . In uno
. . . eodemque alvo castissimae Matris et carnem Christus sibi assumpsit et 'spiritale'
simul corpus adiunxit, ex iis nempe coagmentatum 'qui credituri erant in eum.' Ita
ut Salvatorem habens Maria in utero, illos etiam dici queat gessisse omnes, quorum
vitam continebat vita Salvatoris. Universi ergo, quotquot cum Christo iungimur,
quique, ut ait Apostolus, 'membra sumus corporis eius, de carne eius et de ossibus
eius,' de Mariae utero egressi sumus, tamquam corporis instar cohaerentis cum
capite."

to understand. In loving Christ, Mary rises to an object far above her; in loving mankind, she bends to what is far below. And whereas, in the first case, the Immaculate Conception was needed to enable her worthily to love God; in the second case, it was needed to enable her to love as God loves.

For God loves all that He has created; nothing is too insignificant to be regarded by Him, since nothing exists except as the effect of His loving regard. And it is only by loving them as God does that Mary is able to take into her heart all the children God has given her. The effect of the Immaculate Conception in this regard is a kind of transparent forgetfulness of self which it produced in her, making her wholly docile to the Spirit of Love, Who could incline her heart where He would.

But the children who have been given to the Blessed Mother are not only unworthy of her affection; as sinners, they are positively offensive to it. She is afflicted by nothing except what offends God; but this she feels all the more keenly because of her sinlessness. From this point of view, the Immaculate Conception might appear as an obstacle to Mary's maternal love for the sinner. But it is the paradox of her Immaculate Heart that she is the *Refuge of Sinners* precisely because she herself is without sin; she is merciful to them because she has loved that which they failed to love. For there are two ways to love a sinner: one is as a fellow-sinner would love him, by a kind of sympathy which, in a sense, connives with the sin. Such love does him no good; it harms him. The other way is that of mercy, which perceives the full misery of his condition, and loves him in order to raise him out of it. God's love for the sinner is of this type, and so is Mary's, in virtue of the grace that kept her heart immaculate as regards sin, but overflowing with divine love for the souls to be saved from sin.

We must note, lastly, a difference which the Immaculate Conception makes between Mary's relationship to her children, and that of other mothers to theirs. In other cases, the child's dependence on his mother diminishes as he matures. The strength and wisdom which he acquires normally come, in time, to surpass hers, with the result that it may be the mother, in her declining years, who is dependent on the child. Likewise, the original boundless confidence of the child in his mother becomes tempered as he gradually discovers her faults and limitations.

There is no parallel to this in the case of the Blessed Mother. Because she is immaculate, there are no defects or hidden limitations in her, but only boundless wisdom and power in the service of perfect goodness. The better she is known, the greater the confidence she inspires; and the more one matures in the spiritual life, the more he depends on her.

III

THE HOLINESS OF THE BLESSED VIRGIN:
A DIVINE MYSTERY

In the preceding pages, we have distinguished carefully between the Blessed Virgin's own spiritual life and her influence on the lives of others; and, in the latter case, between her two roles as model and helper. However, the actual Marian piety of the Church, whether considered in the teachings of the most authoritative Marian saints, or in the devotion of the common faithful, seems not to pay a great deal of attention to these distinctions. The attitude of the Church seems to be one of simple affection for its Blessed Mother, as though the distinct roles we have indicated blended into one; or rather, as though she transcended them. Seldom does piety distinguish between imitating her example and invoking her help. Those who imitate her expect by that very fact to obtain her help; their attitude is at one and the same time an effort to conform to her example and a reliance on her assistance.

Similarly, the Blessed Virgin's personal holiness is seldom considered without some reference to one's own spiritual improvement; yet, paradoxically, it is recognized that a powerful means of advancing one's own sanctification is the disinterested contemplation of her holiness. Thus, for example, the enthusiastic lyricism of St. Bernard's Marian sermons or of the Byzantine '*philotheotokoi*,'[49] was primarily a song of praise; its 'moral influence' on the people consisted not merely in stimulating them to go and pray to her, but even more in its effect of putting them directly and immediately into a state of prayer and of spiritual union with her which would itself be sanctifying.

Thus, devotion to the Mother of God, particularly in its highest form, seems to be a simple movement of the heart to her, in which the spirit of the 'devotee,' by its affectionate attachment to that which she is, is conformed to her spirit and draws upon her sanctifying power.[50] Underlying this devotion is the supposition that those who draw near to Mary in prayer are sanctified by contact with her holiness just as those who approach a fire are warmed by its heat. She is thus given a position analogous to that of Christ, of whom it is written, "Power went forth from Him and healed all." (Luke 6:19) Or, rather, she is a kind of sacrament, mysteriously productive in others of that which is symbolized in her own person.

In attempting to formulate this attitude of Christian piety, we must, of

---

[49] Cf. chapter III of the present volume, p. 91 ff., and chapter IV, p. 115 ff.

[50] The language of St. Grignion de Montfort is even stronger: "The soul of the Blessed Virgin will communicate itself to you to glorify the Lord; her spirit will enter into the place of your spirit to rejoice in God, her savior."—*Traité de la vraie dévotion* . . . , ch. VII, art. 5.

course, take care not to attribute to Mary what is a property of God: that of being the First Being, from whom others derive their being and goodness by a kind of participation. Like the Sacred Humanity of Christ, she can never have more than an instrumental role in the communication of grace; and she ranks far below Christ in that, in her case, the instrument is not in the same being and person as the principal cause.

Yet, with all these cautions observed, the Immaculate Conception appears to provide a certain justification for the transcendence which the piety of the Church seems to attribute to Mary with respect to the distinctions pointed out above. For in causing her to possess grace from the beginning of her existence, and with a certain fullness, the Immaculate Conception causes her to possess it *after the manner of a source,* by comparison with those who receive it only partially, and after having already been in existence previously. It makes her, as an individual, a kind of personification or embodiment of grace, from whom others will derive it as participating in her fullness.

Furthermore, as has been pointed out elsewhere in this volume,[51] Mary is, "in virtue of her singular plenitude of grace, a universal principle with regard to common grace." If this be so, it is only normal that the manner of her influence, with regard to grace, should bear a particular resemblance to the influence of Christ, who is the universal cause of all grace,[52] and of God, as the universal cause of being. But it is precisely a characteristic of the divine causality — and one in which it is imitated by the Sacred Humanity — that its *effect* is a participation in that which it *is*; that its influence transcends the distinction between efficient and exemplary causality. The transcendence which the piety of the Church attributes to the Immaculate Virgin would seem to be a reflection, more distant than that of Christ's Sacred Humanity, of this mode of the divine activity.

The Immaculate Conception not only explains this transcendence — if what we have said be admitted — but also provides a striking example of it. A long tradition, which has been given expression in the writings of recent popes, looks upon the victory over Satan which Mary won in her Conception, as mysteriously one with the victory over him which she achieves in those devoted to her. Pope Pius X declares:

> If we trust in Mary as she deserves, particularly now that we are going to celebrate her Immaculate Conception with special fervor, we will discover that she is still today the Virgin Most Powerful, "who has trampled beneath her virginal foot the head of the serpent."[53]

[51] Cf. chapter X, p. 384.
[52] *Ibid.*
[53] Pius X, *Ad diem illum* (Tondini, *op. cit.,* pp. 328-330; Doheny-Kelly, *op. cit.,* p. 148).

. . . The Virgin will not cease to help us in our difficulties, however great they may be, and to carry on the fight fought from her very conception, so that daily it can be repeated: "Today the head of the serpent of old was trampled under her foot."[54]

*   *   *

CONCLUSION

At the beginning of this essay, we pointed out that the term, *spirituality of the Blessed Virgin*, could be referred either to Mary's own spiritual life, or to other lives that are particularly colored by her influence. We then showed that, in the first sense of the term, the "spirituality of the Blessed Virgin" derived some of its most distinctive characteristics from the Immaculate Conception, which is the germ from which it grew.

Now, after pointing out that the Immaculate Conception is also the basis of Mary's influence on others, we have tried to show that this influence, as the piety of the Church seems to visualize it, is not a mere result of Mary's personal holiness, but a kind of participation in it. If this be granted, it follows obviously that the Immaculate Conception is of radical importance for Marian spirituality taken now in the second sense also. If the spiritual life which Mary fosters in others is a reflection of her own, it will necessarily be affected by whatever affects her own.

St. Grignion de Montfort assures that those who take Mary for the road by which they go to union with God will advance "with less bitterness and greater tranquillity" than those who take other roads, which will lead through "dark nights, strange combats and agonies, steep mountains, sharp thorns and terrifying deserts."[55] Does this not say, in effect, that some of the traits which characterize the spirituality of Mary, by reason of her immaculateness, are reflected in those who are led by her? The "child of Mary" is imbued with the spirit of Mary; and the Immaculate Conception is a prime root of this spirit, whether it be considered in her or in him — in the source, or in the derivative.

---

[54] *Ibid.*, TONDINI, pp. 322-324; DOHENY-KELLY, p. 147. Cf. Pius IX, *Ineffabilis Deus.* ". . . beatissima Virgo, quae tota pulchra et Immaculata venenosum crudelissimi serpentis caput contrivit, et salutem attulit mundo." (*Acta Pii IX*, Pars prima, p. 617; DOHENY-KELLY, *op. cit.*, p. 26).

[55] ST. GRIGNION DE MONTFORT, *op. cit.*, ch. V, art. v, n. 1. Cf. ch. VII, art. 6: "By taking the immaculate road which is Mary, and by following the divine practice which I am teaching, a person labors 'by day,' he labors in a holy place, he labors little. *There is no night at all in Mary, because there was no sin in her, nor even the least shadow of it.*"

PART III

SUPPLEMENTARY STUDIES
AND
APPENDICES

XII

Islam and the Immaculate Conception

George C. Anawati, O.P.*

"O Mary, God has chosen thee and has purified thee . . ."
(Koran 3, 41)

One of the aspects of Islam most likely to prove interesting in this Marian epoch is the place occupied by the Holy Virgin in Islamic doctrine. The Koran indeed speaks of her in extremely laudatory terms, recounting some of the circumstances of her birth, and citing the special protection given to her against Satan, the miraculous nurture sent to her, the virgin birth of her son, Jesus and, finally, specifying the first rank she holds among all women, both in this world and in the next.

Indeed a famous *hadîth*[1] is known which assures that:

> Every Adam's son coming into this world is touched by Satan except Mary's son and his mother.

Some Catholic authors think, therefore, that there exists in Islam an intuition, more or less confused, of the dogma of the Immaculate Conception. It might prove fruitful to examine this problem and to determine to what degree such an assertion is valid.

Before plunging *"in medias res,"* it is necessary to stress two points concerning such a study. The first is that we must not forget that *Islam* is a very complex concept, without authoritative unity such as exists in the Catholic Church. The exact meaning and implications of any dogma held by the Church is fixed by Apostolic authority; but in Islam there is no such final court of decision. We are thus obliged, when exposing the "Islamic" point of view, to define, first, whether we are concerned with Shiites or Sunnites; and, after limiting the discussion to Sunnites, to specify whether the point of view being stated is that of the Koran, of the *hadîth,* or of one of the different currents of Islamic thought (juridical,

---

* Director of the Dominican Institute of Oriental Studies, Cairo, Egypt.

[1] A *hadîth* is a saying or deed of Mohammed, transmitted by tradition. This one will be discussed below, at the end of section II.

philosophical, mystical or theological)[2]. It is even possible, on some important questions, to oppose the divergent opinions of different doctors. Therefore there exists in this discussion a factor of uncertainty which allows Moslems to present diametrically opposed solutions, with quite legitimate references to texts of different doctors. Our review of the problem will be limited to the discussion of the common teaching of the great *sunni*[3] commentators and theologians.

The second point to be noted is the necessity of keeping to the expressions borrowed from the Christian vocabulary their precise technical meaning. The Immaculate Conception in the official Catholic doctrine means a very definite dogma, not a vague attribute granted to the Holy Virgin to exalt her position. It means that Mary, from the instant of her conception, has been preserved from the original sin in view of Christ's foreseen merits. To determine therefore whether this doctrine is accepted by Islam, it is necessary, first to examine whether the dogma of original sin and its transmission is taught therein, and then to study the special case of the Holy Virgin[4]. Accordingly, this note will comprise two sections, corresponding respectively to these two questions.

---

[2] There is, for instance, a difference between the "Moslem Brethren" (*al-Ikhwân al-muslimûn*) and the progressive Modernists. The Moslem Brethren are a politico-religious society founded in Egypt by shaykh al-Banna in 1928, with the aim of restoring the (theoretically) primitive Islam in all its integrity and rudeness. On these movements, cf. Ch. ADAMS, *Islam and modernism in Egypt*, Oxford Univ. Press, 1933; L. GARDET, *La Cité musulmane*, Paris, Vrin, 1954, Annexe III and particularly J. JOMIER, *Les tendances de l'exégèse moderne en Egypte: Le commentaire du Manâr*, Paris, Maisonneuve, 1954 and his recent article in *Mélanges*, Cairo, 1954: "Quelques positions actuelles de l'exégèse coranique en Egypte révélées par une polémique récente 1947-1951."

[3] The *sunni*, in opposition to the *shi'i*, are the great majority of Moslems, who recognize the legitimacy of the first four caliphs.

[4] Obviously, it is impossible to give here the more technical details from the point of view of Orientalists. We hope to treat the problem more extensively in volume II of our *Introduction à la théologie musulmane*, which is in preparation. The best synthesis of Islamic Mariology is the precious book of Father J. ABD EL-JALIL, O.F.M., *Marie et l'Islam* (Paris, Beauchesne, 1950, 90 pp.), which is a development of two studies published previously, one in the work *Maria*, edited by H. DU MANOIR, S.J., vol. I (Paris, Beauchesne, 1949, pp. 183-211), the other in *Bulletin des Missions* (Saint André-les-Bruges, 1948, no. 3). Father Abd El-Jalil is a professor at the Institut Catholique in Paris. Among his works, let us also mention: *Brève Histoire de la Littérature arabe*, Paris Maisonneuve, 5e édition, 1947 and *Aspects intérieurs de l'Islam*, Paris, Ed. du Seuil, 1948. Cf. also the article of the famous Catholic scholar, Louis MASSIGNON, one of the best specialists on Islam, "Le signe marial," in *Rythmes du monde*, 1948, No. 3. Other references will be found in the book of Father Abd El-Jalil.

I

DOES THE NOTION OF ORIGINAL SIN EXIST IN ISLAM?

Since we are dealing with the precise sense of the Christian dogma, and in order to allow a fruitful comparison with Moslem doctrine, let us recall the essential aspects of our own doctrine on this point:[5]

A. *The state of original justice,* the principle of which is sanctifying grace. This is a state characterized by the theological virtues and the gifts of integrity: absence of concupiscence, absence of corporal death, impassibility ("paradisiac state") and the gift of infused knowledge.

B. *Adam's sin,* constituted by a formal disobedience to God's order.

C. *The personal consequences of Adam's sin:* the loss of sanctifying grace and of the integrity of nature.

D. *The transmission of this sin to Adam's posterity:* being the father of the human race, Adam bequeathed a sin to his posterity as regards both the guilt and its consequences.

These dry technical specifications as to the official teaching of the Catholic Church will allow us to circumscribe a problem of which only certain elements are found in the Koran. It will thus be possible to see both the common points of the two faiths and their irreducible divergencies.

A. ADAM AND THE ORIGINAL STATE.

1) After the creation of earth, heaven and the angels, God decided to create man. He apprises the angels of his purpose:

The Lord said to the angels, "I shall put on earth a vicar." (2, 28) In contrast with the angels, Adam is composed of clay, earth (*tîn*, 7, 11; *sulalat min tîn* 23, 12; *tîn lazib* 37, 11; *hama' masnûn, salsal,* 15, 26, 28, 33; 55, 13) all expressions which indicate the earthy origin of Adam. After having formed him of clay, God says to him:

"Be!"—and he becomes. (3, 52)—and God gives him of his "spirit." (15, 29; 32, 8; 38, 72)

2) Adam is superior to the angels, who are obliged, on God's order, to recognize his sovereignty (2, 31; 7, 10). This order provokes the revolt of Iblis who refuses to prostrate himself before Adam.[6]

---

[5] For a more detailed account, see the essay of Father M.-J. NICOLAS, O.P., in chapter VIII of the present volume.

[6] Because he is created from fire, whereas Adam is created from earth. God expels him from paradise. Satan obtains a reprieve until the final resurrection: he will pass his time seducing men: "Because thou hast degraded me," says he to God, "I will lay wait for men in thy strait way; then will I come upon them from before and from behind and from their right hand and from their left; and thou shalt not find the greater part of them thankful" (7, 11-17). This action of the evil on the soul is capital in the Moslem conception of the moral struggle in which man is engaged in this world.

3) God gives to Adam a partner, his wife (7, 189). The two are placed in a garden, living in a state of innocence:

Their nakedness was hidden to them. (7, 19)

They do not suffer hunger, thirst, or heat there (20, 116-117); but they are not immortal (7, 19).

4) God makes Adam aware of the "names" of creatures. Commentators see in this a communication of an infused universal knowledge.

B. ADAM'S SIN

1) Adam's fall is reported several times in the Koran. God had placed Adam and his wife in the garden, allowing them to eat as they liked of all the fruits of the garden (2, 33), but forbidding them to eat of the tree of immortality,[7] warning them against Satan, their enemy, who will try to get them expelled from paradise and make them unfortunate (20, 115). Satan, however, succeeds in seducing them:

> "O Adam, dwell thou and thy wife in paradise; and eat (of the fruits thereof) wherever ye will; but approach not this tree, lest ye become (of the number) of the unjust." And Satan proposed to them both, that he would discover unto them their nakedness, which was hidden from them; and he said: "Your Lord hath not forbidden you this tree, [for any other reason] but lest ye should become angels or lest ye become immortal. And he swore unto them [saying]: "Verily, I am [one] of those who counsel you aright." And he caused them to fall through deceit. And when they had tasted of the tree, their nakedness appeared unto them; and they began to join together the leaves of paradise, to cover themselves. And the Lord called to them [saying]: "Did I not forbid you this tree and [did I not] say unto you: 'Verily, Satan is your declared enemy?'" (7, 18-21)

2) Some commentators try to diminish Adam's guilt and want to consider his sin as mere negligence, in order to save the impeccability (*'isma*) of the 'first of the prophets.' Others, however—and this seems to be the prevalent opinion, following the testimony of the Koran itself:

Adam refused to obey his Lord, and was in error. (20, 119)

—consider the disobedience to have been a real fault, which occurred before the prophetic character was conferred on Adam.[8]

---

[7] It is the devil who, when tempting Adam, tells him that the tree from which it is forbidden to eat, is the tree of immortality.

[8] Moslem theology distinguishes between prophet and apostle. The prophet who is only prophet (*nabi*) receives from God a "mission of honor" before men. The apostle (*rasûl*) is commissioned by God to transmit to men a revealed Law. The apostle is necessarily a prophet, but not vice-versa. The apostle enjoys the privilege of impeccability (*'isma*). Cf. *Encl. of Islam*, s. v.; WENSINCK, *The Muslim Creed*, Cambr. Univ. Press, 1932, p. 203 sq.; SWEETMAN, *Islam and Christian Theology*, Lutterworth Press, London, 1947, Part I, vol. 2, p. 122 sq.; ELDER, *Commentary of Taftazani*, Columbia Univ. Press, N. Y. 1950 chap. 14.

C. PERSONAL CONSEQUENCES OF ADAM'S SIN

1) One of the first effects of Adam's disobedience is the apparition of concupiscence:

> And when they had tasted of the tree, their nakedness appeared to them. (7, 21)

2) Adam and Eve lose the advantages they had in paradise; they are obliged henceforth to live on the earth:

> Get down, the one of you an enemy to the other; and you shall have a dwelling place upon earth, and a provision for a season. (7, 23)

3) Nothing is said concerning the destiny of the knowledge given to Adam.

4) Adam and Eve repent of their fault. (7, 22)   God teaches Adam how to express his repentance:

> O Lord, we have dealt unjustly with our own souls and if thou forgive us not and be not merciful to us, we will [surely] be of those who perish. (2, 35; 7, 22)

God accepts his repentance:

> And then the Lord chose him, forgave him and guided him. (20, 120)[9]

5) And so the *personal* punishment of Adam is to leave his life of rest in paradise for a life of work and struggle on the earth.   But this punishment is not such as to deprive him of enjoying the wealth of the earth.

D. RELATION OF ADAM TO HIS POSTERITY: THE PROBLEM
OF THE TRANSMISSION OF HIS FAULT

1) Adam is the father of humanity; from him derive all men.   The Koran distinguishes in man a corporal element, and a spiritual one—his soul, which is a "secret" from God.   While the body comes by generation from Adam, we must inquire about the origin of the soul.

2) This problem has received divergent solutions.   It is said in the Koran that the Lord:

> . . . extracted from Adam's loins his descendants, and he made them bring testimony against themselves saying, "Am I not your Lord?" They said, "Surely, we attest it." (7, 172)

---

[9] Comment. of the *Manâr* t. 1, p. 283. The same author relies upon this text to reject the Christian dogma of original sin: "The pardon given by God to Adam consisted in guiding him in the true path, taking him out of the impasse into which he had fallen. . . . The mention of pardon given by God to man refutes the belief of Christians, who think that God ascribes the fault of Adam both to himself and to his progeniture, till Jesus comes to deliver them. Such a belief is rejected by sane reason and denied by sure Revelation coming to us from many sources." (*Ibid.*)

This is the famous 'Covenant' or *Mîthâq*. Some authors hold that God had in fact created all souls together and had them appear before him to acknowledge this Pact. These souls were kept in store (the *barzakh* according to Ibn Hazm) and then infused into their bodies when the time came. For others, *Mîthâq* only represents one of God's Ideas. Finally, others think that the souls are annihilated after having been created and summoned before God, and are re-created when the bodies are ready to receive them.

Irrespective of the solution given to this problem, the question remains whether, in the Islamic conception of the soul, the notion of a transmission of sin is possible; and, granted that the *guilt* is not transmissible, whether the *consequences* of that guilt could be passed to subsequent generations; i.e. does our soul actually bear the "wounds" of a previous fault of our first parents?

This problem is not easy to solve. Commentators and theologians have not treated it "formally." We are obliged to pick up from here and there dispersed elements of a solution.

Let us remark first that a certain number of terms designate the spiritual reality of the man, that which is responsible for his acts and is the subject of passions and virtues: *nafs* (soul), *rûh* (spirit), *qalb* (heart).

In the Koran, *nafs*[10], when it concerns man designates either the human being himself—and this is its most frequent use (3, 54; 12, 54; 51, 20, 21), or the human soul (6, 93; 50, 15; 64, 16 etc.)

The soul has three characteristics: a) It draws to evil, *ammâra bil-sû'* (12, 53). It murmurs in the ear (50, 15); it is associated with passions, bad desires, *al-hawâ*. Man must master it (79, 40), make it patient (18, 29) and fear its covetousness (59, 9). b) It reproduces and blames, *lawwâma* (75, 2). c) Finally, it is pacified, quieted, *mutma'inna* (89, 27).

The word *rûh*, which later was used to designate the spiritual element of man, receives five uses in the Koran: 1) Allâh breathes of his *rûh* into Adam, giving life to his body (15, 29; 38, 72; 32, 8), and into Maryam for the conception of 'Isa (21, 91; 66, 12). 2) Four verses associate *rûh* with the order (*amr*) of God, but are subject to discussion (17, 87; 16, 2; 40, 15; 45, 52). 3) In 4, 169, 'Isa is named a *rûh* emanated from God. 4) In 97, 4; 78, 38 and 70, 4, *rûh* is associated with the angels. 5) In 26, 193, *al-rûh al-amîn*, the faithful spirit comes down in Mohammed's heart to reveal the Koran. For most commentators, it here represents the angel Gabriel. In 19, 17 Allâh sends of his *rûh* to Maryam. In 16, 104, *rûh al-qudus* has sent the Koran to strengthen the believers. Three

---

[10] For *nafs*, see the excellent article of Mr. CALVERLY in *Encl. of Islam* where he studies also the *rûh*. One of the most detailed Arabic works concerning the origin and the destiny of the soul is the *Kitâb al-rûh.* of IBN QAYYIM AL-JAWZIYYA (several editions in India and in Egypt).

other texts assure that Allâh gives to 'Isa the help of the Holy Spirit (2, 91; 2, 254; 5, 109).

Rûh is never used in the Koran to designate the *ego*, the person, or the soul of a human being.

Qalb (heart) is used very frequently in the Koran (nearly 200 times). Apart from its anatomical meaning, it designates that which is most intimate in man: it is the seat of his faith (16, 108), of the peace of his soul (2, 262; 13, 28), of prophetic inspiration (26, 194), of the understanding of spiritual things (22, 45), of ignorance (7, 178), of blindness (22, 45) and generally of passions and virtues.

Starting from these Koranic data, and under the gradually increasing influence of Greek philosophy, Moslem thinkers tried to elaborate a doctrine of the soul. The first *Mu'tazilites* and *Ash'arites*,[11] attached to an atomistic conception of reality, do not admit immaterial substances, and consider the soul to consist of subtile molecules which die and resuscitate with the body. They practically identify the *rûh*, the *'aql* (intelligence) and the *qalb*, the three words designating the most "spiritual" part of man, the seat of his faith and virtues. However, gradually, beginning with Ghazzâli[12] and under the growing influence of Greek philosophy, some theologians were able to affirm that the soul is spiritual.

Ghazzâli particularly tried to synthesize, from a philosophical and mystical point of view, the multiple data of the Koran and of Tradition. He has consecrated, among other works, a treatise of his *Ihyâ'* to the definition of the four terms: *qalb, rûh, nafs* and *'aql*. We need not enter into the details of this analysis. All we have to know is that to him the *qalb* (heart) means the reality of man: it is what apprehends, praises and questions; it has a mysterious relation with the material organ which bears the same name. The *rûh* (spirit) is materially a subtile body, the source of which is the concavity of the heart, whence it diffuses into the other parts of the body like the light of the lamp in a room. But from the spiritual standpoint it is in fact the correspondent of the "heart," i.e. that in man which knows and perceives (*al-latîfa l-'âlima al-mudrika min al-insân*). It is "the secret coming from God" (17, 87).

---

[11] The *Mu'tazilites* are theologians of rationalistic tendencies; they affirm the objectivity of good, and stress man's liberty in such wise as to affirm that man creates his good actions. *Ash'arism*, founded by Ash'ari (†935), represents the common theology of Islam. In opposition to the Mu'tazilites, the Ash'arites stress the absolute and unconditioned omnipotence of God, Creator of good and evil. They are strictly occasionalists. Cf. GARDET-ANAWATI, *Introduction à la théologie musulmane*, Paris, Vrin, 1948, pp. 39-67.

[12] JUWAYNI (Imâm al-Haramayn, †1085), the master of Ghazzâli, still thinks that the soul is composed of subtile corpuscles (Cf. *Irshâd*, ed. LUCIANI, Paris, 1938, p. 320). GHAZZALI (the Algazel of mediaeval Christian authors), called the "Proof of Islâm," is the greatest Moslem theologian. His most important book is *Ihyâ' 'olûm al-dîn* (*"The revivification of religious science"*). We quote from the Cairo edition (1352 H./1933).

On the same lines, *nafs* also has two meanings: either it means the sensible and concupiscible appetite (this is the sense in which mystics use it), or else it designates man himself, embracing then the three functions of the soul mentioned by the Koran: the pacified soul, the blaming soul and the soul provoking to evil. This third aspect of the soul may be referred to as the carnal soul.

Briefly, we can say that for Moslem doctors there exists in man a material element, the physical body (muscles, nerves, flesh, bones, etc.), and a superior "vital" element, named almost equivalently, *soul, heart, spirit*. This vital element presents a double aspect: the first "passional," designated either as *nafs* without any qualificative, in the senses of "carnal soul," or as soul "provoking to evil" (*nafs ammâra bil-sû'*); the second, spiritual which is the soul in its highest aspirations.

The twofold question set forth above has now to be solved: whether the inner conflict in man is the result of a fault or wound, or constitutes a natural, inborn state.

The Koran itself asserts that man has been created *variable* (or *unquiet, impatient*), *halû'*: depressed when he is touched by misfortune, and insolent when in possession of some riches (70, 19-21). Râzî in his great commentary[13], quoting Bâqillâni, explains that *fear* (*al-hala'*) may designate either the interior state of soul or simply its outward manifestation in words or actions. But as God blames man because of it, He could not have created it directly. If this fear were necessary, it would be impossible for man to get rid of it. These outward manifestations are then due to man. This reasoning may be applied to all the bad tendencies which exist "naturally" in man. The anthologies of proverbs and the moral treatises concerning practical life do not fail to point out the conflict in man between his bad instincts and his inward propensity to good. The violence of the fight varies from person to person, but exists in everyone. But Moslem moralists are likewise unanimous in recognizing that it is precisely the aim of education and religion to restrain these bad instincts, and that they succeed in their efforts.

In the struggle to which the soul is subject, and which is natural to man, two exterior agents play a considerable role: the devil by his solicitations to evil, and the angel by his good inspirations. In fact there exists a vast literature, based on the Koran, concerning the role of Iblis in the temptation of man (*talbîs Iblîs*).[14] We have seen previously that Satan has refused to bow to Adam, thus disobeying God. He obtained from God

---

[13] *Mafâtîh al-ghayb*, Cairo, 1308 H./1890, t. 8, p. 211.

[14] Especially the book of IBN AL-JAWZI (597 H./1200) which bears precisely this title (Cairo, 1928, 412 pages). Ghazzâli devotes a long chapter to this action of the devil on man. Cf. *Ihyâ*, t. 3, p. 23 sq. where he analyzes with care the manifold kinds of temptations.

the permission to stay in this world till the resurrection, in order to perse-
cute men. Tradition attributes to the Prophet the assertion:

Satan circulates in man like his own blood

—suggesting that there is a kind of "infection" of the human soul by evil.

Another *hadîth* says:

Satan has put his trumpet to the heart of man

But the *hadîth* continues:

. . . if this man mentions God's name, the devil goes away; on the
contrary, if he forgets God, the devil swallows his soul.[15]

The Moslem mystics (*sûfîs*) have improved upon this view and con-
tinually warn their disciples of the necessity to fight their hidden passions:

Your most fierce enemy is the soul you bear in your heart.

That this action of the devil is universal, is shown by the famous *hadîth:*

Every Adam's son coming into this world, is touched by Satan, except
Mary's son and his mother.

—which we will discuss in the second section. According to commentators,
this 'touching' by the devil, this 'sting,' consists only in temptation. The
devil finds in human nature itself an ally—its own passions—which he is
very eager to lead astray from the good by all kinds of "cheatings" and
"illusions."

The proof that the conflict is not a disequilibrium irremediably ruining
human nature, and making it unable to resist the devil and accomplish
the good, is found in a series of texts which show that this nature is not
fundamentally bad and that the action of the devil is not irresistible.

Let it be pointed out first, that the Koran insists on the perfect character
of the creation of man:

We have created man the best creation (*taqwîm*).[16]

Râzî glosses that this applies both to the harmony of the body which
stands erect, unlike that of other animals and to the perfection of the intelligence, fitted with knowledge and capable of education etc.[17]

God has further created man in a state of nature (*fitra*) predisposed to
recognize God as his master in the line of true religion. The adolescent
is led astray by his parents—Jews, Christians or Sabeans—who divert him
away from Islam, the natural religion of humanity. In other words, human
intelligence is *naturally* ordained to the true God and the true religion:

[15] *Talbîs Iblîs,* p. 25.
[16] It is true that the verse adds immediately: "and we have put him among the
lowest of the low" (95, 4), but this refers to men who are precipitated into hell.
[17] *Mafâtîh al-ghayb* t. 8, p. 433.

only impropitious circumstances of education or social milieu turn him away from the true way.

Moreover, every soul has signed the "covenant" with God, has appeared before Him in the pre-eternity, a token that "there is a natural religion engraved in all men providing a rational basis for the apostolate in Islam."[18]

Further, when, after his revolt, Satan announces to God that he is going to seduce all men, God tells him:

> You have no power over them—only over those who follow you. (15, 42)

Râzî comments:

> Briefly, Satan wanted to make believe that he had power over some creatures of God. God manifested his lie by saying that he had absolutely no power over any of them.[19]

Ghazzâli, who has finely analyzed the movements of human soul, although seeming sometimes pessimistic as to certain bad instincts of men, does not fail moreover to write:

> The child is a deposit entrusted to his parents. His soul is a precious substance, innocent, denuded of all inscriptions or pictures. He receives all that you engrave on it, and tends in whatever direction you incline him.[20]

The Koran frequently stresses the exclusively personal responsibility of man. It repeatedly (6, 164; 17, 16; 35, 19; etc.) avers that:

> . . . every man is responsible only for his own acts. Souls act for themselves only, and no one will bear the burden of another.

Modern commentators constantly quote these texts in order to reject any idea of redemption being required by reason of original sin. And the most recent Moslem biographer of Mohammed only expresses the common opinion of Islam when he writes:

> The idea of a redemption by a Messiah who [pours out] his blood for the sins of his brothers in Adam is certainly fitting, and what has been written on this subject deserves to be studied from the poetic, moral and psychological points of view. But the principle affirmed by Islam, that "no sinner will bear the burden of another" and that every man, on the day of judgement, will receive a retribution according to his actions—good if he has done good, bad if he has done bad— makes the rational reconciliation of the two faiths [viz. Christian and Moslem] impossible. The logic of Islam is so precise that all efforts of reconciliation will be unsuccessful because the contradiction between

[18] MASSIGNON, *La Passion d'al-Hallâj*, Paris, Geuthner, 1922, t. 2, p. 607.
[19] *Mafâtîh al-ghayb* t.5, p. 280.
[20] Cf. WENSINCK, *La pensée de Ghazzâli*, Paris, Maisonneuve, 1940, p. 64, sq.
[21] Husayn HAYKAL, *Hayât Mohammad*, Cairo 3rd ed. 1939, p. 8.

the idea of redemption and the idea of personal retribution is evident. "No father will be of value for his son and no child will be of value for his father." (31, 32)[21]

*   *   *

At the end of this first section, the results of our investigation can be summarized as follows:

1)   Islam admits an original sin committed by Adam and his wife, our first parents, created first in a state of innocence. But this fall had only personal consequences and they have, moreover, been forgiven. The notion of an original sin transmitted by Adam to his posterity is absolutely opposed to the teaching of Islam.

2)   Man has been created in order to be the vicar of God in the world. He is at the same time soul and body. From this duality results naturally a struggle between the two elements, but this is not the consequence of the original parental sin. The devil takes occasion of this opposition to tempt man and lead him to transgress God's Law. This action of the devil is, however, not a consequence of Adam's original sin: already before Adam's disgrace, Satan had decided to busy himself on earth tempting man.

II

MARY'S CONCEPTION AND BIRTH

The preceding section of this paper has solved, though in an essentially negative way, the first problem which confronted us in the study of the Immaculate Conception in Islam: we found that the notion of original sin transmitted to humanity by its first parents is rejected by Moslem authorities. Now the problem of Our Lady's conception must be investigated directly, by an examination of the texts which describe Mary's birth and its circumstances.

Two texts will retain our attention. The first concerns Mary's birth mentioned by *sûra* 3, *Al-'Imrân* (*'Imrân* designating in the Koran Mary's father):

> God has surely chosen (*istafa*) Adam and Noah and the family of 'Imrân above [the rest] of the world; a race [descending] the one from the other . . . [Remember] when the wife of 'Imrân said, "Lord, verily I have vowed unto thee that which is in my womb, to be dedicated [to thy service]: accept [it] therefore of me; for thou art he who heareth and knoweth." And when she was delivered of it, she said, "Lord, verily I have brought forth a female," and God well knew what she had brought forth—and a male is not as a female. "I have called her Mary. And I commend her to thy protection and also her issue, against Satan, driven away with stones."

Therefore the Lord accepted her with a gracious acceptance and caused her to bear an excellent offspring. And Zacharias took care of the child; whenever Zacharias went into the chamber to her, he found provisions with her: and he said, "O Mary, whence hadst thou this?" She answered, "This is from God, for God provideth for whom he pleaseth without measure."

The second text concerns the Annunciation: the angels say to Mary:

O Mary, God has chosen thee and has purified thee. He has chosen thee above (all) the women of the two worlds. (3, 41)

Before undertaking the analysis of these texts, it must be pointed out that Mary's birth, though associated with special favors from God, remains, unlike that of Jesus, a normal conjugal event. The Koran links her to the lineage of the Prophet through her family, the 'Imrân, by Abraham, Noah and Adam. Commentators will add some details, asserting that she is of Davidic descent. The confusion made by the Koran between Mary, sister of Moses, and Mary, mother of Jesus, is not relevant to our problem.[22] Let us consider the texts themselves.

Some terms deserve special attention. First is the word *"choice"* or *"election."* May we understand its use with regard to Mary as meaning a special grace placing her absolutely above all creatures? Judging by the context, the answer is certainly negative, since the same *sûra* speaks again of the choice of Adam, of Noah, of Abraham's family and of Mary's family. The comprehensive commentary of Alûsi[23] asserts, in commenting on this text, that regarding prophets, the choice consists in a free gift by God of a holy soul with appropriate faculties, and sometimes even of physical perfections, which put the recipient above other creatures. These prerogatives differ from one prophet to another. Mary has had the greatest part (*al-hazz al-awfar*) of some of them, but others had their share also. Adam, for instance, the first of the prophets, was formed by God himself, was given the knowledge of the names of all creatures, received from the angels tribute of honor and, moreover, dwelt near God. Noah is, after Adam, the father of humanity. His prayers for unbelievers and believers were heard. Abraham's family had the great honor of giving birth to Mohammed, and thus received the Revelation of the Koran. The privilege of Jesus and Mary lay in their being given as extraordinary signs (*âyât*) to the 'two worlds,' i.e. this world and the next.

The same term of choice is used again twice in the second text, being

---

[22] In the Old Testament (Ex. 6, 20), 'Amrâm is the father of Aaron and Moses and of their sister Mary. In the Koran, he is the Holy Virgin's Father and the name is read 'Imrân. Further, Mary is addressed in these terms, "O sister of Aaron." Some Moslem commentators think that there exist two Marys, two 'Imrân and even two Aarons, with a separation of eighteen centuries between them. The problem of Aaron's sister could be solved on the lines of that of Christ's brothers.

[23] *Rûh al-m'ânî*, Cairo, 1301 H./1883, t. 1, p. 560.

associated with the word *"purification"*: "God has chosen thee and has purified thee. He has chosen thee above (all) the women of the two worlds." As quoted in the commentary of the *Manâr*, God caused Mary's desire for perfection to grow according to the law of nature (*al-fitra*) and thus elevated her gradually and constantly in spirituality. The first choice, therefore, consisted in admitting her to God's service, which was reserved to men. The second was the privilege granted her to speak with angels, and to keep in perfect accord with God's ways (*kamâl al-hidâya*). Mohammed 'Abduh thought this second privilege to be the giving birth to a prophet without being touched by man.

The purification (*tathîr*) has been interpreted in different ways: 1) it may be conceived as an absence of *menses,* and hence the possibility for her to enter the most reserved place of the temple (*mihrâb*). Fâtima, Mohammed's daughter has been named *al-Zahrâ,*' the Brilliant, because of her amenorrhea. 2) According to al-Jalâl, the purification consisted in the absence of relations with man. Mohammed 'Abduh interprets the term in its widest sense, as purification from all that is bad. It is not useless to point out that this purification of Mary is connected by commentators with the purification of Mohammed's chest. The Koran reports God as saying to Mohammed, "Have we not opened your chest and laid far from you the burden which overpowered your shoulders?" (94, 1) Some authors have materialized this hint and believed the following legend: when Mohammed was only four years old, two angels opened his chest, took out his heart and washed it with snow water[24]. There is here perhaps an attempt of Moslem hagiography to avoid leaving to Jesus and Mary the monopoly of preservation from the devil. The founder of Islam could not be kept inferior to them in this respect.

In the text concerning Mary's birth, her mother, *after* bringing her forth, confided her to God and begged him to keep her and her offspring safe from Satan. It is in explaining this text that commentators quote the famous *hadîth:*

> Every Adam's son coming into this world is touched [or: "stung"] by Satan except Jesus' Mother and her son.

The commentary of the Manâr admits that this *hadîth* is certainly authentic from the point of view of transmission (*isnâd*), being found in the Corpus of the two *shaykhs* (Moslem and Bukhâri) and others. It finds a confirmation of this in the *hadîth* on the purification of Mohammed's heart, which is supposed to mean that Satan's part therein was removed, leaving him no hold at all on the Prophet's heart. When Mohammed was asked whether he also had a devil, he replied, "Yes, but God has

[24] Cf. Tor ANDRAE, *Mahomet, sa vie et sa doctrine* [French trans.] Paris, Maisonneuve, 1945, p. 34-35.

helped me against him. The devil has become Moslem." The text excludes, as far as Mohammed is concerned, not only the possibility of
succumbing to temptation, but even any power of the devil to tempt him.
Mohammed 'Abduh, representing the rationalistic tendency, remarks that
the three *hadîth* (of the sting, of conversion of Mohammed's devil to
Islam and of the purification of Mohammed's heart) are unparalleled
(*âhâd*)[25] and cannot, therefore, compel belief. He thinks it possible to interpret them metaphorically. For others, it is quite useless to seek to penetrate
the way in which this preservation was realized, suffice it to be held for
true, since affirmed by the Prophet. They see in it only his intention to
magnify Jesus and his mother.

It should be pointed out, continues the commentary, that such a privilege does not by itself involve any superiority of any one of the three,
Jesus, Mary and Mohammed, over other creatures; it is indeed possible
that others not so preserved had other qualities which the three who were
purified may have lacked. For instance, Mary is not superior to Abraham
and Moses, because, though the prophets were not preserved from the
sting of Satan from their birth, they have yet received the gift of prophecy,
and enjoyed the divine friendship (*khulla*), conversing with God. These
gifts surpass that of preservation from Satan's attacks.

These qualifications do not in any way diminish the immense respect
and the great place given to the holy Virgin in Islamic doctrine and piety.
Commentators do not fail to remark that she has received a special, mysterious, nurture from God, and the simple faithful have readily expressed
their devotion to the Koranic details telling of the miraculous birth of
Jesus and the gentle care given him by his mother.[26] Since the beginning
of Islam, based on the Koran and on some words of the Prophet, a superiority over other women has always been recognized in Mary. Agreement
is not, however, unanimous on this point. It is known that the prophet's
wives were considered "the mothers of the believers." The Koran says:
"O Wives of the Prophet, you are not like any of women." (32, 32) This
is surely not a question of special grace bestowed on them—of such graces
neither the Koran nor commentators speak—but of a juridical disposition
by which remarriage is prohibited to these women after the Prophet's
death. According to this *hadîth,* the noblest women are Mary, Khadija
(Mohammed's first wife) and Fâtima (his daughter). But in paradise,
Mary is first of all. Indeed Mohâmmed is reported to have said to his
young favorite wife:

You will be the princess of women in paradise, after Mary.[27]

---

[25] A *hadîth âhâd* is a *hadîth* which is transmitted originally from one source only.
[26] For the manifestation of this piety, cf. 'Abd EL-JALIL, *Marie et l'Islam*, p. 79
and sq.
[27] Mentioned by 'Abd EL-JALIL, p. 75 quoting Ibn SA'D, *Tabaqât*, II, II, p. 40.

CONCLUSION

We may sum up the results of our research in the following points:

1. If we hold to the precise technical meaning of the expression, *Immaculate Conception,* i.e. preservation from original sin at conception, we must say that even the *notion* of such a doctrine is absent from the common teaching of Islam in which the dogma of a transmissible original sin is formally denied.

2. It is possible that the Christian belief in the sanctity of Jesus and Mary, and Mary's preservation from original sin, has been diffused in Islamic thought, where it was not correctly understood. Only some elements were kept, the traces of which are found in the Koran and *hadîth.* These echoes of the Christian creed as later interpreted by Islamic doctors, though confirming the eminent position of Jesus and Mary, are however unable to grant them a privilege so irrelevant to the Moslem conception of human nature and of sin.

3. That Catholics, in the light of their faith, can find hidden meanings in the materials lying in some Koranic texts or in a few *hadîth,* and recognize in them the dogma of the Immaculate Conception, is possible. But such a construction constitutes a "Christian interpretation" of Islamic data, building up a "wished-for" Islam distinct from the *de facto* Islam, i. e. from the Islam really lived by Moslem believers, and officially taught by their doctors. As a means of promoting understanding and cooperation, and in order to induce the real Islam to become the "wished-for Islam," such an approach is highly laudable. The success of the Ephesus pilgrimage, the spiritual value of which infinitely exceeds its touristic aspect, is extremely convincing in this respect.[28]

Indeed, the contrary would have been astonishing. If we recall on the one hand, the role of the Holy Virgin in the mediation of graces, and, on the other, the reflections of the Christian faith in Mary so mysteriously preserved both in Islamic texts and in the hearts of Moslem believers, we cannot help seeing in the Marian activity so magnificiently displayed today a providential signpost of the road to be followed. Perhaps God is inviting us to pursue this direction in order that those who are, like ourselves, sons of Abraham, and have such great respect for Mary's holiness, may be brought to know and love fully the Son of her whose most beautiful title, eclipsing all others, is that of "Mother of God," *Theotokos.*

[28] In the city of Ephesus (near Smyrna in Turkey), there exist a grotto of the "Seven sleepers," a church dedicated to St. John the Apostle and another one to the Holy Virgin (Theotokos). A tradition affirms that the tomb of the "Holy Virgins" is also there. Cf. L. MASSIGNON, *"Les fouilles archéologiques d'Ephèse et leur importance religieuse (pour la chrétienté et l'Islam),"* in *Les Mardis de Dar El-Salam,* Le Caire, 1952. Owing to the action of Msgr. Descuffi, Catholic Bishop of Smyrna and M. Massignon, a Marian pilgrimage has been organized at Ephesus and has received encouragement from the Turkish authorities. Even Mohammedan Turks attend the pilgrimage.

Pulchra ut luna

XIII

The Iconography of the Immaculate Conception

Maurice Vloberg

The mystery of the Immaculate Conception is one of the most beautiful, but also one of the most delicate subjects of Marian iconography. It poses difficult problems, and needs to be rendered with precision; at the same time, discretion also is called for. Furthermore, a certain contemplative gift is necessary if one is to "understand" this mystery, to have a "feeling" for it, as its best interpreters did. Along with the Divine Maternity, the Immaculate Conception has inspired arts' purest masterpieces—above all, when the great Spaniards applied their faith and genius to it.

It is well known that in religious art, the evolution of iconography nearly always keeps pace with the evolution of the doctrine and liturgy. We will begin, therefore, by summarizing what is known for certain about the origins of the feast of the Conception.[1]

It was first celebrated by the Oriental Church, beginning in the seventh century.[2] Only later are traces of it found in the West: in England, perhaps also in Ireland,[3] in the tenth century, possibly even in the ninth. From the north it passed into Normandy, where stories of miracles, such as the vision of the Abbot Helsin, and the adventure of the none-too-edifying canon of Rouen,[4] furthered its spread. Numerous documents from the first half of the thirteenth century prove that in the duchy at that time, the feast had very distinctly the sense of *Immaculate* Conception. At the University of Paris, the students from the Nation of Normandy propagated it with such zeal that it was called *Festum Nationis Normanicae*—"the Feast of the Normans."

In the twelfth century, it was adopted and maintained by the Church of Lyons, in spite of the fiery protest against this "novelty" which St. Bernard addressed to the canons of that city (1140). Through the theological debates carried on by the Franciscans and the doctors of the Sorbonne[5]

---

[1] For further details, cf. chapters IV, V, VI, of the present volume.

[2] Cf. chapter III of the present volume, p. 114.

[3] Cf. chapter III of the present volume, p. 125 ff.

[4] Cf. chapter IV, of the present volume, p. 128, and the twelfth century sermon appended below, p. 522 ff.

[5] The seventh centenary of the foundation of which was observed in 1957.

during the thirteenth and fourteenth centuries, the doctrine was made more precise.

The artist cannot claim to express, *with the same precision* as the theologian, this mystery which is, indeed, essentially inexpressible by sensible forms. But the artists attempted at least to make it clear for the mass of the faithful by narrative form, in which the story of the meeting of Anne and Joachim was employed to allude to Mary's privilege.

This primitive manner of suggesting the mystery was gradually replaced by a more subtle manner in which symbolism was used—and also abused —the better to bring out the elements of the belief.

I
NARRATIVE TYPE REPRESENTATIONS

Byzantine art and that of the high Middle Ages represented this mystery solely by the story of the circumstances in which it took place. Some iconographers call these representations *historical,* but this term seems strange in such matter. Like the Fathers, the homelists, and the hagiographers who spoke of this mystery, the artists had no other source of information then the apocryphal gospels—the *Protogospel of James* and the *Pseudo-Matthew*[6] which recount the legend of St. Anne, her sterility and the grief it caused her, and the angel's announcement of Mary's birth.[7]

The epilog of this legend is the *Hypapante,* or the Meeting of Anne and Joachim at the Golden Gate. Oriental art chose this episode[8] as the representative image of what was then the object of the Feast of the Conception—not only the fact itself of Mary's Conception, but still more the holiness of this "first instant" of the *Theotokos,* and its importance in the economy of man's salvation.

To list even the principal works would be too long and tedious.[9] It will be more profitable to consider the image itself. (See the frontispiece, and plates I and II.) Its symbolic value was questionable, because it was liable to be misunderstood: it could lead people to believe that the Blessed Virgin had been conceived by the chaste embrace of her parents at this meeting. In fact, we find engravings in Books of Hours in which precisely such an interpretation of the scene is indicated by the following rubric: *"Taliter concepta est beata Maria*—Thus was the Blessed Mary con-

---

[6] See chapter II of the present volume, pp. 58 f. and 81 f.

[7] The legend of St. Anne, as recounted in the *Pseudo-Matthew* and the *Protogospels of James,* is given below, p. 513 ff.

[8] Note that the episode does not occur in the Greek text of the Protogospel of James but only in the Latin version, i.e., the *Liber de nativitate Mariae;* cf. p. 519.

[9] An abundant list is given in several of the studies cited in the bibliography at the end of this chapter. We will follow this same policy with regard to the other themes treated in this article: complete lists of names would have obliged us to triple its length.

ceived."[10] This recalls the dream of the author of *Romanz de Saint Fanuel*, who was doubtless inspired by the mythical parthenogenesis of the Orient: this Fanuel, who is given as the father of St. Anne, is supposed to have been engendered of the perfume of a flower.[11]

Some iconographers give a similar interpretation to the scene of the *Hypapante*. Msgr. Barbier de Montault, speaking of a representation of this scene on a Vatican ivory, makes the following remark: ". . . Anne and Joachim meet at the Golden Gate, and of their chaste kiss, Mary is conceived, holy and immaculate."[12] Obviously, the reverend archeologist is not giving his personal belief here, but is only explaining the meaning which this image did in fact have.

The mystery would not have been represented thus, if due consideration had been given to the doctrine. In the words of Saint Bernard, ". . . Mary conceived (Jesus) by the operation of the Holy Spirit, but she herself was not conceived in this way. She gave birth while remaining a virgin, but she herself was not born of a virgin."

As a matter of fact, the belief in St. Anne's virginity—"a belief originating in a fable," as Jean Molan characterized it in the sixteenth century[13]— was condemned in 1677 by Pope Innocent XI.

A REALISTIC THEME.

The art of the fifteenth century pushed the narrative style much too far, with a realistic image that strikes us today as in very bad taste: the infant visible in the womb of St. Anne.[14]

[10] Cf. BOURASSÉ, *Summa Aurea*, t. II, c. 948. Cf. FOURNÉE, p. 15 f.

[11] The poem was published by C. CHABANEAU, according to Ms. 350 of Montpellier (Paris, 1889).

[12] *Annales Archéologiques*, XXVII, p. 85.

[13] J. MOLANUS [= VERMEULEN], *De historia sacrarum imaginum et picturarum pro vero earum usu contra abusus*, p. 393.

[14] The use of such 'realistic' images was not confined to those who believed in the Immaculate Conception. The 'maculists' also employed them to represent the sanctification of Mary in her mother's womb. The engraving reproduced in figure 4 appeared in *Rosario della gloriosa Vergine Maria con figure adornato* . . . of the Dominican, Alberto DA CASTELVETRO (Venice, 1616, folio 39v). The maculist sense is made explicit by the commentary on the facing page, which reads: "Contempla quì . . . concetta la gloriosa Vergine Maria nel ventre di Sant'Anna . . . Iddio . . . mandò il Spirito santo nella gloriosa Vergine Maria subito, dapoi che fu unita l'anima rationale al suo corpo virgineo quella mondando da ogni macola di peccato contratto per ogni persona, che è concetto d'huomo e donna."

Figure 3. THE SANCTIFICATION OF MARY BEFORE HER BIRTH.

This overly explicit motif is somewhat spiritualized by the symbolic details of the altarpiece at Frankfort which will be described below.[15] St. Anne appears between two angels with a dove before her breast—symbol of her purity, unless, perhaps, the artist wished thereby to indicate the particular operation of the Holy Spirit in this mystery of Mary's immediate sanctification. Rays of light stream forth from the body of the tiny infant in the mother's womb. Overhead, God appears, addressing to His Elect the words of the Canticle of Canticles (4:7) inscribed on a scroll: *"Tota pulchra es, Amica mea, et macula non est in te."* In the two corners, to the right and to the left, David and Solomon likewise bear appropriate texts: the former, a verse of a psalm (9:36) *"Quaeretur peccatum illius et non invenietur"*—"Her sin shall be sought for, and shall not be found";[16] the latter, a passage from Proverbs (8:24): *"nondum erant abissi et ego jam concepta eram"*—"The depths were not as yet, and I was already conceived."[17]

One of the most beautiful miniatures of the famous Grimani Breviary[18] represents this mystery in the same way. St. Anne, seated on a Gothic throne, between David and Solomon richly robed in chaperons, seems plunged in meditation, attentive to what takes place within her. Before her breast, enveloped in a glory, the Immaculate Virgin is seen in the form of a tiny, naked infant, with hands joined. Two latin inscriptions specify the allusion to the privilege of the exemption from original sin.

The two biblical kings, whose presence was doubtless intended to recall the noble lineage of St. Anne and of her daughter, are found in other mystico-realist compositions. A fifteenth century miniature (plate V) represents them on either side of a throne, before which St. Anne stands with her hands joined and with the child visible within her.[19] They are also in this same place of honor on an illuminated page of an Office inscribed, *"Of the Conception,"* in a folio manuscript containing five Masses by Pierre de la Rue, *Maître de chapelle* of Margaret of Austria.[20] Other drawings on the same and following page represent St. Leo, Alexander V, Sixtus IX, St. Gregory the Great, Nicholas IV, and Innocent V, each holding a parchment on which can be read his declaration of the Immaculate Conception. An analogous composition occurs in

---

[15] P. 487.

[16] The Latin word *illius* can be taken as either masculine or feminine, and so can be translated by *his* or *her*. The context makes it clear that the former sense is intended, and so the Douay-Rheims version reads, *"his* sin." Since, however, the passage is here being applied to the Blessed Virgin, we must translate it, *"her* sin."

[17] G. DE TERVARENT, "Le retable de Sainte Anne au musée de Frankfort," in his *Enigmes de l'art du moyen age*, t. II, Paris, 1941, pp. 39 ff.

[18] Illuminated about 1475.—Venice, Bibl. Marciana. Not all the miniatures of this remarkable manuscript were executed at that time. The Virgin with the biblical symbols (plate XIV), among others, dates from the first quarter of the sixteenth century.

[19] Paris, Bibliothèque Nationale, nouv. acq. lat. 1140, f. 1.

[20] Ms. belonging to the city of Malines.

Figure 4.   ST. ANNE WITH MARY AND JESUS.
Early fifteenth century.

a small painting on wood from the sixteenth century, at the Church of St. Stephen, in Beauvais.

In a tableau attributed to Jean Bellegambe (ca. 1534-1535), in the Museum of Douai, the principal subject is accompanied by a context that is both legendary and allegorical. St. Anne, with her hands joined, is kneeling on a rich prie-dieu, draped and cushioned, in the manner of the noble ladies whose portraits we find in the Books of Hours; the immaculate fruit of her womb, represented as a naked infant in half figure, appears in a glory. On either side, under the shadow of Renaissance structures, a pope, cardinal, and other dignitaries of the Church contemplate her, while various episodes of the legend are enacted on the landscape in the background.

The *Heures a l'usage d'Angers*, bearing the mark of Simon Vostre (1510), present an engraving of this realistic theme with a noteworthy variation. Here the idea of the Immaculate Conception fuses with that of the Divine Maternity: the rays which stream out from St. Anne's lap englobe the Blessed Virgin, who is represented not merely as an infant conceived, but also as one who will conceive: for Mary holds the Child Jesus in her own lap. (Cf. figure 4.) Biblical symbols encircle the group, and their symbolism is supplemented in the text, by such declarations as the following:

> *Celici cives, reges terrae colunt;*
> *Sterilis parit: miratur natura;*
> *Stupet infernus, videns sine labe*
> *Virginem nasci.*

The chisel gave still greater relief to this theme. Let us mention a sixteenth century wood carving in the Church of St. Stephen in Beauvais, and a statue in wood, from the same epoch, the work of an atelier of Verneuil-au-Perche (Orne); the latter is conserved at the Museum of Norman Art at Rouen.[21]

Among the stained glass windows, we may mention that of St. Valerian in Chateaudun (Loire-et-Cher), which represents a girl emerging from a golden glory, with eyes lowered and hands joined.[22]

II

SYMBOLIC REPRESENTATIONS

The narrative type of image, as we have said, not only was insufficient, it suggested an interpretation bordering on the heretical. It was, therefore,

---

[21] Canon PORÉE, *Note sur une statue de sainte Anne,* Mâcon, 1901.

[22] Ch. MÉTAIS, "Un vitrail de Sainte Anne du XVIe siècle," *Bulletin archéologique,* 1903, p. 519.—Curiously enough, this realistic image of the Conception is the only one alluded to by the German visionary, Catherine Emmerich (1824), in her *Life of the Blessed Virgin Mary,* trans. Palairet (Springfield, Ill., Templegate, 1954, p. 61.)

abandoned for other expressions in which exegesis and symbolism intervened to place the emphasis on the true substance of the mystery—Mary's initial, perpetual and perfect sanctity.

These superior formulas were inspired by three figures drawn from

Figure 5. THE SPOUSE OF THE CANTICLE
OF CANTICLES. Fifteenth century.

Sacred Scriptures: the woman of the Protogospel who is to crush the head of the Serpent[23] (cf. plates VII and XVIII), the Woman of the

---

[23] "I will put enmities between thee and the woman, and thy seed and her seed: she shall crush thy head, and thou shalt lie in wait for her heel." (Genesis 3:15, according to the Vulgate, which was the version in use during the period being treated)

Apocalypse[24] (cf. figure 12), and the Spouse of the Canticle of Canticles[25] —the *tota pulchra,* pure of every shadow of stain. (Cf. figure 5.) The attributes of the Woman of the Apocalypse—the rays of the sun, the crown of stars and the crescent moon beneath her feet—were bestowed on the Spouse of the Canticle of Canticles, and the resulting theme, enriched by a selection of biblical metaphors, provided the finest reflection of the doctrine of Mary's original exemption and impeccability.[26]

We will sketch the principle features of this iconography, in which the traditional belief expressed itself more and more firmly during the fifteenth and sixteenth centuries.

THE WOMAN CRUSHING THE SERPENT'S HEAD.

According to a tradition of the church of Verdun—a tradition accepted by the Bollandists[27]—Bishop St. Pulchronius, upon his return from the Council of Chalcedon (451), erected a church in honor of Our Lady

[24] "And a great sign appeared in heaven: a woman clothed with the sun, and the moon was under her feet, and upon her head a crown of twelve stars. And being with child, she cried out in her travail and was in the anguish of delivery. And another sign was seen in heaven, and behold, a great red dragon having seven heads and ten horns, and upon his heads seven diadems. . ." (Apoc. 12:1-3)

[25] Cf. ch. 4, vv. 7, 12, 15: "Thou art all fair, O my love, and there is not a spot in thee. . . . My sister, my spouse, is a garden enclosed, a garden enclosed, a fountain sealed up. . . . The fountain of gardens: the well of living waters, which run with a strong stream from Libanus."—Let us recall here one of the oldest and most beautiful works of art inspired by the Spouse of the Canticle of Canticles: the great mosaic in the apse of Santa Maria in Trastevere, executed during or soon after the pontificate of Innocent II (1130-1143). The majesty of the coronation scene is softened by a gesture of tenderness: Christ lays His hand on the Virgin's shoulder, saying (in words inscribed in the open book which He holds), *"Veni, Electa mea, et ponam te in thronum meum:"* The scroll in Mary's hands reads, *"Leva ejus sub capite meo et dextera ejus amplexabitur Me."* (Cant. 8:3)

[26] It will be observed that little mention is made, in the following pages, of images representing one only of the three biblical figures just mentioned—i.e., the Woman of the Protogospel, the spouse of the Canticle of Canticles, or the Woman of the Apocalypse. This is because, to the best of our knowledge, they are nearly always fused together when used to represent the Immaculate Conception. We must remember that the iconography of this mystery is, as a general rule, pluri-symbolic. It is rare to find, in the sixteenth century, as isolated image of the Woman in the Garden of Eden crushing the head of the serpent. One of the border miniatures reproduced in plate VII (early fifteenth century) does so represent her, but it is not apparently specifically Immaculist. Similarly in Normandy, until the seventeenth century, the Woman of the Apocalypse is ordinarily encircled by the biblical symbols (Cf. Dr. FOURNÉE, *Iconographie de l'Immaculée Conception. . . ,* pp. 22, 24.) Regarding the figure of the *Virgin with the crescent* (cf. figures 2 and 14, and plates XIV-XIX; XXIII-XXV), a derivative of the Woman of the Apocalypse, Emile Mâle declares: "It cannot be doubted that this was the first symbolic representation of the Immaculate Conception." (*L'art religieux à la fin du moyen âge,* 3rd. ed., 1925, p. 211.) As for the Spouse of the Canticle of Canticles, the image remains literal; hence, its Immaculist signification is less striking, and it needs the context of a gloss. (Cf. the theme *Tota pulchra es* discussed and illustrated below.)

[27] *Acta Sanctorum,* February; Anvers edition, 1658, t. III, pp. 12-13.

and had a statue carved, representing her as crushing heresies in the form of a serpent. This would be the oldest example of this theme, were it not more than doubtful that a *Theotokos* had been carved in fifth century Gaul.[28]

Not until the first years of the fifteenth century do we find a certain image of the Immaculate Virgin trampling on the head of the Serpent. In 1407—not 1047, as some iconographers have mistakenly written— Canon Ugo di Summo ordered a wooden statue of the Blessed Virgin for the Church St. Mary of Cremona, specifying that she was to be "crowned with twelve stars and with the ancient Serpent under her feet. . . ."[29]

In this mixed image, in which the Woman of the Protogospel is crowned with the stars of the Woman of the Apocalypse, the Blessed Virgin appears alone, without her Son, as befits her who is not yet Mother of God, but has been prepared for that unique dignity by the unique privilege of exemption from original sin. In affirmation of this privilege, she crushes the head of the reptile who has attempted to "bruise her heel," according to the Vulgate rendering of Genesis 3:15.

This type of *Immaculata*, combining the signs of the two biblical visions, won the favor of the artists. Masters of the seventeenth and eighteenth centuries exerted themselves to the utmost to attain the grandeur of the idea. Francesco Vanni († 1609) recalls in the same painting the Fall and the Promise of Redemption: above the Tree of Eden stands the Virgin Mother, crushing the head of the serpent whose coils descend to the foot of the trunk where the two victims of his deception stand in despair (Louvre). In the following century, Tiepolo († 1770), in his *Immaculata* of St. Pascal of Aranjuez (plate XVIII)—of which a similar painting in the museum of Vicenza seems to be the sketch—gives Mary an expression of almost haughty defiance and assurance of victory as she settles her account with Satan: standing proudly erect, all in white, she scarcely bends her knee as she breaks the back of the long serpent who holds the apple of perdition in his mouth. Scattered upon the clouds, there rise up to her the praises of the biblical symbols—the palm tree, the lily, the fountain, the faultless mirror—details borrowed from the theme, *Tota pulchra es*, which we will describe below. Another *Immaculata* by the same master, but of a different type, is in the museum of Strasbourg.

Among the images of the *Immaculata with the Serpent*, besides this type in which the Virgin appears alone, there is another in which the Son accompanies the Mother. (Cf. plate IX.) Mary holds the Infant Jesus in her arms, while the latter plunges the pointed foot of a long cross into

---

[28] Cf. Msgr. Ch. AIMOND, *Notre-Dame dans le diocèse de Verdun*, Paris [s.d.], p. 42.

[29] BALLERINI, *Sylloge Monumentorum ad mysterium Conceptionis Immaculatae Virginis Deiparae illustrandum.* Rome, 1854, p. 16; Paris, Lecoffre, 1855, p. 17.

the serpent's mouth, with the gesture often given to Him in ancient monuments.[30] This image was zealously propagated by the Franciscans and Jesuits (cf. plate VIII). In an eighteenth century painting in the parish church of Montmédy (Meuse), Jesus looses a bolt of lightning to blast the monster's head. An unusual arrangement is found in a Dominican madonna, the *Virgin of St. Hyacinthe*—an alabaster group conserved at Lwow in Polish Galicia: Mary holds the child Jesus in her left arm, while on her right Christ is crucified at the top of a knotty tree trunk around which the serpent is entwined.

The question whether the Virgin of the Immaculate Conception should be represented with or without the Infant, has been debated by iconographers. Bishop Malou holds for the Virgin alone, while Canon Auber and Father Cahier, as well as Barbier de Montault, are of the contrary opinion. We will speak again of this matter below (section V). In either representation, what counts is the artist's intention; but the type which prevailed is that which shows Mary alone crushing the serpent, for it harmonized better with the logic of the doctrine.[31]

Fig. 6. MIRAC-ULOUS MEDAL.

St. Pierre Fourier, the apostle of Lorraine, distributed medals in which the serpent, placed lower down than Mary's foot—as if the woman most pure could not even touch the unclean beast—encircled from head to foot the terrestrial globe; thus was signified the universal curse from which the Imaculate Virgin escaped.[32] This is the same figuration which St. Catherine Labouré beheld in her vision of the Miraculous Medal (1830; cf. figure 6 and plate XXI).[33]

In a painting by Eustache Le Sueur († 1655), the Virgin appears trampling underfoot an asp, a basilisk, a lion and a dragon. We do not know what has become of this painting, with which we are acquainted only through the

---

[30] There are ivories, mosaics, and miniatures which represent Him holding, as if it were a scepter, a long cross terminating in a spearhead. This majestic attitude was inspired by that of the gods and monarchs represented on the metals and coins of ancient cities. It is even possible that the Christian image derives directly from some official monument executed by order of the emperor Constantine, who had himself represented in the vestibule of his palace as trampling a dragon underfoot and piercing it with the pointed shaft of the labarum. (Cf. my *Vierge Médiatrice*, p. 49.)

[31] In the work cited in the bibliography at the end of this chapter, Father LÉPICIER gives further details concerning this debate (pp. 88-93).

[32] Cf. L. GERMAIN DE MAIDY, "La Vierge Marie et le Serpent," in *Revue de l'art chrétien*, 1901, p. 504.

[33] Note, furthermore, that the figure of the Virgin of the Miraculous Medal was not a purely celestial innovation, a sort of *acheiropoieton* to which human work had not in any way contributed. All the elements of the figure, except for the rays of light descending from the hands, were already known, and in common use in

mention made of it by L. Dussieux.[34] However, the allusion to Psalm 90:13[35] is evident; and according to Miss Mirella Levi D'Ancona, this text was occasionally used between the twelfth (*sic!*) and fourteenth centuries as a source for Immaculist images.[36]

In connection with the triumph of Mary over the Serpent, we may note another theme, of analogous inspiration, in which Mary is contrasted with Eve, the Serpent's first victim. Examples of this theme are not numerous, however, and they occur relatively late. Here we will mention only a few by way of illustration.

One of the *Chants Royaux* of Rouen[37] declares that the Virgin Mary was not "*assise en la chaire de peste*—seated on the throne of the plague" —a metaphor for the state of Original Sin. The miniature which illustrates this text (and which would be indecipherable without it) shows Satan, armed with a club, before a group of naked women, whom he is about to compel to sit, one after another, on the black throne of the plague. Eve looks sadly upon these women—her offspring and victims of her fall; but in the sky appears the triumphant *Reparatrix,* the only one excepted from the lot of fallen mankind.

In the *Sacrum Oratorium* (1634) of the Jesuit, Pierre Biver, an engraving represents Adam and Eve asleep at the foot of the cursed tree, around which a human-headed serpent is entwined. Nearby, God the Father tenderly embraces the Virgin (who wears a crown), saying to her: "*Audi Filia, et vide debita naturae tuae. Evasisti.*" — "*Listen, My daughter, and see thy nature's debts. Thou has evaded [them].*" (Cf. figure 7)

---

religious imagery. The engraver of this medal, cast in 1832, designed the figure of the Virgin according to a type which had been created a century before by a master of the chisel, the royal sculptor, Edme BOUCHARDON († 1762). The latter's work, cast in silver, was placed in the church of Saint Sulpice, in Paris. It disappeared during the Revolution; but a copy, likewise in silver, was afterwards made. (Cf. plate XXII) Bouchardon's Virgin enjoyed great popularity; plaster copies of it were set up, not only in churches and chapels, but also over the fireplaces of thatch-roofed dwellings and on household altars. It was one of them that came to life before the eyes of St. Theresa of Lisieux, smiled on her, and cured her. Is it not noteworthy that this "Smiling Virgin," as she has been called, a modest but faithful copy of Bouchardon's silver Virgin, is the sister, by artistic filiation, of the Madonna of the Miraculous Medal?

[34] L. DUSSIEUX, *Nouvelles recherches sur la vie et les ouvrages d'Eustache Le Sueur,* Paris, 1852, p. 114.

[35] "Thou shalt walk upon the asp and the basilisk, and thou shalt trample underfoot the lion and the dragon." (Ps. 90:13)

[36] Mirella Levi D'ANCONA, *The iconography of the Immaculate Conception in the Middle Ages and early Renaissance,* 1957, p. 23 f. Three instances are cited in this work: a twelfth century psalter in All Souls College, Oxford (Ms. 6, fol. 4), the Psalter of Robert de Lisle (British Museum, Arundel Ms. 83, fol. 131v; reproduced in E. MILLAR, *English Illuminated Manuscripts of the XIV-XV Century,* pl. 101) and the Virgin of the Cathedral of Magdeburg (reproduced in H. GIESAU, *Der Dom zu Magdeburg,* Burg, 1924, p. 65).

[37] Paris, Bibliothèque Nationale, ms. fr. 1537, f. 54.

In a group of statues quite similar to one another, from the fourteenth and fifteenth centuries, the *rapprochement* of the two Eves is equally significant. In Saint-Laud Church at Angers, there is a remarkable statue of the Blessed Virgin, known as *Notre-Dame du Salve,* at whose feet can

DEVS PATER MARIÆ:
Audi Filia, et vide debita naturæ tuæ .Euasisti.

MARIA DEO PATRI:
*Dimitte nobis debita nostra, sicut et nos
dimittimus debitoribus nostris .*

Figure 7. THE IMMACULATE VIRGIN AND OUR SINFUL
FIRST PARENTS. Seventeenth century.

be seen the mother of the human race, biting savagely into the fateful apple. The same detail reappears in an alabaster Virgin of the Church of Saint-Pierre-du-Queyroix, at Limoges. Likewise, on the portal of a Renaissance church at Lampaul-Ploudalmézeau (Finistère) in Brittany, the Virgin-Mother is represented with Eve at her feet. These figures seem to utter, in words carved in stone, the same immaculist argument that is drawn from the parallel between Mary and Eve.[38]

The theme, "Tota Pulchra Es."

Among its initiatives in favor of the development of the belief in the Immaculate Conception, France can lay claim to having composed the

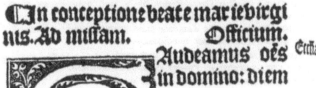

Figure 8. The 'Tota Pulchra Es.'
Sixteenth century.

[38] In a Book of Hours dating from the end of the fifteenth century, the Office of Saint Anne is illustrated by a miniature in which Adam, Eve and the Serpent are

first ideal image of the Immaculate Virgin—an image of the highest fittingness, in which theology is rendered plastically intelligible by the use of consecrated signs and symbols. (Cf. figure 8)

The Virgin stands in the center, upon the clouds, between heaven and earth, while from above God looks down upon her as the perfect realization of His tenderest thought. Symbols taken from Sacred Scripture are scattered round about her or arranged one above the other.[39] An inscription taken from the Canticle of Canticles (4:7) specifies the doctrinal sense of the composition: *"Tota pulchra es, amica mea, et macula non est in te"*—"Thou art all fair, my love, and there is no stain in thee." Hence the title given to this theme,[40] which, incidentally, borrows some of its symbols also from Solomon's poem.[41]

---

sculptured into the gate before which Anne and Joachim embrace one another. V. Leroquais, *Un livre d'heures manuscrit à l'usage de Mâcon*, Mâcon, 1935. The miniature is reproduced on folio 17v.

[39] Ordinarily these symbols are fifteen in number, each accompanied by an identifying scroll, and grouped as follows:

   a) Symbols drawn from the physical world:

   Sun: *Electa ut sol.*
   Moon: *Pulchra ut luna.*   } Ecclesiasticus 50:6-7 (praise
   Star: *Stella Matutina.*   } of the high priest, Simon).

(For the sun, cf. also Wisdom 7:29.—With regard to the star, note that it is nearly always *stella maris* rather than *stella mututina* that is designated in the images; but the *stella maris,* unlike the *stella matutina* (or the *stella Jacob*) has no biblical antecedent.)

   b) Flora of Palestine:

   Cedar of Lebanon: *Sicut cedrus exaltata.* } Ecclesiasticus 24:13-14
   Olive tree: *Oliva speciosa.*   } (praise of Wisdom).
   Rose garden of Jericho: *Plantatio rosae.* }
   Lily among thorns: *Sicut lilium inter spinas.*—Cant. 2:2.

   c) Prophecies, visions, allegories:

   Rod of Jesses *Virga Jesse floruit.*—Isaias 11:1.
   Gate of heaven: *Porta coeli.*—Genesis 28:17.

(It is possible that an allusion to the "Eastern Gate" of the vision of Ezechiel 44:1-2 was also intended in this symbol.)

   City of God: *Civitas Dei.*—Psalm 86:3, and many verses of the "songs of
      ascents"—Ps. 121, 126 and especially 131: 13-14.
   Tower of David: *Turris davidica cum propugnaculis.*—Cant. 4:4.
   Garden enclosed: *Hortus conclusus.*—Cant. 4:12.
   Fountain of the gardens: *Fons hortorum.*   } Cant. 4:15
   Well of living waters: *Puteus aquarum viventium.*   }
   Unblemished mirror: *Speculum sine macula.*—Wisdom 7:26.

Later on (cf. the Bayeux altarpiece, plate XI), this group was enriched with still other scriptural symbols: The Tree of Life (Genesis 2:9), Jacob's ladder (Genesis 28:12), Solomon's Temple (III Kings 6), the Ark of the Covenant (Exodus 25:10-22), Gedeon's fleece (Judges 6:36 ff.).

[40] This emblematic representation of the belief is sometimes designated as the "Virgin of the Litany." From the point of view of iconography, this appelation is improper, or at least misleading, for it gives the impression that the image is a

This image is simply the plastic expression of an idea which already had a very long literary tradition. To say nothing of the glowing comparisons formulated by the Oriental liturgies, there are to be found hundreds of metaphorical epithets and phrases of the Virgin in the Latin hymnals

Figure 9. THE GARDEN ENCLOSED AND THE SEALED FOUNTAIN AS FIGURES OF THE BLESSED VIRGIN. End of the fifteenth century.

representation of the "Litany of Loretto." The fact is that the image is earlier than the litany, the first printed formulas of which date only from the second half of the sixteenth century, and which was approved by Pope Sixtus V in 1587. Cf. U. CHEVALIER, *Notre-Dame de Lorette, Etude historique sur l'authenticité de la Santa Casa,* Paris, 1906, pp. 327-328.

The Little Office of the Immaculate Conception, which has held an important place in private devotion, and is still recited by the Marian Congregations, is of the highest interest for this symbolism, as is well known, for it is wholly composed of biblical metaphors. Cf. P. DEBUCHY, S.J., *Le Petit Office de l'Immaculée Conception. Histoire. Commentaire. Exemples,* 2nd ed., Paris, 1913.

[41] The references are given in note 39.

of the Middle Ages, as well as in the pious poetry of the Romance
languages.[42]

It has been asserted[43] that this suggestive formula occurs in art for the
first time in the *Heures de la Vierge à l'usage de Rome* published at Paris
by Thielman Kerver in 1503. However, it occurs also in the *Heures à
l'usage de Rouen* printed in Paris that same year by Antoine Vérard.[44]
The same design occurs in a woodcut of a more crude execution which
dates perhaps from the end of the fifteenth century. (Cf. figure 10)

Whatever be the case regarding the priority of these works, certain

Figure 10. THE 'TOTA PULCHRA ES.'
Ca. 1500.

[42] See, for example, the text of Peter RIGA given below, p. 528. It should be
compared with the Sequence *In Purificatione Beatae Mariae* of ADAM OF ST. VICTOR
(*PL* 196, 1482-1484). Cf. also the remarks in chapter IV of the present volume,
p. 148 ff.
Figure 9 and plate VII present a number of these symbols applied to the Blessed
Virgin during the fifteenth century and without special reference to the Immaculate
Conception.
[43] By MAXE-WERLY, followed by Emile MALE. Their works are cited in the
bibliography at the end of this chapter.
[44] Paris, Bibliothèque Nationale, vel. 2862.

iconographers have deemed it impossible "that a modest engraving in a Book of Hours should have been the prototype of a mystic figuration of such importance."[45] However, the importance of this first theological image could be explained precisely by its Parisian origin: may it not have been suggested to the publishers Kerver and Vérard by some doctor from the Sorbonne? The latter at that time constituted a learned and devout milieu which was at the head of the Immaculist movement in Paris.[46]

Thereafter this image is reproduced numberless times in stained glass, sculpture, painting (plates X, XI), and engraving, until the seventeenth century. And the literature of the period re-echoes what was to be seen in art; it is not rare to find the biblical titles of the Blessed Virgin chanted in poetry.

Nowhere did this theme have more brilliance than in the stained glass windows of Normandy. That of Conches (Eure), executed about 1540, bears in three different places, on a blue scroll, an inscription which appears at first sight enigmatic:

Seule sans sy dans sa conception

The Old French expression, *sans sy* means "absolutely unique." This inscription is identical with a palinodial refrain of William Tasserie, elected prince of the Palinods of Rouen[47] in 1489. His *"Chant Royal"* (1490) is, incidentally, partially reproduced by the window of Conches:

> Figuree est sa grande preeminence
> Par le blanc lix naissant entre l'espine,
> Par l'esglentier qui donne redollence,
> Par le laurier qui victoire desine
> Et par le jour qui la terre enlumine.
> C'est de la mer l'estoille clere et belle,
> C'est de Noe la pure coulombelle,
> L'arche de Dieu, de bois misterieux,
> L'arche de paix, temple tres gracieux,
> Tres pur, tres nect vaissiau d'election,
> Qu'on doibt nommer maulgre tous envyeux:
> *Belle sans sy en sa conception.*[48]

---

[45] L. Germain de Maidy, in *Revue de l'art chretien,* 1906, p. 336.

[46] Dr. Fournée expresses a different opinion: he wonders whether the German engravers had not preceded those of Paris in the use of this imagery: "German influence," he writes, "is clear in certain works, such as Simon Vostre's *Heures d'Angers* (1510) . . ." *Les thèmes iconographiques. . . ,* p. 60 f. Cf. also the work of Father Lépicier, *L'Immaculée Conception. . . ,* p. 327.

Father Manuel Trens, on the other hand, has called attention to a painting of the *Tota pulchra es* which he dates at 1497 (*Iconografía de la Virgen . . . ,* p. 153), in a church of Artajona. (Cf. plate X) This date, however, must be carefully verified before any conclusion can be drawn.

[47] On these palinods, see the following section of the present article.

[48] "Her greatness is represented by the white *lily,* growing among thorns, by the

Was it in these biblical praises, put into rhyme by a prince of the Palinods, that Vérard received the inspiration for the image in his *Heures de Rouen?*

The engraving which Durante Alberti († 1613) dedicated to Cardinal Orsini in 1577 was distinguished by an interesting interpretation of this theme: on either side of Mary, groups of angels bear her biblical emblems; below and behind her, the ship of the Church, driven by the tempest, makes its way under the patronage of the Immaculate Virgin: *Ecclesia periculis exponitur sed non derelinquetur.*

Were it not for the absence of the characteristic symbols, the most remarkable painted representation of this theme would be a charming little tableau from the fifteenth century, representing the Virgin between heaven and earth with her hands folded and her hair streaming down over her shoulders. Certain critics attribute it to the atelier of the Master of Moulins, and others to a little known primitive, "Master Michel." Here, the Immaculate Virgin, young and "beautiful as the dawn," stands upon the inverted crescent.[49]

In section IV of this article, we will point out how the essence of this theme was retained by the Spanish masters in their paintings of the *Purísima.* One of them, Luis de Vargas († 1567) will represent angelic musicians singing to the *Immaculata* the words of praise inscribed on a scroll: *Tota pulchra es, Amica mea, et macula non est in te.*[50]

THE ALLEGORIES OF THE 'PUYS DE PALINOD'

In the fifteenth and sixteenth centuries, the symbolic imagery of the Immaculate Conception reached a peak of picturesqueness and exuberance, thanks to the *Puys* instituted in Normandy and northern France to defend, promote and celebrate Mary's signal prerogatives.[51] The *Chants Royaux* of the *Puy* of Amiens were accompanied with paintings illustrating the refrains, which latter were ordinarily inscribed on a scroll close to the kneeling figure of the master who had donated them. These paintings, most of which have disappeared today, were reproduced in large miniatures for Louise of Savoy, mother of Francis I. The compositions of this

---

wild rose yielding its fragrance, by the *laurel tree,* symbol of victory, by the *sun* which enlightens the earth. She is the bright and beautiful *star of the sea,* the pure *dove* of Noe, *the Ark of God,* built of mysterious wood, the *rainbow* of peace, the graceful *temple,* the most pure and spotless *vessel of election,* whom we must call, in spite of all (the protests of) the invidious: *The only one beautiful in her conception.*

[49] Anc. coll. Quesnet. Cf. P. DURRIEU, *La Peinture à l'Exposition des Primitifs français,* Paris, 1904, pp. 84-86.

[50] Cathedral of Seville. Cf. LEFORT, *La peinture espagnole,* p. 73.

[51] On the *Puys,* see the note at the end of this chapter.

splendid manuscript[52] are all allegories; the artist must often be given credit for having introduced some degree of clarity into the confusion of the poem which he is illustrating; the *rhétoriquers* of the *Puy* of Amiens cultivated a vague symbolism, obscure when not simply trivial; they delighted in puns and witticisms, often at the expense of good taste.

The *Chants Royaux* of the *Puy* of Rouen are analogous; they are of a quintessence even more forced and subtle. Here, too, the images are worth more than the verses. We speak of the miniatures which illustrate them in two other collections of the Bibliothèque Nationale of Paris— mss. fr. 1537 and 379. The former contains fifty palinods, which won prizes or were presented at the *Puy* of Rouen between the years 1519 and 1528. Each is accompanied by a painting. Although this manuscript is the work of a better artist, its iconography is not so curious as that of manuscript 379.

Of this astonishing imagery, inspired by the *Puys* of Normandy and Picardy, we will mention only a few titles. First of all, in the Amiens manuscript, illuminated for Louise of Savoy, we find: *The Virgin of the "Sainte Ampoule,"* a symbolic recall of the anointing of the kings of France and of their veneration for *Notre Dame; The Virgin of the Cloth,* whose virtues and graces are represented by the pieces of cloth that women gave away to the "naked" poor; *The Virgin of the Hammer and Anvil*—tools of the mystic forge to which the Divine and Virginal Maternity were compared.

The allegory painted in the two manuscripts of the *Chants Royaux* of Rouen are no less curious. The subject of one of them (Ms. fr. 1537, f. 36) has been misunderstood by certain iconographers, who see there the "making of the seamless robe of Jesus Christ." In reality we have here a subtle allusion to the maternity of St. Anne, who wove from her flesh the pure and immaculate flesh of the Virgin Mary, who, in turn, made from her flesh a garment, as it were, for the Humanity of the Word. Such is the meaning of the refrain of the palinod: *"Du Filz de Dieu la Robe inconsutile"*—"The seamless robe of the Son of God," repeated in each strophe of a *Chant Royal* of unknown authorship, crowned in 1520. In this miniature, Joachim holds the skeins while St. Anne feeds out the thread needed for the making of this "seamless and all-perfect robe." This composition of "figurative style," as the author of the poem expresses it, is one of the most original in the symbolic iconography of the Immaculate Conception.

In this same manuscript, the Immaculate Virgin appears, with a palm in her hand, as triumphing over death and sickness: at her feet lies a golden skeleton beside a green dragon rampant, while the seven virtues encircle

[52] Paris, Bibliothèque Nationale, ms. fr. 145.

her and the rainbow which serves as her aureole.[53] The artist of manuscript 379 (f. 2), with a real talent for landscape, rendered the hymn composed by Master Jacques Le Lyeur upon the refrain: *"La Fille Adam, Pélerine de grâce"*—"The Daughter of Adam, Pilgrim of Grace"; the bark of this Pilgrim, i.e. The Immaculate Virgin, is piloted by Jesus Christ, while another bark, which the devil maneuvers with a gaff, tries in vain to accost it.

Since we are dealing with nautical comparisons, let us cite one other work in which this type of image occurs. It must have come quite naturally to the sailor-poet, Jean Parmentier of Dieppe, who died at Sumatra in 1529. His *Chant Royal* on the Immaculate Conception has for its refrain: *"La Forte Nef toute Pleine de Grace"*—"The sturdy ship all full of grace." This ship is *La Marie, which has the Virtues for her crew.*[53a]

Collections of Engraved Symbols or Emblems.

Figurative suggestions of the same sort are not wanting from the mystical works illustrated by engravings. Collections of Marian symbols multiplied during the seventeenth and eighteenth centuries. Sometimes an entire collection was consecrated to the Immaculate Conception in a continuous series, such as the *Conceptus chronographicus* of the Benedictine Zoller. (Cf. figure 12) Sometimes symbols of the Immaculate Conception would be contained in a collection referring to the various mysteries and prerogatives of the Blessed Virgin, as in the case of the *Pium Oratorium* of Father Biver, S.J. (cf. *infra*), the *Pancarpium Marianum* of Father David, S.J., or the *Emblesmes* of Callot. Finally, Immaculist images appear in collections of a more general nature, in which they are occasionally presented in a single group, as in the *Sylloge* of the Jesuit Boschius,[54] who collected over two thousand symbols under the four headings, *Sacred, Heroic, Moral* and *Satiric Symbols.*

All sorts of comparisons abound in these collections, some excellent, some mediocre. We will be content to make a random choice here and there.

The *Sacrum Oratorium* of the Jesuit Biver (Antwerp, 1634) represents the *Divine Eagle and the Immaculate Virgin.* (Cf. figure 11) The idea apparently comes from Deuteronomy 32:11-12:

> Like the eagle enticing her young to fly
> And hovering over them,
> (Jahweh) spread his wings and has taken (His People)
> And carried him on his shoulders.

At the foot of the engraving, the bird of death, on the right, emits his

---

[53] The refrain of the *Chant Royal* which this miniature is intended to illustrate, goes as follows: *"Conception plus Divine que Humaine."*

[53a] Cf. G. Lebas, *Les Palinods et les poetes dieppois. Dieppe,* 1904.

[54] Cf. the bibliography at the end of the present article.

cry of malediction, *Vae,* which is the name *Eva* (= Eve) rearranged; on the left, the bird of life takes up the anagram, but turns it into a greeting and blessing: *Ave.*

One of the most complete of these collections of engravings is that of

Figure 11. THE DIVINE EAGLE AND THE IMMACULATE VIRGIN. Seventeenth century.

the Benedictine Zoller, *Conceptus Chronographicus de Concepta Sacra Deipara* (Augsburg, 1712). The frontispiece (cf. figure 12) represents the Virgin as the Woman of the Apocalypse, encircled with angels and cherubs who carry darts and javelins to use against all those who deny the privilege of the Immaculate Conception; the latter are represented by a seven-headed hydra, designated by the legend, *Draco rufus ad pedes Illibatae.*

The learned Benedictine makes considerable use of the mediaeval *Bestiaries,* and excels in discovering an unexpected parallelism. Among other figurative beasts, he cites: the *looust,* which dares to attack the serpent and pierce its head (Symb. 33); the *lion,* which flees in terror at the singing

Figure 12. THE WOMAN OF THE APOCALYPSE.
Eighteenth century.

of a girl (Symb. 180); the *starfish,* named by reason of its shape and its radiance (Symb. 243); the *eagle,* which, crowned with oak leaves, is not afraid of lightning (Symb. 355). Many other animals are present in this symbolic menagery: the *swan,* which devours snakes; the *salamander,* which is invulnerable to fire, etc. The author draws likewise upon the *plantaria,* astrology, and the phenomenology of nature. Each engraving is surmounted by an explanation in Latin, composing the chronogram, 1712 —the date when the work was published.

Besides complete collections, the volumes of Marian *emblems* contain other subjects akin to the Immaculate Conception. Thus, the engraver Jacques Callot of Lorraine († 1635) represents it also by the *salamander,* who explains his symbolic role in a quatrain:

> I live amid fire without being burned:
> And the Virgin amid the original crime
> By the absolute power of the Eternal Judge
> Has not burned her soul in the common furnace.[55]

In the same class, let us call attention to the engravings of certain theological treatises on this belief. As frontispiece to a work[56] of the Spanish Franciscan, Pedro de Alva y Astorga, there is an image in the worst

Figure 13. THE MYSTICAL ROSE. Eighteenth century.

possible taste: the Immaculate Virgin appears in the form of a naked, hairy infant, cradled in the calix of a flower, as if to suggest the instant of her creation. Fortunately, the symbols which encircle this figure help us somewhat to overlook its ugliness and bad taste.[57] Far preferable is the charming composition engraved in an eighteenth century collection of *Sagradas Quintillas:*[58] at the heart of an unfolded rose, the Immaculate Virgin appears in glory, Queen of virtues as the rose is queen of flowers (Cf. figure 13).

The *Caeleste Pantheon*[59] of the Jesuit Henri Engelgrave gives a *pearl* gleaming in an open oyster shell as a symbol had already served as motif for some of the *Chants Royaux* for

---

[55] *Emblesmes sur la Vie de la Mère de Dieu.* Paris, 1646.

[56] *Monumenta antiqua Immaculatae Conceptionis SS. Virginis Mariae ex novem auctoribus antiquis recollectis,* Lovanii, 1664. This work is not to be confused with

the *Puy de Palinod* of Rouen. One of them, which won the prize in 1612, addresses the Virgin as follows:

> Your beautiful luster, O Pearl of the East,
> By exception to the fatal ordinance,
> Remains incorrupt amid the bitterness of sin.

A master of this same academy had chosen the metaphor for his palinodial refrain: *"The rich pearl in which God took human form."* These words make it clear that a symbol of the Incarnation is intended; and in fact the miniature which illustrates this hymn shows the Savior holding a magnificent pearl in a golden setting.[60] Usually, however, the pearl represents Mary's Immaculate Conception. St. Anne, say the allegorists, was the *Sea Shell* which, under the dew of Heaven, engendered this *Unio*, this Pearl unique for its purity and splendor.[61]

III
THE "DISPUTATIONS" ON THE IMMACULATE CONCEPTION

The bitter controversy over the doctrine of the Immaculate Conception, which lasted for centuries, but, in the end, served the cause of the dogma, is well known.[62] Art intervened in these debates and made itself an apologist. Its reaction was effective above all during the religious crisis of the sixteenth century, when the beliefs most combatted by Protestantism were the most passionately defended. Thus it was with the doctrine of Mary's original purity. Artists affirmed it in compositions which were, in effect, painted or engraved theses, in which texts were unfurled in the hands of Doctors of the Church and champions of the Holy Virgin.

One of the first examples of this formula is the painting of Jean Belle-gambe of Douai, in 1521, in fulfillment of the request of the dying

---

another volume of *Monumenta*, published in the same year and at the same place, *Monumenta Antiqua Immaculatae Conceptionis Sacratissimae Virginis Mariae. Ex variis authoribus antiquis tam manuscriptis, quam olim impressis, sed qui vix modo reperiuntur.*

[57] Cf. Bishop MALOU, *Iconographie de l'Immaculée Conception*, p. 18. However, Father LÉPICIER declares that he is not unduly shocked by this engraving. (*L'Immaculée Conception. . .* , p. 34, n. 18.)

[58] *Sagradas Quintillas a Maria Santissima en el ternissimo mysterio de su Concepcion Inmacalada.* Sévilla, Vasquez (1766-1799).

[59] This book constitutes the third part of a work entitled *Lux evangelica.* The complete title of Part III is: *Lucis evangelicae sub velum sacrorum emblematum reconditae pars tertia, Hoc est Caeleste Pantheon, sive caelum novum in festa et gesta sanctorum . . .* per R. P. Henricum ENGELGRAVE . . . Antverpiae, apud Viduam et haeredes J. Chobbari, 1658. In-4. The *Coeleste Pantheon*, which was put on the Index in 1686, no longer forms part of the work.

[60] Paris, Bibliothèque Nationale, Ms. fr. 1537, f. 89.

[61] Greek homiletic literature makes use of the same metaphor: it occurs notably in the sermons of Elias MINIATIS, preacher and controversialist (1669-1714).

[62] See chapter VI of the present volume.

Marguerite Pottier, called to God on the very eve of her wedding. She had always been devoted to Our Lady's Immaculate Conception, and had made her father promise to present their parish with a painting recalling this privilege. Bellegambe, to whom the commission was given, must have taken counsel of a theologian, for his work is a veritable doctrinal synthesis; perhaps he was instructed by the *De puritate Conceptionis B. Mariae Virginis*[63] of Clichtovaeus, a canon of Chartres. His painting is in the museum of Douai.[64]

About the same date, a miniaturist painted an analogous subject as frontispiece of a collection of palinods:[65] under a green and rose dais, the Immaculate Virgin, all in white, stands modestly upon a golden column, with her hands folded. An emerald dragon is under her feet, while, on either side, prophets and doctors unfurl scrolls which proclaim her spotless Conception.

About 1530, a miniaturist, interpreting a poem of Guillaume Thibaut, *rhétoriqueur* of the *Puy* of Rouen, gives to the subject a form dear to the Normans, that of a court trial (plate XII). He introduces us into a courtroom: before the sovereign judge, Jesus defends the honor of His Immaculate Mother, basing His case on the testimonies of *Grace* and *Honor, Faith* and *Succor;* while the opposing advocate exhibits the proclamation: *"Omnes in Adam peccaverunt"*—"In Adam all have sinned." In the end, as the refrain declares—and as we might have expected—"Mary won her case."[66]

Did the original idea of these compositions in the form of a thesis or scholastic debate come from Flanders? A precise instance already occurs in a panel of the *Altarpiece of St. Anne,* at Frankfort, dating from the end of the fifteenth century, of which we have spoken above.[67] Below the altar, St. Anne is represented with the immaculate infant visible in her womb. Around her, various personages are assembled: St. Augustine, as bishop, with a heart in his hand, holds a crosier from which is unfurled a scroll bearing the famous passage of one of his treatises: *"Nullam prorsus, cum de peccatis agitur, de Maria volumus habere quaestionem"*—"When treating of sin, we have no intention of bringing Mary into the question."[68] Saint Anselm, Archbishop of Canterbury, repeats the words of a sermon erroneously attributed to him: *"Non est verus amator Virginis qui celebrare respuit festum suae Conceptionis"*—"He is no true lover of the Virgin,

---

[63] Published in 1513 by Henri ESTIENNE. We find there, in a wood-cut, the image that had been used in Kerver's Book of Hours: the Immaculate Virgin with the Biblical symbols. (Cf. *supra,* p. 478).

[64] See the works of N. A. CAHIER and Father LEONARD, in the bibliography which follows the present chapter. Jean Bellegambe was elected "Prince" of the *Puy of the Assumption* (also called *Confrérie des Clercs Parisiens*) at Dieppe.

[65] Paris, Bibliothèque Nationale, ms. fr. 19369.

[66] Paris, Bibliothèque Nationale, ms. fr. 379, f. 16.

[67] P. 466.

[68] *De natura et gratia,* XXXVI; cf. p. 70 of the present volume, note 62.

who refuses to celebrate the feast of her Conception."[69]   The pope who stands in the background on the right must be Sixtus IV, the Franciscan whose initiatives greatly contributed to the development of the belief.[70]

Thus we see that in these historico-dogmatic works, if they may so be called, the personages represented are not necessarily the best qualified witnesses to the belief. Neither are they always the same. In the painting of an unknown artist of the sixteenth century (plate XIII), the upper part is a symbolic adaptation of the episode of Esther and Assuerus[71] (Esther 15:13); below, on the right, David and Solomon join their prophetic praises to the encomia of the three saints who face them on the left: Augustine, Ambrose and—on his knees—Anthony of Padua, the last named declaring in Latin: "It seems more probable to attribute to Mary that which does greater honor to her."[72]

The character of thesis and apologetic is evident above all in the great

---

[69] *Sermo de Conceptione B. Mariae,* P.L. 159, col. 322.   A translation of this sermon will be found below, p. 522 ff.   The text in question occurs in the third paragraph from the end, at note 5.   On St. Anselm's views, see chapter V of the present volume, p. 168.

[70] Cf. the work of G. DE TERVARENT, *Enigmes . . . ,* p. 39 f.   See also chapter VI of the present volume, p. 234 ff., and chapter VIII, pp. 275, 298 ff.

[71] When Queen Esther was requested to intercede with King Assuerus for her people who were threatened with death, she was afraid; for "whosoever, whether man or woman, cometh into the king's inner court, who is not called for, is immediately to be put to death without any delay, except the king shall hold out the golden sceptre to him, in token of clemency."   (Esther 4:11)   At length, however, she went to the king.   At the view of his wrathful countenance, she fainted; but the king caressed her, and touched her with the sceptre, saying, "Thou shalt not die; for this law is not made for thee, but for all others." (15:13)   This last text was not infrequently applied figuratively to Mary's exemption from the law of original sin.

[72] *"Videtur probabile quod est excellentius attribuere Marie."*   This is actually a verbatim quotation from the commentary of Duns Scotus on the *Sentences* of Peter Lombard (III, Dist. 3, Qu. 1; cf. chapter V of the present volume, p. 210, note 234).   For this reason, Montgomery CARMICHAEL argues that the kneeling friar in this painting was intended to represent, not the great Franciscan saint, Anthony of Padua, but the great Franciscan doctor, Duns Scotus (*Francia's Masterpiece. . . ,* p. 23).   The painting, designed as an altarpiece for the Confraternity of the Conception in the Franciscan Church of San Francesco, "must have been inspired, designed and controlled," probably even painted, "by the Franciscans themselves." . . . "It is impossible to imagine the friars of San Francesco who had been under the influence of Fra Paolo da Lucca (Paolo Jova), a great champion of the doctrine and author of a 'Symbola de Conceptione Beatae Mariae,' it is impossible, I say, to imagine these friars, full of the subject, introducing Saint Anthony of Padua into a picture of the Conception, and making him use words which would be familiar as being those of Scotus even to their theological students of the first year." (p. 23) It is true that the name *S. Antonius de Padua* appears in the painting beneath the friar, who also holds in his hand the fire which was St. Anthony's emblem.   Carmichael explains this, however, in that "it would have been rash in the extreme in 1480 to represent the uncanonized Scotus with a halo among canonized Saints.   So the friars, resorting to a ruse, wrote underneath the name of Saint Anthony, but introduced the words of Scotus to show all friars, present and to come, who really was intended by that little Franciscan." (p. 26)

This painting closely resembles that by Francesco FRANCIA, also in the town of Lucca, in the Church of San Frediano.   Carmichael believes that Francia's work, compositions insipred by the Counter-Reformation, and called *Disputations on the Immaculate Conception,* by analogy with the famous *Disputazione* on the Eucharist, painted by Raphael in the Vatican. Emile Mâle devotes the following words to the principal works of this type:

> Painters have several times represented these grave assemblies. In a work of Ippolito Scarsella of Ferrara (Milan, Brera), some Fathers of the Church and outstanding theologians hold converse with the stainless Virgin who appears in the sky, encircled with the symbols of the litany. Domenico put only the four great doctors of the Latin Church at her feet (Leningrad, *Hermitage*). In the church of Saint Mary of the People, Carlo Maratta represented St. John pointing out, above the clouds, the Immaculate Virgin whom he had known on earth and had seen in the skies over Patmos; he seems to be communicating his faith and his love to St. Gregory the Great, who is listening to him, while St. Augustine, seen in the foreground, with his eyes raised, is lost in the mystery of that predestined Virgin. The same painting is found in Rome at San Carlo Al Corso.[73]

We must add to this list the suggestive paintings of the great artist of Ferrara, Dosso-Dossi († 1542), in the Dresden Museum: in heaven above, God the Father exempts from the common stain her who had been conceived all pure in his mind from the very beginning; below, the four doctors, Ambrose, Augustine, Jerome and Gregory, contemplate her, or carry on a discussion as if in council.[74]

The artists could not, of course, overlook the sons of St. Francis, the acknowledged defenders of Mary's privilege. As a matter of fact, the latter themselves inspired numerous paintings and prints in honor of the Immaculate Virgin. As was only just, these compositions feature the Order's standard-bearer in this doctrinal battle, Duns Scotus, the *Subtle Doctor*.[75]

Sometimes there was even an excess of zeal on the part these devoted proponents of the doctrine, as is proven by several curious works. In Spain, a terra-cotta craftsman did the following scene in *faience* of Alcora: Pope Alexander VII is represented as a dragon, with the keys of St. Peter clenched in his teeth. He is bridled like a horse, the reins being held by the Blessed Virgin herself, who is in the sky, enveloped in a glory overladen with cherub heads. The instigators of this satire in clay are indicated on the two reins: Philip IV on the one, and *Ordo Seraphicus* on the other.

---

executed between 1511 and 1517, (cf. p. 84), took its inspiration from the other, which he thinks was done not long after 1480 (p. 50).

[73] *L'art religieux du XVIIe siècle,* pp. 46-47.

[74] Concerning the *Immaculatas* of the type inspired by the controversy, see BEISSEL, *Geschichte der Verehrung Marias in Deutschland im XVI und XVII Jahrhundert,* ch. XI.

[75] Cf. *Acta Ordinis Fratrum Minorum Immaculatam Conceptionem B.M.V. concernentia* . . . Ad Claras Aquas, 1904. See also chapter V of the present volume, p. 204 ff., and note 72 of the present article.

The broad leather whip brandished by the Virgin bears the name, *Doctor Subtilis Scotus,* and overhead a scroll proclaims the following profession of faith:

> *Sentada y a mi Pureza*
> *Con este nuovo Bocado*
> *Del antiguo he Discuitado.*[76]

But this belongs to the realm of anecdote. The Iberian peninsula was to proffer testimony of a quite different importance: the pictorial blossoming of the belief in its full beauty.

IV

THE *PURISIMA* OF THE SPANISH MASTERS

The sixteenth century had multiplied the symbolic expressions of the Immaculate Conception. It was the genius of the seventeenth to express the mystery with all possible perfection, surmounting the difficulties of such a plastic transposition.

In this fervent endeavor, the success of Spain surpassed that of Italy and of the other schools. Her masters lived, of course, in a climate of exceptional fervor, in which the cult of the *Inmaculada* was manifested with as much passion by the poor mule driver as by the *conquistador* and the "Discoverer of new worlds."

In the museum of Seville, a painting by Domingo Martinez (seventeenth and eighteenth centuries) represents the Immaculate Virgin with popes on her right and some of the "Catholic kings" on her left.[77] They are there by just title, as sovereigns of a land that has so exalted the privileged exceptions of *Nuestra Señora.* In our day, it is still common for the people there to greet one another with the profession of faith, *"Ave María, Purísima, sin pecado concebida."*

This cult goes back very far in the history of Spain, but it was never more national than in the seventeenth century, when the defense of the prerogative of the Immaculate Virgin became an affair of state, a point of honor for monarch and subject alike. The cause provoked an admirable rivalry in all classes of the people. In 1621, the Cortes of Castile who had come to Madrid to take an oath of allegiance to the new king, Philip IV—so well known through Velasquez' portrait—also made a vow ever

---

[76] This work, belonging to a private collection, was sold in Paris. An engraving of the same image appeared in *Discussio theologica super definibilitate proxima Mysterii Immaculatae Conceptionis Dei-Genitricis* by the Franciscan, Domingo Lossada, Madrid, 1733, and has been reproduced in *Archivo Ibero-Americano,* xv (Enero-Junio, 1955), preceding page 1.—On the iconography of this Franciscan-inspired *Immaculata,* cf. A.-M. Lépicier, *L'Immaculée-Conceptoin...,* chapter XIV.

[77] This painting is reproduced in the Spanish review *Miriam,* January-February, 1954.

to affirm the prerogative of the *Purísima*. In 1624, the University of Alcala de Henarez determined that it would confer no degree thereafter on any candidate who would not swear to defend the "Most Pure Conception." This followed the example of the University of Paris, which had imposed the same rule in 1497.[78] The famous orders of knights—that of St. James in 1650, that of Calatrava in 1652, that of Alcantara in 1653—exacted a similar oath of those being received into their company. And the heart of Spain has not yet ceased to beat for the Immaculate Virgin, not even after the cruel civil war of 1936, which saw the destruction of so many of her holy images.

Hence this "land of the *Inmaculada*" as it proudly calls itself—and with just reason—was destined to produce something much finer than portraits of kings, queens, and *infantes*. Its great masters raised the vision of their genius higher than this. Certainly, they felt their powerlessness before this *chef-d'oeuvre* of God: nevertheless their faith and their love attempted to render the inexpressible Model. Most of them, Juan de Juanés and Montañes among others, when called upon to paint or sculpture her, did not dare to take up brush or chisel until after having fasted, prayed, and received Holy Communion.

The renowned artists of the sixteenth and seventeenth centuries rivaled one another in creating these ideal *Concepciones* in a new and grander style. At Valencia, the pious Juan de Juanés († 1579) painted his work following the vision of a holy Jesuit, his friend, Father Martin Alberro. At Toledo, the somber mysticism of El Greco († 1614) became more gentle for the *Purísima*. All the great names of Spanish art are found upon great works on this same subject: at Valladolid, the sculptor Gregorio Fernandez († 1636); at Naples, Ribera († 1652); at Madrid, Velasquez († 1660); and finally, at Seville, the chosen land of the *Purísima*, the two masters of the chisel, Montañes († 1649) and Alonso Cano († 1667) (cf. plate XIX); and the two painters who here reached their greatest height, Zurbaran († 1663; cf. plate XVI), and Esteban Murillo († 1682; cf. plate XVII).[79]

THE VISIONS OF THESE MASTERS.

It has been said that the type known as *Purísima* belongs properly to Spain, which can lay claim to it as "a national artistic creation." However, without any chauvinism, it can be pointed out that the essentials of this creation are already found in the theme of French origin of which we have already spoken, that of the *Tota Pulchra Es,* in which the Blessed Virgin, who is the principal figure, is encircled with the biblical symbols which

---

[78] Cf. chapter VI of the present volume, p. 239.

[79] Likewise, there were Murillo's imitators of the second half of the century; Juan Escalante, José Antolinez, Valdes Leal and Coello.

prefigured her. The Spanish masters were acquainted with this image,[80] and reproduced it; their merit is to have interpreted it in such a way that, "what was grand only in conception was rendered grand by their style." (E. Mâle)

Of all the *Purísimas* which use the biblical metaphors the one which most resembles the French type is that of Juan de Juanéz (in the Jesuit Church at Valencia). But the features it gives to Mary, and the penetrating gentleness of her expression, betray racial feelings and the circumstances of the painting's origin. It was produced, as we have already said, following a vision. The pious Valencian artist makes a direct allusion to this fact in attributing to the three Divine Persons, who are crowning the Immaculate Virgin, the same words of praise which Father Alberro had been uttering just before his ecstasy: *Tota pulchra es, Amica mea, et macula non est in te.*

We meet the Virgin of the litany symbols in the works of Fray Sanchez Cotán (Museum of Granada), of El Greco (cf. plate XV), of Pacheco (Cathedral of Seville), of Roëlas (Berlin Museum), of Ribera (Augustinian Monastery at Salamanca), of Alonso Cano (two paintings, one in the Cathedral, the other in the monastery San Diego, of Valencia).

But the Spanish masters departed farther and farther from the dogmatic image which was still too abstract, despite the intelligible sense of the symbols. The latter became for them mere accessories, often greatly reduced, and sometimes not employed at all.[81] Their whole effort bore upon the expression and the attitude of the *Inmaculada.* Sometimes she seems to be in flight; other times she stands immobile, an aetherial being, inundated with life. This was the best, if not the only way, in which to suggest the mystery, given so few concrete possibilities.

There are still many particularities that distinguish the *Purísimas* from one another. Usually the Virgin's feet stand upon the crescent moon, but sometimes upon a crown of angel heads, as we see in the statues of Fernandez, of Montañes, and Alonso Cano (plate XIX). The effect of this detail in the painting of Zurbaran (plate XVI) is charmingly comical: the lower folds of Mary's robe make a kind of bonnet for the heads of the heavenly *bambinos* who seem to be delighted.

Rarely does the *Purísima* show the trace of a smile: the solemn gravity of her beauty reflects the concentration of her soul on the mystery of which she is the object. In this attitude of nobility and of intimate conversation with God, no *Inmaculada* is more expressive than the polychrome sculpture of Montañes in the Cathedral of Seville.

Other masters thought, not without reason, that it was fitting to give

---

[80] Cf. plate X.

[81] This transition can readily be observed in plates XIV-XIX; see plates X and XI and figures 8 and 10 for the starting point.

PLATES

For permission to reproduce the following images, we are indebted to the copyright owners, whose names are indicated in the notes accompanying the photographs. For assistance in obtaining the latter, we are indebted to M. Maurice Vloberg, Miss Mirella Levi D'Ancona (who drew our attention to the works reproduced in the frontispiece and plates I-V, VII and XIII), Mlle. Chabrier of the *Service Photographique* of the Bibliothèque Nationale of Paris, Mr. T. J. Brown of the Department of Manuscripts of the British Museum, and Father Bernard Ransing, C.S.C., Assistant General of the Congregation of Holy Cross.

The notes are the work of the editor, on the basis of information supplied in many cases by M. Vloberg.

FRONTISPIECE—THE LEGEND OF ST. ANNE. (Cf. p. 464.) The large miniature represents the legend of Anne and Joachim. In the center, Joachim, arriving at the Temple with his sacrificial lamb, is halted by the high priest. He is then driven away by one of the Temple guards (right), who cries, *"Recede."* Above, an angel appears to Joachim in the pasture and sends him back to the Temple, with the words, *"Va au temple de ierusalem."* Meanwhile, at the left, Anne is directed to the same place by a heavenly messenger, who tells her, *"Va au temple a la porte doree."* Below is represented the meeting of Anne and Joachim at the Golden Gate, with the inscription (taken from the first line of the text), *"nata vero proge.* [= *progenie*].*"* Note the curious alternation between Latin and French in these inscriptions.

The smaller miniatures in the margin represent, from top to bottom: a sermon, a classroom lecture, a discussion between two friars or monks, and (right) another sermon. The preacher, in this last case, is *Lady Wisdom,* according to Canon Astrik Gabriel, O. Praem. We may presume that the Conception of Blessed Mary is the topic of discussion in these four scenes, but no great significance should be attached to them. They are all clichés, and many similar miniatures occur throughout this breviary. The legends are all phrases snatched (with no particular discrimination) from the text under the main miniature (Upper left: *"a quo glorificata in celo."* Middle left: *"proposicionem igitur sequatur."* Lower left: *"iamque refrenamus* [for *referamus*].*"* Lower right: *"dixit eternus ad veterem."*

The Bedford (or "Salisbury") Breviary (Paris, Bibliothèque Nationale, Ms. Lat. 17,294) was made for John of Lancaster, Duke of Bedford, between 1424 and 1435, during the occupation of northern France by the English. It is probably a Parisian work, and closely resembles the Book of Hours made for the same man, from which the miniatures reproduced in plate VII are taken (see the note accompanying that plate). There are 46 such half-page miniatures in the book. (Cf. LEROQUAIS, *Les bréviaires manuscrits des bibliothèques publiques de France,* vol. III, pp. 271-348.)

The page here reproduced is folio 386v. The office of December 8, entitled *"In concepcione b. Marie virg.,"* begins on the recto of the same folio. The text which appears in the photograph is the end of Lesson II and the beginning of Lesson III of Matins.

Canon Astrik Gabriel, O. Praem., Director of the Mediaeval Institute of the University of Notre Dame, was kind enough to examine this page in the original Ms. and verify certain points which were not clear in the photograph.

Reproduced in approximately original size through the courtesy of the *Service Photographique* of the Bibliothèque Nationale.

Plate I

Three versions of this legend are given in the documents appended below, p. 513. Only the third version—that of the *Liber de Nativitate Mariae*—gives the detail of the Golden Gate.

The texts which appear below the miniature are the Introit, Oration and Epistle of the Mass of the Conception. Concerning them, see chapter IV of the present volume, p. 141 ff., especially notes 78 and 82.

Missal from Saint Victor in Paris (end of fifteenth century), f. 23v. (Paris, Bibliothèque Nationale, Ms. Lat. 14,818.)

Plate II (Detail of Plate IV)

THE LEGEND OF ANNE AND JOACHIM. (See note on Plate I.)

Upper left: Joachim, carrying the lamb he intended to sacrifice, is repulsed from the Temple.

Upper right: Joachim, in the pasture with his shepherds and flocks, is consoled by the angel.

Lower left: The meeting of Joachim and Anne at the Golden Gate of the City.

Lower right: The Nativity of Mary.

Plate III (Detail of Plate IV)

THE LEGENDS OF ABBOT HELSIN AND THE CANON OF ROUEN.

These legends are recounted in the twelfth-century sermon given in the documents appended below, p. 522 ff.

Above: THE ABBOT HELSIN. On the right, the Abbot's ship is capsizing under the vehemence of the storm and the action of the devils, and the terrified sailors jettison their cargo. But on the surface of the water there appears a figure clad in episcopal robes and bearing a scroll which reads (so far as can be judged from the somewhat obscure photograph): "Vis . mortem . evadere . Concepcionem . Virginis . celebrabis." On the left, Abbot Helsin, now safe in England, preaches in favor of the feast of the Conception.

Below: THE CANON OF ROUEN. On the right, the Canon is drowning beside his overturned boat, while devils seize his soul. The Blessed Virgin, however, observing the incident from heaven, dispatches angels to the rescue. One of them is already sweeping down through the air, past a devil who recoils, clutching his head, in anticipation of the impending defeat. (Compare the engraving in figure 19.) On the left, the angels have recovered the canon's body and are putting the soul back into it, while the devils flee in rage and chagrin.

Plate IV

ALTARPIECE OF THE VIRGIN MARY (London, National Gallery, 4250).

The *Earlier Italian Schools* catalogue of the National Gallery ascribes this work to the Venetian school; elsewhere, it is sometimes attributed to Jacobello di Bonomo. *Center:* the Virgin and Child. *Predella:* Christ and the twelve apostles. *Left* and *Right:* Scenes symbolic of the Immaculate Conception (see plates III and IV).

Plate V

MARY SANCTIFIED IN HER MOTHER'S WOMB. (Cf. p. 465 ff.)

From the Heavenly Father, rays of divine grace descend upon the tiny Virgin, visible in the womb of St. Anne. On either side stand David and Solomon, who often appear in paintings of the same subject during the fifteenth century. (Cf. plate XIII.) This miniature is found in the Mass of the Conception of the Virgin in a fragmentary manuscript in the Bibliothèque Nationale of Paris (Nouv. acq. lat. 1140, f. 1). LEROQUAIS is of the opinion that it belonged to a Book of Hours done in the second half of the fiteenth century. (*Les livres d'heures manuscrits de la bibliothèque nationale,* tome II, p. 288 f.)

Reproduced (actual size) through the courtesy of the *Service photographique* of the Bibliothèque Nationale.

Plate V

Plate VI

In this late fifteenth-century miniature, Mary, encircled by a kind of halo of glory, appears between heaven and earth, while angels surround her in the background. The arrangement anticipates somewhat the Spanish masterpieces of the sixteenth century. (Cf. plates XV-XIX) The three persons of the Trinity look out from heaven above her, while the unhappy trio, Adam, Eve and the Serpent, look up from the Garden below.

This miniature is the first of thirteen in a Book of Hours which, according to S. DE RICCI and W. J. WILSON (*Census of mediaeval and renaissance manuscripts in the United States and Canada,* vol. I, p. 315), was produced in France about 1470. It does not seem to have been intended explicitly as a symbol of the Immaculate Conception; for the *kalendar* lists the feast of the Conception in the red lettering used for ordinary feasts, whereas the major feasts are inscribed in gold.

Nevertheless there are signs that relate this work to the Immaculist images. The contrast between the authors of original sin — Adam, Eve and the Serpent — and the Virgin, who appears altogether apart in a sphere of her own close to God and surrounded by angels, naturally suggests her spotless holiness, unaffected by the consequences of the fall. Note how Adam and Eve, as well as the Serpent himself, raise their eyes towards her as if in awe and wonder.

Furthermore, the position of Mary with respect to the Trinity is almost precisely that which will reappear in the theme *Tota Pulchra Es,* except that in the latter image the Heavenly Father is unaccompanied by the Son and the Holy Ghost (cf. plates X and XI). It will be recalled that the *Tota Pulchra Es* appeared in France soon after 1500 — that is to say, only about three decades after the composition of the present work (cf. p. 475 ff.). The biblical symbols characteristic of the *Tota Pulchra Es* do not occur here; but in their place is a text from the very chapter of Ecclesiasticus from which many of the symbols were drawn.

However, rather than risk attributing to the artist an intention more precise than that which he actually had, it would seem better to regard this miniature simply as indicative of an intellectual and devotional climate altogether in harmony with the belief in the Immaculate Conception, and even predisposed in its favor, whether or not the belief was as yet consciously espoused.

The text below the miniature is the beginning of St. John's prologue —*"Secundum iohannem. In principio erat verbum . . ."* — with which the Books of Hours commonly opened. It is followed, as usual, by lessons from each of the other three gospels. The present miniature replaces the representations of the four evangelists which usually accompany these lessons. The next miniature, the Annunciation, occurs at Matins; it is followed by the Visitation (at Lauds), the Nativity (at Prime), etc. — an arrangement common in the Books of Hours.

In the margin can be seen a scroll bearing the text, *"Et sic in Syon firmata sum"* ("And thus was I established in Sion" — Ecclesiasticus 24:10). This is from the famous passage in which Wisdom speaks in praise of herself, and which the liturgy has so frequently drawn upon for the praises of the Blessed Virgin. (Cf. p. 476, note 39)

Reproduced (actual size) through the courtesy of the Art Institute of Chicago (no. 17,388).

Plate VI

Plate VII

OLD TESTAMENT SYMBOLS OF THE BLESSED VIRGIN. (See p. 476 ff.)

The miniatures here reproduced ornament the Mass of the Blessed Virgin in an early fifteenth-century Book of Hours. They represent Old Testament figures taken as symbols of Mary. Although such symbols became standard elements of the Immaculist image, *Tota Pulchra Es,* in the following century, they seem to be used here without any specifically Immaculist reference, for the Mass which they ornament is simply the common of the Blessed Virgin, *Salve sancta parens.*

These miniatures occur in the "Bedford" Book of Hours (British Museum Add. Ms. 18,850), so-called because it was made for John of Lancaster, Duke of Bedford and regent of France. (It was likewise for him that the "Bedford Breviary," from which our frontispiece has been taken, was made.) The Book of Hours was made between 1423 and 1430 as a wedding gift from the duke to his wife Anne, daughter of John, Duke of Burgundy. (Cf. *Illuminated Manuscripts of the British Museum,* in which a detailed account of the work is given, as well as a reproduction of one page in color.)

The Mass of the Blessed Virgin in this book runs from folio 282v to 284r, and immediately follows the Mass of St. Gregory, to which the miniatures on folio 282v refer. On each of the three remaining pages, there are two miniatures, one in the outside margin and one in the bottom margin, just as in the half-page reproduced in plate VII. This arrangement seems to be observed throughout the book. The text of the book is in Latin, but at the bottom of each page there are two lines of French explaining the meaning of the two miniatures.

The lower half (or, more nearly, two-thirds) of folio 283r is reproduced in the upper part of plate VII. The miniature in the right margin represents Mary standing upon the dragon and plunging the foot of the Cross into him. *"Une fame te casera la teste"* — "A woman shall crush thy head," reads the scroll in the hand of the Heavenly Father. At the bottom of the page, the inscription referring to this miniature explains: *"Comment la vierge marie fust signifiee en lancien testament et comment elle mist le pied sur sathanas"* — "How the Virgin Mary was symbolized in the Old Testament, and how she put her foot on Satan." This is one of the earliest extant examples of the use of the Protogospel in an artistic representation of the Blessed Virgin. (Cf. p. 471)

The bottom miniature is described by the line, *"Comment la vierge marie fust signifiee par la colombe la quelle aporta bonne nouvelle a larche de noe"* — "How the Virgin Mary was symbolized by the dove that brought good news to Noe's Ark." The scroll within the miniature, which Mary holds, declares, *"je aporte le sauvement a lumain lignage"* — "I bring salvation to the human race."

The miniatures in the lower part of plate VII are from folios 283v and 284r. *Left* (283v, left border): Mary symbolized by Jacob's ladder (*"Comment la vierge marie fust signifiee par lechiele iacob par la quelle les anges montoient & descendoient."*)

Upper middle (283v, lower border): Mary symbolized by the Fountain of Jerusalem (*"Comment la vierge marie fust signifiee par la fontoine de iherusalem, de la quelle david desira"*; cf. II Kings. 23:15). The text within the miniature reads: *"je ta porte leaue de salvac[io]n"*—"I bring you the water of salvation."

Right (284r, right border): Mary symbolized by the olive tree that bore fruit while it was still green (*"Comment la vierge marie fust figuree par labre de lolivier le quel estoit vert et portoit fruit."*)

Lower middle: (284r, lower border): Mary symbolized by the seven-branched candlestick of Zacharias 4:2 (*"Comment la vierge marie fust figuree par le candelabre de vij lampes que vit zacharie le prophete."*)

Several of these symbols will be found used and "explained" in the text from Peter Riga transcribed among the documents given at the end of the present volume.

Reproduced through the courtesy of the Trustees of the British Museum. The reproductions are slightly reduced in size; the original folios are 10⅜ in. in height by 7¼ in. in width.

...llos q̔ muunus voni
ne deus perpetua mentis et corpo
ris sanitate gaudire: et gloriosa
beate marie semper uirginis in
tercessione a presenti liberari tri
sticia et eterna perfrui leticia. Po̅.

Lectio libri sapiencie.
B inicio et ante secula
creata sum et ad futurum seculum
non desinam. et in habitacione sca̅
coram ipo ministraui. Et sic in
syon firmata sum: et in ciuitate

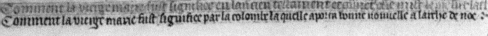

Comment la vierge marie fuit signistee en lancien testament et comment elle mult lende sarl
Comment la vierge marie fuit signifiee par la colombe la quelle aporta bonne nouuelle a laribe de noe

Plate
VII

Plate VIII

A Moslem Immaculate Conception?

Plate VIII

Mohammed's teaching, that "Every Adam's son coming into this world is touched by Satan, except Mary's son and his mother," is discussed in chapter XII of the present volume, p. 447 ff. Perhaps some trace of this belief is expressed in the adjoining miniature, executed in Hindu-Persian style. It probably dates from the reign of the Timourides, the Mongol sovereigns Akbar our Djahângir (sixteenth and seventeenth centuries), when the Moslem artists often drew inspiration from Christian paintings and images introduced by the Jesuit missionaries. (Cp. plate IX, and the Woman slaying the dragon in plate VII, upper right.)

The Urdu inscription in Arabic characters at the upper left proclaims the following words of praise, which are an allusion to the triumph of the Virgin Maryam over Iblîs (Satan):

> From this princess comes the victory, the eternal victory.

Reproduced from a photograph by M. Vloberg of a work in the Bibliothèque Nationale, Paris (Cabinet des Estampes, OD. 44, f. 20).

Plate IX

Christ and Mary triumphing over the Serpent. (Cf. p. 471 f.)

Mary is crowned and enthroned as a Queen. Two of the Apocalyptic symbols appear — the moon at her feet and the crown of stars on her head, not to speak of the stars scattered over her gown. The Christ Child plunges the pointed foot of the Cross into the mouth of the Serpent trodden under Mary's foot, showing that it is through her Son that Mary triumphs over the Enemy of mankind.

The angels in the corners also bear some of Mary's traditional emblems: a star, the sun, and the moon (or perhaps a mirror?). It is not clear from the reproduction whether the fourth angel once held something or not.

The text on the fluted border reads (beginning just left of the Serpent's head, and reading clockwise, except for the last phrase):

EOM:A:ME   COLUMBA   [?]...me. A dove
EST AM[I]CA: MEA ET MACULA   is my beloved. And stain
NON EST IN:ME   is not in me.
SINE:LABE·:·||·:·CONCEPTA·:·   Conceived without sin.

This photograph has been reproduced from the catalog of a Paris auction, in which it is described as, "Plaque hispano-mauresque à reflets métalliques," and dated at the end of the fifteenth century.

Plate IX

Plates X and XI

A very early and a very late example of this theme.

Plate X represents the main altarpiece in the Church *del Cerco* at Artajona (Spain). The altarpiece is dated 1497 by Dom Manuel TRENS, Conservator of the Diocesan Museum in Barcelona. This would make it perhaps the oldest known example of this theme (but cf. the reservations made by M. VLOBERG, p. 479, n. 46).

The usual fifteen symbols appear in the customary arrangement. (Cf. p. 476, n. 39) It will be noted that they correspond exactly to those of the woodcut reproduced in figure 9, p. 477.

Photo Mas, Barcelona.

Plate XI represents the seventeenth century altarpiece (carved in wood) of the Cathedral of Bayeux (France). The traditional theme has here undergone a lavish elaboration. The customary inscriptions have, for the most part, been replaced by interesting variants, which generally omit the name of the object represented (here supplied in parentheses):

(sol) EXORIENS   (porta) COELI
                                        (stella) MARIS
(rosa) SINE SPINA   LUNA PLENA
(lilium) INTER SPINAS   (turris) DAVIDIS
                                        (speculum) SINE MACULA
(puteus) AQUAE VIVAE   (fons) GRATIARUM
                                        (Altissimus) FUNDAVIT (eam - i.e. the
                                            "Civitas Dei"; cf. Ps. 86:5.)

The usual *Flowering Rod of Jesse, Beautiful Olive Tree,* and *Cedar of Lebanon* have been fused into a single *Tree of Life* (ARBOR VITAE).

Five new symbols have been added (cf. p. 476, note 39):

(scala) JACOB
(arca) DOMINI (i.e. Ark of the Covenant)
(templum) SOLOMONIS   (odor) THURI[S]
(vellum) RORE MADENS (i.e. Gedeon's fleece)

Finally, the six Old Testament figures worked into the border (Abraham, David, Solomon, Elias, Isaias and Micheas) add a note from the "Disputation" theme. (Cf. p. 486 ff.)

Plate X

Plate XI

Plate XII

The doctrine of the Immaculate Conception is being tried before a "court of law." Against the theologian who points to the testimony of St. Paul ("In Adam all have sinned" — cf. Rom. 5:12), Christ, as Mary's advocate, brings evidence of her virtues.

Reproduced (actual size) through the courtesy of the *Service Photographique* of the Bibliothèque Nationale, Paris, from *Recueil de Chants Royaux du Puy de Rouen* (ms. fr. 379, f. 6). This miniature illustrates the *Chant Royal* composed by Master Guillaume Tybauld (ca. 1530) on the theme, *"Marie gaigna son proces."*

Plate XII

Plate XIII

"SCHOLASTIC DISPUTATION" IN FAVOR OF THE IMMACULATE CONCEPTION. (Cf. p. 488)

The upper part of the painting is a symbolical adaptation of the episode of Esther and Assuerus. (Cf. p. 488, n. 71) Below, from left to right:

St. Anselm, with the inscription supposedly taken from his writings, *"Non puto esse verum amatorem Virginis qui celebrare respuit festum sue conceptionis."* — "Anyone who refuses to celebrate the feast of the Virgin's Conception is, in my opinion, no true lover of hers." (Cf. references given in note 69 on p. 488.)

St. Augustine, with the text, *"In celo qualis est pater talis est Filius. In terra qualis est Mater talis est Filius secundum carnem"* — "In heaven, the Son is like His Father; on earth, the Son is like His Mother, so far the flesh is concerned." (—Sermo 20 *ad Fratres in eremo; PL* 40, 1267. The sermon is regarded by the editors as not authentic.)

St. Anthony (= *Duns Scotus?* — cf. p. 488, note 72), with the text of Scotus, *"Videtur probabile quod est excellentius attribuere Marie"* — It seems probable that whatever is more excellent should be attributed to Mary."

King David, with the text of Psalm 18:6: *"In sole posuit tabernaculum suum"* — "He pitched His tent in the sun."

King Solomon, with text of the Canticle of Canticles 4:7: *"Tota pulchra es amica mea et macula non est in te"*—"Thou art all beautiful, my beloved, and there is no stain in thee."

The landscape in the background is composed largely of Marian symbols: the *Rose garden in Jericho* and the jars of *Myrrh* and *Balsam* are labeled; the *Cedar* and the *Palm* are obvious; the tree in the center is probably the *Olive.*

Plate XIV
The 'Tota Pulchra Es' in the Grimani Breviary.

The usual elements of the theme (cf. p. 476, n. 39) are here arranged into a landscape. (The tall tree next to the *Tower of David* is doubtless meant for the *Cedar of Lebanon,* although it has no inscription visible on the photograph.) An angel has been introduced to hold the *Flawless Mirror,* as well as two others who place the crown on Mary's head. The *Moon* has been placed under Mary's feet in the manner of the *Woman of the Apocalypse* image. Above the head of the Heavenly Father appears the usual text, *"Tota pulchra es, amica mea, et macula non est in te."* (Cant. 4:7)

This is the last miniature in the Breviary of Cardinal Grimani (Venice, Bibl. Marciana). The work is Flemish, but the date uncertain. It was long supposed to have been done prior to 1489 (which would make it by far the earliest known example of the *Tota Pulchra Es*), but some scholars now consider it possible that the work dates only from the early sixteenth century. (Cf. Giulio Coggiola, *Le Bréviaire Grimani de la Bibliothèque Saint-Marc de Venise,* Leyden, Paris, 1908; and Jean Fournée, *Les thèmes iconographiques . . . ,* p. 60 f.)

We reproduce it here (from a photograph belonging to M. Maurice Vloberg) largely in order to illustrate the transition (not precisely chronological) from the customary *Tota Pulchra Es* (Cf. figure 8, p. 475, and plate X, above), to the great Spanish *Inmaculadas* of the seventeenth century. (Cf. the following plates)

Plate XV
El Greco: The Immaculate Conception (1609-1614; cp. p. 491 f.)

The landscape composed of biblical symbols is retained, but in a secondary role. Note also the variation of the symbols from the usual ones.

Budapest, Nemes Collection.

Plate XVI
Francisco de Zurbaran († 1662): The Immaculate Conception. (Cf. p. 492.)

Only the faintest indication of a landscape is visible along the bottom of the painting. Some of the biblical symbols can be discerned — from left to right: the Temple of Solomon (?), the fountain, the mirror, the gate, the cedar (?), the well, the tower (?).

Reproduced through the courtesy of the Szepmuveszeti Muzeum, Budapest.

Plate XVII
Bartolomé Esteban Murillo († 1682): The San Ildefonso Immaculate Conception. (Cf. p. 494)

The Immaculate Virgin is here completely detached from any landscape, and only four symbols are retained, born by the cherubs.

Madrid, Prado. Photo Mas, Barcelona.

Plate XVIII
Giovanni Batista Tiepolo († 1770): The Immaculate Conception of San Pascual d'Aranjuez. (Cf. p. 471.)

By introducing the Serpent into his Immaculate Conception, the artist has fused together the three great biblical images of Mary: the Woman of the Protogospel, who crushes the head of the Serpent; the Woman of the Apocalypse, who stands on the moon and is crowned with stars; and the Spouse of the Canticle of Canticles, in connection with whom the minor biblical symbols — lily, rose, palm, mirror, etc. — found entrance into Immaculist art. (Cf. p. 470) For good measure, the artist has also added the dove of the Holy Spirit, Who does not appear so frequently in this art (unless one admit the Tree of Jesse as a symbol of Mary's Conception; cf. p. 499 f.).

Madrid, Prado. Photo Mas, Barcelona.

Plate XIV

Plate XV (EL GRECO)

Plate XVI (Zurbaran)

Plate XVII
(Murillo)

Plate XVIII →
(Tiepolo)

Plate XX

Plate XX
Our Lady of Lourdes. (Cf. p. 497 f.)

This is not the well-known statue by Joseph Fabiche, which stands in the niche of the Apparition, but is rather that which used to stand over the old baths left of the Grotto. It was designed (as also was Fabiche's work) in an effort to capture one moment of the scene described by Bernadette:

"The Lady stood upright above the wild rose and was just like she is on the Miraculous Medal. When I asked her the third time, *she looked grave and seemed to become humble. She joined her hands and lifted them to her breast.* She looked up at the sky. . . . Then slowly separating her hands — like this — she leaned down towards me and said in a trembling voice, 'I am the Immaculate Conception.' " (—Michel de Saint-Pierre, *Bernadette and Lourdes*, p. 76 f.)

Note the remarkable resemblance between this figure and the statue by Alonso Cano in plate XIX.

Plate XIX

Plate XXI

During the night of November 27, 1830, this apparition occurred in the chapel of the Filles de la Charité in Paris. Sister Catherine saw Mary standing on a globe inscribed *France*. Under her left foot, the head of the Serpent lay crushed, while rays of light streamed from her hands as a symbol of the graces obtained through her. Above her head appeared the words, "O Marie conçue sans péché, priez pour nous qui avons recours à vous" — "O Mary, conceived without sin, pray for us who have recourse to thee."

Then the vision swung around, as if on a great medal; on the reverse appeared the two hearts (one encircled with thorns, the other pierced with a sword) and the *M* surmounted by the cross. (The present engraving combines these two phases of the apparition into one.)

Mary directed that a medal be made in this likeness, and Sister Catherine communicated this request to her spiritual director, the Vincentian, Father Aladel. The latter put the matter off, and it was not until June 30, 1832, that the medal was actually struck, by order of Mgr. de Quélen, Archbishop of Paris, who had learned of the apparition from Father Aladel. The numerous miracles which at once began to be reported brought wide diffusion to the medal. By the same stroke, popular devotion to the Immaculate Conception was intensified, preparing the way for the Definition of 1854.

Plate XXII reproduces (actual size) an engraving of the apparition which was published by Father ALADEL himself, in his little volume, *Notice historique sur l'origine et les effets de la nouvelle médaille frappée en l'honneur de l'Immaculée Conception de la Très-Sainte Vierge, et généralement connue sous le nom de la Médaille miraculeuse* (Paris, 8ème éd., 1842).

Reproduced through the courtesy of the Marian Library of the University of Dayton.

Plate **XXII**
The Madonna of Edme Bouchardon
(Cf. p. 472, n. 33)

A much-copied eighteenth-century
work, prototype of the Madonna of the
Miraculous Medal (cf. *infra*).
Paris, Treasury of the Church of St.-
Sulpice. Photo Lutetia.

Plate XXIII
MONUMENT OF POPE PIUS IX. (Cf. p. 497.)

This statue, designed by Giuseppe OBICI and cast in the Vatican foundries, was erected in the Piazza di Spagna at Rome to commemorate the definition of the Immaculate Conception. Construction on the monument began on May 6, 1855, and it was dedicated on September 8, 1857. (Cf. Luigi HUETTER, "Il monumento all'Immacolata in Piazza di Spagna a Roma," in *Virgo Immaculata,* XIV, pp. 414-422.)

Photo Felici, Rome.

Plate XXIV
NOTRE-DAME DE GENÈVE.

In 1859, Pope Pius IX gave this statue to Father (later Cardinal) Mermillod for the new church of the Immaculate Conception in Geneva. The Pope is reported to have said that every day since the definition he had prayed before this statue. (Cf. Edmond GONTIER, "Notre-Dame de Genève," in the Canadian review, *Marie,* 1954, pp. 213-216.)

Photo L. Baccheta, Geneva.

Plate XXV
THE LADY ON THE DOME, UNIVERSITY OF NOTRE DAME.

Plate XXV

When the University building burned to the ground in 1879, construction began almost at once on a "new Notre Dame," which was to be surmounted by a great dome supporting a statue of Our Lady. The students of the neighboring St. Mary's College for women volunteered to pay for the statue, which was to be modeled after the one erected in Rome not many years previously by Pope Pius IX, in commemoration of the Definition of the Immaculate Conception. (Cf. plate XXIII) The statue was made in Chicago by Giovanni MELI, and delivered to Notre Dame in the summer of 1880. Pending completion of the dome (which does not appear in the adjoining photograph), the statue was placed over the front porch of the new building. In October of 1883 it was hoisted to its present position. Both statue and dome are covered with gold. The statue originally wore a crown containing lights which illumined it at night; later on, the crown was removed and the lights placed below.

Plate XXIII

Plate XXIV

Plate **XXVI**
Lu Hung Nien: The Immaculate Virgin.

This artist, noteworthy for the noble simplicity of his style, was the disciple of Luke Ch'en, founder of the Chinese neo-Christian school, at the University of Peking.

the *Purísima* all the attractiveness of youth. This was the feeling of St. Teresa of Avila, who experienced sweet tenderness in imagining the Blessed Virgin with the grace of a young girl, *niña*. The painter Pacheco, godfather of Velasquez, echoed the Carmelite saint, in formulating the following rules for the studio:

> This Lady should be painted in the flower of age, as twelve or thirteen years old, as a very beautiful *niña*, with attractive but grave eyes, a marvelously formed mouth and nose, red cheeks, beautiful loose-flowing golden hair—in fine, as well as a human brush can paint her.[82]

These banalities were superfluous for great artists whose contemplation gave them other resources, thanks to which they were able to give the *Purísima* much more than the air of an *infante*.

In this connection, how could we forget that the idea of these painters was one day to take on a living and marvelous reality in the best known of the Virgin's modern apparitions? She here gave her name, in the dialect of Bigorre spoken by the visionary: *"Qué soy era Immaculada Councepciou"* —"I am the Immaculate Conception." She emphasized this name by an appearance of radiant youth: *"Uno petito damizelo,* a little girl, no taller than myself," replied Bernadette to those who questioned her about the Lady of the grotto of Massabielle. But long before this favored shepherd girl, the artists and the mystics of Spain had already glimpsed the Immaculate Virgin in the splendor of her eternal youth.

The "Pintor de las Concepciones"

We have scarcely mentioned the painter *par excellence* of the Immaculate Conception, Esteban Murillo. An exceptionally gifted man, mystic, poet and a magician with colors, he was, with Zurbaran, the master of the ecstasies and miracles of the saints; but in rendering the belief in Mary's original sanctity, he outdid himself. He understood that in the instant in which her life began, God's Elect is a being more of heaven than of earth: as she was conceived in the Divine Thought "before time and its abysses," so was she conceived in the flesh, the flower and *calix* of purity in which God's very holiness would become Incarnate in the person of the Word.

To render this mystery, the Sevillian master simplifies the symbolism of

---

[82] *Arte de la Pintura*, Seville, 1649. Pacheco, who was the master of Murillo, was a personage all the more respected in that he was feared: the Inquisition had made him censor of "all holy paintings found in the shops and public places."

Another Spaniard who composed a sort of 'Painters Guide,' Juan de Ayala, makes similar recommendations, particularly concerning the youthful air which the *Purísima* should have: "in primis depingenda est sacra Virgo aetate, ut mihi videtur, admodum tenera . . . decennis, inquam, aut duodennis: in hac enim purior in Virgine atque emaculatior pulchritudo resplendet."—*Pictor christianus eruditus*, Madrid, 1730, p. 149.

the French image, when he does not suppress it altogether; only two or three of his *Purísimas* maintain the original tradition. He replaces the conventional symbolism of the biblical figures with splendor and radiance of form, enveloped in a golden light. No one else spent beauty as lavishly as he in affirming the belief so dear to the heart of Spain.

He produced numerous *Inmaculadas,* of which eighteen are particularly well known; among these, there are four or five in which he attained the peak of religious art. In his first manner, between the years 1653 and 1665, he painted the two *Purísimas* of the Prado: that of *Aranjuez,* was called, by the poet José Velardo, a "Miracle of Life"; that of *San Ildefonso* (plate XVII) is an exquisite vision such as could have been dreamed by the contemplatives who, like St. Teresa, liked to picture the Virgin in the flower of adolescence: if she were not so solemn she could be taken for the elder sister of the four little angels who bear her emblematic flowers—the rose of charity, the lily of innocence, the palm of martyrdom, the laurel of glory.

Similar little angels hover in a cloud over the *Inmaculada* named after *Maréchal Soult,* the soldier-collector who secured possession of it during Napoleon's expedition in Spain. After being exhibited in the Louvre for a century, this work was restored to its land of origin during the last war. It is considered to belong to the artist's third manner, like the *Walpole* Immaculate Conception in the Hermitage Museum of Leningrad. This last, after having belonged to the English Minister, Horace Walpole, passed into the collection of Catherine of Russia. One of Esteban's daughters is said to have been the model for this painting which is considered to have more strength and feeling than that which was once in the Louvre.

The museum of Seville conserves the *Purísima* painted for the Franciscans of that city. Intended for the triumphal arch of their church, and therefore meant to be seen from a distance, this canvas, eight feet high, is a vigorous piece of work. Its expression and gesture are perfect, its attitude superb. Émile Mâle gives it this enthusiastic acclaim: "It has no equal. . . . It is a cry of ecstasy from Old Spain."[83]

Whatever be our preference among these *Purísimas,* they all suggest the same meditation. They evoke the Immaculate Virgin as the realization of the plan of her sublime predestination, before all creation—spiritual or physical: *Ab aeterno ordinata sum,* she declares in her liturgical office. Mankind is about to receive her, but she has not yet fully departed from heaven. She seems to pause in her descent towards the earth upon waves of light and golden clouds: with her large eyes raised towards her invisible Creator, her hands joined or her arms outstretched, her feet resting on the crescent of the night, she remains for a moment motionless in this limpid and mysterious expanse. She lingers there as if in her natural element,

---

[83] *L'art religieux du XVIIe siècle,* p. 48.

and as if she were to know soon enough this world of darkness and misery in which all that tarnishes and soils will be powerless over her.

Is this too lyrical a judgment upon these *Purísimas*? Are we straining to find in them much more than Murillo was able to put into them? Certain critics have even refused to see in the work of this painter any spirituality whatsoever. In his defense, it is sufficient to point out that for centuries he had been able to hold the constant and unqualified admiration of those who are capable of fervor among both the common people and the elite.

Murillo has been called a visionary. He even surpasses the greater part of the mystics and seers, who are so poor when it comes to describing the excellence of the marvelous supernatural world. There are theologians who think that in certain cases the being who makes an apparition takes on no other form than that of light. Some are inclined to believe that this was the case at Fatima. To explain the immaterial splendor which radiated from the Lady, little Lucia found these words: *"She was light."* Three simple words, but so meaningful! They sum up the magnificent praises which the Church address to *"Her who gave birth to the Light of the World,"* and who is a *"Night of light, bearing her Son, born before the morning star,"* as the liturgy chants in the procession for Candlemas Day.

This is what the pious and magical Sevillian also wished to render with his misty colors and dawnlike gleamings. His *Purísima* is of the same essence as the almost immaterial light that envelopes her. The better element of our sensibility will always be awakened by these blinding appearances of God's Elect, with her great eyes lost in ecstasy and with her long hair that floats, like her heavy blue mantle, in the wind of infinity.[84]

V

HOW SHOULD THE IMMACULATE CONCEPTION BE REPRESENTED?

Mary's Immaculate Conception was defined as a dogma of faith by Pius IX, on December 8, 1854. One might have hoped that this victory of the ancient belief would stimulate art and inspire it to new creations. As a matter of fact, Church authorities did interest themselves in the matter.[85] Bishop Malou of Bruges, in order to forestall the phantasies

---

[84] Another canvas by Murillo, in the Louvre, exalts Mary's same prerogative. Here she appears to some lay people, perhaps students of some university such as that of Salamanca, in which an oath was taken to defend the belief. Cf. *supra,* p. 241. If this hypothesis is correct, this work should be classed among the dogmatico-historical compositions of which we have spoken above (section III).

[85] In the bibliography we cite the dissertation of Cardinal Sterkx, Archbishop of Malines.

of painters who were not very good theologians, published a sort of guide-book in 1856 under the title, *Iconographie de l'Immaculée Conception, — ou de la meilleure manière de représenter ce mystère.* He lays down the principle that a "good image should have all the qualities of a good definition," and, in keeping with this directive, he indicates the features and attitude that should be given to Mary, the form and color of her clothing, and the attributes and symbols which should accompany her.

This author is very well informed about the subject, which he treats in great detail; his judgment is often quite discerning, and his book can be consulted with profit. But his dialectic is too imperative for a domain in which the liberty of the artist also counts. He subjects it to rules that are sometimes arbitrary, a striking example of which is his prohibition of representing the Immaculate Virgin with bare feet. This usage he finds contrary to theology, to good taste, and to iconographic tradition—hence objectionable on three counts.[86] Erudite minds do not always escape being doctrinaire. The learned prelate published his work in 1856; two years later, the Interested Party herself retorted by appearing at Lourdes with nothing on her feet but a rose (cf. plate XX).[87] When, in our own day, Mary appeared to little Mariette Beco at Banneux (Belgium) in 1933, her right foot which alone was visible, was again clothed in nothing but a rose.

Bishop Malou's dogmatism[88] has kept people from appreciating the useful part of his work. Both Catholic and Protestant critics have treated him severely. We may disregard the diatribes of the Protestant minister, Athanase Coquerel, which are directed more against the Roman Church than against the iconographic theories of the Bishop of Bruges;[89] but, while the Jesuit archeologist, Father Cahier, was moderate in his criticism, Canon Auber wrote unsparingly:

[86] *Op. cit.,* pp. 33-35.

[87] The earliest and most important historians of Lourdes, H. LASSERRE, Father CROS, J. B. ESTRADE, Fathers SEMPÉ and DUBOÉ, are unanimous concerning this detail of the *bare feet* of the apparition. However, the *Curé* of Lourdes at the time of Bernadette, Abbé PEYRAMALE, in recounting to his brother the first prodigies of the Grotto, wrote to him that "the Lady had yellow slippers, with a rose on each one." This letter, unknown until recently, is dated March 9, 1858—one month, that is, after the first apparition. How are we to explain it? The Parisian journal *La Croix,* in its issue of September 27, 1957, published the text of this letter, which has been reprinted in *Lourdes: Documents authentiques* edited by René LAURENTIN, Paris, Lethielleux, 1957, vol. I, pp. 229-231.

[88] Still other arbitrary veto's can be observed in the same work. Thus, for example, the Bishop approved the rigorism of Juan de Ayala who is severe towards painters guilty of representing the Blessed Virgin "with head bare, and long hair flowing loose over an ivory neck!" Not even Murillo is absolved by the episcopal iconographer for having committed this fault! (*op. cit.,* p. 39)

[89] See his work cited in the bibliography at the end of this chapter, as well as that of another Protestant of the same opinion, A. STAP.

The worst thing about Bishop Malou's system is that his authority as bishop led some in his diocese to attempt to realize his ideas, which have been abandoned today, and never had much success.[90]

But are the Canon's own ideas any better? He maintains that the Blessed Virgin should never be painted or sculptured without her Son, not even in the mystery of her original exemption.[91] However, there are scenes and events in which Mary obviously cannot be accompanied by Jesus, such as her birth, her education, her marriage, the Visitation and the Annunciation; and it is not at all evident why the presence of the Infant is any more necessary in the mystery of the Immaculate Conception. At best, it could be explained only by some mystical or symbolic reason; and even in this case there arises the danger of confusion about the time and the theme. That is why the figure of Mary alone, with the serpent under her feet, was destined to prevail both in art and in devotional imagery.

Certain theologians, without denying the meaning given by iconography to the figure of Mary and the Serpent, consider it nevertheless to be based on an erroneous exegesis. Such was the judgment of Father Patrizi, among others: for him, the biblical expression, "crush [the Serpent's] head," far from implying an exemption from the original stain, formally excludes it.[92] This opinion is contradicted by the magisterial Act of Pius IX in 1854; for the Bull *Ineffabilis,* along with other biblical arguments, invokes this very text of Genesis foretelling the victory of the Woman over the Serpent. And on September 8, 1857, the same Pope dedicated in the *Piazza di Spagna* at Rome, as a memorial of the dogmatic definition, a bronze statue of Mary Immaculate (plate XXIII): one hand is raised toward heaven, while the other is lowered towards the earth; she stands upon the crescent moon and the globe of the earth, on which the head of the Serpent is crushed under her left foot. Pius IX himself is thought to have indicated this attitude to the sculptor.

And has not the Blessed Virgin a word of her own in this matter? It would seem that she wished to provide the best and definitive model, when she descended among the French Pyrennees in 1858, to ratify, as one may believe, the judgment made four years previously by the Vicar of Christ concerning her prerogative. But whether from indifference or from impotence, the artists have not profited by this remarkable manifestation, which they have left entirely to the makers of popular images. Yet were not the setting of Lourdes, the phases of the apparitions, and the

[90] *Histoire du symbolisme,* Paris, 1871-1872, t. IV, p. 137, n. 2.
[91] *Op. cit.,* pp. 137 ff.
[92] F. X. PATRIZI, *De* אןח, *hoc est, de immaculata Mariae origine a Deo praedicta disquisitio, cum appendice de feminini generis enallage in linguis semiticis usitata.* Rome, 1853, pp. 24-25.

reflections of invisible Beauty upon the ecstatic countenance of Bernadette, so many resources for the brush of a believing soul?

Léon Bloy declared that when we seek to express the mystery of the Immaculate Conception, "we should be fearful of every word."[93] The same can be said, with still greater reason, of lines and colors used to paint it. While the more sublime element of the dogmatic fact, as Pius IX has defined it, transcends the possibilities of art, still there is a certain aspect of the mystery that remains plastically accessible, when it is envisaged according to the concrete and marvelous data of Lourdes.

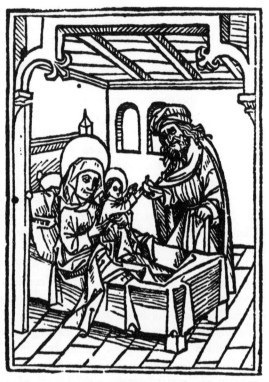

Figure 14. THE NATIVITY OF THE VIRGIN. End of the fifteenth century.

During this centenary of the apparition, religious art should renew its inspiration by the edge of the Gave, in front of the rocky niche of Massabielle. There one can perceive more vividly the beauteous form that ravished the soul of Bernadette; there one can better understand her appearance of extreme youth, chosen, no doubt, for the profound reason grasped by Colette Yver:

> Bernadette saw the Virgin Mary at the age of the Annunciation, as we may believe. Must it not be this age of the Divine Maternity that heaven has eternalized in her glorious person?[94]

Lourdes is ever visible, ever actual; it is a visit from the Immaculate Virgin, who has descended, in the words of Dante, from the "Kingdom of eternal love, of which she keeps the keys and opens the door."

---

[93] *Vie de Mélanie, Bergère de La Salette*, Paris 1919, Introduction.
[94] *L'humble sainte Bernadette*, Paris, 1934, p. 86.

VI

THREE DISPUTED "SYMBOLS OF THE IMMACULATE CONCEPTION"

THE TREE OF JESSE

Many iconographers follow the opinion of Emile Mâle, who declared, "The artists saw an assertion of Mary's original privilege in the simple image of her lineage." But his only argument is that the *Tree of Jesse* illustrates the Office of the Conception in certain printed Books of Hours and Missals. However, the *Tree of Jesse* engraving is accompanied by another—the direct image of the Immaculate Conception with the biblical symbols (the '*Tota Pulchra Es*' described above, in section II).

This association of the two themes is frequent in Norman miniatures, bas-reliefs, and stained-glass windows. As I see it, their juxtaposition is not a reduplication of the same idea, but rather a distinction: the *Tree* illustrates a historical fact—the genealogy of Christ and his Mother; while the Virgin with the Biblical symbols expresses a moral reality: the privilege of original grace.

Figure 15. THE TREE OF JESSE. End of the fifteenth century.

A certain number of *Trees of Jesse* terminate in a *lily* from which emerges the Virgin with the Child. It is to these above all that the Immaculist interpretation is given. According to certain iconographers, this flower, the emblem of innocence, intervenes between the tree, infected in its first root, and its heavenly offshoot; hence the conclusion that the Immaculate Conception was clearly intended. This is plausible; but it is equally possible to recognize in this lily the simple symbol of the most pure Maternity of Mary, according to the words of Isaias on the flowering rod of Jesse (Is. 11:1). Incidentally, it is often from a different flower, notably the rose, that the Virgin and Child emerge.

For that matter, the iconographers who attribute an Immaculist "sap"—if one may put it so—to the *Tree of Jesse,* find it difficult to cite examples that are beyond question. They are obliged to refer to the conjunction of criteria that are only more or less valid. On the other hand, according to the interpretation which seems to have been current during the Middle Ages, the *Tree of Jesse* represented nothing more than the genealogy of Christ and His Mother. A proof of this is furnished by the illuminated manuscripts of the famous *Speculum Humanae Salvationis,* which codified, as it were, the figurative parallelism between the Old and New Testaments. In this work, two miniatures are juxtaposed: on the one hand, the *Tree of Jesse,* and, facing it, the Nativity of Mary. (Cf. figures 14 and 15; another noteworthy example occurs in the beautiful manuscript of Chantilly.)

In conclusion, for the present author it has not been established that the *Tree of Jesse* is an evident and major symbol of the Immaculate Conception.

THE VIRGIN WITH THE UNICORN.

In spite of the opinions and the arguments of iconographers such as Germain de Maidy and Maxe-Werly[95] the Unicorn cannot be regarded as an Immaculist symbol, even by adaptation: the legend of this fabulous beast proves sufficiently that it entered into Marian typology as a figure of *Virginity* of the Mother of God.

Certain *Annunciations,* called the *Hunt for the Unicorn,* are put in a setting composed of the same biblical symbols which are used in, and characterize, the theme *Tota Pulchra Es.* But the similarity of these borrowings is not sufficient reason to classify the unicorn among the types of the Immaculate Conception. The biblical symbols were applied to the iconography of the Annunciation even before their application to that of the Immaculate Conception, and they can be found grouped together in still other Marian themes. Bishop Malou even goes so far as to declare that the symbols which compose the *'Tota Pulchra es'* "are foreign to the mystery of the Immaculate Conception." (*Iconographie.* . . , pp. 96 f. and 134 f.) It would be more accurate to say that these symbols are equally capable of representing other mysteries and prerogatives of the Blessed Virgin.

ST. ANNE WITH MARY AND JESUS.

Studies in the iconography of the Immaculate Conception sometimes associate with the 'realistic' image discussed above (section I) the trilogy, Anne, Mary and Jesus (referred to in German as *Anna selbdritt*), in which Mary holds Jesus in her arms, and is herself held in the arms or in the lap of St. Anne. (Cf. figure 4, p. 468) Sculptured representations of this type are particularly numerous in Brittany. The natural explanation of this fact is to be sought in the ardent devotion which the Bretons have long

---

[95] Cf. the bibliography at the end of this chapter.

had to the grandmother of the Savior. And it seems probable that the intention of such trilogies—whether sculptured or painted—is simply to honor St. Anne in this relationship, without any specific reference to the Immaculate Conception of Mary.[96]

VII

NOTE ON THE *"PUYS DE PALINOD"*

In the course of the fifteenth century, certain confraternities under the patronage of the Conception or some other mystery of the Virgin, gradually lost their original character as simply pious associations, and turned into literary institutions, called "academies." The term *puy* which was used to designate them derived, not from the Latin *puteus* (a well) but rather from *podium,* for the pulpit or platform from which the confreres declaimed their works.[97]

Such *Puys Notre Dame* came into existence all over the North of France and Normandy. They seem to have originated from that of Arras, which was imitated at Lille, Douai, and Valenciennes. The *Puy* of Arras conferred awards on two poems of a laureat who was to become famous as a chronicler, Jean Froissart. The Flemish towns already had identical academies, the *Chambers of Rhetoric.*

The *puys* flourished in Picardy, notably at Amiens and Abbeville. That of Amiens, the statutes of which were drawn up in 1451, comprised craftsmen, merchants and shopkeepers: simple people and, for the most part, great eaters and drinkers. Their patronal feast was that of the Purification of Our Lady: on that day they presented the 'mystery' in the nave of the Cathedral, Mary's role being played by a girl carrying a wax figure of the Infant Jesus. Beginning in 1452, the master elected for the year was re-

---

[96] We agree with the judgment of Bishop MALOU: "These groups do not represent the Immaculate Conception of Mary, but the family of St. Anne." (*Iconographie ...,* p. 737, note.) — On the iconographic theme, *Anna selbdritt,* see Beda KLEINSCHMIDT, O.F.M., *Die heilige Anna. Ihre Verehrung in Geschichte, Kunst und Volkstum,* Dusseldorf 1930. Cf. also his article, "Die Blütezeit des Annakultes," in *Theologie und Glaube* 19 (1927), p. 488 ff., and Paul CHARLAND, O.P., *Madame Saincte Anne et son culte au Moyen Age,* 2 vol., Paris 1911.

[97] In Picardy, the academies of Amiens and Abbeville deliberately "forgot" the etymological meaning of *puy* and adopted the symbol suggested by its homonym, *puits* (well). The equivocation led Nicolas Blasset of Amiens (1600-1659) to carve for the chapel of Notre-Dame du Puy in the cathedral of Amiens a group in which the Virgin, who carries the Infant Jesus in her left arm, reaches out with her right arm to help a naked child out of an octagonal well. The same artist carved another *Virgin of the well* on the marble plaques upon which the names of the masters of the confraternity were inscribed. Similarly, the academy of Abbeville possessed a silver statuette of the Virgin, at whose feet rose the rim of a tiny well, complete with bucket, chain and pulley. This statuette is today conserved in the church of Saint-Vulfran in the same town.

quired, when he took office, to have a painting made, which was to be an allegorical composition inspired by the idea and the refrain of his *Chant Royal*. This painting, erected in the Cathedral, was supposed to be re-placed, the following year, by that of the new master; in fact however, they were all left in place. Unfortunately, only a few of them remain today, in the Picardy Museum, at Amiens. Forty-seven such paintings, with the text of the *Chants Royaux* were reproduced in a splendid manuscript which was offered to Louise of Savoy in 1517, on the occasion of her visit to Amiens with her son, Francis I (Paris, Bibliothèque Nationale, Ms. fr. 145).

The *puys* were no less prosperous in Normandy, at Caen, Dieppe, and Evreux; but the *Puy de la Conception* at Rouen eclipsed all the others. Originating in a pious confraternity dedicated to the cult of the Virgin conceived without stain, it adopted the activities of an *academy* in 1486. Prizes were awarded for the best poems in honor of the Immaculate Con-ception, which was invariably the theme proposed for the contest. The prizes were small golden or silver figures in the form of the biblical attributes of the All Pure Virgin: a rose, a lily, a palm, a laurel branch, a crenelated tower, a gold star, etc. They were worth more than many of the prize-winning poems, as were also the miniatures which illustrate the latter in two remarkable manuscripts of the Bibliothèque Nationale of Paris (Mss. fr. 379 and 1537).

At Rouen, Amiens, and elsewhere, the poems were of various types and meters: ballads, rondeaux, epigrams, *"stances,"* odes, sonnets; but the master-piece was that called *Chant Royal*: after each stanza, the idea of the allegory was repeated in the refrain: hence the name *palinod*—etymologi-cally, "song with a refrain," which is still given to these *companies* and their literary tourneys. Most of these compositions, corsetted in an armature of prosody which smothered all natural feeling, are boring to read today. Nevertheless we must recognize that these *rhétoriqueurs* of the *Puys Notre Dame*, in spite of the redundancy and obscurity of their divine "hodge-podges" (*"fatras"*)—as those of Amiens characterized their *Chants Royaux*, contributed not a little to the spread of the belief.[98]

---

[98] On the *puys*, cf. A.-G. BALLIN, *Notice historique sur l'Académie des Palinods*, Rouen, 1834; Edm. SOYEZ, *Le Puy Notre-Dame. Ancienne confrérie amiènoise.* Amiens, 1906; E. ROBILLARD DE BEAUREPAIRE, *Les Puys de Palinod de Rouen et de Caen*, Caen, 1907; J. DURAND, *Tableaux et chants royaux de la Confrérie du Puy Notre-Dame d'Amiens.* Amiens, 1911; Cr. GUERY, *Palinods ou Puys de Poésie en Normandie,* avec appendices et bibliographie. Evreux, 1916.

BIBLIOGRAPHY

J. M. Abgrall, "L'iconographie de l'Immaculée Conception en Bretagne, in *"Premier Congrès Marial Breton tenu à Josselin en l'honneur de l'Immaculée Conception 21-24 novembre 1904,* Paris and Vannes, 1905, pp. 387-401.

V. Alce, O.P., "L'Immacolata Concezione nell'arte," in *Sapienza* 7(1954), pp. 557-583.

———, "L'Immacolata nell'arte dalla fine del sec. XV al sec. XX," in *Virgo Immaculata,* vol. XV, 1957, pp. 107-135.

M. L. D'Ancona, *The iconography of the Immaculate Conception in the Middle Ages and early Renaissance* (Monographs on archeology and fine arts sponsored by The Archaeological Institute of America and The College Art Association of America). Published by The College Art Association of America in conjunction with The Art Bulletin, [s.l.] 1957.

Juan de Ayala, *Pictor Christianus eruditus.* Madrid, 1730.

Mgr. Barbier de Montault, *L'Office de la Conception à Luçon au XVe siècle.* Vannes, 1888. (Liturgical and iconographic commentary).

———, *Traité d'iconographie chrétienne.* Paris, 1890, pp. 204 ff.

Piero Bargellini, *La Storia dell'Immacolata.* Firenze, 1954. (Gives numerous excellent reproductions of Italian *Immacolatas.*)

L. Battailon, "Les symboles des Litanies et l'iconographie de la Vierge en Normandie au XVIe siècle, in *Revue archéologique,* nov.-déc. 1923.

Ch. de Beaurepaire, *Les Puys de Palinod de Rouen et de Caen.* Caen 1907.

St. Beissel, *Geschichte der Verehrung Marias in Deutschland im XV-XVII Jahrhundert.* Freiburg-im-Breisgau, 1910.

J.-Fr. Bonnefoy, O.F.M., *Quand Séville fêtait la "Purísima." 1614-1617.* Nicolet, Centre Marial Canadien, 1954.

B. Borchert, O. Carm., "L'Immaculée dans l'iconographie du Carmel," in *Carmelus* 2 (1955) fasc. 1, pp. 85-131.

———, "L'Immacolata nella iconografia del Carmelo," in *Virgo Immaculata,* vol. XV, 1957, pp. 158-169.

J. Boschius, S.J. *Symbolographia, sive de arte symbolica sermones septem, quibus accessit: Sylloge celebriorum symbolorum in quatuor divisa classes . . .* Augustae Vindelicorum, 1702. (The *Sylloge* is a collection of engraved emblems grouped under four headings: sacred, heroic, moral and satiric. The seventeen which refer to the Immaculate Conception (nos. 497-573) are explained on p. 35. Cf. *supra,* p. 482.)

Carlo Bricarelli, S.J., "Storia d'un monumento artistico all'Immacolata," in Civiltà Cattolica 1 (1905), pp. 190-197. (Deals with the monument erected by Pope Pius IX in the Piazza di Spagna.)

J.-C. Broussolle, *De la Conception Immaculée à l'Annonciation angélique. Essais de théologie artistique.* Paris, 1908.

Ch. Cahier, S.J., *Iconographie de la Sainte Vierge. Etudes religieuses,* 6e série, t. V, 1880.

M. A. Cahier, *Un vieux tableau du musée de Douai: l'Immaculée Conception de la Sainte Vierge honorée dans Douai à la fin du XVe siècle.* Douai, 1858. (Reprinted from *Mémoires de la Soc. d'Agriculture, Sciences et Arts de Douai,* 2e sér. t. IV.)

M. Carmichael, *Francia's Masterpiece: An essay on the beginnings of the Immaculate Conception in art.* London, 1909.

Carlo Cecchelli, "Note sulla più antica iconografia della Immacolata," in *Virgo Immaculata,* vol. XV, pp. 199-203.

A. Clément, *Iconographie de l'Immaculée Conception. Etudes Mariales.* 1905.

L. Cloquet, "Le seul véritable tableau de l'Immaculée Conception, ou Iconographie démontrant que le plus beau privilège de la Vierge Immaculée est incompris des peintres, et traçant le plan détaillé d'un tableau fidèle, d'après les

Ecritures, les Pères, les Docteurs, les saints et l'encyclique de Pie IX." Cf. *Annales archéologiques* of Didron, t. XXIII, 1863, p. 336.

Ath. Coquerel, *Des beaux-arts en Italie au point de vue religieux.* Paris, 1857. Appendix, pp. 253-290: "Iconographie de l'Immaculée Conception." (Protestant critique of the work of Bishop Malou cited below. The arguments formulated by this Protestant minister were used again by A. Stap, also against the Bishop of Bruges, in his controversial work, *L'Immaculée Conception. Etudes sur l'origine d'un dogme.* Paris, 1869, pp. 205 ff.)

Mgr. Crosnier, "L'Immaculée Conception de Marie proclamée par les iconographes du moyen âge," in *Bulletin Monumental,* 1857, t. XXIII, pp. 57 ff.

Bordona J. Dominguez, "Exposición castellana de arte concepcionista," in *Estrella del Mar,* 1921 and 1922.

J. Durand, *Tableaux et chants royaux de la Confrérie du Puy Notre-Dame d'Amiens.* Amiens, 1911.

Ignacio Elizalde, S.J., *En torno a las Inmaculadas de Murillo.* (Colección Capitel, Serie Azul: Art. I) Madrid, Ed. Sapientia. 164 pp.

J. Fournée, "Les thèmes iconographiques de l'Immaculée Conception en Normandie au Moyen-âge et à la Renaissance," in *Virgo Immaculata,* vol. XV, Romae, Academia Mariana Internationalis, 1957, pp. 18-106. (This work, remarkable both for its precision and its method, had previously been published in Paris in mimeographed form under the title, *Iconographie de l'Immaculée Conception au moyen âge et à la renaissance,* 1953.)

――――, "Les thèmes essentiels de l'Immaculée Conception dans l'art français," in *Sanctuaires et pèlerinages,* mars 1958.

Tommaso Gallino, O.F.M., "L'Immacolata nelle immagini ispirate dai Francescani (Dal Medioevo a tutto il secolo decimosesto)," in *Virgo Immaculata,* vol. XV, 1957, pp. 170-198.

L. Germain de Maidy, *Le Chasse à la licorne et l'Immaculée Conception.* Nancy, 1897.

――――, "La rencontre à la Porte Dorée, première représentation allégorique de l'Immaculée Conception," a series of five articles in the review, *Espérance,* of Nancy, 19 mars - 26 mai, 1897.

――――, "La Vierge et le serpent. Recherches iconographiques," in *Revue de l'art chrétien,* 1894 and 1901, p. 504.

――――, "A propos de l'ouvrage de L. Maxe-Werly sur l'iconographie de l'Immaculée Conception. Quelle est l'origine de la Vierge aux symboles bibliques?" in *Revue de l'art chrétien,* 1906, p. 336. (The problem is raised but not solved.)

――――, *Les types iconographiques de l'Immaculée Conception au XVIe siècle.* Nancy, 1914.

――――, *Un vitrail de la collection Douglas (vers 1526) symbolisant l'Immaculée Conception.* Nancy, 1916.

Manuel Gómez-Moreno, *La Inmaculada en la escultura española.* [Comillas, Univ. Pontif. 1955.] 1, 18 pp., 32 pl.

Joh. Graus, *Conceptio Immaculata in alten Darstellungen.* Gratz, 1905.

Pietro Guidi, *L'Immacolata a Lucca,* Pavia, 1905.

R. M. de Hornedo, "Evolución iconográfica de la Inmaculada en el arte español," in *Razon y Fe* 151 (1955).

E. Hucher, "L'Immaculée Conception figurée sur les monuments du moyen âge et de la renaissance," in *Bulletin Monumental,* t. XXI (1855), pp. 144-148.

N. de la Iglesia, *Flores de Miraflores: jeroglíficos sagrados, figurados, sombras verdaderas del misterio de la Inmaculada Concepción de Nuestra Señora.*

Cécile Jéglot, "L'Immaculée Conception dans l'art," in *Compte-rendu du 2e Congrès Marial National de Lourdes,* Lourdes, 1931, pp. 264-281.

Luigi Huetter, "Il monumento all'Immacolata in Piazza di Spagna a Roma," in *Virgo Immaculata.* Acta Congressus Mariologici-Mariani Romae anno MCMLIV celebrati, Vol. XIV, Romae, Academia Mariana Internationalis, 1957, pp. 414-422.

Al. JANSSENS, Scheut. "De Iconographie van de Onbevlekte Ontvangenis," in *Stand. Maria* 10 (1930), pp. 324-329.

K. KÜNSTLE, *Ikonographie der Christlichen Kunst*, Freiburg-im-Breisgau, 1928, p. 646 ff.

J. LAFOND, "Le thème iconographique de l'Arbre de Jessé," in *Bulletin des Amis des monuments rouennais*, 1911, pp. 153 ff.

———, "L'Immaculée Conception glorifiée par le vitrail," in *Ecclesia*, déc. 1954.

Xavier-Marie LE BACHELET, S.J., "L'Immaculée Conception dans l'Eglise latine après le Concile d'Ephèse," in VACANT-MANGENOT-AMANN, *Dictionnaire de théologie catholique*, tome VII, col. 979-1218, *passim*.

P. LÉONARD, S.J., "L'Immaculée Conception dans l'art. Esquisse d'iconographie," in *Cahiers Notre-Dame*, pp. 22 ff.

J.-J. LE PETIT, "L'Immaculée Conception dans la peinture," in *Premier Congrès Marial Breton tenu à Josselin en l'honneur de l'Immaculée Conception 21-24 novembre 1904*, Paris & Vannes, 1905, pp. 359-383.

A.-M. LÉPICIER, O.S.M., *L'Immaculée Conception dans l'art et l'iconographie*, Spa, 1955.

P. LIGTENBERG, article in *Collect. Francisc. Neerland.* 1927, pp. 1-44.

P. MAARSCHALKERWEERD, O.F.M., "Saggio iconografico della Immacolata," in *Antonianum* 29 (1954), pp. 543-562.

J. DE MAHUET, S.M., "Le thème de Marie Nouvelle Eve dans l'iconographie chrétienne," in *Bulletin de la Société des Études Mariales*, 1957, pp. 27-48.

E. MÂLE, *L'art religieux en France à la fin du moyen âge*. (Several editions. See esp. ch. V, No. 7 and ch. VI, No. 6.)

———, *L'art religieux du XVIIe siècle*. Paris, 1951. See ch. II, No. 3, pp. 41-48 (deals mainly with the *Purisima* of the Spanish masters.)

Mgr. MALOU, *Iconographie de l'Immaculée Conception de la Très Sainte Vierge Marie, ou de la meilleure manière de représenter ce mystère*. Bruxelles, 1856.

Fr. MARTIN, C.M.F., "La Inmaculada Concepción de María en el Arte, in *Virtud y Letras* 13 (1954), pp. 158-160.

L. MAXE-WERLY, *L'Iconographie de l'Immaculée Conception de la Sainte Vierge depuis le milieu du XVe siècle jusqu'à la fin du XVIe*. Moûtiers, 1903. (Reprinted from *Notes d'art et d'archéologie*, sept., oct., nov. 1902.)

A. MUNOZ, *Iconografia della Madonna*. Con 253 illustrazioni. Firenze, 1905. Pp. 90-104.

Abbé NICKERS, "Iconographie de l'Immaculée Conception de la Très Sainte Vierge, in *Namur, Les Fêtes mariales et le congrès marial*, 1904. Pp. 296-304.

Jean DE NICOLAY, S.J., "Murillo, peintre de l'Immaculée Conception," in *Cahiers Notre-Dame*, févr. 1932, pp. 85-94.

G. NIETO, "Una representación de la Inmaculada en el siglo XV," *Boletin del Seminario de Estudios de Arte y Arqueologia*, Fasciculo 37-39, curso 1944-45.

Mgr. PECHENARD, "L'Immaculée Conception et l'ancienne Université de Paris," in *Revue du Clergé français*, janv. 1905.

Luis PÉREZ RUBIN Y CORCHADO, *Ensayo artistico arqueológico sobre el Culto Mariano, y especialmente de la Purisima, en la archidiocesis de Valladolid*. Valladolid, 1906.

PÉREZ Y PANDO, O.P., *Iconografia Mariana Española*. Vergara 1930.

F. PICAUD, "La Vierge de Carado," in *Premier Congrès Marial Breton tenu à Josselin en l'honneur de l'Immaculée Conception, 21-24 novembre 1904*, Paris and Vannes, 1905, pp. 403-408.

J. PLANELLA, "La Purisima de Juan de Juanès," in *Razon y Fe*, Madrid, 1904, p. 152.

Francisco RIOS, *Las Inmaculadas de Murillo. Estudio crítico*. Barcelona, 1948.

ROHAULT DE FLEURY, *La Sainte Vierge. Etudes archéologiques et iconographiques*. Paris, 1878.

A. SALZER, *Die Sinnbilder und Beiworte Mariens*. Linz, 1893.

L. SCHREYER, *Bildnis der Mutter Gottes*. Freiburg-im-Breisgau, 1951.

Edm. Soyez, *Le Puy Notre-Dame. Ancienne Confrérie amiènoise.* Amiens, 1906.

Engelbertus Cardinal Sterkx, *Brevis disquisitio de modo pingendi Ssmam. Dei genitricem Mariam, sine labe originali conceptam.* Romae, 1854.

———, *Courte dissertation sur la manière de représenter par la peinture le mystère de l'Immaculée Conception.* Malines, 1855.

Eva Tea, "L'Immacolata Concezione nell'arte," in *L'Immacolata Concezione, Storia ed esposizione del dogma.* (Anon.) Milano 1954, pp. 145-162.

G. de Tervarent, "Le Retable de Sainte Anne au musée de Francfort," in his *Énigmes de l'art du moyen âge,* t. II, Paris, 1941, p. 39-40.

J. J. M. Timmers, "L'Iconographie de l'Immaculée Conception," in *Carmelus* 1 (1954) fasc. 2, pp. 278-287.

Romanus Tominec, O.F.M., "Immaculata in arte slovenica," in *Virgo Immaculata,* vol. XV, 1957, pp. 136-157.

Elias Tormo, *La Inmaculada y el Arte Español.* Madrid, 1915.

Man. Trens, *María. Iconografía de la Virgen en el arte español.* Madrid, 1946.

———, *Santa María. Vida y Leyenda de la Virgen a través del arte español.* Barcelona, 1954.

Jean Vermeulen (= Molanus), *De historia SS. imaginum et picturarum pro vero earum usu contra abusus.* Edit. Noel Paquot. Louvain, 1771. (In this work, which appeared originally in 1578, Vermeulen, professor at the University of Louvain, attacked the most beautiful themes of mediaeval iconography.)

Virgo Immaculata, vol. XV (1957) contains several articles on the Immaculate Conception in art. For complete table of contents, see *Bibliography* at the end of the present volume, appendix.

M. Vloberg, "L'Immaculée dans le Coran et dans l'Islam," in the review, *Notre-Dame,* février 1921.

———. *La Vierge et l'Enfant dans l'art français.* Grenoble, 1933. (4th ed. 1954.)

———. *La Vierge notre Médiatrice.* Grenoble, 1939.

Jos. Zoller, O.S.B., *Conceptus Chronographicus de Concepta Sacra Deipara, septingentis sacrae Scripturae, SS. Patrum, ac rationum, nec non historiarum, symbolorum, antiquitatum, et anagrammatum suffragiis roboratus.* Augsburg, 1712.

(*Anonymous*) *Iconografía y florilegio clásico de la Inmaculada Concepción,* Madrid, 1904.

Notes on the Figures [1]

We wish to express here our gratitude to those who have kindly assisted us to obtain the engravings described on the following pages: to Sister Mary André, O.S.U., M. Maurice Vloberg, Mrs. Gertrude L. Woodward of the Newberry library, Brother Stanley Matthews, C.M. of the Marian Library at Dayton, Dr. Francis Lazenby of the Mediaeval Library of the University of Notre Dame, Father Edmund Ivers, S.J. of Woodstock College, and Srta. María Lourdes Díaz-Trechuelo y López Spinola of the University Library, Seville. We are indebted likewise to Mr. Robert Lehman and the Indiana Engraving Company, who prepared the plates.

The cover of this volume is the work of Sister Mary André, O.S.U., of Cleveland, and represents the *Garden Enclosed* with the *Lily among Thorns*. It should be compared with the fifteenth century *Garden Enclosed* in figure 9, p. 476. The same artist also made the (unnumbered) engravings of other biblical symbols of the Blessed Virgin on pp. 86, 160, 347, 362 and 462.

Figure 1. (p. 243) The Friars Agree on the Immaculate Conception.
Frontispiece to the *Armamentarium* of Alva y Astorga (Madrid, 1649; cf. the Table of Abbreviations at the end of chapter VII, at the entry Alva). The entire work is a defense of the doctrine of the Immaculate Conception.)
At the foot of the *Tower of David,* on which their armor now hangs at rest, the Friar Preacher and the Friar Minor clasp hands in accord. The sense of the image is indicated by the text of Canticle of Canticles 4:4, inscribed on three shields borne by angels: *"Aedificata est cum propugnaculis, Mille clypei pendent ex ea, omnis armatura fortium"* ("[the tower of David] is built with bulwarks: a thousand bucklers hang upon it, all the armor of valiant men." Overhead, Mary appears in glory with the marks of the Woman of Apocalypse 12:1 (rays of the sun enveloping her, the moon under her feet, and the crown of twelve stars), while she tramples underfoot the apocalyptic dragon as if he were the serpent of Genesis 3:15.
Other common Marian symbols also appear: the burning bush of Exodus 3, with the inscription, *"Veritas Moysi rubus"* ("The Truth is like the bush of Moses"—?), and the rose flowering on a snowy landscape, with the inscription, *"Ab hyeme gratior"* ("Made all the more pleasing by the winter"). The *"vellus victoriae signum"* ("Fleece, emblem of victory") hung from the tower is doubtless intended to contain an allusion also to Gedeon's fleece (Judges 6:36-40).
Reproduced (reduced in size) by courtesy of the Woodstock College Library.

Figure 2. (p. 279) Apocalyptic Virgin, with prayer "of Sixtus IV."
In this print which P. Heitz dates at about 1460, the Virgin is adorned with the symbols of Apocalypse 11:1, except that there are no stars in her crown. The four evangelists occupy the corners of the engraving.
This image was not part of a book, but an isolated print (*Einblatt*) similar to modern "holy cards." The prayer that appears above it was not part of the original engraving, but has been cut from a different sheet and pasted on. However, the very wording of the prayer shows that it was designed to accompany an image of this type as is confirmed by the two similar examples cited below.

---

[1] These notes refer only to the *line cuts* contained in the text. Notes on the halftone plates accompany those plates on the insert in chapter XIII. These notes are the work of the editor, on the basis of information supplied in some cases by M. Vloberg.

The prayer and introductory note read as follows:

Subscriptam Orationem edidit Sixtus papa quartus: et concessit eam devote dicentibus coram imagine beate Marie Virginis in soli. XI. millia annorum indulgentiarum.

Ave sanctissima Maria: mater dei: regina celi: porta paradisi: domina mundi: tu es singularis virgo pura. tu concepta sine peccato concepisti jesum sine macula. tu pepercisti creatorem et salvatorem mundi: in quo ego non dubito: Ora pro me jesum dilectum filium tuum. et libera me ab omnibus malis. Amen.

Translation:

The following prayer was published by Pope Sixtus IV, who has granted an indulgence of XI thousand years to those who devoutly recite it before an image of Blessed Mary the Virgin in the sun. [The allusion here is doubtless to the rays of the sun which envelope the figure of Mary, according to Apoc. 11:1].

Hail, most holy Mary, Mother of God, Queen of heaven, Gate of Paradise, Mistress of the world. Thou art a virgin of unique purity. *Conceived without sin,* thou hast conceived Jesus without stain. Thou hast born the Creator and Savior of the world, in whom I do not lack faith. Pray for me to Jesus, thy beloved son, and free me from all evils. Amen.

This engraving has been reproduced (in reduced size) through the courtesy of the Pierpont Morgan Library, from P. HEITZ, *Einblattdrücke des XV Jahrhunderts,* V, Strasburg, 1906, pl. 5. It is also described in W. L. SCHREIBER, *Manuel de l'amateur de la gravure sur bois et sur metal au XVe siècle,* Berlin, 1891-1911, vol. I, No. 1099. We are indebted to Miss Mirella Levi D'Ancona for drawing our attention to this engraving, and to Professor Kurt Bühler, of the Pierpont Morgan library, who graciously sent us a transcription of the notes in Heitz, which we were not able to consult directly.

Another image of the Virgin Mary holding the Infant Jesus, and accompanied by the apocalyptic symbols (as well as two angels who bear her crown) was printed ca. 1500 by Nikolaus Kessler of Basel. Below it appears a German translation of the same prayer transcribed above, except that the allusion to Mary's sinless conception is wanting. An attribution of the prayer to Pope Sixtus IV very similar to that noted above precedes the prayer in this case also:

Bapst. Sixtus der. iiij. hat dis nach geschriben gebet gemacht: vnd allen denen die ir sund geruuet vnd gebeicht haben vnd es andechtig sprechen vor vnser fronen bild in der sonnen iverlichen [= verleihen] eilff tausennt iar ablas.

Gegriesset siestu aller heiligiste maria du muotter gotes ein kingin des himels du port des paradysz ein frau der erde. Du bist ein besundre reyne iungkfrau. Du hast einpfangen iesum an sund du hast geboren den schepffer und behalter der vuelt dar an ich nit zueyffel: Bit fir mich iesum dinen lieben son: vnd erlesz mich von allen ubel. Amen.

   (—A. SCHRAMM, *Die Bilderschmuch der Frühdrucke.* Leipzig, 1920-23. Vol. 21, Abb. 795; cp. his remarks on p. 21, *ibid.*)

Another image of the Virgin with the apocalyptic symbols accompanied by the prayer *Ave sanctissima* is described in W. L. SCHREIBER, *Manuel . . . ,* vol. I, 1053; the editor there declares, however, that the indulgence is apocryphal. (Cf. chapter VII of the present volume, p. 277, note 29).

Figure 3. (p. 465) THE SANCTIFICATION OF THE VIRGIN.
The figure of Mary being sanctified as an infant in the womb of St. Anne, which is used elsewhere to represent the Immaculate Conception, (e.g. plate V

above) is here used in a maculist sense by the Dominican Alberto DA CASTELVETRO (in other editions: Albert DE CASTELLO) in *Rosario della gloriosa Vergine Maria con figure adornato* . . . Venice, 1616, fol. 39v.

Reproduced (actual size) through the courtesy of the University of Notre Dame Library.

Figure 4. (p. 467) ST. ANNE WITH MARY AND JESUS.

St. Anne opens out her mantle, revealing her daughter, Mary, who, in turn, holds the Infant Jesus in her lap. The composition is somewhat spiritualized by the biblical symbols (cf. p. 476, note 39) which encircle it.

This image was used to illustrate the Office of the Conception of Blessed Mary the Virgin in the *Heures à l'usage de Rouan*, printed in Paris in 1508 by Simon Vostre. In 1510 it was used again in the *Heures à l'usage d'Angers.*

Reproduced (actual size) through the courtesy of the Newberry Library, Chicago.

Figure 5. (p. 469) MARY AS THE SPOUSE OF THE CANTICLE OF CANTICLES.

Christ here addresses Mary with the words which the immaculists adopted as their chief text: "Thou art all fair, O my beloved, and there is not a spot in thee." (Cant. 4:7)

From a fifteenth century xylograph of the Canticle of Canticles, Paris, Bibl. Nat. Reproduced from M. ALADEL, *La Médaille Miraculeuse,* second edition, Paris, 1881, facing p. 58, through the courtesy of the Marian Library of the University of Dayton.

Figure 6. (p. 472) THE MIRACULOUS MEDAL.

This medal was struck (June 30, 1832) according to a model which the Blessed Virgin herself showed to Sister Catherine Labouré in the chapel of the *Filles de la Charité* in Paris on November 27, 1830. (Cf. plate XXII and its accompanying note.)

Figure 7. (p. 474) THE IMMACULATE VIRGIN AND OUR SINFUL FIRST PARENTS.

This engraving is one of a series representing the glories of the Blessed Virgin in the work of Pierre BIVER, S.J., *Sacrum Oratorium piarum Imaginum Mariae,* Antwerp, Plantin, 1634. (Cf. *supra,* p. 482) God the Father says to Mary, "Hear, O daughter, and see [cf. Ps. 44:11] thy nature's debts. Thou hast EVADED [them]." Mary replies, "Forgive us our trespasses as we forgive those who trespass against us."

Reproduced (actual size, through the courtesy of the University of Notre Dame library.)

Another engraving from the same work is reproduced in figure 11, p. 483.

Figure 8. (p. 475) THE 'TOTA PULCHRA ES.'

A typical example of the theme, *'Tota Pulchra Es,'* which came into great popularity after 1500 as a representation of the Immaculate Conception. (Cf. p. 475 ff.) This image should be compared with those in figure 10 and plates X and XI.

Reproduced (actual size) from a *Missale Sacrum* (Paris, Guillaume Merlin, 1555; at the feast of the Immaculate Conception — fol. 3v of Part II) through the courtesy of the Newberry Library, Chicago.

Figure 9. (p. 477) THE GARDEN ENCLOSED AND THE SEALED FOUNTAIN AS FIGURES OF THE BLESSED VIRGIN.

The *Garden Enclosed* and the *Sealed Fountain* of Canticle of Canticles 4:12 are two of the earliest Marian symbols adopted from the Old Testament. They were standard figures of Mary's virginity long before their inclusion among the 'Litany symbols' used to represent the Immaculate Conception. (Cf. p. 477)

The woodcut reproduced in figure 9 is a transitional case. Mary's sanctification rather than her virginity is symbolized, but her sanctification as understood in a maculist sense, or at least one which carefully avoids any immaculist expression, as is evident from the text cited below. It is taken from *Spiegel der Menschlichen Behaltniss* (Augsburg, Peter Berger, 1498; fol. iiij), a German translation-paraphrase of the *Speculum humanae salvationis.* (On the nature of the latter work, see the note on figures 14 and 15, below.)

The meaning of the image is explained by the following text:

Der beschossen [read: *beschlossen*] Gart und der versigelt brunn.canticorum
am iiij.

Von diser säligen tochter Maria het auch Salomon lanng vor gesagt dass sÿ in jrer muotter leib solte geheÿliget werden, Wann er sprach in dem buoch der liebe unn nennet sÿ ein beschlossen garten unnd geleichte sÿ einem versigelten brunnen. wann die weil sÿ jr muoter beschlossen in irem leib truog, da gosz der heÿlig geist in sÿ sein heÿligkeyt unnd versigelt sÿ mitt dem insigel der heÿligen drifaltigkeÿte, also das sÿ in kein unsauberkeÿt mocht fallen. O maria du bist ein warer gart alles gelustes, und ein genuogsamer, ungebrechhaffter brunne der dürstigen selen.[2]

Translation:

The closed Garden and the sealed fountain. IV Cant.

Of this blessed daughter, Solomon long before said that she should be sanctified in her mother's womb, when he spoke in the Book of Love [= Canticle of Canticles] and called her a closed garden and likened her to a sealed fountain. During the time her mother bore her enclosed in her womb, the Holy Ghost poured His holiness into her and stamped her with the seal of the Holy Trinity, so that she might not fall into any impurity. O Mary, thou art a true 'Garden of all delight,' and a useful, unfailing fountain to thirsty souls.

Reproduced (actual size) through the courtesy of the Newberry Library, Chicago (Inc. f. 1918, fol. 4).

Figure 10. (p. 478) THE 'TOTA PULCHRA ES' OF THE BRÉVIAIRE DE BÉTHUNE.
Mary, here holding the Infant Jesus in her arms, is surrounded by the usual fifteen biblical symbols (cf. p. 477, n. 39), except that the customary garden of roses is replaced by the stylized rose which she holds in her hand. Also, instead of the more usual text from Canticle of Canticles 4:7, the image bears the inscription, "Pulchra es et decora Filia Hierusalem — Thou are beautiful and comely, daughter of Jerusalem." (Cf. Canticle of Canticles 6:3)
This is one of a series of 120 woodcuts in the Bréviaire de Béthune (Paris, Bibl. Nat., Cab. des Estampes), which dates from around the beginning of the sixteenth century, perhaps even from the end of the fifteenth. It should be compared with the examples of this same theme in figure 8 and plates X and XI.
Reproduced from a photographic print belonging to M. Maurice Vloberg.

Figure 11. (p. 483) THE DIVINE EAGLE AND THE IMMACULATE VIRGIN.
The mystery of the Conception of the Virgin, as it is represented in the *Sacrum Oratorium piarum Imaginum Immaculatae Mariae* of Pierre BIVER, S.J., Antwerp,

---

[2] In this transcription, the punctuation has been modernized, but the capitals have been retained as in the original. Abbreviated words have been written out in full. We have used the diphthong *uo* (as in *muotter*) to transcribe *u* with a superscript *o*. Professor William Bennett, of the Mediaeval Institute of the University of Notre Dame, was kind enough to review our transcription of the Old German texts cited in these notes.

Plantin, 1634. (Cf. p. 482 above) Another engraving from this same work is reproduced above in figure 7, p. 474.

Reproduced (actual size), through the courtesy of the University of Notre Dame library.

Figure 12. (p. 484) THE WOMAN OF THE APOCALYPSE.

The Immaculate Conception is here symbolized by a detailed representation of the vision described in Apocalypse 12: 1, 3 and 4, which text is cited in the lower part of the engraving. (Cf. p. 469 f.) Michael (lower left) and his angels are derived from verses 7 and 8, which are not cited. On the shields of the angels, the artist has indicated the weapons which are to be used in defense of the Immaculate Conception:

Antiquitas indicabit illibatam.

Peccatum Deiparae negabunt rationes.

Puram Scriptura docebit.

Nec deerunt centum historiae.

Angelica Salutatio ostendet puram.

Plura alludent symbola.

Accedent variae Patrum sententiae.

The dragon is labelled with the scroll, "Draco rufus ad pedes Illibatae."

This image (here reduced in size) was used as frontispiece to the *Conceptus chronographicus de Concepta Sacra Deipara* of Jos. ZOLLER, O.S.B. The capital letters of each inscription, when taken as Roman numerals, add up to 1712 — the date of publication of the volume. Thus, in the title at the foot of the page, the following capitals occur: D,D,C,C,C,C,C,C,V,V,I,I. (For a description of the contents of this work, see pp. 483-485.)

Reproduced (in reduced size) through the courtesy of M. Maurice Vloberg.

Figure 13. (p. 485) THE MYSTICAL ROSE.

Mary, clothed with the apocalyptic emblems, appears in the center of a blooming rose.

From *Sagradas Quintillas a Maria Santissima en el ternissimo mysterio de su Concepcion Inmaculada*, Sevilla, Vasquez, (1766-1799). Reproduced through the courtesy of the University of Seville library.

Figures 14 and 15. (pp. 498 and 499) THE NATIVITY OF THE VIRGIN AND THE TREE OF JESSE.

The Tree of Jesse image takes its origin from the prophecy of Isaias 11:1 ff., which, in the Vulgate, reads: "Et egredietur virga de radice Jesse, et flos de radice ejus ascendet. Et requiescet super eum spiritus Domini . . ." After having been adopted originally in art to represent the genealogy of Christ, it came in time to be used for that of Mary. It is here associated with Mary's Nativity (cf. p. 499), certainly not with any intended reference to the Immaculate Conception, because the document from which it is taken is pretty clearly maculist. (Cf. the note on figure 9, above.)

This document is the *Spiegel der Menschlichen Behaltniss* (Augsburg, Peter Berger, 1498; fol. 4v and 5), a German translation - paraphrase of the *Speculum humanae salvationis*. The latter work, composed apparently by Ludolph of Saxony, O.P. in 1324, is an illustrated history of the work of salvation. In it, scenes from the life of Christ are juxtaposed with their prefigurations in the Old Testament, as well as with symbols drawn from elsewhere; a text beneath explains the illustrations.

The *Spiegel* drew from its prototype with considerable freedom. The cuts reproduced in figures 15 and 16 occur in chapter iiij, which is entitled, "Wie Maria geborn ward" — "Mary's birth." They face one another in approximately the same relative positions as they have in our text. A short paragraph declares that Mary was born of the family of David as Isaias had prophesied. Then follows a long paragraph, entitled, "Die ruot yesse bedeüt Mariam ysaie am xj.capitel" — "The Rod of Jesse signifies Mary; Isaias xi." Here it is declared that Mary is the rod or stem that rose out of the root of Jesse and bore the "aller lustigeste" flower. In the flower one finds seven goods, which signify the seven gifts of the Holy Ghost. The rest of the paragraph is devoted to an exposition of these seven gifts and of their helpfulness against the seven deadly sins.

Reproduced (actual size) through the courtesy of the Newberry Library, Chicago.

Figure 16. (p. 514) The Annunciation to St. Anne.

As the angel speaks to Anne, Joachim's head already appears in the Golden Gate.

This drawing represents a leaden medal found in the bed of the Seine. M. E. Hucher, who published the drawing in *Bulletin Monumental,* Caen, 1855 ("L'Immaculée Conception figurée sur les monuments du Moyen-Age et de la Renaissance"), associates the medal with the shoemakers' guild in Paris and dates it "sur les confins de la Renaissance."

Figure 17. (p. 521) The meeting of Anne and Joachim at the Golden Gate of Jerusalem.

This drawing, reproduced from M. E. Hucher, "L'Immaculée Conception figurée sur les monuments du Moyen-Age et de la Renaissance" (in *Bulletin monumental,* Caen, 1855) represents a medal which is evidently to be associated with a Confraternity of the Immaculate Conception erected in the Church of St. Severin in Paris before 1361, perhaps as early as 1311. (Hucher does not allude to this confraternity, which is described by Henri Lesetre in *L'Immaculée-Conception et l'Eglise de Paris,* Paris, 1904, tome II, p. 60 f., cited by X. Le Bachelet in *Dict. théol. cath.* VII, 1096.)

On the meeting of Anne and Joachim, see chapter XIII of the present volume, p. 464.

Figure 18. (p. 522) The legend of Helsin.

Miniature from the margin of the "Officium de Conceptione beate Marie Virginis," in *Heures à l'usage de Rouan* published by Simon Vostre ca. 1508 in Paris (fol. 83v). It is from this same work that the image of Anne, Mary and Jesus, reproduced in figure 4, p. 468, was taken.

The Old French inscription reads:

> An abbot was about to perish at sea,
> But he recalled
> That the Virgin would save him
> On condition that he would cause to be celebrated
> Her most holy Conception.

Reproduced (actual size) by courtesy of the Newberry Library, Chicago.

Figure 19. (p. 525) The Canon of Rouen.

From the same source as figure 17 (fol. 84r). The inscription reads:

> A cleric led astray by sin,
> On his way to commit fornication,
> Was drowned by some devils,
> But was brought back to life by the Virgin
> Whom he was accustomed to serve devotedly.

Documents

I. THE LEGEND OF ANNE AND JOACHIM
from the *Protogospel of St. James*[1]

I. 1. In the annals of the twelve tribes of Israel we read of a certain man named Joachim, who was very rich. It was his custom to make offerings in double measure, saying, "Let my extra offering be for all the people, and let my atonement offering be given to the Lord to obtain forgiveness of my sins."

2. When the great day of the Lord came, the children of Israel offered their gifts; but Reuben barred the way to Joachim, saying, "You are not permitted to offer your gifts first,[2] because you have not raised up posterity in Israel."

3. And Joachim was exceedingly sad, and went to (the records of) the Twelve Tribes of Israel, saying, "I will look at (the records of) the Twelve Tribes of Israel, to see if I am the only one who has not raised up posterity in Israel." He examined them and found that all the just had had offspring in Israel. And he recalled that God had given a son Isaac to Abraham the patriarch in his old age. 4. Then Joachim became exceedingly sad, and did not return to his wife, but went into the desert and there pitched his tent, and fasted for forty days and forty nights, saying to himself, "I will not touch food or drink until the Lord my God overshadows me. Prayer will be my food and drink."

II. 1. Then his wife Anne made double lamentation, saying, "I shall lament my widowhood, and I shall lament my childlessness."

2. Then the great day of the Lord arrived, and Judith her servant said, "How long will you afflict your soul? Behold the great day of the Lord has come, and it is not fitting for you to grieve. Now take this headband which has been given to me by the mistress of the servants. I may not wear it because I am a servant, and the headband is a sign of royalty."

3. And Anne replied, "Away from me! I shall not take it. Already the Lord has humiliated me exceedingly. I fear that some rogue may have given it to you, and that you have come to make me share in your guilt." And Judith answered, "What evil can I wish upon you, seeing that the

---

[1] On the nature of this document, see p. 58 of the present volume. The present passage has been translated by Rev. James E. Moran, C.S.C., of the Department of Classics of the University of Notre Dame, from the text edited by Emile Amann, *Le Protévangile de Jacques et ses remaniements latins*, Paris, Letouzey, 1910, and represents the first five of Amann's twenty-five chapters.

[2] The word here translated as *first* does not, perhaps, belong to the original text. It was missing from many of the ancient manuscripts, and occurs with several variants in others.

513

Lord has already closed your womb that you may not bear offspring in Israel?"

4. And Anne was very sad. But she took off her sombre garments, washed her head, put on her wedding garb, and went down into the garden about the ninth hour to take a walk. And she saw a bay tree, and sat beneath it, and besought the Lord, saying, "O God of our fathers, bless me and hear my prayer, just as Thou didst bless the womb of Sara and didst give her a son, Isaac."

III. 1. And lifting up her eyes she saw a sparrows' nest in the bay tree; and she grieved and said, "Alas, who begot me, what womb has borne me, since I have become accursed in the sight of the children of Israel. I have been reviled and driven from the Temple of the Lord by their sneers.

2. "Alas, to what have I been likened? Certainly not to the birds of the sky, because even the birds are fertile before Thee, O Lord. Alas, to what have I been likened? Certainly not to the wild beasts of the earth, because the wild beasts of the earth are fertile before Thee, O Lord. Alas, to what have I been likened? Certainly not to these waters, because these waters are fertile before Thee, O Lord. 3. Alas, to whom have I been likened? Certainly not to this earth, because this earth produces its fruits in season and praises Thee, O Lord."

IV. 1. And behold an angel of the Lord stood beside her and said, "Anne, Anne, the Lord hath hearkened to thy prayer. Thou shalt conceive and bring forth, and people throughout the world shall speak of thy child."

And Anne said, "By the living God, my Lord, if I give birth whether to male or female, I shall offer it as a gift to the Lord my God, and it will be dedicated to His service all the days of its life."

2. And behold, two messengers came and said to her, "Behold, your husband Joachim is coming with his flocks. For an angel of the Lord came down to him and said, 'Joachim, Joachim, the Lord thy God has hearkened to thy prayer. Go down from this place, for behold, thy wife Anne shall conceive[3] in her womb.' 3. And Joachim went down, summoned his shepherds and said, 'Bring me ten lambs without stain or blemish; they shall be for the Lord my God. And bring me twelve sleek calves, they shall be for the priests and for the Sanhedrin; likewise, a hundred kids for all the people.'"

4. And behold, Joachim was coming with his flocks, and Anne stood near the gate, and beheld Joachim coming. She ran and hung upon his neck, and said, "Now I know that God has blessed me abundantly. The widow is no longer a widow, and she who is childless will conceive in her womb." And Joachim rested at home that first day.

V. 1. The next day he offered his gifts, saying within himself, "If the Lord God has been propitious to me, the golden ornament of the high

[3] Some manuscripts read, "has conceived." Cf. the remarks of Monsignor Jouassard on p. 59 of the present volume.

priest will give me a sign of favor." And Joachim offered his gifts, and carefully observed the golden ornament of the high priest as he ascended to the altar of the Lord, and he saw no sin in himself.[4] And Joachim said, "Now I know that the Lord has been propitious to me, and has taken away all my sins." And he came down from the temple justified, and returned to his house.

Figure 16. THE ANNUNCIATION TO ST. ANNE.
Late mediaeval medallion.

2. Now the months of Anne were fulfilled, and in the ninth month she gave birth to a child. And she said to the midwife, "To what have I given birth?"

And the midwife answered, "To a daughter."

And Anne said, "This day has my soul been exalted!" And she put the infant to bed. And when the days were fulfilled, Anne was purified, nursed the child, and called her name Mary.

II. THE LEGEND OF ANNE AND JOACHIM
from the *Pseudo-Matthew*[1]

In those days there lived in Jerusalem a man named Joachim, of the tribe of Juda. He was a shepherd, and a simple, good-hearted man, who lived in the fear of God and concerned himself with nothing but his flocks, from the produce of which he gave provisions to all God-fearing men. He gave a double amount to those who lived in the fear and wisdom of God, and single gifts to their servants. Thus, everything he had—whether lambs or sheep or wool—he divided into three parts: one part for the widows, orphans, pilgrims, and the poor; a second part for those who carried on the worship of God; and the third part for his own household.

---

[4] The reference is to the golden disk which the high priest wore on his turban, according to Exodus 29:38. AMANN explains that, due to a later misunderstanding, it was imagined that if the person making an offering saw no stain on the golden disk, this was a sign that God accepted the offering.

---

[1] On the character and significance of this work, see chapter II of the present volume, p. 81 f. Our translation is based on the text edited by E. AMANN, *Le*

2. Because he did this, God multiplied his flocks, so that there was no one like him among the people of Israel. He was fifteen years old when he began to do this, and at twenty he took to wife Anne, the daughter of Issachar, a man of his own tribe, that is, of the family of David. But he did not have any sons or daughters of her, although he lived with her for twenty years.

II. 1. Now on a certain feast day, Joachim was standing with those who were offering incense to the Lord and was preparing his gifts in the sight of the Lord. And a certain temple scribe named Reuben came to him and said, "You must not stand with those who are making sacrifice to God, because God has not blessed you by giving you offspring in Israel." Put to shame in front of the whole populace, Joachim left the Temple in tears; but instead of returning home, he went off to his flocks. Taking his shepherds with him, he went up into the mountains to a distant land, so that it was impossible for Anne to get any news about him for five months.

2. One day Anne was weeping in prayer, saying, "Lord, mighty God of Israel, you have given me no children, why have you now taken my husband from me? Lo, five months have passed since last I saw him. I do not even know if he is dead, that I might at least make a sepulchre for him." And as she wept exceedingly in the garden of her home, she raised her eyes to the Lord in her prayer and saw a nest of sparrows in a bay tree. Then she groaned to the Lord, saying, "Lord, God almighty, Who hast given offspring to every creature—to the beasts and the cattle and the serpents and the fish and the birds, so that they all rejoice over their offspring—hast Thou excluded me alone from the gift of Thy bounty? Thou knowest, O Lord, that at the beginning of my marriage, I vowed that if Thou shouldst give me a son or a daughter, I would offer it to Thee in Thy holy Temple."

3. As she was saying this, an angel of the Lord suddenly appeared before her and said, "Fear not, Anne, for God intends to give you a child.[2] That which shall be born of you shall be an object of admiration in all ages, to the very end." After saying this, he vanished from her sight. She, however, trembling with terror at having seen such a vision and heard such words, went into her room, threw herself on the bed as if dead, and remained an entire day and night in great trembling and in prayer.

---

protévangile de Jacques et ses remaniements latins, Paris 1910, p. 272 ff., and represents the first five of Amann's seventeen chapters. In the following notes, we call attention only to such variants from Amann's text as are relevant to our subject. These are, for the most part, attempts to rid the text of the doctrine of a virginal conception of Mary, which seems to have belonged to the original.

[2] " . . . in consilio Dei est germen tuum." Perhaps the expression here used is inspired, as Amann suggests, by a reminiscence of the scriptural verse, "Dominus possedit me in initio viarum suarum antequam quidquam faceret" (Prov. 8:22), which in time came to be applied to the Blessed Virgin.

4. Then she called her maid and said to her, "You see me desolate in my bereavement and filled with anguish, and were you not willing to come in to see to me?"

The latter replied in a mutter, "If God has closed your womb and taken away your husband, what am I to do for you?" Hearing this, Anne wept all the more.

III.   1. At the very same moment, a young man appeared in the mountains where Joachim was pasturing his flocks and said to him, "Why don't you go back to your wife?"

Joachim replied, "For twenty years I had her, and now, because God did not will to give me any children of her, I have suffered abuse and have had to leave the Temple in shame. Why should I go back to her after having been humiliated and despised once already? So I will stay here with my sheep as long as God sees fit to give to my eyes the light of this world; and by the hands of my servants I will gladly give the poor and the widows and the orphans and those who carry on the worship of God their portion."

2. When he had said this, the young man replied, "I am an angel of God, and this day I have appeared to your wife, as she was weeping and praying, and have consoled her. For know that she has conceived[3] a daughter of your seed. This child will stay in the Temple of God; the Holy Spirit will abide in her, and she will be the most blessed of all holy women, so that not only can no one say that there has ever been anyone like her before, but even after her there will be no one like her in this world. Go down from the mountain, therefore, and return to your wife, and you will find her with child. For God has given her a child,[4] for which you must give Him thanks; the child will be blessed, and (Anne) herself will be blessed, and will be made the mother of everlasting blessing."

3. Prostrating himself before the angel Joachim said, "If I have found grace in your eyes, stay in my tent for a while, and bless your (humble) servant."

And the angel said to him, "Do not call yourself my servant, but rather my fellow-servant; for both of us are servants of the same Lord. But my food is invisible, and my drink cannot be seen by mortal men, and so you must not invite me into your tent. But what you were going to give me, offer as a holocaust to God."

Then Joachim took a spotless lamb and said to the angel, "I would not

---

[3] ". . . quam scias ex semine tuo concepisse filiam." One, however, of the manuscripts used in the preparation of Amann's edition (*Parisinus 5559* — fourteenth century) reads, instead of *concepisse, concipere,* which would have to be translated, "is going to conceive."

[4] ". . . et invenies eam habentem in utero: excitavit enim Deus semen in ea . . ." All this is omitted by *Parisinus 5559.*

dare to offer a holocaust to God if it were not that the priestly power of offering sacrifice has been conferred on me by your order."

And the angel said to him, "And I would not have invited you to make an offering if I had not known the will of the Lord."

And it came to pass that as Joachim was offering the sacrifice to God, the angel rose to heaven along with the odor of the sacrifice, as if with the smoke.

4. Then Joachim fell on his face and lay there from the sixth hour of the day until evening. When his servants and the traders came, they did not know the reason for this, and were terrified, thinking that he wanted to kill himself. They went up to him and with difficulty raised him off the ground. When he told them what he had seen, they were stupefied; then, spurred by their amazement, they urged him to do the angel's bidding without delay, and return quickly to his wife.

And as Joachim was debating within himself whether to return, it came to pass that a deep sleep took hold of him and, lo, the angel that had appeared to him when he was awake appeared to him in his sleep, and said, "I am the angel whom God has given you for a guardian; go down (from this mountain) without any anxiety, and return to Anne, for the works of mercy which you and your wife have done have been recounted in the presence of the Most High, and an offspring has been given to you such as none of the prophets or saints have had from the beginning, nor will have."

And it came to pass that when Joachim awoke from sleep, he called his shepherds and told them his dream. They fell down and worshipped God; then they said to (Joachim), "Do not ignore the angel any longer, but get up and let us be on our way, travelling slowly and pasturing (the flock as we go)."

5. And when they had been on the way for thirty days and were near home, the angel of the Lord appeared to Anne as she stood in prayer and said to her, "Go to the gate called Golden,[5] and meet your husband; for he will come to you today."

Anne went hastily with her maids and, standing in the gateway itself, began to pray. And when she had waited a long time and was losing heart from the long wait, she raised her eyes and saw Joachim coming with his flocks. Anne went out to meet him and threw herself on his neck, giving thanks to God and saying, "I was a widow, and, behold, I am not one

---

[5] The origin of this detail is unexplained. Josephus mentions that some of the gates of the Temple were covered with gold and silver on the inside (*De bell. jud.*, V, v, 3; cf. VI, v, 3); but from the circumstances of the narrative, one would be inclined to suppose, as Amann points out, that the meeting took place at a gate of the city rather than a gate of the Temple. However, no "Golden Gate" seems to have been identified in the walls of Jerusalem.

any longer; I was sterile, and, behold, I have already conceived." [6]   And all her neighbors and acquaintances were overjoyed, so much so that the entire land of Israel rejoiced at the news.

IV.   Nine months later,[7] Anne gave birth to a daughter and named her Mary.   After three years, when the child had been weaned, Joachim and his wife Anne went together to the Temple of the Lord, offered sacrifice to the Lord, and committed their little girl Mary to the convent of virgins who praised God day and night.   And when Mary had been put down in front of the Temple she ran up the fifteen steps without looking back or crying for her parents as children usually do.   At this, everyone was stupefied with amazement, and even the Temple priests marvelled.

V.   Then Anne, filled with the Holy Spirit, declared before them all, "The Lord God of hosts has been mindful of His word, and has visited His people with holy visitation, to humble the nations that were rising against us, and convert their hearts to Himself.   He has opened His ears to our prayers and has turned away from us the insults of our enemies.   She who was sterile has become a mother, and has given birth to joy and rejoicing in Israel.   See, I shall be able to offer gifts to the Lord, and my enemies will not be able to stop me.   May the Lord make their hearts favorable to me, and give me everlasting joy."

III.   THE LEGEND OF ANNE AND JOACHIM
from the *Liber de Nativitate Mariae*[1]

I.   1. The blessed and glorious ever Virgin Mary, of the royal line and family of David, was born in the city of Nazareth and raised at Jerusalem in the Temple of the Lord.   Her father was called Joachim and her mother Anne.   He was from the city of Nazareth in Galilee, she from Bethlehem. 2. Their life was simple and righteous before the Lord, and charitable and irreproachable before men.   For they divided all their possessions into three parts: one part they gave to the Temple and those who cared for it; a

---

[6] ". . . jam concepi." *Parisinus 5559* reads: *concipiam* — "I will conceive."

[7] "Post haec autem, expletis mensibus novem, peperit Anna filiam . . ." *Parisinus 5559* reads: *Post haec autem concepit Anna* — "After this, Anne conceived . . ." Another manuscript (*Laurentianus-Gaddianus 208*) reads: *mensibus iiii* — "four months later." This would imply that the conception had occurred before Joachim's departure, since his sojourn in the mountain country lasted five months, according to chapter II, 1. Amann explains this as a later correction, designed — like most of those noted in *Parisinus 5559* — to avoid the representation of the conception as virginal.

---

[1] Translated from the edition of E. AMANN, *Le protévangile de Jacques et ses remaniements latins*, Paris 1910, pp. 344-350.   The entire work consists of ten chapters, besides a preface.   The present translation corresponds to the first five chapters.   On the significance of this work, see the remarks on p. 82 of the present volume.

second part to pilgrims and the poor; the third part they kept for themselves and their household. 3. Thus, these two, dear to God and good to men, lived a chaste married life for about twenty years, but without having any children. They vowed, however, that if God should give them offspring, they would dedicate it to His service; for this reason they used to go to the Temple of the Lord each year on the feast days.

II. 1. Now it came to pass one year, when the feast of the Dedication was drawing near, that Joachim went up to Jerusalem with some of his compatriots. Issachar was high priest at that time, and when he saw Joachim standing with his offering among the men from his city, he gave him a contemptuous stare and rejected his gifts, asking how one who was sterile dared take a place among those who were fruitful. He also declared that Joachim's gifts were altogether unworthy of God, for God had judged him unworthy to have children, and Scripture says that everyone who has not begotten a son for Israel is accursed. He said therefore that Joachim would first have to be freed from this curse by begetting a child, and then could come into the presence of the Lord with his gifts. 2. Joachim was covered with shame at this reproach and went off to the shepherds who were in his pastures with the flocks; he did not want to return home for fear that he would be branded with the same reproach by his compatriots who had been there and had heard the priest say this.

III. 1. He had been there for some time (*aliquamdiu*) when one day, as he was alone, an angel of the Lord stood beside him in a great light. Joachim was disturbed at the sight, but the angel who had appeared to him calmed his fear, saying, "Fear not, Joachim, and do not be disturbed at the sight of me, for I am an angel of the Lord. He has sent me to you to tell you that your prayers have been heard and that your alms have ascended into His presence. He has indeed seen your shame and has heard you unjustly reproached with sterility. But God is the avenger of sin, not of nature; and so, when He closes someone's womb, He does it in order to open it again all the more marvellously, so that what is born may be recognized as the fruit not of passion but of God's gift.

2. "For was not Sara, the first mother of your race, childless until her eightieth year? And yet in her extreme old age she bore Isaac, in whom all the nations were to be blessed, according to the Promise. Rachel, too, although so pleasing to God and so beloved of holy Jacob, was sterile for a long time; but in the end she bore Joseph, who became not only lord of Egypt, but also the deliverer of many nations that were on the point of perishing from famine. And which of the judges was mightier than Sampson or holier than Samuel? Yet both of these were born of sterile mothers. Therefore, if you are not convinced by reason because of what I said, at least believe that long-delayed conceptions, and births from mothers long sterile, are all the more marvellous.

3. "And so your wife Anne is going to bear you a daughter, whom you

will call Mary. She will be consecrated to the Lord from her infancy, as you have vowed, and she will be filled with the Holy Spirit from her mother's womb (*adhuc ex utero matris*). She will not eat or drink anything unclean, and her life will not be spent among the noisy crowd, but in the Temple, so that no evil can even be suspected, let alone spoken, of her. And just as she herself will be born wondrously of a sterile mother, so, when she has grown up, she will, by an unprecedented (miracle), give birth, while remaining a virgin, to the Son of the Most High, who will be called Jesus. He will be, as the etymology of His name indicates, the Savior of all nations. 4. And this will be to you a sign of what I am telling you: when you come to the Golden Gate at Jerusalem, you will meet there your wife Anne, who is now anxious over your delayed return, and will then be overjoyed to see you." After saying this, the angel left him.

IV. 1. Then the angel appeared to his wife, Anne, saying, "Fear not, Anne, and do not think that what you see is a ghost. For I am the angel who bore your prayers and alms, and those of your husband, to God. Now I have been sent to tell you that a daughter will be born to you. She will be called Mary, and will be the most blessed of women. Filled with the grace of God from her very birth (*a nativitate sua statim Domini gratia plena*), she will remain in her home for the three years that she is being nursed at the breast. Thereafter she will be given over to the service of the Lord, and will not leave the Temple until she comes of age, but will serve God there in fasting and prayer day and night, and will keep herself from everything impure. She will never know man, but, transcending all precedents, without stain, without corruption, without union with man, she, a virgin, will bear a son; she, the servant, will bear the Lord—Him Who, by grace, by title and by works, will be the Savior of the world. 2. Get up, therefore, and go to Jerusalem; when you reach the gate which is called Golden because it is gilded, there, as a sign to you, you will meet your husband, about whose well-being you are now anxious. And when this happens, know that what I am telling you will certainly take place."

Figure 17. THE MEETING AT THE GOLDEN GATE.
Sixteenth century medallion.

V. 1. And so the two of them, in obedience to the angel's order, left the places where they were, and went up to Jerusalem; and when they had come to the place designated by the angel's prophecy, there they met. Overjoyed at the sight of one another, and elated with their assurance of the promised child, they gave due thanks to the Lord who exalts the humble. 2. Then, after adoring the Lord, they returned home and awaited the fulfillment of God's promise with joyous certitude. And so Anne conceived and bore a daughter, and, in accordance with the angel's command, they named her Mary.

IV. A MEDIAEVAL SERMON ON
THE CONCEPTION OF BLESSED MARY [1]

May your charity, venerable brethren, deign to listen to me, as I tell how it has been shown, by many signs that have been observed in England, France and other parts of the world, that the Conception of the venerable Mother of God and ever Virgin Mary ought to be celebrated.

Sur mer vng abbe periſſoit/ mais il cui recordacion/ q̃ lavier ſe le ſauueroit/moyẽ nant q̃ feſter feroit/ ſa treſſaicte cõceptiõ

Fig. 18
HELSIN

For in the days when God, in His goodness, saw fit to correct the evils of the English people and to bring them to a more strict fulfillment of the duties pertaining to His service, the most glorious duke of the Normans, William, subdued their land by warfare. Having become King of the English, William reformed the entire ecclesiastical hierarchy (*ecclesiasticae dignitatis honores*) by the power of God and his own zeal. The devil, the enemy of all good things, hated the works undertaken in this pious intention, and often attempted to obstruct the King's success, through the treachery of his associates, and the attacks of outsiders. But the Lord protected and glorified this king who feared Him, and "the hateful one was brought to nothing." (Psalm 14:4)

---

[1] This work, of unknown authorship, was for centuries attributed to St. Anselm, who for this reason was frequently cited among the authorities favoring the doctrine and the feast of the Immaculate Conception (cf. p. 128 of the present volume, note 44, and the explanatory note accompanying plate XIII). We reproduce it here chiefly because it contains the legends of Helsin and of the canon saved from drowning (the 'Canon of Rouen,' as he is called in other works). These two stories are also presented together in the altarpiece panels reproduced in plate III.

Our translation has been made from the text printed in Migne, *PL* 159, 319-324. The names Helsin and Ramsay, which we give in parentheses, are given in parentheses in Migne, without any further explanation. Another account of the Helsin legend, closely parallel to the present one, has been edited by H. THURSTON and Th. SLATER in *Eadmeri Cantuariensis Tractatus de Conceptione Sanctae Mariae*, Freiburg im Br., 1904, pp. 88-92, followed by two other accounts which are not so similar. A fifth redaction is given by Migne immediately following the one here translated.

When the Danes, however, heard that England had been subjected to the Normans, they were deeply angered, as if an hereditary right had been taken from them. They prepared their arms and made ready their fleet in order to go and expel the Normans from the land which they felt had been given them by God. When William heard of this, being a very prudent man, he sent for a certain monk (Helsin), abbot of the monastery (of Ramsay) and sent him to Denmark to seek out the truth of the matter. The latter, a man of keen intelligence, carried out the King's mission vigorously, and, with his task faithfully accomplished, set sail again for England.

At first the trip went well, and he had crossed the greater part of the sea, when strong winds suddenly arose on all sides, and a terrible storm agitated both the sea and the sky. With the oars broken, the ropes snapped and the sails fallen, all hope was lost by the sailors, who were too exhausted to make any further effort, and were wretchedly waiting to be drowned. Despairing of saving their bodies, they loudly commended to their Creator the salvation of their souls alone, and they called upon the most Blessed Virgin Mary, Mother of God, the refuge of the miserable and the hope of the desperate. Suddenly they saw, in the midst of the waves not far from the ship, a man rather majestically garbed, and wearing a bishop's miter.

He called the abbot (Helsin) to him, and began to address him in these words: "Do you wish to escape from the peril of the sea? Do you wish to return to your country safe and sound?"

When the abbot had tearfully[2] replied that he desired this with all his heart, and looked for nothing more than this, the stranger declared, "Know that I have been sent to you by Our Lady Mary, the Mother of God, to whom you have so readily appealed: and if you are willing to do what I tell you, you and your companions will be saved from the danger of the sea."

The abbot at once promised that he would obey in everything if he should escape this shipwreck.

"Then promise," said the stranger, "to God and to me, that you will solemnly celebrate the day of the conception and creation of the Mother of Our Lord Jesus Christ, and that you will exhort others to celebrate it."

At this, the abbot, being a most prudent man, inquired, "On what day is this feast to be celebrated?"

"You are to celebrate[3] this feast on December 8 (*sexto Idus Decembris*)," was the rejoinder.

"And what office," asked the abbot, "shall we use in the Church services?"

---

[2] Reading *fletu* instead of the *fietu* which occurs in Migne.
[3] Reading *tenebis* instead of the *tenebris* which occurs in Migne.

"The entire office of her Nativity is to be recited for the Conception, except that instead of the word *Nativity,* you are to read *Conception."*

With this he disappeared, and in less time than it takes to tell, the storm died down. A breeze arose and the abbot safely reached the English shore, and made known what he had seen and heard to whomever he could. Moreover, he directed that this feast be celebrated in the monastery (of Ramsay), and until the end of his life celebrated it devoutly.

Therefore, dearly beloved brethren, if we wish to reach the port of salvation, we will celebrate the feast of the Conception of the Mother of God with fitting rites and services, so that we may be rewarded by her Son with a fitting recompense.

Elsewhere we find this festival honored in another way: for in the time of the illustrious Charles, King of the French, there was a certain cleric, who was a deacon, and was related to the King of Hungary. He loved the Mother of Jesus with all his heart and chanted her Hours with great care. On the advice, however, of his parents, he intended to marry a beautiful young girl. On a certain day, after receiving the nuptial blessing from the priest and hearing Mass, he remembered that he had not chanted the hours of the most Blessed Virgin that day, as was his wont; he sent his bride home, compelled everyone else to leave the Church, and remained alone before the altar of the Virgin.

He was singing the Hours of the Mother of the Lord, and was reciting the antiphon, "Thou art beautiful and comely, daughter of Jerusalem," when the Virgin Mary suddenly appeared to him with two angels who were holding her hands, and said to him: "If I am beautiful and comely, why do you send me away, and take another spouse? Am I not exceedingly lovely? Am I not more beautiful than she? Where have you seen anyone so beautiful as I?"

Stupefied, the youth replied, "My dearest Lady, your beauty surpasses that of all the world. Lady, what do you wish me to do?"

"If for the love of me, you put aside the fleshly spouse to whom you intend to cleave," she answered, "you will have me for your spouse in the Kingdom of Heaven; and if you solemnly celebrate the feast of my Conception each year on the eighth day of December, and urge others to celebrate it, you will be glorified together with me in the Kingdom of my Son."

With these words, the Blessed Virgin disappeared. The cleric would not go home, but went, without consulting the advice of his parents, to a certain abbey in another country and there was clothed in the monastic habit. In a short time, by the merits of Blessed Mary ever Virgin, who always rewards with happiness those who love her, he was made Bishop and Patriarch of Aquileia. As long as he lived, he diligently celebrated the feast of the Conception of the Blessed Virgin on the day indicated, as well as its proper octave, and urged that it be celebrated everywhere.

Cing clerc par pecbe
vesuoie, allant en fot
nicacion, fut par plu-
ficurs dyables noie/
par la vierge fut ra-
uoie, quil feruoit par
beuocion.

Fig. 19

THE CANON
OF ROUEN

With the help of divine grace, we will also recount another miracle of this feast, which took place elsewhere. By the French river[4] there lived a certain canon who was a priest, and who used to sing the canonical hours of the Blessed Virgin Mary. One day he was returning from a certain village in which he had committed adultery with another man's wife, and was on his way to the town in which he lived. Desiring to cross the Seine, he got into a boat by himself, and while rowing, began to sing the office of the Mother of the Lord. He was reciting the invitatory, *Ave Maria, gratia plena, Dominus tecum,* and had reached the middle of the river, when, lo and behold, a great horde of demons in the depths of the river, capsized him and his boat, and snatched away his soul for the torments. But three days later the Mother of Jesus came with a great company of angels, to the place where the demons were tormenting him, and said to them, "Why do you thus unjustly afflict the soul of Our servant?"

They answered, "He belongs by right to us, because he was taken doing our works."

"If he belongs to the person whose works he was doing," replied the Mother of Jesus, "then he belongs to Us, because at the moment that you undid him, he was reciting Our Matins; therefore, it is rather you who are guilty for having done injustice to me."

The demons, scattered in every direction by these words, took to flight; and the Blessed Mary restored the man's soul to his body. Then, taking the arm of this man who had been revived from a twofold death, she commanded the water to stand like a wall on either hand, and brought the man safely to the port from the depths of the river. He, overcome with joy, threw himself at the feet of the Blessed Virgin, crying, "Oh, dearest Lady mine, Oh beautiful Virgin, beloved of Christ, what shall I render to thee for the great benefits thou hast bestowed on me? Thou hast delivered me from the lion's mouth, and my soul from the grievous torments of hell."

"I beseech thee," replied the Mother of Jesus, "never again to fall into

---

[4] "In pelago Gallico"—referring doubtless to the river Seine, which is called explicitly a *pelagus* three times in the following lines (besides being referred to once as *flumen*).

the sin of adultery, lest thy last error be worst than the first. Likewise, I beseech thee from now on to devoutly celebrate the feast of my Conception each year on the eighth of December, and to urge that it be celebrated everywhere."

As soon as she had said this, the Blessed Virgin Mary ascended into Heaven, before his eyes. But he became a hermit, and to all who desired to hear, he told what had happened to him. Thereafter, for the rest of his life he solemnly and devoutly celebrated the feast of the Conception, and urged others to celebrate it.

And we, dearly beloved brethren, by our archiepiscopal authority, confirm and prescribe that none of us is in too desperate a state, either as regards temporal affairs, or by reason of his sins, to celebrate each year the Conception of Blessed Mary, the Virgin. For just as her Nativity is honored in the Holy Church, so should her Conception be likewise, since if she had not been conceived she would not have been born. As her Nativity was necessary for the salvation of the human race, so likewise was her conception; she was both conceived and born by God's command. If we can see from this the plan (*ratio*) of God, it becomes clear that the day of her spiritual conception is more deserving of honor than that of her Nativity.

For it was a greater thing for Adam to have been created by God than for Adam's offspring to be born of a mother: there is nothing wonderful, if, by (the operation of) God, a man is born of a mother. Therefore, let those foolish ones be discomfited, who, blinded by the darkness of ignorance, refuse to celebrate such great sacraments and such great mysteries, on the grounds that the union of man and woman was involved in the Virgin's Conception. For if foolish men are unwilling to celebrate the feast of her Conception today, because it was carnal, at least let them be happy to celebrate today that honorable day, that night—although to many unknown —the time, the hour of her spiritual conception, in which the Creator of souls, by the ministry of angels, joined the worthy and most holy soul of his Mother to her virginal body. He who provides for our salvation made this the first day of our reparation and salvation. He it was who chose it, and He sanctified it.

For, as all the learned know, man has a twofold conception: one in which the carnal union of man and woman takes place, and another in which the spiritual soul, new and pure, is, by God's operation, joined to the body. If someone is unwilling to celebrate the carnal conception of the Mother of the Lord, at least he should be willing to celebrate the spiritual creation of her soul, and its union with the body. Oh how great is that day, on which the worthy soul of our Reparatrix (*nostrae reparatricis*) is created, sanctified, and joined to her most holy body! For he who refuses to honor the day of her conception is no true lover of the Virgin.[5]

Likewise, shame on those insane people who do not wish to observe this day, on the grounds that holy Church is not accustomed to honor the conception of other saints. For it is stupid to make a comparison in this matter between other saints and her in whom God took human flesh, and whom He elevated above all the angels and archangels in heaven. For while it has not been granted to other saints to have the day of their conception celebrated, this has been granted by the Holy Spirit to her who is greater and worthier than the rest. It is beautifully fitting for her through whom all the saints are sanctified to have dominion over all the others. For Christ is called *sanctorum Sanctus,* and she *sanctorum Sancta;* and just as the supreme governor of all things conferred on her above all the other saints, this unprecedented dignity of conceiving and bearing the Word made Flesh while a virgin, and of remaining thereafter a virgin, so likewise He gave her, above all the others, this unprecedented dignity, of having the sacred solemnities of her Conception and Nativity celebrated by us in the Holy Church.

But why go on any longer? To honor the conception of the Mother of the Lord is to commemorate the birth of Christ, for with her is conceived the stock from which Christ will spring. This is why the Gospel, "The book of the generation. . ." (*Mat.* 1:1), is sung before morning lauds, and read at Mass, today, as on the Nativity of the Lord, in accordance with a praise-worthy custom. It is with good reason, therefore, that we celebrate both the origin of the Son and the conception of the Mother, for the conception and birth of the Mother is the origin of the Son. Therefore, (dearly beloved) let us celebrate today with due rites these two conceptions of hers—the spiritual and the human, both of which are worthy of veneration —so that by her merits and prayers we may deserve to be rescued from worldly cares and from all evils, and to be brought to eternal joys, through Our Lord Jesus Christ, her Son, Who with the Father and the Son lives and reigns, God, throughout all the ages of ages. Amen.

[5] "Non est enim verus amator Virginis qui respuit colere diem ejus conceptionis." (*PL* 159,322C) This text became famous because so often cited as St. Anselm's *sententia* in favor of the feast. Cf. plate XIII of the present volume, with its ac-companying note, and p. 487 f.

V. THE BIBLICAL SYMBOLS OF THE BLESSED VIRGIN
from the *Aurora* of Peter Riga[1]

129   Archa, columba Noe[2] fuit hec; Moysi rubus,[3] Aaron
        Virga,[4] Iacob scala,[5] septupla spica Ioseph,[6]
        Nubes manna pluens,[7] petra larga fluenta reffundens,[8]
        Pertica serpentis qui medicina fuit,[9]
        Funda Dauid fundens lapidem qui perculit hostem,[10]
        Fons Bethleem cuius ille sitiuit aquam,[11]

135   Prefulgens eboris candore thronus Salomonis,[12]
        Conc[h]a fluens rore per Gedeonis opus,[13]
        Vrceus electri quem[14] uidit in igne Propheta,[15]

---

[1] Peter RIGA (b. *ca.* 1140, † 1209) was a canon of Rheims. The *Aurora,* which he composed between 1170 and 1200, was a paraphrase of the Old and New Testaments, heavily interlarded with legend and allegorical interpretation, all put into verse. Although it enjoyed extraordinary popularity during the thirteenth and fourteenth centuries (several hundred manuscripts are still extant), it has never been printed, except for a few excerpts.

The text given here reproduces that of a manuscript (U.N.D. Ms. 3) in the University of Notre Dame library, folio 176, recto and verso (the verso begins with line 159). Father Paul E. Beichner, C.S.C., who is preparing a critical edition, considers this manuscript to be of late thirteenth-century origin. To facilitate the reading of the document, I have modernized the punctuation, added capitals (which, in the manuscript, are used only at the beginning of each line), and italicized the names of the Marian symbols in the second half of the passage. Otherwise the text has been adhered to faithfully, except for a few corrections based mainly on Father Beichner's transcription of other manuscripts, which are all indicated in the notes (the letter *B* being used to designate the text established by Father Beichner.) Variants occurring in other Mss. are not indicated except where they are of special interest.

The passage reproduced here (lines 129-186 of Riga's New Testament) immediately precedes the account of the Annunciation. In some of the Mss. it is headed by the rubric, *"De commendatione Beate Virginis in eloquiis scripturarum."* Another entitles it: *"De signis Beatam Virginem prenuntiantibus."* I have found no allusion to Mary's conception in the work. The present passage is reproduced here merely as an example of an early listing of Old Testament symbols applied to the Blessed Virgin. Note that five of the symbols which appear in this passage also occur in the miniature reproduced in plate VII: the dove of Noe (line 129), Jacob's ladder (1. 130), the Fountain of Bethlehem (1. 134), the seven-branched candlestick (1. 139), and the green olive tree (1. 140).

[2] Genesis 6-8.
[3] Exodus 3:2 ff.
[4] Exodus 7:8 ff.
[5] Genesis 28:12 ff.
[6] Genesis 37:6 ff.
[7] Exodus 16:14 ff.

[8] Exodus 17:6 ff.
[9] Numbers 21:8 f.
[10] I Kings 17:49.
[11] II Kings 23:15.
[12] III Kings 10:18.
[13] Judges 6:38.

[14] quem: quod B. B's reading fits the scriptural reference better, because it would refer to the *electrum*, the likeness of which Ezechiel saw in the fire. The reading *quem* would refer to the vase; but no vase is mentioned by the prophet. Cf. the following note.

[15] Ezechiel 1:4 f.: "Et vidi, et ecce ventus turbinis veniebat ab aquilone, et nubes magna, et ignis involvens, et splendor in circuitu ejus; et de medio ejus, quasi

In Domini semper ianua clausa domo,[16]
Lampas prerutilans septem uicina lucernis

140   Quam Zacharias uidit,[17] oliua uirens,[18]
Cui decor est nomen de uirgis una duabus,[19]
    Terra creans uermem quo perit umbra Ione,[20]
Solis amicta die mulier cuius caput ornat
Bis sex stellarum luce corona micans.[21]

145   Que modo perstrinxi de Virgine singula currant
    Ordine; uult planum sermo uiator iter.
Vt det sermoni decus ordo decorus, inauret
    Pennam scriptoris, aurea Virgo, sui.

148b   *De specificatione beate Marie.*[22]
Archa Maria fuit: semen seruatur in illa,

150   Et tegit et seruat et regit ipsa suos.[23]
Ipsa *columba* fuit: oculos imitata columbe,
    Simplex et mitis et sine felle mali.
Hec *rubus* est *Moysi:* rubus est inmunis ab igne;
    Virgineum tetigit nulla libido decus.

155   Est Virgo uirga: sine germine protulit illa
    Flores; absque uiro protulit ista Deum.

---

species electri, id est, de medio ignis; et in medio ejus similitudo quattuor animalium." Cf. 1:27. The Hebrew word corresponding to *electri* is of uncertain meaning; many modern translators understand it to refer to glowing or shining metal. The Latin word *electrum,* like the Greek of which it is a transliteration, was used both of amber and of an alloy of gold and silver. (See note 29 below.) It is in this last sense that the term was evidently understood here, as is evident from line 173 below.

[16] Ezechiel 44:2.

[17] Cf. Zacharias 4:2: "Et dixit ad me: Quid tu vides? Et dixi: Vidi, et ecce candelabrum aureum totum, et lampas ejus super caput ipsius, et septem lucernae ejus super illud, et septem infusoria lucernis quae erant super caput ejus."

[18] According to the explanation given below (line 179 f.), this would seem to be an allusion to the oil of the olive. Perhaps, however, the author himself did not understand the significance of this traditional symbol, and drew on St. Bernard (cf. note 30, below) for the best explanation he could find. But "the green olive tree" would be a strange way of referring to olive oil. A more convincing interpretation of the symbol is given by the Bedford Book of Hours: "The olive tree which bore fruit while it was still green." (See the note accompanying plate VII, above.)

[19] Zacharias 11:2: "Et assumpsi mihi duas virgas, unam vocavi Decorem, et alteram vocavi Funiculum . . ." Cf. 11:10.

[20] Jonas 4:7.

[21] Apocalypse 12:1.

[22] This rubric does not seem to belong to the original text. The other manuscripts have various rubrics and at various places.

[23] B: Et regit et seruat et tegit ista suos.

Hec est *scala Iacob,* prece cuius, munere cuius,
Exemplis cuius, scandis ad alta[24] poli.
Septupla spica Ioseph, et cella simul fuit Almo

160   Pneumate concipiens, panis alumpna sacri.
Manna dat hec *nubes,* laticem hec[25] *petra,* dum parit illum
Qui fuit esca poli fonsque perhennis aque.
Pertica Virgo fuit que serpentem tulit illum
Qui nos sanauit[26] nulla uenena ferens.[27]

165   *Funda Dauid* fudit lapidem quo funditur hostis:
Virgo Deum fudit, quo malus hostis obit.
Hec est *fons Bethleem* quam rex siciit, quia panem
Etheris in panis protulit ista domo.
Conc[h]a fluens rore fuso de uellere.   Spreta[28]

170   Gaudet Iudea, Virgo repleta Deo.
Est *thronus* ex ebore *Salomonis,* cella pudoris
Facta Dei sedes, candida sicut ebur.
Est *vas electri,* nitet argento, rubet auro,[29]
Dum parit hunc unum qui Deus est et homo.

175   *Ianua clausa* manet quia uir transire per illam
Non ualuit: Virgo concipit absque uiro.
Hec est quam septem cingebant lumina *lampas:*
Septeno Christi munere plena micans.
Est et *oliua uirens,* quia lux est, esca, medela:

[24] alta: astra B.
[25] hec: omitted by B.
[26] sanauit: saluauit B.
[27] ferens: gerens B.
[28] spreta: This was the original reading of the Ms., and is also preferred by B, on the basis of 6 Mss., including the older and better ones. However, in our Ms., a later hand has added in the margin: "vel presso," and someone has scratched out the word *spreta* leaving only the letters *pr,* as if he intended to insert *presso,* according to the note in the margin. There is great variation in the Mss. collated by B: one reads *spreto,* 5 (including ours) *presso,* 1 *pressa,* 2 *sumpto,* and one has *sumpto* corrected to *spreto.*
[29] At this point (lines 172-175) a later hand has added the following notes, in the left and right margins:

dicitur et electrum quoddam genus gummi quod fluit ab arboribus et durescit in lapidem quod succinum dicitur. dicitur et electrum metallum quod naturaliter invenitur et precio habetur —	tribus partibus argenti et una auri: dicitur electrum. [*This note is fragmentary in the text itself.*]

These three interpretations of *electrum* are the same as those given by St. Isidore of Seville in Book XVI of his *Etymologiae,* c. 24 (Lindsay ed., vol. II; *PL* 82, 590), and some of the very words match Isidore's; but of the third type of *electrum,* Isidore says: "fit de tribus partibus auri et argenti una." In authors of classical antiquity, still other accounts of the metallic *electrum* are to be found.

180   Lux cecis, miseris esca, medela reis.[30]

Est et *virga decens,* quia solis lumen et omnes

Celi candelas Virgo deccore premit.

Terra creat uermen siccans [h]ederam quia[31] Christum

Virgo parit, per quem flens synogoga perit.

185   *Sole nitens mulier* quam bis sex astra coronant,

Bis sex discipulos astra fuisse reor.[32]

---

[30] Cf. St. BERNARD's interpretation of Canticle of Canticles 1:2, "Oleum effusum nomen tuum," as applied to the Holy Name of Jesus: "Est procul dubio inter oleum et nomen sponsi similitudo; nec otiose Spiritus sanctus alterutrum comparavit. Ego autem dico in triplici quadam qualitate olei, quod lucet, pascit et ungit, si vos melius non habetis. Fovet ignem, nutrit carnem, lenit dolorem: lux, cibus, medicina. Vide idem nunc et de sponsi nomine. Lucet praedicatum, pascit recogitatum, invocatum lenit et ungit." (*Sermo XV in Cantica Canticorum, PL* 183, 846B; read in the fourth lesson of matins on the feast of the Holy Name of Jesus).

[31] *quia* has been inserted by a later hand; agrees with B.

[32] Line 186 is replaced in six Mss. by the following:

Mens humilis, flos uirgineus, deuotio pura,

Vera fides, certa spes, geminatus amor,

Et sex uirtutes, alias quas Martha figurat,

Bis sex astra reor que diadema tulit.

Bibliography (1830-1957)

This Bibliography is devoted to theological and historical works on the Immaculate Conception printed in book form between 1830 and 1957, in the following languages: English, French, German, Italian, Latin, Spanish. Hence, it consists essentially of literature occasioned directly or indirectly by the Definition of 1854, although it goes back far enough to take in also the writings that immediately preceded the Definition. 1830 was chosen as the starting point because of the apparition of the Blessed Virgin to Sister Catherine Labouré in November of that year (cf. plate XXI above), which greatly stimulated popular devotion to the Immaculate Conception, and was thus a kind of prelude to the papal pronouncement.

Works on the Immaculate Conception: Not only those which are devoted exclusively to the Immaculate Conception, but also any containing a serious discussion of it (i.e. several pages at least) have been included. Some works which were not available for examination have been included on the strength of their titles, which gave grounds to suppose that the Immaculate Conception would be treated in them.

In book form: This means principally that *articles in periodicals* (journals, reviews, and the like) have *not* been included.[1] Leaflets of only a few pages have also been omitted where they were known to be such; but in a great many cases, the length of a given work was not known. Otherwise, no restriction has been made on the basis of length; booklets, brochures and the like have been included, so long as they met the other specifications.

Theological and historical: Expositions of the doctrine and its history form the principal object of this Bibliography; however, any writings liable to interest theologians and historians of the subject have also been listed. The Bibliography is not limited merely to strictly scientific works; but writings of a purely ephemeral character, such as most popular expositions of the doctrine, have been omitted when they could be detected. As, however, the majority of the works listed were not available for direct examina-

---

[1] The reason for this restriction was purely of a practical order. The sheer quantity of periodical literature on our subject during the nineteenth century was so great that it would be a major project merely to locate it, let alone sift it; and the worth of the literature in question would not merit such attention.

tion, it was not always possible to evaluate their quality; and rather than risk omitting works of some interest, it has been judged better to err on the side of including some that were valueless.

The following categories of works were *definitely excluded:* prayer books; collections of meditations, sermons and "elevations" (including particularly the May Devotions so abundant in Italian and German); poetry; "lives" of the Blessed Virgin; papal encyclicals; works on the Miraculous Medal (except for a few of the earliest) or Marian apparitions or shrines; works on the Immaculate Conception in art.[2]

Manuals of dogma abound during the first 75 years of this period, particularly in the Latin literature. In most of them, the treatise on the Immaculate Conception is merely a routine summary of what is found also in most other manuals. Hence these manuals have not been listed here, except when the unusual length of the treatise (i.e. 20 pages or more) or some other sign indicated that the author had taken special pains with it.

New editions of works written originally before 1830 have not been included unless the work as a whole dealt with the Immaculate Conception.[3] New translations of older works, however, have been treated as new works.

Exceptions have been made to all the above rules when the importance of an individual author or work, or some other circumstance, so dictated. Thus, we have been more open about including works written before 1854 (when they were rare) than those written during subsequent decades, when they were abundant. Similarly, we have been broader about including works written in the English language, not only because they are of special interest to readers in this country, but also because English is about the poorest of these six languages in *Immaculata* literature.

Sources

As far as possible, this Bibliography was established through direct examination by the editor of the relevant material contained in the libraries of the following institutions: the University of Notre Dame, the Catholic University of America, the University of Dayton (Marian Library), Holy Cross College (Washington, D. C.), Woodstock College, Mundelein Seminary, the Dominican House of Studies (Washington, D. C.) — as well as the personal Mariological library of Father Juniper Carol, O.F.M.

Secondly, lists were sent to us of the holdings of other libraries which we were not able to visit. In the first place, mention must be made of

---

[2] The last-mentioned are presented in a special bibliography on p. 503 ff., above.

[3] Hence we have not listed any of the following works, which appear over and over again in most languages all during the period under consideration: *The glories of Mary*, by St. Alphonsus Liguori, *The Mystical City of God*, by Maria d'Agreda, and the *Life of the Blessed Virgin*, by Catherine Emmerich.

Father Lucien Arendt, director of the Marian Library at Banneux, and of Father G.-M. Besutti, O.S.M., director of the Servite Fathers' Marian Library in Rome. Both went to considerable pains to send us an account of the *Immaculata* literature in their libraries. Likewise, reports were made for us on the libraries of the following institutions: the Lateran College in Rome, by Father Constantino Vona; the Gregorian University, by Father Schyns, S.J.; Berchmanskollegs at Pullach, Germany, by Father Walter Brugger, S.J.; the Priesterseminar in Münster, by Msgr. Johannes Weinand, Rector; the Dominican monastery in Vienna, by the Fathers of the monastery; the Priesterseminar in Vienna, by Father Johann Bauderer; the Canisianum in Innsbruck, by Father Hermann Zeller, S.J.; the University of Salamanca, by Father Felix Rodríguez Encinas; the Union Theological Seminary in New York, by Mrs. Hugh M. Foster. We wish to express here our gratitude to all these people for their cooperation, which was indispensable to us.[4]

Finally, we have had recourse to bibliographies compiled by others, the principal ones of which are listed below. Where it was practical, the works mentioned in these sources were verified in national catalogs of printed books.

A work involving so many collaborators and such varied sources will inevitably suffer from inconsistencies and inaccuracies. For this reason, we were tempted for a time to abandon this bibliography, which had been begun by others and taken over by us when they had to give it up; finally we went ahead with it, in the belief that even an imperfect work can still render useful service. We only hope that this will be kept in mind by those who find mistakes in it.

[4] Besides the correspondents mentioned in this paragraph, the following people assisted in the preparation of this Bibliography: Fathers Joseph Papin, Luke Malik, O.P., and John Cibor, colleagues and former colleagues at the University of Notre Dame, were of great help in contacting European libraries and sifting the reports received from them. Father Juniper Carol, O.F.M., founder of the American Mariological Society, Father Eamon Carroll, O.C., professor of theology at Whitefriars' Hall and at the Catholic University of America, and Brother Stanley Matthews, S.M., were most cooperative in responding to requests for information. Fathers Matthew Miceli, C.S.C., and Jaroslav Polc, as well as Messrs. Morris Amen, Nicholas Ayo, Santo Ciatto, Jerome Esper, Dennis Freemal and Richard McInnes, seminarians in the Congregation of Holy Cross, assisted in the examination of the holdings of the Notre Dame University Library and of printed bibliographies. Finally, the trying labor of assembling the material and preparing the manuscript for publication was greatly advanced by the help given generously and painstakingly by Miss Caroline Schmidt, professor of anatomy at St. Scholastica's College, Duluth, and student of theology at the University of Notre Dame. When time came to check the proofs, the editor's brother Joseph spent many hours ferreting out errors. To all, we are profoundly grateful.

BIBLIOGRAPHICAL WORKS[5]

GENERAL

[Sire, Dominique.] *Notice sur la Collection des documents relatifs à la définition du dogme de l'Immaculée Conception de la Très-Sainte Vierge qui sont conservés dans la basilique de Notre-Dame du Puy.* Le Puy, Marchessou, 1860. 128 pp. (Republished in J.-J. Bourassé's *Summa Aurea* . . . , tome VIII, col. 585-612.)

Roskovány, Augustinus. *Beata Virgo Maria in suo conceptu Immaculata ex monumentis omnium seculorum demonstrata.* 9 volumes, Budapestini & Nitriae, 1873-1881. (For further details, see the Latin bibliography below under 1881. The author lists every publication known to him which touches on the Blessed Virgin; but works dealing particularly with the Immaculate Conception are given in separate lists. Unfortunately, the references are frequently inaccurate. We have tried to verify them elsewhere whenever possible; but for many minor works published between 1830 and 1880, we have had to rely on Roskovány as the sole source of information. The more trivial works cited by him have been omitted from the present Bibliography.)

Escard, F. "Biblographie de l'Immaculée Conception," in *Polybiblion* X (1879), pp. 534-538; XI (1880) pp. 78-83. . . . (Photographically reproduced by *Marianum*, Rome, 1947. Escard's work, like Roskovány's, is careless and inaccurate.)

McKenna, Bernard A. *The dogma of the Immaculate Conception* . . . Washington, Catholic University Press, 1929, pp. 573-603. (Separate bibliographies in English, Latin, French, Italian, Spanish, German.)

Roschini, Gabriel Maria, O.S.M. *Mariologia,* tomus II, pars 2, ed. 2, Romae, Belardetti, 1948, pp. 12-19. (Separate bibliographies in Latin, Italian, English, French, German, Spanish.

PARTICULAR LANGUAGES

German:

Kolb, Georg, S.J. *Wegweiser in die marianischen Literatur zunächst für Maivorträge und Vereinsansprachen. Eine Sammlung vorzugsweise deutscher Werke der vier letzten Jahrzehnte, nebst Winken zu deren Benützung und Ergänzung.* Freiburg im Br., Herder, 1888. 224 pp.

————. *Supplement zum Wegweiser in die marianische Literatur, reichend bis Anfang 1900. Ibid.,* 1900. 120 pp.

Polish:

Bruchnalski, Wilhelm. *Bibliografia Maryologii Polskiej od wynalezienia sztuki drukarskiej do r. 1902.* Lwów and Warszawa, 1905. xvi, 314 pp.

Szostkiewicz, Z. & Wesoly, S. "Bibliographia Mariana Polonorum ab anno 1903 ad annum 1905," in *Marianum* 18 (1956), supplement to fascicle 2, v, 76 pp.

Portuguese:

Anaquim, Conego Manoel. *O Genio Portuguez aos pés de Maria.* Lisboa, Livraria Ferreira, 1904. xiv, 306 pp. (Secção da Immaculada Conceição, pp. 1-79.)

Spanish:

Pérez, Nazario, S.J. *La Inmaculada y España.* Santander, "Sal Terrae." Pp. xi-xxxii.

PARTICULAR RELIGIOUS COMMUNITIES

Capuchins

* Eduardus alenconiensis. "Bibliotheca Mariana Ordinis FF. MM. Capuccinorum, seu de operibus a religiosis Ordinis nostri conscriptis quae de B. V.

---

[5] Only the more important bibliographies are listed here; a great number of general expositions of the Immaculate Conception to be cited below also contain short bibliographies.

* Not available for consultation by the present bibliographer.

Maria tractant," in *Analecta Ordinis Minorum Capuccinorum* 21 (p. 27) — 26 (p. 122). (Republished in 1910 with the title, *Bibliotheca mariana Ordinis FF. Min. Capuccinorum, seu catalogus scriptorum ejusdem Ordinis qui de B.V.Maria opera ediderunt vel manuscripta reliquerunt* ab Eduardo Alenconiensi . . . contexta. Accedit dissertatio de prima bibliotheca scriptorum Ordinis Min. Capuccinorum. Romae, apud Curiam Generalitiam. xi, 95 pp.)

Carthusians:

Autore, Stanislaus Maria, O. Cart. *Bibliotheca cartusiana mariana, seu breves notitiae scriptorium sacri Ordinis Cartusiensis, qui de Beatissima Deipara Virgine Maria tractatus et libellos, hymnos aut sermones conscripserunt.* . . . Monstrolii, typis Cartusiae S. Mariae de Pratis, 1898. 70 pp.

Dominicans:

Masson, Reginaldus, O.P. "De Immaculata Conceptione apud Fratres Praedicatores," in *Angelicum* XXXI (1954), pp. 358-406, XXXII (1955), pp. 52-82.

Franciscans:

[Holzapfel, Heribert, O.F.M.] "Bibliographia seu bibliotheca Franciscana de Immaculata Conceptione," in *Acta Ordinis Fratrum Minorum,* Dec. 1904, pp. 70-99.

Huntemann, Ulricus, O.F.M. "Maria Immaculata in der Franciscaner Bibliographie," in *L'Ordine dei Frati Minori al Congresso Mariano Internazionale* (1904), Roma, 1905, pp. 51-56.

(*Anon.*) "Opera anno iubilari definitionis dogmaticae Immaculatae Conceptionis recurrente a Nostratibus circa eamdem Immaculatam Conceptionem publicata," *ibid.* pp. 71-82.

Uribe, Angel, O.F.M., "La Inmaculada en la literatura franciscana Española," in *Archivo Ibero-americano,* XV (1955), pp. 201-495. (Reprinted separately.)

Jesuits:

Sommervogel, Carlos, S.J. *Bibliotheca Mariana de la Compagnie de Jésus.* Paris, Picard, 1885. vii, 242 pp. (IC pp. 47-107.)

de Uriarte, Eugenio, S.J. *Biblioteca de Jesuitas españoles que escriberon sobre la Inmaculada Concepción de Nuestra Señora antes de la definición dogmática de este misterio.* Madrid, G. Lopez y del Horno, 1904. x, 148 pp.

de Letter, P., S.J. "The Immaculate Conception and the Society of Jesus," in *Woodstock Letters* 83(1954), pp. 365-401.

Mercedarians:

* Valenzuela, Pedro Armengaudo, O. de M. *De Intemerato Deiparae conceptu in Ordine ipsi sub titulo Mercede dicato,* Romae 1904. Pp. 218-244.

Symbols, Abbreviations, Etc.

s.d. (*"sans date"*)—the date of publication is not indicated.
s.e. (*"sine editore"*)—the publisher is not indicated.
s.l. (*"sine loco"*)—the place of publication is not indicated.
Each work is entered under the date of its first edition if this is known; otherwise under the earliest known edition. (With regard especially to books dated by the second edition, it should be kept in mind that the "first editions" of professors' manuals were in some cases not printed editions at all, but mimeographed notes or the like. Also, it is not uncommon for a second edition to appear in the same year as the first.) Later editions, when known, are mentioned in the entry of the first edition; they are given separate entries only when they bear a different title from the first edition.

---

* Not available for consultation by the present bibliographer.

Works consisting of several volumes which appeared in different years are entered under the date of the last, except where there is reason to treat each volume as a distinct work.

A date is given in brackets [1885] for books which do not indicate a publication date, but do bear the date of the *Imprimatur,* Preface, or the like. The actual appearance of the book would in many cases occur the year following this.

At the end of each chronological list, we have indicated some books "of date unknown." This does not mean necessarily that these books bear no date; in some cases, it means simply that we have found a reference to the book but with no indication of its date.

ENGLISH[1]

1830 (MIRACULOUS MEDAL APPARITION TO SISTER CATHERINE LABOURÉ, PARIS, NOVEMBER 17; FIRST MEDALS STRUCK, JUNE 30, 1832)

1844 LAMBRUSCHINI, Luigi Cardinal. *A polemical dissertation on the Immaculate Conception of the Most Blessed Virgin Mary.* London, Richardson. 109 pp.
(Translated from the Italian; another English translation appeared in 1855.)

1847 PARETTI, G. B. *Idolatrous worship of the Virgin Mary in 1847.* London, Miller. x, 12 pp.

1848 (COMMITTEE APPOINTED BY POPE PIUS IX TO EXAMINE THE ADVISABILITY OF A DEFINITION, JUNE 1)

1849 (ENCYCLICAL LETTER *Ubi primum* OF POPE PIUS IX, FEBRUARY 2)

1851 MORRIS, John Brande. *Jesus the Son of Mary,* or the doctrine of the Catholic Church upon the Incarnation of God the Son, considered in its bearings upon the reverence shown by Catholics to His Blessed Mother. 2 vol. London, Toovey. IC vol. II, pp. 219-385.

1854 (DEFINITION OF THE IMMACULATE CONCEPTION AS A DOGMA OF FAITH BY POPE PIUS IX, DECEMBER 8)

COSTA, Fr. *Reflections regarding the expected dogmatic definition on the Immaculate Conception.* Translated by George Bowyer. Rome, Propaganda. 28 pp.

1855 BRYANT, J. D. (M.D.) *The Immaculate Conception of the Most Blessed Virgin Mary, Mother of God;* A Dogma of the Catholic Church. Boston. xx, 322 pp.

COXE, A. *The novelty and nullity of the papal dogma of the Immaculate Conception,* preached in Grace Church, Baltimore, 25 March. Baltimore, Watters. [s.d.]

CUDDESDEN, John Jerome. *Cuddesden versus Vatican,* or a Lawyer's demurrer to the Bishop of Oxford's complaint against the Immaculate Conception and worship of the Blessed Virgin Mary. London, Paris, Tours.
(Cf. the entry [WILBERFORCE], below.)

DONAHOE, Patrick. *The Immaculate Conception of the most blessed Virgin Mary,* a dogma of the Catholic Church. Boston.

FABER, Frederick W. *An explanation of the doctrine and definition of the Immaculate Conception,* with a meditation. Baltimore, John Murphy.

[1] We are indebted to Msgr. H. Francis Davis of Oscott College, England, and to Father Kevin McNamara of St. Patrick's College, Maynooth, for information about works in English belonging to their libraries.

1855 (continued)

HUSENBETH, F. C. *The Chain of the Fathers, witnesses for the doctrine of the Immaculate Conception of the Blessed Virgin Mary, Mother of God.* London, Richardson. 34 pp.

LABORDE, Jean Joseph. *The impossibility of the Immaculate Conception as an article of faith.* Philadelphia, Hooker. 5, 160 pp.

LAMBING, Andrew A. *The Immaculate Conception of the Blessed Virgin Mary.* New York, Sadlier. 256 pp.

> Republished by Benziger in 1904, viii, 216 pp.

LAMBRUSCHINI, Louis Cardinal. *A polemical treatise on the Immaculate Conception of the Blessed Virgin.* To which is added a history of the doctrine, by Father Felix, S.J. The French portion of the work trans. by Mrs. J. Sadlier, and the Latin extracts from the Holy Fathers by a clergyman. New York, Sadlier, 256 pp.

> Reprinted *ibid*, 1860, 1886.
> (The original work was written in Italian. Another English translation had appeared in 1844, *q.v.*)

MAGUIRE, Edward. *The new Romish dogma of the Immaculate Conception, or, Trial of the Church of Rome before a jury of Irish Roman Catholics.* Belfast & New York, Maganos. 9, 101 pp.

MASON, Gallagher. *The regard due to the Blessed Virgin Mary,* with an examination of the new Roman dogma. Oswego, Winchester. 3, 162 pp.

RANKIN, Ch. W. *The Blessed Virgin vindicated;* preached in St. Luke's Church, Baltimore, 25 March. Baltimore, Robinson.

RUSSELL and HERFOOT. *The new papal dogma false and superstitious.* Two sermons delivered in the chapel of the College of Saint James (Maryland), one by Russell, the other by Herfoot. [Baltimore]

> (Reference from SIRE. "*Herfoot*" is perhaps a mistake for *Herbert* or *Herford*.)

SKIERS, Edmund. *Illustrations on the Incarnation and Immaculate Conception of the Virgin Mary and the miraculous and mysterious birth of our Saviour, Jesus Christ.* Paris.

SWOPE, Cornelius E. "*Christ and not the Virgin Mary, the Head of the new creation . . ,*" preached in Mount Calvary Church, Baltimore, 25 March. . . . Baltimore, Robinson.

TORMEY, Michael. *The Immaculate Conception.* Dublin, Duffy, x, 236 pp.

> Republished, 1879.

ULLATHORNE, Bishop William B. *The Immaculate Conception of the Mother of God.* An exposition. Baltimore, Murphy. 204 pp.

> *Id.,* revised by Canon Iles, D.D., and with an Introduction by the Bishop of Birmingham. Westminster (Art & Brook); New York, Cincinnati, Chicago, 1904.

WALSH, W. P. *The Immaculate Conception of our Lord and Saviour Jesus Christ.* A sermon preached on the feast of the Nativity, 1854; with some notes on the new Dogma of the Church of Rome. Dublin.

[WILBERFORCE] Samuel, Lord Bishop of Oxford. *Rome: her new dogma and our duties,* a sermon preached before the University at St. Mary's Church, Oxford. Oxford and London, Parker.

> Second edition also 1855.

(*Anon.*) *The Immaculate Conception of our Lady,* a historical sketch of the discussions on this dogma with a preliminary solution of the questions concerning it, by a Catholic priest. Baltimore, Murphy.

(*Anon.*) *Pastoral letter of the Archbishop of Baltimore, and the bishops and prelates of the province of Baltimore, assembled in provincial council, in May, 1855.* Baltimore, Murphy and Co.; Pittsburgh, Quigley. 16 pp.

1856 MEYRICH. *Devotional Theology of the Church of Rome.* The glories of Mary. Oxford.

1858 (Apparitions of Mary Immaculate to Bernadette Soubirous, Lourdes, February 11 - July 16)

1861 Cummings, John. *The Immaculate Conception; its antecedents and consequences.* London, Miller. 3, 11 pp.

1865 Pusey, E. B. *An Eirenicon, in a Letter to the author of the "Christian Year."* London, Oxford, Cambridge. IC pp. 116-198; 351-409.

1866 Harper, Thomas Norton, S.J. "The Immaculate Conception," in *Peace through the truth; or Essays on subjects connected with Dr. Pusey's Eirenicon.* First series. London: Longmans, Green, Reader and Dyer; Burns and Oates. Pp. 285-445.

New and revised edition, with an Introduction by Joseph Rickaby, S.J., London, Burns and Oates, 1919.

Newman, John Henry, of the Oratory (later Cardinal). *Letter to the Rev. E. B. Pusey, D.D., on his* Eirenikon.

(A second edition appeared this same year, as well as an American edition by Kehoe, New York. Republished in *Certain difficulties felt by Anglicans in Catholic teaching*, vol. II, 2nd ed., London, 1876, under the title, "A letter addressed to the Rev. E. B. Pusey, D.D., on occasion of his Eirenicon." Republished in 1901 by the Catholic Book Exchange, New York, under the title, *Mary the Mother of Jesus. . . . Being a letter addressed to Rev. E. B. Pusey, D.D., in 1864* [sic!] *in answer to his objections to the Catholic doctrine and practice concerning Mary, the Mother of Jesus.* Republished s.d. by the Paulist Press, New York, also under the title, *Mary the Mother of Jesus. . . .*

Extracts from this work have also been published many times under various titles.)

1867 Preuss, F. R. E. *The Romish doctrine of the Immaculate Conception traced from its source.* Translated [from the German] by George Gladstone. Edinburgh (Clark) and London. 1, 219 pp.

1868 Melia, Raphael, P.S.M. *The woman blessed by all generations, or, Mary, the object of veneration, confidence, and imitation to all Christians.* London: Green, Longmans. xxiv, 454 pp. IC pp. 73-96.

1869 Pusey, Edward Bouverie. *First letter to the Very Rev. J. H. Newman, D.D., in explanation chiefly in regard to the reverential love due to the Ever-Blessed Theotokos;* with an analysis of Cardinal de Turrecremata's work on the Immaculate Conception. Oxford, Rivingtons. xiii, 1, 3, 520 pp.

(Presented as part II of the *Eirenikon* of 1865.)

1874 Vercruysse, Bruno, S.J. *The Immaculate Conception;* summary of conferences. Dublin, McGlashan. 61 pp. [Translated from the French.]

(*Anon.*) "Immaculate Conception" in *The American Cyclopedia*, edited by Gorge Ripley and Charles A. Dana, New York, Appleton, vol. IX, pp. 194-196.

1875 Bridgett, Thomas E., C.SS.R. *Our Lady's Dowry; or, How England gained and lost that title.* Second edition, London: Burns and Oates. 486 pp. IC pp. 23-38.

Fourth ed., *ibid.* [1890].

1876 Nicolas. *The Virgin Mary according to the Gospel.* Translated by the Vicomtesse de L.S.J., and Sister M. Christopher, O.S.F. Edited by Rev. H. Collins. London, Richardson. IC pp. 112-148.

1880 Bourke, Ulick S. *The dignity, sanctity and intercessory power of the Blessed Virgin Mary, Mother of God.* Dublin.

1881 (*Anon.*) "Immaculate Conception," in *Encyclopedia Britannica*, 9th ed. vol. XII, Boston, pp. 715-716.

(Perhaps appeared already in the eighth edition, 1853-1860.)

1889 PETITALOT, John Baptist. *The Virgin Mother according to theology.* Translated from the third French edition. London, St. Anselm's Society. xxviii, 490 pp. IC pp. 27-69.

1891 LEE, Frederick George. *The sinless conception of the Mother of God.* A theological essay. London, Unwin. xxiv, 168 pp.

SCHAFF, Philip. "Immaculate Conception of the Virgin Mary," in *A religious encyclopedia or dictionary of biblical, historical, doctrinal, and practical theology,* Based on the *Real-Encyklopädie* of Herzog, Platt & Hauck, edited by Philip Schaff, LL.D., New York, Funk and Wagnalls, vol. II, pp. 1064 f.

1895 SIMPSON, W. J. Sparrow. *Lectures on St. Bernard.* With appendix on the doctrine of the Immaculate Conception of the B.V.M. London, Masters. 257 pp.

1902 RICKABY, Joseph, S.J. "The Immaculate Conception, a development of doctrine," in *Oxford and Cambridge conferences. Second Series — 1900-1901,* London, Sands, pp. 76-88.

Reprinted in his *The Lord my Light,* 1915 and 1952.

1903 (*Anon.*) "Immaculate Conception of the Virgin Mary," in *The new international encyclopedia,* ed. D. C. GILMAN *et al.,* New York, vol. IX, pp. 829 f.

1904   (FIFTIETH ANNIVERSARY OF THE DEFINITION)

ANASTASI, S. E., O.P. *The Immaculate Conception with relation to the Dominican Order and the doctrine of St. Thomas.* A paper read at the monthly conference at St. Vincent Ferrer's Convent in New York on the 5th Dec. 1904. [Non-paginated pamphlet; s.l., s.e., s.d.]

BISHOP, Edmund. *On the Origins of the Feast of the Conception of the Blessed Virgin Mary.* London, Burns and Oates. 39 pp. [Appeared originally as an article in 1886.]

Reprinted, with a supplementary note on "The Irish Origins of the Conception," in *Liturgica Historica. Papers on the liturgy and religious life of the Western Church.* Oxford, 1918, pp. 238-259.

LAMBING, Andrew A. *The Immaculate Conception of the Blessed Virgin Mary.* New York, Cincinnati, Chicago, Benziger, 1904. viii, 216 pp.

1905 BALDWIN, Louis, O.F.M. "John Duns Scotus and the Immaculate Conception," in *L'Ordine dei Frati Minori al Congresso Mariano Internazionale (1904),* Roma, pp. 57-63.

DENT, F. *Blessed John Duns Scot and Mary Immaculate.* Rome.

FLEMING, David, O.F.M. "The dogma of the Immaculate Conception and the Franciscan Order," in *L'Ordine dei Frati Minori al Congresso Mariano Internazionale (1904),* Roma, pp. 15-21.

VAUGHAN, *Sinless Mary and Sinful Mary.* London, Burns & Oates, 80 pp.

1906 HUALT, Placid, S.M. *The Mother of Jesus.* Sidney. IC pp. 105-122.

WILLIAMS, J. Herbert. *The Mother of Jesus in the first age and after.* New York (Benziger), London (Kegan) . . . xxiii, 264 pp.; IC pp. 237-264.

1910 HOLWECK, Frederick G. "Immaculate Conception," in *The Catholic Encyclopedia,* ed. C. G. Herbermann *et al.,* New York, Appleton, vol. VII, pp. 674-681.

1911 HEDLEY, John Cuthbert, O.S.B., Bishop of Newport. "The Immaculate Conception," in *Encyclopedia Brittanica,* 11th ed. 1910-1911, vol. 14, pp. 334 f.

1914 POHLE, Rt. Rev. Msgr. Joseph, *Mariology. A dogmatic treatise on the Blessed Virgin Mary, Mother of God.* With an appendix on the worship of the saints, relics, and images, . . . adapted and edited [from the German] by Arthur Preuss. London, Herder. [1914]

Later editions: 1916, 1919, 1926 (185 pp.; IC pp. 39-82), 1930.

1915 TURMEL, Joseph. "Immaculate Conception," in *Encyclopedia of Religion and Ethics*, ed. J. Hastings [*et al*]. New York, Scribner, vol. VII, pp. 165-167.

1919 HARPER, Thomas, S.J. *The Immaculate Conception*. A new and revised edition with an introduction by Joseph RICKABY, S.J. London. viii, 62 pp. (Abridgement.)

1920 HOGAN, S. M., O.P. *Mother of Divine Grace:* A chapter in the Theology of the Immaculate. London, Burns and Oates. 173 pp., IC pp. 28-36.

HURLEY, *The Immaculate Conception*. Dublin.
(Poem accompanied by copious theological notes.)

VASSALL-PHILLIPS, O. R., C.SS.R. *The Mother of Christ;* or, The Blessed Virgin Mary in Catholic tradition, theology, and devotion. London, Burns and Oates, xviii, 524 pp. IC pp. 23-48.
Second edition, 1922.

1923 LUMBRERAS, Peter, O.P. *St. Thomas and the Immaculate Conception.* Notre Dame, University Press. 15 pp.
(Reprinted from *Homiletic Review,* vol. 24, no. 3, December 1923.)

1925 JAGGAR, J. B., S.J. *The Immaculate Conception.* New York, Paulist Press. 15 pp.
Republished: London, Catholic Truth Society [1951]; New York, Paulist Press [s.d.].

STORFF, Hugolinus, O.F.M. *The Immaculate Conception.* The teaching of St. Thomas, St. Bonaventure and Bl. J. Duns Scotus on the Immaculate Conception of the Blessed Virgin Mary. A reply to the article [by Lumbreras], "St. Thomas and the Immaculate Conception. . . ." San Francisco. 272 pp.

1928 FRIEDEL, Francis J., S.M. *The Mariology of Cardinal Newman.* New York, Benziger. xvi, 392 pp. IC pp. 294-311.

1929 McKENNA, Bernard A. *The dogma of the Immaculate Conception.* Historical development and dogmatic fulfillment. A guide for theologian and layman from approved Catholic sources. Washington, Catholic University of America. xv, 653 pp.

WILLIAMSON, E. W. *The letters of Osbert of Clare, Prior of Westminster.* Oxford, University Press. 232 pp.

(Anon.) St. Bonaventure's Seminary Year Book, 13 (1929).
(Numerous articles on the IC.)

1931 LUDDY, Ailbe, O.C.R. *A Bernardine Mariology.* Waterford, Mount Melleray IC pp. 17-26.
(Reprinted from the *Irish Catholic.*)

1934 FLYNN, T. E. "The Immaculate Conception of Our Lady," in *Our Blessed Lady.* Papers read at the Summer School of Catholic Studies held at Cambridge July 29th-August 7th, 1933, edited by C. Lattey, S.J. London, Burns, Oates and Washbourne, 1934, pp. 93-120.

1935 MEYER. *Who is She?* Cincinnati. IC pp. 377-402.

1936 CANICE [BOURKE], O.M.Cap. *Mary. A study of the Mother of God.* Dublin, Gill. x, 339 pp. IC pp. 51-60.
Republished in 1937 (3rd ed.) and 1950.

1939 BRUDER, Joseph S., S.M. *The Mariology of Saint Anselm of Canterbury.* Dayton, Mt. St. John Press. xxii, 211 pp. IC pp. 25-66.

RESCH, Rev. Peter A., S.M. *Our Blessed Mother,* outlines of Mariology. Milwaukee, Bruce. xi, 192 pp. IC pp. 97-111.

RYAN, Im. *The Mother of God.* New York, IC pp. 1-43.

1941 FECKES, Charles. *The Mystery of the Divine Motherhood.* A theological portrait of Mary. London (Coldwell) and New York (Spiritual Book Associates). IC pp. 96-118.

1943 SMITH, Matthew. *Unspotted mirror of God.* A compilation of scriptural, patristic and theological doctrine about the Blessed Virgin Mary. Denver, Register College of Journalism. IC pp. 165-181.

1945 JAMES, O.F.M.Cap. *The Mother of Jesus.* Dublin, Gill. viii, 159 pp.

1946 SCHEEBEN, Matthias Joseph. *Mariology.* Translated [from a Flemish translation of the German original, *scil.* the Mariological section of the *Katholische Dogmatik*] by Rev. T. L. M. J. Geukers. 2 vol. London and St. Louis. Herder. IC vol. II, pp. 32-111.

1948 GARRIGOU-LAGRANGE, Reginald, O.P. *The Mother of the Saviour and our interior life.* Trans. [from the French] by Bernard J. Kelly, C.S.Sp. Dublin, Standard House [1948]. 11, 338 pp. IC pp. 51-71.
    Reprinted: St. Louis, Herder, 1949, 1953.

    MUSSER, Benjamin Francis, O.F.M. (by affiliation). *Florilegium Mariae,* a catena of excerpts from the writings of her devotees early and late. Manchester, "Magnificat." xvii, 548 pp. IC pp. 1-24.

1949 LOSSKY, Vladimir. "Panagia," in *The Mother of God,* ed. E. L. MASCALL, London, Daere [s.d.],pp. 24-36.

1951 GUITTON, Jean. *The Blessed Virgin.* [Translated from the French by A. Gordon Smith, according to the American edition of 1952.] London, Burns and Oates. 190 pp. IC pp. 95-99.
    Republished in 1952 in New York by Kenedy.

1952 CONNELL, Francis J., C.SS.R. "Historical development of the Dogma of the Immaculate Conception," in *Studies in praise of Our Blessed Mother,* edited by J. C. Fenton and E. D. Benard, Washington, Catholic University, pp. 93-99.

1954 CAROL, Juniper, O.F.M. [editor]. *Proceedings of the Fifth National Convention of the Mariological Society of America, held in Washington, D. C., on January 4, 5, 1954.* New York, 233 pp.
    Allan B. WOLTER, O.F.M., "The theology of the Immaculate Conception."
    Armand ROBICHAUD, S.M., "The Immaculate Conception in the Magisterium of the Church before 1854."
    Stephen C. GULOVICH, "The Immaculate Conception in the Eastern Churches."
    Albert KIPPES, O.M.I., "The Immaculate Conception and the preternatural gifts."
    Thomas U. MULLANEY, O.P., "The nexus between the Immaculate Conception and Mary's other prerogatives."

    HINGER, George. *Eadmer's treatise on the Immaculate Conception;* a translation and critical introduction . . . [Thesis], Washington, Catholic Univ. v, 57 pp.

    KEARNEY, Mary Benigna, S.S.N.D. *The American hierarchy and the definition of the dogma of the Immaculate Conception.* [Thesis] Washington, Catholic Univ. ii, 69 pp.

    MATTHEWS, Stanley G. [editor] *The promised woman:* an anthology of the Immaculate Conception. St. Meinrad, Indiana; Grail, 316 pp.

    NEUBERT, Emil, S.M. *Mary in doctrine.* [Translated from the third French edition.] Milwaukee, Bruce, vi, 257 pp. IC pp. 49-180.

    PLASSMANN, Thomas Bernard. *The radiant crown of glory;* the story of the dogma of the Immaculate Conception. New York, Benziger Brothers, 258 pp.

    VOGT, Berard, O.F.M. *Duns Scotus, defender of the Immaculate Conception* A historical-dogmatic study. Paterson (New Jersey), St. Anthony. ix, 30 pp.

1955 BERAUD DE SAINT-MAURICE. *John Duns Scotus, a teacher for our times.*
Translated by Columban Duffy, O.F.M. St. Bonaventure (New York),
Franciscan Institute. IC pp. 214-238.

GRAJEWSKI, Maurice, O.F.M. "The Immaculate Conception according to
Duns Scotus," in *Tribute to Mary,* Papers presented at the Provincial
Marian Congress of the Assumption Province of Franciscans on the
occasion of the Marian Year, edited by Fr. Theodore ZAREMBA, O.F.M.,
Pulaski (Wisconsin), Franciscan Printery, pp. 35-38.

SMITH, Ferrer, O.P. "The Immaculate Conception," in *The Mystery of the
Woman,* ed., Edward D. O'CONNOR, C.S.C., Notre Dame, University
Press, pp. 39-60.

VOGT, Berard, O.F.M. *Duns Scotus, defender of the Immaculate Conception.*
Paterson (New Jersey), St. Anthony. ix, 30 pp.

(Anon.) Virgo Immaculata, volumes IV, V. See below, p. 611 ff.

1956 BURKE, Anselm, O.Carm. *Mary in history, in faith and in devotion.* New
York, Scapular Press. xii, 262 pp.

CAROL, Juniper B., O.F.M. *Fundamentals of Mariology.* New York [et al.],
Benziger. [1956] x, 203 pp. IC pp. 87-121.

(Anon.) Mary in the Seraphic Order. (Franciscan Educational Conference,
vol. XXXV, 1954.) Washington [1956] viii, 550 pp.

Ernest LATKO, O.F.M., "The Franciscan position on the Immaculate
Conception before Duns Scotus." (Pp. 1-78)

Berard VOGT, O.F.M., "Duns Scotus and the Immaculate Conception." (79-86)

Aidan CARR, O.F.M. Conv., "Mary's sanctification according to St.
Bonaventure." (256-267)

Bonaventure CROWLEY, O.F.M., "The Militia of Mary Immaculate."
(376-395)

Carmel FLORA, O.F.M. Cap., "The Chaplet of the Immaculate
Conception." (421-431)

(Anon.) Virgo Immaculata, volume XII. See below, p. 611 ff.

1957 CALKINS, Frank P., O.S.M. "Mary's fullness of grace: Initial fullness," in
Mariology, ed. Juniper CAROL, O.F.M., vol. 2, New York, Bruce, pp.
298-302.

(Anon.) Virgo Immaculata, volumes IX, XI, XIII, XIV. See below, p. 611 ff.

DATE OF PUBLICATION UNKNOWN

HUMMEL, J. *The Immaculate Conception: a short dogmatical and historical
treatise.* 18 pp.

MARTINDALE, C. C. *Mary Immaculate and John Duns Scotus, O.F.M.*

MILDNER, Francis, O.S.M. *The Immaculate Conception in England up to the
time of John Duns Scotus.* A dissertation for the degree of Doctor in
Sacred Theology at the Pontifical University of the "Angelicum." 143 pp.

FRENCH[1]

1830   (MIRACULOUS MEDAL APPARITION TO SISTER CATHERINE LABOURÉ,
        PARIS, NOVEMBER 17; FIRST MEDALS STRUCK, JUNE 30, 1832)

1834 [ALADEL]. *Notice historique sur la nouvelle médaille de l'Immaculée Conception
        de la Très-Sainte Vierge et géneralement connue sous le nom de médaille
        miraculeuse.* Paris.[2]
            Ch. I: "Dévotion à Marie conçue sans péché." 8ème éd. 1842;
        édition revue et augmentée, Paris, 1878.
1836 GUILLOU. *Le livre de Marie conçue sans péché.* Paris.
1839 LE QUÉLEN, Hyacinthe [Archbishop of Paris]. *Mandement au sujet de la fête
        de l'Immaculée Conception de la très-sainte Vierge Marie, Mére de Dieu.*
        Paris.
1841 (*Anon.*) *L'excellence de Marie et da sa dévotion . . .* par un religieux passion-
        iste. Traduit du manuscrit italien. 2 tomes. Tournay, Casterman. IC
        t. I, pp. 113-123; t. II, pp. 9-22.
1842 DE BONALD, Cardinal [Archbishop of Lyons]. *Mandement sur le culte de la
        Sainte Vierge.* Lyon.
        DELORME. "De Immaculata, seu de ratione congruentiae pro Immaculata
        Conceptione," in MIGNE, *Cursus theologicus,* Tome 26, Paris, col.
        659-693.
        WACE. *L'établissement de la fête de la Conception de Notre Dame, dite la fête
        aux Normands.* Publié par Mancel et Trébutien. Caen.
        (A twelfth-century work in Old French.)
1843 LAMBRUSCHINI, Louis, Cardinal. *Sur l'Immaculée Conception de Marie.* Dis-
        sertation polémique. Traduit de l'italien, by J.-M.-A.-Césaire Mathieu,
        Archevêque de Besançon. Besançon, Outhenin-Chalandre. xii, 131 pp.
            Another translation of the same work by Dassance was published
        in Paris this same year, under the same title.
1846 GUÉRIN, L. F. "Conception (Immaculée) de la Très-Sainte Vierge," in
        Encyclopédie Catholique, ed. GLAIRE et WALSH, vol. IX, Paris, Des-
        barres, pp. 60-71.
1847 FÉLIX, Joseph, S.J. *Opuscule théologique du R. P. Perrone sur l'Immaculée
        Conception de la bienheureuse Vierge Marie.* Paris, 32 pp.
            (Cf. Latin bibliography at 1847.)

1848   (COMMITTEE APPOINTED BY POPE PIUS IX TO EXAMINE THE
        ADVISABILITY OF A DEFINITION, JUNE 1)

        BAUDRY, Paul. *La Fête de l'Immaculée Conception de la S. Vierge, ou la fête
        aux Normands.* Rouen.

1849   (ENCYCLICAL LETTER *Ubi primum* OF POPE PIUS IX, FEBRUARY 2)

        LESTANG. *Argument théologique et historique en faveur de l'Immaculée Con-
        ception de Marie à l'occasion de l'encyclique de Pie IX en date du 2
        févr. 1849.* Paris.
        PARISIS, Mgr. Louis, Evêque de Langres. *Démonstration de l'Immaculée Con-
        ception de la bienheureuse Vierge Marie, Mère de Dieu.* Paris, Lecoffre.
        80 pp.

---

[1] Besides the general sources indicated above, in the introduction to the *Bibliography,*
the following were employed in the preparation of this French section: *Catalogue
générale de la librairie française,* Paris, Lorenz (for the years 1840-1925), "*Biblio,*"
Paris, Hachette (for the years 1934-1956).
[2] This is the first printed work on the Miraculous Medal. Subsequent writings
on the same subject, which are fairly numerous, will not be indicated.

1849 (continued)

SAUCERET, Paul. *Culte catholique de Marie, Mère de Jésus.* Ouvrage faisant suite aux *Figures bibliques de Marie.* 3 vol. Paris.

(*Anon.*) *Question de l'Immaculée Conception.* Délibération de la Commission chargée de l'examiner.
(Reprinted in *Pareri* . . . , vol. VII, pp. 137-194.)

(*Anon.*) *Sur la lettre encyclique de N.S.P. le Pape Pie IX, du 2 février 1849, concernant la doctrine de l'Immaculée Conception de la Très-Sainte Vierge.*

(*Anon.*) *Sur l'Immaculée Conception de la Vierge Marie.* Paris.

1850 DONNET, Cardinal [Archbishop of Bordeaux]. "Mandement au sujet de l'Immaculée Conception de la Très-Sainte Vierge," in *Instructions pastorales, Mandements, lettres et discours de S. E. le Card. Arch. de Bordeaux.* Bordeaux, tom. I, p. 139 ff.
(Originally written in 1841.)

GUÉRANGER, Prosper. *Mémoire sur la question de l'Immaculée Conception de la Très Sainte Vierge.* Paris, Lanier & Lecoffre. 147 pp.
(Reprinted in *Pareri*, vol. VII, pp. 1-130.)

LABORDE, Jean-Joseph. *La Croyance à l'Immaculée Conception ne peut devenir dogme de foi, en réponse aux divers écrits qui ont paru de nos jours sur cette controverse.* Paris.
(For revised edition, cf. 1851.)

——. *Discussion de l'origine, des progrès et des fondements de la croyance à l'Immaculée-Conception, en réponse à la Démonstration* [Cf. 1849] *de Mgr. Parisis, évêque de Langres.* Paris, Guyot. 82 pp.
(Condemned by decree of the Holy Office, July 10, 1850.)

1851 LABORDE, Jean-Joseph. *De la croyance à l'Immaculée Conception de la Sainte Vierge,* en réponse aux diverses écrits qui ont paru de nos jours sur cette controverse. Nouvelle édition, suivie du discours sur quelques fausses légendes touchant la dernière partie de la Passion de N. S. J.-C. le tout produit comme mémoire au concile provincial d'Auch. Toulouse, Privat. 164 pp.
(Condemned by the S. Congregation of the Index, Sept. 6, 1852. See 1850 for the first edition.)

PIE, Louis-François-Désiré-Edouard [later Cardinal]. *Mandement de Monseigneur l'Evêque de Poitiers concernant l'Immaculée Conception de la Bienheureuse Vierge Marie.* Poitiers, Oudin, 6 pp.
Republished in *Discours et Instructions pastorales,* vol. I, 1858, p. 445 ff.

1852 DARAS. *Essai historique sur l'Immaculée Conception de la très Sainte Vierge.* Plancy (St. Victor) & Paris (Bray). 103 pp.
Republished at Paris by Jourdan in 1854. (?)

(*Anon.*) *Convenances sociales d'une définition dogmatique sur l'Immaculée Conception de la bienheureuse Vierge Marie.* Paris, Bailly, Divry. 31 pp.
(Translated from the Italian of 1851.)

1854 (DEFINITION OF THE IMMACULATE CONCEPTION AS A DOGMA OF FAITH BY POPE PIUS IX, DECEMBER 8)

COQUEREL, [Athanase], pasteur de Paris. *Un Dogme nouveau concernant la Vierge Marie.* Paris.
Republished the following year by Cherbulliez, 35 pp.

[GRATRY, Auguste Jos. Alphonse]. *Une étude sur l'Immaculée Conception de la Bienheureuse Vierge Marie,* par un membre de l'Oratoire. Paris, Douniol. 99 pp.

1854 (continued)

LABORDE, Jean-Joseph. *La Croyance à l'Immaculée Conception ne peut devenir dogme de foi, en réponse aux divers écrits, qui ont paru de nos jours sur cette controverse,* et *Discours sur quelques fausses légendes, touchant la dernière partie de la Passion de N.S.J.C.* 3ème éd. Followed by letters, reflections, and a dissertation, "Sur l'autorité de la Congrégation de l'Index." Paris, Dentu.

    (Cf. publications of 1850 and 1851.)

——. *Lettre à N.S.P. le Pape Pie IX, sur l'impossibilité d'un nouveau dogme de foi, relativement à la Conception de la S. Vierge, français et latin.* Paris, Dentu. 27 pp.

MAUREL, Antonin, S.J. *L'Immaculée Conception de la Très Sainte Vierge.* Lyon, Girard & Josserand. 64 pp.

    Republished in 1855, 1856, 1866 (= "3rd ed."; 104 pp.).

SISSON, A. *De l'Immaculée-Conception de la Sainte Vierge.* Examen critique des articles du "Journal des Débats." Douniol.

    (Published also in *L'Ami de la Religion,* Paris, t. 166, 1854.)

(*Anon.*) *De l'Immaculée-Conception de la Très Sainte Vierge.* Réflexions à propos de la définition dogmatique de l'Immaculée-Conception de la Très Sainte Vierge. Nantes. 22 pp.

1855 AMERITUS, Christophilus. *Protestation contre le dernier Mandement de l'Archevêque de Malines,* ou Lettre à ce Prélat sur le Culte de Marie et sur le nouveau dogme de l'Immaculée Conception. Bruxelles.

BERTON, Elie. *L'Immaculée Conception et le XIXe Siècle.* Marseille.

——. *Réponse aux critiques de L'Immaculée Conception.* Marseille.

BISSEUX, J. *Réflexions sur le Culte de Marie, et sur le dogme de l'Immaculée Conception.* Paris.

BORDAS-DEMOULIN. "Marianisme substitué au Christianisme," in *Les Pouvoirs constitutifs de l'Eglise,* p. 56 ff. Paris.

BUNGENER. *Rome à Paris: lettre à Mgr. l'Archevêque.* Paris, Cherbulliez. 26 pp.

COLLAËS, F. *L'Immaculée Conception de Marie dans ses figures prophétiques.* Bruxelles. 165 pp.

——. *Trois questions dogmatiques au sujet de l'Immaculée Conception de la Ste. Vierge.* Bruxelles, Fonteyn. 61 pp.

COQUEREL, Athanase. *Le culte de la Vierge*: deuxième sermon sur le nouveau dogme catholique, suivi de notes. Paris.

COSTA. *L'Immaculée Conception considérée dans la doctrine de l'Eglise et dans sa définition dogmatique.* Puy.

DEMALHERBE, Franz. *Rondeau inédit sur l'Immaculée Conception,* publié par G. Mancel. Caen.

    (Seventeenth-century work.)

DONNET [Cardinal Archbishop of Bordeaux]. "Lettre à M. l'Evêque de la Rochelle au sujet de son ouvrage sur l'Immaculée Conception," in *Instructions pastorales, mandements, lettres et discours de S. E. le Card. Arch. de Bordeaux.* Bordeaux, tom. III, p. 184 ff.

DUPANLOUP, Félix-A.-P., Mgr., Evêque d'Orléans. *Instruction pastorale sur l'Immaculée Conception de la SS. Vierge.* Orléans.

DURAND, Louis. *Brève réfutation du nouveau dogme de l'Immaculée Conception.* Bruxelles.

——. *Neuf thèses sur le dogme de l'Immaculée Conception de la Vierge Marie,* avec défi à M. Théodore, Evêque de Liège, et à tout prêtre ou membre de l'Eglise de Rome. Bruxelles.

GOUSSET, Cardinal, archevêque de Rheims. *La croyance génerale et constante de l'Eglise touchant l'Immaculée Conception de la B. V. Marie,* prouvée principalement par les constitutions et les actes des Papes, par les lettres

1855 (continued)

    et les actes des Evêques, par l'enseignement des Pères et des Docteurs de tous les temps. Paris, Lecoffre. 820 pp.

    (Summary of the *Pareri* of 1851-1854.)

[GUETTÉE, Rene-François-Wladimir]. *Observations d'un théologien sur la Bulle de Pie IX relative à la Conception de la S. Vierge.* Paris, "l'Union chrétienne." 75 pp.

——. *Très-humble remontrance à Mgr. l'archevêque de Paris, à propos de son mandement sur l'Immaculée-Conception.* Paris, "l'Union chrétienne."

HAAN, J., S.J. *L'Immaculée Conception de la B.V.M. considérée comme dogme de foi de la S. Eglise Catholique.* Paris.

[LABIS, G.-J.] *Lettre pastorale de M. l'Evêque de Tournay à l'occasion de son voyage à Rome et de la proclamation du dogme de l'Immaculée Conception de la très-sainte Vierge.* Tournai.

LABORDE, J. J. *Relation et mémoire des opposants au nouveau dogme de l'Immaculée-Conception et à la bulle* Ineffabilis. Paris, Dentu.

LE CLÉRIAN. *Lettre à M. Berton.* Marseille.

LE MIRE, Noël. *Lettres sur l'Italie: Souvenirs du VIII Déc. 1854 à Rome.* Lyon et Paris.

PASSAGLIA, Charles, S.J. *Traité sur l'Immaculée-Conception de la Mère de Dieu, toujours vierge* . . . Traduit du latin par l'abbé A.M. Tome 1er. Paris, Vivès.

    (No trace of tomes 2, 3 or 4 has been found by the present bibliographers.)

PEYRAT. *Un nouveau dogme, histoire de l'Immaculée Conception. Portrait de la Vierge. Les visions d'un Jacobin. Lettre Apostolique.* Paris, Librairie nouvelle. 143 pp.

    (Reprinted from *Presse*.)

PIE, Louis-François-Désiré-Edouard. *Mandement de Monseigneur l'Evêque de Poitiers promulguant les lettres apostoliques qui définissent le dogme de l'Immaculée Conception de la Bienheureuse Vierge Marie.* Poitiers, Oudin. 27 pp.

POINSOT, *Réfutation du dogme de l'Immaculée Conception de la Vierge Marie.* Bruxelles.

PRESSENSÉ. *L'Immaculée Conception.* Histoire d'un dogme catholique romain, ou, Comment l'hérésie devient un dogme. Paris.

VERCRUYSSE, Bruno. *L'Immaculée Conception.* Résumé de conférences sur le dogme de l'Immaculée Conception prêchées dans l'église du collège d'Alost. Bruxelles, Wageneer. 35 pp.

    (Republished: Tournai, 1863; Bruxelles, 1879.)

VEUILLOT. *La Sainte Vierge.* Jacques-Bénigne BOSSUET, Sermons sur les mystères et le culte de la Mère de Dieu. Avec une introduction. . . . Paris.

(*Anon.*) *La définition dogmatique de l'Immaculée Conception,* traduit de l'italien par Maréchal. Courtraie. Beyaert.

(*Anon.*) *Gloire à Marie Immaculée,* ou Résumé de la doctrine de l'Eglise catholique sur le dogme de l'Immaculée Conception. Par un serviteur de Marie. Bourges.

(*Anon.*) *Notice historique sur l'Immaculée Conception par deux Orléanais.* Orléans.

(*Anon.*) *Une pensée sur le dogme de l'Immaculée Conception.* Lyon.

1856 BORDAS-DEMOULIN et F. HUET. *Essais sur la réforme Catholique.* Paris, Chamerot. viii, 644 pp.

    P. 478 ff.: "Lettres sur l'Immaculée Conception"; p. 539 ff.: "Etude sur la Bulle, *Ineffabilis Deus*"; p. 596 ff.: "Appel aux Catholiques contre la nouvelle hérésie." Cf. anonymous *Etudes* of 1857.

1856 (continued)

BUNGENER, Felix. *Marie et Mariolatrie.* Genéve.

DE MOSQUERA, Emmanuel Marie. *Apologie de M. Emmanuel Joseph de Mos-quera, mort Archevêque de Santa-Fé de Bogota, et de sa Réponse à l'Encyclique de N. S. Père le Pape Pie IX du 2 fèvrier 1849,* ou Lettre à S. E. le Cardinal Gousset, Archevêque de Reims. Paris.

GODFRAY [=translator?]. *Rome, son nouveau dogme et nos devoirs.* Discours prononcé devant l'Université d'Oxford par le Lord Ev. d'Oxford; traduit de l'anglais. [Cf. the entry *Wilberforce,* below.] Paris.

SPEELMAN, S.J. *La Vierge Immaculée, patronne de la Belgique,* ou Témoignages de foi et de dévotion à l'Imm. Conc. recueillis dans les annales belges . . . Tournai.

WILBERFORCE, Samuel [Bishop of Oxford]. *Sermon sur le nouveau dogme de l'Immaculée Conception.* [Translated from the English.] Oxford.

(*Anon.*) "Conception (Immaculée) de la Sainte Vierge," in *Supplément à l'Encyclopédie Catholique* publié sous la direction de M. CHANTREL . . . et de M. l'abbé ORSE . . . Tome I, Paris, Desbarres [s.d.], pp. 665-672.

(*Anon.*) *Correspondance des Confesseurs de la Foi relativement au nouveau Dogme de l'Immaculée Conception.* Paris.

(*Anon.*) *De l'Immaculée Conception de la Vierge.* Dijon.

(*Anon.*) *Testaments de Notre Seigneur et de la S. Vierge réduits en maximes.* [2nd ed.] Paris.

1857 BRAUN, Thomas [excommunicated priest]. *Actes relatifs à la prétendue définition de l'immaculée Conception.* Lettres de M. Thomas Braun à MM. les rédacteurs de l' "Observateur Catholique" et à M. l'Archevêque de Munich. Paris, Huet. 39 pp.

DE GRANDEFFE, Arthur. *L'Immaculée Conception au point de vue rationel.* Paris, Lecour.

FABER, Frederick William. *Exposition du dogme de l'Immaculée Conception.* (Translated from the English and published as a preface to *Salutations à Marie Immaculèe,* by J. SAGETTE, Paris, Bray, 1857.)

GAGARIN, Jean (= Ivan), S.J. *Lettre à une dame russe sur le dogme de l'Immaculée Conception.* Tournai, Casterman. [s.d.] 31 pp.

——. *Deuxième lettre à une dame russe sur le dogme de l'Immaculée Conception. Ibid.* [s.d.] 32 pp.

——. *Troisième lettre à une dame russe sur le dogme de l'Immaculée Conception. Ibid.* [s.d.] 49 pp.

——. *Quatrième lettre à une dame russe sur le dogme de l'Immaculée Conception. Ibid.* [s.d.] 61 pp.

(Cf. the entry *Gagarin* under 1859.)

[GUETTÉE, René-François-Wladimir.] *Le nouveau dogme en présence de l'Ecriture sainte et de la tradition catholique,* ou Lettres à Mgr. Malou sur son livre intitulé "l'Immaculée-Conception de la bienheureuse Vierge considérée comme dogme de foi." Paris, "l'Union chrétienne."

MALOU, Mgr. Jean-Baptiste, Evêque de Bruges. *L'Immaculée Conception de la B. V. Marie considérée comme dogme de foi.* 2 vol. Bruxelles, Goemaere.

NICOLAS, Auguste. *La Vierge Marie d'après l'Évangile.* Paris, Vaton.

(Republished in 1864 as tome II of *La Vierge Marie dans le plan divin.*)

ROBITAILLE, François J. *Traité historique et dogmatique de la définition du dogme de l'Immaculée Conception de la Très S. Vierge,* dédié à Mgr. Parisis. Arras, Lefranc.

(*Anon.*) [= Ad. STAPPAERTS?] *Etudes sur le nouveau dogme de l'Immaculée Conception.* Publiées par les auteurs des *Essais sur la réforme catholique.* [Cf. 1856.] 2e éd. Paris, Chamerot. 275 pp.

(Cf. revised edition of 1869.)

1857 (continued)

(*Anon.*) *L'Immaculée Conception devant l'Ecriture sainte et la tradition des Pères.* Paris.

1858   (APPARITIONS OF MARY IMMACULATE TO BERNADETTE SOUBIROUS, LOURDES, FEBRUARY 11 - JULY 16)

GAGARIN, J., S.J. *Curieux témoignages en faveur de l'Immaculée Conception.* Paris.

LABRUSSE, J. F. *Exaltation de saint Joseph dans le Mystère de l'Incarnation. Définition réelle du dogme de l'Immaculée Conception de la Vierge Marie. Traité sur les cultes israélite et protestant,* par un laïque. Paris (Dentu) & Besançon. 78 pp.

PARODI, L., S.J. *La Foi et la dévotion à Marie, toujours immaculée, expliquée et proposée d'aprés les sentiments et les paroles des SS. Pères.* Ouvrage traduit de l'italien par H. J. Maréchal. Paris & Tournai, Casterman. xvi, 395 pp.

PERRONE, S. J. *Thèse dogmatique sur l'Immaculée Conception,* qu'il faut ajouter aux leçons de la théologie. Traduit en français par Fournet. Besançon.

PIE, Louis-Edouard-Désiré. *Discours et Instructions pastorales de M. l'Evêque de Poitiers.* Poitiers.

Vol. I, p. 445 ff.: "Mandement de M. l'Evêque de Poitiers concernant l'Immaculée Conception de la Bienheureuse Vierge Marie." [1851]

Vol. II, p. 253 ff.: "Homélie prononcée dans l'Eglise de Notre-Dame à la Messe Pontificale de la Fête de l'Immaculée Conception, le 8 déc. 1854."

1859 BERGIER. "Marie," in MIGNE, *Encyclopédie théologique,* ou Série de Dictionnaires sur toutes les parties de la science religieuse. Paris. Tome XXXV, p. 630 ff.

(Eighteenth-century work.)

CONSTANT, B. H. "Pie IX en définissant l'Immaculée Conception n'a pas contredit ses prédécesseurs, ni rien ajouté à la foi catholique," in: *L'histoire et l'infaillibilité des Papes,* ou Recherches critiques et historiques sur les actes et les décisions pontificales que divers écrivains ont crus contraires à la foi, vol. II, Lyon & Paris, p. 303 ff.

DURAND, Louis. *L'Infaillibilité papale prise en manifeste et flagrant délit de mensonge, ou Le dogme de l'Immaculée Conception cité et condamné au tribunal de l'histoire et des Pères.* Examen de quelques assertions de la Bulle, "Ineffabilis Deus," et réfutation des deux volumes de M. Malou sur le nouveau dogme. Bruxelles, Librairie chrétienne évangélique. 615 pp.

GAGARIN, Jean [= Ivan], S.J. *Quatre lettres à une dame russe sur le dogme de l'Immaculée Conception.* Tournai, Casterman.

(Cf. entries *Gagarin* under 1857.)

GRATRY, A.-J.-A., de l'Oratoire. *Mois de Marie de l'Immaculée Conception.* Paris, Douniol.

Republished in Paris by Tequi in 1916.

SALVADOR, I. "L'Immaculée Conception en 1854, et sa différence d'avec la conception immaculée, ou de quelle manière les dogmes se font et peuvent se défaire," in *Paris, Rome, Jérusalem, ou, La question religieuse au XIXème siècle,* II, Paris. p. 452 ff.

2e éd., entièrement revue et augmentée, 1882.

[SPEELMAN, Edm.] *Belgium Marianum.* Histoire du culte de Marie en Belgique et dans l'ancien territoire de Lille, de Douai, de Cambrai, etc. . . . Tournai.

1860 DE BUCK, V. *Osbert de Clare et l'abbé Anselme, instituteurs de la fête de l'Immaculée Conception de la Sainte Vierge dans l'église latine. Etudes de théologie,* nouvelle série, t. II. Paris.

MORGAËZ, Braulius. *Examen de la Bulle* Ineffabilis *fait et rédigé d'après les règles de la sainte théologie.* Paris, Dubuisson. xxiv, 115 pp.
>   (Cf. work published in Latin in 1858.)

NICOLAS, Auguste. *La Vierge Marie et le plan divin.* Nouvelles études philosophiques sur le christianisme. 2 vol. Vaton. IC vol. I, pp. 362-374.
>   (Republished in 1864 as tomes III and IV of *La Vierge Marie et le plan divin.*)

S ... [= SIRE], Marie-Dominique-Henri. *Notice sur la Collection des documents relatifs à la définition du dogme de l'Immaculée Conception de la Très-Sainte Vierge qui sont conservés dans la basilique de Notre-Dame du Puy.* Le Puy, Marchessou. 128 pp.

(Anon.) *L'Eglise de France et le Decret dogmatique du 8 décembre 1854.* Documents historiques, 1849-1859.

(Anon.) *Le six mai de la Savoie en l'an de grace 1855.* Souvenir national de la promulgation du dogme de l'Immaculée Conception. Chambéry, Imp. du Gouvernement. 228 pp.

1862 BOURASSÉ, Joannes Jacobus. *Summa aurea de laudibus Beatissimae Virginis Mariae . . . ,* Tomus VIII. Paris, Migne.
>   Col. 481-584: MALOU, Mgr. Jean-Baptiste, Evêque de Bruges. "Histoire de la définition dogmatique de l'Immaculée Conception de la Très-Sainte Vierge Marie."
>   Col. 585-612: SIRE, D. "Enumération des documents relatifs à la définition du dogme de l'Immaculée Conception de la Très-Sainte Vierge."
>   (For other articles in the *Summa Aurea* relative to the Immaculate Conception, see below, p. 609 ff.)

1863 RAMIÈRE, S.J. *Les espérances de l'Eglise.* Paris.

(Anon.) "Conception Immaculée de la S. Vierge, in MIGNE, *Première Encyclopédie Théologique,* tome 33, p. 983 ff. Paris.

SPADA, Marianus. *Saint Thomas et l'Immaculée-Conception,* ou Remarques et observations sur l'ouvrage d'illustr. et révér. seigneur J. B. Malou, au sujet du dogme de l'Immaculée-Conception de la B. Vierge Marie . . . [Cf. 1857.] Traduit du latin par le T. R. P. F. J. D. Sicard. Paris, Poussielgue. 299 pp.

1864 BOURDALOUE, Louis, S.J. [1632-1704] *Sur la Conception de la Vierge.* Lyon.
DE GRANDEFFE, Arthur. *L'ordre des Frères Prêcheurs et l'Immaculée Conception.* Bruxelles.

FRÈRE, Edouard. *Approbation et confirmation par le Pape Léon X des statuts et privilèges de la Confrérie de l'Immaculée Conception dite Académie des Palinods instituée à Rouen.* Publiée d'après une édition gothique du XVIe siècle, avec une notice historique et bibliographique ... Rouen.

NICOLAS, Auguste. *La Vierge Marie et le plan divin.* 4 vol. Paris.
>   (Appeared first as three books: *La Vierge Marie dans le plan divin,* 1856; *La Vierge Marie d'après l'évangile,* 1857; *La Vierge Marie vivant dans l'église* (2 vol.), 1860. These became volumes I, II, III and IV of the present work, respectively.
>   Huitième éd. 1875-1880; IC vol. II, 112-149; vol. III, 358-368.)

ROUARD DE CARD, Pie Marie, O.P.: *L'Ordre des Frères Prêcheurs et l'Immaculée Conception de la Très Sainte Vierge.* Lettre adressée à Monseigneur Malou, évêque de Bruges. [Cf. 1857.] Louvain & Paris. 109 pp.

1865 COMBALOT, Théodore. *Le culte de la bienheureuse Vierge Marie, Mère de Dieu.* Nouvelles conférences prêchées à Paris, à Lyon, en Belgique, etc., depuis le decret dogmatique de l'Immaculée Conception. 2 tom. Lyon, Périsse. IC tome I, pp. 217-401.

[GUETTÉE, R.-F.-W.] *De l'Encyclique du 8 décembre 1864,* par un docteur en théologie. Paris, "l'Union Chretienne."

[HAMON] *Notre-Dame de France, ou Histoire de la Sainte Vierge en France, depuis l'origine du christianisme jusqu'à nos jours,* par le curé de Saint-Sulpice. 7 vol.

1866 CASTAING. *Marie et son culte devant la raison du Chrétien.* Paris, Plon. viii, 257 pp. IC pp. 23-47.

DU QUESNAY. *L'Immaculée Conception reconnue dans le Coran.* Paris.

[HIMONET, P. F.] *Marie, ses mystères et son culte,* par un curé du diocèse de Verdun. Tolra. 2 vol.
2ème éd., revue, corrigée et augmentée, 2 vol., Lavoye (Meuse) chez l'auteur.

NEWMAN, John Henry [later Cardinal] *Du culte de la sainte Vierge dans l'Eglise catholique,* lettre au docteur Pusey. Traduite de l'anglais par Georges Du Pré de Saint-Maur. Paris, Douniol.
(Another French translation of this work was published in 1908.)

1867 BARBIER. *La Sainte Vierge d'après les Pères.* 4 tomes. Lyon & Paris: Girard. IC t. I, pp. 247-342.

1868 PETITALOT, Jean-Baptiste, S.M. *La Vierge Mère d'après la théologie.* 2 vol. Paris, Grou.
Deuxième édition, revue et augmentée, 1869. 5ème éd. 1904. IC vol. I, pp. 44-88 of the fifth edition.

1869 STAP, A. [= Ad. STAEPPERTS] *L'Immaculée Conception. Etudes sur l'origine d'un dogme.* Nouvelle édition. Paris, Bruxelles: Librairie internationale. 314 pp.
(For first edition, see the anonymous *Etudes . . .* of 1857.)

1871 GASSIAT, B. "De la Vierge Marie. Etude sur son Immaculée Conception," in *De quelques thèmes théologiques sur le dogme et la morale,* Paris.

1872 (*Anon.*) *Histoire du Culte de la Sainte Vierge à Lyon depuis S. Pothin jusqu' à nos jours.* Par l'auteur des *Grands Souvenirs de l'Eglise de Lyon.* Lyon.

1873 PLAINE, Dom François. *Histoire du culte de la Sainte Vierge dans la ville de Rennes, ancienne capitale de la Bretagne.* Rennes, Vatard. xvi, 380 pp.

1874 BERGIER. *Dictionnaire de théologie.* Approprié au mouvement intellectuel de la seconde moitié du XIXe siècle par l'abbé LE NOIR. Paris, Vives, tome III.
BERGIER, "Conception Immaculée de la Sainte Vierge." (Pp. 82 f.)
LE NOIR, "Conception (La définition dogmatique de l'Immaculée)." (83-98)

1876 GAGARIN, J., S.J. *L'Église russe et l'Immaculée Conception.* Paris, Plon. 103 pp.

1877 BERNARD. *L'Eglise de Lyon et l'Immaculée Conception.* Essai théol. historique. Lyon.

MONSABRÉ, Jacques-Marie-Louis, O.P. *Exposition du dogme catholique. Préparation de l'Incarnation.* (Conférences de Notre-Dame de Paris, Carême 1877.) Paris, Balterweck. IC pp. 289-340; 391-405.

(*Anon.*) [= SIRE?] *Rapport annoté au Très Saint Père le Pape sur les deux collections du Puy et de Rome.* Paris, Plon.

1878 RÉVILLE, A. "Conception Immaculée," in *Encyclopédie des sciences religieuses,* ed. LICHTENBERGER, t. III, Paris.

(*Anon.*) "Conception - Theol." in *Grand Dictionnaire universel du XIXe siècle . . .* par Pierre LAROUSSE, Paris, 1865-1878, tome IV [s.d.] pp. 827-831.

1879 [GUIBERT, Joseph Hippolyte] *Le premier jubilé de l'Immaculée Conception.* Mandement de S. E. le cardinal-archevêque de Paris . . . , avec préface par R. P. LARGENT, de l'Oratoire. Paris, Poussielgue.

  (ESCARD cites also the decrees and letters of the bishops of Avignon, Agen, Arras, Autun, Châlon and Mâcon, Angoulême, Bayonne, Besançon, St-Flour, Langres, Laval, Limoges, Le Mans, Nancy and Toul, Reims, and Vannes on the 25th anniversary of the Definition.)

  MOREAU, W. *L'Immaculée Conception* — à l'occasion du 25. anniversaire de la définition solennelle du dogme . . . Paris.

1880 HILAIRE DE PARIS, O.F.M. *Notre-Dame de Lourdes et l'Immaculée Conception,* à l'usage du clergé et des laiques instruits. Lyon, Pélagaud. xxiii, 565 pp.

  (*Anon.*) [= SIRE?] *Le Puy et Rome.* Monuments du dogme de l'Immaculée Conception (1854-1879). Paris.

1881 LAURAS, M., S.J. *Bourdaloue, sa vie et son oeuvre.* Paris. T. II, pp. 477-500.

  MORGOTT, Franz. *La doctrine sur la Vierge Marie, ou Mariologie de saint Thomas d'Aquin,* d'après le chanoine Fr. Morgott. [Translated from the German by Mgr. BOURQUARD.]

  PERREYVE, Henri. *Etude sur l'Immaculée Conception.* Paris, Gervais. 62 pp. Republished, Paris, Tequi, 1904.

  MERCIER. *La Vierge Marie, d'après Mgr. Pie.* Paris, Oudin. cxxxiv, 485 pp. IC pp. 19-85 & *passim.*

1883 ORRY, A. *Le docteur angélique a-t-il combattu le privilège de l'Immaculée Conception de la T. Sainte Vierge . . . ?* Bordeaux. 29 pp.

1888 DE MARTIGNÉ, Prosper. *La scolastique et les traditions franciscaines.* Paris, pp. 362-387.

  HUET, F. *La révolution religieuse au XIXe siècle.* Paris.

1891 LAGARDE. *Mois de Marie doctrinal.* Paris, Lethielleux. IC pp. 41-114.

1892 RAGEY. *Eadmer.* Paris.

1896 JAMAR, C.-H.-T. *Marie, Mère de Jésus (Act. I,14).* Histoire de la Très-Sainte Vierge d'après la Sainte Ecriture, les monuments de l'antiquité, les écrits des pères et des théogiens. Bruxelles (Devaux), Bois-le-duc (Van Gulick). xvii, 547, 21 pp. IC pp. 61-75.

1898 VOLLET, E.-H. "Marie (La Sainte Vierge) — Immaculée Conception," in *La Grande Encyclopédie,* Inventaire Raisonné des sciences, des lettres et des arts . . . publiée sous la direction de MM. BERTHELOT [*et. al.*], tome XXIII, Paris, [*s.d.*]

1899 DUBOSC DE PESQUIDOUX, Jean-Clément-Léonce. *L'Immaculée Conception.* Histoire d'un dogme. 2 vol. Tours (Mame) & Paris (Lecoffre). (1898, 1899).

  PRADIÉ, Hippolyte, S.J. *La Vierge Marie, Mère de Dieu et chef-d'oeuvre de Dieu.* 2 tomes. Tours, Dubois 1899. IC Tome I, pp. 125-201.

1900 SIRE, Dominique Marie. *De l'Eden par Nazareth à la Rome Papale et à Lourdes. Le dogme de l'Immaculée Conception d'après la Bulle Ineffabilis Deus et les apparitions de la sainte Vierge. Son histoire et son influence manifeste, surtout à Lourdes.* (1850-1890). Amiens, Picard, 320 pp.

  TERRIEN, J. B., S.J. *L'Immaculée Conception.* Paris, Lethielleux. 180 pp. (Extract from *La Mère de Dieu et la Mère des hommes.* [1900-1902])

1901 GOSCHLER, I. "Vierge (L'Immaculée Conception de la Sainte)," in *Dictionnaire encyclopédique de la théologie catholique . . .* publié par les soins du Dr. WETZER . . . et du Dr. WELTE . . . traduit de l'allemand par I. GOSCHLER . . . , Paris (Rondelet) & Montréjeau (Soubiron), tome XXV, pp. 270-283.

  (*Anon.*) *Compte rendu du Congrès Marial tenu à Lyon les 5, 6, 7 et 8 septembre 1900.* Lyon, Vitte. [s.d.] 780 pp.

1902 DOUCHER, Pierre. *La Sainte Vierge et le Saint-Siége.* L'oeuvre de Saint Paul.
TERRIEN, Jean Baptiste, S.J. *La Mère de Dieu et la Mère des hommes d'après les Pères et la théologie* . . . 4 vol. Paris. P. Lethielleux. [1900-1902] IC vol. I, pp. 335-392.
(Later editions: 1902 [2nd], 1933 [6th], 1943, 1954.)
1903 LE BACHELET, Xavier Marie, S.J. *L'Immaculée Conception. Courte Histoire d'un Dogme.* 2 vol., Paris, Blond. 128 pp.
QUINOT, Léopold, des Frères-Mineurs. *Joyeux Cinquantenaire de la proclamation comme dogme de foi catholique de l'Immaculée Conception.* Tamines, Ducoulot-Roulin. 48 pp.
Deuxième édition, revue et augmentée, 1904.

1904 (FIFTIETH ANNIVERSARY OF THE DEFINITION)

BAUMES, Emile. *L'Immaculée-Conception.* Discours prononcé dans l'église de Notre-Dame-du-Port. Nice.
BOURGEOIS, L. Th., O.P. *L'Immaculée Conception, et le cinquantenaire de la proclamation de ce dogme.* Paris, Lethielleux. 64 pp.
CLAVÉ, M.M.J. *Je suis l'Immaculée Conception. Études et Contemplations.* Edition nouvelle, Tournai & Paris: Castermann. 169 pp. [1904]
CUCHE, H.-P.-J., O.F.M. *Marie prédestinée et préservée. Étude sur l'Immaculée Conception d'après la doctrine franciscaine.* Paris, Mlle Royer. 47 pp.
DAVIN, Paul Marie. *L'Immaculée Conception de la Très Sainte Vierge, honorée dans la ville d'Aix-en-Provence.* (Étude d'histoire religieuse locale.) Aix, Makaire.
D'OSUNA, François, Frère Mineur. *L'Immaculée Conception.* Quatre sermons composés en 1532 par François d'Osuna, Frère Mineur, auteur de l'abécédaire spirituel. Traduction du latin par le P. Michel Ange, Frère Mineur Capucin. [1904]
DRIVE, A. *Marie et la Compagnie de Jésus.* Tournai, Castermann. 2ème éd. revue, complétée et illustrée avec fig., 1904. 3ème éd., 1913, 599 pp. (IC pp. 95-162 in the 3rd ed.)
GODTS, F. - X., Rédemptoriste. *La Sainteté initiale de l'Immaculée exposée et défendue selon la doctrine de saint Alphonse.* Bruxelles, Dewit. 292 pp. 2nd ed. 1905; 3rd, 1906.
HOBEIKA, J. *Témoignages de l'Église syro-maronite en faveur de l'Immaculée Conception de la très sainte Vierge Marie.* Traduit en français par son frère, le Père Pierre Hobeika. Basconta (Lebanon).
(64 pp. of French preface and translation, besides the original texts.)
LÉMANN, Augustin. *La Vierge et l'Emmanuel. Cinquantenaire de la définition dogmatique de l'Immaculée Conception.* Paris, Poussielgue.
LESÊTRE, H. *L'Immaculée-Conception et l'Église de Paris.* Paris, Lethielleux. 263 pp.
(A second edition was also published in 1904.)
NOYON, Augustin. *Les origines de la fête de l'Immaculée Conception en Occident (Xe, XIe et XIIe siècles).* Paris, Demoulin. 31 pp.
(Appeared originally in *Etudes,* 20 sept. 1904.)
PAUWELS, P., O.F.M. *Les Franciscains et l'Immaculée Conception.* Malines, Godenne. 278 pp.
PÉCHENARD, Mgr. P. L. *L'Immaculée Conception dans l'ancienne Université de Paris, étude historique.* Paris, 74, rue de Vaugirard.
RANSAN, Otho, O.F.M. *Les Frères Mineurs d'Aquitaine et l'Immaculée Conception.* Bar-le-duc, S. Paul. 44 pp.
SERVAIS, O. C. D. *Immaculata.* Namur, Picard-Balon. 55 pp.
SIRE, Marie Dominique. *Le dogme de l'Immaculée Conception.* Paris, Plon Nurrit.

1904 (continued)

SIRE, Marie Dominique. *L'Immaculée Vierge Mère dans la Bible et dans l'Eglise.* Amiens, Impr. picarde. 425 pp.

VAN DE WALLE, J., S.J. *Du culte de l'Immaculée Conception de la Bienheureuse Vierge Marie dans la province belge de la Compagnie de Jésus au cours des trois derniers siècles.* Louvain, Smeesters. 93 pp.

1905 ADJUTUS, le P., des frères mineurs [pseudonym]. *L'Immaculée Conception et les traditions franciscaines.* Rapport présenté au Congrès Marial de Namur le 13 juillet 1904, suivi d'une étude sur la doctrine de Duns Scot au sujet de l'Immaculée Conception et d'une dissertation historique sur le débat public du même docteur à la Sorbonne. Avec grav. Malines, Saint-François.

BRYSSAC, J. *L'Immaculée Conception dans les ordres militaires de l'Espagne.*

GODTS, F. X. *Vénérables serviteurs de Dieu et théologiens de la compagnie de Jésus, favorables à l'opinion alphonsienne touchant la première grâce de Marie.*

GUYOT, A. M. *L'Immaculée Conception dans la poésie liturgique du Moyen Age et dans les vieux cantiques français.* Vannes, Lafolye.

LE BACHELET, Xaverius Maria, S.J. *Roberti Cardinalis Bellarmini de Immaculata B.M.V. Conceptione Votum aliaque eiusdem argumenti fragmenta inedita* collegit, vulgavit, illustravit L.B. Paris, Beauchesne.

PAOLINI, François-Marie, O.F.M. "L'Immaculée Conception et les missions franciscaines. Discours prononcé au Congrès Marial de Rome à l'Assemblée générale du 3 décembre 1904," in *L'Ordine dei Frati Minori al Congresso Mariano Internationale tenuto in Roma dal 30 nov. al 4 dec. 1904 per celebrare il cinquantenario del dogma dell'Immacolata,* Roma, Artigianelli, pp. 39-49.

SIRE, Marie-Dominique. *Mémorial de mes travaux d'un demi-siècle depuis le 8 décembre 1854 en l'honneur de la Vierge Immaculée, Mère de Dieu.* Pour le Congrès Marial Universel de Rome en 1904. Paris, [s.d.]

——. *Oeuvre catholique poursuivie pendant un demi-siècle sur le dogme de l'Immaculée Conception.* Paris. 56 pp.

VERMEERSCH, A., S.J. *Le Cinquantenaire de Marie Immaculée.* Bruxelles, Société belge de libraire.

(Anon.) *L'Immaculée Conception à l'Institut Catholique de Paris (8 décembre 1904).*

(Anon.) *Namur. Les Fêtes mariales et le Congrès Marial, Juillet 1904.* Namur, Wesmael-Charlier.

DEPIERREUX, "Rapport sur l'Immaculée Conception." (Pp. 77-91)

Alfred LEGRAND, "Le culte de la Sainte Vierge à travers les âges au pays de Namur." (105-154)

ADJUTE, O.F.M. [*Pseudonym*]: "Les Frères-Mineurs et l'Immaculée Conception." (312-326)

(Anon.) *Premier Congrès Marial Breton, tenu à Josselin en l'honneur de l'Immaculée Conception, 21-24 novembre, 1904* (orné de 16 gravures). Vannes (Lafolye) & Paris (Beauchesne). 600 pp.

J.-V. BAINVEL, "L'histoire d'un dogme." (Pp. 39-60)

Jh. VALY, "Exposé théologique de l'Immaculée Conception." (63-89)

A. BLANCHE, O.P., "Le privilège de l'Immaculée Conception et ses conséquences pour la Très-Sainte Vierge." (93-110)

J. BULÉON: Histoire liturgique de l'Immaculée Conception." (113-132)

J. BULÉON & Eug. LE GARREC, "La définition du dogme et ses conséquences pour le culte de S. Joachim et de S. Anne." (157-175)

Joseph ROBILLARD, "Opportunité de la définition du dogme de l'Immaculée Conception." (179-189)

1905 (continued)

A. DE LA BARRÉ, "Les conséquences de la définition du dogme de l'Immaculée Conception." (193-207)

F. SANCHOT, "Les apôtres de l'Immaculée Conception." (269-285)

A.-M. GUYOT, "L'Immaculée Conception dans la poésie liturgique du Moyen-Âge et dans les vieux cantiques français." (295-336)

H. MORICE, "L'Immaculée Conception dans l'éloquence." (339-355)

J. LEPETIT, "L'Immaculée Conception dans la peinture." (359-383)

J.-M. ABGRALL, "L'iconographie de l'Immaculée Conception en Bretagne." (387-401)

[Various authors] "La croyance et le culte" [especially in Brittany]. (413-548)

1906 DELAPORTE, V. *L'Immaculée-Conception et la Compagnie de Jésus* (Notes et Souvenirs). Paris, Retaux.

1907 POURMARIN, C. *Marie, étudiée dans le saint evangile et d'après la théologie et les pères. La France et l'Angleterre.* Paris, Amat.

1908 BOURGEOIS, L. Th., O.P. *La Vierge Marie. Mystères de sa prédestination et de sa vie.* Paris, Lecoffre. viii, 352 pp. IC pp. 77-98.

HERZOG, Guillaume [= J. TURMEL] *La Sainte Vierge dans l'histoire.* Paris, Nourry. IC pp. 98-162.
(Condemned by the S. Congr. of the Index, July 5, 1909.)

NEWMAN, le Cardinal J. H. *Du culte de la Sainte Vierge dans l'Eglise catholique.* Traduction revue et corrigée par un bénédictin de l'abbaye de Farnborough. Avec une préface par dom Cabrol. Paris, Tequi. xii, 252 pp.
(Translation of the "Letter" of 1866; another French translation had appeared in 1866.)

SIRE, Marie Dominique. *Glorie à Marie, l'Immaculée Vierge Mère, en la cinquantaine de son triomphe dans l'Église, 1854-1904.* Saint-Cloud, Belin. 67 pp.

1909 CLÉMENCET, C. *La mariologie de S. Bernard.* Brignais, Sacuny. 123 pp.

STIMART, L. *L'Immaculée Conception et la virginité de Marie.* Paris (Lecoffre, Gabalda) & Bruxelles (L'Action Catholique). [1909] 38 pp. ("Science et Foi")

THIBAUT, J., des Augustins de l'Assomption. *Panégyrique de l'Immaculée dans les chants hymnographiques de la Liturgie grècque.* Étude présentée au Congrès Marial de Rome. Paris, Picard. 52 pp.

1910 PESSION, Pierre-Joseph. "Saint Anselme et l'Immaculée Conception," in *Actes du congrès marial tenu à Aoste à l'occasion du viiie Centenaire de la mort de Saint Anselme, 1109-1909,* Aoste, Imp. Catholique, pp. 37-48.

1912 BERTRET. *Les grandeurs de Marie.* IC pp. 49-64.

GEORGES-EPHREM. *Les solennités de la Sainte Vierge.* Paris, Gabalda. IC pp. 3-90

VACANDARD, E. "Les origines de la Fête et du dogme de l'Immaculée Conception," in *Etudes de critique et de l'histoire religieuse,* III, Paris.

1913 CAMPANA, Emile. *Marie dans le dogme catholique.* Ouvrage traduit de l'italien par A. M. Viel, O.P. 3 vol. Montréjeau, Soubiron & Cardeilhac, [1912]-1913. IC vol. II, pp. 37-275.

DEBUCHY, Paul, S.J. *Le petit office de l'Immaculée Conception.* Deuxième éd. Paris, Lethielleux. 314 pp.

LE BACHELET, Xavier-Marie, S.J. *Auctuarium Bellarminianum.* Supplément aux oeuvres du Cardinal Bellarmin. Paris, Beauchesne. IC pp. 626-632.

1914 ARTAUD, V. D. *La Vierge Marie.* Paris, Beauchesne. 432 pp. IC pp. 17-46. 5th ed., 1921.

1916 FLACHAIRE, C. *La Dévotion à la Vierge dans la littérature catholique au commencement du XVIIéme siècle.* Paris, Leroux. 175 pp.

GARRIGUET, L. *La Vierge Marie.* Sa prédestination - sa dignité - ses privilèges - son rôle - ses vertus - ses mérites - sa gloire - son intercession - son culte. [1916].

5th ed., 1924; 9th ed. Paris, Téqui, 1933: IC pp. 82-108.

LE BACHELET, X.-M., S.J. "Marie, Mère de Dieu — Immaculée Conception," in *Dictionnaire apologétique de la Foi catholique,* sous la direction de A. D'ALES . . . , vol. III, Paris, col. 209-218.

Reprinted in 1926.

1920 TOURNEBIZE, [F.] *L'Immaculée Conception dans les anciennes Eglises Orientales grecque, arménienne, copte, syrienne.* Paris. 9 pp.

1922 BRAUN, François-Marie, O.P. *L'Immaculée Conception. Les erreurs, le dogme.* Bruxelles. 23 pp. (*Etudes religieuses,* no. 69, 25 nov., 1922) (See 1923 for vol. II.)

(Anon.) *Mémoires et rapports du Congrès Marial (sections d'expression française) tenu à Bruxelles, 8-11 septembre 1921.* Premier volume. Bruxelles, "L'action catholique." [1922]

B. CAPELLE, O.S.B., "Notes sur des textes de saint Augustin relatifs à l'Immaculée Conception." (Pp. 84-92)

B. DEL MARMOL, O.S.B., "Quelques précisions sur le culte de la Vierge au XIIe siècle. Influence des moines anglais sur son développement." (Pp. 231-241)

1923 BRAUN, François-Marie, O.P. *L'Immaculée Conception. II. Les Convenances du privilège; les fondements du dogme.* Bruxelles. 36 pp. (*Etudes religieuses,* no. 81., 10 juin, 1923) (See 1922 for vol. I.)

EADMER, Moine de Cantorbéry. *La Conception immaculée de la Vierge Marie.* Introduction et traduction par Dom B. DEL MARMOL. Maredsous. 78 pp. (Collection *Pax*)

VACANT, MANGENOT, AMANN, *Dictionnaire de théologie catholique,* tom. VII. Paris.

Xavier-Marie LE BACHELET, S.J., "L'Immaculée Conception dans l'Ecriture et la tradition jusqu'au Concile d'Ephèse." (Col. 845-893)

Martin JUGIE, A. A., "L'Immaculée Conception dans l'église grecque après le Concile d'Ephèse." (893-975)

Martin JUGIE, A. A., "L'Immaculée Conception dans les églises nestoriennes et monophysites." (975-979)

Xavier-Marie LE BACHELET, S.J., "L'Immaculée Conception dans l'église latine d'après le Concile d'Ephèse." (979-1218)

1924 HEDDE, René, O.P. *Marie-Immaculée, rempart de la foi chrétienne.* Paris, Gabalda. 156 pp. IC pp. 121-135; 136-156.

MARIN-SOLA, Francesco, O.P. *L'évolution homogène du dogme catholique.* 2 vol. Fribourg, St-Paul. IC I, pp. 322-331.

1925 COULANGE, Louis [= Joseph TURMEL]. *La Vierge Marie.* Paris, Rieder. 159 pp.

(Condemned by decree of the Holy Office, Nov. 6, 1930.)

SIGISMOND, O.F.M. *La royauté universelle du Sacré-Coeur et l'Immaculée Conception de Marie d'après la doctrine du bienheureux Jean Duns Scot.* Toulouse, "Les Voix franciscaines." 48 pp.

1926 PÈGUES, Thomas, O.P. *Commentaire français littéral de la Somme Théologique de saint Thomas d'Aquin.* Toulouse (Privat) - Paris (Téqui). 1907-1931. Tome XVI (1926), *La Rédemption.* IC pp. 1-46 [= Summa Th. III, Q. XXVIII].

RENAUDIN, Paul, O.S.B. *La pensée de saint Thomas sur l'Immaculée Conception.* Avignon, Aubanel. 16 pp. (Extrait de la *Revue Thomiste,* 1922, pp. 205-210)

1926 (continued)

RIVIÈRE, J. "Immaculée Conception" in *Dictionnaire Pratique des Connaissances Religieuses* publié sous la direction de J. Bricout. Paris, Letouzey. Tome III, col. 915-920.

1927 DOURCHE, J. M. *La Vierge Toute Sainte*. Bruges, Desclée. [1927] IC pp. 89-152.

SYNAVE, P., O.P. "L'Immaculée Conception," in *S. Thomas d'Aquin, Somme théologique, Vie de Jésus,* tome premier [= III a pars, Qq. 27-34.] Paris, Tournai, Rome (Desclée) [1927], pp. 282-289.

1929 MORINEAU, B.-M., S.M. *La Sainte Vierge*. Paris, Bloud et Gay. 1929.
(*Bibliothèque catholique des sciences religieuses*) IC pp. 45-66.

1931 DILLENSCHNEIDER, Clément, Rédemptoriste. *La Mariologie de S. Alphonse de Liguori. I. Son influence sur le renouveau des doctrines mariales et de la piété catholique après la tourmente du protestantisme et du jansénisme.* Fribourg, Paderborn, & Paris. xvii, 406 pp. (*Studia Friburgensia.*) IC *passim,* esp. pp. 289-302.
(For vol. II, see 1934)

(*Anon.*) *2e Congrès Marial National de Lourdes, 23-27 juillet, 1930.* Compte rendu officiel. Lourdes, Grotte. 316 pp.

Ephrem LONGPRÉ, O.F.M., "Exposition du dogme de l'Immaculée Conception." (Pp. 79-102)

M. P. POURRAT, P.S.S., "Le dogme de l'Immaculée Conception. Histoire de sa définition." (150-169)

AURIAULT, S.J., "La place de l'Immaculée Conception dans la synthèse théologique." (215-224)

1933 ANCELET-HUSTACHE, Mme. *L'Immaculée Conception.* Paris, Flammarion. 187 pp.

BERNARD, Rogatien, O.P. *Le mystère de Marie*. Paris, Desclée. 491 pp.
4ème éd. *ibid.,* 1954: IC pp. 61-78.

DE BLIC. *St. Thomas et l'Immaculée Conception.* Paris. 12 pp.

JÉROME DE PARIS, O.M.C. *La doctrine mariale de Saint Laurent de Brindes.* Etude théologique. Rome (Frères Mineurs Capucins) - Paris (Saint-François). xxvii, 295 pp.
(Appeared originally in *Etudes franciscaines* 42 (1931), pp. 273-298; 43 (1932) pp. 121-142; 285-305; 44 (1932), pp. 407-428.)

NEUBERT, E., S.M. *Marie dans le dogme.*
2ème éd. refondue: Paris, Spes, 1945, 313 pp.

1934 DILLENSCHNEIDER, Clément, Rédemptoriste. *La Mariologie de S. Alphonse de Liguori. II. Sources et synthèse doctrinale.* Fribourg, Paderborn & Paris. (*Studia Friburgensia.*) IC pp. 212-231.
(For vol. I see 1931.)

MONSABRÉ, J. M. L., O.P. *La Vierge Marie*. Paris, Lethielleux, viii, 220 pp. IC pp. 3-17.
(Extracts from the works of this nineteenth century preacher, arranged by Canon J. CHAPEAU.)

1935 BERNARD, St. *L'oeuvre mariale de saint Bernard.* Juvisy, Cerf. [1935] 240 pp.
(The Marian works of the Saint translated by P. AUBRON, S.J.)

MELLET, Marcellin, O.P. *La sainteté de la Mère de Dieu.* (Essai sur la mariologie de Saint Albert le Grand.) Lyon, Bosc. 142 pp.
(Doctoral thesis, Facultés Catholiques de Lyon.)

NOGUES, Dominique. *Mariologie de Saint Bernard*. Paris & Tournai: Casterman. 243 pp.
2ème éd., 1947: IC pp. 27-40.

1937 DEMARET, Gaston, O.S.B. *Marie de qui est né Jésus.* 6 tomes [1937-1942]. Paris, Spes. Tome 2, *L'Immaculée Conception.* 262 pp.

1938 HOFFER, P. *La dévotion à Marie au déclin du 17e siècle.* Autour du jansénisme et des "Avis salutaires de la B. V. Marie á ses dévots indiscrets." Paris, Cerf.

1939 Longpré, E., O.F.M. *La Vierge Immaculée. Histoire et doctrine.* Montréal (Le Devoir) & Paris (Ed. Franciscaines). 60 pp.

1941 Garrigou-Lagrange, Réginald, O.P. *Mariologie.* La Mère du Sauveur et notre vie intérieure . . . Lyon, Ed. de l'abeille. xi, 389 pp. IC pp. 30-82.
Republished: Paris (Cerf) and Montreal (Lévrier), 1948.

1943 Brutsch. *La Vierge Marie.* Neuchâtel, Delachaux & Niestlé. 118 pp.
Rauguel, A., S.M. *La Doctrine mariale de Saint Bernard.* Paris, Spes. 215 pp.

1944 Béraud de St. Maurice. *Jean Duns Scot, un docteur des temps nouveaux.* 2ème éd. 1953, Paris, Gabalda: IC pp. 192-215.

1946 de Monléon, J., O.S.B. *Le dogme de l'Immaculée-Conception.* Libr. de l'Arc, [s.d.] 33 pp. (Collection, *Le Catholique devant les obscurités de sa foi.*)
Dufourcq, A. *Comment s'éveilla la foi à l'Immaculée Conception et à l'Assomption* aux Ve et VIe siècles. Paris, Ed. Franciscaines. 44 pp.
(Also published as vol. IV of *Etudes de science religieuse.*)
Garreau, A. *Histoire mariale de la France.* Paris, Ed. des Saints-Pères. 263 pp.
Janssens, Edgar. *La doctrine mariale de Bossuet.* Liège, Solédi. IC pp. 51-66.
l'Ermite. *La Très Sainte Vierge Marie.* Montréal, Levrier. IC p. 129 ff.
Musters, Anselme (O.E.S.A.) *La Souveraineté de la Vierge d'après les écrits mariologiques de Barthélemy de los Rios O.E.S.A.* Appendice pp. 179-192: "De los Rios et l'Immaculée-Conception." Bruges, Augustins.

1947 Plessis, Armand, S.M.M. *Manuel de Mariologie dogmatique.* Montfort-sur-Meu, Séminaire des Missions. 360 pp.; IC pp. 59-96.

1948 Duhr, J., S.J. *La glorieuse Assomption de la Mère de Dieu.* Paris, Bonne Presse. 1948.
(Chapter entitled, "L'évolution du dogme de l'Immaculée Conception," reproduced from *Nouvelle Revue Théologique,* décembre 1951.)
Francez, J. *Notes historiques sur la dévotion à l'Immaculée-Conception dans les Hautes-Pyrénées.* Tarbes, Bigorre, [s.d.]. 14 pp.

1949 Bonnefoy, Jean-François, O.F.M. *Le mystère de Marie selon le Protoévangile et l'Apocalypse.* Paris, Vrin. 192 pp.
Guitton, Jean. *La Vierge Marie.* Paris [1949]. 224 pp.
Longpré, Ephrem, O.F.M. "L'Assomption et l'Immaculée Conception," in *Congrès Marial du Puy-en-Velay,* pp. 243-282.

1950 Abd-el-Jalil, Joseph Marie, O.F.M. *Marie et l'Islam.* Paris, Beauchesne. 90 pp.
Dehau, Pierre-Thomas, O.P. *Eve et Marie.* Bouvines, Monastère du Coeur Immaculé de Marie. 396 pp.

1951 Blond. "L'Immaculée Conception, grâce initiale de Marie," in *La Sainteté de la Mère de Dieu,* par. Mgr. Soubigou, les chanoines Blond et Catta, les RR. PP. Gerlaud O.P. et Holstein, S.J., Paris, Téqui [1951], pp. 59-65.

1952 Duval, André. "La dévotion mariale dans l'Ordre des Frères Prêcheurs," in *Maria, Etudes sur la Sainte Vierge,* dirigées par Hubert du Manoir, S.J., Paris, Beauchesne, tome II, pp. 737-782.
Jugie, Martin, A.A. *L'Immaculée Conception dans l'Ecriture Sainte et dans la Tradition orientale.* Romae, Academia mariana & Officium libri catholici. ix, 489 pp. (*Bibliotheca Immaculatae Conceptionis. Textus et disquisitiones,* vol. 3)

1953 Longpré, Ephrem, O.F.M. *L'Immaculée Conception, proclamée à Rome le 8 Décembre 1854, manifestée à Lourdes le 25 Mars 1858.* 31 pp.
Moret, Jeanne. *L'Immaculée Conception.* Nicolet (Canada), Centre Marial Canadien 53 pp. (*Tracts marials,* n. 43-44.)
Scheeben, M.-J. *La Mère virginale du Sauveur.* Traduit de l'allemand par A. Kerkvoorde, O.S.B. [= *Die bräutliche Gottesmutter,* from the *Handbuch* of 1882.] Paris, Desclée. IC pp. 126-139.

1954 CASTONGUAY, E., O.M.I. *Elle t'écrasera la tête.* L'Immaculée et le dragon. Montréal-Paris, Fides.

GIAMBERARDINI, Gabriele, O.F.M. *L'Immaculée Conception dans l'Eglise Egyptienne.* Le Caire [s.e.]. 19 pp.

GUELLUY, Robert. *L'Immaculée Conception.* Gembloux, Duculot. 63 pp.

JOURNET, Charles. *Esquisse du développement du dogme marial.* Paris, Alsatia, [1954]. 165 pp. (*"Sagesse et Cultures."*)
 (Cf. the editor's footnote on p. 3 of the present volume.)

LEVACK, D., C.SS.R., et VADEBONCOEUR, P., C.SS.R. *Saint Alphonse-Marie Liguori, docteur de l'Immaculée.* Etudes et principaux écrits à l'occasion du centenaire de la proclamation du dogme de l'Immaculée Conception. Sainte-Anne de Beaupré (Canada), Levack.

(*Anon.*) *La Vierge Immaculée. Histoire et doctrine.* Montréal, Editions franciscaines. xviii, 302 pp.
 MALO, A.-M., "La définition dogmatique de l'Immaculée Conception." (Pp. 1-25)
 POIRIER, L., "La révélation de Marie à travers la littérature patristique." (27-50)
 BOISVERT, E., "L'Immaculée Conception dans la littérature patristique." (51-90)
 COITEUX, F., "Le caractère marial des origines franciscaines," (91-116)
 ROBERT, P., "L'Immaculée Conception au moyen âge." (117-151)
 PARENT, E., "L'intervention de l'Eglise sous Sixte IV." (153-178)
 BLAIS, H., "S. Léonard de Port-Maurice et la définition de l'Immaculée Conception." (179-200)
 BARIL, H., "La préservation de la tache originelle." (201-227)
 PUECH, L.-M., "La plénitude de grâce en Marie." (229-261)
 MALO, A.-M., "Valeur de vie du dogme de l'Immaculée Conception." (267-284)

1955 BOURGUET, Pasteur P. *La Vierge Marie.* L'Ecriture ou la tradition. Berger-Leurault.

RIGAUX, Béda, O.F.M. "Marie Immaculée dans sa conception," in *Actes du Congrès Marial,* Bruxelles [1955], pp. 37-56.

(*Anon.*) *L'Immaculée Conception.* Compte rendu in extenso des travaux du Congrès. Lyon, VIIème Congrès Marial National, 1954. Lyon [s.e.] 445 pp.
 BARRÉ, "De Pie IX à Pie XII, l'Enseignement des Papes sur l'Immaculée Conception." (Pp. 95-112)
 BRAUN, O.P., "Le progrès de la preuve scripturaire à propos de l'Immaculée Conception depuis la Bulle Ineffabilis." (113-130)
 NICOLAS, O.P., "L'Immaculée Conception dans la tradition vivante de l'Eglise." (131-145)
 CAPELLE, O.S.B., "La fête de la Conception de Marie en Occident." (147-161)
 WENGER, A.A., "L'Immaculée Conception dans la tradition orientale." (163-184)
 BONNEFOY, O.F.M., "Marie préservée de toute tache du péché originel." (187-220)
 FRÉNAUD, O.S.B., "La grâce de l'Immaculée Conception." [Reprinted separately [s.d.] at Saint-Rémy by Lacroix.] (221-249)
 DE BACIOCCHI, S.M., "La Mission de Marie et l'Immaculée Conception." (251-263)
 Mgr. JOUASSARD, "La théologie mariale de saint-Irénée." (265-276)

1955 (continued)

(*Anon.*) *L'Immaculée Conception de la Bienheureuse Vierge Marie.* Journées d'études, Cap-de-la-Madeleine, 12-13 août 1954. Société Canadienne d'Etudes Mariales. Ottawa, Ed. de l'Université.

Adrien-M. MALO, O.F.M., "L'économie divine dans la révélation biblique de l'Immaculée Conception." (Pp. 13-35)

Paul-E. VADEBONCOEUR, C.SS.R., "Le dernier docteur de l'Immaculée Conception." (37-96)

Joseph LEDIT, S.J., "L'Immaculée Conception et les Eglises d'Orient." (97-104)

Marcel BÉLANGER, O.M.I., "L'Immaculée Conception et Maternité Divine." (127-150)

Robert MORENCY, S.J., "La libre coopération de Marie à sa grâce initiale." (105-126)

Pierre-E. LACHANCE, O.P., "Immaculée Conception et Association au Sauveur dans l'oeuvre de la Rédemption." (151-164)

(*Anon.*) *Virgo Immaculata,* volumes III, IV, V, VI, VIII/2. (See Latin bibliography under 1958.)

1956 (*Anon.*) *Virgo Immaculata,* volumes II, VIII/3, XII, XVI. (See Appendix below, p. 611 ff.)

1957 (*Anon.*) *Virgo Immaculata,* volumes IX, X, XI, XIII, XIV. (See Appendix below, p. 611 ff.)

DATE OF PUBLICATION UNKNOWN

HOFFET, Emile, O.M.I. *Mgr. C. J. Eugène de Mazenod, évêque de Marseille, fondateur de la Congrégation des Missionnaires Oblats de Marie Immaculée, et la définition du dogme de l'Immaculée Conception.* Liège, Dessain. [s.d.] viii, 119 pp.

(*Anon.*) *La Vierge Marie.* Petite Somme mariale. 5ème éd. rev. et augm. Lyon-Paris, Vitte. 426 pp., 1952.

GERMAN[1]

1830   (MIRACULOUS MEDAL APPARITION TO SISTER CATHERINE LABOURÉ, PARIS, NOVEMBER 17; FIRST MEDALS STRUCK, JUNE 30, 1832)

1831 WAIBEL, Alois Adalbert, O.S.F., *Von der Schöpfung und von dem Sündenfalle der abtrünnigen Engel, und von der Sünde der ersten Menschen.* Eine dogmatische Abhandlung. Augsburg.

1834 SCHEILL, J. *Über die Meinung, Verehrung und Festfeier von der Empfängniss der seligsten Jungfrau Maria.* Ein theologischer Tractat, zugleich eine Beleuchtung der dogmatischen Erörterung über die Würde Mariä. Landshut, Thomann.

(Reprinted from *Die Bonner Zeitschrift,* 1833.)

---

[1] We are grateful to Mrs. Waldemar Gurian for checking the proofs of this section.

1836 [ALADEL] *Geschichtlicher Bericht über den Ursprung und die Wirkungen der neuen Medaille, geprägt zur Ehre der Unbefleckten Empfängniss — allgemein bekannt unter dem Namen: Die wunderbare Medaille.* Nach der 5. franz. Ausgabe. Münster.

(Translated from the French; reprinted in 1839. This work is listed here as being the earliest book on the Miraculous Medal in German that we have found; subsequent literature on this subject, however, will not be given.)

1837 MURATORI, L. A. *Über den rechten Gebrauch der Vernunft in Sachen der Religion.* Aus dem *Lateinischen* [of the eighteenth century] übersetzt [by Biunde and Braun]. Koblenz.

ODILO. *'Ritterus et Balzerus' vapulantes, d.i. Beurtheilung des dogmatischen Gutachtens der Herren Professoren R. u. B. über die ersten XVI Sätze, welche in der Erzdiöcese Köln dem Clerus zur Unterschrift vorgelegt werden.* Mainz. IC p. 45 ff.

(Cf. the following entry.)

[RITTER, Jos. Ign & BALTZER, Joh. Bapt.] *Abdruck eines dogmatischen Gutachtens über die ersten XVI Sätze, welche in der Erzdiöcese Köln dem Klerus zur Unterschrift vorgelegt werden.* Göttingen. IC pp. 31 ff. 43 ff.

(*Anon.*) *Noch ein Gutachten über die XVI ersten Thesen, welche den Neoapprobanden und anderen Priestern der Erzdiöcese Köln zur Unterschrift vorgelegt werden.* Von einem kath. Theologen. Darmstadt, Leske. IC p. 50 ff.

(*Anon.*) *Theologische Beurtheilung der Sätze, welche den Geistlichen der Erzdiöcese Köln zur Unterschrift vorgelegt werden.* Von einem kath. Geistlichen. Frankfurt. IC p. 49 ff.

1838 REBER, Engelbertus. *Beleuchtung der Schrift des Bischofs v. Linz Dr. Gregorius Thomas über die Kölner Thesen.* Köln. IC p. 61 ff.

[ZIEGLER], Gregorius Thomas, O.S.B., Bischof v. Linz. *XVI Thesen, welche der Erzbischof* Clemens Augustus *seinem Clerus zu unterzeichnen vorgelegt hat, mit den Einwendungen gegen dieselben und mit der kath. Dogmatik verglichen.* Linz. IC pp. 73 ff.

1840 KLÖDEN, J. *Zur Geschichte der Marienverehrung, besonders im letzten Jahrhundert vor der Reformation in der Mark Brandenburg und Lausitz.* Berlin, Lüderitz.

1842 DUGUESNE, Arnold. *Die erhabenen Vorzüge Mariens.* Oder Betrachtungen auf die achttägige Feier der Hauptfeste der allers. Jungfrau. Nach dem Französischen bearbeitet und mit einer geschichtlichen Darstellung dieser Feste vermehrt von Laurenz HECHT. Regensburg, Manz. IC Band I, pp. 3-151.

(The original French of Arnauld DUQUESNE appeared in 1791, entitled, *Les Grandeurs de Marie.* It was republished in 1820 and frequently thereafter. Cf. the following entry.)

——. *Die Herrlichkeit Mariä,* oder Betrachtungen auf die achttägige Feier der Hauptfeste der allers. Jungfrau. Augsburg.

(A translation of the same French original mentioned in the preceding entry.)

1843 LAMBRUSCHINI, Cardinal Aloysius. *Polemische Dissertation des Kard. Lambruschini über die unbefleckte Enpfängniss Mariä.* Übersetzt [from the Italian] von M. Zürcher. Schaffhausen, Hurter. 96 pp.

LAMBRUSCHINI, Aloysius, Bischof v. Sabina. *Über die unbefleckte Empfängnis Mariä.* Polemische Dissertation. Mit anmerkungen und Zusätzen von Dr. A. KELLNER. München, Lentner. 128 pp.

1847 (*Anon.*) "Unbefleckte Empfängniss," in *Aschbach allgem. Kirchenlexicon,* II, 574 ff. Frankfurt.

(*Anon.*) "Unbefleckte Empfängniss Mariä," in *Binder allg. Realencyclopädie für das kath. Deutschland.* III, 978 ff. Regensburg.

1848   (COMMITTEE APPOINTED BY POPE PIUS IX TO EXAMINE THE
        ADVISABILITY OF A DEFINITION, JUNE 1)

1849   (ENCYCLICAL LETTER *Ubi primum* OF POPE PIUS IX, FEBRUARY 2)

PERRONE, Johann, S.J. *Ist die unbefleckte Empfängniss der seligsten Jungfrau
Maria dogmatisch definirbar?* Eine theologische Untersuchung. Aus
dem Lateinischen von Dr. Aegid Dietl u. Bernhard Schels. Regensburg,
Manz. 341 pp.
        Republished in 1855.

1850 OSWALD, Heinrich. *Dogmatische Mariologie*, d.i. systematische Darstellung
sämmtlicher die allerseligste Jungfrau betreffenden Lehrstücke. Ein
Versuch. Paderborn, Schöningh. IC pp. 16-40.
        (Condemned by the S. Congr. of the Index, Dec. 6, 1855.)

1851 (*Anon.*) "Mariä Enpfängniss" in *Kirchenlexicon oder Encyklopädie der
katholischen Theologie*, herausgegeben . . . von Heinrich Joseph WETZER
. . . und Benedikt WELTE. . . . Freiburg im Breisgau, Herder, VI, pp.
865-872.

1852 GENTHE. *Die Jungfrau Maria, ihre Evangelien und ihre Wunder*. Ein Beitrag
zur Geschichte des Mariencultus. Halle.

1853 GAILLARD, Georg, P. *Sechs Reden über die Unbefleckte Empfängniss der
allerseligsten Jungfrau Maria*. Soest, Nasse. xii, 82 pp.

HÄNGGI. *Bemerkungen über die Schrift des Probstes und Prof. Leu:* "Warnung vor Neuerungen und Übertreibungen in der kath. Kirche Deutschlands." Solothurn.

KARL VOM HEILIGEN ALOYS. *Die Gottesmutter in ihrem dreifachen Triumphe
über die Welt*, oder Versuch einer Darstellung der wahren Entwicklung
und jetzigen äusseren Ausdehnung der Marienverehrung unter den
Menschen. Regensburg, Pustet. 316 pp.

LEU, Jos. Burkard. *Warnung vor Neuerungen und Übertreibungen in der
kath. Kirche Deutschlands.* Luzern.

1854   (DEFINITION OF THE IMMACULATE CONCEPTION AS A DOGMA OF FAITH
        BY POPE PIUS IX, DECEMBER 8)

COSTA, Fr. *Kurzer Unterricht bezüglich auf die am 8 Dec. 1854 erfolgte
kirchliche Entscheidung über die unbefleckte Empfängniss der seligsten
Jungfrau.* Nach dem Italienischen des Fr. Costa Prof. und Priester in
Rom. Innsbruck.
        (Originally published in *Katholische Blätter aus Tirol*, 1854, p. 1169)

FRANTZ, Cl. *Versuch einer Geschichte des Marien- und Annencultus in der
kath. Kirche*. Halberstadt.

LABORDE. *Der Glaube an die unbefleckte Empfängniss der heil. Jungfrau,
und die Bestrebungen derer, welche diesen Glauben zu einem Dogma
machen wollen, in geschichtlicher und religiöser Hinsicht beleuchtet.*
Nach der dritten französischen Ausgabe. Stuttgart.

LABOULAYE, Eduard. *Die Frage der Unbefleckten Empfängniss.* Nach dem
französischen . . . bearbeitet. Berlin. 55 pp.

LANZ, Franz Carl. *Auswahl alter Marianischer Predigten, Homilien und Unter-
weisungen* für Stadt und Land, mit besonderer Berücksichtigung der
Bruderschaften Mariens. Gesammelt, übersetzt und herausgegeben unter
Mitwirkung mehrerer Freunde. 2 vol. Schaffhausen.
        (Vol. II contains 39 sermons on the IC.)

UHRIG, Adam Jos. *Zur Aufklärung über die berühmte Zeitfrage von der
unbefleckten Empfängniss der heil. Jungfrau Maria.* Dillingen.

WIMMER, G. A. *Papsthum und Christenthum.* Oder Beweis, dass das moderne
Papsthum innerhalb der christlichen Kirche keine Berechtigung habe.
Der gesammten Christenheit zur Beherzigung. Bremen, Kühtmann. VII,
132 pp. 2. Aufl. 1869.

1854 (continued)

(*Anon.*) *Das Geheimniss der unbefleckten Empfängniss in Harmonie mit Offenbarung und Vernunft.* Ein Marienbild gewidmet dem Bedürfniss der Gegenwart, insbesondere dem gläubigen Protestantismus. Vom Verfasser des Adventswortes von 1852: *Die kathol. Kirche in ihrer Freiheit.* Münster. 27 pp.

1855 BRANDES, Karl, O.S.B. *Lehrsatz und Dogma der unbefleckten Empfängniss Mariä.* Zur Feier des 8. Dec. 1854. Einsiedeln, Benzinger. 89 pp.

COSTA, Franz. *Einige Erwägungen in Bezug auf die dogmatische Entscheidung über die unbefleckte Empfängniss der sel. Jungfrau Maria.* Ins Deutsche übersetzt [from the Italian]. Strassburg.

CZERSKI, Johannes. *Offenes Sendschreiben an Papst Pius IX.* Eichstädt Schneidemühl.

[DE PREUX, Peter Joseph.] *Stimme eines Schweizerischen Bischofs über die unbefleckte Empfängniss der heil. Jungfrau und Gottesmutter Maria,* oder Denkschrift des Bischofs von Sitten über die Erbsündlosigkeit der sel. Jungfrau. (Aus dem Lateinischen) Solothurn.

GEISSEL, Card. Erzb. v. Köln. *Empfehlung in den Schutz der unbefleckt empfangenen Gottesmutter Maria.* Münster.

GISSMANN, Augustin. *Der Glaubenssatz von der unbefleckten Empfängniss der allersel. Jungfrau Maria,* in spekulativ dogmatischen Vorträgen. Schneidemühl, Eichstädt.

——. *Des Kirchenfeindes Irrgarten,* eine humoristisch-kritische Antwort auf das offene Sendschreiben des J. Czersky an Papst Pius IX. Schneidemühl.

HAAN, Joseph, S.I. *Die unbefleckte Empfängniss der seligsten Jungfrau und Mutter Gottes Maria als Glaubenslehre der hl. katholischen Kirche.* Paderborn, Schöningh. 152 pp.

(Translated from the French.) 2 verb. Aufl . . . *ibid.,* 1859.

KOLSCHMID, I. "Über die Unbefleckte Empfängniss Mariä," in *Drei kleine Abhandlungen,* Landshut, pp. 49-72.

LÖCHERER, Joseph. *Die Verehrung der allersel. Jungfrau Maria im Allgemeinen, und insbesondere in ihrer unbefleckten Empfängniss.* Zumeist nach den Aussprüchen der Heiligen. Augsburg, Kohlmann. 72 pp.

MING, J. *Die unbefleckte Empfängniss der seligsten Jungfrau und Gottesmutter Maria.* Schaffhausen, Hurter. 178 pp.

NIRSCHL, J. *Das Dogma der unbefleckten Empfängniss Mariä.* Eine fassliche Erklärung und Begründung desselben. Passau, Elsässer und Waldbauer.

PERRONE, Johannes, S.J. *Abhandlung über die dogmatische Definition der unbefleckten Empfängniss der seligsten Jungfrau Maria.* Übers. Dietl und Schels. Regensburg. Manz. 2. Aufl.

(For 1st edition, see 1849.)

RAUSCHER [Archbishop of Vienna]. *Maria, die Königin, ohne Makel empfangen.* Wien.

(Sermon; printed also in *Wiener Kirchenzeitung,* 1855; p. 487 ff., and *Salzburger Kirchenblatt,* 1855, p. 253).

SCHOPF. *Gemeinfassliches über die unbefleckte Empfängniss der allersel. Jungfrau Maria.* Salzburg.

WIERY, Valentin, Domherr v. Salzburg [later Prince-bishop of Gurk]. *Fragen und Antworten über die kath. Lehre von der unbefleckten Empfängniss der allers. Jungfrau Maria.* Salzburg.

WIMMER. *Ehrenrettung der seligen Jungfrau Maria, der Mutter unsers Herrn und Heilandes Jesu Christi, gegen die päpstlichen Verunglimpfungen.* Bremen, 3. Ausgabe, 1876. Kühtmann. 70 pp.

(*Anon.*) *Die Marienverehrung in ihrem Grunde und nach ihrer mannigfaltigen kirchlichen Erscheinung mit besonderer Rücksicht auf die vom Papst Pius IX am 8 Dec. 1854 ausgesprochene Glaubenslehre der Kirche von der unbefleckten Empfängniss Mariens.* Paderborn [Second edition].

1855 (continued)

(*Anon.*) *Papst Pius IX und sein Dogma von der Unbefleckten Empfängniss der Jungfrau Maria.* Nach der Geschichte beleuchtet, von einem Protestanten. Chur & Leipsig. 71 pp.

1856 AMERISTUS, Christophilus. *Über die Verehrung der Maria, und über den neuen Lehrsatz von der unbefleckten Empfängniss.* Protestirende Erwiederung auf den letzten Hirtenbrief des Erzbischofs von Mecheln. Aus dem Französischen übersetzt. Elberfeld.

BRANDT, Chr. C. A. *Paulus oder Papst?* Die neue römische Papst-kirche mit der alten römischen Kirche des Apostels Paulus genau verglichen nach der Epistel S. Pauli an die Römer. Philadelphia, IC pp. 19, 54.

BRAUN, Thomas. *Katholische Antwort auf die päpstliche Bulle über die Empfängniss Mariä.* Ottenburg. 240 pp.

GINAL, J. N. *Die Unbefleckte Empfängniss der seligsten Jungfrau Maria.* Eine dogmatische Abhandlung, zunächst für gebildete Katholiken. Augsburg, Kohlmann. 44 pp.

1857 BRAUN, Thomas. *Der Fall des Papstthums, und die unbefleckte Empfängniss.* Stuttgart.

——. *Die unbefleckte Empfängniss Mariä als Glaubensatz beleuchtet.* Besonderer Abdruck aus der Schrift: *Der Fall des Papstthums,* etc. Stuttgart.

2. Auflage, *ibid.*, 1862.

NICOLAS, August. [See under 1861.]

STEPISCHNEGG, J. [Later Bishop] "Das Dogma der unbefleckten Empfängniss Maria," in *Abhandlungen über Religion und Kirche,* p. 346 ff. Graz.

1858   (APPARITIONS OF MARY IMMACULATE TO BERNADETTE SOUBIROUS, LOURDES, FEBRUARY 11 - JULY 16)

LAURANT, Joannes. *Die Geheimnisse Mariens.* Mainz, Kirchheim. IC Band I, pp. 1-81.

STEITZ, Georg Eduard. "Maria, die Mutter des Herrn, ihre Verehrung und ihre Feste," in HERZOG Johann Jacob. *Realencyclopädie für protest. Theol. u. Kirche,* IX. Stuttgart & Hamburg.
(Cf. the entry ZOECKLER under 1903.)

WEBER, Beda. "Das neue Dogma von der unbefleckten Empfängniss Mariä," in *Cartons aus dem deutschen Kirchenleben,* pp. 753-765. Mainz.

(*Anon.*) *Die unbefleckte Empfängniss der Jungfrau Maria.* Eine historisch-dogmatisch-kritische Abhandlung von einem kath. Geistlichen. Leipzig, Brockhaus. x, 376 pp.

1859 GRATRY, A. *Der Monat Mariä von der unbefleckten Empfängnis.* Regensburg. (Translated from the French. See also the entry *Gratry* under 1934.)

[WILBERFORCE, Samuel]. *Rom, seine neue Lehre und unsere Pflichten.* Eine Predigt, gehalten in der Universität Oxford, am Tage des Festes Mariä Verkündigung 1855 von dem Bischofe von Oxford. Aus der zweiten englischen Ausgabe übersetzt von Prof. de Grüter. Herausg. von Kitchin. London.

1860 MARGOTTI, Jacob. "Die Unbefleckte Empfängniss, oder Sieg der Kirche über den Rationalismus," in *Die Siege der Kirche in dem ersten Jahrzehnt des Pontifikates Pius IX,* 2., beträchtlich verm. Aufl. aus dem Italienischen von Bonifatius Gams. In: *Bonifatius (Pius)* GAMS, O.S.B., *Geschichte der Kirche Christi im 19. Jahrhundert, mit besonderer Rücksicht auf Deutschland* . . . Innsbruck, Wagner.

NICOLAS, August. [See under 1861.]

SCHEEBEN, M. J. *Marienblüthen aus dem Garten der heil. Väter und christlichen Dichter zur besonderen Verherrlichung der ohne Makel empfangenen Gottesmutter gesammelt.* Schaffhausen.

1861 GAGARIN, J., S.J. *Das Dogma von der unbefleckten Empfängniss.* Briefe
an eine russische Dame. Deutsch [from the French] von M. Brühl. Wien,
Mech.-Dr.

NICOLAS, August. *Die allerseligste Jungfrau Maria. Neue Studien über das
Christenthum.* . . . Aus dem Französischen übersetzt von Silvester Hester.
4 Bände. Paderborn, Schöningh. 1856-1861. IC Bd. II (1857), pp.
129-171: Bd. III (1860). 2nd. ed., 1861 ff.

——. *Die Jungfrau Maria und der göttliche Plan.* Neue studien über
das Christenthum. Deutsche, vom Verfasser genehmigte Originalausgabe.
Herausgegeben von Carl B. Reiching. Regensburg, Manz. 3 Bde.
[III in 2 parts.] 1856-1861. IC Bd. II (1857), pp. 108-146; Bd. III,
1 (1860), pp. 309-318.

(This and the preceding entry are two different translations of the
same French original; see French bibliography at 1864.)

1862 HASE, Karl. *Handbuch der protestantischen Polemik gegen die römisch-
katholische Kirche.* Leipzig. xxxii, 665 pp. (IC: pp. 309-335 in the
7th ed.)

1863 BRAUN, Thomas. *Gegen die falschen Propheten des 8. Dec. 1854.* Geharnischte
predigt auf den VII Sonntag nach Pfingsten. St. Gallen.

PARODI, Aloys, S. J. *Der Glaube der heiligen Kirchenväter an Maria, die ohne
Makel der Erbsünde empfangene Jungfrau.* Mit einem Anhang von
Andachtsübungen für das Fest der unbefleckten Empfängniss. Übersetzt
[from the Italian] durch Paul Graf v. Reischach. . . . Mainz, Kirchheim.
xii, 240 pp.

1864 MARTIN, Konrad, Bischof v. Paderborn. *Ein bischöfliches Wort an die
Protestanten Deutschlands, zunächst an diejenigen meiner Diöcese, über
die zwischen uns bestehenden Controverspunkte.* Paderborn, Schöningh.
2 Bde. IC Bd. II, pp. 177-180.

(A second and third edition appeared this same year and a fourth,
unchanged, in 1866, *ibid.*)

PREUSS, Ed. *An den Bischof von Paderborn.* Eine Erwiderung auf dessen
bischöfliches Wort. Berlin.

1865 ANDREAE, U. *Viertes offenes Sendschreiben an den Bischof v. Paderborn,
zugleich ein evangelisches Wort an alle Katholiken über den Marien-
Heiligen und Bilderdienst.* Soёst.

KRÜGER-VELTHUSEN, W. *Maria, die Mutter Jesu Christi.* Barmen, Lange-
wiesche. 287 pp.

PREUSS, E. *Die Römische Lehre von der unbefleckten Empfängniss aus den
Quellen dargestellt und aus Gottes Wort widerlegt.* Berlin.

1866 NEWMAN, Johann [Cardinal]. *Die heilige Maria.* Sendschreiben an
Herrn Pusey. Köln, Bachem. 208 pp. IC pp. 51-58.

(Translated from the English *Letter* . . . of this same year by
Schündelen.)

PREUSS, Eduard. *Komparative Darstellung des Lehrbegriffs der verschiedenen
christlichen Kirchenparteien.* Berlin. IC p. 41 ff.

1867 PARODI, S. J. *Gebete und Betrachtungen zur Verehrung der Unbefleckten
Empfängniss Mariä,* aus den Schriften der heil. Väter zusammengestellt.
Aus dem Italienischen übersetzt und mit Zugaben vermehrt von Jos.
Jungmann, S. J. Innsbruck.

1868 HOFFMANN, W. Gen. Superintendent. *Deutschland einst und jetzt im Lichte
des Reiches Gottes.* Berlin.

SCHNEIDEWIN, G. *Der Bischof von Mainz und die drei Hessischen Super-
intendenten.* Eine Beleuchtung der Erwiderung der drei Superinten-
denten Prälat Dr. Zimmermann, Dr. Simon, Dr. Schmitt, auf die Schrift
des Bischofs von Mainz, "Die wahren Grundlagen des religiösen Friedens."
Mainz, Kirchheim. iv, 80 pp.

1868 (continued)

VON KETTELER, Wilhelm Emmanuel, Bischof von Mainz. *Die wahren Grundlagen des religiösen Friedens*. Eine Antwort auf die von Herrn Prälaten Dr. Zimmermann und der evangel. Geistlichkeit Hessens erhobene Anschuldigung wegen "Verunglimpfung des evangel. Glaubens." 1.-3. Aufl. Mainz, Kirchheim. viii, 87 pp.
(Cf. the entry *Wimmer* under 1855.)

ZIMMERMAN, SIMON, SCHMITT. *Erwiderung auf die Schrift des Herrn Bischofs in Mainz:* "Die wahren Grundlagen des religiösen Friedens." Darmstadt [Zernin]. iv, 76 pp.
2. verm. Aufl. *ibid.*, 1869, iv, 83 pp.

(*Anon.*) *Mariologien,* d.i. vierzig Betrachtungen oder Abhandlungen über das Glaubensgesetz von der Unbefleckten Empfängniss der allers. Jungfrau und Mutter Gottes Maria, auf Grund der dogmatischen Bulle des Papstes Pius IX. und nach verschiedenen Autoren für gebildete kath. Christen bearbeitet. Von einem katholischen Geistlichen. Landshut, Thomann'sche Buchh. iv, 268 pp.

1870 OTT. *Die Glorie der allerseligsten Jungfrau und gebenedeiten Gottesmutter Maria in ihrer unbefleckten Empfängniss*. Regensburg, Pustet.

RUTJES. "Kurzes belehrendes Wort über die Bedeutung und Geschichte des Dogmas der unbefleckten Empfängniss," in, *Leben, Wirken und Leiden des Papst-Königs Pius IX*. Oberhausen. IC p. 1097 ff.

UHLHORN, Gerhard. *Das römische Concil*. Vier Vorträge im Evangelischen Verein zu Hannover gehalten. Hannover. 77 pp.
(The IC is treated in the first *Vortrag*.)

VON SCHAEZLER, Constantin. "Die schönste Erlösersthat Jesu Christi, die unbefleckte Empfängniss seiner Mutter," in *Das Dogma von der Menschwerdung Gottes im Geiste des hl. Thomas dargestellt*. Freiburg, Herder, pp. 324-344.

1873 REINLEIN. *Zu Mariä Verkündigung*. Eine alt-katholische Festpredigt des Papstes Innocenz III. Deutsch mit einigen einleitenden Worten. Erlangen.

1874 BUCHMANN, J. "Der Immaculatismus und das Tridentiner Konzil," in *Vermischte Aufsätze,* Breslau, Fiedler. p. 94 ff.

REUSCH, F. H. *Bericht über die am 14., 15. und 16. September zu Bonn gehaltenen Unions-Conferenzen,* im Auftrage des Vorsitzenden Dr. v. Döllinger herausgegeben. . . . Bonn.
(Thesis X, the discussion of which is here reported, rejects the IC as contrary to the tradition of the first thirteen centuries.)

1876 FRIEDRICH, J. "Die unbefleckte Empfängniss Mariä durch den Georgi-Ritterorden in Bayern gegen Amort vertheidigt," in *Beiträge zur Kirchengeschichte des 18. Jahrhunderts,* aus dem handschriftlichen Nachlass des regul. Chorherrn Eusebius AMORT zusammengestellt, pp. 17-27. München.

MARTIN, Konrad, Bischof von Paderborn. *Irrthum und Wahrheit in den grossen Fragen der Gegenwart*. 1. und 2. Aufl. Mainz, Kirchheim. viii, 190 pp. IC p. 91 ff.

1878 MORGOTT, Franz. *Die Mariologie des hl. Thomas von Aquin*. Freiburg, Herder. 121 pp. IC pp. 67-94.

1879 LENZ, Ant. *Mariologie,* oder: die von der kathol. Kirche tradirte und in ihr aufbewahrte Lehre von der Mutter Gottes. Prag.

MARTIN, Konrad, Bischof von Paderborn. *Die Schönheiten des Herzens Mariä*. Mainz, Kirchheim. 152 pp.

[PREUSS, Eduard] *Zum Lobe der Unbefleckten Empfängnis der Allerseligsten Jungfrau*. Von Einem, der sie vormals gelästert hat [Cf. 1865, 1866]. Mit einem Begleitworte des hochwürdigsten Herrn Dr. Konrad MARTIN, Bischofs von Paderborn. Freiburg im Breisgau. viii, 227 pp.

1880 REUSCH, F. H. *Die deutschen Bischöfe und der Aberglaube.* Bonn.

ZARDETTI, Otto. *Die Unbefleckte Empfängniss Mariä und die Entdeckung des Mississippistromes in Nordamerica.* Ein kleiner Beitrag zum Cultus der *'Immaculata.'* Frankfurt.

1881 KURZ, Anton. *Mariologie,* oder Lehre der katholischen Kirche über Maria, die seligste Jungfrau. Regensburg, Manz. IC pp. 19-107.

1883 KÖRBER, Joh. *Maria im System der Heilsökonomie, auf thomistischer Basis dargestellt.* Regensburg, Manz. 223 pp.

MORGOTT, Franz. *Lehre von der Menschwerdung und Erlösung.* Christologie-Mariologie-Soteriologie. Eichstätt. Per modum manuscripti multi-plicatum. IC pp. 206-223.

1885 TSCHACKERT. *Ev. Polemik.* Gotha. IC pp. 118 ff.; 147 ff.

1886 GAYER, A. *Maria, Ihre Stellung im Reiche Jesu Christi.* Ein Beitrag zur Verehrung der Gottesmutter. . . . Regensburg [*et al.*]. Pustet. 456 pp.

SCHEEBEN, M. J. "Empfängniss, die unbefleckte, der seligsten Jungfrau Maria, Lehre und Fest," in *Wetzer und Welte's Kirchenlexikon* . . . zweite Auflage . . . begonnen von Joseph Cardinal HERGENRÖTHER, fortgesetzt von Dr. Franz KAULEN. . . Freiburg im Breisgau, Herder. IV (1886), col. 456-474.

1887 SCHEEBEN, Matthias Joseph. *Handbuch der katholischen Dogmatik.* 4 Bände, Freiburg-im-Breisgau, Herder. 1873-1903.

    (*Band III,* which treats of the IC pp. 527-558, appeared in three parts between 1882 and 1887. The whole was republished in 1933, and again in 1954 as *Band VI* of the *Gesammelte Schriften.* The Mariological treatise from *Band IV* was edited separately in 1936 by Dr. Carl FECKES, under the title, *Die bräutliche Gottesmutter.*)

1890 WÖRNHART, Leonard. *Maria, die wunderbare Mutter Gottes und der Menschen,* nach allen Gesichtspunkten dargelegt und mit sehr zahlreichen Stellen der Väter und der theologischen Schriftsteller begründet. Innsbruck, Rauch. viii, 447 pp.

1892 SCHNEIDER, Ceslaus Maria. *Die unbefleckte Empfängnis und die Erbsünde.* Erwiderung auf Többes: "Die Stellung des heil. Thomas von Aquin zu der unbefleckten Empfängnis der Gottesmutter." [Cf. the following entry.] Regensburg, Manz. 92 pp.

TÖBBE, Wilhelm. *Die Stellung des heil. Thomas von Aquin zu der unbefleckten Empfängnis der Gottesmutter.* Dogmengeschichtliche Abhandlung. Münster, Theissing. 104 pp.

1896 HITTMAIR, Rudolph. *Die Lehre von der unbefleckten Empfängnis an der Universität Salzburg.* Linz, Ebenhöch. vi, 239 pp.

JAMAR, C. H. T. *Maria, die Mutter Jesu.* Ein Lebensbild der allerseligsten Jungfrau und Gottesmutter auf Grund der heiligen Schrift, der Kirchenväter, der theologischen Schriftsteller. Uebersetzt [from the Latin] von Franz Prim. Trier, Paulinus. 510 pp.

1901 ALBERS, R. *Maria, die Mutter der Gnade,* oder, die drei Kronen und zwölf Ehrenvorzüge Mariä. Steyl, Missionsdruckerei. IC pp. 80-120.

1902 MÜLLER, A. B. *Alphons v. Liguori und der Madonnenfetischismus.* Halle,

1903 HANCK. "Maria," in *Realencyklopädie für protestantische Theologie und Kirche,* Leipzig, vol. XII, pp. 309-336.

POHLE, J. *Lehrbuch der Dogmatik,* Bd. II.

    4th ed., Paderborn, 1908.

SCHÜTZ, J. H. *Summa Mariana.* Allgemeines Handbuch der Marienverehrung für Priester, Theologie-Studierende und gebildete Laien. Herausgegeben unter Mitwirkung von Welt-und Ordenspriestern . . . 4 Bände Paderborn, Junfermann. 1903-1914.

    IC Bd. I, pp. 198 f., 324-326, 336-342.

1903 (continued)

ZÖCKLER. Maria, die Mutter des Herrn," in *Realencyklopädie für protestantische Theologie und Kirche.* Begründet von J. J. HERZOG. In dritter verbesserter und vermehrter Auflage . . . herausgegeben von D. Albert HAUCK. Band XII, pp. 309-336.
(Cf. entry *Steitz* under 1858.)

1904　(FIFTIETH ANNIVERSARY OF THE DEFINITION)

HATTENSCHWILLER, Josef, S.J. *Die Unbefleckte Empfängnis.* Münster, Alphonsusbuchhandlung. 368 pp.

STEMBERGER, Eduard. *Die Unbefleckte und ihre Verehrung in Tirol.* Marianische Vereinsbuchhandlung. 96 pp.

(*Anon.*) *Zur Geschichte der Immaculata-Tradition in der Mainzer Kirche.* Festgabe zur Konsekration und Intronisation S. bischöflichen Gnaden des hochwürdigsten H. H. Georgius Heinrich Kirstein. . . . Im Anhange: "Die Immaculata—Feier zu Rom unter Sixtus IV (1471-1484) . . ." Mainz, Kirchhein. 22 pp.

1905 HUNTEMANN, Ulricus, O.F.M. "Maria Immaculata in der Franciscaner Bibliographie. Vortrag gehalten . . . im marianischen Congress 3ten Dezember, 1904," in *L'Ordine dei Frati Minori al Congresso mariano Internazionale* . . . pp. 51-56. [Cf. Italian bibliography at 1905.]

KÖSTERS, Ludwig, S.J. *Maria, die unbefleckt Empfangene.* Zur Jubelfeier der fünfzigjährigen Erklärung des Dogmas. Geschichtlich-theologische Darstellung. Regensburg, Manz. viii, 274 pp.

KOTTMANN, Dominicus, O.F.M. "Die Verehrung der unbefleckten Empfängniss: Gründe, Schönheit, Vorzüge," in *L'Ordine dei Frati Minori al Congresso Mariano Internazionale* (*1904*) . . . , pp. 7-13. [Cf. Italian bibliography at 1905.]

SCHWEYKART, Alois Joseph, S. J. *Die Verehrung der Unbefleckten Empfängniss Mariä in der Geschichte der Kirche.* Zweiunddreissig Vorträge gehalten in der Universitätskirche zu Wien im Mai 1904. . . . Graz, Meser. vii, 259 pp.

1907 FRIEDRICH, Philipp. *Die Mariologie des hl. Augustinus.* Köln, Bachem. 279 pp. IC pp. 183-232.

1909 BEISSEL, Stephen. *Geschichte der Verehrung Marias in Deutschland während des Mittelalters.* Freiburg, Herder. 678 pp. IC *passim.*

1910 BEISSEL, Stephen. *Geschichte der Verehrung Marias im 16. und 17. Jahrhundert.* Freiburg, Herder. 517 pp. IC *passim.*

1911 NEWMAN, J. H., Kardinal. *Eine Apologie des Marienkultus.* Regensburg.
(Translation by H. Riesch of the *Letter* . . . of 1866. Another German translation had appeared in 1866.)

1912 BARTMANN, B. "Das Dogma von der Unbefleckten Empfängniss," in: *Sechster Internationaler Marianischer Kongress in Trier vom. 3. bis 6. August 1912,* Zweiter Teil, I. Abteilung: "Die deutsche Referate."

1913 ALBRECHT. *Die Gottesmutter.* Freiburg im Breisgau.
(*Anon.*) *Der Glaubenschatz von der Unbeflecten Empfängniss der All. J. M. in den Gebeten der Kirche.* Köln, Kühlen. 178 pp.

1917 GUTBERLET, Dr. Konstantin. *Die Gottesmutter.* Regensburg, Manz. 124 pp. IC pp. 54-66.

HÄNSLER, Basilius. *Die Marienlehre des hl. Bernhard.* Regensburg, Manz. 138 pp.

1918 BARTMANN, Bernhard. *Christus ein Gegner des Marienkultus?* Freiburg-im-Breisgau.

1922 BARTMANN, Bernhard. *Maria im lichte des Glaubens und der Frömmigkeit.* Paderborn, Bonifacius. 406 pp.
3rd and 4th editions, 1925: IC pp. 26-36.

1925 VERMEERSCH, A., S.J. *Die Muttergottesfeste,* deutsch [from the 3rd. French edition] von Th. Metzler. Innsbruck, Marianischer Verlag. 470 pp. IC pp. 54-67; 311-409.

VON NEUKIRCH, Mich., O.Cap. *Kleine theologisch-praktische Mariologie.* Leipzig, "Vier Quellen," 131 pp.

1926 BRUDERS, Heinrich, S.J. *Die Theologie des Rheinlands von 925 bis 1925.* Dogmengeschichtliche Entwicklungsmomente zur Definition der Immakulata und der Unfehlbarkeit . . . Düsseldorf, Schwann. xv, 150 pp. IC pp. 13-18; 37.

1928 DREWS, Arthur. *Die Marienmythe.* Jena, Diederichs. 190 pp. IC pp. 161-181.

1930 GRISAR, H., S.J. *Marienblüten.* Systematische Marienlehre, vorzüglich aus dem grossen Marienwerk des Kirchenlehrers Petrus Canisius, mit Beigaben von ausgewählten Väterstellen. Innsbruck, Rauch. 7, 108 pp. IC pp. 33-50.

1932 GRATRY, A. *Der Monat Mariä.* Translated from the French. (For second edition, see 1934.)

1933 DERCKX, H. *Die Muttergottes, die Erfüllung des Weibes der Uroffenbarung.* (Übers. durch G. von Poppel.] Paderborn, Bonifacius. 202 pp.

1934 BINNEBESEL, Bruno. *Die Stellung der Theologen des Dominikanerordens zur Frage nach der Unbefleckten Empfängis Marias bis zum Konzil von Basel.* Dissertation zur Erlangung der theologischen Doktorwürde der Hochwürdigen Katholisch-theologischen Facultät der Schlesischen Friedrich-Wilhelms-Universität zu Breslau vorgelegt. . . . Kallmünz bei Regensburg, Lassleben. xvii, 86 pp.

DREWNIAK, F., O.S.B. *Die Mariologische Deutung von Gen. 3,15 in der Väterzeit.* Breslau, Nischkowsky. x, 100 pp.

GRATRY, A. *Die unbefleckte Empfängnis.* Betrachtrungen. 2. Aufl. (Re-edition of the work published in 1932.)

1936 SCHEEBEN, Matthias Josef. *Die bräutliche Gottesmutter.* Aus dem *Handbuch der* Dogmatik [vol. III, 1887] herausgegeben und für weitere Kreise bearbeitet von Carl FECKES. Freiburg i. Br., Herder. IC p. 110-126. Republished [1951] at Essen by Fredebeul & Koenen.

——. *Maria, Schutzherrin der Kirche.* Paderborn, Schöningh. 104 pp. (Re-edition, by J. SCHMITZ, of articles published at the time of the Vatican Council.)

1937 FECKLES, Carl. *Das Mysterium der Göttlichen Mutterschaft.* Ein dogmatisches Marienbild. Paderborn, Schöningh. IC pp. 88-110.

1938 COHAUSZ, Otto, S.J. *Maria in ihrer Uridee und Wirklichkeit, die zweite Eva.* Steffen, Limburg. 240 pp.

HAMMERSBERGER, Ludwig. *Die Mariologie der Ephremischen Schriften.* Eine dogmengeschichtliche Untersuchung. Innsbruck, Tyrolia. IC p. 57-71.

1940 TYCIAK, Julius. *Mariengeheimnisse.* Regensburg, Pustet. 124 pp. IC pp. 69-83. (Cf. reprint of 1950.)

1947 DILLERSBERGER, Josef. *Die Stellung Marias in der Heilsordnung nach* "Mystici Corporis" *Pius' XII, Salzburg, Müller.* 257 pp. IC pp. 119-123.

FECKES, C. "Die Gnadenausstattung Mariens," and "Die Anfangsgnade," chapters I and II respectively of *Maria in der Glaubenswissenschaft,* volume II (1947) of *Katholische Marienkunde,* edited by Paul STRAETER, S.J., Paderborn, Schoeningh, 1947-1951. Second edition, 1952.

KOESTER, Heinrich Maria, S.A.C. *Die Magd des Herrn.* Theologische Versuche und Ueberlegungen. Limburg, Lahn-Verlag, xxxi, 506 pp. 2. Aufl., 1954.

1948 Sors, Vladimir. *Das debitum der Erbsünde in der Gottesgebärerin bei Johannes Eusebius Nieremberg, S.J.* (Dissert. Pont. Univ. Greg.) Roma.
1950 Tyciak, Julius. *Magd und Königin. Gedanken zur Teilnahme Mariens am Heilswerk Christi.* Freiburg, Herder. 2. Aufl. 124 pp.
    (= an unaltered reprint of the work published in 1940.)
1952 Mitterer, Albert. *Dogma und Biologie der heiligen Familie nach dem Weltbild des hl. Thomas von Aquin und dem der Gegenwart.* Wien, Herder. IC pp. 31-52.
    Schimmelpfennig, Reintraud. *Die Geschichte der Marienverehrung im deutschen Protestantismus.* Paderborn, Schöningh. 164 pp. IC *passim.*
1953 Newman, John Henry, Kardinal. *Maria im Heilsplan.* Eingeleitet und übertragen von Birgitta zu Münster, O.S.B. (*Zeugen des Wortes.*) Freiburg, Herder. [1953]. 83 pp.
    (Translated from the seventeenth and eighteenth *Discourses to Mixed Congregations,* 1849)
1954 Bossuet, Jacques Bénigne [1627-1704]. *Predigten zum Fest der Immakulata.* Uebertragen [from the French] von Joseph Günster. (*Kleine Marianische Bücherei,* 3.) Paderborn, Schöningh [1954]. 124 pp.
    Eadmerus, O.S.B. *Die Empfängnis der seligen Jungfrau.* Erstmalig übertragen von Carl Feckes. (*Kleine marianische Bücherei;* die Mutter Jesu im Lichte der Überlieferung, 1) Paderborn. Schöningh. [1954]
    Ebner, Friedrich. *Die Unbefleckte Empfängnis Mariens nach der Lehre des Gabriel Biel.* (Excerpta ex dissertatione ad lauream in facultate theologica Pont. Univ. Greg.) Bozen, Athesia. 36 pp.
    Mühle, Erika Maria. *Mutter des Herrn.* Leben Mariä aus den Werken der Väter, der Kirchenschriftsteller und Meister der Predigt. Mödling bei Wien, St. Gabriel. IC pp. 45-73.
    Scheeben, Matthias Joseph. *Immakulata und päpstliche Unfehlbarkeit.* Sedes Sapientiae und Cathedra Sapientiae. Neu hrsg. von Josef Schmitz. (*Kleine marianische Bücherei;* Die Mutter Jesu im Lichte der Überlieferung, Heft 3.) Paderborn, Schöningh [1954]. 94 pp.
    (Originally published in *Periodische Blätter,* 1870, under the title: "Die theologische und praktische Bedeutung des Dogmas von der Unfehlbarkeit des Papstes in seiner Beziehung auf unsere Zeit.")
    (*Anon.*) *Maria in Glaube und Frömmigkeit.* Vorträge des Marianischen Kongresses der Diozese Rottenburg in Stuttgart, 6-8 Juli, 1954. Rottenburg, Bischöfl. Seelsorgeamt. 164 pp.
1955 Schmaus, Michael. *Katholische Dogmatik.* Bd. V. *Mariologie.* München, Hueber. iv, 416 pp.
    (*Anon.*) *Virgo Immaculata,* volumes III, IV, VI. (See Appendix below, p. 611 ff.)
1956 Rahner, Karl. *Maria, Mutter des Herrn.* Theologische Betrachtungen. 2. Auflage. Freiburg im Breisgau, Herder. IC pp. 39-50.
    (*Anon.*) *Virgo Immaculata,* volume II. (See Appendix below, p. 611 ff.)
1957 (*Anon.*) *Virgo Immaculata,* volumes IX, X, XIII, XIV. (See Appendix below, p. 611 ff.)

DATE OF PUBLICATION UNKNOWN
Huber. *Der Jesuitenorden.* IC pp. 315-331.

ITALIAN[1]

1830   (MIRACULOUS MEDAL APPARITION TO SISTER CATHERINE LABOURÉ, PARIS, NOVEMBER 17; FIRST MEDALS STRUCK, JUNE 30, 1832)

1832 OCCHIUZZI, Vito. Discorsi teologici scritturali e morali sull'Immacolato Concepimento di Maria. Napoli.

1834 CINI, Clementino, Minore Osservante. *Discorsi in preparazione alla festa dell'Immacolata Concezione di Maria Santissima.* Roma, Salviucci. vi, 229 pp.
> Republished: Napoli, 1847.

1835 *(Anon.) Novena in onore della Immacolata Concezione di Maria Vergine.* Roma, Ajani. 45 pp.

1836 [ALADEL] *Ragguaglio storico sopra l'origine e gli effetti della Medaglia miracolosa,* scritto da un prete di S. Lazzaro in francese, e tradotto da un altro della medesima Congregazione. Napoli.

> PANINI, Francesco da Gaëtano. *Notizia storica sopra l'origine e gli effetti della nuova Medaglia coniata in onore dell'Imm. Conc. della SS. Vergine.* Modena.

> SPINA, Stefano. *Le glorie del primo istante del Concepimento di Maria.* 2 vol. Palermo.

> *(Anon.) Notizia storica della Medaglia coniata in onore dell'Immac. Conc.* Cremona.

> *(Anon.) Notizie storiche del miracoloso simolacro della salve.* Alexandria.

> *(Anon.) Novena in onore dell'Immac. Conc. di Maria, con un breve racconto sull'origine della Medaglia miracolosa.* Palermo.

> *(Anon.) Le nuove glorie di Maria SS. nella sua Immacolata Concezione.* Notizia tratta da un opuscolo francese e volgarizzata. Aggiuntavi la novena della B. V. Immacolata Concetta. Udine.

>> (Note: Further literature on the Miraculous Medal will not be indicated, but those listed above are noted as being the earliest books on this subject in Italian, so far as we have been able to determine.

1839 SPADA, Mariano, O. P. *Esame critico sulla dottrina dell'Angelico Dottore S. Tommaso di Aquino circa il peccato originale relativamente alla Beatissima Vergine Maria.* Napoli, Giordano. 85 pp.
> Republished, 1848 in SPADA-SALZANO, *La Dottrina dell'Angelico* . . . pp. 1-85, and in *Pareri,* vol. V, pp. 581-660.
> Seconda edizione, riveduta dall'autore, Roma, 1855.

1842 *(Anon.)* "Concezione Immacolata della Beata Vergine Maria," in *Dizionario di erudizione storico-ecclesiastica da S. Pietro sino ai nostri giorni.* . . . Compilazione del Cavaliere Gaetano Moroni Romano, Venezia Emiliana, vol. XV, pp. 140-150.

---

1. Besides the general sources mentioned above, this section of the bibliography is based chiefly on a list compiled at the library of the Academia Mariana and the College of St. Alexius at Rome, by Fathers Martin Wojciechowski and John Lisowski, to whom we are deeply grateful. We have also made considerable use of PAGLIAINI, *Catalogo generale della libreria italiana dall'anno 1847 a tutto il 1899,* Indice per materie, Milano 1915 (s.v. "Maria Vergine"), and his *Catalogo generale della libreria italiana dall'anno 1900 a tutto il 1920,* Indice per materie, Milano 1938 (s.v. "Maria Vergine"). We are also greatly indebted to Father Joseph P. Browne, C.S.C., for verifying a considerable number of references in various Roman libraries, and to Mrs. Nicoletta Hary for helping with the proof-reading.

1843 LAMBRUSCHINI, Luigi, card. *Sull'Immacolato Concepimento di Maria.* Dissertazione polemica. Roma, Propaganda. 124 pp.
> Ed. prima veneta, riv. Venezia, Emiliana, 1844. Reprinted in *Pareri*, vol. V, pp. 123-179.

PERRONE, J. *Sunto Analitico della dissertazione polemica di sua Emza. Ema. il Sig. Card. Lambruschini, Vescovo di Sabina, Bibliotecario di S. Chiesa, ec. ec. sull'Immacolato Concepimento di Maria.* Roma. 30 pp.

1844 BIGONI, Angelo. O.F.M. *In Lode di Maria SS. senza macchia concetta.* Dissertazione panegirica. Roma.
> 2nd ed., Venezia, 1849. Reprinted in *Pareri*, vol. IX, App. II, p. 285-386.

1846 SALZANO, Thomas, O.P. "Sull'Immacolato Concepimento di Maria SS.," in *Corso di Storia Eccles.*, Napoli, t. III, p. 518 ff.

1848   (COMMITTEE APPOINTED BY POPE PIUS IX TO EXAMINE THE ADVISABILITY OF A DEFINITION, JUNE 1)

ANIVITTI, Vincenzo. *De' vantaggi che il culto dell'Immacolato Concepimento ha recato alla scienza, alla letteratura, all'arte e alla civiltà.* . . . Roma, Puccinelli. 23 pp.

BIANCHERI, Pietro, della Congregazione della Missione. *Voto in forma di dissertazione sulla definizione dogmatica dell'Immacolato Concepimento della B.V.M.* Tivoli.
> Reprinted in *Pareri*, vol. V, pp. 181-579.

SPADA, Mariano, O.P. e SALZANO, Tommaso, O.P. *La Dottrina del'Angelico Dottore S. Tommaso di Aquino e la Sentenza del sacro Ordine de' Predicatori a favore dell'Immacolata Concezione della Gran Madre di Dio Maria SS.* . . . da servire di supplemento alla *Dissertazione polemica* ec. di S.E.R. Il Sig. Cardinale Lambruschini ec. e alla *Disquisizione teologica sul dogmatico decreto* ec. del P. Giovanni Perrone. [s.l.] xi, 306 pp.

1849   (ENCYCLICAL LETTER *Ubi primum* OF POPE PIUS IX, FEBRUARY 2)

CAVALIERI, Pietro. *Concordia della ragione con alcune importantissime verità cattoliche ossia propagazione del peccato originale e prova diretta dell'Immacolato Concepimento della Vergine SS.* . . . Bologna, Guidi all'Ancora. 320 pp.
> (Condemned by the S. Congregation of the Index, Dec. 19, 1849.)

[*Anon, O.P.*] *Della Immacolata Concezione della B. Vergine.* Pareri teologici inediti del Card. PALLAVICINO della Comp. di Gesù, e del Card. GOTTI dell Ord. de'Pred. Proëmiati e dati in luce per un Domenicano. Roma [s.e.].

(*Anon.*) *Dissertazione di un prete della Congregazione dell'Oratorio di Venezia, nella quale ritenutosi che Maria SS. sia stata preservata dell'atto d'incorrere nella colpa d'origine nel primo istante della infusione dell'anima sua nel suo corpo, studiasi di mostrare che sia stata preservata altresì da ogni debito di incontrarla.* Venezia, Tip. Armenad. S. Laggaro.
> Reprinted in *Pareri*, vol. V, pp. 663-682.

(*Anon.*) *Voto umilissimo della Trevigiana diocesi, innalzato dal suo vescovo, ad illustrazione e difesa del privilegio specialissimo di un Immacolato Concepimento, conceduto all'eccelsa Nostra Signora.* . . . Treviso, Andreola.
> Reprinted in *Pareri*, vol. V, pp. 99-122.

1850 FONDORA, Cesare. *Cenni sull'Immacolata Concezione di Maria Vergine Madre di Dio e Regina dell'Universo, compilati dall'avv. Cesare Fondora.* Lucca, Torcigliani.
Reprinted in *Pareri,* vol. V, pp. 683-720.

MARTORELLI, Gaetano. *Dissertazione sull'opportunità del tempo di dichiarar dogma di fè l'Immacolato Concepimento di Maria SS.* Recanati, Morici.
Reprinted in *Pareri,* vol. V, pp. 721-733.

1851 BIANCHERI, P. *Esame critico di un opusculo del P.F.G.D.B.B.C. Domenicano* [cf. 1849, Anon, O.P.], editore di due pareri teologici sulla Concezione Immacolata di Maria attributi al Pallavicino ed al Gotti. Velletri, Cappallacci.

NURRA, Emmanuele Marongio, [Archbishop of Cagliari in Sardinia]. *Breve esposizione della mente del Dottore Angelico intorno all'Immacolato Concepimento della B. V. Maria.* Loreto.

(*Anon.*) *Pareri dell'episcopato cattolico* . . . , volumes I-V.
(See appendix below, p. 606 ff.)

(*Anon.*) *Ragionamento, dedicato all'Immacolata Concezione di Maria Vergine.* Torino.
Reprinted in *Pareri,* vol. V, pp. 735-767.

1852 BAGLIONE, Carlo, C.O. *Dilucidazione cronologica dell'Immacolata Concezione di Maria Santissima sempre Vergine distinta in tre parti.* . . . Si aggiungono alcuni miracoli, apparizioni e rivelazioni. Trattato inedito. . . . Firenze, Birindelli. xii, 435 pp.

[CADOLINI, Ignazio, Card. Arciv. di Ferrara, † 1850]. *Parere che in ossequio alla enciclica del 2 Febbraio 1849 intorno all'Immacolato Concepimento di Maria SS., umilia al Santo Padre il Card. Arciv. di Ferrara.* Ferrara, Bresciani. [1852] 51 pp.

COSTA, Giuseppe, Minor. *Breve Narrazione degli omaggi che si praticano dai Siciliani all'Immacolato Concepimento della SS. Vergine Maria, loro principale Patrona.* Palermo.

DA REGNANO, Antonio, M. O. *Novenario e panegirico della Immacolata Concezione di Maria Vergine.* Terza ed. Prato.

GUAL, Pedro, O.F.M. *Della definibilità della Concezione Immacolata di Maria.* Dissertazione teologica . . . volgarizzamento dallo spagnuolo del P. Marcellino da Civezza M. O. Roma, Puccinelli. 151 pp.
Republished in 1856 [s.l., s.e.] and in *Pareri,* vol. VIII, pp. 1-130.

PACIFICO, Agostino di Maria Addolorata, O.F.M. *Della origine, progressi e stato presente del culto e festa dell'Immacolatissimo e santissimo Concepimento della grande genitrice di Dio Maria, e della sua dogmatica definizione.* Ricerche storico-cronologico-critiche. Napoli, Tizzano. xxxii, 901 pp.

(*Anon.*) *Pareri dell'episcopato cattolico* . . . , volumes VI-IX. (See Appendix below, p. 606 ff.)

1853 BRUNI, Mons. Francesco, Vescovo di Ugento. *Breve risposta alle principali obiezioni che si oppongono alla definizione dogmatica del mistero dell'Immacolata Concezione di Maria Santissima.* Roma.

PAGANO, Leopoldo. *Dell'Immacolato Concepimento di Maria Santissima o della sua originaria santità.* Lettera la quale contiene il rendiconto delle opere stampate e dei materiali sinora raccolti, umiliata alla Santità di Pio IX dal canonico Leopoldo Pagano . . . [s.l., s.e.] 100 pp.

(*Anon.*) [= BALLERINI, Antonio, S.J.?] *Breve espositione degli atti della commissione speciale, stabilita dalla Santità di N.S. sull'argomento dell'Immacolata Concezione di Maria Santissima.* Rome, Pontificale. 72 pp.

1853 (continued)

(*Anon.*) *Poliantea cattolica, apologetica, morale ed oratoria.* Milano, Pirotta. 365 pp.

(Contains works on the IC by Luigi SPERONI, Luigi LAMBRUSCHINI, Giacomo Benigno BOSSUET, Nicola S. BERGIER. Republished in 1854, *ibid.*, Redaelli, 254 pp. Cf. 1858: *Biografia.*)

1854 (DEFINITION OF THE IMMACULATE CONCEPTION AS A DOGMA OF FAITH BY POPE PIUS IX, DECEMBER 8)

COSTA, Fr. *Riflessioni in proposito della definizione dommatica sull'Immacolato Concepimento della SS. Vergine.* Roma.

DE MATTHIAS, Michele. *Sulla tradizione asiatica in onore dell'Immacolata.* Lucca.

(Dissertation presented to the *Academia Immaculatae Romana* in 1848.)

LUCIANI, Filippo Maria, O.S.B. *Sull'Immacolato Concepimento di Maria Vergine dimostrato dall'infallibile dogma della divina sua maternità.* . . . Macerata, Mancini. 111 pp.

PIANORI DI BRISIGHELLA, Angelo, O.F.M. *Fondamenti ortodossi per la definibilità dell'Immacolato Concepimento di Maria Santissima.* Cesena, Biasini. 252 pp.

[ROSSI, Filippo, O.M.Conv.] *L'Immacolata Concezione di Maria ed i Francescani Minori Conventuali dal 1219 al 1854.* Cenni vari per un sacerdote umbro. Roma, Salviucci. 152 pp.

SPERONI, Luigi, O.M.I. *Sull'Immacolata Concezione della SS. Vergine Maria.* Istruzione. Milano, Redaelli. 147 pp.

Reprinted in *Poliantea* . . . . (Cf. 1853)

(*Anon.*) *Breve relazione di quanto si è operato dalla Santità di nostro Signore Pio Papa IX, e de'sentimenti manifestati dall'Episcopato e dai consultori, sull'argomento dell'Immacolata Concezione di Maria Santissima.* Roma.

(*Anon.*) *L'Immacolata Concezione di Maria.* Roma, Salviucci.

(*Anon.*) *Lettera di un sacerdote cattolico ai Vescovi della Chiesa di Dio* per rappresentar loro che la sentenza della Immacolata Concezione della B.V.M. non può essere definita dottrina di fede cattolica. Torino.

(Abridgement of the anonymous *Proposta* . . . , *infra.*)

(*Anon.*) *Pareri dell'episcopato cattolico* . . . , volume X and XI. (See Appendix below, p. 606 ff.)

(*Anon.* = BERLETTI?) *Proposta di alcune difficoltà che si oppongono alla definizione dogmatica della Immacolata Concezione.* Torino, Progresso. 64 pp.

(*Anon.*) *Raccolta di prose e versi in onore dell'Immacolata Concezione di Maria Vergine.* Roma.

(Includes works by PASSAGLIA, PERRONE, ANIVITTI, *et al.*) ·

1855 BIANCHI, Pietro. *Lettera a A. Donetti.* Milano.

DI GIOVANNI, Vinc. *Sulla dogmatica dichiarazione dello Immacolato Concepimento di Maria*: discorso. Palermo, Carini.

DONETTI, Atanasio. *Il Dogma dell'8 Dicembre 1854.* Lettere ai veri amatori della religione. Bellinzona.

GUÉRANGER, Prosper, O.S.B. *Sullo Immacolato Concepimento di Maria Vergine.* Memoria . . . aggiuntavi una orazione panegirica dell'abate Agostino Antonio GRUBISSICH. Milano, Wilmant. 154 pp.

IMPELLIZZERI, Santi. *Discorso sulla definizione dogmatica dell'Immacolata Concezione di Maria Vergine.* Palermo, Nocero.

MAINI, Luigi. *Del culto all'Immac. Conc. di Maria nella città di Carpi.* Ricordi con iscrizioni. Carpi.

1855 (continued)

MAJOCCHI, Rod. *L'Università di Pavia ed il dogma dell'Immacolata*: documento. Milano, Ghezzi. 12 pp.

MONICO, Jacopo, Card. Patriarca di Venezia. *Risposta . . . della Enciclica del 2 Febb. 1849 del S.P., Pio IX, intorno alla dogmatica definizione dell'Immac. Conc. di Maria.* Venezia.

NARBONE, Alessio, S.J. *Mistero e Decreto dell'Immacolato Concepimento della Madre di Dio, solennizzati nella reale Cappella Palatina.* Ragionamento storico. Palermo, Lao.

PERRONE. *Discorso recitato in Roma all'Accademia della SS. Concezione.* Reprinted in *Studi teologici spettanti al Cristianesimo e al Protestantesimo*, Milano, 1858, vol. II, p. 267 ff.

TIPALDI, Giuseppe. *La verità del Concepimento Immacolato di Maria SS.* Ragionamento.

VENANZIO DA CELANO, Ministro generale dell'Ordine de' Minori. *Dissertazione sul domma del Concepimento Immacolato della Beatissima Vergine Maria* corredata di note. Recitata . . . nell'Accademia de' Quiriti nella tornata solenne del 29 dicembre 1854. Con l'allocuzione della Santità di N.S. Pio Papa IX nel concistoro segreto del 1. dicembre 1854 e la Bolla dommatica. Roma, Tiberina. 92 pp.

(*Anon.*) *Istruzione sull'Immacolato Concepimento di Maria SS. e sulla dommatica definizione di esso.* Pistoia.

(*Anon.*) *La questione dell'Immac. Concezione della B. Vergine Maria trattata e decisa da S. Bernardo, S. Tomasso, e S. Bonaventura.* Con note ed aggiunte di un sacerdote cattolico. Torino.

1856 ALIMONDA, Gaetano, Cardinale. *Il dogma dell'Immacolata.* Ragionamenti . . . Genova, Schenone. xxv, 450 pp.
    32 ediz., Genova, T. D. Gioventù, 1880. 42 ediz., Torino, 1886.

GAUDE, Francesco, Cardinale. *Sull'Immacolato Concepimento della Madre di Dio*, sulla dogmatica sua definizione, in rapporto specialmente alla scuola tomistica, ed all'istituto dei RR. PP. Predicatori. Dissertazione . . . trad. dal prof. Salv. Cumbo [from the Latin]. Roma, Saenze. 141 pp.

GUALCO, Domenico. *La dommatica definizione dell'Immacolato Concepimento della B.M.V.* Apologetico. 2 vols. Genova, Fassi-Como. 1855-1856.

MAZZOTA DI ANTONINO, Gian Domenico. *L'Immacolato Concepimento, Pio IX, ed il cattolicismo.* Con 31 sermoni del'Immacolata. Cuererra, Napoli. 345 pp.

NICOLAS, A. *La Vergine Maria e i disegni divini.* Nuovi studî filosofici sul cristianesimo. 2 vol. Milano, Guglielmi e Volpato. 419 pp.
    (Translated from the French.)

PARODI, Luigi, S.J. *La fede e la divozione a Maria sempre Immacolata dichiarata e proposta coi sentimenti e colle parole de' SS. Padri.* . . . Roma, Civilta Cattolica. 318 pp.

SAGRINI, Tiberio. *Discorso sul'dogma dell'Immacolato Concepimento di Maria.* Venezia, Gaspari. 22 pp.

(*Anon.*) *La verità e la bugia*, ossia la definizione dell'Immacolata e il libro del prete Atanasio Donetti. Roma, Civiltà cattolica. 132 pp.

1857 CARPANETTI, Giuseppe. *Conferenze pacifiche tra Don Probo e Don Sincero per la soluzione di alcune difficoltà intorno al Dogma dell'Immacolata Concezione* . . . Pavia, Fusi.
    (Reply to the anonymous *Proposta* of 1854.)

DUQUESNE. *Le grandezze di Maria.* Opera nuovamente tradotta da un sacerdote Milanese. Cremona.
    (Translated from the French. The original appeared in 1791 and was republished in 1820 and frequently thereafter.

1857 (continued)

MALOU, Giov. Battista, vesc. di Bruges. *L'Immacolata Concezione della Beata Vergine Maria considerata come dogma di fede.* Torino, Marietti. xix, 376 pp.
(Translated from the French.)

NICOLAS, A. *La Vergine Maria secondo il Vangelo.* Nuovi studî filosofici sul cristianesimo. 2 vol. Milano, Turati.
(Translated from the French.)

RENZONI, Gino. Ma. *Le glorie di Maria SS. nel solenne decreto dell'immortale Pio IX intorno all'Immacolato suo Concepimento.* Rieti, Trinchi.

1858   (APPARITIONS OF MARY IMMACULATE TO BERNADETTE SOUBIROUS, LOURDES, FEBRUARY 11 - JULY 16)

[AQUARONI, L., GRIGNANI, JOS., PARONA, JOS., TENCA, A.] *La Prova di fatto che il Dogma dell'Immacolata non può essere difeso, e l'innocenza dei preti scomunicati di Pavia provata dai loro avversarii.* Torino.

(*Anon.*) *Biografia-Polemica-Conferenze.* Milano.
(Treatises on the IC by SPERONI, LAMBRUSCHINI, BOSSUET, BERGIER, PIUS IX et al. Cf. 1853, *Anon, Poliantea.* . . .)

1860 MASTROIANNI, Domenico, O.P. *Lettera critica teologica conciliante la dottrina di San Tommaso (III, 27, 2) con la verità dell'Immacolato Concepimento della Santissima Vergine.* Reggio.

(*Anon.*) *Compendio di controversie tra la Parola di Dio et la Teologia Romana, ad uso dei Christiani Evangelici.* Torino. IC, art. 23 ff.

1862 BURONI, G. *Discorso per la festa della Immacolata Concezione di Maria sopra lo sviluppo de' dogmi nella Chiesa Cattolica.* Torino.

1863 BASSO, Ant. *Il mistero dell'Immacolato Concepimento di Maria SS.* Nuova ediz. Siena, Baroni. 32 pp.

1864 ANTONELLI, Giovanni. *Un pensiero filiale sulla Concezione Immacolata di Maria V. Madre di Dio,* rispettosamente offerto al Sommo Pontefice Pio IX, in argomento di devozione particolare e di perfetta adesione all S. Sede. Firenze.

1865 GALEOTTI, Melchiorre. *Sull'Immacolato Concepimento di Maria Vergine: Discorso.* Palermo, Amenta. 102 pp.

GAUDE, Francesco. *Sullo Immacolato Concepimento della Madre di Dio.* . . . Roma, Tip. d. Scienze. 141 pp.

PAPA, Gennaro. *Breve istoria del culto di Maria SS. nella città di Napoli.* Napoli.

ROUARD DE CARD, Pie Marie, O.P. *L'Ordine dei frati Predicatori e l'Immacolato Concepimento della Santissima Vergine.* Lettera indirizzata a Mons. Malou, Vescovo di Bruges . . . Prima traduzione italiana del R.P. Vincenzo Giuseppe Lombardo. . . . Noto, Norcia e Morello. x, 96 pp.

(*Anon.*) *La Vergine Maria della Bibbia, e la Vergine Maria della Chiesa Romana.* Firenze.

1867 FOLGORI, Ferd. *Dignità, santità e gloria di Maria Vergine in sè stessa:* considerazioni. 5 vol. Napoli, Fibreno. cxci, 1637 pp.

MANSELLA, Giuseppe. *Il domma dell'Immacolata Concezione della Beata Vergine Maria,* ossia storia e prove di questo domma di fede. . . . 3 vol. Roma, Salviucci, 1866-1867.

1868 TEDESCHI, Fedele. *La Vergine Immacolata e Pio IX.* Catania.

1869 DA NAPOLI, Bernardo. *Il Concepimento di Maria.* Napoli.

ROZZI. *Efeso e Roma,* ovvero il trionfo di Maria Vergine. Bologna.

1870 TRIPEPI, Luigi. *I papi e la Vergine*: Studî. Da S. Pietro a S. Celestino I. Torino (Marietti) & Roma (Monald). 3 vol. 1869-1870.

ZINELLI, Federico Maria. *Lettera pastorale al clero e popolo per la festa dell'Immacolata*. Treviso, Priuli.

1872 COLINI, Ludovico da Castelplanio, O.F.M. *Maria nel consiglio dell'Eterno*, ovvero La Vergine predestinata alla missione medesima con Gesù Cristo. 4 vol. 1872 ff. IC vol. I, pp. 165-200.

Seconda ediz., Napoli, Rondinello & Loffredo, 1904. Republished in 1942, Milano, "Vita e Pensiero."

(*Anon.*) *L'Immacolato Concepimento di Maria SS. dimostrato dalla tradizione costante nella Chiesa cattolica*: Cenni. Bologna.

1872 PAROCCHI, L. M., Vescovo di Pavia. *Omilie ed Orazioni* edite ed inedite, dette dall'8 Dicembre 1871 a tutto il 1872. Pavia. IC p. 383 ff.

1873 PETITALOT, J. B. *La Vergine Madre e la teologia*. Versione [from the French] del teologo Oglietti. 2 vol. Torino, Giuseppi.

1874 ANIVITTI, Vinc. *Opuscoli vari sull'Immacolato Concepimento di Maria Vergine*, raccolti in un solo volume, ne' vicennali del dogma. Roma.

GRIGNANI, Giuseppe. *Risposta all'Orazione di Mgr. Lucido Parocchi Vescovo di Pavia*, detta il giorno 8 Dicembre 1872 e publicata nel 1873 sul' l'Immac. Conc. di Maria; ossia Ripetizione della *Protesta* colla sua giustificazione contro il nuovo e falso dogma dell'Imm. Conc. di Maria, e *Protesta* contro l'altro nuovo e falso dogma del'infallibilità del Papa quando parla dalla Cattedra; che il sacerdote *Giuseppe Grignani*, uno dei preti scomunicati, pubblica anche a nome di altri fedeli cattolici dell'uno e dell'altro scsso. Pavia.

MARIGLIANO, Luigi. *San Tommaso, l'Immacolato Concepimento e l'infallibilità pontificia*.

1875 GIAMBELLI, Siro. *Il mistero della Incarnazione nei suoi rapporti coll'Immacolata Concezione*. Pavia, Fusi.

1876 GIGLI, Andrea. *Magnetismo animale e spiritismo. Matrimonio cristiano e dogma dell'Immacolato Concepimento*. Napoli, Morano.

TRIPEPI. "Il Romano Pontifice glorificatore dell'Immacolato Concepimento di Maria e le speranze delle scienze e delle lettere a'giorni nostri," in *Memorie ed Apologie*, o Scritti religiosi e scientifici intorno ai Sommi Pontefici, Roma. P. 353 ff.

(Reprinted from *Il Papato, pubblicazione di Scienza cattolica*, Roma, 1876.)

1877 LIBERATORE, M., S.I. "Dell'Immacolata Concezione di Maria; Art. I: Congruenza religiosa e civile della definizione dommatica dell'Immacolato Concepimento della B. V. Maria; Art. 2: Definizione dommatica dell'Immacolata Concezione di Maria SS.," in *Spicelegio*, vol. I. Parte Religiosa, pp. 5 ff., Napoli.

MAGNASCO, Salv. *l'Immacolata: trattenimento accademico*. Genova, Arciv. 64 pp.

MORGERA, Giuseppe. *L'Alba ed il meriggio della redenzione*, ossia lo Immacolato Concepimento di Maria Vergine. S. Agnelli.

2a ediz., Napoli, Accattoncelli. 342 pp.

RODINÒ, Luigi. *L'Immacolata: trattenimento accademico*. Genova, Arciv.

1879   (TWENTY-FIFTH ANNIVERSARY OF THE DEFINITION)

ALIMONDA, Gaet. *L'Immacolata e i zoologi fanatici*: prolusione. Roma, Frat. Monaldi.

2a ediz. Roma, Sociale, 1881. 20 pp.

1879 (continued)

Nazari di Calabiana, L., Arcivesc. di Milano. *Lettera pastorale alla diocesi di Milano pel XXV. anniversario della definizione dommatica dell'Immac. Conc. di Maria SS.* Milano.

Riboldi, Vesc. di Pavia. *Lettera pastorale per il 25. anno della definizione della Imm. Conc. di Maria SS.* Pavia.

[Scalabrini, Giovanni Battista]. *Lettera pastorale in occasione del primo giubileo della dogm. defin. dell'Imm. Conc. di Maria SS.* Piacenza.

Vera, Vinc. *Le glorie di Maria SS. celebrate dall'angelico dottore S. Tommaso d'Aquino.* Genova, T. della Gioventù. 142 pp.

1880 Cerri, Domenico. *Maria Vergine SS. predicata Genitrice di Dio dalla teologia cristiana e pagana.* Torino, Camilla e Bertolero. 344 pp.

de Gaudenzi, P. G., Vescovo di Vigevano. *Lettera pastorale per l'Immacolato Concepimento di Maria Vergine.* Vigevano.

Filippi, Luigi, Arcivescovo d'Aquila. *Lettera pastorale per la Concezione.* Aquila.

Gianfrancesco da Venezia, O.F.M. *Del culto alla Immacolata Concezione di Maria in Venezia*: cenni storici. Verona, Merlo.

Oglietti. *La Vergine Madre e la teologia.*

1882 Magani, Fr. *Le grandezze della Madonna secondo S. Tommaso d'Aquino*: discorso. Pavia, Tip. Vescovile. 60 pp.

Morgott, Franz. *Maria nella dottrina di s. Tommaso d'Aquino.* Traduzione [from the German] di Andrea Dolzan. Piacenza, Bertola. 206 pp. IC pp. 117-162.

1883 Licciardello, Fr. *L'Immacolata: discorso accademico.* Catamia, Coco. 44 pp.

1884 Agnoletti, Carlo. *Il culto di Maria nella diocesi trevigiana storicamente illustrato.* Treviso, Scuola apostolica. 256 pp.

Cugia de Litala, Francesco. *Maria Vergine SS. nel mistero dell'Incarnazione del Verbo e Redenzione del mondo considerata dopo la definizione dommatica della Immacolata Concezione.* Studi e pensieri. Alba, Sansoldi. xvi, 694 pp.

1885 Cicuto, Ant. *L'Immacolata Concezione nelle sue attinenze teologiche e razionali*: saggio. Urine, Centoni. 25 pp.

1886 Publio, Lucio. *Nuovi splendori dell'Immacolata Concezione di Maria SS*: dissertaz. teologica. Prato, Natali. 100 pp.

Vespignani, Alf. Ma. *Due memorie relative alla questione circa l'origine dell'anima umana, con una 3a sulla mente di s. Tommaso intorno all'Immacolato Concepimento di Maria SS.* Bologna, Mareggiani. 201 pp.

1888 Giovanzana, Fr. *Il dogma della Immacolata Concezione di Maria SS. propugnato.* Bergamo, Bolis. 44 pp.

1889 Frai, Em. *Dissertazione sulla tesi, "Le dottrine di s. Tommaso, non che contraddire, concordano col domma dell'Immacolata Concezione."* Sorrento, Sorrentina. 30 pp.

1891 Cornoldi, Ioannes Maria, S.J. *Partenio. La creazione e la Immacolata.* Conversazioni scolastiche. Roma, Befani. 243 pp.

1892 Beninati-Cafarella, Gius. *L'Immacolata ed il papato*: conferenza. Siena, s. Bernardino. 122 pp.

Serafini, Mauro M. *Le grandezze di Maria Madre di Cristo e della Chiesa contenute nel Cantico dei cantici.* Parma, Fiacadori. 228 pp.

1894 Vigo, Ilario Maurizio. *La donna ed il serpente*, ossia l'Immacolata Concezione e i suoi nemici in fine del secolo XIX. Torino, t. Artigianelli. 39 pp.

1895 Venzano, Domenico. *Le grandezze di Maria Santissima nel suo Immacolato Concepimento.* . . . in confutazione degli errori sparsi . . . dai novelli apostati del secolo XIX. S. Pier d'Arena, Salesiana. 28 pp.

1897 Milošević, Giuseppe Ma., O.F.M. *L'Immacolata Concezione di Maria difesa dal ven. Giov. Duns Scoto: conferenza.* Padova, Prosperini. 67 pp.

1897 (continued)
  (*Anon.*) *Atti del primo Congresso mariano nazionale tenuto in Livorno nei giorni 18, 19, 20 e 21 Agosto 1895.* Livorno, Fabreschi. x, 208 pp.
1903 Monsabré, J. M., O.P. *L'esposizione del dogma cattolico.* Conferenze, tradotte [from the French] da Mons. Garemia Bonomelli, vesc. di Cremona. Torino, Marietti.

1904   (Fiftieth anniversary of the Definition)

Ballerini, Ant. *Questio an s. Hildefonsus, episcopus toletanus, Conceptae Virginis festum in Hispanis instituerit.* Roma, Pustet.
Bulgarelli-Quartana, Antonino. *La Immacolata Concezione.* . . . Trapani, tip. G. Gervasi-Modica. 8 pp.
Capecelatro, Alfonso, card. arciv. di Capua *La devozione alla Madonna e il cinquantesimo della definizione dell'Immacolato Concepimento di Lei.* Lettera pastorale per la Quaresima del 1904. Milano, Cogliati. 18 pp.
Cappellazzi, Andrea. *Maria nel Dogma cattolico.* Siena, S. Bernardino.
Cascioli, Giuseppe. *L'Immacolata attraverso i secoli.* Pubblicazione nella ricorrenza del cinquantenario dalla definizione dommatica. Roma, Pistolesi. 61 pp.
Cervetto, Luigi Aug. *Genova e l'Immacolata nell'arte e nella storia.* Genova, Lanata. iv, 149 pp.
Ciardi, Franco. *Sull'Immacolata Concezione di Maria Vergine*: componimenti, pubbl. da Fel. Ceretti. Mirandola, Grilli. 35 pp.
Dalla Santa, Gius. *Di alcune manifestazioni del culto all'Immacolata Concezione in Venezia dal 1480 alla metà del secolo XVI*: nota storica. Venezia, Patriarcali. 13 pp.
Diamare, Giovanni Maria, vesc. di Sessa e Aurunca. *L'Immacolata, l'Ordine Serafico e Mons. Caraccioli, vescovo di Sessa nel 1728.* Napoli, Artigianelli. 72 pp.
Filiti, Gaet. *Il dogma della Concezione Immacolata di Maria e la Compagnia di Gesù in Sicilia*: memorie storiche. Palermo, Bondì. 144 pp.
Gargano, Raff. *Appunti di teologia mariana, a proposito del libretto "Scoto e l'Immacolata" di Fr. Filia.* Roma, Pistalesi. 19 pp.
Gazzo, Angelico Fed. *Le magnificenze dell'Altissimo nella Immacolata Concezione di Maria,* esposte in 32 discorsi.
Guerrini, Norberto, O.F.M. *L'Immacolata ed il Verbo Umanato nel concetto di Giovanni Duns Scoto.* Dieci ragionamenti in occasione del 50° annivarsario della definizione dommatica dell'Immacolato Concepimento di Maria. Quaracchi, S. Bonaventura. xxiii, 333 pp.
Hilaire de Paris, O.M. Cap. *Nostra Signora di Lourdes e l'Immacolata Concezione.* Versione [from the French] del sac. Angelo Acquarone. Siena, S. Bernardino. xvi, 384 pp.
Le Bachelet, Saverio Maria, S.J. *La Immacolata Concezione.* Breve storia di un domma. Parte I, *L'Oriente.* (Traduzione ital. sulla 2ª ediz. francese.) Roma, Desclée-Lefebvre. 63 pp. (*Scienza e Religione.* Studi per i tempi presenti.)
    (For *Parte II,* see 1905.)
Manio, Michele. *La Vergine Madre Maria Immacolata al lume della fede, della ragione teologica, della letteratura e dell'arte,* con un'appendice intorno al verginale suo sposo S. Giuseppe. Novara, Salesiana. xvi, 706 pp. IC pp. 112-171.
Mariotti, Candido, O.F.M. *L'Immacolata Concezione di Maria ed i Francescani in occasione del cinquantesimo della dommatica definizione.* Quaracchi, S. Bonaventura. xvi, 272 pp.
Monsabré, J. M., O.P. *L'Immacolata Concezione.* Panegirico. Versione dal francese del P. Giuseppe Benelli del medesimo Ordine. Napoli, Rondinella e Loffredo. 40 pp.

1904 (continued)

MUNERATI, D. *Il culto dell'Immacolata nella vita della Chiesa ed in relazione colla Pia Società Salesiana.* Parma, Salesiana. 117 pp.

PAOLINI, Francesco M., O.F.M. *L'Immacolata e i Francescani di Corsica durante il primo Cinquantenario della definizione del Dogma (1854-1904).* Roma, Artigianelli. 60 pp.

PARISI, Francesco Paolo. *Il Magnificat, canto trionfale di Maria pel suo Immacolato Concepimento.* Note e commento . . . Palermo, Pontificia. 148 pp.

(For 2nd ed., see 1905.)

PAUWELS, Pietro e P. A. A. dei Frati Minori. *I Francescani e la Immacolata Concezione.* Traduzione libera dal francese con prefazione, illustrazioni fuori testo e note per il P. Agostino Molini del medesimo Ordine. Roma, Sallustiana. 300 pp.

RUSSO, Salvatore Petronio. *L'Immacolata e la Sicilia nelle sue più antiche pergamene.* Messina, Trimarchi. xii, 66, cxxxvii pp.

TERRIEN, Jean-Baptiste, S.J. *L'Immacolata Concezione.* Estratto dalla grande opera "La Mère de Dieu et la Mère des hommes." (p. I. L. IV, vol. I). Pubblicato in occasione del 50° anniversario della definizione dommatica dell'Immacolata Concezione di Maria SS. Parigi, Lethielleux. 79 pp.

(Translated from the French.)

VERDONA, Giovanni. *Maria Santissima.* Edizione seconda. Torino. IC pp. 5-75.

VIO, Carlo Silvio. *Adamo e Maria,* ossia il peccato orginale e l'Immacolata. Venezia, t. Patriarcale. 277 pp.

1905 DAL GAL, Nicolaus, O.F.M. *L'opera dei Francescani attraverso i secoli per il trionfo dell'Immacolata.* Dissertatione storico-critica preparata per l'Accademia Provinciale, tenuta nel Convento di S. Bernardino in Verona il 5 Gennaio 1905. Quarrachi, S. Bonav. 69 pp.

LE BACHELET, Saverio Maria, S.J. *La Immacolata Concezione. Breve storia di un domma.* Parte II, L'Occidente. Traduzione italiana sulla 2a ediz. francese. Roma, Desclée-Lefebvre. 65 pp. (*Scienze e Religione* Studi per i tempi presenti.)

(For *Parte I,* see 1904.)

MOLINI, Agostino, O.F.M. *Il dogma della Immacolata Concezione nella storia francescana.* Discorso tenuto nell'adunanza generale del Congresso Mariano del 2 dicembre 1904. Roma, Sallustiana.

Printed also in *L'Ordine dei Frati Minori* . . . [cf. infra], pp. 23-38.

PAOLINI, Francesco Maria, O.F.M. *Di una illustre testimonianza sopra la divina missione del b. Giov. Duns Scoto per insegnare e difendere la dottrina dell'Immacolata Concezione in Parigi.* Roma, Artigianelli. 11 pp.

PARISI, Francesco Paolo. *Il Magnificat applicato allo Immacolato Concepimento di Maria.* Illustrazioni e commenti . . . 2. ed. accr. da una dissertazione: "Il Magnificat rivendicato a Maria." Palermo, Pontificia. xxxii, 148 pp.

(For 1st ed., see 1904.)

SARDI, Vincenzo, Mons. *La solenne definizione del dogma dell'Immacolato Concepimento di Maria Santissima.* Atti e documenti pubblicati nel cinquantesimo anniversario della stessa definizione . . . 2 vol. Roma, Vaticana, 1904-1905.

SCARAMUZZI, Diomede, O.F.M. *L'evoluzione del domma dell'Immacolata nell'Ordine francescano.* Conferenza storica. Quaracchi. 28 pp.

VALLE, Fr. *Discorso dommatico sull'Immacolata Concezione di Maria SS.* Napoli, Cozzolino. 22 pp.

(*Anon.*) *L'Ordine dei Frati Minori al Congresso mariano internazionale tenuto in Roma dal 30 nov. al 4 dec. 1904 per celebrare il cinquantenario del dogma dell'Immacolata.* Roma, Artigianelli. 4, 91 pp.

(Articles in various languages by Domenico KOTTMANN, David

1905 (continued)
>FLEMING, Agostino MOLINI, Francesco M. PAOLINI, Ulrico HUNTEMANN, Louis BALDWIN; for titles, see the pertinent language section of this bibliography.)

1906 MESSINA, Vito. *Catania ufficiale e l'Immacolato Concepimento di Maria nel secolo XVII.* Catania, Pastori. 18 pp.

>(*Anon.*) *Atti del primo Congresso Mariano Sardo, tenuto in Cagliari, 14-15 dicembre, 1904.*

1907 ROSMINI-SERBATI, Antonio. *Voto sulla definizione del dogma del'Immacolata.* Roma, Forzani. 40 pp.

1908 MARINI, Niccolò, Monsignore [later Cardinal]. *L'Immacolata Concezione di Maria Vergine e la Chiesa greca ortodossa dissidente.* Roma, Salviucci. vi, 172 pp.

>ROMANI, Fulvio. *Discorso dell'Immacolata Concezione* recitato ai membri dell'Accademia liturgica il dì 11 dicembre nella Chiesa della Missione di Roma, presso la Curia Innocenziana. Roma, Artero. 30 pp.

1909 BUCCERONI, Ian., S.I. *La Beata Vergine Maria.* Considerazioni sopra i misteri della sua vita. Roma, Pio IX. 134 pp.

>Ed. terza, 1913, Roma, Artigianelli, 356 pp.

>CAMPANA, Emilio. *Maria nel dogma cattolico.* Prefazione del P. Alessio Maria LÉPICIER, O.S.M. Torino, Marietti, xvi, 822 pp. IC pp. 273-417.

>2a. edizione riveduta ed accresciuta. Torino-Roma, Marietti, 1923. Later editions: 1928, 1936, [1945].

>NEWMAN, Giov. Enr. *Anglicanismo, cattolicismo e culto della Vergine*: lettere. Traduzione [from the English] di Dom. Battaini, Piacenza, Apuana. 268 pp.

**

1929 DOURCHE, Joachim M., O.S.M. *La Tutta Santa. Alcuni suoi titoli alla nostra venerazione.* Prima versione italiana autorizzata dall'autore e fatta da una carmelitana del monastero di S. Maria Maddalena de' Pazzi. Roma, "Buona Stampa." 272 pp. IC pp. 74-116.

>(Translated from the French.)

1931 PISANI, Pietro, arcivescovo tit. di Costanza, Roma. "Concezione Immacolata," in *Enciclopedia Italiana*, Istituto Giovanni Treccani, vol. XI, pp. 47-48.

>SCARAMUZZI, Diomede, O.F.M. *L'Immacolato Concepimento di Maria.* Questione inedita di Landolfo CARACCIOLO, O.F.M. (†1351) Firenze, Vallechi.

>(Estratta da *Studi Franciscani*, S. 3a. III (1931), n. l.)

1933 CAMPANA, Emilio. *Maria nel culto cattolico.* 2 vol. Torino-Roma, Marietti. IC vol. I, pp. 157-212.

>Second edition, *ibid.*, 1945.

>SABA, Agostino. *Maria Vergine Immacolata.* Dieci discorsi storici sul dogma di M.I., tenuti nella Chiesa dell'Immacolata ad Andria (Bari). Prefazione di S. Ecc. Mons. Ferdinando BERNARDI, vescovo di Andria. Torino, S.E.I., [1933]. 129 pp.

1935 ISIDORO D'ALATRI, O.M. Cap. *Tra i precursori del dogma dell'Immacolata* [= S. Laurentius a Brundisio]. Conferenze. Grottaferrata, Italo-Orientale. 30 pp.

** For the period between 1909 and 1929, we could find no Italian literature on the Immaculate Conception worth noting. Doubtless there was a certain weariness with the subject after the intense activity devoted to it in 1904 and the following years, coming on top of the abundant literature of the preceding half-century. Then World War I and its aftermath turned men's thoughts to other problems, as well as hindering the publication of books. Nevertheless, this nineteen-year gap is surprising, and is perhaps due partly to the fact that our bibliographical sources were weakest for the period 1920-1930.

1935 (continued)

LAURENTIUS A BRUNDISIO, S. [1559-1619] *Discorsi sulla Immacolata Concezione*. Traduzione del Dr. P. Isidoro da Alatri, O.F.M. Cap. Grottaferrata, Italo-Orientale. xxxii, 103 pp.

1937 BASILONE, Giuseppe. *L'Immacolata Concezione.* 2 vols. in 1. Torino, Internazionale. [1937.]

FRATEA, G. *L'Immacolata in Cantanzaro.* Catanzaro, Bruzia. vii, 163 pp.

1938 GORRINO, Achille. *Maria Santissima Madre di Dio e madre nostra. Grandezze, privilegi, uffici.* Note critiche di teologia. *(Bibl. di Ascetica e mistica.)* Torino, Internazionale. [1938]. 189 pp., IC pp. 30-53.

1939 FOLGARAIT, G., Marianista. *La Vergine Bella in S. Bernardino da Sienna.* Milano, Ancora. xiii, 542 pp.

MANCINI, Vincenzo, O. de M. *Il primo difensore dell'Immacolata Concezione di Maria è stato un Mercedario: S. Pietro Pascasio.* Estratto dalla tesi di laurea: *La Vergine Immacolata nella tradizione del sacro Ordine di S. Maria della Mercede.* (Pontificio Instituto "Angelicum," Facoltà teologica.) Napoli, Raimondi. 59 pp.

1941 EUPIZI, Salvatore, congr. Dott. cristiana. *Il pensiero di Tommaso d'Aquino riguardo al domma della Immacolata Concezione.* Dissertatio ad lauream in Facultate s. Theologiae apud Pontificium institutum "Angelicum" de Urbe. Varallo Sesia. 167 pp.

1942 TUMMINELLO, Giuseppe, O.E.S.A. *L'Immacolata Concezione di Maria e la Scuola Agostiniana del Secolo XIV.* Dissert. Pont. Univ. Greg. Roma, Agostiniana. xvi, 620 pp.

1943 CECCHIN, Andrea Maria, O.S.M. *L'Immacolata nella liturgia occidentale anteriore al secolo XIII.* Roma, *Marianum.* [1943] 73 pp.

CLARET, Antonio M., Arciv. di Cuba. *L'Immacolata.* Trattatello sul mistero dell'Immacolato Concepimento di Maria. Versione dallo spagnolo del P. Giuliano M. Pierazzi, O.S.M. Introduzione e note del P. M. Gabriele M. ROSCHINI, O.S.M. *(Lavori mariani, 7.)* Milano, Ancora. [1943] 82 pp.

1944 BOCCAZZI, Carlo. *Prontuario di teologia mariana.* Cremona, Maffezzoni, [1944]. 231 pp. IC pp. 21-46.

NEUBERT, E. *Maria nel dogma.* Traduzione [from the French] di Leopoldo Cassis. [Alba], S. Paolo, [1944]. 294 pp. IC pp. 77-122.

1948 MONSABRÉ, Jacques-Marie-Louis, O.P. *Esposizione del Dogma Cattolico . . . ,* versione e note di Mgr. Geremia BONOMELLI rivedute e aggiornate dal P. L. CIAPPI, O.P. 18 vol. Torino-Roma, Marietti, 1948-1952. IC vol. 5, pp. 197-231.

1949 LONGPRÉ, Ephrem, O.F.M. *La Vergine Immacolata.* Milano, "Vita e Pensiero." [1949]. xi, 80 pp.

1950 BERTETTO, Domenico, S.D.B. *Maria nel dogma cattolico.* Trattato di mariologia. Torino, Internazionale, [1950]. xv, 528 pp. IC pp. 353-372.

BOSCO, Giacinto, O.P. *L'Immacolata Concezione nel pensiero del Gaetano e del Caterino.* Dalla dissertazione di dottorato in teologia. Pontificio Istituto "Angelicum" — Roma. Firenze, "Il Rosario." ix, 84 pp.

COSTA, Beniamino, O.F.M. Conv. *La Mariologia di S. Antonio da Padova.* *(Pont. Fac. Theol. Fratrum Min. Conv. in Urbe,* Theses ad Lauream — n. 23) Padova, Il Messaggero di S. Antonio. IC pp. 101-125.

MIEGGE, Giovanni. *La Vergine Maria.* Saggio di storia del dogma. Torre Pellice, Claudiana. 220 pp. IC pp. 117-148.

ROSCHINI, Gabriele, O.S.M. *L'Assunzione e l'Immacolata Concezione. Assunta perchè Immacolata. (Studi Mariani, 1)* Roma, Belardetti. 89 pp.

⸻. *La Mariologia di San Tommaso. (Studi Mariani, II)* Roma, Belardetti. IC pp. 193-237.

1951 BERTELLI, Vasco Giuseppe. *L'interpretazione mariologica del Protoevangelo negli esegeti e nei teologi dopo la Bolla "Ineffabilis Deus" di Pio IX (1854-1948)* . . . Excerpta ex dissertatione ad lauream in fac. theol. Pont. Univ. Gregorianae. Romae, [s.e.]. 77 pp.

PAZZELLI, Raffaele, T.O.R. *L'Immacolata Concezione di Maria in P. Francesco Bordoni, T.O.R.* (1595-1671). Roma. 158 pp.

(Reprinted from *Analecta Tertii Ordinis Regularis S. Francisci*, V, 1950-1951.)

ROSCHINI, Gabriele M., O.S.M. *La Mariologia di S. Lorenzo da Brindisi* (*Miscellanea Laurentiana*, II) Padova, Gregoriana. 230 pp. IC pp. 117-140.

ROSCHINI, Gabriele, RAES, Alfonso, LÖW, Giuseppe, LAVAGNINO, Emilio, "Immacolata Concezione," in *Enciclopedia Cattolica*, Città del Vaticano vol. VI [1951], col. 1651-1663.

1952 ALASTRUEY, Gregorio. *La SS. Vergine Maria.* Trattato di mariologia per sacerdoti e laici. 2 vol. (*Collana "Mater Dei,"* 1-2). [Roma], Paoline, [1952]. IC vol. I, pp. 162-287.

(Translated from the Spanish.)

1953 BERTETTO, Domenico, S.D.B. *Maria Immacolata.* Il domma della Concezione Immacolata di Maria nel centenario della sua definizione. 1854 — 8 Dicembre — 1954. (*Collana mariana,* 5) [Roma], Paoline. [1953]. 305 pp.

GIAMBERARDINI, Gabriele, O.F.M. *L'Immacolata Concezione di Maria nella Chiesa egiziana.* Cairo.

LABATE, Antonino. *L'Immacolata nei secoli.* Reggio Calabria, Morello. 134 pp.

ORLINI, Alfonso, O.F.M. Conv. *Pio IX e l'Immacolata. Commemorazione della Bolla "Ineffabilis Deus."* Roma, Santi XII Apostoli. 29 pp.

(Text of a conference given in the *Palazzo della Cancelleria Apostolica*, March 9, 1930.)

PAZZAGLIA, Luigi M., O.S.M. *La Madonna nella poesia italiana. Poesia dell' Immacolata.* Torino, L.I.C.E., Berruti.

ROSCHINI, Gabriele M., O.S.M. *Il dogma dell'Immacolata.* Rovigo, Istituto Padano di Arti Grafiche.

————. *Il Dottore Mariano.* Studio sulla dottrina mariana di S. Bernardo di Chiaravalle nell'VIII centenario del suo glorioso transito. Roma, SEIR— Edizioni cattoliche. xx, 204 pp.

1954 BAJ, Ferdinando. *L'Immacolata.* Milano, Ancora.

BALDUCCI, Antonio. *L'Immacolata nelle diocesi di Acerno e Salerno.* Salerno [Linotipografia Spadafora]. 94 pp.

BARGELLINI, Piero. *La storia dell'Immacolata.* Firenze. 88 pp.

BAUDUCCO, Francesco Maria, S.J. *Storia di un domma. Centenario della definizione dell'Immacolata (1854-1954).* Chieri, Casa S. Antonio. 68 pp.

BERTETTO, Domenico. *Le prove del domma dell'Immacolata Concezione negli atti preparatori alla definizione e nel magistero pontificio.* Torino [etc.], Internazionale [1954] 39 pp. (Biblioteca del "Salesianum," 33).

CAGGIANO, Egidio, O.F.M. *La B.V. Maria Immacolata.* Le encicliche di Pio IX, Pio X, Pio XII sull'Immacolata Concezione di Maria SS.; con introduzione storico-dottrinale. Milano, Vita e pensiero [1954] 111 pp.

CIAPPI, L. "Immacolata Concezione," in *Enciclopedia Mariana "Theotocos"* [Raimondo SPIAZZI, direttore], Genova (Bevilacqua e Solari) & Milano (Massimo), pp. 294-298. 2a ed., 1958.

DA NIVIANO, [et al.] *L'Immacolata nella provincia parmense dei FF. MM. Cappuccini.* Notizie storiche . . . Parma, Fresching [1957]. 168 pp.

GARRIGOU-LAGRANGE, Réginald, O.P. *La Madre del Salvatore e la nostra vita interiore.* Sintesi dommatico-ascetica. [Firenze], Fiorentina, [1954]. 441 pp.

(Translated from the French.)

1954 (continued)

MOSCARELLA, G. *Il primato di Gesù Cristo sulla creazione nella luce dell'Immacolato Concepimento di Maria SS.* Manfredonia. 132 pp.

PERNIOLA, Erasmo, Concezionista. *La mariologia di S. Germano, Patriarca di Costantinopoli.* Presentazione del P. Gabriele M. ROSCHINI, O.S.M. Roma, Padre Monti. xv, 200 pp.

PIANA, C. et al. *L'Immacolata Concezione.* Storia ed esposizione del dogma. VIII. settimana di spiritualità promossa dall'Università Cattolica del Sacro Cuore (Milano, 9-16 maggio 1954) Milano. Vita e Pensiero. [1954]. 177 pp.

Celestino PIANO, "Il privilegio dell'Immacolata nelle battaglie e nelle discussioni dei secoli."

Efrem LONGPRÉ, O.F.M. "La scuola teologica francescana nello sviluppo del dogma dell'Immacolata Concezione."

Carlo COLOMBO, "Il dogma dell'Immacolata nella teologia dogmatica."

Gabriele M. ROSCHINI, O.S.M. "Il dogma dell'Immacolata e la vita della Chiesa."

Giovanni BERTI, "La storia della liturgia e il dogma dell'Immacolata."

Eva TEA, "L'Immacolata Concezione nell'arte."

Francesco OLGIATI, "La definizione del dogma dell'Immacolata e la cultura moderna."

PRETE, Benedetto, O.P. *L'Immacolata e la Bibbia.* Bologna, Studio Domenicano, 63 pp. (Quaderni *Sacra Doctrina*).

————, et al. *Maria Immacolata.* Bologna, Studio Domenicano. 175 pp.

B. PRETE, "I fondamenti biblici del dogma dell'Immacolata." (7-47)

L. CIAPPI, "Genesi, sviluppo e valore degli argomenti teologici in favore dell'Immacolata Concezione." (49-78)

M. GIRAUDO, "Storia della controversia del dogma dell'Immacolata." (79-110)

A. D'AMATO, "L'Immacolata e Satana." (111-127)

R. SPIAZZI. "L'Immacolata e lo spirito della civiltà." (129-144)

V. ALCE, "L'Immacolata Concezione nell'Arte." 145-173)

ROSCHINI, Gabriele Maria, O.S.M. *Il dogma dell'Immacolata.* Istruzioni. Rovigo, Instituto Padano di arti grafiche. [1954]. 225 pp.

————. *La Madonna secondo la fede e la teologia.* 4 vol. Roma, Ferrari, 1953-1954. IC vol. III pp. 6-90.

TOGNETTI, Mariano, O.S.M. *L'Immacolata nelle controversie Tridentine.* Roma, "Marianum." 123 pp.

1955 ANDREAS DE NOVO CASTRO, O.F.M. *De Conceptione Virginis gloriosae.* [Edited by T. SZABÒ.]

(Work originally composed in the fourteenth century.)

ROSCHINI, Gabriele M., O.S.M. *I Servi di Maria e l'Immacolata.* Roma, "Studî storici O.S.M." x, 163 pp.

(Anon.) *L'Immacolata Ausiliatrice.* Relazioni commemorative dell'Anno Mariano 1954. (*Accademia Mariana salesiana,* 3) Torino etc., "Internazionale" [1955]. 434 pp.

(Anon.) *L'Immacolata Concezione.* Lezioni tenute in Assisi al XII. Corso di studi cristiani (*Il simbolo,* vol. XII) Assisi, Pro civitate Christiana. 183 pp.

(Anon.) *Maria Immacolata nella Provincia dei Frati Minori Cappuccini di Lombardia.* A ricordo dell'Anno Mariano 1954. Milano, "Lux de cruce," [1955] 407 pp. tav.

(Anon.) *Virgo Immaculata,* vols. III, IV, V, VI. (See below, p. 611ff.)

1956 SPIAZZI, Raimondo, O.P. *La Regina Immacolata.* Rovigo, Ist. Padano. 269 pp.

1956 (continued)
  (*Anon.*) *Virgo Immaculata,* vols. II, VIII/3, XII, XVI, XVIII.
    (See below, p. 611 ff.)
1957 (*Anon.*) *Virgo Immaculata,* vols. VII/2, VII/3, IX, X, XI, XIII, XIV, XV,
    XVII. (*Ibid.*)
1958 (*Anon.*) *Virgo Immaculata,* vol. VII/1. (*Ibid.*)

DATE OF PUBLICATION UNKNOWN

CAPASSO, G. *Scoto, teologo dell'Immacolata.*

LATIN[1]

1830   (MIRACULOUS MEDAL APPARITION TO SISTER CATHERINE LABOURÉ,
        PARIS, NOVEMBER 17; FIRST MEDALS STRUCK, JUNE 30, 1832)

1837 F.B.I.C. *Censura theologica XVI thesium priorum neoapprobandis et aliis
        presbyteris AD. Coloniensis ad subscribendum nuper propositarum;*
        quam confecerunt aliqui SS. Theol. doctores et professores, adauctam
        vero et in latinum sermonem conversam edidit F.B.I.C. Francof. IC p. 42.

    P.Q. *Responsum de XVI prioribus earum thesium, quae sub titulo:* Theses
        neoapprobandis et aliis presbyteris AD. Colon. ad subscribendum pro-
        positae, *innotuerunt.* In sermonem latinum conversum edendum curavit
        P.Q. Darmstadii. IC p. 36.
          (Cf. German bibliography, 1837.)

1838 CLARI, Mich. Basil., Archiepiscopus Barensis. *Mariologia.* Barii.

1842 DE BERLEPSCH, Augustus L.B. *Anthropologia Christiana.* Moguntiae. xxv,
        261 pp. P. 201: "Estne S. Maria sine peccato originali concepta?"

    DELORME. "De Immaculata, seu de ratione Congruentiae pro Immaculata
        Conceptione," in MIGNE, *Theologiae Cursus Completus,* tomus 26 (1842),
        col. 659-698. Paris, Migne.

1843 PAULUS. [Former Superior General of the Redemptorists.] *Spicilegium
        Marianum.* Neapoli.
          (= Pietro Paulo BLASUCCI, Superior General 1793 - 1817?)

1844 *Episcopus Aquensis in Pedemontio. Epistola pastoralis de Immaculata Con-
        ceptione B. V.*

    FELIX, Joseph, S.J. *Dissertatio de Immaculata B. V. Mariae Conceptione.*
        Laval.

    (*Anon.*) *Opusculum de immaculata Conceptione B. M. V. desumptum ex
        variis Auctoribus.* Matriti.

1845 DE CAROLO, Augustinus. *Theotocologia, seu institutio de Virgine Dei Genitrice
        Maria,* scholastica methodo IV libris concinnata. Accedit *Appendix de
        mysteriis vitae et praecipuis titulis eiusdem Magnae Dei Genitricis:*
        opus Iosephi IANNINI. 2 vol. Neapoli, Cirillo.

    DELORME. *De Immaculata Conceptione.* Claromonte.
          (Cp. work of 1842.)

    MAZZOLA, Fedelis. *De beata Virgine* Disputationes historico-theologicae . . .
        Aug. Taurinorum, Chirio et Mina. 480 pp. IC pp. 22-34; x, 419-420.

---

[1] We are grateful to Father George Bernard, C.S.C., for having helped with this
section of the Bibliography.

1845 (continued)

(*Anon.*) "Conceptio B.M.V. (Articulus novus Casinensis)," in L. FERRARIS, O. Min., *Promta bibliotheca,* Editio novissima opere et studio Monachorum O.S.B. Abbatiae Montis Casini. Vol. II, p. 404.

1846 ANSTRUTHER, Robertus. *Epistolae* HERBERTI DE LOSINGA, *primi Episcopi Norvicensis,* OSBERTI DE CLARA *et* EADMERI, *Prioris Cantuariensis.* Nunc primum e cod. mss. editae. Londini.

BIGONI, Angelus, O. Min. *De Christo Reparatore.* Opus theologicum ex Scripturis et Patribus concinnatum. IC t. I, p. 165 ff.

1847 PERRONE, Ioannis, e societate Jesu. *De Immaculato B.V. Mariae conceptu an dogmatico decreto definiri possit disquisitio theologica* . . . Romae, Marini et Morini, 1847. viii, 287 pp.

Id., Napoli, 1847 (54 pp. folio); Editio altera emendata et brevibus accessionibus ab ipso auctore locupletata, Monasterii Guestphalorum, 1848. Other editions: Matriti, 1848; Olyssipone, 1849; Monasterii Guestphalorum, 1849; Mediolani, 1852; Taurini, 1854. The second edition was also reprinted in *Pareri* . . . , vol. VI, pp. 309-608

1848   (COMMITTEE APPOINTED BY POPE PIUS IX TO EXAMINE THE ADVISABILITY OF A DEFINITION, JUNE 1)

1849   (ENCYCLICAL LETTER *Ubi primum* OF POPE PIUS IX, FEBRUARY 2)

(Note: the replies of cardinals, bishops, etc. to this Letter were published in the work *Pareri* . . . listed in our Italian bibliography under 1854.)

DIEZ DE SOLLANO, Jos. Maria [Later Bishop of Léon] *Theologica de Imm. Conc. B.V.M. dissertatio,* Pont. ac nationalis Universitatis iussu elucubrata, et suis sapientissimis in Commissione collegis, cunctorumque Theologorum Mexicanorum commendatissimo Ordini grato animo oblata, unaque cum praedicta universitate SS. D. N. Pio Papae IX, qui Petri fidem et Sedem tenet, quique suo Brevi huic dissertationi occasionem dedit, pie reverenterque dicata. Mexici, Rafael.

Reprinted in *Pareri,* vol. VI, pp. 217-308.

[SAGGESIUS, Iosue Maria.] *Pro BMV Conceptione Immaculata dogmatice definienda ad Pium IX P.O.M. Aeppi Teatini votum:* quo expenduntur Romanae Sedis ordinationes, Eppatus magisterium, et fidelium sensus; insuper horum omnium invariata praxis. Praecedunt duae supplices Epistolae, sequiturque Romanorum Pontificium Iubilum. Teate, Vella.

Reprinted in *Pareri,* vol. VII, pp. i-lvi.

SOLDATI, Sebastiano. *Ad B. Patrem Pium Papam IX, Humilissimum votum diocesis Tarvisianae ad defensionem Immaculati Conceptus.* Tarvisii, Typ. Andreoliansis.

1850 BIGARO, Petrus. *Purissimae Virginis Mariae Dei Genitricis Conceptus quomodo immaculatus biblico "τοῦ πρωτευαγγελίου" testimonio statuendus brevis disquisitio theologico-critica. Venetiis,* Antonelli.

Reprinted in *Pareri,* vol. VII, pp. lxxxi-cxxiv.

[PARLADORE, Livius] Episcopus *S. Marci atque Bisianensis. Pro solemni ac pridiana commemoratione diei festi Immaculatae Conceptioni Beatae Mariae Virginis dicati, proque ipsomet Immaculato Conceptu dogmatice definiendo; duplex Episcopi S. Marci atque Bisianensis ad Pium P. O. M. votum.* Naples.

1851 CERRI, Dominicus, C.M. *Enchiridion super duodecim momenta fundatum ex quibus exsurgit triumphus B. Mariae Virginis Matris Dei in originale peccatum.* Taurini, Fontana, 221 pp.

Reprinted in *Pareri,* vol. VI, pp. 1-216.

(*Anon.*) *Pareri dell'Episcopato Cattolico* . . . , tomi I-V. (See Italian bibliography at 1854.)

1852 (*Anon.*) *Defensio Immaculatae Conceptionis B.M.V. ex rationibus theologicis.*
   (*Anon.*) *Pareri dell'Episcopato Cattolico . . .* , volumes VI-IX. (See Italian
   bibliography at 1854.)

1853 ALBERTUS A BULSANO [Knoll]. *Institutiones Theologiae seu Dogmatico-Po-
   lemicae.* Taurinae. IC vol. II, pp. 464-499.

   MARTINEZ Y FEBRER, Raymundus. *De utilitati et ratione sufficienti ad dogmaticam definitionem super immaculato Deiparae Mariae Conceptu,* pro
   maiori Dei gloria, B. Virginis laude, totiusque Ecclesiae pace et gaudio
   elucidatio sacra. Interamnae, Saluzi. xii, 533 pp.
      (Extract from volume I of his *De natura . . .* , 1852-1854, with a
   special preface.)

   PATRITIUS [= PATRIZI], F. X., S.J. DE אנה, *hoc est de immaculata Mariae
   origine a Deo praedicta disquisitio* cum appendice de feminini generis
   enallage in linguis semiticis usitata. Romae, Morini. 54 pp.

1854   (DEFINITION OF THE IMMACULATE CONCEPTION AS A DOGMA OF FAITH
         BY POPE PIUS IX, DECEMBER 8)

   BALLERINI, Antonius, S.J. *Sylloge monumentorum ad mysterium Conceptionis
   Immaculatae Virginis Deiparae illustrandum.* Roma (Civiltà Cattolica),
   1854, and Paris, 1855.
      Reprinted as vol. X of *Pareri.*
      (For *Pars II,* see 1856.)

   CAESARI, Theobaldus. *Ordinis Cisterciensis suffragia pro dogmatica ferenda
   sententia super mysterio Immaculatae Conceptionis B.V. Mariae SS.
   D. N. Pio IX P. M. humiliter porrecta atque supplici elucidata libello.*
   Per Dom. Theobaldum Caesari, monac. Cisterc. coenobii D. Bernardi
   in alma urbe Abbatem, totiusque ordinis Procuratorem Generalem.
   Interamnae, Saluzzi. 51 pp.
      (Originally published in volume IX of *Pareri,* 1852.)

   CLARI, Michael Basilius, Archiepiscopus Barensis in Sicilia. *An sententia de
   Immaculata B. Virginis Conceptione in fidei dogma evehi possit.* Dissertatio theologico-polemica. Baren. 56 pp.

   C. J. *De Immaculata B.M.V. conceptione in Genesi praedicta, in Evangelio
   edicta, breve argumentum, utinam grave!* Paris.

   GAUDE, Franciscus, O.P. [later Cardinal]. *De immaculato Deiparae conceptu
   eiusque dogmatica definitione in ordine praesertim ad scholam thomisticam
   et institutum FF. Praedicatorum,* auctore P. M. Francisco Gaude, procurat.
   eiusd. ordin. ac rect. pontificii seminarii Pii. Rome, Bertinelli. 192 pp.

   MARTELLUS, Franciscus. *In B.V. Mariam opera D. Bernardini Senensis, D.
   Anselmi Cantuariensis AEppi, et Eadmeri Monachi, ex eorum scriptis
   diligenter expromta.* Neapoli.

   MARTINEZ Y FEBRER, Raymundus. *De Natura et gratia admirabilis et purissimae
   Conceptionis Deiparae V. Mariae* elucidationes polemicae ad dogmaticam
   proxime ferendam sententiam utiliter congestae, tribusque distinctae
   sectionibus. 6 vol. Interamnae, Possenti. 1852-1854.

   (*Anon.*) *Cardinales S.E.R. Patriarchae, Archiepiscopi et Episcopi in Basilica
   Vaticana adstantes Pio IX Pont. Max. dogmaticam definitionem de
   Conceptione Immaculata Deiparae Virginis Mariae pronuncianti inter
   Missarum solemnia die viii. decembris an. MDCCCLIV.* Romae, Cam.
   Apostolicae. 18 pp.

   (*Anon.*) *Narratio actorum SSmi. D.N. Pii IX, P.M. super argumento de
   Immaculato Deiparae Virginis Conceptu.* Romae. 7 pp. fol.
      Reprinted in *Atti e documenti . . .* , ed. SARDI, 1905 (See Italian
   bibliography.)

   (*Anon.*) *Pareri dell'Episcopato Cattolico . . .* tomi IX, X. (See Italian
   bibliography at 1854.)

1855 BAJZÁTH, Georgius. *Beatissimae V. Mariae Matris Dei Redemptoris de matre sterili immaculate conceptae glorificatio,* dogmate per SS. Papam Pium IX Summum Pontificem edicto die 8 Dec. 1854. Pestini.

[BONACCORSO, Giacomo Salvo.] *De immaculata B.V. Mariae conceptione* tractatus cui accedunt de huiusce dogmatis definitione monumenta. Florentiae, Manuelli. 77 pp.

BROTTO, Pietro. *Dialogus inter Romanum et Callistum de festis Immaculatae Mariae Virginis anno 1855 celebratis.*

GIUNCHI, Antonius. *Theses de Immaculato B.M.V. conceptu.* Romae.

LOPUSSNY, Franciscus. *Sermo academicus,* dum facultas theologica caes. reg. scientiarum universitatis Pestiensis Immaculati Conceptus Beatae Deiparae Virginis Mariae dogmaticam definitionem a sanctissimo domino nostro Pio IX. pont. maximo, exultante universa Ecclesia editam, ii. non. maji 1855 solenni ritu ageret, in aula universitatis majore dictus. Budae, Typ. Univers. 82 pp.

    Reprinted in A. DE ROSKOVÁNY, *Beata Virgo Maria in suo conceptu Immaculata* . . . tom. VI, 1874, pp. 239-349.

MORGAEZ Carillo Braulio, O.P. *Iudicium doctrinale super decreto pontificio diei 8 Dec. anni proxime praeteriti.* Matriti.

PASSAGLIA, Carolus, S.J. *De Immaculato Deiparae semper Virginis Conceptu commentarius.* 3 vols. Romae, Propaganda, 1854-1855.
Id. 2 vol., Neapoli, Dura, 1855.

PERRONE, Joannes, S.J. *Thesis dogmatica de Immaculata B.V. Conceptione* addenda praelectionibus theologicis quas in Coll. Rom. S.J. habebat Joannes Perrone, S.J. Ratisbonae, Manz. 35 pp.

1856 BALLERINI, Antonio, S.J. *De S. Bernardi scriptis circa Deiparae Virginis Conceptionem dissertatio historico-critica* . . . Romae, Propaganda. 117 pp.
    Reprinted in his *Sylloge* (1854-1857), *Pars II,* p. 712 ff.

———. *Quaestio, an sanctus Hildefonsus, episcopus Toletanus, Conceptae Virginis Festum in Hispaniis instituerit.* Romae, Propaganda. 86 pp.
Id. Parisiis, Lecoffre, 1856, 87 pp.

———. *Sylloge monumentorum ad mysterium Conceptionis Immaculatae Virginis Deiparae illustrandum* . . . Pars II. Romae, Propaganda. lxxxvii, 881 pp. [For *Pars I,* see 1854.]
Id. Paris, 1857. (= the Roman edition, corrected and augmented.)

D'ARIA, Paschalis. *Conceptio passiva magnae Deiparae Virginis in sinu B. Annae matris prorsus sancta ac semper immaculata necesariis argumentis asserta.* Neapoli, Vitale.

GOLESSÉNY, Pantaleon, O.F.M. *Sermo de Immaculata Conceptione B.V. Deiparae* ad P.T. patres vocales pro Generali Capitulo totius Ordinis Minorum S.P.N. Francisci Romae in conventu B.M.V. de Ara Coeli sub auspiciis Pii Papae IX congregatos, habitus ibid. die 5 Maii 1856. Posonii, Schreiber. 20 pp.

HAGEN, Hermannus Gerardus. *Disquisitio historico-dogmatica inauguralis de dogmate Immaculatae Conceptionis Mariae.* Traiecti ad Rhenum. xii, 116 pp.

PETRARCHA. *De Immaculato Virginis Deiparae conceptu dialectica diatribe.* Neapoli.

1857 ALLODI, Joannes. *De Immaculato B. Mariae Virginis Conceptu.* Parmae, S. Rossi Ubaldi.

PELELLA, Jos. IUSTINI MIECHOVIENSIS, O.P., *discursus praedicabiles super Litanias Lauretanas BMV.* Edito Neapolitana. Additis huic editioni variis passim ab editore adnotationibus, eiusque discursibus iuxta methodum auctoris super novissimum in litaniis titulum, '*Regina sine labe originali concepta,*' disquisitione theologica Ioannis PERRONE e S.I. denique

1857 (continued)

perraro opere B. ALBERTI MAGNI, cui titulus: *Biblia Mariana.* 2 vol. Neapoli.

(JUSTIN OF MIECHOW's work was composed in the seventeenth century.)

1858 (APPARITIONS OF MARY IMMACULATE TO BERNADETTE SOUBIROUS, LOURDES, FEBRUARY 11 - JULY 16)

HEINRICH, I. "De Immaculata Conceptione Beatae semper Virginis Deigenitricis Mariae," appendix added to Leop. LIEBERMANN, *Institutiones Theologicae.* Moguntiae. 16 pp.

MORGAËZ CARILLO, Braulius, O.P. *Examen Bullae* Ineffabilis *institutum et concinnatum iuxta regulas sanioris theologiae.* Paris, Huet. 104, xv pp. (Apparently a translation from the Spanish of 1857, *q. v.*)

1859 IOANNES DE CARTAGENA, O. Min. *Homiliae Catholicae de sacris arcanis Deiparae Mariae et D. Iosephi eiusdem Sponsi.* Editio prima Neapolitana, addito Promtuario de diversis titulis Marianis a Cartagena praetermissis, auctore Raphaele M. COPPOLA presb. Neap. Neapoli, 5 vol. [Originally published in 1611 at Rome, under title, *Homiliae catholicae in universa christianae religionis arcana. De sacris arcanis aeternae praedestinationis ac Immac. Conceptionis Deiparae Virg. Mariae . . .*]

SARTORIUS. *Soli Deo Gloria.*

SUAREZ, Franciscus, S.I. "Dissertatio de Immaculata Conceptione Beatae Mariae Virginis," in *Opusculis sex ineditis,* primum a Ioanne Bapt. MALOU Eppo. Brugensi vulgatis, Bruxellis et Parisiis, p. 234 ff.

1861 PREUSS, E. "De immaculato conceptu b. Mariae Virginis," Appendix to his edition of Chemnitz' *Examen Concilii Tridentini.* Berlin. Pp. 965-1024.

1862 BOURASSÉ, Joannes Jacobus. *Summa aurea de laudibus Beatissimae Virginis Mariae . . .* Tomi I-XII. Paris, Migne.

(For detailed table of contents, see Appendix below, p. 609 ff.)

PREUSS, Eduardus. "De Immaculato Conceptu Beatae Mariae Virginis," in new edition of Martini CHEMNICII *Examen Concilii Tridentini,* Berolini.

SPADA, Mariano, O.P. *Animadversiones . . . in opus Ill.mi ac Rev.mi domini J. B. Malou episcopi Burgensis de dogmate Immaculatae Conceptionis B. Mariae Virginis.* Romae, Salviucci. v, 96 pp.

TOSCANI, Theodorus, et COZZA, Josephus. *De Immaculatae Deiparae conceptione hymnologia graecorum* ex editis et manuscriptis codicibus Cryptoferratensibus latina et italica interpretatione patrologica comparatione et adnotationibus illustrata. Romae, Propaganda. xxxii, 239 pp.

(*Anon.*) *Tractatus theologicus de Beata Maria Virgine.* Lugduni et Parisiis.

1864 HAINE, Ant. Ios. Iac. Franc. *De Hyperdulia eiusque fundamento dissertatio historico-theologica.* Lovanii.

1866 BOURASSÉ, J. J. *Summa Aurea . . . ,* tomus XIII. (See entry *Bourassé* under 1862, above.)

DE VEGA, Christophorus, S.J. *Theologia mariana sive certamina litteraria de* B.V. Dei Genitrice Maria quae tam apud theologos scholasticos, quam apud sacrorum voluminum interpretes excogitari solent, opus Divini Verbi praeconibus perutile. Editio prima Neapolitana adnotationibus ab editore [= Joseph PELELLA] aucta. 2 vol. Napoli, Bibliotheca catholica Immaculatae Conceptionis. IC vol. I, pp. 66-283.

(Republished in 1867. The work originally appeared in the seventeenth century.)

PETITALOT, I. B. *Coronula Mariana,* seu theologica dissertatio de Beatissima Deipara. Molinis.

1868 CORNOLDI, G. M. *Sententia S. Thomae de immunitate B. Virginis Dei Parentis a peccati originalis labe* . . . Brixiae, Typis Wegerianis, 52 pp.
> Republished *ibid.*, 1869; Napoli, Giannini, 1870; Parma, 1873; Roma, Stefani, 1889.

[DEHO, Hector, S.M.M.] *Tractatus theologicus de B. Maria Virgine* auctore H. D. Societatis Mariae presbytero. [2nd ed.] Taurini, Marietti. 282 pp; IC pp. 121-156.

(*Anon.*) *Responsio Anglicana Literis Apostolicis Pii Papae IX ad omnes Protestantes aliosque acatholicos.* Londini, Oxonii, et Cantabrigiae.

1869 BOUCARUT. *Theologia de SS. Virgine Maria.* Nemausi [= Nemanzin], Goustelle, 1869.
> Republished *ibid.* 1870.

PUSEY, E. B. *Tractatus de veritate Conceptionis B. Virginis,* pro facienda relatione coram Patribus Concilii Basileae A.D. 1437 mense Iulio de mandato Sedis Apostolicae Legatorum eidem S. Concilio praesidentium. Compilatus per R.P.Fr. Ioannem DE TURRECREMATA Card. Ep. Portuensem. Primo impressus Romae 1547. Nunc denuo luci redditus Oxoniis et Londini et Cantabrigiae.

1870 HURTER, H., S.I. *De gloriosa Deigenitrice Maria SS. Patrum opuscula selecta.* Oeniponti.
> (Includes the *Tractatus de Conceptione BMV* then commonly attributed—but not by Hurter—to St. Anselm. Republished at Regensburg in 1894.)

KENRICK, Petrus Richardus [Archbishop of St. Louis, U.S.A.] *Concio in Concilio Vaticano habenda at non habita.* Neapoli. IC p. 43.

1871 IUNGMANN, Bernardus. *Institutiones theologiae dogmaticae specialis. Tractatus de Deo Creatore.* Ratisbonae [etc.], Pustet.
> Ed. 2a. 1875: IC pp. 307-341.

1872 TEISSONNIER. "Tractatus de B. V. Maria," in *Compendium Theologiae Dogmaticae,* II, pp. 569-691. Nemausi.

1873 DE ROSKOVÁNY, Augustinus. *Beata Virgo Maria* . . . , volumes I-IV. (See below, under 1881.)

1874 DE ROSKOVÁNY, Augustinus. *Beata Virgo Maria* . . . , tom. V, VI. (See below, under 1881.)

VAN DEN BERG, P. C., O.P. *Beatissima Virgo Maria, Imago Dei et SS. Trinitatis iuxta mentem D. Thomae Doctoris Angelici.* Buscoduci.

1877 DE ROSKOVÁNY, Augustinus. *Beata Virgo Maria* . . . tom VII. (See below, under 1881.)

MAZZELLA, Camillus, S.J. *De Deo creante* praelectiones scholastico-dogmaticae . . . Romae. Propaganda. IC pp. 738-775.
> Republished: 1880, 1892, 1896.

1878 HURTER, Hugo, S.J. *Mariologia.*

PALMIERI, Dominicus. "De Immaculato conceptu SS. Deiparae," in *Tractatus de Deo creante et elevante,* pp. 666-754. Romae.

1879 (*Anon.*) *Rhythmi et carmina variis e monumentis excerpta, in honorem Mariae Virginis Immaculatae;* anno primi eius iubilaei. Parma, Off. Fiaccadoriana.

1880 DIEZ DE SOLLANO, Ios. María [Bishop of León]. *Theologica disquisitio de mente D. Thomae cum mente S. Ecclesiae comparata circa Immac. Conc. B. V. Mariae.* Mexici.

1881 DE ROSKOVÁNY, Augustinus, episcopus Nitriensis. *Beata Virgo Maria in suo conceptu Immaculata ex monumentis omnium seculorum demonstrata.* Accedit amplissima literatura.
> *Tomus I.* Monumenta et literaturam primorum XVI seculorum complectens. Budapestini, Typis Athenaei, 1873.
> *Tomus II.* Monumenta sec. XVII et XVIII complectens. *Ibid.,* 1873.

1881 (continued)

Tomus III. Literaturam sec. XVII et XVIII complectens. *Ibid.,* 1873.

Tomus IV. Monumenta e sec. XIX, signanter responsa praesulum ad encyclicam P.M. a. 1849 editam ex Italia et Gallia complectens. *Ibid.,* 1873.

Tomus V. Monumenta e sec. XIX, signanter responsa ad encyclicam anni 1849 ex variis regnis ac provinciis complectens, *Ibid.,* 1874.

Tomus VI. Monumenta e sec. XIX, signanter inde a definitione dogmatica anni 1854, et literaturam sec. XIX usque annum 1871 complectens. *Ibid.,* 1874.

Tomus VII. Literaturam supplementarem usque a. 1871, et ulteriorem usque annum 1875 complectens. Nitriae, Siegler. 1877.

Tomus VIII. Literaturam supplementarem, et ulteriorem usque annum 1880 complectens. Nitriae, Schempek & St. Huszár, 1881.

Tomus IX. Monumenta Mariana usque annum 1880, et repertorium in novem tomos complectens. *Ibid.,* 1881.

STAMM, Christianus . . . *Mariologia, seu potiores de S. Deipara quaestiones ex SS. patrum ac theologorum mente propositae.* Paderbornae, Junfermann. xxii, 666 pp. IC pp. 3-67.

1885 BUCCERONI, Gennaro, S.J. *Commentarii de Beata Virgine Maria.* Editio altera, ab ipso auctore recognita, et novis aucta commentariis. Romae, Propaganda, 327 pp. IC pp. 15-36.

For the fourth edition, see 1896.

1888 LEGNANI, Enrico, S.J. *De secunda Eva,* commentarius in Protoevangelium. Venetiis, Aemiliana, 102 pp.

1889 PAQUET, A. A. *Disputatio theologica de Incarnatione Verbi.* Romae (Pustet) and Neo-Eboraci (Benziger). IC pp. 206-309.

1895 MENDIVE, Josephus, S.J. *Institutiones Theologiae dogmatico-scholasticae.* Vallisoleti, Cuesta. 5 vols., IC vol. III, pp. 474-505.

PESCH, Chr. *Praelectiones dogmaticae* . . . Friburgi, Brisgoviae, Herder. IC vol. III, pp. 152-186.

Republished: 1902, 1908, 1909, 1924.

1896 BUCCERONI, Gennaro, S.J. *Commentarii de SS. Corde Jesu, de Beata Virgine Maria et de Sancto Joseph, sponso B.V.M.* Romae, 262 pp.

(The Mariological section constitutes the fourth edition of the work of 1892.)

JAMAR, C. H. T. *Theologia Mariana* juxta probatissimos auctores concinnata ad normam P. SEDLMAYR . . . Lovanii, Fonteyn. IC pp. 45-54.

1898 RAMELLINI, Carolus, C.M. *In Quaest. XXVII. III. P. S. Thomae "De B. Virginis Mariae Sanctificatione" Lectiones.* Accedit Appendix de praeservatione B.M. Virginis I. a peccato originali, II. a fomite peccati in sua conceptione. Placentiae, 144 pp.

1899 DE POIX, Henri. *Tractatus theologicus de Beata Virgine Maria.* Paris, Vives.

1901 HÄNSLER, B. *De Mariae plenitudine gratiae secundum S. Bernardum* . . . Friburgi Helvet. 79 pp.

LÉPICIER, Alexis Henri Marie, Card., O.S.M. *Tractatus de beatissima Virgine Maria Matre Dei* . . . (*Institutiones theologiae speculativae.*) Parisiis, Lethielleux. [1901] xxxii, 484 pp.; IC pp. 86-147.

Republished: 1906 (3rd ed.), 1912, 1926 (Romae; "notabiliter aucta.")

(*Anon.*) *Liber de Immaculatae Beatissimae Virginis Conceptione.* (*Biblioteca de la Revista Lulliana*) Barchinone, Giró.

(Work attributed to Bl. Raymond Lull. Preface by S. BOVÉ.)

1902 JANSSENS, Laurentius, O.S.B. *Summa theologica ad modum commentarii in Aquinatis summam praesentis aevi studiis aptatam.* Friburgi Brisgoviae, Herder. IC vol. V (1902), pp. 30-160.

592　*The Dogma of the Immaculate Conception*

Aquaspartas, Matthaeus, O.F.M., Card. *Questiones disputatae de Immaculata Conceptione Beatae Mariae Virginis.* Quaracchi, S. Bonavent. 156 pp.
(Critical edition of a twelfth-century work.)

Arendt, Gulielmus, S.J. *De Protoevangelii habitudine ad Immaculatam Deiparae Conceptionem.* Romae, S. Joseph. xii, 229 pp.

Canali, Aloisius, O.F.M. *Sermo de Immaculato Mariae conceptu,* in generalibus Ordinis comitiis Romae ad S. Antonium habitis an. 1889 perlectus . . . Editio altera revisa, emendata, notisque illustrata. Ad Claras Aquas, S. Bonavent. 28 pp.

de Bustis, Bernardinus, O.F.M. *Officium et Missa de Immaculata Conceptione B.M.V.* Ad Claras Aquas, S. Bonav.
(Reprinted from *Acta O.F.M.,* 1904, as below.)

Eadmerus Cantuariensis, O.S.B. *Tractatus de conceptione sanctae Mariae* olim sancto Anselmo attributus, nunc primum integer ad codicum fidem editus adiectis quibusdam documentis coaetaneis a P. Herb. Thurston et P. Th. Slater, S.I. Friburgi Brisgoviae, Herder. xi, 104 pp.
(Critical edition of a twelfth-century work.)

Guarra, Scotus, Aureoli. *Quaestiones disputatae de Immaculata Conceptione Beatae Mariae Virginis.* (*Bibliotheca franciscana scholastica medii aevi,* tomus III.) Ad claras aquas, S. Bonavent. xix, 156 pp.
(Works originally published in the thirteenth and fourteenth centuries.)

Palmieri, Dominicus, S.I. *Tractatus de peccato originali et de Immaculato Beatae Virginis Deiparae Conceptu.* 2nd ed. Romae. 355 pp.

Patrizi, Fr. Sav., S.J. *De Immaculata Mariae origine a Deo praedicta disquisitio.* Roma, Pustet. 25 pp.

Ramoni. *Theologia mariana.* 3 vol. Retaux.

Valenzuela, Pedro Armengando, O.d.M. *De intemerato Deiparae conceptu in ordine ipsi sub titulo de Mercede dicato* . . . Romae, [s.e.] 238 pp.

van Rossum, Gulielmus Maria, Card., C. SS. R. *S. Alphonsus M. De Ligorio et Immaculata Conceptio B. Mariae Virginis.* Scripta excerpta a Gulielmo M. van Rossum, Card., C. SS. R. Romae, Propaganda. xii, 240 pp.

(*Anon.*) *Acta Ordinis Fratrum Minorum Immaculatam Conceptionem B.M.V. concernentia.* Anno ab eius definitione recurrente quinquagesimo in lucem edita iussu et auctoritate Rmi. P. Dionysii Schuler. . . . Ad Claras Aquas, S. Bonavent. 99 pp.
(= vol. XXIII, fasc. 12, pp. 385-483 of *Acta Ordinis Fratrum Minorum.* Among the contents are to be noted: "Immaculata Conceptio Beatae Mariae Virginis et Ordo Minorum," pp. 391-398; "Officium et missa de Immaculata Conceptione composita a Ven. Fr. Bernadino de Bustis, O.F.M.," pp. 401-420; "Documenta vetera de Missa Immaculatae Conceptionis," pp. 420-422; "Bibliographia seu Bibliotheca Franciscana de Immaculata Conceptione B.M.V.," pp. 454-483.)

1905 Bellarminus, Robertus. [1542-1621] *De Immaculata B.V.M. Conceptione Votum aliaque ejusdem argumenti fragmenta inedita.* Anno post definitum dogma quinquagesimo . . . Paris, Beauchesne. 82 pp.

Muncunill, Joannes, S.J. *Tractatus de Verbi Divini Incarnatione.* Matriti, Saenz de Jubera. IC pp. 524-551.

Polcari, Innocenzo, S.J. *In Beatam Mariam Virginem a Pio IX P.M. sine labe originis proclamatam.* Libri Septem. Beneventi, de Martini. 186 pp.

Senso Lazaro, Antonio. *De Immaculata Conceptione Mariae Virginis secundum s. Thomam in Summa Theologica.* Scholium in Art. 2. Quaest. 27. Part. 3. Matriti, "S. Cord. Jesu." viii, 114 pp.

1905 (continued)
VALLARO, Stefano. *De sanctitate Beatae Virginis Genitricis Mariae.* Cherii.
(*Anon.*) *Atti del Congresso Mondiale Mariano tenuto in Roma l'anno 1904,* cinquantesimo aniversario della definicione dogmatica dell'Immacolato Concepimento di Maria. Roma.
1906 LEPICIER. *De Virgine Maria.* Parisiis. 544 pp. IC pp. 84-169.
1910 (*Anon.*) *Acta II. conventus Velehradensis theologorum comercii studiorum inter Occidentem et Orientem cupidorum.* Prague.
   M. JUGIE, A.A., "De immaculata Deiparae Conceptione a byzantinis scriptoribus post schisma consummatum edocta." (p. 42 ff.)
   A. PALMIERI, O.S.A., "De academiae ecclesiasticae Kiovensis doctrina B. Mariam V. praemunitam fuisse a peccato originali." (p. 37 ff.)
1912 MANZONI, Ces. *Tractatus de B. Virgine Maria ejusque sponso S. Josepho.* Excerptus e Compendio theologiae dogmaticae.
1913 VAN CROMBRUGGHE, C. *Tractatus de Beata Virgine Maria.* Gandae, Scheerder. IC pp. 109-154.
1918 MÜLLER, Josef, S.J. *De sanctissima Dei matre.* Innsbruck, Rauch. 220 pp. ("Als Manuskript gedruckt.")
1919 DEL PRADO, Norbertus, O.P. *Divus Thomas et bulla dogmatica "Ineffabilis Deus."* Friburgi Helveticorum, S. Paul. lxiv, 402 pp. (Posthumous work.)
1924 IANNOTTA, Antonio Maria, vesc. di Aquino. *Theotocologia catholica* seu scientia de Deipara iuxta doctrinam Angelici Doctoris Divi Thomae Aquinatis methodo scholastica . . . ed. nov. Isola del Liri, Macioce e Pisani. vi, 332 pp. IC pp. 16-22; 58-137.
1931 CARACCIOLO, Landolfo, O.F.M. († 1351). *L'Immacolata Concepimento di Maria.* Questione inedita. . . . [Edited, with introduction and notes in Italian, by Diomede SCARAMUZZI, O.F.M.] Firenze, Vallechi.
   (Estratta da *Studi Francescani,* S. 3a., III (1931) n. 1.)
   JOANNES DE POLLIACO, et JOANNES DE NEAPOLI. *Quaestiones disputatae de Immaculata Conceptione Beatae Mariae Virginis* quas ad fidem codd. mss. edidit Carolus BALIĆ . . . (*Bibliotheca mariana medii aevi,* fasc. I) Sibenici, "Kacić," liv, 110 pp.
   (The original works are from the fourteenth century.)
   MUELLER, F. S. "S. Augustinus amicus an adversarius Immaculatae Conceptionis?" in *Miscellanea Agostiniana,* Testi e studi pubblicati a cura dell'Ordine eremitano di S. Agostino nel XV centenario dall'morte del santo dottore), vol. II, *Studi Agostiniani,* ed. Ant. Cassamosse, Roma, Vaticana, pp. 885-914.
1933 BALIĆ, Carolus, O.F.M. *Ioannis Duns Scoti, Doctoris Mariani, Theologiae marianae elementa* quae ad fidem codd. mss. edidit Carolus Balić, O.F.M. Sibenici.
1934 ALASTRUEY, Gregorius. *Mariologia,* sive Tractatus de Beatissima Virgine Maria Matre Dei . . . , vol. I. Vallisoleti, "Cuesta." IC vol. pp. 175-312.
   Vol. II, *ibid.,* 1941.
   BALIĆ, Carolus, O.F.M. *De Ordine Minorum tamquam duce pii fidelium sensus in quaestione de Immaculata Conceptione B.V. Mariae.* Sermo academicus occasione solemnis inaugurationis novi Athenaei Antoniani die 14 decembris 1933, habitus. Ad Claras Aquas, S. Bonavent. 57 pp.
1935 HUARTE, Gabriel, S.I. *De Deo creante et elevante ac De Novissimis . . .* ad usum privatum auditorum universitatis gregorianae. Editio altera et aucta, Romae apud aedes pontif. univer. gregor. IC pp. 566-618.
   SERRANO, Juan, O. Min. *De Immaculata prorsusque pura sanctissimaque semperque Virginis genitricis Dei Mariae Conceptione,* libri 5. Naples.
1937 JONES, Roger T. *Sancti Anselmi Mariologia.* Dissertatio Doctoralis Praesentata Facultati Theologicae Sanctae Mariae Ad Lacum. Mundelein (Illinois, U.S.A.), Seminarii Sanctae Mariae Ad Lacum. 84 pp. IC pp. 24-47.

1939 MERKELBACH, Benedictus Henricus, O.P. *Mariologia.* Tractatus de beatissima Virgine Mariae Matre Dei atque Deum inter et homines mediatrice, . . . in usum scholarum et cleri. . . . Parisiis, Desclée de Brouwer. [1939] 424 pp. IC pp. 106-142.

ROMERI, Candidus M., O.F.M. *De Immaculata Conceptione Beatae Mariae Virginis apud s. Antonium Patavinum.* (Pont. Athenaeum Antonianum —Facultas theologica. Pars thesis ad lauream in s. theologia obtinendam exhibitae.) Romae, 87 pp.

Id., Romae, Chillemi, 1939.

1940 (*Anon.*) *Clypeus contra jacula adversus sacram ac Immaculatam Virginis Conceptionem volitantia* . . . Lipziae.

(Previously published by Alva y Astorga, in *Monumenta Antiqua* . . . Lovanii, 1664, pp. 479-527.)

[BERNARDINUS A S. JOANNE ROTUNDO, O.F.M. Cap. *S. Laurentius a Brundusio et Immaculata Conceptio.* Isola del Liri, Macioce e Pisani. 147 pp.

1941 BALIĆ, Carolus, O.F.M. *De debito peccati originalis in B. Virgine Maria.* Investigationes de doctrina quam tenuit Joannes Duns Scotus. Romae, Officium libri catholici. vii, 106 pp.

(Reprinted from *Antonianum,* 1941, pp. 205-252; 317-372.)

CHIETTINI, Emmanuel, O.F.M. *Mariologia S. Bonaventurae.* Praefatio P. Caroli BALIĆ, O.F.M. (Pont. Athen. Antonianum, Theses ad lauream, 11. *Bibliotheca Franciscana medii aevi,* III.) Sibenici (Kacić) & Romae. xxvi, 214 pp.

1942 PLESSIS, Armand, S.M.M. *Manuale Mariologiae dogmaticae.* Pontchâteau, Libr. Mariale [1942]. 310 pp. IC pp. 53-93.

ROSCHINI, Gabriele Maria, O.S.M. *Mariologia.* 3 vol. Mediolani (Ancora), *et al.* [1941-1942] IC tomus III, pars secunda, pp. 11-90.

2. ed. rev. et not. aucta, Romae, Belardetti, 1947-1948.

TORTORA, Francesco. *Un grande Mariologo napoletano: Pietro Antonio Spinelli, S.J. (1555-1615).* Napoli, Borsa.

1943 LENNERZ. *Duae quaestiones de Bulla* "Ineffabilis Deus." Rome. 20 pp.

1945 SERICOLI, Cherubinus, O.F.M. *Immaculata B. M. Virginis Conceptio iuxta Xysti IV Constitutiones.* (*Bibliotheca mariana medii aevi,* Textus et disquisitiones, V) Sibenici (Kacić) & Romae (Officium Libri Catholici). xix, 174 pp.

1946 ROSCHINI, Gabriele Maria, O.S.M. *Compendium Mariologiae.* Romae, "Scientia catholica." xi, 512 pp. IC pp. 331-377. (*Cursus theologicus alexianus.*)

1948 CEUPPENS, F. *De Mariologia biblica.* Torino & Roma.

ZUBIZARRETA, V., Arzv. de Santiago de Cuba. *Theologia dogmatica.* Vol. III, Vitoria (El Carmen), pp. 561-588.

1949 GALLUS, Tiburtius, S.J. *Interpretatio mariologica protoevangelii (Gen. 3, 15) tempore postpatristico usque ad Concilium Tridentinum.* Romae, Orbis Catholicus. xvi, 215 pp.

Id. Dissert. Pont. Univ. Greg. Romae, "Pio X." 1949.

1950 BRAÑA ARRESE, Antonius, O.F.M. *De Immaculata Conceptione B. V. Mariae secundum theologos hispanos saeculi XIV.* (*Bibl. Immaculatae Conceptionis,* Textus et disquisitiones, I.) Romae, Academia Mariana & Officium Libri Catholici. xxxi, 176 pp.

MARTINELLI, Alexius, O.F.M. *De primo instanti Conceptionis B.V. Mariae.* Disquisitio de usu rationis. (*Bibl. Immaculatae Conceptionis. Textus et disquisitiones,* 2. Dissert. Pont. Athen. Antonianum.) Romae, Academia Mariana & Officium Libri Catholici. xx, 144 pp.

1951 LERCHER-SCHLAGENHAUFEN. *Mysterium Verbi Incarnati. De Ancilla Domini Salvatoris.* (Institutiones theologiae dogmaticae in usum scholarum, III.) Quinta edición. Barcelona, Herder. 372 pp.

1951 (continued)
LORENZIN, Paschalis, O.F.M. *Mariologia Jacobi a Voragine, O.P.* (*Bibliotheca Mariana Medii Aevi*, VI.) IC pp. 90-119. Romae, Academia Mariana & Officium Libri Catholici. xvi, 200 pp. IC pp. 90-119.

1952 ROSANAS, Juan, S.I. *Mariologia.* Buenos Aires, Poblet. 217 pp. IC pp. 70-93.
ROSCHINI, Gabriel M., O.S.M. *Summula Mariologiae* scholis theologicis accommodata. Romae, Belardetti. IC pp. 123-148.

1953 BERTETTO, Domenico. *Maria Immacolata, 1854-1954.* Rome.
GALLUS, Tiburtius, S.J. *Interpretatio mariologica Protoevangelii posttridentina usque ad definitionem dogmaticam Immaculatae Conceptionis. Pars prior.* Aetas aurea exegesis catholicae a Concilio Tridentino (1545) usque ad annum 1660. Roma, Edizioni di storia et letteratura. xv, 286 pp.
TONUTTI, Bonaventura, O.F.M. *Mariologia Dionysii Cartusiani (1402-1471).* Romae, Academia Mariana & Officium Libri Catholici. xii, 182 pp. IC pp. 120-133.

1954 AMERI, Hyacinthus, O.F.M. *Doctrina theologorum de Immaculata B.V. Mariae Conceptione tempore Concilii Basileensis.* (*Bibliotheca Immaculatae Conceptionis. Textus et disquisitiones*, 4.) Romae, Academia Mariana & Officium Libri Catholici. xxiv, 271 pp.
BALIĆ, Carolus, O.F.M. *Joannes Duns Scotus, Doctor Immaculatae Conceptionis.* I, Textus auctoris. (*Bibliotheca Immaculatae Conceptionis*, 5.) Romae, Academia Mariana & Officium Libri Catholici.
GALLUS, Tiburtius, S.J. *Interpretatio Mariologica Protoevangelii Posttridentina. Pars posterior,* ab anno 1661 usque ad dogmaticam definitionem Immaculatae Conceptionis. Roma, Ediz. di Storia et Letteratura. xxxviii, 383 pp.
KOROŠAK, B., O.F.M. *Mariologia S. Alberti Magni eiusque coaequalium.* (*Bibliotheca Mariana Medii Aevi*, VIII.) Romae, Academia Mariana Internationalis. xxv, 651 pp.
THOMAS DE ROSSY, ANDREAS DE NOVO CASTRO, PETRUS DE CANDIA, FRANCISCUS DE ARIMINO. *Tractatus quatuor de Immaculata Conceptione B. Mariae Virginis.* Studio et cura PP. Collegii S. Bonaventurae. Quaracchi. 412 pp.

1955 BALIĆ, Carolus, O.F.M. *Ioannes Duns Scotus et historia Immaculatae Conceptionis.* Roma, Antonianum. 159 pp.
HENRICUS DE WERLA, O.F.M. *Tractatus de Immaculata Conceptione Beatae Mariae Virginis.* Ad fidem manuscripti in lucem edidit Sophronius CLASEN, O.F.M. (*Opera Omnia*, I. *Franciscan Institute Publications*, Text series, n. 10.) New York (St. Bonaventure), and Louvain (Neuwelaerts). xxvii, 109 pp.
(Works dating from the fourteenth and fifteenth centuries.)
MELCHIOR A POBLADURA, O.F.M. Cap. *Regina Immaculata.* Studia a Sodalibus Cappucinis scripta occasione primi centenarii a proclamatione dogmatica Immaculatae Conceptionis B.M.V. collecta et edita a P. Melchiore a Pobladura, O.F.M. Cap. (*Bibliotheca Seraphico-Capuccina.* Sectio historica, Tom. XV.) Romae, Institutum historicum Ord. Fr. Min Cap. 595 pp.
MODRIĆ, Lucas, O.F.M. *Doctrina de Conceptione B. V. Mariae in controversia saec. XII.* (Pars dissertationis.) Romae, Pontificium Athenaeum Antonianum. viii, 62 pp. (P. Athen. Antonianum. Facultas Theologica. Thesis ad lauream, no. 106.)
ROSSI, J. F., C.M. *Quid senserit S. Thomas Aquinas de Immaculata Virginis Conceptione.* (*Monografie del Collegio Alberoni*, 21.) Piacenza, Collegio Alberoni. 98 pp.
(*Anon.*) *Virgo Immaculata,* vols. III, IV, V, VI, VIII/1, VIII/2. (See below, p. 611 ff.)

1956 (*Anon.*) *De Immaculata B.M.V. Conceptione apud Carmeli Teresiani Ordinem.*
        Doctrina et cultus. Romae, Ephemerides Carmeliticae. 239 pp.
    (*Anon.*) *Virgo Immaculata,* volumes II, VIII/3, XII, XVI, XVIII.
        (See below, p. 611 ff.)
1957 LENNERZ, H., S.J. *De Beata Virgine.* Tractatus dogmaticus. Romae, Gregor.
        IC pp. 73-119.
    (*Anon.*) *Virgo Immaculata,* vols. VII/2, VII/3, IX, X, XI, XIII, XIV.
        See below, p. 611 ff.
1958 (*Anon.*) *Virgo Immaculata,* vols. I, VII/1., (*Ibid.*)

DATE OF PUBLICATION UNKNOWN

FRIETHOFF, Caspar, O.P. *Praelectiones de Mariologia systematice ordinata . . .*
        ad usum privatum RR. DD. Studentium. (Inst. Pont. internat. Angelicum
        —Facultas theologica) [Roma], Copisteria V. Coscia [s.d.]. 147 pp.
        IC pp. 35-95.
HAULIK, Georgius, S.R.E. Card. Archiep. Zagrab. *Selectiores encyclicae literae
        et dictiones sacrae.* Viennae. IC tom. IV, pp. 72-99. (Letter of March
        5, 1855.)
LEONARDO. *Trigeminum Marianae Conceptionis Examen . . .* Wien, Van Ghelen.
        182 pp.
PASCUAL, Antonio Raimundo. *Mens divi Bernardi de Immaculata Virginis
        Concepcione.*
PERIS PASCUAL, Vincente. *Tractatus de Immaculata Conceptione.*
TRAPPERT, Dionysius Maria, O. Cart. [† 1886]. *Tractatus de Immaculata Conceptione
        B. V. Mariae.*
(*Anon.*) *Elucidatio sacra de ratione sufficienti ad dogmaticam definitionem.*
        [s.e., s.d.]

SPANISH[1]

1830   (MIRACULOUS MEDAL APPARITION TO SISTER CATHERINE LABOURÉ,
            PARIS, NOVEMBER 17; FIRST MEDALS STRUCK, JUNE 30, 1832)

1843 LAMBRUSCHINI, Luis. *Disertación polémica sobre la Inmaculada Concepción.*
        Traducción del italiano por D.M.S.M., Pbro. Madrid, Pita. 87 pp.

1848   (COMMITTEE APPOINTED BY POPE PIUS IX TO EXAMINE THE
            ADVISABILITY OF A DEFINITION, JUNE 1)

1849   (ENCYCLICAL LETTER *Ubi primum* OF POPE PIUS IX, FEBRUARY 2)

    PERRONE, J., S.J. *Disquisición teológica, sobre si el misterio de la Concepción
        Inmaculada de la Bienaventurada Virgen María pueda definirse por
        medio de un decreto dogmático.* Barcelona, Piferrer. 247 pp.
        (Translated from the Latin.)

1. Thanks are due to Father Angel SANTOS, S.J., librarian of the University of
Comillas, Santander, Spain, for his generous assistance in the preparation of this
bibliography, and to Father Peter Forrestal, C.S.C., of the University of Notre Dame,
for helping to correct the proofs.

1849 (continued)

SÁNCHEZ, Pascual, O.P. *Dictamen sobre la Concepción de María SS.* Expedido a petición de varios Obispos. Salamanca.

Dictamen de la Comisión del M. I. y V. Deán y Cabildo de la S. Iglesia Catedral de Guadalajara sobre la Inmaculada Concepción de María. Guadalajara, Rodríguez.
(Reprinted in *Pareri,* vol. VIII, pp. 345-435.)

Dictamen de la Universidad Literaria de Guadalajara sobre la Concepción Inmaculada de María Santísima. Guadalajara.
(Reprinted in *Pareri,* vol. VIII, pp. 441-488.)

1850 ÁGUILA, José Rafael. *Dictamen sobre el misterio de la Inmaculada Concepción de María SS.,* presentado por el Dr. José Rafael Águila, al M.J. Y. V. Cabildo eclesiástico, en 25 de Marzo de 1850. Durango.
(Reprinted in *Pareri,* vol. VIII, pp. 299-343.)

DE ROMO, Judas José, Cardenal, Arzobispo de Sevilla. *Discorso sobre la Inmaculada Concepción de María,* dedicado a S.M. la Reina Doña Isabel II (Q.D.G.) . . . Sevilla, Geofrin. 152 pp.
(Reprinted in *Pareri,* vol. VIII, p. 131.)

HERNÁNDEZ, F. M. *Sermón de la Inmaculada Concepción de María SS.* México.

1851 DEL VALLE DE SAN JUAN. *Maria sine labe concepta:* Defensa del misterio de la Inmaculada Concepción de María SS. Madrid.
(Originally published as articles in the review, *La Cruz,* Sevilla.)

1852 ARACENA, Domingo, O.P. *Dictamen del ilustrísimo i reverendísimo Arzobispo de Santiago i del Ilmo. Obispo de la Concepción sobre la declaración dogmática del privilegio de la Inmaculada Concepción de la Santísima Virgen María,* con diversas piezas relativas al mismo asunto, i el de la congregación especial encargada de dilucidar la materia. Redactado por uno de sus miembros, el R.P.M. Fr. Domingo Aracena, de la recolección dominicana. Santiago de Chile, Imprenta de la Sociedad. 6, 247, iv pp.

GARCÍA, Antonius Gonzáles, O.S.Fr. *Triunfo de María SS.* ó sea Folleto contra la Concepción Inmaculada de la Madre de Dios, escrito por . . . Pascual Sánchez 1849, e impugnado por quien le retó. Madrid, Ortigoza.

(*Anon.*) *Pareri dell'Episcopato Cattolico* . . . , vol. VIII. (See Italian bibliography under 1852.)

1854   (DEFINITION OF THE IMMACULATE CONCEPTION AS A DOGMA OF FAITH BY POPE PIUS IX, DECEMBER 8)

GODÍNEZ GARCÍA, Luis, Franciscano Observante. *Triunfo de la Verdad en justa defensa del misterio encumbrado de la Concepción sin mancha de María,* contra un dictamen que pretende negar a la Madre de Dios este privilegio excelso, y su definibilidad. 2 tom. Madrid, Castro Palomino. 1853, 1854.

1855 CASTELLANOS DE LOSADA, Basilio Sebastián. *Reseña histórica acerca de los fundamentos, devoción, controversia y festividad de la Inmaculada Concepción de María Santísima antes de ser definido de fe este misterio por nuestro Santo Padre Pío IX, el 8 de diciembre de 1854; y defensa de esta definición contra sus impugnadores.* Madrid, Alonso. 1st and 2nd editions.
(Cf. work of 1885.)

CLARET Y CLARA, Antonio María [Archbishop of Santiago de Cuba]. [Circular letter of July 16, 1855. Printed in Cuba, Barcelona and Paris. Cf. entry *Claret* under 1954.]

1855 (continued)

J.J. Y T. [= José Jiménez y Teixidó] *Nulidad de la definición dogmática de Su Santidad Pío IX acerca del misterio de la Inmaculada Concepción.* Madrid, "Europa." 52 pp.

(Composed of two articles reprinted from *Europa* and *Iberia*.)

Pulido y Espinosa. *Defensa y validez de la Definición del Dogma de la Inmaculada Concepción.*

(Anon.) *Justo homenaje, que consagra a María SS. la Academia de Santo Tomás de Aquino.* Vich.

1856 Blanco, Fernando. *Sermón de la Concepción Inmaculada de María Santísima,* que en el día 8 de diciembre de 1855 pronunció en la S.A.M. Iglesia Catedral de Santiago el Presbitero Dn. Fernando Blanco. [s.l.] Souto [s.d.] 49 pp.

Roca y Cornet, Joaquín. *María inmaculada.* Recuerdos históricos y afectuosos desahogos que luego después de haberse definido dogmáticamente el misterio de la Concepción Inmaculada de SS. Virgen María. Barcelona, Ribet. 176 pp.

1857 [Morgaez Carrillo, Braulio] *Juicio doctrinal sobre el decreto Pontificio, en que se declara artículo de fe católica que la Gran Madre de Dios fué preservada de la mancha del pecado original.* Escrito por un teólogo de los de Cuatro al Cuarto. [s.l., s.e.]

(Condemned by the S. Congregation of the Index, December 10, 1857.)

Jiménez y Teixidó, José. *Observaciones acerca de la retirada del folleto intitulado "Juicio doctrinal sobre el decreto pontificio en que se declara artículo de fe católica que la Gran Madre de Dios María Santísima fué preservada de la mancha del pecado original,"* por un teólogo de los de Cuatro al Cuarto. Madrid, García Padrón.

1858   (Apparitions of Mary Immaculate to Bernadette Soubirous, Lourdes, February 11 - July 16)

1859 Gual, Pedro. *Triunfo del Catolicismo en la definición de la Inmaculada Concepción.* Lima, Masías.

(Anon.) *Defensa de la Iglesia católica contra la Bula dogmática de Pío IX en 8 Diciembre de 1854.* Por un Americano al Congreso de la Alianza evangélica.

1860 (Anon.) *La España a la Inmaculada,* documento 700. Madrid.

1861 Nicolás, Augusto. *La Virgen María viviendo en la iglesia.* Madrid.

Republished: Lérida, 1868-1871, 2 vol.

1864 Sánchez de Gálvez, Frederico Antonio. *La mujer pura.* Estudio sobre la tradición, la creencia y el dogma de la Inmaculada Concepción de la Madre de Dios en el primer instante de su sér. (*Academia bibliog. Mariana.*) Barcelona, Her. de la V. Pla. 72 pp.

1865 Villarrasa, Eduardo María. *Las dos Inmaculadas,* o sea tratado de las analogías entre la Santísima Virgen y la Silla Apostólica en su destino, concepción, virginidad, maternidad, constancia, triunfos, poder, reino, popularidad e indefectibilidad. Barcelona, Lib. Religiosa. 289 pp.

1866 Nicolás, Augusto. *La Virgen María y el plan divino.* 4 vols. Barcelona. (Translated from the French.)

1867 (Anon.) *Album que la academia bibliográfico-mariana ofrece a su Santidad el sumo Pontífice Pío Nono.* Lérida, Carruez. 368 pp.

(Anon.) *Album en obsequio de la Inmaculada Concepción de la Santísima Virgen María . . .* Madrid, Pérez Dubrull.

1875 CONTENSON, Guillaume de, O.P. *Mariología*, a sea tratado de las grandezas de la Madre de Dios, sacada de la obra teológica del P. Vicente Contenson [1641-1674]. Traducida y anotada por el Dr. D. Juan OCROMINAS. Lérida, Carruez. 267 pp.

1876 PERRIER, M. *La estrella del progreso sobre el monte Pío IX*, ó sea historia del monumento proyectado en honor de los dogmas de la Inmaculada Concepción y de la infalibilidad pontifical. Traducido del francés por D.L.P. y dedicado a Ntra. Sra de la Academia. Lérida, Carruez. iv, 112 pp.

1879 DE LA FUENTE, Vicente. *Vida de la Virgen María con historia de su culto en España.* 2 vol. Barcelona, Montaner y Simón. 1877, 1879.

1882 PIN, L. M. *Consideraciones acerca de la Concepción Inmaculada de María...* Traducido de la 3a edic. francesa por D. Tomás Cortés y Aguiló. Barcelona, "Inmaculada Concepción."

1884 [NICOLÁS, Augusto]. *La Concepción Inmaculada de la Santísima Virgen María Madre de Dios.* Lérida, Mariana. 111 pp.
   (Translated from the French; includes other works also, e.g., 53-62, CASTELLANO Y CARLÉS, Pascual: "Discurso sobre la Inmaculada Concepción de la Santísima Virgen María.")

1885 CASTELLANOS, Sebastián. *La Inmaculada Concepción.* Madrid.
   (Cf. work of 1855.)

1888 GRAVOIS, Marco Antonio, Franciscano Recoleto. *Del origen y progreso del culto y festividad de la Inmaculada Concepción de la bienaventurada Virgen María, Madre de Dios.* Obra escrita en latín . . . traducida al castellano por D. Vicente Calatayud y Bonmantí . . . Lérida, Mariana. 266 pp.
   (The original is from the eighteenth century; cf. p. 323.)

1891 SILÍCEO, Cardenal. *Opúsculos Marianos.* Lérida.

1893 SERRANO Y ORTEGA, Manuel. *Glorias Sevillanas.* Noticia histórica de la devoción y culto que la muy noble y muy leal Ciudad de Sevilla ha profesado a la Inmaculada Concepción de la Virgen María desde los tiempos de la antigüedad hasta la presente época. Sevilla, Rasco. 920 pp. 30 plates.
   (*Anon.*) *Las universidades españolas y la Inmaculada Concepción.* Oficio parvo de la Inmaculada. Plática de San Gonzaga a los estudiantes de Siena. Oficio parvo de S. Luis Gonzaga. Barcelona, De Henrich (*Laus Perennis* II). 91 pp.

1895 [MESEGUER Y COSTA, José, Bishop of Lérida.] *Mística azucena dedicada a la Inmaculada Concepción de María Santísima patrona del seminario conciliar de Lérida* por el Ilmo. Sr. Obispo de la Diócesis . . . Lérida, Mariana.

1896 BOURASSÉ, Juan Jaime. *Summa Aurea de las alabanzas de la Bienaventurada Virgen María Madre de Dios concebida sin pecado.* Tomos IV-VIII. Lérida, Imp. Mariana, 1894, 1896.
   (Translation from the Latin *et al.* For works treating the IC, see Latin bibliography at 1862.)

1899 RODRÍGUEZ, Alonso, San, S.J. [1526-1616] *Devoción a la Purísima Concepción.* Santander, Propaganda Católica. 16 pp.

1901 HERNÁNDEZ VILLAESCUSA, Modesto. *La Inmaculada Concepción y las Universidades Españolas.* 2ª edición. Oñate. vi, 86 pp.

1902 PÉREZ-SANJULIÁN, Joaquín. *Historia de la Santísima Virgen María, del desarrollo de su culto y de sus principales advocaciones en España y en América.* 3 tom. Madrid, Dojas.

1904   (FIFTIETH ANNIVERSARY OF THE DEFINITION)

1904 Arqués y Arrufat, Ramón. *Lo dogma de la Immaculada en la literatura catalana antiga.* Noticies reunides . . . en commemoració del cinquantenari de la definició dogmática. Lleyda, Farré.

Briceño. *La doctrina del angélico doctor sobre la Inmaculada Concepción de la Madre de Dios.* León.

Castellote, Salv. *Memoria histórica sobre las vicisitudes por que ha pasado en España la creencia en la Concepción Inmaculada de María Santísima.* Roma, Artigianelli (also Madrid?) 142 pp.

Costa y Fornagnera, Tomás, arciv. de Tarragona. *Carta Pastoral del Exmo. é Ilmo. Sr. Dr. D. Tomás Costa y Fornagnera* . . . que dirige al clero y fieles de su diócesis con motivo de la celebración del Quincuagésimo aniversario de la definición del dogma de la Inmaculada. Tarragona, Aris. 26 pp.

Gil, Heliodoro. *España y la Inmaculada Concepción.* Madrid, Apostolado de la Prensa.

Hernández, Luis Martín. *Inmaculada!* Colección de artículos referentes al misterio de la Purísima Concepción de la Santísima Virgen . . . Salamanca, Guervos. viii, 135 pp.

Meseguer y Costa, José [Bishop of Lérida, transferred the following year to archiepiscopal see of Granada]. *El primer quincuagenario de la definición dogmática de la Inmaculada ante la sociedad, la Iglesia y España por el Obispo de Lérida.* Lérida, Farré. 15 pp.

Ortega, Angel. O.F.M. *La Inmaculada Concepción y los Franciscanos.* Loreto, San Antonio. [1904] 136 pp.

Pérez de Guzmán y Gallo, Juan. *El primer Certamen Poético que se celebró en España en honor de la Purísima Concepción de María, Madre de Dios, Patrona de España y de la Infantería Española.* (*Sevilla, 26 de Abril de 1615*). Hallado original y autógrafo en el tomo XCII del Fondo de Jesuitas de la Real Academia de la Historia . . . Publicado . . . en conmemoración del primer cincuentenario de la declaración dogmática del sagrado Misterio. Madrid, Fortanet. cxxviii, 36 pp.

1905 Abad, Camilo M., S.I. *El culto de la Inmaculada Concepción en la ciudad de Burgos.* Madrid.

Borondo y Romero, Jorge. *El dogma de la Inmaculada Concepción de la Santísima Virgen María en sus relaciones con el orden moral.* Memoria sobre el tema XVIII del programa del Certamen Científico Literario celebrado en Toledo con motivo de las fiestas jubilares en honor de la Inmaculada. Lema, "Tabernaculum suum Dominus santificavit." Toledo, Rodríguez. 157 pp.

Gazulla, Faustino. *Los reyes de Aragón y la Purísima Concepción de María Santísima.* Barcelona.

Mir y Noguera, Juan, S.J. *La Inmaculada Concepción* . . . Madrid, Sáenz de Jubera. x, 574 pp.

Oller, J. M., S.J. *España y la Inmaculada Concepción de la Santísima Virgen.* Memoria histórica premiada en el Certamen Mariano de Zaragoza. Madrid. xi, 242 pp.

Reyes, Rafael, S.J. *La Concepción Inmaculada según el Nuevo Testamento.* Jerez de la Frontera, Salido. 74 pp.

(*Anon.*) *El rito muzárabe, y la Inmaculada Concepción de María.* Toledo.

1906 Fernández de Castro, Venancio Mª. *Catecismo sobre la declaración dogmática de la Inmaculada Concepción de María.* Valladolid. El Porvenir. 56 pp.

Martín y Campos, Manuel. *Sevilla por el Dogma de la Pureza Original de Nuestra Señora la Virgen María* . . . Trabajo premiado en el **Certamen** celebrado en el quincuagenario de la definición, con un objeto de **arte,**

1906 (continued)
por el Excelentísimo y Reverendísimo Señor Arzobispo don Marcelo Spínola y Maestre. Sevilla, Hidalgo. 62 pp.

1907 DEL PRADO, Norberto, O.P. *Carta a un joven teólogo sobre el dogma de la Inmaculada Concepción.* 24 pp.

SALVADOR, Federico. *Del culto de la Inmaculada.* Granada, Guevara.

1908 BORRAS, J. *María S. y el R. Pontífice en las obras del Bto. Ramón Lull.*

CAPARROSO. *La Inmaculada Concepción de Duns Scoto.* Pamplona.

[DEL PINO, José García] *La fiesta de la Concepción, en la antigua iglesia de Santiago y san Ildefonso de los Españoles en Roma, el año 1715,* según un Ms. inédito de la Embajada de S.M. Cat. cerca de la Santa Sede: con dos apéndices de notas y documentos, y 29 ilustraciones. Monografía histórica . . . [Edited by Ramón DE SANTA MARÍA.] Rome, Propaganda. vii, 113 pp.

DEL PRADO, Norberto, O.P. *Santo Tomás y la Inmaculada.* Carta segunda a un joven teólogo. . . . Vergara, tip. de El Sant. Rosario. 19 pp.

1909 ALUJAS BROS, Moisés. *Santo Tomás y la Inmaculada Concepción de la Virgen María.* Ensayo crítico . . . Premiado en el Certamen celebrado en el Seminario Conciliar de Tortosa, el 9 de Mayo de 1905. Prólogo del M. Iltre. Sr. Dr. D. Salvador Bové . . . Barcelona, Librería Católica Internacional. xxvii, 79 pp.

DEL PRADO N., O.P. *Santo Tomás y la Inmaculada.* Barcelona (Internacional) —Vergara. 250 pp.

FITA Y COLOMER, F., S.J. *Tres discursos históricos. Panegírico de la Inmaculada Concepción. (Colección diplomática.)* 2nd ed. Madrid.

1911 PORTUGAL, José M. de Jesús (Obispo de Aguascalientes, México). *La Inmaculada Concepción de la Virgen Santísima a la luz de la divina escritura, según la enseñanza de los santos padres y de los teólogos católicos.* Barcelona. 472 pp.

1917 ORTEGA, Angel, O.F.M. *La tradición Concepcionista en Sevilla. Siglos XVI-XVIII.* Notas histórico-críticas con motivo de un proyecto de Monumento a la Inmaculada Concepción en esta Ciudad . . . Sevilla, San Antonio. 94 pp.

1918 GARRIGUET, Luis. *La Virgen María.* Su predestinación. Su dignidad. Sus privilegios. Su misión. Sus virtudes. Sus méritos. Su gloria. Su intercesión. Su culto. Barcelona, Bloud y Gay. 458 pp. IC pp. 82-181.

1919 FRÍAS, S.J. *Los Reyes de España y la Inmaculada.* Madrid, "Razón y Fe."

1922 SALAVADOR RAMÓN, Francisco. *Teología Mariana. (Bibliotheca aurea,* série 2, obra 3.) 3 vol. Guadix, "Divina Infantita." 1921-22. IC vol. I, pp. 220-275.

1923 OCERIN JAUREGUI, Andrés, O.M. *Fundamento Doctrinal y relaciones entre el Reino de Cristo y el Reino de la Inmaculada.* Memoria presentada al XXV Congreso Eucarístico celebrado en Lourdes en 1914, Guadix, "Divina Infantita." 18 pp.

(Anon.) Sevilla por la Inmaculada Concepción. El monumento conmemorativo del III Centenario del Voto y Juramento Concepcionista . . . Sevilla, Macía y Flores. 53, 46 pp.

1924 LÓPEZ, Juan. *Concepción y Nacencia de la Virgen.* (Introducción y notas de Luis G. A. GETINO, O.P.) Madrid, "La Ciencia Tomista." cxix, 288 pp. *(Biblioteca Clásica Dominicana, 7.)*
(The original work is from the fifteenth century.)

1926 EGUÍA RUIZ, Constancio, S.J. *María y sus gracias.* Barcelona, "Religiosa." IC pp. 3-16; 63-75.

1928 BAYLE, Constantino, S.J. *Santa María en Indias.* La devoción a Nuestra Señora y los Descubridores, Conquistadores y Pobladores de América. Ilustraciones de Arribas B. Madrid, "Apostolado de la Prensa." 369 pp.

1928 (continued)
TERRIEN, J. B., S.J. *La Madre de Dios y la Madre de los hombres según los Santos Padres y la teología.* Madrid, Voluntad.
(Translated from the French.)

1931 ALTISENT, Juan B. *Lérida y la Inmaculada.* Lérida, "Mariana." pp. 103-202.

LUIS Y PÉREZ, Juan Bautista. "Fiesta de la Inmaculada," in *Cartas pastorales del Obispo de Oviedo Dr. D. Juan Bautista Luis y Pérez.* Oviedo, "La Cruz." 15 pp.

1939 GARCÍA GARCÉS, Narciso, C.M.F., *Títulos y grandezas de María,* o explicación teológico-popular de los misterios y prerrogativas de la celestial Señora. Madrid, Coculsa [s.d.]. xvi, 275 pp. IC pp. 201-208.
2nd ed. *ibid.,* 1952. xv, 536 pp.

1941 DE SOLA, Francisco, S.J. *La Inmaculada Concepción.* Estudio histórico-dogmático-litúrgico. Barcelona, "Lumen." 242 pp.

GOMA Y TOMÁS, Isidro, Card. *María Santísima.* Obra póstuma . . . 2 tom., Barcelona, Casulleras, 1941-1942. T. I, Estudios y escritos pastorales sobre la Virgen. IC pp. 381-394.
2a edic., 1947.

1942 TERRIEN, J. B., S.J. *La Madre de Dios y Madre de los hombres según los santos Padres y la Teología.* Traducción directa de la quinta edición francesa. 4 tomos. Madrid, Fax.

1943 SÁNCHEZ PÉREZ, José Augusto. *El culto Mariano en España.* (Consejo superior de investigaciones científicas; Instituto "Antonio de Nebrija"; Biblioteca de tradiciones populares.) Madrid, [s.e.]. 482 pp., 213 plates.

1944 DE GOICOECHEA Y VITERI, Jesús María, O.F.M. *Doctrina Mariana de Enrique de Gante.* Lima, Scheuch. 76 + xxx pp.

ESCRIBANO, E. *La Virgen Nuestra Señora.* Madrid, "La Milagrosa." 548 pp.

1945 ALASTRUEY, Gregorio. *Tratado de la Virgen Santísima.* Primera versión castellana de la Mariología latina del mismo Autor. Madrid, Católica. xxxvii, 974 pp. IC pp. 140-244; 262-269.
2nd ed. *ibid.,* 1947; 3rd ed. *ibid.,* 1951.

BERNARD, R., O.P. *El Misterio de María.* Buenos Aires.
(Translated from the French.)

1946 PÉREZ, Nazario, S.J. *Historia Mariana de España.* Publicada por entregas de la Obra de la Propaganda Mariana. 3 vol. Valladolid [s.e.]. 1945-46.

1947 GARRIGOU-LAGRANGE, Réginald, O.P. *La Madre del Salvador y nuestra vida interior.* Mariología. Versión castellana [from the French] del Pbro. José López Navío. Buenos Aires, Desclée de Brouwer. [1947] 331 pp. IC pp. 42-71.
2a edic., 1950.

1948 LAGO, Bernardino, O.F.M. "La Asunción corporal de la Santísima Virgen y su Concepción Inmaculada," in *Actas del Congreso Mariano franciscano-español,* Madrid. pp. 167-180.
(= Verdad y vida, VI (1948), en. sept., num. 21-24)

RICART, José. *La mariología del Dr. Torras y Bagés.* Prólogo de Juan PERELLÓ. Barcelona, Católica Casals. 412 pp.

TERRIEN. *La Madre de Dios y la Madre de los hombres.* 4 vols. Madrid.
(Translated from the French.)

1949 CHÁVEZ, Ricardo [Bishop of Oruro] "La Inmaculada Concepción y su influencia en la civilización." In *Primer Congreso Mariano Nacional* . . . La Paz. pp. 161-166.

PÉREZ, Nazario, S.J. *Mariología popular.* La Madre admirable en la mente divina y en el Antiguo Testamento, en su vida mortal, en su vida gloriosa,

1949 (continued)

en la Iglesia y en las almas . . . 2. ed. Valladolid, Gerper. 392 pp. IC pp. 85-123.

(The "first edition" was by parts, in various places, e.g. in *Estrella del Mar*.)

1950 AGUILERA CAMACHO, Daniel. *La Inmaculada y Córdoba*. Loores y leticias literarios, iconografía y culto concepcionistas en la capital y 121 pueblos de la provincia, historiados a través del tiempo. Córdoba, Artística. 333 pp.

(Reprinted from *Revista Universitaria*, of the Universidad Católica de Chile, xxxiv (1949), no. 3, pp. 33-117.)

SAURAS, Emilio, O.P. "La Asunción y el dogma de la Inmaculada," in *La Asunción de la Santísima Virgen*, (*Biblioteca de Tomistas Españoles*, V. XII), Valencia, F.E.D.A. [1950], pp. 426-439.

1951 DE MUÑANA, Ramón J., S.J. *Lecciones marianas*. 2 tom. Bilbao, "El Mensajero del Corazón de Jesús." 1950, 1951. T.I.: *Vida y misterios de María*. IC pp. 31-83.

SEVERINO DE SANTA TERESA, O.C.D. *Vírgenes conquistadoras que Santa Teresa envió a las Américas; la purísima Concepción y nuestra Señora del Carmen*. Historia documentada de estas dos Imágenes y del desarrollo de su culto y devoción en Ibero América . . . Vitoria (El Carmen) & San Sebastián. 774 pp.

(*Anon.*) "Concepción (Inmaculada, de la Santísima Virgen)" in *Enciclopedia de la Religión Católica*. Barcelona, Dalman y Jover, II (1951), col. 926-932.

1952 MOURE, Pedro, S.O.P. *El padre maestro Fr. Domingo Aracena, O.P. y su doctrina acerca de la Inmaculada Concepción de María*. (Pars dissertationis ad lauream in facultate S. Theologiae apud Pontif. Inst. "Angelicum" de Urbe.) Santiago de Chile. ix, 87 pp.

(Reprinted from the *Revista Universitaria* of the Universidad Católica de Chile, xxxiv, 3 (1949) pp. 33-117.)

1954 ALAMEDA, Santiago, O.S.B. *María segunda Eva*. Tratado teológico biográfico sobre la Santísima Virgen. Vitoria, "Estibaliz." IC pp. 221-286.

BARBERO MARTÍNEZ, Luis. *La Inmaculada Concepción y España*. Madrid, Gloria. [1954] 318 pp., with plates.

CLARET, Antonius Maria, S. *María Inmaculada*. Carta pastoral dirigida a sus diocesanos al definirse dogma de fe la Concepción Inmaculada de María. Santiago de Cuba, 1855. Edición cuarta, presentada por el P. FRANQUESA, C.M.F. . . . Madrid, Coculsa [1954]. 184 pp.

FRÍAS, Lesmes, S.J. *Antigüedad de la fiesta de la Inmaculada Concepción en las Iglesias de España*. Dos estudios inéditos del P. Lesmes Frías, S.J. Comillas, Universidad Pontificia. 63 pp.

MAÑARICUA, Andrés E. *La Inmaculada en Vizcaya*. Bilbao, Desclée de Brouwer. 232 pp.

MARTÍNEZ, Pedro de Alcántara, O.F.M. *La Redención y el débito de María* (*Siglos XVII-XVIII*). (Virgo Redempta. Estudio de la teología sobre la redención de la Virgen en los siglos XVII-XVIII. Tesis presentada en la facultad de teología. Universidad de Salamanca.) Madrid, "Verdad y Vida." 110 pp.

MERKELBACH, Benito Enrique, O.P. *Mariología. Tratado de la Santísima Virgen María Madre de Dios y Mediadora entre Dios y los hombres*. Traducido [from the Latin] y notablemente mejorado por el P. Pedro ARENILLAS, O.P. (*Stella matutina*, 2) Bilbao, Desclée de Brouwer. 592 pp.

MONTÁNCHEZ, Jesús. *María, Madre de Dios*. Tratado dogmático teológico. Buenos Aires, Compañía del Divino Maestro. IC pp. 176-185; 205-266.

1954 (continued)

NEUBERT, Emile, S.M. *María en el dogma.* Versión de la 2. ed. francesa por el p. Miguel Fernández de Prada y D. Gregoria Cerio. [Zalla] Ed. Paulinas [1954.] 275 pp.

PÉREZ, Nazario, S.J. *La Inmaculada y España.* Santander, "Sal Terrae." xxxii, 480 pp.

RAMBLA, Pascual, O.F.M. *Tratado popular sobre la Santísima Virgen.* Todos los temas marianos al alcance del gran público. Barcelona, Vilamala. 510 pp.

SEVERINO DE SANTA TERESA, P., O.C.D. *La Inmaculada en la conquista y coloniaje de la América Española.* Vitoria, Carmen. 343 pp.

SIMÓN DÍAZ, José. *Los votos concepcionistas de la Villa de Madrid . . . (Temas Madrileñas,* vol. X) Madrid, Estudios Madrileños, 25 pp.

(*Anon.*) *La Inmaculada en el Carmelo,* por los padres Carmelitas de la antigua observancia (Calzados) de Zaragoza. Zaragoza, Gráficas Salduba. 71 pp.

(*Anon.*) *La Inmaculada y El Carmelo.* (Congreso Nacional Mariano 1954. Sección Carmelitana.) Vitoria, "El Carmen." 214 pp.

(*Anon.*) *La Inmaculada y la Provincia Franciscana de Santiago en el I Centenario de la Definición Dogmática, 1854-1954.* Liceo Franciscano 7. 388 pp.

(*Anon.*) *Primer Centenario de la declaración del dogma de la Inmaculada Concepción.* Discursos leídos en la Junta solemne conmemorativa de 30 de enero de 1954 por los excelentísimos señores D. Lorenzo RIBER CAMPINS . . . D. Luis PÉREZ BUENO . . . y Fray José LÓPEZ ORTIZ . . . Madrid, Góngora. 49 pp.

1955 AGUIREBEITÍA, Severino de Santa Teresa, O.C.D. *Vizcaya por la Inmaculada.* Estudio histórico . . . Vitoria, "El Carmen." [1955] 272 pp.

ANGUITA VALDIVIA, José. *Manuscritos Concepcionistas en la Biblioteca Nacional.* Madrid. Dirección General de Archivos y Bibliotecas. 122 pp.

DEL SDO. CORAZÓN, Enrique, O.C.D. *Los Salmanticenses: su vida y su obra.* Ensayo histórico y proceso inquisitorial de su doctrina sobre la Inmaculada. (Extracto de la tesis doctoral, presentada en la Facultad de Teología.) Madrid, Editorial de Espiritualidad. xxxvii, 277 pp.

PÉREZ DE URBEL, J. "Las advocaciones marianas en España," in *Anuario Católico Español,* Madrid, 1955, pp. 113-590.

(*Anon.*) *La Inmaculada y la Merced.* Secciones Mercedaria y Sudamericana. (Il Congreso Mariológico Internacional.) 2 vol. Roma, Curia generalicia de Mercedarios.

(*Anon.*) *Virgo Immaculata,* vol. VI, VIII/1. (See Latin bibliography at 1958.)

1956 (*Anon.*) *Memoria del Congreso Mariano Nacional de Zaragoza. 1954.* Prólogo y presentación del Excmo. y Revmo. Sr. Dr. D. Casimiro MORILLO Y GONZÁLEZ, arzobispo de Zaragoza. (Estudios Mariológicos.) Zaragoza [Artes gráficas, El Noticiero], 1014 pp.

Em. SAURAS, O.P., "Contenido doctrinal del misterio de la Inmaculada." (Pp. 143-191)

Máximo PEINADOR, C.M.F., "Estudio comparativo de las pruebas de Escritura en favor de la Inmaculada." (193-221)

Jesús SOLANO, S.J., "La Inmaculada en los Padres Españoles." (223-248)

Marc. LLAMERA, O.P., "El problema del débito y la redención preservativa." (249-310)

Antonio HORTELANO, C.SS.R., "La Inmaculada y la Psicología." (311-341)

Basilio DE S. PABLO, C.P., "La Inmaculada y la muerte de María." (343-370)

1956 (continued)

Antonio RIERA, T.O.R., "La doctrina inmaculista en los orígenes de nuestras lenguas romances." (371-416)

Laurentino N. HERRAN, "La Inmaculada en la literatura [i.e. poetic, not theological] de los siglos XVIII-XX." (417-472)

Joaquín ALONSO, C.M.F. (Ponencia), "Constitutivo formal del privilegio de la Concepción Inmaculada de María." (473-498)

Basilio DE PABLOS, "Memoria sobre la Ponencia anterior." (499-513)

A. GELABERT, O.P. (Ponencia), "Ensayo teológico-psicológico sobre la Inmaculada." (515-527)

Jaime Colomina TORNER, "Memoria sobre la Ponencia anterior." (529-580)

Leopoldo BAYO (Ponencia), "Proposiciones de la Concepción Inmaculada sobre la santidad y misión total de María, en orden a fundamentar nuevos avances de la Mariología." (581-588)

Benito PRADA, C.M.F., "Memoria sobre la anterior ponencia." (589-636)

Angel GOENAGA, S.J. (Ponencia), "El folklore inmaculístico español." (637-652)

Vicente TENA (Ponencia), "Anecdotario Inmaculista." (635-661)

Ismael DE SANTA TERESITA, O.C.D., "El Carmelo por la definición dogmática de la Concepción Inmaculada de María." (758-788)

Hno. Manuel RODRÍGUEZ, "La inclusión del 'Mater Immaculata' en la letanía lauretana." (900-912)

Antonio VÁZQUEZ, O. de M., "Inmaculada Concepción y psicología de la Virgen." (914-922)

(*Anon.*) *Virgo Immaculata*, vols. II, VIII/3, XII. (See Latin bibliography at 1958.)

1957 (*Anon.*) *Virgo Immaculata*, vols. IX, X, XI, XIII, XIV. (See Latin bibliography at 1958.)

DATE OF PUBLICATION UNKNOWN

DE LA PEÑA Y LAZCANO, Pablo. *Información histórica y eclesiástica en que se prueba que el glorioso doctor San Ildefonso, Arzobispo de Toledo y Primado de las Españas, afirmó en diversos lugares de sus escritos de la Purísima Virgen María, que fué concebida sin mancha . . .*

DEL PUERTO, Juan. *La tradición concepcionista de Sevilla.*

GUAL, Pedro, O.F.M. *El dogma de la Inmaculada Concepción;* refutación del doctor Vigil.
    (Cf. Italian translation in *Pareri* VIII [1952], p. 1 ff.)

MORERA, Emilio. *El culto de la Inmaculada en Tarragona y su provincia eclesiástica.*

MONTESINO, Alfonso. *Tratado de la Concepción de Ntra. Sra.*

MUÑOZ Y PAVÓN, Juan Francisco. *Llena de gracia.* (Diálogo concepcionista.)

PACHECO, Francisco. *Apacible conversación entre un tomista y un congregado acerca del misterio de la Inmaculada Concepción.* Reimpreso por Asensio.

SAIZ GÓMEZ, Julián. *Antonio Calderón, Arzob. Electo de Granada y la controversia concepcionista del siglo XVII.* [s.d.] 112 pp.

(*Anon.*) *Fundamentos de la definición dogmática de la Inmaculada.* Razón y Fe. Madrid, Rivadeneyra. [s.d.] 269 pp.

APPENDIX TO THE BIBLIOGRAPHY

The contents of the following three collections are given in detail in order to facilitate their consultation by scholars who may have to borrow individual volumes from a considerable distance.

The authors of the individual articles have not been listed in the Index to the Bibliography.

PARERI

Pareri dell'Episcopato Cattolico di capitoli, di congregazioni, di università, di personaggi ragguardevoli ecc. ecc. sulla definizione dogmatica dell'Immacolato Concepimento della B.V. Maria rassegnati alla Santità di Pio IX. P.M. in occasione della sua Enciclica data da Gaeta il 2 Febraio 1849. Roma, Coi Tipi della Civiltà Cattolica [1851-1854].[1]

PARTE PRIMA.
Volume Primo (1851). *Enciclica del Sommo Pontefice [Ubi Primum*—Caietae die 2 feb. anno 1849] alla quale sono date in risposta le lettere contenute in questi volumi. [The rest of the volume is taken up by the replies of archbishops, bishops, patriarchs, vicar apostolics, etc. to the encyclical letter.]
Volume Secondo (1851). [Continuation of the replies as given in volume I.]
Volume Terzo (1851). [Continuation of the replies as given in volumes I and II, followed by indices.]

PARTE SECONDA.
Volume Quarto (1851). [Letters, etc. from other notables, prefaced by a text from Bl. LEONARD OF PORT MAURICE (pp. 5-8); with an appendix of replies from archbishops and bishops received too late for inclusion in Part I.]

PARTE TERZA.
Volume Quinto (1851)
Congruenze sociali di una definizione dogmatica sull'Immacolato Concepimento della B.V.M.; dei Compilatori della CIVILTÀ CATTOLICA. pp. vii-xxvi
Dissertazione, in cui si prova che Maria Vergine sia stata necessariamente concepita Immacolata per necessaria conseguenzà dell'infallibile dogma della Divina sua Maternità; dell'Abate Cassinese D. Gaspare RIVAROLA. (Palermo presso *Lorenzo Dato* 1822) 7-97
Voto umilissimo della Trevigiana Diocesi innalzato dal suo Vescovo ad illustrazione e difesa del privilegio specialissimo di un Immacolato Concepimento concedute all'eccelsa Nostra Signora (Trevisó, dalla Tipografia Andreola 1849) 99-122
Sull'Immacolato Concepimento di Maria; Dissertazione polemica del Card. Luigi LAMBRUSCHINI Vescovo di Sabina, Bibliotecario di S. Chiesa ecc, ecc. (Roma coi Tipi della S. Congregazione di Propaganda Fide 1843) 123-179
Voto in forma di dissertazione sulla definizione dogmatica dell'Immacolato Concepimento della B. V. M. del P. Pietro BIANCHERI Prete della Congregazione della Missione. 181-579

---

[1] The following *partial* list of contents indicates only the more noteworthy documents contained in this collection.

Esame critico sulla dottrina dell'Angelico Dottore S. Tommaso di Aquino, circa il peccato originale relativamente alla Beatissima Vergine Maria del P.M. Fr. Mariano SPADA de'Predicatori, già Reggente del Collegio della Minerva in Roma. Napoli presso *Saverio Giordano* 1839) 581-660

Dissertazione di un Prete della Congregazione dell'Oratorio di Venezia, nella quale, ritenutosi che Maria SS. sia stata preservata dell'atto d'incorrere nella colpa d'origine nel primo istante della infusione dell'anima sua nel suo corpo, studiasi di mostrare che sia stata preservata altresì da ogni debito di incontrarla. (Venezia, dalla Tip. Armena di S. Lazzaro 1849) 663-682

Cenni sull'Immacolata Concezione di M.V. Madre di Dio e Regina dell'universo; compilati dall'avv. Cesare FONDORA. (Lucca Tip. di Tommaso Torcigliani 1850) 683-719

Dissertazione di D. Gaetano MARTORELLI Arcidiacono della Cattedrale di Osimo sull'opportunità del tempo da dichiarar dogma di Fede l'Immacolato Concepimento di Maria SS. (In Recanati pei fratelli Merici Tipografi, 1850) 721-733

Ragionamento dedicato all'Immacolata Concezione di Maria Vergine. (Torino, Tipografia diretta da Paolo De-Agostini, 1851) 735-767

Dissertazione dell'Arciprete Agostino OPITZ nella Diocesi di Vratislavia [translated from the German by the editors of the *Pareri*]. 769-774

Pastorale dell'Emo. Card. Arciv. di Ferrara, in occasione dell'Enciclica di S.S. PIO PAPA IX, intorno all Immacolata Concezione della B.V.M.

Pastorale di Monsig. Vescovo d'Aiaccio, in occasione della Enciclica medesima. 778-782

Estratto dal processo verbale della Conferenze Ecclesiastica tenutasi dai Vescovi di Lombardia a Groppello presso Milano, sotto le Presidenza dell'Arciv. Metropolita il 23 maggio 1849. 783

Circolare del Vescovo di Acqui in Piemonte. 784-787

Volume Sesto (1852)

Enchiridion super duodecim momenta fundatum, ex quibus exurgit Triumphus B. Mariae Virginis Matris Dei in Originale Peccatum; auctore Canonico Hon. Dominico CERRI Theol. Iurisque Canonici Professore emerito, publico et ordinario. (Taurini, Ex. Typis Alexandri Fontana 1851) 1-216

Theologica de Immaculata Conceptione B.V. Mariae Dissertatio, Auctore Iosepho Maria DIEZ DE SOLLANO . . . (Mexici: Ex Typographia R. Rafael. An. 1849) 217-308

De Immaculato B.V. Mariae Conceptu An dogmatico Decreto definiri possit; Disquisitio Theologica Ioannis PERRONE e Societate Iesu in Coll. Rom. Theol. Prof. Editio altera emendata et brevibus accessionibus ab ipso auctore locupletata. (Monasterii Guestphalorum, Typis et sumptibus Librariae Theissingianae 1848) 309-608

Pastorale del Vescovo di Acqui. (die 1 Decembris 1844) 621-637

Volume Settimo (1852)

Mémoire sur la question de l'Immaculée Conception de la très sainte Vierge par le R.P. Dom Prosper GUÉRANGER Abbé de Solesmes. (Paris 1850, Julien et C. éditeurs) 1-130

Question de l'Immaculée Conception. Délibération de la Commission chargeé de l'examiner. [= Commission appointed by Cardinal de La Tour-D'Auvergne, diocese of Arras.] 137-194

Instruction Pastorale de Monseigneur l'Archevêque de Reims à son clergé sur l'Immaculée Conception de la S.V. Marie, Mère de Dieu. (Thomas-Marie-Joseph GOUSSET) . . . le 5 Avril 1849 205-225

Instruction Pastorale de Monseigneur l'Evêque de Langres, Pierre-Louis PARISIS. . . . (le 2 juillet 1849) 254-298

APPENDICE SECONDA AL VOL. IX.
Volume Undecimo (1854)
    Selectae quaedam theses De Immaculata B. Mariae Virginis Conceptione in Universitati catholica Lovaniensi secundum veterem Theologorum Lovaniensium sententiam nuperrime propugnatae.   380-394

SUMMA AUREA

BOURASSÉ, Joannes Jacobus. *Summa aurea de laudibus Beatissimae Virginis Mariae, Dei Genitricis sine labe conceptae*, omnia quae de gloriosissima Virgine Maria Deipara scripta praeclariora reperiuntur in sacris bibliis, operibus sanctorum Patrum, decretis conciliorum, constitutionibus Romanorum Pontificum et libris celeberrimorum doctorum, historica methodo et ordine temporum digesta, complectens; necnon monumenta hagiographica, liturgica, theologica, ascetica, encomiastica, paraenetica, etc. quibus, adstruitur, illustratur, vindicatur dogma catholicum de praerogativis, virtutibus, cultu, intercessione et laudibus Sanctissimae Virginis Deiparae. 13 tomi. Paris, Migne. [Tomi I-XII, 1862; tomus XIII, 1866.]

Tomus I.
    PARS PRIMA. HISTORIA MARIANA.
    Sectio Prima. "Mariae Sanctissimae vita et gesta per dissertationes descripta," auctore Joanne Chrysostomo TROMBELLI.

Tomus II.
    Sectio Secunda. "Historia Deiparae V. Mariae, ad veritatem collecta, et veterum Patrum testimoniis comprobata, accurateque discussa," per P. Christophorum DE CASTRO, S.J.
    Sectio Tertia. "De reliquiis B. Virginis Mariae," auctore J. C. TROMBELLI.
    Sectio Quarta. "De aedibus quas incoluit SS. Virgo," auctore eodem.
    Sectio Quinta. "Iconographia B. Virginis Mariae," eodem auctore.

    PARS SECUNDA. QUAE PRO B. VIRGINE GESSIT DEUS.
    Sectio Prima. "Biblia Mariana, ex pluribus Divinarum Scripturarum commentariis excerpta," per J. DE S. MIGUEL et Barco BURGENSEM, O.P.

Tomus III.
    Sectio Secunda. Mundus Marianus.
    I.   "Symbola Virginea," . . . Rev. D. Philippo PICINELLI . . .
    II. "Hortus Marianus," . . . R. P. Michaele PEXEN-FELDER, S.I.

    PARS TERTIA. QUAE IN HONOREM B. V. MARIAE GESSIT ECCLESIA.
    Sectio Prima. Liturgia Mariana.
    I.   "Kalendarium Marianum," . . . auctore . . . COLVENERIO . . .
    II. "De Festis Beatae Mariae Virginis," auctore BENEDICTO XIV.
    III. SS. Patrum liturgica Mariana.
    IV. Excerpta ex antiquis liturgiis.

Tomus IV.
    V.   "De cultu publico ab Ecclesia B. Mariae exhibito," auctore TROMBELLI.
    Sectio Secunda. Cultus Marianus.

I.   "Annus Marianus," auc. R. Francisco Costero.
II. "Mensis Marianus," pluribus auctoribus.
III. "Quindena Mariana . . . "
IV. "Novendialia Exercitia pro VIII festis principalioribus B. V. M." . . .
V.   "Hebdomada Mariana," opus mariologici Bohemi.

Tomus V.
 Sectio Tertia. "Pietas Mariana," auc. Spinello, Bona, de Cerf.
 Sectio Quarta. "Corona Mariana," pluribus auctoribus.
 Sectio Quinta. "Scapulare Marianum," auct. T. Raynaudo, S.J. et al.

PARS QUARTA. Doctrinalis et Practica.
 Sectio Prima. Theologia Mariana.
  I.   "Testimonia Mariana SS. Patrum, ordine temporum digesta." Collegit
J. J. Bourassé.

Tomus VI. (*Eiusdem continuatio.*)

Tomus VII.
  II. "Bullarium Marianum." Collegit J. J. Bourassé.
  III. "Conciliorum decreta Mariana." Collegit J. J. Bourassé.
  IV. "Scholastica Mariana, sive Theologia Mariana . . . ," auctore P. V.
Sedlmayr, O.S.B. IC col. 867-1040.

Tomus VIII.
   (*Eiusdem continuatio.*)
  [V.] "De duodecim privilegiis B. Mariae Virginis," auctore Alberto
Magno . . .
  [VI.] De Immaculata Conceptione B. Virginis Mariae.
   I.   "De ortu et progressu cultus ac festi Immaculati Conceptus B. Mariae
Dei Genitricis," auctore P. F. M. A. Gravois, Ord. Min. S. Franc.
   II. "Tractatus theologicus de Immaculata Conceptione B. Mariae Virginis,"
auct. Fr. Suarez, S.J.
   III. "Histoire de la Définition dogmatique de l'Immaculée Conception de
la Très-Sainte Vierge Marie," par Mgr. J.-B. Malou, Evêque de Bruges.
   IV. "Enumération de documents relatifs à la Définition du dogme de
l'Immaculée Conception de la Très-Sainte Vierge," par M. l'abbé D. Sire.
   V.   "De Maria Virgine Incomparabili et Dei Genitrice Sacrosancta libri
quinque," auct. P. Canisii, S.J.

Tomus IX.
   (*Eiusdem continuatio.*)
 Sectio Tertia. Paraenetica Mariana.
 "B. Virginis Mariae Corona Stellarum Duodecim, sive conciones duo-
decim . . . " auct. G. Reismyllero.
 Sectio Quarta. Encomia Mariana.
 "Polyanthea Mariana . . . " auctore R. P. H. Marraccio, e Cong. Cler. Reg.

Tomus X.
  (*Eiusdem continuatio.*)
 Sectio Quinta. Familia Mariana.
  I.   "Pontifices Mariani," auct. Marraccio.
  II. "Antistites Mariani," auct. Marraccio.
  III. "Purpura Mariana," auct. Marraccio.
  IV. "Caesares Mariani," auct. Marraccio.

Tomus XI.
  V.   "Reges Mariani," auctore Marraccio.
  VI. "Principes Mariani," auctore Marraccio.

VII. "Fundatores Mariani," auctore MARRACCIO.

VIII. "Heroides Mariani," auctore MARRACCIO.

IX. "Lilia Mariana, seu de candidissimis sacrarum Virginum in Mariam . . . studiis," auctore MARRACCIO.

Sectio Sexta. "Ordines Mariani," auct. Ferreolo LOCRIO.

Sectio Septima. "Confraternitates et Congregationes Marianae."

Sectio Octava. "Regna, Provinciae, oppida sub Patronatu B. Mariae Virginis Deiparae," auct. Ferreolo LOCRIO.

Sectio Nona. "Peregrinationes Marianae. (Atlas Marianus . . .)," auctore G. GUMPPEMBERG, S.J.

Tomus XII.

  (*Eiusdem continuatio.*)

  Sectio Decima. "De Imitatione B. Mariae Virginis libellus," ex P. S. SAILER, S.J.

PARS QUINTA. "BENEFICIA ET MIRA, intercedente B. Virgine Maria, ecclesiae ac fidelibus concessa, sive, Miranda Mariana . . ." a R. P. Ignatio Brentano CIMAROLO, O.S.B.

Tomus XIII.

"Elogia gloriosissimae Virginis Deiparae Mariae ad Litanias ejusdem Lauretanas," auctore BERLENDO.

"Apostoli Mariani . . . (Romae 1643)," auctore H. MARACCIO.

"Expositio nova litteralis cantici *Magnificat* pro mysterio Immaculatae Conceptionis Virginis Mariae," auctore R. P. Petro DE ALVA ET ASTORGA.

Baptistae MANTUANI, Ordinis Carmelitarum, "Parthenice."

Indices.

VIRGO IMMACULATA

Virgo Immaculata. (Acta Congressus Internationalis Mariologici et Mariani, Romae anno MCMLIV celebrati). Romae, Academia Mariana Internationalis. 1955-1958

Vol. I: Congressus ordo et summarium. (1958)

Vol. II: Acta Magisterii Ecclesiastici de Immaculata B.V.M. Conceptione. (1956)

LAURENTIN, René. "L'action du Saint-Siège par rapport au problème de l'Immaculée Conception." (pp. 1-98)

SERICOLI, P. Cherubinus, O.F.M. "Ordo Franciscalis et Romanorum Pontificum acta de immaculata B.M.V. conceptione." (99-152)

GUTIÉRREZ, Constantius, S.J. "La Bula 'Sollicitudo' en favor de la Inmaculada y las gestiones para conseguirla (1659-1661)." (153-173)

CRISÓSTOMO DE PAMPLONA, S.F.M. Cap. "Elaboración de la definición dogmática de la Inmaculada Concepción." (pp. 174-200)

ALFARO, Juan, S.J. "La fórmula definitoria de la Inmaculada Concepción." (201-275)

AUBERT, Roger. "L'épiscopat belge et la proclamation du dogme de l'Immaculée Conception en 1854." (276-309)

BOUDENS, René, O.M.I. "Mgr. de Mazenod et la définition du dogme de l'Immaculée Conception." (310-322)

THILS, Gustave. "La définition de l'Immaculée Conception et l'idée de révélation." (323-336)

FRÉNAUD, Georges, O.S.B. "Dom Guéranger et le projet de bulle 'Quemadmodum Ecclesia' pour la définition de l'Immaculée Conception." (337-386)

SANNA, Ambrogio, O.F.M. Conv. "I Padri G. B. Tonini e Angelo Trullet, O.F.M. Conv., membri delle Commissioni dogmatiche dell'Immacolata (1848-1854.) (387-407)

SCARAMUZZI, Diomede, O.F.M. "Il P. Antonio Fania da Rignano, O.F.M., e il dogma dell'Immacolata." (408-419)

VODOPIVEC, Giovanni. "La definizione dell'Immacolata Concezione e l'infallibilitá Pontificia." (420-434)

SCHWERDT, Karl, S.C.J. "Das Weiterleben der Definierung der Unbefleckten Empfängnis in den marianischen Rundschreiben der Päpste seit dem Jahre 1854." (435-473)

PARENTE, Pietro. "La bolla 'Ineffabilis' e la costituzione 'Munificentissimus.'" (474-488)

FILOGRASSI, Ioseph, S.J. "Progressus dogmatis Immaculatae Conceptionis in litteris encyclicis Pii XII 'Fulgens corona.'" (488-496)

Vol. III: De Immaculata Conceptione in Sacra Scriptura. (1955)

BEA, Augustinus, S.I. "Bulla 'Ineffabilis Deus' et hermeneutica biblica." (pp. 1-17)

BRINKTRINE, Johannes. "Das Protoevangelium (Gen. 3, 15) und die Unbefleckte Empfängnis Mariens." (18-28)

MARIANI, Bonaventura, O.F.M. "L'Immacolata nel Protoevangelo: Gen. 3, 15." (29-99)

COPPENS, Joseph. "La Mère du Sauveur à la lumière de la théologie vétéro-testamentaire." (100-115)

CERFAUX, Lucien. "La vision de la Femme et du Dragon de l'Apocalypse en relation avec le Protévangile." (116-131)

STROBEL, Albert, O.M.I. "L'Immaculée Conception dans la révélation de l'économie actuelle." (132-150)

MALO, Adrien, O.F.M. "L'économie divine dans la révélation biblique de l'Immaculée Conception." (151-173)

PLASSMANN, Thomas, O.F.M. "Uno eodemque decreto (Maria Immaculata praedestinata in Sacra Pagina)." (174-197)

KOEHLER, Théodore, S.M. "Une interprétation théologique de l'Ecce filius tuus' (Jn. 19, 26) d'après l'exégèse et à la lumière du dogme de l'Immaculée Conception." (198-215)

ROMEO, Antonino, "La Donna ravvolta dal sole, Madre di Cristo e dei cristiani, nel cielo (Apoc. 12)." (216-258)

RUSH, Alfred, C.SS.R., "Outlines of Mary's holiness in New Testament Apocrypha." (259-268)

Vol. IV: De Immaculata Conceptione apud SS. Patres et Scriptores orientales. (1955)

SÖLL, Georgius, S.D.B. "Elementa evolutionis in historia dogmatis Immaculatae Conceptionis B.M. Virginis ante Concilium Ephesinum." (pp. 1-9)

KRUEGER, Paul. "Die Immaculata-Frage bei den Syrischen Kirchenvätern." (10-27)

JOUASSARD, Georges. "L'interprétation par S. Cyrille d'Alexandrie de la scène de Marie au pied de la Croix." (28-47)

BOYER, Charles, S.J. "La controverse sur l'opinion de S. Augustin touchant la conception de la Vierge." (48-60)

DIETZ, Ildefons Maria, O.E.S.A. "Ist die Hl. Jungfrau nach Augustinus 'Immaculata ab initio'?" (61-112)

VAN ROEY, Albert. "La sainteté de Marie d'après Jacques de Saroug." (113-132)

VONA, Costantino. "Un argomento filologico a favore dell'Immacolata Concezione in S. Giacomo di Sarug." (133-144)

KOREN, Antonio, S.J. "La devozione mariana ed in specie la fede nell'Immacolata Concezione nei testi liturgici bizantino-slavi." (145-157)

RAES, Alphonse, S.J. "La Sainte Vierge et le cosmos dans la liturgie byzantine." (158-169)

GORDILLO, Maurizio, S.J. "L'Immacolata Concezione e lo stato di giustizia originale nella Mariologia dei palamiti." (170-184)

ELDAROV, Giorgio, O.F.M.Conv. "La dottrina dell'Immacolata nei maestri francescani e nei teologi palamiti dei secoli XIV-XV." (185-195)

WENGER, Jean B., A.A. "L'Eglise orthodoxe russe et l'Immaculée Conception." (196-215)

HOFMANN, Giorgio, S.J. "Le Isole Greche e l'Immacolata avanti il 1854." (216-222)

SCHULTZE, Bernardus, S.J. "Vladimirus Soloviev de Immaculata Conceptione B.M. Virginis." (223-246)

Vol. V: De Immaculata Conceptione in epocha introductoria scholasticae. (1955)

DAVIS, H. Franciscus. "Theologia Immaculatae Conceptionis apud primos defensores, scil. in Anglia, saec. XII." (pp. 1-12)

MODRIĆ, P. Lucas, O.F.M. "Doctrina de conceptione B. V. Mariae in controversia saec. XII." (13-73)

GAGOV, Giuseppe, O.F.M. Conv. "L'ambiente liturgico e culturale inglese a favore dell'Immaculata e Giovanni Duns Scoto, O.Min." (74-89)

GEENEN, Godfried, O.P. "Eadmer, le premier théologien de l'Immaculée Conception." (90-136)

EMMEN, Aquilinus, O.F.B. "Epistola pseudo-anselmiana 'Conceptio veneranda' eiusque auctoritas in litteratura mediaevali de Immaculata Conceptione." (137-150)

BARRÉ, Henri, C.S.Sp. "Immaculée Conception et Assomption au XIIe siècle." (151-180)

PIOLANTI, Antonio. " 'Sicut sponsa ornata monilibus suis'—Maria come 'Sponsa Christi' in alcuni teologi del sec. XII." (181-193)

DEL MARMOL, Boniface, O.S.B. "Marie Corédemptrice. — Eadmer enseigna-t-il que Marie rachetante fut rachetée?" (194-201)

Vol. VI: De Immaculata Conceptione in Ordine S. Dominici. (1955)

CIAPPI, Aloisius, O.P. "De privilegio Immaculatae Conceptionis ac de praedestinatione Matris Dei Salvatoris iuxta doctrinam S. Thomae de motivo incarnationis." (pp. 1-10)

CUERVO, Manuel, O.P. "Por qué Santo Tomás no afirmó la Inmaculada." (11-68)

VERARDO, Raymundus, O.P. "De concupiscentia in transmissione peccati originalis iuxta D. Thomam ac de huius doctrinae momento relate ad progressum dogmatis immaculatae conceptionis B.M.Virginis." (69-91)

DUNCKER, Petrus Gerardus, O.P. "Auctoritas S. Scripturae et praevia sanctificatio Beatae Virginis Mariae iuxta S. Thomam." (92-102)

BROWNE, Michael, O.P. "Circa Immaculatam Conceptionem et Magisterium Ecclesiae apud S. Thomam." (103-107)

GARRIGOU-LAGRANGE, Reginaldus, O.P. "De perfectissima redemptione B.V.Mariae secundum tria principia a S. Thoma admissa." (108-115)

LUMBRERAS, Petrus, O.P. "Personaliter redempta." (116-123)

KOSTER, Mannes Dominicus, O.P. "Relate ad progressum dogmatis immaculatae conceptionis doctrina S. Thomae magni valoris erat." (124-135)

DI FRANCESCO, Salvatore, O.P. "Influsso del Dottore S. Tommaso d'Aquino nello sviluppo della dottrina sull'immacolato concepimento della Beatissima Vergine Maria." (136-145)

BINDER, Karl. "Kardinal Juan de Torquemada und die feierliche Verkündigung der Lehre von der unbeflecktken Empfängnis auf dem Konzil von Basel." (146-163)

HOFFMANN, P. Adulphus, O.P. "De voto Cajetani 'De conceptu B. Mariae Virginis ad Leonem Decimum Pontificem Maximum.'" (164-176)

MASSON, Réginald, O.P. "Les Dominicains favorables à l'Immaculée Conception de Marie." (177-186)

ANDALORO, Ambrogio, M., O.P. "Il P. Mariano Spada, O.P., e l'attività da lui svolta per la definizione dell'Immacolata Concezione." (187-200)

SZCZURECKI, Theophilus, O.P. "De doctrina circa immaculatam conceptionem B.M. Virginis in Ordine Fratrum Praedicatorum in Polonia ante eius sollemnem definitionem proclamatam a Pio PP. IX anno 1854." (201-212)

Vol. VII: De Immaculata Conceptione in Ordine S. Francisci. Fasc. I, Doctrina theologorum saec. XIII et XIV. (1958)

CHIETTINI, Emanuele, O.F.M. "La prima santificazione di Maria SS.ma nella scuola francescana del sec. XIII." (Pp. 1-39)

ROMERI, Candido M., O.F.M. "La santificazione di Maria in S. Antonio di Padova." (40-50)

BALIĆ, Carlo, O.F.M. De significatione interventus Ioannis Duns Scoti in historia dogmatis Immaculatae Conceptionis." (51-171)

BONNEFOY, Jean-Fr., O.F.M. "Duns Scot, défenseur de l'Immaculée Conception de Marie." (172-219)

VOGT, Bernard, O.F.M. "Duns Scotus, defender of the Immaculate Conception (A historical-dogmatic study)." (220-240)

POMPEI, Alfonso, O.F.M. Conv. "L'Immacolata Concezione e i teologi francescani del sec. XIV." (241-272)

Vol. VII, fasc. II: Doctrina auctorum inde a saec. XV usque ad nostram aetatem. (1957)

ABATE, Giuseppe, O.F.M. Conv. "S. Bernardino da Siena, 'esplicito' assertore dell'Immacolato Concepimento di Maria, secondo un sermone finora sconosciuto e attribuito allo stesso santo." (Pp. 1-13)

BERTAGNA, Martino, O.F.M. "L'Immacolata nella predicazione di S. Bernardino da Siena." (14-21)

CLEMENTE DA S. MARIA IN PUNTA, O.F.M. Cap. "S. Lorenzo da Brindisi, teologo dell'Immacolata." (22-43)

MACALI, Luigi, O.F.M. Conv. "La dottrina dell'Immacolata nei grandi scotisti O.F.M. Conv. dei secoli XVI-XIX." (44-98)

CAMBELL, Jacques, O.F.M. "L'Immaculée Conception chez les théologiens franciscains français des temps modernes." (99-165)

APERRIBAY, Bernardo, O.F.M. "La Inmaculada según Fr. Luis de Miranda, O.F.M." (166-181)

PIJOAN, José, O.F.M. "La Inmaculada Concepción en Francisco Guerra y Tomás Francés Urrutigoyti." (182-208)

MARTÍNEZ, Pedro de Alcántara, O.F.M. "La Inmaculada Concepción según las doctrinas de Juan de Cartagena y Juan Serrano (s.XVII)." (209-241)

DI MONDA, Antonio M., O.F.M. Conv. "L'Immacolata nell'opera mariologica dello scotista Angelo Volpi, O.F.M. Conv. († 1647)." (242-273)

STEINHEIMER, Mauritius, O.F.M. "De Immaculata Conceptione juxta theologos franciscanos Provinciae Bavariae." (274-294)

DOIMI, Samuele, O.F.M. Conv. "I predicatori O.F.M. Conv. e l'Immacolata nei secoli XVI-XIX." (295-335)

DI STOLFI, Liberato, O.F.M. "L'Immacolata Concezione nella tradizione dei predicatori francescani." (336-363)

VAN DE WALLE, Albertus, O.F.M. "Le décret de l'Inquisition de 1644 et les théologiens franciscains belges." (364-400)

Vol. VII, fasc. III: De disputationibus publicis et cultu erga Immaculatam Conceptionem. (1957)

PIANA, Celestino, O.F.M. "Un saggio dell'attività francescana nella difesa e propagazione del culto alla Concezione Immacolata." (Pp. 1-41)

COCCIA, Antonio, O.F.M. Conv. "Il culto dell'Immacolata nelle Provincie italiane ed estere O.F.M. Conv." (42-71)

ROTOLO, Filippo, O.F.M. Conv. "I Frati Minori Conventuali e il culto dell' Immacolata in Sicilia." (72-123)

GOETZ, Arnulf, O.F.M. "Die Immaculata und die Franziskaner auf bayerischem Boden (1625-1803)." (124-139)

GRAJEWSKI, Maurice, O.F.M. "The Franciscans of the United States and the cult of the Immaculate Conception (1854-1954)." (140-158)

ANDREOZZI, Gabriel, T.O.R. "L'Immacolata Concezione di Maria nel Terz' Ordine Regolare di San Francesco." (159-170)

UMBERTO, Betti, O.F.M. "Il 'Voto sanguinario' in difesa dell'Immacolata Concezione. L'atteggiamento dei Frati Minori nella controversia suscitata da Ludovico Antonio Muratori." (171-187)

BRLEK, Michael, O.F.M. "De historia et valore iuridico legislationis Ordinis Fratrum Minorum circa Doctorem Immaculatae Conceptionis." (188-226)

VEUTHEY, Leone, O.F.M. Conv. "La spiritualità francescana e l'Immacolata." (227-232)

Vol. VIII, fasc. I: De Immaculata Conceptione in Ordine B.V. Mariae de Mercede. (1955)

SANCHO, Amerio, O. de M. "Sanctus Petrus Paschasius, Episcopus et martyr Immaculatae Conceptionis defensor. (Prima pars)" (pp. 1-35)

AQUATÍAS, Luis del Sagrado Corazón, O. de M. "La Orden de la Merced, defensora de la Inmaculada." (37-51)

LÓPEZ, Fernando, O. de M. "La Inmaculada en la liturgia de la Orden de la Merced." (53-66)

MUÑOZ, Vicente, O. de M. "Francisco Zumel († 1607) y la Inmaculada Concepción." (67-87)

GÓMEZ, Elías. "La Inmaculada Concepción de María, según el Ilmo. Maestro Fr. Pedro de Oña (1560-1607)." (89-101)

DELGADO CAPEANS, Ricardo, O. de M. "La Concepción en gloria." (103-137)

BARRIGA, Victor M., O. de M. "La Inmaculada y la Merced en el Perú." (139-155)

DELGADO VARELA, J. M., O. de M. "La quinta junta de la Concepción y el P. Alonso Vázquez de Miranda." (157-208)

IGNELZI, Vicente, O. de M. "El culto de la Concepción en el Convento de Bonaria." (213-226)

DELGADO VARELA, J. M., O. de M. "¿Fué el P. Diego Tello anticoncepcionista?" (227-279)

HERRADA, Juan B., O. de M. "El P. Cabrera y la Inmaculada Concepción en Chile." (281-349)

BRUNET, José, O. de M. "La Inmaculada y la Merced en la Argentina." (351-362)

PÉREZ, José León, O. de M. "El Rvdmo. P. Fr. Pedro A. Valenzuela y la Inmaculada Concepción de María." (363-381)

Vol. VIII, fasc. II: De Maria Immaculata et reparatione ad mentem Ecclesiae et in Spiritu Congregationis Sacerdotum a Sacro Corde Jesu. (1955)

HARTMANN, Prosperus, S.C.J. "Virgo Immaculata et reparatio in Magisterio ecclesiastico et liturgia." (pp. 6-27)

SCHWERDT, Carolus, S.C.J. "Immaculata conceptio B.M.Virginis et vita nostra reparationis secundum encyclicas Summorum Pontificum marianas et liturgiam." (27-51)

Sánchez-Cremades, Josephus, S.C.J. "De necessitudine inter reparationem in cultu SS. Cordis Jesu et reparationem marianam, imprimis in cultu Immaculati Cordis Mariae, ratione habita apparitionum Virginis Immacultae." (52-105)

Haas, Joannes, S.C.J. "Maria Immaculata et reparatio (Aspectus theologico-psychologicus)." (106-117)

Millet, Henri, S.C.J. "La réparation chez le Père Dehon." (118-127)

Tessarolo, Andreas, S.C.J. "Virgo Immaculata et reparatio apud Leonem Dehon, Fundatorem S.C.J." (127-183)

Middendorf, Henricus, S.C.J. "De methodo in doctrina et cultus et devotionis Immaculati Cordis B.M.Virginis adhibenda." (183-223)

Stockmann, Julius, S.C.J. "De devotione et cultu Cordis Immaculati Beatae Virginis in praxi." (224-240)

Perales-Pons, Eduardus, S.C.J. "Reparatio marialis secundum spiritum Sacerdotum a Sacro Corde Jesu." (241-258)

Dal Lago, Bernardus, S.C.J. "Immaculata et reparatio in mariologia P. Andreae Prévot, S.C.J." (259-270)

Vol. VIII, fasc. III: De Immaculata Conceptione in nonnullis ordinibus et congregationibus religiosis. (1956)

Valvekens, Ioannes B., O. Praem. "De Immaculata Conceptione apud Philippum de Harveng et Adamum Scotum, O. Praem." (pp. 1-18)

Claudio, Catena, O. Carm. "L'Immacolata Concezione nell'Ordine Carmelitano." (19-39)

Couto, S. E. Mons. Gabriele B., O.C.D. "La Inmaculada y la Reforma Carmelitana Descalza." (53-79)

Rossi, P. Alessio M., O.S.M. "Il culto dell'Immacolata presso i Servi di Maria." (80-91)

Capone, Domenico, C.SS.R. "La dottrina di S. Alfonso sulla concezione immacolata di Maria SS.ma." (92-128)

Santonicola, Alfonso, C.SS.R. "Il 'voto di sangue' per l'Immacolata e S. Alfonso di Liguori." (129-150)

Hupperts, Jean M., S.M.M. "L'Immaculée Conception dans la doctrine mariale de S. Louis-Marie de Montfort (1673-1716)." (151-172)

Morabito, Joseph, O.M.I. "Monseigneur de Mazenod, serviteur de Marie Immaculée." (173-192)

Fernández, Félix, S.M. "La Congrégation de l'Immaculée Conception selon l'esprit du P. Guillaume Joseph Chaminade." (193-215)

Neubert, Emile, S.M. "Raisons de la dévotion spéciale envers le mystère de l'Immaculée Conception dans la Société de Marie." (216-228)

Vol. IX: De Immaculata Conceptione aliisque privilegiis B.V.Mariae pro statu Christum natum antecedente et concomitante. (1957)

Nicolas, Marie-Joseph, O.P. "Sublimiori modo redempta." (pp. 1-15)

Martínez, Pedro De Alcántara, O.F.M. "La redención de la Santísima Virgen." (16-41)

Koksa, Giorgio, "La causalità retroattiva del merito di Cristo." (42-69)

Gilbert, Maurice, O.M.I. "Immaculée Conception et justice originelle." (60-70)

Valentinus a Westende, O.F.M. Cap. "De relationibus inter immaculatam B. M. Virginis conceptionem et dona iustitiae originalis." (71-89)

Martinelli, Alexius, O.F.M. "Utrum et qua ratione B. V. Maria cooperata sit ad propriam sanctificationem." (90-115)

Gigon, Andreas, O.P. "De praedestinatione Virginis Immaculatae." (116-123)

Blasucci, Antonio M., O.F.M. Conv. "La dottrina scotistica della predestinazione assoluta di Maria e il dogma dell'Immacolata Concezione." (124-163)

Colomer, Luis, O.F.M. "El porqué de la Inmaculada Concepción." (164-184)

BELANGER, Marcellus, O.M.I. " 'Et misericordia eius a progenie in progenies' (De Immaculata Conceptione principio misericordiae illustrata)" (185-200)

LLAMERA, Marceliano, O.P. "La maternidad divina y la Concepción Inmaculada de María." (201-231)

GERVAIS, Jacques, O.M.I. "L'Immaculée Conception et la maternité divine." (232-247)

VEUTHEY, Leone, O.F.M. Conv. "Fondamenti dogmatici e psicologici del culto dell'Immacolata." (248-277)

HEALY, Kilian J., O. Carm. "The harmony between the Immaculate Conception and the perfect virginity of the Mother of God." (278-285)

ZIBERTA, Bartholomaeus M., O. Carm. "De excedendis rationibus convenientiae et de necessariis inducendis in quaestione de Immaculata Mariae Conceptione." (286-304)

SCHILLEBEECKX, Henricus, O.P. "Mutua correlatio inter redemptionem obiectivam eamque subiectivam B.M.Virginis in ordine ad eius maternitatem erga Christum et nos, ut principium fundamentale Mariologiae." (305-321)

CONNELL, Francis J., C.SS.R. "The initial grace of the Blessed Virgin Mary." (322-332)

GUMMERSBACH, Joseph, S.J. "Mariens Befestigung in der Gnade." (333-354)

Vol. X: De Immaculata Conceptione aliisque privilegiis B.V.Mariae pro statu Christum natum consequente. (1957)

PHILIPS, Gérard. "L'Immaculée Conception dans le mystère de la Rédemption." (pp. 1-26)

CUERVO, Manuel, O.P. "Inmaculada y Corredentora." (27-46)

SIMON, Joseph, O.M.I. "L'Immaculée Conception et le concours salvifique de Marie." (47-68)

MITTERER, Albertus. "Ab Immaculata Conceptione ad mediationem omnium gratiarum." (69-72)

BECQUÉ, Maurice, C.SS.R. "La relation entre l'Immaculée Conception de la B. Vierge Marie et sa corédemption selon la doctrine de saint Alphonse." (73-79)

GALLUS, Tiburtius, S.J. "Ratio quae intercedit inter dogmata Immaculatae Conceptionis et Assumptionis corporalis B.M. Virginis." (80-91)

KOSTER, Mannes Dominikus, O.P. "Die Himmelfahrt Mariens gleichsam die Vollendung ihrer Unbefleckten Empfängnis." (92-114)

GHINI, Giordano G., O.P. "L'Immacolata e l'Assunta." (115-131)

WUENSCHEL, Eduardus, C.SS.R. "De relatione Immaculatae Conceptionis ad Mariae mortem et Assumptionem in doctrina S. Alfonsi." (132-144)

BASILIO DE SAN PABLO, C.P. "Las reclamaciones de la muerte en la Inmaculada." (145-177)

GARRIGOU-LAGRANGE, Réginald, O.P. "La douleur et la mort en Marie Immaculée." (178-190)

GAGNEBET, Rosaire, O.P. "L'Immaculée Conception de la T. S. Vierge et sa mort." (191-202)

LATTANZI, Ugo. "L'Assunzione di Maria SS. Immacolata nel quadro dell'escatologia paolina." (203-207)

LANDUCCI, Pier Carlo. "L'ipotesi della immortalità corporea della Immacolata alla luce del dogma." (208-218)

Vol. XI: De debito contrahendi peccatum originale in B.V.Maria. (1957)

BONNEFOY, Jean-Fr., O.F.M. "Marie indemne de toute tache du péché originel." (pp. 1-62)

DELGADO VARELA, José M., O. de M. "La exclusión de todo débito a la luz de la razón teológica." (63-93)

ALEJANDRO DE VILLALMONTE, O.F.M. Cap. "María Inmaculada exenta del débito del pecado original." (94-136)

Vol. XIII: De relatione Virginis Immaculatae ad Corpus Christi Mysticum. (1957)
QUADRIO, Giuseppe, S.D.B. "L'Immacolata e la Chiesa nell'insegnamento di Pio IX." (pp. 1-24)
GUINDON, Henri-Marie, S.M.M. "Un grand signe: L'Immaculée, victorieuse de toutes les hérésies." (25-36)
DOMENICO, Grasso, S.J. "La Vergine nelle conversioni contemporanee." (37-47)
SCHMAUS, Michael. "Ein neuer Aspekt zur Begründung der Immaculata Conceptio." (48-54)
MULLANEY, Urban. "The Immaculate Conception and the living Church." (55-86)
IRENAEUS, Rosier P., O. Carm. "The significance of Mary's Immaculate Conception for our spiritual life." (87-96)
ARTADI, Juan, S.M. "Comunicación al misterio de la Inmaculada en razón de nuestra filiación." (97-110)
SPIAZZI, P. Raimondo, O.P. "La Vergine Immacolata come tipo della perfezione etica cristiana." (111-127)
FABRO, Cornelio, C.P.S. "L'Immacolata nella storia del mondo." (128-140)
BÉKÉS, Gerardo, O.S.B. "L'umanesimo moderno e l'Immacolata." (141-151)
DOMÍNGUEZ, Olegarius, O.M.I. "Immaculata Conceptio et opus missionarium." (152-167)
ANICHINI, Guido. "L'Azione Cattolica nata e sviluppata sotto gli sguardi di Maria Immacolata." (168-182)

Vol. XIV: De Immaculata Conceptione apud varias nationes. (1957)
JELLOUSCHEK, Carl Johann, O.S.B. "Die Lehre von Marias Empfängnis bei den ältesten Theologen der Wiener Universität." (pp. 1-35)
MARCOS RODRÍGUEZ, Florencio. "La Universidad de Salamanca y la Inmaculada." (35-118)
WILLAM, Franz Michael. "John Henry Kardinal Newman und die Lehre von der Unbefleckten Empfängnis Marias." (119-146)
KOUDELKA, Vladimirus J., O.P. "Quid theologi in Bohemia saec. XIV et XV senserint de conceptione B.M. Virginis." (147-152)
SAKAC, Stephanus, S.I. "Doctrina Laurentii Chrysogoni, S.I., de Immaculata Conceptione Virginis Deiparae." (153-159)
WEIJENBORG, Reinoldus, O.F.M. "Doctrina de Immaculata Conceptione apud Ioannem de Palz, O.E.S.A., magistrum Lutheri novitii." (160-183)
CIRAC ESTOPANAN, Sebastianus. "Martinus García, canonicus caesaraugustanus et episcopus barcinonensis (saec. XV-XVI), maximus praedicator de Immaculata Conceptione Virginis Mariae." (184-213)
MIKLAVCIC, Max. "Johann Ludwig Schönleben, ein slowenischer Mariologe (1618-1681)." (214-241)
SHESTANI, Zif. "L'Albania e l'Immacolata." (242-246)
TATARYNOVIC, Pietro. "La Santissima Vergine Immacolata è la ispiratrice dell'unità cristiana in Biancorutenia." (247-249)
GAGOV, Giuseppe M., O.F.M. Conv. "La fede nell'Immacolato Concepimento di Maria tra i bulgari." (250-253)
CRNICA, Antonius, O.F.M. "Immaculata Conceptio B.M.Virginis apud croatos." (254-299)
EMMEN, Aquilinus, O.F.M. "Doctrina et cultus Immaculatae Conceptionis in Hollandia usque ad Concilium Tridentinum." (300-348)
KADA, Ludwig. "Das Fest der Unbefleckten Empfängnis in der kirchlichen und staatlichen Gesetzgebung Ungarns." (349-359)
BERTAGNA, Martino, O.F.M. "Episodi toscani riguardanti la controversia e il culto dell'Immacolata Concezione." (360-384)
ANREOZZI, Gabriele, T.O.R. "Cesare Borgia e un tempio votivo all'Immacolata Concezione." (385-389)

FREDIANI, Giusseppe. "La Protettrice della libertà (Lucca e l'Immacolata)." (390-413)

HUETTER, Luigi. "Il monumento all'Immacolata in Piazza di Spagna a Roma." (414-422)

RUBIN, Ladislao. "Dottrina e culto dell'Immacolata Concezione in Polonia prima della definizione dogmatica." (423-431)

MROCZEK, Ladislaus, M.I.C. "Cultus Mariae Immaculatae et Congregationes religiosae originis polonae." (432-442)

WELKYJ, Atanasio, O.S.B.M. "L'Immacolata in Ucraina." (443-451)

MORIN, Conrad, O.F.M. "La première Congrégation paroissiale des Filles de Marie Immaculée." (452-483)

OHLMANN, Ralph, O.F.M. "Notes on the cult of the Blessed Virgin and her Immaculate Conception in the United States." (484-505)

HABIG, Marion, O.F.M. "The U.S.A., dowry of Our Lady Immaculate." (506-520)

Vol. XV: De Immaculata Conceptione in litteratura et in arte Christiana. (1957)

SLOOTS, Ephrem, O.F.M. "Autour du tournant du culte de la Vierge au moyen âge." (Pp. 1-17)

FOURNÉE, Jean. "Les thèmes inconographiques de l'Immaculée Conception en Normandie au moyen-âge et à la Renaissance." (18-106)

ALCE, Venturino, O.P. "L'Immacolata nell'arte dalla fine del sec. XV al sec. XX." (107-135)

TOMINEC, Romanus. "Immaculata in arte slovenica." (136-157)

BORCHERT, Bruno, O. Carm. "L'Immacolata nella iconografia del Carmelo." (158-169)

GALLINO, Tommaso, O.F.M. "L'Immacolata nella immagini ispirate dai Francescani (Del Medioevo a tutto il secolo decimosesto)." (170-198)

CECCHELLI, Carlo. "Note sulla più antica iconografia della Immacolata." (199-203)

VAROTTI, Albino M., O.F.M. Conv. "L'Immacolata nella produzione musicale dei maestri compositori O.F.M. Conv." (204-230)

MELLONE, Attilio, O.F.M. "Dante Alighieri e la Immacolata." (231-241)

VITOLO, Attilio, O.F.M. "Omaggio dei poeti francescani alla Vergine Immacolata." (242-265)

MESA, Carlos E., C.M.F. "La Inmaculada en los autos marianos españoles." (266-317)

KUCHARSKI, Casimirus, S. I. "De Conceptione Immaculata B.M.Virginis in canticis religiosis, in poësi et in arte figurativa Polonorum." (318-338)

SWIDER, Ladislaus, "'Horulae Matris Dei' seu Officium Parvum de Immaculata Conceptione B.M.Virginis eiusque mira cum cantu populari per Poloniam expansio." (339-364)

NÁHALKA, Stefano, "L'Immacolata nella letteratura ed arte della Slovacchia." (365-394)

Vol. XVI: De apparitionibus Virginis Immaculatae. (1956)

TRUHLAR, Carolus, S.J. "Principia theologica de habitudine Christiani erga apparitiones." (pp. 1-17)

LAURENTIN, René. "Les apparitions de Lourdes." (18-92)

TROCHU, Francis. "Sainte Bernadette, la voyante de Lourdes." (93-105)

BELLENEY, Joseph. "Guérisons miraculeuses de Lourdes." (106-126)

DEDEBAN, Georges J. "Lourdes, centre de vie théologale ou cité de l'Immaculée, cité de Dieu." (127-151)

LAMBOT, Cyrille, O.S.B. "Le 'Message' de Beauraing." (152-163)

TOUSSAINT, Fernand. "Enquête canonique sur les faits de Beauraing." (164-181)

RANWEZ, E. "Nos raisons de croire aux apparitions de Beauraing." (182-196)

Vol. XVII: De officio Immaculatae Conceptionis nonnullisque aliis quaestionibus marialibus. (1957)

SZABO, Titus, O.F.M. "De officio perusino Immaculatae Conceptionis in breviario Fratrum Minorum et Ordinis S. Benedicti saec. XIV." (Pp. 1-46)

CEYSSENS, Lucien, O.F.M. "Le Petit Office de l'Immaculée Conception: prétendue approbation, condamnation (1678), tolérance (1679)." (47-124)

LYONNET, Stanislas, S.J. "Virginité et maternité divine d'après le récit de l'Annonciation." (125-156)

KRUPA, Ludovicus, O.F.M. "De sanctitate Immaculatae Matris Redemptoris nostri." (157-181)

VASSALLI, Giuseppe, S.S.S. "La cooperazione dell'Immacolata all'opera redentiva dell'Eucaristia." (182-206)

CENTO, Mgr. Fernand. "Dante et la médiation de Marie." (207-215)

CONFALONIERI, Mons. Carlo. "Il Cuore Immacolato di Maria e la vita sociale." (216-230)

VAN DER PLUIJM, Petrus, C.B., M.S.C. "Commentarium de cultu Mariae sine labe conceptae in devotione erga Dominam nostram a S. Corde Iesu." (231-243)

BLASUCCI, Antonio, O.F.M. Conv. "La 'Milizia di Maria Immacolata.'" (244-260)

LANDUCCI, Mons. Pier Carlo. "Valore dell'argomento di convenienza dopo la proclamazione dei massimi dogmi mariani." (261-267)

MULA, Mgr. Paul, M.A. "Comment certains milieux islamiques ont réagi au stimulant de quelques manifestations récentes de la doctrine et de la piété catholiques concernant la personne privilegiée de Marie, Mère de Jésus." (268-282)

Vol. XVIII: Expositionis Marianae catalogus in aedibus 'Palazzo Venezia' ordinatae occasione Congressus Mariologici-Mariani Internationalis. (1956)

Indices[1]

Index to the Bibliography[2]

Abad, Camilo, S.I. S:1905
Abd-el-Jalil, Joseph-Marie, O.F.M. F:1950
Abgrall, J.-M. F:1905
Adjutus (= Adjute), O.F.M. F:1905
Agnoletti, Carlo. I:1884
Aguila, José Rafael. S:1850
Aguilera Camacho, Daniel. S:1950
Aguirebeitía, Severino de Santa Teresa. S:1951 1954 1955
Aladel. F:1834; G:1836; I:1836
Alameda, Santiago, O.S.B. S:1954
Alastruey, Gregorio. I:1952; L:1934; S:1945
Albers, R. G:1901
Albertus a Bulsano. L:1853
Albertus Magnus. L:1857
Albrecht. G:1913
Alce, V. I:1954
Alimonda, Gaetano, Card. I:1856 1879
Allodi, Joannes. L:1857
Alonso, Joaquín, C.M.F. S:1956
Altissent, Juan B. S:1931
Alujas Bros, Moisés. S:1909
Ameri, Hyacinthus, O.F.M. L:1954
Ameristus, Christophilus. F:1855; G:1856
Amort, Eusebius. G:1876
Anaquim, Conego Manuel. 1904 (Cf. p. 535)
Anastasi, S.E., O.P. E:1904
Ancelet-Hustache, Mme. F:1933
Andreae, U. G:1865
Andreas de Novo Castro, O.F.M. I:1955

Anguita Valdivia, José. S:1955
Anivitti, Vincenzo. I:1848 1854 1874
Anstruther, Robertus. L:1846
Antonelli, Giovanni. I:1864
Aquaroni, L. I:1858
Aquaspartas, Matthaeus, O.F.M., Card. L:1904
Aracena, Domingo, O.P. S:1852
Arendt, Gulielmus, S.J. L:1904
Arenillas, Pedro, O.P. S:1954
Arques y Arrufat, Ramón. S:1904
Artaud, V.D. F:1914
Aureoli. L:1904
Auriault, S.J. F:1931
Autore, Stanislaus Maria, O. Cart. 1898 (Cf. p. 536)

Baglione, Carlo, C. O. I:1852
Bainvel, J.-V. F:1905
Baj, Ferdinando. I:1954
Bajzáth, Georgius. L:1855
Balducci, Antonio. I:1954
Baldwin, Louis, O.F.M. E:1905
Balić, Carolus, O.F.M. L: 1933 1934 1940 1954 1955
Ballerini, Antonio, S.J. I:1852 1904; L:1854 1856
Baltzer, Joh. Bapt. G:1837
Barbero Martínez, Luis. S:1954
Barbier. F:1867
Bargellini, Piero. I:1954
Baril, H. F:1954
Barré. F:1955

---

[1] The indices have been prepared by the editor's father, Mr. Edward James O'Connor, with the assistance of Mrs. Frances St. Aoro. It is impossible to thank them sufficiently for doing this trying work with such great care.

[2] This Index covers only the Bibliography on p. 522 ff., and does *not* include the Appendix on p. 611 ff. Only the writers of books, chapters, etc. are indexed; translators, editors who have not contributed to the work itself, and authors of introductions, etc., are not indexed, nor are anonymous works. In the alphabetizing, particles such as *de, von,* etc. have been counted as part of the name, and *J* has been distinguished from *I* even when the entry in the Bibliography uses *I* for *J*.

The letters *E, F, G, I, L, S* refer to the languages, English, French, German, Italian, Latin, Spanish; the subsequent numbers give years under which the author is listed in the language indicated. [?] means that the work is listed under the section entitled, *Date of publication unknown.*

Trappert, Dionysius Maria, O. Cart.
  L:[?]
Tripepi, Luigi. I:1870 1876
Tschackert. G:1885
Tumminello, Giuseppe, O.E.S.A. I:1942
Turmel, Joseph. E:1915; F:1908 1925
Tyciak, Julius. G:1940 1950

Uhlhorn, Gerhard. G:1870
Uhrig, Adam Jos. G:1854
Ullathorne, Bishop William B. E:1855
Uribe, Angel, O.F.M. 1955 (Cf. p. 536)

Vacandard, E. F:1912
Vadeboncoeur, Paul E., C.SS.R. F:1954
Valenzuela, Pedro Armengaudo, O.de M.
  1904 (Cf. p. 536)
Vallaro, Stefano. L:1904
Valle, Fr. I:1905
Valy, Jh. F:1905
Van Crombrugghe, C. L:1913
Van Rossum, Gulielmus Maria, Card.,
  C.SS.R. L:1904
Van de Walle, J., S.J. F:1904
Van den Berg, P.C., O.P. L:1874
Vásquez, O. de M., Antonio. S:1956
Vassall-Phillips, O. R., C.SS.R. E:1920
Vaughan. E:1905
Venanzio da Celano, O.F.M. I:1855
Venzano, Domenico I:1895
Vera, Vinc. I:1879
Vercruysse, Bruno. E:1874; F:1855
Verdona, Giovanni. I:1904
Vermeersch, A., S.J. F:1905; G:1925
Vespignani, Alf. Ma. I:1886
Venillot. F:1855

Vigo, Ilario Maurizio. I:1894
Villarrasa, Eduardo María. S:1865
Vio, Carlo Silvio. I:1904

Virgo Immaculata. See p. 611 ff.
Vogt, Berard, O.F.M. E:1954 1955
Vollet, E.-H. F:1898
Von Ketteler, Wilhelm Emmanuel.
  G:1868
Von Neukirch, Mich., O. Cap. G:1925
Von Schaezler, Constantin. G:1870

Waibel, Alois Adalbert, O.S.F. G:1831
Wace. F:1842
Walsh, W. P. E:1855
Weber, Beda. G:1858
Wenger, A. A. F:1955
Weninger, S.J. E:1862
Wesoly, S. 1956 (Cf. p. 535)
Wiery, Valentin. G:1855
Wilberforce, Samuel. E:1855; F:1856;
  G:1859
Williams, J. Herbert. E:1906
Williamson, E. W. E:1929
Wimmer, G. A. G:1854 1855
Wolter, Allan, O.F.M. E:1854
Wörnhart, Leonard. G:1890

Zardetti, Otto. G:1880
Ziegler, Gregorius Thomas, O.S.B.
  G:1838
Zimmerman. G:1868
Zinelli, Federico Maria. I:1870
Zöckler. G:1903
Zubizarreta, V. L:1948

Index to Scriptural Citations

631

General Index[1]

ABELARD, PSEUDO–171 172 174 175 181
183 185n 186n
ABSALOM SPRINCKIRSBACENSIS 170
Acceptance of the faithful *ix* 249 263
268 270 415. See also *Sensus Fidei.*
"Active conception" 133 150 172 **332f**
ADAM: creation of 449; Blessed Virgin
compared with 110 357 417; Blessed
Virgin descended from 53 94 147 153
174 183 199 206; and Christ 53 178
373 400; grace and gifts of 43 420
426 458; punishment of 146 149 449;
sin of 35 373 **450ff**; source of sin to
mankind *vi* 41 42 153 166n 168 181
186 192 193 219f 221 224 252 257
258f 262 293 298 **328ff** 373 447 449
ADAM AND EVE 180 340 473 475n 509
plate VI
ADAM OF ST. VICTOR 171n 478n
ADAM OF SOISSONS 226
ADE, John 226
AEGIDIUS DE PRAESENTATIONE 253 259n
260 270
AEGIDIUS ROMANUS (=GILES OF ROME)
189 197n **221**
AELRED REIVALLENSIS 170
AGATHO, Pope St. 292n
ALAN OF LILLE (=ALANUS DE INSULIS)
170
ALBERRO, M. 491 492
ALBERT THE GREAT, St. 44 189 191
197 390
ALBERT OF PADUA 222
ALBERTI, D. 480
ALBERTINUS 253
ALCUIN 80 162n
ALEXANDER V, Pope (=Peter of Candia)
223 304n 466
ALEXANDER VI, Pope 260 263 300
ALEXANDER VII, Pope **286f** 288 **302ff**
307 308 315 320n 379 489. See also
Sollicitudo.
ALEXANDER VIII, Pope 297n
ALEXANDER OF ALEXANDRIA, St. **57** 63n
ALEXANDER OF HALES 44 187n 189 191n
ALPHONSUS OF LIGUORI, St. **269**
ALVA Y ASTORGA, P. de 216 239 256
273 274n 308 321 485
AMADEUS OF LAUSANNE, St. 170n 407f
AMBROSE, St. 57n **68** 69 70n 71 72 84n
153 154n 244n 261 488 489

AMBROSIASTER 67
AMPHILOCHIUS OF ICONIUM 58
Analogy of faith **17** 23 38
ANASTASIUS OF SINAI 89
ANDREAS, A. 218ff 256
ANDREW, St. (the Apostle) 157
—— Canon of 120n
ANDREW OF CRETE, St. **93** 103 114 118
Animation 142 334 335
ANNE, St. 93n 97 **465ff** 481 487 **500**
509; devotion to 138f 240
Anne and Joachim, legend of 59 110
118 134 149 **464ff** 475n **512 513ff 515ff**
519ff frontispiece, plates I, II. See also
Blessed Virgin — Sanctification
Annunciation 25 26 27 28 31 53 101
105f 108 120 122 143n 165; feast of
90; homilies on, chapter III *passim.*
ANONYMOUS I 171n 183n 184n 185n
186n
ANONYMOUS II 171n 185n
ANONYMOUS III 171n 185n
ANSELM, St. 129 130 137n 157 **168ff**
171n 177 180 187n 188 193 204 205
336 402 487 522n plate XIII
ANSELM OF BURY-ST. EDMUND's 134
ANSELM THE YOUNGER 128 129 135
ANTHONY OF PADUA, St. **196n** 488 plate
XIII
ANTIPATER OF BOSTRA 62
ANTIS, V.J. 239
ANTONINUS OF FLORENCE St. 216 233
Apocalypse, Woman of. See *Symbols of
the BVM — Woman . . .*
Apocrypha **81** 132 134 432 464
Apostles 6-15 *passim,* 20 24 38 54 304n
Aragon, Kingdom of **227f** 232 233 277n
295
Arianism 28
ARISTOTLE 369n 387 391n 392 394n
396 405 412
ARNOBIUS 67
ARS, CURÉ OF 423
ATHANASIUS, St. **57** 58 63n 64 68
AUGUSTINE, St. xi 5 9n 32n 33 43 44
68 **69ff** 77 78 84 152 154n 162 171n
186n 204 205 215n 244n 252n 385n
387 393 395 405 408n 420 487 488
489 plate XIII

---

[1] Modern authors are not as a rule listed here; most of them however will be
found in the Index to the Bibliography, p. 622 ff.

References to plates refer primarily to the notes accompanying those plates in
the insert following p. 492.

Chronological Table

of the chief persons and events in the history of the doctrine.

Dates indicate periods of chief activity, etc., unless designated date of death by the sign †.

Approx. date	Western Church	Eastern Church	Magisterium	Life, practice of Church
c. 150		Protogospel of St. James (c. 150)		
200	Irenaeus (202/203), Tertullian (c. 210)			
c. 254		Origen († c. 254)		
300				
c. 365 / 372		Athanasius (c. 365), Ephraem († 372)		
390, 392	Ambrose (390, 392)			
415, 428 / 431	Augustine (415, 428), Pseudo-Matthew		Ephesus (431)	
c. 500				New Marian feasts appear in Orient: Nativity, Annunciation, Purification, Dormition.
638		Sophronius († 638)		
c. 700				Feast of Conception of St. Anne (Orient)
720? 740? / 733 / 749 / 735	Bede († 735)	Andrew of Crete († 720? 740?), Germanus of Const. († 733), John Damascene († 749)		
c. 800				Calendar of Naples
c. 865	Paschasius Radbertus († c. 865)			
883 / 897?		Joseph the Hymnograph († 883), Photius († 897?)		
c. 1000				Feast of Mary's Conception celebrated in England
1079?		Michael Psellos († 1079?)		

Year					
1100	Anselm († 1109?) Bernard (c. 1130)	Eadmer († 1124?) "Friends of the feast"	John Phournes Th. Prodromus		
1200	Alex. of Hales († 1245) Albert († 1280) Bonaventure († 1274) Thomas Aquinas († 1274) Henry of Ghent († 1293)	Grosseteste († 1255) Wm. of Ware (ca. 1293)	Germanus II († 1240)		
1300	John of Pouilly (1309) John of Naples (1317)	Scotus († 1308), Lull († 1316) Auriol, Giles of Rome P. Thomas, A. Andreas, Rubio Mayron, Baconthorp D'Ailly, Vitalis	Palamas († 1359) Cabasilas († after 1396)	Conception celebrated by Roman Curia	
1400	Eymeric (1357-1399) Montson (1387-1389) Torquemada (c. 1437)	Gerson (1401, 1415) Segovia (1435 ff.) Nogarolo (1477) De Bustis (1480) Sorbonne (1497)	Paleologus († 1425) Bryennius († c. 1435) Scholarios († after 1472)	Woman and Serpent in art (1407) Nogarolo's Office adopted in Roman books (1477)	Basel (1439) Sixtus IV (1477, 1482, 1483)
1500	Bandelli (1474 ff.) Frickenhausen (1489 f.) Cajetan (1515) Spina (1533)	Catherinus (1528, 1532)		"Tota pulchra Es" Puys de Palinod Nogarolo's Office sup- pressed (1568, 1570)	Alexander V (1502) Leo X (1512-1517) Trent (1546) Pius V (1570)
1600	Widenfeldt (1673) Launoy (1676) Baillet (1694, 1701)	John of St. Thomas (1637) Alva y Astorga (1648-1660)		Feast major double (1602) Votive Mass (1609) Title Conception (1622) Murillo († 1682) Second class feast (1693)	Paul V (1617) Decree of 1644 Alexander VII (1661, 1665)
1700	Muratori (1714; 1740-1747)	Alphonsus Liguori (1748, 1750)		Feast of obligation (1708)	
1800				Miraculous Medal (1830) Lourdes (1858) Office of Pius IX (1863) First class feast (1879)	Gregory XVI (1831-1846) Definition (1854)
1900					

ERRATA

Accented foreign names, such as BALIĆ and ROSKOVÁNY, appear without the accent in the early chapters of this book, and with it in the later ones. This is due to the fact that certain characters not ordinarily used in English were unavailable at the printer's when the typesetting began, but became available in the course of the two years over which the work extended.

Plate XIII is reproduced by the permission of Fratelli Alinari, Florence.

CPSIA information can be obtained
at www.ICGtesting.com
Printed in the USA
LVHW030535090322
712938LV00012B/2038